THE SCHUBERT READER

THE
Schubert Reader

A Life of Franz Schubert in Letters and Documents

By OTTO ERICH DEUTSCH

Translated by ERIC BLOM

BEING AN ENGLISH VERSION OF
FRANZ SCHUBERT: DIE DOKUMENTE SEINES LEBENS
REVISED AND AUGMENTED WITH A COMMENTARY
BY THE AUTHOR

W · W · NORTON & COMPANY · INC · New York

First Edition

This book was published in England
under the title
Schubert, A Documentary Biography

To
VIENNA'S PAST AND FUTURE

CONTENTS

ILLUSTRATIONS

Half-tone

ILLUSTRATIONS

Line

PREFACE

THIS is a book of facts—the impress of a life left on its contemporary world. Unlike other biographies it does not select events and testimonies that become known to an author, who then makes it his business to fill up gaps and to link the whole together in a literary or scientific way. It is rather a fairly complete collection of all the known biographical raw material, on which the labour of a lifetime has been spent, together with such explanations as may be required. These explanations themselves are dealt with objectively, so far as that is humanly possible: there are no personal elaborations, and prejudices have been kept in check. The book, in short, is intended to be not a biography of Schubert, of a kind that will doubtless continue to be written by others, but the plain record of his life—an unheroic monument such as befits one of the heroes of human culture.

Whether the system that produced this book was due to the material itself—the modest account of one who died young—or to the peculiarities of its author, who lacks the gift of analysis and, probably for that reason, dislikes the aesthetic approach to matters of art, he himself can no longer tell. The former circumstance caused one of Schubert's friends, the poet Eduard von Bauernfeld, to say with a sigh in 1857 that this life showed "so few tangible biographical marks" that it could perhaps be described only by means of "a kind of poetical outline"—as indeed it frequently has been in our time. As late as 1897 Max Friedlaender, one of the most meritorious of Schubert scholars, declared that "material for a biography was, and still is, wanting." As for the second circumstance, it has done away with this deficiency: ever since 1914 it has been difficult, not so much to write a Schubert biography, as to refrain from writing one. If this book has been not unprofitably drawn upon for the last thirty years by Schubertian scholars and writers in its fragmentary German edition, this definitive version should prove even more useful, for all that it is a translation. It may, therefore, be accompanied in its new career with a blessing free of covetousness or envy: *Vivant sequentes!*

.   .   .   .

The present edition, which the author regards as the finally valid one, has been augmented not only by a commentary never published in German, which amounts to about two-fifths of the whole, so far as the number of words goes: as the 'Summary Comparison' (Appendix VIII) shows, more than 160 documents and more than seventy facts have been newly added. The ninety facts previously given in the German edition have been brought into line with the new ones by being deprived of numbers, now reserved exclusively for actual documents, and set in the smaller type. Some seventy-five documents, most of which are criticisms amounting to little more than variants of those retained, have been discarded as being superfluous, but are duly mentioned in the commentary. Many documents have been translated from more accurate sources than those which served for the German edition, and several previously given in incomplete extracts have been amplified. Among the new pieces are the five preliminary documents, marked A to E, and the obituary documents numbered I to XLVI.

Seventy-one letters from Schubert's hand are extant (eleven of which appear only in the English edition), and his other writings amount to seven poems, an allegorical tale, two fragmentary diaries and about thirty-five characteristic dedications and notes on manuscripts. In addition there are some fifty letters addressed to him, with about 230 passages in letters and nearly 300 entries in diaries concerning him. (In the case of the brothers Franz and Fritz von Hartmann the author may have been somewhat too generous in drawing upon their diaries, but they seemed to him important as a contribution to the description of the biographical background.) At least three diaries kept by contemporaries of Schubert's are lost: those of Anselm Hüttenbrenner, Leopold von Sonnleithner and Johann Baptist Jenger, all of which were clearly destroyed intentionally. The documents printed during Schubert's lifetime include programmes, advertisements and criticisms. Moreover, there are all sorts of family documents and official testimonials, poetic effusions by friends and admirers, and so on.

The fact that the commentary was written for English readers, who are necessarily even less conversant with the daily life of old Vienna than their contemporaries on the Continent, may have made it more loquacious, but also more informative. The necessity of explaining everything, if possible, including even things that may be supposed well known (though that is not always the case), produced more detailed annotations than might have been called for in a complete German edition. The commentary also aims at making mention of everything of biographical importance that does not happen to emerge from the contemporary documents.

Although the German edition, unfinished as it was, contained no references to sources, their authenticity was never doubted by any one. The author's present circumstances have made it impossible in various ways to make good this omission, and the whole of his correspondence relating to the matter was destroyed. It may, however, suffice to say that most of the sources were discovered in Vienna. Among their chief owners were the descendants of Schubert's brothers and sisters, the Archives and Library of the City of Vienna, the National and University Libraries, the Household, Court and State Archives, the Archives of the Ministries of the Interior and of Education, the Registries of some other offices, and the collections of the Philharmonic Society (Gesellschaft der Musikfreunde) and other associations. Those who personally contributed to the undertaking are too numerous to mention; instead a list of Schubertians is given here with whose descendants, heirs or successors the author was in communication:

Artaria & Co.; Bibl, Bocklet, Breitkopf & Härtel, Breuning, Bruchmann; Clodi, Craigher; Diabelli, Doblhoff; Ebner, Enderes, Count Esterházy; Grob, Karl Magnus Gross, Sir George Grove; Hardtmuth, Franz and Therese von Hartmann, Josef Hauer, Holzapfel, Hönig, Josef Huber, Hugelmann, Hüttenbrenner; Kenner, Kienreich, Princess Kinsky, Kleyle, Koller, Kreissle, Leopold von Kupelwieser, Kurzrock; Franz Lachner, Leidesdorf, Leitermayer, Löwenthal; Mayerhofer von Grünbühel, Mayssen; Pachler, Pinterics, Pompe, Pratobevera, Probst, Prokesch; Rieder; Sauter, Schellmann, Schlechta,

Schnorr, Schober, Franz Schubert of Dresden, Schweighofer, Schwind, Seidl, Siboni, Sonnleithner, Josef von Spaun, Albert Stadler, Streinsberg; Teltscher, Traweger; Umlauff; Count Weissenwolff.

The author personally visited all the places to which Schubert went, except Ochsenburg Castle near St. Pölten, Steyregg Castle near Linz and Wildbach Castle near Graz. In addition he went, for example, to the places of Schober's birth and death: Torup Castle near Malmö and his last lodgings at Dresden.

To do honour to those who to some extent anticipated the labour embodied in this work, a chronological list of previous Schubert biographers is given here (some of these, marked *, did not get beyond making private collections of material; others, marked †, not beyond sketches for a biography):

Alois Fuchs*	Ferdinand Luib*
Anton Schindler†	Heinrich Kreissle von Hellborn
Ludwig Gottfried Neumann†	Konstant von Wurzbach
Franz Derffel*	Sir George Grove
Josef Wilhelm Witteczek*	Max Friedlaender†
Franz Liszt†	Richard Heuberger
Alois Fellner*	

Friedlaender and Heuberger gave kind advice to the author, while Ludwig Scheibler and Eusebius Mandyczewski, who published but little in the way of Schubertian biography, were friends always willing to help.

The German edition, published by Georg Müller of Munich, was to have consisted of four parts: Vol. I. Grove's biography, translated and revised (printed, but never published), and a complete Schubert bibliography (edited separately by Willi Kahl in 1938); Vol. II, Part I. The documents from birth to death (published in 1914); Part II. Obituaries and eulogies printed up to 1830, and recollections, with a commentary and an index to both parts (not published); Vol. III. The life in pictures (published in 1913); Vol. IV. Thematic Catalogue (not published).

The English edition not only includes an enlarged and corrected collection of documents covering Schubert's lifetime, but also a number of prenatal and posthumous ones. It is illustrated with the accredited portraits of Schubert and a selection of other pictures from the iconographical third volume of the German edition; besides, there are several new illustrations, especially maps that should be of much use to English readers. The thematic catalogue of Schubert's works, which is the first complete one to be published, was finished in the course of the preliminary work done for the translation of the documents. The work-numbers cited in this book, however, are those of the complete edition (e.g. i. 1.= Series I, No. 1, etc.)

. . . . . .

A personal note to conclude.

During the first European war my one anxiety was to return home in order to complete my Schubert labours; but it never came to that. Then, during the present war, in exile from Vienna, I had the happiness of bringing my work to its conclusion at Cambridge. For this I am indebted above all to the Society for the Protection of Science and Learning.

Another stroke of good fortune furthering my undertaking was the transfer of my Schubert collection, rescued from New York harbour, to the Cambridge University Library, thanks to the help of several friends and the kindness of the Librarian and the Syndics of that library.

To the publishers of this book I should like to tender my special thanks for the confidence shown me when they commissioned it, and for their indulgence during the period of its making. They were acquainted only with the German fragment, and the English work in the end considerably exceeded the size at first estimated.

I am lastingly indebted to Mr. Eric Blom, who suggested this book and recommended it to its publishers. He has not merely been its translator, but has acted as interpreter between my English readers and myself.

O. E. D

CAMBRIDGE,
Summer 1944.

TRANSLATOR'S FOREWORD

THERE is little to say by way of explanation and, I hope, not much more by way of excuse. These translations are meant to speak for themselves. I trust they speak, as they were intended to do, like English originals, not necessarily literary originals, but the kind of thing English-speaking people resembling the writers of these documents would have written in similar circumstances.

Not that I could allow this to be my only consideration. It would have been impossible even to attempt doing justice to this task by merely aiming throughout at a reasonable average of decent English style. Here and there I felt called upon to sacrifice this deliberately—and I can only hope that whenever anything sounds bad the reader will conclude that it was contrived on purpose. For one thing, something had to be done to vary the colour of the writing in a book gathering together material from the pens of so many different people, as well as legal and official documents, commercial advertisements and a variety of poetry of sorts. For another, it seemed sometimes advisable to retain the German characteristics of this or that writer where they help to give a picture of the period or of a personality.

In the case of the pompous and patronizing critic of the Leipzig 'Allgemeine musikalische Zeitung,' for example, it would have been easy to demolish those endless and tortuous sentences and build them up again into a semblance of human speech; but it was only by at least sometimes reproducing his manner as closely as possible that some idea could be given to English readers of what this priggish humbug was like. Elsewhere some writer or other may have wielded a clumsy or a blunt pen, and it would have been misleading to translate him so as to give an impression that he wrote as elegantly as did Baron von Schönstein to Count Esterházy. And there seemed to be no reason for not showing the dry manner of C. F. Peters, the publisher, Josef von Spaun's awestruck, stilted way of addressing Goethe, and so on.

So with the far more difficult problem of the verse. Little of it, so far as I am any judge of German poetry, is good verse and

B
xvii

some I am quite sure is doggerel. In cases of the latter I had no hesitation in indulging my own talent for that species of versification, but where the original poet did better, I at least tried to approach his own quality. There is one really first-rate piece of poetry among the documents: the long and beautiful one by Grillparzer. With that I took a great deal of trouble; but I am bound to confess that here, as indeed in other cases, I did not hesitate to substitute single rhymes for double ones for the sake not only of achieving greater ease and flexibility, but also of keeping the clauses as nearly as possible in their proper places. No doubt the words could have been worried into double rhymes, but there seemed to be no point in producing an exact reproduction of the shape of the original at the risk of thereby damaging its spirit or lowering its significance.

Except for some regional idioms produced by regional conditions the English language is, of course, more than adequate to the expression of anything whatever that can be said in German. Still, there is one special difficulty. The German habit of immediately qualifying a statement as soon as it has been made has produced an apparatus of words like "zwar," "allerdings," "eigentlich," "jedoch," "immerhin," etc., to serve that special purpose. Even the positively affirmative "ja" has acquired a secondary, qualifying sense. In English, where it happens to be a virtue not to write down a statement unless it is really meant, it is sometimes very difficult to reproduce these tricks without a good deal of circumlocution. I am bound to confess that I have occasionally given up the struggle in such cases, though only where I found that to sacrifice these little words was to do no harm to the sentence at all and merely to prove their essential superfluity.

The author and I had several consultations about the manner of presenting the titles of Schubert's works, particularly of the songs. We came to the conclusion at last that, although Schubert's own titles are, of course, sacrosanct, it would be disturbing if German titles kept cropping up in our text, since this is, after all, an English book. It would be absurd, for instance, to translate "Vogl sang den 'Erlkönig'" otherwise than "Vogl sang the 'Erl King.'" The final arrangement was that any German title that needs trans-

lating should follow the English in brackets the first time it occurs
—e.g. 'Eulogy of Tears' ('Lob der Tränen')—and that afterwards
the English was to be used alone. But of course German titles
reappear in the appendices where works are listed, as well as in the
index, where cross references can be found at a glance; also sometimes in the commentaries.

For a few English titles which I preferred to my own I am indebted to Mr. Arthur Hutchings, who uses them in his Schubert
volume in Dents' 'Master Musicians' series. Thus I originally
had 'Warrior's Premonition' for 'Kriegers Ahnung' and 'Old
Man's Song' for 'Greisengesang,' but I was glad to adopt Mr.
Hutchings's much better 'Warrior's Foreboding' and 'Veteran's
Song.' One or two very familiar titles are retained, however, for
greater ease of identification, such as 'Chronos the Charioteer'
and 'The Wanderer,' though 'Postilion Chronos' and 'The Wayfarer' are far preferable. Everybody knows the 'Wanderer' song
and we really cannot at this time of day begin to talk of the 'Wayfarer Fantasy'; but in other connections (e.g. 'Wanderers Nachtlied' and 'Der Wanderer an den Mond') I have adopted "wayfarer,"
and it seems obvious that 'Das Wandern' ought never to be called
'Wandering,' which suggests mental aberration rather than
anything else.

Immense difficulties arose over the translations of the many offices
and titles, some of which are, or were, peculiar to Austria, and
therefore have no equivalents in English. I cannot pretend that I
was always able to render them by anything more accurate than
whatever may come fairly close to them in British officialdom, and
it is to be feared that some of them at least will quite unavoidably
look fancifully "Ruritanian" in translation. Scarcely less perplexing were the Czech, Slovak, Polish, Hungarian and Croatian names,
etc., all of which appear in the original documents in German
spellings, as they were written in the Austrian Empire of Schubert's
time. But many place-names are no longer so written in the world
at large, while others yet remain familiar in German, so that con-
sistency was impossible to achieve. Lemberg, for instance, has
loomed large in present-day war news in the Polish form of Lwów
(not to mention transliterations from the Russian like Lvov and

Lvoff); Laibach has hardly been heard of at all, but its Slovenian name of Ljubljana has; on the other hand neither the original Hungarian Poszony nor the new Slovak Bratislava is as familiar as the German Pressburg. Even more perplexing were the names of persons. One of the composers listed among the contributors to the 'Vaterländischer Künstlerverein' of 1824, for instance, is there called W. (for Wenzel) Tomaschek; but as he lived in Prague and is justly claimed as a Czech national composer, he ought to be called Václav Tomášek. At the same time there were many Czechs (and others) settled in Vienna who regarded themselves as Austrians and signed their names in the German way with their own hands. There is Wittassek, the original form of whose name might be hard to discover, and Worzischek, who might not be recognized as Voříšek. Yet again there is Czapek, whose name has been made very familiar by Karel Čapek. This problem, then, had to be given up as impossible to solve to everybody's satisfaction; but the commentary will be found to do something to help.

Like Professor Deutsch, I want to end with a personal note, for I wish to thank him publicly for his unfailing patience in helping me with explanations where my linguistic knowledge forsook me or where I failed to understand some local allusion or other; also, and more particularly, for the forbearance he showed me whenever I ventured to make a suggestion or asked for an elucidation which I felt English readers would like to see included in his commentary. I am afraid I asked him hundreds of questions (even though I knew the answers to some). I do not think he failed to reply to one of them. Everything has gone into the commentary that either he or I could think of; but I take the very minimum of credit for that, for I am well aware that, except in perhaps a dozen cases or so, every point would have been met by him even if I had never raised it.

Another debt of gratitude I must not omit to pay is that which I owe to my friend Mr. John F. Crowder, who very generously cast an eye over the legal documents and made a number of valuable corrections in their terminology. But he must not be held responsible for any mistakes that may still remain, for he saw only the proofs I submitted to him, not those of the whole book.

E. B.

INTRODUCTORY NOTES

AUSTRIA AND VIENNA IN SCHUBERT'S TIME

At the second Annual Dinner of the Anglo-Austrian Society, held in London on 24th April 1925, Sir Henry Hadow, the author of 'The Viennese Period,' vol. v of 'The Oxford History of Music,' said: that to all who loved music Vienna was in very truth a sacred city. If they considered the three greatest artistic periods in the world's history, he would place first Periclean Athens; second, Elizabethan England; and, without any doubt whatever, he would place third Vienna in the latter half of the eighteenth and the first quarter of the nineteenth century.

'The Times,' 25th April 1925.

WHEN Francis of Habsburg-Lorraine was crowned emperor in 1792 he immediately became involved in war with revolutionary France. In the spring of 1796 Austria was attacked on the Rhine by two armies, which were resisted by the Archduke Karl, the emperor's brother, and in Italy by one victoriously led by Bonaparte. At New Year 1797 Austria strove to relieve Mantua, only to be first defeated at Arcola and then, on 14th January, at Rivoli. This was seventeen days before Schubert's birth (31st January 1797).

In the autumn of 1796 already Vienna had called up a volunteer corps. When its second division left to join the Italian army on 17th November, the day of the battle of Arcole, Beethoven wrote the 'Song of Farewell to the Citizens of Vienna,' which he dedicated to the commander of the corps, Major Karl von Köwesdy.

At the end of 1796 the Government, following England's example, had commissioned from Haydn the 'People's Hymn,' which on 12th February 1797 was sung in all the Austrian theatres.

After the fall of Mantua on 21st February, at which the Viennese volunteers were forced to surrender, Inner Austria itself was menaced. Bonaparte traversed the eastern Alps, occupied Graz, the capital of Styria, and threatened to push on towards Vienna across the Semmering.

On 4th April the storm troops were called up all over Austria, and on the 14th Beethoven brought out his 'Austrians' War-Song.' Three days later, on Easter Monday, the corps called up in Vienna assembled in the parade-ground on the glacis. After a field mass they marched with military music down the roads to Währing and Nussdorf, so well known to-day, passing Schubert's birthplace and making for the outer ring of fortifications. This was the first public musical performance heard by the composer—aged seventy-six days.

This music, however, which doubtless included the new people's hymn, did not actually lead to battle. The seven brigades did not reach beyond the frontiers of the two districts above and below the Vienna Forest (which were part of Lower Austria); the University brigade went as far as Kritzendorf and the commercial corps, which followed on 18th April, as far as Klosterneuburg on the Danube. For on that day Bonaparte, fearing to be cut off, concluded the preliminary peace of Leoben (Styria) with Austria. On 3rd May the Viennese detachments returned, probably by the same route. Before the month was out Bonaparte returned to northern Italy, and in October 1797 the peace of Campo Formio was concluded, which cost Austria the territories of Lombardy and Flanders, but let Venetia fall to her share.

In the third War of Coalition Joachim Murat, the Emperor Napoleon's brother-in-law, conquered the capital of Austria and of the German Empire during the month of the victory of Trafalgar, October 1805. Napoleon took up residence at the pleasance of Schönbrunn. At the peace of Pressburg (Poszony) in Hungary Austria lost further territories. The Emperor Francis, who had already assumed the title of a hereditary emperor of Austria in 1804, resigned that of German emperor in 1806, thus marking the end of the old German Empire.

In 1809 Austria attempted to free Europe single-handed from the French yoke, while Napoleon appeared to be held fast in Spain; but by May he occupied Vienna for the second time and continued to hold it even after his defeat at Aspern (Lower Austria). His victory at Wagram (July) led to the Peace of Vienna in October, which once more involved Austria in territorial losses. But in April 1810 Napoleon married the Emperor Francis's daughter, the Archduchess Marie Louise.

In 1812 Francis was compelled, like the King of Prussia, to do homage at Dresden to Napoleon before his Russian campaign. The following year, however, Frederick William III called for a war of liberation, which united Austria, Prussia and Russia against France. The battle of Leipzig in October 1813 and the entry of the Allies into Paris in March 1814 decided Napoleon's doom, sealed afterwards by the battle of Waterloo.

The impressive Congress of Vienna (September 1814 to June 1815) restored all her possessions to Austria with the exception of Flanders and the so-called Rhine provinces. The Austrian Empire, as the monarchy was called since 1804, comprised roughly the territory of the later Austro-Hungarian monarchy, with Venetia, Milan and other possessions in northern Italy in addition, some 250,000 square miles in all. The fourteen provinces had more than 30,000,000 inhabitants, including about 15,000,000 Slavs and 6,000,000 Germans. Nearly 27,000,000 were Catholics. In the Napoleonic wars Austria had lost nearly a million men.

After Napoleon's frustrated *coup d'état* his son, later known as the Duke of Reichstadt (Bohemia), went to live in Vienna, where he remained until his early death in 1832.

Francis, the first as Emperor of Austria (1768–1835), was married for the fourth time in 1816, to the former consort of the Crown Prince of Württemberg, Karolina Augusta of Bavaria (1792–1873), who was belatedly crowned Queen of Hungary as well at Pressburg in 1825. He played the domestic tyrant to the family of his people, thinking and taking care of everything, but in a petty way, much concerned about the loyalty of his subjects and ruthless in his persecution of elements dangerous to the throne, whether real or, as in the case of the "Jacobins" and the freemasons, imaginary. His counsellor from 1809 was Clemens, Prince Metternich, an astute but not a wise chancellor, whose system led to revolution in 1848, not only in Austria but in Europe at large. Metternich's tool from 1817 was the chief of police, Josef, Count Sedlnitzky, and the two were not particularly fastidious in the choice of ways and means. The censorship of books (including music with words) and newspapers, the prohibition of gymnastic associations, the surveillance of the universities, etc., were proposed by Metternich to the ministerial conference of the new German Federation at Carlsbad in 1819 and sanctioned by the federal diet at Frankfort-on-Main.

The upper nobility, which preserved a certain degree of independence towards the court, consisted of princes and counts as well as *Freiherren* (barons) of the older order. In the Vienna of 1825 there were about twenty princely, seventy lordly and sixty baronial families. The income of a princely house amounted to 100,000–150,000 florins a year in assimilated coinage (in which ten florins were worth about £1); that of a wealthy lordly house was 20,000–80,000 florins. The secondary, so-called Leonine (meaning approximately "silk-and-cotton") nobility consisted of knights, squires, *Edle von* and *Herren von*, and consisted mainly of officers and officials, but also included ennobled manufacturers, wholesale merchants and bankers, who would not be acknowledged by the old high aristocracy even if, like Fries, they attained to the rank of count. The ennobled merchants were mostly immigrants from Switzerland and Germany who had embraced Catholicism.

The court had a Lord High Steward, to whom, among others, the members of the court chapel and of the court library as well as the "Court Music Count" were subordinate; also a Lord Chamberlain, who among other things supervised the art collections and the court theatres.

The administration of the autocratic system was in the hands of three court chancelleries in Vienna: the United (Austro-Bohemian, Galician and Italian), the Royal Hungarian and the Royal Transylvanian; and further in those of the governments of the fourteen counties and provinces. There were government, county and municipal officials, who in Vienna alone numbered 4,000–5,000.

Austria-Hungary. Section of a Map, designed by K. J. Kipferling, engraved by F. Reisser. Vienna 1803

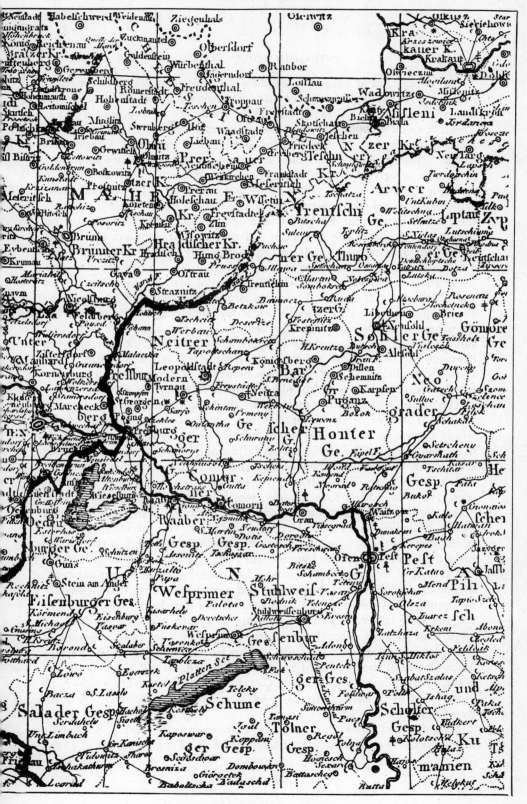

The population of Vienna (excluding the garrison), which had already reached 270,000 by 1788, but had temporarily gone down as far as 230,000 during the following war years, amounted to 290,000 in 1824. About 50,000 people lived in the inner city, and they included the picturesque figures of non-German inhabitants, especially Greeks and Turks. The number of foreigners settled permanently in Vienna amounted to 40,000 as early as 1802. The city, a semicircle cut off by the Danube Canal, a regulated branch of the river, was fortified. The wall and moat, called bastion and glacis, dated back to the Middle Ages, and it is said that the English ransom for Richard Cœur de Lion had helped to pay for the fortress, which was the European bulwark of Christendom against the heathenish oriental perils. It served particularly against the Turks from 1529 onwards, and it was due to them that in 1704 the suburbs too were included in the fortified area, which was surrounded by the outer ring of walls, called the *Linienwall*, forming a larger semicircle and joining on to the Danube itself. The Leopoldstadt alone, including the Prater and the Augarten, which lies between the Danube and the canal and was often subject to inundations, remained largely unfortified and, like the outlying districts, had to be left in the lurch when there was serious trouble. The French demolished part of the bastion before their departure in 1809, but it was restored in 1816–17 to relieve a serious shortage of work.

The glacis, which is now replaced by the Ringstrasse, was 600 paces in width. The area of the inner city was about 400,000 and that of the whole town some 8,500,000 square fathoms (roughly four times as much in square yards). The 127 streets and alleys of the inner city were narrow; they comprised about 1,200 houses (not counting churches), most of which were tall. Through the twelve gates in the bastion radiating roads led to the thirty-four suburbs, which had more than 7,000 houses. These roads continued through the gates of the outer wall (now replaced by the "Girdle" and by the city railway) farther out into the outer districts, most of them villages at the foot of the Vienna Forest, a spur of the eastern Alps ending on the Danube near Nussdorf (one of those villages).

The cost of living on the Continent had risen by ten to fifteen per cent, owing to the Napoleonic wars, yet still remained below that in Britain by about twenty-five per cent. In spite of the dearths of 1803 and 1809 and the state bankruptcy of 1811, living in Vienna was cheaper again by 1820 than in most other large continental cities. In 1825 a pound of beef cost 6 kreuzer (c. 2½d.)—in London nearly three times as much—lunch at one of the good inns 20–40 kreuzer (8d.–1s. 4d.), at one of the better eating-houses 2–4 florins, A.C. (4s.–8s.). A tankard of beer—c. 2½ pints—cost 6–14 kreuzer (c. 2½d.–6d.), according to quality. (A florin was divided into 60 kreuzer.)

Lodgings and firewood alone were comparatively dear. Schubert's furnished room on the glacis cost 6 florins, A.C., (12s.) a month in 1825.

Vienna in those days had eighty-four coffee-houses—the meeting-places most favoured by men—where all kinds of hot and cold refreshments but no meals were to be had. Genuine coffee, temporarily cut off since 1810 by Napoleon's continental blockade or by special import bans, was obtainable again from 1813 onwards. There were some two thousand private carriages, over six hundred cabs, sixty unnumbered four-wheelers for hire, twelve hundred open wagonettes plying outside the outer walls and twenty middle-class coaches for single passengers to drive into the country. Sedan chairs were reduced to thirty-seven, but there were also new omnibuses running out of the city.

Catholic Vienna had eighteen churches and eight convents in the inner city, and thirty churches and eight convents in the suburbs. The sixteen convents included thirteen monasteries and three nunneries. The fee at the elementary schools, of which there were five within and fifty-five without, was 3 florins (6s.) a year.

There were five theatres in Vienna in those days: the court theatre near the imperial residence (*Burg*), called the Burg Theatre for short, which was the best German theatre for spoken plays; the court theatre next to the Carinthian Gate (*Kärntnertor*), known as the Kärntnertor Theatre, which was an opera-house subject to strong Italian influences and possessing a good ballet; the Theatre on the Wien (a tributary of the Danube), called *Theater an der Wien* and built by Schikaneder to take the place of his former Theatre on the Wieden (*Freihaus-Theater* or *Theater auf der Wieden*); the Leopoldstadt Theatre; and the smaller Josefstadt Theatre. These last three suburban theatres were privately owned, and cultivated both spoken plays—mainly comedies—and opera, often amounting to no more than plays with incidental music. The place of the Viennese clown Johann Laroche, whom Nelson applauded at the Leopoldstadt Theatre as late as the year 1800, was taken by Ferdinand Raimund with his fairy-tale plays, for which music was furnished by various composers, including the highly gifted Wenzel Müller. Prices of admission varied between about 20 kreuzer and 1 florin, A.C. (8d.–2s.).

Concerts were held in the large and the small assembly hall (*Redouten-saal*), the court ballrooms of the Hofburg; at the great hall of the University (facing the old Jesuit college housing the new City Seminary); in the County Hall (*Landhaussaal*), where the Lower Austrian County Council held its sessions; also in the Philharmonic Society's hall or at the Roman Emperor Inn (*Zum römischen Kaiser*). Admission was usually 1–2 florins (2s.–4s.).

The foreign languages most assiduously cultivated were Italian (among artists) and French (among the aristocracy). English had considerably declined since Mozart's time, or more precisely since about 1785, when there had been an English colony in Vienna and the native snobs had indulged in fits of Anglomania. On the other hand English fashions in furniture and dress (at any rate among men) had to a great extent ousted French. In portraiture the best Viennese painters, such as Füger and Daffinger in miniature and the two Lampi and Amerling in oil-painting, were pupils of the English masters. "Ossian," Shakespeare and Scott were translated and much read. Shakespeare was made topical at the Burg Theatre by the political censorship, which even in such works as 'Richard III' and 'King Lear' took exception to anything that might be thought to allude even remotely to contemporary circumstances, particularly those prevailing in the reigning house.

The indigenous dance of the Viennese was the waltz, which had driven back the French minuet and was soon to do the same with the écossaise, as also with the polonaise, which had become fashionable at court during the Congress. Dancing was so much the rage that on the Thursday before Carnival Sunday of 1821, for instance, sixteen hundred balls took place in a single night. This did not include the inns, where there was, especially in the suburbs, music daily and, of course, dancing too during the carnival. In the spring of 1818 the first theatre *ridotto* was held at the Theater an der Wien, then the largest of Vienna's playhouses. To the assembly halls, which were opened for public masked balls, had been added the hall at the Sperl in the Leopoldstadt and the sumptuous Apollo Rooms on the Schottenfeld. At private balls, even in the aristocratic houses, dancing during the carnival generally went on until six or eight in the morning.

The cultivation of the sciences had a mainly practical aim under Francis I's matter-of-fact reign. Literature, at any rate German literature, did not arouse any particular interest in Austrian aristocratic society, which inclined far more towards the plastic arts and, needless to say, towards music. For all that the romantic school of German literature flourished especially in Vienna, and Austria's own poetry, with Grillparzer at the head, began to unfold itself. Classical literature, and Goethe in particular, was probably better known to the new bourgeoisie of the *Vormärz*, the pre-revolutionary period of 1815 to March 1848, than to the aristocracy.

In the cultivation of music the educated bourgeoisie had begun to enter into competition with the nobility, and it came to assume leadership there. Every house had a pianoforte; the banker von Geymüller, who was blessed with many daughters, had no fewer than five of these instruments. The emperor was no enthusiastic patron of music, though he played in a string quartet of his own. The noble families rarely had their own orchestras, as in the eighteenth century, and their chamber music was no longer performed by musical servants, but by professional musicians invited for the purpose. The place of the "Society of Associated Cavaliers" (consisting of three princes and three counts), which had begun the cultivation of Handel in Vienna in 1786–91 with Gottfried van Swieten as secretary, was taken by the middle-class Philharmonic Society (*Gesell-*

schaft der Musikfreunde), which likewise began its functions with Handel in 1814. But instead of a small body of performers listened to by a select audience in the stately hall of the court library, the new events were monster concerts held for monster audiences in the huge winter riding-school at the Hofburg. Opposed to this was the bourgeoisie's cultivation of music, which was maintained not only in the family circle (as in the Schuberts' home), but also by groups of friendly amateurs which often developed into veritable musical *salons*. Leopold von Sonnleithner, in his 'Musikalische Skizzen aus Alt-Wien,' refers to five such *salons* as dating back to the eighteenth century and to eighteen that were newly formed. Between these extremes there were semi-public organizations like the Philharmonic Society's evening entertainments or gatherings of connoisseurs like the *Concert spirituel*; and besides there was Catholic church music of high excellence, especially in the court chapel. Add to this the vigorous music publishing, the competent instrument making (particularly on the part of pianoforte manufacturers), the serenades favoured ever since the eighteenth century, the music of the military bands, the little string orchestras conducted by the elder Strauss and by Lanner, the harp players in the Prater and organ-grinders on the high roads, the musical boxes in public places and private houses, and it will be understood that Vienna had truly become the musical metropolis in Schubert's time. And that proved to be more lastingly impressive than the honour of being the capital of a great country, or even of two great countries.

Austria's Coat of Arms

SCHUBERT'S ANCESTORS

Franz Schubert is regarded, apart from Johann Strauss, as the only native Viennese among the numerous masters who have made Vienna the metropolis of music. Yet his parents, like those of so many great Viennese of the eighteenth and nineteenth centuries, had migrated to the capital from the Austrian provinces.

Schubert's father originated from Moravia, his mother from Austrian Silesia. Both were brought to Vienna by fortuitous circumstances. That they met there was one of musical history's strokes of good fortune.

The name Schubert means shoemaker, and it can be traced back to the fifteenth century. Franz's earliest ancestor is attested in the year 1629: the patriarch Kaspar Schubert of Waltersdorf in northern Moravia, in the region of the Spieglitzer Schneeberg. His second son, Christoph, moved with his family to the neighbouring Neudorf (near Schönberg in the Altstadt district of Moravia) c. 1665 and advanced from the station of cottager to that of farmer. Hans, the youngest of his nine children, became Franz's great-grandfather. Hans Schubert, who also had numerous children, seems to have been a woodman. In the *Auenhäusl*, at the edge of the Hochwald, of which he later became the owner, yet another son was born to him: Karl, Franz's grandfather, who in 1754 married Susanna Mück, bought his father's house and later his father-in-law's farm land. From 1780 onward this prosperous and pious citizen of Neudorf also filled the office of senior juror. Only four of his thirteen children survived the high rate of infant mortality of the time, among them Karl, who was born in 1755, and as first-born should, according to the custom of those days, have followed his father as farmer; and a younger son, Franz Theodor Florian, born in 1763—the composer's father.

A peasant's son of Seibersdorf, in the parish of Neudorf, Andreas Becker by name, migrated to Vienna about 1765 and became a schoolmaster in the Leopoldstadt suburb. He married there the daughter of his predecessor at the Carmelite School. Becker may have induced Karl Schubert to follow the same path. He did it so thoroughly that in 1778, as Becker's successor, he married his widow, Anna, who was almost twice Karl's age. About 1783 Franz Theodor Florian followed his brother; he was, in 1784-5, his school assistant, but already in 1785 we find him lodging in the Liechtental suburb. In that year he married Elisabeth Vietz, who was his senior and bore him fourteen children, Franz being the twelfth. (The composer's father had five surviving children of that union, and four out of the five of his second marriage; his son Ferdinand had twenty-eight children of two marriages, twelve of whom survived.) Three months after Anna Schubert's death Karl married, in 1792, Maria Magdalena Vietz, Elisabeth's younger sister. She bore him seven children, and when he died in 1804 two daughters survived him, one of whom, Magdalena, lived to become the composer's playmate. Franz's father, in fact, took his dead brother's family into his school house in the Säulengasse, Himmelpfortgrund, and for a time also his brother-in-law Felix Vietz and his family. Maria Magdalena Schubert remained there when Franz Schubert, senior, migrated into the Rossau suburb and died in 1829 at the family house, which had already been sold.

The Vietz family, Schubert's maternal ancestors, can be traced back to 1590 as citizens of the old mountain town of Zuckmantel in northeastern Silesia. They were smiths at first, and Martin Vietz, Franz Schubert's forefather, was called "Master of the Smithy" in 1654. His son Christoph was Franz's great-great-grandfather and had one son among others who became a locksmith and gunmaker. This Valentin Vietz, Franz's great-grandfather, married a huntsman's daughter. Her brother was town organist for forty years and his son a *virtuosus fidicen*. Valentin, too, like his father, had several sons, and Franz Johann, Schubert's grandfather, was likewise a locksmith and gunmaker; but in later years he advanced to the dignity of head toast-master to the locksmiths and blacksmiths, and even of sheriff. Franz Johann Vietz, who also, like his forbears, followed the subsidiary calling of farmer, endured even greater strokes of ill fortune than they—wars and fires—that befell the township. The Seven Years War between Austria and Prussia, between Maria Theresa and Frederick the Great, thrust him deeply into debt, and in his despair he yielded to the temptation of tampering with the guild moneys, which was a capital crime. He was imprisoned on trial, kept long in the municipal jail, and even threatened with torture. Although he was never convicted, he had to leave his old family home in disgrace and reached Vienna in beggary, where he died soon afterwards (about 1770). His wife and children seem to have followed him there immediately: the wife probably died on the way; the aforesaid son Felix became a weaver in Vienna, while the two daughters went into domestic service. The fact that the brother and sisters settled in the neighbourhood of Liechtental may have been due to its flourishing weaving trade. It was here that Elisabeth Vietz came to know and to love the school assistant Franz Schubert senior.

The Vietz family were more sanguine than the Schuberts and more artistically gifted, even if only as craftsmen. The Schuberts were the pious and respectable part of the mixture. To these two families we owe Franz Schubert, and, above all, to the fate which brought those two immigrants together in Vienna. Schubert never saw his parents' home; he never visited Moravia and Silesia, nor Bohemia.

N.B.—In 1928, when the centenary of Schubert's death was celebrated, about 150 descendants of his brothers and sisters were alive, among them the well-known pianist Miss Carola Geisler-Schubert in London. For this computation, as also for most of the data concerning Schubert's ancestors, we are indebted to Herr Franz Köhler of Vienna.

Vienna's Coat of Arms (1461)

PRENATAL RECORDS

1785-96

A. FROM THE MARRIAGE REGISTER of the Parish of 'The Fourteen Friends in Need' in the Viennese suburb of Liechtental

17th January 1785.

Josephus Hollpein, sen., Co-operator.

Bridegroom: Franz Schubert, a school assistant, native of Neudorf in Moravia, farmer's son, Liechtental No. 152, 25 years.

Bride: Elisabeth Vietz, native of Zuckmantel in Imp. Silesia, master locksmith's daughter, Liechtental No. 152, 28 years.

Witnesses: Ignaz Wagner, shoe-maker, Karl Schubert, a schoolmaster.

Franz Schubert, sen., who in those days was still assistant schoolmaster at his brother Karl's in the Leopoldstadt suburb (Brunngasse), is here actually described as "instructor." It may be that, having himself passed through six grammar-school classes, he was already giving supplementary lessons in Latin in order to augment his income. He lived at Liechtental with his bride, now 20 Badgasse (rebuilt).

B. FROM THE 'REGISTER OF BIRTHS AND DEATHS in the Family of the Schoolmaster Franz Schubert'

(1) Ignaz Franz, born 8th March 1785, 5.30 a.m.

(2) Elisabeth, born 1st March 1786, 5.45 a.m., died 13th August 1788, 7 a.m.

Franz Schubert, sen., is appointed schoolmaster in the Himmelpfortgrund, No. 12, on 13th June 1786.—He had been assistant for five years, three of them probably in his Moravian homeland and two in Vienna. The school was probably situated already in the Säulengasse (later No. 10, now No. 3), and the house was called "The Black Horse" ("Zum schwarzen Rössel"). It is said that not till 1796 did the elder Schubert move from Liechtental to the Himmelfortgrund, to the house No. 72 in the Upper High Street (now 54 Nussdorferstrasse), called "The Red

Crayfish" ("Zum roten Krebsen"), Schubert's birthplace, the court-yard and garden of which are preserved. On the first floor a museum has been maintained by the City of Vienna since 1912. The suburbs of Himmelpfortgrund—86 houses in 9 streets with more than 3,000 inhabitants—Thury, Althan and Michelbeurn'scher Grund, also belonged to the parish of Liechtental, but their elementary school was in the Him-melpfortgrund. It had a bad reputation when the elder Schubert suc-ceeded to it, so that he had for the most part to instruct poor children gratis. The name of the suburb (literally Ground of the Heavenly Gate) is explained by the fact that canonesses at the "Himmelpforte," a convent in the inner city (disestablished under Joseph II), had been granted proprietary rights in the land of the village formerly named Sporkenbüchel, destroyed by the Turks in 1529.

(3) Karl, born 23rd April 1787, 1.30 p.m., died 6th February 1788, 7 a.m.

On 16th December [recte 24th] 1787, at 3.30 a.m., died my dearly loved and venerated father Karl Schubert.

A small inheritance was swallowed up in the costs of fitting up the school (96 florins) and the rent for it; indeed the elder Schubert was obliged to borrow additional money for this.

(4) Franziska Magdalena, born 6th June 1788, 1.30 a.m., died 14th August 1788, after 11 o'clock in the evening.

(5) Franziska Magdalena, born 5th July 1789, 2 a.m., died 1st January 1792, 8.30 a.m.

(6) Franz Karl, born 10th August 1790, 6 p.m., died 19th September 1790, 10.45 a.m.

(7) Anna Karoline, born 11th July 1791, 11.15 a.m., died 29th July 1791, 7 a.m.

Mozart dies, 5th December 1791.

C. FROM THE MARRIAGE REGISTER of the Parish of St. Joseph at the Carmelites in the Leopoldstadt Suburb

7th May 1792.

Father Adolphus Dobera, Co-operator.

Bridegroom: Schubert, Karl, civil schoolmaster, No. 408, here, Catholic, 38 years.

Bride: Maria Magdalena Vietz, legitimate daughter of
             Karl (*recte* Franz Johann) Vietz, master locksmith
             of Zuckmantel in Silesia and Elisabeth Riedl,
             No. 408, 27 years, Catholic.

Witnesses: Anton Sterzing, Scribe to the Lower-Austrian
             Government; Franz Schubert in the Himmel-
             pfortgrund.

D. FROM THE FAMILY REGISTER OF SCHUBERT'S FATHER

(8) Petrus, born 29th June 1792, 1.15 a.m., died 14th January
                1793, 5.30 a.m.

Beethoven comes to Vienna, early November 1792.

E. FROM THE FAMILY REGISTER OF SCHUBERT'S FATHER

(9) Josef, born 16th September 1793, 12.15 a.m., died 18th
              October 1798, midnight.

(10) Ferdinand Lukas, born 18th October 1794, 3.30 a.m.

(11) Franz Karl, born 5th November 1795, 12.15 a.m.

Franz Schubert, sen., applies unsuccessfully for the schoolmaster's
post at St. Leopold, in the Leopoldstadt suburb, Grosse Pfarrgasse,
31st January 1796.

Coat of Arms of the Vienna Suburb
Himmelpfortgrund (1825). Lithograph by Anton Jung (1829)

THE LIFE

1797-1809

1. From the 'Register of Births and Deaths in the Family of the Schoolmaster Franz Schubert'

(12) Franz Peter, born 31st January 1797, 1.30 p.m., baptized 1st February.

Schubert's sister, Maria Theresia Schneider, wrote in October 1865 to her daughter Therese Krasser that her father told her his first fourteen children were born in an alcove on the first floor. The room was probably one adjacent to the courtyard.

2. From the Register of Births of the Parish of 'The Fourteen Friends in Need' at the Liechtental Suburb

Name of the Baptist: Rev. Wanzka.

Year, Month, Day: 1797, February, 1st.

Domicile and No. of House: Himmelpfortgrund, No. 72.

Name of the Baptized: Franz Peter.

Religion, Catholic: 1 [yes].

Sex, male: 1.

Legitimate: 1.

Parents:

 Father's Name and Station or

  Character: Schubert, Franz, schoolmaster.

 Mother's Christian and Sur-

  names: Elisabeth, *née* Vietz.

Godparents, Name: Karl Schubert.

   Station: Schoolmaster.

Remarks: [None].

Franz Schubert, sen., applies, again unsuccessfully, for a post at the school of St. Augustine in the Landstrasse suburb, 15th March 1797.

Franz Schubert, sen., applies without success for a post at the school of St. Stephen in the City, 16th December 1797.

Schubert's brother Josef dies, 18th October 1798.

3. FROM THE FAMILY REGISTER of Schubert's Father

(13) Aloisia Magdalena, born 17th December 1799, at 3.15 a.m., died 18th December 1799, after 6 a.m.

The school in the Himmelpfortgrund assigns the sum of 25 florins 58 kreuzer, collected by its catechist, the co-operator Martin Rössner, and the schoolmaster Franz Schubert, to the German Chief School Inspectorate for the army under a new levy for the defence against Napoleon (official 'Wiener Zeitung,' 31st January 1801). Josef Lanner born, 11th April 1801.

4. FROM THE REGISTER OF PROPERTY, Municipality of Vienna

Franz Schubert and Elisabeth, his wife, are granted the use and occupation of a house on the manor of Sporkenbüchl, *sub No. 14*, called the Black Horse, situate between the houses of Matthias Rutner and Matthias Schwindl. For the which they are to pay the Imperial and Royal Estate of Himmelpforte annually at Michaelmas 45 Kreuzer, and no more. Further they will pay five florins per annum regularly in rent, in addition to all other estate, sovereign and customary fees. . . . For the said premises . . . Elisabeth Mölzer was formerly alone responsible in the Register of Property, but she assigned the said premises, in accordance with a purchase contract entered into under date of 14th May 1801 . . . to the persons named above against a purchase exchange of 3,200 florins. Vienna, 27th May 1801. . . .

If Maria Theresia Schubert (*see* No. 5) was born in the old lodgings, the family cannot have moved to their own house before the autumn of 1801 at the earliest. Schubert, of course, went to his father's school (*c.* 1803–8).

5. FROM THE FAMILY REGISTER of Schubert's Father

(14) Maria Theresia, born 17th September 1801, 2.45 a.m.

Johann Strauss I born, 14th March 1804.
Schubert's uncle, Karl Schubert, dies, 29th December 1804. Schubert's father applies, again without success, for the post thus vacated to the Carmelites in the Leopoldstadt, March 1805.

Vienna is occupied by the French, 13th November 1805 to 13th January 1806. Napoleon resides at the palace of Schönbrunn.

Schubert's grandmother, Susanna Schubert, dies at Neudorf, 6th August 1806, aged 75.

6. From the Official 'Wiener Zeitung,' 28th May 1808

ANNOUNCEMENT

Two boy choristers' appointments having to be newly filled in the I. & R. Court Chapel, those who wish to obtain these posts are to present themselves on 30th September, at 3 p.m., at the I. & R. Seminary, 796 Universitätsplatz, and to undergo an examination, as regards both the progress made by them in their studies and such knowledge as they may have already gained in music, and to bring their school certificates with them. Competitors must have completed their tenth year and be able to enter the first grammar class. Should the boys received at the Seminary distinguish themselves in morals and studies, they are to remain there, according to Imperial decree, after mutation of the voice; otherwise they are to leave after mutation of the voice. Vienna, 24th May 1808.

I. & R. = Imperial & Royal (actually K.k. = Imperial Royal).

7. From the Official 'Wiener Zeitung,' 3rd August 1808

VACANT POST FOR A SOPRANO IN THE I. & R. SEMINARY

At the end of the present school-year the post for a soprano will fall vacant at the I. & R. Seminary. Whosoever wishes to obtain this place for his son or ward is to prove to the directorate of the said Seminary, where an examination is to be held on 1st October, at 9 a.m., that the candidate is fit to enter the first Latin class, possesses a good voice and has been well instructed in singing. For the present, however, certificates are to be submitted to the said directorate concerning the candidate's progress during the last two terms and his bodily health, as also that he is past the danger of small-pox.

From the I. & R. Lower-Austrian Government. Vienna, 11th July 1808.

Jos. Schürer v. Waldheim, Secretary.

The I. & R. City Seminary (K.k. Stadtkonvikt) was founded in 1803
by Francis II (Francis I as Emperor of Austria from 1804) as an educational
institution.   It was to replace the earlier Imperial Seminary at St.
Barbara, governed by the Jesuits, which, like all other similar establish-
ments, had been dissolved by the Emperor Joseph II.   (The name of
"Konvikt" was derived from the Latin *convictorium*=a communal house.)
The new institution, named after the inner city to distinguish it from the
Löwenberg Seminary for scholars of the nobility in the Josefstadt suburb,
restored as early as 1801, was housed in the old university building
opposite the new hall and next to the Jesuit church.   It was, like the
Löwenberg Seminary, under the direction of the holy order of the
Pii Fratres (Piarists).   The seminarists, most of them foundationers, were
primary scholars who attended the neighbouring grammar-school (preparatory school for the university) and undergraduates at the university,
medical students excepted.   The teaching of the grammar-school was done
by the prefects of the Seminary, i.e. the brethren of the order.   Among
the seminarists were also the choir-boys of the court chapel in the imperial
palace, sent by the court, as well as older singers and musicians supplied
by two special endowments, and required to furnish tenors, basses
and violinists to the church in the square called "Am Hof."   There
were some 130 boarders, many of them sons of noble army officers
and officials, divided into seven houses.   Each house had a room for
the prefect, a hall for study and a dormitory.   There was an insignificant library and a collection of minerals (actually various specimens of
nature belonging to the grammar-school and only housed here).   French
and Italian were not obligatory subjects: neither were drawing, calligraphy and music.   For the choir-boys, however, music was of course
obligatory, and as the director, Dr. Franz Innocenz Lang (born Marchegg,
Lower Austria, 1752), though not a musician himself, was a great music-
lover, he soon saw to it that instruments and music were procured.
(The collection of music, which had a bookplate of its own, was also
contributed to by Josef von Spaun, who sometimes went hungry in order
to be able to procure new works, and who in 1808 returned home to
Linz on foot because he had sacrificed the money for his journey for two
Beethoven symphonies.)   Almost daily there were musical practices
at fixed hours, and the City Seminary soon had an orchestra that was
worth hearing, and was indeed gladly listened to on the University
Square through the open windows.   Once, shortly before Schubert's
admission, it even played at Schönbrunn palace before the Archduke
Rudolf and Beethoven, who was visiting his imperial pupil.   The
seminarists had a uniform of their own, not so much as a distinction
as for the purpose of their control in the streets.   It consisted of an
old-fashioned, low three-cornered hat, a white neckerchief, an open
coat of dark brown colour with a small gilt epaulet on the left shoulder,

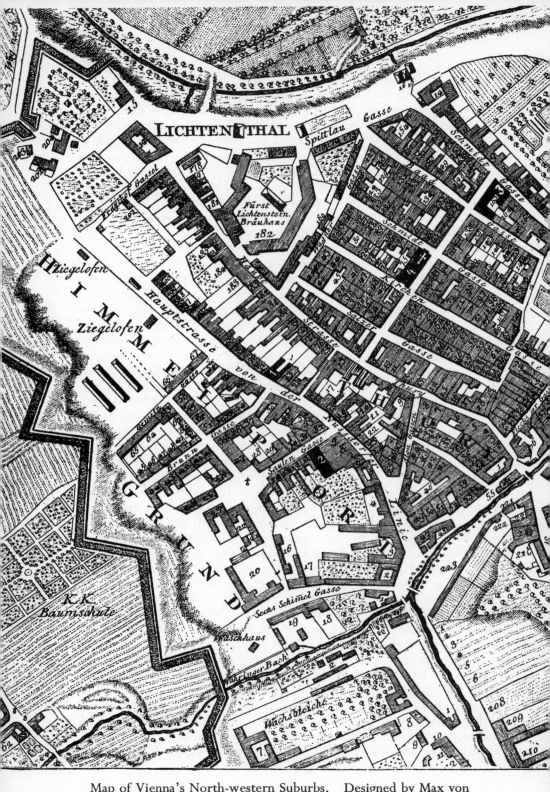

Map of Vienna's North-western Suburbs.   Designed by Max von Grimm, engraved by Hieronymus Benedetti.   Vienna 1797

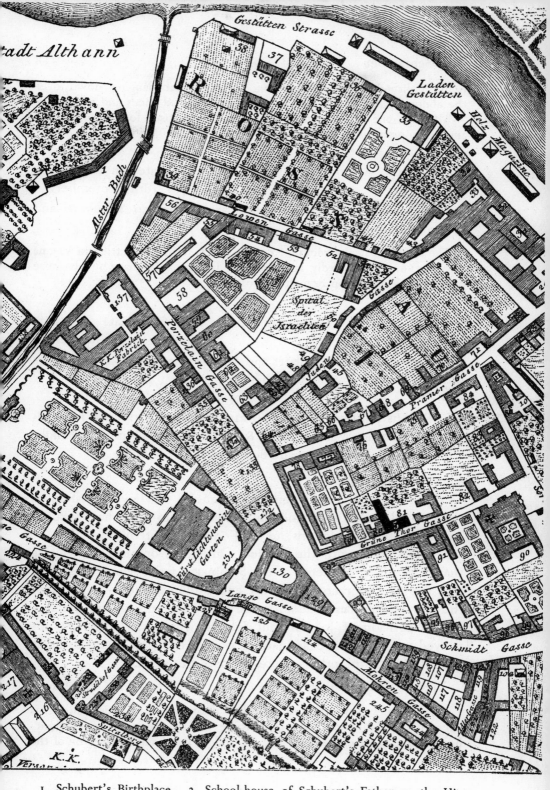

1. Schubert's Birthplace.   2. School-house of Schubert's Father on the Himmelpfortgrund.   3. House of Therese Grob's Mother.   4. Liechtental Church.
5. School-house of Schubert's Father in the Rossau

light, polished buttons, an outmoded waistcoat hanging down over the abdomen, knickerbockers with straps, buckled shoes and no sword. —Although one soprano and one alto were advertised for in No. 6 here another soprano is required.

8. From Antonio Salieri's Lost Certificate (in Italian)
1808 (?) 30th September.

The best among the sopranos are Francesco Schubert and Francesco Müllner. . . .

The court musical director, Antonio Salieri, although settled in Vienna since 1766, spoke hardly anything but Italian, a language much more current in Vienna than French in those days.

9. From Innozenz Lang's Lost Certificate
1808 (?) 1st October.

The two sopranos Schubert and Müllner also excel all the others in preliminary knowledge.

10. To His Serene Highness Prince Ferdinand von Trautt-mansdorff-Weinsberg, I. & R. Conference Minister, Knight of the Golden Fleece and Supreme High Steward

Your Serene Highness,
Three places having fallen vacant among the boy choristers of the Court Chapel, an examination of competitors was held according to existent regulations, to wit, on 30th September.

I enclose herewith the Musical Director's opinion, as well as that of the Rev. Director of the Seminary; from which it is clear that the two sopranos, Schubert and Müllner, and next to them the alto Maximilian Weisse, merit preference among the others.

The petition of Johann Paul Schurz, whose son, although not proved useless at his examination, was nevertheless found to be as yet inferior to the others, is re-enclosed herewith.

Vienna, 4th October 1808.   Count v. Kuefstein.

Three places were thus to be filled altogether. Antonio Salieri, as court musical director, was responsible for the examination of choir-boys of the court chapel (*see* No. 8), and so was Lang as director of the

Seminary (*see* No. 9). Maximilian (later Ritter von) Weisse (born 1798 at Ladendorf, Lower Austria), for whom Schubert during his period at the Seminary wrote an overture for pianoforte, now lost, became a distinguished astronomer. Johann Ferdinand, Count Kuefstein (born 1752), an amateur composer, was "Hof-Musikgraf" at the time, a court appointment held by a count with musical leanings. Trauttmansdorff (born Vienna, 1749) had been Supreme Court Chamberlain since 1807. —At his examination Schubert wore a pale grey, whitish suit, so that he was thought to be a miller's son.

11. INTIMATION from the Lord High Steward's Office to the I. & R. Court Musical Count Ferdinand Count von Kuefstein

8th October 1808.

The competitive examination for the three vacant posts for boy choristers in the Court Chapel having taken place on the 30th ult., and the two sopranos Franz Schubert and Franz Müllner, as well as the alto Maximilian Weisse, having been found most suitable according to the certificates of the I. & R. Court Musical Director Salieri and the Seminary Director Lang returned enclosed, their admittance is subject to no objection.

In accordance with this the Court Musical Count will attend to all further requirements, inform the directorate of the Seminary and at the same time send a report here stating the reasons for the instructions given to Seminary Director Lang last year that—according to his statement—no altos are to be admitted, but only sopranos.

Mosel.

Ignaz Franz Mosel, with whom Schubert later came into closer touch, was then a probationer in the Lord High Steward's office.

12. LOST LETTER from Count von Kuefstein to Lang
[Middle of October 1808.]

Information that during the examination for the three vacant posts for boy choristers in the Court Chapel held on 30th September 1808 the two sopranos Franz Schubert and Franz Müllner and the alto Maximilian Weisse were found to be the most suitable and accepted for admittance to the Seminary.

Johann Georg Albrechtsberger dies, 7th March 1809.

13. ATTESTATION to the Moral Conduct and the Progress in their Studies and in Music of the Court Chapel Choir-Boys in the I. & R. Seminary, 1st Term, 1809

Name	Morals	Studies	Singing	Pianoforte	Violin	Remarks
Schubert Franz	v. good	good	v. good	good	v. good	A musical talent

Vienna, 17th April 1809.   Lang,
                                        Director of the I. & R. Seminary.

14. COUNT KUEFSTEIN to Prince Trauttmansdorff

Your Serene Highness,

The Director of the Seminary has forwarded me the enclosed attestation to the moral conduct and the progress in their studies and in music of the Court choir-boys for the first term of this year, which I humbly submit to Your Serene Highness for your gracious perusal, with the remark that most of them have so far rendered themselves worthy of full satisfaction. The two boys Weisse and Müllner, who in some respects still figure as no more than mediocre, are those who were admitted last, so that it would seem reasonable to hope that they too will endeavour, as they go on, to equal their colleagues.

Vienna, 20th April 1809.   Count v. Kuefstein.

The progress of the court choir-boys was reported to the court in special statements, apart from the ordinary school certificates. Both certificates were made out twice a year, according to the two Austrian school-terms. Holidays occurred in the autumn, but the choir-boys were sent home only in rotation.

> Vienna is again occupied by the French. After a short siege, 9th–13th May 1809, they enter the city and remain until 20th October. During the bombardment of the inner city the building of the Seminary is pierced by a howitzer grenade in the evening of 11th May 1809. Napoleon again resides at Schönbrunn. During that time the orchestral practices at the Seminary are interrupted.

In September 1809 Schubert's friend Josef von Spaun leaves the Seminary.

Haydn dies, 31st May 1809.

15. CATALOGUE FOR THE SCHOOL-YEAR 1809 concerning the Scholars of the First Grammar Class at the University Preparatory School. For the First and Second Terms. By the Professors of Religion, Josef Tranz, of Grammar, Pius Strauch, and the Preceptors of Mathematics and Natural History, Walch, and Geography and History, Rittmannsberger

Name and Age of the Youth	Country, Birthplace, Domicile	Name and Occupation of Parents	Morals	Application	Progress						Stipendiary, Foundation Scholar, Paying Scholar	Remarks
					Religious Instruction	Latin Language and Style	Mathematics	Natural History and Physics	Geography and History	Greek		
Schubert Franz 11	Orientation No. City 796	Franz, School-master	1 1	1 1	1 1	1 1	1 1	1 1	1 1	— —	Foundation Scholar, I. & R. Seminary	

The catalogues of the preparatory school were also preserved in print. The houses in the inner city, about 1,000 of them, were numbered consecutively, not street by street; so were those of the separate suburbs.

16. LIST OF THE CHOIR-BOYS of the I. & R. Court Chapel in Respect of their Morals and their Application to Studies and the Various Branches of Music, Second Term, 1809

Name	Morals	Studies	Singing	Violin	Pianoforte	[Remark]
Schubert Franz	g.	g.	v. g.	v. g.	v. g.	A special musical talent

[29th October 1809.]   Lang,
                              Director of the I. & R. Seminary.

17. Lang to Count Kuefstein

Right Honourable Court Music Count,

I have the honour to forward enclosed for your kind further conveyance the list of the choir-boys of the I. &. R. Court Chapel in respect of their morals and their application, with the observation that the pianoforte master Ruzicka continued even in this agitated half-year, with his usual commendable zeal, especially to instruct the boys by means of extra lessons in the various branches of music, for their better advancement.

Vienna, 29th October 1809.   Lang,
Director of the I. & R. Seminary.

Wenzel Ruzicka, viola player at the Burg Theatre and court organist, was piano and organ master at the Seminary; he also instructed the boys in viola and cello playing, as the case might be, and even in thorough-bass (Schubert, 1811). For this he received 100 florins to begin with. He visited the institution twice daily, and had established the Seminary orchestra, which he conducted, later to be replaced at times by Schubert, of whom he said: "This one's learnt it from God." The violin was taught by Ferdinand Hofmann at the Seminary, and singing by Philipp Korner. In the orchestra, which played a symphony and one or two overtures each evening, at first without trumpets and trombones, Schubert soon played first violin; Josef van Spaun played second; Anton Holzapfel of Vienna, grammar-school boy and later law student, also played second violin at first, and later the cello; among the violins were also Anton Hauer and Leopold Ebner, the latter a Tyrolese; the first flute was Franz Eckel, the first clarinet Josef Kleindl. Max von Spaun, a cellist, and the future composer Benedikt Randhartinger, who looked after the drums presented by the vice-director Franz Schönberger, entered only after Schubert had left. According to George von Thaa, a seminarist of the time, the orchestra consisted of 6 first and 6 second violins, 2 cellos, 2 double basses, 2 flutes, 2 oboes, 2 clarinets, 2 bassoons, 2 horns, trumpets (!) and drums. Among Schubert's closer associates were also Michael Rueskäfer, Josef Kenner, Albert Stadler, Franz Werner and Josef Beskiba. Some of these grammar-school pupils and undergraduates had come from the Seminary of the Kremsmünster monastery in Upper Austria, and they formed the nucleus of the first Schubert circle.

18. COUNT KUEFSTEIN to Prince Trauttmansdorff

Your Serene Highness,

By the enclosed list the Director of the Seminary has informed me, in accordance with the regulations, of the application of the ten choir-boys in the I. & R. Seminary, with the observation that the pianoforte master Ruzicka continued with his usual commendable zeal, even in this troublous half-year, to give special instruction in the various branches of music by means of extra lessons.

Although Ruzicka is under no obligation to work at anything beyond the pianoforte, it does this man the more honour that, apart from that instrument, the I. & R. Seminary is indebted to him for a tolerably well organized band, including even wind instruments.   I therefore feel it to be incumbent on me to recommend him to the good graces of Your Serene Highness.

Vienna, 10th November 1809.   Count v. Kuefstein.

19. INTIMATION to the I. & R. Court Music Count
28th November 1809.

. . . Johann Wisgrill is to be commended for good progress in his studies and Franz Schubert for his exemplary application to the art of music, whereas Franz Müllner and Max Weisse are to be seriously enjoined to make themselves worthy of similar satisfaction by greater industry.

The news of the laudable zeal of the pianoforte master Ruzicka is welcomed as being agreeable.

Mosel.

20. LOST LETTER from Count Kuefstein to Lang
[4th December 1809.]

Information that in accordance with the gracious Imperial decision arrived at with regard to the statement of the application of the choir-boys of the Court Chapel housed in the Seminary, forwarded to the Lord High Steward's Office, Johann Wisgrill and Franz Schubert are to be commended, i.e. the former for good progress in his studies, the latter for his exemplary application to the art of music.

1810

Fantasy for Pianoforte Duet (ix. 30), 8th April–1st May.

---

21. CONCERNING THE MORAL CONDUCT and Progress in their Studies and in Music of the Court Choristers in the I. & R. Seminary, First Term, 1810

Name	Morals	Studies	Singing	Pianoforte	Violin	Remarks
Schubert Franz	g.	g.	v. g.	v. g.	v. g.	A musical talent

[Early May 1810.]   Lang,
Government Counciller and Director
of the I. & R. Seminary.

22. COUNT KUEFSTEIN to Prince Trauttmansdorff

Your Serene Highness,
Enclosed I have the honour of forwarding, according to the regulations, the statement concerning the application of the ten boy choristers in the I. & R. Seminary, handed to me with the list by the Director of the Seminary.

Vienna, 7th May 1810.   Ferdinand, Count v. Kuefstein,
Court Music Count.

23. INTIMATION to the I. & R. Court Music Count
7th May 1810.

The statement concerning the application of the Court choir-boys in the I. & R. Seminary, enclosed with the [Court Music Count's] report of even date, is retained for official use, and Johann Wisgrill as well as Franz Schubert is to be commended

16

by the directorate of the I. & R. Seminary, whereas Max Weisse is to be reprimanded for his lack of industry.

Mosel.

24. CATALOGUE FOR THE SCHOOL-YEAR 1810 Concerning the Scholars of the Second Grammar Class in the University Preparatory School. First and Second Terms

The Teacher of Religion, Josef Tranz.
Schönberger,   of Grammar, Pius Strauch.
Vice Director.   of Geography and History, Rittmannsberger.
                      of Mathematics and Natural History, Walch.

Name and Age of the Youth	Country, Birthplace, Domicile	Name and Occupation of Parents	Morals	Application	Religious Instruction	Latin Language and Style	Mathematics	Natural History and Physics	Geography and History	Greek	Stipendiary, Foundation Scholar, Paying Scholar	Remarks
							Progress					
Schubert Franz	Orientation No. City 796	Franz, School-master	I	I	I	I	I	I	I	—	Foundation Scholar,	
12			em	I	I	I	I	I	I	—	I. & R. Seminary	

25. CONCERNING THE MORAL CONDUCT and Progress in their Studies and in Music of the Court Choristers in the I. & R. Seminary. Second Term, 1810

Name	Morals	Studies	Singing	Pianoforte	Violin	Remarks
Schubert, Franz	v. g.	g.	v. g.	v. g.	v. g.	A musical talent

Vienna, 23rd September 1810.

Lang,
Government Councillor and Director
of the I. & R. Seminary.

26. INTIMATION to the I. & R. Court Music Count
26th September 1810.

. . . Johann Wisgrill is apprised of the satisfaction felt here with the continuation of his praiseworthy assiduity, and care is to be taken [by the Court Music Count] that especial attention should be paid to the musical education, of Franz Schubert, since he shows so excellent a talent for the art of music.

Mosel.

'Shepherd's Complaint' ('Schäfers Klagelied'), Op. 3, No. 1 (1814). Engraved Vignette from Karl Czerny's Arrangement of Schubert's Song for Pianoforte Solo. Vienna 1838–9

1811

String Quartet in D Major (lost).
Song, 'Hagar's Lament' ('Hagars Klage'), 30th March.
Overture for String Quintet (unpublished), 29th June–
12th July.

———

Count Joseph Karl Dietrichstein is appointed curator of the City
and Löwenberg Seminaries 25th January 1811.—Owing to the
bankruptcy of the Austrian State caused by the wars with
France an emergency currency was introduced on 15th March
1811. Paper money was reduced to one-fifth of its nominal
value, and converted into a new State paper currency, the so-
called Viennese Currency (abbreviated V.C. hereafter). The old
Assimilated Coinage (abbreviated A.C.), established by a State
treaty with Bavaria in 1753, was based on the 20-florin standard
(20 florins coined from a pure Cologne Mark, i.e. about half a
German pound in weight). There were 60 kreuzer to the florin, in
the new as in the old currency. But 5 florins, V.C., were worth
only 2 florins, A.C. For 100 florins in old treasury notes 250 florins
in "exchange notes" or "sham money" were now to be had; for
100 florins, V.C., accordingly, 40 florins, A.C. (V.C. [in German
W.W. for "Wiener Währung"] was derisively called "Weh!
Weh!"="Woe! Woe!") Both currencies were used side by side
for a long time. (Later on £1 equalled about 10 florins, A.C.)

27. CONCERNING THE MORAL CONDUCT and Progress in their
Studies and in Music of the Court Choristers in the I. & R.
Seminary. First Term, 1811

Name	Morals	Studies	Singing	Pianoforte	Violin	Remarks
Schubert Franz	v. good	good	v. good	v. good	v. good	—

Vienna, 25th April 1811.

Lang,
Government Councillor and Director
of the I. & R. Seminary.

19

28. INTIMATION to the I. & R. Court Music Count

28th April 1811.

. . . Franz Schubert and Franz Müllner are to be praised for their good progress in all subjects.

Mosel.

Schubert hears, (?) on 8th July 1811, Joseph Weigl's opera, 'The Swiss Family' ('Die Schweizerfamilie') at the Kärntnertor Theatre. The date accepted by Sir George Grove for his famous article on Schubert in his 'Dictionary of Music and Musicians' is uncertain. He also gives 12th December 1810 as the date of the first opera Schubert is supposed to have heard, Weigl's 'The Orphanage.' Josef von Spaun, who invited Schubert to the fifth tier at the Kärntnertor Theatre (part of the Vienna Court Opera) to hear his first operas, contradicts himself in two different records about the priority of these two Weigl operas. In any case, however, he was absent at Linz at the end of 1810 and did not return to Vienna until March 1811.

29. CATALOGUE FOR THE SCHOOL-YEAR 1811. Concerning the Scholars of the Third Grammar Class in the University Preparatory School. First and Second Terms

Alois Vorsix [Professor of Grammar].
The Teacher of Religion, Josef Tranz.
Rittmannsberger, Professor of Geography and History.
The Teacher of Mathematics and Natural History, Walch.

Name and Age of the Youth	Country, Birthplace, Domicile	Name and Occupation of Parents	Morals	Application	Religious Instruction	Latin Language and Style	Mathematics	Natural History and Physics	Geography and History	Greek	Stipendiary, Foundation Scholar, Paying Scholar	Remarks
Schubert Franz	Austria, Vienna, City No. 796 in I. & R. Seminary	Franz, School-master	1 em	g.	1	1	1	1	1 em	—	Foundation Scholar, in I. & R. Seminary	
13			1 em	g.	1	1	1	1	1	—		

30. CONCERNING THE MORAL CONDUCT and Progress in their Studies and in Music of the Court Choristers in the I. & R. Seminary. Second Term, 1811

Name	Morals	Studies	Singing	Pianoforte	Violin	Remarks
Schubert Franz	v. g.	good	v. good	v. good	v. good	Fiddles, and plays difficult pieces at sight

[Middle of September 1811.]

Lang,
Government Councillor and Director
of the I. & R. Seminary.

31. INTIMATION to the I. & R. Court Music Count

28th September 1811.

. . . Hellmesberger is to be given an emphatic rebuke in the name of the Lord High Steward's Office for insufficient application to his studies;

to Franz Schubert, on the other hand, an expression of the satisfaction felt here with the excellent progress he has shown in all subjects, and the praise they deserve is to be meted out to the music teachers recommended by the Director, particularly to the piano master Ruczizka.

Mosel.

Johann Georg Hellmesberger (born Vienna, 1800), who was a seminarist and court choir-boy only in 1810–12, became a celebrated violinist.

The choir-boys of the Court Chapel take part in the concert called 'Collin's Celebration' at the large University Hall, in four choruses for Heinrich von Collin's tragedy, 'Polyxena,' composed by Abbé Stadler, Sunday, 15th December 1811. The net proceeds of the event are intended for the monument to the poet to be erected in the Karl church at the instigation of Moritz, Count Dietrichstein.

The choir-boys again sing in the same work at a concert in the Burg Theatre in aid of the new Maria Hospital at Baden near Vienna, organized by the Society of Noblewomen for the Promotion of Good and Useful Deeds, 24th December 1811.

A similar celebration in memory of the dead poet was held at the Burg Theatre on 3rd April 1812, with the collaboration of the opera singer Anna Milder and the court chapel bass Leopold Pfeiffer; but it is unlikely that the choir-boys took part in this. They were debarred by the regulations from appearing in public; the supposition is therefore untenable that they could have taken part in 1808 in the festival performance of Haydn's 'Creation' in the hall of the University or—with Schubert—in one of the oratorios organized by the Society for Musicians' Widows and Orphans. The two performances mentioned above were exceptions: the first time Count Moritz Dietrichstein, who organized that celebration, probably intervened; on the other occasion Princess Karoline Lobkowitz, who was president of that ladies' society, then newly founded, wrote to the Lord High Steward on 18th December 1811 a request for release of the "*jeunes garçons* of the Seminary" (Vienna State Archives). The performers were amateurs. The boys were conducted by their singing-master, Philipp Korner (born 1761). He was a tenor in the court chapel, a lean man who still wore a long, thin pigtail and often treated the lads to cuffings or pulled their ears (Holzapfel's report). By the way, Franz Xaver Stumreiter, who was leader of the Seminary orchestra until 1807, in 1809 set to music eight 'Warriors' Songs' by Heinrich von Collin, the poet of Beethoven's 'Coriolan.'

'First Loss' ('Erster Verlust'), Op. 5, No. 4 (1815). Engraved Vignette from Karl Czerny's Arrangement of Schubert's Song for Pianoforte Solo. Vienna 1838–9

1812

Overture in D major (ii. 2) finished 26th June.
'Salve Regina' in F major (published 1928), 28th June.
Sonata Movement for Pianoforte, Violin and Violon-
   cello in B flat major (published 1923), 27th July–
   28th August.
'Kyrie' in D minor (xiv. 14), 25th September.

An otherwise unknown schoolfellow of Schubert's at the Seminary,
Ignaz Spenn (born *c.* 1795), who was also friendly with Josef von
Spaun, Holzapfel and Kenner, as well as with Körner, Schober and
Mayrhofer, whom we shall not meet until later, kept a diary in
1811–12, in which Schubert is mentioned several times. This
diary, in the possession of Anton von Spaun's descendants in Vienna,
has not been published so far. Spenn was in the Seminary in 1805–12,
became conveyancer in the Vienna State Archives, and died early,
on 6th January 1813. Among his poems is a farewell to Schober,
dated 31st October 1812.

32. CONCERNING THE MORAL CONDUCT and Progress in their
   Studies and in Music of the Court Choristers in the I. & R.
   Seminary.   First Term, 1812

Name	Morals	Studies	Singing	Pianoforte	Violin	Remarks
Schubert Franz	v. g.	g. .	v. g.	v. g.	v. g.	—

Vienna, 20th April 1812.   Lang,
                                 Director of the I. & R. Seminary.

33. FROM THE FAMILY REGISTER of Schubert's Father

1812, 28th May, on Corpus Christi Day, at 4 p.m., died my
deeply cherished wife Elisabeth, *née* Vietz.

That Schubert was previously banished from the paternal house and was
allowed to come home only for the funeral of his mother is a supposition of Alois Fellner's (drawn upon in W. Dahms's biography of Schubert,
first edition, 1912), due to his interpretation of Schubert's tale, 'My
Dream,' of 3rd July 1822 (No. 298).

34. FROM THE REGISTER OF DEATHS of the City of Vienna
[Vienna,] 28th May 1812.

Schubert, Herr Franz, official schoolmaster and I. & R. almoner, his wife Elisabeth, *née* Vietz, born in Silesia, at the Black Horse, 10 Himmelpfortgrund, of typhus, aged 55 years.

Wolf.

35. FROM THE LIECHTENTAL PARISH REGISTER (Death)

Died 28th May 1812 Elisabeth Schubert, *née* Vietz, 10 Himmelpfortgrund. Franz Schubert, schoolmaster and almoner, his wife Elisabeth, aged 55 years; of typhus, interred 30th May.

In this document and the foregoing (No. 34) the cause of death is given as "nervous fever"; but this meant nothing else than typhus abdominalis, of which Schubert himself died.

36. REMARK on a Musical Exercise by Schubert

(A *cantus firmus* by Salieri with a counterpoint by Schubert.)

Counterpoint begun, 18th June 1812, 1st species.

Schubert visited Salieri twice a week. Undated counterpoint exercises of his (Prussian State Library, Berlin) show on two pages of oblong octavo the working-out of points 15 and 16 of paragraph 41 of an unidentified text-book, and the beginnings of paragraph 43. Later on Schubert used the 'Harmonie- und Generalbasslehre' by Josef Drechsler (born 1782 at Wällisch-Birken in Bohemia) in its second edition published by Tobias Haslinger in 1828 (copy in possession of the Krasser family in Vienna). It had been written about 1816 for the training-school in Vienna which Schubert frequented in 1813–14.

37. FROM THE REGISTER OF PROPERTY, City of Vienna

Franz Schubert, schoolmaster in the Himmelpfortgrund, is granted sole use and occupation of a dwelling *sub* No. 10 in the Himmelpfortgrund, known as the Black Horse. For the which are to be paid to the I. & R. Estate of Himmelpforte annually

45 Kreuzer for ground lease, as well as a rent of 5 florins in addition to all the subsisting estate, sovereign and customary fees.

The wife of the lessee, Elisabeth Schubert, was formerly responsible for half the dues on the aforesaid dwelling, but after her demise the said premises have, according to negotiations entered into this day, been absolutely assigned at the value of 5,200 florins to the aforementioned Franz Schubert.

Vienna, 16th July 1812.

38. FROM THE REGISTER OF PROPERTY, City of Vienna

Copyhold on the Himmelpfortgrund, House No. 10 . . . Statutory References: . . . *Lit. F.* 307, 16th July 1812 for Ferdinand, Karl, Franz and Theresia Schubert à 204 fl. 1/11 kr., 816 fl. 1 2/4 kr.

The hereditary portions were merely credited in the Register of Property. It is remarkable that the first-born son, Ignaz Schubert, has no share. He was born (*see* B. 1) as early as seven weeks after marriage. He played the pianoforte and the violin and helped his father with the first musical instruction of his younger brothers. Franz was taught the violin by his father and the pianoforte by Ignaz, while the choirmaster Michael Holzer (born 1772 in the Himmelpfortgrund suburb) instructed him in singing, organ playing and counterpoint. Already in his student days Ignaz helped his father, in whose school he was the first assistant master from 1805 to 1830, when he became his successor as master. Although a freethinker, he sometimes had to deputize for the catechist in the religious teaching, and was also made to take Sunday school. His brother Ferdinand, the next born, was in practice regarded as the future head of the family.

39. DECREE

To the I. & R. Court Musical Director Herr Josef Eybler.

Following the announcement made by the I. & R. Court Musical Director that the two boys in the I. & R. Court Chapel, Franz Schubert and Franz Müllner, have suffered mutation of their voices, the admittance of new ones has been arranged by means of an announcement for a competition to be held on 28th September of this year and an insertion in the 'Wiener Zeitung' . . .

Vienna, 21st July 1812.

40. NOTE at the End of the Third MS. Alto Part of Peter Winter's First Mass, in C major, in the I. & R. Court Chapel, in Schubert's Hand

Schubert, Franz, crowed for the last time, 26th July 1812.

41. NOTE on the Fourth Alto Part (List of the Performing Choir-boys) in Weisse's Hand

Hellmesberger, Boyer, Huber, Oehlinger, Müllner, Fuchs, Kinast, Schubert, Weisse, Chimani. 26th July 1812. Weisse.

These are the ten court choir-boys of 1812, of whom Schubert still was one. Apart from Müllner, Weisse and Hellmesberger, the following are now first given their full names: Georg Boyer, Ferdinand Huber, Johann Oehlinger, Franz Fuchs, Johann Kinast and Alois Chimani.

42. FROM THE OFFICIAL 'WIENER ZEITUNG,' 29th July 1812

ANNOUNCEMENT

of Vacant Endowments for Musical Posts in the I. & R. Seminary.

At the beginning of the coming school-year two endowed places for boy choristers are to be filled at the I. & R. Seminary in this city. Candidates must be aged 10, capable of entering the first year of the Latin school, gifted with a good voice and well instructed in singing. Such parents and guardians as wish to enter their sons or wards for these places are to present them for examination to the directorate of the said Seminary on 29th September of this year, at 9 a.m., having previously submitted school certificates to the directorate.

Vienna, 10th July 1812.

43. CATALOGUE FOR THE SCHOOL-YEAR 1812 concerning the
   Scholars of the Fourth Grammar Class at the University
   Preparatory School.   For the First and Second Terms

   > Josef Tranz, for Religion.
   > Matthias Rebel, for Grammar.
   > Benedict Lamb, for Greek.
   > Rittmannsberger, for Geography and History.
   > Walch, for Mathematics.

Name and Age of the Youth	Country, Birthplace, Domicile	Name and Occupation of Parents	Morals	Application	Progress							Stipendiary, Foundation Scholar, Paying Scholar	Remarks
					Religious Instruction	Latin Language and Style	Mathematics	Natural History and Physics	Geography and History	Greek			
Schubert Franz	Vienna City 796	Franz, School-master	1	1	1	1	1	—	1	1	Pupil of the I. & R. Seminary	
14			1	1	1	1	1	—	1	1		

44. CONCERNING THE MORAL CONDUCT and Progress in their
   Studies and in Music of the Court Choristers in the I. & R.
   Seminary.   Second Term, 1812

Name	Morals	Studies	Singing	Pianoforte	Violin	Remarks
Schubert Franz	good	good	v. good	v. good	v. good	Voice broken

Vienna, 16th September 1812.   Lang,
                              Director of the I. & R. Seminary.

45. COUNT KUEFSTEIN TO PRINCE TRAUTTMANSDORFF
Your Serene Highness,
   . . . For the admittance of three new choirboys the competitive
examination has been fixed for Monday next, the 28th, Schubert's

and Müllner's voices having broken and Hellmesberger being dismissed. I shall not fail to report on this further.

Vienna, 26th September 1812.   Kuefstein.

Alexander Holz, Benedikt Randhartinger and Augustin Gment were the three new court choir-boys admitted in the place of those named.

> Schubert hears, (?) on 1st October 1812, Spontini's opera, 'The Vestal,' at the Kärntnertor Theatre. The date is uncertain (*see* 8th July 1811). Schubert is supposed to have heard the following operas also about this time: Cherubini's 'Medea,' Boïeldieu's 'Jean de Paris,' Isouard's 'Cinderella' and Mozart's 'Magic Flute.'

46. SCHUBERT TO HIS BROTHER (?) FERDINAND

24th November 1812.

Straight out with what troubles me, and so I shall come to my purpose the sooner, and you will not be detained by any precious beating about the bush. I have long been thinking about my situation and found that, although it is satisfactory on the whole, it is not beyond some improvement here and there. You know from experience that we all like to eat a roll or a few apples sometimes, the more so if after a middling lunch one may not look for a miserable evening meal for eight and a half hours. This wish, which has often become insistent, is now becoming more and more frequent, and I had willy-nilly to make a change. The few groats I receive from Father go to the deuce the very first days, and what am I to do for the rest of the time? "Whosoever believeth on Him shall not be put to shame." Matthew, iii. 4. I thought so too.—How if you were to let me have a few Kreuzer a month? You would not so much as know it, while I in my cell should think myself lucky, and be content. I repeat, I lean upon the words of the Apostle Matthew, where he says: "He that hath two coats, let him give one to the poor," &c. Meanwhile I hope that you will give ear to the voice that calls unceasingly to you to remember

Your

loving, poor, hopeful

and again poor brother

Franz.

This first preserved letter of Schubert's may perhaps have been addressed to his elder brother Ignaz, although Ferdinand Schubert had already been assistant schoolmaster at the Vienna orphanage since 1809, and therefore had a small income.   Schubert was on the best of terms with both these brothers, as well as with the third, Karl; but his favourite was certainly Ferdinand, who, as indicated above (see No. 38), was the actual head of the younger generation.   This letter is a mild specimen of similar complaints addressed to Franz von Schober at Kremsmünster between the end of 1813 and the beginning of 1814 by Franz von Schlechta (born 1796 at Pisek in Bohemia), a new seminarist who had come from there (at the same time as Max von Spaun), concerning the evils at the Seminary (Vienna City Library, published in 'Die Quelle,' Vienna, April 1928, pp. 487-8).   Schubert too, it is true, is said to have called the Seminary a prison in 1809.   His biblical quotations are wrong and probably deliberately invented, not as to wording but as to sources: instead of Matthew iii. 4 it should be St. Paul to the Romans x. 11, and instead of the unspecified St. Matthew quotation it should be St. Luke iii. 11: "He that hath two coats, let him impart to him that hath none."   It was not unusual for the seminarists to receive pocket money from their relatives.

Schubert's Note on the Third Alto Part of Peter Winter's First Mass, C major (1812). *See* p. 26

1813

Trios and Canons (in xix and xxi), 15th April—15th July.
Octet for Wind Instruments, Minuet and Finale preserved (iii. 2), finished 18th August.
'Drinking Song' ('Trinklied'), for Bass Solo with Male Chorus and Pianoforte Accompaniment (xvi. 16), 29th August.
Symphony in D major (i. 1) finished 28th October.
Minuets and German Dances for Orchestra (ii. 8–9) begun 19th November.
30 Minuets for Pianoforte (10 lost, the remainder xii. 30).

———

47. FROM THE OFFICIAL 'WIENER ZEITUNG,' 30th January 1813

ANNOUNCEMENT

In the I. & R. City Seminary the following endowments are vacant and open for re-admission, according to a decree of the I. & R. Court Educational Commission dated 23rd October of last year: . . . 5) One Meerfeld Endowment for impecunious youths of good family, presented by the Lower-Austrian Government. . . .

Vienna, 26th January 1813.

Leopold, Freiherr v. Cazan,
I. & R. Lower-Austrian Government Secretary.

Balduin Franz von Meerfeld, an Austrian aulic councillor, had in 1771 presented the earlier Seminary with 26,250 florins for the education of youth. In accordance with this endowment eight foundationers were to receive annually 150 florins on condition that they should once a month recite a rosary for the founder and his family (*Freundschaft*), and confess and communicate on the anniversary of his death. The further condition that these foundationers should all be minors and orphaned sons of respectable parents left without means seems to have fallen into disregard.

48. FROM THE FAMILY REGISTER of Schubert's Father

On 25th April 1813 I was married for the second time, to the esteemed spinster Anna Kleyenböck, born 1st June 1783.

49. FROM THE PARISH REGISTER of the Church of St. Giles at Gumpendorf

Married on 25th April [1813] by Kolumban [Daigele], Co-operator: Franz Schubert, Householder and Schoolmaster at Himmelpfortgrund, born at Neudorf in Moravia, legitimate son of the late Karl Schubert, a farmer, and Susanna, *née* Mick. Resident for 27 years at 10 Himmelpfortgrund. Catholic, 49 years of age, widower.—Anna Kleyenböck, legitimate daughter of Anton Kleyenböck, citizen and silk manufacturer, and Anna, *née* Zeiner. At Gumpendorf, No. 160, for 6 months. Catholic, 29 years of age, single.—Witnesses: Johann Kunert, manu-facturer at Gumpendorf. Michael Wagner, territorial judge at Himmelpfortgrund.

Anna Kleyenböck was one of four daughters. The silk industry flourished in Vienna at that time. Gumpendorf is a suburb in the south-west of Vienna. At the church of St. Giles (Aegidius), which belonged to the Scottish monastery, Haydn's funeral service had been held in 1809. The priest, Daigele, was a cousin of the bride. The statement that the elder Schubert had been resident in the Himmelpfortgrund for twenty-seven years counts in his residence at Liechtental since 1785. His witness, Wagner, persued the same calling as the bride's father; the acquaintance may have been due to him. Schubert's stepmother was kind to him, and later often helped him out of her housekeeping money.

50. POEM BY FRANZ SCHUBERT

TIME (in May 1813)

Unrelenting does she fly,
Once departed, never tarrying.
Thee, O fair companion of our days,
To our resting-place we shall be carrying.

But a breath!—for such is Time.
Let this breath sing worthy measures.
To the throne of justice go thou forth,
Voicing songs of virtue's heav'nly treasures!

But a sound!—for such is Time.
Let this sound be music's treasure.
To the seat of mercy go thou forth,
Pouring out repentance without measure.

Unrelenting does she fly,
Once departed, never tarrying.
Thee, O fair companion of our days,
To our resting-place we shall be carrying.

The occasion of this poem is unknown.　Holzapfel, who kept a copy of it, told Ferdinand Luib in 1858 that Schubert had written yet another poem at that time, in the style of Klopstock's odes, on God's omnipotence in creation.　This is lost.

51. COMIC POSTSCRIPT to the Fragmentary Octet for Wind
Instruments (iii. 2), 18th August 1813

Finished wi' th' *Quartet*, the which has been composéd by Franz° Schubert, Chapel Master to the Imp. Chinese Court Chappppelll at Nanking, the world-famous residence of His Chinese Majesty.　Written in Vienna, on a date I can't tell, in a year which has a 3 at the end, and a oner at the beginning, and then an eight, and another oner: that is to say—1813.

This playful inscription indicates that this octet was intended for the Seminary orchestra.　The allusion to a Chinese Austria reads as if Schubert were acquainted with the documents Nos. 52 ff., which had begun to circulate as early as 6th August 1813.

Theodor Körner falls in battle at Gladebach and Johann Baptist Wanhal dies, 26th August 1813.—Theodor Körner (born Dresden, 1791), the poet of the Wars of Liberation, who had lived in Vienna —lastly as dramatic poet to the Burg Theatre—from August 1811 to March 1813, and there became engaged to be married to the court actress Antonie Adamberger, was musical, sang bass in the new Philharmonic Society and is said to have taken part with a guitar in the Viennese serenades of his friends, who included Josef von Spaun.　Spaun took Schubert to hear Gluck's 'Iphigenia in Tauris' (not therefore as late as 1815, as Grove supposed), met Körner there and introduced Schubert to him.　They dined together at the "Hunter's Horn" in the Dorotheergasse near the Graben, and were full of enthusiasm about Anna Milder and J. M. Vogl, who sang Iphigenia and Orestes. That evening, it is said, Körner confirmed Schubert in his intention to stick to music. In Körner's letters from Vienna Schubert's name is not mentioned, which leads to the conclusion that their meeting did not take place until early in 1813. Körner appears to have lived in the Wipplingerstrasse near the old town hall, at Frau Anna Sanssouci's, who later became Mayrhofer's, Schubert's and Josef Hüttenbrenner's landlady. Her son Franz was another of the seminarists at that time. Her husband, who died in 1814, had been a wine merchant and jeweller. She became a tobacconist. It is significant that Schubert, soon after that octet with the comic postscript (see No. 51), wrote a 'Little Mourning Music' for wind instruments, including a double bassoon (thus evidently not for the Seminary orchestra), dated 19th September 1813. It is absurd to suppose that this work had anything to do with his mother's death in May 1812, and the later inscription from another hand, "Franz Schubert's Funeral Ceremony," cannot be regarded as giving any indication of its original purpose. It seems quite possible that it was intended as a tribute to Körner, in whose honour, by the way, his friend Theodor von Sydow organized a memorial performance in Vienna on 14th March 1814.

52. FROM A REPORT of the Educational Court Commission of 6th August, presented on 13th September 1813, suggesting the Occupation of six Endowments of Windhag, one of Meerfeld and one of Goldegg at the Seminary in Vienna

. . . The directorate of the Seminary declares: . . . For the second, third, fourth and fifth Windhag place the following are proposed according to regulations, being no longer available as choir-boys owing to mutation of their voices: Josef Andorfer, Josef Kleindl, Franz Schubert and Franz Müllner, in order to relieve the Seminary's funds of their maintenance as soon as possible.

The Lower-Austrian Government can see no better use for its rights of proposal than to agree entirely with this conscientious recommendation, which is wholly in accord with the rules, the letters of endowment and the regulations . . .

The curator of the Seminary, Count Dietrichstein . . . observes

. . .: it seems to him that the said choir-boys should succeed to the vacated endowment places only on condition that they possess the same qualities, particularly as they are favoured in any case by their admission, when they are considered not so much for progress in their studies as for fine voices. . . . The four proposed choir-boys should therefore enter only when the next vacancy occurs, and even then only if their other qualities conform . . .

The Commission of Studies draws attention to the following: . . . As regards the admission of these four choir-boys to the Windhag Endowment, the majority of votes . . ., and further, Government Councillor Lang regards it as necessary and as being in accord with the meaning of the most exalted instructions that the present opportunity should be seized to bestow the Windhag Endowment places on those four singers maintained at the expense of the free funds. . . . Four of the vacated six Windhag places might thus be occupied by the aforesaid four choir-boys, Andorfer, Kleindl, Schubert and Müllner, who were all distinguished the preceding year with top marks, three being given preference in morals and Kleindl also in three subjects, and who thus possess the sufficient capacities required by the letters of Endowment, as well as Christian and virtuous conduct . . .

Teplitz, 23rd September 1813.

Dittmann.

[Certificate from the Court Physician Andreas von Stifft:]

. . . There appears thus to be no objection to the succession of the four broken-voiced choir-boys to the Windhag Endowment places.

24th September 1813.   Stifft.

[Imperial Resolution:]

We assign the Windhag Endowment places to Anton Hayek, Mathias Winter, Rieger Wenzel and to the three of the four choir-boys Josef Andorfer, Josef Kleindl, Franz Schubert and Franz Müllner who have most distinguished themselves in studies and morals, the Meerfeld Endowment place going to the fourth of the said choir-boys, unless that Endowment should offer greater advantages than the Windhag . . .

Komotau, 10th October 1813.

Franz.

Johann Joachim, Count Windhag, had left in 1670 a capital sum for several endowments to the earlier Seminary, and these now fell due again. There were sixty of them, amounting to 200 to 300 florins each; but they were primarily intended for poor students of philosophy who had distinguished themselves, and occasionally for secondary scholars.—The endowment for poor and talented students founded in the old Seminary by Johann Matthias, Freiherr von Goldegg, in 1657, did not concern Schubert.—The fact that the document was signed at Teplitz recalls the battle of Kulm and Nollendorf, where General Vandamme was beaten by the Russians and Austrians on 29th and 30th August 1813.—Andreas Josef, Freiherr von Stifft (born 1760), a doctor of medicine, was also a state and conference councillor.—The emperor, who concerned himself with the smallest details of statesmanship, was at Komotau in Bohemia a week before the battle of the nations at Leipzig.

53. CATALOGUE FOR THE SCHOOL-YEAR 1813 concerning the Scholars for the First Humanities Class at the University Preparatory School. For the First and Second Terms
For Elocution and Greek, Benedikt Lamb.
For Religious Teaching, Josef Tranz.
For Geography and History, Rittmannsberger.
For Mathematics, Walch.

Name and Age of the Youth	Country, Birthplace, Domicile	Name and Occupation of Parents	Morals	Application	Religious Instruction	Latin Language and Style	Mathematics	Natural History and Physics	Geography and History	Greek	Stipendiary, Foundation Scholar, Paying Scholar	Remarks
Schubert Franz	Austria Vienna I. & R. Seminary	Franz, School-master	1	1	1	2 (1)	1	—	1	1	I. & R. Seminary	
15			1	1	1	1	2	—	1	1		

The grammar-school's *studia inferiora* at that time comprised four grammar and two humanities classes; the actual university studies were preceded by another two years of philosophy, or *studia superiora*. In Latin, the chief subject at the grammar-school, Schubert had improved during the second term; but he fell a victim to mathematics at the end of the year, like many other pupils at the Seminary, including Johann Nestroy. The marking was "1 em[inent], 1, 1–2, 2."

54. FROM THE PRINTED CATALOGUE

Juventus Caesareo Regii

Gymnasii Academici

Viennae

E Moribus et Progressu in Litteris

censa

exeunte anno scholastico

MDCCCXIII . . .

In I. humanitatis classe:

Schubert Franc. Austr. Vienn. e C.R. Conv.	E Moribus	E Doctrina Religionis	Ex Auct. Interpr. et Stylo	E Graecae Linguae Studio	E Geogr. et Histor.	E Mathesi
	1	1	1	1	1	2

One of the *Catalogi inferiorum*, preserved by descendants of the Schubert family, is here reproduced. In the Vienna "Akademisches Gymnasium" the four older printed catalogues in which Schubert's name appears are likewise preserved: they are, of course, identical with the hand-written certificates. The last catalogue containing Schubert's name also tallies with the general register of foundationers written in German supplied by the director, Lang. Among Schubert's closer associates during this last Seminary year were Maximilian Löwenthal, Franz Sanssouci (*see* note on Körner, p. 33) and Josef von Streinsberg, of whom we shall hear more. Among his comrades in a wider sense were Johann Nestroy, the great satirical playwright, and Josef Othmar (later Ritter von) Rauscher (born 1797), a future prince-archbishop of Vienna. The Viennese comrades were mostly day scholars, i.e. they attended the grammar-school without living at the Seminary. But among the seminarists there were some paying boarders, called *Kostgeher*.

55. PROPOSAL from the Lower-Austrian Marshal of the Province and Curator of the Seminary, Josef Karl, Count Dietrichstein, dated 26th September, presented 30th September 1813

Wherewith the aforesaid submits the . . . class registers of . . . the boarders at the I. & R. Seminary for the second half of the school-year of 1813, with the following observations:
. . . To Franz Schubert, scholar in the First Humanities Class, formerly choir-boy of the Court Chapel; and furthermore . . ., who during the two terms of the year dropped to the second rank, further residence in the Seminary might be granted in such a way that the former should raise himself above second grade after vacation . . . ; Schubert, an excellent youth, being praised by the Court Musical Director Salieri for his superior musical talent and as the composer of several good musical pieces . . .

Teplitz, 3rd October 1813.

Dittmann.

[Certificate from the Court Physician Andreas von Stifft:]
As regards the foundation scholars, . . . Franz Schubert . . . Your Majesty might grant the Curator's proposals.
4th October 1813.

Stifft.

[Imperial Resolution:]
In regard to the foundation scholars . . . Franz Schubert . . . We grant your proposals on condition that they shall be incontinently dismissed if they do not rise above the second rank after vacation or relapse into the second rank after next term's examination, since singing and music are but a subsidiary matter, while good morals and diligence in study are of prime importance and an indispensable duty for all those who wish to enjoy the advantages of an Endowment.

Rötha, 21st October 1813.

Franz.

Rötha is in Saxony. The emperor signed his decision concerning the foundationers two days after the Allied victory at the battle of Leipzig. On 15th November 1813 Schubert wrote a canon for three male voices,

'On the Victory of the Germans,' to the first verse of an anonymous poem which he also set the same year in its entirety for one voice with accompaniment for two violins and cello.

56. Words of Schubert's 'Cantata for his Father's Name-Day'

'Terzetto' (xix. 4)

Resound, my lyre,
My songs inspire!
Apollo, come, descend,
This feast thy presence lend!

Long live our belovèd Father Franz!
Long endure his chain of happy days!
Like a wreath of flowers and bays
Fortune shall his life entrance.

Joy shall embrace him, laughing with pleasure,
Never his happy future aggrieve.
Never shall sorrow and trouble assail him
Till Elysium's shades him receive.
Come, repeat it, say it, precious lyre,
Sing it gently on this festive day,
Sing it yet again another season:
Father Franz's happiness for aye!

Fine, 27th September 1813.

For my Father's Name-Day!!!

[Franz Schubert.]

In the Catholic countries of central Europe the name-day, i.e. the day of the saint after whom a person is named, is celebrated more than the birthday. The name-day of Schubert's father (and his own) was 4th October. The cantata, for which Schubert also wrote the words, is for three male voices (2 tenors and bass) with guitar accompaniment. This is the only time Schubert actually wrote a part for this instrument, although many of his songs were later published with alternative guitar accompaniments. He is supposed to have played it. (The so-called guitar Quartet of 1814 is a Notturno for flute, viola and guitar by Wenzel Matiegka, Op. 21, for which Schubert wrote only an additional cello part—? for his father.) The vocal parts were evidently sung by his three brothers, Ignaz, Ferdinand and Karl, since his own voice was just then undergoing mutation. Possibly that canon of 15th November 1813 was also sung by his brothers at home.

57. DECREE of the I. & R. Court Educational Commission to the I. & R. Lower-Austrian Government, 1813

His Majesty has been graciously pleased to command, concerning the Government report of 24th May received on 10th June of this year, enclosures to which are returned herewith, and also concerning the most humble proposal accordingly submitted to H.M., that the following be granted: The 6 vacant Windhag Endowments to Anton Hayek, Matthias Winter and Wenzel Rieger, as well as to three of the 4 choir-boys, Josef Andorfer, Josef Kleindl, Franz Schubert and Franz Müllner, who have most distinguished themselves in morals and studies, while the Meerfeld Endowment is to go to the fourth of the said choir-boys, unless the latter endowment should be more advantageous than the Windhag Endowment, and the Goldegg Endowment to Franz Graf. Moreover, that, since the Windhag Endowments warrant the attainments of their beneficiaries, they may in any case at all times be granted to the best of the students, so long as there are none especially appointed for grants by the founder; that, therefore, even the choir-boys who are now receiving such may have them withdrawn if other endowments can be assigned to them and if, according to the aforesaid gracious pleasure, more suitable choir-boys should be found than the above, who may then be granted other endowments.

The Government is forthwith to do what is necessary for the execution of this gracious decision, and the choir-boys whose voices have broken, Josef Kleindl, Josef Andorfer and Franz Müllner, are to be assigned to the Windhag Endowment, but Franz Schubert to the Meerfeld Endowment, and future cases are to be handled according to Imperial decree.

Count Laczanzky.

From the I. & R. Court Educational Commission

Vienna, 22nd October 1813.

Stainer.

Prokop (II), Count Laczansky (born 1771), an amateur singer, was attached to the Court Educational Commission as Bohemian-Austrian court chancellor.

58. LOST LETTER from Josef Karl, Count Dietrichstein, to the Directorate of the Seminary

> Communicating the Imperial consent of 21st October 1813 that Franz Schubert may remain in the City Seminary, on condition that he should make good during vacation the second-class mark obtained by him.

59. REMARK AT THE END of the Autograph Score of the Symphony No. 1, in D major (i. 1), 28th October 1813

Finis et fine.

It was said that this first Symphony was written for the birthday (28th July) or name-day (? 4th October) of Director Lang. It was too late for either. Perhaps Schubert dropped the idea because he was going to leave the Seminary. In any case he later dedicated to Lang the manuscript of his second Symphony of 1814–15.

60. NOTE ON THE TITLE-PAGE of one manuscript of the Magic Opera, 'The Devil's Pleasaunce' (xv. 1), begun on 30th October 1813

. . . Pupil of Herr Salieri, First Court Musical Director in Vienna.

61. LOST LETTER from Count Dietrichstein to the Directorate of the Seminary

(6th November 1813.)

> Information that the Court Educational Commission has assigned the Meerfeld Endowment to the choir-boy Franz Schubert.

62. GOVERNMENT DECREE to the Directorate of the Seminary

Very Urgent   Decree.
and to be delivered without   To the Directorate of the
fail by the 29th inst.   I. & R. Seminary.

[The first two paragraphs communicate the contents of No. 57.]

While the Directorate of the I. & R. Seminary is given the required intelligence to this effect, the newly elected beneficiaries are being informed of the matter, with the exception of those whose voices have broken, who are to be apprised in due form by the Directorate; . . . Finally, Franz Schubert having renounced the Meerfeld Endowment, according to information just received from the Curator of the Seminary, his place is to be regarded as vacant and its assignment to be arranged according to regulations . . .

Kraus *m. p.*   23rd November 1813
                                                    [illegible].

Schubert had thus resigned and left the institution. A disciplinary affair, in which he was not directly involved, may have had something to do with it (report from the curator of the Seminary to the emperor, 29th August 1813, printed in 'Die Quelle,' Vienna, April 1928, pp. 485–7). The Court Finance Office had paid the Seminary during the past five years some 1,500 florins, A.C., for Schubert. The fact that he was now to leave was not due to the mutation of his voice, but to his failure in his studies and the circumstance that he did not wish to advance conditionally to the second humanities class, where a Meerfeld endowment awaited him. Presumably his father was not in favour of this course either, but decided that it was time for Franz to make a change in his career. He was now to enter his father's profession, like his brothers. He therefore went home first of all and afterwards, during the school year of 1813–14, frequented the teachers' training-school of the so-called "Normal-Hauptschule" in the Annagasse (in the inner city), where those intended for assistant teachers were trained in a model elementary school. It had been established in the reign of Maria Theresa by Josef Mesmer, a brother of the magnetist, and there were affiliated institutions in the provinces.—Anton Josef Emanuel Kraus (later Ritter von Elislago) was Councillor to the Lower Austrian Government.

1814

Operetta, 'The Devil's Pleasaunce' ('Des Teufels Lustschloss') (3 acts,
Kotzebue) (xv. 1), 30th October 1813—22nd October 1814.
Mass in F major (xiii. 1), 17th May–22nd July.
Song, 'Margaret at the Spinning-Wheel' ('Gretchen am Spinnrade'),
19th October.

_____

63. FROM THE FAMILY REGISTER of Schubert's Father

(15) Maria Barbara Anna, born 22nd January 1814, 9.30 p.m.,
baptized 23rd January, at 4 p.m.

Schubert hears, (?) on 23rd May 1814, Beethoven's 'Fidelio' at
the Kärntnertor Theatre. This was the first performance of the
final version. That Schubert sold his school-books in order to be
able to attend may be gathered from a report of Moritz von Schwind,
who, it is true, did not make his acquaintance until later. (Ludwig
Nohl, 'Beethoven,' · Leipzig, 1867, vol. ii, p. 569.) Cf. 3rd
November 1822.

64. INSCRIPTION WITH CHRONOGRAM on the House of Schubert's Father at the Entry of the Emperor Francis I on his Return from Paris in the Evening of 16th June 1814

Illumination at 10 Himmelpfortgrund. In the Säulengasse.
At the House of Herr Schubert, Schoolmaster.

Oh could I, as I would,
Do honour, as we should,
To our good Emperor Franz!
My loyal heart is welling
With love, though on this dwelling
But tapers meet your glance.

FRANCISCO MAGNO, VICTORI
REDEVNTI!

Literally the original says that although only candles are seen burning,
sprigs of laurel are sprouting from his heart.

65. FROM THE LIST of Secular Candidates at the I. & R. Training College, examined on 19th August 1814

THEORETICAL KNOWLEDGE

Name and Studies	Principles of Instruction	German Writing	Latin Writing	Clerical Writing	Orthography	Pronunciation	German Grammar	Arithmetic	Geography	Style	Religious Instruction
Schubert Frz. 17 yrs. ditto [future assistant]	m	g	m	m	g	g	g	g	—	—	m

PRACTICAL KNOWLEDGE

Knowledge of Letters	Spelling	Reading	Calligraphy / Orthography	Dictation / German Grammar	Arithmetic	Geography / Style	Religion	Industry / Morals	Remarks
			g	g		—		industr.	
g	g	g	g	g	m	—	bad		as assistant

[Josef Peitl.]

The director of the training-school was Dr. Wilhelm Bauer (born 1779), who, like his predecessor, Josef Mesmer, had been acquainted with Mozart. Josef Peitl (born 1789, at Hohenwuppersdorf, Lower Austria) was a teacher there at that time and director of the school in 1825–6; Ferdinand Schubert became a teacher there in 1824 and director in 1851. Peitl taught pedagogic methods with exercises in practical instruction.

66. REMARK AT THE END of the First Movement, *Allegro ma non troppo*, of Schubert's Quartet in B flat major (v. 8)

(5th September 1814.)

Done in $4\frac{1}{2}$ hours.

First performance of the Mass in F major (xiii. 1), 16th October

1814, under Schubert's direction in the church at Liechtental, for its centenary; choirmaster—Michael Holzer, organ—Ferdinand Schubert, solo soprano—Therese Grob.

The parish church of Liechtental, in whose choir Schubert was quite at home, actually celebrated its jubilee as early as 25th September 1814, a week after which a second high altar had been consecrated there. Zacharias Werner (born 1768, at Königsberg), the converted priest and poet, who had not long been in Vienna, had preached at the church on Friday, 9th October. (He had come into fashion during the opening of the Congress of Vienna.) The 16th of October, the day after St. Theresa's Day, was also a Friday. This Mass was the first work by Schubert to be performed. Apart from his parishioner friends, Josef Mayseder (born Vienna, 1789) took part as first violinist. Salieri was present.

Second performance of the Mass in F major, 26th October 1814, at St. Augustine's Court Church under Schubert's direction; solo soprano—(?) Therese Grob.

There is no doubt that this performance was attended by several foreigners who were in Vienna for the Congress of 1814–15. Schubert's father, proud of his son's success, is said to have presented him at that time with a five-octave pianoforte from Konrad Graf's workshop.

Josef von Spaun introduces Schubert to Johann Mayrhofer, December 1814.

Schubert had set Mayrhofer's poem 'By the Lake' ('Am See') on 7th December 1814, and it was this which led to the acquaintance. Mayrhofer, born in 1787 at Steyr in Upper Austria, had been a clerk for four years at the monastery of St. Florian, studied law in Vienna from the autumn of 1810 and in 1820 was appointed revisor at the Central Book Censorship Office, i.e. third censor. In spite of his love of freedom he took his post seriously, and was regarded as a strict censor. He was taciturn, sarcastic and a misogynist. Among his favourite books was Young's 'Night Thoughts.' His friendship with Schubert remained cordial until 1824. He was musical, sang and played the guitar.

K. K. Convict

N.º 140.

Ex libris of the Music Collection of the City Seminary (*Stadtkonvikt*). Aria from the Vocal Score of Beethoven's 'Fidelio,' Vienna 1814, bearing the Stadtkonvikt Library Label

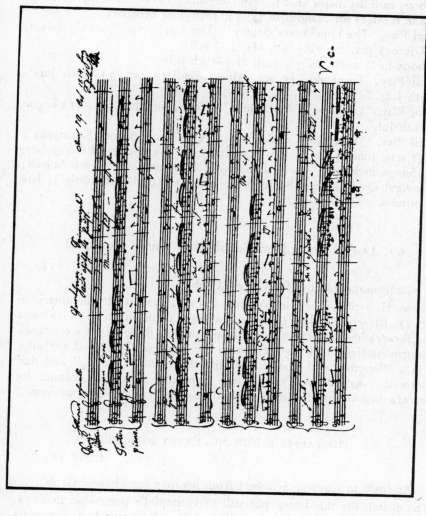

'Margaret at the Spinning-Wheel' ('Gretchen am Spinnrade'),
Op. 2.   First Page of the Autograph (1814)

1815

Symphony in B flat major (i. 2), 10th December 1814—24th March 1815.

Sonata in E major for Pianoforte (x. 1), 18th–21st February.

Musical Play, 'The Four-Years' Sentry' ('Der vierjährige Posten') (1 act, Körner) (xv. 2), 8th–19th May.

Symphony in D major (i. 3), 24th May–19th July.

Musical Play, 'Fernando' (1 act, Albert Stadler) (xv. 3), 27th June–9th July.

Musical Play, 'Claudine of Villa Bella' (3 acts, Goethe) (xv. 11) begun 26th July.

Musical Play, 'The Friends of Salamanca' (Die Freunde von Salamanka') (2 acts, Johann Mayrhofer) (xv. 4), 18th November–31st December.

c. 145 Songs, including 'The Hedge-Rose' ('Heidenröslein'), 19th August; several Ossian songs, September; and 'Erl King' ('Erlkönig'), late autumn.

---

67. LOST LETTER from Schubert to Anton Holzapfel

Early 1815.

Confession of his love for Therese Grob.

Anton Holzapfel, born in Vienna in 1794, was at the Seminary in 1805–17, latterly as a law student. In notes dating from 1858 (Vienna City Library) he writes that it was characteristic of Schubert's reticence to inform his friend of his inclination for Therese Grob, not verbally, but in a "lengthy, enthusiastic and unfortunately lost letter," and that he himself "endeavoured to dissuade him in a ridiculous manner by means of a didactic epistle which at that time seemed to me full of wisdom."

68. HOLZAPFEL'S MISSING REPLY to Schubert

Early 1815.

Attempt to dissuade Schubert from his love for Therese Grob.

The sketch for this letter was still in Holzapfel's possession in 1858. He describes Therese Grob, whom he had himself known for a few years before 1815, as "not by any means a beauty, but well shaped, fairly buxom, with a fresh, childlike little round face and a fine soprano voice extending to D in alt." Therese Grob, born in Vienna in 1798, and a brother, Heinrich, two years younger and also musically inclined, were the

46

children of a widow, Therese Grob, who ran a small silk factory near the Liechtental church. Their father had been an immigrant from Switzerland. Therese's aunt, Wilhelmine (born 1785), was married to the medal engraver Leopold Hollpein (born Berlin, c. 1785), after whose death she married Schubert's elder brother Ignaz. The Schuberts and the Grobs were often godparents to each other's children. Schubert wrote 'The Girl from Afar' ('Das Mädchen aus der Fremde') on 16th October 1814, 'Margaret at the Spinning-Wheel' on 19th October and many love songs in May 1815. He does not seem to have given up hope of marrying Therese until three years later, and in 1820 she married the master baker Johann Bergmann. Schubert afterwards discussed the matter with Anselm Hüttenbrenner, to whom he described her as "not particularly pretty, with pock-marks on her face, but very good-hearted." He wrote a few of his smaller church music works for her, and for her brother, who played the cello among other instruments, the 'Adagio and Rondo concertante' in F major for piano quartet (vii. 2), dated October 1816. Heinrich's descendants have preserved a collection of autograph songs by Schubert, mostly of 1816, including three never yet printed, a set known as "Therese Grob's Album." If Hüttenbrenner's recollections of 1858 (Vienna City Library), doubtless wrong in some details, are correct in this respect, Schubert was unable ever to forget Therese Grob, and finally renounced marriage on her account. The reason why she did not become his wife seems to have lain in his hopeless material circumstances at that time.

69. TITLE AND NOTE at the End of the Manuscript of the Ten Variations in F major (xi. 6)

X Variations pour le Forte-Piano composés [sic] par François Schubert, Ecolier de Salieri, prémier [sic] Maître de la Chapelle imperiale [sic] et royale de Vienne . . . 15th February 1815.

The three mistakes of gender and accentuation in two lines of a French title show that Schubert's knowledge of that language was defective, and his school certificates prove that it was not among his subjects at the Seminary. Many of his later works appeared with French title-pages, as was indeed usual at that time both in Austria and in Germany, but although they were often wrongly spelt by him or by his publishers, they will hereafter usually be given in their correct form. Schubert remained Salieri's pupil after he left the Seminary, whence he had visited him twice a week, and did not leave him until 1816 at the earliest.

First performance of the Mass in G major (xiii. 2), Spring 1815, in the church of Liechtental.

70. FROM THE FAMILY REGISTER of Schubert's Father

(16) Josefa Theresia, born 8th April 1815, 7.45 a.m., baptized
9th April, 5 p.m.

This stepsister of Schubert's had her mother's cousin, Kolumban
Daigele, for godfather.

71. REMARK on the Manuscript of the *Singspiel*, 'Fernando' (xv. 3)

(27th June 1815.)

. . . Pupil of Herr v. Salieri.

The libretto of 'Fernando' was by Schubert's schoolfellow Albert
Stadler, born at Steyr in 1794. He entered the Vienna Seminary in 1812,
and until June 1817, when he went to Linz, copied all the songs by
Schubert on which he could lay hands.

72. REMARK on the Manuscript of the *Liederspiel*, 'Claudine von Villa Bella' (Libretto by Goethe) (xv. 11)

(26th July 1815.)

. . . Pupil of Herr v. Salieri.

The songs in this play of Goethe's were first set to music by Ignaz von
Beecke, and it was performed thus in Vienna in 1780. Among other
composers who set them was (Berlin, 1789) Goethe's friend Johann
Friedrich Reichardt (born Königsberg, 1752).

73. FROM THE UNSUCCESSFUL PETITION of Schubert's Father to the Prelate of the Scottish Order, Andreas, for the Vacant Teacher's Post at the Elementary School of the Monastery

(25th August 1815.)

Above all does he regard this gracious promotion as desirable
on account of his four sons, all of whom are already in the service
of the elementary school organization, one of whom, while being
drawing master at the Girls' Institute at the Hof [square], frequents
the Drawing Academy (where last year he obtained the first

prize in figure-drawing), the other incidentally practising composition with success under the kind guidance of the first I. & R. Court Musical Director, Herr von Salieri; so that they should be brought appreciably nearer their further education and final destination, each in his own way.

The so-called "Scottish monastery" was founded in the twelfth century by Heinrich Jasomirgott ("Ja, so mir Gott helfe!" = "Aye, so help me God!"), Duke of Babenberg, for the use of Irish Benedictines. Its designation as "Scottish," which has persisted down to our own time, is therefore incorrect.—The drawing-master was Karl Schubert, the youngest of Franz's three brothers.

> Franz von Schober comes from the Seminary of the Monastery of Kremsmünster to Vienna, Autumn 1815.—Franz, Ritter von Schober, was born in 1796 at Torup Castle near Malmö in Sweden, as the son of Aulic Councillor Franz von Schober (ennobled 1801, died 1802), of Saxon extraction, who was manager of the castle estates, and of his wife, Katharina, née Derffel, 1764, a native of Vienna. He had watched Nelson's bombardment of Copenhagen with his telescope in 1801, was educated at Salzmann's famous Institute at Schnepfental in 1802–6, then at the Seminary attached to the monastery of Kremsmünster in 1808–15, and was now studying law in Vienna. He had a brother and two sisters, the elder of whom, Ludwiga, died as early as 1812 by an accident with a pistol after only two years of married life with the singer Giuseppe Siboni (born Forli, 1780).

74. Note on the Manuscript of the Play with Songs, 'The Friends of Salamanca' (xv. 4), 18th November 1815

. . . Pupil of Herr Salieri, 1815.

The libretto of this opera, by Johann Mayrhofer, is lost. Following Kreissle its title is sometimes given as 'The Two Friends of Salamanca' ('Die beiden Freunde . . .'): actually there are three friends, who are in league against a vainglorious count.

75. Josefa von Spaun to her Son Josef

Linz, 24th November 1815.

The Écossaises, which Anton has already studied a little, are very fine.

Josefa, Edle von Spaun, née von Steyrer, 1757, widowed for the second time, her first husband having died on the wedding-day, lived at Linz with her daughter and some of her sons. She was very musical, sang Zumsteeg's and later Schubert's songs particularly well, and her children inherited her love of music. The écossaise, a country dance, was favoured as a ballroom dance in Vienna as well as in Paris, as a change from the waltzes, German dances and *Ländler* in 3–4 time, and as a counterpart to the galop in 2–4. The later name, *Schottisch*, which is simply the German translation of the original, became familiar in Britain, spelt "schottische"; but it has no special connection with Scotland. It would seem as if these 'Écossaises,' whose composer is not named, had been the first of Schubert's works to become known outside Vienna. Frau von Spaun's son Josef, Schubert's friend, had evidently sent her the '12 Écossaises' Schubert had written for her daughter Marie (born 1797) on 3rd October 1815 (xxi. 29 and 'Die Musik,' Berlin, 1st September 1912, 8 and 4 dances respectively). Anton von Spaun, another brother, was at that time a county official at Linz.

'Huntsman's Evening Song' ('Jägers Abendlied'), Op. 3, No. 4 (1816). Engraved Vignette from Karl Czerny's Arrangement of Schubert's Song for Pianoforte Solo. Vienna 1838–9

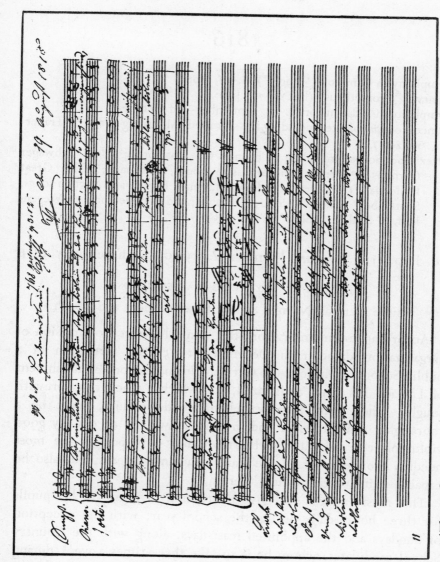

'The Hedge Rose' ('Heidenröslein'), Op. 3, No. 3. First Page of the Autograph (1815)

11

1816

Symphony in C minor ('Tragic') (i. 4), April.
Cantata, 'Prometheus' (lost), 17th June.
Symphony in B flat major (i. 5), September–3rd October.
Dances for Pianoforte, including the so-called 'Mourning Waltz' ('Trauer-walzer').
Over 100 Songs, including 'Chronos the Charioteer' ('An Schwager Chronos') opening, more Ossian songs, February; 'The Great Hallelujah' ('Das grosse Halleluja'), June; Harper and Mignon songs, September; 'The Wanderer,' October; and 'Cradle Song' ('Wiegenlied,' " Schlafe, schlafe "), November.

---

76. From the Official 'Wiener Zeitung,' 17th February 1816

FILLING of the MUSIC MASTER'S POST

at the German Normal School Establishment at Laibach

According to an order from the Central Court Commission of Organization dated 11th December 1815, the formation of a public School of Music at the German Normal School Establishment of Laibach has been authorized, for which a teacher is herewith sought, who, apart from excellent good conduct, must be a thoroughly trained singer and organist as well as an equally good violin player, and must furthermore not only possess the most needful knowledge of all the usual wind instruments, but also be capable of instructing others therein.

This music master will give instruction in music to his pupils for three hours daily during the school-year, with the exception of Sundays and the appointed feast-days, along with the Country School candidates, whom he is to take three times a week during their six-monthly preparatory course, for at least an hour at a time; in consideration of which he is to receive a salary of 450 florins A.C. per annum out of the Provincial funds for the regular musical scholars, but in regard to the Country School candidates an annual remuneration of 50 florins A.C. from the Normal School funds; in addition to which he is to hold the rank of a Normal School teacher and to be at the same time allowed to devote his remaining hours to private teaching, but on no account to such occupations whereby the reputation of an official teacher might be endangered.

Whosoever desires to obtain this teaching post is therefore enjoined to submit authentic testimonials of his age, birthplace, present occupation, state of knowledge, and the fact is to be stated whether he is single, married, widowed, a parent, and if so of how many children, or childless, and at the same time authentic testimonials are to be submitted as to his thorough musical knowledge and corresponding teaching capacity, as well as a certificate of good morals attested by the spiritual and political authorities of his place of residence; and the applications, accompanied by the above testimonials, are to be presented before 15th March of this year to the Hon. I. & R. Lower-Austrian Government, so far as applicants are resident in Lower Austria.

From the I. & R. Provincial
Government.
Laibach, 19th January 1816.

At Laibach, too, the capital of the Austrian crown land of Carniola (now Ljubljana in Yugoslavia), there was a training-school for "German" (i.e. elementary, as distinct from Latin) teachers. The post, which would have meant a considerable improvement on the small salary Schubert received as sixth assistant in the bottom form of his father's school, may perhaps have been desirable also in view of his wooing of Therese Grob. He must have felt, however, that such a post would come nearer to fulfilling his vocation than his father's profession could ever do. The advertisement appeared also at Laibach, Klagenfurt, Graz and Prague.

77. SCHUBERT to the Vienna Captaincy of the Civic Guard

(April 1816.)

Right Hon. I. & R. Captaincy of the Civic Guard,

The undersigned most submissively begs that the vacant post of Musical Director at Laibach may be graciously assigned to him.

He supports this request with the following reasons:

1. He is a pupil of the I. & R. Seminary, ex-choir-boy of the I. & R. Court Chapel and composition scholar of Herr von Salieri, first I. & R. Court Musical Director, on whose benevolent advice he desires to obtain the said post.

2. He has gained such knowledge and skill in all branches of composition, in performance on the organ and violin, and in singing that he is declared to be the most suitable among all the applicants for this post, according to the enclosed testimonials.

3. He promises to use his qualifications in the best possible way to do the fullest justice to a gracious consent to his petition.

Franz Schubert

at present assistant teacher at his

Father's school in

Vienna, 10 Himmelpfortgrund.

The captaincy of the Viennese Civic Guard was a kind of district office, which however subsisted only up to 1820. The remark that Schubert was called the most suitable of all the applicants cannot refer to Spendou's lost certificate (*see* No. 80), but is probably to be explained by the fact that Schubert had not himelf seen Salieri's testimonial. The house-number of the school, 10, was formerly 14, and later 12.

78. Salieri's Testimonial for Schubert (in Italian)

I, the undersigned, assert that I support the application of Franz Schubert in regard to the musical post at Laibach.

Antonio Salieri,

First Musical Director of the

I. & R. Court.

Vienna, 9th April 1816.

79. Anton von Spaun to his Betrothed, Henriette von Vogelsang

Vienna, 12th April 1816.

I still have to tell you in what state I write this letter. I sit in a small room, at Schober's, with my brothers, Kreil, Schubert, &c.,

standing about and hardly able to hold out until I have finished this letter; at last, in order not to disturb me, they go into the next room, and Schubert begins to play the pianoforte, which confuses me even more.   Yet his tones set my heart longing more ardently —and altogether I feel even happier here than before, if possible, when I see the restless, empty, wrong-headed strivings of the people here, where the best of them ceaselessly complain that the most cherished wishes of their hearts are granted no fulfilment, indeed not even a hope of it.

Anton von Spaun (born 1790) was in Vienna on a visit.   His brother Josef (born 1788) was an official in the lottery office there, another, Franz (born 1792), was in the Court Chancery, and the youngest, Max (born 1797), was an external scholar of the Vienna Seminary, which he hated, living at Linz with his mother, and coming to the capital only for examinations.   Schober and his younger sister Sofie (born 1795) lived with their well-to-do mother in the Landskrongasse in the inner city, at a house called "The Winter."   Josef Kreil (born 1792), who also came from Linz, was at that time tutor in the household of Court Chancellor Prokop (II), Count Laczansky, and active as an author.

80. FROM THE VIENNA CAPTAINCY of the Civic Guard to the Lower-Austrian Government

The enclosed petition by Franz Schubert for the post of Musical Director at Laibach is herewith conveyed to the constituted authority, following the report of the undersigned dated 3rd April 1816 concerning the similar applications of Hanslischek and Wöss.

The applicant has not been required to undergo a new examination of his musical capabilities, for the reason that he enclosed with his petition a testimonial from the I. & R. Court Musical Director Anton Salieri, dated 9th April 1816, which declares him to be fit for the solicited post.

Since it is Salieri himself who also examined the remaining applicants for this post, his judgment greatly honours Schubert.

No less commendatory is the report from Government Councillor and German Head School Inspector Canon Josef Spendou concerning the applicant's method of dealing with children.

Schubert having been a pupil of the I. & R. Seminary and a boy chorister in the I. & R. Court Chapel, and being at present still acting as assistant teacher at Himmelpfortgrund, these circumstances should serve, according to the view of the undersigned, to redound to his credit and advantage.

Vienna, 14th April 1816.

Mertens.   Freiherr v. Haan.   Unger.

Before Salieri, who was concerned only with Viennese and Lower Austrian candidates, encouraged Schubert to compete belatedly, he had issued certificates to Jakob Schauff, then to Peter Anton Hanslischek and Josef Wöss, as well as to Schauff a second time, who finally defeated the others.   The certificate from Spendou, the Schubert family's special patron, is lost.

81. JOSEF VON SPAUN TO GOETHE

Your Excellency,

The undersigned ventures by these presents to rob Your Excellency of a few moments of your valuable time, and he takes upon himself so great a liberty only in the hope that the enclosed set of songs may be deemed by Your Excellency to be a not altogether unwelcome gift.

The poems contained in the present fascicle are set to music by a musician aged nineteen, Franz Schubert by name, whom nature endowed from the tenderest childhood with the most pronounced leanings towards the art of music, gifts which Salieri, the Nestor among composers, brought to fair maturity with the most unselfish love of art.   The general acclamation accorded to the young artist for the present songs as well as for his other, already numerous compositions by severe critics of the art no less than by the inexpert, both men and women, together with the general desire of his friends, have at last induced the modest youth to open his musical career by the publication of part of his compositions, whereby he will doubtless shortly take his place in that rank among German composers which his pre-eminent talents assign him.

A beginning is now to be made with a selection of German songs,

56

to be followed by sizable instrumental works. It is to comprise eight books. The first two (of which the first is enclosed as a specimen) contain poems by Your Excellency, the third contains poems by Schiller, the fourth and fifth by Klopstock, the sixth by Matthisson, Hölty, Salis, &c., and the seventh and eighth contain songs from Ossian, these last excelling all the others.

These songs the artist now wishes to be allowed to dedicate most submissively to Your Excellency, to whose glorious poetry he is indebted not only for the origin of a great part of them, but also, in all essentials, for his development into a German song-writer. Himself too modest, however, to regard his works as worthy of the great honour of bearing a name so highly celebrated throughout the reach of the German tongue, he lacks the courage to request so great a favour of Your Excellency in person, and I, one of his friends, permeated as I am by his melodies, thus venture to ask it of Your Excellency in his name. An edition worthy of such a favour shall be assured. I refrain from any further recommendation of these songs, which may speak for themselves, but will only add that the succeeding books by no means yield to the present one as regards melody, but on the contrary may perhaps even exceed them, and that the pianoforte player who is to interpret them to Your Excellency should want nothing in skill and expression.

Should the young artist be so fortunate as to obtain the approval of one whose approbation would honour him more than that of any other person in the wide world, may I request that the solicited permission may be graciously intimated in two words,

To him who remains in boundless veneration

Your Excellency's most obedient servant,

Josef Edler von Spaun.

Vienna, 17th April 1816.

Resident at Landskron-Gasse, No. 621, 2nd floor.

Josef von Spaun, Schubert's most faithful friend, who lived near Schober, received no answer from Goethe. The specimen book of songs, however, was returned. Like the second book of Schubert's Goethe songs, it is preserved in a fair copy, although not quite complete. Book I (March 1816), which now contains sixteen songs (Prussian State Library, Berlin), probably began with 'Chronos the Charioteer' ('An

Schwager Chronos') or the 'Scene from Goethe's Faust,' and includes
'Shepherd's Complaint' ('Schäfers Klagelied'), 'The Hedge-Rose' ('Heidenröslein'), 'Margaret at the Spinning-Wheel' ('Gretchen am Spinnrade'),
'Restless Love' ('Rastlose Liebe'), etc., concluding with 'Erl King'
('Erlkönig') in its third version with an accompaniment in even quavers
instead of the difficult triplets. Book II, dating from May 1816 (partly
in the Paris Conservatoire Library, and partly in the Vienna City Library),
contained twelve songs, including 'Only he who sorrow knows' ('Nur wer
die Sehnsucht kennt') and 'To the Moon' ('An den Mond').   None of the
important Goethe songs among the thirty-four Schubert had written in
1814–15 was thus missing. It is interesting to note that Schubert's
friends at that time planned an edition of his songs arranged according to
the poets; but the Ossian songs alone appeared together in 1830 as
vols. i–v of 'Posthumous Poems.' Spaun's letter and the accompanying consignment are mentioned neither in Goethe's diaries nor in his correspondence with Zelter (born 1758), in which indeed Schubert's name
never occurs at all. According to Eckermann's testimony, Goethe preferred not replying at all to making empty phrases. He was of course overwhelmed with musical offerings; but his disregard of this particular letter
may have had something to do with the fact that an uncle of Spaun's, the
eccentric Franz Seraphicus von Spaun (born Vienna, 1754) in Munich, had
turned from a profound Goethean scholar into a malicious opponent of the
poet.   But even later on, at any rate during Schubert's lifetime, Goethe
never repaired his error.—Spaun moved in May 1816 to the house of Josef
Wilhelm Witteczek, who was himself a tenant of his future father-in-
law, Professor Heinrich Josef Watteroth (born 1756, at Worbis near
Kassel), in the Landstrasse suburb, Erdberggasse, No. 97. Beethoven
was a visitor at the adjoining house of Frau Johanna Antonia Brentano,
but the two circles did not intersect.

82. FROM THE SCHOOL-INDEX of the Lower-Austrian Government, 1816

13910 *Civic Gd. Cptncy. 14 April ad* . . . concerning the petition
of Franz Schubert—To the Government of Laibach with all [other]
petitions . . . 18th April.

83. ANTON VON SPAUN to Henriette von Vogelsang
[Vienna, *c.* 20th April 1816.]

Schubert I have heard—that is something quite extraordinary, of which I had no conception whatever. I shall bring with me some of the lighter and wonderfully glorious new songs.

84. SCHUBERT'S REMARKS at the Opening and Close of a Manuscript of Six Ecossaises, only partly preserved (xii. 27), written (?) for Fräulein Marie von Spaun

Composed while confined to my room at Erdberg, May 1816 . . . God be praised and thanked.

Schubert too was at that time staying at the Watteroth's house, probably during the Whitsun holidays. There is a legend, by the way, that Richard Cœur de Lion was arrested in the Erdberggasse in 1192, before he was imprisoned in the castle of Dürnstein on the Danube. Schubert, of course, was confined only in fun, perhaps in order to compel him to write these Écossaises, just as his former schoolfellows locked him up in the study during divine service when he visited the Seminary on Sundays round about 1814. The first note, with the date, which Kreissle professes to have seen, is not to be found on the Vienna Philharmonic Society's MS. (cf. p. 50).

85. ATTESTATION from the Directorate of the Philharmonic Society at Laibach concerning the Applicant Schubert

Schubert Franz, assistant schoolteacher in Vienna.
Birthplace: unknown.
Musical Qualifications: A. Organ, violin and singing, very commendable; is also a composer; wind instruments, unknown.
Morals: B. very good.
Remarks: This applicant, whose age is nowhere mentioned, is a pupil of the Imperial and Royal Seminary: was a choir-boy in the Court Chapel and may be supposed to be still very young, and single. He was declared fit for the post of music master by Salieri, the Imperial and Royal Musical Director of the Court Chapel, and is highly recommended by the civic authorities and the School Inspectorate in Vienna.

26th May 1816.

A. and B. refer to the two certificates, of which Spendou's is lost, as mentioned above. Schubert's age and circumstances (whether he was single, married or widowed, or had children) were unknown at Laibach. His number among the twenty-one applicants was 18.

86. FROM SCHUBERT'S DIARY

[Outside:]

DIARY

Vienna, 14th June 1816.

Franz Schubert.

[Inside:]

13th June 1816.

A light, bright, fine day this will remain throughout my whole life. As from afar the magic notes of Mozart's music still gently haunt me. How unbelievably vigorously, and yet again how gently, was it impressed deep, deep into the heart by Schlesinger's masterly playing. Thus does our soul retain these fair impressions, which no time, no circumstances can efface, and they lighten our existence. They show us in the darkness of this life a bright, clear, lovely distance, for which we hope with confidence. O Mozart, immortal Mozart, how many, oh how endlessly many such comforting perceptions of a brighter and better life hast thou brought to our souls!—This Quintet is, so to speak, one of the greatest of his lesser works.—I too had to show myself on this occasion. I played variations by Beethoven, sang Goethe's 'Restless Love' ['Rastlose Liebe'] and Schiller's 'Amalia.' Unanimous applause for the former, less for the latter. Although I myself think my 'Restless Love' better than 'Amalia,' I cannot deny that Goethe's musical poet's genius contributed much to the success. I also made the acquaintance of Mme Jenny, an extraordinarily fluent pianist, who however seems to be somewhat lacking in true and pure expression.

Only a few leaves from Schubert's diary are preserved (cf. Nos. 450 ff.); but in any case he probably made few entries in it. The musical party he attended on 13th June 1816 cannot be determined. The violinist who took part in the Mozart string Quintet—probably the G minor, K. 516—is said to have been the Bohemian Martin Schlesinger (born at

Wildenschwert in 1751), who was musical director to Count (? Josef) Erdödy and died in Vienna in 1820. The pianist, Mme Jenny, was probably the Frau von Jenny mentioned by Beethoven on 19th April 1817 in a letter to Charles Neate. She must have been one of two ladies, Therese and Susanna von Jenny, who, in 1820, were supporting members of the Philharmonic Society. As Therese joined it together with the violinist Gabriel von Jenny, it may be supposed that Susanna was the wife of the wholesale merchant Rudolf, Edler von Jenny. Which set of Beethoven's variations was played by Schubert cannot be discovered.

87. FROM SCHUBERT'S DIARY

14th June 1816.

I took an evening walk for once, as I had not done for several months. There can be scarcely anything more agreeable than to enjoy the green country on an evening after a hot summer's day, a pleasure for which the fields between Währing and Döbling seem to have been especially created. In the uncertain twilight and in the company of my brother Karl, my heart warmed within me. "How beautiful," I thought and exclaimed, standing still delightedly. A graveyard close by reminded us of our dear mother. Thus, talking sadly and intimately, we arrived at the point where the Döbling road divides. And, as from the heavenly home, I heard a familiar voice coming from a halting coach. I looked up —and it was Herr Weinmüller, just alighting and paying us his compliments in his cordial, honest voice.—In an instant our conversation turned to the outward cordiality of people's tone and language. How many attempt vainly to show their upright disposition by means of cordial, honest language; how many would thus only expose themselves to derision. Such a thing may not be regarded as an acquisition, but only as a natural gift.

Währing and Döbling were north-western urban districts of Vienna, easily reached from the Himmelpfortgrund. The cemetery passed by the two brothers was the general one of Währing outside the Nussdorf gate, where Schubert's mother was buried, and where his father too was to be interred later. (The gates called Linien [e.g. Nussdorfer Linie] were in the outer ring of fortifications bounding the suburbs of Vienna. A toll was charged at these gates for food coming into the town.) The present

Billrothstrasse branches off to Döbling from the Döblinger Strasse.—Karl
Friedrich Weinmüller (born 1874, at Dillingen near Augsburg), who had
sung Rocco in 'Fidelio' in 1814, was a bass at the Kärntnertor Theatre and
in the Court Chapel, and also acted as producer.   He had a villa at Ober-
döbling.   Schubert had already known him in the Court Chapel.

88. From Schubert's Diary
15th June 1816.

It is quite common to be disappointed in one's expectations.
This happened to me when I saw the exhibition of Austrian paintings held at St. Anna's.   Among all the pictures a Madonna and
Child by Abel appealed to me most.   The velvet cloak of a prince
deceived me completely.   For the rest, I admit that it is necessary
to see such things several times and at leisure, if one is to discover
the proper expression and receive the right impression.

At "St. Anna," formerly a Jesuit monastery in the inner city not only
the training-school but also the Academy of Fine Arts was housed.
Annual exhibitions were held there from 1813.   The catalogue of 1816
mentions as No. 73 in Room II a picture by the historical and portrait
painter Josef Abel (born 1764, at Aschach, Upper Austria), "The Virgin
Mary showing her sleeping Child to the angels with motherly delight."
The picture has not been preserved, but it was thus described as early as
1811: "A Madonna with the sleeping Child, surrounded by four angels.
Life-size figures."   ('Paris, Vienna and London,' Rudolstadt, 1811,
vol. i., p. 88.)   In 1817 Abel painted Frau Marie Leopoldine Pachler, the
amateur pianist at Graz.   The portrait of the prince whose velvet cloak
was so realistically painted may have been by Johann Baptist, Ritter von
Lampi, sen.

89. Words of the 'Contribution to the Fiftieth Anniversary of
     Herr von Salieri, First Imperial and Royal Court Musical
     Director in Vienna, from his Pupil Franz Schubert' (xvi. 44,
     xix. 5), 16th June 1816

> Oh thou, sagacious,
> Eminent, gracious!
> The tears I have to shed,
> The art by which I 'm fed,
> I dedicate to thee,
> Who gave them both to me.

Kindness and wisdom flow from thee,
As God's own image thou 'rt to me,
As an angel thou art good,
Fain I 'd give thee gratitude.

Grandsire to us all thou art,
Not for long from us depart!

[Franz Schubert.]

The fiftieth anniversary celebrated was that of Salieri's arrival in Vienna. It fell on a Sunday. After a service attended at the Italian Minorite Church with his four daughters Salieri went to the Lord High Chamberlain, Prince Trauttmansdorff, who presented him with the civil gold medal of honour in the emperor's name and in the presence of Count Kuefstein, the musical representative of the court, and the staff of the Court Chapel. Salieri then conducted high mass in the Court Chapel with music of his own, and this was followed by luncheon in the company of his children and several friends. In the evening the celebration arranged by his pupils took place in Kuefstein's presence at Salieri's home. He sat at the pianoforte, surrounded by his past and present pupils in two semicircles, fourteen women on his right and twelve men on his left. Hummel and Moscheles, who were not in Vienna, had sent vocal compositions, and each of the pupils present had brought a dedicatory composition. The evening began with a thanksgiving chorus with words and music by Salieri, and concluded with some numbers from his oratorio 'Gesù al limbo' (1803, words by Luigi Prividali). Salieri's pupils included Karl, Freiherr von Doblhoff, Josef Weigl, Josef Hartmann Stuntz, Ignaz Assmayr, Julius Cornet, Anselm Hüttenbrenner and Schubert for composition (also Liszt later on), and Josef Mozatti as well as the ladies Betty Vio, Karoline Unger, Therese Rosenbaum, Katharina Canzi and Fortunata Franchetti for singing (also Cavalieri in earlier days). Schubert's contribution had at first been begun as an unaccompanied vocal quartet, but was later turned into a trio with pianoforte, perhaps for reasons of casting. (At that time Schubert regularly took part in male-voice quartets, especially those of Weber and Kreutzer, with Assmayr, Hüttenbrenner and Mozatti, but Hüttenbrenner was absent on this occasion.) The second part is an aria with pianoforte accompaniment, the third a three-part canon; the whole is for male voices.

90. FROM SCHUBERT'S DIARY

16th June 1816.

It must be beautiful and refreshing for an artist to see all his pupils gathered about him, each one striving to give of his best for his jubilee, and to hear in all these compositions the expression of pure nature, free from all the eccentricity that is common among most composers nowadays, and is due almost wholly to one of our greatest German artists; that eccentricity which joins and confuses the tragic with the comic, the agreeable with the repulsive, heroism with howlings and the holiest with harlequinades, without distinction, so as to goad people to madness instead of dissolving them in love, to incite them to laughter instead of lifting them up to God. To see this eccentricity banished from the circle of his pupils and instead to look upon pure, holy nature, must be the greatest pleasure for an artist who, guided by such a one as Gluck, learned to know nature and to uphold it in spite of the unnatural conditions of our age.—

Herr Salieri celebrated his jubilee yesterday, having been fifty years in Vienna and nearly as long in the imperial service; he was awarded a gold medal by His Majesty and invited many of his pupils, male and female. The works written for the occasion by his composition students were performed from top to bottom, according to the order in which they came under his tuition. The whole was framed by a chorus and an oratorio, 'Jesu al Limbo,' both by Salieri. The oratorio is worked in a genuinely Gluckish manner. The entertainment interested everybody.

"One of our greatest German artists" is clearly Beethoven. "Eccentric" (*bizarr*) was Amadäus Wendt's word for "Beethoven's manner" in the Leipzig 'Allgemeine musikalische Zeitung' (1815, cols. 387–9). Judgments of this kind were thus in the air; but we may suppose that in those days Schubert was under the influence of Salieri, who may possibly have said something of the kind himself, in his broken German, in the course of his address early in the evening. "From top to bottom" means that the youngest pupils came first.

91. FROM SCHUBERT'S DIARY

17th June 1816.

To-day I composed for money for the first time. Namely, a cantata for the name-day of Professor Wattrot [Watteroth], words by Dräxler. The fee is 100 florins, V.C.

Concerning the cantata *see* note under 24th July 1816.

Schober's departure for Sweden, 1816. He passed his first, and probably last, examination in law only in 1817. Meanwhile he went with his uncle, probably the syndic Franz Derffel, to Malmö to attend to matters of inheritance.

92. ANTON VON SPAUN to his Brother Josef in Vienna

Linz, 14th July 1816.

. . . First we had music last night: Lugo, adjutant to General Bentheim, who was Arneth's lieutenant and sings very well, sang Schubert songs: 'Longing' ['Die Sehnsucht'], 'The Minstrel' ['Der Liedler'] and others. . . .

Lugo cannot be identified. His general was Friedrich Wilhelm Belgicus, Prince of Bentheim-Steinfurt. Lugo's subordinate was probably Josef von Arneth, one of the Linz circle of friends in Vienna (*see* note to No. 709), who had taken part in the Wars of Liberation in 1813.

93. DEDICATION to Michael Holzer on the Lost Manuscript Title-page of the Mass in C major (xiii. 4)

Mass in C major by Franz Schubert for Herr Holzer.   July 1816.

At the Schubert Exhibition held in Vienna in 1897 the autograph of a Kyrie dedicated to Holzer was shown with the putative date of July 1810. This must have been a mistake, for there is no church music by Schubert dating from that year. This Kyrie was evidently part of the present Mass, which again bore the dedication to Holzer, his first music-master, when it was published in 1825, shortly before the latter's death.

93A. SUGGESTIONS FOR AN APPOINTMENT from the Episcopal Consistory of Laibach to the Government of Carniola, 16th July 1816

Among the competitors from elsewhere, none of whom is known to the Consistory, which therefore attempts only with the greatest diffidence to determine their order of merit, the following three appear to be the most suitable for the post of music master, to judge by the testimonials submitted by them: viz. Kubick, Franz, cathedral chapel-master at Görz; Sokoll, Franz, music teacher at Klagenfurt; and Schubert, Franz, school assistant in Vienna. Their musical qualifications are entered in the table of competitors and, as in the case of other testimonials, may be found in greater detail in the enclosed certificates.

The Consistory had a strong preference for the choice of Josef Miksch, who worked at Laibach, but made these three suggestions as alternatives. The description of Schubert in the table is that of No. 85.

24th July 1816. First performance of the cantata, 'Prometheus,' words by Philipp Dräxler (later von Carin), music by Schubert, in the garden of Professor Heinrich Josef Watteroth, Vorstadt Landstrasse, No. 97, Erdberggasse. Organized by law students, with Philipp von Mannagetta at their head. Rehearsals in the consistorial hall at the University. Originally intended for the host's name-day, 12th July, but postponed owing to bad weather. Address by Konstantin, Count Wickenburg. Performers: Conductor, Schubert; soloists, Fräulein Marie Lagusius (later married to Griesinger) (Gaea), Franz Pechaczek or Josef Götz (Prometheus); chorus and orchestra, students, including Anton Müllner, Franz von Schlechta, Leopold Sonnleithner and Albert Stadler.

This performance took place at a serenade organized by the law students of the fourth year before they left. It was rehearsed in the consistorial hall at the "old University building," now Sonnenfelsgasse, where the university proctor's man lived next door to the Jesuit church. The Watteroth house, which has also been preserved, has a courtyard and garden not unlike those of Schubert's birthplace. The author of the poem, who was of the same age as Schubert, had written it during a walk to Baden near Vienna. He, as well as Mannagetta and Wickenburg, who delivered the address on that evening, later achieved great distinction as an official. Marie Lagusius (born c. 1796), who belonged to the family of the botanist Jacquin, which had been on friendly terms with Mozart, married (?) the Haydn biographer Georg August von Griesinger,

counsellor to the Saxon legation in Vienna. Pechaczek was a
city official, an amateur singer and pianist (not to be confused with
his namesake, who was then deputy leader at the Theater an der
Wien, nor with a composer of the same name who died in Vienna
soon afterwards).   Josef Götz, an official in Prince Josef Johann
Nepomuk Schwarzenberg's household, was a bass whom we shall
frequently meet again.   Leopold Sonnleithner, who was to mean
much for Schubert, made his acquaintance on this occasion.   He
too, like Josef von Spaun, was a pupil of the jurist Watteroth.
It is noteworthy that 12th July is not the Catholic name-day of
Josef, but the Protestant one of Heinrich.   It looks as though the
Catholic students wished to honour their freethinking teacher, who
was himself brought up as a Catholic, in the Protestant manner,
although the celebration of the name-day is unusual with Protestants.
Schubert's cantata was lost, probably not until about 1828.   Sonnleithner at least left us a few of its themes, written down from
memory ('Zellners Blätter für Theater, Musik und bildende Kunst,'
Vienna, 5th March 1867).   While Kreissle in 1865 named Götz in
the part of Prometheus, Sonnleithner says it was sung by Pechaczek.
The work was undivided, and lasted three-quarters of an hour.
(Other musical pieces followed.)   Schubert had himself copied
out the parts; like the score, they were lost.   There were no
separate arias: the solos consisted mainly of accompanied recitatives.   The only elaborate solo piece was a duet for Gaea and
Prometheus (see below).   There were three choruses, the first of
them, "Ye nymphs and ye naiads come hither," rather gay and not
so much concerned with the hero's fate as with the occasion (see
p. 68).   The second, sung by the "Pupils of Prometheus," was
doubtless a poetic allusion to the professor's students.   The close
consisted of a triumphal chorus for mixed voices with instrumental
accompaniment.   There must therefore have been ladies among
the performers, perhaps including the daughter of the house, Wilhelmine (born 1800), who married Witteczek in 1819.   Schubert
frequented the Watteroths' during the following years, and later
the Witteczeks'.

Ihr Nymphen her-bei und Na-ja-den, her -

Ihr Nymphen her-bei und Na-

- bei, ihr seid al-le ge-la-den!

-ja-den, her - bei, ihr seid al-le ge-la-den!

94. FROM THE VIENNA 'ALLGEMEINE THEATERZEITUNG'
(published 27th September 1817)

TO HERR FRANZ SCHUBERT

(For the Performance of his Cantata, 'Prometheus')

Deep and vibrant thrills of tone,
    And the strings' exultant singing,
Echoes of a life unknown
    In my bosom set a-ringing.

Wave on wave of plaint, unending,
    Clamour forth man's sorry plight—
But in wrath and strife descending
    Doth Prometheus break the night!

Joy and splendour then my sadness
    Lightened with a wondrous start;
From on high a ray of gladness
    Fell into my throbbing heart!

And while tears and exaltation
    Rent my breast with sweet sensation,
Gladly in Promethean strife
    Had I sacrificed my life!

FRANZ VON SCHLECHTA.

This was the first time Schubert's name appeared in a periodical. The poem was printed a year too late, because Schlechta did not become a contributor of this journal until the summer of 1817. He was born in 1796 at Pisek in Bohemia, first attended the Seminary at Kremsmünster, and then, much to his sorrow, that in Vienna, later becoming a law student. Schubert first set a poem of his to music in 1815, 'To a Cemetery' ('Auf einen Kirchhof'). Schlechta did not enter the Vienna Seminary until Schubert had left it.

95. JOSEF VON SPAUN TO SCHOBER

Vienna, 19th August 1816.

My brother [Franz] . . . is comfortable at Ried . . . but his days in Vienna and Linz still hover before him like lost felicities; and daily before he goes to bed he sings with his violin the beautiful song, "Thou, who hast from heav'n descended," whereupon sweet peace sometimes comes over him and gently closes his eyes after a sad day's work done . . . Mayrhofer, Kreil, &c., all send you greetings, also our dear minnesinger, whose big cantata has been performed with much success.

Schober was at that time in Sweden. Franz von Spaun had become district commissary at Ried in Upper Austria. The song, 'Der du von dem Himmel bist,' is Goethe's 'Wayfarer's Night Song' ('Wanderers Nachtlied'), composed in 1815. The minnesinger is, of course, Schubert. It is remarkable that later on, when the friends nicknamed each other according to the figures in the Nibelungs' Saga, Schubert was called Volker the Minstrel.

96. FROM THE SCHOOL INDEX of the Lower-Austrian Government, 1816

33711 Government at Laibach, 20th August, 9107 *ad* 13910. That this post has been assigned to the local musician Franz Sokol.— To the Civic Guard in Vienna— . . . for the information of the applicants. . . . 7th September.

This document proves that there is no truth in the tradition according to which Salieri secretly favoured Schauff behind Schubert's back. The first suggestion of three candidates made by the Laibach Consistory (*see* No. 93A) had mentioned Kubick, Sokoll and Schubert. It was declined by the Government of Carniola. The second suggestion of 11th August

1816 mentioned Schauff, Sokoll and Kubick, Sokoll being the victor. But he was not "local," for he lived at Klagenfurt, not at Laibach. He came from Salzka in Bohemia (born *c.* 1780). Schubert, by the way, was probably the youngest of the competitors, though the authorities were not aware of this. Schauff, after an initial failure, had submitted to a second examination by Salieri on 28th March 1816 (together with Hanslischek and Wöss). Salieri at that time called him the best of the applicants examined by him. Only then came Schubert, whom he encouraged and had no need to examine. There is thus no question either of betrayal or of dissension.

97. JOHANN MAYRHOFER TO SCHOBER

Vienna, 7th September 1816.

Schubert and several friends are to come to me to-day, and the fogs of the present time, which is somewhat leaden, shall be lifted by his melodies.

Mayrhofer lived in the Wipplingerstrasse, next door to the old town hall. It is possible that the ideas expressed in the following extract from Schubert's diary were suggested by the melancholy and introspective Mayrhofer.

98. FROM SCHUBERT'S DIARY

8th September 1816.

Man resembles a ball, to be played with by chance and passion. This sentence seems extraordinarily true to me.

I have often read authors to the effect that the world is like a stage on which each human being plays a part. Applause and censure follow in the next world.—But as a stage part is assigned, so is our part assigned to us, and who is to say whether he has played it well or ill?—It is a bad producer who gives his actors parts they are unable to play. Neglect is unthinkable here, for the world has no example of an actor who was dismissed for bad elocution. If only he is given an apt part, he will play it well; whether he receives applause or not will depend on a public subject to a thousand different moods. Up there, praise or disapproval depends on the stage-manager of the world. Thus public censure is suspended.

Natural disposition and education determine mankind's mind and heart. The heart *is* the ruler, but the mind *ought* to be. Take people as they are, not as they should be.

Blissful moments brighten this dark life; up there these blissful moments become continual joy, and happier ones still will turn into visions of yet happier worlds, and so on.

Happy he who finds a true man-friend. Happier still he who finds a true friend in his wife.

To a free man matrimony is a terrifying thought in these days: he exchanges it either for melancholy or for crude sensuality. Monarchs of to-day, you see this and are silent. Or do you not see it? If so, O God, shroud our senses and feelings in numbness; yet take back the veil again one day without lasting harm.

Man bears misfortune without complaint, but feels it the more keenly.—Wherefore did God give us compassion?

Light mind, light heart. Too light a mind usually means too heavy a heart.

Urban politeness is a mighty antithesis to the sincerity of human relationships.

The greatest misfortune of the wise and the greatest fortune of the foolish rests upon convention.

To be noble and unhappy is to feel the full depths of misfortune and happiness, just as to be noble and happy is to feel happiness and misfortune.

I can't think of any more now. To-morrow I shall think of something more. Why is that? Is my mind duller to-day than to-morrow, because I am sated and sleepy?—Why does my mind not think when the body is asleep?--It goes for a walk, no doubt? —For surely it cannot sleep?—

What are all these questions?
'Twill not do to dare it.
No, 'tis not enough:
We must grin and bear it.
And so to bed
Till morn shines red.

71

This page was written on an Austrian holiday, the feast of the Birth of the Virgin. The second idea shows a certain resemblance to a passage in Marcus Aurelius (who died in Vienna A.D. 180): ". . . as though the master of the show, who engaged an actor, were to dismiss him from the stage." (A. S. L. Farquharson's translation.) The thoughts on marriage do not seem to have been produced by any particular case.

99. SECRET

TO FRANZ SCHUBERT

[Composed by Schubert in October 1816, xx. 269.]

Say who made thee a singer
So tender and so sweet,
To draw down heaven's blessings
The earth's dull cares to meet?
In mist and vapour shrouded
But erst the country lay;
Yet spring's delight and sunshine
Thy songs to us convey.

The ancient decked with rushes,
Who ceaseless pours his urn,
Thou see'st not, only waters
In meadows thou 'lt discern.
So too the singer wonders
At all that meets his gaze:
Like thee, what gods have given
He views as in amaze.

JOHANN MAYRHOFER.

This poem was probably written during an excursion to Lilienfeld in Lower Austria, made by Mayrhofer in September with Watteroth's son Hermann (born 1801). The harmless composition of this song in praise of himself recalls Haydn's settings of similar adulatory poems: Dr. Henry Harington's 'What art expresses' and Mrs. Anne Hunter's 'O tuneful voice.'

First performance of the Symphony in B flat major (i. 5), "without trumpets and drums," at Otto Hatwig's in the Schottenhof, autumn 1816.—Hatwig, who was born in 1766 at Grulich (Bohemia), was a member of the Burg Theatre orchestra, teacher of the piano-forte and violin, and a composer. In 1815–18 he conducted the domestic concerts which had originated in the string quartet practices at the house of Schubert's father and until the autumn of 1815 had been held at the house of the merchant Franz Frischling.

100. FROM THE FAMILY REGISTER of Schubert's Father

(17) Theodor Kajetan Anton, born 15th December 1816, at 3 a.m., baptized 15/12, at 4.30 p.m.

This stepbrother of Schubert's died as an infant in 1817.

101. REMARK REPEATED on the Manuscript of the Songs, 'Song of Life' ('Lebenslied') and 'Sorrow of Parting' ('Leiden der Trennung') (xx. 284, 285)

(December 1816.)

At Herr v. Schober's lodgings.

After Schober's return from Sweden Schubert had moved to his lodgings in the Landskrongasse, perhaps only temporarily for the Christmas holidays. It looks, however, as though he had already at that time escaped from school service for a period and that he found his first refuge with Schober from the autumn of 1816 to the autumn of 1817. That was doubtless why he twice emphasized this address on one and the same manuscript.

'Secret Loving' ('Heimliche Lieben'), Op. 106, No. 1 (1827). Engraved Vignette from Karl Czerny's Arrangement of Schubert's Song for Pianoforte Solo. Vienna, 1838–9

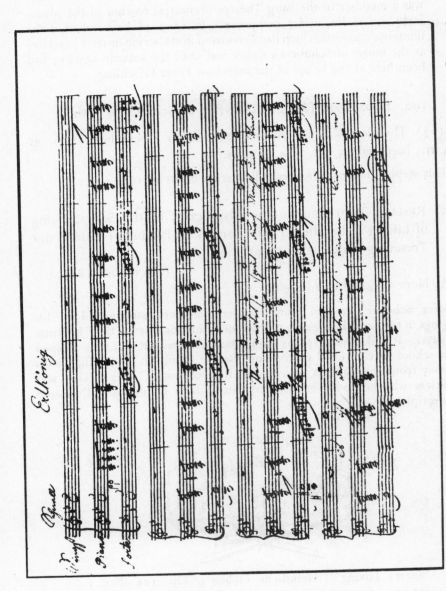

'Erlking' ('Erlkönig'), Op. 1. First Page of the Fair Copy written for Goethe (1816). *See p.* 58

1817

7 Sonatas for Pianoforte (x. 3–7, xxi. 9–10), May–August.
2 Overtures in the Italian Style, D major and C major (ii. 5 & 6), November.
Nearly 60 Songs, including 'Death and the Maiden' ('Der Tod und das
   Mädchen'), February; 'Ganymede,' March; 'To Music' ('An die
   Musik'), March; and 'The Trout ('Die Forelle').

Schubert.   Unsigned Silhouette (1817).   Formerly
in the Possession of Anton Holzapfel.   *See* p. 927

A few of Schubert's friends edit a kind of literary annual in 1817
and 1818, 'Beiträge zur Bildung für Jünglinge,' published by Franz
Härter in Vienna.   A copy has been preserved in the Viennese
National Library.   The collaborators were Anton von Spaun, Anton
Ottenwalt, Josef Kenner, Josef Kreil and Johann Mayrhofer.   The
authorities took some exception to this publication and to the association behind it, because the latter suspiciously resembled the
German "League of Virtue."   But no prohibition ensued: the
annual became extinct from lack of interest.

Schober introduced Schubert to Johann Michael Vogl, February or
March 1817.   The meeting seems to have taken place in Schober's
lodgings, where Schubert too was living.   Schober had connections
with the Kärntnertor Theatre through his brother-in-law Siboni,
who, it is true, had left Vienna as early as 1814.   Vogl, born in 1768
at Steyr in Upper Austria, had been active at the German Opera
since 1794, sang principal tenor-baritone parts there, and also

acted as producer. He was a gentleman, tall, well educated and uncommonly well read. He had been a pupil at the grammar-school of Kremsmünster, and was first intended for the law. Apart from the classical languages he knew English, and is said to have copied Epictetus's 'Enchiridion' in four languages, including German. Marcus Aurelius was one of his favourite authors. He appreciated Flaxman, and in his diary there is a tribute to Scott. He composed songs, including Desdemona's Willow Song, and wrote a treatise on singing, which however remained unfinished. He was somewhat gruff, and at this first meeting with Schubert he remained rather sceptical, but later became his warm friend and advocate. It appears that his performance of Schubert's songs was unforgettable owing to his splendid declamation. However, he permitted himself certain alterations of what the composer had written, and his play with an eyeglass, when seated beside the piano, was a little foppish. He was the first Pizarro in the final revision of 'Fidelio' (1814).

Schubert or Josef von Spaun writes to Breitkopf & Härtel in Leipzig offering them 'Erl King,' Spring 1817.

102. FRANZ SCHUBERT OF DRESDEN to Breitkopf & Härtel in Leipzig

Dresden, 18th April 1817.

Most valued Friend,

. . . I have further to inform you that some ten days ago I received a valued letter from you in which you enclosed the manuscript of Goethe's 'Erl King' alleged to be set by me. With the greatest astonishment I beg to state that this cantata was never composed by me. I shall retain the same in my possession in order to learn, if possible, who sent you that sort of trash in such an impolite manner and also to discover the fellow who has thu misused my name. For the rest, I am greatly obliged to you for so kindly sending me this, and remain with the most perfect respect,

Your most grateful friend
and brother!!!
Franz Schubert,
Royal Church Composer.

[Remark on the outside:]

Replied 23rd May and asked for return of the MS.

The Dresden Schubert, born in 1768, was in the service of the Saxon court as double-bass player and composer. His son, a violinist born in 1808, became better known as a composer (his 'L'Abeille' ['The Bee'] is often taken as being by our Schubert even now). This son became a friend of Schober's later on, and thus his family came into possession of several Schubert manuscripts, now in the Saxon State Library. The elder Dresden Schubert was a freemason, like Gottfried Christoph Härtel, the head of the firm of Breitkopf & Härtel in those days. This firm, then nearly a hundred years old already, published Schubert's complete works at the end of the nineteenth century, but accepted nothing of his in his lifetime. The manuscript of 'Erl King' was returned to Schubert by the publishers. It is worthy of note that in 1817 this firm published a setting of 'Erl King' among the Goethe songs by Petersen Grönland (born Schleswig, 1760).

103. Anton von Spaun to Schober

[Linz,] 15th May 1817.

Do you see Schubert frequently? Have you written no new poems?

104. Dedication on an Album Leaf by Schubert, with an Ecossaise in E flat major and a German Dance in A flat major (c. 1817)

Hop and skip you with this Ecossaise
Through weal and woe for all your days!

Your best friend
Franz Schubert.

[Overleaf:]

Take this waltz to have a go at,
Be you Muscovite or Croat.

The above friend.

To whom this leaf was dedicated is not known. The German Dance (waltz) was later published as Op. 9, No. 3. In the original Schubert rhymes "Wohl und Weh" with "écossaise," spelt properly in the feminine form (but with two c's). This shows that he must have pronounced the word wrongly, as though its form were masculine ("écossais").

The Overture in B flat major (ii. 3) is played at the Orphanage under Ferdinand Schubert's direction, 22nd June 1817. *See* note to No. 137.

105. ANTON VON SPAUN to his Brother Josef

Linz, 19th July 1817.

That Münch is with us you probably know . . . He . . . always breakfasts with us; then we have music until he goes to the office . . . in the afternoon he again drinks coffee with us, when we generally have music until office-time. If you could send me a Schubert song for bass, I should be greatly pleased. Oedipus ['Antigone and Oedipus'], which is set for a bass, pleases him extraordinarily.

Münch is probably Konstantin, Freiherr Münch von Bellinghausen, who had been district commissioner at Ried together with Franz von Spaun, was now evidently residing at Linz and later became government concillor and district captain at Teschen in Silesia and an honorary member of the Linz Musical Society (1823). The song in question was not written until March 1817.

106. ANTON VON SPAUN to his Brother Josef

Linz, 27th July 1817.

Thank you very much for the strings and the songs; let me know what the former cost—the latter I have not yet been able to try as we have not by any means sized up the earlier ones yet. What pleases me much is 'Silence of the Sea' ['Meerestille']—and particularly still the 'Erl King' ['Erlenkönig'—*sic*]—Leni Diemer [?], however, prefers the 'Shepherd's Complaint' ['Schäfers Klagelied'?] and the 'Huntsman's Morning Song' ['Jägers Morgenlied']; the 'Nearness of the Beloved' ['Nähe des Geliebten'] also is splendid—'To Mignon' we did not manage properly, and the 'Song at the Grave' ['Grablied'] we have not yet been able to try, as I sent it to Mama—as well as 'Adelaide.' If you were here, I should have enough to tell you about each separate one, but as it is it won't quite do, unless I wrote at once as I rise from the fortepiano; but perhaps you will receive a detailed report all the same.

The lady named by Spaun is unknown. The 'Huntsman's Morning Song' he mentions was probably the 'Huntsman's Evening Song' ('Jägers Abendlied') set to a poem by Goethe in 1816, or the 'Singer's Morning Song' ('Sängers Morgenlied'), words by Körner, of 1815. 'To Mignon' must be one of the two versions written in 1815 (Op. 19, No. 2). 'Song at the Grave' may be the 'Grablied auf einen Soldaten' of 1816. Spaun's mother was then staying with her son Franz at Ried, together with her daughter Marie.

107. FROM THE FAMILY REGISTER of Schubert's Father

[Theodor Kajetan Anton,] died 30th July 1817, at 7.30 a.m.

108. SCHUBERT TO FRANZ VON SCHOBER

(Set to music xx. 586.)

24th August 1817.

FAREWELL

For the Album of a Friend.

Fare thee well, my dearest friend!
Going to a distant land,
Hold true friendship's hallowed band
In a firm and faithful hand!
Fare thee well, my dearest friend!

Fare thee well, my dearest friend!
Hark, how in a plangent song,
My heart's beats together throng,
Mourning sadly, loud and long.
Fare thee well, my dearest friend!

Fare thee well, my dearest friend!
"Parting" is a bitter word:
Woe to us, for thou hast heard
Calls from where thou art preferred.
Fare thee well, my dearest friend!

Fare thee well, my dearest friend!
If this song may touch thy heart,
Friend, thy shadow, where thou art,
Music will to me impart.
Fare thee well, my dearest friend!

[Franz Schubert.]

Schober had gone to meet his ailing brother Axel (born 1789), who was an Austrian first lieutenant and adjutant in the tenth Hussars regiment, then on his way back from France. He died at Dillingen near Saarlouis on 6th September 1817, before his brother's arrival there. Axel, the eldest of the family, was, like Franz, educated at Schnepfental, took to flower-painting, had been in Vienna during the Congress in 1814–15, and was now due there on leave. Schubert had to give up his room at Schober's to him, and went back to his father. Axel's French valet, Claude Étienne, who later became a teacher of his language in Vienna, wrote an account of his master's end for Frau von Schober. Although Schubert's poem sounds like a farewell for a long time, we know nothing of any intention on Schober's part of remaining abroad. It is possible that he meant to leave for Sweden again after a meeting with his brother, and that he was obliged to return home by the latter's death.

109. ANTON OTTENWALT TO JOSEF VON SPAUN in Vienna

Linz, 7th October 1817.

. . . My greetings to our Mayrhofer and, alas! as yet unbeknown, to Schubert, who has given me great pleasure by having got at one of my poems. I greatly look forward to hearing the song soon.

Anton Ottenwalt, born at Linz in 1789, was an official in the Upper Austrian county council. He was a particularly cultivated and sensitive man, serious, somewhat awkward and good-hearted. He wrote several plays and a number of poems, some of which were already published at that time. He knew Latin and French, but not English, so that in 1826 Bruchmann had to procure him a translation of Byron's 'Cain.' (Bruchmann had cursed that work.) The song mentioned is 'The Boy in the Cradle' ('Der Knabe in der Wiege'), entitled 'Cradle Song' ('Wiegenlied') in its second, incomplete version of November 1817.

110. Anton Holzapfel to Albert Stadler at Linz

Vienna, 17th October 1817.

. . . I promise you upon Schubert's soul that he will improve and really let you hear something from him.

Stadler was employed in 1817–20 at the district government of Steyr his birthplace, and only in 1821 went to Linz as an official in the count council.

> First performance of one of the two Overtures in the Italian Style, D or C major (ii. 5, 6) at Hatwig's in the Schottenhof (end of 1817). Schubert wrote these two overtures under the influence of the Rossini craze that had begun to rage in Vienna in 1816. They were composed in November 1817, as a challenge rather than as a tribute.

111. Album Leaf for Anselm Hüttenbrenner

Exiguum nobis vitae curriculum natura circumscripsit, immensum gloriae.

Cicero ex Orat.

Vindobonae, 16/12, 1817.   .   *pro Rabirio*

Francisc. Schubert.

Schubert wrote down this quotation in the last month of the year during which he had most assiduously cultivated poetry with subjects from antiquity: poems by Mayrhofer, Schiller and Goethe. Anselm Hüttenbrenner, born at Graz in 1794, was educated first at the grammar-school there, then as a monk in the Cistercian monastery of Rain near Graz, and finally at the university there, where he studied law. From April 1815, at the recommendation of Count Moritz Dietrichstein, he finally studied music with Salieri in Vienna, where he spent the winter, living at Graz during the summer. He wrote his first compositions at that time.

112. The Schoolmaster Franz Schubert in the Himmelpfortgrund

N: C: $\dfrac{3445}{556}$

By Government Decree of 6/16 December of this year, Z. 52148, the transfer of the schoolmaster in the Himmelpfortgrund, Franz Schubert, to the Rossau has been agreed and resolved. The same is expected to enter on duty at the Rossau school

F

without delay and to make himself worthy of this favour on the part of the constituted authority by diligent performance of all his duties.

> Matth. Paulus, Bishop of Antioch.
> Ex Consistorio Archieppli.
> Vienna, 24th December 1817.

The Rossau suburb, near Liechtental, was a little nearer the inner city. The school there had not been opened until the preceding year, and its first teacher, Valentin Rosen, had been dismissed for a breach of discipline. The elementary schools were under the supervision of the Archiepiscopal Consistory. Bishop of Antioch was, of course, a mere title, assumed for one of the unoccupied sees of the Catholic Church.

'At the Erlaf Lake' ('Am Erlafsee'), Op. 8, No. 3 (1817). Opening Bars of the First Schubert Song published (1818). *See* pp. 84 f.

1818

Symphony in C major (i. 6), October 1817—February 1818.

---

113. ADMISSION FORM [for Conscription] in the Year 1818,
Rossau, No. 147, School House, Dwelling I

Franz Schubert * 1763, commissioned schoolmaster.

His spouse Anna * 1783.

Son Ignaz * 1786, accredited school assistant, born in the Himmelpfortgrund, is hunchbacked.

Son Ferdinand * 1795, commissioned schoolmaster at the Orphanage at Spitalberg, married.

Son Karl * 1796, landscape painter, according to certificate, [later addition:] received on 23rd July 1818 a year's pass into the conscripted Hereditary States, married, tall.

Son Franz * 1797, master of music, measures 4 feet, 11 inches, 2 lines and is weak, [addition:] received on 7th July 1818 a five months' pass into Hungary, [later addition:] died 21st November 1828, [earlier addition:] according to a report from the Chief Inspectorate of 12th August 1819, the same is employed as school assistant in the Rossau.

Rubric: Totally unserviceable according to their qualifications:
1 [yes]

Son Andrä * 1823 [addition].

Son Anton * 1826 [addition].

Daughter Theres * 1801.

Daughter Marie * 1814.

Daughter Jos[ef]a * 1815.

Not all these admission forms for conscription have been preserved in Vienna. This is the first that remains for Schubert, and one of the only two still extant (see No. 417A). He had, of course, been enrolled already at the Himmelpfortgrund, and probably again at Schober's in the inner city at the beginning of 1817. But the present document proves that he was at home again, perhaps as his father's school assistant once more. It is not true that he was already free of military

duty at that time and became a teacher to evade that duty (cf. No. XLVI):
only assistant teachers who had passed the examination were exempt
in all the city schools, and that would have applied at best—since
Ignaz Schubert was not eligible—to the second assistant and certainly
not to the sixth.   The fact is that Schubert was then, as in earlier days,
short of the required minimum stature, i.e. less than five feet tall.   He
measured 157 centimetres, but the measurements were entered only for
men who were eligible for military duty.   This duty applied to men from
the age of eighteen to forty-five; the time of service was fourteen years!
Those exempt were the clergy, the nobility (Beethoven escaped as a rule
thanks to his prefix ''van''), officials, holders of various honours, barristers,
doctors, privileged wholesale merchants, actors in a regular company,
artists with good academic testimonials, musical performers and composers, and they only by virtue of a certificate renewable triennially and
issued by some political authority testifying to their profession and its
importance, their morals, etc.   Among those temporarily exempt were
schoolmasters and capable university students.   The Schubert brothers
were partly ineligible and partly exempt.—The asterisks before the years of
birth stand for the word ''born.''   Ignaz's age had been lowered by a
year, with the obvious purpose of concealing his birth less than two months
after his parents' marriage.   Ferdinand had been a teacher (formerly school
assistant) at the orphanage in the Alsergrund suburb, near the Himmelpfortgrund, since 1816, in which year he had married Anna Schülle at
the Liechtental church, where he was still organist (c. 1810–20).   Karl,
who had no acknowledged profession, did not marry until 1823 and,
as we shall see, travelled in 1818, like Franz.   Next to his sister Therese,
who later married the teacher Matthias Schneider, and Schubert's two
half-sisters, the younger half-brothers were entered in the register later
on.   Marie died single; Josefa first married one Zant, and secondly
Johann Bitthan, a teacher in the Rossau.   Andreas became financial
councillor and married Anna Fleurriet.   Anton became a priest in the
Scottish monastery in Vienna under the name of Pater Hermann.

114. From the Official 'Wiener Zeitung,' 6th February 1818

> (Advertisement of the 'Mahlerisches Taschenbuch für Freunde
> interessanter Gegenden, Natur- und Kunst-Merkwürdigkeiten der
> Oesterreichischen Monarchie.' Edited by Dr. Franz Sartori.
> Year VI. With 5 Copper-plates. Vienna, 1818. Paper covers,
> 6 florins.)

What again appeals most agreeably to the responsive reader this
year are [the travel descriptions and] the two delicate, sensitive

poems by Johann Mayrhofer, 'On the Danube' and 'At the Erlaf Lake' ['Am Erlafsee'], the last of which is accompanied by music by Schubert that is as ingenious as it is lovely. . . . The copperplates are both surprising and masterly, and make the reading of the work most pleasurable.

This was the first work to be published by Schubert himself, and the advertisement is the first announcing such a work. It was not unusual for musical supplements, especially songs, to appear in periodicals or almanacs; generally, as here, in set type. This volume contained among other things 'The Journey to Lunz' on Lake Erlaf and a copperplate depicting that lake (in Lower Austria, near the Styrian shrine of Maria-Zell). It is now called Erlauf. Sartori (born 1782) was Mayrhofer's chief as head of the Central Book Censorship Office. Apart from this 'Picturesque Pocket-Book,' which was here published for the last time by A. Doll, he also edited other works, including the 'Vaterländische Blätter für den österreichischen Kaiserstaat.'—Schubert had written nearly 350 songs by the time this was published as the first.

115. DEDICATION OF A TRIO for Pianoforte (xii. 31) to Ferdinand Schubert

Trio, to be regarded as the prodigal son of a minuet by Franz Schubert, written down expressly for his beloved brother in Feb. 1818.

Although Ferdinand is not named, this trio section of a lost minuet was more likely rewritten from memory for him than for Ignaz. It is to be supposed that the Minuet in C sharp minor (xxi. 27) was the one here thought to have been lost.

116. LOST LETTER FROM SCHUBERT to Albert Stadler at Linz, 19th February 1818

The contents of this letter, which is mentioned in No. 117, are not known.

117. ANTON HOLZAPFEL TO ALBERT STADLER at Linz
Vienna, 19th February 1818.

. . . To-day I collected Schubert's and Hölzel's missives as well.

"Hölzel" was probably Heinrich Josef Hölzl, a colleague of Mayrhofer's, who about 1820 was second examiner in the Book Censorship Office.

118. DEDICATION OF A COPY OF 'THE TROUT' (xx. 327b) to
     Joseph Hüttenbrenner, 21st February 1818.   Midnight

Dearest Friend,

It gives me extraordinary pleasure to know that you like my songs.
As a proof of my most devoted friendship I am sending you another,
which I have just now written at Anselm Hüttenbrenner's at midnight.   I trust that I may become closer friends with you over a
glass of punch. *Vale.*

Just as, in my haste, I was going to send the thing, I rather
sleepily took up the ink-well and poured it quite calmly over it.
What a disaster!

'The Trout' ('Die Forelle') had been composed as early as 1817.
There are five different versions of it, the last dated 1821. The manuscript with the large ink-blot which is in question here is lost, but has
been reproduced. Schubert's story is a little misleading. He had not
"just now written" the song, but only copied it out again. After
addressing the recipient as "dearest friend" ("Teuerster Freund"), it is
rather odd that he should wish to "become closer friends" with him.
But this was all written at midnight after several bottles of Szegzárd (a red
Hungarian wine).—Josef Hüttenbrenner, born at Graz in 1796, was a
younger brother of Anselm. He was at that time a farmer, and had made
the acquaintance of Schubert, who had already sent him the songs 'Minona'
and 'Restless Love,' in the summer of 1817 in Vienna, where he finally
settled in December 1818 to become an official in the registry of the
Ministry of the Interior. He was an amateur singer and a composer in a
modest way; there is a 'Wanderer' by him, written before Schubert's,
but not published (Schubertbund, Vienna). He became Schubert's
"prophet, singer, friend and pupil," as he wrote to A. W. Thayer about
1860. Unfortunately, having been Schubert's factotum in the 1820's, he
became after the latter's death an equally enthusiastic herald of his brother
Anselm's supposed genius.—Anselm said in his Schubertian recollections
(written for Liszt in 1854) that Schubert got hold of the ink-well instead
of the sand-box, which made the opening bars almost illegible. Anselm
lived at the time at the "Neubad" near the Kohlmarkt as tenant of the
bookseller Josef Geistinger. Schubert sometimes spent the night there.

First performance of the Symphony No. 1, in C major (i. 6), at
Hatwig's in the Schottenhof, early 1818.

119. FROM THE VIENNA 'ALLGEMEINE THEATERZEITUNG,' 26th February 1818

(Notice of a concert and recitation in the hall of the "Roman Emperor," organized by the violinist Eduard Jaëll, member of the orchestra at the Theater an der Wien, Sunday, 1st March 1818, at 5 p.m.)

Part II: An entirely new Overture by Herr Franz Schubert.

This was the first public performance of a work by Schubert. The hall of the hotel "The Roman Emperor" (the house still exists) was much in favour; the hotel was small, but first-class. Eduard Jaëll, the father of the pianist Alfred Jaëll, included among his occupations that of leader at Hatwig's musical evenings and later of the Laibach Philharmonic Society. The overture was no doubt one of the two in the Italian style, probably that in C major. Another overture played at this concert was by Philipp Jakob Riotte (born at Trier in 1776, in Vienna since 1809, and at that time conductor at the Theater an der Wien). The pianist Leopoldine Blahetka, aged seven, took part in the concert.

120. FROM THE 'THEATERZEITUNG,' 14th March 1818

The second part began with a wondrously lovely overture by a young composer, Herr Franz Schubert, a pupil of our much-venerated Salieri, who has learnt already how to touch and convulse all hearts. Although the theme was surprisingly simple, a wealth of the most astonishing and agreeable ideas developed from it, worked out with vigour and skill. It is to be wished that this artist will quite soon delight us with a new gift.

[? Franz von Schlechta.]

Apart from this notice others appeared in the Vienna 'Allgemeine musikalische Zeitung' of 7th March 1818, and in the Dresden 'Abendzeitung' of 28th April 1818 (German edition, Nos. 119 and 121). The latter was the first foreign criticism of any work by Schubert.

121. FROM THE 'THEATERZEITUNG,' 24th March 1818

(Notice of the private concert and recitation held by the retired I. & R. Court actor Karl Friedrich Müller, at the "Roman Emperor," 12th March 1818.)

A beginning was made with an overture for two pianos, eight

hands, by Franz Schubert, performed by the Fräulein Therese and Babette Kunz and Herren Schubert and Hüttenbrenner. The reviewer regards it as his duty to draw special attention to the young artist, Herr Schubert, since he has several times had an opportunity of admiring his rich gifts. Profound feeling, disciplined yet spontaneous force and appealing charm mark his every work, large and small, and once practice, that mother of all human perfection, has done her own work with him, they will without a doubt find their favoured place among the productions of the day. The performance too deserved all praise.

F. v. S.

[Franz von Schlechta.]

Müller, a member of a well-known family of Viennese actors, was also a composer: while retired as an invalid (until 1828) he published some collections of Viennese dances. Which of Schubert's overtures was performed is not known, but it was probably again one of the two in the Italian style, since he had himself arranged them for pianoforte duet (ix. 9 and 10). Nothing is known of an arrangement for eight hands. The two ladies named Kunz, doubtless sisters, twice recur in these documents later, but Viennese musical history has otherwise ignored them. The fourth performer, Hüttenbrenner, was Anselm. The programme further contained Variations for violin, played (and ? composed) by Bernhard Molique, born at Nuremberg in 1802, recently settled in Vienna, a violinist at Hatwig's evening concerts and a composer (in London after 1840); Beethoven's 'Adelaide,' sung by Franz Jäger; Variations for guitar by Mauro Giuliani (and ? played by him); and a Rondo for four hands by Moscheles (? played by the Kunz sisters). The Leipzig 'Allgemeine musikalische Zeitung' had a note on Schubert's overture, but no criticism (German edition, No. 123).

122. SCHUBERT'S DEDICATION on a Copy of the 'Mourning Waltz' ('Trauerwalzer') (xii. i, No. 2)

Written down for my coffee, wine and punch brother Anselm Hüttenbrenner, world-famous composer. Vienna, 14th March in the year of Our Lord 1818, in his very own most exalted diggings at 30 florins V.C.

The so-called 'Trauerwalzer,' too, had an early origin, i.e. in 1816, and Schubert here only recopied it for Anselm Hüttenbrenner. But what

Hüttenbrenner tells us about it in his Schubert memoirs is incorrect in one respect: the waltz had never been attributed to Beethoven before, for this happened only in 1821, when it appeared in the first book of Schubert's dances, Op. 2 (see No. 384). The title is not Schubert's own, but was an invention of his publisher's.

123. DEDICATION of the same German Dance to Ignaz Assmayr, March 1818

Here is a German,
My dearest Asma'r!
I'll make you squirm, an
Accursèd Asma'r!

Illustrissimo, doctissimo, sapientissimo,
prudentissimo, maximoque Compositori
in devotissima humillimaque
reverentiae expressione
dedicatum oblatumque
de
Servorum Servo Francisco Seraphico vulgo Schubert nominato.

Assmayr, Schubert's fellow-pupil with Salieri, was born at Salzburg in 1790, and at first studied with Michael Haydn. He had been organist at St. Peter's church there (1808–15), and now lived in Vienna as a pianoforte teacher.

124. SCHUBERT TO ANSELM HÜTTENBRENNER
[Vienna, 17th or 18th March 1818]

[Outside:]

To

Herr von Hüttenbrenner, Composer

in

Vienna.

[Inside:]

Dear Hüttenbrenner,

I beg you instantly to be at home on Thursday afternoon, that is on the 19th of the month of March at 3 o'clock, so that I may fetch you and we may visit the Kunz people together. If you should not have time—which would be most inconvenient—leave me a message with your landlord.   All of which is urgently asked of you by your friend

Franz Schubert.

Letters were folded and sent without any envelope, generally sealed; the address was written on the outside.   Within Vienna they were delivered by the "little post" for 2 kreuzer and franked with a rubber stamp.—The "Kunz people" are the family of the two pianists (*see* No. 121); Hüttenbrenner's landlord was the bookseller Geistinger (*see* No. 118).

> Leopold Kozeluch dies, 7th May 1818.   In the Seminary, when a symphony by Kozeluch was performed, Schubert once defended him to the disadvantage of Krommer, whose symphonies enjoyed greater favour there.   Kozeluch was a pianoforte teacher, composer and music publisher, and the last of the Masters of the Emperor's Chamber Music (as Mozart's successor).

125. From the Vienna 'Allgemeine Musikalische Zeitung,' 6th June 1818

> (Notice of the midday concert and recitation organized by the violoncellist Anton Schmid, 17th May 1818, at Müller's hall.)

Herr Schubert's overture pleased greatly; it is modelled upon the Italian taste and its most recent dictator, Herr Rossini.   (The orchestra was not quite sufficiently in tune throughout.)

> Anton Schmid, a pupil of Alois Linke's, was an amateur musician, his profession being that of an official in the financial accountancy.   (He must not be confused with Dr. Anton Schmidt, an amateur violinist who was on friendly terms with Mozart, and who had prophetically praised the earliest minuets by Schubert.   He was related by marriage to the Spauns, and in 1815 became a member of the Philharmonic Society committee, but later emigrated to Kiev.   His daughter Marie was one of the Viennese clairvoyants who, in 1825, engaged the attention of Friedrich von Schlegel and Ludwig von Schnorr.)   This time the overture may have been the one in D major.

126. From the Leipzig 'Allgemeine Musikalische Zeitung,' 24th June 1818

> (Notice of the same concert.)

Better than the leading personage were all the other ingredients: viz. a quite interesting overture by Herr Schubert, Salieri's pupil . . .

> The "leading personage" was, of course, the concert-giver.

127. Lost Letter from Josef Doppler to Schubert

Request to compose a 'Rondo brillant' for Leopoldine Blahetka. 1818.

Josef Doppler (not to be confused with two other musicians, Josef and Franz Doppler) affirmed to Grove that he had been present at Schubert's christening. He was certainly a friend of the Schuberts, and as early as 1814 took part in their domestic quartet practices, playing viola (like Franz). At Frischling's, where this amateur party developed into an orchestra, he played clarinet, and he was also conversant with the bassoon. In 1828 he presented the Philharmonic Society with copies of the parts of Schubert's first two Symphonies (those of No. 2 copied in June–July 1816, probably for the orchestra at Hatwig's). Later he became manager of the publishing house of C. A. Spina, A. Diabelli's successor.

128. Anton Ottenwalt to Josef von Spaun in Vienna

Linz, 3rd July 1818.

. . . The hospitable place where you liked to sit with us, the castle garden, is now less frequented; we have moved down. Mayrhofer will tell you that he spent several evening hours with us at the newly chosen place, and there spoke with fine enthusiasm of Goethe's songs and Schubert's melodies for them.

The castle of Linz, which later became a barracks, had a public garden on the Danube.

Schubert receives a passport to Hungary for five months, 7th July 1818. —Johann Karl Unger, the father of the singer Karoline Unger, had introduced Schubert in Vienna to Count Johann Karl Esterházy of Galánta as music-master to his two daughters. Unger, born in 1771 in the county of Zips, had been a theological student, then studied law and became professor of national history at the Theresian Academy of Knights in Vienna, later tutor in the household of Ignaz, Freiherr von Forgács, and in 1810 councillor of domestic economy to Josef, Freiherr von Hackelberg-Landau. He was also a writer and poet, an editor of almanacs and a member of the Philharmonic Society as an amateur singer. At the Theresianum he became friendly with Esterházy. The latter was born in 1775. In 1801 he went on a tour in Germany to complete his education, visiting Weimar among other places. He did not meet Goethe, but made the acquaintance of Wieland, to whom later on he sent wine from his vineyard near Buda (Ofen). He was a cultivated and well-read

man, although he once described himself as "a son of nature,
barbarously brought up." He sang bass, and in 1807 Wenzel
Matiegka, oddly enough, dedicated to him that Op. 21—with a
"zingara" movement—which Schubert in 1814 converted into a
guitar Quartet (*see* note to No. 56). The count, descending from
the Altsohl line of the Esterházys (Galánta, their ancestral seat, is
situated near Diószeg in the county of Poszony [Pressburg, Bratislava in Slovakian]), had in 1802 married the charming Countess
Rosine Festetics de Tolna (born 1779), with whom during the
winter he lived at Penzing, a suburb of Vienna. She called
herself "Rose of the Heath" ("Röschen auf der Heide"), after
Goethe's (not yet Schubert's) 'Heidenröslein,' and sang contralto.
Her children, three surviving out of six, were nearly all born at
Penzing: Marie on 27th December 1802, Karoline on 6th September 1805 (not 1811, as is usually said) and Albert on 15th
June 1813. Marie sang soprano, Karoline contralto, and both played
the pianoforte. Schubert may have taught them already before his
first visit to Hungary in Vienna, where the family then lived on the
second floor in the Herrengasse, City No. 40, at the corner of the
Landhausgasse (now No. 2). The summer residence was the castle
of Zseliz on the Gran (Garam in Hungarian, Hron in Slovakian) in the
county of Bars. The small château in its enormous park and lands,
which were cut up when the village was transferred to Czechoslovakia
under the name of Želiezovce, lies north of Gran (Esztergom), the
residence of the Primate of Hungary: that is to say, on the waterway
from Vienna (via Pressburg) to Budapest a little before the Danube
bend is reached. The castle was built in 1787, and has a single
story with a French mansard roof and surrounds a quadrangular
courtyard. It is overgrown with wistaria, and has delightful views
into the park and the flat landscape down to the river. Thanks to
special circumstances it has remained almost unchanged and still
contains the original furnishings, including the Pressburg grand pianoforte of Schubert's time. The small family archives are a model of
chronicling. The auxiliary buildings in use for agriculture, cattle-
breeding, wine-growing and coursing are in the park and in the
village, where the family vault may be found near the Catholic
church, holding the remains of all the family except Marie, who is
buried in the castle of Grafenegg (Lower Austria), and the count,
whose heart alone lies at Zseliz while his bones rest at Galánta.
The village populace speaks Hungarian; the count's family and some
of the servants also knew German.—Schubert journeyed to Zseliz at
the beginning of July, by stage coach (fourteen stages), probably
alone.

N.B.—Sir Henry Hadow relates in his unfortunate pamphlet on Haydn, 'A Croatian Composer' (p. 27), that he travelled from Vienna to Eisenstadt in 1897, the year of Schubert's first centenary celebrations, and discovered on that occasion that the residence of Haydn's Esterházy princess and the little castle of Schubert's were identical, the Slavonic name being Zeljez. The fact is that Eisenstadt (Kis-Marton in Hungarian) is Zelesno in Croatian, and Zseliz (Zelczov in Slovakian) only later received the name of Želiezovce. Apart from the family names of the owners these two musical places have thus no connection, except that they are both in Hungary east of Vienna; to be exact, Eisenstadt is about twenty-five miles south-south-east and Zseliz more than a hundred miles due east of the Austrian capital.

128A. Lost Letter from Schubert to his Parents, Zseliz, *c.* 1st August 1818

129. Schubert to Franz von Schober and his other Friends

Zseliz, 3rd August 1818.

Best and dearest friends,

How could I forget you, you who mean everything to me? How are you, Spaun, Schober, Mayrhofer, Senn? Are you well? I am quite well. I live and compose like a god, as though that were as it should be.

Mayrhofer's 'Solitude' ['Einsamkeit'] is ready, and I believe it to be the best I have done, for I was without a care. I hope that you are all merry and in the best of health, as I am. Thank God I live at last, and it was high time, otherwise I should have become nothing but a thwarted musician. Schober had better pay my respects to Herr Vogl, to whom I will soon take the liberty of writing. If possible, make him consider if he will not be so kind as to sing one of my songs at the Kunz concert in November—whichever he likes. Greetings to all the acquaintances you can think of. My profound respects to your mother and sister. Write to me soon, for I cherish every syllable from you all.

Your ever faithful friend

Franz Schubert.

The Spaun mentioned here is Josef.—Johann Chrisostomus Senn, Schubert's schoolfellow at the Seminary in 1808–13, was born in 1795 at Pfunds in the Tyrol. He had already made Schober's acquaintance in 1807. He studied in more than one faculty at the University of Vienna, and later made a living as private tutor.—The song 'Solitude,' set to a poem by Mayrhofer, is a solo cantata of which the rough draft has not been preserved.—The freedom Schubert enjoyed may be explained by his having again shaken off the burden of teaching he had once more taken upon himself in the autumn of 1817. It was no doubt due to his engagement at Esterházy's that he was able to escape from it.—Babette Kunz gave a concert of her own on 23rd December 1818, at noon in Müller's hall, and called it a "private musical entertainment." Vogl, who would there have sung a Schubert song in public for the first time, did not take part after all.—At the close of the letter Schubert sends greetings to Frau von Schober and her daughter Sophie.

130. Ignaz Schubert to Karl Schubert at Linz

Vienna, 10th August 1818.

Dearest Brother,

. . . About Franz I must inform you that he wrote and that according to his letter he is as happy as a god, also that he charged us particularly to send his greetings to you, his twofold brother, as he puts it. You will hear further news of him in Vienna . . .

Yours loving brother
Ignaz Schubert.

Karl Schubert had gone travelling in Upper Austria, a little later than Franz. In the lost letter he wrote home Schubert had evidently used the same phrase as in that to his friends ("like a god"). He there called Karl his "twofold brother" because they were both artists.

130A. Lost Letter from Schubert to his Parents, Zseliz, c. 8th August 1818

131. Schubert to his Brother Ferdinand

24th August 1818.

Dear Brother Ferdinand,

It is half-past eleven at night, and your German Requiem is finished. It made me sad, believe me, for I sang it from the depth of my soul. Add what is missing, i.e. write in the words below the music and the signs above it. If you wish to make a number of repeats, do so, without writing to Zseliz to ask me about it.   Things are not well with you: I wish I might change with you, so that you might be happy for once.   You would then find all heavy burdens cast off your shoulders.   I could wish this for you with all my heart, dear Brother.—My foot is going to sleep, much to my annoyance. If the dolt could write it could not go to sleep. . . . Good morning, dear little Brother: I have now slept together with my foot and continue my letter at 8 a.m. on the 25th.   In exchange for your request I have another: love to my dear parents, brothers and sisters, friends and acquaintances, not forgetting Karl in particular.   Did he not remember me in his letter? . . . Kick my city friends mightily, or have them kicked, to make them write to me.   Tell Mother that my laundry is very well looked after, and that her motherly care greatly touches me.   (But if I could have more apparel, I should be extremely glad if you were to send me an extra supply of handkerchiefs, scarves and stockings.   Also I am much in need of two pairs of—cashmere trousers, for which Hart may take the measure where he will.   I should send the money for them at once.)   My receipts for the month of July, including the travelling expenses, amounted to 200 florins.—It is beginning to get cold here already, yet we shall not leave for Vienna before the middle of November.   I hope next month to go for a few weeks to Freistadtl, which belongs to Count Erdödy, my count's uncle.   They say the country there is extraordinarily pretty.   I also hope to get to Pest, as we are going for the vintage to Pócs-Megyer, which is not far from it.   It would be uncommonly agreeable for me if I were to meet the administrator Daigele there.   But altogether I look forward to all the vintages, about which I have been told a lot of such nice things.   The harvest too is very fine here.   The corn is not put into barns here, as in Austria, but enormous stacks are erected, which they call *Tristen*.   They are often some 80 to 100 yards long and 100 to 120 feet high. They are stacked with such skill that the rain, which is made to run off, can do no damage.   Oats and the like is buried in the earth, too.—Well and happy as I am here, and kind as the people are, I look forward with immense pleasure to the moment at which the word will be "To Vienna, to Vienna!"   Indeed, beloved Vienna, thou holdest all that is most dear and cherished in thy narrow space, and nothing but the sight of this, the heavenly sight, will appease my yearning. Requesting once again the fulfilment of the wishes mentioned above,

A hearty greeting to my Aunt Schubert and her daughter.

I remain, with true affection for you all,
Your sincerely faithful Franz.
A thousand greetings to your good wife and your dear Resi.

The "German Requiem" ('Deutsche Trauermesse') was one of the compositions written by Schubert for his brother Ferdinand, who was a composer in a modest way, in order to help him in his profession. Ferdinand evidently performed it as a work of his own in September 1818 at the chapel of the Vienna orphanage, and he also used it on 23rd December 1819 at his examination in musical theory. This small and insignificant work was published by A. Diabelli & Co. at New Year 1826 in parts under Ferdinand's name (publishers' Nos. 2068–9), dedicated to the vice-director of the orphanage, Johann Georg Fallstich. In 1928 it was republished by Eduard Strache of Vienna as a work by Schubert.—With his stepmother, whom he calls "mother" here, Schubert was on the best of terms.—The request for handkerchiefs, etc., in brackets is addressed directly to the stepmother in the polite third person plural "Sie," which it was then usual for children to use to their parents; Schubert also addressed his father in this way.—A tailor, Bartholomäus Hardt, appears after Schubert's death among his creditors (see No. XXII): he is probably the "Hart" mentioned here.—The journey from Vienna to Zseliz by stage coach cost about 5 florins, A.C., reckoned by the number of stages. As in 1824 Schubert received only 100 florins a month from Esterházy (see No. 485), it must be supposed that this was in A.C., but the 200 florins mentioned here were doubtless in V.C., so that in 1818 he would have received about 75 florins, A.C., per month. In September and October 1819 Leopold Czapek was music-master in the count's household, and received 300 florins, probably in Viennese currency.—Freistadtl (Galgócz in Hungarian) on the Waag, between Pressburg (Poszony) and Pistyan, was a property belonging to Count Josef Erdödy of Monyorókerék and Monte Claudio, who was related to the Festetics family by marriage (cf. No. 86). It lies to the north-west of Zseliz. Whether Schubert really went there is not known. Neither can we tell whether he ever went to Count Esterházy's vineyards at Pócs-Megyer on an island in the Danube opposite Waitzen (Vác), or indeed to Pest itself, which was then still politically separated from Buda (Ofen) on the opposite bank of the Danube. The wine there—which Michael Kelly called "Hofner"— was red, like that of Szegzárd (county of Tolna), which Schubert had learnt to appreciate already in Vienna. That he was not averse to the expensive Tokay we know not only from his song 'In Praise of Tokay' ('Lob des Tokayers'), set in 1815 to a poem by Gabriele von Baumberg, whose married name was von Bacsanyi, a friend of Countess Esterházy.—Kolumban Daigele (*see* No. 49) was a cousin of Schubert's stepmother, born in 1782 at Aletshausen near Ulm (Württemberg), who from 1810 to July 1818 was co-operator at St. Giles's church in the Gumpendorf suburb, which belonged to the Scottish monastery, and was at the time of the present letter manager of the estate of Telki near Buda, and priest at Jenö, both of which belonged to the same foundation.— The haystacks were so piled up that the required quantity could be cut off without spoiling them.—The aunt is Maria Magdalena Schubert, *née* Vietz, uncle Karl's widow, who lived at the family house in the Säulengasse with her daughter Magdalena (born 1797), who in 1820 married Michael Sandler, a draughtsman attached to the natural history collection belonging to the court. The mother remained in the house even after the removal of the school.—On Resi *see* note to No. 138.

132. KARL SCHUBERT TO HIS BROTHER FRANZ

[? Gmunden, 1818.]

Traweger, who was very obliging and kind towards me, as your brother, sends you hearty greetings and asks that you should think of him if you should have any male-voice partsongs for four or eight voices.

This note, reproduced from Kreissle, was quoted twice in different forms, and in neither case in strict accordance with the present wording, by Ferdinand Luib in letters to Eduard Traweger and Albert Stadler in 1858. The discrepancies, however, are unimportant. Ferdinand Traweger was a merchant at Gmunden in Upper Austria, with whom Schubert was to lodge later. When and how he became acquainted with him cannot be discovered.

133. FRANZ SCHUBERT, SEN., TO HIS SON KARL at Linz

Vienna, 27th August 1818.

Dear Son,

. . . On the 10th inst. I again had a letter from your brother Franz. He is so well as to regard himself as very fortunate; he speaks in a very cordial tone, full of feeling and affection; and remembers each one of us by name. . . . My mother-in-law and her daughter Therese, wife of the baker Obermeyer, left for Hungary on the 20th inst. to visit our cousin, Herr Daigele, endowment administrator at Telki. . . .

Your devoted Father Franz Schubert,
Schoolmaster in the Rossau.

The letter from Schubert to his family mentioned here (No. 130A) is lost, like that of about a week earlier (No. 128A).—The elder Schubert's second mother-in-law was Anna Kleyenböck, sen., *née* Zeiner. Therese Obermeyer was one of the three sisters of Schubert's stepmother. Her husband, a baker in the Himmelpfortgrund, is not identical with the baker Leopold Obermayer at Gumpendorf, the brother-in-law of Beethoven's brother Johann.

134. SCHUBERT TO SCHOBER and his other Friends

8th September 1818.

Dear Schober, dear Spaun, dear Mayrhofer, dear Senn, dear Streinsberg, dear Waiss, dear Weidlich,

How infinitely the letters from you, all and sundry, delighted me is not to be expressed! I was just attending a deal in oxen and cows when your nice, portly letter was handed to me. As I broke it open, loud cries of joy burst from me on beholding the name of Schober. I read it in a neighbouring room, with continual laughter and childish pleasure. It was as though I were laying my hands on my dear friends themselves. But I will answer you in good order:

Dear Schobert,

I see we shall have to keep to this transformation of the name. Well then, dear Schobert, your letter was very welcome and precious to me from beginning to end, especially the last sheet. Yes, indeed, this last sheet gave me sheer delight. You are a magnificent chap (in Swedish, of course), and believe me, my friend, you will not succumb, for your understanding of art is the purest and truest imaginable. That you should have regarded this alteration as a small one pleased me very much, for after all you have long had one foot in our pandemonium.—That the opera

people in Vienna should be so idiotic as to perform the finest
operas just now, when I am not there, makes me not a little furious.
For at Zseliz I am obliged to rely wholly on my self. I have to be
composer, author, audience, and goodness knows what else. Not
a soul here has any feeling for true art, or at most the countess
now and again (unless I am wrong). So I am alone with my beloved and have to hide her in my room, in my pianoforte and in
my bosom. Although this often makes me sad, on the other hand
it elevates me the more. Have no fear, then, that I shall stay
away longer than is absolutely necessary. Several songs have
materialized these days—very good ones, I hope. That the Greek
bird [Vogl] flutters about in Upper Austria does not surprise me,
since it is his native country and he is on holiday. I wish I were
with him, then I should certainly make the most of my time. But
that you, such an intelligent fellow by nature, should think that
my brother is fluttering in the same place without either guidance
or agreeable acquaintance surprises me very much, firstly because
an artist is happiest in his own company, secondly because there
are too many beautiful districts in Upper Austria for him to find
the loveliest, and thirdly because he has a very pleasant acquaintance
in Herr Forstmeyer at Linz. He is thus certainly in the right
place.

If you could bring yourself to remember me to Max without
depression, it would give me great pleasure. And since you are
also soon to see your mother and sister, please pay my respects
to them. It is possible that this letter will no longer find you in
Vienna, for I did not receive yours until the early days of September,
when you were due to leave. I shall have it forwarded on to
you.—By the way, I am very glad that for you Frau Milder is irreplaceable; I feel just the same. She sings more beautifully than
anybody—and trills worse.

Now a description for everybody:

Our castle is not one of the largest, but very neatly built.
It is surrounded by a most beautiful garden. I live at the inspectorate. It is fairly quiet, save for some forty geese, which at times
cackle so lustily together that one cannot hear oneself speak.
Good people around me, all of them. It must be rare for a

count's retinue to fit so well together as these do. The inspector,
a Slavonian, is a good fellow, and has a great opinion of his former
musical talents. He still blows two German dances in 3–4 time
on the lute, with great virtuosity. His son studies philosophy,
is here on holiday just now, and I hope I shall take to him. His
wife is a woman like all women who want to be ladies. The
steward fits his office perfectly: a man with an extraordinary insight into his pockets and bags. The doctor, who is really accomplished, ails like an old lady at the age of 24. Very unnatural.
The surgeon, whom I like best, is a venerable old man of 75,
always cheerful and happy. May God give every one so happy an
old age! The magistrate is an unassuming, excellent man. A
companion of the count, a merry old fellow and a capable musician,
often keeps me company. The cook, the lady's maid, the chambermaid, the nurse, the manager, &c. and two grooms are all good folk.
The cook rather a rake; the lady's maid 30 years of age; the
chambermaid very pretty and often my companion; the nurse a
good old thing; the manager my rival. The two grooms are more
fit for traffic with horses than with human beings. The count is
rather rough, the countess haughty but more sensitive; the little
countesses are nice children. So far I have been spared dining
with the family. Now I cannot think of any more; I hardly need
tell you, who know me, that with my natural candour I hit it off
quite well with all these people.

Dear Spaun, I was truly most heartily glad that you will be able
to build palaces one day for junior court officials to jump about in.
I suppose you mean a vocal quartet. Remember me to Herr
Gahy.

Dear Mayrhofer, my longing for November will hardly be less
than yours. Cease ailing, or at least dabbling in medicines, and
the rest will come of itself.

Hans Senn kindly read as above.

Friend Streinsberg appears to be dead by now: he may therefore
not write. Friend Weidlich may set his hand to someone else's
letter.

The good Waiss remembers me with gratitude, and is thus a
good man.

And now, dear friends, the very best to you all. Only write to me very soon. My favourite and most valued entertainment is to read over your letters a dozen times.

Greetings to my dear parents, whom please tell that I long for a letter from them. In eternal affection, your faithful friend

Frz. Schubert.

c/o Count Johann Esterházy

Via	at
Raab	Zseliz.
&	
Dorog.	

Josef Ludwig von Streinsberg, born in 1798 (? in Vienna), was another of Schubert's schoolfellows at the Seminary, and became friendly with him through the influence of Josef von Spaun. In June 1818 Schubert had written a 'Funeral Song for [Streinsberg's] Mother.'—"Waiss" is probably the Maximilian Weisse we have already met (*see* No. 10).— Weidlich is said to have been a friend from the monastery of Krems-münster. He is probably identical with the military official Josef Weid-lich, who helped Nikolaus Zmeskell von Domanowitz, Beethoven's friend, with his book on a chronometer.—The cattle auctions were held in the farmyard at Zseliz. They included horses and sheep as well. They were first proclaimed in the village, and the county gentry and officials who put in an appearance were invited to lunch by the master of the house.— Schober was apparently on the point of departure again, but he remained in Vienna. He had now given up the law and tried to become a landscape painter, one of the many callings he took up, only to drop them again. He was not unskilled in drawing, but never became anything more than a dilettante.—Only three songs of that time are preserved: the 'Solitude' ('Einsamkeit') of July already mentioned, 'The Flower-Letter' ('Der Blumenbrief') and 'The Picture of Mary' ('Das Marienbild') of August 1818. ('The Litany of All Souls' Day' ['Litanei auf das Fest Aller Seelen'] had been written before 1817.)—Vogl is called the "Greek" because of his Hellenic enthusiasms; perhaps, too, because of his parts of Orestes in Gluck's 'Iphigenia in Tauris' and Creon in Cherubini's 'Medea.' The "bird" (German *Vogel*) is, of course, an allusion to his name.— Leopold Forstmeyer, whom Karl Schubert visited, was a government official at Linz.

The second part of the letter is addressed to Josef von Spaun.—Pauline Anna Milder, whose married name was Hauptmann, born in 1785 at Con-stantinople, was a pupil of Vogl's and of Salieri's, first sang at the Theater

an der Wien (1803–4), and was engaged from 1805 as first soprano at
the Vienna Court Opera. She had gone to Berlin in 1815. Like Vogl,
she had aroused the greatest enthusiasm in Schubert and his friends at the
Kärntnertor Theatre.—The inspectorate, where Schubert was housed on
this occasion, is directly in front of the castle park.—The archives of
Zseliz permit of a fairly certain identification of the persons named by
Schubert.   The inspector was Johann Már, whose son's name was Ignaz;
the steward was Andreas Pschorner (who was burdened with a long lawsuit beginning in 1822); the doctor Stefan Brach; the surgeon Dr. Ignaz
Losbiegler; the magistrate Paul Grünwald; the count's musical companion
probably a certain Fröhlich (Salieri's pupil), who sang, played the guitar
and also composed; the cook Georg Buchmayer (he drew the largest of the
salaries, 1,000 florins; his successor is said to have been the ancestor of the
famous Viennese *restaurateurs*, the Sacher family); the lady's maid Therese
Tschekal; the chambermaid Pepi Pöckelhofer (Pepi being the diminutive
of Josefine, as of Josef); the nurse for little Albert, Barbara Steiner; the
estate manager Johann Röhrer (whose house, in the park, later occupied
by a stewardess, is adorned with a symbolic owl); the two grooms Anton
Toss and Kaspar Döntz.   In addition there were, of course, a valet, huntsmen, officials, women cooks, laundresses, gardeners, cellarers, coachmen,
etc. etc.   The inspector's blowing upon the lute is a joke, needless to
say.—The pretty chambermaid, probably an Austrian, with whom Schubert
may or may not have had a more or less serious love affair (he does mention
a rival), became lady's maid in 1818, and later married the new valet Josef
Rössler (probably not till about 1830).   In the end she became waiting-
woman and was pensioned off in 1845.—The countess played in her own
life something like the part of her equal and namesake in Mozart's 'Figaro.'
The young Countess Marie was then seventeen, pretty and intelligent; her
sister Karoline, aged thirteen, was unpretentious, shy and not Marie's
match in music either.—Schubert, who in July 1818 wrote two-part vocal
exercises with figured bass for the two young countesses, was evidently not
asked to eat at his master's table during this first sojourn at Zseliz.—Josef
von Spaun, after serving in the hated lottery office, had become conveyancer in the Court Chamber in 1816; he may already have built castles in
the air about marriage and children, perhaps even about four musical sons.
—Josef (later von) Gahy, born in Hungary in 1793, was employed in the
same office.   He was very musical, playing the violin and more particularly
the pianoforte.   He too had been introduced to Schubert by Spaun, and
the Rondo in D major of January 1818, inscribed "Notre amitié est invari-
able," was probably written for him, whom Schubert favoured as partner
in pianoforte duets.   Gahy played Schubert's dances so as to "electrify"
the dancers.—Mayrhofer already inclined towards hypochondria.—The
high road by which the post conveyed these letters led from Vienna on

the south bank of the Danube by way of Raab (Györ) and Dorog to Gran (Esztergom).

The Polonaise in B flat major for violin (played by Ferdinand Schubert) and orchestra are performed at the Orphanage as a work by Ferdinand, 29th September 1818.—*See* note to No. 137.

135. FROM THE 'THEATERZEITUNG,' 17th October 1818

(Notice of the midday concert and recitation arranged by Herr Josef Scheidel, retired member of the I. & R. Court Theatre Orchestra, 11th October 1818, at the County Hall.)

We also heard, instead of the overture by Schubert chosen for the opening, that for the opera, 'Così fan tutte,' by Mozart, and by no means without displeasure.

— — r.

Scheidel was born in 1751 and died in the spring of 1819; he had been a violinist in the court chapel.—The overture that was replaced was that to Goethe's play with music, 'Claudine von Villa Bella' (*see* No. 137).

136. IGNAZ SCHUBERT TO HIS BROTHER FRANZ

[Vienna,] 12th October [1818.]

Dear Brother,

At last, at long last, as you will think, one sets eyes on a few lines. But indeed, I believe you would have seen nothing even now, had not the welcome vacations arrived in the end, much to my relief, and given me leisure enough to write a decent letter, undisturbed and without any irksome thoughts.

You happy creature! How enviable is your lot! You live in sweet, golden freedom, can give free rein to your musical genius, may let your thoughts stray where they will; you are loved, admired and idolized, while the likes of us wretched scholastic beasts of burden are abandoned to all the roughnesses of wild youngsters and exposed to a host of abuses, not to mention that we are further humiliatingly subjected to an ungrateful public and a lot of dunderheaded bigwigs. You will be surprised when I tell you that it has got to such a pitch in our house that they no longer even dare to laugh when I tell them a funny yarn about superstition in the Scripture class. You may thus easily imagine that

in these circumstances I am often seized by a secret anger, and that
I am acquainted with liberty only by name.   You see, you are now
free of all these things, you are delivered, you see and hear nothing
of all these goings-on, much less of our pundits, about whom it is
surely unnecessary to recall Herr Bürger's consolatory verse to you:

> Nay, envy not the massive skulls
> Of consequential people,
> For most of them as hollow are
> As knobs upon a steeple.

Now for something else.   Our Papa's name-day was solemnly
celebrated. The whole Rossau school staff with their wives,
brother Ferdinand and his wife, together with our little aunt and
Lenchen and the whole Gumpendorf crew, were invited to an
evening party, where we all guzzled and drank with a will and had
a good time altogether.   On this occasion I for once collected
my modest poetic wits and offered the old gentleman the following
toast:

> Long may our Father Franz still live amid us;
> To-day we beg that he again will bid us
> Another year to come and dine
> On chicken, fritters, sweets and wine.

Before the repast we played quartets, but keenly regretted not
having our master Franz in our midst; so we soon put an end to it.
The next day the feast of our holy patron-saint Franciscus
Seraphicus was kept with great solemnity. All the scholars had
to be taken to confession, and the bigger ones had to gather at
3 o'clock in the afternoon at school before the saint's image; an
altar had been erected, and two school banners were displayed right
and left; a short sermon was preached which several times reiterated
that it is needful to learn to "decide" between good and evil,
and that much gratitude was due to the "troublesome" teacher.
Also, a litany was addressed to the saint—a litany the oddity of
which astonished me not a little.   At the end there was singing,
and a relic of the saint was given to all present to kiss, whereupon
I noticed that several of the grown-ups crept out at the door,
having no desire, perhaps, to share in this privilege.
Now just a few words about the Hollpein family.   Both he and

she send you hearty greetings and ask whether you do sometimes think of them.   They hope to see you again soon, although they suppose that after your return to Vienna you will not visit them as often as you used to, because your altogether new circumstances may prevent you.   They often regret this, for they are fond of you, as of us all, from the bottom of their hearts and often express their sincerest pleasure about your happy condition.

If I do not say anything about your name-day, you will guess why from our sentiments.   I am attached to you, and always shall be, and that's that.   You know me.

Now good-bye, and come soon, for I could tell you a great deal more, which however I will keep for verbal discussion.

Your Brother Ignaz.

If you should wish to write to Papa and me at the same time, do not touch upon any religious matters.   The little aunt as well as Lenchen also send heartfelt greetings.

The school holidays occurred in the autumn.—Schubert's father was strictly religious, but Ignaz was a freethinker.—Gottfried August Bürger's poem 'An Göckingh,' running to twenty-seven verses, begins at this point with the words "Doch neid' ich nicht . . ." not, as Schubert has it, "Beneide nicht. . . ."—Although the name-day for Franz falls on 4th October, the celebration took place on the preceding evening.— The service was held in the neighbouring Servite church.   The priest, Father Kandidus Lösch, protested the following month, with the support of Schubert's father, against the projected establishment of an amateur theatre in the hall at "The Green Gate" ("Zum grünen Tor"), which adjoined the school.—The Hollpeins (see No. 67) lived at Liechtental, next door to the Grobs.   They had four children, one of whom died immediately; the youngest was then only six months old.   Their son Heinrich, born in 1814, became a sound portrait painter among whose works was a likeness of Ignaz Schubert, his future stepfather.—Schubert's "new circumstances" were his life in the city among friends and patrons of superior rank.—Two other letters were evidently enclosed with this one: Ferdinand's (No. 137) and one from Therese Schubert, which is lost.

137. FERDINAND SCHUBERT TO HIS BROTHER FRANZ

[Middle of October 1818.]

Dear Brother Franz,

. . . I am heartily glad that you are quite well.   Only see to it that you return soon, for everybody asks me how much longer you are to stay away. Our excellent Father told me that even your little sisters (Marie and Bebi [Pepi]) find time hanging heavily and inquire day after day "When is Franz coming at last?"—And it is just the same with all the friends of your songs. If you can fix the day of your arrival, do so.

Your city friends could not be sought out, as they were all in the country. But Papa let Mayrhofer read your last letter, and the secret that Schober is devoting himself to landscape painting is kept no longer.

Among other things I shall have to tell you about a few musical happenings. Your overture for 'Claudine,' which was already to be done earlier at one of Jaëll's concerts at Baden, comes in for much criticism, so Doppler tells me. The wind parts are said to be so difficult as to be unplayable, particularly those for the oboes and bassoon. Others say, though (including Radecki), it is too difficult only for the Baden orchestra. Now it was to be given on 11th October of this year at the County Hall in Vienna, according to the official bills, and yet nothing came of it. This must be very disagreeable for you, I fancy; and doubtless you may thank Doppler for it. Then they began to say the same thing about it here, as above, and a certain Scheidel, I have it from Jaëll, wanted to make out that the effect was not properly calculated, and that there were some cribs in it.

Now something else: at a prizegiving at the orphanage your overture to Hoheisel's cantata was played with much success, and afterwards my examination song was quite well sung. Then came the distribution of the school prizes and of 12 silver medals; three of them were insignia of honour with gown and ribbon, which, after having been worn by the winning scholars for a certain time, have to be surrendered again, while the 9 others remain the property of the respective pupils; moreover, one of them was presented with a watch. At the end the national anthem was sung.

The director's name-day I wanted to celebrate with a grand concert. However, as I was short of both singers and funds, it turned out a very small one. The whole orchestra, which included only oboes and horn apart from the string instruments, amounted to a mere 13 individuals. Therese Grob refused to sing: she wanted to be only a listener this time. I wanted to do the overture to your 'Prometheus' and the chorus following it, together with other big works; but as it was, the music consisted of the following pieces: 1. Overture to Mozart's 'Idomeneo' 2. Two Songs of the Orphans by Ferdinand Schubert; 3. Polonaise in B flat for violin by Franz Schubert, played by Ferdinand Schubert; 4. First movement from a Symphony by Rosetti; 5. Overture to Mozart's 'Figaro.' And that was all.

One more thing: my fortepiano is being sold, and now I should like to acquire yours. If you agree, will you fix the price? Cash will follow.

And now take 1,000 kisses, and when you come to Vienna, see that I am not the last you look up. You will be welcome here in any case, and doubly so if you wish to spend the winter at my home. With true affection,

Hearty greetings from my   Your sincerely devoted brother
    people, also from Father,   Ferdinand.
Mother, brothers, sisters
and friends.

P.S. Father asks me to warn you not to send any money without keeping a receipt, since it is uncertain as a rule whether it will get here.

The opening of this letter, which is preserved only in a copy, has been tampered with. The explanation will be found at the beginning of Schubert's reply (No. 138): it was Ferdinand's confession that he had passed off the 'German Requiem' (*see* No. 131) as a work of his own, and performed it thus at the orphanage, not as a composition dedicated to him by his brother.—Marie and "Bebi" (Josefa) are Schubert's youngest step-sisters.—Baden is a watering-place with an ancient sulphur spring south of Vienna.—Radecki must be Friedrich Hradezky, born in Bohemia in 1776, a horn player at the Kärntnertor Theatre and the Court Chapel.—On Scheidel's concert *see* No. 135.—The prizegiving took place at the end of the school year, this time on 16th September. The cantata (xvii. 2) was set to words by Johann Baptist Hoheisel in September 1816 in honour of Josef Spendou as founder and president of the institute for the widows of Viennese elementary schoolmasters. The overture to it, not indicated in the complete edition, is probably that in B♭ major dating from the same month (ii. 3). It is missing in the first edition of the cantata, a vocal score made by Ferdinand Schubert, published in 1830 as Op. 128, but is specially mentioned in Anton Schindler's list of Schubert's works, from particulars given by Ferdinand. The work had very likely been performed on the twentieth anniversary of the foundation of that institute, at the orphanage, on 22nd January 1817; but on this occasion only the overture was repeated. Spendou (*see* No. 80) was born in 1757 at Möschnach in Carniola; he was a prelate, provost at St. Stephen's cathedral, chancellor of the university, inspector-in-chief of the elementary schools until 1816, etc. It was at his instigation that the teaching of thorough-bass was introduced at the training-school. Hoheisel, born in 1768, was an official in the school-book administration and wrote, apart from some poetry, German language primers. Schubert, on the manuscript of the cantata, calls him "Professor." The same overture was again performed by Ferdinand at the orphanage on 16th August 1829, at a celebration in honour of the new director, Johann Georg Fallstich (*see* No. 131).— Ferdinand's 'Song of the Orphans on the Day of their Examination' was composed on 16th September 1817 (autograph owned by the Philharmonic Society in Vienna) and published, with similar songs, in his Op. 3 by A. Diabelli in Vienna in 1826.—The national anthem, "Gott erhalte Franz den Kaiser," is, of course, Haydn's hymn, written about the time of Schubert's birth.—The name-day (Michael) of the director of the orphanage, Franz Michael Vierthaler (born in 1785 at Mauerkirchen in Upper Austria), fell on 29th September.—Therese Grob had clearly sometimes sung at the church of the orphanage before.—For the 'Prometheus' cantata *see* note on pp. 66–7.—Schubert's Polonaise for violin and orchestra, dated September 1817, has been recovered only recently, and was published in 1928 by E. Strache of Vienna. It was one of several works Schubert wrote for Ferdinand, who played the solo part, while his colleagues and the pupils made up the orchestra, in which the bassoon parts had to be given to other instruments. But the Polonaise had evidently been played already on Vierthaler's name-day in 1817. The 'Namensfeier' cantata of 1815 (xii. 4), dedicated by Ferdinand to his director in a manuscript (Salzburg City Library) purporting to be his own work, had originally been intended for Vierthaler. In print, however, he dedicated to him only his Op. 3.—Short symphonies by Francesco Antonio Rosetti (*recte* Franz Anton Rösler, born at Leitmeritz in 1750, died at Ludwigslust in 1792, court chapel master at Schwerin) had been played in the autumn of 1815 by the amateur orchestra at the merchant Frischling's house.—The "fortepiano" was probably that which Schubert had been given by his father in 1814 (*see* note preceding No. 67).—Ferdinand Schubert lived at the orphanage at that time (*see* No. 113).—Schubert, who does not seem to have wished to return to the new school-house, appears to have sent home some of his savings, or at least to have expressed a wish to do so.

138. SCHUBERT TO HIS BROTHERS FERDINAND AND IGNAZ AND HIS SISTER THERESE

Zseliz, 29th October 1818.

Dear Brother Ferdinand,

The sin of appropriation was forgiven you from the time of the very first letter, so that you had no cause to defer writing so long, except possibly your tender conscience. So my German Requiem pleased you, and you cried over it, perhaps at the very word over which I wept myself. Dear brother, that is my greatest reward for that gift: on no account mention any other.—If I did not day by day get to know the people around me better, things would be as well with me as at the beginning. But now I see that I am lonely among them after all, with the exception of a couple of really kind girls. My longing for Vienna grows daily. We shall be off by the middle of November. Affectionate remembrances and kisses to those dear little creatures, Pepi and Marie, as also to my excellent parents. The city friends are the limit! Now that Schober's wish is no longer a secret, I breathe again.

The musical affairs left me pretty cold. I merely marvel at the blind and wrong-headed zeal of my rather clumsy friend Doppler, whose friendship does me more harm than good. As for my feelings, I shall never be calculating and politic: I come straight out with what is in me, and that 's that.

Do take my fortepiano; I shall be delighted. The only thing that troubles me is that you imagine your letters to be disagreeable to me. It is too terrible even to think your brother capable of such a thing, let alone to write about it.—I hate your always talking about payment, reward and thanks—to a brother, fie, for shame!—Kiss your dear wife and your little Resi for me. And so good-bye.

I was most sincerely pleased to receive letters from you, Ignaz and Resi. You, Ignaz, are still quite the old man of iron. Your implacable hatred of the whole tribe of bigwigs does you credit. But you have no conception what a gang the priesthood is here: bigoted as mucky old cattle, stupid as arch-donkeys and boorish as bisons. You may hear sermons here to which our most venerated *Pater Nepomucene* can't hold a candle. They chuck about black-guards, riffraff, &c. from the pulpit, something lovely; they put a death's head on the pulpit and say: "Look here, you pock-pitted mugs, that's how you will look one day." Or else: "There, a fellow takes a slut into the pub, they dance all night, then go they to bed tight, and when they get up there are three of 'em," &c. &c.—Whether you thought of me while you were guzzling I don't know.—And you, dear Resi, you often think of me—how charming!—I send 99 kisses to all the Hollpeins, man as well as wife, and Resi and Heinrich and Karl, also his godfather together with his future spouse. Whether I have thought of them will be answered in person by

Franz.

The beginning of this letter refers to the lost opening sentences of Ferdinand's latest letter (No. 137). Grove had remarked as early as 1880: "It fixes the Trauermesse [German Requiem] as his [Franz Schubert's], which before was considered as Ferdinand's" (letter to Miss Carola Geisler-Schubert, quoted in Charles L. Graves's biography of Sir George Grove, London, 1903, p. 260).—The "kind girls" were, of course, among the maids.—Pepi and Marie are Schubert's half-sisters.— Schober's wish was to become a landscape painter.—Resi is Ferdinand's first child, Therese, born in 1816.—It is curious that Schubert, who did not know Hungarian, should mention a sermon evidently delivered at Zseliz, where the priest, Nikolaus Horvath, of course preached in Hungarian. It was perhaps translated for him by one of the domestics. The *"Pater Nepomucene"* is perhaps the catechist Father Maria Johann Nepomuk Priegl in the Rossau, the subordinate of Father Lösch.—"Dear Resi" is Schubert's sister Therese.—The other Resi is probably Therese Grob and Heinrich her brother. Karl is the Hollpeins' youngest son (*see* No. 136), to whom Schubert's brother Karl stood godfather in the spring of 1818. Karl Schubert's future wife was yet another Therese, Fräulein Schwem-minger, born in 1799. (She too had a brother Heinrich, but Schubert would hardly have mentioned her twice.)

139. Anton Holzapfel to Albert Stadler at Linz

Vienna, 7th November 1818.

. . . I shall soon write you something about Schubert. I no sooner knew that he had gone away than I hear that he is due back. All the same, we shall be torn away from our pleasant union.

The "pleasant union" may be that of Schubert's schoolfellows, dissolved now they were grown up. Only a few of his fellow seminarists played a part in his later career.

140. From the Official 'Wiener Zeitung,' 21st November 1818

Foreign and Native Arrivals. 19th November: . . . Count Johann Karl von Esterházy, I. & R. Chamberlain, and family, from Hungary (City, No. 40).

Schubert, who was still at Zseliz in November, when he wrote the song 'Sunset Glow' ('Das Abendrot'), probably for the count, must have returned to Vienna at the same time as the Esterházys.

'Slumber Song' ('Schlummerlied'), Op. 24, No. 2 (1817). Engraved Vignette from Karl Czerny's Arrangement of Schubert's Song for Pianoforte Solo. Vienna 1838–9

1819

Music for the Farce, 'The Twin Brothers' ('Die Zwillingsbrüder') (1 act,
     George Ernst von Hofmann) (xv. 5), end of 1818–January 1819.
Overture in E minor (ii. 7), February.
Pianoforte Quintet ('The Trout') (vii. 1).
Song, 'Prometheus,' October.

Second performance of the Cantata, 'Prometheus,' with pianoforte
accompaniment, at a musical practice at Ignaz Sonnleithner's, who
himself sings the part of Prometheus, at the Gundelhof; Gaea—
Fräulein Eleonora Staudinger; among the choral singers is Josef
Hüttenbrenner: 8th January 1819.—Ignaz Sonnleithner, born in
Vienna in 1770, was a barrister and professor of commercial
law.   He lived on the third floor of the Gundelhof on the "Brandstätte" in the city, where from 1815 to 1824 he regularly held
domestic concerts.   Each Friday evening, and later every other
Friday, more than 120 music-lovers gathered there during the
winter months.   Schubert was introduced into this house by
Sonnleithner's son Leopold (born 1797), whom he had met at
the first performance of the 'Prometheus' cantata (see note on
pp. 66–7).   The elder Sonnleithner was a brother of the poet
Franz Grillparzer's mother.—Eleonora Staudinger died in 1821.

141. SCHUBERT TO JOSEF HÜTTENBRENNER, (?) early 1819

Dear Hüttenbrenner,

   I am and remain yours.   I am extremely glad that you have
finished with the symphony.   Bring it to me to-night, at 5 o'clock.
I live in the Wipplingerstrasse, at Mayrhofer's.

   Josef Hüttenbrenner, who in December 1818 had left his father's
property of Rothenturm near Judenburg, in Styria, to become an official
in Vienna, lived at first in the "Citizens' Hostel" (Bürgerspital), an
enormous tenement in the city.   Schubert did not return to the Rossau
in November 1818, but moved to Mayrhofer's in the Wipplingerstrasse,
next door to the old town hall, where they both lived in a single room

on the third floor at Frau Sanssouci's (*see* note on pp. 32–3). This widow of a French emigrant had become a tobacconist, a trade carried on under a State monopoly in Austria. She was born in 1779 and her son Franz, formerly Schubert's schoolfellow at the Seminary, in 1799. The house, owned by Franz Irrsa, was No. 387 in the city.—The Symphony mentioned is Schubert's first, in D major, which had been arranged for pianoforte duet by Josef Hüttenbrenner. Schubert is said to have played this arrangement with him on an old grand pianoforte, perhaps at Maria Theresia von Oettel's (*née* Countess Saurau), Hüttenbrenner's landlady, who, like Frau Sanssouci, subscribed for Mayrhofer's poems in 1824. Schubert may have needed this pianoforte arrangement for the sisters Kunz (*see* note to No. 121).

142. SCHUBERT TO ANSELM HÜTTENBRENNER

[Outside:]

                    To

                         Herr Anselm Hüttenbrenner

                                                    at

                                                         Graz.

[Inside:]

                                        Vienna, 21st January 1819.

Dear old Friend,

Are you still alive? I may well ask, when I consider how long it is since you left us, how long since you last wrote, and how faithlessly you have abandoned us.

Now the last hope of your return has vanished. What holds you at that accursed Graz with such fanatical tenacity? Is there a magic ring round you to fetter you so terribly that you forget all the world? True, I felt as I kissed you good-bye that you would not soon return.

So you have composed two symphonies—a good thing. But you let us see nothing of them: *not* a good thing. After all, you ought to give news to your old friend now and again.

But where are the many hours I spent so happily with you? Perhaps you no longer remember them. But I do. For the rest, you will have heard that I am quite well.

I wish the same to you, with all my heart.
Remain my friend and do not forget

Your

Schubert.

Write to me quite soon.

As soon as his brother Josef had moved to Vienna, Anselm Hüttenbrenner had returned to Graz in the autumn of 1818, having completed his legal studies. He remained there for a year in the district office. His first Symphony, in E major, was performed by the Styrian Musical Society on 18th September 1819. He wrote six symphonies in all.

143. FROM THE 'THEATERZEITUNG,' 4th March 1819

(Notice of Eduard Jaëll's concert and recitation, 28th February 1819, at 5 p.m., at the "Roman Emperor.")

Part I. . . . 3. 'Shepherd's Complaint' ('Schäfers Klagelied'), by Goethe, with music by Herr Franz Schubert, sung by Herr [Franz] Jäger, opera singer at the Theater an der Wien. A beautiful composition, sung most feelingly in Herr Jäger's enchanting voice.

This was the first of Schubert's songs to be sung in public. Franz Jäger, born in Vienna in 1796, was engaged as tenor at the Theater an der Wien in 1817–20, then at the Kärntnertor Theatre, and he went to Berlin in 1824 and to Stuttgart later. He had begun his career as assistant schoolmaster in the Viennese suburb of Lerchenfeld, and he ended it as singing-master at the Württemberg Court Opera. He also wrote songs.—The programme contained among other things an overture and bravura variations for pianoforte, violin and orchestra by Eduard, Freiherr von Lannoy (born at Brussels in 1787, settled in Vienna since 1813), and the declamation of a 'Jeremiad of a Wandering Virtuoso' by Ignaz Franz Castelli.

144. FROM THE 'WIENER ALLGEMEINE MUSIKALISCHE ZEITUNG,' 6th March 1819

3. 'Shepherd's Complaint' ('Schäfers Klagelied') by Goethe, music by Franz Schubert, sung by Herr Jäger . . . The vocal pieces were found amusing.

145. FROM THE BERLIN 'GESELLSCHAFTER,' 22nd March 1819

A vocal piece, 'Shepherd's Complaint,' composed by young Schubert and sung by our valiant tenor Jäger, proved the most enjoyable. We look forward, indeed, to a larger work by this hopeful artist which is now preparing for our delectation.

—S.—

The larger work, rumours of which had been circulating in Vienna since the end of 1818, was the play with music, 'The Twin Brothers' ('Die Zwillingsbrüder'), not performed until 1820.—Another notice of that first song appeared in the Leipzig 'Allgemeine musikalische Zeitung' on 24th March 1819 (German edition, No. 146).

146. FROM MATTHIAS FRANZ PERTH'S DIARY, 14th March 1819

(Concerning the twelfth concert of the Society of Amateurs at Müller's Hall.)

6. Overture by Fr. Schubert.

Perth (born 1788) was conveyancer at the Supreme Court and Constabulary Administration. For nearly fifty years he kept a diary of Viennese events, especially theatrical and musical, but only fragments of it have been published.—This Society of Amateurs (*Dilettanten-Gesellschaft*) may have been identical with the United Private Musical Society (*Vereinigte Privat-Musikgesellschaft*), established in 1818. (Nestroy sang for the first time there, in Handel's 'Alexander's Feast,' entitled 'Timotheus' in its Viennese version, used since 1812.) Ferdinand Schubert had been elected an honorary member and orchestral conductor of this society. It may have been he, therefore, who conducted the overture, probably the new one in E minor of February 1819 (ii. 7). The concert took place in the hall near the Red Tower by the Danube canal in the city, where Josef Müller (*recte* Count Deym von Stritetz, 1750–1804) finally established his art collection, which had at first been merely a museum of plaster casts from antique sculpture, including copies of Sir William Hamilton's Etruscan vases, but developed gradually into a panopticon for the mechanical instruments of which, now lost, Mozart, Haydn and Beethoven had written music. His sister-in-law, Countess Therese von Brunsvik, was one of Beethoven's "immortal beloveds," with whom Schober later came into touch in Hungary, where she occupied herself with charitable work in connection with nurseries for small children.

147. From the Dresden 'Abendzeitung,' 7th June 1819

(Notice of a concert in the Theater an der Wien for the benefit of the poor of the theatre, 25th March 1819.)

8. 'Shepherd's Complaint' ('Schäfers Klagelied'), by Goethe, with music by Schubert, sung by Jäger.

[Höhler.]

The Theater an der Wien, then the largest playhouse in Vienna (which still exists) had been opened in 1801 by Emanuel Schikaneder as the successor of his Theater auf der Wieden, and was now under the direction of Count Ferdinand Pálffy of Erdöd. "Wieden" is the name of a suburb, formerly, as the name implies, a meadow or pasture; "An der Wien" was the name of a nearby suburb, called after the Wien, a tributary of the Danube.—The concert, given on the day of the Feast of the Annunciation, was badly attended.

Performance of Haydn's 'The Seven Words of Our Saviour' at Anton von Pettenkoffer's, in the Bauernmarkt, No. 581, 6th April 1819, in which Schubert takes part.

Pettenkoffer, the father of the painter August von Pettenkofen (the name was changed in passing from father to son), was born in 1788 at Szöny in Hungary. He was a wholesale grocer and landowner. He had taken over from Hatwig the musical society originally founded by the elder Schubert, which in the years 1819–20 met at his house each Thursday evening. Schubert still frequently played the viola there.

148. From the Vienna 'Allgemeine Musikalische Zeitung,' 17th April 1819

(Notice of the concert given by the violinist Pietro Rovelli, 12th April 1819, at noon, in the County Hall.)

Herr Jäger sang with true expression Herr Schubert's sensitive setting of Goethe's poem, 'Shepherd's Complaint.'

The council chamber in the County Hall (Landhaus), the parliament house of the Lower Austrian province, was much in favour as a concert hall in those days.—Rovelli, born at Bergamo in 1793, Bavarian chamber virtuoso, was in Vienna in 1817–19, and there married a daughter of the composer Emanuel Alois Förster.

The Esterházy family, at whose Viennese residence Schubert had probably continued to teach music during the winter, returns to Zseliz in April 1819, without him.

149. Schubert to Anselm Hüttenbrenner

Vienna, 19th May 1819.

Dear Friend,

You are a rogue, and no mistake!!! It will be a decade before you see Vienna again. Now one girl, now another turns your head: well then, may the deuce take all girls, if you allow them to bewitch you in this manner. For heaven's sake, get married, and there's an end of it!—Of course you may say, like Caesar, you'd rather take first rank at Graz than second in Vienna. But be that as it may, I really am in a tearing rage because you are not here. The above proverb applies to Cornet even more than to you. God bless him for it. I shall end by coming to Graz too, and become your rival.—There is little news here; if one hears anything good, it is always the same old things.—Recently Rossini's 'Otello' was given here. Apart from Radicchi, it was all quite well done. This opera is far better, that is to say more characteristic, than 'Tancredi.' You cannot deny him extraordinary genius. The orchestration is most original at times, and the vocal parts too occasionally, except for the usual Italian gallopades and several reminiscences of 'Tancredi.'—In spite of Vogl it is difficult to outwit such *canaille* as Weigl, Treitschke, &c.—That is why instead of my operetta they give other rot, enough to make your hair stand on end.

Catel's 'Semiramis' is to be given soon, with absolutely glorious music.—Herr Stümer, a tenor from Berlin, who has already sung in several operas, is also to appear in it here. His voice is rather weak, with no depth and continual falsetto up above.—I can't think of any more. Keep on at composition and let's see something of it.

All the best. Your true friend

Vienna, 19th May 1819. Franz Schubert.

Anselm Hüttenbrenner did not marry until 1821, when he had succeeded to his father's lands. His wife was Elise von Pichler, the daughter

of a Russian councillor of state.—Schubert here varies Caesar's exclamation at the sight of a miserable little Alpine town, reported by Plutarch:
"Rather first here than second in Rome!"—Julius Cornet, born in
1793 at San Candido in the Tyrol, a tenor, Salieri's pupil in 1816–17,
was engaged in Vienna in 1818 and at Graz in 1819–20.—"The same old
things" are the same old operas.—Rossini's 'Otello' was first given at the
Kärntnertor Theatre on 29th April, but had already been performed at
the rival Theater an der Wien on 19th January; both theatres did it in
German.—Julius Radicchi (born 1763), who had been Beethoven's
Florestan in 1814, was a tenor at the Kärntnertor.—Vienna had already
heard Rossini's 'Tancredi' in Italian in 1816 and in German in 1818; it
marked, after 'L'inganno felice,' the beginning of the Rossini craze.
Meanwhile, in 1817, 'L'Italiana in Algeri' had also been given.—Josef
Weigl, born at Eisenstadt in 1766, was an opera composer and had been
court theatre conductor since 1790.—Georg Friedrich Treitschke, born
at Leipzig in 1776 and living in Vienna since 1800, was producer and
librettist at the Kärntnertor Theatre. He had taken a share in the final
version of the 'Fidelio' libretto.—Schubert's operetta was 'The Twin
Brothers' ('Die Zwillingsbrüder'), the composition of which was
finished on 19th January 1819. Its libretto was by Treitschke's future
successor, Georg von Hofmann.—Charles Simon Catel's 'Semiramis' had
already appeared in German at the Theater an der Wien in 1806 and at
the Kärntnertor in 1815. It was revived on 22nd May 1819, with Heinrich
Stümer (born 1789) from Berlin as guest artist in the part of Arsoz. He
had appeared on 6th May as Pylades in Gluck's 'Iphigenia in Tauris,'
but was not engaged. He was the first Max in Weber's 'Freischütz.'
(Alfred Einstein, in his 'Meisterbriefe,' suggests that Schubert's description of Catel's music as "absolutely glorious" was meant ironically, but there is no good reason to suppose so.)

150. JOSEF HÜTTENBRENNER to his Brother Heinrich

[On the reverse of the preceding letter.]

Dearest Heinrich,

    Your excellent letter gave me much pleasure. I went to the
Prater on Sunday, lay down in the grass and read it over several
times.—You shall have an outline of my present year before long.
—I am content, so far as one may be so.—Since I took to reading
Plato on Socrates I see more and more clearly.—How I enjoy life
—and youth: this is the happiest time.—The idea that it is to
vanish so soon is sad and becomes ever harder. In seven years

I shall be already half-way; I shall have to make the most of all my powers now, for then it will be all over with the joys of life.— The time of love, the fairest on earth, will be over, and with it all hope of a better world.—However, I trust in the Father of us all, for whom it is an easy thing to bestow eternal life on us. For the present, make it your business to write an opera libretto for Schubert—and tell Schröckinger the same.—There is a fee to be had at the same time.—Your names will be known all over Europe.—Schubert will actually shine as a new Orion in the musical heavens.—Heartiest greetings to André and the dear sisters.—Write soon about your decision concerning Schubert.— Fare you well.

Your

Josef.

You must certainly come to Vienna for the coming term—a place is already being looked for.

Heinrich Hüttenbrenner, another of the four Graz brothers, was born there in 1799, and went to Vienna in 1819 to study law, like his father and his brothers Anselm and Andreas. Later he became professor of Roman and church law at Graz, but died as early as 1830. He tried his hand at lyric poetry from his youth, and in Vienna he was a contributor to the 'Theaterzeitung.'—The Prater, an imperial deer-park in earlier days, is the famous recreation and pleasure ground of the Viennese, on the island between the Danube and the Danube canal, on which the Leopoldstadt suburb also lies.—Seven years later Josef Hüttenbrenner would be thirty. He remained single.—Heinrich wrote no libretto for Schubert, neither did Karl Johann Nepomuk Schröckinger, who was born at Graz in 1798, studied law and also went to Vienna in September 1819, but died there at the end of that year.—Andreas (later Ritter von) Hüttenbrenner, born in 1797, was the third of the four brothers. He remained at Graz and gained much distinction as a lawyer. He played the flute and had been one of the founders of the Styrian Musical Society in 1815. —Of the Hüttenbrenner sisters no details are known.—In 1819 Salieri gave a certificate to Anselm Hüttenbrenner, who may at that time have wished to secure an appointment as conductor or operatic manager.

151. Anton Holzapfel to Albert Stadler at Linz

Vienna, 24th May 1819.

. . . I will write to you about Schubert. We did not meet often, though fairly so. *Physice* he is quite well, *quoad exterius atque interius.* *Musice* he is alive too; that is to say he writes, at Vogl's instigation and therefore not without purpose, operas, operettas for performance and other big things. I neither know nor hear them, but it is so. I was introduced to Vogl by Schellmann. His reception of me was most flattering, Schubert and especially Schellmann having indeed spoken most favourably about me. Mayrhofer, who seems to be a friend of the house, also came just then. We talked—however, one always speaks with some constraint and embarrassment even with the most cultivated men, to whom Vogl unquestionably belongs, if one feels, or thinks one feels, the superiority which art and great knowledge of the world imparts to them.

'The Twin Brothers' ('Die Zwillingsbrüder') had been composed at the instigation of Vogl.—The Schellmanns were a barrister's family at Steyr, Vogl's birthplace (*see* No. 154).

152. ANTON HOLZAPFEL TO ALBERT STADLER at Linz

Vienna, 17th June 1819.

. . . Schubert, then, is to come to Steyr: happy he and happy you!—Schubert has so much praise for Rossini's 'Otello'; talk to him about it. I have not yet heard it.

Stadler lived in 1817–20 as an official of the district office at Steyr, his birthplace.

153. FRAGMENT OF A PETITION (not sent) from Franz Schubert, sen., to the Prince-Archbishopric, (?) 1819

. . . The undersigned therefore begs most obediently that his son Franz Schubert, who a year ago interrupted his school service for reasons worthy of consideration in order to develop an artistic talent recognized by experts, may again be graciously confirmed as sixth assistant at his school; more especially as according to the annual school reports he had already [served] four years as school assistant to the entire [satisfaction] . . .

This petition, which was preserved only as a fragment by the Schubert family, seems to have been kept back and torn, perhaps after a violent altercation between father and son. It is not dated, so that its chronological place is merely conjectural. If it was really written in the spring of 1819 the four years during which Schubert acted as assistant teacher must be the time between 1814 and 1818, which it is true he had not devoted continuously to that profession. We may, however, fix the period autumn 1814 to autumn 1816 and autumn 1817 to spring 1818 as being certain. But by the time at which we have now arrived Schubert's service at his father's school was unquestionably over. There is no evidence that this led to a prolonged rupture between father and son, extending over as much as three years.

154. Schubert to his Brother Ferdinand

Steyr, 13th July 1819.

Dear Brother,

I have reason to believe that this letter will find you in Vienna and that you are well. What I am really writing for is to ask you to send me, as soon as possible, the 'Stabat Mater,' which we want to perform here. So far I am pretty well, only the weather refuses to be favourable. We had a very violent thunderstorm here yesterday the 12th, which struck Steyr, killed a girl and paralysed the arms of two men. At the house where I lodge there are eight girls, nearly all pretty. Plenty to do, you see. The daughter of Herr v. K[oller], where I and Vogl eat daily, is very pretty, plays the pianoforte well and is going to sing several of my songs.

Please forward the enclosed letter. As you see, I am not quite so faithless as you may imagine.

Remember me to my parents, my brothers and sisters, your wife and all acquaintances. Whatever you do, don't forget the 'Stabat Mater.'

Your

The country round Steyr   ever devoted
is inconceivably lovely.   Brother Franz.

It may have been about the beginning of July that Schubert went to Steyr with Vogl, who liked to spend his opera vacation in his native town. This, situated very picturesquely at the confluence of the Steyr and the Enns, about ninety miles west of Vienna, is one of the finest towns in Austria, with a splendidly preserved central square, in which some of the houses date back to the fifteenth century. There had been a manufacture of armour at Steyr since the Middle Ages, and later on of fire-arms.—

Schubert stayed at the house of Dr. Albert Schellmann, sen., an expert in mining law born in 1759 at Steinbach in Upper Austria, not actually with him on the first floor of his house in the central square (now No. 34), but on the second, where his nephew Stadler lived with his mother. Schellmann had three sons and eight daughters, five of whom lived at home. They were therefore not the eight girls mentioned by Schubert: three of these were the daughters of the district commissary Weilnböck, who lived next door to the Stadlers, and one of whom, Antonie, was to become Stadler's wife. (The adopted daughter of Dr. Franz Xaver Krugluger, Karoline Eberstaller [born Steyr, 1812], who lived with the doctor at Schellmann's house, boasted in old age of having been Schubert's friend.) As Schubert took the only pianoforte in the house into his room, the girls had to give up dancing during his visit.—The iron merchant Josef von Koller, born at Steyr in 1780, lived in the central square (now No. 11) with his wife and his daughter Josefine (born 1801), who sang and played the pianoforte. She took part in a quartet performance of 'Erl King,' Schubert singing the father, Josefine the child and Vogl the spectral king, Stadler playing the pianoforte part.—What the enclosed letter contained is not known.—The 'Stabat Mater,' probably intended to be performed at the fifteenth-century city parish church (well known through Bruckner's association with it as organist), may have been the German one in F minor, composed in 1816 to words by Klopstock (xiv. 13).

155. CANTATA

(For Johann Michael Vogl's birthday, 10th August 1819, composed by Schubert at Steyr [xix. 3] and sung by Josefine von Koller, Bernhard Benedict and Schubert, with Stadler at the pianoforte.)

From thy heart proceeds thy singing,
To our hearts a message bringing,
Holding us within its power,
Though as gentle as a shower
Sent, refreshing thirsty fields,
When God's grace in mercy yields.

In these hills that saw thee growing,
Here thy heart, first burning glowing,
To an artist's high endeavour
Didst thou dedicate for ever;
And from Nature hast received
What no art has yet achieved.

There we saw Orestes parting,
Jacob from his sorrow smarting,
Saw the doctor vault hope's barrier,
Pity move the water-carrier.
Saw him on a lover's quest
Climb for brides a mountain's crest.

To be known to song and story
Worthy standst thou in thy glory
At the temple of the Muses,
Where applause thy daily use is;
Yet nor wreath, nor rhyme, nor sword
Is the artist's true reward.

Later, when the years oppress thee,
When old age's pains distress thee,
To thy homeland then return us,
Leave to others the cothurnus!
Only keep, as thou hadst done,
Faith like Agamemnon's son.

May God from thy dear existence
Keep all evils at a distance;
Clear and pure its joys be ringing,
As thy splendid, soulful singing.
Then, though silent be thy throat,
Still our souls shall hear its note.

　　　　　　　　　　　　　　Albert Stadler.

This cantata was performed by Josefine von Koller, Bernhard Benedict, a local singer, and Schubert at Koller's house.—The first two lines of Stadler's poem recall Beethoven's motto on the 'Missa solemnis,' "From the heart; to the heart may it return!" which is roughly contemporary. It may not have been original in either case.—The third stanza refers to various parts sung by Vogl on the operatic stage. Orestes is that in Gluck's 'Iphigenia in Tauris,' Jacob is in Méhul's 'Joseph,' the "doctor" is the regimental physician Berg in Gyrowetz's 'Oculist' ('Der Augenarzt'), the "water-carrier" the Savoyard Micheli in Cherubini's 'Les Deux Journées' ('Der Wasserträger' in German). The "lover" is Jakob

Friburg in Weigl's 'Swiss Family' ('Die Schweizerfamilie') and one of the "brides" in line 6 of the translation is the heroine in that work, Emeline, called by the pet name of "Lina" in line 5 of the original. It should be noted that Vogl's birthday, not his name-day (Michael, 29th September), was celebrated, doubtless because the latter did not occur during his holidays.

> The School Inspectorate informs the Conscription Office that Schubert is employed as School Assistant in the Rossau, 12th August 1819.

By this time Schubert was probably an assistant schoolmaster only nominally. The journey to Upper Austria would hardly have been possible had he still remained in office.

156. SCHUBERT TO JOHANN MAYRHOFER

Linz, 19th August 1819.

Dear Mayrhofer,

If you are as well as I am, you must be in the best of health. I am at Linz just now and have been at the Spauns', where I met Kenner, Kreil and Forstmayer, made the acquaintance of Spaun's mother and of Ottenwalt, to whom I sang his 'Cradle Song' ['Wiegenlied'], composed by me. At Steyr I had an excellent time, and shall again. The country is heavenly, and near Linz too it is lovely. We, that is Vogl and I, are to go to Salzburg in a few days. How I look forward to——! I greatly recommend you the bearer of this letter, a student of Kremsmünster named Kahl, who is passing through Vienna on the way to his parents at Idria, and I beg you to let him have my bed for the few days he is there. Altogether, I hope you will look after him in the friendliest manner, for he is a very excellent, pleasant fellow.

Kindest regards to Frau von S[anssouci].—Have you done anything yet? I hope so.—Vogl's birthday festivities we celebrated with a cantata written by Stadler and composed by me, which was quite a success. Now good-bye until the middle of September.

Vogl sends you his   Your
greetings. Regard to   Friend
Spaun.   Franz Schubert.

Mayrhofer had been seriously ill in 1818–19.—It was from Steyr that Schubert for the first time visited Linz, the capital of Upper Austria, where he had good friends and was to find more of them.—Josef Kenner, born in Vienna in 1794 and educated first at Kremsmünster and then at the Vienna Seminary, had been since the middle of 1816 an official in the Linz magistracy. He was gifted as a draughtsman and a poet, and later married Anna, the sister of the brothers Kreil.—The Kreil mentioned here may have been Karl's brother Franz Sales (later Ritter von) Kreil, who was a state official.—Ottenwalt married Marie von Spaun in November 1819.—The plan of going to Salzburg from Linz was not carried out by Vogl and Schubert at that time.—Philipp Kahl, who came from Idria in Carniola, had been at the Seminary of Krems-münster until that time. He was among the subscribers to Mayr-hofer's poems in 1824, but nothing else is known about him.—Schubert's inquiry probably concerns a new libretto by Mayrhofer, since 'The Friends of Salamanca' ('Die Freunde von Salamanka') and probably the fragment of 'Adrast' as well had been set to music by Schubert earlier.— The Spaun mentioned here is Josef.

157. ALBUM LEAF by Schubert and Vogl for Katharina Stadler

Steyr, 14th September 1819.

Ever enjoy the present wisely: thus will the past be a fair re-membrance for thee and the future hold no terrors.

[Franz Schubert.]

On earth naught can such pleasure give
As in the hearts of friends to live.

[J. M. Vogl.]

This joint album leaf was probably written at the farewell on the occasion of Vogl's and Schubert's second visit to Steyr.—Grove quotes, as a counterpart to Schubert's (? own) thought an English entry (? a quotation) written by Mozart in a Viennese freemason's album in 1787: "Patience and tranquillity of mind contribute more to cure our dis-tempers as [sic] the whole art of medicine."   (National Library, Vienna.) (Grove erroneously says "an English freemason.")

158. SALIERI'S TESTIMONIAL FOR SCHUBERT

That Herr Franz Schubert has completely learnt the art of com-position and already furnished very good compositions both for the church and for the stage; and that he is therefore entirely suited to any chapel master's post, in regard to his thorough knowledge as well as his moral character, is herewith confirmed in praise of him.

Ant. Salieri,

I. & R. Musical Director of the Court

Vienna, 21st September 1819.   Chapel.

This testimonial, written by Salieri soon after a similar one for Anselm Hüttenbrenner (23rd May 1819), does not appear to have served any special purpose. It is possible that at this period Salieri furnished several of his pupils with attestations of this kind or that Schubert and Hüttenbrenner asked for them for future use about the same time.

159. ANTON HOLZAPFEL TO ALBERT STADLER at Steyr

Vienna, 14th November 1819.

. . . That you all, yourself, Schubert, Vogl, Paumgartner, &c. have led a joyous life—must have been visible in your faces.

Sylvester Paumgartner, who is here mentioned for the first time, was the musical patron of Steyr. Born c. 1763, assistant manager of the chief mines, an amateur wind player and cellist, he had furnished a musical drawing-room on the second floor of his house in the central square (now No. 16), decorated with symbolic emblems and portraits of musicians, and containing numerous instruments as well as a copious collection of music. Performances took place there regularly, not unlike those at Sonnleithner's house in Vienna, except that Paumgartner was the only musical patron at Steyr. He had commissioned the "Trout" Quintet that year, but was able to give only a modest account of the cello part.

160. REMARK ON A MISSING MANUSCRIPT of Schubert's Overture in F [Introduction in F minor] for Pianoforte Duet (ix. 8), 1819

Written in November, in Herr Josef Hüttenbrenner's room at the "Citizens' Hostel," within three hours, and lunch neglected over it.

Schubert had first played one of Beethoven's overtures as a pianoforte duet with Josef Hüttenbrenner, said to have been in the same key (F major), though there is no such thing. However, Schubert's introduction

is in F minor, the key of Beethoven's 'Egmont' overture.—"Citizens'
Hostel" (*Bürgerspital*) was merely the name of the house in which
Hüttenbrenner had rooms.

First performance of the Male-Voice Quartet, 'The Little Village'
('Das Dörfchen) (xvi. 4) at Ignaz Sonnleithner's; sung by Josef
Barth, Josef Götz, Wenzel Nejebse and Johann Karl Umlauff,
19th November 1819.—Josef Barth, born in 1781 at Grosslippen in
Bohemia, had come to Vienna in 1807 as an official in the household
of Prince Josef Schwarzenberg, and was a tenor in the court chapel.
—Josef Götz, born in 1784 at Krumau (Bohemia), had also been
one of Prince Schwarzenberg's officials since 1812. He was a bass
in the court chapel, joined the Kärntnertor Theatre in the second
half of 1821 (Bartolo in Rossini's 'Barber' was his best part) and
died in 1822 of venereal disease.—Wenzel Nejebse, born in 1796
at Karlstein (Bohemia), a state official, first in the censorship and
later in the exchequer, was a bass.—Johann Karl Umlauff (later
Ritter von Frankwell), born in 1796 at Schönberg in Moravia, who
was to become a judge, had been in Vienna since 1816, but remained there only until the summer of 1821. He was a tenor,
a pupil of Vogl's, and played the guitar.

Anton Ottenwalt marries Marie von Spaun at Linz, 25th November
1819.

Karl Johann Nepomuk Schröckinger dies in Vienna, 23rd December
1819. Schubert and the brothers (Anselm, Heinrich and Josef)
Hüttenbrenner follow his hearse to the Währing cemetery, 25th
December 1819.

'Lay of the Imprisoned Huntsman' ('Lied des gefangenen
Jägers'), Op. 52, No. 7 (1825). Engraved Vignette
from Karl Czerny's Arrangement of Schubert's Song for
Pianoforte Solo. Vienna 1838–9

1820

Music for the Melodrama, 'The Magic Harp' ('Die Zauberharfe') (3 acts, Hofmann) (xv. 7), 1819–20.
Easter Cantata, 'Lazarus' (first and part of second action preserved) (xvii. 1), February.
Song, 'Faith in Spring' ('Frühlingsglaube').
String Quartet Movement in C minor (v. 12), December.
Psalm 23 for Female Choir (xviii. 2), December.
Song, 'To Diana in Anger' ('Der zürnenden Diana'), December.

---

161. FROM PERTH'S DIARY, 2nd March 1820

(Concerning a musical entertainment at Anton von Pettenkoffer's.)

8. Overture by Schubert.

Probably the E minor Overture again.

162. REPORT FROM HIGH COMMISSIONER of Police von Ferstl, March 1820

Concerning the stubborn and insulting behaviour evinced by Johann Senn, native of Pfunds in the Tyrol, on being arrested as one of the Freshmen Students' Association, on the occasion of the examination and confiscation of his papers carried out by regulation in his lodgings, during which he used the expressions, among others, that he "did not care a hang about the police," and further, that "the Government was too stupid to be able to penetrate into his secrets." It is also said that his friends, who were present, Schubert, the school assistant from the Rossau, and the law-student Streinsberg, as also the students who joined later, the undergraduate Zechenter [sic] from Cilli and the son of the wholesale dealer Bruchmann, law-student in the fourth year, chimed in against the authorized official in the same tone, inveighing against him with insulting and opprobrious language. The High Commissioner of Police reports this officially, in order that the excessive and reprehensible behaviour of the aforesaid may be suitably punished. The Chief Constable observes that this report will be taken into considerstion during the proceedings against Senn; moreover, those individuals who have conducted themselves rudely towards the High Commissioner of Police during their visit to Senn will be called and severely reprimanded, and at the same time the Court Secretary Streinsberg as well as the wholesale dealer Bruchmann will be informed of their sons' conduct.

[Outside:]

Arrest of Johann Senn,
excessive conduct of the same
as also of the students
Streinsberg
Zehentner [sic]
Bruchmann and
the School Assistant Schubert.

To make this report clear it should be said that ever since the murder of the dramatist August von Kotzebue, a devotee of absolutism, by the student Karl Ludwig Sand in 1819, student life in Germany had been under strict supervision under the terms of the so-called Carlsbad Resolutions. All undergraduate unions were under suspicion. The influence of German students had made itself felt in Austria by way of Prague, but none of the investigations made there led to any serious discoveries. Johann Senn, Schubert's former schoolfellow at the Seminary, was one of the first and most gravely affected victims of the new measures instituted by the Austrian chief of police, Josef, Count Sedlnitzky, who, in 1819, had written to the lord burgrave of Prague: "The outbreak of this evil spirit abroad makes it incumbent on us to see that our State is preserved from the horrors of political fanaticism." Leopold Ferstl, the commissary of the Supreme Constabulary, proceeded in the spirit of Sedlnitzky, who, in a report to the emperor dated 29th March 1820 (Vienna State Archives) and entitled 'Emulation of German Student Life by some Students of Vienna University,' says that "The names of the known participants will be found in the special list enclosed; and it is probable that their number will yet increase. They are for the present disclosed by the Supreme Constabulary for the local students' directorate to take the necessary measures." (The list is lost.) Senn, like his pupil Anton, Freiherr von Doblhoff-Dier, had come under suspicion by attending gatherings at an inn. The search of his lodgings was the result. The friends named in the report were present on that occasion, but Schubert can hardly have been among the frequenters of that place. That it was he, and not his brother Ignaz, who was meant by the designation of "school assistant" is clear from the rest of the company, with which Ignaz had nothing to do. Streinsberg, whose name is spelt "Steinsberg" in the report, was identified by his father, the court secretary Josef, Edler von Streinsberg. Zechenter, or Zehetner, is probably the future husband of Schober's sister Sophie, Johann Baptist, who it is true was born at Seitenstätten in Lower Austria. He had been to school at Kremsmünster, and became a surveyor. Franz Seraph, Ritter von Bruchmann (born 1798), was a son of the wholesale merchant Johann Christian von Bruchmann, who had migrated to Vienna from Cologne; he had met Schubert through Streinsberg. In his 'Confessions,' written for Senn in 1827 (published at Innsbruck in 1930), Bruchmann mentions this event only allusively: "After a wildly spent night, during which we gave ourselves up to joy without a care and had no inkling of the impending disaster, you were torn from our midst in the early morning, never to return." Senn remained under detention during a fourteen months' trial, and was then deported to the Tyrol, his career ruined. He at first became a barrister's clerk, then a soldier, an instructor at a cadet school and finally held officer's rank in 1828–32. He never saw Schubert again, but according to a letter from Schwind to Schober he once dreamt of him in 1830. Senn was a lyric poet of importance: his poem of the Napoleonic war of 1809, 'The Red Eagle of the Tyrol,' became famous.— The assertion that Mayrhofer and Leopold Kupelwieser had anything to do with this affair is untrue. Nor was the arrest of a few Swiss and a few Prussian students in Vienna about the same time connected with it, although Gustav Ignaz, Count Chorinsky, who was mixed up with the Prussian disturbances, is mentioned as an intermediary in a letter of 1825 from Bruchmann to Senn.—Schubert escaped with a black eye. In Sedlitzky's decree to the Supreme Constabulary, dated 25th March 1820, the only names still mentioned, besides Senn's, are those of Bruchmann and Streinsberg.

163. NAME-DAY SONG

(On the name-day of Josef von Koller, 19th March 1820, for his daughter Josefine, composed by Schubert [xx. 157].)

Father, lend a willing ear,
From my lips an anthem hear!
'Tis to thee my thanks I bring,
Without thee I could not sing;
Bounteously thou didst thy part,
Paving me a way to art.

See, the grateful tears will flow!
Let me kiss this hand; I know,
More than music did it give:
All the happy life I live.
In my grateful glances read
For thy love my humble meed.

From thy blessings' richest store,
Heav'n, the richest on him pour!
Shine for him, fair Fortune's sun!
Founts of joy, abundant run!
And from ev'ry splendid flow'r
Bind we wreaths to grace this hour!

Pray we God that in thy hair
Such a crown may be for e'er,
And I crave it with a tear
That a second may appear,
Blue and gold, for 'tis our lot
All to ask: Forget-me-not!

Albert Stadler.

Schubert's manuscript is dated Steyr, March 1820, but the work was, of course, not written there.

164. TITLE AND INSCRIPTION on the Antiphons for Palm Sunday (xiv. 18), 28th March 1820

1820. Frz. Schubert. . . . In the I. & R. Orphanage.

Schubert had evidently written this work before 28th March at the orphanage, i.e. at his brother Ferdinand's, who had just become choir-master at the church of the western suburb of Alt-Lerchenfeld. He at first met with opposition from the resident musicians there, and Schubert clearly helped him on the following Sunday as well to make an impression. In 1821 Ferdinand also became a teacher in that suburb and went to live in the school there. The church of "The Seven Refuges" was then having a new organ by Christoph Erler installed.

Schubert conducts on Easter Sunday, 4th April 1820, Haydn's so-called "Nelson" Mass in the church of Alt-Lerchenfeld. This

Mass, in D minor, better known in England as the "Imperial" or "Coronation" Mass, was performed at Eisenstadt in 1800 on the occasion of Nelson's visit there, but had been written earlier, in July and August 1798.

165. From a Graz Concert Programme, 7th April 1820

(Grand Concert given by Eduard Jaëll with several members of the Styrian Musical Society in the Assembly Hall.)

Part I, No. 1.   New Overture by Herr Franz Schubert.

The Assembly Hall (*Redoutensaal*) is in the County Theatre (*Landständisches Theater*).—The overture was probably again that in E minor, the last written by Schubert as a separate composition.   This was the first performance of a work by Schubert outside Vienna.

Haydn's 'Creation' is performed at Pettenkoffer's on 13th April 1820, probably with Schubert among the performers.

Project for a performance of the cantata, 'Prometheus,' at the Augarten, under Schubert's direction; cancelled by himself after unsuccessful rehearsals: Spring 1820.—The Augarten is a public park in the Leopoldstadt belonging to the old Favorita, an imperial summer palace, where already in Mozart's time Sunday morning concerts were held in the spring season.

166. Ottenwalt to Josef von Spaun in Vienna

Linz, 3rd May 1820.

You will [if you are transferred here] have to let the pianoforte, which is heard so rarely, resound with many a Schubert song.

Spaun was not transferred to Linz until the autumn of 1821.

167. Programme of the Vienna Court Opera

New Farce with Songs

This Day, Wednesday, 14th June [1820], to be performed . . .: (In the Theatre by the Carinthian Gate.)

By the I. & R. Court Opera Singers:

For the First Time:
THE TWIN BROTHERS.

['Die Zwillingsbrüder.']
Farce with Songs in One Act.
The Music is by Herr FRANZ SCHUBERT.
Dramatis Personae:

The Mayor	Herr Meier
Lieschen, his Daughter	Mlle Vio
Anton	Herr Rosenfeld
The Bailiff	Herr Gottdank
Franz Spiess ⎫	
Friedrich Spiess ⎬ Invalids	Herr Vogl
Country Folk.	

(The action takes place at a village on the Rhine.)

(Im Theater nächſt dem Kärnthnerthore.)
Von den k. k. Hof-Operiſten:
Zum erſten Mahle:
Die Zwillingsbrüder.
Poſſe mit Geſang in einem Aufzuge.
Die Muſik iſt von Herrn Franz Schubert.

Perſonen:

Der Schulze	. . .	Hr. Meier.
Lischen, deſſen Tochter	. . .	Dlle. Vio
Anton	. . .	Hr. Rosenfeld
Der Amtmann	. . .	Hr. Gottdank.
Franz Spieß. ⎫		
Friedrich Spieß, ⎬ Invaliden .		Hr. Vogl.
Landleute. ⎭		

'The Twin Brothers' ('Die Zwillingsbruder')
Play-bill of the First Performance (1820)

Subsequently:
THE TWO AUNTS, OR: THEN AND NOW.
Comic Ballet in Two Acts, devised by Herr Aumer,
Ballet Master of the I. & R. Court Theatres.

The Music is by the Musical Director, Herr Gyrowetz.

.   .   .   .   .

Herr Mayseder will have the honour of playing the violin solos.

Free List suspended for the Day.

To commence at 7 o'clock.

This, at last, was the first sizable work by Schubert to be performed in public. The libretto, by Georg, Edler von Hofmann (born 1771), had not appealed to Schubert particularly. It is said, by the way (*see* No. 170), to have been written on a French model. This would square with the fact that Hofmann, Treitschke's successor as librettist to the Kärntnertor Theatre, was still translating libretti from the French in 1835, together with Josef von Seyfried. He also wrote several libretti for Weigl and Gyrowetz, as well as the melodrama 'The Magic Harp' ('Die Zauber-harfe') for Schubert; and it is said that the words for the musical numbers in the supposed trial work submitted to the Kärntnertor Theatre in 1826 (the Nannette Schechner affair) were also by him.—The playbills of that time, of double width, gave the programmes of both the court theatres side by side, thus including the spoken plays at the Burg Theatre.— "Meier" is probably Friedrich Sebastian Meyer (or Meier or Mayer), born in 1773 at Benediktbeuern in Bavaria, Josefa Hofer's second husband and thus Mozart's posthumous brother-in-law, a bass singer and actor, first at the Freihaus Theatre, then at the Theater an der Wien (where he sang Pizarro in 'Fidelio' in 1805) and lastly at the Kärntnertor Theatre. He was a great Handel propagandist and sang extracts from that master's works at his farewell concert on 1st May 1828.—Betty (Elisabeth) Vio, born in Vienna in 1802, a niece of the theatre manager Wilhelm Vogel, had been engaged since the summer of 1819 at the Kärntnertor Theatre, and in the spring of 1824 went to the Theater an der Wien.—Viktor Rosenfeld, born in Prague in 1790, had been at the Court Opera since 1815, and was soon to go to Dresden.—Josef Gottdank (born 1779) had at first been at the Theater an der Wien, and since 1806 at the Court Opera, where he became producer later on.—Mayseder had been appointed director of the violins at the court chapel and was also active as solo violinist at the court theatres.

168. FROM THE TRAVEL DIARY of Wolfgang Amadeus Mozart, jun.

Vienna, 14th June 1820.

In the evening I saw at the Kärntnertor Theatre a little operetta, 'The Twin Brothers,' with music by Herr Schubert, a beginner.

The composition contains some quite pretty things, but is kept a little too serious.

Mozart's youngest son, who bore his father's Christian names, born in the year of the master's death (1791), was a pianist and composer. He travelled in 1819–22, and later became musical director at Lemberg (Lwów in Galicia). Two of Schubert's friends appear in his autograph album: Johann Baptist Jenger inscribed himself at Graz on 8th July 1820 and Josef von Spaun on his departure from Lemberg on 18th April 1826.

169. From Josef Karl Rosenbaum's Diary, 14th June 1820

Kärntnertor Theatre. For the first time: 'Twin Brothers.' Farce in 1 act by Hoffmann. Music by Schubert.—'2 Aunts' . . . To the Kärntnertor Theatre. The operetta has nothing to recommend it, yet Schubert's friends made a lot of noise while the opposition hissed—at the close there was a fuss until Vogl appeared and said: "Schubert is not present; I thank you in his name."

Josef Karl Rosenbaum (born 1770) had been secretary to Count Karl Esterházy, and had married the opera singer Marie Therese Gassmann, a pupil of Salieri's who had been a friend of Haydn's.—Schubert, as usual, sat in the gallery with Anselm Hüttenbrenner, and was not to be induced to exchange his old frock-coat for Anselm's evening tail-coat, in order to take a call. He smilingly listened to Vogl's thanks, and then went with his friends to Achatius Lenkay's wine-shop in the Liliengasse (near St. Stephen's Cathedral), where they drank a few pints of "Nessmüller" (a cheap Hungarian wine) to his success (cf. No. 518).

170. From the Vienna 'Allgemeine Musikalische Zeitung,' 17th June 1820

Just as the earliest years determine the whole character of a person and decide the happiness or misfortune of his life, so the first steps taken by a disciple of art and his first success or failure give a firm direction to the long succession of his later years, furthering or impeding his career, at any rate frequently, for one can think of exceptions. The critic is thus bound in such cases to weigh each word and to do no injury to the tender blossom, the more so because he lacks time and opportunity to deliver an· exhaustive judgment, and it is difficult to fix in his mind sounds which have only fleetingly passed his ears once, in such a manner that they may be subjected to the operations of his power of judgment. Moreover, another circumstance arises in this case: it is a question here of indigenous, home-grown art, and that alone would call for discretion. Let us therefore pronounce our views openly but indulgently; as we see it, *faciant meliora potentes*, so to say. Herr Schubert, with whom we are mainly concerned, has so far been known to us only by a few meritorious romances; his opera, which he let appear modestly under the name of "farce," was talked about as early as the end of 1818, but we never caught sight of it until now, in spite of all the influence that was exerted. It attests its composer as a gifted mind, full of force and invention —a major advantage, since everything else can be acquired; but it also shows at the same time that Herr Schubert's abilities lie in the direction of tragedy rather than comedy, for which reason we urgently advise him to choose the former category, at any rate for the present. The music for 'The Twin Brothers' has much originality and many interesting passages, and the declamation is correct; but it is a blot on the work that the sentiments of simple country folk are interpreted much too seriously, not to say heavy-handedly, for a comic subject. *Medium tenuere beati*. Little as one is inclined to countenance heroes who sing polonaises and who weep in bravura passages, one can no more allow the passions to be tragically conceived in a light operetta. We will say nothing here of the German composers and Mozart, that paragon of romantic and of the only true music; but even if we take the Frenchmen as models, we shall find a vast gulf between Méhul's 'Two Foxes' ['Une Folie'] and his greater works, or between Cherubini's masterpiece, 'The Days of Peril' ['Les Deux Journées'] and his 'Medea,' which is quite a different composition. Comic music, it seems to us, does not take at all kindly to a very close adherence to the words, or to the composer's taking refuge in a modulation whenever pain, for instance, is mentioned; and both kinds, the higher and the lighter music, demand shapely pieces, each of which has its exposition, its development and its unravelling, like the scenes of a spoken play—for which see Mozart's operas. Herr Schubert is too much wedded to details of the text, and this chases him and his hearer restlessly through modulations and allows of no point of repose; he tries to express words in music instead of painting the nature of a whole speech by means of the character of a whole piece, which, as Mozart proves, is the only way of attaining to the highest aims of art and of conquering its greatest difficulties, by producing regular, rounded-off pieces and yet by making the whole call forth the required feeling. For this Herr Schubert has allowed himself to be led too far astray by his laudable endeavour to go his own way, and he has done away too drastically with the concluding formulas of musical numbers. Is a letter to be regarded as unoriginal because it is subscribed "Your obedient servant"? To this habit, which makes suddenly ending pieces appear hacked off to us, the greatest of living composers, Beethoven, has perhaps succumbed most thoroughly; but is he a less original mind for that? Generally speaking one should even avoid the appearance of wanting to be original: one must simply be so. Now what often makes the unprepared and therefore hard modulations seem even more cutting is the too scattered orchestration. Let the string or wind instruments follow what figuration or what subsidiary voice-part they will, one part or another must hold the thread of the harmonies and not let it go until another takes it up, and the whole must have unity. This defect was particularly noticeable in the overture (D major). The introduction in B flat major that follows (chorus with tenor solo) is both melodious and harmonious, and it was repeated by general request; what, however, is the meaning of the minor chord that comes several times immediately before the cadences, only to be resolved again, we cannot conceive; it seemed merely odd to us. In the duet (a few bars of G major and the rest in E flat major) the voices are admirably led, but surely there is an excess of modulations. The same may be said of the soprano aria in G major, which has a sparkling motif, but is quite devoid of repose; it would surely have pleased better, with its refrain, if it had been worked strophically. The mariner's quite fine aria in C major can be barely apprehended before it is finished; it comes too suddenly to be properly grasped. The quartet in B flat major might have given rise to canons and other contrapuntal turns; but although it is not used in that way, it has repose and unity, and it pleased. This last is true also of the trio in E major, which is vigorous and significant. The aria which introduces the gentler Spiess is excellent in parts, which however, differently handled by the composer, might have moved us even more. About the chorus in D major little can be said, about the finale nothing, and so we have finished our analysis—if memory has been faithful and omitted no number—and thus given the author proof of our attention. The subject is taken from a French vaudeville, 'Les Deux Valentins', we believe, though it is not at hand to enable us to be more precise. There is nothing new in it, little that is good, and it contains some coarse jests and much that is tedious. The performance went well; Herr Rosenfeld and Mlle Vio distinguished themselves in acting and singing. Herr Vogl did the two brothers Spiess very artistically, without exaggeration if therefore also with correspondingly less comic effect. The close gave occasion for party strife, Schubert's friends wishing to call him and a great many serpents hissing their dissent. The greater part of the audience remained quiet during this squabble, which really had nothing to do with art, for the composer merited neither the one nor the other, but simply encouragement. Herr Vogl, to whose care and nurture we are mainly indebted for this young composer, appeared, announced that Herr Schubert was not present and thanked us in his name.

This was the first detailed criticism Schubert received.—Cherubini's opera had three different titles in German: 'The Water-Carrier' ('Der Wasserträger'), 'Count Armand' and 'The Days of Peril' ('Die Tage der Gefahr').—The "mariner" is one of the twin brothers in the play, Franz Spiess. The "gentler Spiess" is Friedrich.—The critic did omit one number: the second duet between Lieschen and Anton, No. 7 in the score.—That the libretto was modelled on the vaudeville in question is affirmed in the second notice (No. 171).—The first notice reproduced here may have been by Josef, Ritter von Seyfried, born in Vienna in 1779, then the editor of this periodical.

171. FROM THE VIENNA 'CONVERSATIONSBLATT,' 20th June 1820

. . . After what has been said, the general verdict on Schubert can only be favourable, although not to the point to which his numerous friends endeavour to force it. He will do great and beautiful things, and it is in this hope that we welcome the modest artist very cordially.

B. S.

172. FROM THE VIENNA 'SAMMLER,' 22nd June 1820

. . . The music [for 'The Twin Brothers'] is the neat minor product of a young composer. It must have been preceded by very fair studies in composition, for the style of this opera is pretty pure and shows that its author is no novice at harmony. Many of the melodies, however, are a little old-fashioned, and some even tuneless. . . .

173. FROM THE DRESDEN 'ABENDZEITUNG,' 14th August 1820

. . . This gifted young man too might be reminded of the age-old saw, "Excess is unhealthy," for the public acclaimed the operetta like a great masterpiece, which it is not. . . . As regards the performance, that master of ours, Vogl, accomplished little this time. He played the two twins in such a way that one knew only too well it was the same actor who interpreted them; and he too is not very much at home in comedy.

[? Höhler.]

174. FROM THE LEIPZIG 'ALLGEMEINE MUSIKALISCHE ZEITUNG,' 16th August 1820

. . . In this first dramatic essay he seems to attempt to fly as high as Beethoven and not to heed the warning example of Icarus. Little true songfulness is to be found, whereas hardly any repose is to be met with in confused and surcharged instrumentation, anxious striving after originality and continual modulation. Only the introductory chorus, a quartet and a bass aria proceed clearly and intelligibly . . . That Herr Schubert has many friends willing to work on his behalf was shown at the first performance; but they must have forgotten that there is an enormous difference between a *fiasco* and a *furore*, as the Italians have it, that the best and most beneficial reward for a beginner is friendly encouragement and that, here as anywhere else, the middle path is surely always the best.

The Vienna 'Hof-Theater-Journal' for the year 1821 mentions only the bare fact that the performance took place (German edition, No. 176).

175. KARL SCHUBERT to his Betrothed, Therese Schwemminger

16th June 1820.

Dear Resi,

In spite of very necessary work, I am incapable of staying away from the second performance of 'The Twin Brothers.' Should you, to my intense pleasure, be able to accompany me, I shall gratefully await your decision (about calling for you).

I remain, most respectfully,

Your faithful friend

Karl Schubert.

176. FROM THE PROGRAMME of the Kärntnertor Theatre,
16th June 1820

THE TWIN BROTHERS

.   .   .   .

To be followed by

ALFRED THE GREAT

Heroic-pantomimic Ballet in three Acts, devised by Herr Aumer, Ballet Master of the I. & R. Court Theatres.
The Music is by Count W. Robert von Gallenberg.

There are two playbills of the same theatre, dated 21st June and 8th July 1820, announcing the same two works.

176A. JOHANN KARL UNGER TO JOHANN KARL, COUNT ESTERHÁZY

Vienna, 27th June 1820.

Schubert has done himself honour with his first little opera,

'The Twin Brothers,' without as yet standing on the summit of Parnassus.

Schubert had already written six operas and plays with songs before 'The Twin Brothers,' not to mention two unfinished works.

177. REMARK ON THE AUTOGRAPH OF 'MORNING SONG' ('Morgenlied') (xx. 379)

N.B. To the singer P. [Pepi von Koller] and the pianoforte player St. [Albert Stadler] I recommend this song most particularly!!! 1820.

178. FROM THE PROGRAMME OF THE KÄRNTNERTOR THEATRE, 14th July 1820

THE TWIN BROTHERS

. . . . . .

To be followed by

ACHILLES

Heroic Ballet in two Acts, devised by Herr Aumer, Ballet Master of the I. & R. Court Theatres

The Music is by Herr Karl Blum.

Karl Ludwig Blum, born in Berlin in 1786, producer at the Royal Opera there, had studied for a time with Salieri.

Sybille von Bruchmann dies of consumption, 18th July 1820, at Hütteldorf near Vienna: one of Franz von Bruchmann's three sisters (born 1799). It is said that the words of Schubert's song, 'Sister's Greeting' ('Schwestergruss') of November 1822, by her brother, were addressed to her.

179. FROM THE PROGRAMME OF THE KÄRNTNERTOR THEATRE, 21st July 1820

THE TWIN BROTHERS

. . . . . .

To be followed by

ALINE, QUEEN OF GOLCONDA

Grand Ballet in three Acts, by Herr Aumer, Ballet Master of the
I. & R. Court Theatres

The Music is by Herr Karl Blum.

This was the sixth and last performance of 'The Twin Brothers.'

180. PROGRAMME OF THE THEATER AN DER WIEN

New Magic Play.

This Day, Saturday, 19th August 1820,

will be given

at the I. & R. Privileged Playhouse by the Wien,

For the First Time:

THE MAGIC HARP.
[Die Zauberharfe]

Magic Play with Music in Three Acts.

Music by HERR SCHUBERT.

The New Scenery is by Herr Neefe.

The New Machinery is by Herr Roller.

The New Dresses are by Herr Lucca Piazza.

Dramatis Personae:

Arnulf, Count of Montabor . . .	Herr Rüger
Melinde, Arnulf's Wife	Mme Gottdank
Ida of Brabant, Arnulf's Niece . . .	Mlle Botta
Folko, the Eagle ⎫ . . .	Herr Heurteur
Ryno, the Bear ⎬ Knights of the Round Table	Herr Spitzeder
Alf, the Dolphin ⎭ . . .	Herr Demmer
Sauville ⎫ . . .	Herr Hann
Marin ⎬ Knights of Brabant . . .	Herr Leeb
Tirecour ⎭ . . .	Herr Stadelmeyer
Palmerin, a Minstrel	Herr Schimon
Sutur, a Fiery Spirit	Herr Küstner

Knights, Ladies, Pages, Minstrels, Genii.
Masques, Guards, People.
Free list suspended.

Lottery tickets for this Theatre are to be had from its office
during the usual business hours, and in the evening at the
box office.
To commence at 7 o'clock.

The words were again by Georg von Hofmann.   Schubert was indebted
for this commission to the scene-painter Hermann Neefe, a son of Christian
Gottlob Neefe, Beethoven's teacher at Bonn.   He was born there in
1790, went to Vienna in 1804, where he worked at first at the Leopoldstadt Theatre, and from 1814 at the Theater an der Wien.   He had
married Regina Lutz (born 1799) in 1819, and through her became later
on a brother-in-law of the painter Leopold Kupelwieser, Schubert's
friend, who married her sister Johanna.   Besides Neefe, who was also a
friend of Rosenbaum's, the producer Friedrich Demmer (born 1786)
had a share in Schubert's commission.   The machinist Andreas Roller
was an important man at that theatre, which luxuriated in elaborate
productions; and so, of course, was the costumier, Lucca Piazza.   The
artists in the cast were Karl Erdmann Rüger, born at Zossen (Silesia) in
1783; Josefa Gottdank, *née* Schlögl, in Vienna in 1792, the wife of Josef
Gottdank; Fräulein Botta, about whom nothing is known; Nikolaus
Heurteur, born in Vienna in 1781, a producer; Josef Spitzeder, born at
Bonn in 1795, a *basso buffo* who was to marry Betty Vio as his second wife;
Demmer, the producer mentioned above; Herren Hann, Leeb and Stadel-
meyer, otherwise unknown; Ferdinand Schimon, born at Pest in 1797,
a singer and portrait painter (a well-known portrait of Beethoven is by
him); Josef Küstner, born in 1787, a producer who committed suicide in
November 1821.—Count Pálffy, born in Vienna in 1774, who since 1813
had been the owner of the theatre, which was deeply sunk in debt, had
advertised a lottery, the draw of which took place soon afterwards.   The
winner of the theatre, however, a poor Hungarian wine-merchant, contented himself with a share, so that the count made an appreciable profit
from the lottery; but he used this for structural alterations and speculations which only plunged him into new debts.

181. From Eduard von Bauernfeld's Diary, 19th August 1820

In the Theater an der Wien: 'The Magic Harp.'   A Spectacular
Play.   Music by Franz Schubert.   Excellent.

Eduard von Bauernfeld, born in Vienna in 1802, had been to the grammar-school attached to the Scottish monastery, and was now studying philosophy. He was to become a good friend of Schubert's.

182. FROM ROSENBAUM'S DIARY, 19th August 1820

W. Th. [Wieden Theatre]. First Time, 'Magic Harp.'—Wretched trash, quite failed to please, the machinery jibbed and went badly, although nothing remarkable. Nobody knew his part: the prompter was always heard first.

182A. JOHANN KARL UNGER TO JOHANN KARL, COUNT ESTERHÁZY

Vienna, 20th August 1820.

Schubert has composed fine music for 'The Magic Harp,' a spectacular opera given at the Wieden Theatre. Schimon, an ex-Jew, is a promising tenor there.

183. FROM THE 'THEATERZEITUNG,' 26th August 1820

First a few words on the book of this melodrama or, as it prefers to call itself, magic play; and unfortunately, with the best will in the world, nothing very edifying may be said about it. Alas! though the witchery might pass, with what distressing tedium does it overflow, as it were, still affecting one's memory and paralysing even the most fluent critical pen!—Those lamentations of old Count Arnulf, those extravagant promises of the idle knights Eagle, Bear and Dolphin, thus named by heroic deeds which no mortal has seen—though it is plain enough that they can drink—those discussions and disputations between the gentle sorceress Melinde and the barbaric fire-spirit Sutur, that shallow pathos and unending length of the monologues and dialogues—where is the human patience whose threads are not snapped by it all at last, be they as stout as hawsers?—Even the hand and heritage of the Brabantian princess, which are to be the prize of the knight who succeeds in destroying the sorceress Melinde, are nothing wonderful. Eagle and doves, genii and monsters appear—all in vain, for there is no entertainment! Even a bat is to be seen, big enough in all conscience to be taken for a vampire.—Well, the vampire is not too bad!—Out with it: we know, we know.—The tale from which these rare things are culled may have its significance and the presentation may be attractive; still, everything here is left to the music, the settings and the machines. Yet even these united forces are incapable of overcoming a flood of boredom. If only some scenes had been, I will not say cut out, but at least cut down! True, there is the music—and real music! Many good ideas, forceful passages, cleverly managed harmonic pieces, insight and understanding; but also inequalities in abundance, commonplaces side by side with originalities, a mixture of light and far-fetched, valuable and frivolous things; so that one cannot, in spite of better moments, do otherwise than regard the whole as perfunctory. Not that it deserves censure, but it is to be wished that the talented composer will in future find a better subject and a full measure of deliberation.

Herr Schimon, as the minstrel Palmerin, sang his arietta with great tenderness. The roundness of his low notes and the softness of his falsetto made an agreeable contrast, and his simple delivery of a song well calculated to suit the peculiarities of his voice earned him encouraging applause.

The three scenic artists . . . had expended much industry and skill in order to compensate by outward finery for the lack of content. Let us here record only the transformation of a crescent moon into a full-moon gloriole, with an arc of stars each of which expanded to reveal a genius in the centre; the last setting but one, which showed the demon Sutur in a welter of fire; and the brilliant final tableau, representing a magnificent fairies' temple, in whose enchanting blend of colours was mirrored the whole exquisite fancy of the ingenious Neefe. To him, together with Herren Roller and Lucca Piazza, the third performance was assigned as benefit, and lovers of the stage, mindful of their delightful and indefatigable efforts, vied in demonstrating their gratitude, so that on the whole the success was commensurate with modest expectations.

Palmerin's "arietta" is a romance, "Was belebt die schöne Flur?" It occurred before the final chorus at the end of the second act, and was cut after the first performance on account of Schimon's insufficiency. Although Schubert later somewhat altered the piece for concert use, both versions are missing in the complete edition, and the first has appeared only in vocal-score form, arranged by Josef Hüttenbrenner, in vol. vii of Peters's 'Schubert Album.' Schubert, by the way, later used the piece purely instrumentally at the end of the first act.

184. FROM THE VIENNA 'ALLGEMEINE MUSIKALISCHE ZEITUNG,' 26th August 1820

. . . If it is considered that here [in 'The Magic Harp'] the young composer tried his hand at a higher species for the first time, it is only fair to do full justice to his praiseworthy endeavour to remain original and one day to attain to a significant rank in art in this only possible way. . . .

Although a manuscript of this criticism in Mayrhofer's hand was found among Josef Hüttenbrenner's remains, it is hardly credible that he wrote it. More probably he merely made a copy of it.

185. FROM THE 'SAMMLER,' 26th August 1820

. . . So far we had heard only of a Man in the Moon; but this magic play increases our sidereal knowledge by teaching us that there are also Maids in the Moon. There is a sorceress who looks evil enough, but is not really as bad even as some of our human enchantresses. . . . In our opinion the monotony of a magic play ought to be relieved for the spectators by the addition of a comedian, as used to be done by the often unjustly censured Schikaneder, Hensler and others, and which that accomplished stage craftsman, Kotzebue, did not disdain in his 'Lady in the Forest'; moreover the accompanying music should continue the action instead of holding it up; and furthermore the gentlemen actors must learn their parts nicely at home, to save the audience paying for a rehearsal (honourable exception must, here again, be made of the ladies). . . .

Much might be said of the score if 'The Magic Harp,' being a magic play, also had magic music. In that case the title at any rate would have preserved the three unities, more or less as with *ci-devant* Aristotle.

. . . For this we should have needed a composer who is a magician in his art, capable of breaking down barricades and fortresses, at any rate in our hearts. For that a knowledge of all the secrets of nature and the spirit-world is needful. But that is to be acquired only by initiates by a long, faithful and exacting service in the realm of great Alidoro, for he understands the true abracadabra with which musicians too have to reckon . . . Lastly, Alidoro teaches the use of the instruments which are to be used for magic plays. Those who do not know him are liable to use a magic wand like a whip-handle or the bass trombone like a toy trumpet. Only let one of those airy spirits of trombonists try it! And yet many composers expect it of them, especially the composer of 'The Magic Harp.'

. . . Study of the rules of melodrama is thus very important, and the question of the cadence according to the strictest rules of true recitative must be considered. Here the great magician Alidoro will as yet see much to find fault with in the style of 'The Magic Harp,' particularly in the part of the Spirit.—Spirits, if only for their relationship, are much in favour of spirit in composition, and since they discard their own invisibility, they are particularly vexed when they see it playing hide-and-seek and refusing to show itself. They also demand a certain force and cannot abide anything that is weak, characterless, commonplace and ordinary in music. But the 'Magic Harp' music is often thin, insipid and stale in taste. . . .

Emanuel Schikaneder, born at Ratisbon in 1751, the librettist of 'The Magic Flute' and founder of the Theater an der Wien, died in Vienna in 1812 in poverty and bereft of reason.—Karl Friedrich Hensler, born at Schaffhausen in 1761, another writer of popular plays, was manager of the Theater an der Wien in 1817, having first managed that in the Leopoldstadt and later that in the Josefstadt.—Kotzebue's 'The Wise Lady in the Forest, or The Dumb Knight' was a magic play published in 1801.—Alidor is the prince's tutor and—in place of the usual pantomime fairy—the wizard astrologer in Isouard's 'Cinderella' (libretto by Charles Guillaume Étienne), produced in Paris in 1819, and given in Vienna at the Theater an der Wien in 1811 and at the Kärntnertor in 1815, both times in German.

186. From the 'Wiener Zeitschrift für Kunst, Literatur, Theater und Mode,' 29th August 1820

If this magic play is considered in its length and its breadth—for these two dimensions may properly be taken for granted—it is seen to show two properties in effective union, and to distinguish itself thereby above many others of the kind: nonsense and tediousness. . . .

The music, not very effective to begin with, is not shown to advantage by its scattered melodramatic passages. The choruses are unequal and in part negligently worked. On the other hand one becomes aware of an attempt to cause surprise by glaring and overloaded discordant progressions, and the composer's weaker side reveals itself in faulty use of the instruments, so that isolated good ideas and well-managed movements pass by ineffectually in a stream of affectations and commonplaces. . . . The Minstrel's romance is uncommonly appealing, and Herr Schimon delivered it especially safely and pleasingly, although his voice had failed him once or twice before. . . .

187. From the Vienna 'Conversationsblatt,' 29th August 1820

. . . what a pity that Schubert's wonderfully beautiful music has not found a worthier subject. . . . In the present work the overture begins with an uncommonly lovely *andante*, which is very delicately scored and merges into a quick *allegro* whose theme is taken from the melodrama in Act I. . . . We think, too, that the overture has greater merit as a composition pure and simple than as a connection with this melodrama, and might as well be played before an opera as before a fairy-tale. . . . Palmerin's romance in D is an infinitely heart-felt piece, overflowing with loveliness. True, the singer gave us a mere inkling of what the composer aimed at, but even this pale reflection proved touching. Why Palmerin, for whose voice the romance was in any case too high, should have taken the thankless trouble of adding clumsy ornamentations at the end of it which took him up to high C sharp is incomprehensible . . . the final chorus of the second act . . . should have had an accompaniment of the full orchestra with a harp, but this was unfortunately omitted—without the composer's consent, we hear. . . . The introduction to the third act, by the way, is so like dance music that one is scarcely able to conceal one's astonishment, although this piece is otherwise quite pretty. . . .

B. S.

The overture (there is another before the third act) was published c. 1827 as the overture to 'Rosamond' (in an arrangement for pianoforte duet, see No. 628), although in 1823 Schubert used that originally written for the opera 'Alfonso and Estrella' for 'Rosamond.' The overture to 'The Magic Harp,' which is sometimes wrongly said to have taken the place of a 'Rosamond' overture that was in fact never written, appears properly in the complete edition.—This notice reports furthermore that the drinking chorus (No. 5) had to be repeated.—The orchestral accompaniment of the final chorus in the second act included two harps. The "introduction to the third act" is the second overture mentioned above.

188. From the Dresden 'Abendzeitung,' 30th September 1820

. . . The music, written by the young composer Schubert, once again proves his talent. He knew how to accompany the words very suitably, and the choruses have force and life. The only thing with which he might be reproached is that he has too often interrupted the words with music.

[? Höhler.]

189. From the Leipzig 'Allgemeine Musikalische Zeitung,' 4th October 1820

. . . The score shows talent here and there; but on the whole it lacks technical resource and wants the grasp which only experience can give; most of it is much too long, ineffective and fatiguing, the harmonic progressions are too harsh, the orchestration redundant, the choruses dull and feeble. The introductory adagio in the overture and a romance for tenor are the most successful pieces and appeal by feeling, sincere expressiveness, noble simplicity and discreet modulations. A subject of an idyllic nature should suit the young composer's individuality infinitely better, and one might call it a mistake to try his hand at a species where it will never be possible to do anything effective without the most intimate knowledge of the inmost secrets of stagecraft.

The overture does not begin with an *adagio*, but with an *andante* (leading to *allegro*).

190. FROM ROSENBAUM'S DIARY, 20th August 1820

W. Th. [Wieden Theatre]—the ill-fated magic play, 'The Magic Harp,' from the French, by Hofmann.

It is here that the positive statement occurs that this piece, like 'The Twin Brothers,' was taken from the French.

The benefit performance mentioned below was announced by Count Pálffy in the official 'Wiener Zeitung' and in the 'Wanderer' (German edition, Nos. 195–6) on 18th August 1820.

191. FROM THE PROGRAMME OF THE THEATER AN DER WIEN, 21st August 1820

For the Benefit of Herren Neefe, Roller and L. Piazza

For the third time:

THE MAGIC HARP

. . . . . .

| Knights | . | . | Herren Jüngling, Marchard, Meyer, Riter, Schlager, Weber, Macho, Bauernschober. |
| Minstrels | . | . | Herren Dunst, Bock, Baduscheck, Glossy, Ibner, Mick, Schmidt, Simser. |

. . . .

Boxes and Stalls are to be had in the Spiegelgasse, No. 1164, to the right of the main entrance, at the usual hours of the morning and afternoon.

. . . .

Even the supernumeraries were named on this programme because they too gave their services for the sake of the beneficiaries.

192. From Rosenbaum's Diary, 21st August 1820

Benefit of Neefe, Roller, Piazza, third performance of the unsuccessful magic play, 'The Magic Harp.'—We took box No. 17
and four seats in the second tier, and I gave 30 florins—Wohlfarth
20 florins.—It was very empty, 8 boxes unoccupied, the gallery
empty.—Prince Kaunitz alone gave 5 ducats. They can hardly
have taken as much as 1,500 florins.

Josef Anton (? von) Wohlfahrt was a friend of Rosenbaum's.—Alois
Wenzel, Prince Kaunitz-Rietberg (born 1774), was a diplomat.—The
Dresden 'Abendzeitung' of 4th October 1820 (German edition, No. 198)
also reports that the takings were small.

193. From Rosenbaum's Diary, 22nd August 1820

W. Th. [Wieden Theatre.]—'Magic Harp.'

Three exactly similar entries in Rosenbaum's diary, dated 23rd
and 24th August and 15th September 1820. For this last day the
'Wanderer' of 15th September 1820 erroneously announced a
revival of 'The Twin Brothers.'

194. Poem by Schubert, September 1820

The Spirit of the World

Leave them but in their conceit,
Tossed on stormy brine:
Though their boat be insecure,
Thus they still are mine.

Thus the Spirit of the World
Spake: let them but chase
After dark and far-off goals,
And with wrangling fill their days;

Yet no harm it be for them
Short of truth to fall:
Frail and human is their world,
Godlike understand I all.

This poem, wrongly assigned by Bauernfeld to the year 1824 and reprinted by Schumann, reappeared in 1860 as having been in the possession of "a recently deceased friend of Schubert's" with the additional remark "after a reading of 'Faust'" and was more recently considered by Walter Dahms as alluding to Senn's fate. Yet another explanation emerged in the end: an original manuscript written in pencil on the back of a handsome breakfast bill of fare (now the property of the Schubertbund in Vienna) of the Seitzerhof Inn in the city was found by the family of a friend of Schubert's who did not die until 1870, Josef Huber, born in 1794 at Aggsbach in Lower Austria, who had been to school at Kremsmünster, and became conveyancer in the court war accountancy. He was called "tall Huber" on account of his height, was often caricatured by Schwind because of his long nose, and his clumsiness generally made him the butt of his friends. Schubert, who is said to have written this poem for him, lived with him in 1823–4 on the Stubentor bastion (city No. 1187). For all that the poem does seem to date from 1820. Another copy, almost wholly identical and also written in pencil, bears that date. It was given by Ferdinand Schubert to Schumann in 1838 during the latter's visit to Vienna, and sold by auction in Berlin in 1932.

195. FROM THE OFFICIAL 'WIENER ZEITUNG,' 13th September 1820

Announcement of W. G. Becker's 'Pocket-Book of Sociable Pleasure,' edited by Friedrich Kind, for the year 1821, Leipzig, G. J. Göschen, to be had in Vienna of Carl Gerold. Price, 2 florins, 45 kreuzer, A.C., the *édition de luxe*, 4 fl., 30 kr., A.C.

Contents: . . . IV. Song Compositions by . . . Fr. Schubert . . .

The musical supplements of that year, which included the very first printed copies of a number from Weber's 'Freischütz' (words by Kind, then the editor of the almanac founded by Becker), were not published, but Schubert's song, the first version of 'Reflection' ('Widerschein'), poem by Schlechta, was actually printed. So was the Weber number, the girls' chorus, "Wir winden dir den Jungfernkranz," issued for a single voice as a "Folksong from the 'Freischütz'" (a copy of which is in the possession of Hans Harold Rath in Vienna). The Schubert supplement, printed from type on a double sheet twice folded, is now to be found in the Vienna City Library. Evidently none of the supplements was ready in time for publication. The almanac in its ordinary edition is adorned with an arabesque from the "Baths of Titus," and in the *édition de luxe* with Raphael's "Four Seasons."

196. FROM THE VIENNA 'CONVERSATIONSBLATT,'
28th September 1820

. . . Further pleasant supplements to the 'Pocket Book' are the musical compositions by . . . Franz Schubert of Dresden, . . . and Franz Schubert of Vienna. Among those who showed themselves less happy are . . . and especially Franz Schubert of Dresden, who cannot bear comparison with his Viennese namesake.

B—r.

The song by the Dresden Schubert was entitled 'The Life-Companions' ('Die Lebensgefährten'), poem by A. von Nordstern.

Schubert's cousin Magdalena marries Michael Sandler, 9th October 1820.

197. FROM ROSENBAUM'S DIARY, 12th October 1820

W. Th. [Wieden Theatre.]—'Magic Harp.'

The eight performances of 'The Magic Harp' are mentioned also in the manuscript diaries of the actor Friedrich Henning and the composer Ignaz von Seyfried, both of which deal with events at the Theater an der Wien (Vienna City Library). Josef Lanner (see note preceding No. 415) is said to have attended one of the repeat performances and to have particularly praised the overture.

198. FROM THE LIECHTENTAL PARISH REGISTER (Wedding)

November 21st 1820. Therese Grob, married to Johann Bergmann, master baker.

Johann Bergmann, citizen master baker, born at Neubau, legitimate son of Friedrich Bergmann, master baker, and Dorothea, née Kassimir, resident at 831 Stadt;

Grob, Theresia, born at Liechtental, legitimate daughter of Grob, Heinrich, citizen silk manufacturer, and his wife, née Männern, 22 years of age.

[Witnesses:] Michael Kassimir, citizen master baker at the Strozzigrund, and Johann Wagner, citizen silk manufacturer and magistrate at L[iechtental, No.] 166.

Neubau and Strozzigrund were suburbs of Vienna.—Johann Michael
Wagner, to give his full name, had also been a witness at the second
marriage of Schubert's father in 1813.

First performance of 'Erl King' (xx. 178) by August R. von
Gymnich, at Ignaz Sonnleithner's; Anna Fröhlich at the pianoforte: 1st December 1820. August, Ritter von Gymnich (born
c. 1786), was registrar in the Court Chamber and representative
of the Philharmonic Society. He sang tenor and died early, in the
autumn of 1821. It is said to have been he who introduced Grillparzer
(born Vienna, 1791) to the Fröhlich sisters, the four daughters of a merchant, formerly a nobleman, who lived by themselves in the Spiegelgasse (near the Graben). Only one, Barbara, married. Grillparzer,
the beautiful Katharina's friend, lodged with them later on.
(Bauernfeld at that time punningly called them "Grillparzen,"
Parzen being the German name for the Greek Fates.) They were
all musical, and in 1841 the 'Allgemeine Wiener Musikzeitung'
wrote about them that "they may well have done more for art, and
particularly for singing, than many an Amazon of the throat of
European fame." Maria Anna (born 1793), a pupil of Johann
Nepomuk Hummel's, sang soprano, and in 1819 became a teacher
of singing at the Philharmonic Society's Conservatory (third form
for female singing-students). Barbara (born 1798), the most
gifted of the sisters, sang mezzo-soprano. In 1816 she appears to
have briefly tried a career at the Theater an der Wien, but became a
painter as a pupil of M. M. Daffinger; in 1825 she married the
flautist Bogner, and later taught drawing. Katharina (born 1800)
sang soprano. Grillparzer later wrote about her in his diary:
"As drunkards in wine, so she intoxicates herself in music. She
loses all power over herself on hearing good music." (She remained the poet's "eternal beloved.") Josefine (born 1808)
sang contralto. Having been Anna's pupil at first, she was at the
Kärntnertor Theatre from the summer of 1821 to the beginning of
1822, and later appeared as a concert singer, abroad as well as at
home, went to Copenhagen, where she became Siboni's pupil and
became chamber singer to the Danish court. Early in 1826 she
reached the summit of her talents, and later she became a teacher
of singing and pianoforte.—The daughters of the legendary glass-
maker Tschöll (Veit in the English version), living on the Melk
bastion in Vienna, in R. H. Bartsch's Schubert novel 'Schwammerl'
and in Heinrich Berté's musical play 'Das Dreimäderlhaus' ('Lilac
Time'), may have been suggested in their outline by the Fröhlich
sisters, but they are pure figments, as is also "Baron" Schober in
the part of Schubert's rival.

199. FROM THE DRESDEN 'ABENDZEITUNG,' 30th January 1821

(Vienna correspondence of early December 1820.)

The young composer Schuberth has set to music several songs by the best poets (mostly Goethe), which testify to the profoundest studies combined with genius worthy of admiration, and attract the eyes of the cultivated musical world.   He knows how to paint in sound, and the songs, 'The Trout,' 'Margaret at the Spinning-wheel' (from 'Faust') and 'The Combat' ['Der Kampf'] by Schiller, surpass in characteristic truth all that may be found in the domain of song.   They are not yet engraved, to my knowledge, but go from hand to hand only in manuscript copies.

Höhler.

Two songs by Schubert had actually appeared already, though printed from type, not engraved: 'At the Lake Erlaf' ('Am Erlafsee') and 'Reflection' ('Widerschein').   The third was to follow at once (*see* note below).

> 'The Trout' ('Die Forelle'), Op. 22 (xx. 327), appears as a supplement to the 'Wiener Zeitschrift,' 9th December 1820.   The 'Wiener Zeitschrift für Kunst, Literatur, Theater und Mode,' called briefly the "Modezeitung," edited by the draper Johann Schickh (born Vienna, 1770), was founded in 1816 and contained as supplements engraved fashion-plates (mostly from French models) and folded sheets of music printed from type, generally songs, among them a series by Schubert printed for the first time, some of which were afterwards reprinted separately on four pages with a special title-page.—'The Trout' appeared here in its fourth version —the last but one.

'Norman's Song' ('Normans Gesang'), Op. 52, No. 5 (1825).
Engraved Vignette from Karl Czerny's Arrangement of
Schubert's Song for Pianoforte Solo.   Vienna 1838–9

Heute Samstag den 19. Auguſt 1820,
wird in dem k. k. priv. Schauſpielhauſe an der Wien
gegeben:

Zum erſten Mahle:

Die Zauberharfe.

Zauberſpiel mit Muſik in drey Aufzügen.

Muſik von Herrn Schubert.

Die neuen Decorationen ſind von Herrn Neefe.

Die neuen Maſchinerien von Hrn. Roller.

Das neue Coſtume von Hrn. Lucca Piazza.

Perſonen:

Arnulf, Graf von Montabor	· · ·	Hr. Rüger.
Melinde, Arnulfs Gemahlinn	· · ·	Mad. Gottdank.
Ida von Brabant, Arnulfs Nichte	· · ·	Mlle. Botta.
Folko, der Adler)	· · ·	Hr. Heurteur.
Ryno, der Bär) Ritter der Tafelrunde	· · ·	Hr. Spitzeder.
Ulf, der Delphin)	· · ·	Hr. Demmer.
Sauville,)	· · ·	Hr. Hann.
Marin,) Brabantiſche Ritter	· · ·	Hr. Leeb.
Tirecour)	· · ·	Hr. Stabelmeyer.
Palmerin, ein Troubadour	· · ·	Hr. Schimon.
Sutur, Feuergeiſt	· · ·	Hr. Küſtner.
Ritter, Damen, Pagen, Troubadours, Genien.		
Larven, Wache Volk.		

Freybillete ſind ungültig.

Der Anfang iſt um 7 Uhr.

'The Magic Harp' ('Die Zauberharfe'). Play-bill of the First
Performance (1820). *See* pp. 142 f.

'Reflection' ('Widerschein'), First Version. First Page of the Second
Schubert Song published (1820). *See* pp. 152 f.

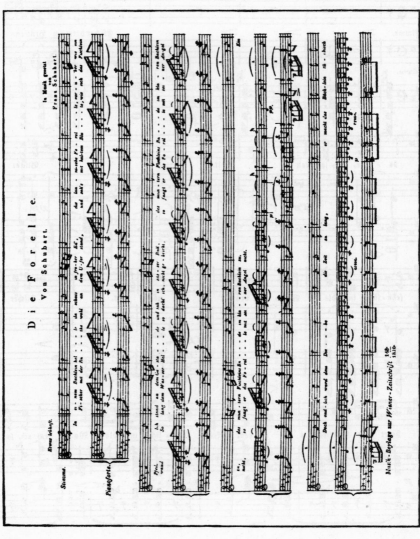

'The Trout' ('Die Forelle'), Op. 32 (1817). Opening Bars of the Third Schubert Song published (1820). *See p. 155*

1821

'Song of the Spirits over the Waters' ('Gesang der Geister über den
    Wassern') for 8 Male Voices with String Quintet Accompaniment
    (xvi. 3), February.
Songs, 'Suleika' I & II, 'Greetings to thee' ('Sei mir gegrüsst').
Sketch for a Symphony in E minor (published in arrangements only),
    August.

200. MOSEL'S TESTIMONIAL FOR SCHUBERT

I hereby testify that Herr Franz Schubert, former pupil of the
First I. & R. Court Musical Director Herr Anton Salieri, possesses
not only a profound knowledge of theoretical and practical harmony, but also the required auxiliary sciences acquired by himself
for the purpose of vocal composition, as well as an excellent talent
that makes him one of the most hopeful of our young composers,
from all of which opera in general and particularly the I. & R.
Court Opera Theatre, to which he wishes principally to devote his
labours, may promise themselves the most gratifying art-products.

Vienna, 16th January 1821.

> Ignaz Franz, Edler von Mosel,
> Acting I. & R. Court Secretary.

The testimonials Nos. 200, 201 and 203 may have been solicited by
Schubert to submit to the directorate of the Court Opera, then due for
re-election, in order to introduce himself either as composer or as conductor. They may even have been intended for a petition to the
emperor. The "Court Opera Theatre" was the Kärntnertor, situated
near the Carinthian Gate in the city (behind the recent opera house). It
originally belonged to the city, and was long used as a playhouse, then
alternately with the later theatre in the Hofburg, the so-called Burg
Theatre, as an opera house as well, only to be entirely devoted to the
latter purpose in the end. Since Dietrichstein was elected supreme
court theatre director on 12th February 1821, with Mosel for his
secretary, Schubert, to whom this may have come as a surprise, could not
use these two men's testimonials as a recommendation to themselves.
It seems more credible that the leasing out of the Opera, which took place
at the end of the year, was already foreseen in January. But as the new

management was Italian, Schubert could hardly be eligible for the Opera any longer.—Ignaz Franz, Edler von Mosel, whom we have already met as an official attached to the former "Court Music Count" (*see* No. 11), was born in Vienna in 1772; he had in the meantime become court secretary, and followed his new chief, Moritz, Count Dietrichstein, to the Opera. He was musically active as composer and writer, and had done excellent work for the cultivation of Handel in Vienna since 1812.

August von Gymnich sings 'The Wanderer' (xx. 266b) at Ignaz Sonnleithner's, 19th January 1821.

201. DIETRICHSTEIN'S TESTIMONIAL FOR SCHUBERT

Induced as much by inclination as by duty to seek out excellent musical talents in our own country for preference, and to further their noble efforts to the best of my ability, I take especial pleasure in declaring hereby that Herr Franz Schubert, who received his first musical education at the Seminary, so long as he remained there as chorister in the I. & R. Court Chapel, has since, in the course of few years, given the most eloquent proofs of profound knowledge based on innate genius, diligent study of strict counterpoint and frequent excellent preliminary work, as well as of feeling allied to taste; so that it only remains to hope that this estimable man will find the opportunity of unfolding such fair blossoms, in the interests of art in general and of dramatic music in particular.

24th January 1821.   Moritz, Count Dietrichstein,
                                        I. & R. Court Music Chamberlain.

Moritz, Count Dietrichstein-Proskau-Leslie (born 1775), had become "Court Music Count" in 1819, in succession to Kuefstein, and was, in addition, since 1815, deputy Lord Chamberlain to Napoleon's son, the Duke of Reichstadt, in Vienna. As a song composer he was, like Niklas, Freiherr von Krufft, a modest Viennese precursor of Schubert.

202. FROM THE PROGRAMME of the Eighth Musical Evening Entertainment held by the Philharmonic Society (Gesellschaft der Musikfreunde) at the Gundelhof, 25th January 1821

[4.] 'Erl King' by Goethe, set to music by Fr. Schubert, sung by Herr von Gymnich.

Schubert's Birthplace.   From the Bird's-eye View of Vienna and its Suburbs,
1769–74, designed by Josef Daniel von Huber and engraved by Various Hands.
Vienna 1776.   By Courtesy of the Trustees of the British Museum

The house, Himmelpfortgrund No. 42 (later 72), is just opposite the side-
turning of the main street (now Nussdorferstrasse), in the centre of this section
of the map.   There are two wings adjoining the court and a little garden behind
it, overlooking the suburb of Liechtental.   The staircase on the left leads to
the church.   See pp. 4 and 929

PLATE II

The Trout Fountain (*Forellen-Brunnen*) in the Court
of Schubert's Birthplace.   Marble by Josef Müllner
(1911).   *See* p. 929

PLATE III

These evening entertainments held by the Philharmonic Society (as the *Gesellschaft der Musikfreunde* is literally translated throughout this work), also known as the "Little Society," were not open to the public. From 1818 onwards they took place in the society's chancellery, at first at "the Red Apple" in the Singerstrasse, and now in the Gundelhof, below Sonnleithner's dwelling. On this occasion Schubert or Anna Fröhlich accompanied, and Gymnich, who was a member of the society since its foundation in 1812, introduced Schubert.

203. Weigl's and Salieri's Testimonial for Schubert

Ex off°   TESTIMONIAL

That Herr Franz Schubert, by reason of his renowned and much-promising musical talent, which distinguishes itself especially in composition, has already been employed, and is to be further employed, in this branch by the I. & R. Directorate of the Court Theatre, to the general satisfaction, is hereby attested by

Vienna, 27th January 1821.   Josef Weigl,
For and on behalf of the Chan-   Director of the I. & R. Court
cellery of the I. & R. Court   Opera.
Theatre Directorate, Vienna,   Antonio Salieri,
29th January 1821.   I. & R. Court Musical Director.
Leopold Pfersmann von Eichthal,
I. & R. Court Secretary
and Director of Chancellery.

Coram me:
Johann, Count Barth-Barthenheim,
Lower Austrian Government Secretary,
noe. Captain of the Civic Guard.

The Court Opera, where Weigl had been "Musical Director" since 1805, only once enlisted Schubert's services, on the occasion of 'The Twin Brothers.'—This collective testimonial includes attestations from the musical director of the Court Opera, the chancellery of the two court theatres and—witnessed by the civic guard of Vienna—the master of the court chapel.

204. Dietrichstein to Vogl (? January 1821)

I request you, dear friend, kindly to hand this to honest Schubert. May it prove of some advantage to him, for ever since I have fathomed the genius of this young, vigorous, extraordinarily promising composer, it is among my dearest wishes to work for him *sub umbra alarum tuarum*, in so far as it is in my power.   Good morrow, dear friend, *rara avis in terra*, or rather *rarissima*.

The letter refers to No. 201, a testimonial that had evidently been requested by Vogl.

205. Josef Huber to his Betrothed, Rosalie Kranzbichler, at St. Pölten

Vienna, 30th January 1821.

What a pleasure it was for me to hear from Fräulein Schober that, greatly to her surprise, she found you much better than she had imagined. . . . As for me, I am now always pretty well. Last Friday I had excellent entertainment: as [Fräulein] Schober was at St. Pölten, Franz invited Schubert in the evening and fourteen of his close acquaintances.   So a lot of splendid songs by Schubert were sung and played by himself, which lasted until after 10 o'clock in the evening.   After that punch was drunk, offered by one of the party, and as it was very good and plentiful the party, in a happy mood anyhow, became even merrier; so it was 3 o'clock in the morning before we parted.   You may imagine how agreeable the enjoyment of so many cultivated men, which I missed for so many years, must be for me, and that it is further enhanced by the recollection of my student-years.   For this I would gladly leave all that is called entertainment.

St. Pölten lies to the west of Vienna, in Lower Austria.—Sophie von Schober, Franz's sister, was a friend of Huber's betrothed, who was consumptive, and died soon after.   She and her mother sometimes stayed at St. Pölten with relatives.—This party, though exclusively male, is the first recorded "Schubertiad," a kind of evening party among friends and their families at which music by Schubert alone was to be heard, even, when ladies were present, the dances, which he, who was not a dancer, himself played on the pianoforte, often improvised on the spur of the moment.

206. FROM THE PROGRAMME of the Tenth Evening Entertainment
held by the Philharmonic Society, 8th February 1821

4. 'Longing' ['Die Sehnsucht'] by Schiller, set to music by
Franz Schuberth.   Delivered by Herr Götz.

207. FROM PERTH'S DIARY, 8th February 1821

(On a musical entertainment at Pettenkoffer's.)

7. Ballad, 'The Erl King'; set to music by Schubert.

> Sophie Linhart sings 'Margaret at the Spinning-Wheel' (xx. 31) at
> Ignaz Sonnleithner's, 2nd March 1821.   She was a soprano who
> later sang under her married name of Schuller; a pupil of Anselm
> Hüttenbrenner's.

208. SCHUBERT TO HIS BROTHER FERDINAND [? early 1821]

Dear Brother,

As I was seedy to-day on account of yesterday's dissipations, I
did no work on the Offertory, and it is therefore not ready.   What
is more, Anselm Hüttenbrenner is here, with whom I have made
an appointment for 6 o'clock to-night.   If you should feel inclined
to be with us, come to Frau von Sanssouci's in the Wipplinger
Strasse, where I used to live, and perhaps inquire below in the
tobacco vaults, about 6 o'clock.   If not, we shall meet to-morrow
at the Cross Inn.

Franz.

It is possible that "yesterday's dissipations" were the evening at
Schober's on 26th January 1821.—The offertory was probably Schubert's
second, of 1815, to which, however, he did not add the new wind parts
until 1823.   Anselm Hüttenbrenner, it is true, had joined the Military
Judicature in Vienna already in 1820, serving there as conveyancer for
about a year.   He may have gone home for the Christmas holidays.   The
only evidence for the date of this note is Schubert's removal from Frau
Sanssouci's house and from his joint lodging with Mayrhofer to another
house in the Wipplingerstrasse, No. 380 (later No. 21) in the city, at
the corner of the Tiefer Graben in the former building of the Theatine
monastery.   In 1821 Schwind made a pen-and-ink drawing of his room
there, with a pianoforte (*see* p. 204).—Frau Sanssouci, who lived on

the third floor, kept her (vaulted) tobacco shop below; but all shops in Vienna were apt to be called "vaults" because they were usually vaulted to support the upper structure.—"The Red Cross" in the Himmelpfort-grund, Obere Hauptstrasse (now Nussdorferstrasse), near Schubert's birthplace, hard by the steps leading down to the Liechtental, was one of the family's accustomed haunts. The fact that the brothers still met there indicates that Ferdinand, though he was to move to Alt-Lerchenfeld during the year, was still living at the orphanage at that time.

209. FROM THE PROGRAMME of the Kärntnertor Theatre, 7th March 1821, at 7 p.m.

(Grand Concert with recitations and tableaux, organized by Josef Sonnleithner for the Society of Ladies of the Nobility.)

Part I: . . .

6. 'The Little Village' ['Das Dörfchen'], poem by Bürger, set for two tenor and two bass voices by Herr Franz Schubert, performed by Herren Götz and Barth, in the service of H.H. the Reigning Prince von Schwarzenberg, and Herren Nejebse and Umlauff . . .

Part II: . . .

12. 'Erl King,' poem by Goethe, set to music by Franz Schubert, performed by Herr Vogl, I. & R. Court Opera Singer, accompanied on the Pianoforte by Herr Anselm Hütten-brenner. . . . .

15. 'Song of the Spirits over the Waters,' poem by Goethe, set for four tenor and four bass voices by Herr Franz Schu-bert, performed by Herren Götz, Barth, Nejebse, Umlauff, Weinkopf, Frühwald and two Choristers.

This concert, held on Ash Wednesday, when the theatres were closed, was an important event for Schubert. It was organized by the "Society of Ladies of the Nobility for the Promotion of the Good and the Useful," founded in 1811 by Karoline, Princess Lobkowitz (see note of 24th December 1811, on p. 22) and Princess Babette Odescalchi, with Josef Sonnleithner (Ignaz's brother) as secretary. He was born at in 1766, and was a Lower Austrian government councillor and court agent, old enough to have had dealings with Mozart. He took a share in the foundation of the Philharmonic Society and, as theatre poet, in the libretto of Beethoven's

'Fidelio,' and he had at various times been a music publisher and a court theatre secretary. He collected material for a history of music and musicians' portraits, which he had specially painted for the most part (now the property of the Philharmonic Society in Vienna).—The society of those 160 ladies had published 'Evening Entertainments for the Winter of 1815–16,' which had included poems by Ottenwalt and Schlechta (National Library, Vienna). The society's Ash Wednesday concerts, which celebrated their 125th anniversary in 1936, were at that time under the special protection of Therese, Landgravine Fürstenberg. Josef Sonnleithner had taken a special interest in this particular programme. It contained a tableau after Van Dyck's "Hagar," in which Vogl took part, a Mozart aria sung by Wilhelmine Schröder (later Schröder-Devrient), another sung by Karoline Unger (later married name Sabatier), a poem recited by the tragedienne of the Burg Theatre, Sophie Schröder, Wilhelmine's mother, a duet from Rossini for the two singers, and at the end another tableau in which appeared the later world-famous dancer Fanny Elssler, then aged ten and already at the end of a three years' engagement. Adalbert Gyrowetz, born in 1763 at Budweis in Bohemia, the former conductor of the court theatre, conducted the music, and the court theatre costumier, Philipp von Stubenrauch, born in Vienna in 1784, arranged the tableaux.—'The Little Village' was the first vocal quartet by Schubert to receive a public performance. It is unaccompanied. According to Anselm Hüttenbrenner's recollections Schubert, at the rehearsal, interpolated a few bars into the accompaniment of the 'Erl King' here and there at Vogl's request, to give the singer time to breathe. Being too shy to accompany on the new Graf grand pianoforte at the performance, he is said to have turned pages.—The vocal octet written specially for this performance (? also unaccompanied) received too little rehearsal, according to Leopold Sonnleithner.—Johann Michael Weinkopf (born 1780) was at first at the Theater an der Wien (the first Don Fernando in 'Fidelio') and had been engaged at the Kärntnertor Theatre since 1814 as a bass. Josef Frühwald (born 1783), a tenor, had a similar career (he was the first Jaquino in 'Fidelio' in 1805), and in addition was Korner's assistant and later his successor as singing-master to the choir-boys of the court chapel and at the singing-school of the Conservatory. He was in touch with Schubert during the latter's last years as intermediary in the matter of projected performances of the 'Prometheus' cantata, especially at Göttweig, his birthplace in Lower Austria.

210. From Rosenbaum's Diary, 7th March 1821

3 musical pieces by Schubert—of which the last, 'The Spirits above the Waters,' went under completely.

211. FROM THE VIENNA 'ALLGEMEINE MUSIKALISCHE ZEITUNG,' 21st March 1821

The performance of the ballad, 'Erl King,' music by Schubert, showed our master of declamatory song—Herr Vogl—in all his greatness. The music shows much imagination. Several successful passages were justly acclaimed by the public. A vocal quartet by the same composer also pleased greatly, and had to be repeated. Herr Barth's fine tenor voice distinguished itself.

On the other hand Herr Schubert's eight-voice chorus was recognized by the public as an accumulation of every sort of senseless, disordered and purposeless musical modulation and sidetracking. In such works a composer resembles a drayman who drives eight-in-hand, and swerves now right, now left — in other words, avoids collision—then turns back, and goes on with the same game without ever getting along the road.

Before this criticism another had appeared in the 'Wiener Allgemeine Theaterzeitung' of 13th March 1821; afterwards the 'Sammler' of 27th March also published a notice of the evening (German edition, Nos. 221 and 223).

212. FROM THE DRESDEN 'ABENDZEITUNG,' 26th April 1821

A few songs, set to music by the young and talented composer Schubert, attracted most attention there. What pleased above all was the 'Erl King,' which Vogl performed with his accustomed mastery, and which had to be repeated. This splendid composition cannot fail to seize [the hearer]; it has now appeared in print here, at Cappi & Diabelli's, and I am convinced that I shall earn the gratitude of any reader who wishes to procure this masterpiece for having drawn his attention to it.

[? Höhler.]

This criticism appeared after the publication of 'Erl King' (*see* No. 219). Another foreign one came out in the Leipzig 'Allgemeine musikalische Zeitung' of 2nd May 1821 (German edition, No. 225).

213. FROM THE PROGRAMME of the Fourteenth Evening Entertainment held by the Philharmonic Society, 8th March 1821

[2.] 'Group from Tartarus' by Schiller, set to music by Franz Schubert, sung by Herr [Josef] Preisinger.

Preisinger, born in Vienna in 1792, an official of the Bank Registry, sang bass and played the pianoforte. He was engaged as *basso buffo* by the Kärntnertor Theatre early in 1824.

214. AS SHE SAT LISTENING AT THE CLAVIER

(To Katharina Fröhlich as Schubert's listener, March 1821.)

So still she sat, of all the fair the fairest,
   She listened, giving neither blame nor praise;
The sombre wrap had dropt from off her bosom,
   Which gently did its filmy covering raise;
Her head inclined, the body forward bending,
As if the fleeting tones attendance lending.

Fair, did I say? But beauty is a picture
   Which paints itself and has no other claim;
Yet higher things perceive I in these features,
   Where, like a poet's lettering, whose aim
Is not to please by signs, but touch our senses,
She heavenly grace and tenderness dispenses.

So sat she there, with scarce a feature moving,
   A spasm only in her tender cheek,
The lashes trembling, shading radiant glances,
   The lips' soft play sweet to behold, and meek,
Like crimson shutters, now apart, now hiding
Conflicting thoughts that yield no other tiding.

And while the music grew more agitated,
   Involved in strife with only half a truce,
Now plangent, like lost doves in grief complaining,
   Now thundering as tempests breaking loose,
I saw how joy and pain in her contested,
And how each note emotion from her wrested.

In pity then I longed to stay the artist,
  To cry "Oh cease to lacerate her breast!"
When suddenly harsh dissonance was over,
  And tones of grief gave way to gladness blest;
Like Neptune's trident fiercest storms allaying
A triad rose, the music's turmoil staying.

And as the sun in radiance throws his lustre
  Into the scattered tempests of the night,
Her eye, still wet with tears, beheld I beaming
  With dazzling rays as of a heavenly light;
A gentle sigh from her sweet lips escaping,
She looked to see how others' thoughts were shaping.

This roused me: I resolved that she should hear it,
  Should know what long I had in silence borne;
But she, solicitous for the musician,
  With noiseless signals did my ardour warn;
And yet again I saw her ear inclining,
Again condemned was I to silent pining.

Franz Grillparzer.

The occasion of this poem is said to have been Grillparzer's second meeting with Kathi Fröhlich at the house of the banker Johann Heinrich Geymüller in the Wallnerstrasse (city), whose wife, Barbara, had her numerous daughters taught music by Anna Fröhlich. That Schubert was the pianist at this silent love-scene is merely a tradition. A sketch for the poem bears the inscription: "To Katty Fröhlich." It appeared in Vienna as early as the end of 1821 in the 'Aglaja' almanac edited by Josef Sonnleithner and Josef Schreyvogel. That same March Grillparzer also wrote an album leaf for Kathi. Her gesture of raising her finger to command silence is also described in a letter from Grillparzer to his friend Georg Altmüller of the spring of 1821, but in this case in a jocular manner. From that day the poet was spellbound by the coy beauty for the rest of his life.

215. MOSEL TO JOSEF HÜTTENBRENNER, 17th March 1821

Aware of the benevolent disposition of His Excellency, Count Moritz von Dietrichstein, towards the talented composer Herr

Franz Schubert, I have no doubt whatever that His Excellency will accept the dedication of the poem, 'The Erl King,' set to music by Herr Schubert.

In order to print a dedication the composer of any music about to be published had to obtain the dedicatee's written permission, which had to be submitted to the censorship authorities. Mosel, being the secretary in Dietrichstein's office, answered on behalf of his chief at the Court Opera, and he was right in his assumption that the count would accept the dedication (*see* No. 219).

216. FROM THE 'THEATERZEITUNG,' 29th March 1821

(Notice of the concert given by the pianoforte virtuoso Karl Schunke, 25th March 1821, at noon, in the County Hall. Part II.)

Herr [Franz] Ruess sang the glorious 'Erl King' by our so greatly promising Schubert, not without merit; but all those who have heard this sublime piece at its first performance, amid that assembly of true and worthy music-lovers, will retain the indelible impression they then received from a soulful and spirited delivery.

Mpr.

Karl Schunke, who belonged to a family of musicians, was born in 1801 at Magdeburg, and his later concert tours included London.—Ruess was engaged as tenor by the Leopoldstadt Theatre in 1823. The allusion to his precursor refers to Vogl (*see* No. 209).—A short discussion of the same concert appeared in the 'Wiener Zeitschrift für Kunst, . . .' on 3rd April 1821 (German edition, No. 230).

217. LEOPOLD SONNLEITHNER TO JOSEF HÜTTENBRENNER

Herr von Hüttenbrenner,

I beg you to be sure to see that Schubert comes to Fräulein Linhart to-morrow, in order to rehearse the 'Youth' with her, which she is to sing at our house; further, that Schubert comes to us on Wednesday at 11.30, to rehearse his Chorus of Spirits. I rely on your kindness in making sure that Schubert will come to these rehearsals. Indeed I am surprised that Schubert never appears at our house at all, although I urgently need to speak to him about his 'Erl King' and other matters.

Your respectfully devoted

S. H. [?], 26th March 1821.   Leop. Sonnleithner.

These rehearsals are connected with the concert at Sonnleithner's on 30th March (Friday). 'Erl King' was just about to be published.— "S. H." may stand for Schottenhof, for Sonnleithner was court judge at the Scottish monastery.

> At Ignaz Sonnleithner's Barth, Götz, Gymnich, Umlauff, Krebner, Nejebse, Preisinger and Hardt twice sing the 'Song of the Spirits over the Waters' (xvi. 3) and Sophie Linhart 'The Youth on the Hill' ('Der Jüngling auf dem Hügel') (xx. 285), 30th March 1821. —George Krebner, secretary to the trusteeship of the Habsburg properties, was a member of the Philharmonic Society's committee and sang tenor.—Albert Hardt, who sang bass and played the violin, seems to have been a professional musician.

218. From the 'Sammler,' 31st March 1821

Just published by Cappi & Diabelli, in the Graben, and to be had for 2 florins V.C.: 'Erl King,' ballad by Goethe, set to music by Franz Schubert.

This ballad, sung on 7th March by the renowned Court Opera singer, Herr Vogl, at the concert organized by the Society of Ladies of the Nobility for the benefit of its charities, pleased so much by its music that it had to be repeated by general request. The same piece had already been performed at the foremost houses where music is cultivated, and everywhere Herr Schubert's composition earned the merited—that is to say the most resounding —success. The favour with which music-lovers have received it appears to be justified by the judgment of the most excellent local connoisseurs of art, according to which Goethe's words have been most justly conceived by the young composer and their characteristic features have been reproduced with an arresting truthfulness in this thoroughly original composition.

Musical Vienna, on its executive side, can thus but ardently welcome the fact that the setting of the above ballad is now to enjoy a larger publicity, and it is the less doubtful that the editor will be favoured with success because the subscribers already amount to a sufficient number to cover the costs of publication.

[Josef Hüttenbrenner.]

After a vain attempt with Breitkopf & Härtel of Leipzig (*see* No. 102), Leopold Sonnleithner offered the 'Erl King' to the Viennese publishing house of Steiner & Co.; but this too declined to publish the song on account of the composer's obscurity and the difficulty of the pianoforte accompaniment. Thereupon Leopold Sonnleithner, Josef Hüttenbrenner and two other music-lovers, Johann Schönauer and Johann Nepomuk Schönpichler, clubbed together to publish the work by subscription, the new publishing firm of Cappi & Diabelli acting as agents only. These four men had collected the necessary sum of money, but when copies were offered at one of Ignaz Sonnleithner's domestic concerts (perhaps already on 1st December 1820), a hundred were at once subscribed for, and this paid also for the engraving and printing of the smaller Op. 2 ('Margaret at the Spinning-Wheel'). Thus the books of Schubert's songs Opp. 1–7 and 12–14 were published by subscription. The price was 1 florin 30 kreuzer, except for Nos. 1 and 14, which cost 2 florins each. All these books bear Schubert's control number and initials: 1–7 are signed "Sch." with the number following, while on 12–14 the signature "Schbt." follows the numbers in the right-hand bottom corner of the last blank page. About 600 copies of 'Erl King' were published in this way in three issues, about 500 of 'Margaret at the Spinning-Wheel' in two issues and about 400 of the mixed Goethe songs, Op. 3, in two issues. The editions of the other seven opus numbers may have amounted to about 300 copies each.—Schönauer (born 1778) was proctor's man at the university, and at the same time, until 1807, a tenor in the court chapel; he had already taken part as a boy chorister in Gottfried van Swieten's private Handel concerts in Vienna under Mozart's direction. Schönpichler (born c. 1771) was a manorial land steward, a member of the Philharmonic Society's committee and a violinist.

219. FROM THE OFFICIAL 'WIENER ZEITUNG,' 2nd April 1821

At the House of Cappi & Diabelli, Graben, No. 1133, is newly published and to be had:

ERL KING

Ballad by Goethe, set to music and reverentially dedicated to the Hon. Herr Herr

MORITZ, COUNT VON DIETRICHSTEIN,

by

FRANZ SCHUBERT.

Price . . . . . 2 florins, V.C.

The value of this composition has already been so favourably and advantageously expressed in the ingenious young composer's honour by the public verdict at the concert given in the I. & R. Court Opera theatre last Ash Wednesday, where, delivered by our celebrated Court Opera singer, Herr Vogl, its repetition was unanimously demanded, as well as by several public journals, that any further recommendation should be as superfluous as its appearance in print and its possession by every connoisseur and lover of song at home and abroad should be welcome.

[Josef Hüttenbrenner.]

Dietrichstein had himself set several Goethe poems to music.—It is remarkable that the opus number (1) is not mentioned in either of the two preceding advertisements, although it is on the title-page of the first issue.

220. From Rosenbaum's Diary, 4th April 1821

(Concerning the first private subscription concert of the vocal quintet of Johann Sedlatzek, Ernst Krähmer, Wenzel Sedlak, August Mittag and Friedrich Hradezky in the County Hall at noon.)

A Quartet by Schubert.

Sedlatzek, born in 1789 at Oberglogau in Silesia, and living in Vienna since 1810, was flautist at the court theatres; he also played in London in 1826. Krähmer, born at Dresden in 1795, living in Vienna since 1815, was first oboist at the Kärntnertor Theatre, and later in the court chapel. Sedlak (born 1776) was clarinettist in Prince Liechtenstein's orchestra. Mittag (born 1795) was bassoon player at the court theatres and professor at the Conservatory. The horn player Hradezky has already been mentioned (*see* No. 137).—The male-voice quartet by Schubert was 'Das Dörfchen' ('The Little Village').

221. From the 'Wiener Zeitschrift für Kunst,' &c., 24th April 1821

. . . This was followed by the well-known vocal Quartet by Herr Schubert, which was well sung and, as always, favourably received.

"As always" no doubt refers to the following concert as well.

222. FROM THE MS. PROGRAMME of the Third of the Annual
Concerts given by the Vienna Philharmonic Society in the
Large Assembly Hall, 8th April 1821, at Noon (Conductor,
Vincenz Hauschka)

5. 'The Little Village' [Das Dörfchen'], poem by Bürger, set
for 4 male voices by Franz Schubert and delivered by Herren Barth,
[Peter] Lugano, [Johann] Nestroy and Götz.

A printed programme of this concert has been preserved (reproduced
in the iconographical volume appended to the German edition of this
work, p. 157).   It included the first chorus of the Trojan women and the
antiphonal chorus in Collin's 'Polyxena,' composed by Stadler (see 15th
December 1811, note on pp. 21–2).—On Hauschka, see No. 712.—
Lugano was an amateur singer.—Nestroy, born in Vienna in 1801, went
to the academic grammar-school in 1810–13.   In the autumn of the latter
year he, like Schubert, failed in mathematics, but Nestroy had a bad report
for conduct as well.   He was just then attempting to enter a legal career,
only to embrace that of a singer before long.   He became later a character
comedian and, as a playwright, the greatest satirist of the Austrian stage.

223. FROM THE 'WIENER ZEITSCHRIFT FÜR KUNST,' &c.,
26th April 1821

The Quartet by Schubart [sic] on Bürger's song, "I love my
little village here," performed by male voices, had to be repeated.
The pleasing delivery by the tenor and the vigorous tone of the
bass deserve special mention.

The praise is doubtless intended for Barth and Götz.

224. LEOPOLD SONNLEITHNER TO JOSEF HÜTTENBRENNER

Herr von Hüttenbrenner,
I have just received the enclosed chit from Diabelli.   As you
have introduced the matter, I beg you urgently to see to the
necessary.   If Count Fries accepts the dedication, the title might
run as follows:

Margaret at the Spinning-Wheel,
A Scene from the Tragedy, 'Faust,' by Goethe
Set to music and reverentially dedicated to
the Hon. Herr Herr
Moritz von Fries, Count of the Realm,
Knight of the I. & R. Order of Leopold, &c. &c.
by Franz Schubert
(Work 2).

Should Fries not have accepted the dedication, the engraver might still begin the plate in the meantime and leave room for the name. Please speak to Diabelli about it. Your devoted

13th April 1821.   Leopold Sonnleithner.

The "matter" was once again the permission required from the deci-catee, which it fell to the publishers, as agents for the work, to seek. Anton Diabelli, born at Mattsee near Salzburg in 1781, had been Peter Cappi's partner since 1818, but in 1824 he became sole head of the firm. —Count Fries (born 1777) was the head of the banking concern of Fries & Co., director of the Austrian National Bank, a great art collector and Maecenas, and incidentally a patron of Anselm Hüttenbrenner.—The title of Op. 2 was somewhat differently worded on publication.

225. FROM THE 'THEATERZEITUNG,' 21st April 1821

(Notice of Sedlatzek's third subscription concert, 15th April 1821, at noon, in the County Hall.)

We heard a charming composition by our greatly promising Schubert, in the performance of which the tenor, Herr Barth, particularly distinguished himself.

B. v. M—s—r.

[Benedikt, Freiherr von Möser.]

This was 'The Little Village' again.

226. FROM THE PROGRAMME of the Kärntnertor Theatre, 22nd April 1821

(Evening entertainment for the benefit of public charities.)

Part II. . . . 4. 'The Nightingale,' a poem by K. Unger, set for voices especially for this evening by Herr Franz Schubert and

performed by Herr Barth, singer in the I. & R. Court Chapel,
with Herren Götz, Umlauff and Nejebse.

This concert took place on Easter Sunday. The evening began with
Goethe's pastoral play, 'The Lover's Caprice' ('Die Laune des Verliebten'), following Cherubini's 'Medea' overture. Hellmesberger played
two movements from a violin concerto by Charles Philippe Lafont. There
was also a trio from Rossini's 'Riccardo e Zoraide' and, of course, a
tableau at the end.—Unger, Count Esterházy's friend, wrote the words for
a few vocal quartets, among them 'Evening' ('Der Abend') for Anselm
Hüttenbrenner, much in favour at Zseliz (see No. 617). 'The Nightingale' ('Die Nachtigall') was given in its first version, unaccompanied.

227. FROM BAUERNFELD'S DIARY

22nd April 1821.

Kärntnertor Theatre: Goethe's 'Lover's Caprice' ['Die Laune
des Verliebten'] is not favoured by fortune. The best is a quartet
by Schubert. A splendid fellow! I shall have to make his
acquaintance.

Bauernfeld did not get to know Schubert until 1822.

228. FROM THE DRESDEN 'ABENDZEITUNG,' 29th July 1821

'The Nightingale,' a vocal quartet by Schubert, had to be repeated. It is in fact an excellent composition. . . . The excellent
song-writer Schubert is said to be occupied at present with the
composition of a grand romantic opera.

The opera is probably 'Alfonso and Estrella,' although Schubert did
not begin its composition until the autumn of 1821.—Other notices of
the Easter concert appeared in the 'Sammler' of 28th April, in the
'Theaterzeitung' and the 'Wiener Zeitschrift für Kunst, . . .' on 1st
May, in the Vienna 'Allgemeine musikalische Zeitung' on 16th May and
in the Leipzig 'Allgemeine musikalische Zeitung' on 30th May 1821
(German edition, Nos. 243–7).

229. OTTENWALT TO JOSEF VON SPAUN in Vienna

Linz, 28th April 1821.

Marie practises beside me playing the Schubertian marches.
Although it is only the bass, and on aunt's pianoforte, I yet have

difficulty in resisting so charming an interruption; even my writing fingers try to follow the changing bars.

None of Schubert's marches for pianoforte duet is dated. It may here be a question of the 'Three Heroic Marches,' Op. 27.—Spaun's aunt, Marie Berndt, was a widow.

230. FROM THE PROGRAMME of the Sixteenth Evening Entertainment held by the Philharmonic Society, 29th April 1821

[2.] 'Longing' ['Sehnsucht'] by Schiller, set to music by Franz Schubert. Sung by Herr Götz.

At this concert Götz sang for the last time before his death.—The programmes for the evening entertainments of 1821–2 have not been preserved.

231. FROM THE OFFICIAL 'WIENER ZEITUNG,' 30th April 1821

At the House of Cappi & Diabelli,
Art and Music Dealers, Graben, No. 1133,
is newly published and to be had:

MARGARET AT THE SPINNING-WHEEL.

From Goethe's 'Faust.'

Composed for One Voice with Pianoforte Accompaniment
and reverentially dedicated to
the Hon. Herr Herr
MORITZ VON FRIES, Count of the Realm,
Knight of the Austrian Imp. Order of Leopold, &c. &c.
by
FRANZ SCHUBERT
Work 2.   Price, 1 Florin 30 Kreuzer, V.C.

Already this song has invariably been received with the most decisive approbation at the most excellent local private concerts. It may moreover justly be said of it that it deserves to be regarded as one of the most interesting of songs. Its possession will thus be greatly welcomed by all lovers of art, and especially by ladies who like singing.

Also to be had:

'Erl King.' Ballad by Goethe, composed for one voice with
pianoforte accompaniment by Fr. Schubert. Work 1. Price
2 florins, V.C.

Do. for do. with guitar accompaniment.   1 florin 30 kreuzer.

Most of the editions with guitar accompaniments, which are not authentic, did not appear until a little later.

232. FROM THE VIENNA 'SAMMLER,' 1st May 1821

At Cappi & Diabelli's, on the Graben, has just been published:
'Margaret at the Spinning-Wheel,' from Goethe's 'Faust,' by
Herr Franz Schubert. Price 1 florin 30 kreuzer, V.C. This
composition has been distinguished by unanimous applause at
several private concerts, and every lover of song has looked forward eagerly to the public appearance of a composition which does
so much honour to a pupil of the great masters Salieri and Vogl.

Margaret's state of mind, in which the feelings and sensations
of love, of pain and of rapture take turns, are so affectingly depicted by Schubert's music that a more heart-stirring impression
than that left by his musical picture is scarcely imaginable. Apart
from that, the composition is also remarkable for its pianoforte
part, which so successfully sketches the motion of the spinning-
wheel and develops its theme in such a masterly way. The little
song, 'Margaret at the Spinning-Wheel,' must in fact be con-
ceded to have as much originality and uniqueness as Beethoven's
'Adelaide' and Mozart's 'To Chloe' and 'Evening Musings'
['Abendempfindung'].

The work is dedicated to Count of the Realm Moritz von Fries,
a lover of the arts, which have found in him one of the most
generously-minded connoisseurs and protectors.

—nn—

[Josef Hüttenbrenner.]

233. JOSEF VON SPAUN TO SCHOBER

Linz, 11th May 1821.

. . . But of you too, of my friends, I hear less than I should like. As regards Schubert, I have to look to the newspapers for the best information about his doings. The day before yesterday Derffel positively refreshed me with detailed news and quite transported me among you at the Crown Inn and the Wasserburger café. I am glad that it has fallen to Hosp to follow his inclination, and I wish him every success. A pity that he cannot take you and Schubert with him, for I am, greatly afraid for him if he is left without guidance and encouragement.

Spaun was probably at Linz only temporarily. Franz Derffel, jun., Schober's cousin, was a Viennese official, on a visit to Linz. — The "Hungarian Crown" Inn, known already to Mozart, who played billiards there, was at the corner of the Himmelpfortgasse and Seilerstätte in the city, Leopold Wasserburger's café in an Seilerstätte close by. At the inn (called after its former owner, an Archbishop of Gran) there was a reserved room on the ground floor where Schubert and his friends gathered about 1822. It is there that the nickname of "Canevas" is said to have originated, Schubert being in the habit of asking "Kann er was?" ("Can he do anything?") whenever a newcomer was introduced, which was punningly turned into "Canevas," .meaning the canvas used for embroidery.—Hosp, about whom no details are known, was tenor at the Leipzig Theatre in 1823.

234. FROM THE VIENNA 'ALLGEMEINE MUSIKALISCHE ZEITUNG,' 12th May 1821

. . . The triplet accompaniment [in 'Erl King'] keeps the whole alive and gives it more unity, as it were; but one could wish that Herr Schubert had occasionally transferred it to the left hand, and thus facilitated performance; for the ceaseless striking of one and the same note in triplets throughout whole bars tires the hand, if the piece is to be taken at the rapid pace demanded by Herr Schubert. . . .

235. SCHUBERT'S DEDICATION on a Manuscript of German Dances, Op. 18, Part I, Nos. 5 and 8, May 1821 (one Waltz cut off)

German Dances for Countess Caroline [Esterházy].

These two dances (the first in E♭ minor instead of, as it is now, in E minor) are written down on the back of the song 'Restless Love' ('Rastlose Liebe') as transposed for Karl, Freiherr von Schönstein, a friend of the Esterházys', who was a baritone. The dedication is vigorously crossed out, as though in a fit of pique.

236. SATIRICAL POEM on Anselm Hüttenbrenner's 'Erl King' Waltzes, published in the Vienna 'Allgemeine Musikalische Zeitung,' 16th May 1821

ATTRACTION.

Question:

Tell me, thou exquisite wight, what seekst thou in verses by Goethe?

Answer:

Titles I look for, and see! Erl King for waltzes I found.

THREE-FOUR TIME.

Question:

How is the spirits' dread world to be rendered in Germany's dances?

Answer:

Cannot no matter what song serve us for dancing to-day?

FEELING.

Question:

Say, doth the world of to-day direct to its legs its emotions?

Answer:

Yea, in these tight-lacing days hearts have sunk nearer the boots!

F. A. Kanne.

Hüttenbrenner's waltzes did appear shortly afterwards, issued by Schubert's own publishers (see note on p. 187). No trace of this production has remained, but it was evidently a travesty of Schubert's song in waltz form. Friedrich August Kanne (born 1778), a poet, musician and critic living in Vienna since 1808, was editor of this periodical in 1821–4, and published several satirical distichs in it. Schubert copied that couplet and sent it through Josef Hüttenbrenner to Anselm in Styria. After Schubert's death Diabelli published 'Erl King' galops under the composer's own name (about New Year 1829). In 1824, by the way, Steiner & Co. of Vienna published 'Euryanthe' waltzes, and about 1826 J. C. Gombart of Augsburg 'Wanderer' waltzes, both anonymous.

237. PYRKER TO SCHUBERT

Much-to-be-honoured Sir,

Your kind proposal to dedicate to me the fourth book of your incomparable songs I accept with the greater pleasure, since it will now frequently recall to my memory that evening when I was so much moved by the depths of your being—particularly through the sounds of your 'Wanderer'! I am proud to belong to the same country as you and remain with the highest esteem

Your most devoted

Venice, 18th May 1821.   Johann L. Pyrker,
Patriarch.

Johann Ladislaus Pyrker of Felsö-Eör, born in 1773 at Lángh in Hungary, went to the Cistercian monastery at Lilienfeld in Lower Austria in 1792, became Bishop of Zips (Hungary) in 1818, having become abbot in 1812, and Patriarch (i.e. Archbishop) of Venice in 1820. He was a poet and had made Schubert's acquaintance at Matthäus von Collin's. Collin, Heinrich's brother, born in Vienna in 1779, was tutor to the Duke of Reichstadt, editor of the 'Jahrbücher der Literatur' and a poet. He had met Schubert at Josef von Spaun's, who was his cousin, and then invited him to his own house with Vogl. There Schubert met Mosel, Count Moritz Dietrichstein, Josef, Ritter von Hammer-Purgstall, Karoline Pichler and Pyrker. It is said that on that evening Schubert performed his 'Wanderer' and, with Anselm Hüttenbrenner, the Variations in E minor, Op. 10, on the romance of Queen Hortense. This was probably in 1820.

238. FROM THE 'THEATERZEITUNG,' 22nd May 1821

At Cappi & Diabelli's have newly appeared: 'Shepherd's Complaint' ['Schäfers Klagelied'], 'The Hedge-Rose' ['Heidenröslein'], 'Huntsman's Evening Song' ['Jägers Abendlied'] and 'Stillness of the Sea' ['Meeresstille'], four poems by Goethe, set to music by Franz Schubert. Each of these songs has its own character, according to the poet's intention; delightful melodies and a noble simplicity, alternating with original force and elevation, unite them into a glorious wreath of song, which joins worthily on to the earlier excellent achievements of this talented

composer. The little work is dedicated to the Hon. Aulic
Councillor and Court Theatre Vice-Director Herr Ignaz, Edler
von Mosel.

—i—

239. FROM THE OFFICIAL 'WIENER ZEITUNG,' 29th May 1821

At the House of Cappi & Diabelli,
Art and Music Dealers, Graben, No. 1133,
are newly published and to be had:

THE WANDERER
['Der Wanderer']
by
Schmidt of Lübeck.

MORNING SONG ['Morgenlied'] by Werner, and
WANDERER'S NIGHT SONG
['Wanderers Nachtlied']
by Goethe.

Set to Music for One Voice with Pianoforte Accompaniment
by FRANZ SCHUBERT.

Work 4. Price, 1 Florin 30 Kreuzer, V.C.

SHEPHERD'S COMPLAINT, THE HEDGE-ROSE,
['Schäfers Klagelied'] ['Heidenröslein']
HUNTSMAN'S EVENING SONG and STILLNESS OF THE SEA
['Jägers Abendlied'] ['Meeresstille']
by Goethe.

Set to Music for One Voice with Pianoforte Accompaniment
by FRANZ SCHUBERT. Work 3. Price, 1 Florin 30 Kreuzer, V.C.

The publishers feel induced by frequent requests to submit these
two books also to friends of German song. The choice of the
poems alone betokens the composer's poetic disposition; but the
manner in which he conceives masterpieces of poetry and repro-
duces them musically testifies to the young artist's surpassing genius.

Op. 4 is dedicated to Pyrker.

First performance of the magic opera in three acts 'The Magic Bell' ('Das Zauberglöckchen'), 20th June 1821, after E. G. M Théaulon de Lambert, by Friedrich Treitschke, music by Louis J. F. Hérold, in the theatre at the Kärntnertor, with two extra vocal numbers by Schubert (xv. 15).—Schubert's name was not mentioned on the playbill, but his authorship of the two additional numbers commissioned by the management (? to words by Treitschke) was known at any rate to the critics. The first extra was a comic duet for the Chinese bridegroom Bedur (Franz Siebert) and his companion Zedir (Josef Gottdank) in the second act. The other was an aria for Azolin (Franz Rosner) at the beginning of the third act. Siebert, born in 1793 at Einsiedeln in Switzerland, was a bass at the Kärntnertor Theatre in 1818–21. Rosner (recte Rosnik), born in 1800 at Waitzen in Hungary, was a tenor there in 1819–24. Vogl, to whom the commission was probably due, sang the part of the Sultan.

240. FROM THE VIENNA 'ALLGEMEINE MUSIKALISCHE ZEITUNG,' 4th July 1821

(On 'The Magic Bell')

The characteristic duet in B flat major, invented by Herr Schubert, is to be praised for its management of the voices as well as instrumentation. The bass has quite a piquant figure in two places. The performance by Herren [Franz] Siebert and [Josef] Gottdank was admirable. The shades of *forte* and *piano* could not have been heard to better advantage. Their due was loud applause. But——!

. . . The aria in E, for Prince Azolin, is also of Herr Schubert's invention. However, we are compelled to speak quite otherwise of this piece than of the pretty duet mentioned above. For one thing, the voice-part continually lies high, even in *forte*, and what is even more damaging is the frequent repetition of one and the same high note. It is clear that Herr [Franz] Rosner is incapable of singing it properly to the end. Drastic changes of tempo, by the way, disturb its unity. E trumpets should be used only in the lower registers.

Further notices appeared in the 'Wiener Zeitschrift für Kunst, . . .' on 30th June, in the 'Sammler' on 3rd July and in the Leipzig 'Zeitung für die elegante Welt' on 3rd September 1821 (German edition, Nos. 258,

259 and 261). The Leipzig paper did not mention Schubert's name. Josef von Spaun reports that Schubert's music overshadowed Hérold's.

Second performance of 'The Magic Bell,' 22nd June 1821.

241. FROM THE POSTSCRIPT to Vol I of the Vienna 'Eichenblätter'

For the pleasure of music-lovers and the increase of subscribers to this work, moreover, the composers of genius, Herren W. Tomaschek in Prague and Franz Schubert in Vienna, have kindly taken turns in composing the musical supplement added to each volume.

Vol. II will appear towards the end of October 1821.

Vienna, 27th June 1821.   The Editors.

Of this almanac, dedicated to the Society of Noble Ladies, only the first year's issue appeared with a musical supplement, 'The Father's Death' ('Des Vaters Tod') by Wenzel Johann Tomaschek (Vaclav Jaroslav Tomašek), born in 1774 at Skutsch in Bohemia. An organist and musical educationist, he was a forerunner of Schubert's lyrical pianoforte pieces. The almanac was published by Leopold Grund in Vienna. Its editor may have been Karl Friedrich Weiss, the author of the dedicatory poem. The first year's issue was not announced in the official 'Wiener Zeitung' until 4th August 1821 (German edition, No. 271).

'To Emma,' Op. 58, No. 2 (xx. 26) appears in the 'Wiener Zeitschrift,' 30th June 1821.

242. SCHUBERT TO JOSEF GROSS [? Middle of 1821]

Dear Gross,

Kindly hand to the bearer of this all my German Dances which are in your keeping, as they are to be engraved.

Your

Schubert.

Gross, secretary to the court exchequer, a friend of Josef von Spaun's, was a good pianoforte player. His wife, Kamilla Ellmaurer, a pupil of Vogl's, married after Gross's death (1834) Karl, Ritter von Enderes, another Schubertian.—Schubert had evidently lent Gross his single manuscript of these German dances, which he then published as Op. 9. The bearer of this note was Josef Hüttenbrenner, whom Schubert had introduced

to Gross.   All three lived in the Wipplingerstrasse at that time: Schubert at the Hohe Brücke, Hüttenbrenner with his landlord Irrsa below
Mayrhofer's and Gross opposite the town hall.

Third performance of 'The Magic Bell,' 1st July 1821.

243. From the Official 'Wiener Zeitung,' 9th July 1821

At the House of Cappi & Diabelli,
Art and Music Dealers, Graben, No. 1133, are newly
published and to be had:

Restless Love,
['Rastlose Liebe']
Nearness of the Beloved,   The Fisherman,   First Loss,
['Nähe des Geliebten']   ['Der Fischer'] ['Erster Verlust']
and The King in Thule
['Der König in Thule']
Poems by Goethe.

Set to Music for One Voice with Pianoforte Accompaniment
by Franz Schubert.
Work 5.
Price, 1 Florin 30 Kreuzer, V.C.

The works by this composer require no recommendation, since
their intrinsic value expresses itself too clearly for any lover of art
not to feel and each connoisseur unconditionally to acknowledge it.

Goethe's masterly poetry could hardly be clothed in music
more worthily than it is done in the carefully chosen and grouped
compositions here submitted.

Op. 5 is dedicated to Salieri.   The fact that the songs were settings of
German poems, although by Goethe, may have disappointed him.

Schubert at Atzenbrugg, July 1821.   The property of Atzenbrugg,
then belonging to the Klosterneuberg monastery, lies on the river
Perschling between Tulln and Traismauer, but on the south bank of
the Danube, some twenty-three miles west-north-west of Vienna.
Schober's uncle, Josef Derffel, sen., a brother of Franz Derffel
already mentioned, was a superior official of the monastery and
steward of the property.   It was he who about 1820 offered
hospitality to the Schubertians at Atzenbrugg for a few days each

year. Lists are preserved of the circle which met there for con-
vivial gatherings, called Atzenbrugg feasts, dating from 1817 to 1822
(copies were in the possession of Max Kupelwieser in Vienna). We
first find in them Schober, his sister Sophie, his cousins Franz and
Therese (children of Franz Derffel, sen.), Josef von Spaun and Gahy;
later the philosopher and doctor Philipp Karl Hartmann, the
military surveyor Ferdinand Mayerhofer von Grünbühel and his
colleague Johann Zechenter (Sophie von Schober's future husband),
Emilie Stöger (who later married the Aulic Councillor von Werne-
kingh) and Frau Derffel, probably Josef's wife; and lastly Josef
Gross, Elise Stöger (Emilie's sister) and Louise Johanna (called
Jeannette) Cuny de Pierron (Anton von Doblhoff's betrothed, who
died early). Schubert first appeared in the circle's lists in 1820,
so that he must have been at Atzenbrugg already in the summer of
that year. With him emerges the painter Leopold Kupelwieser,
born in 1796 at Piesting in Lower Austria, with whom again Schubert
had become acquainted through Josef von Spaun. Kupelwieser in
July 1821 drew separate portraits of Schubert and Schober at
Atzenbrugg, and for the latter the two water-colours (now in the
Schubert museum in Vienna), one of which depicts an excursion
by carriage to the nearby Aumühle, the other a scene from a charade
played by half of those present and, according to a letter by Schober
(14th February 1876), based not only on a riddle, but also on a pun:
the first half of the word "Rheinfall" (Rhine Falls) having been
punningly changed into "rein" (pure), the second half being
presented as the fall of man. The picture (*see* coloured plate) shows
the representation of the fall of Adam and Eve, Schubert accompanying the scene on the pianoforte. In 1821 the circle was joined by the
painter Ludwig Mohn, born in 1797 at Halle o/S., who etched a game
of ball with Schober and Schwind at Atzenbrugg. (Schwind, to whom
Schubert was introduced in 1821 by Josef Kenner, did not belong
to the circle until 1823.) Axel von Schober's former valet, Claude
Étienne, also turned up in 1821. In the following year, the last in
the lists, came Anton, Freiherr von Doblhoff, Max Josef Gritzner
and his wife Josefa and their daughter Jenny (the later owners of the
Aumühle), the landscape painter and violinist Ludwig Kraissl and
tall Josef Huber. There were, moreover, a few people of whom no
details are known.—Schubert's sojourns at Atzenbrugg are attested
by his 'Atzenbrugg Dances' ('Atzenbrugger Tänze'). It has been
stated but never proved that Ernst, Freiherr von Feuchtersleben
(born Vienna, 1806), wrote his poem 'Es ist bestimmt in Gottes
Rat' (later set by Mendelssohn) at Atzenbrugg in 1825 as a
farewell to Schober.

244. Occasional Poem by Schober [? Atzenbrugg, 1821]

(On the occasion of a *jeu d'esprit*, at which F. Schubert was present, on the words Wit, Ball, Pen, Heath, Frog, Art, Food and Assuagement.)

Dearest brethren, dearest brethren,
What is it that holds us captured?
Why are we, though music beckons,
But by wit's dull game of ball,
But by pen and ink and all,
Not by streams of song enraptured?

Many steal away from feasting
And from merry social pleasure
To the heath, by rushes bordered,
To the woods of darkling oak,
Where the frog emits his croak
And the cuckoo pipes his measure.

Yet the conjurer in music,
Of high art the food withholding,
Sits unheard in our assembly;
No assuagement does he give.
Come, do not kill time, let live
Melodies in song unfolding!

The party game called "wording" (*Worteln*), which consisted in making poems from a number of given words, had reached the Schubertians in Vienna from Kremsmünster. It corresponds with Schwind's assiduously practised game of making drawings from a number of given dots and, as we shall see, to Schubert's attempt on 1st March 1828 at composing a German dance from given notes (*see* No. 1033).

245. From the Vienna 'Allgemeine Musikalische Zeitung,' 18th July 1821

(Concerning the cultivation of music at Steyr.)

Vocal chamber music has suffered much through the departure of several valued persons, and little or nothing can be offered at

present, apart from a private house where Franz Schubert's fair
young Muse is at home. Yet Steyr rejoices in being the cradle
of the celebrated singer Michael Vogl, who, born at a small house
in the suburb of Ennsdorf, as a child received his first musical
instruction at Steyr, and even now, at the height of his mastery,
does not neglect frequently to see his cherished home again and,
in it, his friends and admirers.

A. St[adler].

The private house is most likely Paumgartner's.—Stadler moved in
1821 from Steyr to Linz, where he became an official in the county council.

Fourth performance of 'The Magic Bell,' 22nd July 1821.

246. FROM F. H. BÖCKH'S REGISTER of Musicians living in and
around Vienna, including the Foremost Amateurs, with
Particulars of their Domiciles, Summer 1821.

SCHUBERT, Franz, Composer.   Wipplingerstrasse, City of
Vienna No. 350.

Franz Heinrich Böckh, born c. 1787 at Klagenfurt in Carinthia, was
manager of the court and state printing works. His handbook, of which
the musicians' register is but a section, bore the title of 'Vienna's Living
Authors, Artists and Amateurs in the Faculty of Arts.' A second issue
with a new title-page appeared in 1823 as 'Curiosities of the Capital
and Residence of Vienna, . . .' with a supplement, in which Schubert,
however, is not named.—Schubert's lodgings mentioned here are the
second he occupied in the Wipplingerstrasse, at the Hohe Brücke. Mayrhofer was still at the old address there, previously shared with Schubert.

247. FRANZ VON BRUCHMANN to August, Count Platen, at Erlangen

Vienna, 2nd August 1821.

. . . Write to me, too, by what opportunity you wish to have
books and whether you have at Erlangen a middling or perhaps
even a good singer and pianoforte player, for I should then send
you some poems by Goethe gloriously set to music by Schubert,
which could not fail to enrapture all your friends. Is not Dr.
Engelhardt musical? Did I not see a pianoforte at his house?

Bruchmann had gone to Erlangen at the end of 1821, in order to hear
at the university there the lectures, 'Initia universae philosophiae,' given

by the philosopher Friedrich Wilhelm Schelling, whom Senn had revered already before 1820. Such visits to the universities in Germany were no longer permitted to Austrian students after 1819, so that Bruchmann had to make this educative journey secretly. He made friends at Erlangen with the poet August, Count Platen-Hallermünde, born in 1796 at Ansbach in Bavaria, who had been in Vienna in September 1820, without however coming into touch with the Schubert circle. His 'Ghazals' appeared in 1821, and on 31st March of that year he wrote a sonnet into a copy given to the departing Bruchmann, in which he says:

> Thou hatest all who chatter by convention,
> Thou striv'st to grasp the meaning of all matter,
> And steel'st thy mind with opposites' contention.

In Vienna Bruchmann procured for Platen copies of Persian manuscripts from the court library with the aid of Hammer von Purgstall and the orientalist Vincenz von Rosenzweig.—Platen began to learn the pianoforte in November 1821.—Veit Engelhardt, born 1791 at Neustadt in Franconia, had been professor of theology at Erlangen since 1820.

Anselm Hüttenbrenner's 'Erl King' Waltzes (in G minor) are on sale at Cappi & Diabelli's, 13th August 1821.

248. From the Official 'Wiener Zeitung, 23rd August 1821

At the House of Cappi & Diabelli,
Art and Music Dealers, Graben, No. 1133,
are newly published and to be had:

Memnon, Antigone and Oedipus,

by J. Mayrhofer,

and

At Anselmo's Grave,
['Am Grabe Anselmos']

by Claudius.

Set to Music for One Voice with Pianoforte Accompaniment
and reverentially dedicated to the Hon.
Herr Michael Vogl,

Member and Producer of the I. & R. Court Opera Theatre,

by Franz Schubert.

Work 6. Price, 1 Florin 30 Kreuzer, V.C.

This book joins on worthily to its predecessors. It is dedicated by permission to the valued producer and singer of the I. & R. Court Opera Theatre, Herr Michael Vogl, whose favourite songs are here gathered together. This circumstance guarantees their excellence.

A later edition (the fourth issue) of this book is adorned with an engraved vignette from Leopold Kupelwieser's pen-and-ink drawing for the song 'At Anselmo's Grave,' perhaps intended for the presentation copy for Vogl (iconographical volume, p. 194).

249. FROM THE MS. PROGRAMME of an Examination at the Vienna Conservatory, 30th August 1821, at the Gundelhof

Part III. . . . 14. Four-part Psalm by Schubert, performed by women pupils of the 3rd class.

Schubert had composed the Twenty-third Psalm, "The Lord is my shepherd," in Moses Mendelssohn's translation in December 1820, for Anna Fröhlich's pupils. It appeared posthumously as Op. 132 (xviii. 2). —On the same occasion the final sextet from Mozart's 'Don Giovanni,' long neglected on the stage, was sung with Nestroy and Nejebse among the singers.

250. FROM THE LEIPZIG 'ALLGEMEINE MUSIKALISCHE ZEITUNG,' 26th September 1821

Psalm by Schubert, sung by four women pupils of the third class. A pleasing but somewhat long-drawn composition.

251. FROM THE VIENNA 'ALLGEMEINE MUSIKALISCHE ZEITUNG,' 29th September 1821

A four-part psalm by Schubert, performed by lady pupils of the third class, Mlles Fabiani, Heinrich, Devils and Fleischmann, pleased by the interesting part-writing which it shows.

The four singers were Louise Fabiani, Emerenzia Heinrich (later married name Reichel), Amalie Tewilis (not Devils) and Josefine Fleischmann.

252. BRUCHMANN TO PLATEN

Vienna, 5th September 1821.

[Books sent to Platen:]

. . . 6th) Goethe songs (Schubert has not yet received yours, as he is not here).

The first song composed by Schubert to words by Platen was 'Love hath lied' ('Die Liebe hat gelogen'), early in April 1822. He only set one other, the ghazal 'Thou lov'st me not' ('Du liebst mich nicht'), in July 1822 (*see* Nos. 259 and 265).—Schubert may have stayed at Atzenbrugg again at the beginning of September 1821 (*see* No. 258).

> Fifth to seventh performances of 'The Magic Bell,' 9th, 19th and 25th September 1821

> Josef von Spaun, appointed assessor to the Upper Austrian Excise Revenue Office, removes to Linz, 23rd September 1821.

253. TO FRANZ

Autumn 1821.

I.

Thou lov'st me! Deeply have I felt it,
Thou faithful youth, so fair and true;
Then let our courage never falter,
So nobly steeled betwixt us two!
Let life but press on us its burden,
True friendship's concord be our guerdon.

Yet, truth for thy reward I offer:
My very self I 'd have thee learn;
Thy goodness leads thee to ideals
For which, alas! we vainly yearn;
And if thou deem'st with life I bubble,
'Tis but endeavour's toil and trouble.

I have but lisped some poor reflections.
Have ever I a true thing wrought?
Whate'er I wrote, 'twas but a body
Of which I scarce the spirit caught.
Did e'er I grasp the sense of history
And clothe it in a poet's mystery?

Yet let us, till to match endeavour
Our strength and knowledge prove their worth,
As brothers quietly united
Strive for a freer, better earth.
Be this my theme, the plan I cherish,
Which once attained, my song may perish!

II.

['In the High Alps,' from 'Heliopolis,' composed by Schubert,
April 1822 (xxi. 405).]

Rock piled up on rocky masses,
Solid earth, majestic height;
Waterfalls and sweeping tempest,
Oh, unfathomable might;
Solitude and sunset glories,
Castle ruins fraught with stories,
Let it sink into my brain:
Naught the poet sees in vain!
Breathe we then the holy ether
And the beauteous world adore;
To the great and noble only
Give our labours evermore.
Let the passions but assail us,
Rend our ears with hideous chords:
Only where the tempest's raging
Shall we find concordant words!

III.

A source is gushing
And gently rushing
Through flowered meadows;
Floods of the river
Through darkness shiver
In forest shadows.

With the corn's abundant treasure
Spread the hilly, sunlit leas,
And unto the western breeze
Yields the greenery with pleasure.
In the hills the tempest lours,
Lightning strikes the ancient towers;
Yet th' unheeding stars on high
Pass us by.
Thee and me protects the Sire
Of the Universe,
Who one day with Judgment's fire
Darkness shall disperse.
Let us then embark with daring,
Through a sea of perils faring.
Voyages of bitter duty
We 'll adorn with love and beauty!

Johann Mayrhofer.

The three parts of this poem are translated here as they appear in Ernst von Feuchtersleben's edition of Mayrhofer's poems (1843). The manuscript of Mayrhofer's poetic works, which came into the possession of the Vienna City Library from Schober's remains, dates the second part, which Schubert composed, September–October 1821. In the manuscript and the first edition of the poems (1824), which contain only Part II, there is a variant in lines 5 and 6, as there is also in Schubert's setting.— The Franz addressed in the title seems to be Schober rather than Schubert.

254. PLATEN TO COUNT FRIEDRICH FUGGER

Göttingen, 3rd October 1821.

In the winter you will have to bring an instrument with you or hire one at Erlangen. I am to receive, through Bruchmann, a collection of Goethe songs said to have been wonderfully set to music by a Viennese composer (Schubert), which you will have to play for us.

Friedrich, Count Fugger-Hoheneck (born 1795), was Platen's intimate friend and later the editor of his works. He himself set poems by Platen to music and in 1821 he lived at the garrison of Dillingen near Augsburg.

August von Gymnich dies, 6th October 1821.

City Seminary (*Stadtkonvikt*). Part of the Old University of Vienna, where Schubert received his Secondary Education (1808-13). *See* p. 929

PLATE IV

Court Chapel (*Hofkapelle*), in the Imperial Palace, where as a Boy Schubert
sang in the Choir (1808–12)

PLATE V

255. FROM THE PROGRAMME of the Kärntnertor Theatre,
8th October 1821
(Concert for the benefit of the dancer Theodora Rozier)

3. 'Erl King,' by Goethe, set to music by Herr Franz Schubert,
sung by Herr Vogl and accompanied by Herr Karl Schunke.

Madame Rozier, a daughter of the ballet-master J. Aumer, and a dancer
at the Kärntnertor Theatre since 1814, had married her colleague Jean
Rozier in 1818.—The programme of this performance included Beethoven's 'Prometheus' overture and the ballet 'The Swiss Dairymaid' by
the new ballet-master Filippo Taglioni (born 1777), with music by
Gyrowetz.

256. FROM THE 'WIENER ZEITSCHRIFT FÜR KUNST,' &c.,
16th October 1821

The favourite poem by Goethe, 'Erl King,' with the valued
music by Herr Franz Schubert, sung by Herr Vogl, failed this time
to make the expected effect, much as the singer's art sought to
penetrate it, for the accompanist at the fortepiano, Herr K.
Schunke, was incapable of supporting the voice-part with the
accompaniment.

Eighth performance of 'The Magic Bell,' 19th October 1821. This
was the last performance of Hérold's opera with the extra numbers
by Schubert.

257. SCHUBERT TO JOSEF VON SPAUN

Vienna, 2nd November 1821.

Dear Friend,

Your letter gave me much pleasure, and I hope that you continue
keeping well.—But now I must tell you that my dedications have
done their work: that is to say, the Patriarch has forked out 12
ducats and, through Vogl's intervention, Fries 20, which is a
very good thing for me.

Will you be good enough, therefore, to close your correspondence with the Patriarch by a message of thanks suited both to

him and to me?—Schober's opera has already progressed as far as the third act, and I do wish you could be present at its production. We have great hopes of it.—The Kärntnertor and Wieden Theatres are actually leased to Barbaja, and he takes them over in December. Now good-bye. Greetings to all acquaintances, especially your sister and brothers.

Your friend
Frz. Schubert.

Write quite soon to Patr. and to us.

P.S. Send me Ottenwalt's 'Cradle Song.'

The patriarch is Pyrker (*see* No. 237).—A ducat was worth 4 florins 30 kreuzer, A.C.—The opera is 'Alfonso and Estrella.' Schober wrote concerning it to Schubert's brother Ferdinand on 18th March 1848 that the libretto had been produced "in a state of very happy enthusiasm, but with great innocence of heart and mind."—Domenico Barbaja (born 1778), impresario at Naples and Milan, had leased the Kärntnertor Theatre from 1st January 1822, but taken it over already on 1st December 1821. He received an annual subsidy of 160,000 florins, A.C., from the court. Pálffy assigned him the Theater an der Wien on lease. This first Viennese period of Barbaja's lasted until 31st March 1825. Soon after his arrival several of the Viennese singers, including Vogl, left the Court Opera.—Schubert's abbreviation in the first postscript, "an Patr.," caused some commentators to take it as meaning *ad patrem*, and to deduce therefrom that Josef von Spaun had brought about a reconciliation between Schubert and his father, who were said to have been estranged again since the autumn of 1818, the son being cast out by the father. Yet in the middle of the letter Schubert expressly asks Spaun to thank the patriarch, whose favours he had procured for him.—Schubert appears to have left his setting of Ottenwalt's 'Cradle Song' ('Wiegenlied') at Linz in 1819 (*see* No. 156).

258. SCHOBER TO JOSEF VON SPAUN

(On the second sheet of the preceding letter.)

[4th November 1821.]

Dear Friend,

Schubert and I have now returned from our half country and half town holiday, and we have brought back recollections of a lovely month. At Ochsenburg we were much taken up with the truly beautiful surroundings, and at St. Pölten with balls and concerts; in spite of which we worked hard, especially Schubert, who has done nearly two acts, while I am on the last. I only wished you had been there to hear the glorious tunes as they arose: it is wonderful how once again he poured forth rich and teeming ideas. Our room at St. P. was particularly snug: the twin beds, a sofa next to the warm stove, and a fortepiano made it all very domestic and cosy. In the evenings we always compared notes on what we had done during the day, then sent for beer, smoked our pipes and read, or else Sophie and Nettel came across and there was singing. There were a couple of Schubertiads at the Bishop's and one at the Baroness Münk's, of whom I am quite fond, where a princess, two countesses and three baronesses were present, all most generously ecstatic. Now we have come here with my mother. At Heiligen-Eich we were entertained to dinner, and for a travelling present Heaven sent us the first of the glorious days that have gladdened us till now, i.e. for a matter of a week. The Bishop too has now followed us, so that St. P. has been transferred to Vienna. He and Mother are well. They are more than usually cheerful and send you their greetings. That we have sadly missed Kuppel, who had promised to follow us but did not, and you too, you can imagine; for we should have been particularly glad to make you two judges of our work. Altogether, I feel like one who has looked into the sun and now sees everywhere those confounded black spots—so disturbing is your departure for me. The "Crown" we found utterly desolate. Derffel is now wholly obsessed by the demon of whist: he has established two regular days for it at home, yet plays as usual at Hugelmann's, at Dornfeld's, at the coffee-house—in short all the time. Waldl [Mayrhofer] too, as well as Huber, is a prey to the same devil, and both absent themselves, too, because they live in the suburbs. Gahy is quite lost without you. I found him thoroughly sad. He does not know what to do, and in his despair watches the gambling. I shall try to look after him again. Kuppel is always at the Belvedere, where he copies the "Io"; so he hardly ever comes, but sleeps at Schnorr's, who still lives in the Heugasse. His "Faust" was bought for 2,500 A.C. Yesterday Weber's

'Freischützen' [sic] were done, but did not please much. I am very glad Max is so well. Götz and his wife are charming and in the seventh heaven. The other day they kept walking straight on through the boundaries of the suburbs, &c., until at last, when hunger made itself felt too late, they found themselves in a neighbourhood where they could hardly procure a crust of bread. My compliments to all. You must not think things will always continue as now. As I am working at the opera, I do not think I shall be able to write anything else.

Your Schober.

If Ottenwalt still has the poem I once gave him with an iron bas-relief, kindly copy it for me—but soon, please. Ask Max to write. Zwerger, Hosp's principal, has gone bankrupt for a million. Hosp is thus at liberty and has to go on the stage.

In the autumn Schubert and Schober stayed at St. Pölten on the river Traisen (about twenty-eight miles west of Vienna) and in the neighbouring castle of Ochsenburg, which belonged to the Bishop of St. Pölten, at that time Johann Nepomuk, Ritter von Dankesreither, who was related to Schober, probably on the side of the latter's mother. Dankesreither was a patron of the association of Upper Austrian youths (*see* note on p. 73). Frau von Schober and her daughter Sophie seem often to have been guests at this episcopal residence, as also at the bishop's palace on the cathedral square in the town. This time Schubert and Schober profited by the bishop's hospitality, with whom they had probably sought a refuge for the purpose of working together. It appears that both had returned to Atzenbrugg early in September, and had gone from there to St. Pölten, which lies not far off to the south-west. If Schubert wrote the first act of the opera there, the dates on its manuscript, 20th September to 16th October, may give us roughly those bounding his stay on the banks of the Traisen. The second act, dated 18th October at the beginning, was started at St. Pölten and finished in Vienna early in November. Schober was, of course, ahead of him with the libretto.—It may be that at St. Pölten itself the two friends did not stay with the bishop, but possibly at the inn of the "Three Crowns" on the Herrenplatz.—Sophie von Schober was on friendly terms with Anna (Netti) Prunner, with whom Schwind later fell in love, but who married another in 1824.—Josefa, Freiin von Münk (Schober writes Mink), *née* von Holzmeister in 1798, Schwind's aunt and wife of the district forest commissary Ignaz, Freiherr von Münk, was an authoress: several of her poems were set to music, but none by Schubert. —The other six aristocratic ladies cannot be identified with certainty; but one of them may have been the wife of the retired General Karl Mack, Freiherr von Leiberich (Naples, 1799; Ulm, 1805).—Heiligeneich lies near to Atzenbrugg and Aumühle, so that apparently the two friends and Schober's mother returned from St. Pölten to Vienna by way of Atzenbrugg once more.   They arrived in Vienna about 28th October. —Kuppel (cupola) was the usual abbreviation for the name of Kupelwieser, but only in the case of Leopold the painter.—The "Crown" is the "Hungarian Crown" Inn.—Derffel is Franz, jun.—Josef Hugelmann, born in Vienna in 1768, was an official in the court exchequer and an amateur musician; he played the pianoforte, composed, and published a pianoforte duet arrangement of Mozart's string quintets.—Anton, Ritter von Dornfeld (born 1772), the elder brother of the district captain of Steyr, was secretary to the Lower Austrian Government in Vienna.— "Waldl" was Mayrhofer's nickname. It is known that when he and Schubert lived together, the latter sometimes jestingly attacked Mayrhofer with a stick, uttering the alliterative magic formula, "Waldl, Waldl, wilder Verfasser!" but the origin of this nickname is doubtful. Waldl =Waldmann, a south German dog's name (cf. note to No. XXIX). —Huber is Josef Huber, a fairly close friend of Mayrhofer's. Both were fond of a game of whist. They clearly did not eat in the city at that time, but had a table reserved in one of the suburbs.—In the upper Belvedere (once Prince Eugene's summer palace) the imperial picture gallery was housed, including Correggio's famous "Jupiter and Io," or briefly "Io." The Belvedere lies on the Rennweg near the Heumarkt, where lived Ludwig Ferdinand von Schnorr, born at Königsberg in 1788, who had been in Vienna since 1804, and was one of the leaders of the romantic school of painters, Schwind's master and a friend of Friedrich von Schlegel. His most famous picture is "Faust in his Study," bought in 1818 by the gallery, whose custodian he became later on.—'Der Freischütz' had been given for the first time in Vienna on 3rd November 1821, at the Kärntnertor Theatre.   (Grillparzer, who could see no more than a happy accident in this opera, took Rossini's side against Weber.)—Max is Spaun's brother. —Götz (Schober writes Görz) is probably the bass of that name who had returned from Bohemia in December 1820 and was engaged by the Court Opera in the summer of 1821. But he fell ill, had to give up singing at the end of the year and died in the spring of 1822. — The boundaries of the suburbs (*Vorstadtlinie*) were an outer wall of the city's fortifications with a gate for each suburb at which toll was levied on incoming food. — Of Zwerger nothing is known. — For Hosp *see* No. 233.

259. Bruchmann to Platen

Vienna, 8th November 1821.

. . . Schubert is setting not only the little poem you sent me, but also several others of your 'Lyrical Leaves,' including the two wintry songs.

'Lyrical Leaves' ('Lyrische Blätter') was the title of one of Platen's sets of poems.   There is a 'Winter Song' ('Winterlied') and a 'Winter Sigh' ('Winterseufzer') in it, neither of which was set by Schubert, so far as we know.

260. From the MS. Programme of the Second Annual Concert held by the Philharmonic Society, 18th November 1821, at Noon, in the Large Assembly Hall (Conductor, Leopold Sonnleithner)

4. Overture in E minor by Herr Franz Schubert, Member of the Society.

This concert, one of the society's public ones, opened with Beethoven's seventh Symphony.   At the close was sung "part of the last finale from Mozart's 'Don Giovanni,' which is omitted at the performances in the I. & R. Court Theatre," that is to say, the final sextet again.—In the printed programme (see the iconographical volume of the German edition of this work, p. 162) Schubert's membership is, of course, not mentioned; but the indication in the society's minutes is important, for it disposes of the ancient legend according to which Schubert was ineligible as a professional musician.   In any case, he may quite easily not have been regarded as such a musician, since he held no appointment of any kind. In the society's manuscript register he does not appear until the following March (see note preceding No. 278) and in a Viennese directory published early in 1823 he is expressly named as a practising pianoforte and viola player attached to the society (see No. 346).

261. From the Leipzig 'Allgemeine Musikalische Zeitung,' 2nd January 1822

At the second "Society" concert we heard: . . . 4. Overture by Schubert . . . All went well together.

262. FROM THE PROGRAMME of the Second Annual Concert held by the Private Musical Society at the "Roman Emperor," 18th November 1821 (4 p.m.)

5. 'The Wanderer,' poem by Goethe, music by Schubert.

The day on which Schubert was performed at noon and in the afternoon was a Sunday. The concert was organized by the United Private Musical Society (see No. 146), which now held its performances here and was managed by Friedrich Klemm, an executive member of the Philharmonic Society. It closed with Rossini's overture to 'The Barber of Seville.'— The poem 'The Wanderer' is, of course, by Schmidt of Lübeck.

263. FROM THE OFFICIAL 'WIENER ZEITUNG,' 27th November 1821

At the House of Cappi & Diabelli,
Art and Music Dealers, Graben, No. 1133, are newly published:

THE OVERBLOWN LIME-TREE   THE FLIGHT OF TIME
['Die abgeblühte Linde']   ['Der Flug der Zeit']
Poems
by Count Ludwig von Széchényi.

DEATH AND THE MAIDEN by Claudius
['Der Tod und das Mädchen']

Set to Music for One Voice with Pianoforte Accompaniment by FRANZ SCHUBERT. Work 7.

Price, 1 Florin 30 Kreuzer, V.C.

Such of Schubert's compositions are here assembled as combine with their intrinsic excellence the advantage of an easily performable accompaniment as well as a moderate extent of the vocal compass. This circumstance imparts to the present book the additional value of general utility.

Also to be had are the same composer's
'Memnon,' 'Antigone and Oedipus,' for One Voice with Accompaniment of the Pianoforte. Work 6. Price 1 Florin 30 Kreuzer.

'Restless Love' ['Rastlose Liebe'], 'Nearness of the Beloved'
['Nähe des Geliebten'], &c.   Work 5.   1 Fl. 30 Kr.

'The Wanderer,' 'Morning Song,' &c.   Work 4.   1 Fl. 30 Kr.

'Shepherd's Complaint' ['Schäfers Klagelied'], 'The Hedge-Rose'
['Heidenröslein'], &c.   Work 3.   1 Fl. 30 Kr.

'Margaret at the Spinning-Wheel' ['Gretchen am Spinnrade'],
Work 2.   1 Fl. 30 Kr.

'Erl King,' by Goethe.   Work 1.   2 Fl.

N.B. Several of these are also to be had with guitar accompaniment.

Op. 7 is dedicated to the poet of the first two songs.   Louis, Count
Széchényi of Sárvár-Felsö-Vidék, was born in 1781 at Horpács in Hungary.
He was high steward to the Archduchess Sophie (the mother of the future
Emperor Francis Josef) and a member of the Philharmonic Society.
Randhartinger later became his private secretary.

264. FROM THE OFFICIAL 'WIENER ZEITUNG,'
29th November 1821

At the House of Cappi & Diabelli,

\rt and Music Dealers, Graben, No. 1133, are newly published:

ORIGINAL DANCES
for the Pianoforte,
Composed by FRANZ SCHUBERT.
Work 9.   Book I, 1 Florin 30 Kreuzer.   Book II, 1 Florin
30 Kreuzer, V.C.

The next book of songs, Op. 8, did not appear until the spring of 1822
see No. 287), but the assumption that this was due to the numerous
Viennese editions of Weber's 'Freischütz' music is arbitrary.—Op. 9,
Schubert's first book of instrumental music, contained waltzes, later
entitled 'First Waltzes.'   The 'Mourning Waltz' ('Trauerwalzer') was
among them, appearing as No. 2 among the thirty-six, and it was so
entitled in the book, though not by Schubert himself.   Schubert's dances,
written for domestic entertainments, were published by him, if at all,
only in their original pianoforte versions.

265. PLATEN TO HIS MOTHER (in French)

Erlangen, 2nd December 1821.

He [Fugger] is a musician and has composed several of my songs very prettily, and they please everybody.   A noted composer in Vienna, Mr. Schubert, has also set some of my songs, which I am to receive some time.

See note to No. 252.

266. FROM PERTH'S DIARY

(Concerning a concert of the Private Musical Society at the "Roman Emperor," 2nd December 1821, 4 p.m.)

5. 'The Youth' ['Der Jüngling'], poem, set to music by Schubert.

This was the third annual concert given by this society; the programme has not been preserved.   The song, the title of which Perth does not give accurately, was evidently 'The Youth on the Hill' ('Der Jüngling auf dem Hügel'), to words by Heinrich Hüttenbrenner, composed in November 1820, the first of the Op. 8 set, which was unquestionably ready to go to press by this time.

267. LEOPOLD SONNLEITHNER to the Concert Committee of the Philharmonic Society

Vienna, 3rd December 1821.

Being prevented by illness from attending the meeting to-day, I request that the following observation may receive attention:

I recommend the following pieces for the third of the Society's concerts: . . .

2. A vocal quartet or chorus by Schubert or Assmayr.

The first of Sonnleithner's suggestions was acted upon: Schubert's 'Spirit of Love' ('Geist der Liebe') was performed (*see* No. 275).

268. FROM THE MINUTES of the Philharmonic Society (Meeting of the Society Concert Committee, 3rd December 1821)

Leopold von Sonnleithner, as conductor of the third concert, proposed: . . .

2. A vocal quartet or chorus by Schubert or Assmayr.

It is to be wished that those by the valued Herr Schubert should not be too gloomy. If the quartet by Seyfried is to be had, it is to be preferred, and in any case to be chosen for the fourth concert.

Ignaz Xavier, Ritter von Seyfried, born in Vienna in 1776, a pupil of Mozart's, had been conductor at the Freihaus Theatre and was now at the Theater an der Wien. He was both a composer and an author. His vocal quintet was not after all sung at the fourth concert either.

'The Flowers' Sorrow' ('Der Blumen Schmerz'), Op. 173, No. 4 (xx. 399) appears in the 'Wiener Zeitschrift,' 8th December 1821. Schubert spends Christmas Eve with Heinrich and Emilie Anschütz, 24th December 1821.—The Christmas tree, a Protestant custom, had only recently been introduced to Catholic Vienna. Heinrich Anschütz, born in 1785 at Luckau in Lusatia, had come from Breslau to Vienna in the summer of 1820, and was engaged at the Burg Theatre since the summer of 1821 as actor and producer. His second wife, Emilie, née Butenop, born at Stuttgart in 1797, shared his engagement.

'Fisherman's Ditty' ('Fischerweise'), Op. 96, No. 4 (1826). Engraved Vignette from Karl Czerny's Arrangement of Schubert's Song for Pianoforte Solo. Vienna 1838–9

Morgen Mittwoch den 7. März 1821
wird
in dem k. k. Hoftheater nächst dem Kärnthnerthore
mit hoher Bewilligung,

eine große musikalische Akademie

mit Declamation und Gemählde - Darstellungen

verbunden, gegeben werden.
Die einzelnen Gegenstände sind folgende:

Erste Abtheilung:

1. Die Ouverture des Schauspiels: Die Templer auf Cypern.
2. Ein Tableau: Die von Abraham verstoßene Hagar, nach Danhök, dargestellt von Dlle. Heurteur, k. k. Hofschauspielerinn, Mad Vogel, k. k. Hofopernistinn, Hrn Vogl, k. k. Hofopernisten, Dlle. Kraft d. ält, Dlle. Dichler, Herren Pfeiffer, Segatta, Rossi und andern Mitgliedern des Balletcorps.
3. Eine Arie von Mozart, gesungen von Dlle. Wilh. Schröder.
4. Der erste Satz des zweiten Violinconcertes von L. Spohr, gespielt von Hrn. Leon de St. Lubin dermaligem Schüler des Hrn. Professors der Violine, Joseph Böhm.
5. Der kleine Gernegroß, ein Gedicht von Langbeins vorgetragen von Mad. Wilhelmine Korn, k. k. Hofschauspielerinn.
6. Das Dörfchen, ein Gedicht von Bürger, für zwey Tenor- und zwey Baßstimmen gesetzt von Hrn Franz Schubert, vorgetragen von den Herren Gott und Barth, in Diensten Sr. Durchlaucht des regierenden Herrn Fürsten von Schwarzenberg, und den Herren Nesehle und Umlauf.
7. Variationen für das Pianoforte, componirt von Hrn Hugo Wortzisch, auf zwey Instrumenten gespielt von den zwey Dlles Schadt.
8. Ein Tableau. Sokrates vor seinen Richtern, nach Juger, dargestellt von dem Aichinger Vater und Sohn, Reiperger d. ält, Dettelani, Rossi, Jos. Kobindera, Pfeiffer, Wie senberg, Segatta und anderen Mitgliedern des Balletcorps.

Zweyte Abtheilung:

9. Die Ouverture der Oper die Zauberglocke (la Clochette, von Boieldieu.
10. Eine Arie von Mozart: Da ich einsam vor die Stehe, gesungen von Dlle. Unger, k. k. Hofopernistinn.
11. Die Gräfin Spadara im Erdbeben von Messina, 1785, ein Gedicht, vorgetragen von Mad Sophie Schröder, k. k. Hofschauspielerinn.
12. Der Erlkönig, Gedicht von Göthe, in Musik gesetzt von Franz Schubert, vorgetragen von Hrn Vogl, k. k. Hofopernisten, auf dem Pianoforte begleitet von Hrn Anselm Hüttenbrenner.
13. Adagio und Rondo für das Violoncell von Bernhard Romberg, gespielt von Hrn Pechatschef.
14. Duett aus der Oper: Ricardo e Zoraide, von Rossini (Invasio tu lingi, ingrata), gesungen von den Dlles Schröder und Unger.
15. Der Gesang der Geister über den Wassern, Gedicht von Göthe, für vier Tenor- und vier Baßstimmen gesetzt von Hrn Franz Schubert, vorgetragen von den Herren Gott, Barth, Nesehle, Umlauf, Weinkopf, Fruhwald und zwey Chorsängern.
16. Ein Tableau: Aurora, nach Guido Reni, dargestellt von Hrn Taglioni, erstem Tänzer der k. k. Hoftheater, und den Dlles Neuwirth, Mayer, Krebah, Kreutzer, Wittwer, Chiesa, Dichler, Kraft d. ält, Fanny Ehier und anderen Mitgliedern des Balletcorps.

Herr Kapellmeister Gyrowetz hat die Leitung dieser Akademie, und Herr Philipp von Stubenrauch die Anordnung der Tableaux übernommen

Die Einnahme wird von der Gesellschaft adeliger Frauen zur Beförderung ihrer wohlthätigen Zwecke verwendet.

Sämmtlichen Personen, welche mit der menschenfreundlichsten Bereitwilligkeit ihre Talente und Bemühungen gewidmet haben, wird hiermit der verbindlichste Dank abgestattet.

Die Eintrittspreise sind wie gewöhnlich. Die Freybilleten sind ohne Ausnahme ungültig. Die gesperrten Sitze sind an der k. k. Hoftheater Casse, die Logen aber bey der Frau Therese Landgräfinn von Fürstenberg, geb. Fürstinn von Schwarzenberg, in der Himmelpfortgasse im Christenbergischen Hause Nro. 952 im 2. Stock zu haben.

Der Anfang ist um 7 Uhr.

Programme of the First Representative Concert including Schubert
Songs (1821). See p. 164

Schubert's Room with Piano, Wipplingerstrasse, corner of Tiefer
Graben. Pen-and-ink drawing by Moritz von Schwind (1821).
See p. 930

1822

Opera, 'Alfonso and Estrella' (3 acts, Schober) (xv. 9), 20th September
1821—27th February 1822.

'God in Nature' ('Gott in der Natur') for Female Choir (xviii. 3),
August.

Mass in A flat major (xiii. 5), November 1819—September 1822.

Symphony in B minor ("Unfinished") (i. 8) begun 30th October.

Fantasy for Pianoforte (" Wanderer " Fantasy) (xi. 1), November.

Song, 'The Muses' Son' ('Der Musensohn'), December.

---

269. To Herr Josef Spaun, Assessor at Linz
(Composed by Schubert [xx. 588], January 1822.)

And ne'er a letter?
Are we quite forgotten?
Wilt thou be silent for eternal time?
Is it that other friends have claimed allegiance?
Is it that prosecutions, writs and crime
So bulky and so tedious fill thy days
That ne'er again thou wilt Parnassus climb?
Yet no! our lot alone to be neglected!
This silence and oblivion 's but for us.
Alone we starve and pine without a message.
No other comrades hast thou treated thus.
To others sendst though letters by the yard:
While they came flying to them in all haste,
Us cruelly didst thou from thy heart discard.

Soar aloft, then, our complainings,
Out from our indignant breast,
By melodious strains be wafted
To his faithless heart addressed!

> This from us in sorrow tell him,
> Let him answer what he will:
> "Though forgotten, we thy friendship
> Lovingly remember still."
>
> Matthäus von Collin.

This "missive" consists of a recitative and aria parodying the pathetic manner of Italian opera.

270. From the Vienna 'Allgemeine Musikalische Zeitung,' 19th January 1822

The new books of songs by Franz Schubert, again published by Cappi & Diabelli and containing 'The Overblown Lime-Tree,' 'The Flight of Time' and 'Death and the Maiden,' the poem of the first two by Count Széchényi, of the last by Claudius, give us a welcome opportunity thoroughly to recommend to the musical public not only these, but far more particularly the earlier songs published by the same artistic house and written by a young composer with a rich lyrical gift, and openly to express our respect for his excellent talent.   Not often has a composer had so large a share of the gift for making the poet's fancy so profoundly impressive for the receptive listener's heart.   This is shown with especial felicity by Goethe's song for Margaret at the spinning-wheel, where the vivid imitation of the sound of a spinning-wheel makes a most characteristic background in a Rembrandtesque chairoscuro for the description of the profoundest depths of a woman's being, lost now in gloomy visions of the present and the future, now in sweetly melancholy recollections of the past.   No feeling heart can follow the changes of the unhappy Margaret's emotions depicted here without being seized by sadness and by the foreboding of the fearful proximity of the evil powers which ensnare her.   Equally excellent, both in the voice-parts and in the characteristic accompaniments, are 'Memnon' and 'Antigone and Oedipus' (both to poems by Mayrhofer).

'Memnon,' considered as a poem, is a masterly delineation of a noble mind wrapped up in itself and afflicted by profound grief, into whose agitated soul falls a soothing ray of dawning hope from another world.

In 'Antigone and Oedipus' the poet shows us the blind old man asleep in the grove of the Eumenides, his loving daughter at his side addressing pious prayers to the gods on her father's behalf. Oedipus wakes and is seized by sorrow at the recollection of his former royal glory stirred up by his dream.

Both these excellent poems have true poetic inspiration.

It is to be regretted that the poet's line, "The gentle breath of consolation let Oedipus' great soul invade," should have been changed to the following words, and the sense be thus wholly disfigured: the composer makes the poet say "the father's soul invade"; for this means a direct injury to the metre, although the original words would not have damaged the cantilena in the least. The treatment of a text should show the same respect for a poet's work with which we honour a composer's creation.

These beautiful poems Herr Schubert has reproduced by music of stirring truthfulness. The introduction to 'Memnon' conjures up the magic sounds of the famous Egyptian statue. No womanish plaint desecrates the heroic king's mournful words. The pain that burns in his breast blazes up into wild flames which at last die down in rapt anticipation.

Antigone's prayer is kept in a melodic style full of childlike piety and most touchingly expresses the sentiments of the daughter who willingly offers to sacrifice herself for her father. It is interrupted by two connecting bars alternating with short recitatives and most expressively describing the uneasy groans of the awakening old man. The song of Oedipus which now follows is truly royal and elevated, closing worthily with the spirits' call accompanied by terrifying chords. In the same book with 'Memnon' and 'Antigone' is to be found Claudius's sorrowful plaint, 'At Anselmo's Grave,' a song full of moving expression which must find its echo in every responsive heart. Herr Schubert has dedicated the three last-named songs to our excellent Court Opera singer Vogl, and could truly not have entrusted them to better hands, as will surely be cordially granted by every one who was privileged to enjoy their performance by this great master of song in a small but select circle of receptive music-lovers.

We pass over the gifted composer's remaining songs; not because they fall behind those mentioned above (for we need only recall his admirable 'Wanderer,' his 'Wayfarer's Night Song' by Goethe, 'Erl King,' &c.), but because we believe we have done enough to draw our readers' attention to the production of this eminent talent and thus to have rendered an agreeable service to all lovers of truly expressive song.

We know several other songs by the same author, still in manuscript, the public appearance of which promises our musical circles many another great enjoyment.

This first detailed criticism of songs by Schubert is perhaps by Kanne, the new editor of this periodical. The author seems to have known Schubert and Mayrhofer, for he speaks of manuscript songs and accurately quotes from the poem 'Antigone and Oedipus,' which appeared in print only in 1824 among Mayrhofer's collected poems (but not in the edition of 1843). Whether the change he mentions was sanctioned or merely tolerated by the poet is not known.

271. FROM BAUERNFELD'S DIARY

22nd January 1822.

Had an evening with Fick at Weintridt's yesterday. The composer Schubert was present and sang several of his songs. Also the friend of my youth, Moritz Schwind, who brought Schubert with him. The painter Kupelwieser, Professor Stein, Count Lanckoroński, Stadion, &c. We remained until midnight.

Josef Fick, born in Vienna in 1800, was an author and became a teacher of history (later to the future Emperor Francis Josef). He knew English, and Bauernfeld learnt that language from him when they both worked on the Viennese edition of Shakespeare.—Vincentius Weintridt, born in Vienna in 1778, was a professor of theology, but, being a freethinker, was relieved of his appointment early in 1820. He went to Retz in Lower Austria as a deacon in 1824. Bauernfeld and Schwind, his disciples, were devoted to him.—Anton Stein, born in 1759 at Bladen in Upper Silesia, was professor of classical philology and literature at the University of Vienna, Grillparzer's and Bauernfeld's teacher and a friend of Weintridt's.

—Kasimir, Count Lanckoroński-Brezie (born 1802) had been Bauern-feld's schoolfellow at the Scottish monastery.—Stadion, Weintridt's pupil, is probably Walter Wilderich, Count Stadion-Warthausen (born 1799), then a lieutenant.—Moritz von Schwind, born in Vienna in 1804, one of Schubert's most faithful friends, was the son of a court secretary who died in 1818 and had also been a pupil of the grammar-school of the Scottish monastery. He lived with his mother and several brothers and sisters in the Wieden suburb, near the Karl church, in the so-called "Moonshine House" (*Mondscheinhaus*), which belonged to his parsimonious grandmother (Franziska von Holzmeister, sen.) and was popular until 1824 on account of its dance-hall. Schwind was an enthusi-astic youth who grew later into a cheerful but somewhat caustic man. Schubert, who made his acquaintance through Josef von Spaun in 1821, called him his "beloved," and there really was something rather feminine about him in his adolescence. He was gifted especially as a draughtsman and water-colourist, but less as an oil and fresco painter. His strong point was composition, and as an illustrator of German fairy-tales he was never surpassed. He was very musical; his motto was "One should take a spoonful of music daily." He was to become a violent opponent of Liszt and Wagner. It is interesting that the great German historian Karl Lamprecht styles him a belated early romantic, but Schubert a late romantic.

271A. THE DIRECTOR OF THE THERESIAN ACADEMY OF KNIGHTS to its Curator, Master of the Ordnance August Picot Beccaduc, Freiherr von Herzogenberg

Sir,

The assistant teacher of aesthetics at the I. & R. Theresianum, Deinhardstein, has written for the celebration at the Musical Entertainment a hymn in the manner of 'God keep our Emperor Francis,' which has been set to music by Schubert and is to be sung by a choice of academic pupils on the eve of His Majesty's most exalted birthday-feast. The most obediently-disposed directorate submits the same to your Grace's condescending inspection and requests the sanction and exalted signature necessary for forwarding the same to the censorship and the printer.

Vienna, 23rd January 1822.

Peter Brukner,
Director.

The Theresianische Ritter-Akademie, called Theresianum for short, was housed in the so-called New Favorita, an imperial country seat on the Wieden, as a school for youths of the nobility. It was founded by the Empress Maria Theresa. Its director was a cleric.—Johann Ludwig Ferdinand (later Freiherr von) Deinhardstein, born in Vienna in 1794, was assistant teacher, later professor of aesthetics and classical literature at the Theresianum. He had in 1816 edited an anthology, 'Poetry for Orators' ('Dichtungen für Kunstredner'), in which Schubert found the poem 'The Wanderer.'—The commission came to Schubert through Leopold Sonnleithner. As early as 23rd December 1821 Brukner had written to Herzogenberg that the lawyers and philosophers of the Theresianum wished to celebrate with a concert the birthdays of the emperor and the empress (Maria Caroline, born 1792, the fourth consort of Francis I) on 7th February 1822. This project was later confined to the emperor alone, and the date was altered. The prologue, in verse, written by Friedrich von Hentl (born c. 1800), a former pupil of the institution, had been submitted by Brukner on 19th January 1822. It was printed as well as the lithographed score of Schubert's hymn, of which only a proof copy has been preserved.

272. FROM THE OFFICIAL 'WIENER ZEITUNG,' 11th February 1822

At the House of Cappi & Diabelli,
Art Dealers, Graben, No. 1133, is published and to be had:
LATEST DANCE MUSIC for the CARNIVAL 1822
For the Pianoforte.

. . . . .

Schubert, Fr. Original Dances for the Pianoforte. Books I & II, 1 Florin 30 Kreuzer each.

. . . . .

For the Violin and Other Instruments.

. . . . .

Schubert, Fr. Original Dances for flute or violin and guitar. 1 Florin 30 Kreuzer.

It was the fashion in Vienna to publish a number of new dances for the carnival each year. Haydn, Mozart and Beethoven had written seasonable minuets and German dances for the two assembly rooms in the Hofburg, where every season at least a few such sets of new dances appeared. —A copy of the spurious arrangement of Op. 9 was preserved by the Philharmonic Society, and republished in 1920 by J. Zuth in Vienna.

273. FROM THE PROGRAMME of a Concert held to celebrate the Birthday of the Emperor Francis I by the Pupils of the I. & R. Theresian Academy of Knights, 11th February 1822, at the Academy

4. 'Erl King,' Ballad by Goethe, set to music by Franz Schubert. . . .

10. Chorus, poem by Deinhardstein on the occasion of H.M. the Emperor's Birthday Celebrations, set to music by F. Schubert [xvii. 3].

Leopold Sonnleithner conducted. Hentl recited his prologue himself.

> Karl Maria von Weber pays a visit to Vienna, 17th February 1822.—
> Weber went on the same day to a performance of Weigl's 'King
> Waldemar.' On 18th February the opening performance under
> Barbaja's new management took place. On 7th and 9th March
> Weber conducted his 'Freischütz,' which had been in the Court
> Opera repertory since 1821, and it was at last given without cuts.
> At the end of one of these evenings, according to the custom of the
> time, an adulatory poem addressed to Weber was scattered from the
> gallery. The author was Schober and the title read 'To Karl Maria
> von Weber, after a performance of "Der Freischütz," with a wreath.'

274. ANTON HOLZAPFEL to Albert Stadler at Linz

Vienna, 22nd February 1822.

. . . Schubert, as they say, made *bruit*, and he will likewise, as they say, make his *sort*. I rarely see him, nor do we hit it off very well, his world being a very different one, as it should be. His somewhat gruff manner stands him in very good stead and will make a strong man and a ripe artist of him; he will be worthy of art. . . . Schubert is working at an opera, the words of which are by Schober, a work at which they are said to have both laboured together in mutual understanding.

> Schubert induces Weber to hear Friedrich Schneider's oratorio,
> 'The Last Judgment,' at Franz Xaver Gebauer's *Concert spirituel*,
> 24th February 1822, at noon, in the County Hall, where Karl Gott-
> lieb Reissiger as soloist delights Weber by his voice and delivery.—
> Gebauer, born in 1784 at Glatz in Silesia, was choirmaster at the

court church of St. Augustine and had founded the *Concert spirituel* in 1819 for the performance of short pieces of church music as well as symphonies. The concerts were first held at the hotel "Zur Mehlgrube," in the Neuer Markt. The oratorio by Schneider (born in Silesia in 1786) had already been heard in Vienna in 1821. On this occasion the singers under Gebauer's direction were Therese Klieber, Marie Mathilde Weiss, Barth, Reissiger and Nestroy. Karl Gottlieb Reissiger, born in 1789 at Belzig in Saxony, a bass singer and pianist, later court musical director at Dresden, lived in Vienna around 1822. He knew Schubert, but when he revisited Vienna in 1825 he was unable to see him, Schubert being ill (letter to Luib, 1857, Vienna City Library).

275. FROM THE PROGRAMME of the Third of the Annual Concerts held by the Philharmonic Society, 3rd March 1822, at Noon, in the Large Assembly Hall (Conductor, Leopold Sonnleithner)

2. 'The Spirit of Love' ['Der Geist der Liebe'], poem by Matthisson, set for 4 male voices by Franz Schubert [xvi. 6].

Cf. Nos. 267 and 268. The quartet, written for this concert (January 1822), was sung unaccompanied, probably by Barth, Lugano, Nestroy and Nejebse (Götz was dying). The concert began with a C major Symphony by Mozart, probably the 'Jupiter.' After Beethoven's 'Egmont' overture it concluded with the finale from Weber's opera 'Silvana.' Weber may have been present.—This was the third and last of the Philharmonic Society's public concerts at which anything by Schubert was performed during his lifetime (cf. Nos. 206 and 260). Schubert's quartet is mentioned in a notice of the concert in the Leipzig 'Allgemeine musikalische Zeitung' of 8th May 1822 (German edition, No. 309).

276. JOSEF VON SPAUN TO SCHOBER

Linz, 5th March 1822.

. . . Winter has gone by since then, and much that is of interest must have happened among you all, of which you should not deprive your far-off dear one. I am so very anxious to know all that the poetic-musical-painting triumvirate has produced. It cuts me to the soul that Schubert has ceased to sound for me.

A song recently found by Max in the 'Modezeitung,' entitled 'The Flowers' Sorrow' ['Der Blumen Schmerz'], was a veritable feast for me.   Persuade him to send me a few new songs one day; there might be a good opportunity now through Frau von Schmith . . . Where have there been any Schubertiads this winter?   How are things at the "Crown," to whose people I send greetings?   Does the mechanical clock play Schubert's song already? . . . On the whole I am well content, only nothing can make me forget the happy, sociable hours I spent with you all, and which Schubert so often beautified; I fear they will never return so happily for me.

The "triumvirate" were Schober, Schubert and Kupelwieser.—For the song *see* note on p. 202.—Helene, the niece and adopted daughter of the widow Berndt (*see* No. 229), had at first been married to Karl Mayrhofer, sen., after whose death she became the wife of Dr. Anton Schmidt (*see* No. 125).   It may be mentioned here that Marie Berndt had been a pupil of Mozart's and Schmidt, her son-in-law, a friend of his.   Helene Schmidt, Spaun's cousin, incidentally, was not related to the poet Mayrhofer through her first husband.—At the "Hungarian Crown" Inn there was from 1820 onward a mechanical clock which played a song by Schubert in 1822, and later a few of his waltzes (*see* No. 483).   The song may perhaps have been 'The Hedge-Rose' ('Heidenröslein') or 'Shepherd's Lament' ('Schäfers Klagelied').   Such clocks, with flute or cornet stops, or both combined, had been favoured in Vienna since the end of the eighteenth century (*see* note to No. 146); the musical quality of the Viennese mechanical clocks, which were produced mainly by Czech artisans, was first-rate.

277. From Anton Prokesch's Diary

[Vienna,] 5th March 1822.

At Pichler's for lunch.   Schubert played several songs set by him with a wealth of feeling and profundity.

Anton Prokesch, later Freiherr and finally Count von Osten, born at Graz in 1795, was first lieutenant in the general quartermaster staff. He was a stepson of the historian Julius Franz Schneller, married Irene von Kiesewetter in 1832 and became a diplomat.—Karoline Pichler (*see* No. 237), *née* von Greiner, Vienna, 1769, was an authoress and ran a literary *salon* in the Alserstrasse; she translated parts of Walter Scott's 'Lady of the Lake,' which, however, were not those used by Schubert.

> Schubert becomes a member of the Philharmonic Society, March 1822. In the society's manuscript register of 1844 is the entry: "In March 1822. Franz Schubert, . . ." (cf. No. 260).
>
> Weber leaves Vienna, 20th March 1822.

278. FROM THE 'WIENER ZEITSCHRIFT FÜR KUNST,' &c., 23rd March 1822

A GLANCE AT SCHUBERT'S SONGS
[Opp. 1–7]
By Friedrich von Hentl

Having undertaken to throw light on Schubert's songs, I intend above all to lay stress on the spirit which unifies the whole, the poetry which animates it and the organization which imparts living expression to it. Others will judge the theoretical aspect of these works and say how far justice is done to the technics of an art where no lapse may be tolerated, since definite rules exclude wilfulness. Schubert's songs raise themselves by ever undeniable excellences to the rank of masterpieces of genius, calculated to restore the present debased taste; for never has the true force of genius failed in its effect on heart and mind. Let the divine spark be buried never so deep under the ashes smouldering upon the altar on which we sacrifice to the idol of sensuality, it will blaze up into the brightest flame of enthusiasm on being fanned by the breath of genius, which we can never describe, but only profoundly feel.

In the greatest work by our composer, the 'Erl King,' it is neither the melodic expression nor the succession of notes in the voice-part which gives organic unity to the whole, but rather the harmonic expression, the tone, imparted to the work by the accompaniment. This is the foundation here, on which the tone-picture is laid, and indeed quite in accordance with the text, where night and tempest and the father on horseback with his child compose the background. With profoundly moving truth the melodic expression characterizes the inner meaning of the action, the changing emotions of the father, the child and the erl king, while its outward aspects, such as the galloping horse and the intermittent howling of the gale, are outlined by the most appropriate figures of accompaniment.   Such a treatment was the only possible one in this case, since the uniform romance-like tone of the poem demanded a similarly uniform tone in the musical representation.   In order to weave this tone into the whole, without sacrificing anything of the necessarily different characteristics in the words of the acting exponents, the separate melodies, the disparate parts of the significant vocal expression, had to be unified by the accompaniment.   The latter thus did not only serve as a foil to the voice-part, but also as musical painting outlining the atmosphere.

As in the 'Erl King' our emotion is prepared and subjected to the impression even before the voice delivers the words

> Who rideth so late through night and wind?

and only reinforces the picture suddenly brought before us, so we have a presentiment of the unhappy man descending from the mountains in 'Wanderer's Morning Song' [*recte* 'The Wanderer'] where even before the voice has entered the words begin to dawn in our soul:

> From heights I come into the dale,
> Storm on the sea, mist in the vale!

Overwhelming expression animates the following verses:

> With little joy I wander there,
> And ever ask I, sighing, "Where?"

The impression is too intense to be wholly sadness, yet not sharp and concentrated enough to be wholly pain, which is the highest degree of sadness.

As the most solemn ardour accompanies the line:

> Storm on the sea, mist in the vale,

and takes the most unforced turn into an expression of sadness, so the melancholy expression loses itself in that inner void and stunned staring into an empty world that has nothing more to give, at the words:

> The sun appears to me so cold,
> The blossoms dead, and life so old;
> Their words are neither here nor there:
> I am a stranger ev'rywhere.

With profound satisfaction our feelings accept the succeeding expression of longing, bursting violently from the heart with the question:

> Where art thou, my belovèd land, &c.,

where the quicker tempo and the bitter-sweet melody are entirely appropriate to the psychological progress of the words and join the sadness of longing to the brightness of the thought of all that the heart desires.   Only one thing might offend refined feelings, namely that this more cheerful expression, which lies perhaps mainly in the quicker pace, also accompanies the line

> Where all my dead will rise again.

Here one might have expected a decided damping of the joy in the thought of the resurrection of the beloved dead by the pain of the unhappy man's first having to seek the land where they are to rise again and by the solemnity of the thought of death and re-surrection.   Such transitions from one emotion to another, where each word has to be given its own particular meaning without dis-turbing the organic life of a melody, is among music's most difficult problems.   Here too Mozart stands alone and unrivalled.   In the monologue from Goethe's 'Faust,' 'Margaret at the Spinning-Wheel,' as in 'Erl King,' the accompaniment makes a wonderful foundation for the heart-rending expression of sounds wherein the pain and the rapture of love are steeped; it is the strong cord which holds together the tonal row of pearls and with its uniform motion, resembling the turning of the spinning-wheel, it makes a most moving contrast with the impassioned mood of the whole and the changing emotions in the voice.

Any further comment is not called for by this masterpiece.   Only those who are capable of seizing and feeling the whole depth of Goethe's poem will find it again in this song; they will clearly perceive, from the first bar to the last, what is felt by a childlike soul possessed by first love.

No less splendid is 'Shepherd's Complaint.'   Here everything conspires to make a perfect musical work.   The peculiar pastoral tone is admirably suggested; the melody expresses it, to begin with.   The accompaniment is suitable and holds together the melodies differentiated by the characteristic changes. These melodies are delightful in themselves and have their effect as aesthetic notions even apart from the words and the harmony. Each note must remain where it is if the melody is not to be ruined—a sure touchstone of its organic constitution! The characterization is so incisive as to require no analysis in order to be generally felt. The transitions between one characteristic expression and another, too, are most natural and affecting here.

Dramatic songs, worked chiefly in recitative, are 'Memnon' and 'Oedipus and Antigone' [*sic*]. The former strikingly weaves the sounding of Memnon's statue into the accompaniment, giving tone and shape to the whole. The original character of the tune should also be noticed: it represents, as a departure from the usual sentimental manner, something like the antique way of feeling by seriousness and a quieter tone of complaint, and with the more reason because it is Memnon who laments. The other composition might be reproached with sacrificing a higher poetic unity to far-fetched musical painting of details.

An all the more splendid gift is the song 'At Anselmo's Grave,' which, simple and unadorned, touches one profoundly.

In the 'Overblown Lime-Tree' Schubert has given pure and beautiful melody even to general phrases which do not express any particular mood, such as

Change is the child of Time.

Altogether this is an especially excellent composition, full of well-chosen themes and delicately matching the sense of the poetry.

If together with these compositions one thinks of the song 'Restless Love,' captivating by its passionate, superbly invented and realized expression, as well as the two Goethe romances, 'The Fisherman' and 'The King in Thule,' both kept in the true romance tone, the latter especially moving by its naïvely sorrowful expression; if one considers the original treatment of Werner's 'Morning Song' from 'The Sons of the Valley,' the depth of expression of Goethe's 'Wayfarer's Night Song,' the charming, innocent tune of 'The Hedge-Rose,' the apt characterization in 'Huntsman's Evening Song,' the rich expression in Goethe's 'First Loss' and the profoundly affecting treatment of the poem by Claudius, 'The Maiden and Death' [*sic*], one cannot fail to congratulate German music on a genius who, deploying himself in rich profusion, is capable of endowing the masterpieces of German musical poetry with the highest significance in unerringly and exhaustively characteristic works.

Whoever is inclined to doubt whether Schubert can write pure melody and to reproach him with relying for the effect of many of his songs on harmony and characteristic expression alone by means of excessive accompaniments, as for instance in 'Margaret,' has only to hear his lovely and extremely simple 'Hedge-Rose,' to take up 'Shepherd's Complaint' or the tender 'Cradle Song,' to consider the melodic passages in 'Erl King,' 'The Wanderer,' &c.

I believe that I have said enough and need therefore not proceed from particulars to the general characteristics of Schubert's Muse. His works will reveal to every one at a first glance the marks of genius and of a thinking artist, and if the cultivated mind, deeply touched, declares that here music expresses in perfect truth and beauty what has been said in the same way in poetry, it will be better to snub niggling reasoning, should it wish to put the question whether this is really the proper manner of doing it, whether there might not be another, and whether this or that master had proceeded in the same way or not. Each genius bears his own measure within himself and is inspired by feelings which pour the deepest inner consciousness, the highest wisdom and the only true sources of perception into works of great and noble art.

Hentl had evidently made Schubert's acquaintance at the celebration in the Theresianum (*see* Nos. 271A and 273). He mentions Schubert in his 'Gedanken über Tonkunst und Tonkünstler,' published in 1868.— The "divine spark," probably a commonplace, recalls the exclamation attributed to Beethoven when he came to know several of Schubert's songs in the last year of his life through the intermediary of Anton Schindler: "Truly, in Schubert stirs a divine spark!"—Hentl confuses the two titles of 'The Wanderer' ('Der Wanderer') and 'Wayfarer's Night Song' ('Wanderers Nachtlied') in Schubert's Op. 4, although later on he expressly discusses the second of these songs as well. He also misquotes the titles of 'Antigone and Oedipus,' 'At Anselmo's Grave' and 'Death and the Maiden.'—The 'Morning Song' ('Morgenlied') by Zacharias Werner does belong to his drama 'The Sons of the Valley'

('Die Söhne des Tals'), i.e. to its first part entitled 'The Templars on Cyprus' ('Die Templer auf Cypern'), Act i, Scene ii, where Philip, Duke of Anjou, disguised as a gardener, sings this song, which in the play has no title. 'Cradle Song' (*Wiegenlied*) may be a misprint for 'Morning Song' (*Morgenlied*).

Rossini's arrival in Vienna, 23rd March 1822.

279. SCHUBERT TO ANTON DIABELLI

[Spring 1822.]

[Outside:]

Anton von Diabelli, Esq.

[Inside:]

As Baron Schönstein was not to be found, and I do not know of any other way in which I might obtain a form of authorization, in Heaven's name take this letter for its representative.

Frz. Schubert.

Schubert must have received Esterházy's consent in writing to dedicate to him the five songs, Op. 8, but the formal authorization for the censorship could not be obtained in good time from Schönstein as Esterházy's representative (*see* No. 235). If it had been intended to publish this book in its proper chronological place as early as the winter of 1821–2, Esterházy could surely have been found in Vienna. It is possible, however, that its appearance was delayed precisely by the absence of a form of authorization.

280. FROM THE LEIPZIG 'ZEITUNG FÜR DIE ELEGANTE WELT,' 16th May 1822

(Vienna correspondence of spring 1822.)

A fair prospect opens up before the friends of German opera, since there are to be produced, by next autumn at the latest, ['Aesop at Court' by Kreutzer, a new opera by Weber and] another by the talented Schubert (whose songs breathe such an infinity of loveliness and delicacy).

'Aesop at the Court of King Croesus' was not performed in Vienna. The opera had been written in 1808 as 'Aesop in Phrygia,' and was performed under the above title at Donaueschingen in 1821, and at Stuttgart in 1822 as 'Aesop in Lydia.' Konradin Kreutzer, born in 1780 at

Möskirch in Baden, had been repeatedly engaged as theatre conductor in
Vienna and first became deputy conductor at the Kärntnertor in 1825.
—Weber's opera commissioned by Barbaja is, of course, 'Euryanthe.'—
It is said that Barbaja also commissioned the libretto of 'Fierabras' for
Schubert from Josef Kupelwieser (born 1791), Leopold's elder brother,
who had been secretary to the Court Opera since 1821 (*see* No. 369).
The work was not performed, neither was 'Alfonso and Estrella,' which
seems to be meant here (*see* No. 328).

281. FROM THE LEIPZIG 'ALLGEMEINE MUSIKALISCHE ZEITUNG,' 29th May 1822

(Notice of a concert for the benefit of the official charities held at
the Kärntnertor Theatre on 7th April 1822.)

4. 'Spring Song' ['Frühlingsgesang'], set to music as a vocal
quartet by Herr Fr. Schubert [xvi. 7].

The programme of this Easter Sunday concert has not been preserved.
Schubert's quartet was clearly sung without accompaniment, probably
by the singers engaged for the concert noticed below.

282. FROM THE 'WIENER ZEITSCHRIFT FÜR KUNST,' &c., 25th April 1822

(Notice of the concert given by Josef Merk, violoncellist in the
I. & R. Court Chapel and member of the Court Opera Orchestra,
15th April 1822, at the County Hall.)

The new Schubert Quartet ['Spirit of Love' (xvi. 6)] was
excellently delivered by Herren Barth, [Ludwig] Tietze, Nestroy
and Nejebse, and had to be repeated. It is a pity that, as we have
already remarked recently, owing to the close proximity in which
the four voices lie as well as the exertion to which the first tenor
has to submit, compositions of this kind bear in themselves the
seed of a smaller effect than they would have were they set for
the proper four voices.

Particulars of this concert too are known only from criticisms, another
of which appeared in the Vienna 'Allgemeine musikalische Zeitung' on
4th May 1822 (German edition, No. 315).—Merk, born in Vienna in
1795, was also a professor at the Conservatory. About 1833 he dedicated
"to his friend Schubert" his Op. 11, '20 Exercices pour le Violoncelle.'

—Anton Haizinger, sen., took the first tenor part in place of Barth. Born in 1796 at Wilfersdorf in Lower Austria, he was a pupil of Mozatti, and in January 1822 was engaged by the Court Opera, where soon afterwards he sang Florestan in 'Fidelio.' His wife was the actress Amalie Haizinger of the Burg Theatre and his son Anton, a superior officer, became a famous amateur singer of Schubert's songs.—Ludwig Tietze (born 1797), in Vienna since 1821, and later assistant proctor's man at the university, was now becoming one of Schubert's favourite tenors.—What the critic had "remarked recently" may refer to male-voice quartets in general rather than to Schubert.—The quartet may this time have been sung with its accompaniment (*see* Nos. 290–1).

283. From the 'Theater-Zeitung,' 30th April 1822

6. New Quartet by Herr Schubert, sung by Herren [Anton] Haizinger, Tietze, Nestroy and Nejebse, pleased much and had to be repeated.

S—t.

284. Bruchmann to Platen

Vienna, 17th April 1822.

. . . Enclosed you will find your poem, set to music as desired. Consequently I have done my share.

The song was 'Love hath lied' ('Die Liebe hat gelogen') (*see* No. 252).

285. From the Official 'Wiener Zeitung,' 19th April 1822

At the House of Cappi & Diabelli,
Art and Music Dealers in the Graben, No. 1133,
is newly published and to be had:

VARIATIONS

on a French Song, composed for Pianoforte, 4 Hands,
and dedicated to Herr Ludwig van Beethoven by
his Worshipper and Admirer Franz Schubert.

Work 10.   Price, 3 Florins 30 Kreuzer, V.C.

The French song is the romance 'Le Bon Chevalier' ("Reposez-vous, bon chevalier, laissez là votre armure"), supposed to be by Queen Hortense of Holland, the mother of Napoleon III (born Paris, 1783), who published it as No. 5 of her 'Romances' (Paris, 1813; Leipzig, 1817; London, 1825). Schubert had found the song in the Leipzig edition at Zseliz. These romances are said to have been actually written by the court flautist Louis Drouet (born Amsterdam, 1793), who stayed in Vienna in the summer and autumn of 1822, and unsuccessfully wooed Karoline Unger.—Schubert is said to have taken a copy of the work, for the dedication of which he had doubtless obtained Beethoven's permission, to the master next door to the Auersperg palace in the Josefstadt, but not to have met him. Josef Hüttenbrenner (letter to Luib, May 1861, Vienna City Library) reports from communications of Beethoven's nephew Karl and of Anton Schindler, that the work had Beethoven's approval, and that he played it through with Karl during the following months "almost daily." The fact that Schubert may have seen Beethoven in the music shop of Steiner & Co. in the Paternoster-Gässchen off the Kohlmarkt, as Anselm Hüttenbrenner says, or at an inn (*see* No. 299), does not necessarily suggest any communication between them. It looks rather as though Schubert had seen Beethoven only on his deathbed in the company of the two Hüttenbrenners and the painter Josef Teltscher, who made a sketch of the master. Schubert had evidently always been too shy to approach Beethoven.

286. FROM PROKESCH'S DIARY

24th April 1822.

At Pichler's, where I met Schubert, who sang some things to me.

'The Rose,' Op. 73 (xx. 408), appears in the 'Wiener Zeitschrift,' 7th May 1822.

287. FROM THE OFFICIAL 'WIENER ZEITUNG,' 9th May 1822

At the House of Cappi & Diabelli,
Art and Music Dealers, in the Graben, No. 1133,
is newly published and to be had:

.   .   .   .   .

Further is newly published:

The Eighth Book of Schubert's Songs, with pianoforte accompaniment, containing the following poems: 'The Youth on the Hill' ['Der Jüngling auf dem Hügel'] by H. Hüttenbrenner, 'Longing' ['Sehnsucht'], 'Erlaf-See' ['Lake Erlaf'] and 'By the River' ['Am Strome'], by Mayrhofer. Price 2 Fl.

Connoisseurs and amateurs have already honoured Schubert's works as they deserve; this book will thus require no further recommendation.

288. JOSEF VON SPAUN TO SCHOBER

Linz, 13th May 1822.

It gave me much pleasure to hear many things about you all from him [Kandler]; I am very glad that you still gather together so numerously and merrily at the "Crown." But do let me hear something more about you, from yourselves.—How about the Atzenbrugg festival? I hope all is well, else I should have to bury my hopes of seeing you again before long.—As regards the Atzenbrugg funds, I am just on the point of making some suggestions about my arrears to the treasurer, which he may then lay before you.—What has Schubert done and Kuppel [Kupelwieser] painted?

Franz Sales Kandler (born 1792) had been a court choir-boy before Schubert, and was now a military official and musical scholar. He was in service in Italy in 1817–26, and must have been in Vienna and Linz on holiday.—The meetings at Atzenbrugg were called "feasts." In order to cover the costs "slip-of-the-tongue groats" were collected between whiles: that is to say, whoever made a slip had to pay a forfeit of a groat (1 groschen was worth 3 kreuzer, A.C.) into the "society's" funds. It was there that Spaun was in arrears. He hoped to visit Atzenbrugg from Linz in the summer of 1822.

289. BRUCHMANN TO PLATEN

Hütteldorf, 22nd May 1822.

. . . The prices of Schubert's music are given in 20-gulden valuation, but I have bought it cheaper at 24-francs valuation; they are engraved on the music itself, and I must ask you to be kind enough to work them out, as I do not remember them.

Hütteldorf was a village near Vienna, where the Bruchmann family had rented a summer residence.—The prices were given on the music both in Viennese currency and in assimilated coinage. Bruchmann made a slip of the pen in the second place, where he meant to say "24-gulden valuation," the so-called Realm Valuation (*Reichsfuss*), which was in use in Bavaria.

290. FROM THE PROGRAMME of the Kärntnertor Theatre, 26th May 1822

(Concert for the benefit of the official charities.)

4. 'Spirit of Love' ['Geist der Liebe'], by Matthisson, set to music by Fr. Schubert, sung by Herren Barth, Tietze, Nejebse and Nestroy.

This was Whit Sunday. As may be gathered from a notice in the Leipzig 'Allgemeine musikalische Zeitung' of 10th July 1822 (German edition, No. 323), Schubert's quartet was done with pianoforte accompaniment. The musical part of this performance was under the direction of the Court Opera conductor Michael Umlauf (born Vienna, 1781), who was among those dismissed by Barbaja. The pianist Franz Schoberlechner (born Vienna, 1797), musical director at the court of the Duchess of Lucca, took part. A horn player "imitated various instruments" in a set of variations.

291. FROM THE VIENNA 'ALLGEMEINE MUSIKALISCHE ZEITUNG,' 15th June 1822

4. 'Spirit of Love' by Matthisson, set to music by Herr Schubert, sung by Herren Barth, Tietze, Nejebse and Nestroy.—This Quartet, although it seems already to have been frequently heard, failed to take to-day, in spite of a very good performance.

292. FROM THE PROGRAMME of the Concert given by Louis Drouet, Chamber Musician and First Flautist to H.M. the King of France, 3rd June 1822, at 12.30 p.m., in the County Hall

3. 'Spirit of Love' ['Geist der Liebe'], by Matthisson, set to music by Franz Schubert, sung by Herren Barth, Tietze, Nejebse and Nestroy.

The King of France at that time was Louis XVIII.—The concert opened with Mozart's overture to 'La clemenza di Tito,' and included, apart from the *Andante* from Beethoven's seventh Symphony, two of Drouet's own compositions.

293. FROM THE 'THEATERZEITUNG,' 13th June 1822

A pleasant Schubert vocal Quartet was very spiritedly sung by Herren Barth, Tietze, Nejebse and Nestroy.

Another notice appeared in the Vienna 'Allgemeine musikalische Zeitung' of 15th June 1822 (German edition, No. 325).

K—t.

The Twenty-third Psalm (xviii. 2) sung by female voices at Ignaz Sonnleithner's, 9th June 1822.

294. FROM THE OFFICIAL 'WIENER ZEITUNG,' 12th June 1822

New Music
published by and to be had of
Cappi & Diabelli,
Art and Music Dealers, in the Graben, No. 1133:

.   .   .   .   .   .

Further is newly published:

Schubert, Fr.   Vocal Pieces for 4 Male Voices, with Pianoforte or Guitar Accompaniment.   Work 11.

No. 1. 'The Little Village' ['Das Dörfchen'], by Bürger, 2 Fl., V.C.
No. 2. 'The Nightingale' ['Die Nachtigall'], by Unger. 2 Fl., V.C.
No. 3. 'Spirit of Love' ['Geist der Liebe'], by Matthisson. 2 Fl., V.C.

This work is dedicated to Barth. The accompaniments to these quartets are *ad libitum*. The fashionable guitar accompaniments, which even appear in the complete edition of Schubert's works, are certainly not his own.

295. PLATEN TO COUNT FUGGER

Ansbach, 28th June 1822.

. . . For the present I beg you to write to me forthwith how much the music books by Schubert come to, as I wish to pay Heyder for Bruchmann immediately on my return. You need never send them back: I herewith make you a present of them.

Cf. No. 289.—Heyder was a bookseller at Erlangen.

296. SCHUBERT TO JOSEF HÜTTENBRENNER

[1822.]

Have the goodness to bring me the opera out there act by act for correction.

I should wish, too, that you would see to my present account with Diabelli, as I need money.

Schubert.

Schubert at this time had 'Alfonso and Estrella' (finished on 27th February 1822) copied at Cappi & Diabelli's, for which 100 florins, V.C., was charged to him out of the proceeds of the music sold on commission (after deduction of the commission fee). Schubert asks that the copy should be sent ''out there'' (*hinaus*); on 31st October 1822 (No. 322) he says ''out here'' (*heraus*). He probably refers both times to his lodgings at the school-house in the Rossau, where he stayed temporarily while he was actually living at the Schober family's new dwelling in the Göttweigerhof (at the corner of the Spiegelgasse and the Göttweigergasse in the city), viz. in 1822 and the first half of 1823. ''Out there'' indicates that this letter was written in the city before he walked out to the suburb.

297. COUNT FUGGER TO PLATEN

Dillingen, 1st July 1822.

. . . The songs, for which I thank you most sincerely, cost altogether 4 florins currency, therefore 4 florins 48 kreuzer in our money.

Bruchmann's consignment evidently comprised Opp. 1–5, the first books of Goethe songs, which cost 1 florin for Op. 1 and 45 kreuzer each for Opp. 2–5, 4 florins, A.C., in all, or 4 florins 48 kreuzer in Bavarian money.—Bruchmann subscribed in 1822 for fifty copies of Platen's 'New Ghazals' ('Neue Ghaselen') and bought a further forty copies for Viennese friends.

298. ALLEGORICAL TALE BY SCHUBERT

3rd July 1822.

[MY DREAM]

I was the brother of many brothers and sisters. Our father and mother were good people. I was deeply and lovingly devoted to them all.—Once my father took us to a feast. There my brothers became very merry. I, however, was sad. Then my father approached me and bade me enjoy the delicious dishes. But I could not, whereupon my father, becoming angry, banished me from his sight. I turned my footsteps and, my heart full of infinite love for those who disdained it, I wandered into far-off regions. For long years I felt torn between the greatest grief and the greatest love. And so the news of my mother's death reached me. I hastened to see her, and my father, mellowed by sorrow, did not hinder my entrance. Then I saw her corpse. Tears flowed from my eyes. I saw her lie there like the old happy past, in which according to the deceased's desire we were to live as she had done herself.

And we followed her body in sorrow, and the coffin sank to earth.—From that time on I again remained at home. Then my father once more took me to his favourite garden. He asked whether I liked it. But the garden wholly repelled me, and I dared not say so. Then, reddening, he asked me a second time: did the garden please me? I denied it, trembling. At that my father struck me, and I fled. And I turned away a second time, and with a heart filled with endless love for those who scorned me, I again wandered far away. For many and many a year I sang songs. Whenever I attempted to sing of love, it turned to pain. And again, when I tried to sing of pain, it turned to love.

Thus were love and pain divided in me.

And one day I had news of a gentle maiden who had just died. And a circle formed around her grave in which many youths and old men walked as though in everlasting bliss. They spoke softly, so as not to wake the maiden.

Heavenly thoughts seemed for ever to be showered on the youths from the maiden's gravestone, like fine sparks producing a gentle rustling. I too longed sorely to walk there. Only a miracle, however, can lead you to that circle, they said. But I went to the gravestone with slow steps and lowered gaze, filled with devotion and firm belief, and before I was aware of it, I found myself in the circle, which uttered a wondrously lovely sound; and I felt as though eternal bliss were gathered together into a single

moment. My father too I saw, reconciled and loving. He took
me in his arms and wept. But not as much as I.

[Franz Schubert.]

This tale has been preserved in the original and in a copy. The
original, written in pencil, bears a title and signature added in ink by
Ferdinand Schubert: "My Dream. Franz Schubert." Ferdinand presented the manuscript to Schumann on 7th January 1839, during the
latter's visit to Vienna. The copy, probably in Schober's hand, is preserved by the family of the Dresden musician Schubert (*see* No. 102),
whom it undoubtedly reached through Schober. The story, an em-
bodiment of ideas in the style of Novalis (Friedrich Leopold von Harden-
berg, born 1772) has been psycho-analytically and otherwise speculatively
interpreted. Alois Fellner, it is true, whose explanation was accepted
by Walter Dahms for his Schubert biography (first edition), alleged
a statement of Schubert's stepbrother Anton (*see* No. 113) to the effect
that Schubert had been twice expelled from his parental home. No other
trustworthy evidence exists, however. Very likely this figment is merely
the literary effusion of a contemporary of German romanticism. The
letters of Schwind's youth and even his early works of art speak a similar
language. Let who will believe that Schubert is really referring to his
mother's death, that he vowed his vocation of song-writer at St. Cecilia's
tomb, and so on; but the description of his father's school first as a place
of revelry and then as a pleasure garden carries no conviction.

299. JOHANN FRIEDRICH ROCHLITZ to his Wife and Gottfried Christoph Härtel at Leipzig

Baden [near Vienna], 9th July [1822].

About a fortnight later [after a first meeting with Beethoven],
when I was just about to have a meal, I came across the young
composer Franz Schubert, an enthusiastic admirer of Beethoven.
The latter had mentioned me to him. If you wish to see him more
unconstrained and happy, said Schubert, you need only this
moment eat at the inn where he always goes for the same purpose.
—He took me there. The chairs were mostly taken: Beethoven
sat surrounded by several of his acquaintances, who were strangers
to me. He really did seem to be happy. . . .

Rochlitz, born at Leipzig in 1769, was a writer on music and novelist,
and had been editor of the Leipzig 'Allgemeine musikalische Zeitung'
(published by Breitkopf & Härtel) until 1818. He stayed in Vienna from

24th May to 2nd August 1822, and made an excursion to the nearby Baden.—Rochlitz's first meeting with Beethoven took place in Steiner's shop at Whitsun. The scene described here also occurred in Vienna. There is no other contemporary witness to the disputable fact of Beethoven's speaking to Schubert. (Rochlitz's letter first appeared in September 1828, and thus still within Schubert's lifetime, in his book 'For Quiet Hours' ['Für ruhige Stunden'].) The inn may have been the "Little Flower-Pot" ("Zum Blumenstöckl") in the Ballgasse, behind St. Stephen's Cathedral. It is significant that Schubert appears to have only conducted Rochlitz there and not entered the place. The possibility, already envisaged by Thayer, that this letter is a forgery, remains open. Rochlitz may later have taken a novelist's licence with it, if indeed he did not invent it altogether. Probably it was he, by the way, who fabricated the famous Mozart letter to a Baron X. (? van Swieten), which betrays its falsity by Saxon turns of phrase, though it contains a brilliant description of the process of musical creation.

300. FROM THE BERLIN 'GESELLSCHAFTER,' 21st September 1822

(Vienna correspondence of July 1822.)

Maria von Weber, Spontini, Weigl, Umlauf, Schubert and Baron Poissl have been commissioned in the most flattering manner to furnish compositions for this [Kärntnertor] theatre, in order to give new impetus to the love for national music and worthy occupation to these valiant composers.

While Barbaja held a season at the Kärntnertor Theatre under Rossini's direction from 13th April to 14th July 1822, and by turns gave other operas at the Theater an der Wien, a committee of management was co-opted on 1st July under the presidency of the composers Count Wenzel Robert Gallenberg (born Vienna, 1783, since 1803 husband of Beethoven's pupil Giulietta Countess Guicciardi) and Josef Weigl. At the Theater an der Wien the actor and dramatist Wilhelm Vogel (born Mannheim, 1772) took the reins as general secretary to Count Pálffy. While the Wien also cultivated drama, which was Vogel's special preserve, that committee at the Kärntnertor may have been expected to look especially after the interests of German opera.—Weber's 'Euryanthe' was already talked of, and of Weigl's works 'The Iron Portal' ('Die eiserne Pforte') was given in 1823. The other commissions came to nothing. Johann Nepomuk Poissl (born 1783 at Haunkenzell in Bavaria) was intendant of the Bavarian court music and Gasparo Spontini (born 1774) Prussian musical director-general.—For Schubert's opera *see* No. 280.

301. ANTON VON SPAUN to his Wife, Henriette, at Linz

Steyr, 20th July 1822.

I very much wish, too, that Pepi would come soon. Vogl is already looking forward to meeting him and would have a lot to talk about with him. To me Vogl is extremely pleasing. He told me his whole relationship to Schubert with the utmost frankness, and unfortunately I am quite unable to excuse the latter. Vogl is very much embittered against Schober, for whose sake Schubert behaved most ungratefully towards Vogl and who makes the fullest use of Schubert in order to extricate himself from financial embarrassments and to defray the expenditure which has already exhausted the greater part of his mother's fortune. I wish very much that somebody were here who would defend Schubert at least in the matter of the most glaring reproaches. Vogl also says Schober's opera is bad and a perfect failure, and that altogether Schubert is quite on the wrong road. Please tell Pepi all this as soon as possible.

The District Captain and the old Dornfeld lady too I have already visited, as well as Koller, at whose house Vogl is wont to sing as a rule. About the recent evening party at Hintermayr's Nona Kindinger will have told you by now. 'Memnon' and 'Antigone' enoaptured me in spite of my bad accompanying. To-night I shall probably play at Dornfeld's.

Anton von Spaun, who was registrar to the Upper Austrian Common Law office, married in 1818 Henriette von Vogelsang (born 1798). He was only temporarily at Steyr, where Vogl was on holiday.—Pepi is Josef von Spaun.—No details are known of Vogl's estrangement from Schubert, which must have changed for the better very soon. A hint at it will be found in No. 328. It is interesting that Schober, who lived above his means, is here represented as Schubert's parasite; but it is not clear whether he is supposed to have taken advantage of him in the way of cash, possibly from the receipts of his song publications, or indirectly by enlisting his help in approaching others for loans. Schubert lived with him at that time. Both before and after that Schober was represented by intimates as having lured several of his friends, Schubert included, into loose living. Kenner wrote to that effect to Anton von Spaun as early as 1815 and to Luib in 1858 (Vienna City Library), Ottenwalt to Josef von Spaun in 1816, 1817 and 1825, and lastly Holzapfel

to Luib in 1858 (Vienna City Library).   A friend of Schober's, Antonio
Mayer, wrote to him from Breslau in 1826 about the former's Turkish
upholstery, Arabian carpets and Persian pipes, to match which he wished
to obtain a Persian dressing-gown from Breslau.   (It is easy to understand
that Schober was a friend of Liszt's, and the wonder is that he did not
become friendly with Wagner too.)   His influence on the Schubert circle
was undoubtedly great and dominating.—Johann Nepomuk, Ritter von
Dornfeld, born at Linz in 1773, was district captain of the district office
of Traunviertel at Steyr; his wife Katharina was of an age with him.
She may be called the "old lady" here because her daughter Friederike,
born in 1804, was better known to the Schubert friends.—Hintermayr,
Edler von Wallenberg (whose Christian name cannot be discovered), was
head inspector to the Lamberg estate at Steyr.—Nina (Anna) von
Kindinger was a cousin of the brothers Spaun.

Rossini's departure from Vienna, 22nd July 1822.

'The Quail's Call' ('Der Wachtelschlag'), Op. 68 (xx. 401), appears
in the 'Wiener Zeitschrift,' 30th July 1822.

302. FROM PROKESCH'S DIARY

6th August 1822.

Supped at the inn, where I came across the composer Schubert.
Musical discussions.   He saw me home.

Prokesch, who soon afterwards vanished from Schubert's circle again,
met him this time at the ale-house next to the Kärntnertor Theatre,
in the so-called Komödiengässchen (Comedy Alley).

303. FROM PROKESCH'S DIARY

8th August [1822].

To the inn.   Schubert.

304. BRUCHMANN TO PLATEN

[Summer 1822.]

Some of these first Ghazals will be set by Schubert, to which I look
forward with much pleasure; how did you like his setting of
your song? . . . I have just heard Schubert sing your Ghazal,

"I 'm broken-hearted, thou lov'st me not," which has quite be-witched me. If there is to be another, and you should write to me about him in the meantime, you shall have both.

The song 'Thou lov'st me not' of July 1822 opens with the words: "Mein Herz ist zerrissen, Du liebst mich nicht."

305. JOSEF HÜTTENBRENNER TO KARL FRIEDRICH PETERS in Leipzig

Vienna, 14th August 1822.

. . . Among the newer local composers Vienna again possesses a talent to-day which has already attracted general attention and enjoyed the resident public's favour—in short, and without exaggeration, we may speak of a "second Beethoven." Indeed that immortal man says of him: "This one will surpass me."

The house of Peters was formed by the amalgamation of Franz Anton Hoffmeister and Ambrosius Kühnel in 1813.—Josef Hüttenbrenner is not to be trusted about details any more than Rochlitz (*see* No. 299). Yet these two letters seem to indicate that after Schubert's dedication of the Variations, Op. 10, to him (*see* No. 285) Beethoven did take notice of Schubert in 1822.

306. FROM THE PROGRAMME of the Theater an der Wien, 27th August 1822

(Evening entertainment for the benefit of the dancer Angioletta Mayer.)

Part III . . . 8. Vocal Quartet, with guitar accompaniment, by Schubert, performed by Herren Jäger, [Josef] Spitzeder, [Jakob Wilhelm] Rauscher, Ruprecht and [Josef] Schmidt.

Angioletta Mayer (born 1807, later married name Hopfen), a member of Friedrich Horschelt's notorious children's ballet, had appeared at the Theater an der Wien at the age of five. Later she was engaged at the Kärntnertor for eight years and returned to its ballet in 1833.— Which of Schubert's quartets was sung on this occasion is unknown; probably it was 'Spirit of Love' once again.—Jakob Wilhelm Rauscher, born in 1803 at Wilfersdorf in Lower Austria, was at the Theater an der Wien at that time and at the Kärntnertor in 1822–4, where he sang Jaquino in 'Fidelio.' Ruprecht (Christian name unknown) too went to the Court Opera in 1822. The guitar player may have been the actor Josef Schmidt (born 1797) of the Theater an der Wien, who went to the Burg Theatre in 1828.

307. Bruchmann to Schober

Innsbruck, 8th September 1822.

. . . Remember me to Schwind and Schubert.

Bruchmann was on a walking tour by way of Linz and Salzburg to Innsbruck, where he no doubt met Senn.

308. From a Graz Concert Programme, 8th September 1822

(Grand vocal and instrument concert held by the Styrian Musical Society for the benefit of its funds, in the Assembly Hall.)

Part II, No. 4. Vocal Quartet for pianoforte accompaniment ('The Little Village'); by Fr. Schubert.

The singer Maria Theresia Sessi (see No. 311) took part in this concert. Of the singers in the quartet only Fausky (Christian name unknown) is mentioned (see No. 309). The suggestion of this Schubert performance may have come from Anselm Hüttenbrenner, but more probably from Johann Baptist Jenger, a military official born in 1792 at Kirchhofen in the Breisgau (still Austrian at that time), who was secretary to the Styrian Musical Society and a good pianoforte player.

309. From the Official 'Grazer Zeitung,' 14th September 1822

Schubert's vocal quartet, 'The Little Village,' made a great sensation, here as in the capital. It had to be sung more than once. A wholly perfect, thoroughly original composition, it cannot fail to be speedily accepted everywhere. Herr Fausky delighted us in it by his still very agreeable tenor voice.

310. From the Official 'Grazer Zeitung,' 12th September 1822

(Preliminary notice of the concert next mentioned.)

Herr Ruess of Vienna will perform, at the express desire of numerous and excellent lovers of art, the 'Erl King' by Goethe, with pianoforte accompaniment, by our German song-writer

Schubert.   The literary interest of this short poem and the masterly
musical painting are known to all friends of poetry and music, and
will be the more sure to appeal because the vocal quartet by the
same master, 'The Little Village,' had to be repeated by general
request at the last concert.

311. FROM A GRAZ CONCERT PROGRAMME, 13th September 1822

(Grand vocal and instrumental concert given by the singer Maria
Theresia Sessi, with the collaboration of the Styrian Musical Society,
at the Assembly Hall.)

Part I, No. 3, Vocal Quartet: 'The Nightingale,' by Schubert
. . . Part II, No. 7. 'Erl King,' poem by Goethe, music by
Schubert, sung by Herr Ruess.

Sessi was born in 1796, began her career at Parma in 1805, went to
the Vienna Court Opera in 1812 and became a teacher of singing.   She
was not one of the four well-known Sessi sisters.—On Ruess *see* No. 216.
—Another notice of this concert appeared in the Vienna 'Theaterzeitung'
on 10th October 1822 (not in the German edition).

312. FROM THE OFFICIAL 'GRAZER ZEITUNG,' 21st September 1822

In order to give more variety to the concert, a vocal quartet by
Schubert, 'The Nightingale,' and the same composer's favourite
'Erl King' with pianoforte accompaniment were performed.   The
latter vocal piece demands a clear-sighted singer and pianoforte
player, capable of properly conceiving the spirit of this great
composition.   Herr Ruess delivered his part according to all
the rules of declamatory song, and knew how to move us, especially
at the close.   The pianoforte accompaniment, which calls for all
a player's powers, was undertaken by Herr Anselm Hüttenbrenner,
who carried out with the certainty and force of a master the task
of vividly conceiving the romantic-tragic spirit of the poem and the
characteristic music.

313. FROM THE PROGRAMME of the Fourth Society Concert held by the Linz Musical Society, 15th September 1822, at 11 a.m., in the Assembly Hall

3. Vocal Quartet: 'The Nightingale.' Poem by Matthisson, with Pianoforte accompaniment by Schubert.

The member of the Linz Musical Society who was active on Schubert's behalf was Albert Stadler, who became its secretary in 1823. The concert is mentioned also in the society's first printed annual report. The accompanist is not named there either.

314. FROM THE PROGRAMME of the Kärntnertor Theatre, 24th September 1822

(Concert given by the violinist Anton Bohrer, Royal Prussian Concert Master, and the violoncellist Max Bohrer, virtuoso to the King of Prussia.)

4. Vocal Quartet with guitar accompaniment, by Schubert, sung by Herren Haizinger, Rauscher, Ruprecht and [Josef] Seipelt.

Anton Bohrer was born in 1783, and Max Bohrer, his brother, in 1785 at Munich. The guitar player is not named. The quartet was 'Spirit of Love' once more. Josef Seipelt, born in 1782 at Raika in Hungary, was a bass singer at the Theater an der Wien, and went to the Court Opera at the end of 1822. He had a nasal voice. In 1824 he sang the solo bass part at the first performance of Beethoven's ninth Symphony. Later he became a choirmaster and music teacher.—The concert included a grand military 'Sinfonie concertante' for violin and cello with orchestral accompaniment by the brothers Bohrer. In the concluding "Anacreontic Divertissement" by Taglioni there was a *pas de trois* composed by Mayseder, who played a violin solo in it.

315. FROM THE 'WIENER ZEITSCHRIFT FÜR KUNST,' &C., 1st October 1822

A vocal quartet with guitar accompaniment, by Schubert, sung by Herren Haitzinger, Rauscher, Ruprecht and Seipelt, is well known. What has been said about it before is still true. Two tenors and two basses do not produce the best effect. The *stretta*, owing to the quick enunciation of the words, requires much practice, and this indeed shows itself in the happy agreement between the singers, who also deserve praise for their clear articulation.

The critic refers to No. 282.

316. [Lost Letter from Josef Hüttenbrenner to the Publisher Peters concerning Schubert's Works, 18th October 1822.]

Peters had evidently answered No. 305 (*see* No. 325).

317. From a Graz Concert Programme, 18th October 1822

(Concert given by the violoncellist J. B. Amerbacher in the County Theatre.)

Part II, No. 4. The vocal quartet, 'The Little Village,' by Schubert, received here with general acclamation, sung by Herren Stefan and Franz Dunst, Forti and Krebs.

Amerbacher was professor at the Prague Conservatory.—Stefan Dunst, a tenor, was probably a brother of Franz Xaver Dunst, who had been at the Court Opera and later became producer at the Josefstadt Theatre. Of Forti (tenor) and Wilhelm Krebs (bass) no details are known. All these four singers were members of the Graz theatre company.—On the same evening the deceased poet Karl Schröckinger's drama 'The Shepherd Lad' ('Der Hirtenknabe') was given.

318. From the 'Theaterzeitung,' 29th October 1822

Herr *Kapellmeister* Stauffer enjoyed a deserved success with Herren Stefan and Franz Dunst, Forti and Krebs, who very meritoriously performed the vocal quartet, 'The Little Village' ['Das Dörfchen'], by Schubart [*sic*].

P. . .

[Adalbert Prix.]

About this Stauffer nothing is known.

Schubert, with Josef Hüttenbrenner, visits the Leopoldstadt Theatre: 'Aline, or Vienna on Another Continent,' magic play by Adolf Bäuerle, music by Wenzel Müller, 19th October 1822.—The first performance of this popular piece had taken place ten days earlier.

Bäuerle, born in Vienna in 1786, was a successful writer of popular plays and editor of the Vienna 'Theaterzeitung.'—Wenzel Müller, born in 1786 at Tyrnau in Moravia, was a prominent composer of folksong-like theatre airs, many of which have actually become folksongs, and conductor at the Leopoldstadt Theatre. Hans Költzsch thinks that the waltz theme in the scherzo section of Schubert's "Wanderer" Fantasy, written during the following month (November 1822), was derived from the duet for Zilli and Bims in 'Aline,' beginning "Was macht denn der Prater, sag', blüht er recht schön?" and containing the familiar tag: "Ja, nur ein' Kaiserstadt, ja, nur ein Wien!" Bauernfeld, in a Schubert article of 1869, writes: "We tried to prove to Schubert that certain passages in the 'Maid of the Mill' songs recalled an old Austrian grenadiers' march or Wenzel Müller's 'Wer niemals einen Rausch hat g'habt.'" This theatre air of Müller's also became a folksong, as did his song 'Kommt ein Vogerl geflogen.'

319. From Maximilian Löwenthal's Travel Diary
(Concerning his visit to Goethe at Weimar.)

[20th October 1822.]

The subjects of the short conversation . . . were . . . the "undesirability of entering into new relationships, and an increase of duties in old age" (to which he was brought by my remark that he had never been in Vienna), and "the enormous quantity of music there must be in Vienna; if only because the fine instruments which are made there must tempt thereto" (this upon my mention of Schubert's settings of his poems, which he did not know). He said but few words on all this, and they were short.

Maximilian (later von) Löwenthal, born in Vienna in 1799, had been to the academic grammar-school at the same time as Schubert. He was court conveyancer and an author. In 1822 the comedy 'The Friends According to Fashion' ('Die Freunde nach der Mode'), adapted by him from one of Arthur Murphy's plays, was performed in Prague. He had just concluded a journey through France, England and Germany, which he described in his 'Sketches' of 1825. The present diary entry is quoted there, so that Schubert may have read it. In Goethe's diary the following occurs on the same day: "Löwenthal, a traveller from Vienna, returning from his journey through France and England." (For Goethe's disregard of Schubert's first approach to him see No. 81.)

320. Franz Ignaz von Holbein to Josef Hüttenbrenner

[Outside:]

>Prague.
>>Jos. Hüttenbrenner, Esq.,
>>>Official in the Registry of the I. & R.
>>>Austrian-Bohemian United Court
>>>Chancellery in Vienna.
>>>To be left at the I. & R. Court Chancellery.

[Inside:]

Sir,

It gives me particular pleasure to smooth the usually rough path of young talents. Kindly send me the book and music of 'The Devil's Pleasaunce' ['Des Teufels Lustschloss'].

Should it correspond to what you say, nothing shall hinder its performance.

I regret that during my sojourn in Vienna, between 20th September and 19th October, I did not have the pleasure of making your and your talented friend's acquaintance.

>>>>Yours respectfully,
22nd October 1822.   v. Holbein.

Holbein, Edler von Holbeinsberg, born in 1779 at Zistersdorf in Lower Austria, was a dramatist and theatre manager in Prague. Josef Hüttenbrenner had offered him, among other managers, Schubert's youthful opera 'The Devil's Pleasaunce.' The case was a peculiar one: Hüttenbrenner had received the second, definitive version of this work (1814), in which Schubert was no longer interested, in return for a small outstanding debt. It is possible, however, that this did not happen until after the copying of the work, for which Hüttenbrenner charged Schubert early in 1823 (see No. 339). It is certain that Schubert, since he had to pay for the copying, did not intend to give up his rights in the work together with the autograph. According to Hüttenbrenner's information to Kreissle he at that time also offered this weak musical play to Count Gallenberg for the Kärntnertor Theatre, to Hensler for the Josefstadt Theatre, newly opened on 3rd October 1822, and to Peter von Winter (born Mannheim, 1754) for the Munich Opera; all in vain. Schubert, who said of Hüttenbrenner: "This one is pleased with anything of mine!" may have only passively endured these efforts. The information that the

management of the Josefstadt Theatre had promised a production and
that Gallenberg had demanded a guarantee of 10,000 florins (? V.C.)
may once again be attributed to Hüttenbrenner's lively imagination.

321. MORITZ VON SCHWIND TO SCHOBER

[Vienna,] 22nd October 1822.

The Misses Bruchmann very much desire to hold a Schubertiad
on 10th November, i.e. the eve of their mother's birthday, in
order to dispel as far as possible the sorrowful recollection of the
departed Sybille, which insists on returning on such a festive day.
They rely on you for this without fail.   Please make sure that you
will be there.

Justine von Bruchmann, *née* Weis in Vienna, 1774, had three daughters
apart from her son Franz.   The eldest, Sybille (*see* note preceding No. 179),
had died in 1820, and the song 'Sister's Greeting' ('Schwestergruss')
was written in this very November 1822.   Isabella, born in 1801, was
jestingly called "Princess Tea-kettle," and later, as Frau von Streinsberg,
the "Hofrätin" (aulic councillor's wife).   Justina, born in 1805, became
secretly engaged to Schober, who before that had wooed Marie von Spaun,
but later married Rudolf, Ritter von Smetana.   Schwind later called the
two surviving sisters the "Bruch children" (*Bruchkinder*).   Their father,
born at Cologne in 1768, was a wholesale merchant and director of the
Austrian National Bank; he bore the nickname of "old Shylock."   The
family lived in the Weihburggasse, in the city.—Schwind at that time still
addressed Schober in the distant third person plural, but he soon became
the most devoted of his friends, only to give him up in later years.

322. SCHUBERT TO JOSEF HÜTTENBRENNER

Dear Hüttenbrenner,

As I have to make very important alterations in the songs handed
to you, do not give them to Herr Leidesdorf yet, but bring them
out to me.   Should they have been already sent, they must be
fetched back immediately.

Frz. Schubert.

Vienna, 31st October 1822.

The publishing house of Sauer & Leidesdorf was founded only in
1822.   Ignaz Sauer, born *c.* 1759, was musical director at the orphanage,
and had since about 1800 run an art and music publishing business under

the name of "The Seven Sisters" (his daughters). Maximilian Josef Leidesdorf, born in Vienna in 1788, whom Beethoven punningly called "Dorf des Leides" (village of sorrow), was more assiduous both as composer and as publisher than his old partner. The shop was in the Kärntnerstrasse. The firm, so Josef Hüttenbrenner said, made an agreement with Schubert when he withdrew from Cappi & Diabelli, according to which he was to supply it with songs for two years for the sum of 1,200 florins, V.C. The first book of his was Op. 20, dedicated to Frau von Bruchmann, and published in the spring of 1823. It contained three songs, the second of which, the famous 'Faith in Spring' ('Frühlingsglaube'), exists in an earlier version in B flat major, dating from 1820, whereas the familiar version dates from November 1822. It is to this that the present note refers. Incidentally, such afterthoughts are rare with Schubert.

323. JOSEF HÜTTENBRENNER TO HOLBEIN (Draft)

Autumn 1822.

A prolonged absence and intervening obstacles are the reason why I have so far failed to thank you most cordially for your kind readiness to take my friend, our gifted young composer Schubert, under your protection, and at the same time to send you the opera ('The Devil's Pleasaunce').

[At the back of this draft:]

Even though an eminent talent like X.'s is almost exclusively applauded, is it commendable to sacrifice time, trouble and strength to the rise of another composer, since art is so manifold that no finality is conceivable and no fully achieved aim, no *non plus ultra*, can be imagined.—For this reason the offering of a new composer who seeks celebrity should be welcomed by any opera company as well as by any audience, and he should at least be allowed to look for a calm and therefore just appraisal of such developed powers as may be shown by the work he has supplied. For each new talent stimulated to a creative flight can only be a fair and honourable gain to art, provided that it possesses true force and bears the stamp of originality, even though his success may not always be marked by the most brilliant applause.—For one thing, a true genius requires time, to begin with, to be forgiven by his contemporaries for the great audacity with which he dares to go his own way, and for another, it is by no means always the worst morsels which begin by appearing somewhat unpalatable to the world.

The second part of this draft, in which Hüttenbrenner clearly alludes to Rossini, was hardly intended for Holbein, but more likely for some periodical. It too, however, may refer to the opera. Both parts are on the same sheet of paper.

324. LOST LETTER from Karl Maria von Weber to Josef Hütten-brenner dealing at some length with Schubert's opera, 'Alfonso und Estrella,' autumn 1822 (?)

Weber's letter, which Josef Hüttenbrenner says was addressed to him, but whose postage dues were charged to Schubert (see No. 339), is described as "very promising" by the latter (No. 328). Salieri and Mosel, the latter of whom wrote to Weber about 'Alfonso and Estrella,' are said to have spoken favourably of this opera. Wilhelmine Schröder, born at Hamburg in 1805, the famous soprano who in 1823 married the actor Karl Devrient at Dresden, is said to have handed the libretto to Weber there. She had begun her career in the ballet at the Kärntnertor Theatre, continued as an actress at the Burg Theatre and in 1821 joined the Court Opera as a singer. She was particularly successful as Pamina in 'The Magic Flute,' as Leonore in 'Fidelio' and as Agathe in 'Frieschütz,' and it was she who at last, in 1830, made Goethe appreciate the 'Erl King.'

Schubert goes with Louis Schlösser to Beethoven's 'Fidelio,' revived in a new production at the Kärntnertor Theatre, 3rd November 1822. —Schlösser, born at Darmstadt in 1800, who had studied in Vienna with Mayseder and Ignaz von Seyfried and become violinist in the court chapel, later court musical director at Darmstadt, stayed in Vienna again from the spring of 1822 to the end of May 1823, and visited Beethoven there. His recollections, published in 1883, relate that he visited Schubert in the Rossau, and that he wrote compositions for a certain Count Stefan X., a cousin of Count Esterházy's, which his customer gave out as his own. This is untrue. He also says that after the performance of 'Fidelio' Schubert pointed out Beethoven to him as the master returned home with Schindler and Stephan von Breuning. At this performance Wilhelmine Schröder sang Leonore, Haizinger Florestan, Nestroy Don Fernando and

Anton Forti Pizarro. Forti was born in Vienna in 1790 and is said to have caused Vogl's premature retirement by trying to prejudice Moritz, Count Dietrichstein, against him.

Schubertiad at the Bruchmanns', 10th November 1822.

325. PETERS TO JOSEF HÜTTENBRENNER

[Outside:]
The Right Honourable
Herr Josef Hüttenbrenner,
Official in the I. & R. Court Chancellery,
Wipplinger Strasse, No. 389, 3rd Floor,
in
Vienna.

Franked.
[Inside:]

Leipzig, 12th November 1822.

Herr Hüttenbrenner in Vienna.

I trust that an accumulation of business at the moment may excuse my somewhat belated reply to your favour of 15th October.

I am much obliged to you for your information concerning Herr F. Schubert, several of whose song-compositions are favourably known to me, and they strengthen my confidence in what you tell me to that artist's advantage. I shall be glad to contribute to a wider dissemination of this composer's works than the Viennese firms are able to achieve; but before I commit myself to anything, allow me to give you a short outline of the conditions of my trade.

From the moment at which I entered upon my present business I conceived the plan of distinguishing myself favourably as a publisher by never printing anything that is bad, but on the contrary as much as possible of what is good. To carry this out completely is out of the question, since it is impossible to obtain as many manuscripts as I require from the most excellent artists alone, and moreover we publishers are often forced by circumstances to print many things of a kind which I at least should not otherwise undertake; nay, we are even obliged to issue much that is superficial and thus to cater for every section of the public, for with classical works alone our activities would be very much restricted, connoisseurs being, as you know, not by any means in the majority. Nevertheless, I did not allow myself to be enticed by mere love of gain to deal in more profitable but empty fashionable trifles, but have seen to it that even works intended for the masses were not bad. Moreover, I have always worked towards my favourite purpose and aimed chiefly at the publication of superior works, an endeavour that will become more and more apparent as time goes on, since each year I enter into new and good relations, while my increasingly favourable economic position will allow me to maintain them.

Two things now arise from this which have often hampered me. The first is time, which almost always holds me in check. In order to obtain as many good works as possible, I was obliged to seek intercourse with good artists and to consolidate it, not only by trying to satisfy them, but by offering myself as an ever-ready publisher, which is good and agreeable for both parties; and indeed my relations with most of the composers I value, such as Spohr, Romberg, Hummel, &c., have become most friendly, so that it is now doubly incumbent on me to publish everything such friends and good artists send me, even where, as is often the case, there may be something among it which I know from the first to be unprofitable.

Now these obligations make a great many claims on my time. It is not only that these artists keep me continually occupied, but that I must also reserve some time for works that may come un-expectedly, as may happen nowadays in the case of several of them. The remaining time then rarely suffices me for the publication of other equally necessary things, so that I am nearly always prevented from entering into relations with new composers, simply because I have no time for their works.

The second point arising from the above is the newness and, in my own sphere, the obscurity of a coming composer which makes new connections difficult for me. I am often reproached with being reluctant to contribute to the propagation of the works by new composers, who cannot become known because the publisher will have nothing to do with the circulation of their music; but this is quite unjust, for I cannot do everything, and one must follow one single plan if anything of value is to result. I aim at the works of artists already acknowledged, and although I print many other things, I can obtain enough from them, so that I must leave the introduction of new composers to other publishers, who may also do something; and many like doing that, fighting shy of the fees asked by the older and more expensive artists. But once the new composer has made a name and his works are recognized as good, then I am his man, for then the publication of his works accords with my plan, which is based on honour rather than on gain; and I would rather obtain his works at a dearer price then than have them cheaply at the beginning.

You will thus see that it is difficult for me to fall in at once with your suggestion concerning Herr Schubert, my very limited time being the chief reason. However, from what I gather about the young artist, I should not like to refuse his wish either. As a compromise I would therefore suggest that Herr Schubert should send me a few of the works he intends for publication to look at. For I do not print anything by a composer who is as yet little known without having seen it. If a great and well-known artist writes a bad work, then the blame is his, for I relied upon his name; but if I issue anything by a new artist that fails to please, it is my own fault, for why should I print anything of the quality of which I am not myself convinced? In such a case the composer's name affords me no protection.

There can be no question that Herr Schubert would entrust his works to good hands if he sent them to me. He is secure from any sort of trickery with me. If they are what I want, I will keep what I can of them; on the other hand, Herr Schubert must not resent it if there should be something I do not like. I shall be quite frank, since plain speaking is most likely to lead to a good understanding.

I must ask, furthermore, that he should send me only the best works. Not that he would wish to publish anything he does not regard as successful, I fancy; but be that as it may, one work is apt to turn out better than another, and I must have the best—I mean if I am to introduce a composer to a very extensive public;

not in order to make sure of a profit, but for my own credit.   I have taken great pains to perfect my business as far as possible, so that I am by now in many places reaping the reward for it in the particular confidence shown to my firm.   People are accustomed to my issuing many good works, and if now and again I appear with a new author, he is regarded with the better faith because it is assumed that he must be good if I have him in hand. I admit that I have made more than one mistake, but this has made me more and more cautious, for I wish to retain and further consolidate my hard-earned reputation.   It is for this reason that I ask a new author to supply me with his best.   In this way I may at once recommend him thoroughly, and my recommendation will justify itself.   What is more, it is often the first impression which opens up a career for the whole future, for which reason coming composers cannot be often enough told the precept that they should go to work as carefully as possible with the publication of their music.   Let them compose much, but have little printed until they have established their fame.

Spohr has published only 58 works, Andreas Romberg only 66 and Bernhard Romberg only 38, while many other artists nowadays, though they are much younger, already have over a hundred in print.   These acknowledged artists too have written a great deal more, but have refrained from publication; and if it should be attempted to set up against them such fertile and yet sterling figures as Mozart, Haydn, Beethoven, &c., I declare these to be rare examples who should certainly be taken as models, but to whom one should not compare oneself unless justified by experience.   And what masses of earlier works by Mozart and others have never been printed!

Kindly discuss with Herr Schubart [sic] the contents of this letter and deal further with such conditions as he may wish to make on his side, concerning which I shall be glad to hear from you, for it is disagreeable for me to dictate in the matter of the products of another's mind.   As for my terms, they will give rise to no objections.   The constancy with which my authors remain with me alone proves that I am not difficult to get on with, so that I may give myself this testimony; besides which I imagine that the young artist's stipulations will hardly be so extravagant as to prove unacceptable.

That a work by Herr Sch. will sell 300 copies in Vienna alone I am ready to believe, provided that it has been printed there; but I should scarcely dispose of 100 there, although I deal with all the shops. You will hardly understand this, and I shall not set forth the reasons for you; but you may believe that it is so, and experience confirms it only too clearly, exceptions being very rare.

With my compliments, I remain very respectfully,

Your obedient servant,
K. F. Peters.

If Herr Schub. should send songs, those with a name, like Beethoven's 'Adelaide,' and so on, are preferable to plain songs, for so many songs and partsongs appear now that such a title no longer attracts sufficient attention.

Josef Hüttenbrenner, who had for some time shared the second floor of Irrsa's house with the latter, now lodged in Mayrhofer's room at Frau von Sanssouci's.—Louis Spohr had been leader in the Theater an der Wien orchestra in 1812–15.—Andreas Romberg, the violinist, had died at Gotha at the end of 1821.—Johann Nepomuk Hummel, born at Pressburg in 1778, a pupil of Salieri's and very famous as a pianoforte virtuoso and composer for his instrument, had taught in Vienna in 1811–16, and now lived at Weimar.—Bernard Romberg, a cousin of Andreas, was born in 1767 at Dinklage in Oldenburg. He was a cellist, conductor at the Kärntnertor Theatre in 1822 and later in Berlin.—Some 300 copies of 'Erl King' may have been disposed of by the autumn of 1822.—Beethoven's 'Adelaide' was one of Schubert's favourite songs.—The negotiations with Peters came to nothing. His letters resemble in style those which he wrote to Beethoven about the same time.

326. Schubert's Album Leaf for Albert Schellmann (jun.)

Vienna, 28th November 1822.

Who loves not wine, maidens and song,
Remains a fool his whole life long.
Martin Luther.

For eternal remembrance.   Franz Schubert.

[Reverse:]

> One thing will not do for all.
> Let each live in his tradition,
> Each consider his own mission,
> And who stands, beware a fall.
>   Goethe.

For remembrance.

The younger Schellmann was born at Steyr in 1798, had been to the Kremsmünster Seminary and became a barrister, like his father. He was a good pianoforte player, and Vogl sometimes preferred him to Schubert as an accompanist.—The first quotation (which should properly read "wine, woman and song") is generally but wrongly attributed to Luther. Johann Strauss, jun., drew from it the title of his waltz, 'Wein, Weib, Gesang.'—The Goethe verse is the last of his poem 'Beherzigung.'

327. FROM PERTH'S DIARY, 1st December 1822

(At the third of the annual concerts of the Private Musical Society, at the "Roman Emperor," at 4 p.m.)

6. 'Spring Song' ['Frühlings-Gesang'], vocal quartet by Franz Schubert.   Pleased inordinately and had to be repeated.

328. SCHUBERT TO JOSEF VON SPAUN

[Outside:]   From Vienna.

To Herr Josef, Edler von Spaun, Financial Assessor at Linz.

[Inside:]   Vienna, 7th December 1822.

Dear Spaun,

I hope to give you some little pleasure by the dedication of these three songs, which indeed you so very much deserve that I really and *ex officio* ought to offer you an enormous one, and should in fact do so if I were able.   For the rest you will like their choice, for I selected those which you indicated yourself.   Apart from this book two others appear at the same time, one of which is already engraved, so that I enclose a copy of that too; the other is

now in the engraver's hands.   The first of these contains, as you
will see, the three songs of the Harper, the second of which,
'Who never ate his bread with tears,' is new, and is dedicated to
the Bishop of St. Pölten.   The other includes, as you won't see,
the 'Suleika' and 'Secrets' ['Geheimes'], and is dedicated to
Schober.   Apart from these I have composed a Fantasy for pianoforte, two hands, which is also to appear in print, inscribed to a
certain wealthy person.   Moreover, I have set some new Goethe
songs, such as 'The Muses' Son' ['Der Musensohn'], 'To the
Distant One' ['An die Entfernte'], 'By the River' ['Am Flusse'],
and 'Hail and Farewell' ['Willkommen und Abschied'].—With the
opera I did not get on in Vienna.   I asked to have it back, and it
came.   Vogl has really left the theatre, too.   I shall shortly send
it either to Dresden, whence I had a very promising letter from
Weber, or to Berlin.—My Mass is finished, and is to be produced
before long.   I still have my old notion of dedicating it to the
emperor or the empress, as I think it a success.—Now I have told
you all the news that could be told of me and my music.   Now
just one thing about somebody else.   'Libussa,' a grand opera by
K. Kreutzer, has been given for the first time these days, and it
pleased.   The second act is said to be particularly fine, but I heard
only the first, which left me cold.

And now, how are you?   I was able to leave the question so late
because I have the certain hope that you are well.   How is your
family?   What about Streinsberg?—Do write to me soon about
everything.   I should be pretty well, if only the miserable business
of the opera were not so galling.   With Vogl I have taken up again,
now that he has left the theatre and I am no longer embarrassed
in that respect.   I even think I may come up there with him again,
or after him, this summer; a thing to which I look forward with
pleasure, as I shall then see you and your friends again.—Our
companionship in Vienna is quite agreeable now.   We hold
readings at Schober's three times a week as well as a Schubertiad,
at which Bruchmann too makes an appearance.   And now, dear
Spaun, farewell.   Do write to me soon and at length, so as to
mitigate somewhat the gaping void your absence will always
make for me. — Most cordial greetings to all your brothers,

also to your sister and Ottenwalt, as well as Streinsberg and many others, &c.

Your faithful friend,

Franz Schubert.

Make out the address to the school house in the Rossau, Grünthorgasse, as I live there now.

The songs in question are Op. 13 (*see* No. 330); they are dedicated to Spaun.   Op. 12 too was ready, but Op. 14 was still printing.   No. 2 of Op. 12 was not written till 1822, but the other two Songs of the Harper had been composed in 1816, and were thus known to Spaun.   Schubert several times set all the songs of the mysterious harper and the Italian dream-child Mignon in Goethe's romantic novel of 'Wilhelm Meister's Prentice Years,' but not those of the frivolous actress Philine.   Wilhelm Meister (to whose unstable character Bauernfeld compared that of Schober) had rescued little Mignon from a troupe of rope-dancers; she and her strange companion (the old man whom the Viennese artists represented in the imaginary likeness of Ossian) join the small actors' company into which Meister had strayed by accident.   He becomes her protector and idol. She dies of a broken heart, and only then does it appear that she was the crazed old man's child.—The Bishop of St. Pölten was Dankesreither.— The two songs 'Suleika' and 'Secrets' came from Goethe's Hafiz songs, the so-called 'Westöstlicher Divan.'   The words of this first 'Suleika' song, also called 'Eastern Wind,' were, like those of the second, 'Western Wind' (Op. 31), by Marianne von Willemer (*née* Jung, 1784, at Linz), written at Frankfort o/M., and Goethe had added the two poems by his friend to his collection with her consent.   This, however, was unknown to Schubert, for the authoress did not disclose the matter until 1856 or 1857.—The Fantasy was the so-called "Wanderer" Fantasy, Op. 15 (*see* No. 351); the dedicatee was Emanuel Karl, Edler Liebenberg de Zsittin, born 1796, a Jew baptized in 1819 and ennobled in 1821, a landowner and a pianoforte player who had been a pupil of Hummel's.—'To the Distant One' was first composed in 1815; it is the second version that bears the date of December 1822.—The opera is 'Alfonso and Estrella,' which had thus really been submitted to the Kärntnertor Theatre.   Vogl had left the Court Opera on 30th November 1822.—Schubert sent the libretto to Dresden and a copy of the score to Berlin later on.—The A flat major Mass was begun in November 1819 and finished in September 1822 in a second version entitled 'Missa solemnis'; it remained unpublished until 1875.   On 23rd February 1823 Moritz, Count Dietrichstein, wrote to Moritz, Count of the Realm Lichnowsky (born 1771, Beethoven's friend and Josef

Hüttenbrenner's patron): "At the same time I am sending you here-with the score of a Mass by Reutter [jun.]; the truth is that H.M. the emperor likes that style. . . . H.M. likes fugues to be very thoroughly developed, yet not too long; the Sanctus with the Osanna as short as possible in order not to hold up the transubstantiation." It was probably unconsciously that Schubert deferred to these demands.—'Libussa,' to a libretto by Josef Karl Bernard (born 1780), had its first performance on 4th December 1822. The libretto was intended for Beethoven, among others.—Streinsberg was at that time conveyancer to the customs office at Linz.—As Vogl had no great opinion of 'Alfonso and Estrella' (*see* No. 301), he cannot have pressed its claims at the Court Opera, where his views counted for something. (The part of Troila in the work had been intended for him.)—"Readings" began at this time to be a favourite pursuit in the Schubert circle, and they were of considerable use to the composer.—From the end (? autumn) of 1822 Schubert lived for some time, probably until the spring of 1823, at his father's schoolhouse.

329. [LOST LETTER from Schubert to Johann Nepomuk Dankesreither, *c.* 7th December 1822]

This letter referred to the dedication of Op. 12 (*see* No. 331).

330. FROM THE OFFICIAL 'WIENER ZEITUNG,' 13th December 1822

At the House of Cappi & Diabelli,
Art and Music Dealers, 1133 Graben,
are newly published and to be had:

SONGS OF THE HARPER
from
'Wilhelm Meister,' by Goethe.
Set to Music
For One Voice with Pianoforte Accompaniment by
FRANZ SCHUBERT
Work 12.   Price, 1 Florin 30 Kreuzer, V.C.

THE SHEPHERD AND THE HORSEMAN
['Der Schäfer und der Reiter']
By Fr. B[aron] de la Motte Fouqué.

EULOGY OF TEARS
['Lob der Tränen']
by A. W. von Schlegel, and

THE ALPINE HUNTER
['Der Alpenjäger']
by J. Mayrhofer.

For One Voice with Pianoforte Accompaniment.

Set to Music by FRANZ SCHUBERT.

Work 13.   Price, . . . 1 Florin 30 Kreuzer, V.C.

SULEIKA and SECRETS
['Geheimes']
From Goethe's 'Westöstlicher Divan.'
For One Voice with Pianoforte Accompaniment.

Set to Music by FRANZ SCHUBERT.

Work 14.   Price, 2 Florins, V.C.

The public is herewith offered three books of the choicest songs by the ingenious composer who in so short a time has become a favourite with connoisseurs and amateurs. The songs from Goethe's 'Wilhelm Meister' have, it is true, been set several times, but rarely have they been interpreted with so much feeling, so truthfully and so appealingly. No less attractive are the other two books: Fouqué's and Mayrhofer's poems will surprise every hearer in this musical guise. But it is the songs from Goethe's 'Westöstlicher Divan' which are set in the most original spirit. Oriental passion is matched in them with such tenderness that they cannot fail to produce the greatest effect. These three books will thus be an ornament for every connoisseur's desk and cannot fail to receive the warmest sympathy, especially from the tender sex.

The following works by the same author are still to be had: [List of Opp. 1 to 11 in inverse order.]

According to Franz von Hartmann's recollections Schwind had drawn a vignette for Op. 14 ('Suleika') with a portrait of Anna Hönig, which was clearly not used. As, however, Anna Hönig does not appear in our circle until later, and Schwind wrote to Schober on 19th November 1823 that he had finished a 'Suleika,' his lost drawing appears to have been made after the publication of the book in question.

331. JOHANN NEPOMUK DANKESREITHER TO SCHUBERT

Sir,

You have done me a truly unmerited and quite exceptional honour in dedicating to me the twelfth work of your universally esteemed and popular musical art-products. Please receive my most cordial thanks for such a distinction and attention and for the copies of this excellent work sent to me with your kind dedicatory letter; together with the confession that I regard myself as being very much in your debt. I at once gave a copy to my secretary, Herr Giessriegl, and another to Professor Kastl, both of whom were highly delighted with them.

God, from whom all blessings flow, has invested you preferentially with so rare and exalted a musical talent that you may be sure of staking your happiness firmly on its further cultivation and application. In wishing you such lifelong felicity with all my heart, I remain most respectfully and gratefully

St. Pölten, 14th December   Your obedient servant
      1822.   Johann Nep., Bishop.

Karl Giessriegl was born in 1789 at Langenlebarn in Lower Austria. Johann Kastl, born in 1788 at Malsching in Bohemia, was professor of ecclesiastical history in the episcopal seminary of St. Pölten; he had in 1814 written a Latin poem to return thanks for a fortepiano presented to him by the Bishop of Kreutz in Croatia.

332. FROM THE PROGRAMME of the Fifth Evening Entertainment held by the Philharmonic Society, 19th December 1822, at the "Red Hedgehog."

4. 'Group in Tartarus,' Poem by Schiller, set to Music by Schubert, performed by Herr von Preisinger.

The "Red Hedgehog" ("Rote Igel") was a house in the Tuchlauben ("Unter den Tuchlauben," or briefly Tuchlauben, a street in the city), where the Philharmonic Society had at last found a permanent home in the autumn of 1822. The house backed on to the square called "Brandstätte" (so called after a fire there in 1276), and in it was a tavern of the same name which was later frequented by Brahms.

333. FROM A MANUSCRIPT REGISTER of Viennese Musicians,
End of 1822

Schubert, Fr. Composer—Spiegelgasse—Göttweigerhof next to
the Kochgasse, at Herr Schober's, merchant, No. 1089, 2nd floor.

Schubert had left his room at the Schobers' by this time (*see* No. 328).
The family remained there until the autumn of 1823. The house belonged to the Göttweig monastery, and was altered in 1828. The indication "next to the Kochgasse" is incomprehensible. Schober was not
a merchant at that time, but he may have called himself that, failing any
other profession.

334. [SCHUBERT'S REPUTED PETITION to the Vienna Philharmonic
Society to be Elected as a Performing Member in the
Capacity of Viola Player (?).   End of 1822]

This and the following document are suspect. Kreissle had the particulars from Gustav Nottebohm, but later on doubted them himself
(according to his private copy of his Schubert biography). Dahms
deduced from them that Schubert sought admission in order to get the
unfinished Symphony performed by the Philharmonic Society; but we may
be sure that such a possibility never occurred to him. Again, he had
been a member of the society since March 1822 (*see* the first note on
p. 214). The fact is that a regulation debarring professionals from
membership did exist, for Götz, Nestroy, Karoline Unger and (temporarily) Josefine Fröhlich left the society when they were engaged by
the Kärntnertor Theatre. But this may have been the rule only for
singers, and perhaps for instrumentalists who made a living with their
art, not for composers who, like Schubert, were not public performers.

335. [REPUTED REPLY from the Philharmonic Society to Schubert,
declining his application on the ground that according to
regulations only amateurs are admissible, not persons who
make a living by music.(?).   End of 1822]

336. PROKESCH'S MEMORANDUM [written some years later]
Schubert. Composer. Vienna, 1822

Introduced to at Pichler's house. Young man of great hopes
for music. There is something original, deeply appealing about

his songs, which explains the wide popularity they have found, as for instance the passage in 'Erl King,' "Wilt, tender boy, thou go with me?" &c. The cradle-spell that speaks from the melody, and yet at the same time the sinister note, which repels while the former entices, dramatize the poet's picture. I was much with Schubert, for although he is not cultivated, he is yet agreeable by reason of his frankness, his sane understanding and his enthusiasm. He sang most of his compositions to me. Many an evening did we spend in the most animated conversation at an ale-house near the Kärntnertor Theatre.

These notes, entitled 'Encounters and Relationships' ('Berührungen und Verhältnisse') were written by 1830 at the latest. In 1870 Prokesch wrote, in other notes, on Schubert: "Great music slumbered in him, but it never came to such an awakening as he himself dreamt of and listened to in his soul." On the question of Schubert's culture cf. No. 574.

337. FRIEDRICH VON SCHLEGEL to Ludwig Schnorr von Carolsfeld, Vienna, c. 1822–3

. . . Be sure you come to-night; but should it be your Schober and Schuber [sic] Tuesday to-day, then come earlier for preference; but in that case let me know the time by bearer.

Friedrich von Schlegel (born Hanover, 1772), like Zacharias Werner a convert from Protestantism to Catholicism, had lived in Vienna since 1808 as legation councillor. Bruchmann was in touch with him. Vogl esteemed his brother August (born 1767), another leader of literary romanticism and translator of Shakespeare, even more highly than Friedrich. Schwind came under the indirect influence of Friedrich as a pupil of Schnorr's. This letter is the only evidence of a loose connection between the Schubert and Schlegel circles. Nothing is known of a more intimate relationship of Schubert and Schober with Schnorr. The fact that the friends met at Schober's on Tuesdays is probably true only of the weekly Schubertiads (see No. 328).

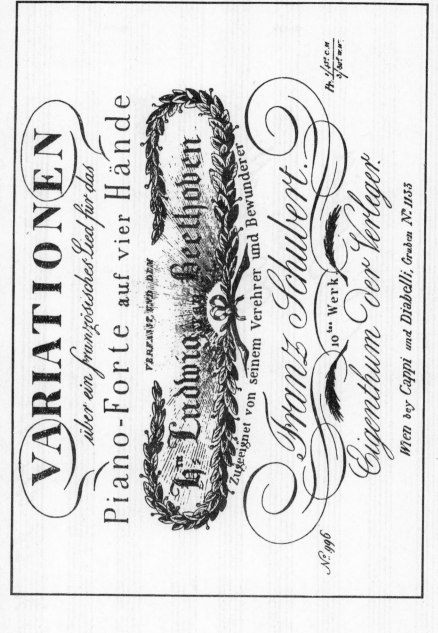

Variations for Pianoforte Duet, E minor, Op. 10 (1818), dedicated to Beethoven.
Title-page of the First Edition. See p. 221

The Unfinished Symphony (1822). Title-page of the Autograph

1823

Sonata in A minor for Pianoforte (x. 8), February.
Operetta, 'The Conspirators' ('Die Verschworenen'), later called
    'Domestic Warfare' ('Der häusliche Krieg') (1 act, Castelli) (xv. 6),
    April.
Opera, 'Fierabras' (3 acts, Josef Kupelwieser) (xv. 10), 23rd May–
    2nd October.
Song Cycle, 'The Fair Maid of the Mill' ('Die schöne Müllerin'), May–
    November.
Music for the Drama, 'Rosamond' ('Rosamunde') (4 acts, Helmina von
    Chézy) (xv. 8), late autumn.
Songs, 'Thou art repose' ('Du bist die Ruh'), 'The Dwarf' ('Der Zwerg'),
    'To be sung on the Water' ('Auf dem Wasser zu singen').

———

338. New Year's Eve 1823 in a Circle of Friends

The Ages dance, eternally encircled,
And hover in the round of changing years.
No sooner has the one from us departed,
Another, younger, in our midst appears.

Thus do we witness one about to vanish,
Who long companioned us with kindly thought.
A beaker she presents us, full of sweetness,
As her last sacred offering to us brought.

And so she leaves.—Yet let us with a question
Arrest her as she lightly turns to go:
"What were thy days?   What didst thou offer to us?
What wilt thou take from us?   What gift bestow?"

The goddess turns in silence as she passes,
A gentle smile upon her radiant face;
Confidingly she looks around our circle,
And from her lips pour forth these words of grace:

"You favoured ones of mine, why need you question?
Did I not all your path with roses strow?
Do your own hearts not tell you with assurance
What to my love and vigilance you owe?

"The fairest gifts I singly send and rarely
Into the world at a propitious time,
You found, united, ordered them together,
Tied as you were by friendship's bond sublime.

"The silent lips I knew how to unseal you,
How your emotions to awake to speech,
And how to lure a host of magic fancies
From cunning hands to you I sought to teach.

"Melodious strains I wakened in the singer:
Still are you moved this moment by their sounds; *
And the philosopher I taught to fathom
The spirit's life which in all things abounds.

"And not in yearning and afflicting anguish
Of dreaded loneliness did you create;
I filled your hearts with friendship's true devotion,
Your souls I taught how to appreciate.

"Then saw you noble forms of gentle beings,
With majesty and beauty richly crowned,
Bind wreaths and garlands for your richer glory,
To prove how greatly is your work renowned.

"Continue then in all your high endeavour:
I know, a mother were you giv'n in me!
My sister too may grant you newer favours;
If not—be steadfast, and remember me!"

So turned she, moved and loth to pain and shame us,
Removing step by step her lovely frame.
Twelve of them heard we, then apace she vanished,
And after her an utter silence came.

* Schubert had just sung a series of new songs.

258

Long may our gratitude to her be given
For all the favours she on us bestowed:
We thank her, as we thank so many true ones
To whom for love and trust so much we owed!

And should her Sister come from outer spaces
To look upon us, haply, with a frown,
Perhaps to cleave our circle without pity
And coldly what we builded to cast down,

Or should she rend in twain the happy union
By which the other held us in her thrall,
Compelling each in solitude to nourish
The deep affection that united all,

Then let us all remember the departed,
As she forsook us with consoling speech,
Let memories of her for long refresh us
And heal the grievous, the unwelcome breach;

So shall we still enjoy our constant friendship,
Again and yet again we 'll meet in joy,
And each shall of a happy past prove worthy
And strive that naught our union shall destroy.

                                        Franz von Schober.

The New Year celebration, held on the evening of the so-called St.
Sylvester's Day, is a widespread custom on the Continent. It takes the
form of merry conviviality and drinking, particularly at midnight, and
extends to the streets, where in Vienna the chimney-sweep, the sucking-
pig and a symbolic clover-leaf appear as mascots. Special church services
are held there on New Year's Eve, as on Christmas Eve.—Stanza 7 probably
refers to poets, i.e. Schober himself, as well as to painters, i.e. Schwind and
Kupelwieser.—Schober's footnote, added to the later printed version of the
poem, unless he erroneously thought of the 'Fair Maid of the Mill' cycle
(not written till [May–November] 1823), refers very likely to the four
Goethe songs composed in December 1822: 'The Muses' Son,' 'To the
Distant One,' 'By the River' and 'Hail and Farewell.'—The "philosopher"
may be Bruchmann, who in his confession to Senn, written in 1827, says:
"The following winter [1822–3], which brought with it a brilliant life

enhanced by music and poetry, quite bewitched me.''—Stanza 10 seems
to refer to the absent ladies of the circle, including for instance Bruchmann's sisters.　But the ''Sister'' in stanza 14 is, of course, the new year.

339. JOSEF HÜTTENBRENNER's FIRST ACCOUNT, early 1823

Expenses for Schubert, 1822

For the Opera, 'The Pleasaunce' ['Des Teufels Lustschloss']	90 fl.
	100 fl.
	———
Letter from Weber and Reply	1.10
Letter to Winter	.35
do. from Holbein	.25
Oct 7th paid	1.40
9th paid	.40
Binding of Opera Score	6.——
Written to Peters and Reply 18th Oct.	2.——
19th—Leopoldstadt Theatre	1.——
Oct. 21st	4.——
For Copying of Mass and Paper Nov. 14th lent	1.——
10th	5.——
10th	5.——
	———
	25 f. 30
Received of Diabelli	10 f.
	———
	15
Given on 3rd January	20 f.

Josef Hüttenbrenner at that time temporarily looked after Schubert's
modest cash.　This account is connected with that shown in No. 348,
which it partly overlaps.　It is reckoned in Viennese currency.　The first
two amounts are to be taken separately: 100 florins had been received by
Cappi & Diabelli for their commission on music-books and 90 florins were
the fee for the copying of the opera 'The Devil's Pleasaunce,' deducted by

the firm. The difference of 10 florins appears near the end of this account and the other. The first total is wrong (a florin was worth 60 kreuzer): it should be 28 florins 30 kreuzer. The second total is meant to be only approximate: it should be 18 florins 30 kreuzer. Schubert seems to have settled this debt with 20 florins, so that he should have had 1 florin 30 kreuzer to his credit.—For Weber's letter and the reply cf. No. 324, and for the letters to Winter and Holbein cf. No. 320.—The item of 1 florin 40 kreuzer, which also appears in the second account, is not specified, but that of 40 kreuzer is there, as having been lent to Schubert.—"Binding of opera score" seems to be the meaning of the obscure German *Opernverband*: this may mean "operatic association," which, however, would be meaningless; perhaps the score of 'Alfonso and Estrella' had been bound.—For the postage for the letters from and to Peters *see* No. 325.— The two expenditures of 18th and 19th August (for the performance of 'Aline') appear in the second account also.—The debt of 21st August there appears as 5 florins.—The costs of the paper for (4 florins 30 kreuzer) and the copying of (15 florins) the A flat major Mass appear only in the second account.—The debt of 14th November is shown in both.—The two items of the 10th may belong to October, November or December.—The whole seems to have been a memorandum for Hüttenbrenner's own use; the first account actually handed to Schubert was that of February 1823, although that too was found among Hüttenbrenner's remains.

340. From the Leipzig 'Literarisches Konversations-Blatt,' 18th January 1823

(Vienna correspondence, early 1823, concerning the musical entertainments at Ignaz von Mosel's.)

I found there, too, the Musical Director Schubert, a modest young man, whose songs are very original, among them Margaret's song at the distaff in Goethe's 'Faust,' which is particularly distinguished by originality.

64.

The title of Musical Director (*Kapellmeister*) is here quite arbitrarily given to Schubert, perhaps for the sake of politeness, which required some title or other.—Mosel, who lived at the Melkerhof, had married for his second wife the pianist Katharina Lembert (born Klosterneuburg, near Vienna, 1789), a pupil of Hummel's, who was also a composer and authoress; his daughter of the first marriage, Babette, whose later married name was Lagusius, sang.—The figure 64 is a cipher, used as a kind of pseudonym.

341. FROM THE PROGRAMME of the Eighth Evening Entertainment held by the Philharmonic Society, 9th January 1823

4. 'Spirit of Love' ['Geist der Liebe'], Vocal Quartet by Schubert, performed by Herren Barth, Tietze, [Johann] Leschetitzki and Kiesewetter.

The quartet, written in 1822 for the public Philharmonic concerts, was here repeated privately.—Johann Leschetitzky sang bass as a member of the society. So did Rafael Georg Kiesewetter von Weisenbrunn (born 1773 at Holleschau in Moravia), chairman of the Court War Council, vice-president of the Philharmonic Society and an amateur flautist. He also cultivated musical research and at his house in the Salzgries regularly gave performances of old music from 1816 until the 1840s. These amateur concerts were directed at the pianoforte, first by Hugo Worzischek, later by Jenger (both of them professional colleagues of Kiesewetter's) and lastly by Anna Fröhlich. (Her recollection, according to which the 'Erl King' was first submitted for subscription at Kiesewetter's, is incorrect.)

342. FROM THE OFFICIAL 'WIENER ZEITUNG,' 10th January 1823

At the House of Sauer & Leidesdorf,
I. & R. Privileged Art and Music Dealers in Vienna, Kärntnerstrasse, No. 941, are newly published:
New Dance Music
CARNIVAL 1823
A Collection of Original German Dances
for the Pianoforte.
In Two Books.
By
K. Czerny, Horzalka, Leidesdorf, Pamer, Payer,
Pensel, Pixis, Preisinger, Schoberlechner,
Stein, Schubert and Worzischek.
Book I .   .   .   .   . 2 Florins, V.C.
Book II .   .   .   .   . 2 Florins, V.C.

These waltzes will shortly appear arranged for pianoforte 4 hands and other instruments.

It had become the fashion, especially in Vienna, to issue as New Year gifts special collections of dances for the carnival as well as music-books of varied contents.   All these books have now become extremely rare, the reason being that dance music easily deteriorated in use.   (This is why Schubert's books of dances too have become rare in first editions, whereas his church music has done so on account of the small editions in which it was issued.)   This was the first of seventeen Viennese collective works in which Schubert was represented either by original contributions or by reprints.   Several of them have disappeared without a trace.— Karl Czerny, born in Vienna in 1791, is the well-known pianoforte teacher, the master of Liszt (who went to Vienna at the age of ten and also had a few lessons from Salieri in 1821–3) and composer of a thousand works, most of them published.—Johann Evangelist Horzalka, born in Moravia in 1798, settled in Vienna about 1810, set a poem by Mayrhofer to music in 1824 and after Schubert Grillparzer's 'Serenade' ('Ständchen'), was in touch, according to Schindler, with Vogl, Karl Pinterics and Frau Katharina Lászny-Buchwieser, played pianoforte duets with Schubert and in 1832 became *répétiteur* at the Theater an der Wien.—Michael Pamer, born 1782, was musical director at the "Swan" hall in the Rossau suburb and, as a dance composer, a precursor of Josef Lanner.—Hieronymus Payer, born at the Meidling suburb in 1787, was leader at the Theater an der Wien and the teacher of Leopoldine Blahetka.—Johann Pensel, born c. 1794, died before Schubert in 1828.—Johann Peter Pixis, born at Mannheim in 1788, was in Vienna for several years from 1820.—For Preisinger *see* No. 213, for Schoberlechner No. 290.—Karl Andreas Stein, born in Vienna, 1797, was a pianoforte maker and composer.— Johann Hugo Worzischek, born in 1791 at Wamberg in Bohemia, had been conveyancer in the Marine Department of the Court War Council since 1813; in 1823 he became second, in 1824 first court organist.—Schubert's contribution appeared in Book II: three German Dances (xii. 14).

343. FROM THE MINUTES of the Philharmonic Society

(Meeting of the Committee for the Society Concerts, 11th January 1823.)

Pieces to be performed: . . .
At the 5th Concert . . .

2. Vocal Quartet by Schubert.

It was a question of an additional concert to be given by the society during the season of 1822–3.   Nothing of Schubert's was performed. It is possible that the following letter is connected with the matter.

344. SCHUBERT TO LEOPOLD SONNLEITHNER (undated)

[Outside:]

Leopold von Sonnleithner, Esq.

[Inside:]

Dear Herr von Sonnleithner,

You know yourself how the later quartets were received: people have had enough of them. True, I might succeed in inventing some new form, but one may not count with certainty on anything of the kind. But as my future fate greatly concerns me after all, you, who take your share in this, as I flatter myself, will yourself admit that I must go forward cautiously, and that I cannot therefore by any means accept such an invitation, much as it honours me, unless your honoured Society should consider itself well served by the romance from the 'Magic Harp,' sung by Jäger, in which case I should remain contentedly

Your most devoted
Frz. Schubert.

It is, of course, a question of male-voice quartets, for none of Schubert's string quartets had so far been publicly performed. He became a fore-runner hardly to be equalled in the domain of the German male-voice quartet, as well as in that of the song. The 'Gondolier' ('Gondelfahrer') of 1824 might perhaps be regarded as a new type.—The romance from 'The Magic Harp' (*see* No. 183), in which Schimon had failed, had been put into shape for concert performance, and Jäger must have sung it with ease. It was of no significance in Vienna that this letter was addressed to Leopold *von* Sonnleithner, although he was not ennobled until 1828 (cf. No. 268). Jäger, by the way, left Vienna for Berlin as early as 1824 (until 1828).

345. SCHUBERT TO (?) JOSEF PEITL (undated)

[Outside:]

To the Hon. Herr Herr
von Bäutel
his
Own Hands.

[Inside:]

Most valued Herr von Bäutel,

Since I actually have nothing for full orchestra which I could send out into the world with a clear conscience, and there are so many pieces by great masters, as for instance Beethoven's Overture to 'Prometheus,' 'Egmont,' 'Coriolanus,' &c. &c. &c., I must very cordially ask your pardon for not being able to oblige you on this occasion, seeing that it would be much to my disadvantage to appear with a mediocre work.   Forgive me, therefore, for having accepted too rashly and unthinkingly.   Your most devoted

Frz. Schubert.

If, as we may suppose, Schubert's Mr. "Bäutel" is identical with his teacher, Peitl, of 1813–14 (see No. 65), the occasion was perhaps a pupils' concert at the training-school, for which Schubert had promised to furnish an orchestral piece.   He was evidently anxious not to supply any of the works written before 1820.   (The misspelling of the name, incidentally, would be explained by the tendency in Viennese dialect to pronounce "äu" very much like "ei.")—The overture to Heinrich von Collin's drama 'Coriolan' was represented to Schubert as being unconsciously quoted by him in the pianoforte accompaniment to his 'Trout' when he took that new song to the Seminary, whereupon he was only with difficulty dissuaded from tearing it up (Leopold Ebner's report).   This had doubtless something to do with the 52nd bar of the overture and the resemblance of the middle parts in both works, in a by no means uncommon passage.

346. From Anton Ziegler's Directory of Composers, Amateurs, Court, Chamber, Theatre and Church Musicians, &c., in Vienna; January 1823

PHILHARMONIC SOCIETY IN THE AUSTRIAN IMPERIAL STATE:
Performing Members:
Pianoforte—Herren: . . . Schubert, Franz, domiciled in the City, Spiegelgasse, Göttweigerhof. . . .
Viola—Herren: . . . Schubert, Franz, domiciled in the City, Spiegelgasse, in the Göttweigerhof.
COMPOSERS AND AUTHORS:
Schubert, Franz, [as above].
Cf. No. 260, note preceding No. 278 (also Nos. 334 and 335); concerning the address see No. 333.

347. FROM THE OFFICIAL 'WIENER ZEITUNG,' 5th February 1823

At the House of Cappi & Diabelli,
Art and Music Dealers, in the Graben, No. 1133,
are newly published and to be had:
WALTZES, COUNTRY DANCES AND ECOSSAISES
for the Pianoforte,
composed by FRANZ SCHUBERT.
Work 18.

Part I, 1 Florin 30 Kreuzer. Part II, 1 Florin 30 Kreuzer, V.C.
This most recent work by the ingenious tone-poet, who excels
eminently by originality and delightful ideas, will not fail to be an
agreeable novelty for his numerous admirers.

348. JOSEF HÜTTENBRENNER'S SECOND ACCOUNT, February 1823

Account for Schubert.

October 7th, '22	1 f. 40 kr.
9th Music Paper for the Mass	4.30
for Sandbichler I on a/c for copies	3.—
Schubert	—.40
Oct. 18th do.	2.—
19th do. do. Admission Leopoldstadt [Theatre]	1.—
21st do. cash	5.—
Nov. 4th. Sandbichler, costs of copying	5.—
14th do. Schubert, cash	1.—
19th	1.—
Feb. 5th. Master-Tailor Titze for additional demands	5.—
Cash in February	20.—
Paid the Copyist at Prince Schwarzenberg's for the Mass	15.—
	69 fl. 50 kr.
Received of Cappi & Diabelli	10 f.
Remainder	59 f. 50 kr.

Received thereof 1 gold ♯

Cf. No. 339. The first total is wrong once more: it should be 64 florins 50 kreuzer. The following items are new: the copying, probably of smaller works, done by Sandbichler (perhaps Florian Sandbichler, a student from the Tyrol, who later became a judge at Dornbirn), paid for on 9th August, together with the music-paper for the Mass, and on 4th September 1822; apart from the 4 or 5 florins on 21st August, another florin on 14th September and a further 20 florins in February 1823 for Schubert personally, who thus took back the sum paid by him on 3rd January; the outstanding balance of the tailor's bill on 5th February. Like the music-paper, the copying of the Mass is only now entered properly. (Schubert may have made the copyist's acquaintance through Barth.) The remainder paid by Cappi & Diabelli is again deducted from Hüttenbrenner's expenditure. If he received a gold ducat, i.e. the value of 4 florins 30 kreuzer, Schubert still owed him 55 florins 20 kreuzer, or rather 50 florins 20 kreuzer, for which he may have assigned him the autograph of the second version of 'The Devil's Pleasaunce.'

349. From the Programme of the Thirteenth Evening Entertainment held by the Philharmonic Society, 20th February 1823

2. 'Margaret at the Spinning-Wheel,' poem by Goethe, set to music by Schubert, sung by Fräulein von Linhart.

350. Schubert to Anton Diabelli

[Outside:]

To the Hon.
Herr von Diabelli.

[Inside:]

Vienna, 21st February 1823.

Herr von Diabelli,

Herewith I am sending you the Quartet together with the pianoforte accompaniment.

The appearance of the two books of waltzes, &c., seemed to me somewhat strange, for it was not carried out quite according to arrangements. An adequate remuneration seems to be only indicated.

Furthermore I should like to ask you kindly to let me see the account for the last three books, for I intend to draw my balance

and will let you have them, if you wish, for your own property
for 300 florins, V.C.

I should also like to ask you for a few more copies of the Fantasy.

Franz Schubert.

Diabelli was the real head of the firm of Cappi & Diabelli.—The quartet
was 'Enjoyment of Nature' ('Naturgenuss') of May 1816, published as
Op. 16 in the autumn of 1823, together with 'Spring Song' ('Frühlingsgesang'). The accompaniment was newly added for the purpose,
probably at the publishers' request. Although the four male-voice
quartets, Op. 17, appeared at the same time without accompaniment, and
both came out after Op. 18, it may have been the question of the accompaniments which delayed the appearance of both books.—The two books
of waltzes were Op. 18, 'Waltzes, Country Dances and Écossaises.' What
was the cause of Schubert's dissatisfaction cannot be discovered, but it
seems to have been something touching his material interests, since he
expected to receive compensation. It seems likely that the Écossaises
ought to have been published separately in a third book.—The last three
books (after the "Wanderer" Fantasy) were three sets of songs, Opp.
12–14, which, like Opp. 1–7, were published as author's property.
Schubert had probably already sold his rights in these first books to the publishers, and was now on the point of resigning these later ones too, that is to
say, of selling plates, stocks and rights of publication outright for a lump
sum. He is said to have received 800 florins, V.C., for Opp. 1–7, and was
now asking 300 florins for Opp. 12–14, a price to which, however, he
seems to have been beaten down, which may be the reason for the temporary breach between Schubert and Cappi & Diabelli. Leopold Sonnleithner was by no means in favour of this transaction. Schubert had withdrawn from his surveillance, although it had brought him in some 1,000
florins for those ten books, that is, together with the settlement of about
1,000 florins, on the average 200 florins, V.C., for each opus, which was
most advantageous, and would probably have become even more so had
Schubert been willing or able to wait. It is possible, of course, that the
publishers' account did not meet with his approval, that he had no confidence in it and did not wish to be vexed by it any longer.—The delayed
song-book, Op. 8, for which Esterházy may have paid him, the two double
numbers of dance-books, Opp. 9 and 18, the pianoforte Variations,
Op. 10, and the three male-voice quartets, Op. 11, had already appeared
as the publishers' normal property. So later on did the deferred quartets,
Opp. 16 and 17, as well as the Goethe book, Op. 19, which did not come
out until 1825. All these were bought by Cappi & Diabelli, but there
was a pause in Schubert's relations with this firm.

351. From the Official 'Wiener Zeitung,' 24th February 1823

At the House of Cappi & Diabelli,
Art and Music Dealers, in the Graben, No. 1133,
is newly published and to be had:
Fantaisie pour le Pianoforte,
composée et dédiée
à Monsieur Em. Noble de Liebenberg de Zittin
par
François Schubert.
Œuvre 15.   Price, 4 Florins, V.C.

The fantasy has always been recognized as that kind of musical
piece in which the composer's art, freed from the shackles of
form, may most clearly unfold itself and wholly prove its worth.
Herr Schubert has certified his master-hand in this latest work, in
which he has shown that he not only possesses the gift of invention,
but understands how to develop his felicitous themes according
to all the exigencies of art.   The present Fantasy stands worthily
side by side with similar works by the foremost masters and therefore merits in every way the attention of all artists and lovers
of art.

This opus, too, was published with some delay.   Schubert had received
his author's copies a few days earlier, but evidently no more than twelve,
instead of the promised twenty.

352. Schubert to Mosel

[Envelope:]
            To the
                Hon. Aulic Councillor,
                Edler von Mosel
                    in
                        Vienna
                    to be delivered
                        at the Melkerhof.
269

[Inside:]

Sir,

Kindly forgive me if I am compelled to incommode you with another letter so soon, the circumstances of my health still forbidding me to leave the house.

I now have the honour of sending you, Sir, the third and last act of my opera together with the overture to the first act, with the request that you will be so good as to let me know your valued opinion of them.   Should I not be so fortunate by that time as to have been able to visit your Honour in person, I would only ask that you will very kindly let me know when I may send for your highly esteemed verdict, together with the whole opera.   If I might, perhaps, Sir, remind you of your kind promise to accompany it with a benevolent letter to Weber, I would even venture to ask, if your Honour will not resent this, to be good enough to add to my opera a similar letter to Freiherr von Könneritz, who according to Weber is in charge of the directorship of the Dresden theatre, and to send it to me.

And now, since I have importuned your Honour with so many requests already, I humbly and in God's name add a last one: whether you would be so kind, Sir, as to let me in the meantime have the libretto intended for my humble self, which I assure you most solemnly will be faithfully guarded by me and not allowed to be seen by any one.

With the greatest respect, I am,

Your Honour's

Most humble servant

Vienna, 28th February 1823.   Franz Schubert.

A letter from Schubert to Mosel, written somewhat earlier, seems to have been lost.—We here for the first time learn something of an illness, which seems to have attacked Schubert already at New Year.—The opera is 'Alfonso and Estrella,' the copy of which he sent to Mosel for perusal. For his letter to Weber *see* No. 324.—Hans Wilhelm Traugott von Könneritz, born 1753, was intendant of the Royal Opera at Dresden.— Mosel had himself written music, including the opera 'Cyrus and Astyages' to a libretto by Matthäus von Collin (1818) based on Metastasio; but he was also a dramatist.   It looks as though Schubert was interested in one of his libretti, or professed to be so.

353. FROM THE PROGRAMME of the Fifteenth Evening Entertainment held by the Philharmonic Society, 6th March 1823
(Conductor, Herr [Johann] von Schmiedel)

2. 'The Overblown Lime-Tree' ['Die abgeblühte Linde'] (Song
by Schubert), performed by Herr Ruess.

Johann Baptist Schmiedel, born in Vienna in 1790, a junior in the
court chamber, was a bass and a pianoforte player, a former pupil of
Ruzicka's, member of the Philharmonic Society's committee and conductor of its concerts, later choirmaster at the court church of St. Augustine.   At Pettenkoffer's he had conducted Handel's 'Alexander's Feast'
('Timotheus'), among other works.—Schubert's song had been inserted
in place of a duet by Spontini.—On Ruess see Nos. 216 and 311.

'Urge into the Distance' ('Drang in die Ferne'), Op. 71 (xx. 424),
appears in the 'Wiener Zeitschrift,' 25th March 1823.

354. ANTON DOBLHOFF TO SCHOBER

[? Hajan near Brno, ? Spring 1823.]

We have the vilest weather—rain, snow-drifts, the roughest of
north winds—and we are in the country!—How could I more
effectively defy all this blustering than by taking my bit of imagination in hand and transferring myself nicely and pleasantly to the
Wasserburg and my dearly loved friends? For was it not then
cold winter too?   Yet in that small room my heart always opened
so warmly, nay glowingly and bloomingly, so that now I want to
be with you again for good and not part with you until the sun
shines sweetly and lures me into the pine forest.—Josef, a black
coffee and a long Turkish pipe! And to-day there will be no
chess-playing, my dearest Schober, to-day we are too cosy together.—It will all be decided by now, dear Bertel: the fair
Estrella will doubtless soon reward our patiently endured expectation— . . . —but you are all so chary of words, so mono-
syllabic; indeed you don't say anything—alas! you are not here at
all, and unhappily all this is a dream—but was it not a fair one, and
have I not so often lived it in reality? And is not reality that is
overpast fulfilled only in renunciation and made glorious by

remembrance?   Therefore will I even now be content and blessed. —I have a full library at my disposal and there is a resonant voice that knows how to sing Schubert's inspiringly melodious tunes.

Anton, Freiherr von Doblhoff, born in 1800, once Senn's pupil, was the betrothed of Jeannette Cuny de Pierron. He had been suspected by the police since 1820, but later became a statesman and was Austrian minister several times. He was also a writer on agriculture.—The property of Hajan in Moravia, south-west of Brno, had until 1810 belonged to Leopold von Smetana, Rudolf's father, and had remained in the family's possession. Doblhoff stayed there at this time.—The "Wasserburg" is Wasserburger's café. Josef was the name of a waiter there.—Bertel is an earlier nickname given to Schubert, made from the second half of his surname.—Estrella is, of course, the opera.

Farewell party for Franz von Bruchmann, 8th April 1823 (cf. No. 361).

355. From the Official 'Wiener Zeitung,' 10th April 1823

At the House of Sauer & Leidesdorf,
I. & R. Privileged Dealers in Art and Alabaster and Music Publishers in Vienna, Kärntnerstrasse, No. 941, have just been published:

THREE SONGS

('Greetings to Thee'—'Faith in Spring'—'The Linnet's Wooing')
['Sei mir gegrüsst'—'Frühlingsglaube'—'Hänflings Liebeswerbung']
for One Voice with Pianoforte Accompaniment, by

FRANZ SCHUBERT

Work 20. . . . 1 Florin 30 Kreuzer, V.C.
The same Songs with Guitar Accompaniment,
1 Florin 15 Kreuzer, V.C.

This opus is dedicated to Frau von Bruchmann. It was the first not published by Cappi & Diabelli.

356. Schubert to Cappi & Diabelli

Sirs,

Your letter was a surprise indeed, since according to Herr von Cappi's own statement the account appeared to me to be settled altogether. Having by no means discovered the most honest intentions in my publishers' earlier transactions on the occasion of

the issue of the waltzes, I was well able to understand this second
procedure, from which, gentlemen, you will easily explain to
yourselves my reasons for entering into a permanent arrangement
with another art dealer.   What I do not quite understand, by the
way, is your indication of a debt of 150 florins, V.C., since according to your statement the copying of the opera amounted to only
100 [florins], V.C.   Be that as it may, however, it seems to me
that the exceedingly small sale [price] of my earlier things, as well
as that of the Fantasy at 50 florins, V.C., should have long ago
liquidated a debt unjustly charged to me.   But as I doubt very
much whether you take this all-too-human view, I take the liberty
of drawing your attention to the fact that I am still entitled to
demand 20 copies of the later and 12 of the earlier books, and may
even more justifiably ask for the 50 florins of which you managed
to deprive me in such a subtle manner.   If you will kindly add
all this up, you will find that my demand is not only the greater,
but also the more just, although I should nevertheless have refrained from making it had you not so disagreeably reminded me
of it.   The debt having long been settled in this way, as you will
please acknowledge, there can be no question whatever of any
publication of songs, which once again you could not estimate
cheaply enough, for I am now in a position to obtain 200 florins,
V.C., per book, and Herr von Steiner has repeatedly conveyed to
me an offer to publish my works.   In conclusion I have still to
request you to be good enough to send me all my manuscripts, of
the engraved as well as the unengraved works.

Respectfully,

Frz. Schubert
Composer.

10th April 1823.

N.B. I request an exact account of copies delivered to me since
our first agreement of sale, as I find that my statement greatly
exceeds yours.

[Receipt:]

Received MSS of 1 Sonata, 2 books of songs and 2 songs on one
single sheet, returned.

Jos. Hüttenbrenner.

This cutting letter followed the still reticent No. 350. The song-book had, in the meantime, been published by Sauer & Leidesdorf (*see* No. 355). —Schubert had clearly gone to see the publishers on receipt of their reply to No. 350 and, in Diabelli's absence, had arrived at a new arrangement with Peter Cappi, which was then revoked by another letter. He had, of course, already come to terms with the other firm before this disappointment, which must have been one of the grievances voiced in Cappi & Diabelli's second letter. The costs of copying, of which Schubert learnt only now, would not have been excessive for 'Alfonso and Estrella,' the publishers having charged 90 florins for that of 'The Devil's Pleasaunce.' The "earlier things" may be Opp. 1–7 and 12–14, now sold for a lump sum. The Fantasy is, needless to say, the "Wanderer," and the 50 florins are the sum paid outright for it. The "earlier books," of which Schubert had not even received the twelve author's copies agreed upon, were probably Opp. 8–11 and 18. The 50 florins of which he was "deprived" are possibly the difference between Schubert's demand of 300 florins for the liquidation of Opp. 12–14 and a smaller sum of some 250 florins paid him instead. Without the publishers' lost letter it is impossible to establish Schubert's calculation exactly.—If Schubert was now to receive a fixed fee of 200 florins for each book of songs, he had undertaken to supply six books a year (*see* No. 322), or if the sum of 1,200 florins mentioned by Josef Hüttenbrenner referred to two years, at the rate of three books each.—Siegmund Anton Steiner, born 1773, was the proprietor of the house of Steiner & Co., shared by Tobias Haslinger since 1810. Nothing else is known of any offer made to Schubert by this firm at that time.—The "first agreement of sale" probably refers to the assignment of Opp. 1–7.—The confirmation at the end is written by Josef Hüttenbrenner, who must have visited the firm after their reply to collect the manuscripts. He did not receive them all (*see* note to No. 576). The Sonata may have been that in A minor of February 1823, which after all appeared at Diabelli's, though not till 1839, as Op. posth. 143. The two books of songs and the separate sheet were doubtless works already published.

357. Proposal made by Johann Baptist Jenger at a Committee Meeting of the Styrian Musical Society, 10th April 1823

With reference to § 9 of the Statutes I take the liberty of proposing the composer, Herr Franz Schubert of Vienna, for admittance as a non - resident honorary member, the said composer, although still young, having already proved by his compositions that he will one day take a high rank as tone-poet, and be sure to show gratitude to the Styrian Musical Society for having first made him an honorary member of a not unimportant association.

This was the first of the few honours offered to Schubert in his life-time. Although his fame had certainly penetrated beyond the confines of Vienna, it was due mainly to personal friends.—Paragraph 9 of the Statutes of 1821, of which Schubert received a copy, together with the Diploma of Honour (No. 359), reads thus: ". . . superior musical artists at home and abroad may be proposed by any member of the com-mittee as honorary members *in absentia* . . . they are expected to do their best to further the Society's welfare, even at a distance." The society, founded in 1815, had among others elected Mosel, Diabelli, Moscheles and Lannoy as such members in 1820 and Beethoven, Salieri, Mayseder and Hellmesberger in 1821. The same honour was accorded to Professor Schneller, Castelli and Jaëll at the same time as to Schubert, and later also to Haslinger, Kiesewetter, Abbé Stadler, Josef Sonnleithner, Jäger and Eybler. Anselm Hüttenbrenner and Jenger probably became only "participating honorary members," whose diploma differed from that of the "extraneous" ones in its wording and appearance.

358. THE COMMITTEE of the Styrian Musical Society to Schubert, Middle of April 1823

Sir,

The services you have so far rendered to the art of music are too well known for the Committee of the Styrian Musical Society to have remained unaware of them. The latter, being desirous of offering you a proof of their esteem, have elected you as a non-resident honorary member of the Styrian Musical Society. A diploma to that effect as well as a copy of the Society's Statutes is enclosed herewith.

On behalf of the Committee:
Kalchberg. Jenger.

Johann Nepomuk, Ritter von Kalchberg, born in 1765 at Pichl in Styria, was county deputy a representative of the society, and a poet and historian.

359. SCHUBERT'S DIPLOMA OF HONOUR from the Styrian Musical Society

The Musical Society in Styria, most graciously sanctioned by His I. & R. Majesty,
which endeavours to attain to the goal of moral improvement and religious elevation of the mind in our Fatherland, through the development and perfection of the art of music by way of the flowery path of spiritual recreation, has the honour of apprising you, Franz Schubert, Esq., by the present diploma of your nomination as a non-resident honorary member, in full recognition of your already generally acknowledged merits as a musical artist and composer.

Graz, 6th April 1823.

Ignaz, Count of Attems,
     President.

                  Johann, Knight of Kalchberg,
                       Chairman.

                             Johann Baptist Jenger,
                                 Secretary.

The diploma, which has been preserved by descendants of the Schubert family, resembles that presented to Beethoven on 1st January 1822 (Vienna City Library). The differences in the wording are as follows:

Beethoven:	Schubert:
Euer Hochwohlgeboren	*Euer Wohlgeboren*
. . . to do honour to the high merits of the greatest composer of this present century. . . .	. . . fully honouring your already generally acknowledged merits as tone-poet and composer. . . .

At the beginning the phrasing in Beethoven's case contains a reference to the society's "exalted goal," but in Schubert's only to its "goal"; but this was an error, for the lithographed forms for members and participating honorary members also have "exalted goal." The diplomas bear a vignette on the left with the names of Ossian and Homer, and on the right one with those of Haydn and Mozart. A wafer shows the society's seal with the motto "UT RElevat MIserum FAtum SOLitosque LAbores."—Ignaz Maria, Count Attems (born 1774), was governor of Styria.—If the other two documents (Nos. 357 and 358) are correctly dated in the society's history, this diploma must have been ready before the committee meeting, whose resolution was in that case a mere formality. The diploma was delivered to Schubert through Anselm Hüttenbrenner (Graz) and his brother Josef (Vienna).

360. From the Vienna 'Allgemeine Musikalische Zeitung,' 30th April 1823

FANTASY BY FR. SCHUBERT, OP. 15. CAPPI & DIABELLI. A fantasy is a musical piece in which a composer may allow perfectly free deployment to the wings of his imagination, unite the most curious forms into the greatest possible unity, and thus present our minds with a picture capable of engaging our powers of emotion in the most interesting manner by means of vivacity of colour, shape and arrangement as well as variety organized into a satisfactory whole.

This is by no means to say that he may neglect all the laws of musical art and perhaps create for himself a norm of what is eternal, fixed and necessary in art—beauty. It means rather that he is left far freer of restraint by the contrasts which differentiate various species of style, and that he is at liberty, indeed even enjoined, to unfold the spell of an individual and diversified world within the narrow frame of his picture.

A fantasy is thus a piece of music where an abundance of musical inventiveness is not subject to any such constraint of form and may, as it were, meander through the most delightful fields of musical art like a stream running in all directions and in any ramifications, freed of all obstructions.

Such a piece of music may for that reason be best suited to a faithful reception and reproduction of the feelings which inspired the composer at the time of its creation; nay, it may properly be regarded as a mirror of his soul. Seeing that a composer like Herr Schubert, who had already betrayed such profound sentiments in his generally esteemed songs, presents us with a soul-image of this kind, the musical world can only rejoice.

The Fantasy announced above begins *allegro con fuoco*. The introduction is a short, simple movement, which serves as a basis for the whole composition and, almost teasing, disappears and unexpectedly reappears by turns, always surprisingly, only to be replaced by an *adagio* at last, where the author comes forward with lovely melodies and besides offers the pianoforte player the opportunity of proving his agility in the most brilliant manner, both here and in the succeeding *presto* in 3–4 time.

The texture is fairly pure; but it may be permitted to offer the esteemed author the observation that he has really gone too far here and there in the matter of chord progressions, all of which may not be found tolerable by every ear. This may be seen, for example, at the very beginning, in the second stave, bars 2 and 4, a passage which is repeated later on; just as the continuous striking of A on page 6, staves 2–3, is not based on harmonic principles and might very properly be replaced by other notes, as for instance the minim A in the last bar of the second stave, where G might do, since it would indicate an appropriate chord of the sixth, and so on; for the whole of this passage is by no means to be explained as a *tasto solo* or a pedal-point.

In conclusion it must be said that some mistakes have presumably obtruded in the course of the engraving: witness, among several others, no doubt, the last note in the right hand on that page 6 mentioned above, stave 2, bar 2.

The most glaring engraver's mistakes in the first edition are mentioned in the editor's report of the complete edition. The first of them, however, revealed itself as Schubert's own version. The original manuscript, now in America, was not accessible until after the reprint in the complete edition.—This notice may be by the editor of the periodical, Kanne.

361. BRUCHMANN TO SCHOBER

30th April 1823.

. . . These leave me together with a letter to my mother, requesting her to reserve you and Schubert for a month a few rooms in the Caprice, on the terms discussed . . . Is there to be a Schubertiad in the Caprice on 13th May?

Bruchmann was on his way from Styria to Upper Austria. The "Caprice" (*Mutwille*) was a solidly built summer-house on the country estate of Hütteldorf, repeatedly occupied by the Bruchmanns during the summers of 1819–23. It appears in several illustrations. The Bruch-manns rented it from Prince Karl Paar, in whose English park it was situated. It had a single floor with five prettily furnished rooms, one of which had a wall-screen reflecting the beautiful surrounding landscape by means of a periscope in the roof. Hütteldorf (*see* No. 289) was a village to the west of Vienna and the park still exists in the Rosental (now 15 Dehnegasse); not so the "Caprice," however. Whether Schubert and Schober took the opportunity of staying there before the Bruchmanns occupied it for the summer and, if so, whether they gave a party there on 13th May, is not known. (The 11th was the birthday and the 12th the day of baptism of Sybille von Bruchmann, who had died there in 1820.)

362. POEM BY SCHUBERT

MY PRAYER

With a holy zeal I yearn
Life in fairer worlds to learn;
   Would this gloomy earth might seem
   Filled with love's almighty dream.

Sorrow's child, almighty Lord,
Grant Thy bounty for reward.
   For redemption from above
   Send a ray of endless love.

See, abased in dust and mire,
Scorched by agonizing fire,
   I in torture go my way,
   Nearing doom's destructive day.

Take my life, my flesh and blood,
Plunge it all in Lethe's flood,
   To a purer, stronger state
   Deign me, Great One, to translate.

8th May 1823.   Frz. Schubert.

This poem may have been written under the influence of the illness that had befallen Schubert (*see* later, *passim*).—No credence can be given to Ludwig Stark's (born Munich, 1831) assertion that Schubert wrote it (or copied it) on 2nd July 1825 on the Kranabeth-Sattel near Ebensee in Upper Austria for an unnamed great-uncle of Stark's at Traunkirchen.

It is true that Schubert was somewhere near the Höllengebirge about that time, but nothing is known of a visit to that particular spot; moreover, he was then in a very different mood from that of 1823, and had doubtless long forgotten the poem. Stark, by the way, supplied music for the three songs in the 'Fair Maid of the Mill' cycle which Schubert did not set, and he also completed the master's unfinished pianoforte Sonata in C major (published as 'Reliquie' in 1861).

363. FROM THE OFFICIAL 'WIENER ZEITUNG,' 27th May 1823

At the I. & R. Privileged Art, Alabaster and Music Establishment
of Sauer & Leidesdorf in Vienna,
Kärntnerstrasse, No. 941,
are newly arrived and to be had:

. . . . . .

THE DWARF and MELANCHOLY.
['Der Zwerg']   ['Wehmut']
Two Poems by Matthäus, Edler von Collin.
Set to Music
for One Voice with Pianoforte Accompaniment
by
FRANZ SCHUBERT
Opus 22.   1 Florin 30 Kreuzer, V.C.
The same with Guitar Accompaniment are in the press.

This opus is dedicated to the poet. The first issue, with the wrong publisher's number 337, contains several mistakes, and numerous expression marks are missing. The second issue of the first edition, numbered 357, has additional markings.

364. ANTON VON SPAUN TO SCHOBER

[Linz,] 4th June 1823.

We have recently heard Vogl sing several Schubert songs at St. Florian, among others 'The Dwarf' ['Der Zwerg'], 'Old Man's Song' ['Gesang des Greisen'='Greisengesang'], 'Night and Dreams' ['Nacht und Träume'], &c., which are truly divine songs. A comic scene occurred with tall Huber on that occasion. The bass Linder here was a schoolfellow of Vogl's and burned with desire to see him again for the first time after 36 years. But by mistake he got Huber instead of Vogl by the neck and, in spite of resistance, pressed him so vehemently to his breast that he [Huber] had hardly enough breath left to protest.—Now, while Linder kept on asking whether he no longer recognized his old school-friend after a separation of 36 years, and Huber insisted that he must be making a mistake, Vogl intervened and solved the riddle; however, it is not difficult to imagine that neither Huber nor Vogl felt flattered by this blunder.

St. Florian is an Augustinian abbey to the south-east of Linz, founded in the Middle Ages, well known in connection with Anton Bruckner, who is buried in the crypt. It has a famous organ. The Spaun brothers were always welcome there and often stayed with the prelate, at that time Michael von Arneth (born 1771), who had not long been appointed.— "Tall Huber" is Josef Huber once more. Franz Xaver Linder, a retired estate manager, was a member of the Linz Musical Society's committee.

365. From the Official 'Grazer Zeitung,' 7th June 1823

It looks as though the art of music were now gaining a firm foothold in our county-town. Apart from the Musical Society, which takes the keenest interest in its prosperity, smaller musical circles are forming, whose endeavour it is to practise classical works. To be heard there are . . . male-voice quartets by Schubert . . .

Anselm Hüttenbrenner.

This notice appeared in the literary supplement of the official journal known as 'Der Aufmerksame,' and was reprinted on 2nd July 1823 in the Vienna 'Allgemeine musikalische Zeitung.'

Bishop Dankesreither dies at St. Pölten on 10th June 1823.

366. From the Vienna 'Allgemeine Musikalische Zeitung,' 11th June 1823

(In a notice of six songs by Johann Spech.)

. . . True, there are poems which, owing to their awe-inspiring depths and their mystic, profound significance, must be intentionally treated in such a way by the composer that their melody appears abrupt and square-cut rather than pliant, and many a noble work has been given us as an example of this in the songs by the inspired Schubert.

Spech, born at Pressburg in 1768, had been living as music-teacher in Vienna for several years, and he published numerous books of songs. —This notice too may have been by Kanne (*see* No. 360).

367. FROM THE OFFICIAL 'WIENER ZEITUNG,' 19th June 1823

At the I. & R. Privileged Art, Alabaster and Music Establishment
of Sauer & Leidesdorf
in Vienna, Kärntnerstrasse, No. 941, have just appeared:

ON THE DANUBE   THE BOATMAN
['Auf der Donau']   ['Der Schiffer']
ULFRU FISHING
['Wie Ulfru fischt']
Poems by J. Mayrhofer.
Set to Music for a Bass Voice, with Pianoforte Accompaniment
by
FRANZ SCHUBERT

Work 21.   Price, 1 Florin 30 Kreuzer, V.C.

Fr. Schubert, 'The Dwarf' and 'Melancholy'; set to music for one voice with pianoforte accompaniment.   Price, 1 Fl. 30 Kr.

These two books will shortly appear with guitar accompaniment.

This opus again appeared out of order, possibly because once more the permit for the dedication could not be obtained in good time; for the work is dedicated to the poet, who was on holiday.

368. ANTON VON SPAUN TO SCHOBER

[Linz,] July 1823.

Is Mayrhofer in Upper Austria; are Schubert and Kupelwieser or Schwind coming?

Mayrhofer was probably staying with Josef Huber in Upper Austria, having first been to Steyr. He arrived at Linz on 25th July. Schubert followed later.

369. TITLE-PAGE OF THE MANUSCRIPT LIBRETTO of 'Fierabras'

Presented: Vienna, 22nd July 1823.

Letocha mp.

I. & R. High Police Commissioner,

acting as

Commissioner of Theatrical Censorship.

FIERABRAS

Heroico-Comic Opera in Three Acts,

1823.

For the I. & R. Court Theatre next to the Kärntnertor.

Vienna, 21st July 1823.   J. Kupelwieser.

[at the end:]

The performance is sanctioned *om. del.*

From the I. & R. Police-Court Office.

Vienna, 19th August 1823.

Zettler mp.

The libretto, said to have been commissioned by Barbaja, was by Josef Kupelwieser, who was secretary to the Kärntnertor Theatre in 1821–3. Its subject is a mixture of the old French romance 'Fierabras' and the German legend of 'Eginhard and Emma.' The title is usually spelt with two r's, but the Spanish word is *fierabras*, which means boaster or swaggerer. Schubert had already begun the composition at the end of May, and he had finished more than half the work before the censorship passed the libretto for the Court Opera. The manuscript libretto, which was preserved by descendants of the Schubert family and bears the number 179 of the Court Opera Library, was submitted to the censorship by the poet in his capacity of theatre secretary, received there by Philipp Letocha, the chief commissary of police for the Carinthian quarter (the city was divided into quarters, and his was near the Carinthian Gate [*Kärntnertor*]), and in due course dealt with by the court conveyancer, Alois Zettler, who later became court secretary to the police and censorship. Zettler, born in 1778 at Brüx in Bohemia, had settled in Vienna in 1799 and was himself a poet. His poems were published posthumously in 1836 by Christoph Kuffner. Schubert himself had set a 'Drinking-Song' ('Trinklied') of his in 1815. The formula *om. del.* (*omissis deletis*) indicates that the passages deleted by the censorship are to be omitted in performance. In the list of *dramatis personae*, under the name of Boland, Prince of the Moors, this character's second appellation of "Hispanic Admiral" was removed, and in Act II. Scene ix, in Roland's sentence, "*Confidingly* amid these knights, *the king's and realm's exalted kinsmen*, I come to you to bid you peace," the words in italics were objected to, and it was later replaced by "Us sendeth Charles, my lord, king of the Franks, to offer unity and peace unto you." Thus it was not religion this time, but politics which swayed the censor.—Grillparzer once wrote in Beethoven's conversation book: "Musicians, after all, cannot be affected by the censorship; if only they knew what you think when you write your music!" Soon afterwards he wrote in Moscheles's album a poem on the freedom of music, one verse of which runs thus in Walter Scott's translation:

> But music speaks a loftier tone
> To tyrant and to spy unknown,
> And free as angels walk with men
> Can pass unscathed the gaoler's ken.

370. BRUCHMANN TO SCHOBER

[Hütteldorf, ? July 1823.]

If you wish to bring Schubert out here before his departure, I shall approach my father to fix the day.

The Bruchmanns were again at Hütteldorf during the summer. Franz had returned from his small journey at the end of June.

371. LEOPOLD KUPELWIESER TO SCHOBER

[Baden, near Vienna, 26th July.]
St. Anne's Day 1823.

At Collin's I heard yesterday that Schubert is ill; they say Bradesky brought the news.

Collin is Matthäus von Collin.—Bradesky is probably identical with the Steyr ironmaster Brandetzky, who lived in Vienna and is described as a sharp-tongued wag. His name also appears as Brandeysky, Steyr merchant.—Schwind had been on a visit to Sophie von Schober at Baden at the end of June.

> Josef von Spaun and Albert Stadler introduce Schubert and Vogl at Friedrich Ludwig von Hartmann's at Linz, in the afternoon, where they perform several Schubert songs for the enthusiastic family, 28th July 1823.
> Schubert may have travelled to Upper Austria about 25th July, probably direct to Linz, where he met Vogl.—Friedrich Ludwig von

Hartmann (born 1773 at Ulm in Württemberg) was on the board of the Upper Austrian County Council. His wife was Maria Anna, born 1779. Their children were Anna, born 1800; Fritz, born 1805; Franz, born at Würzburg in 1808; Ludwig, born 1810; and Therese, born 1812. (The elder Hartmann possessed the manuscript of Mozart's earliest work, Köchel No. 1.)

Schubert, Vogl and Josef von Spaun visit the von Hartmann family and go with them to the Castle Inn garden in the evening, 30th July 1823.

372. FROM THE OFFICIAL 'WIENER ZEITUNG,' 4th August 1823

At the I. & R. Art, Alabaster and Music Establishment
of Sauer and Leidesdorf

In Vienna, Kärntnerstrasse, No. 941, are newly published:

LOVE HATH LIED	SELIGE WELT
['Die Liebe hat gelogen']	['Blessed World']
SWAN SONG	THE TREASURE HUNTER'S DESIRE
['Schwanengesang']	['Schatzgräbers Begehr']

Four Poems.

Set to Music for One Voice with Pianoforte Accompaniment
by
FRANZ SCHUBERT.
Work 23. Price, 1 Florin 30 Kreuzer, V.C.

THE DWARF and MELANCHOLY
Two Poems.

Set to Music for One Voice with Pianoforte Accompaniment
by
FRANZ SCHUBERT.
Work 22. Price, 1 Florin 30 Kreuzer, V.C.

.　.　.　.　.　.

The same with Guitar Accompaniment, 1 Fl. 15 Kr., V.C.
(To be continued.)

Op. 23, like the earlier books of dances, Opp. 9 and 18, appeared without any dedication.

373. From the Leipzig 'Zeitung für die Elegante Welt,' 6th September 1823

(Vienna correspondence concerning the serenade on the bastion given by the German opera company in honour of Domenico Barbaja's name-day, 4th August 1823.)

. . . But it was Schubert's 'Nightingale' that pleased most.

374. Schubert to Schober

Steyr, 14th August 1823.

Dear Schober,

Although I write rather late, I hope that this letter will still find you in Vienna. I correspond busily with Schäffer and am fairly well. Whether I shall ever quite recover I am inclined to doubt. Here I live very simply in every respect, go for walks regularly, work much at my opera and read Walter Scott.

With Vogl I get on very well. We were at Linz together, where he sang a good deal, and splendidly. Bruchmann, Sturm and Streinsberg came to see us at Steyr a few days ago, and they too were dismissed with a full load of songs. As I shall hardly see you before your return, I once again wish you the best of good fortune in your enterprise and assure you of my everlasting affection, which will make me miss you most sorely. Wherever you may be give news of yourself from time to time to

Your friend
Franz Schubert.

Kupelwieser, Schwind, Mohn, &c. &c., who have also . . . [illegible] been written to, I all greet heartily.

My address:

City of Steyr, to be delivered at the Square, at Herr von Vogl's.

After Dankesreither's death Schober had probably gone to St. Pölten, and he went soon afterwards, perhaps with the aid of an inheritance from the bishop, to Breslau, where he stayed for two years in order to become an actor.—After a few earlier hints we find here the first definite mention of a serious illness suffered by Schubert. There is no doubt that it was venereal, probably syphilis. (A clear distinction between gonorrhoea and syphilis was made possible only in 1837–8 by Philippe Ricord, the chief surgeon of the Hôpital du Midi for syphilitics in Paris.) Kenner, in a letter to Luib of 1858 (Vienna City Library), mentions "an episode in Schubert's life which only too probably caused his early demise, and certainly accelerated it."—August von Schaeffer (born 1790), Schubert's first physician, with whom he kept in touch even while he was away from Vienna, had been to the Seminary before him, and qualified as a doctor in 1816. He also treated two of Josef von Spaun's brothers in Vienna.—The opera is 'Fierabras.'—Scott was mentioned earlier by Karoline Pichler, in a partial translation of 'The Lady of the Lake,' as being Vogl's favourite poet. Schober wrote a poem on him, and he had been the fashion in Vienna as well as in Germany since 1815. Just as the Prince and Princess of Orange had given an 'Ivanhoe' fancy dress ball at Brussels in 1823, so the British ambassador, Sir Henry Wellesley (the Duke of Wellington's brother), gave a Scott and Fouqué masked ball in Vienna during the carnival of 1826, in which the high nobility took part, and which was repeated at court. What Schubert, who knew no English, read at that time, and in whose translation, we do not know. When he set Scott to music in 1825–7 he used the translations of Adam Storck, Sophie May and S. H. Spiker.—With Vogl, it will be noticed, Schubert was on good terms again.—Bruchmann was on a new journey to Erlangen, where he wished to hear Schelling's lectures on mythology; but he stayed there only a fortnight, probably because he was recalled home by his father. The police had heard of this forbidden visit to a German university, and Bruchmann's prospects of becoming a state official were thus frustrated.—Ignaz Alois Sturm was a doctor of medicine, later district physician at Wels.—Streinsberg was employed at Linz.—Doblhoff too visited Schubert at Steyr (see Nos. 378 and 391).—Schubert and Vogl may have stayed with Paumgartner, as in 1825.

Bruchmann goes to Erlangen, 15th August 1823.

375. DEDICATION OF AN ÉCOSSAISE (xii. 2, No. 2, second version)
to Seraphine Schellmann, (? August) 1823

Hop merrily with this Écossaise
Through your woes for all your days!

Franz Schubert.

Schubert now wrote an album-leaf for Seraphine Schellmann, who married his schoolfellow Ebner, as he had done for her brother Albert in 1822 (*see* No. 326). This couplet is but a variant of that written in 1817 (*see* No. 104).

376. BEETHOVEN'S NEPHEW KARL in the Composer's Conversation Book, August 1823

They greatly praise Schubert, but it is said that he hides himself.

377. LOST DIPLOMA OF HONOUR FOR SCHUBERT from the Linz Musical Society, (? August) 1823

Together with Schubert, Vogl became an honorary member of the Linz Musical Society, of whose committee Hartmann, sen., Josef von Spaun and Albert Stadler were members. This organization, not founded till 1821, found in Schubert the first important musician it was able to enrol among its honorary members.

> Schubert and Vogl at Linz, with the von Hartmanns and their daughter Anna, visit Anton and Marie Ottenwalt, and in the evening go to the Castle Inn with this company, 23rd August 1823.

> Schubert and Vogl make music at Ottenwalt's in the Fügerhof near Linz, where Friedrich Ludwig von Hartmann is also visiting, 25th August 1823.—On this afternoon, when the hostess was Spaun's mother, who was also staying with the Ottenwalts during that summer, Josef von Spaun wrote in his family recollections: "A small party had been invited. After the performance of a few melancholy songs the female part of the audience began to howl, so that the sobs brought Vogl's and Schubert's concert to a premature end. Good coffee and cakes, as well as Schubert's and Vogl's humour, restored order to the company. For both artists, who were particularly honoured by those tears, this day, which ended only after moonrise, remained unforgettable."

> Schubert's sister Therese marries Michael Schneider in the parish church of Rossau, 31st August 1823.—Schneider, born in 1788, was a teacher at the secondary school of the orphanage, where he also taught singing and cello playing; later he became headmaster in the St. Ulrich suburb. Therese had probably made his acquaintance through her brother Ferdinand.

Liechtental Church, where Schubert conducted his First Mass, F major, 1814

PLATE VI

Therese Grob in Later Life.   Schubert's First Love.   Oil Painting by
(?) Heinrich Hollpein

PLATE VII

378. Josef von Spaun to Schober

Linz, 8th September 1823.

Schubert was and Doppelhof [Doblhoff] is here. I was sorry I was hardly ever able to be alone with the former.

379. Konradin Kreutzer to Louis Spohr

Vienna, 16th September 1823.

. . . Apart from these [Weber's 'Euryanthe' and an opera by Kreutzer] we shall also have a few new original German operas— one by Halm, another by Schubert—and moreover Beethoven sets Grillparzer's 'Fair Melusina.' . . .

Kreutzer's opera was probably 'The Diver' ('Der Taucher,' see No. 383), to a libretto by Georg von Hofmann based on Schiller's ballad, which had already been performed at Prince Nikolaus Esterházy's in 1809, and was to be given at the Kärntnertor Theatre on 24th January 1824 (see also No. 280).—Anton Halm, born in 1789 at Wies in Styria, living in Vienna since 1812, had been an officer, and was now a pianoforte teacher and composer, but above all a pianist, and a friend of Beethoven's. No opera of his was performed, if he ever wrote one.--Schubert's is 'Fierabras.'—Grillparzer had written the libretto of 'Melusina' for Beethoven, but it was eventually set by Kreutzer and first performed at Berlin in 1833. (After this performance Mendelssohn wrote a 'Melusina' overture independently. Schwind later glorified the fairy-tale in a cycle of paintings.)

Bruchmann and Doblhoff visit Senn at Trient, autumn 1823.

380. Schubert to the Styrian Musical Society

Gentlemen of the Musical Society,

I am very greatly obliged by the diploma of honorary membership you so kindly sent me, and which, owing to my prolonged absence from Vienna, I received only a few days ago.

May it be the reward of my devotion to the art of music to become wholly worthy of such a distinction one day. In order to give musical expression to my sincere gratitude as well, I shall

take the liberty before long of presenting your honourable Society
with one of my symphonies in full score.

> With the highest regards, I remain,
> Your honourable Society's most grateful,
> devoted and obedient servant,

Vienna, 20th September 1823.   Franz Schubert.

Schubert, who perhaps paid a visit to the Kremsmünster monastery
as well, returned to Vienna in the middle of September at the latest.—
Whether he was at that time still considering the completion of the sketch
for the Symphony in E minor and major of 1821 or of the B minor Symphony is not known. The fact that he sent the unfinished manuscript
of the latter work of 1822 to Anselm Hüttenbrenner through his brother
Josef later on, thus reversing the channel through which he had received
the diploma from Graz, makes it seem probable that he did not intend it
for his friend, who kept it locked up for some forty years, but for the
Graz society. It does not seem credible, however, that Schubert should
have thought of the possibility of a performance of the work in its fragmentary state, or could have imagined that in spite of this it would become
a world success, in fact the most frequently performed symphonic work
a hundred years after its presentation.

Weber arrives in Vienna, 21st September 1823.

381. SCHWIND TO SCHOBER at Breslau

Linz, 3rd October 1823.

He [Kenner] was greatly pleased with the sketches for the
'Minstrel' ['Der Liedler'] and could hardly get done with sheer
looking . . . The covers for the 'Minstrel' are already sketched,
and so I shall start it on white paper.

Schwind, then, had after all gone to Upper Austria that year (see No. 368).
He lived at Streinsberg's.—Schubert had set Kenner's ballad 'The
Minstrel' already in 1815, but it did not appear until 1825, as Op. 38,
dedicated to the poet. Schwind could hardly have planned the publication of his illustrations with the music. But the "covers," which have
not been preserved, seem to indicate that he intended to publish them
in some form. Only seven of his twelve sepia drawings remain (iconographical volume, pp. 195–201), No. 5 of which may perhaps be regarded
as intended for a cover. Three of these sketches were also executed in
stippled pencil drawings, which are perhaps the form he finally planned
for this cycle.

382. FROM THE OFFICIAL 'WIENER ZEITUNG,' 9th October 1823

At the House of Cappi & Diabelli,
Art and Music Dealers, Graben, No. 1133,
are published and to be had:

SCHUBERT'S LATEST SONGS

for Four Male Voices
with Accompaniment for Pianoforte or Guitar.

No. 1. 'Spring Song ['Frühlingsgesang'], by Schober.

No. 2. 'Joy in Nature' ['Naturgenuss'], by Matthisson.

Work 16.   4 Florins 30 Kreuzer, V.C.

FOUR SONGS FOR FOUR MALE VOICES

unaccompanied.

('Youth's Delight'—'Love'—'For a Round Dance'—Night')
['Jünglingswonne'—'Liebe'—'Zum Rundetanz'—'Die Nacht']

Work. 17.   2 Florins, V.C.

These two delayed opus numbers appeared without any dedications.
They were published, like Op. 11, with an additional *ad lib.* guitar
accompaniment, which is not by Schubert, although it was included in
the complete edition.—The title of the first quartet in Op. 16 is wrongly
printed as 'Frühlingslied' on the outside, but the inside heading is 'Frühlingsgesang,' as in the advertisement.

383. FROM THE 'THEATERZEITUNG,' 11th October 1823

In addition to Weber's 'Euryanthe' and Kreutzer's 'Diver' the
I. & R. Court Theatre next to the Kärntnertor is shortly to present
the first grand opera by the much-promising Schubert, the ingenious composer of 'Erl King': 'Fierobras' [*sic*], after Calderón,
by the Court Theatre Secretary, Herr Kupelwieser. It is also
said that Herr Schubert is composing a short opera.

Calderón's play 'La puente de Mantabile' (1635), which appeared in
translation in August Wilhelm von Schlegel's 'Spanisches Theater' in
1809, is related in content to the old French romance 'Fierabras,' which
appeared in the same year in Büsching and Hagen's 'Buch der Liebe,'
where the play is mentioned (cf. No. 369).—Schubert's short opera was
evidently 'The Conspirators' ('Die Verschworenen') (*see* No. 398).

384. FROM THE 'HARMONICON,' London, October 1823

(Review of Karl Czerny's 'Variations upon the Favourite Vienna Waltz,' Vienna, published by Steiner & Co., imported by Wessel & Stodart, Soho Square.)

. . . The waltz is so graceful and expressive, that we are induced to insert it in this place. [Follows Schubert's 'Trauerwalzer,' slightly altered and without the trio.]

This was the first (and in Schubert's lifetime the last) mention in a non-German foreign journal, and also the first reprint of a work of his there. True, Schubert's name did not appear with this commendation, the 'Harmonicon' was in its first year of publication. Karl Czerny had issued his variations on Schubert's "Mourning" Waltz without the composer's name as Op. 12 of his endless series of works soon after the publication of Schubert's Op. 9, in which it was No. 2. It was this anonymity of the waltz which made it easy to ascribe it to Beethoven under the title of 'Waltz of Longing' ('Sehnsuchtswalzer'), in an extended form where it appeared as a trio section together with Friedrich Heinrich Himmel's (died 1814) 'Favourite Waltz' ('Favorit-Walzer'). Beethoven vainly fought against this (as Schubert did not), so that Czerny's popular variations on the "Mourning" Waltz were still printed fifty years later with the indication that the theme was "by Beethoven." But William Gardiner had already wavered in 1838, in his book 'Music and Friends,' where he attributed the "Mourning" Waltz to Czerny himself and the combined "Longing" Waltz to Beethoven. "The popular Vienna waltz," which the London periodical probably also ascribed to Czerny, had been used by that composer in a somewhat altered form, so that it first appeared in London in a corrupt version. This quickly popularized waltz, whose composer's name Czerny may have suppressed because of its inaccurate quotation, adding it only to the fourth edition of his Variations published by Tobias Haslinger, was later used by others for numerous sets of variations for different instruments, and it was repeatedly turned into songs by the addition of words, last of all in the notorious 'Lilac Time' (the English version of 'Das Dreimäderlhaus'), where the words are "I ask the spring, blossom-laden."—The 'Harmonicon,' by the way, discussed, together with Karl Czerny's work, the Variations by Josef Czerny (born in 1785 at Horsitz in Bohemia, the teacher of Leopoldine Blahetka and no relation of Karl's) on "une Écossaise favorite de M. F. Schubert" (named "Monsieur François Schubert" in Steiner's Vienna edition), dedicated as Josef's Op. 25 to a Mlle Charlotte Friedlaender. But this colourless notice had nothing to say on Schubert's Écossaise (Op. 18, Part I, No. 4, published in February 1823).

385. From the Stuttgart 'Morgenblatt für gebildete Stände,' 5th December 1823

(Vienna Correspondence, October 1823.)

Frau von Chézy is at work on a new opera libretto, to be composed by a young local tone-poet. A drama, 'Rosamunde,' has already been completed by her. . . .

Helmina von Chézy, born in 1783 as Wilhelmine Christine von Klencke in Berlin, had been married for a few years to the orientalist Antoine Léonard Chézy in Paris. In the summer of 1823, doubtless because of the production of 'Euryanthe,' she visited Austria with her two sons and at Baden near Vienna, where the elder of them took the waters, wrote the drama of 'Rosamond' ('Rosamunde,' *see* No. 409). The librettist of 'Euryanthe' did not at that time write another opera-book; only a comedy from her pen, 'Der Wunderquell,' was performed shortly after 'Rosamond' at the Burg Theatre and had a similar ill success. It is worthy of note that one of her two sons, the painter Max von Chézy (born Paris, 1808), had lived at Linz about 1820 and was a friend of Anton von Spaun's. The elder of the two, Wilhelm (born Paris, 1806), became an author, like his mother, his grandmother and the ancestress Frau Karschin, and he was introduced to the Schubert circle by Ernst von Feuchtersleben.—It is possible that Helmina was originally intended to write an opera libretto for Schubert. He can hardly have received the commission for the 'Rosamond' music until after October 1823, and it is not likely that the authoress had anything to do with any other young Viennese composer. Bauernfeld described her in 1825 as "extremely good-natured, somewhat ridiculous; cleanliness not her cardinal virtue."

386. Schwind to Schober at Breslau

[Linz,] 16th October [1823].

I hear that Schubert's opera has already been submitted, so that presumably it will soon be performed. Pepi Spaun is afraid for it, because of the orchestration. But I cannot be induced to abandon my good hopes. I have so far done, apart from a small drawing for Frau von Kenner, three for the 'Minstrel.'

Schwind stayed at Linz until 26th October. Apart from some drawings for Kenner's 'Minstrel' (*see* No. 381) he had also made a drawing there for the birth of the latter's first son, Karl, on 6th October (iconographical volume, p. 430).

First production of Weber's 'Euryanthe' at the Kärntnertor Theatre, in the composer's presence, 25th October 1823.—It is said that the next day, 26th October, Schubert met Weber, who stayed at the "Hungarian Crown," and, on being asked, told him frankly that he had liked 'Der Freischütz' much better (cf. No. XXIII). If Weber was estranged from him by this, it is nevertheless impossible that he could have predicted the failure of 'Rosamond' at that time, when the music had not been so much as commissioned. It seems more likely that he may have warned Schubert not to set a libretto by Helmina von Chézy.

387. FROM THE OFFICIAL 'WIENER ZEITUNG,' 27th October 1823

At the House of Sauer & Leidesdorf,
I. & R. Art, Alabaster and Music Dealers in Vienna,
Kärntnerstrasse, No. 941, have just appeared:
GROUP FROM TARTARUS by Fr. Schiller.
['Gruppe aus dem Tartarus']
SLUMBER SONG by Mayerhofer [sic].
['Schlummerlied']
Two Poems,
Set to Music for one Voice with Pianoforte Accompaniment
by
FRANZ SCHUBERT.
Work 24.   Price, 1 Florin 30 Kreuzer, V.C.
In the press, and to appear next week:
Franz Schubert, first grand Sonata for pianoforte duet, Op. 30.

This opus bears no dedication. The second song is entitled 'Schlaflied' on the inside heading. Opp. 25–9 appeared after Op. 30, which did not come out until the end of December. It would therefore be curious if the opus number 26 had already been reserved for the vocal numbers in 'Rosamond.'

388. FROM ROSENBAUM'S DIARY, 28th October 1823

With Weber, Th[erese]. and Etzelt to Reimann, to hear Goll's pianofortes.—Count Mayláth and Schubert joined Th. and Etzelt. —Kreutzer came down, also played. All were tried—pleased by their tone and their safe mechanism; then with Weber to Danhauser.

This encounter between Schubert and Weber, on the day on which the former is said to have judged 'Euryanthe' disparagingly to its composer in the music shop of Steiner & Co., proves that there was no serious disagreement between the two.—The scenes described by Rosenbaum all took place in the Wieden suburb.   Therese was his wife, a daughter of Florian Gassmann's, born in Vienna in 1774, and a pupil of Salieri's. She was at the Kärntnertor Theatre until 1824.—Her friend Etzelt was perhaps the wife of the banker Josef Etzelt, president of the Lower Austrian Savings Bank.   Johann Reimann was a cabinet maker and at the same time Goll's companion; his house was in the Paniglgasse.—Johann Jakob Goll, of Zürich, had constructed a new pianoforte with a sound-board above the strings, for which he had received a five-years' privilege in June 1822, extended to ten years in November 1823.   Rosenbaum ordered one made of coco-nut wood.   He was an eccentric who culti-vated a model garden and did not scruple to take part in the desecration of graves in order to procure an interesting skull, as, for instance, Haydn's, which even to-day has not been reunited with the rest of his skeleton.— Johann, Count Mayláth, born at Pest in 1786, was an author, a sketch for a libretto by whom, with the incomplete title of 'The Salt Mines of . . .' was found among Schubert's remains.—Josef Danhauser, born 1805, the son of a furniture manufacturer on the Wieden, was an ex-cellent genre painter and played the violin well (*see* No. 615).

389. FROM THE FAMILY REGISTER of Schubert's Father

(18) On 7th November 1823, at 8.30 a.m., was born Andreas Theodor.

390. SCHWIND TO SCHOBER

[Vienna,] 9th November [1823].

The day before yesterday Kupelwieser left for Rome.   On the eve of that day we finished by holding a kind of bacchanal at the "Crown," where we all dined, except Schubert, who was laid up that day.   Schaeffer and Bernhardt, who visited him, declare that he is well on the way to recovery and already talk of a space of four weeks after which he might be quite restored.   Apart from us there were Smirsch, Goldhahn, Kuppel [Kupelwieser] from the theatre, which however he has now left, and riding-master Eibo, who showed himself very amiable and sympathetic.   The table was fuller than ever, and all very jolly; after dinner came two violins and a guitar, and soon after a capital punch, two delights which brought mirth to its culmination. Bruchmann drank brotherhood with us all, whereupon a general fraternizing, and at last a fierce bombardment of glasses began. Your health, Schubert's, Senn's and Professor Redl's was drunk with enthusiasm.

The painter Leopold Kupelwieser, whom the Russian Alexis Beresin had taken with him on a journey to Italy to illustrate a projected literary account, was away until August 1825. He did draw a large number of landscapes, buildings and folk costumes, but the work was never published owing to Beresin's sudden death.—The "Crown" is the "Hungarian Crown."—J. Bernhardt, Matthäus von Collin's father-in-law, was Schubert's second doctor at that time. His Christian name is unknown. —Johann Karl Smirsch, born in Vienna in 1801, was chief cashier to the I. & R. private exchequer and an amateur still-life painter. He deputized as teacher during Kupelwieser's absence.—"Goldhahn" is probably Franz Goldhann, an iron merchant, collector of antiques and amateur draughtsman and painter.—"Theater-Kuppel," is, of course, Leopold Kupelwieser's ("Kuppel's") brother Josef. On 9th October he had resigned his post as secretary to the Court Opera, apparently because of the arrogance of the Italian singers.—Nothing is known of "Eibo"; this may have been a nickname for the master of the horse Maximilian von Weyrother, Franz von Bruchmann's future father-in-law.—Drinking brotherhood is a custom in Germanic countries on occasions when acquaintances who become closer friends take a suitable opportunity of proposing the intimate address of "thou" to each other; this is usually done by the elder of the two, and the younger is scarcely in a position to refuse.— Josef Redl, born in Vienna in 1774, was a classico-historical painter and professor at the Academy of Fine Arts.

Schubertiad at the Bruchmanns', 11th November 1823.

391. DOBLHOFF TO SCHOBER

Vienna, 12th November 1823.

From Amstetten I turned via Seitenstetten to Steyr to visit our dear little Tubby [Schwämmelein: Schubert]. I found him seriously ill at the time, but you know that anyhow. Vogl gave me the pleasure of singing a series of beautiful songs, which are amongst the most valued travelling allowances on my journey . . . [Senn at Trient] seems to be avoiding any sort of detailed recollection. For all that, he showed ardent sympathy with you and

Schubert . . . At Bruchmann's we have already once enjoyed the great pleasure of a Schubertiad, at which Vogl sang. We have also begun our readings, for which Smetana, Hönig and Mayer have joined us as "Heinrich IV," "Folko von Montfaucon" and "Etzel."

Schubert seems at last to progress properly towards recovery; his 'Fierabras,' however, has been deferred by Kupelwieser's withdrawal from the theatre.

Amstetten lies some seventy miles to the west of Vienna, between St. Pölten and Steyr. Seitenstätten, a Benedictine abbey, is between Amstetten and Steyr.—"Schwämmelein" is a diminutive of "Schwammerl," the more usual nickname given to Schubert by his friends (translated as Tubby hereafter). It alluded to his figure, not to his inclination towards tippling, as was supposed later because Schwammer is Viennese dialect for "tipsiness." As it happens, the minstrel of the king of the Huns, Attila, was named Swämlîn; but as Schubert was also nicknamed Volker, after the minstrel of the Burgundian princes in the 'Nibelungenlied' (see No. 401), this explanation too fails to convince.—The Schubertiad at the Bruchmanns' had taken place on the previous day, the mother's birthday (see No. 401).—Rudolf, Ritter von Smetana, born in Vienna in 1802, was then a law student. Only in later years, when he had become a priest, does he seem to have tried his hand at poetry. There is no connection between him and the Czech composer.—Karl Hönig too was a law student.—This Mayer (whose Christian name is not known) was also nicknamed "Hungarian Mayer," perhaps because of his moustache, and this was connected with his other nickname of "Etzel." Whether he is identical with the merchant of Tyrnau in Hungary of the same name, who as a consequence of his success in the lottery of 1819 became one of the owners of the Theater an der Wien (see No. 180), is uncertain. —The names were taken from the 'Nibelungenlied' and other works (see Nos. 396 and 401): "Heinrich IV" (recte V) from Shakespeare's 'King Henry V'; "Etzel" is Attila in the 'Nibelungenlied'; "Folko von Montfaucon" is a knight in Fouqué's novel 'Der Zauberring' (1813), on which Schubert had already drawn for his three romances entitled 'Don Gayseros' in 1814. The same figure occurs in Fouqué's novel 'Sintram und seine Gefährten.' Both these novels were soon translated into English, for Fouqué was almost as popular in Britain as Scott was in the Germanic countries. ('Sintram and his Companions,' London, 1820; 'The Magic Ring,' Edinburgh, 1825.) At the Viennese fancy-dress ball of 1826 (see No. 374) Count Josef Hunyadi appeared as Folko von Montfaucon.

392. FROM THE PROGRAMME of the Second Evening Entertainment
    held by the Musical Society, 13th November 1823

2. 'The Dwarf' ['Der Zwerg']. Poem by M. Collin, set to
music by Schubert, performed by Herr von Preisinger.

393. NOTE on a Programme Copy of the Words of the above Song

Sung and played by Preisinger.

394. FROM THE REPORT of the Committee of the Linz Philharmonic
                              Society
for the second year of business from 18th November 1822 to
                    18th November 1823.

Honorary Members:

. . . .

Schubert, Franz, Composer.
Vogl, Michael, retired I. & R. Court Opera Singer and Producer.

395. JOHANNA LUTZ TO HER BETROTHED, Leopold Kupelwieser,
                              in Italy

                              Vienna, 18th November 1823.
    Last Saturday there was a meeting at Mohn's, where the readings
were fixed for Mondays and Thursdays. Two new members have
been admitted, that is to say Hönig and the doctor who is always
at the Bruchmanns'. Schubert is already well again. . . .
Father has given me a few Schubert songs I had not had.

    Johanna Lutz, born 1803, was, on the side of her mother (born in
Vienna in 1764 as Maria Regina Putz), a cousin of Leopold Sonnleithner's;
her sister Regina, born in 1799, was the wife of the theatre painter
Neefe (see No. 180). Her father, Johann Adam Lutz, born in 1757 at
Glatz in Silesia, was registrar at the Foundation and Court Accountancy.
—Mohn lived in the Grasgasse in the Landstrasse suburb.—By "the
doctor" Smetana seems to have been meant, although he did not qualify
as a doctor of law until 1827.

396. Schwind to Schober

[Vienna,] 19th November [1823].

Readings at Mohn's have started again; Mayer, Hönig and Smetana, as King Attila, Folko von Montfaucon and Prince Henry V are new members. Huber, however, is not to be seen there. The smoking Kreuzer are abolished, the time is 7 o'clock Mondays and Thursdays.

. . . The readings are beginning to become somewhat different. Through Mohn, Steiger has been introduced as Kaspar von Thorringer and Goldhahn (!) as Doctor Faust. The crowd and the mixture of guests is irksome, and I do not feel at home.

Schwind is doubtless right in writing "Henry V" and Doblhoff wrong in making it "Henry IV" (*see* No. 391), but it should of course be 'King [not Prince] Henry V.'—Huber is Josef Huber once again.— "Smoking Kreuzer" were forfeits, like the "slip-of-the-tongue groats" that went into the Atzenbrugg cash-box, and they may have been devoted to the same purpose.—Johann Steiger von Amstein, born in 1803, was a mining expert.—'Kaspar der Thorringer' was a popular romantic drama by Josef August, Count Törring; it was a forerunner of Goethe's 'Götz von Berlichingen.'—Doctor Faust is the figure in the puppet play.

397. Schwind to Schober

[Vienna,] 24th [November 1823].

Last night we were at your mother's—Frau von Bruchmann with the children, the Hugelmanns, Fräulein Jakobi and a wild, pert thing, whom I had not seen before, with her mother, Schubert, Vogl, Étienne, Derffel, Huber and I. After a small Schubertiad followed a meal and afterwards a little dance till midnight.

Frau von Schober had just moved into new quarters (? still in the Göttweigerhof).—A Fräulein Hugelmann, probably Josef's niece (*see* No. 258), lived at Graz and went on a visit to Vienna in 1823. She was on friendly terms with Anselm Hüttenbrenner, Mayrhofer, Franz and Therese Derffel (whose aunt Frau von Schober was). Therese Hugelmann, born in 1798 as Franz Xaver's daughter, married Claude Étienne (*see* No. 108) in 1824.—Nothing is known of Fräulein Jakobi.

398. From the 'Theaterzeitung,' 29th November 1823

The short Schubert opera is Castelli's 'Conspirators' ['Die Verschworenen']. 'Fierobras' [*sic*] is not to be performed for the present.

Ignaz Franz Castelli, born in Vienna in 1781, was Lower Austrian accountancy officer, editor of the 'Konversationsblatt' and a dramatist. In his almanac 'Dramatisches Sträusschen' he had published in February 1823 the one-act libretto of 'The Conspirators,' written in 1820 and based on Aristophanes's 'Lysistrata.' It was later called 'Domestic Warfare' ('Der häusliche Krieg') by order of the censorship. In the preface Castelli wrote: "The German composers' complaint is usually this: 'Indeed, we should gladly set operas to music, if only you would supply us with the books!' Here is one, gentlemen!" (cf. No. 383).

399. Schubert to Schober

Vienna, 30th November 1823.

Dear Schober,

For some time I have been itching to write to you, but I have never managed to do so. You know how it happens.

First of all I must pour out a lament over the condition of our circle as well as all other circumstances; for with the exception of the state of my health, which (thank God) seems to be firmly restored at last, everything goes miserably. Our circle, as indeed I had expected, has lost its central focus without you. Bruchmann, who has returned from his journey, is no longer the same. He seems to bend to the formalities of the world, and by that alone he loses his halo, which in my opinion was due only to his determined disregard of all worldly affairs. Kupelwieser, as presumably you already know, has gone to Rome (but is not best pleased with his Russian). As for the others, you know better than I. True, as a substitute for you and Kupelwieser we received four individuals, namely: the Hungarian Mayer, Hönig, Smetana and Steiger, but the majority of such individuals make the society only more insignificant instead of better. What is the good of a lot of quite ordinary students and officials to us? If Bruchmann is not there, or even ill, we go on for hours under the supreme direction of Mohn hearing nothing but eternal talk about riding, fencing, horses and hounds. If it is to go on like this, I don't suppose I shall stand it for long among them.—

With my two operas things go very badly, too. Kupelwieser has suddenly left the theatre. Weber's 'Euryanthe' turned out wretchedly and its bad reception was quite justified, in my opinion. These circumstances, and a new split between Pálffy and Barbaja, leave me scarcely any hope for my opera. Besides, it would really not be a great stroke of fortune, as everything is done indescribably badly now.

Vogl is here, and sang once at Bruchmann's and once at Witzeck's [Witteczek]. He is taken up with my songs almost exclusively. He writes out the voice-part himself and, so to speak, lives on it. He is therefore very polite and docile with me. And now let's hear from you. How are you? Have you already appeared before the world's eyes?

Please be sure to give some news of yourself very soon, and still my longing for you to some extent at least by letting me know how you live and what you do.—I have composed nothing since the opera, except a few 'Maid of the Mill' songs. The 'Mill' songs will appear in four books, with vignettes by Schwind.—

For the rest, I hope to regain my health, and this recovered treasure will let me forget many a sorrow; only you, dear Schober, I shall never forget, for what you meant to me no one else can mean, alas!

And now keep well and do not forget

Your eternally affectionate
friend
Franz Schubert.

My address:
Stubentor-Bastei,
No. 1187, first floor.

The two Schubert operas are 'Alfonso and Estrella' and 'Fierabras.'— Pálffy, the owner of the Theater an der Wien, clearly did not agree with the division of work between that theatre and the Court Opera; but no breach with Barbaja, who, it is true, had withdrawn somewhat from the Theater an der Wien in the middle of 1822 (*see* No. 300), occurred at that time.   The supreme court theatre directorate was transferred as an official post from Moritz, Count Dietrichstein, to Johann Rudolf, Count Czernin, during this November.—Vogl, who had retired two years before, had evidently stayed longer at his summer resort of Steyr.— Josef Wilhelm Witteczek, born at Troppau in 1787, a doctor of law and conveyancer at the Privy State Chancellery, was married in 1819 to Wilhelmine Watteroth, born 1800 (*see* No. 81).   He had made Schubert's acquaintance through Josef von Spaun, and became one of his most ardent admirers.   For more than forty years he held Schubertiads at his house, and after Schubert's death he collected fair copies of all his songs, piano-forte works and chamber music, having previously purchased Pinterics's collection of songs in 1831.   He left his albums to Josef von Spaun.— Schober was preparing himself for his appearance as an actor at Breslau.— The cycle of 'The Fair Maid of the Mill' was written partly at the general hospital, where in 1823 Schubert stayed temporarily on account of the state of his health.   The work appeared in 1824 in five books, but without the vignettes projected by Schwind.   The anonymous and feeble title vignette on a later edition published after Schubert's death is not by him. —From the autumn of 1823 to the spring of 1824 Schubert lived with Huber at the Stubentor bastion, near the present Stadtpark, where Mayrhofer lived in 1825–6.

400. SCHWIND TO SCHOBER

[Vienna,] 2nd December [1823].

I am on the point of resigning from the readings, for the reading is so stifled by business affairs and pranks that even to gather together undisturbed is impossible.   If you or Senn suddenly appeared in our midst, we should be truly ashamed of such company. Schubert will stick to me.

401. BRUCHMANN TO LEOPOLD KUPELWIESER

Vienna, 2nd December 1823.

On 11th November we had a Schubertiad at home, at which Vogl took over the singing.   Those present were Mohn, Doblhoff, Kraissl, Mayrhofer, Schwind, Rieder, Dietrich, Eichholzer, Hönig, Schubert, Vogl and I; also the Liedern and Pierron girls, Julie and my sisters.   V. was much pleased with himself and sang glori-ously; we others were merry and bright at table, and our first health was drunk in your honour in Moselle.

That evening Huber was still much teased about the hazel-hen, and when Schwind drew his naked form on the table at the Wasserburg, he was so upset that he has for some time been lost to our gatherings . . .

On the 17th we had the first reading at Mohn's. We restarted 'Tasso.' Mohn and Dietrich retained their old dignities, and I mine as reader. The chief changes that took place are the election of five new members: Mayer with the name of Etzel, Hönig with the name of Folko von Montfaucon, Smetana with the name of Prince Henry V, Steiger with the name of Kaspar der Thorringer, Goldhahn with the name of Doctor Faust.—The readings are, but twice a week, on Mondays and Thursdays from 7 p.m. until 10 or 11 o'clock. It is quite jolly there, yet we sorely miss our original members and the more intimate ones often remember past times *sub rosa*. It was the same at the Schubertiad where it was secretly felt that we are no longer as sound at the core as before.

On 20th November Kupelwieser had sent Bruchmann a letter addressed to all the friends.—Mohn is called by his nickname, Mone, in the original. —Wilhelm August Rieder, born in 1796 at Döbling near Vienna, was a good portrait painter to whom we owe the best contemporary likeness of Schubert.—Anton Dietrich, born in Vienna in 1799, was a good sculptor, who is said to have made a bust of Schubert, of which no trace remains.—Michael Eichholzer, a painter and lithographer, was a colleague of Schwind's, who, however, could not bear him.—About Fräulein Liedern (or Lindner, as Schwind calls her in 1824) nothing is known. She seems to have been a friend of Justina von Bruchmann's, who was present at this party with her sister Isabella.—For Jeannette Cuny de Pierron cf. the note on pp. 184–5.—Juliana (Julie), Edle von Weyrother, the daughter of the Master of the Horse Maximilian von Weyrother (*see* No. 390), was Bruchmann's betrothed. The Weyrothers had been Masters of the Horse in Austria for the last hundred years. Gottlieb, Ritter von Weyrother, now inspector of the court riding-school, had been in touch with the Mozarts at Salzburg; he was no doubt Juliana's grandfather.—The story of the hazel-hen, which seems to have proved so embarrassing to Huber, who was often made the butt of his friends, is unfortunately unknown.—The "Wasserburg" is Wasserburger's café.— Goethe's drama 'Tasso' had clearly been begun during the preceding season, when Bruchmann had also read from Johann Heinrich Voss's translation of Homer.—Mohn and Dietrich evidently took the chair by turns at these meetings.—We unfortunately learn nothing of the older members' nicknames from these letters; but we know that Leopold Kupelwieser was "Rüdiger von Pöchlarn," Schwind "Giselher the Child," Bruchmann (probably) "Gunther," Schober "Grim Hagen," Doblhoff "Dietrich von Bern" and Schubert "Volker the Minstrel"; all these came from the 'Nibelungenlied,' which at that time occupied many of the best minds, among them especially Anton von Spaun's.

402. JOHANNA LUTZ TO LEOPOLD KUPELWIESER

Vienna, 9th December 1823.

Towards noon, when I am alone, I usually play Schubert songs. They are so very beautiful. The 'Treasure Hunter' ['Schatzgräbers Begehr'] and 'Praise of Tears' ['Lob der Tränen'] are quite uncannily beautiful, but I cannot really tell which . . . Schubert is now pretty well and already begins to show a desire to give up keeping to his strict regimen. If only he does not hurt himself! Oh, there again, how good it would be if you were here!

Johanna Lutz played the pianoforte and her sister Regina Neefe sang, both as amateurs.

403. LEOPOLD KUPELWIESER TO JOHANNA LUTZ

Venice, 10th December 1823.

To-day I dined at the patriarch's . . . After dinner we went into his room and he showed me a copy of Schubert's 'Wanderer,' which is dedicated to him. I revealed myself as the author of the accompanying drawing.

The Patriarch of Venice was Pyrker. The drawing that adorned his copy of the 'Wanderer' (cf. No. 248) has disappeared. It is not identical with the vignette on an edition published after 1828, drawn by Schubert's brother Karl, and engraved by Adolf Dworžak.

404. JOHANNA LUTZ TO LEOPOLD KUPELWIESER

Vienna, 16th December 1823.

Ever since you left there has been only one Schubertiad at Bruchmann's, but there are said to be many gatherings to which your friends do not get.

405. SCHWIND TO SCHOBER

[Vienna,] 17th December [1823].

I recently drew a few satirical sketches on our billiard-playing company . . . I gave it to Bruchmann, who is the only one, apart from Schubert and Eichholzer, who remains faithful. Even Doblhoff indulges in distractions like Bruchmann. Dr. Bernhardt is said to have written a poem in which he makes your spirit reprove these vulgarities, but I have not got to know it yet.

The letter also gives a description of the lost sketches, which satirize the world as a combination of a riding-school and a coffee-house, and the time between 10 a.m. and nightfall as being occupied by coffee, billiards, horses, hounds, tobacco-pipes, etc.—Dr. J. Bernhardt and his melancholy son, a conveyancer in the General Court Chamber, were amateur poets. The poem in question never became known.

406. FROM THE VIENNA 'SAMMLER,' 18th December 1823

Benefit announcement. Frau Helmine von Chézy has delivered to the directorate of the I. & R. privileged Theater an der Wien a new drama with choruses: 'Rosamond of Cyprus.' The music for it is by the favourably known, talented composer, Herr Fr. Schubert, and the first performance, taking place on Saturday, 20th December, has been granted for the benefit of Mlle Neumann, an actress at this theatre. The names of the authoress and the composer assure this artist by the choice arrived at the worthy reception of a work which for its sterling qualities may properly be ranked with the more excellent plays of recent times.

Josef Kupelwieser, who was attractive and frivolous, had fallen in love with a minor actress named Emilie Neumann, who later married her colleague Karl Lucas. It is said that Kupelwieser persuaded Schubert to write the music for Helmina von Chézy's play in order to oblige and help his friend. The play, by the way, has nothing in common with Joseph Addison's 'Rosamond' libretto, composed by Thomas Clayton, T. A. Arne and Samuel Arnold (as a Cologne dissertation of 1937 asserted), nor with Wieland's 'Rosamund,' composed by Anton Schweitzer. Helmina's piece is said to have a Spanish model, which, however, is not to be discovered. The contents of the play are known only from the criticisms, for the libretto, of which there were two versions, both unpublished, has been lost.—Advertisements similar to those in the 'Sammler' (the 'Collector') appeared on the same day in the 'Theaterzeitung' and in the 'Wiener Zeitschrift' (not in the German edition).

407. FROM THE OFFICIAL 'WIENER ZEITUNG,' 19th December 1823

NEW CHRISTMAS and NEW YEAR PRESENTS '
which are to be had at the Privileged Art and Music Establishment of Sauer & Leidesdorf,
Kärntnerstrasse, No. 941:
Album musical
A Collection of new Pianoforte Compositions, Songs with German, French and Italian Text, and Dances.
Property of the Publishers.
Parisian Format,
bound in elegant cover and adorned with vignettes.

Price	3 Fl., A.C.
boxed, with gilt edges . .	5 Fl., A.C.
in silk with gold . . .	8 Fl., A.C.

Germany has so far been deprived of a similar present for the New Year, as well as for other festivals. The above should therefore enjoy an especial success for its novelty and exceptional elegance alone, but still more for its carefully selected contents. Not wishing to hold out the bribe of pompous words and recommendations, we are content merely to announce its contents.

Count Gallenberg, New Cotillon for the Pianoforte.
Fr. Schubert, *Air russe* for the Pianoforte.
Auguste Louis, *Plaisanterie sur des thèmes originaux espagnols.*
Rossini, New Cavatina.
Mme Fodor-Mainvielle, Two French Romances.
M. J. Leidesdorf, 'The Maiden's Heartbeats,' romance.
New Waltzes, Quadrilles, Mazur, &c. &c.

This album, in oblong octavo, was planned and decorated on the basis of a Parisian model (perhaps Gustave Dugazon's 'Danses nationales,' published by Gide *fils*).   Of this first year's issue only two copies of the medium edition have been preserved (Frau Helene Obersteiner, Vienna, and Anthony van Hoboken, Lausanne).—Of Schubert's two contributions one was the pianoforte piece here entitled 'Aire [*sic*] russe,' which later appeared as No. 3 of the 'Moments musicals' [*sic*], Op. 94, and was re-printed in the London almanac 'Le Cadeau' for 1831 as 'Russian Air'; the other is one of the 'New Waltzes,' reprinted in the complete edition as xii. 18, No. 2, and dated January 1824, according to a later fair copy made with another German dance.—Nothing is known about Auguste Louis.—Joséphine Fodor-Mainvielle, *née* Fodor, Paris, 1793, was married to the French actor Mainvielle-Donadio and had since 1823 been with the Italian company at the Court Opera.   Johann Karl Unger published her biography in 1823, in French and German.

408. FROM THE PROGRAMME of the Theater an der Wien, 19th December 1823

THEATRICAL ANNOUNCEMENT

His Excellence, Count Ferdinand von Pálffy, Proprietor of the I. & R. Privileged Theater an der Wien, has granted the under-signed a performance for her benefit; she has therefore the honour of obediently informing the high Nobility and the revered public that this performance will be held on Saturday, 20th December, at the I. & R. Theater an der Wien, and that on this day will be given:

For the First Time:

ROSAMOND, PRINCESS OF CYPRUS.

Grand Romantic Drama in Four Acts, with Choruses, Musical Accompaniment and Dances, by Helmine von Chézy, *née* Freiin Klencke.

Music by Herr SCHUBERT.

Emilie Neumann,
Actress at the I. & R. Privileged
Theater an der Wien.

A brief preliminary announcement appeared also in the 'Wanderer' of 20th December 1823 (German edition, No. 423).

409. Programme of the Theater an der Wien
20th December 1823

I. & R. Privileged Theater an der Wien.

For the Benefit of Mlle Emilie Neumann:

(Subscription suspended!)   For the First Time:

Rosamond, Princess of Cyprus

Grand Romantic Drama in Four Acts, with Choruses, Musical Accompaniment and Dances, by Helmine von Chézy, *née* Freiin Klencke.

Music by Herr Schubert.

Fulgentius, Governor of Cyprus . .	Herr Rott
Clarabella, his Daughter . . .	Mlle Eichenhoff
Alfons, Prince of Candia . . .	Herr Palmer
Albanus, Burgomaster . . .	Herr Klein
Axa, a Sailor's Widow . . .	Mme Vogel
Rosamunde, her adopted Daughter .	Mlle Neumann
Drogut, Captain of the Pirates . .	Herr Demmer
Camalvo ⎫	Herr Hann
Lavegnia ⎬ Pirates	Herr Posinger
Feramör ⎭	Herr Vollkommen
The Commander of Fulgentius's Watch .	Herr La Roche
First ⎫	Herr Wille
Second ⎪	Herr Sandner
Third ⎬ Citizen	Herr Urban
Fourth ⎪	Herr Renner
Fifth ⎭	Herr Willax
An Old Man	Herr Mayerhofer
A Servant	Herr Tomaselli

Ladies and Gentlemen of the Court. Pages. Retinue.
Citizens. Huntsmen. Shepherds and Shepherdesses.

The Scene is laid on Cyprus.

Box Office open at 5 — Begin at 7 — End at 9.30.

It is well known that Schubert wrote the following musical numbers for this play, the original title of which was 'Rosamunde, Prinzessin von

Cypern': act-tune following Act I, in B minor; ballet in B minor for Act II
and act-tune in D major to follow it; for Act III the contralto romance for
Axa, a chorus of spirits for male voices and act-tune in B flat major; for
Act IV the shepherds' melody in B flat major, the shepherds' chorus and
hunting chorus for mixed voices, and the ballet in G major. For the overture *see* Nos. 187 and 411.—Moritz Rott, *recte* Rosenberg, born at Prague
in 1793, was an actor and producer, also an author.—Georg Palmer was
one of the more eminent actors of the company.—Katharina Vogel, *née*
Düpont, was the business manager's wife (*see* No. 300) and worked also
as singer at the Court Opera.—Friedrich Demmer (*see* No. 180) was
opera producer at both theatres.—Adolf Vollkommen, later named Voll-
komm, born in 1797, went to the Burg Theatre in 1824.—Julius Laroche,
born in Berlin in 1781, went to the Burg in 1827. So did Franz Mayerhofer, born in Vienna in 1786, who was also a homoeopath.—About the
other participants no details are known.

410. FROM ROSENBAUM'S DIARY, 20th December 1823

W. Th. [Wieden Theatre]—Benefit of Emilie Neumann.
'Rosamond, Princess of Cyprus,' play in 4 acts by Wilhelmine von
Chézy.—Empty, tedious, unnatural.—Paid 10 florins for my seat.

According to the full playbill (iconographical volume, p. 168) the most
expensive seats cost 1 florin, A.C., or 2 florins 30 kreuzer, V.C., so that
Rosenbaum had paid considerably in excess for Emilie Neumann's benefit.
(The abbreviation at the head of this entry shows that the Theater an der
Wien was still thought of by some people as the Theater auf der Wieden.)
—In Ignaz von Seyfried's manuscript journal of the theatre (Vienna City
Library) the first performance is also mentioned.

411. SCHWIND TO SCHOBER

[Vienna,] 22nd [December 1823].

The day before yesterday the Theater an der Wien produced a
piece by the wretched Frau von Chézy, 'Rosamond of Cyprus,'
with music by Schubert. You may imagine that we all went to
it. As I did not go out all day on account of my cough, I could
make no arrangements and sat alone in the third tier while the others
were in the pit. Schubert has taken over the overture he wrote
for 'Estrella,' as he thinks it too "homespun" for 'Estrella,' for
which he wants to write a new one. It pleased so much that, to

my great joy, it had to be repeated.   You may imagine how I
followed the basses and the scoring.   You were worried about
them, I know.   I noticed that the flute, to which half the theme is
given, comes in a bit too soon, but that may have been due to the
player.   Otherwise it is easy to understand and well balanced.
After the first act there was a piece which proved not sufficiently
brilliant for the place it occupies, and too repetitive.   A ballet
made no impression, nor did the second and third entr'actes.
Well, people are accustomed to talking immediately the curtain
has dropped, and I do not see how they can be expected to notice
such serious and lovely things.   In the last act was a chorus of
shepherds and huntsmen, so beautiful and so natural that I cannot
remember ever hearing the like before.   It was applauded and
repeated, and I believe it will deal the chorus in Weber's 'Euryanthe' the sort of blow it deserves.   An aria, too, though most
atrociously sung by Mme Vogel, and a little bucolic piece were
applauded.   A subterranean chorus could not be heard and even
the gestures of Herr Rott, who was brewing poison the while,
could not make it materialize.

Helmina von Chézy was regarded as a literary blue-stocking.—No
overture was written especially for 'Rosamond' (*see* No. 187).   To make
confusion worse confounded, the overture to 'The Magic Harp,' in a
pianoforte duet arrangement, was published as the 'Rosamond' overture before Schubert's death (*see* No. 628).—He did not write a new
overture for 'Alfonso and Estrella.'   The complete edition placed the
'Alfonso' overture erroneously in front of 'Rosamond,' as the crowning cause of perplexity.—It is not true that the overture had to be twice
repeated at the first performance, as Josef Hüttenbrenner told Kreissle.—
Schober, of course, knew the 'Alfonso' overture, since he was the
librettist of the opera.—The bucolic piece was the instrumental shepherds'
melody.   The chorus of spirits was sung under the stage.

412. FROM THE 'THEATERZEITUNG' 30th December 1823

The curiosity of all lovers of the stage cannot fail to have been
stirred in the liveliest manner when they read the announcement
of a work bearing two famous names at its head.   Frau von Chézy
is known throughout Germany as a pleasant teller of tales and a

gracious writer of lyrics, and her reputation in these branches of poetry is assured. As a dramatist the said lady had so far remained unknown to us, and her 'Euryanthe,' where lyricism may have impaired dramatic qualities, has not predisposed us to expect a great deal of her in that respect. It was in this frame of mind that the reviewer went to see the piece in question, the plot of which is as follows:—The former Prince of Cyprus, advised on his deathbed by his faithful burgomaster Albanus (Herr Klein), had his daughter Rosamond (Mlle Neumann) conveyed to the sea-coast by a secret passage and placed in the care of the trusty fisherman's wife Axa (Mme Vogel), so that she

> Withdrawn from haughty arrogance's crags
> Be schooled by trials of meek lowliness
> To noble duties of her princely state.

There she was to remain until her eighteenth year, only then to reappear and offer her hand to Prince Alfonso of Candia. In the meantime Fulgentius (Herr Rott) reigned as all but absolute governor of Cyprus. The appointed time passed. Rosamond, anxious to bring aid from her hut to the shipwrecked, by accident comes across the only survivor, Alfonso of Candia, who had sailed hither and let himself be stranded on the coast of Cyprus for the purpose of secretly observing his future wife! In the meantime citizens assemble at the secret invitation of Albanus, and Fulgentius (Herr Rott) and his daughter Claribella (Mlle Eichenhoff) also arrive. Axa introduces Rosamond, who after many objections on the part of Fulgentius is acknowledged as princess. Alfonso joins the governor's retinue under the name of Manfredi.—The second act develops the change which the sight of Rosamond has wrought in the governor's heart. He loves her inexpressibly and endeavours to fascinate her by festivities. Corsairs hide in the palace garden in order to abduct Rosamond, but she happens to have playfully changed her princely robe with Claribella. The pirates thus precipitate themselves upon Claribella; Manfredi saves her; the pirates fall, a single wounded one remaining alive. Fulgentius entreats Rosamond to say if she can love him, but she shudderingly confesses that she abhors him. Fulgentius, whose love, having reached its culmination, turns to its opposite, departs in fury. Paying no heed to Claribella's pleas, Fulgentius's followers arrest Rosamond on the pretext that she had known of the corsairs' plot and purposely changed her princely robe with Claribella, the wounded pirate being said to have told this tale.—In the third act, the pirate having been forced to confess that he was bribed to make the above declaration, Rosamond, who has been delivered by the people, returns to Axa, firmly resolved never to part with her again.—Fulgentius, who had already revealed himself as a skilled alchemist, now appears in his laboratory and prepares the strongest of poisons, with which he writes a letter the mere reading of which is deadly. This he gives to his apparent confidant Manfredi with the promise that, provided that he hands the lethal letter to Rosamond, he is to receive Claribella and the Cyprian throne as a reward.—In the fourth act Rosamond appears among her flocks in an idyllic valley. Manfredi tells her the purpose of Fulgentius's letter. Fulgentius appears and suspects betrayal, but Manfredi persuades him that Rosamond has already perused the letter and imbibed death in a gentle madness in which she fancies herself a shepherdess. Fulgentius resolves to nourish that madness by pastoral songs and dances. During this festivity Albanus in disguise takes Alfonso aside and gives him a document which, he says, only needs Rosamond's signature in order to save the situation immediately. As Rosamond writes, Fulgentius rushes in and wrestles with Alfonso for the document; but by accident he gets hold of his own letter, reads it and—dies of his own poison. —I regard it as my duty to draw attention as far as possible to the advantages of a work which, perhaps by accident, found more opposition than it deserves. These consist in pure and cultivated iambics; a pleasant romantic atmosphere; a few vigorous moments and some appealing lyrical passages. According to rumour the piece has already been accepted by many theatres abroad, where it is to be given shortly; and we are curious to hear what sort of success it will have on those stages, proportionately to that accorded it here.—The music by Franz Schubert, our honoured compatriot, is truly excellent in several of its numbers, and it arouses even greater expectations of this composer's latest production, 'Fierabras' (libretto by Herr Kupelwieser), which has been erroneously announced in these pages as having been withdrawn, for it is to appear as early as the end of January. The overture had to be repeated, and the same compliment was paid to the rustic chorus in the last act. The song at the beginning of Act III and the chorus in the same are excellent. Herr Schubert was unanimously acclaimed. —The lady whose benefit it was played bravely and was loudly called, for which she offered modest thanks.—Herr Rott furnished a very successful performance, which enhanced the piece.— Mme Vogel and Herr Klein did their share.—Herr Palmer appeared to have taken his part at short notice.—The choreography in the second act had barely a few good moments and was performed with little precision.

S. S.

[Siegmund Saphir.]

The information that the piece was already accepted by many theatres abroad (i.e. in Germany) was doubtless due to a piece of wishful thinking on Frau von Chézy's part. After a single repeat performance on 21st December 1823 it disappeared for ever.—More unfortunately Schubert's 'Fierabras' (see No. 398) was not given at the Court Opera, either in January 1824 or at any later date. It was not performed at all until 1897, at Karlsruhe, and it was given in French at Brussels in 1926.

413. From the Vienna 'Sammler,' 30th December 1823

. . . Herr Schubert showed originality in his composition, but unfortunately also eccentricity. This young man is as yet in a period of development; it is to be hoped that it will proceed happily. For once he received too much applause; may he never have to complain about too little! . . .

The word "eccentricity" (Bizarrerie), which Schubert had applied to Beethoven in 1816 (see No. 90), now recoiled upon himself.

414. From the 'Wiener Zeitschrift,' &c., 3rd January 1824

. . . The musical accompaniment by Schubert left no doubt as to this popular master's genius. . . .

These last two Viennese criticisms (Nos. 413 and 414) were as detailed as the preceding one (No. 412). On the other hand the Leipzig 'Allgemeine musikalische Zeitung' of 15th January 1824 contented itself with saying that the work "was not satisfactory in any respect." The Stuttgart 'Morgenblatt' of 24th January never mentioned Schubert's name. The Berlin 'Gesellschafter' of 16th February remarked, like the Stuttgart paper, that the actors, expecting a failure, had not even troubled to learn their parts. Höhler, the critic of the Dresden 'Abendzeitung,' regretted on 8th April that he had been unable to go to the first two performances and that there was no later opportunity of seeing the piece. (German edition, Nos. 430–3.)

'Rosamond' performed for the second and last time, 21st December 1823.—This performance is mentioned by Rosenbaum and by Ignaz von Seyfried. Four days of Christmas holiday followed, during which the theatre was closed.

Franz Lachner becomes organist at the Protestant church, 22nd December 1823.—Franz Lachner, one of three musical brothers, was born in 1803 at Rain-am-Lech in Bavaria, and went to Vienna in the autumn of 1822. He soon made friends with Schubert, whom he met at lunch at the Haidvogel Tavern in the Stefansplatz. There is a story that Josef Lanner said at the Partridge Tavern, where he played with his string quintet, on seeing Schubert and Lachner after the latter's success in the competition for the organist's post at the Protestant church: "Yes, indeed, all these little Francises do have something in their little heads!"

415. SCHWIND TO SCHOBER

[Vienna,] 24th [December 1823].

Schubert is better, and it will not be long before he goes about with his own hair again, which had to be shorn owing to the rash. He wears a very cosy wig. He is much with Vogl and Leidesdorf. The dratted doctor is often with him, too. He is now thinking (the doctor) of a concert or a public Schubertiad. If it comes off, I 'll write to you.

Schubert's loss of hair was connected with the secondary stage of his illness, perhaps with some special treatment for it.—The "dratted [verzwickte] doctor" is Bernhardt.—The idea of a concert of Schubert's own works also turns up in a letter of his to Kupelwieser of the spring of 1824 (No. 456), but nothing came of it until the spring of 1828.

416. Schwind to Justina von Bruchmann

29th December 1823.

The picture which shows me yourself and Schober and Schubert around me, and the garden with everlasting flowers, holds no deception for me.

This letter is preserved in a copy by Justina for Schober.—The style of this one sentence is characteristic of Schwind's letters of that time, especially those addressed to Schober; it has the romantic obscurity of Jean Paul's literary manner. Schwind thought of himself as being in the confidence of the lovers, Justina and Schober. The garden with the everlasting flowers may be a symbol for these four people's friendship.

417. From the Official 'Wiener Zeitung,' 30th December 1823

At the House of Sauer & Leidesdorf in Vienna,
Kärntnerstrasse, No. 941, has just been published:

Première grande Sonate
pour le Pianoforte à quatre mains,
composée
par Fr. Schubert.

Œuv. 30.   Price, . . . 5 Florins, V.C.

This Op. 30 appeared immediately after Op. 24, the numbers in between being deferred. It was dedicated to Count Pálffy, the proprietor of the Theater an der Wien, which may have had something to do with the performance of 'Rosamond.' The designation as '*Première Grande Sonate*,' although given in the present announcement, does not occur on the title-page until the second issue. This must therefore have been a belated afterthought on Schubert's part.

'To be Sung on the Water' ('Auf dem Wasser zu singen'), Op. 72 (xx. 428), published in the 'Wiener Zeitschrift,' 30th December 1823.

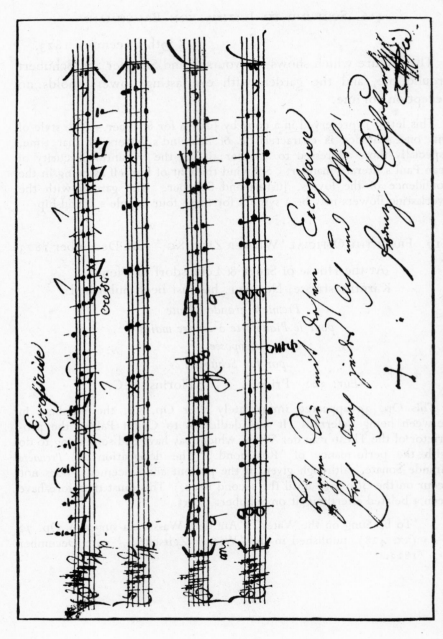

Album Leaf for Seraphine Schellmann (1823).   See pp. 287 f.

Theater = Anzeige.

Se. Excellenz Herr Graf Ferdinand von Pálffy, Eigenthümer des
k. k. priv. Theaters an der Wien, bewilligten der Unterzeichneten eine
Vorstellung zu ihrem Vortheile; dieselbe gibt sich demnach die Ehre,
einen hohen Adel und das verehrungswürdige Publikum gehorsamst zu
benachrichtigen, daß diese Vorstellung Samstag den 20. December
1823 im k. k. priv. Theater an der Wien Statt finden, und an die-
sem Tage gegeben werden wird:

Zum ersten Mahle:

Rosamunde,
Fürstinn von Cypern.

Großes romantisches Schauspiel in vier Aufzügen, mit Chö-
ren, Musikbegleitung und Tänzen, von Helmine von Chezy,
geborne Freyinn Klencke.

Musik von Herrn Schubert.

Die gesperrten Sitze sind an der Theaterkasse, Kärntnerstraße Nro.
1038, nächst dem Kärnthnerthore, im ersten Stock, zu den gewöhnlichen
Amtsstunden zu haben.

Die (P. T.) Herren Abonnenten, welche ihre Logen und gesperrten
Sitze für diesen Abend zu behalten gesonnen sind, werden höflichst er-
sucht, den Tag vor der Vorstellung gütigst Meldung davon geben zu
lassen.

Emilie Neumann,

Schauspielerinn des k. k. priv. Theaters an der Wien.

Handbill Announcing 'Rosamunde' (1823).   *See* p. 307.

1824

Octet in F major (iii. 1), February–1st March.
String Quartet in A minor (v. 13), February–March.
Sonata in C major for Pianoforte Duet ('Grand Duo') (ix. 12), June.
'Divertissement à la Hongroise' for Pianoforte Duet (ix. 19).

417A. FROM THE CONSCRIPTION SHEET, Early 1824

City 1187 [lodging at No.] 2   .

Franz Schubert [born] 1796 [*sic!*].

Musical artist of Vienna.

    Schubert is entered in the visitors' list, i.e. as a lodger (cf. No. 113).

418. FROM THE 'THEATERZEITUNG,' 1st January 1824

We esteem it a most agreeable duty to inform the art-loving
public of an increase of the New Year presents that have so far
appeared by a musical gift, 'Album musical' (at the art establishment of Sauer & Leidesdorf).   Vienna's artistic beauties will now be
able to greet the earliest hours of the year with enchanting melodies
owing their gracious existence to well-known tone-poets.   For
this happily chosen souvenir, the first of its kind in Germany,
contains a new Cotillon for the pianoforte by Count Gallenberg,
a Russian melody by Herr Frz. Schubert, a musical jest on original
Spanish themes by Herr Louis, two French romances by Mme
Fodor-Mainvielle, a new cavatina by the celebrated Rossini, as
well as dances and several smaller pieces, also a romance feelingly
sketched by Herr M. J. Leidesdorf, 'The Maiden's Heartbeats.'
—Outwardly this little work presents an appearance worthy of its
fair purpose.   Genuine Basle paper, clean engraving and printing,
with copper-plates, in addition to an elegant binding, make it a
welcome New Year's gift fit to expect due acknowledgment as a
truly brilliant novelty.

See No. 407.

419. SCHWIND TO SCHOBER

[Vienna,] 2nd January [1824].

Our New Year's Eve festivity went off happily. We gathered at Mohn's. Bruchmann and Doblhoff returned on the stroke of twelve from the city, where they had expected and sought Schubert. You, Senn and Kupelwieser, Bruchmann and everybody's sweethearts all had their health drunk. Soon afterwards Schubert and Dr. Bernhardt announced themselves by a small target-shooting match. Schubert hit, and the shattered window-pane set everybody astir. With the doctor I have fraternized, which should suit me well. I got home at 4.30 a.m. It was all a bit crude and common, but better than we might have expected. Bruchmann danced with Eichberger, Mohn and myself. . . . To-day I brought her [Justina] the news I gathered from Schubert's letter.

"Fraternized" (*schmolliert, see* No. 390).—"Eichberger" is a mistake for Eichholzer.—"Schubert's letter" was one written by Schober to him, which is lost.

420. DOBLHOFF TO SCHOBER

Vienna, 7th January 1824.

All are quite well and thought of you with intimate joyousness on the festively celebrated New Year's Eve which, although in many respects inferior to that of last year, far surpassed [it] in free, unrestrained pleasure and harmony of the most resounding joy. We met at Mohn's at 11 o'clock: Bruchmann, Schwind, Schubert, Bernhardt, Hönig, Smetana, Kraissl, Dietrich, Eichholzer, Steiger, Kiesewetter, Mayer and I. Six Bruchmannish bottles of Moselle precipitated themselves and us and all our splendid absent friends into the new year, and although a little impetuously, this nevertheless developed no other feeling than that of love and friendship, and so we will hope the best of the year which has come of age . . . Schubert is almost completely well and in nearly constant communication with Bernhardt and Leidesdorf.

Kiesewetter is probably Karl von Kiesewetter, the elder son of the aulic councillor (*see* No. 341). About 1820 he had participated or been interested in Senn's students' association (*see* No. 162); Sedlnitzky mentions him in his report of 29th March 1820 (Household, Court and State Archives, Vienna). He had been living for some time with his maternal grandparents at Heidelberg, which drew on him the suspicion of the Viennese police because of the university there.

421. KARL MARIA VON WEBER to Ignaz Franz Castelli in Vienna

Dresden, 8th January 1824.

Bäuerle sent a violent notice of the failure of 'Rosamond' to the 'Abendzeitung,' c/o my address. He probably thought this would give me pleasure, but it has only increased my embarrassment. Winkler, of course, refused to print it, which suited me very well.

Bäuerle (*see* note preceding No. 319), the editor of the 'Theaterzeitung,' had sent this notice unsolicited to the Dresden 'Abendzeitung,' whose Vienna correspondent, Höhler, it is true, had missed 'Rosamond,' as indeed he reported to his paper on 8th April (*see* No. 414). K. G. T. Winkler, born in 1775 at Waldenburg in Saxony, who wrote under the pseudonym of Theodor Hell, was the author of the libretto for Weber's 'The Three Pintos' (later on the German translator of his 'Oberon') and editor of the 'Abendzeitung.' For the strained relations between Weber and Schubert after the performance of 'Euryanthe' *see* notes preceding No. 387 and following No. 388. Weber was clearly reluctant to show his feelings in the matter of 'Rosamond' on account of both Helmina von Chézy and Schubert.

422. FROM THE OFFICIAL 'WIENER ZEITUNG,' 12th January 1824

New Dance Music for 1824,
published by Sauer & Leidesdorf,
Kärntnerstrasse, No. 941:

. . . .

LET 'S STICK TOGETHER
['Halt's enk z'samm']
A Collection of Original Austrian Country Dances for the Pianoforte
by Payer, Pensel, Leidesdorf and others.

Book I.   Price, 1 Florin 15 Kreuzer
do. for 4 Hands, 2 Florins.

Schubert's Brother Ignaz.   Oil Painting by his Stepson, Heinrich Hollpein

PLATE VIII

Schubert's Brother Ferdinand. Ivory Relief by Norbert Schrödl (1845)

PLATE IX

These waltzes are already in the press in arrangements for violin and pianoforte as well as for several other instruments, which will appear in a few days.

This was the first of three dance collections published under the title of the "Egerland" march (which in 1938 became a political song for the Sudeten Germans), 'Halt's enk z'samm' (dialect for "Haltet euch zusammen"), adorned with an etching by Schwind.   This vignette shows a Viennese ballroom and, in the orchestra, a wind player on the right-hand side who is a caricature of "tall Huber" with his long nose seen in profile.— The book contains twelve dances, six by Payer, two by Pensel, one by Leidesdorf and three anonymous.   Schubert was not represented in it, but appeared in Book II (see No. 431).

423. FROM THE 'WIENER ZEITSCHRIFT,' 13th January 1824
EXPLANATION AND THANKSGIVING

The esteemed reviewer of this periodical was unable to grasp the context of my drama, 'Rosamond,' quite correctly and in its most important constituents, and similarly a notice in the 'Theater-zeitung' contains an error here and there; but neither is due to the reviewer, for truly, had the piece not remained clear in my mind, I should myself have been unable to discover its meaning at the performance.   This may also be the reason why the article in the 'Sammler' contains an incorrect report of the story of the piece.

I may possibly decide before long to issue my poem of 'Rosamond' in print, until which time I must beg all those who have seen it performed or read the notices to reserve their judgment.   The breakneck speed with which 'Rosamond' was staged was no part of the directorate's plan, but due to accessory circumstances which need not be mentioned here.   To this one calamity were added several others, as for instance the fact that the dances were re-hearsed for the first time 48 hours before the performance, the last musical pieces had arrived equally late and, for a crowning mis-fortune, a brand-new prompter made his first trial run in 'Rosa-mond.'   On the other hand the producer, Herr Demmer, who is so well accredited as a thinking artist, took such honest and arduous trouble at the rehearsals that I feel it to be incumbent on me to express my sincerest thanks to him in public. The orchestra did wonders, though it was able to go through Schubert's glorious music but twice at a single rehearsal, and performed the overture and most of the other numbers with precision and devotion. A majestic stream, winding through the poem's complexities like a sweetly transfiguring mirror, grandiose, purely melodious, soulful, unspeakably touching and profound, the power of its tones carried away every soul. Nay even those members of the public who since last autumn have been hunting wolves and leopards on the banks of the Wien, would have succumbed to this all-conquering flood of euphony, if they had strayed in to 'Rosamond,' no matter what anti-melodic partisan spirit had crept in among the masses. Those who have seen 'Preciosa' and other weighty pieces at the Theater an der Wien will agree with me that I was entitled to believe I was risking nothing by writing a piece to which I had myself set bounds, and which has been sent abroad in a form differing considerably from that in which it was seen here. The writing of spectacular pieces is a task for which I am as little fitted as a sprig of ivy would be to support a tower or a butterfly to carry a knightly palace on its wings. I was thus able to satisfy the directorate only with a romantic poem made of those deeper echoes of an inner world and of an old subject that offered itself; of art there could be no question, since no time remained me for that in the five days during which I sketched and wrote the piece, in order that it might be staged in all haste. In such circumstances it would be sheer ingratitude to deny recognition to the judicious performance of Mme Vogel, the unmistakable devotion with which Herr Rott enhanced his part, the valiant acting of Mlle Neumann, particularly on the first night, and to that which many others did on its behalf. It is to be hoped that the confidence with which I offered the company a piece of work done with love and exertion, though hastily, will be even better justified later on by renewed study and greater unity in the casting, as well as a worthier production than that which the precipitancy of the whole undertaking permitted.

Vienna, 4th January 1824.   Helmina von Chézy, *née* von Klencke.

The notices in the 'Wiener Zeitschrift' and the 'Sammler' mentioned here are partially quoted in Nos. 414 and 413, that of the 'Theaterzeitung' appears complete in No. 412.—The words of 'Rosamond' were never printed and are not extant even among Helmina von Chézy's manuscripts.—In October 1823 the Theater an der Wien produced a magic play, 'Der Wolfsbrunnen,' by Josef Alois Gleich (born Vienna, 1772) with music by Franz de Paula Roser, in which an actor (Leopold Mayerhofer) represented a she-wolf, much to the delight of the public which loved "animal pieces," in which monkeys and leopards also appeared. —"Partisan spirit" may refer to Weber's Viennese following. His music for Pius Alexander Wolff's drama 'Preciosa' had been used at the same theatre on 5th July 1823.—One of the "spectacular pieces" was Wilhelm Vogel's 'Der böse Krollo,' a drama of ancient Swiss knights drawn from the tragedy 'Fredolfo' by the Irish "terror novelist" Charles Robert Maturin, given on 5th December 1823 for the benefit of the actor Palmer. —That Frau von Chézy could have written her play in five days is hardly credible, for it was already talked of in October 1822 (see No. 385), although Schubert was unable to write some of his music until just before the performance. It is improbable, too, that it could have been sent in an improved version to foreign theatres (i.e. theatres in Germany) as early as the beginning of January, if the original version had not been written before December 1823. Even more questionable is Wilhelm von Chézy's information that the play had been accepted and paid for by a few other theatres.—There was no "renewed study."

424. FROM THE DRESDEN 'ABENDZEITUNG,' 1st May 1824

(Vienna Diary, early January 1824.)

The Carnival again brought us sundry and not a little comically entitled dances: . . . 'Let's stick together,' original Austrian country dances . . .

[? Höhler.]

Schubertiads at Count Weissenwolff's at Linz, January–April 1824.— Johann Nepomuk Ungnad, Count Weissenwolff, born 1779, had been married to Sophie Gabriele, Countess Breuner, born 1794, since 1815 and lived at the castle of Steyregg some five miles to the east of Linz. He was a lieutenant-colonel and in 1825 became head of the family estate and steward of the patrimonial domain in Upper Austria; his wife sang contralto and became an enthusiastic adherent of Schubert's. Both were members of the Linz Musical Society.

425. FROM THE PROGRAMME of the Eleventh Evening Entertainment held by the Philharmonic Society, 15th January 1824

4. 'The Nightingale' by Unger, music by Schubert, for 4 male voices, sung by Herren von Barth, Tietze, Nejebse, [Adalbert] Rotter.

Adalbert Rotter, born 1800, was a bass (*see* No. 465).

426. FROM THE DRESDEN 'ABENDZEITUNG,' 3rd May 1824

(Vienna Diary, middle of January 1824.)

At Sauer & Leidesdorf's appear a collection of new pianoforte compositions, songs and dances under the unsuitable title of 'Album musical.'

[? Höhler.]

Anna von Hartmann sings to her brother Ludwig, who has just undergone an operation, songs by Schubert, at Linz, 18th January 1824.

427. SCHWIND TO SCHOBER

[Vienna,] 19th [January 1824].

To-night we had a kind of Schubertiad at Mohn's. There has only been one at Bruchmann's all this winter.

The Bruchmann Schubertiad had taken place on 11th November 1823.

428. SCHWIND TO SCHOBER

Vienna, 20th January 1824.

The greatest things known to me on earth are love, beauty and wisdom. You have yourself ranked me with you and Schubert, and I could not bear the delight of it. Thus has pain cleansed me, so that to be third among you means everything to me.

429. BRUCHMANN TO SENN at Trient

[Vienna,] 22nd January 1824.

Of Schober we know that he was not engaged at Breslau; he goes to Posen or Stettin. Schubert is fairly well.

Schober's attempt at appearing on the stage at Breslau met with difficulties. He therefore intended to go to Sweden, but did not carry out the plan.

430. Johanna Lutz to Leopold Kupelwieser

Vienna, 25th January 1824.

I am quite frightened, for there is all sorts of vexation in your circle again. You would be much annoyed by the stupid tittle-tattle that always goes on among the men, and I am so afraid of it that I shall be quite glad when Thursday will be over.

Mohn is a good fellow enough, but he is always upsetting our undisturbed propriety and then takes offence at every trifle.all the same.

Last week Schwind was here and brought me Schubert's Russian air. I much look forward to playing it to you.

Schwind is an excellent great baby and likes you very much. That pleases me well, but I should have liked it much better if Kraissl had brought me the music, as he had promised; but you can never trust his promises much.

The "circle" is the friends' reading circle. Its evenings were Monday and Thursday.—The "Russian air" is the 'Air russe' (*see* No. 407).—On Kraissl Bauernfeld wrote that same month, on the occasion of a ball at the printer Josef Trentsensky's: "A mediocre landscape painter who fiddles heavenly waltzes. He looks like a bandit. Pale, with long, black drooping hair, moustache and imperial" (cf. iconographical volume, p. 308, a self-portrait of his earlier years). He was the drawing-master of Kupelwieser's betrothed.

431. From the Official 'Wiener Zeitung,' 29th January 1824

New Dance Music for 1824
published by Sauer & Leidesdorf,
Kärntnerstrasse, No. 941:

. . . . .

Let's stick together

Collection of Original Austrian Country Dances for the Pianoforte by Payer, Pensel, Leidesdorf and others.

For Pianoforte solo . . 1 Fl. 15 Kr.
For Pianoforte Duet . . 1 Fl. 30 Kr.
For Pianof. and Violin *concertante* 1 Fl. 15 Kr.
For 2 Violins and Bass . 1 Fl. 30 Kr.

This is still the first book of the collection (*see* No. 422), which appeared. in several arrangements (now lost).

432. From the Programme of the Thirteenth Evening Entertainment held by the Philharmonic Society, 29th January 1824

2. 'Restless Love' ['Rastlose Liebe'], poem by Goethe, music by Schubert, sung by Herr Tietze.

433. Schwind to Schober

[Vienna,] 2nd February 1824.

Justina read to me from your letter that you [appeared] with success, and what you write about me. That was on Schubert's birthday. We had a feast at the "Crown," and though we were all fuddled, I wished you were present, if only for the sake of Schubert's pleasure over your good fortune. In my consummate tipsiness I was able to see them all as they are. They were all more or less idiotic, and Schubert asleep. Bruchmann alone, although [he] remembers nothing of all this, was 'like someone filled with enthusiasm. He embraced me passionately, drank Julie's health with me alone, and with Schubert and me wished you good health with a warm, everlasting handshake.

Schwind was the confidential messenger between Schober and Justina von Bruchmann.—The word "appeared," which is only a supposition, was crossed out by Schober, together with all the other traces of this stage interlude in his life. He had thus made an appearance after all.—Schubert's birthday was 31st January.—Julie was Bruchmann's betrothed, Fräulein von Weyrother.

434. Helmina von Chézy to Frau Sarah Kaskel

Vienna, 4th February 1824.

I wish I could enclose for Jettchen the entrancing tune for the song in 'Rosamond,' written by Schubert; in this splendid young artist the hope of a great Mozart blossoms for us; indeed he is infinitely valued and liked here.

Frau Kaskel was a banker's wife at Dresden; Jettchen (Henriette) was her daughter, and both were friends of Frau von Chézy's.—For the "song" *see* No. 449.

435. Schwind to Schober

[Vienna,] 13th February [1824].

Schubert now keeps a fortnight's fast and confinement. He looks much better and is very bright, very comically hungry and writes quartets and German dances and variations without number.

The works mentioned were probably the A minor string Quartet, Op. 29, some lost waltzes of January 1824 and the Variations for flute and pianoforte on "Ye flow'rets all" (from the 'Fair Maid of the Mill' cycle) dating from the same month.

436. From the Official 'Wiener Zeitung,' 17th February 1824

At the House of Sauer & Leidesdorf,

Kärntnerstrasse, No. 941, is newly published:

The Fair Maid of the Mill
['Die schöne Müllerin']

A Cycle of Songs, Poems by W. Müller.

Set to Music for One Voice with Pianoforte Accompaniment by Franz Schubert.

Work 25, Book I.   2 Florins, V.C.

True to our opinion that every excellent work carries its own laudatory recommendation with it, we prefer to refrain from any emphatic praise of these songs, and merely remark that the most favourably known tone-poet has succeeded in these songs to an unusually high degree in combining the novelty of his melodies with that intelligibility by which a musical work of art at once favourably appeals to the connoisseur of art as well as to the educated musical amateur.

The second book of this publication is to appear in a week.

These songs are shortly to follow with guitar accompaniment.

·   ·   ·   ·   ·   ·

Further songs with pianoforte accompaniment, as follows:

Schubert, 'Group from Tartarus' ['Gruppe aus dem Tartarus']

and 'Slumber Song' ['Schlummerlied'] by Fr. Schiller. Work 24.   1 Fl. 30 Kr., V.C.

―――― 'Love hath lied' ['Die Liebe hat gelogen'], 'Blessed World' ['Selige Welt'], 'Swan Song' ['Schwanengesang'], 'The Treasure Hunter's Desire' ['Schatzgräbers Begehr']. Work 23.   1 Fl. 30 Kr.

―――― 'The Dwarf' ['Der Zwerg'] and 'Melancholy' ['Wehmut']. Work 22.   1 Fl. 30 Kr.

―――― 'On the Danube' ['Auf der Donau']. 'The Boatman' ['Der Schiffer']. 'Ulfru Fishing' ['Wie Ulfru fischt']. Work 21.   1 Fl. 30 Kr.

―――― 'Greetings to Thee' ['Sei mir gegrüsst']. 'Faith in Spring' ['Frühlingsglaube']. 'The Linnet's Wooing' ['Hänflings Liebeswerbung'].   Work 20. 1 Fl. 30 Kr.

―――― The same with guitar accompaniment.   1 Fl. 15 Kr.

Op. 25 appeared after Op. 30.   It was dedicated to Karl, Freiherr von Schönstein (see No. 235).   He was born in 1797 at Ofen (Buda) in Hungary, was court secretary to the General Court Chamber in Vienna, sang baritone and had made Schubert's acquaintance through the Esterházys c. 1820.   He had previously sung only Italian arias, but became Schubert's song interpreter among the Viennese nobility.   It is noteworthy that Schubert transposed three of the songs in the cycle for Schönstein: 'Impatience,' 'Morning's Greeting' and 'The Miller's Flowers.'—Wilhelm Müller, born at Dessau in 1794, father of the Oxford philologist Max Müller, was called "Greek Müller" on account of his enthusiasm for the Greek wars of liberation.   He wrote in his diary on 8th October 1815: "I can neither play nor sing, yet when I write verses I sing and play after all.   If I could produce the tunes, my songs would please better than they do now.   But courage! a kindred soul may be found who will hear the tunes behind the words and give them back to me."   In a letter of thanks dated 15th December 1822 and addressed to the gifted song-composer Bernhard Josef Klein (born Cologne, 1793, musical director of Berlin University) Müller had written on the publication of two books of Klein's settings from his poems (including 'Trockne Blumen' and 'Der Neugierige') concerning "the musical animation of my verses": "For, indeed, my songs lead but half a life, a paper life of black and white . . . until music breathe life into them, or at least calls it forth and awakens it if it is already dormant in them.   You it is, too, choosing my songs for preference for composition, who penetrate most deeply into them. . . ." The pity is that Müller, who died in 1827, never knew how much more completely his wishes had been fulfilled. The appearance of 'The Winter Journey,' the second of Schubert's cycles set to his words, he did not live to see, and it is doubtful whether he ever saw, let alone heard, 'The Fair Maid of the Mill,' the current German name of which, "Müllerlieder," has a double meaning, since it refers both to the poet's name and to the miller's journeyman who is its protagonist. The poems in their original form were written for a play with songs for Müller's Berlin friends and first set to music by Ludwig Berger (born Berlin, 1777). Which of the ladies of that circle may have been the prototype of the "fair maid" cannot be determined now. Schubert, of course, was not inspired by any maid, or any mill, but simply by Müller's poems. Müller was also a translator from English, especially of Marlowe's 'Faustus' (1818). It is thus particularly interesting to note that the words of 'Impatience' ("I'd carve it in the bark of ev'ry tree") recall Edmund Spenser's 'Colin Clout's come home again' of 1591 ("Her name in every tree I will endosse").—The second book of the cycle did not appear till 24th March 1824.

437. FROM THE OFFICIAL 'WIENER ZEITUNG,' 21st February 1824

At the House of Sauer & Leidesdorf,

in Vienna, Kärntnerstrasse, No. 941, is newly published:

The Favourite New Dance-book

GALOPS AND ÉCOSSAISES

for Pianoforte

by Franz Schubert and M. J. Leidesdorf.

Price, 1 Fl. V.C.

Of the National Austrian Country Dances entitled

LET'S STICK TOGETHER,

by Schubert, Czapek and Leidesdorf,

Book II for Pianoforte solo. 1 Fl.

The actual title of the first collection, in the usual faulty French, was 'Nouvelles Galoppes favorites et Ecossaises'; it contained three Écossaises by Schubert (xii. 25, Nos. 3 and 6, and one newly reprinted in 'Die Musik,' Berlin, 1st September 1912). Only one copy of this book is known: it is in the archives of the Vienna Philharmonic Society.—The second book of the country-dance collection (Vienna City Library and Anthony van Hoboken's collection now at Lausanne) contains Schubert's Op. 127, No. 2, and xii. 10, No. 6.

438. Schwind to Schober

[Vienna,] 22nd February [1824].

Schubert is quite well. He has given up his wig and shows a charming cygnet's down. He has a lot of the finest German dances again. Of the 'Maid of the Mill' songs the first book has been published.

On Schubert's temporary baldness *see* No. 415.—His dances are often undated, so that it is impossible to say which of them Schwind refers to here. In any case the Carnival of 1824 seems to have produced more German dances than have been preserved.

439. Johanna Lutz to Leopold Kupelwieser
(Reading circle at Frau Gritzner's.)

Vienna, 24th February 1824.

Schubert was there also. He was very nice, too. He was quite merry, which gave me much pleasure.

If there is a ball at Schober's, I shall make an excuse to remain at home, although the whole company is reconciled once more.

Josefa Gritzner was an acquaintance at Atzenbrugg (*see* note on pp. 184–5).

440. From the Programme of the Seventeenth Evening Entertainment held by the Philharmonic Society, 4th March 1824 (Conductor, Herr von Pockh)

4. Vocal Quartet ('The Nightingale') by Schubert, sung by Herren Barth, Tietze, Nejebse and Rotter.

Josef and Leopold Pockh were bass singers in the Philharmonic Society; it is not clear which of the two is meant.

441. Schwind to Schober

[Vienna,] 6th March 1824.

Justina wrote before she went to the ball at your mother's. . . . Franz [Bruchmann] was here . . ., but not Schubert, nor

Dr. Bernhardt, presumably because he had promised . . . Schubert is pretty well already. He says that after a few days of the new treatment he felt how his complaint broke up and everything was different. He still lives one day on panada and the next on cutlets, and lavishly drinks tea, goes bathing a good deal besides and is superhumanly industrious. A new Quartet is to be performed at Schuppanzigh's, who is quite enthusiastic and is said to have rehearsed particularly well. He has now long been at work on an Octet, with the greatest zeal. If you go to see him during the day, he says, "Hullo, how are you?—Good!" and goes on writing, whereupon you depart. Of Müller's poems he has set two very beautifully, and three by Mayrhofer, whose poems have already appeared, 'Boating' ['Gondelfahrt' (sic)]; 'Evening Star' ['Abendstern'] and 'Victory' ['Sieg']. The last, indeed, I never knew well, but I always remember it as a rich, teeming, almost fairy-like poem, but now [it] is serious, ponderously Egyptian and yet so warm and round, very grand and genuine. Apart from that some twenty German dances, each finer than the last, courtly, charming, bacchic and fugal, O God! I go to see him nearly every evening, he intends to write to you, but I secretly wish he would not do so, to let you see how disagreeable it is to expect letters; but no, do not write to me, I do not wish it. . . . You and she [Justina] and Schubert and myself. I've felt it, as in a holy dream, . . . I hover above you.

There had thus really been a ball at Frau von Schober's, for which her daughter Sophie had returned from St. Pölten. Among those present were Bruchmann, Hönig, Smetana, Steiger, the painter Josef Kriehuber, Gahy and the mysterious "Eibo" (see No. 390), also all the Atzenbruggers who happened to be in Vienna. It lasted until 6 a.m., which was not unusual during that mad season. Trentsensky, who was just then undertaking a Viennese edition of Shakespeare, gave a ball that same month which lasted twenty-four hours.—Dr. Bernhardt had begun to give Schubert a new treatment.—The performance of the A minor string Quartet was postponed from 7th March to the 14th (see following note). —The Octet for strings and wind, Op. 166, was written in February and finished on 1st March 1824. It was commissioned by Ferdinand, Count Troyer (born 1780), chief steward to the Archduke Rudolph, who had dedicated to him a Sonata for clarinet and pianoforte, for Troyer was a good clarinettist.—Which two of the Müller songs Schwind wished to emphasize we cannot even guess.—Mayrhofer's poems had appeared in Vienna early that year, but Schubert is conspicuously missing among the subscribers: the two friends may have been estranged at that time, or shortly before.   (Mayrhofer, as in 1818–19, was seriously ill and could walk only with the aid of a stick and support.)   Schwind wrongly writes 'Boating' ('*Gondelfahrt*') for 'Boatman' or 'Gondolier' ('*Gondelfahrer*'). 'Victory,' called "Egyptian" by Schwind, perhaps reminded him musically of 'Memnon.'

442. LEOPOLD KUPELWIESER TO SCHOBER

Rome, 8th March 1824.

There is no music to be heard here at all; we Germans sing often and much, and I also treat myself to a Schubertiad now and again.

There was a German artists' colony in Rome composed mainly of painters belonging to the so-called group of "Nazarenes."

First performance of the Quartet in A minor (v. 13) at Schuppanzigh's twelfth Subscription Concert, in the hall of the Philharmonic Society at the "Red Hedgehog," in the afternoon: first violin, Ignaz Schuppanzigh; second violin, Karl Holz; viola, Franz Weiss; violoncello, Josef Linke.   14th March 1824.—Schuppanzigh, born in Vienna in 1776, to whom Schubert dedicated this Op. 29, was conductor of the May Day concerts at the Augarten hall, formerly leader of the string quartet kept by Prince A. K. Rasumovsky, the Russian ambassador in Vienna, and he later founded his own quartet, one of the earliest teams to win fame as such.   He was, moreover, a member of the court chapel and later leader at the Kärntnertor Theatre.—Holz, born in Vienna in 1798, was cashier in the Chancellery of the Lower Austrian County Council, and thus an amateur player.—Weiss, born in Silesia in 1778, lived in the Rasumovsky palace and was something of a composer.— Linke was also a Silesian, born in 1783.   He had worked at the Theater an der Wien and was now at the Kärntnertor, also a member of the court chapel.

443. SCHWIND TO SCHOBER

[Vienna,] 14th March 1824.

Justina dances to-day at [Frau] Lindner's.   As I went from Schuppanzigh's to Wasserburger's, I saw the carriage in front of

the house. I went up too and found the [Bruchmann] children
still there . . . Schubert's Quartet has been performed, rather
slowly in his opinion, but very purely and tenderly. It is on the
whole very smooth, but written in such a way that the tune remains
in one's mind, as with the songs, all feeling and thoroughly expressive. It got much applause, especially the minuet, which is extraordinarily tender and natural. A mandarin next to me thought it
affected and devoid of style. I should just like to see Schubert
affected! A single hearing, what can that mean to the likes of
us, let alone to such a gobbler-up of notes? Afterwards we had
Beethoven's famous Septet.

Frau Lindner was probably the mother of the "Fräulein Liedern"
mentioned by Bruchmann (*see* No. 401).

444. FROM THE VIENNA 'ALLGEMEINE MUSIKALISCHE ZEITUNG,' 27th March 1824

1) New Quartet by Schubert. This composition must be heard
several times before it can be adequately judged.

445. FROM THE LEIPZIG 'ALLGEMEINE MUSIKALISCHE ZEITUNG,' 29th April 1824

In the afternoon of 14th March, in the hall of the Philharmonic
Society: 12th Subscription Quartet Concert given by Herr Schuppanzigh: Quartet No. 1 by Schubert; not to be despised as a first-born.

Actually Schubert had written about sixteen string quartets before this,
and only two more were to follow. The present one, in A minor, was
however the first to be performed in public and to be printed in Schubert's
lifetime (*see* No. 495).

446. FROM THE 'OESTERREICHISCHE BEOBACHTER,' 19th March 1824

(Announcement of the concert given by the pianist Leopoldine
Blahetka on 21st March 1824, at 12.30 p.m. in the County Hall.)

4. Vocal Quartet by Schubert, sung by Herren Barth, Tietze,
Nejebse and Rotter.

Leópoldine Blahetka (*see* No. 119), born in 1810 at Guntramsdorf in Lower Austria, was now aged thirteen. She studied the pianoforte with Karl Czerny and composition with Sechter, and had taken part in the concerts at Hatwig's.—The same announcement appeared on 21st March in the 'Theaterzeitung' and the Vienna 'Allgemeine musikalische Zeitung.'—The vocal quartet announced was probably 'The Nightingale.'

447. FROM THE VIENNA 'ALLGEMEINE MUSIKALISCHE ZEITUNG,' 27th March 1824

5) Instead of the vocal quartet announced Herr Tietze sang Schubert's 'Erl King' very meritoriously.

448. FROM THE 'THEATERZEITUNG,' 1st April 1824

Owing to a sudden emergency Herr Tietze was so obliging as to sing Schubert's ingenious song of the 'Erl King' without any preliminary rehearsal whatever, and Herr Hüttenbrenner to take on its by no means easy pianoforte accompaniment. Herr Tietze once again delighted by an ingratiating, heart-piercing voice, and Herr Hüttenbrenner showed solid, accomplished musicianship.

S. S.

[Siegmund Saphir.]

The accompanist was probably not Josef but Anselm Hüttenbrenner, who may have been on a visit to Vienna, perhaps at Salieri's, who had been ill since the beginning of the year.—The 'Theaterzeitung' published a supplementary notice on 10th April (German edition, No. 466); others appeared in the 'Wiener Zeitschrift' of 27th March and in the 'Sammler' of 27th April (German edition, Nos. 464 and 467).

449. FROM THE OFFICIAL 'WIENER ZEITUNG,' 24th March 1824

At the House of Sauer & Leidesdorf,
Kärntnerstrasse, No. 941, have just been published:

AXA'S ROMANCE

From the Drama, 'Rosamond,' by Wilhelmine von Chézy.

Set to Music for One Voice and Arranged with Pianoforte
Accompaniment
by
Franz Schubert
Work 26.   Price, 1 Florin, V.C.

The Overture and Interludes for Pianoforte Duet, as well as
the Choruses and other Musical Numbers to appear
shortly.

THE FAIR MAID OF THE MILL
['Die schöne Müllerin']
A Cycle of Songs, Poems by Wilhelm Müller.
Set to Music for One Voice with Pianoforte Accompaniment
by
FRANZ SCHUBERT

Work 25.   Book I, 2 Fl., V.C.
          Book II, 2 Fl., V.C.

The esteemed stage directorates who wish to obtain the score
of the music composed by Herr Franz Schubert for the Drama of
'Rosamond,' written by Frau Wilhelmine von Chézy (performed
here), are requested to address themselves to the Art and Music
Establishment of Sauer & Leidesdorf.

Op. 26, published after Op. 30, was probably intended to include
the other musical pieces from 'Rosamond.' The overture to 'The
Magic Harp,' arranged for pianoforte duet, did appear at M. J. Leidesdorf's about 1827. The act-tunes Nos. 1 and 3 were not issued (in
full score) until 1866; No. 2 as well as the 'Shepherds' Melody' not
till 1891 in the complete edition; the ballet music Nos. 1 and 2 (in
full score) only in 1867, after the rediscovery of the parts of the whole
'Rosamond' music by Grove and Sullivan during their visit to Vienna;
but the choruses of huntsmen, of spirits and of shepherds came out soon
after the Romance as Nos. 2–4 of Op. 26, all in vocal score; No. 3 also
(separately) with wind accompaniment at Leidesdorf's in 1828.—No
manuscript copies in full score are preserved; they were probably not
intended to be written out until interest began to be shown in the work.
The original score of the Romance and the three choruses is lost. The
parts of the Theater an der Wien, after being mislaid until 1867, went
from Schubert's nephew, Eduard Schneider, to Max Friedlaender and
then to the archives of the Vienna Philharmonic Society.

450. FROM SCHUBERT'S LOST NOTE-BOOK OF 1824

March 25th.

Pain sharpens the understanding and strengthens the mind; whereas joy seldom troubles about the former and softens the latter or makes it frivolous.

What I hate from the deepest bottom of my heart is that one-sidedness which makes so many wretches believe that only what they happen to be doing is best, everything else being worthless. One kind of beauty should hold man's enthusiasm all through his life, it is true; but the glow of that enthusiasm should light up everything else.

The entries in this note-book, which may have contained nothing else, have been preserved only as published by Bauernfeld. In his diary there is a mention of it in 1826 (*see* No. 701), where he also refers to verses of Schubert's "own making," evidently the poem of September 1820 (*see* No. 194), which Bauernfeld published in his obituary of Schubert in 1829, together with these notes (*see* No. XXXIII). Schubert may have recopied the poem in 1824.

451. FROM SCHUBERT'S LOST NOTE-BOOK OF 1824

March 27th.

There is no one who understands the pain or the joy of others! We always imagine we are coming together, and we always merely go side by side. Oh, what torture for those who recognize this!

What I produce is due to my understanding of music and to my sorrows; that which sorrow alone has produced seems to give least pleasure to the world.

The first entry may be connected with the estrangement between Schubert and Mayrhofer. The second is quoted in the opposite sense by Kreissle (p. 323): ". . . seems to give most pleasure to the world"; and he also misplaced the word "music." As Kreissle gives no source, it is evident that he merely used and altered Bauernfeld. Heine's similar words are familiar: "Out of my greatest sorrows make I my little songs," so are Shelley's: "Men learn in suffering what they teach in song."

452. From Schubert's Lost Note-Book of 1824

March 28th.

From the greatest enthusiasm to the utterly ridiculous there is but one step, as from the deepest wisdom to the crassest stupidity.

It is with faith that man first comes into the world, and it long precedes intelligence and knowledge; for in order to understand anything, one must first believe in something; that is the higher basis on which feeble understanding first erects the pillars of proof. Intelligence is nothing else than analysed faith.

Ideas similar to that in the first entry are in Wieland's 'Abderiten' (1781) and Thomas Paine's 'The Age of Reason,' also in what Napoleon said on the retreat from Russia.

453. From Schubert's Lost Note-Book of 1824

March 29th.

O imagination! thou greatest treasure of man, thou inexhaustible wellspring from which artists as well as savants drink! O remain with us still, by however few thou art acknowledged and revered, to preserve us from that so-called enlightenment, that hideous skeleton without flesh and blood!

454. From Schubert's Lost Note-Book of 1824

[No date.] 2 o'clock at night.

Enviable Nero! Thou who wert strong enough to destroy a loathsome people to the strains of strings and voice!

Bauernfeld said in 1869, in further recollections of Schubert, that the occasion for this note was a violent altercation between Schubert and members of the Court Opera orchestra. They asked Schubert, who had just come from Grinzing to his habitual café with some friends, for a new work for a concert. When he hesitated to comply, they grew presumptuous. "I think we are as good artists as you," said one of them. "Artists? Musicians is what you are! That's all! . . . I am the artist, I am! . . . And if art is the word, we are talking about me,

not about you worms and insects, who ask for solos I shall never write
for you. . . ." This, and more, is what Schubert is said to have told
them after a final glass of punch at Bogner's café. He then wrote the
desired piece for them after all, "and they kiss [or "will kiss"] my hand
for it! I know these people!" Thus Bauernfeld; but unfortunately he
did not become closely acquainted with Schubert until 1825, and in 1824
Bogner's café was not yet his usual haunt. Therefore this story is either
pure invention or else it has nothing to do with that allusion to Nero which
Bauernfeld tried to connect with it.—That Schubert once fell into a rage
as a youth at the Flower Pot Tavern when a university professor at the
next table made fun of Milder and Vogl in Gluck's 'Iphigenia in Tauris' is
attested by Josef von Spaun—who was not a poet.

455. SCHWIND TO SCHOBER

[Vienna,] 30th March 1824.

Yesterday I went to Bruchmann's, the first time that Franz
has invited me. He read me a letter from Senn of 6th March . . .
"Schober must by now have gone to Sweden via Pomerania."

Cf. note to No. 429.

456. SCHUBERT TO LEOPOLD KUPELWIESER

[Outside:]

M. Signor Leopoldo
Kupelwieser
pittore tedesco.
recapito al caffè grecco [sic]

Roma.

[Inside:]

31st March 1824.

Dear Kupelwieser,

For a long time I have felt the urge to write to you, but I never
knew where to turn. Now, however, Smirsch offers me an
opportunity, and at last I can once again wholly pour out my soul
to someone. For you are so good and honest, you will be sure
to forgive many things which others might take in very bad part

from me.—-In a word, I feel myself to be the most unhappy and
wretched creature in the world. Imagine a man whose health
will never be right again, and who in sheer despair over this ever
makes things worse and worse, instead of better; imagine a man,
I say, whose most brilliant hopes have perished, to whom the
felicity of love and friendship have nothing to offer but pain, at
best, whom enthusiasm (at least of the stimulating kind) for all
things beautiful threatens to forsake, and I ask you, is he not a
miserable, unhappy being?—"My peace is gone, my heart is sore,
I shall find it never and nevermore," I may well sing every day
now, for each night, on retiring to bed, I hope I may not wake
again, and each morning but recalls yesterday's grief. Thus, joy-
less and friendless, I should pass my days, did not Schwind visit
me now and again and turn on me a ray of those sweet days of the
past.—Our society (reading circle), as you probably know already,
has done itself to death owing to a reinforcement of that rough
chorus of beer-drinkers and sausage-eaters, for its dissolution is
due in a couple of days, though I had hardly visited it myself since
your departure. Leidesdorf, with whom I have become quite well
acquainted, is in fact a truly thoughtful and good fellow, but so
hugely melancholy that I am almost afraid I owe him more than
enough in that respect; besides, my affairs and his do badly, so
that we never have any money. The opera by your brother (who
did not do any too well in leaving the theatre) has been declared
unusable, and thus no claim has been made on my music. Castelli's opera, 'The Conspirators' ['Die Verschworenen'], has been
set in Berlin by a local composer and received with acclamation.
In this way I seem once again to have composed two operas for
nothing. Of songs I have not written many new ones, but I have
tried my hand at several instrumental works, for I wrote two
Quartets for violins, viola and violoncello and an Octet, and I
want to write another quartet, in fact I intend to pave my way
towards grand symphony in that manner.—The latest in Vienna
is that Beethoven is to give a concert at which he is to produce
his new Symphony, three movements from the new Mass and a
new Overture.—God willing, I too am thinking of giving a similar
concert next year. I will close now, so as not to use too much

paper, and kiss you 1,000 times. If you were to write to me about your present enthusiastic mood and about your life in general, nothing could more greatly please

	Your
In that case my address would be:	faithful Friend
c/o the Art Establishment of	Frz. Schubert.
Sauer & Leidesdorf,	
as I go to Hungary with Esterházy	Fare well!
at the beginning of May.	Very well!!

The Café Greco was the German artists' meeting-place in Rome.— Smirsch (*see* No. 390) was probably just writing to Kupelwieser, and Schubert handed him his own letter for transmission at the same time.— Schubert's despondency about his health he had expressed already in August 1823 (*see* No. 374), but only in the shape of doubts. It now cast its shadows even over his friendships.—The quotation is, of course, from Goethe's 'Faust'—a passage which occurs in Schubert's song 'Margaret at the Spinning-Wheel.'—Schubert's complaints about the reading-circle, which was now about a year old, had begun in November 1823 (*see* No. 399). It was suspended on 1st April (*see* No. 460), but continued to exist a little longer (*see* No. 491).—The unnamed opera is 'Fierabras.' —'The Conspirators,' set to music by Georg Abraham Schneider (born 1770), conductor at the Berlin Opera, had been produced there on 6th January 1824, but was only once repeated, thus sharing the fate of 'Rosamond.' Franz de Paula Roser (born Naarn, Upper Austria, 1779), another theatre conductor, submitted his setting of this opera to the Josefstadt Theatre in 1829, where, however, the work was not done.— The new songs referred to are probably the three on poems by Mayrhofer (*see* No. 441) and a fourth, 'Dissolution' ('Auflösung'), which also dates from March 1824.—The two string Quartets are the one in A minor already mentioned and the D minor ('Death and the Maiden') written in March 1824. These, together with a third never composed, were intended to complete Op. 29; but only the A minor eventually appeared under that designation, as Op. 29, No. 1.—By "grand symphony" he did not mean a particular work, but the type of composition he wished to culti-vate as distinct from his youthful works of this species and in regard to his two fragments, the E minor and major Symphony of 1821 and the B minor of 1822.—Beethoven's concert took place on 7th May 1822 at the Kärnt-nertor Theatre with a programme including the first performance of the ninth Symphony, parts of the 'Missa solemnis' given as "Three Grand Hymns with solo and choral voices," and the Overture 'Consecration of the House,' Op. 124, written for the renovation of the Josefstadt

Theatre celebrated on 3rd October 1822.—For the plan to give a concert of his own cf. No. 415.—Count Esterházy had already gone to Zseliz on 24th March, probably with the whole of his family.

457. ANTON SCHINDLER in Beethoven's Conversation Book, Spring 1824

Best one! Do not trouble in the least about me in the matter of the quarrel with M. Weber. Schubert and I have the right man in front of us.

The conversation books which Beethoven in his deafness used with visitors usually show but one side of the talk and are thus often obscure. M. (? Monsieur) Weber is probably Karl Maria von Weber, but this passage cannot be interpreted. It is not even clear whether by the "right man" Weber was meant or somebody else who may have stood by Schubert in his quarrel.

> First performance of the Octet (iii. 1) at Count Ferdinand Troyer's, who commissioned it, in Spielmann's house on the Graben. Performers: Ignaz Schuppanzigh (1st violin), (?) Johann Sina (2nd violin), Franz Weiss (viola), Josef Linke (violoncello), Josef Melzer (double bass), Count Troyer (clarinet), Friedrich Hradezky (horn) and (?) August Mittag (bassoon); spring 1824.—Count Troyer's lodging was on the Graben, in Anton, Freiherr von Spielmann's (later Jakob Josef Fischer's) house (now No. 13), where Pennauer's shop was also to be found. It is not certain whether it was Sina (born 1778) or Holz who played the second violin.—Melzer was double bass and double bassoon player in the court chapel.

458. FROM THE INVITATION to the Private Evening Concert given by the Violinist Georg Hellmesberger, Professor at the Vienna Conservatory, 1st April 1824, in the Philharmonic Society's Hall at the "Red Hedgehog," at 7 p.m.

4. Vocal Quartet by Schubert, sung by Herren Barth, Tietze, Nejebse and Rotter.

The quartet may again have been 'The Nightingale.'—The programme contained, apart from an aria by Paer sung by Fräulein Marie "Weiss" (probably the soprano Marie Pauline Weis, later married as Freiin von Rokitansky), new Variations for the violin composed by the concert-giver, a former schoolfellow of Schubert's.

459. FROM THE VIENNA 'ALLGEMEINE MUSIKALISCHE ZEITUNG,' 10th April 1824

After an aria by Paer . . . followed a vocal quartet by Schubert, sung by Herren Barth, Tietze, Nejebse and Rotter. All three pieces pleased. The quartet had to be repeated.

Another notice appeared in the 'Theaterzeitung' of 20th April (German edition, No. 478).

460. DOBLHOFF TO SCHOBER

Vienna, 2nd April 1824.

Yesterday our reading circle was formally suspended. It had grown so much that in the end it devoured itself; there was disorder in the club rules, revolt among some members—in short, the holy zeal which imparts dignity and permanence disappeared, and moreover Bruchmann was often prevented from coming by his studies, and who could replace him? Thus the institution, so flourishing a year ago, has been dragging out a shadowy existence for some time, until yesterday we gave it a grave and repose. Oh, where are those serene and happy times? Where is the unity of all those noble ones? Many are abroad, many have buried themselves in pandects and codes, and but rarely do we still gather a little nosegay from that Paradise which blossoms on in our memory.—The only faithful Wasserburgians are Schubert and I, but Bernhardt, Smetana and Hönig also come there daily, Bruchmann sometimes and the others rarely.—Schubertiads are hardly mentioned any more, Schubert himself cannot sing and Vogl will sing only in agreeable and respectable society. *O tempora nec sonora.*
. . . Bernhardt has almost wholly recovered from a pretty severe illness, Schubert still complains of pains in his bones, the others are all well.

At his father's desire and in view of his engagement to Julie von Wey-rother Bruchmann had begun to study law.—The "Wasserburgians" are, of course, the frequenters of Wasserburger's café.—The observation that "Schubert cannot sing" doubtless means no more than that his *voix de compositeur* was not suited to performance.

461. Johanna Lutz to Leopold Kupelwieser

Vienna, 7th April 1824.

The day before yesterday my father brought me two books of 'Maid of the Mill' songs, which have just appeared. They gave me very much pleasure. How wondrously beautiful they are I simply cannot tell. There are several among them which you do not know yet. Oh, if only you could hear them, then they would give me twice as much joy.

462. Schwind to Leopold Kupelwieser

Vienna, 10th April 1824.

Schubert is almost wholly well; he sends you many greetings. He was recently confined to the house with a very stringent regimen, and therefore very industrious. For several evenings we took pleasure in the thought that we might all three live together on your return. It remains to be seen whether we shall have that felicity before long.

This letter was continued on 31st May and 9th June (*see* Nos. 475 and 477).

463. Schwind to Schober

Vienna, 14th April 1824.

Schubert is not very well. He has pains in his left arm, so that he cannot play the pianoforte at all. Apart from that he is in good spirits. . . . Justina is now to sing 'To Music' ['An die Musik']. That will be unique. If only she could manage 'Suleika' for me! I simply cannot understand why people cannot sing everything if they have enough voice; but her singing is like growing grass, and I think of it with a secret shudder—until she finally becomes free.

'Suleika' may be either of the two Suleika songs from Goethe's 'West-östlicher Divan.'—The last sentence means doubtless that Justina will sing even more movingly once she has been set free of her home by becoming Schober's wife.

464. JOHANNA LUTZ TO LEOPOLD KUPELWIESER

Vienna, 15th April 1824.

The reading circles have now come to an end very quickly. It was easy enough to see it coming, for there were too many [meetings] for it to last.

465. REMARK ON THE AUTOGRAPH of the Song, 'Longing' ['Sehnsucht'] (xx. 357)

Received as a souvenir from Herr F. Schubert.

Vienna, 24th April 1824.   Adal. Rotter.

The song is that to Schiller's poem.—For Rotter *see* No. 425 and cf. No. 501.

466. FROM THE VIENNA 'ALLGEMEINE MUSIKALISCHE ZEITUNG, 12th May 1824

(Notice of Schuppanzigh's grand musical morning concert, 1st May 1824, in the I. & R. Augarten Hall.)

A vocal quartet (entitled 'The Nightingale') by Schubert, sung by Herren [Adalbert] Herz, [Josef] Hüttenbrenner, [Johann] Hoffmann and Decani, pleased.

Schuppanzigh continued the May Day concerts at the Augarten hall, which he had already conducted in 1798. Herz, at a concert given by him in 1825, performed a vocal quartet by Anselm Hüttenbrenner for a similar team, with Josef as second tenor. Hoffmann, born in Vienna in 1805, went as a bass to the Kärntnertor Theatre in 1826, but remained only for two months and went on tour. In 1855 he became director of the Josefstadt Theatre and the Thalia Theatre, a summer stage attached to it; there he produced 'Tannhäuser,' the first Wagner opera to be given in Vienna.—Of Decani no details are known.

467. FROM THE 'THEATERZEITUNG,' 18th May 1824

7. New vocal quartet by Schubert, in which a dilettante, Herr Herz, had an opportunity of placing his fine, metallic voice into the

light of day.   A handsome appearance, combined with a significant
if not yet developed store of vocal equipment, make him particularly useful to an operatic establishment.   It is to be wished that
he will soon be heard in something more important.

S. S.

[Siegmund Saphir.]

Fritz von Hartmann and Josef Hüttenbrenner sing in the choir at
the first performance of Beethoven's ninth Symphony in the Kärntnertor Theatre, 7th May 1824.—Schubert was certainly at this
concert (see No. 456), at which Henrietta Sontag (born Coblenz,
1803), Karoline Unger, Haizinger and Seipelt sang the solo quartet.
Schindler and Hüttenbrenner are said to have seen the exhausted
Beethoven home afterwards.   In any case Beethoven asked about
Josef before long, and Schindler answered in the conversation
book with his usual unreliability: "He is called Hüttenbrenner,
employed at Count Sauerma's office and come from Graz as
an acquaintance of Lichnowsky's.   He is a good musician and
sang in the choir at the concert."   Franz, Count Saurau, one of
the subscribers to Mayrhofer's poems, was Minister of the Interior,
and Hüttenbrenner was employed in his ministry.   (Saurau's sister,
Maria Therese von Oettel, had been Hüttenbrenner's first landlady
in Vienna.)   Moritz, Count of the Realm Lichnowsky (see note on
pp. 249–50), came from Grätz in Silesia, and Hüttenbrenner, who
came from Graz in Styria (formerly also called Grätz), twice met
Beethoven at his house in Vienna.

468. Leopold Kupelwieser to Johanna Lutz

Rome, 8th–12th May 1824.

The child Giselher, my son-in-law, has not written to me yet,
nor has Smirsch, nor Bruchmann.   The good Schubert alone
complains to me that he is ill again.   I wrote to him recently, and
as I did not know whether, according to his indications, the letter
would still find him in Vienna, since he said he intends to travel to
Hungary with Esterházy, I enclosed the letter with one to Rieder.

Giselher (see note on p. 304) is Gunther's son-in-law in the Nibelung
Saga.—Schwind's letter of 10th April (No. 462) had not yet been sent off.
—Schubert's letter was that of 31st March (No. 456).—Kupelwieser's
reply to Schubert has not been preserved.

469. FROM THE 'ÖSTERREICHISCHE BEOBACHTER,' 8th May 1824

(Announcement of the concert given by the cellist Friedrich Wranitz-ky, member of the Court Opera Orchestra, on 9th May 1824, in the Small Assembly Hall.)

4. Vocal Quartet, composed by Herr Schubert, sung by Herren Haizinger, Rauscher, Seipelt and Ruprecht.

Friedrich Wranitzky was the son of Anton Wranitzky, who had died in 1819. One of his sisters, Karoline Seidler, had been in touch with Countess Esterházy and her daughter Marie in Vienna in 1816.—The quartet may have been the new 'Gondolier' ('Der Gondelfahrer').

470. FROM THE 'THEATERZEITUNG,' 1st June 1824

. . . We observed with condolence that this composition lacks that originality, that fire of enthusiasm and that lyrical force which usually distinguish Schubert's works. The performance was *à peu près.*

Another notice, in the Vienna 'Allgemeine musikalische Zeitung' for 2nd June (German edition, No. 488), mentions that the quartet "had already been performed in other places for our delectation" by the same artists; this may have occurred in private, possibly at Frau von Lászny's. These four singers had only once before sung a quartet by Schubert in public: 'Spirit of Love' in September 1822 (*see* Nos. 314 and 315).

471. FROM THE PROGRAMME of the First Society Concert given by the Philharmonic Society of Linz, 23rd May 1824, at 11 a.m., in the Assembly Hall

2. 'Spirit of Love' ['Der Geist der Liebe']. Vocal Quartet by F. Schubert.

This second performance of a work by Schubert at Linz is mentioned also in the society's third annual report, p. 10 (not in the German edition).

472. KARL, FREIHERR VON SCHÖNSTEIN TO JOHANN KARL, Count Esterházy

Vienna, 25th May 1824.

. . . but it is a fact that every one now is enthusiastic only about Rubini, even our little Schubert, for all that he knew how

to put even David in his place. He may therefore tell you more
about Rubini, for he will probably be with you the day after to-
morrow, having left here to-day, as I believe.

Schönstein and Esterházy were ardent adherents of Italian opera in
Vienna.—Giovanni Battista Rubini, born in 1795 at Romano near Bergamo, had been in Vienna as tenor since 20th May 1824. Giacomo David,
born in 1750 at Presezzo near Bergamo, who had sung at the London
Handel Commemoration in 1791, had appeared as tenor as the Kärntnertor Theatre in 1822–4. His son, Giovanni, born at Milan in 1789,
who did not go to London until 1829, was also a tenor under Barbaja;
but Schönstein evidently refers to the father.

473. JOHANNA LUTZ TO LEOPOLD KUPELWIESER

Vienna, 26th May 1824.

Your letter found Schubert still here.

But he must have gone by now, for the windows of his lodgings,
which were always closed, are now wide open. The books which
Schubert had from you are now with Giselher, and when he has
read them he will bring them to me. He was here last week to
fetch a Rieder and Böhm for copying. He often brings me Schubert songs and German dances. I like that very much, for otherwise
I hear nothing at all.

The letter to Schubert was mentioned in No. 468.—He may actually
have departed for Zseliz by the ordinary mail-coach on 25th May.—His
room was on the Stubentor Bastion, in full view of the Glacis.—Giselher
is Schwind (see Nos. 401 and 468).—"A Rieder and Böhm" seem to be
paintings or drawings Schwind wished to copy. The latter was perhaps by
Josef Daniel Böhm, born in Hungary in 1794, a medal-sculptor.

474. [LOST LETTER from Schubert to his Father, Zseliz, 30th May 1824]

475. SCHWIND TO LEOPOLD KUPELWIESER

[Vienna,] 31st May [1824].

Schubert has left for Count Esterházy's in Hungary. He has an
opera libretto with him, on the subject of the enchanted rose,

worked up by Dr. Bernhardt, and he has also resolved to write a symphony. He sends you many greetings and hopes to see you in Vienna. Be sure you come to us!

The favourite epic 'Die bezauberte Rose' by Ernst Schulze had been used for a libretto by Bernhardt, which Schubert did not set. Bauernfeld too worked at the same subject for Schubert later on (*see* Nos. 540 and 663). In stanza 41 of the second of the three cantos in that work there is a curious anticipation of Schober's poem 'To Music' ('An die Musik') made so famous by Schubert. Schubert's only settings of Schulze's own work, however, are those from the latter's 'Poetic Diary' ('Poetisches Tagebuch').—The projected Symphony was not written at Zseliz, but at Gmunden and Gastein in 1825, and it is lost.

Josef Eybler becomes First Musical Director of the Court Chapel in succession to Salieri, 6th June 1824.

476. From the Official 'Wiener Zeitung,' 9th June 1824

At the House of Anton Diabelli & Co.,
Art and Music Dealers, Graben, No. 1133
(late Cappi & Diabelli)
is quite newly published and to be had:

Patriotic Artists' Association
['Vaterländischer Künstlerverein']
Variations for the Pianoforte,
on a Given Theme,
Composed by the Most Excellent Composers and Virtuosi
in Vienna and the I. & R. Austrian States.

Part I, containing 33 Variations by L. van Beethoven.
Work 120. Price 5 Florins 30 Kreuzer, V.C.

Part II, containing 50 Variations on the same theme by the following Composers, namely:

Assmayr, Ig.; Bocklet, K. M. von; Czapek, L.; Czerny, K.; Czerny, J.; Dietrichstein, M. von, Count; Drechsler, J.; Förster, E.; Freystädtler, J.; Gänsbacher, J.; Gelinek, Abbé; Halm, A.; Hoffmann, J.; Horzalka, J.; Huglmann, J.; Hummel, J. N.; Hüttenbrenner, A.; Kalkbrenner, F.; Kanne, Fr. A.; Kerzkowski,

J.; Kreutzer, K.; Lannoy, E., Baron; Leidesdorf, M. J.; Liszt, F.; Mayseder, J.; Moscheles, Ig.; Mosel, J. von; Mozart, W. A. jun.; Panny, J.; Payer, H.; Pixis, P.; Plachy, W.; Rieger, G.; Riotte, P.; Roser, F.; Schenk, J.; Schoberlechner, F.; Schubert, F.; Sechter, S.; (S. R. D.) Stadler, Abbé; Szalay, J. von; Tomaschek, W.; Umlauf, M.; Weber, Dionys; Weber, F.; Weiss, F.; Winkhler, K. A. von; Wittassek, J.; Worzischek, J. H.; Coda by Karl Czerny.   Price, 10 Florins, V.C.

(Property of the Publishers.)

The art establishment opening under the new name of A. Diabelli & Co. esteems itself fortunate to inaugurate its career with the publication of a new musical work which is unique in its kind and will, according to its nature, remain so.   All the well-known indigenous living composers and pianoforte virtuosi, to the number of fifty, were brought together to write each one variation upon one and the same theme submitted to them, thus demonstrating in the most interesting and instructive manner their ingenuity, taste, individuality and artistic outlook, as well as the treatment of the pianoforte peculiar to each.   Our great Beethoven (the musical Jean Paul of our time) had already earlier used the same theme for 33 variations (published by us), which form the first part of this work and plumb all the depths of genius and of art by its masterly and original treatment.   How interesting must it be, therefore, if all the other musical artists who at present flourish on Austria's classic soil develop their talents on this same subject and thus endeavour by their contributions to make this significant work not only a competitive task, but at the same time an alphabetical lexicon of all the names, some of them long celebrated, others still greatly promising, of a time which so irradiates the history of art.

It would lead too far to detail the separate achievements here, and we content ourselves with incidentally drawing attention to the fact that the late Emanuel Förster, so unhappily torn from us, here deposited the last labour of his noble spirit; that several highly esteemed dilettanti had the goodness to adorn this collection; that Herr Kalkbrenner, too, kindly furnished a contribution during his visit to Vienna; that the public will not without interest find in this set the first essay in composition by the richly gifted boy of eleven years, Liszt; and lastly that Herr Karl Czerny, apart from his alphabetical contribution, at our suggestion added a developed finale to round off the whole. The outward appearance is worthy of the contents.

The theme was Diabelli's own. The commission dates back to 1820. Beethoven may have begun his famous Diabelli Variations as early as February of that year; they had appeared alone at first and were now re-printed, in a third issue, as Part I of the complete work. The National Library in Vienna possesses thirty-seven of the forty-nine manuscripts by the other composers, among them alternative variations by the younger Mozart and by Rieger (also published in the meantime). Schubert's contribution is dated March 1821, and Hüttenbrenner's piece too dates from that year. Sechter's and Roser's manuscripts date from 1823, Kalkbrenner's from 1824, and Wittassek likewise did not write his variation until early in 1824. Among the fifty "Austrian" composers a few visitors to Vienna had been admitted as well as, of course, ten or eleven Bohemians, some of whom germanized their names after settling down in Vienna.—Karl Maria von Bocklet, born in Prague in 1801, went to Vienna c. 1817, became a violinist at the Theater an der Wien and later a pianoforte virtuoso.—Emanuel Alois Förster (see No. 148), born in 1748 at Neurath in Austrian Silesia and settled in Vienna as pianoforte teacher since 1799, had died in November 1823.—Jakob Freystädtler, born in 1768, was another music teacher.—Johann Baptist Gänsbacher, born in 1778 at Sterzing in the Tyrol, chapel master at St. Stephen's Cathedral, was a close friend of Weber's.—Abbé Josef Gelinek, born in 1758 at Seltsch in Bohemia, pianoforte teacher and virtuoso, was domestic chaplain to Prince Nikolaus Esterházy.—Joachim Hoffmann, born in 1788 in Lower Austria, was pianoforte teacher and choirmaster.—Friedrich Wilhelm Michael Kalkbrenner, born at Cassel in 1788, had given a piano-forte recital in Vienna early in 1824; he lived in London for ten years and spent much of his life in Paris.—"Josef Kerzkowski" is perhaps identical with the Warsaw violinist Kaczkowski.—Liszt's contribu-tion may have been written early in 1823.—Josef Panny was born in 1794.—Wenzel Plachy, born in 1785 at Klopotowitz in Moravia, living in Vienna since 1811, was organist at the Piarist church in the Josefstadt suburb.—Gottfried Rieger was musical director at Brno. —Johann Schenk, born in 1753 at Wiener Neustadt in Lower Austria, the composer of the successful comic opera 'The Village Barber' ('Der Dorfbarbier'), taught Beethoven theory and Bauernfeld the piano-forte. The latter introduced him to Schubert later on, and "the old classic did full justice to the new romanticism."—Simon Sechter, born in 1788 at Friedberg in Bohemia, living in Vienna since 1804, master of music at the Blind Institute, was Vienna's great theorist.—Abbé *Commendatore* Maximilian Stadler (*see* note following No. 31), born in 1748 at Melk in Lower Austria, had returned to Vienna in 1815, was a church composer, honorary prebendary of Linz, abbot and canon of Kremsmünster. S. R. D. (S. S. R. D. on the title-page) is an abbreviation of the title Sua Reverentia Dominus.—Josef (not Julius) de Szalay, born *c.* 1806, a pupil of Förster, Hummel and Salieri, had appeared as pianist in Vienna at the early age of nine; it is said that Schubert played duets with him at Josef Gross's.—Dionys F. Weber, born in 1771 at Welchau in Bohemia, was director of the Prague Conservatory.—Franz Weber was an official and a pianist.—For Franz Weiss *see* note preceding No. 442.— Karl (Charles) Angelus von (de) Winkhler was an amateur composer at Pest.—Johann Nepomuk August Wittassek, born in 1771 at Melnik in Bohemia, was chapel master of St. Vitus's Cathedral in Prague.—The second book too still bears the plate-mark of the firm of Cappi & Diabelli engraved before it changed its style. Copies are extremely rare (Philharmonic Society, Vienna; Royal College of Music, London; Paul Hirsch Library, Cambridge).

477. SCHWIND TO LEOPOLD KUPELWIESER

[Vienna,] 9th June! [1824.]

Seeing how I sought you and Schubert and Bruchmann for long, and was almost ashamed of this seeking, and trembling at the thought of finding, how I came among you and found myself loved, while I dared wish for nothing more than to see you, how then should I have become different from what I was? Now that all are away, affection sinks down underground, and as gay reunion has vanished, I hold on directly to appreciation and the essence of things, which is eternal and unshakable.

This second continuation of the letter dated 10th April (*see* Nos. 462 and 475) shows Schwind treating Kupelwieser to his romantic style, which he otherwise reserved for his letters to Schober, who curiously enough is not mentioned here.

478. KARL HAAS TO MAX CLODI at Ebenzweyer

[Linz,] 18th June 1824.

. . . The one who fared worse with the weather was my sister Therese, who, as you may remember, recently drove to Gmunden and Ischl with Countess Weissenwolff, with whom she is at present enjoying an extremely agreeable country sojourn at Steyregg. . . . According to all these reports the countess seems to have as much feeling for nature as she evinces for art and especially for Schubert's music . . . Although she had already called on us repeatedly in town, I was the more pleased to visit her yesterday in her charming neighbourhood, where I myself witnessed the goodness and the engaging, natural demeanour of the countess, whom now, best of all, I heard sing Schubert's 'Maid of the Mill' songs and his most recent and surpassingly glorious compositions, whereby, it is true, Nancy Hartmann's performance was mightily put into the shade, for only now do I believe that I have begun to feel the significance of the Schubertian song. You may imagine how greatly my brother, with whom I went out there, and Josef Spaun, whom we met there, exult in such a patroness for their friend.

Karl Haas, born 1804, a medical student and amateur pianoforte player, was one of several children of Marie Haas at Linz, the widow of a government councillor. He died three months before Schubert. His sister Therese was adored by Max von Spaun and a friend of the Countess Weissenwolff.—Gmunden and Ischl are in the Austrian Salzkammergut.— Nany (Nancy) or Nanette was Anna von Hartmann, who that same year married Count Anton Revertera (born 1786) and became an honorary member of the Linz Musical Society.—Karl Haas had two brothers, Ferdinand and Josef; the one alluded to here was probably Josef, born at Hall in 1803, a priest at Ansfelden and later canon at St. Florian.—The addressee, Max Clodi, born 1804, a law student in Vienna, was the eldest of the three sons of the owner of Ebenzweier Castle on Lake Traun. Anton von Spaun soon afterwards arrived on a visit to that castle and met Vogl either there or at Gmunden. At Steyr, where Vogl spent the summer as usual, a fire broke out on 21st June which destroyed the castle of Lamberg.

479. FROM THE LEIPZIG 'ALLGEMEINE MUSIKALISCHE ZEITUNG,'
24th June 1824

'On the Danube' ['Auf der Donau']. 'The Boatman' ['Der Schiffer']. 'Ulfru fishing' ['Wie Ulfru fischt']. For a Bass Voice. Op. 21.

Zseliz Castle, where Schubert stayed, with the Family of Count Esterházy, in the Summers of 1818 and 1824

Music Room at Zseliz Castle, with the Pianoforte bought *c.* 1810 from Karl Schmidt, Pressburg

PLATE XI

Market Place at Steyr, showing some of its Beautiful Houses where Schubert stayed in the Summers of 1819, 1823 and 1825. *See* p. 121

PLATE XII

'The Dwarf' ['Der Zwerg']. 'Melancholy' ['Wehmut']. For One Voice. Op. 22.

'Love hath lied' ['Die Liebe hat gelogen']. 'Blessed World' ['Die selige Welt']. 'Swan Song' ['Schwanengesang']. 'The Treasure Hunter's Desire' ['Schatzgräbers Begehr']. For One Voice. Op. 23.

'Group from Tartarus' ['Gruppe aus dem Tartarus']. 'Slumber Song' ['Schlummerlied']. For One Voice. Op. 24.

All songs with pianoforte accompaniment composed by Franz Schubert. Vienna, Sauer & Leidesdorf. Each book, 45 Kreuzer, A. C.

The composer of these songs proves himself a respectable talent which, with the fresh courage of youth, disdains the old, well-trodden ways and clears a new path, which it logically follows. Who would blame him for this? None who is fair-minded enough to allow each artist his views of art and his ways and means of expressing himself in and through it; none who has sufficient modesty to admit that his own way may not be the only way to salvation. Yet, fair-mindedness and modesty may also frankly voice their opinion and are entitled to compare their own way with that of others. The reviewer therefore takes the liberty of dealing more thoroughly with the four books named above than is usual with works of this kind.

Herr F. S. does not write songs, properly speaking, and has no wish to do so (though those which come more or less near to it are No. 3 in Op. 21, No. 2 in Op. 22, Nos. 1–3 in Op. 23 and No. 2 in Op. 24), but free vocal pieces, some so free that they might possibly be called caprices or fantasies. In view of this intention the poems, most of them new but greatly varying in quality, are favourably chosen and the translation of them into music is praise-worthy in general, for the author succeeds almost throughout in laying out the whole and each detail according to the poet's idea; but not nearly so well in execution, which seeks to make up for the want of inner unity, order and regularity by eccentricities which are hardly or not at all justified and by often rather wild goings-on. But without these qualities, indeed, no artist's work can become a fine work of art, for their lack quite decidedly produces only bizarre and grotesque things. The voice-part, usually declamatory, is sometimes too little singable and not seldom unnecessarily difficult, and it has the peculiarity that the composer often writes even a soprano part in octaves with the instrumental bass. The harmony is pure as a rule—to hunt after consecutive fifths and octaves, false relations, and suchlike, of which there is no lack, which indeed occur pretty frequently, is quite rightly no longer the fashion—modulation is free, very free, and sometimes rather more than that. This reviewer at any rate knows no composition of this kind, indeed perhaps no composition of any sort, which goes, he will not say farther, but even as far. Op. 21 No. 1, for example, begins in E♭ major, which has disappeared at the seventh bar; then comes C minor, A♭ major and minor, C♭ major, &c., and F♯ minor, where it stays for some time and closes. Op. 22 No. 2, in D minor, has in the eleventh bar a formal cadence in F♯ major, and later the bass that has become celebrated from the first finale in Rossini's 'Tancredi': B♭ D F—B♭ E♭ G♭—B♭ D♭ F♭ G♭—B D♯ F♯, and so on, the same four or five times, always a semitone higher, which is a neat little cobbler's patch and may be recommended to pianoforte tuners to test purity of intonation. Whether in Op. 23 No. 1 the progressions in the third bar from the end were intentionally written as being truly new and original, although sufficiently hideous, or whether they are misprints, the reviewer dare not venture to decide, for all that he has some reason to believe the former. The following chords and modulations, however, the first example of which is remarkable only for the strange notation (it cannot be called orthography), are not misprints: E♭ G♭ C♭—F♭ G C♭ D—D♭ ; C♯ E♯ G♯ C♯—B♭ G B♭ D, and this three more times repeated, each time a semitone higher— F♯ A♯ C♯—F♯ E♭ A C—G D G C, &c. Whoever likes this, may go and play it and sing it and imitate it. Op. 21 [No. 2], bars 13–14, instead of C♭ F D—B♭ F D—A F D would surely be better C♭ G♭ E♭—B♭ G♭ E♭—A G♭ E♭—or rather, it could hardly be anything else. The simple 'Slumber Song' (Op. 24 No. 2) must for the sake of logic endure a few desperate modulations towards the middle, &c. In Op. 23 No. 2 even the most remote modulations are mild and therefore praiseworthy, and Op. 23 No. 4 deals with them easily.　Op. 24 No. 1 illustrates at the beginning, but does it very well, and although the modulations are very glaring, they are excusable, perhaps even justifiable here.— Thirteen shakes in the instrumental bass (Op. 21 No. 1), the abbreviation of four bars into two at the repeat of the last line in Op. 21 No. 2 and a few other things are details about which it is not worth while making words.　But the reviewer deems himself entitled to speak in greater detail about the unwarrantably strong inclination to modulate again and again, with neither rest nor respite, which is a veritable disease of our time and threatens to grow into a modulation-mania to which unfortunately even famous composers succumb, either willingly or for the sake of following the fashion.　He knows that not many listen and pay heed to the preacher in the wilderness, but hopes that a few will nevertheless hear his voice, and if the former, deeming that it is precisely there that their genius and learning, &c., shows itself, rise up in their arrogance and think or say of us others "They are not comfortable except where all is flat," he will remind the latter for their consolation that such modulatory exercises may indeed have their use, but only for the students of harmony; that all composition pupils begun by being wild and foolish, but later on modulate less and less, from which we may surely conclude that such aimless and purposeless straying is but the consequence of clumsy inability to remain comfortably in the place in which one happens to be; and finally that in the glorious works by the greatest masters of all times simplicity, repose, order and clarity are regarded as not their least qualities.　Here too, as in nearly everything, Mozart is the model, and will remain so, even if later scribblers, whom nobody knows, for all that they have the face to name themselves, deny him any power of mind and judgment, granting him only artistic instinct.—*Risum teneatis amici!*

The four books discussed are outwardly well and decently presented.　A few misprints are not important.

[? G. W. Fink.]

For Rossini's 'Tancredi' cf. No. 149.

480. SCHUBERT'S FATHER and Stepmother to Franz

[Vienna, End of June 1824.]

Dear Son,

Your letter of the 31st ult. I received on the 3rd inst. We are all heartily glad that you are in good health and have been so well received in the count's household. Endeavour, therefore, to care for and maintain your health, the first among all earthly possessions, and make it your business to deserve the love and respect of all who mean well by you.

You know that, as a teacher of youth, I am always apt to moralize; but believe me, it is not from habit, but from a profound conviction that nobody can be truly happy who is not continually in touch with God and keeps steadfastly to His holy will. We may, nay we should even, moderately enjoy the innocent joys of life with hearts grateful to God; but we must not let our spirits sink in gloomy circumstances either, for sorrows too are a blessing of God and lead those who manfully endure to the most glorious goal.

Where in history is to be found a great man who did not attain to triumph through suffering and unflinching perseverance? That is why I should like to persuade those I love best to such a disposition!—

In Vienna everything goes on as usual. That Herr von Salieri has been retired with full salary and Herr von Eybler has succeeded him as first Court Musical Director in his place must be already known to you. Your brother Ferdinand spoke to Herr von Leidesdorf and got from him for correction the songs of yours he is about to publish, which Leidesdorf was on the point of sending you for that purpose.

The weather here is always much mixed with cool rain, hailstorms and gales, and leaves little hope for the wine-growers.—Herr Mohn has not yet put in an appearance here.—

Herr von Jeckel, the apothecary at Döbling, aged 58, died suddenly on the 15th inst. of apoplexy; he said to his wife half an hour before he died: "I feel I shall die before the day is out"; and when she replied: "Don't you believe that, and don't frighten me so," he said: "Well, well, I can't help you."

Herr Kopp, too, the landlord at St. Anna (formerly at the "Lime-Tree" in the Liechtental), has died suddenly of a stroke on the 19th inst.

I and mine are all well, thank God.   A thousand greetings and blessings from your brothers, sisters, relations and acquaintances; and so we remain, with the others, your well-meaning parents,

Anna and Franz Schubert.

Ferdinand will soon write to you separately.

In place of the ailing Salieri Josef Eybler was employed from March 1824; born at Schwechat near Vienna in 1765 and deputy chapel master at court since 1804, he was not promoted to the first chapel master's post until 6th June 1825.—The proofs of the songs mentioned are probably those of books 3–5 of 'The Fair Maid of the Mill' (*see* No. 489).—For Mohn cf. No. 483, in Ferdinand Schubert's letter.

'Song to Death' ('Lied an den Tod'), Vol. 17, No. 3 of posthumous songs (xx. 326), appears as supplement to the Vienna 'Allgemeine Musikalische Zeitung,' 26th June 1824.

481. NOTE BY SCHUBERT, 1824

'Domestic Warfare' ['Der häusliche Krieg'], composed at father's, censored and passed for performance at the Court Opera.

It is possible that this chit was written at the beginning of the year. The opera was finished in April 1823, and already on 31st March 1824 Schubert had given up all hope of succeeding with it in Vienna or anywhere else (*see* No. 456).   However, the new title here appears for the first time: in deference to the Vienna censorship 'The Conspirators' ('Die Verschworenen') was turned into 'Domestic Warfare.'   The court theatre's own censorship had passed the libretto, but nothing came of it.

482. JOHANN GABRIEL SEIDL TO SCHUBERT

Vienna, 1st July 1824.

Valued Sir and Friend,

In Heaven's name make haste with the 'Short Cloak' ['Der kurze Mantel']. Demmer, who rules the roost now that Vogel has been dismissed, will give it as his first autumn production and clamours for the music.—Money is sure to come now, namely 50,000 [florins], A.C. from Rothschild on account of the run, which certainly ought to succeed; you may therefore count upon the *nervus rerum* too.—New forces we shall have as well: Mlle Vio for Blanche; Herr Wächter instead of Spitzeder, for which reason please compose only the additional arias; the (four) female voices are [among] the following:

> Mlle Schwarzböck,
> Mme Kneisel,
> Mme Vogel,
> Mme Raimund,
> Mme Wächter.

That is more than we need.

It now all depends on you.—Do not let yourself regret your promise; the theatre, after Vogel's fall, now seems to regain some credit, and much is to be expended on the outward appearance of the [Short] Cloak.

Reply soon and reliably to your

J. G. Seidl.

Gärtnergasse, No. 36. 2nd floor, left.

Seidl, born in Vienna in 1804, was a teacher and numismatist, and he was called, somewhat ironically, a "patriotic" poet. He was soon to undertake a Viennese edition of Calderón, a counterpart to the Vienna Shakespeare edition. The popular dramatic fairy-tale 'The Short Cloak,' in three acts with choruses, songs and dances (based on Benedicte Neubart's 'Neue Volksmärchen der Deutschen'), was his first stage piece. The manuscript in the Vienna City Library still bears the remark "The music by Franz Schubert," who had indeed promised it; but this note was later altered into "Act I—P. J. Riotte, II—Josef von Blumenthal, III—Ignaz, Ritter von Seyfried." Blumenthal, born at Brussels in 1782, worked in the orchestra of the Theater an der Wien. The piece was actually produced there on 6th November 1824, repeated eight times and followed by a parody at the Josefstadt Theatre, 'The Short Cloaks' ('Die kurzen Mäntel'), by Karl Meisl with music by Franz Josef Gläser.—Wilhelm Vogel was obliged to resign the management of the theatre on 31st May 1825.—Pálffy was again trying to restore his ill fortunes by a lottery and evidently hoped for an advance from Salomon Mayer, Freiherr von Rothschild, born at Frankfort o/M. in 1774, the head of the Vienna branch of that house.—The part of Blanche was actually sung by Frau Therese

Wächter.   The other female parts were given to Louise Raimund, the playwright Ferdinand Raimund's divorced wife, Frau Palmer and Fräulein Beatrix Schwarzböck; the male ones to Herren Rott, Jäger and Johann Michael Wächter.   Thekla Kneisel, *née* Demmer in Vienna, was a singer and later an actress at the Burg Theatre.

483. FERDINAND SCHUBERT to his Brother Franz

[Envelope:]

> Herr Franz Schubert,
>   Composer,
>   to be delivered at Count
>   Esterházy of Galánta's
>   at Zseliz.

[Inside:]

Vienna, 3rd July 1824.

Dearest Brother,

"At last a letter from Ferdinand, once in a way!—What a lazy fellow, what a cold-blooded creature, to take no notice of his brother for weeks and weeks!"—That is probably how you think of me.—But leave it alone and do not be angry with me.   I have often had an illusion of your company, for I have begun playing your quartets again * and hear various things from your works at least once a week from the clock at the "Hungarian Crown."   This clock surprised me not a little the first time I heard it play several of your waltzes at lunch.   I felt so strange at that moment, I hardly knew where I was; it did not cheer me up by any manner of means; rather did it strike my heart and soul with such an anxious pain and longing that at last melancholy threw its veil over me and I involuntarily shed—.

Now, dear Franz, write to me to say how you are (but expressly addressed to me); whether you are quite well, how you are occupied and how you pass your spare time.

I have to-day handed in the Bach fugues and the libretto of 'The Short Cloak' ['Der kurze Mantel'] to Herr von Leidesdorf

---

* These quartets, played at my house, are done by the following: first violin, myself, second violin, brother Ignaz, viola, friend Mayssen, violoncello, our dear brother-in-law Schneider.

for transmission to you.   Do see to it that a big work of yours will soon appear on the operatic stage.

Four weeks ago I was visited by Herr von Mohn, to whom I handed copies of the following ten songs:

1. 'The Secret' ['Geheimnis'] by Schiller, 1823.
2. 'To Spring' ['An den Frühling'], 1817.
3. 'Melodies of Life' ['Die Lebensmelodien'], 1816.
4. 'In Windy Weather' ['Beim Winde'], by Mayrhofer, 1819.
5. 'Cheerfulness' ['Frohsinn'], 1817.
6. 'Wayfarer's Night Song' ['Wanderers Nachtlied'] II.
7. 'Consolation' ['Trost'], 1817.
8. 'Spring Song' ['Frühlingslied'], 1816.
9. 'Orestes Abducted' ['Der entführte Orest'] [sic], 1820.
10. 'Language of Love' ['Sprache der Liebe'] by Schlegel, 1816.

A few days later I handed Herr von Kupelwieser, at his request and in exchange for your assignment, the score of your new opera.

Apart from these two gentlemen Herr Hugelmann came too, asking me to return to him his scores of Mozart's quartets which you had given me to keep.   However, as I did not find them after searching three times, I could not satisfy his request.   After that he came to me twice more, once in the training-college corridor and once at my home, where he gave me not a little annoyance by inveighing so violently against your thoughtlessness, blustering, screaming and using such coarse expressions that I very much cursed the honour of his acquaintance.   Be good enough, therefore, to let me know where the music in question might possibly be, so that I may pacify this raging monster.

But now I shall have to inform you of my health, which I do the more gladly because, thank God, I am feeling quite well. My appointment gives me a great deal to do, of course, but I am quite content, and my position satisfies me.   Out of school hours I have to give much time to the revision of home-work, preparing, &c., but the hours of recreation are the more welcome, which for the most part I spend in the company of my dear Rieder, my only real friend.

He (as well as his brother Wilhelm) sends you hearty greetings and plans to perform your latest Mass, needless to say in a manner fit to redound to its honour, and not before you are back in Vienna again.

Now farewell! Write to me quite soon, have a good time and keep well until you are seen again by

Your

devoted brother
Ferdinand.

My wife and our children also send you hearty greetings and a thousand kisses; our well-beloved brother Ignaz and brother-in-law Schneider with his people do no less, as well as our friend and brother Mayssen.

Address me thus: F. S., &c., living at Maria-Trost, No. 20, at the "Golden Serpent," 2nd floor, door on the left, Vienna.

The address is preserved only in a copy made by Kreissle; the letter itself, now in the Vienna City Library, seems thus for once to have been enclosed in an envelope.—Josef Mayssen, born at the village of Hernals near Vienna in 1790, was a school-teacher and choirmaster there. In the garden-house of his dwelling there Schubert composed a 'Tantum ergo' on 16th August 1821.—The clock at the "Hungarian Crown" Inn had played a song by Schubert as early as 1822 (see No. 276). It seems in the meantime to have acquired a few more cylinders with Schubertian melodies, such as dances from Opp. 9 and 18, including doubtless the "Mourning" Waltz.—The Bach fugues were those in one of the early editions of 'The Well-tempered Clavier.'—Seidl must already have left the libretto (see No. 482) with the Schubert family in June; it was left behind there. This may be the reason why Schubert never began the composition at all.—For what purpose Schubert had the manuscripts of these ten songs handed to the painter Mohn, of course only on loan, is not known. It does not seem impossible that they were a pledge given for some monetary debt.—'The Secret' (xx. 431) was the second version, of May 1823; so was 'To Spring' (xx. 107b), dated October 1817. The autograph of 'Melodies of Life' is lost, as also the evidently undated manuscript of 'Wayfarer's Night Song' No. 2 ("another," as Goethe calls it), the famous "Über allen Gipfeln," composed early in 1823; and the same is true of 'Consolation' by an unknown poet beginning "Nimmer lange weil' ich hier" (there is another song of the name). 'Orestes abducted' ('Der entführte Orest'), as Ferdinand writes (see No. 484), is, of course 'Orestes absolved' ('Der entsühnte Orest'). This manuscript, too, like that of 'Language of Love' (poem by August Wilhelm von Schlegel), is lost. It is remarkable how closely Ferdinand observed the dates, or at any rate the years, of the manuscripts.—Josef Kupelwieser had become secretary to the Graz theatre in the spring of 1824 and probably hoped to get 'Fierabras' performed there.—Hugelmann (*see* No. 258) had probably lent Schubert his manuscript or printed scores of Mozart's five string Quintets (not "Quartets," cf. Schubert's correction in No. 484), perhaps one of the octavo editions published by André and by Pleyel.—Ferdinand had become teacher at the training college of St. Anna in 1824; but he was still living in the suburb. His friend was Johann Rieder, a school-teacher, choirmaster and municipal official in the Währing suburb, the son of the composer Ambros and brother of the painter Wilhelm August Rieder.—Schubert's latest Mass was that in A flat major, begun in November 1819 and finished in September 1822. The performances in the churches of Vienna cannot be definitely established.—"Friend and brother" may be merely an extra emphasis, but it may have reference to the fact that Mayssen (*see* above) was also a school-teacher and choirmaster.—Maria Trost, or St. Ulrich, was a western suburb nearer to the inner city; Ferdinand had moved there from Alt-Lerchenfeld.

484. SCHUBERT TO HIS BROTHER FERDINAND

Zseliz, (16th or 17th to) 18th July 1824.

Dearest Brother,

That I really was a little hurt to have received a letter so late, both from home and from you, you may believe word for word. Neither do I hear anything from Leidesdorf, though I wrote to him. Be good enough to keep an eye on him for a bit at his art shop, to get him to send me what I asked for.* You might also inquire about the publication of Book III of the 'Maid of the Mill' songs, for I see nothing in the paper. About your quartet party I am the more astonished because you were able to rope in Ignaz!!! But it would be better if you stuck to other quartets than mine, for there is nothing about them, except that perhaps they please you, who are pleased with anything of mine. Your thinking of me is what I like best about it, especially as they do not seem to grip you as much as the waltzes at the "Hungarian Crown." Was it only the pain of my absence which made you shed tears, and could you not trust yourself to write the word? Or did you feel, on thinking of my person, oppressed by an ever incompre-

* You will have to urge him properly, for he is rather negligent by nature.

hensible longing, that its dismal veil was enfolding you too?
Or did all the tears come to your mind which you have seen me
weep? Be that as it may, I feel more clearly than ever at this
moment that you, and you only, are my truest friend, bound to my
soul with every fibre!—Not to let these lines mislead you into
believing that I am not well or cheerful, I hasten to assure you
of the contrary. True, it is no longer that happy time during which
each object seems to us to be surrounded by a youthful gloriole,
but a period of fateful recognition of a miserable reality, which I
endeavour to beautify as far as possible by my imagination (thank
God). We fancy that happiness lies in places where once we were
happier, whereas actually it is only in ourselves, and so, although
I had an unpleasant disappointment by renewing here an experience already undergone at Steyr, I am better able now to find
happiness and peace in myself than I was then.—A grand sonata
and variations on a theme of my own, both for 4 hands, which I
have already written, shall serve you as proof of this. The variations have met with a special success. As regards the songs you
handed to Mohn, I comfort myself with the thought that only a
few of them seem good to me, e.g. those included with 'The
Secret,' the 'Wayfarer's Night Song' and 'Orestes absolved,' not
"abducted," an error that made me laugh very much. Try to
get back those I have named, at least.

Did Kupelwieser not mention what he intended to do with the
opera? Or where he is sending it??——

The quintets (not quartets) belonging to that arch-donkey
Hugelbeast have accompanied me here by mistake, and, by Heaven!
he shall not have them back until he has atoned for his vulgar
rudeness by a written or verbal apology. If, moreover, an opportunity occurs to administer a vigorous scrubbing to this unclean
pig, I shall not fail to give him a substantial dose. But enough
of that wretch!—

That you are quite well gives me the more pleasure because
I hope to enjoy that same well-being in myself in the coming
winter.

Remember me most lovingly to the parents, brothers, sisters
and friends! Be yourself kissed 1,000 times, together with your

good wife and children.   Write to me as soon as possible and keep very, very well!!!

N.B. How are Karl and Ignaz?   If only they would write to me.
Ever affectionately your
Brother Franz.

N.B. Has Resi perhaps made the world the happier by a new inhabitant already???

No letter from Schubert to Leidesdorf is preserved.—For the reference to other composers' work ("other quartets than mine") cf. No. 345.— The deprecating remark "pleased with anything of mine" was also applied by Schubert to Josef Hüttenbrenner.—It is very curious that Schubert should not only have wept in front of Ferdinand (probably not long before), but that he goes to the length of reminding him of it.—At Zseliz much had changed in the six years since his last visit, needless to say.   The young Countess Marie was as good as engaged to be married: her future husband, August, Count Breunner-Enkevoerth, was just leaving Vienna for Zseliz on 18th July, while Countess Rosine Esterházy went to the capital on the 24th. Marie, who taught Karoline the pianoforte, as the latter did little Albert, had reached such perfection as to be specially described in a Viennese directory of 1823 as "a dilettante in pianoforte playing."   Countess Karoline too was now grown up, being almost twenty years of age; but she remained so much a child that her mother sent her to play with her hoop when she was thirty.   She was particularly attached to Zseliz, and is said to have once declared that "If it is not quite as beautiful in heaven as at Zseliz, I do not wish to go to heaven at all."   Between her and Schubert a kind of friendship had developed which may have seemed to the lonely young man to resemble love.   As for his more realistic friendship with the chambermaid Pepi Pöckelhofer, it was probably not renewed during this visit.   He lived at the castle itself this time, in one of the guest-rooms off the corridor built round the courtyard.   We know that the 'Prayer' ('Gebet'), a quartet for mixed voices, was ordered by the countess at the family breakfast table, and was ready for the rehearsal in the drawing-room on the evening of the very same September day. Schönstein, who sang the tenor part, had come from Vienna in August. The countess regarded the work as her own property and did not allow Schönstein to have it printed until 1838, when it was published by Diabelli with a dedication to him.—The depression expressed in this letter was already felt by Schubert at Steyr in 1823, where he was no longer as happy as he had been in 1819; but it is true that he was ill during the later visit.—The "grand sonata" is the Duo in C major, Op. posth. 140, for pianoforte four hands, which Schumann supposed to have been the first version of the lost Symphony, more usually said to have been written at Gastein, and which Joachim for that reason scored for orchestra. The Variations are those in A flat major, Op. 35. Both works were written in the summer.—The songs "included with 'The Secret'" may mean that and 'The Pilgrim' of May 1823, which were united in a single manuscript (the second of these Schiller songs is now incomplete); possibly, in addition, the 'Forget-me-not' on Schober's poem, which now exists in a separate manuscript.—"Hugelbeast" ("Hugeltier") is a scornful perversion of "Hugelmann."—After his other two brothers Schubert mentions at the end his sister Therese ("Resi"), whose first child, a daughter, did not survive, for she died within a month of her birth (see No. 500).

484A. [LOST LETTER FROM SCHUBERT to his father, end of July 1824]

485. FROM THE BALANCE SHEET of the Esterházy Family's Receipts and Expenses for 1824

In the country, monthly: . . .
Schubert   f. 100.

For this salary cf. note to No. 131. According to Josef Doppler's information to Kreissle Schubert received two gulden a lesson from Esterházy; but that could have referred only to the lessons given in Vienna. The budget at Zseliz allowed for the following per month, in A.C.: 300 florins for the little count, 250 florins and 150 florins for the two young countesses respectively, 430 florins for the servants, 433 florins for the kitchen, which amounted, with Schubert's salary and petty cash "for the household in general," to 1,700 florins at the countess's disposal. In order to make 48,000 florins per annum do, 25,762 florins was estimated for the five months spent in Vienna and 22,238 florins for the seven at Zseliz.

486. FROM THE OFFICIAL 'WIENER ZEITUNG,' 2nd August 1824

AT THE LITHOGRAPHIC INSTITUTE,
Michaelsplatz, No. 2, is newly published . . .:

· · · · · ·

Schubert, Franz, 'Song to Death' ['Lied an den Tod'] ("Death thou terror of Nature''), with Pianoforte Accompaniment. 20 Kreuzer, V.C.

This was a separate issue of the supplement to the Vienna 'Allgemeine musikalische Zeitung' (*see* note on p. 357).

487. SCHUBERT TO HELMINA VON CHÉZY, Early August 1824

If your honour could delight me with a copy of the revised 'Rosamond,' you would greatly oblige me.

Most devotedly,

Franz Schubert.

This seems to have been a sketch for the letter No. 488, not used by Schubert, or a first brief reply which he followed up by the other.

488. SCHUBERT TO HELMINA VON CHÉZY

Madam,

Convinced of the value of 'Rosamond' from the moment I had read it, I am greatly pleased to find that you, Madam, have without a doubt succeeded in remedying in the most favourable manner a few insignificant faults which only an unsympathetic audience could have so conspicuously censured, and I account it an especial honour to become acquainted with a revised copy. As regards the price of the music, I feel unable to fix it at anything less than 100 florins, A.C., without damage to it. Should that nevertheless be too high, however, I should like to ask you, Madam, to decide yourself, but without departing too far from what I have indicated, and kindly to forward the matter in my absence to the enclosed address. With the deepest respect,

Most devotedly yours,

Zseliz, 5th August 1824.   Franz Schubert.

Address: [c/o] Franz Schubert, Schoolmaster in the Rossau, at the School House

in

Vienna.

Schubert had clearly received a letter from Helmina von Chézy in-forming him that she had revised her play and asking what he would take as a lump sum for his music (which had probably been paid for by the Theater an der Wien for its performances). The 100 florins, A.C., he demanded were exactly the amount she had received for the play from that theatre. It looks as though she had really purchased the rights in his music from him and received a copy of it, for she later (c. 1830) offered the revised play with the music to theatres at Stuttgart and Karlsruhe, which declined it. This is mentioned by her in a petition of 1837 to King Ludwig I of Bavaria, to whom she commended 'Rosamond' for the Munich court theatre, once again without success.—The address given by Schubert at the end is, of course, his father's.

489. FROM THE OFFICIAL 'WIENER ZEITUNG,' 12th August 1824

At the House of Sauer & Leidesdorf,
I. & R. Privileged Art, Alabaster and Music Establishment in Vienna,
has just been published and dispatched to all Book and Music Dealers:

THE OARSMAN
['Der Gondelfahrer']
Poem by Mayrhofer

Set to Music for 4 Male Voices with Pianoforte Accompaniment
by FRANZ SCHUBERT.
Op. 28.   3 Florins, V.C.

THE FAIR MAID OF THE MILL
A Cycle of Poems by Wilhelm Müller
Set to Music for One Voice with Pianoforte Accompaniment
by FRANZ SCHUBERT.
Op. 25.   Five Books complete, 2 Florins, V.C., each.

The same work with guitar accompaniment to be published shortly.

Op. 28 appeared after Op. 30. Books 3–5 of 'The Fair Maid of the Mill' came out together.

490. SCHUBERT'S FATHER, STEPMOTHER AND BROTHER IGNAZ TO FRANZ

Dear Son,   Vienna, 14th August 1824.

Your letter, which the complaisant chambermaid personally handed to me on the 31st ult., gives especial pleasure to me and all of us. You have touched the right string with Mother, and she was gladly and harmoniously in tune, for according to your good wishes thunderstorms, and more especially death, will long keep away from her.

I rejoice the more in your present well-being because I conclude it means chiefly that you foresee a pleasant future from it. Indeed it is my daily prayer to God that He may enlighten and strengthen me and mine, that we may ever become more worthy of His goodwill and His blessings.

On the 12th inst. appeared in the 'Wiener Zeitung' the announcement of your 'Oarsman' and the 'Fair Maid of the Mill.'

Your brother Ferdinand is much occupied by the forthcoming examinations, the more so because he is visiting examiner at several schools; but he will write to you as soon as possible. Your other brothers and sisters, and all of us, greet and kiss you lovingly with a thousand blessings, and hope soon to have more pleasant news of you. Is it a long time since you wrote to Herr von Vogl?

How do you stand about your honorary distinctions by diploma from the Styrian and Linz Musical Societies?

If, contrary to all expectation, you should not yet have done so, let me urge you most earnestly to thank them in a worthy manner. These noble societies show you exceptional love and respect, which may be very important for you.

We now commend you to the protection of God, being your faithful parents,

Anna and Fr. Schubert.

A few lines from me too, dear Brother. I am unconscionably pleased that you are keeping in good health; as far as I am concerned, I am hale and hearty also. No need to inform you that I have for some time been an honourable member of a small musical society. Only I shall have to tell you that these musical evening entertainments may not be altogether wrongly compared with a coach which often overturns and could at times hardly be set on its way again without its excellent driver. The latest is that a rabid suicide-mania is the fashion here, as though people were quite sure of jumping straightway into Heaven yonder. Now farewell, write soon or, better still, come soon and enjoy yourself again with your sincere brother

Ignaz Schubert.

It appears that Pepi Pöckelhofer, the "complaisant chambermaid," who may have gone to Vienna (? her home) on holiday, was still on friendly terms with Schubert. His father probably knew nothing of his earlier relations with her or did not take them seriously.—Schubert had congratulated his stepmother on her name-day (Anna, 26th July, an especially popular one in Vienna).—The reminders, in the style of Leopold Mozart, to write to Vogl and to thank the two musical societies, are significant of the elder Schubert's conscientiousness. But he was clearly not thinking of mere letters of thanks, of which Schubert had already sent one to Graz in the autumn of 1823 (*see* No. 380) and of which another to Linz may have been lost, but of dedications to these societies. —Ignaz, who is reticent in his postscript on account of his father, alludes to his participation in Ferdinand's string quartet (*see* No. 483).

Ferdinand, Karl Schubert's son (Franz's nephew) born, 15th August 1824. This nephew of Schubert's became a well-known historical painter.

491. SCHUBERT TO SCHWIND

[Envelope:]   From Zseliz.

Moritz von Schwind, Esq.,
Painter, at the Wien,
at the Moonshine Tavern

Via Dorog   in
  and Raab.   Vienna.

[Inside:]

Zseliz, August . . . 1824.

Dear Schwind,

"At last, a letter from Schubert," you will say, after three months!—True, it is a pretty long time, but as my life here is as uneventful as possible, I have little material for writing to you or the others. And if I were not only too anxious to know how you and the other close friends are faring, especially how things are with Schober and Kupelwieser, perhaps—forgive me—I should not

P   369

have written even now. How does Schober's enterprise prosper? Is Kupelwieser in Vienna or still in Rome? Are the literary meetings still held or have they gone quite to pieces, as I assume? Now, what are you working at??? . . . I am still well, thank goodness, and should be quite comfortable here, if only I had you, Schober and Kupelwieser with me, but as it is I often long damnably for Vienna, in spite of the certain attractive star. By the end of September I hope to see you again. I have composed a grand sonata and variations for four hands, which latter are having a particularly great success here; but as I do not wholly trust the Hungarians' taste, I leave it to you and the Viennese to decide.—How is Leidesdorf? Are things progressing or has he got the wrong sow by the ear? Please answer all these questions most particularly and as soon as possible. You cannot believe how I long for a letter from you. And since so much is to be got from you about our friends in Vienna and a thousand other matters, but nothing from me, it would not have hurt you to let me know a few things, that is if you had my address. Above all I lay it on your conscience to scold Leidesdorf *scandaleusement*, for he has neither answered my letter nor sent me what I asked for. What the devil does he mean by it? It's a very slow business with the 'Maid of the Mill' songs, too: a book comes dragging out once every three months. And now farewell and remember me to whomsoever you may think concerned, and (I tell you) do write to me soon, else you shall . . .

Your

faithful friend

Frz. Schubert.

My address:

    Zseliz in Hungary,

    via Raab and Dorog,

        c/o Count Johann Esterházy of Galánta.

The "Moonshine House" ("Zum Mondschein"), in which there was a tavern and a dance-hall, was next to the Karl church on the glacis. The Schwind family lived in one of the courtyards at the back, and their home was called "Schwindia" ("Schwindien").—Schubert did not at once insert the date, either because he could not remember it at the moment or because he intended to continue the letter later.—He addresses his friend as "Swind," both outside and in, probably in jest.—Schober's "enter-

prise" is his attempt to become an actor.—Kupelwieser was still in Italy.—
For the reading-circle see No. 456.—The "certain attractive star" is usually said to have been the young Countess Karoline, with whom Schubert
may have had some friendly relations of sorts during the past years in
Vienna, though he could certainly not have aspired to her heart, much less
her hand; but the reference sounds rather casual, and in any case
speculations are profitless. It is true that Bauernfeld later wrote quite
definitely that

> In love was Schubert, a countess, no less,
> For a pupil of his did he smart.
> But to quite another he gave himself,
> To banish the one from his heart.

But see No. 454 for Bauernfeld's unreliability, and it should be borne in
mind how easy it is for a young man to sentimentalize and exaggerate a
slight attachment in conversation with another after a lapse of time. On
the other hand it is more than improbable that Schubert would have
referred to the chambermaid Pepi as a star, even if his former relations
with her were renewed.—For the works mentioned cf. No. 484.—The
Viennese phrase used in reference to Leidesdorf, "or is the dog losing
his hair?" cannot well be literally translated, since it is not proverbial in
English. It alludes to the state of Leidesdorf's business.—Schubert's
lost letter to Leidesdorf has been mentioned in No. 484.—Schubert had
not yet received the concluding books of the 'Fair Maid of the Mill' cycle.

492. SCHWIND TO SCHOBER

[Vienna, 20th August 1824.]

Schubert has written. He is quite well and busy. As far
as I know with a symphony. . . . I have the opportunity, which
gives me much pleasure, of frequently [hearing] things by Schubert
at the house of a certain Herr von Pinterics, whose acquaintance
I made at Vogl's. He is an excellent and enterprising man,
confiding, active and cluttered up with old German works of art.

In Schubert's letter (No. 491) there is no mention of a symphony.
But he probably had one in mind on leaving Vienna (see No. 456 and cf.
note on the "grand sonata" for pianoforte duet in No. 484).—Karl
Pinterics was private secretary at Prince Josef Pálffy's in the Josefplatz.
He sang bass, played the pianoforte very well, cut silhouettes and collected
German engravings. It was he who showed Schwind Dürer's "Triumphal
Procession of the Emperor Maximilian," which influenced the latter's
cycle "Figaro's Wedding Procession," though it is true that a German

performance of Mozart's opera on 14th December 1823 and the Italian one on 28th August 1824—the latter in order to reconcile the two operatic parties in Vienna—did as much to fire him. (At the end of September 1824 successive performances were given of Rossini's 'Barbiere' and Mozart's 'Figaro,' partly with the same Italian singers in the chief parts.) Pinterics had been acquainted with Beethoven since 1817 and with Schubert since 1821. He eagerly collected the latter's songs until his death in 1831 and assembled 505 of them, which was much the greater part. It is said that in 1824 Pinterics dissuaded Schubert from taking lessons in theory from Sechter, which the composer nevertheless intended to do shortly before his death. Pinterics, like Schwind, lived near the Karl church, in the so-called "Confectioner's House" ("Zuckerbäckerhaus").

493. SCHWIND TO SCHOBER

[Vienna,] 21st August [1824].

Nothing excels the peace which thinking of you can give, and nothing the hope of being with you. If only Schubert were here by now! There's another for you, and the good Kuppel [Kupelwieser]; I know for certain they will be very different from all those—one is servile, another doubtful, a third insipid, and a whole lot of them are nothing at all.

Schwind, who at that time saw a good deal of Bauernfeld, wished to go to Linz and Salzburg, and had an even greater desire to meet Schober at Dresden. The latter, already much disillusioned about his new actor's profession, also wanted to visit Weimar (where he was to become chamberlain later on).—The people of whom Schwind was so weary were partly members of the reading-circle and partly fellow-students of his at the Academy of Fine Arts.

494. JOHANNA LUTZ TO LEOPOLD KUPELWIESER

Vienna, 30th August 1824.

Schubert wrote to Schwind to find out whether you have already arrived here, and what Schober is doing. Schubert will be back by the end of September.

Schubert actually remained in Hungary until the middle of October; the present allusion to his earlier return may refer to his first intention.

Anton Bruckner born, 4th September 1824.

495. FROM THE OFFICIAL 'WIENER ZEITUNG,' 7th September 1824

At the House of Sauer & Leidesdorf

in Vienna, Kärntnerstrasse, No. 941, has just appeared, and has been dispatched to all the Book and Music Dealers (at Pest, to be had of K. Lichtl):

· · · · · · ·

Trois Quattuòrs
pour deux Violons, deux Altos et Violoncelle
par François Schubert.
Œuv. 29.   No. 1.   6 Florins, V.C.

Karl Lichtl was agent for the Vienna music publishers at Pest.—''Deux Altos'' is, of course, a misprint in the advertisement: there was only one viola. For Op. 29, cf. No. 456. It, too, was published after Op. 30.

496. SCHWIND TO SCHOBER

[Vienna,] 10th September [1824].

Of Schubert's songs I am sending you the 'Maid of the Mill' songs. The others he may send himself, it costs him nothing. . . . As regards the 'Freischütz,' 200 copies are to go to England. If they make a sensation, I shall take up 'Hamlet' at once.

Schwind had doubtless informed Schober before that the second year's issue of the 'Album musical' (*see* No. 510) was to contain, apart from two contributions by Schubert, a small set of etchings he had made for Weber's opera. The intention to sell a part of the issue to England, which resembles Schubert's plan for the Walter Scott songs in 1825, probably had some connection with the first London performance of 'Der Freischütz' (22nd July 1824), but does not seem to have been realized. Schwind nevertheless soon began to work on Shakespeare, for he collaborated in the illustration of the Viennese edition.

497. JOHANNA LUTZ TO LEOPOLD KUPELWIESER

Vienna, 13th September 1824.

What Schwind really came for was to fetch a few books of the 'Maid of the Mill' songs he had left here, Schober having asked him to send them to him.   But he was still short of one book, and as I have it, I gave it to him.   It gave me pleasure.   I am sure you too would have gladly given it to him, and so I imagined I was taking your place a little after all.   It 's childish of me, isn't it?

On that day Schwind went to Steyr and Linz for three weeks, and also visited the castle of Ebenzweier.

498. SCHUBERT TO SCHOBER

[Outside:]   From Zseliz.

To Franz von Schober, Esq., Knight,
                                Ohlauer Gasse
Via Dorog,   at the ''Golden Hatchet,''
    Vienna, &c.   2nd floor,
                                c/o Herr von Schall,
                                Breslau.

[Inside:]

Dear Schober,   2 1st September 1 8 2 4.

I hear you are not happy and have to sleep off the frenzies of your despaïr.   So Schwind writes to me.   Although this makes me extraordinarily sad, it does not surprise me in the least, since such is the lot of almost every sensible person in this miserable world. And what ever should we do with happiness, misery being the only stimulant left to us?   If only we were together, you, Schwind, Kuppel [Kupelwieser] and I, any misfortune would seem to be but a light matter; but here we are, separated, each in a different corner, and that is what makes my wretchedness.   I want to exclaim with Goethe: ''Who only will bring me back an hour of that sweet time!''   That time when we sat so snugly together and each disclosed the children of his art to the others with motherly shyness, not without dread expecting the judgment to be pronounced by affection and truth; that time when one inspired the other and thus united striving after the highest beauty enlivened us all.   Now I sit here alone in the depth of the Hungarian country, whither I unfortunately let myself be enticed a second time, without having a single person with whom I could speak a sensible word. I have written hardly any songs since the time you went away, but tried my hand at several instrumental things. What is to happen to my operas Heaven knows! Notwithstanding that I have now been in good health for five months, my cheerfulness is frequently damped by your absence and Kuppel's, and I often live through days of great misery; in one of those clouded hours, when I particularly keenly felt the idle and insignificant life that characterizes our time, the following verses escaped me, which I communicate to you only because I know that you blame even my weaknesses with affection and indulgence:

COMPLAINT TO THE PEOPLE

Youth of the present time, where art thou gone?
Ye who, the strength of countless folk o'erthrowing,
Each one, another's features scarcely knowing,
In empty insignificance stalk on!

Too great my pain, which at my vitals gnaws,
As a last vestige of that power clinging.
Me too these times are fast to ruin bringing,
Wherein all greatness to exhaustion draws.

Sick and decrepit do the people creep,
The deeds of early youth they call but dreaming,
And golden poetry, once noble seeming,
They no more see as beauteous, strong and deep.

But thee, O sacred art, the gods yet will
In effigy to picture ancient glory,
To soften with the pow'r of song and story
The fate which ne'er our present grief can still.

With Leidesdorf things have gone badly so far: he cannot pay, nor does a single soul buy anything, either my things or any others, except wretched fashionable stuff.

I have now acquainted you pretty well with my present situation and I long to hear about yours as soon as possible. What I should like best is your returning to Vienna.   That you are well I do not doubt.

And now fare you very well, and do write to me as quickly as possible.

Your
Schubert.

My address: Adieu!!!

   Zseliz in Hungary,
     via Raab and Dorog
c/o Count Johann Esterházy.

Karl Schall, born at Breslau in 1780, was editor of the 'Breslauer Zeitung.'   He was just then publishing, with two friends, a German translation of the 'Arabian Nights' at Max & Co.'s (see No. 631), the second edition of which (1827) was embellished with vignettes by Schwind, and which attracted Goethe's attention.—Schubert still stuck to the spelling of "Swind."—The Goethe quotation comes from the song 'First Loss' ('Erster Verlust'), set by Schubert in 1815 (Op. 5, No. 4).—That Schubert had found nobody in Zseliz with whom he could "speak a sensible word" is not incompatible with his amorous preoccupations.—Up to 1823 (inclusive) Schubert had written 450 of his 600 odd songs.—The operas are 'Alfonso and Estrella,' 'Domestic Warfare' and 'Fierabras.'—Schubert's health seems to have been restored by the spring of 1824, i.e. in eighteen months.—The second verse of the poem, the best and most personal, may allude to Schubert's struggles with the large forms of opera and symphony, of which he nearly despaired.

499. LEOPOLD KUPELWIESER TO JOHANNA LUTZ

Palermo, 2 5th September 1824.

What pleases me greatly is that I have a Viennese friend at Palermo. You probably do not know him.   Laurin was articled clerk in the Exchequer, and I made his acquaintance at Frau Witteczek's in the Schubertiads, where I always liked him on account of his spontaneously acute judgment of Schubert's songs.   He is now Austrian consul at Palermo, and I am very glad to be reminded by conversation with him of those days when Schubert's beautiful songs, then so new and surprising, made such a wonderful impression on me.

Kupelwieser and Beresin (*see* No. 390) had been in Rome nearly seven months and were taken ill with malaria during the crossing to Sicily in the middle of August.   Beresin succumbed to it at Girgenti towards the end of the year.—The post of Austrian general consul at Palermo being vacant, it was delegated to Anton Laurin at Messina; but he may have stayed at Palermo in 1824.—It may be mentioned in this connection that Johann Karl Umlauff (*see* note preceding No. 161) had sung Schubert songs with French and "Moldavian" words at Suczawa in Moldavia in 1821–4.

500. Ferdinand Schubert to his Brother Franz

Dear Brother,

You are quite right to be rather annoyed with me, for it really was a little negligent of me not to have written to you long ago. It is true that I could not have answered you at once, as I was very busy preparing for the examinations, not wishing, as a newcomer to this institution, to fall below my colleagues.   Moreover, I had to spend the first half of September visiting eight suburban schools, to make reports on them, and so on.   I did not finish until 17th September, whereafter indeed I should have had time enough to write; but then I had several small journeys to go on again, namely to Mödling, Weidling, Klosterneuburg, Kalksburg, Duttenhof, Leobersdorf, Hainburg and even Pressburg.

I did think of you quite often, especially at Pressburg, since there I too was in the land of the mustachios, and thus nearer to you. At Hainburg I had bed and board at Herr Reinberger's, the amiable town pastor.   This truly dear, good man did all he could to entertain me.   The first day he took us (for Mayseder was there too) to the local castle hill and castle garden, &c., the second day to Pressburg; on the morning of the third titlarks were caught in a lovely meadow, about two hundred of them, and in the afternoon hares were hunted and shot on the so-called Hainburg hill.   On that occasion, too, he introduced me to the local choirmaster and his son, who is a schoolmaster there.   Another couple of excellent people.   The former invited me to a service that took place the following Sunday, on the fourth day of my visit; and when I asked him what Mass he had chosen, he answered: "A very fine one, by a well-known and famous composer—only I can't think of his name at the moment.''—And what do you think the Mass was?—If only you had been there; I know you too would have been greatly pleased; for it was the B flat Mass by—yourself!—You may well imagine how I felt, and also what kind and uncommon people these must be, who took the trouble to touch my feelings in such an agreeably surprising manner.—What is more, the Mass was done with a great deal of enthusiasm, and really very well. The choirmaster conducted and set the tempos so correctly that they could not have been better; his son, who is a clever violinist, and the priest were at the head of the firsts, while the colonel of the local sappers, whose musical band took the wind parts, led the seconds; I played the organ, as usual. The choral parts were also quite well filled; only the tenor was a little anxious, and vocally weak.

It rained almost incessantly that day; so we spent the afternoon at home and amused ourselves with string and vocal quartets, and in the evening with riddles, charades and suchlike. On the morning of the fifth day we inspected the great tobacco works, and in the afternoon we at last went back to Vienna.

As regards the publication of your works, I may not tell you anything, for the announcements in the papers have preceded me— I apologize!

I have not set eyes either on Herr von Mohn or on Herr von Kupelwieser since I handed them the music indicated to you.

Your last letter gave much pleasure to our excellent father, and he even asked me to tell you so, and to add that he greatly looks forward to your speedy return.

Brother Karl has been blessed with a little Ferdinand, to whom I stood godfather, and who is still alive; but Resi, who gave birth to a strong and healthy girl, was not granted that happiness for long, for the infant lived only twelve or fourteen days. Grief at the death of her first-born nearly turned into raving madness and confined her to the sick-bed for several weeks. Fortunately she has now got past the danger of serious trouble and seems to be resigned to her fate.

We all, dear brother, look forward happily to the moment when you will reappear in our midst; and now take cordial greetings from Father, Mother, brothers and sisters, and my wife and children.

Farewell, until you are in the arms of
                    Your
                    Ever affectionate brother
Vienna, 6th October 1824.   Ferdinand.
P.S. Do not forget the Bach fugues.

Cf. letters Nos. 484 and 490.—Ferdinand was new to his post at the training-school.—The resorts named by him (he has Leobendorf) are all, with the exception of Pressburg, in Lower Austria, not far from Vienna. (Walking-tours to more distant places were as yet unusual, and mountaineering parties as good as unknown.)—Pressburg, then the Hungarian Poszony and now the Slovakian Bratislava (*see* note preceding No. 129), lies on the Danube, some thirty-five miles east of Vienna. About ten miles upstream from Pressburg is Hainburg, which has considerable remains of the city walls dating from the Babenberg times and a ruin on its wooded castle mount, where in the so-called "castle garden" there was an inn, as at all such places in Austria.—The Hungarians were often teased about their traditional moustaches, which were polished with pomade and foppishly twirled.—Pressburg was in the direction of Zseliz.—At Hainburg Haydn had gone to school.—Schubert's Mass in B flat major did not appear until 1838; a manuscript copy must thus have got to Hainburg without Ferdinand's knowledge.—*Mineurs* were technical troops trained in mining, now a branch of the engineers.—The tobacco works on the Danube still exist; since the eighteenth century the Austrian State itself has held a tobacco monopoly.—For Mohn and Josef Kupelwieser *see* No. 483.—Schubert seems to have answered his father's letter (No. 490), but if so, this is another Schubert letter that has not been preserved. —For Schubert's sister Resi (Therese) cf. the postscript to his letter, No. 484.—For Bach's fugues *see* No. 483.

501. ADALBERT ROTTER'S REMARK on the Autograph of the Song, 'Longing' ['Sehnsucht'] (xx. 357)

On 12th October 1824 'Longing' was sung by Herr Vogl, retired Imperial and Royal Court Opera Singer.

Cf. No. 465. This second setting of Schiller's 'Longing' was written about 1820 for a bass voice, but appeared in 1826 in the treble clef. Where Vogl sang the song in 1824 is not known; perhaps at Frau von Lászny's.

Schubert drives to Vienna with Baron Schönstein, 16th October 1824.

502. BARON SCHÖNSTEIN TO COUNT ESTERHÁZY

Vienna, 20th October 1824.

Dear Friend,

On Sunday the 17th I arrived here safely, thanks to kind Providence and to your four bays.   About the vicissitudes of my journey I have nothing further to say that is of much moment, since for the greater part of our drive Morpheus cradled us in welcome slumber, disturbed only by the darkness by which we were caught on the first evening, and thus by the constant fear of being overturned. We got as far as Diószeg on the first day, for all that one of the forward horses grew bandy owing to a bad shoe and had to be taken to a blacksmith at Verebély to be newly shod.—As we had so far driven for the most part with closed eyes, and so did not feel particularly sleepy, we spent the evening making up a card party [Tarteln und Mariage]. . On the second day we set out early and were at Pressburg by ten o'clock, where I stayed only long enough for the change of horses.—The coachman in charge must have had an inkling of my generosity, for he accordingly drove so admirably that already by four o'clock we were inside the great capital.— Accept my renewed thanks, dear Hansi, for the good conveyance as far as Pressburg.   May Heaven reward you in your children for these fair impulses of your noble heart.—I found my parents well enough on my arrival, but at this moment my mother pays with gastric convulsions for her impatience to see me, having immediately after dinner and until my appearance stood at the open window in the most dreadful cold.   Talking of cold weather, I nearly forgot to tell you that on the second day of our caravan we suffered from the most appalling cold.—Schmetterling nearly froze to death, and if on this occasion he really had been a butterfly, he would probably have flown for the rest of the journey here, and no god could have kept him on the coachman's box.—To crown it all, the lackadaisical Schubert managed to smash the window at the back of the coach as soon as we were out of Diószeg, whereby the ghastliest of cold winds was given free play about our ears.— However, I dare say there never was a journey without some small

380

fatality, and as otherwise it went off well, we soon got over this mishap.

No sooner had we arrived in the capital than I had to hear the saddest of news, which unfortunately is but too true, namely that Barbaja's lease is now definitely to come to an end on 1st December. Even if he still had individual contracts lasting beyond that date, all hope of having an Italian opera this winter would be frustrated by the mere notice served to Barbaja of the lapse of his own, as well as by the further circumstance that the Kärntnertor Theatre is to be closed altogether from 1st December onwards. As regards the latter, we might console ourselves for the loss of the German opera, for after the Italians it would in any case have become indigestible; but that all ballet too is thereby to cease, and my charming Rozier is thus to be lost to me for all time, that indeed is too hard.—

They pretend to believe that we shall have German operas just the same, and that in connection with drama at the National Theatre. Whoever wants to hear another Italian opera and the divine David here in his life had better make haste about it during the month of November.—For the rest, as I have no doubt that the Kärntnertor Theatre will be used for coach-houses or stables (for what else could be done with it?), I shall take good care that you will find quarters there at least for Fuchs and Gentleman against a reasonable rent, being aware in any case that you are somewhat embarrassed about accommodation for your horses.— *Quo devenimus! Eheu proh dolor!!*

The day before yesterday the new gate at the Burg was opened by H.I. & R.H. the Crown Prince: it is indeed a magnificent piece of work, though it fits in with the rest as chalk with cheese. In order at last to make things quite clear to you about Fanny Hügel's condition, the matter stands as follows: Fanny H., then, was knocked over (to use plain language), without looking outwardly any the worse for it; but she received such a violent contusion as to be incapable of any movement, either with her hands or with her head.—The latter gives her much excruciating pain towards the nape of the neck, and it is feared that it will result in desiccation of the spinal marrow, and that at any rate she will not completely recover. . . . But now be kind enough, dear Hansi, to grant my urgent request—i.e. to write soon

To your sincere friend,

Sch.

Schönstein had left Zseliz on 16th October in his own carriage, but with Esterházy's horses, and had taken Schubert with him.   Their route, to the north of the Danube, was shorter than the post road.   They spent the night at Diószeg.—*Tarteln*, or *Tatteln*, is a card game for two, each player being dealt nine cards, the rest being gradually taken up after each trick.   A run of three cards is called a *Tattel*, one of four a *Quart*, one of five a *Fuss*.   *Mariage*, so called because its aim is the reunion of the king and queen of the same suit, is for two players and is played for points with piquet or "German" cards.—Hansi is a diminutive of Johann (Esterházy).—From Pressburg onward Schönstein used post horses, or perhaps his own.—His father, Franz Xaver von Schönstein, was aulic councillor of the Hungarian Court Chamber in Vienna, and died as early as 1825.—"Schmetterling" may have been a small dog of Schönstein's.—Barbaja's first lease was after all extended to the end of March 1825, and the Kärntnertor was therefore not closed during the winter of 1824–5. —For Mme Rozier, who remained there until 1828, *see* No. 255.   Ludwig Rellstab, who visited Vienna in 1825, wrote later: "Ever since the Italians got such a firm footing here, all that is best has been ousted.   For the nobility the ballet is all that matters: it has a taste only for horses and dancers."—For David *see* No. 472.   In this connection a Viennese jest is worth mentioning, which circulated in the capital at the end of 1822, in the second year of Barbaja's lease, and made fun of the German company. Johann Karl Unger reported it thus to his friend Esterházy: "Vogl— *maestoso*, Forti—*vivace con espressione*, Grünbaum—*capriccioso*, Rosner— *dolce*, Unger—*crescendo*, Schütz—*grazioso*, Schröder—*affettuoso*, Jäger— *amoroso e cantabile*, Weinmüller—*sostenuto*, Haizinger—*allegretto con variazioni*, . . . Vio—*a piacere* . . . Gottdank—*non troppo e ben marcato* . . . Mme Vogel—*sforzando*, Nestroy—*rinforzando* . . . Fröhlich— *tace* . . . Gyrowetz—*un poco più vivace* . . ."—The new Burg gate at the western end of the city, which now faces the museums in the Ring-strasse, had been begun in 1821 and was finished in 1824, replacing a gate outside the outer palace square destroyed by the French in 1809.   It was built by Pietro von Nobile; the opening took place at the commemora-tion of the People's Battle at Leipzig.   It was now one of the gates lead-ing to the inner city through the bastion.   In 1934 it was altered inside and turned into a heroes' monument.—The crown prince was the future Emperor Ferdinand, born in 1793.—Fanny von Hügel, whom Schubert is said to have praised as an interpreter of his songs, and for whom in

1819 he wrote the vocal quartet 'Rest' ('Ruhe'), died insane, although not in the way foreseen here.

Karl, Ferdinand Schubert's son (another nephew to Franz), born 3rd November 1824.—The two brothers Ferdinand and Karl had stood godfather to one of each other's sons. The younger Karl Schubert followed his father in his profession: he became assistant schoolmaster in the St. Ulrich (Maria-Trost) suburb, later professor and finally vice-director of the St. Anna training school.

503. SCHWIND TO SCHOBER

Vienna, 8th November 1824.

Schubert is here, well and divinely frivolous, rejuvenated by delight and pain and a pleasant life.

9th inst.

Schubert sends many kind regards.

Schwind had returned to Vienna from Linz in the early days of November with the brothers Fritz and Franz von Hartmann.—Schubert's high spirits are doubtless explained by his pleasure in being back in Vienna and among his friends. There is no sign of his having been made unhappy by anything like the unattainability of the Countess Karoline. He again returned to his father's school-house in the Rossau this time, and remained there until early in 1825.

504. JOHANNA LUTZ TO LEOPOLD KUPELWIESER

Vienna, 15th November 1824.

Schubert is back here. He is said to be very well, and is much in Schwind's company. This is good, for if they are not of much use to each other, they do each other no harm, and that alone is a good deal in Schwind's case, since he is so easily influenced by his environment. A male friend would be good for him.

505. FROM THE PROGRAMME of the Fourth Concert held by the Linz Musical Society in the Large Council Chamber of the County Hall, 15th November 1824

4. Tenor aria by F. Schubert for the Opera, 'The Magic Bell.'

The assembly hall was being rebuilt, so that the society had to find another place.—As a modest return for the distinction conferred on him Schubert seems to have sent to Linz a copy of the score and parts of this aria (*see* note preceding No. 240), which are preserved there. This performance is mentioned also in the society's annual report. It was the last of a work by Schubert given there in his lifetime.

506. SCHWIND TO SCHOBER

[Vienna], 20th November 1824.

I recently talked with Doblhoff. Time hangs unbearably heavy, if I do not discuss you with any one but Schubert or my companions, who worship you in their stupidity, but know nothing else about you . . . Towards you he [Bruchmann] has, so to speak, become passive, but he takes much interest in Schubert and me.

Schwind's companions are evidently his fellow-students at the Academy of Fine Arts.

Matthäus von Collin dies, 23rd November 1824.

First performance of the Sonata for Pianoforte and Arpeggione (viii. 8) by Vincenz Schuster in Vienna, end of 1824.—The arpeggione, also called bowed guitar, violoncello guitar or *guitare d'amour*, was a stringed instrument with six strings tuned in two octaves ranging from E below the stave in the bass clef and a fretted fingerboard, in use for only about ten years. It was first made in 1823 by Johann Georg Stauffer in Vienna and played by Vincenz Schuster. It was the latter, no doubt, who had asked Schubert for this Sonata, which he played in private, and in 1825 he published at Diabelli's a guide to the playing of the instrument. The picture of an arpeggione on the title-page is reproduced in the iconographical volume, p. 50a, and an earlier picture had appeared at Mainz in 1824, in the magazine 'Cäcilia.' An original instrument is in the Heyer Museum at Leipzig and another in the museum of the Carolino-Augusteum at Salzburg. The name "Arpeggione" is found in Schubert's hand on the autograph of the Sonata, written in November 1824. (An *ad lib.* violoncello part appeared in the very first edition, Vienna, 1871. Violin, viola and viola d'amore parts, too, were used by turns in place of that for the arpeggione. The pianoforte part has been more than once replaced by an orchestral arrangement.)

Court Opera (Kärntnertor-Theater), where Schubert's First staged Opera, 'The Twin Brothers' ('Die Zwillingsbrüder'), was performed in 1820.   Water-colour by Emil Hütter (c. 1860)

PLATE XIII

"Lazarus, or The Feat of Resurrection" ("Lazarus, oder Die Feier der Auferstehung"). Illustration to August Hermann Niemayer's Poem, set to Music by Schubert in 1820. Etching by Daniel Nikolaus Chodowiecki (1778)

PLATE XIV

507. SCHOBER TO SCHUBERT

Dearest Schubert,   [Breslau, 2nd December 1824.]

You will not have made much of my letter sent to Zseliz, which I wrote in the worst possible situation. My good, ever true friend, you continue to value my affection, you have cared for me for my own sake, just as my Schwind and Kupelwieser also will be faithful to me. And are not we precisely those who have found our life in art, while the others only found entertainment in it— those who alone and with certainty understood ourselves, as only Germans can understand? I feel it now: I devoted myself too much to all sorts of things and people, and wasted myself and my time. I had to be dragged out of it, to clarify my environment, to make myself active. Now the one is done and the other is about to be, so that on the whole I am able to contemplate an advance into a better state of things and shall, even if all fails, return more worthily and at least as lovingly to your arms, you who now are the only beings I care for. I have some remote hope to see you before the end of this winter, which would be a beautiful, yet a comic dream. Baron V[aerst], who dotes on adventurous and uncommon things, wishes to go to a ridotto in Vienna for one night, for the sake of an assignation he made this summer at Carlsbad, simply going by express post, remaining for the night, and returning in the same way. He has asked me to go with him, if it should come off, and having just come from Carlsbad, he was full of the scheme. However, being involved in a lot of other things, he seems to have cooled down again. But if it should come to pass, I should let you know the place where you would have to expect me, and we should spend a glorious night.

Now as to your affairs. What about your operas? Has the Castelli one been performed already, and the Kupelwieser one? Have you heard nothing at all from K. M. Weber? Do write to him, and if he does not give you a satisfactory answer, ask for its return. I have means of getting at Spontini; would you like me to make an attempt at seeing if he could be induced to give a performance?—for they say he is difficult! I am sure it is only a matter of doing a complete work to revive popular enthusiasm for you, but it would certainly be a good thing if it happened soon. So Leidesdorf did not succeed? I really am very sorry, and your 'Maid of the Mill' songs too failed to make a sensation, did they? These hounds have no feelings or minds of their own and they blindly follow the noise and the opinions of others. If only you could secure a few noisy drummers among the reviewers, to talk for ever about you in all the papers, it would be easy enough. I know some quite unimportant people who have become famous and popular in that way, so why should not the one who most deserves this have recourse to such methods? Castelli writes for several papers abroad. You have set an opera of his to music: let him open his mouth. Moritz has sent us the 'Maid of the Mill' songs, and do send me anything else that has appeared. How glad I am that you are quite well again! I too shall be soon. Many thanks for the poem, which is so truly felt and has made a great impression on me. Yes indeed: "Sick and decrepit do the people creep!" Good-bye and love me well. We shall certainly be united again. More in Moritz's letter.

Ever your
Schober.

Schober's letter to Zseliz has not been preserved.—If the Austrians, to whom Schober belonged, in spite of his Swedish birth, called themselves Germans, this had no political but only a racial significance, connected with the common language.—Friedrich Christian Eugen, Freiherr von Vaerst, born at Wesel in 1792, is still known by his 'Gastrosophie'; he lived at Breslau and did not go to Vienna with Schober.—The operas are 'Domestic Warfare' and 'Fierabras'; Schober refers to 'Alfonso and Estrella' (his libretto) only indirectly by his mention of Weber and Spontini (cf. No. 498).—Moritz is Schwind. His letter is one written to him by Schober.

508. FROM THE PROGRAMME of the Fourth Evening Entertainment held by the Philharmonic Society, 2nd December 1824 (Conductor, Herr Pockh)

4. 'The Wanderer.' Song by Schubert, performed by [Georg] Hoffmann.

Georg Hoffmann, a conveyancer, who subscribed to Mayrhofer's poems, was an amateur tenor.

509. From the 'Theaterzeitung,' 9th December 1824

(Concerning the concert of Gottfried Schunke, Royal Chamber Musician of Württemberg and first horn player, and his two sons, Ludwig and Ernst, in the County Hall, 5th December 1824, at noon.)

6. Vocal Quartet, composed by Schubert, and sung with the most agreeable voices and charming interpretation by Herren Jäger, Seipelt, Wächter and Weber.

Gottfried Schunke was born in Saxony in 1777. Ludwig, born at Cassel in 1810, was for a time a rival of Liszt's as a pianist and later a friend of Schumann's. Ernst was born at Cassel in 1812. (Karl Schunke [see No. 216] was the son of the horn player Michael, who was one of Gottfried's four brothers.)—The quartet was 'The Nightingale,' sung unaccompanied. The singer Weber cannot be indentified.—Other notices appeared in the 'Wiener Zeitschrift' on 11th December and in the Vienna 'Allgemeine musikalische Zeitung' on 15th December (German edition, Nos. 524 and 525).

510. From the Official 'Wiener Zeitung,' 11th December 1824

At the House of Sauer & Leidesdorf,

Kärntnerstrasse, No. 941, is newly published, and dispatched

to all Book and Art Dealers (in Pest, to be had

of K. Lichtl):

Christmas and New Year's Present

Album musical

Recueil de Compositions

pour Pianoforte seul et Pianoforte et Chant.

Seconde Année.

Bound with gilt edges, with 6 Vignettes representing Scenes from the Opera, 'Der Freischütz,' on Basle Vellum.

Price, 3 Florins, A.C.

Contents:

. . . . .

Les Plaintes d'un Troubadour, par Fr. Schubert.

. . . . .

'The Apparition' ['Die Erscheinung'], set to Music by Fr. Schubert.

. . . . .

Album musical

Premier [*sic*] *Année.*   Price, 3 Florins, A.C.

Contents:

. . . . .

Themes [*sic*] *russe, par François Schubert.*

Of this second year's issue of the 'Album musical,' which is advertised only in its plain edition (*see* No. 407), two copies are preserved (Paul Hirsch, Cambridge, and Anthony van Hoboken, Lausanne). For Schwind's contribution *see* No. 496. It also contained a pianoforte fantasy on themes from 'Le Franc Chasseur' by Auguste Louis (cf. No. 407). Schubert's contributions were the later No. 6 of the 'Moments musicaux,' Op. 94 (*see* No. 3 in the first year's issue of the album under the title of 'Air russe,' now called 'Thème russe'), and the song later published as 'Recollection' ('Erinnerung'), Op. 108, No. 3.

511. ANNA MILDER TO SCHUBERT
Franz Schubert, Esq.,

in

Vienna.

During my sojourn in Vienna Herr Schickh promised that I should have the pleasure of making your personal acquaintance. I waited in vain and unfortunately had to leave without seeing my wish realized. Allow me now to tell you in writing how very much your songs enchant me and what enthusiasm they call forth among the circles to whom I sing them. All this emboldens me to send you a poem which I would earnestly beg you to compose for me, if your Muse will permit it. You would make me infinitely happy thereby, since I desire to perform it at concerts, for which reason I take the liberty of making the single suggestion that the composition should be addressed to a wide public. I heard that you have written several operas and should like you to let me know whether you would not be inclined to have an opera performed in Berlin, and whether I may, or ought to, use my influence with the office of the intendant on your behalf. I have addressed the same question to Vogl on the subject. Probably friend Vogl is not in Vienna, or I should have received an answer about it; should you see him, please give him my kind regards and tell him that I should be very happy to have news of him.

In anticipation of an early and favourable reply. I have the honour of subscribing myself respectfully,

Your

most obedient servant,

Anna Milder.

Berlin, 12th December 1824.

Anna Milder (*see* No. 134) had left her husband, a court jeweller, who did not wish to follow her to Berlin, and a daughter behind in Vienna, and visited the latter again in the autumn.—Schickh was Josef Kilian Schickh, a nephew of Johann (*see* note on p. 155), who had been a schoolfellow of Schubert's at the grammar-school and was now a playwright. Schubert had clearly still been in Hungary when Schickh wished to introduce him to Anna Milder.—The poem sent to Schubert by Frau Milder was probably that mentioned later (*see* No. 538) as 'The Moth' ('Der Nachtschmetterling'), which seems to be identical with Karl Gottfried von Leitner's (born Graz, 1800) 'The Youth and the Moth' ('Der Jüngling und der Nachtschmetterling'). In 1823 Johann Schickh had given Schubert Leitner's poem 'Urge into the Distance' ('Drang in die Ferne') for composition and published the song in the 'Wiener Zeitschrift' (*see* note on p. 271). Although later on Marie Pachler made another attempt to bring the two men together, Schubert never met Leitner, several of whose poems he set, and who in 1826 was professor at the grammar-school of Graz, but had become professor at Cilli in Styria by the time Schubert visited Graz the following year.—Schubert's reply to Frau Milder is lost. He did not set the song, but sent her a copy of the second Suleika song ('Western Wind') with the request to allow him to dedicate it to her, also a copy of the full score of the opera 'Alfonso and Estrella,' which, however, did not reach the Berlin Court Opera, or at least did not remain there, but at late as 1842 still lay unused at the Königstadt Opera in Berlin.

512. FROM THE OFFICIAL 'WIENER ZEITUNG,' 18th December 1824

At the House of Sauer & Leidesdorf
in Vienna, Kärntnerstrasse, No. 941, is newly published,
and dispatched to all the Book, Art and Music Dealers:
(Pest, K. Lichtl)

Trois Marches héroïques
pour le Pianoforte à 4 mains
par Francois Schubert.

Œuvre 27.   Price, 3 Florins.

Op. 27 appeared after Opp. 29 and 30, without any dedication. The
two parts of the first march, with the trio section added later, were
originally the introduction to a setting of Schiller's poem 'The Combat'
('Der Kampf'), preserved in two sketches dated 1815 and 1816. These
and the later marches for pianoforte duet, all with special titles given
them by the publishers, were repeatedly orchestrated after Schubert's
death. There is no reason, however, to suppose that Schubert thought
of them as military marches for wind instruments, but published them
only in pianoforte arrangements. Most of his works for pianoforte duet
(and he is the most prolific of composers for this medium) have an
orchestral quality in common. "A tendency to write orchestrally,"
observed by Eusebius Mandyczewski in Schubert's string quartets, is
characteristic of him and is explained by his "mighty urge always to
express himself as fully and completely as possible."

513. FROM THE OFFICIAL 'WIENER ZEITUNG,' 22nd December 1824

At T. Weigl's Art and Music Establishment,
(Graben, No. 1144, next to the "King of England")
is newly to be had:

MUSICAL SOUVENIR
['Musikalisches Angebinde']
for the New Year.

A Collection of 40 New Waltzes
for the Pianoforte
by
L. van Beethoven, K. Bettlach, J. Bibl, L. Blahetka, K. M. von
Bocklet, Josef Böhm, Leopold Böhm, F. Clement, L. E. Czapek,

Karl Czerny, Josef Czerny, J. Drechsler, J. Faistenberger, F. Grutsch, A. Gyrowetz, G. Hellmesberger, J. Hoffmann, E. Kessler, K. Kreutzer, J. F. Limmer, M. J. Leidesdorf, Léon de Saint-Lubin, K. F. Müller, F. A. Neumann, M. Pamer, J. Preisinger, B. Rand-hartinger, J. Riotte, F. Schubert, I. Schuster, M. Schwarz, I. R. von Seyfried, J. Stadler, F. Stegmayer, M. Umlauf, Ant. Volkert, F. Volkert, F. Weiss, J. Wilde, A. Wranitzky.

Together with a Final Waltz with Coda by F. Lachner.

Price, 3 Florins, V.C.

This collection, dedicated to the actor and producer Demmer by the editor, K. F. Müller, has been preserved in three copies, owned by the National Library in Vienna, by the Vienna Philharmonic Society and by Anthony van Hoboken at Lausanne. Schubert's contribution, appearing as No. 29, is the Country Dance, xii. 10, No. 17, also preserved for four hands as ix. 27, No. 1, both probably dating from 1824, the version for two hands, however, being written later, in November, for the present collection.—Karl Bettlach was a bassoon player in Prague.—J. Bibl is probably a mistake for Andreas Bibl, born in Vienna in 1797, a schoolfellow of Schubert's, later court organist.—Josef Michael Böhm, born at Pest in 1795, in Vienna since 1815, was a violinist, professor at the Conservatory and member of the court chapel, later Joachim's master.—Leopold Böhm, the youngest of Josef's brothers, was among the first violins in the Theater an der Wien.—Franz Clement, born in Vienna in 1780, who had been in London as a child prodigy in 1791, and for whom Beethoven wrote his violin Concerto, had for long been leader at the same theatre.—Franz Seraph Grutsch, born in Vienna in 1800, was a colleague of Leopold Böhm's there.—Erasmus Kessler was born in Vienna in 1808.—J. Franz Limmer was born there about 1808.—Léon de Saint-Lubin, born at Turin in 1805, in Vienna since 1819, had been a pupil of Spohr's.—Ignaz Schuster, born in Vienna in 1779, an actor and bass singer at the Leopoldstadt Theatre and singer in the court chapel, became famous in the traditional stage-part of "Staberl."—Matthias Schwarz was organist at the Karl church.—Josef Stadler, born in Vienna in 1796, was violinist at the Leopoldstadt Theatre, St. Stephen's Cathedral and the court chapel.—Ferdinand Stegmayer was born in Vienna in 1803.—Antonia Volkert, born 1812(!), was probably the daughter of Franz Volkert, who was born in 1778 and was conductor at the Leopoldstadt Theatre and a stage composer. As early as 1815 Franz had produced an opera, 'Ernst, Count of Gleichen,' on a libretto by Gleich dealing with a subject that later occupied Bauernfeld and Schubert as well as Schwind.—Josef Wilde, born in 1778, was a church and dance composer and musical director at the large assembly hall.—Anton Wranitzky, jun., was in the Court Opera orchestra.—Several among these forty musicians, Johann Faistenberger among them, cannot be clearly identified.—The advertisement also appeared on the same day under the name of the "Lithographic Institute," which however acted only as agent for the sale of the book.

514. Schwind to Schober

[Vienna, Christmas Eve, 1824.]

Perhaps Schubert is coming out here too, he came to see me in the morning with Josef Spaun, who is here on leave for a few weeks.

At his maternal home in the Moonshine House Schwind had prepared a large Christmas tree for an evening party of twelve, hung with little drawings with verses and, among other things, a copy of Bauernfeld's translation of 'The Two Gentlemen of Verona' from the new Viennese Shakespeare edition, in which it was the first new German version.

515. From Bauernfeld's Diary

[End of] December 1824.

Moritz [von Schwind] with me, and I [was then] with him on Christmas Eve. His brothers and friends. Merriest conviviality.

See No. 514.—Schwind had three sisters and two brothers: August, born in Vienna in 1800, conveyancer in the Lower Austrian Administration of Public Property, and Franz, born in 1805, a mining expert, who went to the salt works at Lake Traun in Upper Austria.

516. From the Vienna 'Allgemeine Musikalische Zeitung,' 29th December 1824

(Concerning the musical supplements of this journal for 1824.)

No. 5, 'Song to Death' ['Lied an den Tod'] by Franz Schubert. The author shows his mastery of harmony in this short song.

Ed.

See notes on p. 357 and to No. 486.

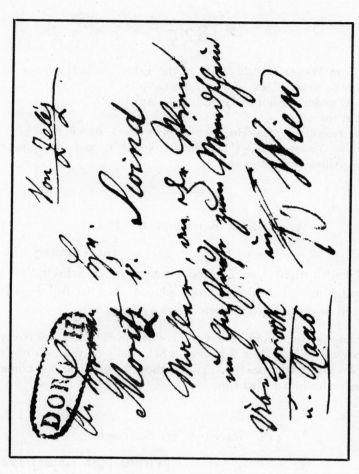

Envelope of a Letter written by Schubert to Schwind (1824). *See* p. 369

1825

7 Songs from Walter Scott's 'Lady of the Lake,' including 'Ave Maria'
    (xvi. 10; xviii, 1; xx. 471–5), March–July.
Sonata in C major (unfinished) (xxi. 14), April.
Sonata in A minor (x. 9).
Symphony (so-called "Gastein" Symphony) (lost), summer.
Songs, 'The Young Nun' ('Die junge Nonne'), and 'Omnipotence'
    ('Die Allmacht'), August.

---

517. From Bauernfeld's Diary

[6th] January 1825.

On Twelfth-night Eve masked procession at Schwind's. Myself as pilgrim. The three kings played dice in full regalia. I
distributed poems, Moritz made a drawing for me.

According to Bauernfeld's entry in his diary in February (*see* No. 529),
he seems again to have met Schubert at Schwind's on the eves of Christmas and Twelfth Night (*see* No. 271), without however having come into
close touch with him at that time.

518. Schwind to Schober

[Vienna,] 7th January 1825.

For the rest I paint all day and rarely go out. Now and again I
go to Schubert on the hop, or to Vogl or the Hönigs . . . If only
you could see Schubert and me for once, when I go to him in the
Rossau early or when we spend a Sunday afternoon together. It 's
a veritable calamity. But the funniest thing in the world, too.
A week ago he came to Hönig's with me, after having already accepted ten times and failed us ten times. We met at six, but did
not want to go until 7 o'clock, as the mother was then going out.
What was there to be done in the meantime? He would not

go to any coffee-house, so we went to Lenkay, where he had
always gone with Senn. Half a bottle of Tokay was served, and
when half of that had gone it was not advisable without great
danger to go on drinking. The remainder was poured into a
little flask and taken with us. As there was nobody about who
could have kept it for us, I took it with me to Hönig's, where it
was brought out with much laughter and drunk up. Schubert
enjoyed himself quite well and wants to go back soon, for he likes
Nettl very well. She is a sweet poppet, too.

Schubert lived at his father's that winter. He does not seem to have
worked on Sunday afternoons.—For Lenkay see No. 169. There only
Hungarian wines were to be had, including the expensive Tokay. Half a
bottle was a *Seitel*, about half a pint. A *Seitel* of Tokay cost at least
3 florins, A.C.—Nettl is Anna Hönig (*see* No. 330). She was born in 1803,
the daughter of the barrister Dr. Franz Hönig (born 1766), whom Schwind
called "old Priam," and his wife Anna. They lived in the so-called
"Trienterhof" in the Kleine Schulerstrasse, near St. Stephen's Cathedral—
and near Lenkay's wine-shop. For their son Karl *see* No. 391. Anna was
"not particularly pretty, but graceful, well-educated, domesticated and
middle-class rather than artistically gifted" (Bauernfeld). She was
given the nickname of "sweet Anne Page." Schwind fell in love with her.

519. FROM THE OFFICIAL 'WIENER ZEITUNG,' 8th January 1825

At the House of Cappi & Co.,
Privileged Art Dealers in the Graben, No. 1122, are to be had:

DANCE MUSIC FOR THE CARNIVAL OF 1825.

GERMAN DANCES AND ÉCOSSAISES
for the Pianoforte composed
by FRANZ SCHUBERT.

Work 33. Price, 1 Florin 30 Kreuzer, Vien. Cur.

For Cappi & Co. *see* note to No. 532.—Op. 33, followed by Op. 32,
but not yet by Op. 31, was Schubert's third book of dances. Like Op. 18
it appeared during the carnival, without dedication.

520. FROM THE OFFICIAL 'WIENER ZEITUNG,' 13th January 1825

At the House of Anton Diabelli & Co.
Art and Music Dealers in the Graben, No. 1133, are newly
published, and to be had at the same price of K. Lichtl
in Pest:

.   .   .   .   .

THE TROUT.
['Die Forelle']
Poem by Schubart.
Set to Music
for One Voice with Pianoforte Accompaniment
by FRANZ SCHUBERT.

Price. . . . . 1 Florin, V.C.
(Property of the Publisher.)

This famous song had already appeared in the 'Wiener Zeitschrift' in
1820 (*see* note on p. 155). In the meantime Schubert had written a
final version of it in October 1821, with five bars of introduction added
(not in the complete edition). The song appeared at first without its
opus number (31) as No. 152 of Diabelli's collection entitled 'Philomele.'

521. FROM THE PROGRAMME of the Ninth Evening Entertainment
held by the Philharmonic Society, 13th January 1825
(Conductor, Herr [Johann] Fischer)

4. 'Erl King,' poem by Goethe, music by Schubert, performed
by Herr Tietze.

522. FROM THE OFFICIAL 'WIENER ZEITUNG,' 27th January 1825

At the House of Sauer & Leidesdorf
in Vienna, Kärntnerstrasse, No. 941, has just appeared:
New Dance Music.
LET 'S STICK TOGETHER.

Original Austrian Country Dances by Payer, Schubert, Pensel,
Leidesdorf, Czapek.
For Pianoforte solo.
Three Books, each 1 Fl. Vien. Cur.
The Same for 4 Hands, each Book 1 Fl. 30 Kr., V.C.
The Same for Pianoforte and Violin, 1 Fl. 15 Kr., V.C.
The Same for two Violins and Bass, 1 Fl. 30 Kr., V.C.

The first two books of this collection, of which the second included two
dances by Schubert, had already appeared early in 1824 (*see* Nos. 422,
431 and 437). The third, which probably contained nothing by Schubert,
has been lost. The first originally cost 1 florin 15 kreuzer.

523. FROM THE PROGRAMME of the Eleventh Evening Entertainment held by the Philharmonic Society, 27th January 1825
(Conductor, Herr [Franz] Kirchlehner)

4. 'Longing' ['Die Sehnsucht'] by Schiller, set to music by
Schubert, performed by Fräulein [Josephine] Fröhlich.

Kirchlehner was a manufacturer who sang bass and played the violin.

Schubertiad at Karl von Enderes and Josef Witteczek's, 29th
January 1825.—Karl, Ritter von Enderes (*see* No. 242), born at
Teschen in 1787, was conveyancer in the Ministry of Finance and
lived in 1824 in the Neuburgergasse (near the Neuer Markt), in
the Klosterneuburgerhof. But according to Franz von Hartmann's
family chronicle Enderes seems to have lived at this time (1825)
at Witteczek's, who about then may have moved from the house of
his father-in-law, Watteroth, in the Landstrasse suburb, to his own
quarters at the corner of the Kärntnerstrasse and the Wallfischgasse.
Josef von Spaun had introduced Enderes to Schubert. He was
an amateur botanist, and later made friends with Ludwig von
Köchel, the author of the Mozart catalogue.

524. FROM THE PROGRAMME of the Twelfth Evening Entertainment held by the Philharmonic Society, 3rd February 1825
(Conductor, Herr [Johann] Fischer)

2. 'The Flowers' Grief' ['Der Blumen Schmerz']. Poem by
Count Mayláth, set to music by Schubert, performed by Herr
[Karl Maria] Gross.

525. From the Official 'Wiener Zeitung,' 7th February 1825

At the House of Pietro Mechetti, qm. Carlo,

has just appeared and is also to be had of K. Lichtl in Pest:

TERPSICHORE.

A Collection of 50 wholly new German Dances,
composed for the Pianoforte by

Eduard von Arbter, Knight, Ignaz Assmayr, Julius Benedict, Leopoldine Blahetka, Johann Nepomuk Breitschädel, L. E. Czapek, Karl Czerny, Josef Czerny, Peter von Decret, Johann Ferdinand Doleczalek, Josef Fischhof, Josef Förster, Adalbert Gyrowetz, Anton Hackel, Johann Horzalka, Josef Hüttenbrenner, Anselm Hüttenbrenner, Franz Janda, L. Jansa, Michael Janusch, Johann Kaltenmarker, Joseph Kerzkowsky, V. Konizek, Karl Krause, Konradin Kreutzer, August Krippner, Franz Lachner, Eduard Freiherr von Lannoy, Josef Lanz, K. Georg Lickl, Alois Linke, Léon de Saint-Lubin, Ignaz Maschek, Michael Pamer, F. Paur, Johann Pensel, W. Plachy, P. J. Riotte, Franz Schubert, Matthias Schwarz, Simon Sechter, L. S——, Franz Stadler, Friedrich Starke, Josef von Szalay, Johann von Vesque, Knight, Franz Weber, Freiherr von Wodniansky, Karl Würth, D. R. von Zepharovich.—Final Coda by L. E. Czapek.

In four Books.   No. 1 . . . . 2 Fl. — Kr.

No. 2 . . . . 1 Fl. 45 Kr.

No. 3 . . . . 2 Fl. — Kr.

No. 4 . . . . 2 Fl. — Kr.

The four Books complete . . 6 Fl. — Kr.

Pietro Mechetti, born at Lucca in 1775, was one of the Italian art and music dealers in Vienna, who in 1811 had succeeded his uncle Carlo as publisher.—Of this collection too, which may have contained a now unknown German Dance by Schubert, no copy is known to exist.—Julius Benedict, born at Stuttgart in 1804, was vice musical director at the Kärntnertor Theatre in 1823–5, having gone to Vienna with his master, Weber. He became conductor in London in 1835, and was a pianoforte player and opera composer.—Breitschädel was a pianist.—Peter, Edler von Decret, had played the pianoforte at Frischling's and the kettle-drums at Hatwig's. —Johann Ferdinand Dolezalek does not seem to be identical with Johann Nepomuk Emanuel Dolezalek, whom we are to encounter later on (*see* note preceding No. 1159).—Fischhof, born in 1804 at Butschowitz in Moravia, had gone to Vienna as a medical student in 1822, but became a pianoforte teacher.—Hackel, born in Vienna in 1799, was an accountancy official and a sentimental song composer; his father, Johann Christoph Hackel, who had been physician at the Seminary and also composed, became blind.—Janda, born at Wildenschwert in Bohemia in 1797, a violinist, had gone to Vienna in 1817, and was a member of the court chapel; he became Schuppanzigh's successor in his quartet and professor at the Conservatory, and later went to London as performer and teacher.—Janusch was a flautist, in Prague at first.—Lanz, born in 1797 at Michaelnbach in Upper Austria, eleven days before Schubert, was also a schoolmaster's son; he became first violinist at St. Peter's church at Salzburg, where at this time he was pianoforte teacher, and later went to Vienna. He, too, will reappear during Schubert's last days (see note preceding No. 1158).—Lickl, born in Vienna in 1801, was a church composer and virtuoso on the fashionable Physharmonika.—Linke, born c. 1801, a violinist, died in 1830 by a fall from the bastion.—L. S—— may be Leopold Sonnleithner, who certainly fits into the alphabetical order.—Franz Stadler, born in 1760 at Lewin in Bohemia, had gone to the Vienna court theatres in 1804 and played violin and oboe. —Starke, born in 1774, was bandmaster of the 33rd Infantry Regiment and had edited a 'Viennese Pianoforte School,' in which a work by Beethoven was printed for the first time: the 'Bagatelles' Nos. 7–11 from Op. 119.—Johann Vesque von Püttlingen, born in 1803 at Opole in Poland, was taken to Vienna as early as 1810; he became an official and later composed under the pseudonym of J. Hoven.—Several of the composers listed cannot be identified.

526. From the Official 'Wiener Zeitung,' 9th February 1825

At the House of Sauer & Leidesdorf

in Vienna, Kärntnerstrasse, No. 941, is just published and to be had:

Variations pour le Pianoforte à 4 mains
par Fr. Schubert.

Œuvre 35. Price, 3 Florins 45 Kreuzer, V.C.

These Variations on an original theme, written at Zseliz in 1824, were dedicated to Count Anton Berchtold von Ungarschütz, a chamberlain born in Vienna in 1796. Schubert was not in close touch with him; the dedication was probably paid for. Opp. 35 and 36 appeared before Opp. 31 and 34.

Schubertiad at Enderes and Witteczek's, 10th February 1825.

527. From the Official 'Wiener Zeitung,' 11th February 1825

At the House of Cappi & Co.,
Privileged Art and Music Dealers, Graben, No. 1122,
are newly published and to be had:

DIANA IN ANGER and NIGHT PIECE
['Die zürnende Diana']   ['Nachtstück']
Poetry by J. Mayrhofer,
set to Music for One Voice with Pianoforte Accompaniment
by FRANZ SCHUBERT.
Work 36.   2 Florins 30 Kreuzer, V.C.

The excellence of Schubert's songs is already so generally acknowledged that they no longer require any recommendation. The publishers have chosen, from the numerous musical works by this composer of genius the present two songs, which have already gained full recognition and merited distinction in several of the choicest private circles with their classic performances by the retired I. & R. Court Opera singer, Herr Vogl, that coryphaeus of German vocal art.   The publishers therefore flatter themselves that they are offering a welcome gift to all friends of indigenous art.

Schubert, F., German Dances and Écossaises for the Pianoforte.
Work 33.   1 Florin 30 Kreuzer.
—— the same Dances arranged for pianoforte duet.   2 Fl. 30 Kr.
—— the same Dances arranged for violin and pianoforte.   2 Fl.

The first of these two songs was at first wrongly entitled 'Diana in Anger' ('Die zürnende Diana'), not only in print, but also in Schubert's first draft and fair copy.   It was only later that the poet's own title, 'To Diana in Anger' ('Der zürnenden Diana'), was restored.   This opus was erroneously marked "Work 35" at first, but this was corrected in the second issue.   It is dedicated to Frau Katharina von Lászny, née Buchwieser at Coblenz c. 1789; she was first married to a Herr Hrzon and now to Ludwig, Edler Lászny von Folkusfálva, land steward to Prince Anton Pálffy.   Kathinka, as she was also called, was a daughter of Balthasar Buchwieser, third conductor at the Theater an der Wien about 1815, and she too had been engaged there.   In 1809–17 she had been at the Court Opera, where her principal parts were Susanna in Mozart's in Mozart's 'Figaro' and the Princess (Cattinka) in Boïeldieu's 'Jean de Paris.' About 1810 she was in correspondence with the romantic novelist Ernst Theodor Amadeus Hoffmann (Offenbach's tale-teller). At the time of the Congress she was said to be involved in love affairs with two princes.—Vogl had probably first sung the two songs at her house.—The arrangements of Op. 33 were not made by Schubert himself.

528. SCHWIND TO SCHOBER

[Vienna,] 14th [February 1825].

Schubert is well and busy again after a certain stagnation. He has recently come to live next door to us, where the ale-house is, on the second floor, in a very pretty room. We meet daily, and as far as I can I share his whole life with him. In the spring we intend to move to Dornbach, into the house of a good friend of mine. There is a Schubertiad at Enderes's each week—that is to say, Vogl sings. Apart from him the company consists of Witteczek, Esch, Schlechta, Gross, Riepl—a mixture of nothing but similar faces. Mayerhofer and Gahy often put in an appearance also. The new Variations for 4 hands are something quite extraordinary. The theme is as grandiose as it is languid, as purely set—don't laugh—as it is free and noble. In eight variations these pages are quite independently and vitally developed, and yet each again seems to reveal the theme. The character of the marches and the unheard-of depth and loveliness of their trios would astonish you. He is now doing songs. If you were inclined to make an operetta or opera out of David and Abigail, or anything else, he would like to have a libretto, but not a wordy one. So you may imagine. 'Diana in Anger' and the 'Night Piece' have appeared and are dedicated to Frau von Láscny, Fräulein Buchwieser that was. What a woman! If she were not nearly twice as old as I and unhappily always ill, I should have to leave Vienna, for it would be more than I can stand. Schubert has known her a long time, but I met her only recently. She is pleased with my things and with myself, more than anybody else except you; I had quite a shock the first time, the way she spoke to me and went on with me, as though there were nothing about me she didn't know. Immediately afterwards she was taken ill again and spat blood,

so that I have not seen her for a long time; but we are to eat there
to-morrow. So now I know what a person looks like who is in
ill repute all over the city, and what she does.

Here is a table of the documents in which Schubert's illness is mentioned
between the beginning of 1823 and the end of 1824: Nos. 352, 362, 371,
374, 390, 391, 395, 399, 402, 415, 420, 429, 433, 438, 441, 456, 460,
462, 463, (474), 480, (484A), 490, 491, 492, 498, 503, 504. Later
references to his state of health will be found in Nos. 569, 572, 615, 957.
(Numbers in brackets refer to lost Schubert letters alluded to elsewhere,
in Nos. 480 and 490.)—Schubert had shortly before moved into Johann
Fruhwirth's house next to the Karl church, where he lodged with the
cooper Georg Kellner. The roomy "Fruhwirthaus" looked across the
glacis towards the city and from the courtyard to the Karl church on
the left and the "Schwindian" Moonshine House on the right. Schubert
remained there until the summer of 1826, the only interruption being
the long summer trip of 1825.—In the spring Schwind moved to the
village of Dornbach near Vienna.—Karl Esch was court secretary in
the Ministry of Finance, where he was the superior of the court con-
veyancers Enderes, Grillparzer and Schlechta.—Gross is Josef Gross
(see No. 242).—Riepl may be the technologist Franz Xaver Riepl,
born at Graz in 1790, professor at the Vienna Polytechnic Institute.
—Ferdinand Mayerhofer, Freiherr von Grünbühel (see note preceding
No. 244), born in Vienna in 1798, who had been a schoolfellow of
Schubert's for a year (1808) and was nicknamed "Sindbad," was
a military surveyor. He was stationed from December 1824 until the
autumn of 1825 at Wiener Neustadt (some thirty miles south of Vienna),
but probably often visited the capital. He collaborated in the Viennese
Shakespeare edition, and was a particular friend of Bauernfeld's. (Considering Schwind's rather careless way of writing, it is just possible that
he referred to Mayrhofer, who, however, was already somewhat estranged
from the Schubert circle. Franz von Hartmann, on the other hand, who
in his family chronicle does not mention Esch, Mayerhofer and Riepl as
being of the party, speaks of [Max] Clodi and [Franz] Derffel.)—The
Variations are Op. 35; Schwind is discussing the printing.—The marches
Schubert played with Gahy were probably those of Op. 27 already
published, not Op. 40 now in preparation.—Schwind himself used the
story of David and Abigail later for a cartoon, of which no trace remains.
Schober did not write another libretto for Schubert.—Frau Lászny was
then about thirty-six and Schwind twenty-one.—Schwind does not
mention Schober's sister Sofie, the last surviving of his brothers and
sisters, who had been married to Zechenter since 1823, and who died of a
pulmonary disease early in 1825.

529. From Bauernfeld's Diary

February 1825.

Schwind came to see me in the evening with Franz Schubert, with whom I had been only distantly acquainted so far. I read the drama of 'Madera' to these friends, at their request and played duets with Schubert. Then to the inn and coffee-house.

The friendship between Schubert and Bauernfeld begins here.—The latter's curtain-raiser, 'Madera,' dating from August 1823, remained unpublished and unperformed.—Whether the habitual meeting-places were still the "Hungarian Crown" and Wasserburger's café is uncertain.

530. From Sophie Müller's Diary

24th February 1825.

Vogl and Schubert ate with us for the first time to-day; afterwards Vogl sang several of Schiller's poems set by Schubert.

Sophie Müller, born at Mannheim in 1803, had been playing juvenile leading ladies at the Burg Theatre since the spring of 1822, and she sang her musical interpolations herself, as Antonie Adamberger had done at the same theatre before her. According to Anselm. Hüttenbrenner the bewitching Sophie sang Schubert's girls' songs "most touchingly." After her mother's death early in 1824 she lived alone with her father in the village of Hietzing near Vienna. She kept a diary and an autograph album which bears as motto a quotation from 'Hamlet' in the original language, which she knew, and also contains an English poem, entered by Cecilia Livesay in Vienna in 1825 or 1826. The Viennese adored Sophie, who died young in 1830.

531. From the Programme of the Thirteenth Evening Entertainment held by the Philharmonic Society, 24th February 1825 (Conductor, Herr [Ferdinand] Bogner)

'Diana in Anger,' poem by Mayrhofer, set to music by Schubert, performed by Herr [Johann] Hoffmann.

Bogner, who that year married Barbara Fröhlich (*see* note preceding No. 199), born in Vienna in 1786, was a flautist and professor at the Conservatory.

Schubertiad at Enderes and Witteczek's, after which the company goes to Leibenfrost's coffee-house, and then to Neuner's; Schubert

and Schwind drink brotherhood with the brothers Fritz and Franz
von Hartmann, 26th February 1825. The Café Josef Leibenfrost was
in the Neuer Markt (called Mehlmarkt earlier), obliquely opposite
the Café Ignaz Neuner in the Neuburgergasse (now Plankengasse),
where Vogl lived in the same house. Its later name was the "Silver
Coffee-House" because of its sterling cutlery and its silver coat-
hangers. A room admitting ladies was opened on the first floor,
where smoking was forbidden, and about 1835 its ground floor
became Vienna's literary café, frequented by Lenau, but cultivating
a tone which Schober disliked.—The two Hartmann brothers from
Linz studied law in Vienna.

532. FROM THE OFFICIAL 'WIENER ZEITUNG,' 28th February 1825

At the House of Cappi & Co.,
Art and Music Dealers, Graben, No. 1122,
are newly published:

Schubert, F., 'The Pilgrim' ['Der Pilgrim'] and 'The Alpine
Hunter' ['Der Alpenjäger'], poems by Friedrich von Schiller,
set to Music for One Voice with Pianoforte Accompaniment.
Work 37.   2 Florins, V.C.

—— Overture in F major for Pianoforte Duet. Work 34.
2 Fl. 30 Kr.

In 1824 Johann (Jean) Cappi readmitted his nephew Peter, who had
parted company with Diabelli: the firm was now styled Cappi & Co., but
the name was changed to Cappi & Czerny in 1826, when Josef Czerny
joined it; by 1828 Czerny alone was left.—Op. 37 is dedicated to the
painter Ludwig Schnorr von Carolsfeld (see No. 258), Schwind's teacher,
Schubert calling him "his friend."—For the Overture see No. 160.

533. FROM SOPHIE MÜLLER'S DIARY

1st March 1825.

Vogl and Schubert came in the afternoon and brought new songs
from 'The Pirate,' also 'The Rose.' Vogl sang from memory the
'Scene from Tartarus' by Schiller; glorious.

Although Sophie Müller always speaks of "new songs" when she means
those which are still new to herself, Norna's song from Walter Scott's

'Pirate' must obviously date from early 1825, not from 1827, as is assumed in the complete edition.   'The Rose' was written as early as 1822.— The "Scene" should, of course, be 'Group from Tartarus.'

534. FROM SOPHIE MÜLLER'S DIARY

2nd March 1825.

After lunch Schubert came; I sang with him until nearly six o'clock, then drove to the theatre.

535. FROM SOPHIE MÜLLER'S DIARY

3rd March 1825.

After lunch Schubert came and brought a new song, 'The Young Nun' ['Die junge Nonne']; later Vogl came, and I sang it to him; it is splendidly composed.   Old Lange then visited us too.   We had music until towards 7 o'clock, when the gentlemen left.

'The Young Nun' was certainly a newly written song.—"Old Lange" is Mozart's brother-in-law, Josef Lange, born at Würzburg in 1751, an actor, producer, portrait painter, pianoforte player and composer, who was re-engaged at the Burg Theatre in 1817–21.

536. JOHANNA LUTZ TO LEOPOLD KUPELWIESER at Naples

Vienna, 7th March 1825.

I really am very curious to know what Franz [von Bruchmann] will write to you about Schober.

It pained me much, because of you, that the whole circle was so delighted.   Alas! how grievous is all parting!

Yet it has its advantages.   For when you and Schober had left, the whole circle shaped itself differently, if no better, and had to be dissolved altogether.   However, the better ones always find each other again, and then not much is lost.

I can only say what I have heard from the Bruchmanns and from Schwind, the two opposing parties, who no doubt both exaggerated a great deal, and draw my conclusions from that.

Rieder, Dietrich, Schubert and Schwind are as close together, or as far apart, as before—but their attitude towards the Bruchmanns is very different.

Rieder and Bruchmann are not hostile towards each other, but they do not meet. Schubert and Schwind are in open feud with Bruchmann. They both seem to me like children, and indeed they give vent to their hatred childishly. They do not meet any more at all, cut each other dead and behave like great enemies. It is true, Justina has been weak and vacillating, and Franz deliberately acted badly towards Schober, for he was quite aware of all the facts. And of course Schober's bad side was easier to see than the good. But after all it is none of it their business.

If they do not care for him, that is their affair. But their conduct is infantile.

Yet their affection for Schober is nice.

Schubert is now very busy and well-behaved, which pleases me very much.

The Bruchmanns now have a very small circle. Smetana and Eichholzer are very often there. The latter is making great artistic progress and has the full support of the whole household. Eichholzer's and Schwind's mutual hatred is schoolboyish on both sides. I cannot understand, especially in regard to the two girls, why they have retained no spark of gratitude for all the affection everybody showed them, for they said themselves (when I made their acquaintance) that it was their happiest time when they joined that circle, which opened a new life to them. But, like the others, they look for all the possible faults in order to make excuses for themselves and to gloss over their fickleness.

Mohn does not associate with the others at all. Nor do I know which party he adheres to.

Doblhoff, Hönig and the others are looking for appointments, and each goes his own way.

You will have some trouble, when you come, in making your choice, for they will probably all be unchanged towards you. Still, you will then best be able to judge how matters stand. There are only a few, after all, to whom one can be close, and no doubt they can always be found. I at least firmly believe that true love and friendship must prevail.

O Leopold, if once you are back here, everything else will adjust itself, and I rejoice infinitely that everything will take new shape about us and our love always remains the same.

The situation so obscurely dealt with by Johanna Lutz was that Franz von Bruchmann, actuated partly by Schober's doubtful choice of the actor's profession, had disclosed the secret engagement between him and his sister Justina and insisted on its being broken off. Some of the friends seem to have expressed unwelcome glee at Schober's discomfiture. Schwind, of course, was on his and Justina's side, and Schubert at least on Schober's.—Smetana was Justina's future husband. The second girl is, of course, her sister Isabella. Both had withdrawn from most of their brother's friends on account of these dissensions about Schober.—Doblhoff, like Bruchmann and Hönig, was preparing for the doctorate in law, which he took in 1826–7 in the north of Italy ruled by Austria, the soil of Vienna appearing too dangerous to him. This doctorate was, needless to say, an indirect means of seeking employment.

537. From Sophie Müller's Diary

7th March 1825.

Vogl came before lunch, and with Schubert at 5 o'clock; they brought several new songs, among which a 'Scene from Aeschylus,' 'Her Tomb' ['Ihr Grab'], 'The Trout' ['Die Forelle'] and 'The Solitary' ['Der Einsame'] are excellent. They left at 7.30.

Here again it is for the most part a question of songs that were new only to Sophie Müller. The "Scene," which should be 'Fragment from Aeschylus,' dates from 1816, 'Her Tomb' probably from 1822, 'The Trout' in its last version from 1821 and even 'The Solitary' (see note preceding No. 540) possibly from 1823, although the complete edition assigns it to the present year: Kreissle asserts that this song was written in hospital.

538. Anna Milder to Schubert

[Envelope:]

Franz Schubert, Esq.

in the Rossau,　　　　　　　　　　　　　in
at the School-house,　　　　　　　　　Vienna.
franked.

[Inside:]

Most honoured Herr Schubert,   Berlin, 8th March 1825.

I hasten to inform you that I received your opera, 'Estrella and Alfonso,' as well as 'Suleika's Second Song' with infinite pleasure. I thank you sincerely for your complaisance. 'Suleika's Second Song' is heavenly and moves me to tears every time. It is indescribable: you have infused into it all the possible magic and longing, as in 'Suleika's First Song' and 'Secrets.' The only regrettable thing is that all this endless beauty cannot be sung to the public, since the crowd wants only treats for the ear. Should the 'Moth' ['Nachtschmetterling'] not be suited to the making of somewhat brilliant music for the voice, I would ask you to choose another poem in its place, if possible by Goethe; one which can be sung in a variety of measures, so that several emotions can be represented. Such as, for instance 'Diverse Feelings in One Place' ['Verschiedene Empfindungen an einem Platz'] * or a similar one, which I will leave to you, so that there may be a brilliant ending.

However many songs you may wish to dedicate to me, this can be only most agreeable and flattering for me. I leave here on 1st June, and if I could have such a desirable song from you for my tour and concerts, it would make me indescribably happy; that is to say, if you will put in some suitable passages and flourishes.

As regards 'Alfonso and Estrella,' your opera, I am very sorry indeed to have to say that its libretto does not accord with local taste, for people here are accustomed to grand tragic opera or French comic opera. Judging by the said taste, you will yourself see that 'Alfonso and Estrella' could not possibly make its fortune here. If I should have the pleasure of being able to appear in one of your operas, it would doubtless have to be suited to my individuality and contain, for example, a part for a queen, a mother or a peasant woman. I should therefore advise you to write something new, if possible in one act, namely an oriental subject with a principal part for the soprano, which you ought to do splendidly, as I gather from [your settings of] Goethe's 'Divan.' With 3 characters and chorus you could be sure of a good performance here, i.e. 1 soprano, 1 tenor and 1 bass. Should you find such

* To be found in Goethe's poems.

a subject, I would ask you to let me know, so that we may negotiate further.   I should then do everything in my power to get the thing staged.   Please let me know what I am to do with your opera of 'Alfonso.'

Kindly give all my hearty greetings to my friend and teacher Vogl; I am very sorry indeed that he is so suffering; but I am little better myself.   Tell him I shall have to go to Wiesbaden this year.   I should be infinitely happy to have a few lines from him.

Please also give my friendliest greetings to Frau von Lászny. I wish I could sing your songs to that amiable and art-loving lady.

Commending myself to your goodwill, I am,

Your

most devoted

Anna Milder.

Schubert's reply to No. 511 has not been preserved.—'Secrets' ('Geheimes'), from Goethe's 'Westöstlicher Divan,' had appeared with the first Suleika song; the second was not yet out.—'Diverse Feelings,' describing the emotions of four different persons, was not set by Schubert. —Anna Milder did not leave until 30th June, going first to Ems (not Wiesbaden) for a cure and then to Paris (*see* No. 563).—Schubert was not to write another one-act stage piece.—If he did ask for the return of 'Alfonso and Estrella' (whose title was at first reversed by Frau Milder), he certainly never had the score back.   Schubert had probably asked her to pass the manuscript on to the Königstadt Theatre.—Frau Milder and Frau von Lászny (as Fräulein Buchwieser) had for a time appeared together at the Kärntnertor Theatre.

539. From the 'Österreichisches Bürgerblatt für Verstand, Herz und gute Laune,' Linz, 11th March 1825

(On the Linz Carnival of 1825)

The cotillon again remained the favourite dance this year, and will yet long remain so, it is to be hoped; but by the uncommonly beautiful German Dances by the composer of genius, Franz Schubert, arranged as cotillons by Herr Schiedermayr, this tasteful dance was ennobled into a more elevated pleasure.

S.

[? Albert Stadler.]

This was the first orchestration of Schubertian dances, so far as we know. They were very likely the German Dances from the new Op. 33. This arrangement did not appear in print. Johann Baptist Schiedermayr, born in 1779 at Pfaffenmünster in Bavaria, was chapel master and cathedral organist at Linz, *maestro al cembalo* to the Linz Musical Society and singing-teacher at its school.

'The Solitary' ('Der Einsame'), Op. 41 (xx. 465), appears in the 'Wiener Zeitschrift,' 12th March 1825.

540. FROM BAUERNFELD'S DIARY

March 1825.

Much with Schwind and Schubert. He sang new songs here. The other day we slept at his place. As we were short of a pipe, Moritz fitted me up something of the kind from Schubert's eye-glass-case. Fraternized with Schubert over a glass of sugar-water. He wants an opera libretto from me and suggested 'The Enchanted Rose.' I said I had a 'Count of Gleichen' in my head.—Visit to the singer Vogl. An odd old bachelor. He reads Epictetus and is a treasury of pleasant dandyism. Moritz behaved with studied rudeness towards him. Schubert is always the same, always natural.

In March 1825 Schubert had set his first poem, 'In the Forest' ('Im Walde'), by the poet of the epic 'The Enchanted Rose,' Ernst Schulze. Schubert, after failing to use Dr. Bernhardt's libretto (*see* No. 475)—if indeed it had been written—now urged Bauernfeld to try his hand at it. But before the latter seriously began to work at it, he learnt in the summer of 1826 (*see* No. 663) that it was too late. The libretto of 'The Count of Gleichen,' however, was really written and its composition sketched by Schubert. Schwind, by the way, dealt with this subject in a picture later on.—After Schubert's death Schwind made fun of Vogl's mannered performance (*see* No. 1030), but he repeatedly made drawings of him and Schubert at the pianoforte.

541. FROM THE PROGRAMME of a Concert given by Georg Hellmesberger, Professor at the Vienna Conservatory, 20th March
1825, at Noon, in the County Hall

5. 'The Flight' ['Die Flucht,' xvi. 26], new Vocal Quartet (for male voices, by F. Schubert.

The concert included a violin Concerto by Hellmesberger. Betty Schröder was to have sung an aria by Cocchi, but her mother recited an ode by Klopstock instead. Betty was born at Hamburg in 1806, the second daughter of the tragedienne Sophie Schröder (*see* No. 209), was engaged at the Burg Theatre in 1819–22 and later became an opera singer.

542. From the 'Sammler,' 5th April 1825

Apart from the pieces mentioned above a new vocal quartet for male voices was produced under the title of 'The Flight' by F. Schubert. Once again a work by our justly and generally liked song-writer must be described as very fine; but it is extremely difficult to perform, for which reason the execution was actually somewhat faulty.

543. From Sophie Müller's Diary

30th March 1825.

Schubert and Vogl came for the last time to-day. Vogl leaves to-morrow for his country seat at Steyr.

Vogl went to Steyr the next day; Schubert did not follow till the end of May. They again stayed at Paumgartner's.

544. Schwind to Schober

[Vienna,] 2nd April 1825.

To-morrow I shall show it [Schwind's series of pen-and-ink drawings to Mozart's 'Marriage of Figaro'] to Netty Hönig, who is much —concerned in it, I meant to write yesterday, but then Schubert and Bauernfeld turned up with a very amusing stranger. To-day we began to look at it, when whom should the devil send us but Hieber and Smetana? So 'Figaro' was hidden and I stole away. Isn't it a misery when such legitimate pleasures are spoilt by that sort of rubbish? Schubert was to come early in the afternoon, but has let me down; I went to sleep first, then I smoked and now I mope over the sight of my spoilt Easter . . .

Schwind had finished his cycle of thirty pen-and-ink drawings, entitled "Figaro's Wedding Procession," in March (*see* No. 492). Both seriously and playfully he attempted in this first large-scale work of his a fanciful illustration of the finale in the third act of Mozart's opera. One-third of it is devoted to imaginary wedding guests and masqueraders, among whom are figures from Friedrich von Schlegel's notorious novel 'Lucinde' (which was "highly esteemed" by Justina von Bruchmann), from the legend of the Count of Gleichen (*see* No. 540), from Mozart's 'Don Giovanni' (the serenade) and 'Magic Flute' (Papageno and his family, Monostatos with two slaves), from Haydn's 'Seasons' (with the figure of Winter which later became popular), etc. As was his wont, Schwind introduced a self-portrait into this, not in the figure of Cherubino, to whom his friends liked to compare him, but that of a youthful burgess in medieval German costume. The musicians who lead the procession following the herald are very characteristic of Schwind, with their different types of players suiting the nature of their instruments. The work was reproduced in facsimile in Vienna in 1904. The original, which Beethoven had with him during his last days, was last in the possession of Professor Josef Hupka in Vienna.—Netti Hönig is probably portrayed as the gardener's daughter Barbarina, seen in an arbour with the page Cherubino, away from the procession.—Who the "amusing stranger" was is not known.—"Hieber," often mentioned by Schwind about this time, may be Josef Huber, who was known as a bore.—Easter Sunday fell on 3rd April.—This letter was interrupted and not completed until the 18th (*see* No. 548A).

545. FROM THE 'THEATERZEITUNG,' 28th April 1825

(Notice of Johann Rüttinger junior's concert, 10th April 1825, at noon, at the "Red Hedgehog.")

Herr Tietze sang Schubert's 'Alpine Hunter' with so much applause that he had to repeat it.

Rüttinger, the son of a member of the Burg Theatre orchestra, was born in 1803 and had played clarinet there since 1823.—The song, sung as No. 5, was clearly the setting of Schiller's 'Alpine Hunter' ('Der Alpenjäger'), not Mayrhofer's, for it had appeared shortly before as No. 2 of Op. 37 (*see* No. 532).

546. From Bauernfeld's Diary

April 1825.

At Weintridt's at Retz with Moritz [von Schwind], who painted us both on the jobmaster's sign.—Grand Schubertiad with friends, musicians and painters. The cask of Retz wine we had brought with us was the occasion.

For Weintridt *see* No. 271.—Retz, about forty-three miles north-west-by-north from Vienna, now on the Czech frontier, is a small town whose fortifications are still partly standing. The central square, in which stands a house with the finest *sgraffiti* in Austria, is traversed by deep cellars in which the much-favoured wine of the neighbourhood is stored. (This wine is mentioned by Hugo von Hofmannsthal in the libretto for Richard Strauss's 'Rosenkavalier,' in the conversation between Ochs and the princess in Act I.)—Apart from the post there were, since about 1822, private stage-coaches, which could be stopped anywhere. The jobmaster of this coach between Vienna and Retz had a sign on his house which Schwind painted for him (now lost, but used about 1860 for the oil painting of "Schwind and Bauernfeld on a country jaunt") and for which he probably paid with a cask of Retz wine. Schubert doubtless took pleasure in a share of this in Vienna.

547. From Bauernfeld's Diary

April 1825.

I am still in love with Clotilde, as Moritz is with his Nettel. Schubert sniggers at us both, but is not quite heart-whole himself.

Clotilde, a young woman whose surname he successfully withheld from his biographers, had been Bauernfeld's mistress since 1821.—Nettel is Anna Hönig.—Schubert's heartbreak may or may not have been on account of Karoline Esterházy, to whom Bauernfeld's verse (*see* note to No. 491) certainly referred later on. "Quite another" in its third line seems to be a disparaging reference to the chambermaid Pepi.

548. Marianne von Willemer to Goethe

[Frankfort o/M.,] 16th April 1825.

Early in the morning I sent to a music shop and had the splendid song by Beethoven, 'Heart, my heart, what will befall thee,' fetched, and they sent me at the same time a quite pretty melody on the East Wind and 'Secrets' from the 'Divan.'

The title of the Goethe song set by Beethoven is 'New Love, New Life' ('Neue Liebe, neues Leben'). It appeared in Beethoven's Op. 75, but was also reprinted separately. There were two printed versions of it; the well-known second one is evidently meant here.—The book sent with it unrequested was the unnamed Schubert's Op. 14, containing the first Suleika song to Marianne von Willemer's own words, published as Goethe's, and to the latter's 'Secrets' ('Geheimes'). The first Suleika song was known also as 'East Wind,' the second (Op. 31) as 'West Wind.' Frau Willemer, who had been an actress before her marriage, was a friend of Anna Milder's (*see* No. 558). Schubert is not mentioned in the correspondence between Goethe and Frau Willemer, nor does this song appear in it again.

548A. Schwind to Schober

Vienna, 18th [April 1825.]

I always visit Schubert early in the morning, and for the rest of the day each of us sees how best to use it. He is much with his brothers, I much with Bauernfeld, but as a rule I am at home. The good Frau Láscny is so ill that nobody is allowed to visit her, for she is not allowed to talk. I am so infinitely sorry for her, and no doubt she misses us, and I should certainly not let her speak a word. I have often been there and have always understood her, although she was allowed to say nothing; I do not know how, but she was always pleased about it. But I must hope that she will be better. She is the only one about whom I care to talk to you, for she is a decisive and splendid person, who in the greatest welter of temptation and licentiousness remained true to herself and who knows to what she owes respect . . . God keep you for me, for the excellent Schubert and my pious girl-friend.

At that time Schubert clearly went for walks to the outlying villages with his brothers in the afternoons and during the Easter holidays, perhaps sometimes to drink the *Heurige*, as "this year's" wine was called, though the word meant the latest vintage and refers to last year's. The wine was retailed by the vintners themselves in the wine-growing villages near Vienna, especially at Grinzing. The vineyards are on the slopes of the Wiener Wald. The so-called *Heurigen-Musik* was not introduced until the second half of the nineteenth century (*see* No. 928).   In Schubert's time only stray players like harpers appeared, and guests used to come only on Sunday afternoons, not in the evenings during the week. Incidentally, the proverbial bush ("good wine needs no bush") is still to be seen hanging outside the houses where new wine is to be had.—The pious girl-friend is Netti Hönig, who was a strict Catholic.

549. FROM SOPHIE MÜLLER'S DIARY

20th April 1825.

Schubert came to-day; I tried several new songs: 'The Solitary' ['Der Einsame'], 'The Evil Colour' ['Die böse Farbe'], 'Urge into the Distance' ['Drang in die Ferne'].

Schubert's visit to Sophie Müller on 7th March (*see* No. 537) was thus not the last before his summer excursion.—'The Solitary' she had received already on that occasion; 'The Evil Colour' from 'The Fair Maid of the Mill' and 'Urge into the Distance,' written in 1823, were new only to her.

550. ALBERT SCHELLMANN, JUN., TO SCHUBERT

Dear Schubert,   [Vienna, end of April 1825.]

To say good-bye, to fetch the gloves I left with you and the book you are lending me—these are the reasons for my being here— yet all to no purpose, except for the book, half of which I found. Farewell, remember me to all at Steyr, my parents, Vogl, Fräulein Pepi, and especially my sweetheart, whom you will easily identify. Take this leaf with you—it will remind you of a promise.

Schellmann.

V.S.
[Reverse:]

THE STARLET

A starlet would I be
So bright and clear to see,
And if perchance, as well she might,
She from her window looked at night—
How friendly would I beam then—
To her how pleasing seem then.

And what my lips not dare
Audaciously declare
Of love's intolerable smart,
I 'd let it shine into her heart,—
The starlet there above her
Would tell how much I love her.

                                                        Schl.

Schellmann (*see* No. 326) had come to Vienna to take his doctor's degree in law. His father (*see* No. 154) was married to Barbara Reutter (born 1770).—"Pepi" is Josefine von Koller (*see* No. 154).—Schellmann's "sweetheart" may have been identified by Schubert at Steyr; we cannot do the same so late in the day. She may have been the addressee of the poem, which Schubert did not set to music, however. Being written on the back of the letter, it could not have been intended for presentation without music.

551. FROM THE OFFICIAL 'WIENER ZEITUNG,' 7th May 1825

At the House of Sauer & Leidesdorf,
Art and Music Dealers in Vienna, Kärntnerstrasse, No. 941,
has just appeared, and is to be had at the prices quoted
(in Pest, at Karl Lichtl's):

*Schubert (Fr.), Six grandes Marches et Trios pour le Pianoforte à 4 mains.
Œuv. 40, Cah. I.*   2 Fl. 45. Kr.

Op. 40, which was published before Op. 39, and the second book of which did not appear until the autumn (*see* No. 592), was dedicated by Schubert "en marque de reconnoissance à Son ami Monsieur J. Bernhardt, docteur en médecine," the doctor who had treated him in 1823–4. The first book contained the marches Nos. 1–3.

Salieri dies, 7th May 1825.

552. FROM THE OFFICIAL 'WIENER ZEITUNG,' 9th May 1825

At the House of Cappi & Co.,
in Vienna, Graben, No. 1122, is just published and to be had

THE MINSTREL
['Der Liedler']

The Hungarian Crown Inn (Gasthof "Zur ungarischen Krone"), Seilerstätte, where a Mechanical Clock played some Schubert Tunes in 1822–4.

See p. 361

PLATE XV

Schubert.   Pencil Drawing by Leopold Kupelwieser (1821).   *See* pp. 185
and 928

PLATE XVI

Ballad by Kenner,
set to Music by
FRANZ SCHUBERT.

Work 38.   Price, 2 Florins 30 Kreuzer, Vien. Cur.

This ballad, the first by the ingenious Schubert to be issued to
the public, not only succeeds worthily to the celebrated ballads
by Zumsteeg, which in their time provoked general enthusiasm,
but even excels them in vivacity of expression and originality.
At the same time the said ballad is written in simpler and more
comprehensible style than other compositions by Schubert, and
will thus doubtless be a welcome publication for all lovers of expressive song.   The words, written by a native and as yet too little
known poet, are no less valuable and interesting, so that this work
may in every respect claim general approval.

For 'The. Minstrel' *see* No. 381.—It is significant that this song was
described as Schubert's first ballad, if only as the first published one.   Yet
the 'Erl King' had been expressly designated as a ballad in Schubert's own
edition.—The work is dedicated to Kenner.

Wilhelm August Rieder paints Schubert's portrait, early May 1825.
This best-known portrait, which was considered to be a very good
likeness, is said to owe its existence to chance.   Rieder, who lived
not far from Schubert in the Wiedner Hauptstrasse, took refuge
at Schubert's, so the story goes, during a shower and whiled away
the time by making a sketch of him, which he afterwards elaborated
at several sittings.   The water-colour bears Schubert's signature
and the date of his death added in Rieder's hand.   It became the
basis for most of the posthumous portraits.

553. FROM BAUERNFELD'S DIARY

May 1825.

Schubert to Steyr.   Moritz complains about him.—"If anything is done expressly to spite me, I can only feel disgusted!"
he said.   (The cap fitted me too.)

Schubert had left for Upper Austria before 20th May, at first for Steyr,
where he stayed on the 20th–24th.   For Schwind's ill-humour with
Schubert *see* No. 563.

Josef von Spaun removed from Linz to Lemberg, 20th May 1825.—
By a decree of January 1825 Spaun had been transferred to Lemberg
(Lwów) as assessor to the administration of customs duties.   He
remained there for about a year.

Schubert and Vogl at Ottenwalt's at Linz, 24th and 25th May 1825.—
Vogl, who had come to Linz from Steyr with Schubert, had already
visited the Ottenwalts on 17th May.   From Linz Schubert made
an excursion to St. Florian and returned to Steyr via Kremsmünster
(27th May), remaining until 4th June.

554. FROM A GRAZ CONCERT PROGRAMME, 2nd June 1825

(Grand vocal and instrumental concert organized by the Styrian
Musical Society for the benefit of needy widows and orphans of
country school-teachers, at the County Hall.)

Part I, No. 2. 'To Diana in Anger' ['An die zürnende Diana'].

Vocal Piece with Pianoforte Accompaniment; by Franz Schubert.

The same charitable cause was served by the concert at Graz in 1827,
in which Schubert took part (see No. 939).—The title of the song here
comes closer to the poet's original one, using the dative, though not yet
in its correct form.   The singer's name is not known.

555. FROM THE DRESDEN 'ABENDZEITUNG,' 19th August 1825

(Vienna Diary, early June 1825.)

The young, talented tone-poet Schubert, whose song compositions betoken the musical painter, continues to do excellent work
in that unfortunately much neglected species.   All his compositions
testify to profound feeling, combined with considerable musical
theory.   His songs find many purchasers.

[? Höhler.]

Josef von Spaun, as the guest of Count Anton and Countess Anna
(née von Hartmann) Revertera on his way through Przemysl early in
June 1825, hears there marches by Schubert (Op. 27 or Op. 40,
Book I) arranged for wind instruments, played by the band of the
Zach Regiment (bandmaster, Franz Wyskoczyl).—Count Revertera
(see No. 478), who had been married to Anna Hartmann since 1824,
was a captain in the infantry regiment No. 15, owned by Anton,

Freiherr von Zach. That regiment's bandmaster, Wyskoczyl, became an honorary member of the Linz Musical Society in 1822, as did Countess Revertera in 1824. The regiment had gone from Linz to Przemysl, an Austrian fortress west of Lwów in Galicia (now belonging to Poland). After Schiedermayr's orchestration of German Dances by Schubert at Linz (*see* No. 539) this arrangement of his marches, probably Op. 27 (*see* 512), for military band was the first known attempt at doing what was both obvious and promising; but this arrangement was not published.

556. FROM THE OFFICIAL 'WIENER ZEITUNG,' 6th June 1825

At the House of Diabelli & Co.,
Art and Music Dealers, in the Graben, No. 1133, are newly published,
and to be had of K. Lichtl in Pest at the same price:

CHRONOS THE CHARIOTEER
['An Schwager Chronos']
("Hasten thou, Chronos! onward with clattering speed!")

TO MIGNON
("Carried over vale and river")

GANYMEDE
("As in dawn's ray thou beamest on me!")
Poems by Goethe.
Set to Music
for One Voice with Pianoforte Accompaniment,
and reverentially dedicated to the Poet,
by FR. SCHUBERT.

Work 19. Price, 2 Florins 30 Kreuzer, V.C.
(Property of the Publishers.)

It was only now, after a delay of about two years, that Op. 19 appeared, perhaps because Goethe's consent to the dedication had been requested. It was certainly never expressly given, but it is doubtful whether permission to dedicate anything to him had to be obtained from the Viennese censorship.—On the title-page the price is given as 1 florin 15 kreuzer, A.C.

557. Schubert to Goethe

[Early June 1825.]

Your Excellency.

If I should succeed in giving evidence of my unbounded veneration of Your Excellency by the dedication of these compositions of your poems, and possibly in gaining some recognition of my insignificant self, I should regard the favourable fulfilment of this wish as the fairest event of my career.

With the greatest respect, I am,

Your most devoted servant,

Franz Schubert.

With this missive two special copies with the title printed in gold on satined paper were sent to Goethe at Weimar (now in the County Library there). Schubert's letter had evidently been written before his departure to Upper Austria, and left with the publishers until the work and the special copies were ready. Like Josef von Spaun's letter to Goethe (No. 81), this remained unanswered. Goethe was under the influence of Zelter and Reichardt; he regarded the simple strophic song of the so-called Berlin school as the only proper form, and was thus unable to find much pleasure in Schubert's solution of the problem. Nevertheless, when Wilhelmine Schröder-Devrient sang him the 'Erl King' in 1830— or perhaps because it was she who sang it—he acknowledged it to be an uncommon achievement. *See* No. 561.

558. From the 'Berlinische Zeitung' (Voss), 9th June 1825

(Announcement of Anna Milder's concert of 9th June 1825.)

We are greatly pleased to be able to announce to the public that Mme Milder has kindly promised us to sing, at her concert to-day, Goethe's 'Erl King' and 'Suleika's [Second] Song' from the 'Westöstlicher Divan,' both composed by Franz Schubert.

——r.

559. From the 'Berlinische Zeitung' (Voss), 11th June 1825

Rich enjoyment was afforded by the musical evening entertainment given by the Court singer, Mme Milder, at Jagor's hall on the 9th inst., which was numerously and brilliantly attended . . .

What we best like to hear from this singer's grandiose voice . . . is simply noble and sustained song, such as Mme Milder delivered in the two Goethe songs, 'Suleika's Second Song' and 'Erl King,' which she transmitted from heart to heart with true mastery.

Franz Schubert of Vienna is a thoughtful song composer, fond of modulation, who set 'Suleika' from the 'Westöstlicher Divan' to music especially for Mme Milder and dedicated the manuscript to her. Although this tone-poem exceeds song form and the five stanzas of the beautiful poem are turned into a continuous composition, its oriental spirit is nevertheless successfully captured and reflected by the music. The tender vocal melody, rendered with profound feeling by Mme Milder, is set into a brighter light by the very peculiar pianoforte accompaniment (executed with much skill by the singer's sister, Mme Bürde, *née* Milder). The blowing of a gentle west wind and the longings of tender love are admirably symbolized by this music. The 'Erl King' is highly original, treated with tragic seriousness, and the orchestral triplet figures in the very difficult pianoforte accompaniment are constantly maintained. Night and dread, storm and terror are painted with gruesome fantasy in this nocturnal piece. This song too was excellently performed according to its nature.

To say that the second Suleika song was written for Anna Milder is, doubtless, a journalistic exaggeration. The autograph has not been preserved; but Witteczek in his Schubert collection dates the song 1821, and the first Suleika song, probably written at the same time, the autograph of which has been recovered, dates from March of that year, when Schubert did not yet know the singer personally.—Jeannette Antonie Bürde, Milder's younger sister, was born in 1799 at Hütteldorf near Vienna; she became a pianoforte player, singer and song composer, later teacher of pianoforte and singing.—Other notices of this concert appeared in Spener's 'Berlinische Nachrichten' on 11th June and in the Leipzig 'Allgemeine musikalische Zeitung' of 3rd August 1825 (German edition, Nos. 581 and 582). The criticism in Spener's paper, which describes German song as Goethe's creation on the one hand and as Zelter's and Reichardt's on the other, though without denying Schubert's achievement, was found among the remains of Frau Willemer, to whom Frau Milder had perhaps sent it.

560. From Bauernfeld's Diary

June 1825.

Walk with Moritz.   A few days later he announced to me the arrival of his highly important friend Schober.

Schober left Breslau at the end of June.

561. From Goethe's Diary

16th June 1825.

Consignment from Felix [Mendelssohn] of Berlin, quartets. Consignment from Schubert of Vienna, compositions of some of my songs.

Mendelssohn, aged sixteen, having been recommended to Goethe by Zelter, had three weeks earlier played his pianoforte Quartet, Op. 3, to the poet, to whom it was dedicated, and had sent him the three pianoforte Quartets, Opp. 1–3, from Berlin on 9th June.   To him Goethe sent a detailed letter of thanks on 21st June.

562. Therese Clodi to her Brother Max in Vienna

Ebenzweier, 22nd June 1825.

That Vogl and Schubert have already come to see us I think I have told you.   I should so much like to invite them, yet do not know as yet how to do it quite properly.   Twice I have heard Vogl sing and Schubert play: it is and remains a divine pleasure to hear those two.

Ebenzweier Castle, about three miles from Gmunden on Lake Traun, dates from the thirteenth century.   It was last in the possession of Don Alfonso Carlos of Bourbon-Habsburg-d'Este (born London, 1849), and is mentioned in Sacheverell Sitwell's book 'A Background for Domenico Scarlatti' (London, 1935).   Florian Maximilian Clodi, whose son Max we have already encountered (see No. 478), born in 1740, had purchased the castle and domain of Ebenzweier in 1802.   He had four children, Therese, Max, Josef and Franz.   They were the children of her father's second wife, Josef von Spaun's aunt Therese, whom he had married in 1800, and who died in 1814.   He became blind and gouty.   His daughter, the amiable Therese (born *c.* 1803), managed the property as householder and administrator. She was called the châtelaine, or preferably the "lady of the lake." Franz von Schwind (*see* No. 515) worshipped her.—Schubert had first been at Steyr for about a fortnight and then stayed for six weeks, from 4th June to 15th July, at Gmunden, where Vogl was with him at least for a time. Gmunden, about a hundred and twenty miles south-west by west of Vienna and thirty from Steyr, lies at the influx of the river Traun into its lake, in the Upper Austrian Salzkammergut. On a hill near by is Cumberland Castle, where the last Duke of Cumberland and last King of Hanover died in 1923. Schubert and Vogl stayed with the merchant Ferdinand Traweger (*see* No. 132) in the Badgasse, near the landing-stage. Stadler called him Gmunden's Paumgartner, and he was thus a patron of music. He and his wife Elisabeth had two daughters and a son, Eduard, who was not born till 1820, and in whom Schubert took much pleasure. He taught him the song "Guten Morgen, schöne Müllerin" from 'The Fair Maid of the Mill' and presented him with a silver toothpick as a reward for his good behaviour on being bled with leeches (iconographical volume, p. 53). Traweger was particularly fond of male-voice quartets, and Schubert is said to have written the Latin drinking-song 'Edit nonna' for him. —Schubert does not seem to have stayed at Ebenzweier Castle during that visit. At Gmunden he was also in touch with the schoolmaster Johann Nepomuk Wolf, whose daughter Anna (Nanette), born at Hallstatt in 1808, played the pianoforte and sang. Schubert may have played duets with her at the house of Aulic Councillor Franz Ferdinand, Ritter von Schiller (born Ponteba, 1773), who had been head steward of the Gmunden salt mines since 1824. Nanette, whose later married name was Böhm, about 1830 became a friend of the poet Nikolaus Lenau, who also appears in Schubert's life at Karoline Unger's and Sophie von Kleyle's.

563. ANNA MILDER TO SCHUBERT

Most honoured Herr Schubert,

I cannot neglect giving you news of my musical evening entertainment, which took place on the 9th inst.; for I sang the 'Suleika' in public after all, and in fact I was requested to do so, as you see. The 'Erl King' and 'Suleika' pleased infinitely, and it gives me much pleasure to be able to send you this newspaper, which I wish and hope will give you joy also. There is a desire for 'Suleika' to be obtainable soon, and I presume that it has already appeared. In

Berlin Trautwein is the most reputable music dealer, a man whom I recommend to you, should you wish to bring out 'Suleika' here.

How about the 'Diverse Feelings in One Place' by Goethe? Have you thought about it?

I leave here on the 30th inst. and shall probably not receive anything from you before I go, much to my regret. In August I shall be at Ems for my health; should you possibly have an opportunity of sending me anything of your latest compositions there, or to Paris, where I shall be for two months, September and October, it would give me endless pleasure.

How is Vogl? I hope well, and indeed very well, if he is as I wish. Please give him no end of greetings from me; I am still sorry to have been in Vienna without being fortunate enough to see him. Kindly let it be known that I am going to Paris, but shall on no account sing there, although the public appears to know more about it than I. Fare very well, and when you compose do not forget

Your most devoted

Berlin, 28th June 1825.   Anna Milder.

See Nos. 558 and 559 for the press notices sent to Schubert by Anna Milder.—Traugott Trautwein founded a music-publishing firm in 1820. He reprinted 'The Trout,' which, with the second Suleika song issued by his colleague F. S. Lischke in Berlin, was almost the only reprint published in Schubert's lifetime.—The Goethe poem, which so far as we know Schubert never set, has already been mentioned (*see* No. 538). —Schubert did in the end write for her the concert piece 'The Shepherd on the Rock' ('Der Hirt auf dem Felsen'; October 1828, op. posth. 129. *See* No. XVII).

564. SCHWIND TO SCHUBERT

[Vienna,] 2nd July 1825.

My dear Schubert,

I almost think my last letter must have contained something that was disagreeable to you. Let me be frank and confess to you what it is that still rankles. You will no doubt remember that you did not come to Hönig's last time. I should be quite idiotic if I took offence, nay if I even allowed it to annoy me, if you do as you please and take no notice of what I happen to want. Still, had you thought of how much affection was awaiting you, you would have come. Little as I shall allow myself to be deterred from meaning to you and doing for you what had so far always been acceptable to you, I am almost afraid of getting as much pleasure from you, seeing how ill I have succeeded all these years in overcoming your mistrust and your fear lest you should not be loved and understood. That may be the reason for some malicious pranks which I was unable to refrain from, much as they hurt me myself. It is no doubt altogether this sort of thing which is responsible for that accursed spirit of mockery. Why should I not say it? Ever since I knew you and Schober I have been accustomed to find myself understood in all things. Then others come, mocking and spying out associations and thoughts of which they have caught some glimpse or other; we let them carry on at first, then take part in it ourselves, and, man not being made of diamond, we lose irreplaceable things for the despicable price of merely tolerable intercourse. If that is too bitter, I was unhappily often too complaisant. I beg you to give me your answer to this, as rude and candid as I am myself, for anything is better than these torturing thoughts, of which I cannot rid myself.

I hear you are expecting me soon, but unfortunately there is nothing in it. I can no longer defer devoting myself wholly to painting, and a whole summer is the least I can add to my previous attempts, if I am to attain to any mastery at all. I must also wait for Schober and shall not be able to run away at once, for he will be sufficiently annoyed as it is not to find you here. For the rest, I often go to Grinzing, where I am able to forget many an arduous week. I wanted to write about something else, but I can positively hear you sneer, for all that you know as well as I, or better, how beneficial and delightful an association may be where one finds oneself and one's friends understood. The enclosed news-sheet is sent you by Netty. You will notice what pains she took to damage your friendship with Tietze, on whom, of course, you bestowed sundry honorary titles in her presence. Everybody sends you many greetings, and there is no end to recollections and reminiscences of the time you were here.

I do not know whether I wrote to you that I had been to see Grillparzer. He showed much pleasure in my "Marriage" and assured me that in ten years he would still remember every figure in it. Since, in default of a Duke of Weimar to protect and to pay us, we can ask nothing better than the spiritual judgment or important people, you may imagine in what a happy frame of mind I went home. Anyhow, he was very friendly and talkative, chiefly about the imperfect and affected tendencies of certain artists and scholars known to us. That his view of the "Marriage of Figaro" is so entirely like my own was no little triumph for me. Of his opera nothing will come, for it is no longer his own, and he is therefore not quite at liberty to do as he likes. For compensation he hopes to secure you an opera for the Königsstadt Theatre in Berlin, whose manager he knows, and who is looking for an opera. He repeated several times that he was really anxious about it. Bauernfeld studies and wishes to be remembered to you. Many remembrances to Herr von Vogl, who is on no account to forget to lure the two drawings from the most beautiful Fräulein Amalia during some occasional pastoral hour. I have not got them myself, and as I wish to begin painting soon, I need them urgently. Frau von Láscny I am still unable to visit. And that is . . . If you get to Ebenzweier, my best regards, and give the kindest messages you can think of from me. Only write to me very soon how you are, what you are doing, how you like it and whether you think that what I told you is true. Remember me to Councillor Schiller as nicely as you know how: if I think of last year, I can only regard even my most submissive compliments as still being rude. Have you no news of Fritzi Dornfeld, from Linz and Florian? I shall step forth mightily when I have finished here. Fare you well.

Your Schwind.

The earlier letter mentioned here has not been preserved. Kreissle asserts that the present one was addressed to Gmunden and forwarded to Schubert at Steyr, whither however he did not return until 25th July, whereas he remained at Gmunden until the 15th.—The disagreement between Schubert and Schwind has already been referred to (*see* No. 553). It arose on account of Anna Hönig, in whose album, however, Schubert had inscribed a waltz (xxi. 31) on 16th April. (Schwind wrote a pianoforte composition of his own in it in 1827). Schwind again referred to the difference on 1st August (*see* No. 575).—Of the sentence containing the words "glimpse" and "diamond" Schubert made fun in his lost letter (cf. No. 575).—Grinzing was a wine-growing village near Vienna.— Tietze, who according to Josef Hüttenbrenner's later reports was hostile to Schubert and whom, of course, Anna Hönig had done nothing to turn in Schubert's disfavour, had last sung a Schubert song on 10th April. The criticism of it (No. 545) may have been the cutting she caused to be sent to Schubert.—Grillparzer, a great admirer of Mozart, was in love with the figure of Cherubino, probably on account of the singer Henriette Teimer (1798–1818), who was married to Anton Forti and had appeared in the part.—Karl August, Grand Duke of Weimar, Goethe's protector, was a patron of the arts.—Grillparzer's opera libretto was 'Melusina' (cf. No. 379). It appears that there was a scheme for putting it in Schubert's way if Beethoven should reject it and before it went to Kreutzer. Grillparzer hoped to procure for Schubert the commission for an opera for the Königstadt Theatre in Berlin, which had been opened in 1824 under the management of Karl Friedrich Cerf, who had engaged Henriette Sontag (the first Euryanthe), Spitzeder and his wife, Jäger and Wächter of Vienna. The Königstadt Theatre, which expected 'Melusina' from Beethoven and in the end received it from Kreutzer, seems to have also received Schubert's 'Alfonso and Estrella' from Frau Milder, without making any use of that opera.—Bauernfeld was preparing for the State examination in order to become an official.—Fräulein Amalia was the daughter of Aulic Councillor von Schiller (cf. No. 562). Schwind must have left these drawings with her in the autumn of 1824.—For Fritzi (Friederike) von Dornfeld *see* No. 301.—(St.) Florian is the monastery near Linz.

565. Ottenwalt to Josef von Spaun at Lemberg

Linz, 2nd July 1825.

. . . who knows whether you will not succeed in imparting life to the Galician forests and stones with our Schubert's songs.

The original has "Sarmatian forests and stones." In ancient times Sarmatia was the region between Germania and Dacia on the one side and the Don on the other.

566. Schubert's Father to Franz

Dear Son,

Mme Milder's father brought me this letter for you and let me read from the Berlin newspapers a great many laudatory things about the evening entertainment given by his daughter on 9th June, where your compositions too are very much praised.

I and all the relations wonder very much why we hear nothing at all from you. I am to send you blessings and friendly greetings from all and sundry. Your last landlord too has been asking for news of you through his servant-girl. I and all our kindred are well, thank God, and in anticipation of a gratifying reply from you, I wish you all that is truly and lastingly good.

Your faithful father,
F. Schubert.

My heartiest respects to the much-to-be-reverenced Herr von Vogl, your exalted well-wisher.

Vienna, 8th June [for July] 1825.

Felix Milder, the singer's father, was at first a confectioner and café proprietor in Constantinople, afterwards interpreter in Bucharest and finally Austrian embassy courier before he settled at Hütteldorf near Vienna c. 1800. About 1825 he seems to have been an antechamber doorkeeper. —He brought the letter No. 563, but without leaving the cuttings Nos. 558 and 559 (*see* Schubert's reply to his father, No. 572).—Kellner, with whom Schubert lodged in Fruhwirth's house, was anxious to know whether he would again occupy the room in the autumn.

567. FROM BAUERNFELD'S DIARY

July 1825.

Schober has arrived from Breslau, where he saw much of Holtei, Steffens, Karl Schall and other men of parts, such as Baron Vaerst, &c. He led a somewhat adventurous life and was for a time an actor *à la* Wilhelm Meister. He is five or six years older than we, also a kind of man of the world possessed of blarney and disputatiousness, and a favourite with women, in spite of his rather crooked legs. We at once began an agreeable relationship.— Klementine Russ called him the God Mahadeva. But she did not desire him to lift her up with arms of fire. Moritz too worships him like a god. I find him pretty human, but interesting.

Schober returned after an absence of nearly two years.—Karl von Holtei, born at Breslau in 1798, was an actor and playwright, just then busy working for the Königstadt Theatre in Berlin.—Henrik Steffens, born in 1773 at Stavanger in Norway, settled at Breslau in 1811, was professor of physics and philosophy there, also a poet who acted as a link between the Breslau and the Scandinavian intellectuals.—For Schall *see* No. 498, for Vaerst No. 507, for 'Wilhelm Meister' No. 328.—Schober was about six years older than Bauernfeld; Schwind was eight years and Schubert one year younger than he.—Klementine, the pretty daughter of the historical painter Karl Russ, custodian of the imperial picture gallery, was an amateur painter and poetess. She and Schwind had drawn Schober's portrait in 1824 in playful competition in her sketch-book.— Mahadeva (Mahadö) is "the lord of the earth" in Goethe's poem 'Der Gott und die Bajadere,' set by Schubert in 1815.

568. THERESE CLODI TO HER BROTHER MAX

[Ebenzweier,] 19th July 1825.

Vogl and Schubert have left Gmunden again. Schubert, I hear, has been at Linz; where Vogl is I do not know myself; but they told me they would both come again in the autumn.

Schubert had left for Linz on Friday, 15th July.

569. ANTON OTTENWALT TO JOSEF VON SPAUN at Lemberg.

Linz, 19th July 1825.

We are enjoying an agreeable time and wish very much you could enjoy it with us.—Schubert is here, so far alone. He came to us first on Friday, but immediately went to Steyregg in the afternoon. Thence he returned this morning and will, we hope, spend some days here, until Vogl calls for him to go to Steyr, presumably towards the end of this week. Schubert looks so well and strong, is so comfortably bright and so genially communicative that one cannot fail to be sincerely delighted about it. He is to-day going to occupy the room where you had your sleeping quarters for some time. His trunk is being taken there to-day, a writing-table set up, and he will be supplied with books, and so on. I am thoroughly proud of such a guest, believe me, and all the affection and honour we show him is meant for you too. How glorious it would be if we had you here! But it gives me much pleasure that Schubert seems to be so much at home among us, for all that you are not here; he even played something from his marches with Marie after dinner to-day. Of his songs he told us that several from Scott's 'Lady of the Lake' have materialized since—not translated by poor Ferdinand, but by another. By the way, he had worked at a symphony at Gmunden, which is to be performed in Vienna this winter. Of you he speaks with much warmth, and recently, when he came to talk about the hours he spent with you in Vienna, he fairly took fire. About your decision to go to Lemberg he shakes his head in amazement, and when we opined that you would not find any contentment there even in time, he eagerly retorted that this would indeed not behove you either, for you ought never to like it there. For Max his visit was a feast: he is with him as much as possible. In the evenings we go for a walk to Jägermayr's, then sup at the "Castle," where the ladies join us. He has not sung us anything yet, although he has not refused to do so; but he did play the German Dances Marie had practised: they take on incredible life under his hands.—

That we know such people and may even have them with us we owe to you; thus do you still permanantly beautify our lives.

[Postscript by Marie Ottenwalt]

If only you could spend these days with us still, how much would I wish to-day that you could hear the glorious new songs which Schubert composed and sang! The words are from 'The Lady of the Lake.'—He read through with much affection those letters of yours which have by now grown into something like a book.— To-day Vogl is to come too; however, he may at once go on to Steyregg and will probably take Schubert away from us; still, I hope to keep him here a few days longer, in any case. . . . Schubert sleeps at the same place where you lay here.

For Steyregg Castle and its owners, Count and Countess Weissenwolff, *see* note preceding No. 425.—The marches for four hands were probably from the new Op. 40, half of which were published in the spring.—In the spring and summer of 1825 Schubert composed five songs and two partsongs from 'The Lady of the Lake'—Lake Traun taking the place of Loch Katrine in his imagination (as also in Schwind's vignette for the vocal score of Rossini's 'La donna del lago,' Sauer & Leidesdorf, c. 1824). The single dated song among them, the 'Lay of the Imprisoned Huntsman,' was, it is true, written as early as 4th April 1825 in Vienna. The translation was not that by Ferdinand Haas (born Salzburg, 1799), a member of the Linz family on friendly terms with the Spauns, which appeared only in 1828, but that of the Bremen professor Ph. Adam Storck (died 1822), which had come out in 1819.—The first documentary information about the lost Symphony written that summer at Gmunden and Gastein occurs here. The projected performance was also mentioned by Schwind on 14th August (see No. 581). Moreover, both Josef von Spaun and Bauernfeld refer to this Symphony as the "Gastein" Symphony in their obituaries of Schubert (see Nos. XXX and XXXIII). Sir George Grove did not know these passages in the letters when he inquired after the existence of a "Gastein" Symphony ('Daily News,' 27th September 1881) and provisionally settled the matter in a discussion with his friend Karl Ferdinand Pohl ('Athenaeum,' 19th November 1881).—Max is Josef von Spaun's brother, who was then employed at Linz, a rather shy and unlucky fellow, bent on improving the world. —Jägermayr's is a tavern in the Stadtwald on the Freinberg to the west of Linz; its garden offers an extensive view. The "Castle" on the Danube, another place of refreshment, has already been mentioned (see No. 128).—The German Dances were probably from Op. 33.—Spaun's letters were those written by him from Galicia.—Schubert, who had already paid a visit to Steyregg from 15th to 19th July, went there with Vogl for a few days, from 22nd to 24th July.

570. SCHUBERT TO JOSEF VON SPAUN

Linz, 21st July 1825.

Dear Spaun,

You may imagine how annoyed I am at having to write a letter to you from Linz to Lemberg!!! Devil take accursed duty, which cruelly tears friends asunder when they have scarcely sipped the goblet of friendship. Here I sit at Linz, half dead with sweating in this frightful heat, with a whole book of new songs, and you are not here! Aren't you ashamed? Linz without you is like a body without a soul, like a headless horseman, or like a soup

without salt.   If Jägermayr did not keep such good beer and they
had not a passable wine on the Castle Hill, I should have to hang
myself on the promenade with the legend: "From sorrow over
the departed soul at Linz."   As you see, I was positively unjust
towards the rest of Linzdom, since after all I am quite happy in
your mother's house and in the company of your sister, Ottenwalt
and Max, and seem to see your spirit flash from the body of many
another Linzer.   Only I fear that this spirit will gradually flash
itself away entirely, whereupon one would like to burst with
vexation.   Altogether, it is a veritable misery how everything
becomes petrified into insipid prosiness everywhere, how most
people look on at this quite unconcernedly, or even feel comfortable
with it, and how they quite calmly glide over this slime into the
abyss.   To go upwards is harder, of course; and yet this rabble
could be driven in pairs easily enough, if only something were done
from up above.   Well, do not let your hair turn white at being
so far from us: defy silly Fate and in her despite let your rich soul
blossom like a flower-garden, in order that you may spread the
warmth of life in the cold North and prove your godlike descent.
Sorrow is unworthy to creep into a noble heart; throw it off and
trample under foot the vulture before it eats into your soul.

Of Schober we had some odd, almost comical news.   To begin
with, I read in the Vienna 'Theaterzeitung' of "a female with
the pseudonymous name of Torupsohn"???   What does that mean?
Surely he has not married?   That would be a bit of a joke.   Secondly,
Punchinello in the travestied 'Aline' is said to be his star part.
Rather a steep descent from the heights of his plans and expectations!
And thirdly, he is said to be returning to Vienna.   Now I ask you,
what is he to do there?   However, I greatly look forward to seeing
him and hope he may bring a more alive and intelligent spirit into
the circle again, much as it has shrunk.   I have been in Upper
Austria since 20th May and was vexed to hear that you had left
Linz a few days earlier.   I should have so much liked to see you
once more, before you delivered yourself to the Polish devil.
At Steyr I stayed only a fortnight, whereupon we (Vogl and I)
went to Gmunden, where we spent a full six weeks quite agreeably.
We lodged at Traweger's, who has a magnificent pianoforte and is,

as you know, a great admirer of my littleness. I lived very pleasantly and freely there. At Councillor von Schiller's we had much music, among other things some of my new songs, from Walter Scott's 'Lady of the Lake,' of which especially the 'Hymn to the Virgin Mary' appealed generally. I am very glad that you meet young Mozart; remember me to him.

And now farewell! My dear good Spaun!

Think often of your

sincere friend

P.S. Do write to me at Steyr.   Franz Schubert.

Schubert also complained in a letter to his father about that summer's heat (*see* No. 572).—The book of new songs must be the manuscript of the 'Lady of the Lake' songs.—The promenade planted with plane-trees on the south side of the castle in the place of the old city fortifications was due to Spaun's father, the County Syndic Franz Xaver, Edler von Spaun, who died in 1804.—Frau von Spaun, like the Ottenwalts, lived at the Grosser Bürgerhof in the Herrengasse, where Schubert was the Ottenwalts' guest.—The 'Theaterzeitung' of 23rd April had published the following report from Breslau, dated 25th March, which was also cited almost word for word in a letter from Anton to Josef von Spaun: "From the Austrian theatres we have engaged . . . and the pseudonymous Torupson, who here makes her first appearance on the stage" (signed Karl Barbarina). There must have been a mistake here, for it is a question of a man—Schober himself, who had adopted this pseudonym for his late and brief stage career, based on the name of his birthplace, the castle of Torup near Malmö in Sweden. He had appeared about New Year 1825 as Hubert in Holtei's play 'Die Wiener in Berlin.' The clown's part of the ship's barber Bims in Bäuerle's 'Aline' (*see* note preceding No. 319), however, was played at Breslau by Karl Stawinsky, of whom Schober himself made a lithographed portrait with Fräulein Kupfer as Zilli. The piece was called "the travestied 'Aline'" because it was based on Berton's opera 'Aline, Reine de Golconde' (Paris, 1803; Vienna, 1804).—Spaun left Linz on the day on which Schubert arrived at Steyr.—The 'Hymn to the Virgin Mary' is, of course, Ellen's third song, 'Ave Maria.'—Mozart's son (*see* No. 168) was a pianoforte teacher at Lwów. Spaun was introduced by the Reverteras to the house of the Government Councillor Ludwig Kajetan Baroni von Cavalcabo, the maiden name of whose wife, a patroness of the younger Mozart, was Josefine Countess Castiglioni.

571. From the Official 'Wiener Zeitung,' 25th July 1825

At the House of A. Pennauer,

I. & R. Privileged Art and Music Publishers in Vienna, are newly published and to be had at their Establishment, Lower Bräunerstrasse, at Fischer's House, as well as of all Book, Art and Music Dealers at Home and Abroad:

The Young Nun and Night and Dreams
['Die junge Nonne']   ['Nacht und Träume']
Two Poems
set to Music for One Voice with Pianoforte Accompaniment by Franz Schubert.

Work 43.   Price, 1 Florin 45 Kreuzer, V.C.

The same with guitar accompaniment, 1 Fl. 30 Kr. V.C.

Op. 43 appeared before Opp. 41 and 42, without a dedication.

572. Schubert to his Father and Stepmother

Steyr, 25th July 1825.

Dear Parents,

I justly deserve the reproach which you made me concerning my long illness; but as I do not like writing empty words and our present time offers little of interest, you will forgive me for giving you news of me only in reply to your affectionate letter. I was very glad to hear that everybody is well, and I may say the same of myself, thanks to the Almighty. I am back at Steyr again, but have been at Gmunden for six weeks, the environs of which are truly heavenly and deeply moved and benefited me, as did its inhabitants, particularly the excellent Traweger. I lived at Traweger's, very free and easy. Later, when Councillor von Schiller was there, who is the monarch of the whole Salzkammergut, we (Vogl and I) dined daily at his house and had music there, as we also often did at Traweger's house. My new songs from Walter Scott's 'Lady of the Lake' especially had much success. They also wondered greatly at my piety, which I expressed in a hymn to the Holy Virgin and which, it appears, grips every soul and turns it to devotion. I think this is due to the fact that I have never forced devotion in myself and never compose hymns or prayers of that kind unless it overcomes me unawares; but then it is usually the right and true devotion. From Gmunden we went via Puschberg, where we met some acquaintances and stayed a few days, to Linz, where we remained a week, which we spent by turns at Linz itself and at Steyregg. At Linz I took up my quarters at the Spauns' house, where they still greatly lament the removal of Spaun (the one you know) to Lemberg. I read a few letters from him, written at Lemberg, which sound very dejected and betray unmistakable homesickness. I wrote to him to Lemberg and rated him soundly over his womanish demeanour, but should probably feel even more lamentable in his place than he does. In Steyregg we called on Countess Weissenwolf, who is a great admirer of my littleness, possesses all my things and sings many of them quite nicely. The Walter Scott songs made such an excessively good impression on her that she even let it be guessed that the dedication of them would be anything but disagreeable to her. But I intend to use a very different procedure with the publication of these songs from the usual one, which yields so very little, since they bear the celebrated name of Scott at their head and may in that way arouse greater curiosity, and might also make me better known in England by the addition of the English words. If only some decency might be expected of those —— of art dealers! But the wise and benevolent dispensations of the State have well and truly seen to it that an artist shall ever remain the slave of every wretched huckster.

As regards Mme Milder's letter, the favourable reception of 'Suleika' gave me great pleasure, although I wish I could have had a sight of the criticisms myself, in order to see if something could not be learnt from them; for however favourable a verdict may be, it may at the same time be equally laughable if the critic lacks the required understanding, which is not altogether rarely the case.

In Upper Austria I find my compositions everywhere, especially at the monasteries of Florian and Kremsmünster, where with the aid of a gallant pianoforte player I produced my four-handed Variations and marches with notable success. What pleased especially were the variations in my new Sonata for two hands, which I performed alone and not without merit, since several people assured me that the keys become singing voices under my hands, which, if true, pleases me greatly, since I cannot endure the accursed chopping in which even distinguished pianoforte players indulge and which delights neither the ear nor the mind. I am at the moment at Steyr again, and if you intend to make me happy with a letter soon, it will still find me here, as we shall stay only 10 to 14 days, whereafter we shall leave for Gastein, one of the most famous watering-places about 3 days distant from Steyr. To this journey I look forward with extraordinary pleasure, since I shall thus get to know the finest country, and we shall visit Salzburg on our return, which is so famous for its glorious situation and surroundings. As we shall not return from this journey until the middle of September, and have promised to go to Gmunden, Steyregg and Florian again then, I am hardly likely to arrive in Vienna before the end of October. By the way, please rent my quarters near the Karl church for me and kindly deposit the 28 florins, V.C., which I shall gratefully refund you on my return, seeing that I had promised it, and it is possible after all that I may arrive sooner than I think. The weather here was very unsettled all through June and half of July, then very hot for a fortnight, so that I positively grew thin from sheer perspiration, and now it has been raining for 4 days almost without stopping. Kindest remembrances to Ferdinand and his wife and children. I suppose he still crawls to the "Cross" and cannot get rid of Dornbach; also, he has doubtless been ill 77 times again, and has thought 9 times that he was going to die, as though dying were the worst that can happen to a man! If only he could once see these heavenly mountains and lakes, the sight of which threatens to crush or engulf us, he would not be so attached to puny human life, nor regard it as otherwise than good fortune to be confided to earth's indescribable power of creating new life. What is Karl doing? Is he going to travel or not? He must be busy now, for a married artist's duty is to supply works of nature as well as art, and if he succeeds in both kinds, he will be very praiseworthy, for that is no small matter. I renounce it myself. Ignaz is presumably at Hollpein's just now; for as he is there only in the mornings, afternoons and evenings, he will hardly be at home. I cannot cease to admire his perseverance, only it is difficult to tell whether it is really a merit or not and whether he deserves more of heaven or of hell thereby. I wish he would enlighten me about it. Schneider and his Schneideress are to look out for the coming little Schneider or little Schneideress, so that the Schneiders may become as numerous as sand by the sea, only let them see to it that there is no superfluity of liars [*Aufschneider*], cutters [*Zuschneider*], slanderers [*Ehrabschneider*] or cut-throats [*Gurgelabschneider*]. And now I must end this chatter at last, though I felt that I must substitute a long letter for a long silence. Marie, Pepi and little Probstl Andre I kiss 1,000 times. Besides, please remember me most kindly to all who are rememberable. In expectation of a speedy reply, I remain, with all my love,

Your

most faithful son

Franz.

The dating of this letter, of which the autograph is lost, wavers between 25th and 28th July. Schubert and Vogl did not arrive at Steyr until late on the 25th, and the next four days were spoilt by rain. The letter may thus have been begun on the 25th and finished on the 28th.—The number of Schubert's sacred (not church) songs is quite considerable.—"Puschberg" is probably Puchberg near Wels in Upper Austria, between Gmunden and Linz.—The letter to Spaun is No. 570.—Op. 52 actually was dedicated to Countess Weissenwolff. The intention to let the words appear in two languages was really carried out, with the exception of 'Norman's Song,' although the metres of the German translation did not quite fit the English originals (*see* Nos. 573 and 577; cf. No. 596). Schubert's plan to become known in England recalls that made by Schwind for his "Freischütz" etchings (*see* No. 496): neither was realized. Karl Czerny, by the way, also published German and English words in his setting of the 'Romance' ("Not faster yonder rovers' might" from 'The Lady of the Lake') with Steiner & Co.—The pianoforte player at Kremsmünster was Father Heinrich Hassak, born 1789, dean of the monastery, who possessed a porcelain bowl with Schwind's vignette for Schubert's trio 'The Wedding Roast' ('Der Hochzeitsbraten,' published in 1829), which however he can hardly have received from Schubert at that time, since the piece was not written until 1827.— The pianoforte duet Variations are Op. 35, the marches probably Op. 40

and the new Sonata is Op. 42, in A minor (written in the spring of 1825).
—The spa of Gastein, or Bad Gastein, is about eighty-seven miles south-
west of Steyr.—Salzburg was not visited on the return journey, but on the
way there.—Schubert did go to Steyr once more, but left for Vienna
early in October.—The rent amounted to only 25 florins (*see* No. 591);
"28" may have been due to a mistake on the part of the second editor
of this letter, Ludwig Gottfried Neumann (born at Graz, 1813), who
was the first to prepare a Schubert biography about 1842. Ferdinand
Schubert, who printed the letter earlier, omitted this sentence.—
The "Red Cross" tavern (cf. No. 208) was owned by Michael Weigert;
Schubert did not like it, for he suspected the wine to be adulterated.—
Dornbach, a village near Vienna, was well known for its new wine (*see*
No. 548A), although not as famous as Grinzing.—On Wilhelmine Holl-
pein, *née* Grob, whom Ignaz married soon afterwards, cf. No. 68.—
Schneider is Schubert's brother-in-law, Matthias Schneider, whose name,
meaning tailor, here serves him for all manner of puns.—Maria, Josefine
(Pepi) and Andreas are Schubert's stepsisters and stepbrother (*see* No.
113). He calls Andreas, who was then hardly two years old, "little
provost," because he was fat and reminded him of a well-nourished cleric.

573. FRANZ HÜTHER TO SCHUBERT

[Outside:]

Herr Michael von Vogl,
Member of the I. & R. Court Chapel and Chamber Singer,
for Franz Schubert, Esq.
City of Steyr.

[Inside:]

Vienna, 27th July 1825.

Herr F. Schubert at the City of Steyr.

Most honoured Friend,

On my return from Leipzig I heard that you had already left
for Upper Austria, but nobody could let me have an exact address,
for which reason I had until this day to forgo the pleasure of inquir-
ing after your health, and of entering into negotiations with you
concerning your new compositions. Only to-day have I heard
from Herr von Bindritsch [Pinterics] of your sojourn at Herr von
Vogl's, and I seize this opportunity of sending you these lines.

I can only suppose (knowing the company you are in) that you are well, and will thus at once pass on to business, taking the liberty of asking what you have written in the course of these recent times and what thereof you would feel inclined to bring before the public.   I would further beg you to let me know how many songs from Walter Scott's works you have composed, whether the German translation keeps to the metre of the English original and both texts could therefore be set under your music.   Kindly fix the most exact price you can ask of a beginner and be assured that I shall contribute my utmost towards the production of a very fine edition and the dissemination of your compositions.   Those of your works I have published are the book containing 'The Young Nun,' a second book of songs to appear next month, and the Sonata, which is already engraved as well and for the dedication of which I daily expect the Archduke Rudolph's permission, in September. Please let me know in which way I may send you copies of your songs.   I hope you will be satisfied with the edition, and although after three proofs a few insignificant mistakes have remained in the two books, these have nevertheless been immediately corrected, and only the first twenty copies, which have not even all been sold, have remained faulty.   I shall by some private opportunity send you an offprint of the Sonata c/o Herr von Vogl, with the request to look it through carefully, for I am very anxious that the works issued by me should be free from mistakes.   Would you be kind enough to indicate to me how much longer you intend to be away from Vienna?   What would please me greatly is the news that you have written a work for four hands, and I would ask you to bear this in mind, should you feel inclined to write a fairly brilliant work of not too large dimensions, such as a grand polonaise or rondo with an introduction, &c., or a fantasy.—

Once again I beg for your most favourable conditions concerning the W. Scott songs and would ask you to send your kind letter to us merely with the address of A. Pennauer, Art Dealers in Vienna. I wish you very fine and favourable weather, so that you may without hindrance make excursions in the glorious environs of your place of sojourn, requesting you to convey our most respectful compliments to Herr von Vogl and now and again to remember

those poor, now wholly forsaken Viennese. Pray accept the
assurance of my especial regard and attention, with which I remain,
your most obedient servant,

Fr. Hüther.

P.S. It may interest you to hear something about our theatres.
I am able to tell you for certain that Barbaja has taken on the management of the Opera for 10 years and that Duport is already in the
act of re-engaging the choral singers. But German opera!!—is
finished altogether; I am told there is to be only ballet and *opera
italiana*. Count Pálffy would like a partner with a great deal of
money; the wish is good, but may be difficult of realization.—
The fate of that theatre is still quite uncertain, but in the meantime
Herr Carl of the Bavarian Theatre has leased it for three months
on trial and will begin playing on 15th August.—

This letter was sent through Vogl because Schubert's exact address was
not known to the writer, and the famous singer was easily to be found at
Steyr.—Hüther was the manager of the music publishing house of Anton
Pennauer, founded in 1820, but not registered till 1825.—Leipzig was
even then the centre of German publishing, including Austria, and annual
fairs were held there.—To Pinterics (*see* No. 492) Schubert's three songs,
Op. 65, were dedicated in 1826, when they were published by Pennauer.
—Already before his departure Schubert had evidently offered this firm
the Scott cycle he had only just begun, and he even then had the idea,
later expressed in No. 572, of issuing it in two languages; but it was
Matthias Artaria who eventually carried this out.—The word "beginner"
used to be interpreted as referring to Schubert, but it alludes to the
new establishment of the firm. (Translation here makes all the difference:
the original *may* mean either the "price you can ask as a beginner" or
"of a beginner.")—For 'The Young Nun' cf. No. 571.—The other "book
of songs" was the delayed Op. 31, 'Suleika's Second Song' (*see* No. 580).
—The Sonata in A minor, Op. 42, dedicated to the Archduke Rudolph,
Cardinal-Archbishop of Olomouc (Olmütz) in Moravia (born Florence,
1788, Beethoven's pupil and patron, protector of the Philharmonic
Society), did not appear at the usual Michaelmas term (end of September), but only at the beginning of 1826.—For Op. 43 Schiller instead of Matthäus von Collin was named on the title-page as the author
of the poem 'Night and Dreams' ('Nacht und Träume'); Op. 31 had,
apart from the publisher's number 130 instead of 133, "East-western"
instead of 'West-eastern Divan' by Goethe.—It cannot be ascertained with
certainty whether Schubert wrote a new work for pianoforte duet before

the end of 1825.—Barbaja's first lease had expired on 26th March 1825. In the spring and summer the company of the Josefstadt Theatre had given two visiting seasons at the Kärntnertor Theatre. The latter was closed from the end of July until the end of April 1826, when at last a new four years' lease of Barbaja's began. His authorized representative was the dancer and ballet-master Louis Antoine Duport, born in 1783, who himself became a lessee of the Vienna Court Opera later.—The Theater an der Wien had been closed since 1st June 1825. From August 1825 until March 1826 Karl Carl (*recte* Karl Andreas Bernbrunn, born at Cracow in 1787) appeared as guest there with his Munich company. He leased the theatre after it was sold by auction on 15th December 1826, and in 1835 he purchased it.

574. Anton Ottenwalt to Josef von Spaun

Linz, 27th July 1825.

Of Schubert—I might almost say of *our* Schubert—there is much I should like to tell you. No doubt, though, his letter will tell you the best of it. Never perhaps, except in the case of playing the fraternal host, have I yet experienced the joys of hospitality as I did during the days he spent with me, was our guest at lunch and passed the evening with us at the "Castle". The fact is that he stayed only a few days at S. [Steyregg] (the count was at Ischl), then came to us again for a few days, until Vogl appeared one morning and, after both had eaten with us, took his friend with him to Steyregg once more; in the end both returned on Sunday evening, again were our guests at midday on Monday (25th), together with Stadler and Therese Haas, who appeared by accident, and, departing after the meal, left us with the hope of possibly seeing them once more on their return from Gastein. We heard Vogl three times, and Schubert himself condescended to sing something after breakfast among ourselves, and also played his marches, two- and four-handed variations and an overture on the pianoforte, compositions of such significance that one cannot trust oneself to discuss them. And if I cannot do so worthily with his latest songs on W. Scott, I cannot keep silent about them either. There are five in particular: 1. 'Ave Maria,' Ellen's evening song and prayer for her father in the wilderness, where they live in hiding. 2. 'Soldier, rest,' a captivating slumber song of the kind

Armida might sing for Rinaldo to her magic harp. 3. 'Huntsman, rest,' another slumber song, more simple and touching, I feel; in the accompaniment, the tune of horns, I should say, like the echoes of a hunting-song in a fair dream. 4. 'Lay of the Imprisoned Huntsman': "My idle greyhound loathes his food, My horse is weary of his stall, And I am sick of captive thrall." . . . Accompaniment—ah, how shall I describe those angrily throbbing, briefly cut-off chords? I am almost ashamed again at having taken it into my head to write about it. And what of the last, 'Norman's Song'? The warrior with his sacrificial torch, the summons to arms, sings as he fares across the country. Hurrying without respite, he thinks of his errand, of the bride he has left at the altar, of the morrow's combat, of victory, of reunion. The tune and the accompaniment you will have to imagine. Schubert himself regards this as the best of the Scott songs. Vogl himself interprets it heavily (a syllable, often a word, to each note), but splendidly. The most generally appealing, by the loveliness of its melody and its rocking horn music, is 'Huntsman, rest.' My dear fellow, how we wished each time that you could hear it! If only we could send those tunes into your dreams, as we ourselves hear them around us deep into the night!

Schubert was so friendly and communicative, not only with Max, which goes without saying, but with us too. On Sunday, after Vogl had left at 9.30, he remained with us: there were Max and I, Marie and Mama, who retired between 10 and 11 o'clock. We sat together until not far from midnight, and I have never seen him like this, nor heard: serious, profound and as though inspired. How he talked of art, of poetry, of his youth, of friends and other people who matter, of the relationship of ideals to life, &c.! I was more and more amazed at such a mind, of which it has been said that its artistic achievement is so unconscious, hardly revealed to and understood by himself, and so on. Yet how simple was all this!—I cannot tell you of the extent and the unity of his convictions—but there were glimpses of a world-view that is not merely acquired, and the share which worthy friends may have in it by no means detracts from the individuality shown by all this.

That is why I am so glad that he seemed to like being near me and was inclined to show us that side of him, which one shows only to kindred spirits; and hence my desire to write to you about it.

Schubert's letter to Spaun is No. 570.—Stadler is Albert Stadler.—The marches were probably Op. 40, the variations for pianoforte solo the *andante* from the Sonata, Op. 42, those for pianoforte duet Op. 35 and the Overture (for four hands) Op. 34.—The Scott songs are Ellen's third, first and second song, the 'Lay of the Imprisoned Huntsman' and 'Norman's Song' from 'The Lady of the Lake.' The two choruses, 'Boating Song' ('Bootsgesang') for four male voices and 'Coronach' for three female voices, which complete the opus, were doubtless also finished by this time.—The subject of Armida and Rinaldo, often used in opera, comes from Tasso's epic 'Gerusalemme liberata.' Schwind later painted among the lunettes in the foyer of the new Vienna Opera an oil illustrating Gluck's 'Armida.'—Vogl left Linz for Steyr on 24th July, Schubert on the 25th.

575. SCHWIND TO SCHUBERT

[Address:]   From Vienna.
                    To

                    Franz Schubert, Esq.,
                         at Steyr in Upper Austria,
                              c/o Herr von Vogl.

[Inside:]

Dearest Schubert,   1st August 1825.

I must have written a fair packet of nonsense, as I gather from that farrago of "diamond and glimpse," in which I cannot find any connection at all. But be that as it may, I did hear something that could not have come to me in my wildest dreams—that somebody insulted you at Hönig's. I do not believe it of Netti, and neither do you, I hope, and it would surprise me very much in the others. If only you had told me at once, the whole thing would have been different, or I should not for a moment have expected you to go there; also, you will believe that I myself should no longer have any desire for company of this sort. In the meantime I shall, in the deuce's name, turn the house upside down to see if there is anything resembling your accusation or a definite withdrawal of it. But I can assure you by all the saints that I cannot imagine anything of the kind.

The 6th.

I asked Netti in a roundabout way, but as explicitly as possible, and the very thought was so far from her that, I warrant you, there was nothing queer, much less equivocal in her behaviour. I hope you will not think of the matter any more on your return.

Schober is here. He sends you a thousand greetings. He is quite the same, even more alive and fresh. From Kuppl [Kupelwieser] a letter came from Padua to-day; he should be here in no more than three weeks. 'The Young Nun' has appeared. I have a lot to do, so that I cannot tell when I shall be able to leave, but I confidently hope to see you. Farewell and write to us soon. Bauernfeld works at examinations and at 'Lebensblätter' by turns, and we live quite merrily together, so far as we may do so without you. If you see Resi Clodi, remember me to her, and I look forward very much to seeing her again. My compliments to Herr von Vogl, and remind him of the two drawings which Mali has. Pinterics, Doblhoff and all send their greetings.

Your Schwind.

I almost forgot the most important thing. Schober has spoken to Tieck, who has become theatre court councillor at Dresden, about your opera of 'Alfonso.' You must write at once whether it is still at Dresden, or where else, for Tieck is waiting for news. I have no more time. Many kind regards.

The opening refers to No. 564, near the end of paragraph 1.—It is not known what the insult offered to Schubert at the Hönigs' may have been. —Leopold Kupelwieser, who had also been absent since the autumn of 1823, returned to Vienna as early as 7th August.—Bauernfeld passed his examination in law brilliantly on 16th August. 'Lebensblätter' is doubtless his 'Poetic Diary in Tame Epigrams,' begun in 1820 and continued until 1886, first published in 1887.—Resi is Therese Clodi, whom Schwind had visited at Ebenzweier in the autumn of 1824. Mali is Amalia von Schiller (see No. 564).—Ludwig Tieck, born in Berlin in 1773, the writer of fairy-tales, on whose 'Phantasus' Schwind based a whole series of paintings filling a room in the royal palace at Munich, had early in 1825 become dramaturgist at the Dresden court theatre and, incidentally, paid a visit to Vienna in the spring.

576. From the Official 'Wiener Zeitung,' 4th August 1825

At the House of Anton Diabelli & Co.,
Art and Music Dealers, Graben, No. 1133, is newly published,
and to be had of K. Lichtl in Pest at the same price:

Second Offertory
(Salve Regina)

Solo for soprano, accompanied by two Violins (two Clarinets,
two Bassoons, ad lib.), two Horns, Double Bass and Organ;
composed by Franz Schubert.

Work 47.   Price, 2 Florins 30 Kreuzer, V.C.
(Property of the Publishers.)

Opp. 44–51, including four church works, had clearly all been composed
before April 1823, and acquired by the firm of Diabelli before Schubert's
breach with it (see No. 356), and they now appeared irregularly, with opus
numbers newly agreed upon (see No. 577), between the middle of 1825 and
the beginning of 1827, the first offertory, 'Totus in corde,' Op. 46, after
the second. Whether these works had already been paid for by the general
settlement of 1823 cannot be determined. In the spring of 1827, at any
rate, there was some kind of reconciliation between Schubert and this
firm, although even then (1827–8) it published for the most part earlier
works by Schubert and was no longer his exclusive publisher.

577. Ferdinand Schubert to his Brother Franz

Vienna, 4th August 1825.

Dearest Brother,

I am sorry to have to begin this letter with a reproach. But
you quite certainly deserve it for going so far from Vienna, and for
so long, without celebrating with me the hour of parting, as we
had arranged!—You know, surely, how precious each moment of
your company is to me. However, let it rest there for the
moment, in the expectation that you will think of me the more
on your return.

That you have already visited the Salzkammergut is more than
I had supposed, since I hoped you would travel through that
wondrously beautiful region with me only at the beginning of

September. As it is (and also on account of those wretched money matters) I think I shall have to make the most of Lower Austria again this year.

But the longing I have for Upper Austria is indescribable. Would that the gods might soon grant me the fulfilment of that wish!—

For not only the fine country but also its excellent inhabitants interest me very much, as I hear these good people being praised on every hand. Even Vierthaler talks about it in his work on geography, after a description of the many-sided industry of these mountain-dwellers, in the following words: "The results of that many-sided industry show themselves not only in the prosperity but also, incomparably better still, in the high degree of morality by which the inhabitants of these mountain regions distinguish themselves from others. Murder, robbery, theft and fraud they know but by name. If ever a crime of this kind is committed, it is nearly always found that the culprit was a vagrant stranger. In this splendid way the old truth here once again proves itself that industrious people are also virtuous people." Dear, good Traweger had already grown [attractive] for me by your verbal description, so that I much like to hear news of him. Is the old peasant still alive who carved the stick decorated with foliage?

That your songs should be so well received there is quite natural, of course, for good souls can be moved and inspired only by the works of one who is good himself. And that a hymn to the Holy Virgin, composed by you, should stir every hearer to devotion will be no surprise to those who have heard your Mass in F, your first 'Tantum ergo' and your 'Salve Regina.' For such pious compositions must inspire anybody in whom there is but a spark of feeling for religious contemplation.

It would long ago have been a good thing to proceed differently with the publication of your songs; but I particularly like your plan for the Walter Scott songs, i.e. to let them appear with English words as well.—I am already dreaming of your reception in England, where, by means of larger works, such as symphonies, oratorios and perhaps operas, you will climb to the same heights among German composers as the Egyptian Joseph did among his brethren.

I also gathered from your letter that you went to the monastery of St. Florian. The organ there is said to be the largest and best in the whole of Austria, and to play on it would be no small delight to me. That is why I too should like to get to St. Florian one day. But then, when will this happy hour strike?—

Oh, you fortunate brother! Even beautiful Salzburg with its glorious environs and the famous, wild watering-place of Gastein, discovered as long as 1,000 years ago, will be visited by you.— Well, I shall ask you for a nice, detailed description of the latter. I too have been on a journey, but a very insignificant one compared with yours, although some valleys, mountains, rocks and passes greatly astonished me. It was a trip to Gutenstein. The company consisted of several respectable men, among whom were the favourite children's writer Chimani and an extremely liberal magistrate named Tuscher.

We spent the first night at Pottenstein, at a collier's, who entertained us capitally. He also described a thunderstorm for us which took place in the neighbourhood the day before: "It were zimmerin' vor halv an hour, like, and then it give one zingle thunnerclap." On the second day we came to the Muckendorf waterfall, which is exceedingly fine and was just then in spate, and I was therefore greatly astonished at seeing such a wonder of nature. Thence we again returned to Pernitz, and then as far as Gutenstein. Having taken lunch, we climbed the Klosterberg, which offered us the most varied views on mountains and valleys. Especially close to us was the king of this mountainous region, the Schneeberg, which showed itself quite brightly and clearly for a few minutes, but soon after wrapped itself in clouds. In the evening we descended again to Gutenstein market, from there by way of a pass between immense masses of rocks piled up on either side, across a long bridge below which the streamlet called Piesting flows. Here the castle of Gutenstein, towering sky-high on precipitous rocky walls, offers a terrifying sight. Particularly wonderful is the daring build of a Gothic arch, which spans a great gap in the rocky wall and supports the armoury. For a long time I gazed at that awe-inspiring antiquity, until the fall of night forced me to go back.

Well, now I must cease, otherwise this letter might not find you at Steyr any more. You will find a few poems enclosed, which were handed me by Diabelli with the remark that they are by Councillor Kleinschmid, as you have already been informed.

And now, farewell, dear, good Franz, and be remembered 1,000 times by all who are capable of remembering; but especially father, our brothers and sisters, and by my wife and children. (My little Karl, who is only 9 months old, already shows musical inclinations, for he sometimes sings quite melodiously.)

God keep and shield you until you are again embraced by your

faithful brother,

Ferdinand.

(Resident in the Viennese suburb of Maria Trost, No. 20, at the "Golden Serpent," 2nd floor, on the left.)

Vierthaler (*see* No. 137) had published a 'Geographie von Salzburg' in 1796. Ferdinand Schubert also brought out a few geographical school-books among his pedagogic writings, some of them illustrated by his brother Karl.—For Traweger *see* No. 132. Whether Schubert went to Gmunden and visited Traweger there in 1819 or 1823 is not known; neither is the story of the old peasant and the carved stick.—The Mass in F is that of 1814; the 'Tantum ergo' is Op. 45 (dedicated to Tietze), and the 'Salve Regina' Op. 47, both of which appeared soon after Op. 46.— The principal organ in the church of the St. Florian monastery, built in 1770–1 by Franz Xaver Chrisman (born *c.* 1725) and finished only in 1837 by Johann Georg Fischer, is still regarded as one of the best and most beautiful in Austria (*see* No. 364 and note preceding No. 709).—The spa of Gastein was visited for its waters at least as early as the Middle Ages. ("The efficacy of the 18 different hot springs [113°–120° F.] in cases of nervous affections, gout, rheumatism and debility is ascribed to the radio-activity of the water."—Baedeker.)—The romantically situated Gutenstein, the favourite resort of Ferdinand Raimund, the author of fairy-tale plays, lies about thirty miles to the south-west of Vienna, on the river Pernitz.—Leopold Chimani, born in 1774 at Langenzers-dorf in Lower Austria, was an administrator for the national distribution of school-books and a children's author, possibly the father of the former choir-boy Alois (*see* No. 41). He published in 1829 'My Excursion on Foot from Vienna through the Country below and above the Enns' (i.e. Lower and Upper Austria).—Matthias Tuscher, born *c.* 1775, a member of the Philharmonic Society committee, sang tenor and in 1814 had commissioned from Beethoven the 'Abschiedschiedsgesang' for a

Schubert at the Piano, with Kupelwieser's Dog Drago.   Detail of Leopold
Kupelwieser's Water-colour, "Party Game of the Schubertians" ("Gesell-
schaftsspiel der Schubertianer") 1821

PLATE XVII

"Game of Ball at Atzenbrugg, or The Feast at Atzenbrugg" ("Ballspiel der Schubertianer in Atzenbrugg, oder Das Atzenbrugger Fest"). Coloured Etching by Ludwig Mohn (c. 1820) after a Drawing by Franz von Schober (Landscape and Architecture) and Moritz von Schwind (Figures)

Schubert, with his long pipe, sitting in shirt sleeves in the foreground; Schober, with stock, on Schubert's right; Kraissl, playing the violin, on his left; the Atzenbrugg Castle in the background

PLATE XVIII

friend emigrating to Steyr.—Pottenstein is to the south-west of Baden. Muckendorf is near Pernitz; the waterfall is now called "Mirafälle." "Klosterberg" should read Mariahilfer Berg (2,300 feet). The Schneeberg, south of Gutenstein, is 6,800 feet high. It is the loftiest mountain in Lower Austria (of which Schubert knew very little). Like the Mariahilf mountain, on which is a pilgrims' chapel, the ruin of the Gutenstein castle, "accessible by the Steinapiesting gorge, on a precipitous rock," has a fine view. According to Seidl's book on 'The Environs of Vienna' (1826), it was regarded as "already very dangerous to climb."—The necessary connection with Diabelli seems to have been maintained by Ferdinand, at least during Franz's absence.—Friedrich August Kleinschmid, born in 1749 at Steinheim in Württemberg, settled in Vienna since 1776, was director of the police station there, and a poet and art collector. Schubert set none of his poems.—On the youngest Karl Schubert *see* note on p. 383.

578. BRUCHMANN TO PLATEN

Vienna, 5th August 1825.

. . . Even your latest wish, for Schubert's songs, I am unable to gratify now, as Schubert is not here and has, so far as I know, set very little of yours. One song you did receive, I think. One is printed, and yet another might be available in manuscript. But I have no precise knowledge about it until he comes.

After the two songs of 1822 Schubert never again set a poem by Platen. One of these was published as part of Op. 23 in 1823, the other not till 1826, in Op. 59.

579. FROM THE OFFICIAL 'SALZBURGER ZEITUNG'

Franz Schubert, musical composer from Vienna, alights at the Blackamoor Inn on 11th August 1825 with Herr Johann Michael Vogl, Court Opera singer, from Steyr.

Schubert and Vogl drove by way of Kremsmünster, Vöcklabruck, Frankenmarkt, Strasswalchen, Neumarkt and the Waller Lake to Salzburg (*see* No. 587), where they remained until 14th August. The supposition that they lodged with the merchant Pauernfeind (*see* No. 587), just opposite the inn, in the narrow Judengasse in the old town on the left bank of the Salzach, has proved to be erroneous. (There is a memorial tablet there; the inn is now known as "Mor'n Sitz"="The Moor's Seat.")

580. FROM THE OFFICIAL 'WIENER ZEITUNG,' 12th August 1825

At the House of A. Pennauer,

I. & R. Priv. Art and Music Publisher in Vienna, Lower Bräunerstrasse, in Fischer's House, is to be had:

SULEIKA'S SECOND SONG

['Suleikas zweiter Gesang']

by Goethe,

Set to Music for One Voice with Pianoforte Accompaniment

by FRANZ SCHUBERT

Op. 31.   Price, 1 Florin 30 Kreuzer.

The same with Guitar Accompaniment, 1 Fl. 15 Kr.

This work, not published until after Op. 47, is dedicated to the "Royal Prussian Court Opera Singer" Anna Milder (*see* No. 538).

581. SCHWIND TO SCHUBERT

[Address:]

From Vienna.

To Franz Schubert, Esq.,

c/o Herr von Vogl

in

Steyr.

In case of absence kindly forward to Herr von Vogl.

[Inside:]

14th August 1825.

Dear Schubert,

Although I do not know where you are, I take it this letter will be duly forwarded to you. That Schober has arrived already you will know from my last letter, if you received it. But now Kupelwieser too has been here for the last week. According to the latest letters we were not to expect him for three weeks. He looks splendid and has a perfect head of hair, without which he had to do for a long time owing to typhus. They all send you a thousand greetings. Nothing is wanting except your returning at last. Schober and Kuppel live together.

Your landlord would like to know for certain whether you wish to take up your lodgings again this winter without fail. Write to me definitely about it, so that I may tell him. If certain negotiations materialize as I desire, I am resolved to live by myself, and that probably on the Wieden. Rieder has an appointment as professor at the Engineering Academy at 600 florins, but for that he is under suspicion of intending to get married. If you apply seriously for the court organist's post, you may succeed equally well. There will be nothing for you but to live decently, for otherwise, considering the complete and decisive poverty of your friends, you will have to satisfy your fleshly and spiritual needs—or rather, your need of pheasants and punch—in a solitude that will yield nothing to life on a desert island, perhaps in the manner of Robinson Crusoe. The stage now seems altogether out of the question, at least as regards operas, and as Wasserburger has no wind instruments for the winter season, we may go and whistle to ourselves. How I look forward again to the first Schubertiad! About your Symphony we may be quite hopeful. Old Hönig is dean of the faculty of jurisprudence, and as such is to give a concert. That will afford a better opportunity of having it performed; indeed we count upon it.

1st September.

I was rather unhappy in the meantime, but now feel bright again. As long as one keeps the courage to be frank, one can put up with anything. Not that I can come, for I have too much to do. But so as not to let you believe I am held by certain people, I let you know that I still intend to go to Merkenstein, and then to Atzenbrugg, where Schober is, to enjoy country life. Although I do not yet have it from your own lips whether you are reconciled again by now, I nevertheless flatter myself that it may be one more reason for your coming back earlier that I and Bauernfeld cannot go up there. Kuppel [Kupelwieser] is very busy and Schober seems seriously to prepare to be the same, but although in this way each is happy, we are not joyously united without you. You may rely on finding a larger life than that which you left. Netti Hönig, the only one whom you doubt, shows her endless devotion to you and your cause so frequently and naturally that, if I deserve some credence, I can answer for it that you could not easily live and sing before any one who thinks more highly of you or is capable of feeling more sincere sympathy or deeper pleasure.

Worzischek is at his last gasp, and the Court organistship must be sought after in all seriousness. So far as I can gather, to make a success of it will be a matter of grinding the organ on a given theme. There must surely be an organ at Gmunden on which you can practise.

In conclusion I would ask you to pay all my possible respects to Herr Vogl and at the same time to importune him day and night to capture and bring with him the two drawings in question. I hope I and my art will be of more value to him than that lady, be she never so amiable, and in whose favour and friendship I wish him every unselfish effort in my power. I should like to paint those things and cannot regard any one as my friend who hinders or refuses to help me in this.

I remain yours so long as I do not forsake myself, and wish for myself, as well as for all who love you, a speedy reply or return.

Your Schwind.

Many kind things from Pinterics, Doblhoff, Randhartinger and, upon my troth, the sincerest messages from the little person. Letter will reach me from home, wherever I may be.

This letter was evidently forwarded to Gastein.—Schwind's earlier letter is No. 575.—Kupelwieser, who had had malaria (described as "nervous fever," which at that time could mean almost anything to the layman), brought home a thick fair head of hair in place of the lost reddish one.—Schober now lived with his lonely mother in the Obere Bäcker-strasse, near the Seminary, and Kupelwieser, who was soon to be married, went to lodge with him temporarily.—For Schubert's landlord cf. Nos. 566 and 572.—Rieder, who had also been in Italy, remained single for the time being.—Worzischek (see No. 342), first court organist since 1824, was taken ill and had gone to Carlsbad for a cure. He died in the autumn of 1825. The post was not advertised, but filled internally: Sechter, who had been second court organist since 1824, became first in 1825, and Assmayr second in 1826. Schuppanzigh regretted at that time that Worzischek's place was not given to Beethoven. Schubert could have been considered only for the second post. In this connection it is worth mentioning that in 1822 Sechter and Ferdinand Schubert, among others, had competed for that place with Worzischek. Dietrichstein, in agreement with

Salieri and Eybler, had proposed Worzischek and obtained him the appointment. He is said to have suggested to Schubert's father in 1825, through Josef Hüttenbrenner, that Schubert should apply for the post (the second, no doubt), which he would hardly have done.—For Vienna's operatic activities *see* No. 573.—The allusion to wind instruments (*Harmonie*) at Wasserburger's café probably had a double meaning. The German technical term for a team of wind players is "harmony." Actually there was no music at that café, but only at two other places in the city, the "Partridge" (*Rebhuhn*), a tavern, and the "Oak-Tree" (*Zur Eiche*), an ale-house. Even there Lanner's and Strauss's small bands were confined to strings. What Schwind seems to mean is that, as they no longer had any opera and not even any harmony (which may mean "wind music" or "concord") at Wasserburger's, they may go and whistle to themselves, which again may have an equivocal meaning.—For the Symphony cf. No. 569.— Franz Hönig (*see* No. 518) was dean of the faculty of jurisprudence, which gave an annual musical and declamatory performance in the hall of the university for the benefit of the widows and orphans of former members. Unfortunately the Symphony was not performed there on 30th April 1826, which may have been one of the reasons why it went astray.—Merkenstein is a tripper's place west of Baden and Vöslau (south of Vienna), where there is a ruined castle, and since 1829 a new one. Beethoven celebrated the place in a song.—The parish church at Gmunden did possess an organ, and Schubert returned there for another week; but it is unlikely that he did anything to prepare himself for the competition.—The lady is once again Amalia von Schiller (*see* Nos. 564 and 575); the drawings may have been those for Schwind's later pictures "Erl King" and "Chronos the Charioteer," or "Katie of Heilbronn" and "Hour of Dawn" ("Morgenstunde"): the sketches of these early years.—Randhartinger (*see* No. 17), born in 1802 at Ruprechtshofen in Lower Austria, court choir-boy in 1813–19 and since 1825 private secretary to Count Louis Széchényi (*see* No. 263), was a composer. As he advanced in years he overrated the extent of his relations with Schubert more and more, so that all his recollections are unreliable, particularly those of the first try-out of 'Erl King' at the Seminary and the origin of the 'Mill' cycle and the song 'The Dwarf.'—The "little person" is, of course, Anna Hönig.

582. From the Official 'Wiener Zeitung,' 3rd September 1825

At the House of Anton Diabelli & Co.,
Art and Music Dealers, in the Graben, No. 1133, is newly published,
and to be had of K. Lichtl in Pest at the same price:

Mass in C

for four Voices, 2 Violins, 2 Oboes or Clarinets,

2 Trumpets, Drums, Violoncello, Double Bass and Organ,
composed and dedicated for kind remembrance to
Herr Michael Holzer,
by FRANZ SCHUBERT

Work 48.   Price, 9 Florins, V.C.
(Property of the Publishers.)

N.B. Parts for doubling at will are issued separately.

This Mass had been composed in 1816, when Schubert was still in close touch with the Liechtental church and its choirmaster.   The autograph lacks a title-page, but Schubert wrote a special one for Ferdinand's copy, which served for the engraving.   It bears the dedication, but the work is still designated Op. 42.   In October 1828, shortly before his death, he wrote a new Benedictus, which Diabelli published and recommended for use "in default of a good soprano singer."   Holzer died in 1826.

583. FROM THE MANUSCRIPT REGISTER of Eligible Members of
the Philharmonic Society in the Austrian Imperial State,
3rd September 1825

Eligible, contributing and executive members:
. . . Schubert, Fr.

This list, which is in manuscript, was found in the archives of the Philharmonic Society.   The date indicates the day of the election.

584. FROM THE VISITORS' BOOK of Bad Gastein
(Left on 4th September 1825:)

Joh. Michl. Vogl, I. & R. retired Court Opera Singer.
Franz Schubert, Composer.

Schubert and Vogl drove to Gastein by way of Hallein, Golling, the Lueg Pass and Werfen on 13th or 14th August (see No. 593).   They were thus there for about three weeks.   Among the visitors taking the waters was Pyrker, the Patriarch of Venice (see No. 237), whose poem 'Homesickness' ('Das Heimweh') Schubert set there.   Mozart's widow, Konstanze von Nissen, who knew Vogl, was also there.   Since Schubert wrote the D major pianoforte Sonata, Op. 53, at Gastein during that August, it is hardly credible that the lost Symphony, long known as the "Gastein" Symphony, also originated there.   The fact is that it was merely finished there, so that it would be much better called the "Gmunden-Gastein" Symphony, or better still just the "lost Symphony." The two friends may have stayed at the so-called "Straubinger-Hütte" (now the Hotel Straubinger). Schubert, who did not take the waters, must certainly have made the most of the natural beauties and the intoxicating air of Gastein, and not done an excessive amount of work. Vogl suffered from gout. He went to Italy soon afterwards, but not with Pyrker, who left on 3rd September.

585. FROM THE 'THEATERZEITUNG,' 6th September 1825

On 8th September, *i.e.* the Feast of the Blessed Virgin, at the Church of St. Ulric on the Platzl, a society of friends of music will perform, at 10 o'clock, a new Mass with a 'Tantum ergo,' Gradual and Offertory by the composer of genius, Herr Franz Schubert, to which all lovers of church music are courteously invited. The said Mass, as well as the 'Tantum ergo' and Offertory, are already engraved and to be had in a very handsome and correct edition at the Art Establishment of Ant. Diabelli in the Graben, No. 1133.

A. Diabelli & Co.

At this church, also known as Maria Trost, with which Ferdinand Schubert was closely connected, a Requiem Mass was held for Schubert at the end of 1828, and his E flat major Mass was performed there in 1829. After the 'Tantum ergo' (Op. 45, xiv. 6), published at the beginning of September, Diabelli also brought out the Gradual or first Offertory (Op. 46, xiv. 1) in mid September, but saved himself the cost of advertisements in the 'Wiener Zeitung.' The second Offertory (Op. 47, xiv. 2) appeared in August, the C major Mass (Op. 48, xiii. 4) in September (cf. Nos. 576 and 582).

586. JOHANN MICHAEL VOGL TO ALBERT STADLER at Linz

[Gmunden, early September 1825.]

. . . Do remember us to all who are fond of us, and assure them that we shall be at Linz in about 3 weeks.

Schubert and Vogl returned to Gmunden by way of Werfen, and after that perhaps via Hallstatt, Attersee and Ebensee on the south shore of Lake Traun, about 10th September. They remained there, with a break for a visit to Ebenzweier, until about the 17th. Linz they did not reach until after another fortnight at Steyr, about 1st October.

Gmunden, 12th September 1825.   ·

Dear Brother,

According to your challenge I should certainly like to give you a detailed description of our journey to Salzburg and Gastein, but you know how little gifted I am for narratives and descriptions; yet as I should in any case have to tell you on my return to Vienna, I prefer after all to sketch in writing now, rather than verbally later, a feeble picture of all those extraordinary beauties, since I may hope to do the former better than the latter, all the same.

We left Steyr, then, about the middle of August and went by way of Kremsmünster, which indeed I had often seen before, but can never bear to miss on account of its beautiful situation. For there is a view over a very lovely valley, interrupted by a few small and gentle hills, to the right of which rises a not inconsiderable mountain; on its summit the extensive monastery offers the most magnificent view even from the high road, which leads across a brook opposite, a view enhanced especially by the ''mathematical'' tower. Here, where we have been known for some time, particularly Herr von Vogl, who studied here, we were very kindly received; we did not stay, however, but continued our journey, which does not call for special mention, as far as Vöcklabruck, where we arrived in the evening: a sorry hole. The next morning we went by way of Strasswalchen and Frankenmarkt to Neumarkt, where we lunched. These places, which lie already in the county of Salzburg, are distinguished by the peculiar architecture of the houses. Nearly everything is of wood. Wooden kitchen utensils stand on wooden trestles fixed on the outside of the houses, round which run wooden galleries. Also, there are shot-up targets hanging on the houses everywhere, kept as trophies of victories won long ages ago; for they often bear the dates of 1600 or 1500. Bavarian money begins to be used here, too. From Neumarkt, which is the last postal stage before Salzburg, summits of mountains in the Salzburg valley may already be seen, just then covered with snow. About an hour out of Neumarkt the country begins to become amazingly beautiful. The Waller Lake, which spreads its bright, blue-green water to the right of the road, animates this delightful landscape most gloriously. The altitude is very high, and thenceforward it drops continually towards Salzburg. The mountains rise higher and higher, and especially the legendary Untersberg rises from amid the others as by magic. The villages show traces of former affluence. At the meanest farmhouses everywhere one finds window-frames and door-posts of marble, and even sometimes stairs of red marble. The sun darkens and heavy clouds run across the black mountains like nebulous spirits; but they do not touch the Untersberg's brow, they creep past it as though terrified of its dreadful interior. The wide valley, looking as if speckled with isolated castles, churches and farmsteads, grows ever more visible to the enchanted eye. Towers and palaces gradually show themselves; at last one drives past the Kapuzinerberg, whose immense rocky wall rises sheer up hard by the road and frowns down fearfully upon the traveller. The Untersberg and its retinue grow gigantic, their size almost crushing us. And now we enter the town itself through some splendid avenues. Fortifications built all of rough-hewn stone surround this famous seat of the former electors. The city gates proclaim by their inscriptions the vanished powers of clericalism. Nothing but houses of four and five stories fill the rather wide streets, and past the curiously decorated house of Theophrastus Paracelsus we cross the bridge over the Salzach, which rushes past turbidly, darkly and mightily. The city itself made a rather gloomy impression on me, because dull weather darkened the ancient buildings still more and, moreover, the fortress, situated on the highest summit of the Mönchsberg, sends its ghostly message into every street in the town. As unfortunately it began to rain immediately after our arrival, which is very often the case here, we were able to see very little apart from the many palaces and glorious churches we caught sight of as we drove by. Through Herr Pauernfeind, a merchant well known to Herr von Vogl, we were introduced to Count von Platz, president of the assizes, by whose family we were most kindly received, our names being already known to them. Vogl sang some of my songs, whereupon we were invited for the following evening and requested to produce

our odds and ends before a select circle; and indeed they touched
them all very much, special preference being given to the 'Ave
Maria' already mentioned in my first letter.   The manner in which
Vogl sings and the way I accompany, as though we were one at such
a moment, is something quite new and unheard-of for these people.
Having climbed the Mönchsberg the following morning, from which
a large part of the city may be surveyed, I could not help being
amazed at the number of wonderful buildings, palaces and churches.
Yet the inhabitants here are few: many buildings are empty and some
are occupied by only one family, or at most two or three.   In the
squares, of which there are many, grass grows between the paving-
stones, so little are they frequented.   The cathedral is a heavenly
building, after the pattern of St. Peter's Church in Rome, but of
course on a smaller scale.   The length of the church is in the form
of a cross, surrounded by four enormous courtyards, each of which
forms a large square.   At the entrance stand the Apostles carved
in stone, gigantic in size.   The interior of the church is supported
by many marble columns, adorned with portraits of the electors
and in truth perfectly beautiful in every detail.   The light, falling
through the dome, penetrates into every corner.   This extraordinary brightness has a divine effect and might be recommended to all churches.   In the four squares surrounding the
church are large fountains decorated with the most superb and
daring figures.   From here we went to the monastery of St. Peter,
where Michael Haydn resided.   That church too is most wondrously
fine.   Here is also to be found, as you know, M. Haydn's monument.   It is rather pretty, though not well placed, but put into a
remote corner.   Also, the slips of paper littered about look rather
childish.   His head is kept in the urn.   It hovers round me, I
thought to myself, thy tranquil, clear spirit, thou good Haydn,
and if I cannot myself be so tranquil and clear, there is no one in
the world, surely, who reveres thee so deeply as I.   (A heavy
tear fell from my eye, and we moved on.—)   We lunched at Herr
Pauernfeind's, and in the afternoon, when the weather allowed us
to go out, we climbed the Nonnberg, which is not high, but affords
the finest of views, for one overlooks the inner Salzburg valley from
there.   To describe you the loveliness of that valley is almost

impossible. Think of a garden several miles in extent, with
countless castles and estates in it peeping through the trees; think
of a river winding through it in manifold twists and turns; think
of meadows and fields like so many carpets of the finest colours,
then of the many roads tied round them like ribbons; and lastly
avenues of enormous trees to walk in for hours, all enclosed
by ranges of the highest mountains as far as the eye can reach, as
though they were the guardians of this glorious valley; think of all
this, and you will have a faint conception of its inexpressible beauty.
The rest of Salzburg's curiosities, which I shall see only on my
return journey, I shall leave until then, for I wish my description
to be chronological.

Ferdinand's request for a detailed description of his brother's journey,
at any rate of Gastein (which he never received), is expressed in
No. 577. Schubert did not post this letter, which he continued at
Steyr (No. 593) without ever finishing it; but he brought it home with
him. Ferdinand first printed it, somewhat edited, in his book 'Der
kleine Geograph,' illustrated by his brother Karl (Vienna, 1833, vol. ii,
pp. 55 ff.); and later in Schumann's 'Neue Zeitschrift für Musik' (Leipzig,
5th February 1839). This reprint too being incomplete, and the original
being lost, the text given here, like that of No. 572, also draws on Ludwig
Gottfried Neumann's compilation, 'Lebensbilder aus Oesterreich'
(Vienna, 1843, pp. 218 ff.).—The departure from Steyr had taken place on
10th or 11th August.—The journey (see No. 579) went in a west-south-
westerly direction; but on that route Frankenmarkt is reached before
Strasswalchen.—Kremsmünster, long known to Schubert through friends
who had been educated there, was founded in 777 and is, after St. Peter's
at Salzburg, the oldest abbey in the Austrian Alps. The buildings date
mostly from the seventeenth and eighteenth centuries, among them the
"astronomical" or "mathematical" tower, an observatory of the middle
of the eighteenth century (not unlike that which used to be next to the
Vienna Seminary). The grammar-school of Kremsmünster had been
founded as early as 1549.—Bavaria had a 24-florin valuation, i.e. one
mark of Cologne silver was worth 24 florins, not 20 florins, as in Austria.—
The Untersberg marble is reddish in colour.—The Kapuzinerberg was
overlooked from Schubert's window at the Blackamoor Inn (Zum Mohren),
giving on to the Salzach.—The archbishops of Salzburg (798–1803)
were primates of the Church of Rome in Germanic countries; but they
were also secular princes, and as such electors of the empire. After the
secularization of the Salzburg county it first went to Bavaria and in 1816

to Austria.—The house named after the famous physician and naturalist Paracelsus (the hero of Browning's poem), who died there in 1541, is on the "Platzl" near the main bridge.—On the Mönchsberg, on the right bank of the Salzach, is the old fortress of Hohen-Salzburg.—Johann Christian Pauernfeind had been burgomaster of Salzburg and was now a representative of the merchant interests with a watching brief in the Salzburg court of exchange.—Maria Hieronymus, Count Platz, born at Radstadt in 1777, was president of the town and county court, as well as of the criminal, mercantile and exchange courts at Salzburg.   He had been brought up by Katharina Gilowsky as his governess: Mozart's "Gilowsky Katherl."—Among the songs Vogl sang there was probably the setting of Schiller's 'Alpine Hunter' ('Der Alpenjäger'; see Nos. 597 and 616).—The city of Salzburg was still suffering from the change of government.—The cathedral, in an early baroque style, was built in the first half of the seventeenth century; it is regarded as the best example of Italian architecture in the north.   There are really only three squares with two fountains round the cathedral.—The nearby Benedictine abbey of St. Peter was founded in 696.   Its collegiate church dates from the twelfth century, but was rebuilt in 1760 with an interior in the rococo style.   Michael Haydn, Joseph's younger brother, born at Rohrau in 1737, had been organist at St. Peter's and concert-master to the prince-archbishop.   His monument, in the *Biedermeier* style, was erected only in 1821.   The "slips of paper" are actually of stone and bear the titles of some of his more important works.   His bones repose in the abbey's famous churchyard just outside.   Whether Schubert felt especially closely bound to Michael Haydn on account of his male-voice quartets, forerunners of his own, cannot be determined.   It seems that about 1815 Schubert sang canons by Michael Haydn (as well as one by F. J. Otter, written in the latter's honour); the second tenor part, which Holzapfel sang, has been preserved by descendants of the Schubert family.   Schubert copied the organ part of M. Haydn's well-known 'German High Mass' ("Here lies before Thy Majesty"; cf. Schubert's 'German Requiem,' No. 131, and his 'German Mass,' No. 962).   In 1840 Ferdinand Schubert composed, as his Op. 33, a chorus 'To Michael Haydn, in the place where he enjoyed many a glad hour,' i.e. at St. Peter's abbey.—The Nonnberg too (Schubert writes "Nonnenberg") is on the left bank of the Salzach; it has a Benedictine nunnery founded about 700, with a Romanesque-Gothic church.

588 BAUERNFELD TO SCHUBERT

[Address:]

Franz Schubert, Esq.

at

To be delivered at   Steyr

Herr von Vogl's.   in Upper Austria.

[Inside:]

Vienna, 13th September 1825.

Dear Friend:

I hardly know whether you are acquainted with the hand of him who is writing to you here, or whether you will not have to take refuge in the signature for your better guidance. Know it then: I am Bauernfeld—I greet and kiss you heartily—but to proceed at once to the most necessary, since you must receive this letter as soon as possible and it must go to the post in a quarter of an hour:

First: write at once whether you wish to retain your room, for your landlord keeps on asking;—

Secondly: Moritz von Schwind and I suggest to you to take a proper lodging and to stick together, the three of us; if you agree, confirm it with a gracious "yes";

Thirdly: the said plan is not to be carried out at once, but only in October or November. Until then I shall live at Schober's, and you anywhere. Do answer all this at once, clearly and explicitly . . .

How are you, fattest of friends? I suppose your belly will have increased; may God preserve it and let it prosper! Schober is at Atzenbrugg; Schwind went there yesterday; I shall probably follow him soon, but only for a few days. Only write to me quickly, and add this to the address: to be delivered at the lithographic vaults of Jos. Trentsensky at the Zwettelhof. Farewell, farewell, farewell!

If you write to me nicely, I may perhaps oblige you with a sensible and weighty letter.

Your friend

Bauernfeld.

For Schubert's landlord see Nos. 566, 572 and 581.—For the friends'
plan concerning their lodgings see No. 591.—Bauernfeld actually moved
to Schober's in October, evidently in place of Kupelwieser, and remained
there until February 1826. Schubert lived there temporarily in the
autumn of 1826.—Although Schubert himself thought he had grown thin
owing to the heat in Upper Austria (see No. 572), Bauernfeld's jocular
allusion suggests rather that he had become fat.—Schober had been at
Atzenbrugg ever since August, but no "feasts" seem to have been held
there any longer. Schwind had probably been at Merkenstein and had
met Bauernfeld at Mayerhofer's at Wiener-Neustadt.—Josef Trentsensky (see No. 430) was the owner of a lithographic establishment, founded
in 1824, in which his brother Matthias, a pensioned officer and the inventor of litho-stereotype plates, was also interested. The shop in the
Zwettelhof still exists under the name of their successors. The firm
became famous through its "Mandel-Bogen," sheets with figures (Mandel,
dialect for Männchen=little men) for cutting out, the models for which
were drawn by noted artists, including Schwind. They were chiefly
toy-theatre pictures in the style of Skelt's (later Redington's, finally
Pollock's) "penny plain, twopence coloured," which were somewhat
earlier. In order to exploit Matthias's invention this firm was now also
bringing out the Viennese edition of Shakespeare (and later a similar one of
Calderón), first issued in forty-three small duodecimo volumes (1824–6) and
later in a single quarto printed from the same plates (1825–6). The nominal
publisher was Johann Paul Sollinger, originally only a printer, Trentsensky evidently having no publishing licence. Bauernfeld and a few
youths of his acquaintance had undertaken the translations, which
were to be added to a reprint of the already familiar ones by August
Wilhelm von Schlegel. Bauernfeld undertook 'The Two Gentlemen of
Verona,' 'King Henry VIII,' 'The Comedy of Errors' and the poems
'The Rape of Lucrece' and 'The Passionate Pilgrim'; and in collaboration
with Fick (see No. 271) 'Coriolanus' and with Mayerhofer 'Antony and
Cleopatra.' Fick alone translated 'The Taming of the Shrew,' Mayerhofer 'Love's Labour 's Lost,' Franz Eduard Hermann von Hermannsthal
(born Vienna, 1799) 'Timon of Athens' and 'Titus Andronicus,' Karl
Spina (born Brno, c. 1801) 'Measure for Measure'—placed by Shakespeare in Vienna—and Andreas Schumacher (born Vienna, 1803)
made an excellent version of the sonnets, first allotted to Bauernfeld,
as well as of the poems 'Venus and Adonis' and 'A Lover's Complaint.'
Bauernfeld, as editor, added a dedicatory poem to Shakespeare. The
plays newly translated had been done only in prose in the earlier Viennese
edition published by Pichler in 1811. The covers, lithographed by
Jakob Hyrtl, were designed by Schwind, as well as two vignettes for the
great quarto edition. The title vignettes of the duodecimo edition,

however, are simply copies of those by John Thurston in the London edition of 1814. It was from Bauernfeld's edition that Schubert took the words of his three Shakespeare songs of 1826.

589. FROM BAUERNFELD'S DIARY

September 1825.

With Schober and Schwind at Atzenbrugg. Lodging with the lady at the Aumühle. We slept all three in a wide bed.

The lady at the Aumühle was its owner, probably not yet Frau Josefa Gritzner (*see* note preceding No. 244), to whom it did not belong till 1827. Her uncle, Weigert, later became estate manager of Atzenbrugg.

590. SCHUBERT TO JOHANN STEIGER VON AMSTEIN

[Gmunden, middle of September 1825.]

Dear Steiger,

I am very sorry not to be able to accompany you back to Clodi's, as we drive to Atter Lake to-day and cannot put off this trip, Vogl having decided to leave Gmunden *to-morrow*!! I only learnt this early to-day, wherefore you will forgive me. Do not be angry, for I much regret it. In the evening I hope I may still see you both at your tavern.

In regard to the viewing of the salt mines, you have only to ask for Herr von Kinesberger at the salt board of trade, who spoke to us yesterday.

Yours

Schubert.

For Steiger *see* No. 396.—His companion was Louis Hönig (*see* No. 591). —The letter was probably written on 16th or 17th September.—Kinesberger was an official in the "Kufen" Board of Trade, named after the "Kufe," an Austrian salt measure.

591. SCHUBERT TO BAUERNFELD

[Outside:]

J. Bauernfeld, Esq.,

in

Vienna.

To be delivered at
Herr Jos. Trentsensky's
Lithographic Institute
in the Zwettelhof.

[Inside:]

Steyr, 18th or 19th September 1825.

Dear Friend,

Your scribbling had indeed gone quite out of my head, all-destroying Time and your almost rudely hasty hand having caused this. In this last matter I propose to do the same to you. — As regards the lodgings in Fruhwirth's house, I intend to keep them, and have already tried to inform him of this through my family. But whether this has been forgotten or whether he is so anxious and fussy, please be kind enough, one or all of you, to hand him 25 florins, V.C., in my name and to assure him that I shall come for certain at the end of October.—As for living together, it would suit me very well, of course, but as I know something about such bachelors' and students' plans, I should not like to find myself between two stools in the end. Should anything suitable turn up, however, I shall still find means of parting from my landlord in a decent manner. The aforesaid 25 fl., which I shall most punctiliously repay on my arrival, would have to be paid him for October.—To Schober and Kupelwieser I look forward with curiosity, to the former as to a man whose plans have miscarried and to the latter as wearing the look of one coming from Rome and Naples.—Schwind is a regular tool-player and wool-teaser, for I do not know which of the two letters he wrote to me is the more confused. Never yet had such a rigmarole of sense and nonsense come my way. Unless he has done some very fine things these days, such brainless chatter is not to be forgiven him. My greetings to those 3, also to Rieder and Dietrich, if you should

see them.   To Rieder I send my congratulations on his professorship.—Steiger and Louis Hönig visited me at Gmunden, which
gave me much pleasure.   If you had added by an iota to the rest
of your admirable brains, you too would have honoured me with
your presence.   But that is not to be expected of fellows who are
over head and ears in love.   How often you must have been unhappy again, and have drowned your sighs and complaints in beer
and punch!   Ha! ha! ha! ha!   I nearly forgot to tell you that I
have been at Salzburg and Gastein, where the country surpasses the
wildest imgination.

Farewell!

Your

Write to me, but write   Schubert.
sense, perhaps a musical   Greetings to all friends.
poem(?)!

P.S. Vogl is just telling me it is possible that he may go to Italy
with Haugwitz at the end of this month or beginning of October;
in that case I too should come earlier, at the beginning of October.

"J." in Schubert's address is an error for "E." Bauernfeld.—For the
lodgings in Fruhwirth's house see Nos. 566, 572, 581 and 588.—Schubert
still thought that he would not return until the end of October.—"Tool-
player" and "wool-teaser" are approximate equivalents of the collo-
quialisms Harn-Freund and Garn-Haspel.   The former is probably a slip
of the pen (H for G) which Schubert did not trouble to correct; the latter,
sometimes Haspel alone, meant something like "queer fellow."—
Schwind's two letters are Nos. 575 and 581.—For Rieder cf. No. 581.—
Louis Hönig, a schoolfellow of Bauernfeld's, was a nephew of Franz
Hönig; his father's name was Ludwig.—A musical poem is, of course,
one suitable for composition.   Schubert set only two of Bauernfeld's
poems, 'The Father with his Child' ('Der Vater mit dem Kind,' 1827)
and the lost 'Little Shroud' ('Totenhemdchen').—Vogl did go to Italy.
Eugen Wilhelm, Count Haugwitz, born at Brno in 1777, was a superior
officer, commandant at Naples in 1815–18; he became a friend of Vogl's
at that time, and was also one of Ludwig Friedrich von Hartmann's (see
note preceding No. 372).   He played the harp and sang Schubert's songs.

our eyes from such disheartening views, and let us rather see to it that we escape from this hole. After a longish descent, during which the two rocky walls come ever closer and the road, together with the river, becomes narrowed to 2 fathom, the road turns here, where you least expect it, below an overhanging rock where the constrained Salzach rages furiously, to the traveller's agreeable surprise. For now your path goes on wider and level, although still enclosed by sky-high mountains. At noon we arrived at Werfen, a market town with an important fortress built by the Salzburg electors and now being improved by the emperor. On our return we climbed it: it is d——d high, but affords a splendid view of the valley, bounded on one side by the immense Werfen mountains, which can be seen from as far as Gastein. Heavens, and the devil and all, the description of a journey is something frightful, and I can no more. As I shall be in Vienna about the early days of October, I shall hand you this screed myself and tell you the rest verbally.

For the first part of this letter *see* No. 587.—The "following morning" was 13th or 14th August.—The valley is the Nonntal.—The Month's Castle, built in 1615 in the course of a single month (though not, as the story goes, for the archbishop's beautiful mistress, Salome Alt), is in the park of the pleasance of Hellbrunn (1613) and now accommodates a museum for folklore.—The journey was continued southward.—The proper name of the Hallein Salzberg, whose salt mines yield 20,000 tons a year, is Dürnberg.—The "rat-hole" is *Ratzenstadl* in the original, the popular name of the Magdalenengrund suburb of Vienna, and Viennese dialect for a place infested by rats.—"A." may be Johann Georg Albrechtsberger (1736–1809), although the original of this letter too is lost and may have been altered in the first reprints.—The Lueg Pass, south of Golling, "is a grand ravine by which the Salzach pierces the barrier of the Salzburg Limestone Alps, between the Tennen-Gebirge on the east and the Hagen-Gebirge on the west. The pass, first fortified in ancient times, is frequently mentioned in the records of the campaign of 1809" (the fight of the Tyrolese under Father Joachim Haspinger—the patriot-hero Andreas Hofer's friend—against the Bavarians, who were allied with the French in the Napoleonic wars).—The first reprint has "rothes Kreuz" ("red cross," in the old spelling), which is almost certainly a misprint for "rohes Kreuz" ("rough cross").—Werfen, also on the river Salzach, is surmounted by Hohenwerfen Castle (2,231 feet), built in 1077, renovated five hundred years later and again restored in recent times.

594. OTTENWALT TO JOSEF VON SPAUN

[Linz,] 27th September 1825.

Schubert we hope to see here soon.   He is at Steyr.   Vogl is said to be going to Italy with Count Haugwitz.

During the last days of his holiday, which Schubert spent at Linz round about 1st October, he again visited Count and Countess Weissenwolff at Steyregg Castle.   Stadler, who accompanied him, shared his bedroom and saw him for the last time in those days, described their companionship in a letter to Luib in 1858 (Vienna City Library).   Vogl does not seem to have gone to Steyregg with them.   He went to Italy for six months.

'The Quail's Call' ('Der Wachtelschlag') (Op. 68) is reprinted in the 'National Calendar for the German United States for the Year 1826,' edited by Christian Karl André and published by J. G. Cotta at Stuttgart, autumn 1825.

Vogl and Schubert perform, at Anton von Spaun's at Linz, on the occasion of his wife Henriette's birthday, the latest songs, of which those from 'The Lady of the Lake' please particularly, 3rd October 1825.

Schubert and Josef von Gahy drive from Linz to Vienna in a hired one-horse carriage, within three days, early October 1825.   Henriette, *née* Vogelsang, was the wife of Anton von Spaun (*see* No. 301). Franz von Spaun (*see* No. 79) had married Louise Wanderer, the daughter of a surgeon at Nussdorf near Vienna, in 1824.   Her mother, Babette Wanderer, had paid a visit to Upper Austria in September with her other two daughters, Babette and Josephine, and Gahy had escorted them.   Schubert thus had company on the return journey home.

595. FROM BAUERNFELD'S DIARY

October 1825.

Schubert is back.   Inn and coffee-house gathering with friends, often until two or three in the morning.

> Shamefully, we confess,
> Every night
> Drinking and laziness
> Give us delight. .

Schober is the worst in this.   True, he has nothing to do, and actually does nothing, for which he is often reproached by Moritz.

Whenever Schubert was of the party, it was unusual for him to stay after midnight.   This probably happened only in the first days of his reunion with Schober and Kupelwieser, after a separation of two years.— The rhyme, which sounds rather like a students' song, resembles others of the kind written by Bauernfeld in 1821 in his 'Poetic Diary.'— Schober's good intentions, noted by Schwind (Moritz) on 1st September (*see* No. 581), were thus not carried out.

596. From the Diary of Jakob Nikolaus Craigher, Freiherr von Jachelutta

Sunday, 23rd October 1825.

Schwind, the painter, and
Schubert, the composer.—

To-day was truly a day of joy for me.   Schwind and Schubert came to breakfast with me and remained here from 9 until towards eleven o'clock.   The former brought his wondrously splendid new work, 'Zrinyi's Sortie near Szigeth,' with him.   I never imagined anything more beautiful of its kind.   The nationality of the Turks and the Magyars is represented as characteristically as possible in the figures of this picture.   I regard it as far surpassing Krafft's great painting.   The hero Zrinyi especially has turned out extremely well, for his spirit spreads, so to speak, over all his fellow combatants.   The manifold characters among the Turks' heads, among which the various Asiatic races may be distinguished, as it were, are most attractive.   On the right, at the foot of the picture, an archer shows himself as a magnificent figure and, on account of the extremely fine drawing, occupies the eye most particularly.   Schwind, provided he concentrates with the utmost ardour on the technique of art, may become one of the greatest painters who have ever lived.—Schubert has entered into an agreement with me according to which I am to supply him with a number of songs by English, Spanish, French and Italian classics with German translations in the metres of the originals, which he will then set to music and have published with the original text. I myself can only gain thereby, the more so because this may bring about a closer connection between us, which could not fail to be in every respect beneficial to us both. Besides, Schubert is too splendid a person for me not to do my utmost to draw him nearer to us.—He also took a few new songs of mine with him, which he will probably set to music.

Craigher, born in 1797 at Ligosullo in Venetia, had gone to Vienna from Pest in 1820. He became an accountant, but was also an assiduous lyric poet and on terms of friendship with Friedrich von Schlegel and Ludwig Ferdinand von Schnorr. He published his poems, written in 1818–24, as 'Poetic Contemplations in Leisure Hours' ('Poetische Betrachtungen in freien Stunden') in 1828 under the pseudonym of Nicolaus, with a preface and a introductory poem by Schlegel. The volume includes the poems set by Schubert in 1825, 'The Young Nun' ('Die junge Nonne') and 'Gravedigger's Homesickness' ('Totengräbers Heimweh'), but not Craigher's translation of Colley Cibber's 'The Blind Boy,' which Schubert had already set early in 1825. This poem (an English setting of which is in Bickham's 'Musical Entertainer') had already been translated by Mayláth (see No. 388) and set by Franz Lachner and Sechter in that version. It looks as though it was this translation of Craigher's that led to the agreement mentioned in the letter, which, however, came to nothing. Neither did Schubert set any further poems by Craigher.—Schwind's sepia drawing, the correct title of which is 'Zrinyi's Last Sortie from Szigeth,' is one of those pictorial broadsheets for the young (an historical, not a theatrical one in this case) which he drew for Trentsensky. They appeared lithographed as illustrations to the country's history. The theme of the defence of the Hungarian fortress by Zrinyi against the Sultan Soliman II in 1566 had become familiar through Körner's drama of 'Zriny' (as the name is spelt in German), and Johann Peter Krafft (born Hanau, 1780), one of Schwind's masters at the Academy of Fine Arts, popularized it by a picture.

597. GEORG NIKOLAUS VON NISSEN TO ALBERT STADLER
at Linz

Salzburg, 23rd–24th October 1825.

. . . But I am heartily glad that my guardian spirit still gives the means into my hand at the right hour to recompense you for everything, indeed for all your trouble. It counsels me, that is, to give you the pleasure of affording me yet another great pleasure. I am (and *sapienti sat*) quite enamoured of a portion of a song of Schubert's composition which Vogl sings. The song is a colloquy between mother and daughter. The latter says: "Mother, mother, let me go!"; but that does not attract me—only the few single strophes sung by the mother; both words and composition. Both seem to me wondrously gentle, sweet and beautiful. But I did not hear all the words; yet the melody continues to ring in my ear and heart.

Nissen, born in 1765 at Hardisleben in Saxony, was a retired Danish state councillor and lived at Salzburg with his wife Konstanze, Mozart's widow. Vogl had met them at Gastein (cf. No. 584) and introduced Nissen to Stadler, who possessed a Mozartian autograph, received by him from Dr. Anton Schmidt (*see* No. 125). He lent this to Nissen, together with the copy of a lost minuet; for Nissen was just then preparing his biography of Mozart. This led to a correspondence in which Nissen came to mention Schubert. He may have heard the song, the setting of Schiller's 'Alpine Hunter,' Op. 37, which was already published, at the house of Count Platz at Salzburg (*see* No. 587). The poem is, of course, not a colloquy between mother and daughter: the words quoted are spoken by a lad.

Johann Strauss, jun., born, 25th October 1825.

Schubert receives from Matthias Artaria a fee of 200 florins, A.C., for the 'Seven Songs from Walter Scott's Lady of the Lake' (Op. 52), 29th October 1825. Schubert had thus come to no agreement about this work with Pennauer (*see* No. 573) and had given it to Matthias Artaria. The latter was a son of the younger Domenico Artaria, one of the heads of the firm of Artaria & Co., with which Schubert came finally into touch. Matthias had married the widow of the publisher Daniel Sprenger, whose concern he had taken over in his own name in 1822. The shop was on the corner of the Kohlmarkt and the Paternoster-Gässchen. His lost account book (1824–31) was kept in A.C.

598. The Dance

(Cantata for Irene Kiesewetter [xvii. 14], 1825.)

The young of to-day, ne'er thinking aught else,
To parties and dances go flying;
When, suddenly reaching a treacherous goal,
We hear them complaining and sighing.
A pain they feel here and an ache they have there,
All heavenly pleasure has vanished for e'er.
"But this time I pray Thee my health to restore!"
They fervent and hopeful kind Heaven implore.

Thus did a young lady quite recently feel
The Fates her life's thread meant to sever;
Yet busily still runs her destiny's wheel,
More joyously lives she than ever.
For which, her companions, let's burst into song
And wish dear Irene may live very long.
Oft may she remember how fickle is chance,
But never misfortune shall trouble her glance.

                                        Schnitzer.

Irene von Kiesewetter, the handsome daughter of the aulic councillor (see No. 277), was born in Vienna in 1811. Although but fourteen years of age, she was already a good pianoforte player; she accompanied Schubert sometimes at this period and Schönstein frequently later on. The poem, the second verse of which is missing in the complete edition, was intended to combat the girl's passion for dancing and had doubtless been commissioned by her father. The writer is probably identical with K. A. F. Schnitzer, a translator from the French and the Greek, or with the amateur musician Kolumban Schnitzer, later von Meerau (possibly one and the same person in any case).

599. From the Programme of the First Evening Entertainment held by the Philharmonic Society, 10th November 1825

3. 'Spirit of Love' ['Geist der Liebe'] by Schubert for 4 male voices. Tietze.

The quartet was inserted in place of Variations for violin and pianoforte composed jointly by Peter Pixis and Josef Böhm. The latter was to play them with Bocklet, but could not appear owing to illness.

600. From Johann Pezzl's 'Description of Vienna,' 7th Edition, November 1825

Among the local musical artists the following deserve honourable mention:

Schubert, Franz, composer, resident at Fruhwirth's house next to the Karl Church on the Wieden.

601. From the Berlin 'Allgemeine Musikalische Zeitung,' 21st December 1825

(Vienna correspondence, late autumn 1825.)

The young composer Schubert continues indefatigably to write songs.   His first-fruits, especially the 'Erl King,' found a public, which however seems to be gradually diminishing.   Diabelli has also published a Mass from his pen.   At ballads he is better.

The Mass was that in C major, Op. 48.

602. From the Programme of the Second Evening Entertainment held by the Philharmonic Society, 17th November 1825 (Conductor, Herr Karl Fradl)

4. 'The Boatman' ['Der Gondelfahrer,' xvi. 9], Vocal Quartet by Schubert, performed by Herren Suchy, Karl Maria Gross, Nejebse and [Alois] Fuchs.

Alois Fuchs, born in 1799 at Raase in Austrian Silesia, living in Vienna since 1816, was an official in the Court War Council, a bass singer and cellist, and an ardent collector of musical autographs.

Johann Hugo Worzischek dies, 19th November 1825.

603. From the Official 'Wiener Zeitung,' 21st November 1825

Latest Dances
for the Pianoforte for the Carnival of 1826,
which are published by
Anton Diabelli & Co.,
Art and Music Dealers, in the Graben, No. 1133, and to be had of
K. Lichtl in Pest, at the same price:

*Valses sentimentales pour le Pianoforte
composées par François Schubert.*
Œuvre 50. Cah 1. 1 Fl. 30 Kr. Cah. 2. 1 Fl. 30 Kr., V.C.

*Galoppe et Écossaises pour le Pianoforte
composées par Fr. Schubert.*
Œuvre 49. 1 Fl., V.C.

These two works appeared without dedications. The faulty French in the title of Op. 49 (*Galoppe* instead of *Galop*) was changed into German in the next issue: 'Galoppe [*sic*: it should be "Galopp," as there was only one] und Ecossaisen für das Piano-Forte,' "performed at the society balls in the ballroom at the 'Seven Electors' at Pest, in the Carnival of 1826." Thereby hangs the following tale: The work had been anonymously scored for these dances of the Pest nobility at the Seven Electors Hotel and played, according to the custom prevailing there, concert-wise on Twelfth Night, after which it was repeatedly used as dance music until Ash Wednesday. It was Karl Lichtl, Diabelli's agent at Pest, who caused the second issue to be printed with the German title and the additional remark; and it seems that this issue, or rather part of it, was printed in Vienna at Lichtl's expense. Thereupon another Pest music dealer, Karl Theodor Müller, brought out the Galop separately, without Schubert's or a publisher's name, printed on a single sheet. Lichtl sued him before the city magistrate of Pest on 2nd March 1826. The verdict of 10th April was a caution to Müller. His reprint, reputed to have been confined to a mere twenty-seven copies, is preserved in a single copy in the Budapest City Archives. Schubert is not likely ever to have heard of this petty lawsuit.—It appears that this same Galop was also reprinted in 1826 by Karl Gustav Förster at Breslau; the 'Musikalische Eilpost' of Weimar that year described the Galop published at Breslau as "quite an agreeable trifle."

604. HANS GEORG NÄGELI TO CARL CZERNY

Zürich, 24th November 1825.

The sonata undertaking is to be for our time what the 'Répertoire des Clavecinistes' was a quarter of a century ago. I shall explain myself circumstantially concerning it in a printed circular addressed to composers as well as to the public.

Nägeli, born in 1773 at Wetzikon in the canton of Zürich, a Swiss composer and musical pedagogue, founded his music publishing house at

Zürich in 1791.   Between 1803–11 he had published the fine series mentioned by him, containing the first edition of Beethoven's Sonata in G
major, Op. 31, No. 1.   He was now embarking on a new one, which later
received the name of 'Musical Portal of Honour' ('Musikalische Ehrenpforte,' *see* No. 665).   Three days before he wrote this letter, on 21st
November 1825, Nägeli wrote the preface for his 'Lectures on Music'
(*see* No. 624).

605. ANTON OTTENWALT TO JOSEF VON SPAUN

Vienna, 27th November [1825].

. . . It is said that he [Schober] is planning the publication of
his poems.

He has no following; Schwind is attached to him with absolute
devotion, and Schubert too still likes his company; a certain
Bauernfeld shares his lodgings.

Of Schubert I could tell you nothing that is new to you and to
us; his works proclaim a genius for divine creation, unimpaired
by the passions of an eagerly burning sensuality, and he seems to
have truly devoted sentiments for friends.   He is cheerful and
therefore, I hope, well too. . . . He [Kupelwieser] is . . .
living more by himself,' so that Schubert and Schwind complain
about the good fellow as well as, in general, about the decline
of the old circle.

[Postscript by Marie Ottenwalt:]

At Schober's . . . we spent an evening too, where Schubert
sang quite beautifully and played with Gahy. . . . A young Frau
von Anderes was there, who knows you too; I think her name is
Marie, and she was probably still single then.   About Schubert
I am bound to complain very much, for he did not once come to
see me, which was very noticeable compared with the assiduous
visits of the others, and yet he had seemed so at home with us at
Linz; yet when I saw him again at Schober's, and so friendly, I
could not be angry with him after all: one must make allowances
for such a genius.

The Ottenwalt couple were on a visit to the Wanderers at Nussdorf
(*see* note preceding No. 595).—In the spring of 1826 Schober published
with Max & Co. at Breslau (*see* No. 631) a small volume of poems entitled
'Palingeneses: From Holy Writ of the Old Testament' ('Palingenesien:

Aus den hl. Büchern des alten Bundes'), a series of sonnets on biblical themes.   This brochure was given only the "Transeat" authorization by the Vienna censorship, which meant that it was not allowed to be advertised in the papers.   Later on he added this set to a collection of poems which he submitted to censorship at Pest in 1841, but published at Stuttgart in 1842; a second, somewhat altered edition appeared at Leipzig in 1865.   Apart from this he published nothing during his long life except a pamphlet, 'Letters concerning Liszt's Sojourn in Hungary' (where he had been his secretary), which came out at Berlin in 1843.—Bauernfeld had been living temporarily with Schober since 20th October (see No. 588).—Frau Marie Anderes may be identical with a Frau von André, who held musical drawing-rooms.

606. From Sophie Müller's Diary

6th December 1825.

Jenger brought the Freiburg singer and an excellent flautist with him to-night.   Schubert came too, and so we had music until half-past nine.   A four-handed overture from Schubert's opera and his latest compositions from Walter Scott's 'Lady of the Lake' pleased me much.

Jenger (see No. 308) had just migrated from Graz to Vienna as assistant to the Lower Austrian General Command in the Court War Council.   He came from the Breisgau.   Who was the singer from Freiburg, his compatriot, is not known; perhaps Franz Xaver, Freiherr von Andlau (see No. 935).   The flautist may have been Bogner (see No. 531).—The overture, played by Jenger with Schubert, was doubtless that to 'Alfonso and Estrella' (performed with the 'Rosamond' play in 1823), arranged for four hands by Schubert and published early in 1826 (see No. 628).

607. From the Official 'Wiener Zeitung,' 9th December 1825

At the House of Cappi & Co.,
I. & R. Priv. Art Dealers, in the Graben, No. 1134,
is just published:
The Extremely Good Likeness
of the Composer
Franz Schubert
painted by Rieder.
3 Florins, V.C.

The composer of genius, sufficiently well known to the musical world, who has so often enchanted his hearers with his vocal compositions in particular, appears here, engraved in copper by Herr Passini's cunning hand, as a speaking likeness, and we therefore believe we have presented Schubert's numerous friends and admirers with a welcome gift.

This engraving, which testifies to Schubert's growing fame, was made by Johann Nepomuk Passini (born Vienna, 1798) after Rieder's water-colour of May 1825 (*see* note preceding No. 553).

608. FROM THE OFFICIAL 'WIENER ZEITUNG,' 9th December 1825

At the House of Sauer & Leidesdorf,

I. & R. Privileged Art and Music Dealers in Vienna, Kärntnerstrasse, No. 941, are just published and to be had:

Guirlandes,

as a Christmas and New Year's Present;

Elegantly bound in three books;

containing:

Original Compositions by several Favourite Masters, such as:

Count Gallenberg, Schubert, Pixis, Auguste Louis,

Leidesdorf and others.

Book   I: Compositions for the Pianoforte   . 3 Fl. — Kr.

Book II: Songs with Pianoforte Accompaniment 2 Fl. 30 Kr.

Book III: Various Dances   .   .   .   . 2 Fl. — Kr.

The three books of this collection are not preserved in any known copies; but they only contained pieces from the two annual volumes of the 'Album musical' (*see* Nos. 407 and 510), i.e. the reprints of Schubert's Op. 94, No. 6 (in vol. i), Op. 108, No. 3 (in vol. ii) and xii. 18, No. 2 (in vol. iii). The 'Air russe,' i.e. Op. 94, No. 3, was probably not printed again. It may be supposed that the publisher used the old plates over again for this collection.

609. From Bauernfeld's Diary

10th December 1825.

My relationship with Fick and Spina at last became extremely oppressive to me . . . [Fick's] moral prudery went too far in the end . . . Of Spina I had a sort of horror later on. . . . How different my present circle of friends!

Bauernfeld had been living in 1823–4 with Fick and Spina, friends of his youth (*see* Nos. 271 and 588). They were collaborators in his Shakespeare edition.

610. From Franz von Hartmann's Diary

Linz, 20th December: Spax brings Schubert's splendidly hit-off portrait.

"Spax Maun" was a nickname for Max von Spaun. The portrait is that advertised in No. 607.

611. From the Official 'Wiener Zeitung,' 28th December 1825

At the House of Sauer & Leidesdorf,
I. & R. Privileged Art and Music Dealers in Vienna, Kärntnerstrasse,
No. 941 (Pest, at K. Lichtl's), are newly published and to be had:

DANCES OF GOTHAM FOR THE PIANOFORTE;
['Krähwinkler Tänze für das Pianoforte']
in two Books, with a suitable Vignette; as a Continuation of
the much-favoured
LET'S STICK TOGETHER
['Halt's enk zsamm']

Book I: Waltzes, with black Vignette, 1 Fl. 20 Kr.,
coloured, 1 Fl. 30 Kr., V.C.

Book II: Écossaises and Galops, do., 1 Fl. 20 Kr.,
coloured, 1 Fl. 30 Kr., V.C.

These books, later assembled into a single volume, No. 1 of three volumes, are here mentioned only for the continuation of the series. They

contained nothing by Schubert.   A copy is preserved in the Vienna City
Library.   The title-page shows an anonymous lithograph representing a
game of double meanings (*see* No. 1018).   "Krähwinkler" were the
inhabitants of the imaginary small town of Krähwinkel (like Abdera or
Schilda, or Gotham in English), whose foolishness was derided by jests
of this kind.   Such *Krähwinkeladen* were practised particularly by the
graphic arts.   There is, for instance, an original lithograph by Schwind
on the cover of a pianoforte Trio by Léon de Saint-Lubin entitled 'Das
Konzert in Krähwinkel,' where all the instruments are played the wrong
way round (cf. No. 754).

612. From the Official 'Wiener Zeitung,' 29th December 1825

Just published
and to be had on commission from Sauer & Leidesdorf
(Kärntnerstrasse, No. 941):

Be Welcome for the Second Time!
['Seid uns zum zweiten Mal willkommen!']
(Continuation of the favourite 'Musical Souvenir' for 1825.)

Containing:
50 New Waltzes with Coda,
together with an Introduction on the above Theme from the
'Magic Flute.'

To Her Most Serene I. & R. Highness
The Archduchess Sophie of Austria,
née Princess Royal of Bavaria,
most reverentially dedicated
by
the Editor, K. F. Müller,
composed by
L. van Beethoven, Leopoldine Blahetka, Leopold von Blumenthal,
Leopold Böhm, Karl Czerny, J. Förster, F. Fraus, F. Gläser,
A. Gyrowetz, F. Grutsch, G. Hellmesberger, I. Hirtl, J. Hoffmann,
J. Horzalka, J. Hüttenbrenner, J. N. Hummel, E. Kessler,

J. Kinsky, K. Kreutzer, Karol[ine]. Krähmer, F. Lachner, E.
Freiherr von Lannoy, M. J. Leidesdorf, M. Count von Lichnowsky,
K. G. Lickl, J. F. Limmer, L. de Saint-Lubin, Adolf Müller, K. F.
Müller, Wenzel Müller, F. A. Neumann, M. Pamer, W. Plachy,
J. Preisinger, B. Randhartinger, P. J. Riotte, F. Schubert, M.
Schwarz, I. R[itter]. v[on]. Seyfried, J. Stadler, F. Starke, F.
Stegmayer, J. Triebensee, M. Umlauf, F. Volkert, F. Dionys Weber,
F. Weiss, A. Wranitzky, W. Würfel, J. Zäch.

The especial success gained by the first annual collection of
waltzes by various composers has induced the editor again to issue
this year, by general request, a similar gathering of blossoms from
the musical Hesperides garden of the most esteemed tone-poets
for presentation to the art-loving public.

The eminent name which this collection bears at its head should
be the safest guarantee that no empty phenomenon comes to life
here, which will be proved without further recommendation
by an enumeration of the names of the most considerable composers,
whose procession is led by the Prince of Music, our genius, Beethoven. Moreover, owners of last year's collection will note
that the editor has endeavoured to make this work even more
interesting by the addition of important composers at home and
abroad who were absent from the first issue.

Price, 4 Florins, Vien. Cur.

Also:

SERIOUSNESS AND PLAYFULNESS.

['Ernst und Tändelei']

A Collection of Minuets, Écossaises, Quadrilles,
Cotillons and Galops.

To Her Most Serene I. & R. Highness
The Archduchess Maria Dorothea of Austria,
née Princess of Württemberg,
(Consort to His I. & R. Highness the Archduke Palatine)
most reverentially dedicated
by the Editor, K. F. Müller.

Minuets

by A. Gyrowetz, Baron Lannoy, M. J. Leidesdorf, L. de Saint-Lubin, M. Pamer, F. Weiss.

Écossaises

by L. van Beethoven, Leopoldine Blahetka, Leopold Böhm, Karl Czerny, F. Gläser, I. Hirtl, J. Hüttenbrenner, J. N. Hummel, K. Kreutzer, Karol[ine]. Krähmer, K. F. Müller, Wenzel Müller, W. Plachy, P. J. Riotte, I. R[itter]. v[on]. Seyfried, F. Starke, J. Triebensee, F. Volkert.

Quadrilles

by J. Horzalka, F. Lachner, Adolf Müller, F. A. Neumann, B. Randhartinger, A. Wranitzky.

Cotillons

by L. von Blumenthal, J. Förster, J. Hoffmann, R. Leser, F. Schubert, J. Spoth, Dionys Weber, J. Zäch.

Galops

by F. Grutsch, E. Kessler, F. Limmer, M. Schwarz, J. Stadler, J. Wilde.

At the *thés dansants*, the fashion of to-day, where it is desired that music should be performed merely by amateurs on the grand pianoforte, the need is the more general for a collection uniting all those society dances which serve to enliven sociable circles.

The editor believes he has supplied this need, and although, as in the case of the collection of waltzes, the dedication graciously accepted by Her I. & R. Highness may serve as the best recommendation, the editor feels, this collection being the first of its kind, that he may rely on the support of the musical public to whom he has endeavoured to show his regard by the publication of these two books. Price, 3 florins 30 kreuzer, V.C.

Of the first annual, entitled 'Musical Souvenir for the Year 1825' and containing 40 waltzes by the most esteemed composers, copies are likewise still obtainable at 3 florins, V.C.

The first of these sets is preserved in the National Library in Vienna and in Mr. Anthony van Hoboken's collection at Lausanne. It was published by Müller himself (*see* No. 121), who also brought out its predecessor (*see* No. 531). The title is, of course, a quotation from 'The Magic Flute': these words open the trio of the genii in the second act.—The Archduchess Sophie, born in 1805, married to the Archduke Franz Karl the preceding year, was later the Emperor Francis Joseph's mother.—Leopold von Blumenthal, a brother of Josef's (*see* No. 482), was a violinist at Pressburg.—Franz Josef Gläser (*see* No. 482), born in 1799 at Ober-Georgental in Bohemia, was stage conductor at various theatres, at that time at the Josefstadt Theatre; in 1824 Diabelli published an 'Erl King' march from his comic fairy play 'Der Erlenkönig' (cf. No. 236).— Of Ignaz Hirtl no details are known.—Josef Kinsky (actually Kinky), born in 1789 at Olomouc in Moravia, was conductor at the County Theatre of Graz.—Karoline Krähmer, *née* Schleicher in 1794 at Constance, the wife of the oboist Ernst Krähmer (*see* No. 220), played the clarinet.—Adolf Müller, sen., born in 1801 at Tolna in Hungary, had lived in Vienna since 1823, became a singer at the Kärntnertor Theatre in 1826 and conductor at the Theater an der Wien in 1828, where in 1834 he produced a grand romantic drama, 'The Erl King, or The Vow,' with a moving dream-tableau (shifting scenery long before Wagner's 'Parsifal'), using Schubert's song arranged for chorus and orchestra.—Josef Triebensee, born in Vienna in 1760, was oboist and theatre conductor, formerly at Brno and later in Prague.—Wilhelm Wenzel Würfel, born in 1791 at Planian in Bohemia, had been musical director at the Kärntnertor since 1820 and became conductor-in-chief there in 1828.—Josef Zäch was an amateur violinist. —Some of the names cannot be identified.—Schubert's contribution, No. 37, was a waltz, not reprinted till 1st December 1925, in the 'Moderne Welt' in Vienna.—The second of these collective books is preserved in two copies: by the National Library in Vienna and by the Vienna Philharmonic Society.—The Archduchess Maria Dorothea, born in 1800, was the third consort of the Archduke Josef, Viceroy of Hungary.—Of Robert Leser no details are known.—Josef Spoth, a son of the Bohemian musician Josef Nikolaus Spoth, was organist at the Karl church in Vienna.—Schubert's contribution was No. 5 of these forty-four dances, a cotillon (xii. 22).—The title-page enumerates 6 minuets, 6 quadrilles, 6 (instead of 18) écossaises, 8 cotillons and 6 galops, in that order.

613. FROM A CONCERT PROGRAMME (? about 1825)

Musical pieces represented:

· · · · · ·

3. 'Spirit of Love' ['Geist der Liebe'], by Matthisson, set to music by Franz Schubert, sung by Herren Gottfried, Tietze, Nejebse and Edler von Mayer.

· · · · · ·

5. 'Spring Song' ['Frühlingsgesang'], set to music by Franz Schubert, sung by the above-mentioned gentlemen.

· · · · · ·

The whole under the direction of Herr Clement.

Danhauser (*see* No. 388) played Variations by Mayseder on the violin. —Vincenz Franz Gottfried may be identical with a choir-boy who was at the Seminary a year before Schubert and later became a merchant; he sang tenor.—For Clement *see* No. 513.

The Vienna Shakespeare Edition. Title Vignette of the Quarto Issue (1826). Drawing by Moritz von Schwind, lithographed by Jakob Hyrtl. *See* p. 462

Schubert and Vogl performing a Song.   Pen-and-ink
Drawing by Moritz von Schwind.   Cf. Plate facing
p. 784

1826

String Quartet in D minor ('Death and the Maiden') (v. 14), March
    1824—January 1826.
String Quartet in G major (v. 15), 20th–30th June.
'Rondo brillant' for Pianoforte and Violin (viii. 1).
3 Shakespeare Songs, including 'Hark, hark' and 'Who is Silvia?', July.
Sonata in G major (x. 12), October.
'Songs for the Celebration of the Holy Rite of the Mass' (so-called
    "German Mass") (xiii. 7).

---

614. Bauernfeld's Skit on the Schubert Circle
(Read at Schober's on New Year's Eve 1826.)

The Outcasts

(An attempt to Represent a Dumb-Show in Words,
in 3 Acts and a Prologue.)

Prologue

(The personages in the dumb-show are seen through a glass door,
gathered in a sorrowful group.)

(Enter the Theatre Manager [Trentsensky] and the Poet
[Bauernfeld] of the play.)

Poet: My dear sir, you have decided and resolved, then, to
dismiss the worthy actors in your dumb-show?

Manager: That is so, sir. They may still draw this month's pay,
and then they may see for themselves how they get on. Sorry as
I am for this branch of our art, I cannot do otherwise. Once and
for all, the public does not like monotony, and my box-office
cannot do with empty houses.

Poet: You will not think it unnatural in me to take an interest
in these excellent people, and not wonder at my being more than
a little pained to know them all to be penniless. At the same time
I have your advantage at heart, my dear sir. If only I could find
means of satisfying both interests!

Mana.: Where could you discover such means? Faith, I cannot live without money. If only these wretched dumb-show actors were less one-sided! Admit it, sir.

Poet: True, true.—But will you not give me some hope to take them back when circumstances change?

Mana.: Dear me! I shall be heartily glad to do all I can; and believe me, I find it hard myself to part with people to whom I have been accustomed for years. If only they had more versatility!

Poet: There are excellent talents among them. Indeed, I seem to have noticed a particular versatility in one or two of them. That Pantaloon from Przelavtsch especially—I shall be very much surprised if there is not a world-shaking gift in that man.

Mana.: Very well, then. Take them under your wing; see what you can do with them. If they have studied other branches of dramatic art, I shall welcome them. If I find that something comes of it, my support shall not be wanting.

Poet (embracing him): Most excellent man! I am infinitely obliged to you. You are the paragon of all managers, and the history of art will gratefully set your name next to those of the stars of the stage!—I look into the future: that noble unselfishness of yours will bear the most glorious fruit for the whole nation. Many an undeveloped great talent will ripen in the gentle sun of your fatherly generosity. You will have the reputation of having formed none but Garricks and Schröders.

Mana.: But see to it that these people really do something. In their own lives, among themselves, they must practise; their whole life must be a continual drama. For that I rely wholly on you.

Poet: Pray, have no fear that . . .

Mana.: They are not all equally industrious. I believe in that Pantaloon, and Harlequin may pass, but I am afraid for Pierrot: he is likely to give way to his laziness too readily. And the womenfolk are not what they should be either, by a long way. However, as I say, I rely on you . . .

Poet: You may rest assured.

Mana. Be their producer; try to bring home to them the dignity of their calling.—Well, you know all this better than I.

Poet: Most excellent man! You are the most important; but I shall do all that lies in my poor powers, needless to say.—Come hither, you pleasant artists, you harmless creatures! Embrace the knees of the kindest manager on earth, and praise his gracious and noble ways with clamorous hymns!

(The dumb-show actors approach the glass door.)

Mana.: Leave that alone, pray! Anything but a sentimental scene! Besides, I have a rehearsal. (Exit hastily.)

(The Poet follows him with raised hands, motioning to the dumb-show actors to follow him.)

Curtain.

THE DUMB-SHOW ACTORS' LIFE

Dramatis Personae:

Pantaloon of Przelavtsch [Schober of Breslau]
Harlequin [Schwind]
Pierrot [Schubert]
Columbine's [II] Betrothed [Mayerhofer]
Columbine [I, Anna Hönig]
Another Columbine [II, Jeannette von Mitis]
Supernumeraries

Act I

Scene i

(Pantaloon, lying in bed and smoking a very long pipe.)

Scene ii
(Enter Harlequin.)

Pantaloon of Przelavtsch: Good morning to you.
Harlequin: The same to you.
Pant.: Fill a pipe.

(Harlequin does so.)
(They smoke. Pause.)

Harl.: As a matter of fact, great Pantaloon, I have come to discuss something with you.

488

Pant.: Speak out, dear Harlequin. You know that there is no end to my endeavour to contribute to your development.

Harl.: Who does not know what you have done to shape me? And yet I regret that I am still such an unpolished lout.

Pant.: There you do yourself an injustice, my good Harlequin. A certain unconstrained behaviour suits your fresh youth, though the common herd may not have the refinement to distinguish it from boorishness.

Harl.: Not that I really mind.—But let me come to the point. —You see, I do not know whether you have noticed it yet; I am not indifferent towards Columbine.

Pant.: Noticed it? Believe me, your inner fibres have some sort of unfathomable connection with mine: if a nerve of yours is touched, I seem to feel it.

Harl.: Thank you.—But look here: I simply cannot do without the girl, and yet I would not for anything fall in love with her, if it should displease you.

Pant.: Fall in love? And why just that? Can you not have some other relationship with her? Must I recall my own example to you?

Harl.: Well, if you only knew—little Columbine is too, too charming.

Pant.: I admit she is attractive, although you do not see things properly. For there's not a doubt of it, her bosom lacks the buxom fullness and roundness that is absolutely indispensable to a Columbine. You should have seen our Columbine at Przelavtsch!

Harl.: But, you see . . .

Pant.: And then her manner is too close, too—how shall I put it?—too little forthcoming, in a word, too self-contained. Her steps are too short by a third at least. Altogether, I should not care to praise her figure. The worst of it all is, really, that, to judge by the general proportions of her body, her thighs are certainly two inches too short.

Harl.: Oh, fie, fie! Who'd think such things?

Pant.: Where it is a matter of perfection, no detail is negligible. —Moreover, I am afraid this love does not a little to keep you from training your talents. You are no doubt a Harlequin who will one day draw the admiration of the world upon himself, and if our injudicious manager lets you slip through his fingers now, imprudently enough, you will be all the more stared at by all and sundry later on, provided that your gifts mature, a thing for which peace and incessant studies are needed.

Harl.: Yes, but Columbine . . . ?

Pant.: Visit her, talk to her, live with her, but do not make her the centre of your being.   You dally too much.

Harl.: I 'd rather be no Harlequin than one without Columbine.

Pant.: That is just what I blame in you: that Columbine means more to you than art, more than I.

Harl.: Never believe that.   If you ask it, I will give her up . . . only she is too, too pleasant.

Pant.: You are not aware yourself that she has already absorbed you entirely.   You no longer have any regard for your talent and your training.

Harl.: What an idea!

Pant.: Believe me.

Scene iii

(Enter Pierrot.)

Pant.: Look, here 's Pierrot!—Would you like to smoke? Here, lie on the floor next to Harlequin.

Pier.: No sooner said than done!—To tell you the truth, it is very tiresome, not knowing what to do.

Harl.: We are supposed to train.

Pier.: Train?   I am trained enough for a Pierrot, and I shan't become anything else.   I shall not let any one take off my wide trousers.

Pant.: There you are right, and I shall not alter my way of life either, as I was used to it at Przelavtsch, not by a hair's breadth.

Pier.: If I don't know what else to do, I drink, and when I 've drunk, I go to sleep.

(They laugh.)

Pant.: It 's easy for you.   Your art really consists of nothing but long, measureless strides in time to the music, of huge grimaces and an enormous laugh fetched up from the depth of your chest. It isn't easy to forget these things. But for little Harlequin to learn all those quips and cranks, those somersaults, those hand-stands and aerial flights, that tripping and trembling, that rolling and spinning, takes endless time and trouble, and almost as much is needed to keep in practice.

Pier.: Ha, ha! Harlequin, yours is a hard calling.

Pant.: I am not afraid for him, if only love does not play him any pranks.

Pier.: I know, Columbine.

Pant.: How do you like her, Pierrot?

Pier.: She is not so bad.

Pant.: Of course not; but who goes and loses his head immediately over every girl who isn't so bad?

Pier.: Ha, ha, ha, ha! Our Harlequin is an amorous fellow!

(They laugh and smoke; then Harlequin practises a little. The scene changes.)

Scene iv

(The second Columbine and Anselmo, her betrothed.)

Columbine II: My beloved, I do not know whether it is as sweet a sensation for you to be betrothed as it is for me.

Anselmo: Oh, most certainly, dearest Columbine; I would not change it for any sensation in the world!

Col. II: You dear, good fellow!—Come, give me a kiss!—Give me another kiss!—Give me yet another kiss!

Ans.: What a sweet little rogue you are!

Col. II: My Anselmo, if you only knew how I should love to marry you!

Ans.: Oh, believe me, I you too, no less.

Col. II: No, you cannot possibly have such an urge and such a talent for it as I. I have a veritable rage for marriage.

Ans.: If only that cursed manager had not taken my bread away! For I don't set much store by his promises. We shall have to go on being betrothed for some time yet, no doubt.

Col. II: No matter—it's not bad either.

491

Ans.: You splendid girl!—Now you shall kiss me for a change.

Col. II: And now you me.

Ans.: And you me.

Col. II: You me.

(They exchange kisses.)

Ans.: I wish you were not always knitting.

Col. II: But look here, my good Anselmo, you have feet on which you have to come to me, and those feet must have whole stockings, after all . . .

Ans.: I know, I know, but . . .

Col. II: Come, come, these are indiscreet thoughts. You have made them a habit in the rather unceremonious company of Pantaloon and Harlequin.

Ans.: You 'll make me angry. Didn't I explain to you . . .?

Col. II: Yes, well, but you are much colder with me.

Ans.: The idea!

Col. II: Well, never mind. But you must come and see me nice and often.

Ans.: Never fear.—But let me go now. I have new hopes for us. They say a god has arrived these days to whom I have been warmly recommended. I hope he will do something for me. Good-bye.

Col. II: Good-bye. You 'll come back soon?

Ans.: In half an hour.

(They kiss.)

Col. II: I shall accompany you as far as the stairs.

(Exeunt.)

Scene v

(Pantaloon's Room.)

(He lies in bed ⟨still or again⟩, smoking and thinking. A knock.)
Pant. Enter!

Scene vi

(Enter the Poet.)

Poet: Good morning, dear Mr. Pantaloon. Well, do you think you will soon be able to do something for our stage?

Pant.: I think that while we develop life, we develop the stage with it imperceptibly. And I am bound to confess to you that I am myself very near to exposing clearly an important conception of life by my own example and teaching.

Poet: Excellent, excellent! You know how much I have always thought of you. Do what you can, only you must try to incite the other people too. I know there are talents among them.

Pant.: Great talents! I suppose you have brought our pay with you?

Poet: Yes; but I had not a little trouble to talk the manager into giving it to me. He swore till all was blue it would be the last if he were not soon to see results.

Pant.: Where have you got the money?

Poet: In this purse.

Pant.: Good. Give it to me.—I must tell you, I 'm not averse to writing a tragedy.

Poet: Pray do so; we can expect nothing but glorious things from your pen.

Pant.: I had a plan even before I left for Przelavtsch. I shall write it down at the first opportunity.

Poet: Only do it soon, very soon!

Pant.: Quite soon.

Poet: I wish you good day.

Pant.: Your servant.

(Exit the Poet.)

Scene vii
(Pantaloon alone. He continues to think.)

Scene viii
(Enter Harlequin, Pierrot and Anselmo.)

(Greetings, whereupon Pantaloon makes the following speech:)

Pant.: I must tell you, my friends, that although all human endeavour is remarkable, and I did more than any one, both here and during my stay at Przelavtsch, to get to know it all and to take part in most of it, only now, in the course of my studies, has the inmost and highest meaning of life become perfectly clear and intelligible to me.   For I see the true significance of life in repose. Do not misunderstand me: not in that dead repose and insensibility which characterizes stone, although its more noble species show by the sparkle of their colours that they lead a true inward and spiritual existence—but be that as it may—the symbol of the repose I mean is a plant.   It remains in that place on earth where the radiance of the sun and the fertilizing spring of water has lured it forth, and by no arbitrary movement does it disturb the highest harmony of its tender being.   To the friendly Zephyr alone it allows to rock it in the glorious morning air and to accompany the pensive magic of its thought with a softly whispering breath. A Boreas, too, may uproot it, like Fate's mighty arm, and hurl it raging to the four winds.   But it does not move from its place of its own will: it toils not, neither does it spin—it only allows us to behold it.   But do not think therefore that it wants motion or lacks inward life.   It dispenses odours all around — that is its motion—nay, it even lends itself to action, though only one single action, as indeed there only is *one* action: namely, it permits its male seed to mingle with the female, and thus to procreate its pure, glorious, divine race.   This, ye friends, shall henceforth be my life.   I disdain position, occupation, industry.   On this bed I shall remain lying, on my flower-bed—nothing shall disturb me—I shall receive mankind purely spiritually and thus react upon it.   Business, however spiritual, is unworthy of me—only the eternal substance of man and of woman shall I keep ever before me, and so lead back life to its pure, primeval condition.

Ans.: Very original, I must say, . . . very fine and true!

Harl.: Oh, glorious, divine, superhuman!

Pier.: Ah, that is really extraordinary!

Harl.: Unheard-of, immense!—Well, now you will soon have your great tragedy finished?

Pant.: What are you thinking of?   Writing a tragedy, too, is an action, and therefore below my dignity.

Harl.: But I thought . . .

Pant.: It may be possible—in fact I gave some hope to the poet,

494

but, as I say, only as a matter of secondary importance and as an insignificant study.

Harl.: Even so, it is and remains extraordinary.

Pier.: Yes, indeed.

Ans.: I hope to see you before long, dear Pantaloon; I am only going to see my Columbine for a short time.

Pant.: Until later, then.

Pier.: I too have some small business.   I am coming with you.— We shall meet at the ale-house, shall we not?

Pant.: In my opinion, I shall no longer visit any ale-house, for I shall not move away from my bed.   So you had better all come to me.

Pier. and Ans.: We shall.

Harl.: I shall come a little earlier.   Meanwhile, good-bye, excellent Pantaloon.   I shall endeavour to form my ideas after your great thoughts.   Farewell!

Pant.: Good-bye, good-bye!

(Exeunt Harlequin, Pierrot and Anselmo.   Pantaloon remains
in bed.)

Curtain.

ACT II

Scene i

(Enter Manager and Poet.)

Mana.: Well, how goes it with our people?

Poet: I hope all will go well.

Mana.: So do I; all the same, they will be put on half-pay.

Poet: Those excellent artists?

Mana.: They are too poetical for me; such fantastic people must not be encouraged.

Poet: As you think.

Mana.: Believe me, I know the ropes.

(Exeunt.)

495

Scene ii

(Harlequin and Columbine I ⟨but not on the Alps⟩.)

Har.: You know his grand, all-conquering manner.

Col.: I should like to call him father.

Harl.: In the dumb-show you are actually his daughter.

Col.: Yes, but he tries to tear you from me.

Harl.: Only in the dumb-show?

Col.: No, in reality . . .

Harl.: What's the matter with you?

Col.: Very foolish lovers, indeed—and I do not know if I am right to treat them all so scornfully.

Harl.: Oh, certainly!

Col.: Dear Harlequin, you are too intolerant. I have been alarmed about them more than once.

Harl.: But my dear little Columbine, ought you to have none of the art of ill-treating those fellows.

Col.: No.

Harl.: But it must be done.

Col.: My conscience pricks me sometimes, when I have looked askance at one of them.

Harl.: You will have to get out of that.

Col.: If only I can!

Harl. (taking her by the lobe of the ear): Well, well, it must be done!

Col. (skipping): Cannot, cannot!

Harl. (hopping): Must, must, must!

Col. (skipping): No, no, no!

Harl. (gliding): Yes, yes, yes!

(They laugh and pull each other by the hands. Then exit Columbine.)

Scene iii

Harl. (alone): She's nice enough to eat—but not to marry. I should go mad with joy if I were her real lover—and yet, it is a hard thing to find all we want in one of them. *Vedremo!* (Exit.)

Scene iv

Pant. (in dressing-gown and slippers): I ache a little on one side from lying down. Well, it's possible to lead a worthy life even in a dressing-gown. (Smokes.)

Scene v

(Columbine II and Anselmo.)

Ans.: The god has not come yet, and if I do not receive any adequate pay, at least I can be idle for compensation.

Col. II: You know what, my dearest, we can try to give each other a thousand kisses to-day. I shall make a mark after each tenth, if you agree.

Ans.: That suits me.

Col. II: Go ahead, then. (They begin.)

Scene vi

(Harlequin and a Rabble of Louts.)

Harl.: Well now, you understand that Pantaloon is the greatest man the world has ever produced?

Louts: We do.

Harl.: Then go your ways and incommode somebody else with your visit; I think I have contributed enough to the entertainment of society.

Louts: We thank you, dear Harlequin. (Exeunt.)

Harl.: These oafs are proper loons. (Exit into his room.)

Scene vii

(A hall at the naked lady's.)

(There is a gathering of people seated between Harlequin and Pierrot, who allow themselves by turns to be led about by the nose by them.)

Scene viii

(Pantaloon lying in bed. Harlequin and Pierrot sit with him, smoking.)

Pier.: That seems to me rather a mouthful.

Pant.: Not at all.

Harl.: You might allow yourself to be let in for that.

Pier.: That really is queer! Why shouldn't a man . . ., it 's the most natural thing in the world, after all.

Pant.: For you, Harlequin, and for all the others with whose inward disposition it is not at variance, although it would be easy to prove that p—— is not the duty of any man whatever. For if we are created for living, all the conditions of living must be given us at the same time, and there must be no disturbances either in our spiritual or in our physical functions; therefore we are under no obligation to make any effort to eliminate impurities from our bodies.

Pier.: Then in the end we should not even be allowed to drink.

Pant.: Certainly not.

Pier.: But I like it.

Pant.: Then it 's your duty.

Harl.: It is doubtless merely a spirit of contradiction that prevents you from doing, or rather not doing, that which it makes you ill to omit doing.

Pant.: Not at all: it is against my inner conviction.

Harl.: Here comes our manager.

Scene ix

(Enter Manager and Poet.)

Mana.: Nice goings-on! A pretty kettle of fish! There is the other Columbine and that fine fellow, her lover, both taken ill. They wanted to give each other a thousand kisses and got as far as the nine hundredth; but they became so heated that it was like cross-firing in the end—crash, bang, crash, bang! Fortunately we both intervened. We tore them apart. Now they are prostrated and miserable, with lips swollen as high as steeples.—Now, and about you, gentlemen?—How, Pantaloon, still in bed? What about the promised training?

Poet: Only give him time.

Pant.: My dear manager, cherish no hope that I shall ever tread your boards again.

Mana.: Indeed?

498

Pant.: For quite apart from the fact that dumb-show by far surpasses your stage, I have given up all acting now.

Mana.: Indeed!

Pant.: What 's more, all this has made me ill.

Mana.: Begad! Devil take all these confounded comedians!—But let me tell you, not another groat shall you get from me, not a groat! And furthermore, if there 's any justice left in this world, I shall wheedle back my advances out of you . . .

Poet.: My dear man . . .

Mana.: You keep quiet! For you are the cause of my having again had dealings with this riff-raff. A pox on you all! (Exit at a run.)

Pant.: Follow him and try to pacify him!

Poet: I will do what I can. (Exit.)

Pant.: What shall we do with our good Anselmo and his betrothed? If he is really ill, we shall have to visit him. I shall get myself carried there and first perform that action which human frailty seems to necessitate.

Harl.: Heaven be praised! (Exeunt omnes.)

Scene x

(Columbine II and Anselmo lie at the last gasp.)

Col. II: My Anselmo!

Ans.: Dearest Columbine!

Col. II: Give me your hand!

Scene xi

(Enter Pantaloon, Pierrot and Harlequin.)

Harl.: But, my dear children!

Col. II: You arrive to witness our end, Harlequin.

Harl.: Oh, surely not!

Pant.: Kissing has probably excited their living spirits too much and caused an inflammation of the soul. I have seen a similar case at Przelavtsch.

Harl.: Their souls have caught the rheumatics.

Pier.: Ha, ha, ha!

499

Col. II: If we die together, as we must assume, the world will have an example of true and pure love before it.

Pant.: I do not think it's very dangerous: take a homoeopathic cure.

Col. II.: O my Anselmo!

Scene xii

(Enter Columbine I.)

Col. I: What do they tell me? Dear Columbine . . .

Col. II: How good of you not to forsake me. You see before you the victims of true love.

Col. I: Good heavens! this is truly dreadful. You here too, Harlequin?

Harl.: Good evening, dear Columbine.

Pant.: My friends!—We may no longer stand before this thing as idle spectators. For firstly, these are our best friends who suffer, and moreover the same fate that made them wretched is also the source of their misery. I therefore cannot doubt that it would be wrong, nay in a certain sense criminal, to deny them the help they seem so sorely to need. I am convinced that you share the feelings which overwhelm me at the sight of these unhappy victims of the purest passion, and I therefore have the less doubt that you will prove willing.

(Columbine II and Anselmo give up the ghost.)

Dear Columbine, dear friend Anselmo, I thus propose to you to have you carried to my lodgings, where you will receive more care and comfort than anywhere else in the world.

Harl.: They do not answer.

Col.I: Heavens! they are dead.

Pant.: Is it possible?

Harl.: Sit down, Columbine; you will have an attack of nerves.

Pant.: An excellent pair!—He was an admirable fellow, although, if the matter is carefully weighed, he did not really love Columbine: she was for him rather a compensation for some lost wordly goods, a kind of symbol, a sort of moral currency.—But Columbine was all love, all devotion, and although a certain sentimentality might be blamed in her, she nevertheless expressed herself through it in a way to which no blame attached.

Harl.: But come, we will do our friends the last honours.

(Exeunt omnes.)

Curtain.

ACT III

(Pantaloon's Apotheosis.)

He is laid on a high sofa and a long pipe is placed into his hand. Harlequin at his feet with a spill. Enter Pierrot with a chorus of smokers. At a given sign all the pipes are lighted. A crowd fills the stage. Accompaniment of suitable music.

The End.

Cf. No. 615. The identification of the characters given there is supplemented in the manuscript of this "skit," which is really a satire, by the remark that the betrothed intended for the second Columbine is Mayerhofer, who, however, in 1832 married the first. It is a matter of tradition that the Theatre Manager was Trentsensky, who brought out the Vienna Shakespeare edition, and that the Poet was Bauernfeld himself, who later became a good writer of comedy.—Schubert was prevented by illness from being present on that New Year's Eve; he probably read the satire later on. It is important not only because it characterizes him, but also on account of Schober, at any rate as regards Bauernfeld's view and mockery of them both.—Przelavtsch is an arbitrary Slavism for Breslau, the place where Schober had been living for two years.—Friedrich Ludwig Schröder was about as famous as a Shakespearian actor on the German stage of the eighteenth century as Garrick was in England. —Jeannette von Mitis, the sister of one of Bauernfeld's schoolfellows, was until the autumn of 1829 engaged to be married to the military surveyor Ferdinand, Freiherr von Mayerhofer (see No. 528).—Schwind is represented as the wooer of Anna Hönig and slavishly devoted to Schober, who had to give up Justina von Bruchmann in 1824.—Schwind had endeavoured early to master the graphic representation of soaring, and occasionally that of acrobatics.—The scenic direction "but not on the Alps" (ii, ii) is inexplicable.—The louts are doubtless the unwelcome members of the former reading-circle.—The "naked lady" may be Katharina Lászny, but the allusion is obscure.—The fact that Bauernfeld

was able to read his satire to Schober shows that the latter had enough
sense of humour to bear being made fun of.   (In a comic drawing that has
never been explained, made by Schwind in 1849, Schober appears as
Harlequin and Schwind as Pierrot, *see* iconographical volume, p. 269.)

615. FROM BAUERNFELD'S DIARY

2nd January 1826.

New Year's Eve at Schober's, without Schubert, who was ill.
A dramatic parody on all the male and female friends read after
midnight, with great success.   Moritz appears in it as Harlequin,
Netti as Columbine.   Schober is Pantaloon, Schubert Pierrot.
—Moritz and I slept at Schober's, and I remained with him until
midday.

What was wrong with Schubert is not known; probably it was only a
passing indisposition.

The Galop and 8 Écossaises, Op. 49, are performed, arranged for
orchestra, in the hall "The Seven Electors" in Pest, 6th January
1826.—*See* note to No. 603.

616. NISSEN TO STADLER

Salzburg, 7th January 1826.

Forgive me for assaulting you again.   But one is so important
to oneself, and my present wish is so innocent.   True, I have no
right to burden you with its fulfilment; but you have been so
courteous to me that I could not fail to detect therein one of your
chief inclinations.

You had the goodness to apprise me that I should come across
a certain song in any music shop.   But that is certainly not the case
in the Salzburg one.   All that they offer me is Schubert's Op. 13,
which however contains nothing (apart from two other songs)
but the 'Alpine Hunter' *by Mayrhofer*.

With your permission I shall therefore repeat my request to
take the trouble, if it is feasible for you (and if you have the words
and music at hand or in your memory), to [address yourself] to

some convenient cop[yist] or other and to send me a copy, with or
without the music, of the 2 or 3 strophes sung by the mother
(only what the mother sings, including, I believe, the first: "Wilt
thou not the lambkin guard?").

In order to save unnecessary postage expenses, the copy or
copies might be on the same paper which contains your accompanying letter, thus obviating all enclosures and envelope.

Kindest greetings from me and my wife to you and all our other
good acquaintances at Linz.

Cf. No. 597.—Schubert had set Mayrhofer's 'Alpine Hunter,' as well
as Schiller's, in 1817, but the former had appeared already at the end of
1822 (*see* No. 330), as No. 3 in Op. 13.

Josef Ludwig Streinsberg marries Isabella von Bruchmann, 7th
January 1826.—Streinsberg, who had returned from Linz in 1824,
was now an official in the General Court Chamber.

616A. Bauernfeld to Seidl

10th January [1826].

Schubert will come to-night [to Schober's in the Bäckerstrasse].
You are hereby invited to a "feast of song."

This note might also have been written in 1827, for Schober lived in
the Obere Bäckerstrasse with his mother from the autumn of 1825 until
February 1827. But Schubert was in close touch with Seidl in 1826:
it was then that he wrote most of his settings of Seidl's poems.

617. From Sophie Müller's Diary

11th January 1826.

In the evening Desprès, Wedekind, Betty Schröder, Scherer,
Ditz, Jenger, Teltscher. There was singing. 'Evening,' quartet
by Hüttenbrenner, a duet by Carafa, a duet by Schubert, an aria
by Rossini, 'Suleika,' 'Maid of the Mill' songs, until 9.30, then
I had Betty driven home. Teltscher brought Schubert lithographed.

This party had been postponed from 10th to 11th January because Betty Schröder was detained (*see* No. 541).—Margarete ("Gretl") Desprès was a friend of Sophie Müller's; so were Sophie Wedekind and Charlotte ("Lotti") Scherer, an indigent colleague.—Ditz is probably a mistake for Tietze.—Josef Teltscher, born in Prague in 1801, was a very gifted portraitist. He was skilled in lithography, water-colour and miniature painting on ivory. He became a good friend of Schubert's, of whom he made several portraits, including the lithograph mentioned here. Among his sitters was the Countess Karoline Esterházy.—'Evening' ('Der Abend'), a vocal quartet for S.A.T.B. to words by Johann Karl Unger (cf. No. 226), had already been sung at one of the Philharmonic Society's evening entertainments on 19th November 1818 by Karoline Unger, Marie Mathilde Weiss, Mozatti and Nestroy before Anselm Hüttenbrenner published it himself in 1823; it had also become known at Zseliz.—Michele Carafa, born in 1787, was the composer of the opera 'Gabriella di Vergy,' which reached Vienna in 1824.—The Schubert duet may have been 'Mignon and the Harper,' composed that month.

618. From the Programme of the Ninth Evening Entertainment held by the Philharmonic Society, 12th January 1826

2. 'Restless Love' ['Rastlose Liebe'] by Goethe, set to music by Schubert, performed by Herr [Josef] Illem.

On 23rd February Kreutzer's setting of the same poem was sung there. —Illem organized a funeral ceremony for Schubert at Linz on 27th December 1828.

619. From Bauernfeld's Diary

16th January 1826.

The day before yesterday sausage ball at Schober's. Schubert had to play waltzes.

A sausage ball (*Würstelball*) was a dance entertainment at which, instead of the usual supper, sausages were served to the men by the ladies (who no doubt had some themselves). The sausages, which were strung in pairs and eaten hot, were called "Frankforters" in Vienna, where they were introduced about 1810, while at Frankfort o/M. they were "Vienna sausages."

620. FROM THE OFFICIAL 'WIENER ZEITUNG,' 20th January 1826

At the House of Sauer & Leidesdorf in Vienna,
Kärntnerstrasse, No. 941, is to be had by commission:

FIFTY NEW WALTZES,
Edited and dedicated with profoundest respect and submission
to her I. & R. Highness, the most exalted
Archduchess Sophie of Austria,
née Princess Royal of Bavaria,
by K. F. Müller,
composed by 50 of the most excellent tone-poets, among whom are
L. van Beethoven, Karl Czerny, J. N. Hummel, F. Schubert, together with a Coda by Franz Lachner.

Price, 4 Florins, V.C.

Further:
SERIOUSNESS AND PLAYFULNESS
a Collection of Various Sociable Dances,
Edited and dedicated with profoundest respect and submission
to Her I. & R. Highness, the most exalted
Archduchess Maria Dorothea of Austria,
née Princess of Württemberg,
by K. F. Müller,
likewise by the most excellent composers.

These "Fifty New Waltzes" are identical with the set "Be Welcome
for the Second Time!" published, like its companion volume, at the end
of 1825 (*see* No. 612). It is interesting to note that Schubert's name is
emphasized as that of one of the four best-known pianoforte composers
among fifty. The coda to the first book, by the way, was not mentioned
before.

621. FROM SOPHIE MÜLLER'S DIARY

24th January 1826.
Teltscher, Jenger and Hüttenbrenner came at midday; they
brought me the lithographed portrait of Schubert.

Hüttenbrenner is Josef.—Sophie Müller soon afterwards had a lithographed portrait of herself made by Teltscher.

622. FROM SOPHIE MÜLLER'S DIARY

25th January 1826.

Call, Jenger and Schubert ate here. The last sang new songs from Ernst Schulze poems composed by him.

Karl, Freiherr von Call, born in 1771 at Eppau in the Tyrol, was a gallant major.—Schubert had set three songs from Schulze's 'Poetic Diary' (*see* No. 475) about New Year: 'To my Heart' ('An mein Herz'), 'The Lovely Star' ('Der liebliche Stern') and (in January) 'Deep Sorrow' ('Tiefes Leid'); there were others before and after.

First rehearsal of the D minor Quartet (v. 14) at the brothers Karl (violin) and Franz (viola) Hacker's, Schönlaterngasse, No. 673, third floor, with Josef Hauer (violin) and the Court Opera violoncellist Bauer, under Schubert's direction and from freshly copied parts still requiring frequent corrections. Listeners: Anton Holzapfel and Benedikt Randhartinger. 29th January 1826.

Second rehearsal of the D minor Quartet, 30th January 1826. This Quartet, with variations on the song 'Death and the Maiden' for its second movement, had been begun as early as March 1824, but was only now finished. At the rehearsal Schubert cut part of the first movement and made other alterations.—Franz Hacker was a law student; his brother Karl died early, in 1830.—Josef Hauer, born in 1802, who had also been at the City Seminary (near the Schönlaterngasse), was studying medicine and later became physician to a factory at Öd near Leobersdorf in Lower Austria. He was a great lover of music, collected first editions and helped Köchel with his Mozart catalogue. His daughter Ottilie, who married one Ebner and was a good amateur singer, later became a friend of Brahms.—Holzapfel (*see* No. 67) was otherwise no longer in touch with Schubert.

623. FROM THE 'THEATERZEITUNG,' 31st January 1826

(Concerning the dance-music collections 'Be Welcome for the Second Time' and 'Seriousness and Playfulness.')

We find as coryphaei the immortal Beethoven, . . . Hummel, and names like Karl Czerny, Gläser, Gyrowetz, Hellmesberger, Kreutzer, Lannoy, Leidesdorf, Würfel, Riotte, Schubert, Seyfried,

Umlauf, &c. and those of so many other favourite composers in good repute throughout the country . . .

R——t.

Schubert receives 300 florins, V.C., from Matthias Artaria, as a fee for the D major Sonata (Op. 53) and the *Divertissement à la hongroise* (Op. 54), 31st January 1826. Nottebohm, who saw Matthias Artaria's cash-book (*see* note preceding No. 598), expressly says "W.W." (Viennese currency). The payment was made on Schubert's birthday.

Ambros Rieder's 'Preludes and Fughettas for the Organ or the Pianoforte,' Op. 82, appear, "respectfully dedicated to the valued composer, Herr Franz Schubert," early 1826.

Schubert's Sonata in A minor, Op. 42, published by A. Pennauer, with a dedication to Cardinal Rudolph, Archduke of Austria, early 1826.—The work had already been prepared for publication in the autumn of 1825 (*see* No. 573), but was advertised only in the spring of 1827 (*see* No. 833); the criticism No. 632 and its mention in Schubert's letter No. 670 prove, however, that it must have appeared near the beginning of 1826 at the latest, though delayed (? by the authorization form). A brown cover bears the title of 'Bibliothèque musicale de nos contemporains. Recueil de compositions originales pour Pianoforte . . . Nr.1.' The description on the title-page, which names "François Schubert de Vienne," as "Première grande Sonate" should be compared with that of the pianoforte duet Sonata in B flat major, Op. 30 (*see* No. 417).

624. FROM NÄGELI'S 'LECTURES ON MUSIC'

[Early] 1826.

. . . the lover of art . . . will . . . doubtless also agree with me, who count . . . among the pianoforte composers now living . . . all the following among the good and inventive, and those apt to increase the artistic blessings of our time: . . . Joseph Czerny, Kalkbrenner, . . . Leidesdorf, Neukomm, Reissiger, . . . Friedrich Schneider, Xaver Schnyder, Schubert, Sechter, . . . and finally the boy Mendelssohn. . . .

Nägeli's ten lectures had been held in the first half of 1824 at Karlsruhe, Darmstadt, Frankfort o/M., Mainz, Stuttgart and Tübingen. For the edition in book form, dedicated to the Archduke Rudolph, whose preface is dated from Zürich 21st November 1825 and which appeared at Tübingen in 1826, Nägeli had written some "supplements" and made some interpolations. The passage quoted here is in the ninth lecture, concerning artistic education. Among the vocal composers Schubert is not mentioned.—Sigismund, Ritter von Neukomm, born at Salzburg in 1777, a pupil of Michael and Josef Haydn's, had lived in Vienna from 1798 till 1806.—Xavier Schnyder, born in 1786 at Wartensee in Switzerland, had lived in Vienna about 1812.

> Performance of the D minor Quartet at Josef Barth's, 1st February 1826.—Barth lived at Prince Schwarzenberg's winter palace on the Neuer Markt, and by turns also at the summer palace in the Heugasse, in the Landstrasse suburb.

625. FROM THE FAMILY REGISTER of Schubert's Father

19) On 3rd Feb. 1826, at 6.45 a.m., was born Anton Eduard *signo* Capricorn.

For Anton Eduard Schubert *see* No. 113.

626. FROM THE OFFICIAL 'WIENER ZEITUNG,' 6th February 1826

At the House of Cappi & Co.
Graben, No. 1134, [is] . . .
to be had:

.   .   .   .   .   .

F. Schubert, 'The Minstrel' ['Der Liedler'], for voice with guitar.   1 Fl. 45 Kr.

For 'The Minstrel' *see* No. 552.

627. FROM THE OFFICIAL 'WIENER ZEITUNG,' 8th February 1826

At the House of A. Pennauer,
Art Dealer, in the Graben, No. 1122, are just published:
Grande Marche funèbre,
à l'occasion de la mort de S.M. Alexandre I.
pour le Pianoforte à quatre mains,
par Fr. Schubert.

Œuvre 55.   Price, 1 Florin 30 Kreuzer, Viennese Currency.

LONGING
['Die Sehnsucht']
Poem by Fr. Schiller,
for One Voice with Pianoforte Accompaniment,
by FRANZ SCHUBERT.

Op. 39. Price, 1 Fl. 30 Kr., V.C.

Alexander I, born in 1777, tsar since 1801, had died on 1st December
1825; the news reached Vienna on 14th December. He had been there
during the Congress, had revisited Vienna at the end of 1818 and again in
the autumn of 1822. Cf. Nos. 676 and 700.—Op. 39 was a late-comer
once again; but it appeared without any dedication. On the title is the remark: "This song-piece is also to be had with the accompaniment arranged
for the guitar." This arrangement was, of course, apocryphal. The
Leipzig 'Allgemeine musikalische Zeitung' mentions this song on 10th
May 1826 as having been performed at the Vienna Philharmonic Society's
evening entertainments (season 1825–6), but says nothing of those shown
in Nos. 618 and 640. This is clearly an error.

> Performance of the D minor Quartet at Franz Lachner's in the
> Landstrasse suburb, (?) February 1826.—Lachner was in 1826–8
> one of the assistant conductors at the Kärntnertor Theatre.

> Schubert's melodrama with pianoforte accompaniment, 'Farewell
> to the Earth' ('Abschied von der Erde,' xx. 603), is privately per-
> formed at the close of Adolf von Pratobevera's one-act parody,
> 'The Falcon' ('Der Falke'), on the birthday of the author's father,
> 17th February 1826.—Adolf von Pratobevera, later Freiherr von
> Wiesborn, born in 1806 at Bielitz in Austrian Silesia, was a law
> student. His father, Karl Josef von Pratobevera, was vice-president
> of the supreme court of appeal and the criminal court in Lower
> Austria; he lived in the so-called Bürgerspital, a large apartment
> house, near the Kärntnertor.—On the same evening Josefine Fröhlich,
> who had just returned home, gave a concert at the County Hall,
> assisted by her brother-in-law Bogner.

628. FROM THE OFFICIAL 'WIENER ZEITUNG,' 20th February 1826

At the House of Sauer & Leidesdorf

I. & R. Priv. Art and Music Dealers in Vienna, Kärntnerstrasse,

No. 941, is just published and to be had
(Pest, at K. Lichtl's):

. . . . .

Schubert (Fr.), Overture to the Opera 'Alfonso and Estrella,'
arranged for Pianoforte Duet, 2 Florins.

Cf. No. 606. The overture appeared, with a dedication to Anna
Hönig, as Op. 52. As this number, however, had already been allotted
to the cycle of Scott songs from 'The Lady of the Lake,' published by
Matthias Artaria, it was later numbered Op. 69 when Diabelli took it
over. The arrangement of the overture, which draws upon themes from
the opera, is said to have been made jointly by Schubert and Josef Hüttenbrenner. The manuscript, in the market in 1890, is however in Schubert's hand. The editors of the complete edition altogether overlooked
this pianoforte duet transcription, which has therefore never been
republished.

629. FROM BAUERNFELD'S DIARY

21st February 1826.

On Sunday with Schubert at the Assembly Hall. The D major
Symphony and 'Egmont.' Then ate with him; after dinner to
Schuppanzigh's. Quartets by Haydn and Beethoven, quintet by
Mozart. Everything heavenly. Grillparzer was present too. . . .
The friends saddled me with the nickname of "Troglodyte"
["Spelunk"], because I am said to emerge rarely from my Cave
on the High Road [Landstrasse suburb].

Sunday was 19th February. The works performed at noon in the
assembly hall at one of the Philharmonic Society's concerts were Beethoven's second Symphony and 'Egmont' overture, and the programme
also included the "Hallelujah Chorus" from Handel's 'Messiah.'—The
afternoon concert (4.30 to 6.30) in the Philharmonic Society's hall at the
"Red Hedgehog" under the Tuchlauben included a string Quartet by
Haydn, Mozart's C minor Quintet and the pianoforte Sextet by Georges
Onslow (born at Clermont-Ferrand in 1784), who was professor at the
Paris Conservatory and had been in Vienna for several years; but nothing
by Beethoven.—Bauernfeld had not long removed to the Beatrixgasse
in the Landstrasse suburb, and his friends called these lodgings the "hovel"
(Spelunke).

Franz Schubert, sen., receives, as schoolmaster and almoner, the freedom of the city of Vienna, 23rd February 1826.—The decree, dated 9th February, mentions his forty-five years' school service and his seventeen years' work for charity. The honour had been petitioned by the parish and community of Rossau. On 23rd February the elder Schubert took the burgess's oath, which cost him 24 florins, A.C., in taxes. In the announcement of his death in 1830 his widow called him by mistake a freeman of the City of Vienna.

630. FROM SOPHIE MÜLLER'S DIARY

28th February 1826.

Official Holiday. In the evening Koberwein with Betty and Minna here. Betty Schröder, Winterberg with Alexander Tettenborn and little Prince Wittgenstein. Desprès, Teltscher, Jenger, Ditz, Hüttenbrenner uninvited, Call; Schubert did not come. Music, dancing, very gay until half-past 10.

Josef Koberwein, born in 1774 at Kremsier in Moravia, was a court actor; one of his daughters, Betty, born in Vienna in 1809, whose later married name was Fichtner, was also engaged at the Burg Theatre since 1822.—Winterberg cannot be identified.—Alexander is probably a son of the ambassador of Baden, Karl, Freiherr von Tettenborn.—Wittgenstein is perhaps Adolf, Prince von Sayn-Wittgenstein, the Hessian ambassador to Vienna.—Ditz is Tietze once again; Hüttenbrenner is Josef.

631. FROM RICHARD OTTO SPAZIER'S BOOK, 'Jean Paul Friedrich Richter in his Last Days and in Death'

(On the autumn weeks of 1825 at Bayreuth; Breslau, end of February 1826.)

Nearly every evening in that last period of his life, when the day was done, he longingly asked for song . . . He was moved above all by these passages from Schubert's splendid composition of Goethe's 'Erl King': "Thou tender child, come, go with me" and "They rock and they dance and they sing thee to sleep"; the premonition of secret bliss, suggestively promised by the voice and the accompaniment, drew him, like every one else, with magic power towards a transfigured, fairer existence.

Jean Paul Friedrich Richter, known as "Jean Paul," born in 1763 at Wunsiedel (Bayreuth), the romantic novelist, had died on 14th November 1825. His nephew Spazier, born in 1803, who translated Scott's poems, published this book of recollections with the Breslau firm of Josef Max & Co. (*see* Nos. 498 and 605). The title of Schober's 'Palingeneses' had also been used by Jean Paul (1798), who had been at Erlangen at the end of August 1823, where he met Platen and possibly also made the acquaintance of Bruchmann. In the 'Contributions to the Education of Youths' ('Beiträge zur Bildung für Jünglinge,' *see* note following No. 101) extracts from Jean Paul's 'Titan' and 'Hesperus' had appeared in 1817. The days referred to by Spazier are roughly between 24th October and 8th November 1825. Jean Paul, who was blind during his last years, also appreciated Reichardt's setting of Mignon's song, "Know'st thou the land," and Zelter's of the harper's song, "Who never ate his bread with tears."

632. From the Leipzig 'Allegemeine Musikalische Zeitung,' 1st March 1826

Première grande Sonate pour le Pianoforte, comp. . . . par Franç. Schubert. Œuv. 42.   Vienne, chez Pennauer.   (Price, 1 Thaler, 8 Groschen.)

Many musical pieces nowadays bear the name of Fantasy, though fantasy has had very little share in them, if any at all, and they are so called only because the title sounds well and because the child of the composer's fancy, running off on every side like wild waters, refuses to fit into any regular form. Here, on the contrary, a composition for once bears the name of Sonata, though it was fantasy, quite evidently, which had the largest and most decisive share in it. Indeed it seems to bear it only because it falls into the same movements and generally keeps to the same outward pattern as a sonata; apart from that, in the matter of expression and technique, although it preserves a praiseworthy unity, it moves so freely and originally within its confines, and sometimes so boldly and curiously, that it might not unjustly have been called a Fantasy. In that respect it can probably be compared only with the greatest and freest of Beethoven's sonatas. We are indebted for this uncommonly attractive and also truly significant work to Herr Franz Schubert, who is, we hear, a still quite young artist of and in Vienna. To us, as doubtless to northern Germany in

general, he is known only by his extremely diversified songs for
one or more voices, with or without pianoforte accompaniment;
and in these we have taken note with pleasure of an admirable
talent, even though their large number betrays great differences
of content and value and they are not without eccentricities of
various kinds which may even now and again be described as
blunders—a talent made of spirit and feeling, with genuine originality in invention and execution, and an endeavour to go his own
way which, though sometimes tempting him from the proper
path, is in itself worthy of respect and not seldom surprisingly
seizes upon the right thing.   Both the merits and the defects of
these songs had led us to suppose that Herr Schubert would be
even happier with a species which need obey no laws but those
governing good music in general — with instrumental music,
especially in its larger and freer forms; and this supposition is fully
confirmed by his first great Sonata now under discussion.   It is
rich in truly new and original melodic and harmonic inventions;
equally rich and even more many-sided in expression; ingenious
and persevering in workmanship, particularly in the conduct of
all the parts; and withal it is genuine pianoforte music throughout.
It is easy to see that these inventions are often somewhat odd, and
that their exposition is even more curious (particularly in the
first movement, where for example the principal theme, which is
almost dry in itself, is not only intentionally introduced in a dry
manner, but often, and clearly of set purpose, repeated in the same
way); also, that the composer now and again hardly knew the ins
and outs of the sometimes strange harmonies that visited him
(even as regards grammatical writing); and there are other things
of the sort over which one can hardly refrain from shaking one's
head a little.   But once it has been shaken and one has thus
acknowledged the rules by the confession that it might be wished
that the composer had done full justice to them as well as to his
work as it now stands (as a whole, be it understood), one cannot
after all refrain from accepting it with pleasure as it is and to make
the best of what may strike one's insight, one's ear or one's eye
as singular.   Better is better—no question of that; but spirit and
soul are best of all—no doubt of that either.   Still, if it behoves

the impartial judge to admit the second half of this sentence, it is also incumbent on the artist to take the first to heart.   However, we promise those of our readers who are capable of coming to terms with this work rich and rare enjoyment, so far as spirit and soul are concerned.   Until experience has fulfilled this promise, they may perhaps believe it the more willingly if we proceed to describe the work for them in some detail, movement by movement—and this shall be done.

First Movement: *Moderato*, A minor, ₵.—The predominant expression is a suppressed but sometimes violently erupting sombre passion, alternating with melancholy seriousness.   Great steadiness of execution and many truly ingenious combinations which are by no means conventional.   Those oddities in minor details need not be insisted on further.   The movement is not short, which is as one would wish if one would remain in this mood without growing weary of it.—Second Movement: *Andante poco moto*, C major, 3–8.—A simple, songful, gently serene theme, finely imagined and harmonized with pleasant fluency in all four parts. It is the more agreeable at this particular juncture, where it makes its effect most suitably.   It is varied five time in the course of the movement, freely but not discursively in the matter of expression, and the final variation is worked into a developed coda.   The harmony too is pure and clear.   The whole resembles in its invention, expression and workmanship the andantes with variations in the quartets of J. Haydn's later years; and every one knows that this implies no small praise.—Third Movement: *Allegro vivace*, *scherzando*, A minor, Trio F major.—The former is long and wholly thematic, the latter short and free.   Restrained passion breaks out hastily and violently in the scherzo; the trio brings some calm, which however is dispelled again by the repeat of the first part.   If the preceding movement could be called Haydnish, the present one might be described as Beethovenian, without, be it understood, any intention to dispute the composer's originality. What, to the stimulated mind, would be the most natural sequel after all these changing emotions?   Surely a generalized and elevated mood, so to say, not vehement but very lively, not sad but not light or merry either—a mood of strong, manly brightness, mixed of a greater part of seriousness and a smaller of jesting. And that is the very expression of the long and technically very well-knit Finale: *Allegro vivace*, A minor, 2–4.—It is in itself a praiseworthy piece of work, but it must be commended the more as a fitting close for the whole.

Should this short description of the work have drawn the readers' attention to it and at the same time have made it easier for them to grasp and to enjoy it according to the composer's intentions, it will have done what it set out to do. In order to perform it adequately this Sonata does not so much demand virtuoso playing (as it is commonly understood) as rather a painstaking performance, somewhat like that demanded by the largest sonatas by Beethoven or by Cramer. The instrument too should be good, capable of the most diverse modifications of loud and soft as well as of *legato*, sustained tone and accurate damping. The engraving is fair, though not as good as it is in the case of several musical works of far smaller significance recently brought out by the same publisher. A special prettily decorated and coloured cover describes this Sonata as *Cah. I.* of a *Bibliothèque musicale de nos contemporains*, &c.

[? G. W. Fink.]

Cf. note preceding No. 624.

633. JOSEF PREISINGER TO ANNA FRÖHLICH

Pressburg, 1st March 1826.

Is Betty married by now and is Bogner already feeling in a state of good hope? How is Kathi, how does Grillparzer, Holz, Piringer, Schubert, Wille, Kaufmann, &c.?

Preisinger (*see* No. 213) was engaged by the theatres of Graz and Pressburg, which were run jointly, in 1825–6. Betti (Barbara) Fröhlich had been married to Ferdinand Bogner since 1825 and expected her first child in August. Kathi is her other sister. Ferdinand Piringer, born in 1780 at Unterrötzbach in Lower Austria, was assistant director in the Court Chamber Registry, a violinist and in 1819–22 deputy conductor for Gebauer of the "Concert spirituel," succeeding him in 1824; but he shared this work with Johann Baptist Geissler (born *c.* 1785), an official in the Lower Austrian accountancy and a cellist.—For Holz *see* note preceding No. 443.—For Wille *see* No. 409.—Kaufmann is perhaps Grillparzer's friend Johann Kaufmann (born 1788), professor of Roman law at the Theresian Academy of Knights.

634. FROM FRANZ VON HARTMANN'S DIARY

Linz, 5th March 1826: Louis plays German Dances by Schubert.

Louis is Franz von Hartmann's brother (*see* No. 637).

635. FROM BAUERNFELD'S DIARY

8th March 1826.

Schober surpasses us all in mind, and much more so in speech! Yet there is much in him that is artificial, and his best powers threaten to be suffocated in idleness.—Schwind's is a glorious, pure nature—though always fermenting, as if he were going to burn himself out.—Schubert has the right mixture of the idealist and the realist. The world seems fair to him.—Mayerhofer is simple and natural, for all that Schober asserts that he is a kind of easy-going intriguer.—And I? Ah, if one could know oneself! Until I have done something worth while I am no human being.

These meditations are a serious sequel to the satire No. 614.

636. FROM THE MINUTES of a Meeting of the Philharmonic Society

1. Meeting of the Committee for Biography and Bibliography of Music, 14th March 1826 . . .

Councillor Sonnleithner read . . . a list of several musicians whose biographies might be furnished gradually by members of this committee: namely, . . . Schubert . . . Thereafter the following artists were selected, with whose biographies the members of the committee entered below have agreed to deal; and according to the rules agreed upon they will either furnish these biographies within three months or else specify the hindrances by reason of which delivery has been made impossible . . .

Herr von Jenger — — — Schubert Franz.

The councillor is Josef Sonnleithner.—Cf. No. 666.

637. FROM FRANZ VON HARTMANN'S DIARY

Linz, 19th March 1826: Louis plays German Dances by Schubert at Ottenwalt's.

See No. 634.

638. FROM FRANZ VON HARTMANN'S DIARY

Linz, 28th March 1826: At Spax's . . . Discussed Vogl and Schubert.

Spax is Max von Spaun.

639. FROM BAUERNFELD'S DIARY

End of March 1826.

Schubert and I hold faithfully together against many a Schoberish folly.   Moritz wavers.

Schober's follies are hinted at in the satire and in the diary (*see* Nos. 614 and 635).

640. FROM THE PROGRAMME of the Sixteenth Evening Entertainment held by the Philharmonic Society, 30th March 1826

4. 'The Wanderer,' set to music by Schubert, performed by Herr J. Hoffmann.

For Johann Hoffmann *see* No. 466.

641. FROM SOPHIE MÜLLER'S DIARY

31st March 1826.

Zedlitz was here this evening, until 7 o'clock, then left. The Koberweins, she and two daughters, Betty Schröder, Guste, Marie Wolf, Fräulein Pracht, Desprès, Teltscher, Dietz, Jenger, Schubert, Call. Quite an enjoyable evening.

Josef Christian, Freiherr von Zedlitz-Nimmersatt, born in 1790 at the castle of Johannesberg in Austrian Silesia, was an officer and a lyric poet. His poem, 'The Nocturnal Review' ('Die nächtliche Heerschau'), was often set to music, but both Schubert and Mendelssohn declined its composition.—Sophie Koberwein, *née* Bulla at Karlsruhe in 1783, was Josef Koberwein's wife.—Auguste (Guste) Schröder, born at Hamburg in 1810, whose later married names were first Gerlach and afterwards Schloenbach, was Betty Schröder's sister and also an actress.—Of Marie Wolf and Fräulein Pracht nothing is known.—Dietz (called Ditz before) is Tietze once again.

642. FROM THE 'HARMONICON,' London, April 1826

(Foreign Musical Report, Vienna.)

. . . The novelties from our musical press are but few; among the most interesting is a new set of variations for the violin by Mayseder. The young composer Schubert continues to labour indefatigably in the composition of songs. The first offspring of his fancy, and particularly his cantata 'Der Erlenkönig,' were very popular, and some of his later productions are marked with great beauty and feeling.

The Viennese reporter is unknown. He calls the ballad 'The Erl King' a "cantata" and gives it the wrong title, 'Erlenkönig' for 'Erlkönig' (cf. No. 612).

643. FROM SOPHIE MÜLLER'S DIARY

4th April 1826.

Home at 7 o'clock . . . Second half of Schubert's songs [from] Walter Scott's 'Lady of the Lake'—2 Florins 24 Kreuzer.

Cf. No. 644. Sophie Müller bought only the second book; the first had perhaps been given to her. The price was a little below normal (2 florins 24 kreuzer, instead of 2 florins 30 kreuzer).

644. From the Official 'Wiener Zeitung,' 5th April 1826

At the House of Matthias Artaria,
Art and Music Dealer, in the Kohlmarkt, No. 258,
is newly published and to be had:

Seven Songs
from Walter Scott's 'Lady of the Lake,'
set to Music
with Pianoforte Accompaniment
by Franz Schubert.

Op. 52. Book I, Price, 3 Fl. 30 Kr., Book II, 2 Fl. 30 Kr., V.C.

Op. 52, which appeared after Op. 55, was "most respectfully dedicated to Frau Sophie, Countess von Weissenwolf [sic], née Countess von Breunner." Book I contained four vocal pieces, including the two choruses, Book II three, including the 'Ave Maria.' It was only in the advertisement published five days after Schubert's death (24th November 1828), which also offered Opp. 53 and 54 again, that the fact was mentioned that the work was engraved "with English and German words"—at any rate in part (see No. 572). The alternative note-values are not always distinguished by different size, although as a rule they are smaller for the English words.

645. From the Official 'Wiener Zeitung,' 6th April 1826

At T. Weigl's Art and Music Establishment,
in the Graben, No. 1144 (next door to the "King of England"),
are quite newly published:

Hector's Farewell—Emma
['Hektors Abschied'—'Emma']
The Maiden's Plaint
['Des Mädchens Klage']
Poems by Fr. von Schiller,
set to Music
for One Voice with Pianoforte Accompaniment
by
Franz Schubert,
Work 56. Price, 2 Florins, V.C.

Furthermore:

Schubert, Fr., 'The Butterfly' ['Der Schmetterling'] and 'The
Mountains' ['Die Berge'], by Fr. von Schlegel. 'To the
Moon' ['An den Mond'], by Fr. von Hölty. Set to
music for one voice with pianoforte accompaniment.

Work 57.   Price, 1 Fl. 30 Kr., V.C.

The appearance of these latest works by the valued composer
occasions the remark that he has directed his attention particularly
to the elimination of any difficulty in the pianoforte accompaniment.

Thaddäus Weigl, born in 1776, a composer like his elder brother
Josef, had opened a publishing establishment of his own in 1803.—
Opp. 56 and 57 appeared before Opp. 53 and 54. The opus number 56,
however, having in the meantime been given to Pennauer (*see* Nos. 672
and 676), Weigl's Op. 56 had to be changed into Op. 58. The three
songs of Op. 57 are given the numbers 4, 5 and 6 as a continuation to
Op. "56," and the six songs of both works were so engraved that they
could also be sold separately. Hölty's name did not have the prefix
"von" and his Christian names were Ludwig Heinrich Christoph.—The
note at the end of this advertisement is not to be found, as Grove thought,
on the title-page of Op. 57; it too refers to Op. 58 ("56").

646. Schubert to the Emperor Francis

Your Majesty, Most Gracious Emperor,

With the profoundest veneration the undersigned ventures to
present the most submissive petition for the most gracious bestowal
of the vacant post of vice Musical Director to the Court Chapel,
and bases this application upon the following grounds:

1. The same is a native of Vienna, son of a schoolmaster, and
aged 29.

2. He enjoyed the most gracious privilege of being for 5 years
a pupil of the I. & R. Seminary, as a boy-chorister of the Court.

3. He received, according to Enclosure A, thorough instruction
in composition from the former first Musical Director of this
Court Chapel, Herr Anton Salieri, whereby he is rendered capable
of filling any chapel-master's post.

4. By his vocal and instrumental compositions his name has
become favourably known, not only in Vienna, but throughout
Germany, and he also has in readiness

5. five Masses with accompaniments for larger and smaller orchestras, which have already been performed in various Viennese churches.

6. Finally, he has not the advantage of employment and hopes by means of an assured career to attain fully to his intended artistic goal.

To do complete justice to the most gracious assent to his supplication will be the most earnest endeavour of the

Most submissive servant
Franz Schubert.

Vienna, 7th April 1826.

[By another hand:] Pres[ented] 9th April 1826.
[Enclosure A: *see* No. 158.]

When Salieri was pensioned off in March 1824 Eybler was elected as his successor in the post of first court musical director, but was not confirmed in it until June 1825 (*see* No. 480). That of second musical director, hitherto held by Eybler, had thus been vacant since 1824. Moritz, Count Dietrichstein, the "Court Music Count," had suggested Michael Umlauf for it as early as the beginning of 1825. Early in 1826 the emperor chose Wittassek, who, however, declined it. A kind of competition had therefore been organized, which Dietrichstein could not see through to the end because on 30th May he became director of the court library, Karl Leonhard, Count Harrach, becoming his successor.— The testimonial enclosed by Schubert was No. 158. For the further development of this competition cf. Nos. 747, 783, and 787.

647. FROM THE OFFICIAL 'WIENER ZEITUNG,' 8th April 1826

At the House of Matthias Artaria,
Art and Music Dealer, in the Kohlmarkt, No. 258,
are newly published and to be had:

Seconde Grande Sonate
pour le Pianoforte,
composée
par François Schubert.

Œuvre 53.   Price, 5 Florins, V.C.

Divertissement à la hongroise
pour le Pianoforte à quatre mains
composée [*sic*]
par François Schubert.

Œuvre 54.   Price, 6 Florins, V.C.

Opp. 53 and 54 appeared after Op. 57.   The Sonata written at Gastein
was dedicated to Karl Maria von Bocklet (*see* No. 476).   The 'Divertissement à la hongroise,' probably written at Zseliz in 1824, Schubert dedicated to Frau Lászny, *née* Buchwieser, her husband being a Hungarian.
The last of its three movements, the *Allegretto*, was written for two hands
at Zseliz on 2nd September 1824 as a 'Hungarian Melody'; it was the germ
of the whole work (not published till 1928, by Eduard Strache of Vienna).
Liszt, who arranged the whole for two hands, with another version "in
easier style," did not know the two-hand version of the *Allegretto*.   He
also, by the way, transcribed the second movement for orchestra and
entitled it 'Marcia.'

648. Josef von Spaun to Schober

Lemberg, 16th April 1826.

The friends, but particularly Bertl, I greet most cordially.

Bertl is Schubert.—Spaun had been appointed third assessor to the
Lottery Direction in Vienna and left Lemberg on 20th April.

Michael Holzer dies, 23rd April 1826.

649. From the Official 'Grazer Zeitung,' 26th April 1826

(On a concert of the Styrian Musical Society, 19th April 1826,
in the County Knights' Hall.)

Among the eight concert pieces given the poem of 'The
Wanderer,' set to music by Franz Schubert, was especially well
received and had to be repeated.   That artistically cultivated,
sensitive and, to us, unforgettable singer, Herr Rauscher, delivered
it; Herr Anselm Hüttenbrenner accompanied him upon the pianoforte with a profound understanding of the ingenious composition.

For Jakob Wilhelm Rauscher *see* No. 306.

650. Bauernfeld to Schober

Klagenfurt, 27th April 1826.

To Schubert I'll write shortly; I therefore request the exact address of an art establishment to which I can send the letter; do. Schwind's address.

First Lieutenant Mayerhofer von Grünbühel had been sent to Carinthia for surveying and map-making purposes. "As he travels by relays and receives allowances, he suggested that I should accompany him, which I seized with both hands," Bauernfeld writes in his diary. After a farewell dinner on 14th April he left on the 15th.—Klagenfurt is the capital of Carinthia, about 150 miles south-west of Vienna.

651. Johann Friedrich Rochlitz to Mosel

Leipzig, 30th April 1826.

[On Beethoven's ninth Symphony.] On the other hand, several new compositions by your Schubert have won my interest and affection. Perhaps that highly gifted artist needs only a scientifically trained friend to enlighten him gently about himself: concerning that which he is, has and aims at; from which, it is to be hoped, he would himself deduce what is expected of him.

Rochlitz (see No. 299), who kept up a correspondence with Mosel for many years (National Library, Vienna), does not otherwise mention Schubert there. The present occasion was a derogatory criticism of Beethoven's ninth Symphony.

652. From Bauernfeld's Diary

Paternion in Carinthia, 2nd May 1826.

Farewell dinner with Schwind, Schober, Schubert, Feuchtersleben and other friends. On the 15th, on a glorious spring morning, the "journey into the blue" was begun . . . "Greetings to thee, boredom, mother of the Muses!"—Thus I thought of the libretto for Schubert and set to work on 'The Count of Gleichen.' Dramatic and musical contrasts: orient and occident, janissaries and knighthood, romantic wooing and wedded love, &c.—in short, a Turkish-Christian outline. The verses flow pretty easily for me.

Paternion is on the river Drau, between Villach (to the west of Klagen-furt) and Ober-Vellach, which is south of Gastein.—Bauernfeld was on friendly terms with Ernst von Feuchtersleben (*see* note preceding No. 244) and his elder stepbrother Eduard. The one mentioned here is probably Ernst, who became a physician, a lyric poet and a moral philosopher; he was a pupil of Philipp Karl Hartmann (*see* ibid.), whose two once well-known books, 'The Teaching of Happiness' ('Glückseligkeitslehre') and 'The Human Spirit' ('Der Geist des Menschen'), influenced Feuchters-leben's successful book, 'Of the Soul's Dietetics' ('Zur Diätetik der Seele').—The legend of the Count Ernst von Gleichen, who brought home a second wife from the east and reconciled her with the first, is substan-tiated by a gravestone at Erfurt with the inscription: "Hic ossa cubant comit. Ernesti de Gleichen ejusque uxorum. R. i. p." Bauernfeld, who as a boy had been incited to deal more seriously with this subject by Volkert's opera (*see* No. 513) at the Josefstadt Theatre, based his libretto on the fairy-tale 'Melechsala' by Johann Karl August Musäus. After Volkert this subject, which received frequent musical treatment, was used also by Karl Eberwein (born 1786), whose opera, written in 1822, was produced at Weimar on 1st May 1824.—Bauernfeld's libretto (pub-lished in 1907 by Karl Fromme of Vienna) gives the titles of 'Orient. Spring. Morning' for the first Act and 'Occident. Autumn. Evening' for the second.

653. BAUERNFELD AND MAYERHOFER TO SCHUBERT
(Fragment)

[Villach, early May 1826.]

. . . you after last year's vintage, he after—the year before last's. All right. Here they have no proper wine at all; nothing but Italian, which tastes like something between cider and wine. Greetings to your fellow-drinkers, to Rieder, Perfetta, &c. How is Bocklet? I can never forget his playing, and I long for him. Imagine, I have not yet found a pianoforte, except one in a Klagen-furt coffee-house; there are only two dulcimers here. Most of the numbers in 'The Count of Gleichen' I have composed and sung as well.—To let you see how we live, here is a description:

THE MERRY MEN OF VELLACH

Saturday we left the city
And, continuing the race,
With the tall surveyor's table,
We proceed from place to place;
And on Sunday, with our cronies
Stay at home and mope we can't,
So we roam about and gamble
Shabby whist at foul Fragant.

Monday is for the surveyor;
We at drawing spend the day.
Tuesday, when the weather 's rainy,
At the groaning board we stay.
Wednesday the agent's visit
Makes a wholly welcome change,
So much that the guard and huntsman
Seem on Thursday almost strange.

Friday is a day of riot:
See the maidens all around!
Let the world cry shame and scandal,
We and they will stand our ground.
Saturday temptation 's over,
And to duty back we go,
Nor shall we be let off lightly,
For quite thickly lies the snow.

Thus our joys and raptures closely
Follow other pleasures still,
So that in the end we wonder,
Truly, what it is we will.
Drinks and games, good friends and damsels,
They go to our heads like wine—
Leave the Viennese folk their Prater,
Villach, Vellach—there it 's fine!

Or this ending:

> Swilling, gobbling, friends and damsels,
> What worse sequels, would you know?
> Viennese folk, where is your Prater?
> Villach, Vellach—woe, woe, woe!!!

Many kind regards to you and, if possible, do as I told you. In any case I should like to have the address for Kremsmünster, Linz, &c. Farewell. A greeting and kiss to Schober.

Your

Bfld.

One more thing: Imagine, two very lovely girls of 16 and 17 here—or rather they were, for they both died a year and a half ago (daughter of the châtelaine here), isn't that the devil's own luck?

B.

Dear Schubert,

Bauernfeld has left me but little room; therefore, to the point. Whatever you do, emerge from your Viennese fox-hole; it would give much pleasure to Feldel.—Address your reply to me, in any case. Schober will give you the address. — I am as well as a weaned lover can be expected to be—work distracts me and my companion cheers me up, so that I often forget that there is a greater space between Upper Vellach and the Trattnerhof than between Grinzing and Nussdorf. Write to me, too, if you will, or rather save it up until I am quite alone—for I shall need it the more then. Good-bye.

Your Mayerhofer.

The first part of this letter has not been preserved. It was addressed c/o Leidesdorf and began with an invitation to meet Bauernfeld in Upper Austria, as well as with a jocular recollection of a wine-drinking party at Grinzing (*see* Nos. 656 and 658).—Martin Perfetta, a registrar in the Court War Accountancy, was given the nickname of "The Pedant." He was an amateur musician and acquainted with Grillparzer.—Bauernfeld, of course, had merely imagined the music for his libretto.—The poem is a parody of Goethe's poem 'The Merry Men of Weimar' ('Die Lustigen von Weimar'); some of the words, or even lines, are taken over as they stand (e.g. "Lasst den Wienern ihren Prater"). Instead of "Villach,

Vellach . . ." Goethe has "Weimar, Jena—da ist's gut!" There is
nothing in Goethe to correspond to the third verse.—Fragant is to the
west of Ober-Vellach.—The châtelaine is the mistress of the castle of
Mörtenegg, or Wertenau. Bauernfeld writes in his diary on 22nd May:
"The estate manager's wife at Villach (in the castle) is as pretty as she is
agreeable. The forester is a bright fellow."—Feldel is Bauernfeld(el).
—Mayerhofer calls himself a "weaned lover" because he had to leave
Jeannette von Mitis behind in Vienna. It was she, no doubt, who lived
at the Trattnerhof, a superior block of flats in the Graben in Vienna.

654. FROM SOPHIE MÜLLER'S DIARY

13th May 1826.

Two Hüttenbrenners, Teltscher and Schubert ate here.

Anselm Hüttenbrenner was in Vienna on a visit.

655. BAUERNFELD TO SCHWIND AND SCHOBER

Upper Vellach, 24th May 1826.

We both really live quite agreeably on the whole, and if I am
not taken away by force, I dare say I shall remain a few more
weeks (4–5) at M.'s [Mayerhofer], before I undertake my further
journey; the plan of this journey, by the way, is outlined in a
letter to Schubert (at Leidesdorf's), which he must by now have
had long ago, and in which I also announce that I have written an
opera for him (N.B. the first act on 1st May) and invite him to
come here. A passage in your letter, dear Schwind, makes me
conclude that you too wish to come; which pleases me even more
than it surprises me; whether you both come, or one, or the other
—it would give me infinite pleasure; fix a place for the congress,
and I will wander to it like a devout pilgrim. Oh, whoever has
it in his power to dream away a spring season, let him not by any
means neglect doing so! . . . The letter to Schubert also contains
a poem describing our condition.

I am visited by a great many poetical thoughts . . . Apart from
the opera (done . . . on a few working-days on which I did not
go with M.) a very moderate number of poems . . .

Greetings to Schubert.

There are some indications here of the lost contents of the beginning of No. 653.—Schwind's letter to Bauernfeld is lost. It evidently contained information to the effect that he and Schubert had gone to live for some time in the Währing suburb (*see* No. 658), with Schober, who had been obliged to leave his town dwelling with his mother at short notice owing to the billeting of a Milanese diplomat and his family.

656. SCHUBERT TO BAUERNFELD AND MAYERHOFER

[Vienna, end of May 1826.]

Dear Bauernfeld,
Dear Mayerhofer,

Your having done the opera is a clever move; only I could wish to see it before me already. They have asked for my libretti here, to see what they can do with them. If your book were ready by now, I could submit that to them, and if its value were recognized, which I do not doubt, I might begin on it, D.V., or send it to Mme Milder in Berlin. Mlle Schechner has appeared here in 'The Swiss Family' and pleased exceedingly. As she looks very much like Milder, she might be good enough for us.—Please don't stay away so long, it is very sad and miserable here—boredom has taken the upper hand too much already. Of Schober and Schwind one hears nothing but lamentations, far more heart-rending than those we heard during Passion Week.—At Grinzing I have been hardly once since you left, and with Schwind not at all . . . From all this you may "divide up together" a nice little sum of mirth for yourself. 'The Magic Flute' was done quite well at the Theater an der Wien. 'Der Freischütz' very badly at the I. & R. Kärntnertor Theatre. 'Herr Jacob and Frau Baberl' are incomparable at the Leopoldstadt [Theatre]. Your poem, published in the 'Modezeitung,' is very beautiful, but even finer is the poem in your last letter. The elevated fun, or funny elevation, and especially the tender note of pain at the end, where you make masterly use of the good city of Villach—"woe, woe!"—is among the best models of that species.—I am not working at all. —The weather here is truly appalling, the Almighty seems to have forsaken us altogether, for the sun simply refuses to shine. It is

May, and we cannot sit in any garden yet.   Awful! appalling!!
ghastly!!! and the most cruel thing on earth for me!   Schwind
and I intend going to Linz with Spaun in June.   We can arrange
a meeting there or at Gmunden, only let us know for certain—as
soon as possible.   Not in two months' time.

    Farewell, both!

    Schubert actually addresses Bauernfeld only, although he includes
Mayerhofer's name, wrongly spelt Mayrhofer.—Barbaja had begun his
new lease of the Kärntnertor Theatre at the end of April, for a term ending
in April 1828.   Duport was his authorized representative.   Mosel, the
champion of German opera, in June 1826 became director of the two
court theatres (of which he had been vice director); but in the case of
the Opera this had a purely nominal significance.   It was at this time that
Schubert is supposed to have applied, and been examined for, the post of
assistant conductor at the Kärntnertor.   It is said that he composed the
fragment of a libretto written for him by Hofmann (*see* No. 167) and
conducted a rehearsal of it, but that he refused at that rehearsal to make
the alterations demanded by the prima donna, Nanette Schechner, and
left the house in a rage.   That there is no truth in this story is proved by
the fact that it includes the information that Schechner's voice had then
begun to decline.   This singer, a pupil of Weber's, about whom Schubert and his friends were enthusiastic (*see* No. 663), was born at Munich
in 1806, so that she was then just twenty, and she had made her first
appearance only on 22nd May, as Emeline in Weigl's 'Swiss Family.'   She
went to Berlin in 1828 and to the Theater an der Wien in 1829.   It is
possible that at the time of her early retirement, in 1835, her voice may
have become what Schindler, the witness for the prosecution in that
doubtful case, represented it to have been at the beginning of her career.
She became engaged to the attractive singer Ludwig Cramolini, but
married in 1832 the painter Karl Waagen.   Schubert visited her with
Anselm Hüttenbrenner in 1826, and Anselm has nothing to report about
any rupture, but only about the Bavarian *Dampfnudel*, a sweet dish her
mother cooked particularly well.   Another untruth is Schindler's
assertion that Schubert was to succeed Karl August Krebs (real name
Miedke, born in 1804 at Nuremberg), who was newly engaged only at
that time and conducted such works as Boïeldieu's 'Dame blanche' with
Schechner as Anne (6th July 1826).   The fact is that by the departure of
Benedict (*see* No. 525) and of Kreutzer (*see* No. 280) a place had been
vacated, and that it was given to Krebs.   Josef von Spaun says that Schubert
was to have become conductor, but showed no desire to do so.   That
probably is the whole truth of the matter.—The Theater an der Wien,
built by Schikaneder when he gave up the Freihaus Theatre, still regarded

'The Magic Flute' as its own chief work and took pride in outdoing the Kärntnertor in its production. It is true, however, that its revival on 15th May was given by the company of the Josefstadt Theatre.—'Herr Jacob and Frau Baberl' is a mistake for 'Herr Josef and Frau Baberl' (Baberl = Babette), a farce with songs in three acts based on Schikaneder's comedy, 'The Butcher of Sopron' ('Der Fleischhauer von Oedenburg'), freely adapted by Gleich, with music by Wenzel Müller. The production had taken place on 11th May, with Therese Krones (born 1801 at Freudental in Austrian Silesia) and Ignaz Schuster in the leading parts. Another play by the same authors, 'Jacob at Home' ('Jakob in der Heimat') had been produced at the same theatre on 14th February. This may explain Schubert's mistake.—Bauernfeld's poem, which had appeared in the 'Wiener Zeitschrift,' known as the 'Modezeitung,' is 'Life's Favour' ('Die Gunst des Lebens'). That the other poem was a parody of Goethe does not seem to have been immediately noticed by Schubert and his two friends in Vienna. For that matter, the fact has also been overlooked by writers on Schubert.—Josef von Spaun went to Linz for three weeks on 7th July, butwith out Schubert and Schwind.—Schubert forgot to sign this letter.

657. ANTON VON SPAUN TO HIS WIFE

[Vienna, May] 28th [1826].

Schubert, Vogl, &c., I have not seen at all yet, but a Schubertiad has already been arranged.

Anton von Spaun had gone to Vienna in order to go to Carlsbad for a cure with Johann Mayrhofer. In Vienna he kept in touch with Schubert, Kupelwieser, Schwind and Mayrhofer, and it may be through him that the last-named temporarily came nearer to the circle again. Anton von Spaun left on 4th June and was away for nearly two months.—Cf. No. 659.

658. FROM BAUERNFELD'S DIARY

9th [? 29th] May 1826.

At Upper Vellach.—The opera finished in a week. Reported on it to Schubert, who replied without delay. He burns for the libretto and is bored at Währing with Schwind.

This entry clearly bears too early a date. That Schubert was at Währing with Schwind is not mentioned in his letter (No. 656), but may have been in the lost one from Schwind to Bauernfeld.

659. Anton von Spaun to his Wife

31st May [1826].

A Schubertiad at Enderes's, to which more than 20 persons have been asked.

Schober was probably absent, for he was ill at the end of May. He seems to have moved to his mother's at Währing only in June when Schubert and Schwind had returned thence. But they evidently visited the Schobers again in the summer.

660. From Franz von Hartmann's Diary

Linz, 6th June 1826: Trip to Walding. Sang the finest of Schubert's songs on the way there.

Walding is near Schwanenstadt, south-west of Linz.

661. From the Official 'Wiener Zeitung,' 10th June 1826

At the House of Cappi & Czerny,
Priv. Art Dealers, in the Graben, No. 1134, are newly published, and to be had of K. Lichtl in Pest at the same price:

Veteran's Song
['Greisengesang']
from the 'Eastern Roses' ['Oestliche Rosen'] by F. Rückert,
and
Dithyramb
by F. von Schiller,
set to Music
for a Bass Voice with Pianoforte Accompaniment,
by Franz Schubert

Work 60.   Price, 2 Florins, Viennese Currency.

Op. 60 appeared before Op. 59, which also contains songs on poems by Rückert.—Friedrich Rückert, born in 1788 at Schweinfurt, was an exceedingly prolific lyric poet, of whose thousand and more poems only a part was printed. He published his cycle 'Eastern Roses' in 1822, and Schubert took five poems from it. The edition of Rückert's collected poems (1834 ff.) gives it incomplete, in vol. i; 'Veteran's Song' and 'Greetings to thee' ('Sei mir gegrüsst') are among the 'Ghazals' of 1837; 'That she hath been here' ('Dass sie hier gewesen') is not in the collection at all.—Op. 60 bears no dedication.

662. Anton von Spaun to his Wife

Carlsbad, 13th June 1826.

I could not resist the temptation and have hired a fortepiano for a fortnight, for which I pay 10 fl. including transport to and fro. Mayrhofer sings many a Schubert song and delights in my German and Country Dances.

Carlsbad is the well-known spa in Bohemia (see No. 657).

663. Schober to Bauernfeld

[Währing near Vienna, June 1826.]

In matters theatrical I inform you only that Mlle Schechner revolutionizes the town by her wonderful singing in German. Since the Milder it is said that no such voice has set the air vibrating, and she is still youthful, pretty and vivacious into the bargain. Schubert has heard her and chimes into the hymn of praise. If only he would write an opera for her; perhaps yours may be suitable. If only he were not quite such a naïve barbarian. When I asked him recently why he had not come to see me during the whole of my illness, he answered quite innocently: "But you are never to be found at home." 'The Enchanted Rose' has already been taken from you: the burgomaster of Teplitz has treated it operatically . . . To-day Schubert is to come out here; I hope he will keep his word . . . Schubert has written four-handed marches, which are said to be very fine again; among the new songs 'In the Open' ['Im Freien'] is my favourite now.

The party in favour of German opera in Vienna was glad that it had become possible once again to oppose a prima donna of high quality to the ladies of the Italian opera.—Schulze's epic (cf. Nos. 475 and 540) had been made into a libretto by E. H. Gehe, which was composed by

Josef Maria Wolfram (born 1789 at Dobrzan, Bohemia), the burgomaster
of Teplitz, under the title 'Maja and Alpino, or The Enchanted Rose'
('. . ., oder Die bezauberte Rose'). The opera was first performed at
Prague on 24th May.—Schubert must have been living alternately in town
and at Währing.—The autographs of all the pianoforte duet marches have
disappeared, so that we have no dates for any of them; those mentioned
here may have been the pair published in 1830 as Op. 121, under the
title of 'Deux Marches caractéristiques.'—The song 'In the Open'
(Op. 80, No. 3), on a poem by Seidl, was written in March 1826.

664. From the Official 'Wiener Zeitung,' 17th June 1826

At T. Weigl's Art and Music Establishment
(Graben, No. 1144, next to the "King of England")
is just published:

Divertissement
en forme d'une marche brillante et raisonnée
pour le Pianoforte à quatre mains,
composé sur des motifs origineaux [sic] francais
par Francois Schubert.

Price, 3 Fl., V.C.

This work appeared as Op. 63, No. 1 (before Opp. 56, 59, 61 and 62),
without a dedication. (The word *raisonnée* in the title seems to mean
constructed according to the rules of the art.) It was to be continued with
two other movements on "French original themes" (never identified and
thus probably of Schubert's own invention) which appeared in the summer
of 1827 under the title of 'Andantino varié et Rondeau brillant,' Op. 84
(*see* No. 916). This divertimento in three movements, the manuscript of
which has not been preserved, has remained separated to the present day
owing to the arbitrary procedure of its original publisher, Thaddäus Weigl.

665. Nägeli to Karl Czerny

Zürich, 18th June 1826.

Sir,

I tender you my most cordial thanks for your kind promise to
lend a hand in the promotion of my undertakings, and take the
liberty of at once taking you at your word. Artists of your rank and
in your position, who have distinguished and wealthy pupils, are

best able to further the subscriptions to 'The Portal of Honour' ['Ehrenpforte']. To this end I therefore enclose the announcement (as well as that of two other enterprises on behalf of which you may perhaps be able to do something). That in such a matter you are also thinking of the advantage and the fame of your fellow-artists is for me a pleasurable proof of your high-minded attitude. Which therefore encourages me to approach you with questions and demands in regard to Viennese artists.

a) The pianoforte composer Schubert I count decidedly among the good, indeed the excellent ones. The first movement of his A minor Sonata (at Pennauer's) seems to me a capital piece. Should you be personally acquainted with him, please assure him that I should very gladly receive him among the contributors to 'The Portal of Honour,' as soon as the subscription list is assured, in which he might perhaps also collaborate. If I am to write to him direct, only give me a hint.

b) Who among the composers Joseph Czerny, Lannoy. Halm, Plachy, Kanne, &c. would be the most capable and worthy collaborator for 'The Portal of Honour'? You may rely on my discretion in this matter.

Cf. No. 604. A manuscript copy of the prospectus for the 'Musical Portal of Honour' is preserved in the possession of Professor Rudolf Hunziker at Winterthur in Switzerland. Nägeli's other two "undertakings" are 'Siona' and 'The Contrapuntists of the Nineteenth Century,' both published to follow the series of 'Musical Works of Art in the Strict Style by J. S. Bach and Other Masters' (1801 ff.), and they both started in 1826.—The sonata is Op. 42 (*see* note preceding No. 624).—*See* No. 670.

666. From the Minutes of a Meeting held by the Philharmonic Society

2. Meeting of the Committee for Musical Biography and Bibliography, 21st June 1826 . . .

In arrears from the first meeting . . . :

Herr Jenger . . . . Schubert Franz.

Newly assigned . . . to Herr [Josef] Hüttenbrenner: . . . Schubert Ferd.

Cf. No. 636. Jenger, who had also undertaken Anselm Hüttenbrenner's biography, did write this, but unfortunately not Schubert's.
Neither does Josef Hüttenbrenner appear to have written any biography
of Ferdinand Schubert.

667. FROM SOPHIE MÜLLER'S DIARY

26th June 1826.

Vogl, the singer, marries [Kunigunde] Rosa.

Vogl, then fifty-eight, had become engaged to be married in April,
after his return from Italy. Kunigunde, "not very young either," was a
daughter of the former first custodian of the picture gallery in the Belvedere, the painter Josef Rosa (actually Roos, 1760–1822). The Vogl
couple had a daughter Henriette (born in 1827 or 1828), to whom her
widowed mother wrote a letter from Steyr about 1850, containing some
vague recollections of Schubert (Fitzwilliam Museum, Cambridge). The
mother and daughter had read English books with Vogl.

668. SCHUBERT TO FRANZ SALES KANDLER

[Outside:]

H. von Kandler, Esq.,
into his own hands.

[Inside:]

Sir,

I would politely request you kindly to have my Mass, which is
at your house, sent to the art establishment of Herr Leidesdorf
or Herr Pennauer.

Your most devoted

Vienna, 30th June 1826.   Frz. Schubert.

For Kandler *see* No. 288. In the spring of 1817, before Kandler left
for Italy, Schubert had written the third of the five versions of the song
'The Trout' into his album (now in the possession of Frau Marie Floers-
heim, Wildegg, Aargau, Switzerland). Now, after Kandler's return,
Schubert had evidently handed him the Mass in A flat for criticism in the
Vienna or the Leipzig 'Allgemeine musikalische Zeitung.' But Kandler,
though he was a reviewer for several journals, did not write about it.
The Mass was not published until 1875, by Diabelli's successor, Friedrich
Schreiber in Vienna. Schubert could have deposited the manuscript

with either of the two publishers named without exciting jealousy.   He probably wanted it only for performance in a church.

> Performance of the Quartet, 'Spirit of Love' ('Geist der Liebe'), Op. 11, No. 3 (xvi. 6) at Laibach, ? 1826.—The performance may have been brought about by Eduard Jaëll (*see* No. 119), who had been orchestral leader at Laibach since 1821.

669. Karl Holz in Beethoven's Conversation Book, 1826

Schubert was just with him, and they were reading one of Handel's scores.   He was very pleasant, and at the same time rendered thanks for the pleasure *milord's* quartets gave him.   He was always present.—He has great powers of conception in song.   Do you know the 'Erl King'?—He always talked very mystically.

> Thayer thought that Schubert's interlocutor was either Matthias Artaria or Mosel, but it is more likely, as Dahms (Fellner) supposed, that it was Kiesewetter.—"My lord Falstaff" was Schuppanzigh's nickname, alluding to his figure.   His quartet had given the first performance on 21st March 1826, at his last subscription concert of that season held in the Philharmonic Society's hall, of Beethoven's new string Quartet in B flat major, Op. 130 (from the manuscript), and, with Halm, the pianoforte Trio in the same key, Op. 97.   Schubert seems to have been present at all the concerts of Schuppanzigh's quartet during the preceding months.

670. Schubert to Nägeli at Zürich

Vienna, 4th July 1826.

Sir,

Through Herr Karl Czerny you have transmitted to me the honourable commission to write a pianoforte sonata for you, to be included by you in a collection of various keyboard compositions (under the title of 'Portal of Honour' ['Ehrenpforte']), having made friends with me through my A minor Sonata.   Not only the favourable reception of that Sonata, but also your most flattering wish, make me entirely willing to satisfy your desire as soon as you like.

In that case, however, I should ask you to remit me the fee, viz. 120 florins, A.C., in advance in a draft on Vienna.

For the rest, it was very agreeable for me to have entered into correspondence with so old and famous an art establishment.

I remain, with all respect.

Your devoted

My address is   Franz Schubert.

Auf der Wieden, No. 100, in Fruhwirth's house,
5th staircase, 2nd floor.

Cf. Nos. 604 and 665; *see also* No. 677.

671. FROM THE OFFICIAL 'WIENER ZEITUNG,' 8th July 1826

At the House of Cappi & Czerny,
Priv. Art Dealers, in the Graben, No. 1134, is newly published, and to be had of K. Lichtl in Pest at the same price:

SIX POLONAISES
for Pianoforte Duet
composed
by FRANZ SCHUBERT.
Work 61.
(Property of the Publishers.)

Price of Book I .   .   . 2 Fl., V.C.
Price of Book II .   .   . 2 Fl., V.C.

Op. 61 appeared after Op. 63, without a dedication.

672. FROM THE FRANKFORT 'ALLGEMEINER MUSIKALISCHER ANZEIGER,' 8th July 1826

'Hail and Farewell' ['Willkommen und Abschied']. Poem by Goethe. 'To the Lyre' ['An die Leier'] (after Anacreon). 'In the Grove' ['Im Haine']. Poems by Bruchmann. Set to music for one voice with pianoforte accompaniment, &c., by Franz Schubert. Op. 56. Books I and II. Vienna, Pennauer. 12 Groschen each book.

By means of these books we make the acquaintance of a very noteworthy song composer, who has grasped the chosen poems truly poetically and reproduced them in sound in a moving and characteristic way. His compositions are therefore hardly among those likely to be acquired by many, but they will certainly make respectable friends. The musical representation sometimes tends, perhaps a little too much, towards the domain of the dramatic, for which Herr Schubert seems to us to have an especial inclination. We think much the same, or *vice versa*, of the

Seven Songs from Walter Scott's 'Lady of the Lake'
by the same composer, with pianoforte accompaniment. Op. 52.
Books I and II.
Vienna, Artaria. 1 Fl. 45 Kr.

except that these, conforming to the words, are more sombre by nature and must derive their historical and in great part also their musical interest from that romance. They will not lack friends either, considering the great number of Walter Scott's admirers. Herr S. shows everywhere a remarkable technical accomplishment; but cases like that on p. 7, double stave 3, bar 3, in the first book, being evidently wrongly written, must strike one the more. Herr S. should certainly have written the whole first movement of that book and its repeats in C♯ instead of D♭, for so he would at the same time have avoided other ineptitudes.

The genuine Op. 56, dedicated by Schubert to his friend Karl Pinterics, may already have appeared in the spring of 1826. It was apparently not advertised till the middle of July (No. 676); but this review proves that it had been ready some time before.—The bar to which the reviewer takes exception and the notation of D flat for C sharp in 'Ellen's First Song' are retained in their original form in the complete edition.

673. SCHUBERT TO BAUERNFELD

[Outside:]
To Herr von Bauernfeld.

[Inside:]
Vienna, 10th July 1826.
Dear Bauernfeld,

I cannot possibly get to Gmunden or anywhere else, for I have no money at all, and altogether things go very badly with me. I do not trouble about it, and am cheerful.

For the rest, come to Vienna as soon as possible. As Duport wants an opera from me, but the libretti I have so far set do not please at all, it would be splendid if your libretto were favourably received. Then at least there would be money, if not reputation as well!

Schwind is quite in the dumps about Nettel! Schober is privileged business man. *Vogl is married!!!*

Please do come as soon as possible!

Because of your opera.

At Linz you need only name my   Your
name to be well received.   Schubert.

The incomplete address seems to indicate that this letter was en-closed in another, probably one to Clodi at Ebenzweier. (This was the first of Schubert's letters to be sold by auction: the first German auction of autographs held by Artaria & Co. in Vienna on 2nd April 1838, from the collection of the bookworm Franz Gräffer, to whom it had been given by Bauernfeld. He was then anxious to purchase this "confidential letter of somewhat compromising content" back again, but was too late, for the editor Johann Paul Kaltenbaeck had already acquired it for 30 kreuzer. Later on the letter went from J. von Radowitz's collection to the Prussian State Library in Berlin.)—In the course of that July Schubert wrote his three Shakespeare songs at Währing. They are in a little book in which the staves are drawn in pencil. It also contains the 'Song of Hippolytus' from Johanna Schopenhauer's novel 'Gabriele.' There is a story according to which Schubert wrote them —or at any rate 'Hark, hark, the lark'—on the back of a bill of fare in the garden of the Beer-Sack Inn ("Zum Biersack," cf. No. 194); but the manuscript refutes this. On the other hand there seems to be some truth about the inn, for Schober wrote to Bauernfeld about that time that next to the garden attached to his lodgings was another belonging to an inn, where he was disturbed by trumpet music and other noises. In the same letter he surprises Bauernfeld with the news that he drove into town from Währing at half-past eight each morning, "to engage in business, which prospers pretty fairly." He managed the 'lithographic institute' founded in 1817 by Count Adolf Pötting and owned in 1826 by Countess Therese Trauttmansdorff.—For Duport cf. No. 656.—Schwind had written to Bauernfeld in June that Anna Hönig had read him "the Riot Act" because of his "want of religion," and that he had replied: "Go and fall in love with the Pope!" Bauernfeld thought this capital, and later put the phrase into the mouth of Herr Sittig, a character in his comedy 'Bourgeois and Romantic' ('Bürgerlich und Romantisch').

674. From Bauernfeld's Diary

10th July 1826.

Across the Mallnitz Tauern to Gastein. Mayerhofer still came with me as far as Salzburg, then I went back with him to Golling. He went off after further work, I to Hallein to Eduard Feuchtersleben, who received me most hospitably. Stayed with him a few days. Sent the larger luggage in advance to Gmunden, where I hoped to meet Schubert. To Ischl with a knapsack on my back.

From Ober-Vellach the route goes via Mallnitz northward to Gastein, and thence in the same direction via Golling and Hallein to Salzburg. On 7th July the two friends wrote verses in the "book of honour" at Gastein (*see* No. 584).—Eduard von Feuchtersleben (cf. No. 652), born at Cracow in 1798, the son of a mulatto mother, was a mining expert and lived at Hallein for professional reasons.—For Gmunden, which Schubert was not to see again, cf. Nos. 656 and 673.—Ischl lies east of Hallein, Gmunden north of Ischl.—Bauernfeld probably took about the same way from the county of Salzburg to Upper Austria as Schubert had done in 1825.

675. From Franz von Hartmann's Diary

Linz, 11th July 1826: Louis and Betty play marches by Schubert.

Louis is Hartmann's brother; Betty (Babette) is perhaps Fräulein Wanderer, Franz von Spaun's sister-in-law (*see* note preceding No. 595). The Marches were Op. 27 or Op. 40.

676. From the Official 'Wiener Zeitung,' 14th July 1826

At the House of A. Pennauer,
Priv. Art and Music Dealer, in Vienna, in the Graben,
No. 1122, in Fischer's House, are quite newly published:

HAIL AND FAREWELL.   TO THE LYRE.
['Willkommen und Abschied']   ['An die Leier']

IN THE GROVE.
['Im Haine']

540

Three Poems
set to Music for One Voice with Pianoforte Accompaniment
by FRANZ SCHUBERT

Op. 56. Two Books, each 1 Fl. 30 Kr., V.C.

Grande Marche funèbre pour Piano seul
à l'occasion de la mort
de S. M. Alexandre I., Empereur de toutes les Russies,
par François Schubert.

Œuvre 55.   Price, 45 Kr., Vien. Cur.

The same for 4 hands.   Price, 1 Fl. 30 Kr., V.C.

Cf. No. 672. These songs were published "with Italian words printed below," evidently for singers versed in that language. The translation may have been by Craigher (*see* No. 596).—The arrangement of Op. 55 (*see* No. 627) for two hands is, of course, not by Schubert.

677. NÄGELI TO KARL CZERNY

[?] July 1826.

I shall now write invitations to Schubert, Lannoy, Halm and Kanne; to the first unconditionally, but to the others with the proviso that the. matter turns out fairly satisfactorily.

This letter is preserved only in fragmentary form. It may have been written before Nägeli received Schubert's letter (No. 670). We know that he did not ask Beethoven to take part in his new enterprise, the 'Portal of Honour,' probably because of his experience with the G major Sonata, Op. 31, No. 1, into which Nägeli had rashly interpolated four bars; but he did invite Weber (who died in London on 5th June) and Mendelssohn, who both declined, as well as Karl Czerny, Ferdinand Ries (born Bonn, 1784), Friedrich Kuhlau (born Hanover, 1786) and Moscheles, whose contributions were already announced, and Spohr, Hummel and Bernhard Romberg. While of the 'Siona' collection only one book appeared, and four of 'The Contrapuntists,' two of 'The Portal of Honour' were published, containing the Sonatas Op. 141 by Ries and Op. 124 by Czerny. No agreement with Schubert was arrived at before the series came to an end. Nägeli's letter to him is lost.

678. From Bauernfeld's Diary

16th July (evening) 1826.

At Ebenzweier. At Therese Clodi's. Recommended to her by letters from the Viennese friends. I live in the small castle. The girl is stewardess and châtelaine in one. The father, blind and gouty, is bedridden. My room faced the lake and the Traunstein.—Letter from Schubert, found at Gmunden. He complains about the friends, longs for me, has no money!—Just what happened to me.—To-morrow I shall leave.

The Traunstein (5,500 feet) is on the opposite shore of Lake Traun, facing Ebenzweier.—Schubert's letter is No. 673.

679. From the Official 'Wiener Zeitung,' 19th July 1826

At the House of Ant. Diabelli & Co.,
Art and Music Dealers, in the Graben, No. 1133, is newly published,
and to be had of K. Lichtl in Pest at the same price:

Continuation of the Periodical Work:

APOLLO AT THE LADIES' DRESSING-TABLE.
['Apollo an der Damen-Toilette']
Light and Agreeable Melodies
for the Guitar,
edited by A. Diabelli.

Books V and VI, each 1 Fl. 30 Kr., V.C.

The fifth book contains: March from 'Gabriella' by Carafa; Funeral March from 'Achille' by Paer; Favourite Theme by Rovelli; Mourning Waltz by Schubert; Fandango; *Menuet à la reine* with Gavotte; Kalamaika; Mazur; *Tempête*; Galopade; Minuet from 'Don Giovanni'; March of the Priests from 'Iphigénie en Tauride' by Gluck.

No copy of this collection is known.—Ferdinando Paer was born in 1771.—Schubert's waltz is Op. 9, No. 2.

680. From the Leipzig 'Allgemeine Musikalische Zeitung,' 19th July 1826

'Longing' ['Die Sehnsucht'], poem by Schiller, set to music for one voice with pianoforte accompaniment by Franz Schubert. Work 39. Vienna, Pennauer. (Price, 45 Kreuzer.)

Herr S., among the considerable number of his songs at the pianoforte, has supplied several very good and some excellent pieces. He seems to be less gifted for song, properly speaking, than for continuously composed pieces, for four voices or for one with an independent, sometimes perhaps excessively full accompaniment. Thus his Goethe 'Erl King,' for example, may be a highly surcharged piece of work very difficult to perform; but it does contain spirit and vitality in general as well as a certain secret devilry of expression. Now here, in Schiller's 'Longing' (likewise continuously set, with an independent and by no means sparing accompaniment), he has been more restrained, it is true, but nevertheless, in our opinion, has done too much in painting a number of details and, for that very reason, too little to keep to what the poet maintains as the fundamental tone — sentiment throughout. For all that, the piece is interesting, at least in some of its sections, without however matching the much earlier composition by Konradin Kreutzer, which is of the same kind. Can it be that this, perhaps Kreutzer's very best in that species, is unknown to Herr S. or that he supposed to have surpassed it? Surely the former is the case! All the same, his little work will, quite rightly, be sung and listened to with pleasure! It is actually for a bass or contralto voice, but may also be performed by a low soprano. It is difficult neither for the singer nor for the player.

[? G. W. Fink.]

By "song properly speaking" the strophic song was still understood at that time.—The work by Kreutzer which Schubert especially valued was the 'Nine Roaming-Songs by Uhland,' Op. 34 (*see* No. XXX).—Next to Schubert's setting of Schiller's 'Longing,' that by Leidesdorf had also become familiar in Vienna (the Philharmonic Society had performed them both by turns at New Year 1824, cf. No. 618); not so much Kreutzer's, however. Schubert's song, by the way, was written for a bass, not for a contralto.

681. From Bauernfeld's Diary

Linz, Sunday, 23rd July 1826.

Recapitulation. The lady of the lake kept me back so long at Ebenzweier, much as I longed to get home . . . Excursion to Kremsmünster . . . At St. Florian a few agreeable hours with the Swede Mayr . . . Here at Linz a circle of friends connected with that in Vienna. The Spauns, Ottenwalts, Mayrhofer.

The "lady of the lake" is Therese Clodi.—Bauernfeld had remained almost a week longer than he had intended.—Theophil Friedrich Mayr (Bauernfeld writes Maier), born in 1793 at Stockholm and therefore known as "the Swedish one" (to distinguish him from others named Maier, Meier, Mair, Meir, Mayer, Meyer, Mayr and Meyr), although at the Kremsmünster Seminary there was next to him another, slightly older Stockholmer, Friedrich Gottlieb Mayer. Theophil was now a canon at St. Florian.—Karl Maurus (or Karl Maria) Mayrhofer, born in Vienna in 1801, the son of Spaun's cousin Helene (*see* No. 276), was a medical student.

682. From Bauernfeld's Diary

24th July 1826.

Dined at Ottenwalt's, who pleases me much. Mayrhofer is a bear.

Bauernfeld, who missed the next concert, left for Vienna by the Danube on the same day, by the "Ulm Ordinary," the regular post-boat, which left Ulm in Württemberg for Vienna each Saturday, taking eight or nine days and charging from 4 to 15 florins per person. (Steamboats at that time plied between Vienna and Pest only since 1823.)

683. From the 'Theaterzeitung,' 19th August 1826

(Correspondence from Linz about the grand musical midday entertainment given by F. X. Arming of Vienna in memory of Their Majesties' visit and for the benefit of the Blind Institution of Linz, at the Assembly Hall there, 25th July 1826.)

3. 'The Wanderer' by Schubert. Sung by a member of the local Musical Society. Received with just applause.

R.

Arming may have been a son of Franz Arming, a comptroller of the Lottery Administration, who was a guarantor of the Linz Musical Society. —The singer is unknown. He was accompanied by the conductor, Schiedermayr (*see* No. 539).

684. FROM BAUERNFELD'S DIARY

[End of] July 1826.

When we landed at Nussdorf in the evening, Schwind and Schubert ran to meet me out of the coffee-house. Great rejoicing!— "Where is the opera?" asked Schubert.—"Here!"—I solemnly handed him 'The Count of Gleichen.'—To Schober at Währing. According to the old custom, we all spent the night together, and how much we had to tell!—Poetry is over, the prose of life begins anew.

The boats, especially the freighters, plying on the Danube above Vienna landed mostly at Nussdorf, the Danube canal being too narrow for most of them and the river itself being too far from the city. At the landing-stage was a pretty building with Knorr's favourite coffee-house. The two friends came from the nearby Währing to meet Bauernfeld, who had contracted an eye complaint through snow blindness.—This summer trip of Bauernfeld's was made shortly before his entering his profession: in September he became equity draughtsman to the Lower Austrian County Government.

685. JOHANN BAPTIST JENGER TO MARIE LEOPOLDINE PACHLER
at Graz

Vienna, 1st August 1826.

. . . Perhaps it will yet happen this autumn, and if I cannot get away, friend Schubert and the painter Teltscher will certainly come, both of whom, dear lady, will present themselves to you.

During his stay at Graz Jenger had made friends with Frau Pachler. She was born at Graz in 1794 under the name of Koschak, had married the brewer and barrister Dr. Karl Pachler in 1816, was a good pianoforte player and in 1817 became a friend of Beethoven's at Vöslau (near Baden, south of Vienna). Schubert's visit to Graz did not materialize until September 1827. In 1826, as in 1828, he had no money for such a journey.

686. MINUTES OF THE MEETING of the Conservatory Committee, 1st August 1828

. . . For the performance of this year's examination concert held by the Conservatory pupils 7th September is fixed . . . The musical pieces to be performed on that occasion, according to the professors' proposals, are the following:

. . . Vocal Quartet by Schubert with pianoforte accompaniment . . .

See No. 696.

687. FROM THE OFFICIAL 'WIENER ZEITUNG,' 7th August 1826

At the House of Ant. Diabelli & Co.,

Art and Music Dealers in the Graben, No. 1133, are newly published and to be had of K. Lichtl in Pest at the same price:

Trois Marches militaires
pour le Pianoforte à 4 mains,
composées par François Schubert.

Œuvre 51.   Prix 2 Fl. 30 Kr. Viennese Currency.
(Propriété des Éditeurs.)

Op. 51, published after Op. 63, bears no dedication. It was one of Diabelli's belated issues. These most popular of Schubert's marches have been often and variously arranged.

688. SCHUBERT TO H. A. PROBST at Leipzig

[Outside:]

[H. A.] von Probst, Esq.,
Art Dealer

in

Leipzig.

[Inside:]

Vienna, 12th August 1826.

Sir,

In the hope that my name may not be wholly unknown to you, I most politely inquire whether you would not be disinclined to acquire some of my compositions at reasonable terms, being very desirous of becoming as well known as possible in Germany. You may take your choice among songs with pianoforte accompaniment, string quartets, pianoforte sonatas, 4-handed pieces, &c. &c. I have also written an Octet for two violins, viola, violoncello, double bass, clarinet, bassoon and horn. Esteeming it an honour in any case to have entered into correspondence with you, I remain, in the hope of a speedy reply, with all respect,

Your devoted
Franz Schubert.

My address: On the Wieden,
No. 100, next to the Karl Church,
5th staircase, 2nd floor.

This is almost identical with No. 689: Schubert was preparing an attack on Germany.—Heinrich Albert Probst (born Dresden, 1791) had founded a new music publishing house at Leipzig in 1823, a partner in and later owner of which was F. Kistner.—*See* No. 694.

689. SCHUBERT TO BREITKOPF & HÄRTEL

[Outside:]   From Vienna.
                    To the Art Establishment
                        Breitkopf *et* Härtel
                                    at
                                        Leipzig.

[Inside:]
                                    Vienna, 12th August 1826.
Sirs,
    In the hope that my name may not be wholly unknown to you, I most politely inquire whether you would not be disinclined to acquire some of my compositions at reasonable terms, being very desirous of becoming as well known as possible in Germany. You may take your choice among songs with pianoforte accompaniment, string quartets, pianoforte sonatas, 4-handed pieces, &c. &c. I have also written an Octet. In any case I should regard it as a special honour to enter into relations with so old

and famous an art establishment.   In anticipation of a speedy reply, I remain, with all respect,

Your devoted

My address: On the Wieden,   Franz Schubert.
No. 100, next to the Karl Church,
5th staircase, 2nd floor.

Cf. No. 102.   The Dresden Franz Schubert had died in 1824. —*See* No. 695.

690. FROM BAUERNFELD'S DIARY

August 1826.

I am to translate Shakespeare's poems and sonnets for Sollinger. So be it!   Schubert ailing (he needs "young peacocks," like Benvenuto Cellini).   Schwind morose, Schober idle, as usual. In myself there's still travel-fever and blood!

Cf. No. 588.—Cellini (born 1500), the famous craftsman and sculptor, whose autobiography was translated by Goethe, liked to shoot peacocks for the table.   But this has nothing to do with the fact that he too suffered from syphilis, and this remark can hardly be taken to suggest a relapse in Schubert's case.—Schober's business zeal had abated already.

691. FROM BAUERNFELD'S DIARY

August 1826.

Schubert liked the opera very much; but we are afraid of the censorship. . . . Schober and Schwind disagree.   Poor Moritz suffers from being in love and finds no recognition in his art. Schubert is penniless, like the rest of us.

The subject of the Count of Gleichen was looked at askance by the censorship, especially that of the court theatres, on account of his bigamy. —Schwind had just then for the first time exhibited a picture which afterwards came into Schober's possession, a representation of Katie of Heilbronn espied asleep by her master, the knight Wetter von Strahl.   Heinrich von Kleist's romantic drama on the subject was produced at the Theater an der Wien in 1810.

692. FROM THE 'THEATERZEITUNG,' 22nd August 1826

(On twelve songs by Friedrich August Kanne to words by Johann Gabriel Seidl.)

. . . A special interest may attach to these compositions because many of these poems have been composed also by Fr. Schubert, B. Randhartinger, Fr. Lachner and others; to be engraved and published shortly and thus offering a comparison that will be both interesting and useful.

J. G. S.
[Seidl.]

This was a kind of self-advertisement by the poet, for Kanne's songs set to his poems had not yet appeared either. They included 'In the Open' ('Im Freien'), which Schubert had also used for a song in March 1826, and 'Grave and Moon' ('Grab und Mond,' here called 'Mond und Grab'), which he was to set as a male-voice quartet in September 1826.

Therese Grob, sen., dies, 22nd August 1826.—Her son Heinrich married a month later.

693. FROM THE FRANKFORT 'ALLGEMEINER MUSIKALISCHER ANZEIGER,' 26th August 1826

Première grande Sonate p. 1. Pianoforte composée par François Schubert de Vienne. Op. 42. Vienne chez Pennauer. 2 fl.

A significant, original work, requiring no pianoforte virtuoso in the ordinary sense of the word, but a player of insight and feeling. Many will fail to grasp it, but then, many do not understand even Goethe, who, one would think, should be comprehensible to all.

694. H. A. PROBST TO SCHUBERT

[Outside:]

Franz Schubert, Esq.,
Tone-Poet and Composer.
Vienna,
On the Wieden, No. 100,

Franked.   next to the Karl Church,
5th staircase.   2nd floor.

[Inside:]

Franz Schubert, Esq.,
Vienna.

Leipzig, 26th August 1826.

It was in truth an honour and a pleasure for me to make your acquaintance by your esteemed letter of the 12th inst., and thanking you cordially for your confidence, I am very gladly prepared to contribute towards the dissemination of your artistic reputation so far as it lies in my power.   Only I must frankly confess to you that our public does not yet sufficiently and generally understand the peculiar, often ingenious, but perhaps now and then somewhat curious procedures of your mind's creations.   Kindly, therefore, bear this in mind on sending me your MSS.   Selected songs, not too difficult pianoforte compositions for 2 and 4 hands, agreeable and easily comprehensible, would seem to me suitable for the attainment of your purpose and my wishes.   Once the path has been cleared, everything will find access, but to begin with a few concessions must be made to the public.   Please forward your MSS. to me through Herr Lähne, book-keeper at Artaria & Co.'s. Receive the highest respects of   Your devoted

H. A. Probst.

Cf. No. 688.—Probst was agent for the house of Artaria & Co. for Germany, and Robert Lähne was its book-keeper.—See No. 777.

695. BREITKOPF & HÄRTEL TO SCHUBERT

[Outside:]

Franz Schubert, Esq.,
famous Composer
in
Vienna,
On the Wieden, No. 100, next to the Karl Church,
5th staircase, 2nd floor.

[Inside:]

Sir,   Leipzig, 7th September 1826.

You kind inclination to consign to us for publication some works composed by you we reciprocate with our sincerest thanks and with the assurance that it would be very agreeable to us to enter into a pleasant mutual relationship of publishing with you. As, however, we are as yet wholly unacquainted with the mercantile success of your compositions and are therefore unable to meet you with the offer of a fixed pecuniary remuneration (which a publisher can determine or concede only according to that success), we must leave it to you to decide whether, in order perhaps to bring about a lasting relationship by a trial, you will facilitate the matter for us and accept merely a number of copies as a return for the first work, or works, which you will send us. We do not doubt your consent to this, since for you, as for us, the question cannot be that of the publication of a single work so much as of the inception of a continued relationship. In that case we propose to you to begin by sending us one or two pieces for the pianoforte, solo or duet. If our hopes of a favourable success are in any way fulfilled, so that we may be able to offer you a decent cash remuneration for the following works, we shall esteem it a pleasure to have thereby made relations with us agreeable for you. We are, Sir, with the deepest respect,

Devotedly,

Breitkopf & Härtel.

Cf. No. 689. This one letter marked the premature conclusion of a tentative transaction between Schubert and Breitkopf & Härtel, the oldest music publishing house in Germany, which attempted to treat him as a beginner. The connection was not resumed until 1839, when the firm acquired the great C major Symphony (see No. XLV), and the years 1884–97 (the latter Schubert's centenary), when the firm carried out the critical complete edition of his works in twenty-one series divided into thirty-nine folio volumes, mainly with the aid of Eusebius Mandyczewski and under the patronage of Brahms.

696. FROM THE PROGRAMME of the Pupils' Examination of the Vienna Conservatory, 7th September 1826, at 3.30 p.m., in the County Hall

12. Psalm XXIII, set to music for 4 voices with fortepiano accompaniment, by Franz Schubert, sung by the lady pupils of the third vocal class.

Cf. No. 686.—It was for Anna Fröhlich's pupils once again that Schubert wrote this work (see No. 249).

697. From the 'Sammler,' 26th September 1826

The male and female pupils of the first, second and third vocal classes performed four-part vocal choruses—for 2 sopranos and 2 altos—by Seyfried, Gyrowetz and Schubert; the last especially, which was also artistically on a higher level, with firm intonation, warmth, feeling and vitality. Schubert's 23rd Psalm, 'The Lord is my shepherd,' is a deeply felt, thoughtfully conceived hymn, but not too easy to perform on account of its modulations, and the supporting pianoforte thus by no means appears as a mere stop-gap.

The Psalm, sung by eight girl students, had to be repeated. Further notices appeared on 28th September in the 'Theaterzeitung,' on 25th October in the Berlin 'Allgemeine musikalische Zeitung' (agreeing almost word for word with that in the 'Sammler'), on 8th November in the Leipzig 'Allgemeine musikalische Zeitung' and, without a date, in the Weimar 'Musikalische Eilpost' of 1826 (German edition, Nos. 706–9).

698. From the Weimar 'Musikalische Eilpost,' 1826

Quintetto pour deux Violons, deux Altos et Violoncelle, par G. Onslow. Op. 23. 1 thl. 16 gr. Vienne chez Sauer et Leidesdorf and
Trois quatuors pour deux Violons, Alto et Violoncelle, par François Schubert de Vienne. Œuv. 29. No. 1. Prix 1 thl. 16 gr. Vienne chez Sauer et Leidesdorf.

True to our journal's tendency, which forbids extensive reviews, we may very well combine the announcement of these two works, if we regard them from the point of view of the highest artistic endeavours, which are clearly expressed. Profound feeling, force and charm, significance and vitality and poetic fire characterize both; whoever has any appreciation for this species—and it still survives in many—will certainly enjoy them more than once, and each time with heightened interest.

The new Quintet by Onslow (*see* No. 629) had been played, from parts published in Paris, at Franz, Edler von Pickher's, in Vienna, about 1825. Pickher, Holzapfel's superior, was county councillor to the Lower Austrian county courts and an enthusiastic collector of chamber music. He held weekly musical sessions at his apartments in the Bürgerspital, with programmes ranging from Handel to the latest publications and including preferably symphonies arranged for string quintet. Holzapfel played the cello there.

699. From the Weimar 'Musikalische Eilpost,' 1826

'Longing' ['Die Sehnsucht']. Poem by Schiller, set to music for one voice with pianoforte accompaniment by F. Schubert. Work 39. Vienna, A. Pennauer. 45 Kreuzer.

A fantasy which, conceived in a fortunate hour, streams onward, suffused with life, in one single outpouring and as a whole produces a very beautiful impression. For that reason one may well over-look a few small transgressions against declamation and a certain melodic stiffness on p. 6.

700. From the Official 'Wiener Zeitung,' 14th September 1826

At the House of A. Pennauer,
I. & R. Art and Music Dealer, in the Graben, No. 1122,
at Fischer's House, is just published:

Grande Marche héroïque
pour le pianoforte à quatre mains,
à l'occasion du Sacre de Sa. Maj.
Nicolas I,
Empereur de toutes les Russies, etc. etc. etc.,
par François Schubert.

Œuvre 66.   Price, 2 Fl. 45 Kr., V.C.

The same arranged for pianoforte solo, 1 Fl. 45 Kr., V.C.

Nicholas I, born in 1796, the dead Tsar Alexander's brother, had ascended the throne on 24th December 1825. It is said that Schubert offered the two marches, Op. 55 (*see* No. 627) and Op. 66, to Steiner & Co. at first; but as Steiner's firm was taken over, on 11th March 1826, by his partner and was now known as Tobias Haslinger, both marches must have been written earlier. Schubert probably composed them in suc-cession. The first was orchestrated by Wilhelm Kienzl, the second by

Rimsky-Korsakov (performed by Balakirev at St. Petersburg on 5th May 1868).—Op. 66 appeared before Opp. 62, 64 and 65.

> Leopold Kupelwieser marries Johanna Lutz, 17th September 1826.—Schubert played for dancing at the wedding and would not let anybody else go near the pianoforte.   Schwind made a speech on the bride, whom he apostrophized as "the master's lady."   Doblhoff arrived too late owing to the illness of his betrothed, Jeannette Cuny de Pierron.

701. FROM BAUERNFELD'S DIARY

18th September 1826.

A very curious note-book of Schubert's for the year 1824 has been found, in which the following passage occurs:
"Enviable Nero!. Thou who wert strong enough to destroy a loathsome people to the strains of strings and voice!"
Also verses of his making.

> Cf. Nos. 450–4.—Bauernfeld had received his employment decree on 10th September.   "I feel as though I were going to be hanged," he wrote the next day in his diary.

702. FROM THE OFFICIAL 'WIENER ZEITUNG,' 21st September 1826

At the House of Sauer & Leidesdorf,
Art and Music Dealers, in Vienna, Kärntnerstrasse, No. 941,
(Pest, at K. Lichtl's) is just published and to be had:

. . . . . .

SCHUBERT, FRANZ, FOUR POEMS ['Thou lov'st me not' ('Du liebst mich nicht')—'That she has been here' ('Dass sie hier gewesen')—'Thou art repose' ('Du bist die Ruh')—'Laughing and Weeping' ('Lachen und Weinen')] by F. Rückert and Count Platen, for One Voice with Pianoforte Accompaniment. Work 59.   2 Florins.

> Op. 59, the first song of which is on a poem by Platen, appeared after Op. 66.   That there was some uncertainty to the last about its numbering is shown by the fact that it was inserted into the title-page afterwards. There is no dedication.

703. From the Frankfort 'Allgemeiner Musikalischer Anzeiger,' 30th September 1826

Franz Schubert's Songs with Guitar Accompaniment. Work 21. Vienna, Sauer & Leidesdorf. 12 Groschen.

Three good songs for a bass voice. The accompaniment is difficult at times.

Cf. No. 367.

704. From Sophie Müller's Diary

2nd October 1826.

Vogl here, back from Steyr day before yesterday, for Schubert —2 florins.

Vogl had this time been to his home-town with his new wife.—The payment "for Schubert" was probably for a copy of Op. 59 (*see* No. 702).

705. Copy of the Agreement for the Sale of Schubert's Paternal House

Under date of the day and year below written the following contract of sale and purchase has been concluded between Herr Franz Schubert, owner of the house No. 10 in the Himmelpfortgrund as vendor of the one part and Herr Jakob Rickel and his wife Josefa as purchasers of the other part:

Firstly the said Herr Franz Schubert doth sell to the said Herr Jakob Rickel and his wife Josefa the dwelling-house of his own property No. 10 Himmelpfortgrund as bounded and fenced by walls and planks together with all that is earthed and walled riveted and all winter windows against an agreed purchase price of six thousand four hundred florins (say 6,400) in assimilated coinage and two hundred florins key money in assimilated coinage (say 200 fl., A.C.).

Secondly the purchasers will pay the agreed purchase price as follows, viz.

a) forthwith on account four hundred florins in A.C.,   say 400 fl., A.C.
the correct receipt whereof is hereby acknowledged,

b) at Lady Day 1827 the sum of three thousand florins, A.C.,   say 3,000 fl., A.C.
and two hundred florins, A.C., as key money say   200 fl., A.C.

c) at Lady Day 1831 the remainder of three thousand florins, A.C.,   say 3,000 fl., A.C.

According to which the purchase price including key money is fixed at   6,600 fl., A.C.

Thirdly the purchasers promise to pay interest at five per cent by quarterly payments on the above-mentioned 3,000 fl., A.C. commencing on Lady Day 1827 and thereupon to hypothecate at their expense this remainder of the purchase price of 3,000 fl., A.C. in the purchased house No. 10 Himmelpfortgrund.

Fourthly is the conveyance of the house to be completed at Lady Day 1827 until which time the vendor is to have the whole use of it and also to defray all costs concerning the house such as rates taxes and other duties whatsoever they may be called.

Fifthly the vendor Herr Franz Schubert will deliver on Lady Day 1827 on payment of 3,200 fl., A.C., the conveyance title-deeds and whatever other documents may be required for the conveyance and will stand security for any charge that may arise and likewise will convey the house free of all encumbrances.

Sixthly is there no repining either on the part of the vendor or on the part of the purchaser.

As witness &c. . . . Vienna, 5th October 1826.

Cf. Nos. 4, 37 and 38; *see also* Nos. 808 and 887. Although the value of the house had risen from 5,000 florins to 6,600 florins since 1812, Schubert's share of c. 200 florins may have been only nominally redeemed by his father.—Other entries concerning this transfer of property are also to be found in the records "D" of the Himmelpfort Convent (Property Register No. 342), fol. 206, verso, and in the Himmelpfortgrund extracts, fol. 42 f., in the archives of the City of Vienna.

706. FROM THE 'WIENER ZEITSCHRIFT FÜR KUNST,' &c., 7th October 1826

TO FRANZ SCHUBERT FROM THE RIVER RHINE

What of two kings to us thou hast related;
What held your Margaret at the Spinning-wheel;
The songs at Müller's waterfall resounding;
The hallelujah-bell's familiar peal;
Your Restless Love, with joy and rapture thrilling;
The Solitary and his cricket's squeal;
All this we heard it in a Morning Song:
With Urge into the Distance thou shalt long.

Oh let us, Wanderer, see thee at our river,
Come, Minstrel! thou great Danube's worthy son.
Not as Imprisoned Huntsman shalt thou meet us:
Like Norman's shall thy glorious prize be won.
An Ave! shall we quire aloud to greet thee,
The Spirit's Tones then shall in this wise run:
At home not more with us, abroad not less,
There, where thou, Harper, art, is happiness.

Julius Velox.
[Schneller.]

Julius Franz Borgias Schneller (*see* No. 277), born at Strasburg in 1777, had gone to Vienna about 1797. He became professor of history at the Lyceum of Linz in 1805 (where he taught Josef von Spaun) and professor of philosophy at the Lyceum of Graz in 1806. In 1817–20 he published a history of Austria, which made him unpopular there, so that at the end of 1823 he went to Freiburg i/B., where he became professor of philosophy at the university. He made friends with the Pachlers and with Jenger at Graz.—His dedicatory poem, containing a fruitless invitation to come to the Rhine, alludes to a number of Schubert's songs. The "two kings" are the 'Erl King' and the 'King in Thule' sung by Margaret in 'Faust'; "Müller" (whom Schneller calls Müllner) is the poet of 'The Fair Maid of the Mill' (though there is a brook in it, not a "waterfall"); the "hallelujah-bell" is in 'The Young Nun'; 'Restless Love' is 'Rastlose Liebe' and 'The Solitary' is 'Der Einsame'; 'Morning Song' is Zacharias Werner's 'Morgenlied' and 'Urge into the Distance' is 'Drang in die Ferne.' The 'Wanderer' in the second verse is the poem by Schmidt of Lübeck, which is paraphrased in the last line and the third from the end; the 'Minstrel' is 'Der Liedler'; the 'Imprisoned Huntsman' and 'Norman' are two of the Walter Scott songs, while the 'Ave (Maria)' is Ellen's third song, also from 'The Lady of the Lake'; the 'Harper' is the singer of three of the songs from Goethe's 'Wilhelm Meister.'

707. FROM SOPHIE MÜLLER'S DIARY
7th October 1826.

Beer, Max, Vogl beefsteak, Jenger, Schubert.　At noon Gretel.

Michael Beer, born in 1800, Giacomo Meyerbeer's brother, was a playwright who lived by turns in Paris and Munich, later at Bonn, and was in Vienna on a visit.—Max may be the younger son of Helmina von Chézy (see No. 385).—Vogl perhaps expressed a preference for beefsteak. —Gretel is Fräulein Desprès (see No. 617).

708. FROM SOPHIE MÜLLER'S DIARY
9th October 1826.

Vogl, Schubert, Jenger dined.

This was in the evening.

Antonie Adamberger (married name, von Arneth) sings before Grillparzer at the monastery of St. Florian songs from 'The Fair Maid of the Mill' and from 'Wilhelm Meister,' including the 'First Song of the Harper,' and in the evening at the Monastery Church, accompanied by the organist Anton Kattinger, the 'Ave Maria,' early October 1826.—This singer, born in Vienna in 1790 as the daughter of the tenor Valentin Adamberger (died 1804), engaged to Theodor Körner in 1812 (see note preceding No. 52), had been at the Burg Theatre in 1807–17, where in 1810, as Klärchen in Goethe's 'Egmont,' she was the first to sing Beethoven's songs "Freudvoll und leidvoll" and "Die Trommel gerühret." She had since married the numismatist Josef Cales von Arneth, born in 1791, custodian of the Cabinet of Coins and Antiquities (see No. 92), and become reader to the Empress Karolina Augusta. Thayer compared her loss to the Viennese stage to that of Elizabeth Anne Linley when she married Sheridan. The prelate of St. Florian (see No. 364) was her husband's brother.—Grillparzer was on his way back from Weimar, where he had visited Goethe.—Kattinger (born c. 1800) was Bruckner's master later on (see No. 577).—Antonie's sister, Mimi Adamberger, sang two Schubert songs at St. Florian on 26th August 1928 (Franz von Hartmann's family chronicle).

709. SCHUBERT TO THE PHILHARMONIC SOCIETY

[Early October 1826.]

To the Committee of the Austrian Musical Society.

Convinced of the Austrian Musical Society's noble intention to support any artistic endeavour as far as possible, I venture, as a native artist, to dedicate to them this, my Symphony, and to commend it most politely to their protection.

With all respect,
Your devoted
Frz. Schubert.

It may be supposed that this was the lost "Gastein" Symphony. It is hardly likely that Schubert would have gone back to one of his youthful symphonies for a dedication that must have been suggested to him; and he had written no other symphony than this, with the exception of the two fragments in E major and B minor (the latter probably at Graz already).

710. FROM THE CATALOGUE of Exhibits of the Philharmonic Society in the Austrian Imperial State, Early October 1826

SCHUBERT (Franz, Composer). The same dedicated a Symphony to the Society, composed by himself. (1826.) Fascicle: Library. No. of the Piece: 105.

The society has preserved no symphony by Schubert dating from that time.

711. LOST REPORT on the Committee Meeting of the Philharmonic Society, 9th October 1826

(The vice-president Rafael Georg von Kiesewetter reports that Schubert wishes to dedicate a symphony to the society. A resolution is passed, without reference to this offer, to have a remuneration of 100 florins, A.C., paid to him, for his services to the society and for further encouragement. The secretary, Josef Sonnleithner, declares himself ready to advance the sum, should the society's present cash balance be insufficient.)

712. KIESEWETTER TO VINCENZ HAUSCHKA

The composer Herr Franz Schubert has been granted, as a token of the Society's gratitude, the sum of One Hundred Florins, A.C., which please remit him with the enclosed letter, and book to expenses.

On behalf of the Committee of Management.

To   Vienna, 12th October 1826.

Herr Vincenz Hauschka,   Kiesewetter.

I. & R. Councillor of Finance,

Treasurer of the Society.

[Outside:]

No. 208

─────────

1826.

Hauschka (*see* No. 222), born in 1766 at Mies in Bohemia, had gone to Vienna in 1792 and became a financial councillor in the Administration of Public Property. He was very musical and founded the evening entertainments of the Philharmonic Society, of which he was treasurer.

713. KIESEWETTER TO SCHUBERT

You have repeatedly given proof of interest in the Philharmonic Society in the Austrian Imperial State, and exerted your excellent composer's talent on its behalf and particularly that of the Conservatory.

Knowing how to appreciate your decided and excellent worth as a composer, it desires to tender you a commensurate proof of its gratitude and esteem and requests you to accept the enclosed, not as a fee, but as a token of the Society's sense of obligation towards you, and of the thanks with which it acknowledges the interest you have shown it.

On behalf of the controlling Committee of the Philharmonic Society in the Austrian Imperial State.

Vienna, 12th October 1826.   Kiesewetter.

It is curious that no thanks are offered for the Symphony, although there is a hint that the present is not regarded as payment for the dedication.

714. **From the Catalogue of Exhibits** of the Philharmonic Society

Schuberth (Composer).   Concerning the 100 florins, A.C., assigned as fee to the same.   (1826.)   Fascicle: Library.   No. of the Piece: 130.

The present enclosed in No. 713 is here called a "fee."   It is remarkable, too, that a library number is given, although not the same as in No. 710.

715. **From the Catalogue of Exhibits** of the Philharmonic Society

Schubert (Franz, Composer).   Concerning the remuneration of 100 florins, A.C., presented to the same.   (1826.)   Fascicle Protocol: 178.

The amount is here called a "remuneration," as in No. 711, and as it appears by implication in Nos. 712 and 713.

716. **From Bauernfeld's Diary**

October 1826.

The libretto prohibited by the censorship.   Schubert wants to compose it all the same.

Cf. No. 691.—Schubert had actually begun the composition of 'The Count of Gleichen,' but the only date in his sketches is 19th June 1827, on the introductory chorus in the first act.   It is worthy of note that the libretto included Goethe's song, 'Delight in Woe' ('Wonne der Wehmut'), which Schubert had already set with pianoforte accompaniment in 1815, but which was only published posthumously as No. 2 of Op. 115 in 1829.

717. **Bauernfeld to Schober**

[Vienna, October 1826.]

When I read the chit, I thought it too blunt myself, and I had some slight qualm lest I should be misunderstood.   I communicated it to Schubert (who as a matter of fact knew as good as nothing of the affair, but only about my being bored), and as it pleased him, I let him have it.

At a gathering of the friends—without Schubert—Bauernfeld had flown into a passion over Schober's and Schwind's injustice to Haas (probably Ferdinand, *see* No. 569) and over the circle's tediousness. He then indulged in satirical doggerel on Schober's conduct, which he first showed to Schubert and then left at Schober's, who replied by letter: "If ideas, or my ideas, mean nothing to you, you had better avoid me." Bauernfeld then wrote a conciliatory letter to Schober and Schwind, with half-humorous variants of the verses, enclosing the present leaf, which led to a reconciliation.

718. From Franz von Hartmann's Diary

Linz, 17th October 1826: Stadler and Gahy play [at the Hartmanns'] glorious Schubertian marches and Schubert's overture to 'Alfonso and Estrella.'

Stadler is Albert.—The overture was marked "Op. 52," but was really Op. 69 (*see* No. 628). Cf. note preceding No. 720.

719. Schubert's Receipt for the Philharmonic Society

Acknowledgment

of One Hundred Florins, Assimilated Coinage, which I have been granted on 12th October of this year as a courteous distinction from the Austrian Musical Society, and the receipt of which I confirm herewith.

Franz Schubert,
Composer

For 100 Fl., A.C.
Vienna, 20th October 1826.

[Outside:]

ad 208
_____
1826.

The file number corresponds to that of No. 712.—The receipt is written on the Neusiedel paper used in the Philharmonic Society's chancellery: Schubert clearly made it out on the spot, having called for the money.

> Gahy and Stadler play piano-duet pieces, particularly by Schubert, at the Ottenwalts' at Linz, before the Hartmanns and Spauns, 20th October 1826.   Cf. No. 718.

720. From Sophie Müller's Diary

6th November 1826.

Schubert, Teltscher, Jenger, Hüttenbrenner *gratula*[*ntur*] Father Carolus.

> Karl Müller, Sophie's father, was born at Mannheim in 1763 and had been an actor at the court of Baden.   He was celebrating his birthday. (The Müllers were Protestants.)

721. From the Programme of the First Evening Entertainment held by the Philharmonic Society, 16th November 1826 (Conductor, Herr Schmiedel)

4. Psalm XXIII, set to Music for 2 Sopranos and 2 Altos by Franz Schubert.

> This quartet was sung by the Conservatory girl students once again (*see* No. 696).

722. Note on the above Programme

[Anna] Fröhlich.

A series of the printed programmes of these evening entertainments, or private concerts, held by the "Little Society," contains notes in the hand of an unknown participant, probably one of the pupils of Anna Fröhlich, who accompanied them on the pianoforte.

723. From Franz von Hartmann's Diary

Vienna, 17th November 1826: At 10 o'clock we went with Ferdinand Sauter to the "Anchor," where Spaun came too, also Schober, Zechenter's brother-in-law and Bruchmann's former friend. We remained there until 12 o'clock.

Franz von Hartmann, who had already studied law in Vienna in 1824–5, went to live in the capital again early in November 1826 with his brother Fritz, who had been at the university since 1823. His diary, and from 1827 onward Fritz's as well, gives many details of the Schubertians' daily life.—Here we are told for the first time of a new habitual gathering-place, which may have been frequented by the friends for some time before, the "Anchor." It was in the Grünangergasse, from which it derived its later name by a mispronunciation (*Der grüne Anker* instead of *Der grüne Anger*=the green meadow). Even to-day, under half Italian management, it is known as "Ancora verde." It is near St. Stephen's cathedral, near the Singerstrasse.—Ferdinand Sauter, born in 1804 at Werfen in the Tyrol, was called "Dinand" by an abbreviation of his name. He went to Vienna in 1825 and became a stationer's assistant. He was a very gifted lyric poet, but was ruined by drink. Not long after his introduction to the Schubert circle, evidently by the Hartmann brothers, Schober turned against him by declaring that "he has nothing to contribute to the association." (Cf. Schubert's question, already current: "Kann er was?")—Zechenter was Sophie von Schober's (*see* No. 162) widower.—Schober too, whom the Hartmanns then met for the first time, had fallen out with Bruchmann.

724. From Franz von Hartmann's Diary

19th November 1826: With Fritz to the "Anchor," where there was a large gathering, including Schwind, who presented me with a small nosegay, Schubert and Bauernfeld. Spaun joined us later, too. At 11.30 we parted.

725. From Franz von Hartmann's Diary

21st November 1826: At 10 o'clock to the "Anchor," where were Spaun, Schubert, Schober, &c., very jolly. Ferdinand Sauter also came later on. At 11.40 every one at last went home.

725A. Schubert to Ignaz von Seyfried

[Outside:]

I. von Seyfried, Esq.
Knight & Musical Director,
Here.

[Inside:]

Sir,

I politely request you to let me know by the bearer of this
whether my overture to 'Rosamond' has been found.   As it is
to be given on December 2nd, I should find myself in a
dreadful embarrassment.   I therefore once again beg you to let
me have a speedy reply.

I remain, with all respect,

Your most devoted

Frz. Schubert.

Vienna, 23rd December [*recte* November] 1826.

The overture played with 'Rosamond' in 1823, i.e. that for the opera
'Alfonso and Estrella' (*see* Nos. 411 and 628), had evidently been kept by
the Theater an der Wien or was lent to that theatre again for some unknown purpose.   It may be supposed that Seyfried, then serving the
last year of his conductorship there, returned the manuscript—probably
score and parts—in good time for use at the concert (*see* No. 731).
When Schubert wrote the duet arrangement of the Overture in 1825, he
must have had a manuscript of the full score at hand.

726. From the Programme of the Second Evening Entertainment
held by the Philharmonic Society, 23rd November 1826
(Conductor, Herr [Johann] Schönpichler)

2. 'The Solitary' ['Der Einsame'], poem by Lappe, set to music
by Fr. Schubert, sung by Herr Tietze.

For Schönpichler *see* No. 218.—Karl Lappe, born in Pomerania in
1773, was an insignificant representative of the German romantic school,
a schoolmaster whose 'Hütte in Pütte' (named after his favourite resort)
became very popular.   Schubert wrote two songs and a male-voice
quartet on poems of his.

727. FROM THE OFFICIAL 'WIENER ZEITUNG,' 24th November 1826

At the House of Cappi & Czerny,

Priv. Art Dealers, in the Graben, No. 1134, are just published, and to be had of K. Lichtl in Pest at the same price:

A BOATMAN'S SONG TO THE DIOSCURI

['Lied eines Schiffers an die Dioskuren']

by J. Mayrhofer;

THE WANDERER

['Der Wanderer']

by A. W. Schlegel;

To HELIOPOLIS

by J. Mayrhofer;

set to Music for One Voice with Pianoforte Accompaniment

by FRANZ SCHUBERT

Work 65.   1 Florin 30 Kreuzer, V.C.

Op. 65 appeared, without a dedication, before Op. 64 and after Op. 66. The poet's name of No. 2, 'The Wanderer,' is wrongly given on the title-page as well as August Wilhelm instead of Friedrich Schlegel.—The second 'Heliopolis' poem (*see* No. 253) was probably, like the present one, composed in April 1822.

728. FROM FRANZ VON HARTMANN'S DIARY

25th November 1826: To the "Anchor," where I hoped to meet Spaun. Later, however, came Schober and Bauernfeld, with a gawky Bavarian. Schober is quite interesting; Bauernfeld very dull. I stayed until 11.40.

The gawky Bavarian may have been Franz Lachner (cf. No. 735).

729. MARIE OTTENWALT TO JOSEF VON SPAUN

Linz, [? November] 30th [? 1826].

Perhaps Max will bring us some new things by Schubert, to which we look forward already.

Max von Spaun was on a visit to Vienna from 8th to 23rd December.

730. From Franz von Hartmann's Diary

30th November 1826: Fritz fetched me to the "Anchor," as Spaun was there. It was quite jolly there. Home at 11.15.

731. From the Programme of the Grand Concert for the Benefit of the Brothers Eduard Konstantin and Josef Rudolf Lewy, Horn Players at the Kärntnertor Theatre, 2nd December 1826, there

1. Overture by Schubert.

Édouard Constantin Lewy, born in 1796 at Saint-Avold (Moselle), was settled in Vienna. His brother Joseph Rodolphe, later known as Lewy-Hoffmann, was born at Nancy in 1804, and did not remain in Vienna. He seems to have been the inventor of the valve horn.—Schubert's overture (*see* No. 725A) was given no title: it had lost its name in all this confusion.—The programme also contained the hunting-chorus from Weber's 'Euryanthe' and finished with a ballet.

732. From the 'Theaterzeitung,' 14th December 1826

An overture by our favourably known song composer Schubert began the concert. The orchestra performed this overture valiantly, and the public showed its approval.

The 'Theaterzeitung' had already published a short notice of the concert on 12th December, where the overture was described as "well written and effective." A criticism of it, in the 'Sammler' of 23rd December, mentioned it in similar terms (German edition, Nos. 743 and 746).

733. From the Berlin 'Allgemeine Musikalische Zeitung,' 28th February 1827

The introductory overture, by Schubert, may well promise more on paper than it fulfils in reality!—

734. From the 'Harmonicon,' London, June 1827

. . . In another concert, given by the brothers Lewy, the novelties were, a revived Overture by Schubert, full of striking effects, and worthy of being better known.

735. From Franz von Hartmann's Diary

5th December 1826: I went to the "Anchor," where Schober, Schubert and Lachner (a composer from Bavaria) were at first, and only late and unexpectedly Pepi Spaun, with whom we then remained there until midnight; he telling us splendid stories of his and his brothers' youth.

736. From Franz von Hartmann's Diary

7th December 1826: To the "Anchor" at 9.45; Schober, Pepi Spaun and Schubert there.　Home at 11.30.

737. From Franz von Hartmann's Diary

8th December 1826 (Immaculate Conception): At 8.30 I went to Spaun's, where the two brothers and Fritz were at first.　Then came Schubert and played a magnificent but melancholy piece of his own composition.　At last Schwind, Bauernfeld, Enderes and Schober came too.　Schubert and Schwind then sang the most lovely Schubert songs.　In the end we supped splendidly. All were very lively and wide awake.　At last everybody began to smoke.　Spax, naturally enough, very often dozed off.　At 12.45 we parted.　We saw Schober home.

The "melancholy piece" may have been a movement of the G major Sonata, Op. 78, written in October and dedicated to Josef von Spaun, who had liked the first movement (cf. No. 740A).　Spaun lived in the Teinfaltstrasse, near the Scottish church, at official lodgings colloquially called the "nags' stables" (Klepperställe).—Spax is Max von Spaun.— Schober lived again in the Obere Bäckerstrasse, where Schubert was his guest in the autumn, after spending the summer at Währing.　He had probably lost his lodgings at Fruhwirt's house through his visits to Währing, and now found new quarters on the bastion near the Karolinentor, opposite the present Stadtpark, where he remained until February 1827, when he joined Schober in his new lodgings for a longer time.

738. FROM FRANZ VON HARTMANN'S DIARY

9th December 1826: I betook myself to the "Anchor," where I found the two Spauns, Enk, Schwind, Schober, Enderes, the two Lachners and a novice conveyancer. It was quite amusing, as by chance we (Spax and I) brought the guessing game on the tapis. At 11.15 everybody went home.

Karl Enk von der Burg, born in 1800 at Salzburg, had studied law and became an important educationist. He was a private tutor and worked with Johann Baptist Hörwarter, whom we are yet to meet, on a prose translation of Dante's 'Divine Comedy,' finished in 1829 and published at Innsbruck in 1830–1.—Franz Lachner's brother Ignaz, born in 1807, became organist of the Protestant church in 1824, succeeding his brother, and in 1826 he also became assistant conductor at the Kärntnertor Theatre.— The unnamed "novice" was a conveyancer, i.e. an academically educated probationer in some official post.

739. FROM FRANZ VON HARTMANN'S DIARY

11th December 1826: We went to Bruchmann's, who was ill, and where juridical matters were very amusingly talked about and abused, in a way I have scarcely ever heard before . . . I went with Fritz to Bogner's coffee-house (Singerstrasse) and there met the Spauns, Schober and Enderes; Schwind came too. Pepi told very interesting things about Poland and played billiards splendidly with Enderes. I lost a turn with Max, but was two up on Schober for compensation. Having been there until 9.30 (!), we went to the "Anchor," where we looked at the 'Lampe' illustrations, and everything was good fun. Home at 11.30.

Bruchmann, like the brothers Hartmann, was a law student. He had undergone a great change at the end of August 1826, when he became converted to positive Christianity, as Streinsberg and his wife Isabella, Bruchmann's sister, had been before him. Franz von Hartmann, who had been in Vienna from the middle of August to the middle of September for examinations, had then made Bruchmann's acquaintance, probably through Smetana.—Bogner's café, near the Anchor Tavern, on the corner of the Singerstrasse and the Blutgassel, now used for other purposes, had, like the latter, recently become one of the friends' habitual haunts. It was owned by Karl Bogner and had only two small guest rooms and a kitchen, all on the ground floor. In the corner room, which was the larger, there was a billiard table. Schwind, to pay off his score, painted a Turkish man and woman as inn-signs there. A waiter at Bogner's café, possibly the only one, had taken the friends' fancy by always passing on an order for a Bavaroise (tea with syrup) as "Brsss." In the Viennese cafés, where the authorized German, French, Italian and English newspapers were to be seen, there were coffee, tea, chocolate, rosolio, punch, lemonade, milk of almonds, *chaudeau* and liqueurs, also ices in summer (no food). Chess and cards were played.—'The Lantern' or 'The Lamp' ('Die Lampe') was a manuscript newspaper edited and illustrated by Kenner, first called 'The Morning Star' ('Der Morgenstern'). (There is a copy in the Upper Austrian County Archives at Linz.) At the house of the Hartmanns' parents at Linz a society of early risers had been formed in the autumn of 1824 under the name of "Eos." It was also devoted to smoking and chess playing. The members wore oriental costumes at their meetings, three of the female ones functioning as "slaves." It was under the patronage of Karl Maurus Mayrhofer (*see* No. 681); its president was the Hartmanns' father, while Fritz was the leader of the Viennese branch. The members were called Memnonides, but there were also honorary Memnonides, like Kenner, and Memnonides-friends, like Enk and Sauter.

740. From Franz von Hartmann's Diary

12th December 1826: Spax and I went to see Streinsberg in vain . . . I went to Bogner's coffee-house, where I saw Spax, Schober and Derffel, and fetched Fritz. We stayed there until 6.40. Then we called for Pepi Spaun, who paid for us at the Burg Theatre, where 'The Settlement of Succession' ['Der Erbvertrag'], after Hoffmann's tale of the same name, was splendidly and staggeringly performed. Anschütz as Daniel played especially movingly. We then went to the "Anchor," where Enderes, Schober and Schubert were too. Home at last towards midnight

Derffel is Schober's cousin.—'The Settlement of Succession,' a dramatic poem in two acts based on E. T. A. Hoffman's story by Wilhelm Vogel (*see* No. 300), had been in the Burg Theatre's repertory since 1825 and was published in 1828.

Fritz and Franz von Hartmann look at pictures at Schober's, including Kupelwieser's 'Party Game at Atzenbrugg,' 13th December

1826.—For the picture *see* note preceding No. 244. Schober had in his handsome home a small collection of paintings and engravings, most of them by friends of his, the contents of which he gradually enlarged and kept until his death (1882).

740A. JOSEF VON SPAUN'S PERMISSION for the Dedication of the Sonata, Op. 78 (X. 12)

It is with sincere pleasure that I accept the dedication so flatteringly intended for me by Herr Franz Schubert of his fourth Sonata for the pianoforte.

Vienna, 15th December 1826.   Josef Edler von Spaun.

Cf. No. 737. This is the only permission that has been preserved (at any rate for Schubert's dedications). It was enclosed with the autograph, which by a circuitous route came into the hands of Mr. Ernest Perabo of Boston, Mass., and thence reached the British Museum, unfortunately without Spaun's note. The manuscript is entitled "IVth Sonata," according to Schubert's arbitrary enumeration. It did not appear till the spring of 1827 (No. 847).

741. FROM FRANZ VON HARTMANN'S DIARY

15th December 1826: I went to Spaun's, where there was a big, big Schubertiad. On entering I was received rudely by Fritz and very saucily by Haas. There was a huge gathering. The Arneth, Witteczek, Kurzrock and Pompe couples, the mother-in-law of the Court and State Chancellery probationer Witteczek: Dr. Watteroth's widow, Betty Wanderer, and the painter Kupelwieser with his wife, Grillparzer, Schober, Schwind, Mayrhofer and his landlord Huber, tall Huber, Derffel, Bauernfeld, Gahy (who played gloriously *à quatre mains* with Schubert) and Vogl, who sang almost 30 splendid songs. Baron Schlechta and other Court probationers and secretaries were also there. I was moved almost to tears, being in a particularly excited state of mind to-day, by the trio of the fifth March, which always reminds me of my dear, good mother. When the music was done, there was grand

feeding and then dancing.   But I was not at all in a courting mood.
I danced twice with Betty and once with each of the Witteczek,
Kurzrock and Pompe ladies.   At 12.30, after a cordial parting
with the Spauns and Enderes, we saw Betty home and went to
the ''Anchor,'' where we still found Schober, Schubert, Schwind,
Derffel and Bauernfeld.   Merry.   Then home.   To bed at
1 o'clock.

This was the first festive Schubertiad at Spaun's, represented by
Schwind's famous sepia drawing of 1868, though in a free variant.—
Fritz is Hartmann's brother; Haas is probably Karl, the third brother of
the Linz family (*see* Nos. 478 and 569), born in 1804, who was a medical
student.—Johann Baptist von Kurzrock was court conveyancer at the
United Court Chancellery; his wife, Anna, *née* Schlauker in 1801, nicknamed ''the fair Jessica,'' became a friend of Grillparzer's, Bauernfeld's
and Schwind's.   Short dresses being then unknown, Grillparzer made a
frivolous punning epigram on her name, and when she died at Graz in
1877 her daughters laid in her grave drawings by Schwind which she had
treasured.—Josef Pompe (born *c.* 1788) was director of the Lottery Office
and thus Josef von Spaun's superior; his wife was Johanna, *née* Sebald.—
Mayrhofer, who reappears in this circle after a long absence from it, at
that time lived with Huber on the Stubentor Bastion, in the same house,
probably in the same room, as Schubert had occupied from the autumn of
1823 to the spring of 1824.—The march, which seems to have greatly
impressed Hartmann's mother, is Op. 40, No. 5, called 'Funeral March'
in Liszt's orchestration.—Enderes was then living with Spaun and is
therefore not named among the guests.   The same is, of course, true of
Max von Spaun.

742. FROM THE FRANKFURT 'ALLGEMEINER MUSIKALISCHER ANZEIGER,' 16th December 1826

*Divertissement en forme d'une Marche brillante et raisonnée (?) pour le
Pianoforte à 4 mains composé sur des motifs originaux français par
François Schubert. Œuv. 63.* No. 1. Vienna, Weigl.   1 Reichstaler.

A rather broad, often difficult, but not uninteresting little work,
and outwardly most excellently presented.

For ''*raisonnée (?)*'' see No. 664.

743. From Franz von Hartmann's Diary

16th December 1826: Spax fetched us to the coffee-house, where were also Pepi, Schwind, Schubert, Schober, Bauernfeld and Derffel. These we accompanied to Hönig's, where there was a Schubertiad, parted at the gate and went home.

Pepi is Josef von Spaun.—The Hartmanns had not been introduced at the Hönigs'.

744. From Bauernfeld's Diary

17th December 1826.

A party at Josef Spaun's the day before yesterday. Vogl sang Schubert songs with mastery, but not without dandyism. Frau Arneth (Adamberger) was present, also Grillparzer, to whom I was introduced. He was very amiable. I do not know whether I particularly pleased him.

Cf. No. 741.

745. From Franz von Hartmann's Diary

17th December 1826 (Sunday): To Spaun's, where Gahy played splendid brand-new German dances by Schubert (entitled *Hommage aux belles Viennoises*, much to S.'s annoyance). Breakfast. An artillery officer, Rueskäfer's brother, came too. Also a certain Heerdegen, a student, who was at Linz during vacation a few years ago. Then guests of the Wanderers drove off to Nussdorf in two carriages: Pepi Spaun, Schubert, Derffel and Fritz in the first; Enderes, Spax, Gahi(di) and I in the second. An excellent lunch was taken at the extremely kind and charming Wanderers', where we had great fun. Two things dear Pepi Spaun said were taken up and held against him as equivocal. 1. That his brother Franz had shot a bolt on his wife's plans to spend another summer at Nussdorf; 2. that Fritzi Dornfeld looked as though a worm were gnawing at her. After lunch came the Kurzrocks and Frau von

Kurzrock's three adorers—Schober, Schwind and Bauernfeld. The last two played and sang Schubert songs quite lamentably, after we had been dancing, when Betty was extremely affectionate. But "I am no longer in love." There was also a medical student named Haller from Steyr. When all these afternoon guests had gone, the old cosiness returned, and Schubert sang splendidly, especially 'The Solitary' by Lappe and 'Dried Flowers' from the 'Maid of the Mill' songs. Betty too sang three of those songs charmingly. Then Schubert and Gahy again played enchantingly, whereupon there were general gymnastic and conjuring feats, and at last we parted unwillingly. We drove back in the same order in which we had come, except that Derffel and Gahy changed places. We gossiped for a while at Spaun's and went from the Freiung as far as the "Anchor" in pairs, Fritz and Max at the head, then Enderes and Gahy, then Schubert and Pepi Spaun, and lastly Derffel and I. In front of the "Anchor" Derffel took his leave; but Schober took his place later. There I got back my old hat, and we spent the rest of the evening most merrily by telling Scheibiads [?] and anecdotes. Pepi Spaun finished by declaring he had stood us the drive to Nussdorf and became almost angry when we insisted on paying up all the same. At 11.30 we all parted cordially and went to bed.

These sixteen country dances (*Ländler*) were announced, with two Écossaises, only in February 1827, as Op. 67 (*see* No. 802), but were evidently printed by December 1826. Their composition probably dates much farther back, doubtless to before April 1823, when Schubert broke with Diabelli. The title was the publisher's.—Michael Rues- käfer's (*see* No. 17) brother, Friedrich, was a first lieutenant.—Of Heerdegen nothing is known.—Fritz is Hartmann's brother.—Gahy's nickname, Gahidi, may be connected with the onomatopoetic open- ing of the song 'Linnet's Wooing' ('Hänflings Liebeswerbung,' Op. 20, No. 3, words by Friedrich Kind): "Ahidi, I love."—For Wanderer *see* note preceding No. 595. Franz von Spaun was the surgeon's son- in-law.—For Fritzi (Friederike) Dornfeld *see* No. 258.—Betty (Babette) was the unmarried one among the three daughters of the house; Franz von Hartmann seems to have courted her for some time.—Adam Haller, born *c.* 1807 at Steyr, lived with Vogl in 1825–6; he remained in Vienna until he took the doctor's degree (1831) and became first city physician of Linz.—The Freiung is the square in front of the Scottish church, near Spaun's lodging.—Max is Spaun's brother.—The expression "Scheibiads" cannot be interpreted, unless it has something to do with target (*Scheiben*) shooting.

746. FROM FRANZ VON HARTMANN'S DIARY

18th December 1826: Spax came. We discussed Betty Wanderer. Then went to Bogner's coffee-house, where Schober, Schwind and the painter Führich from Prague were. Spax and Schober went to the Schubertiad at Witteczek's.

Spax is Max von Spaun.—Josef Führich, born in 1800 at Kratzau in Bohemia, was an important Catholic painter of religious subjects, just then on his way from Prague to Italy, where he remained two years. Schober and Schwind had given Anton von Spaun letters of recommendation to him when he went to Bohemia in the spring; they must therefore have known Führich before. With Schubert he does not seem to have come closely in touch. (Karl Kobald, in his popular books on Schubert, repeatedly mentions the painter Führich's autobiography; but he quotes from the Schwind biography by the art historian Lukas von Führich, 1871.) —The Hartmanns were not yet introduced at the Witteczeks'.

747. COUNT KARL HARRACH to the Lord High Chamberlain, Prince Ferdinand Trauttmansdorff

Your Serene Highness, my Lord,

As is well known, Vice Chapel-Master Eybler was advanced to the post of the I. & R. Court Chapel-Master Salieri vacated by the latter's incapacity for service, viz. in March 1824, and the post of Vice Chapel-Master has so far remained unoccupied.

It is true that my predecessor, Count Moritz Dietrichstein, had proposed for the occupation of the Vice Chapel-Master's post, under date of 24th January 1825, the certainly commendable pensioned Court Theatre conductor Umlauf; but this suggestion has not so far been carried into effect, and I deemed it advisable to let some time elapse before liquidating the proposal made under date of 24th January 1825—the more so because I had been entrusted for only a few months with the honourable care of the I. & R.

Court Chapel—in order to do full justice to the service of the I. & R. Court Chapel under the direction of the worthy and generally esteemed Court Chapel-Master Eybler.

In the circumstances, however, it being not unthinkable that Court Chapel-Master Eybler might be incapacitated by illness and I, to my utmost embarrassment, should be hard pressed to know to whom I might entrust the direction of the orchestra in case of service; and a number of petitions for ministration having been forwarded to me from the Lord High Steward's Office from applicants to the Court competing for this Vice Chapel-Master's post; I regard it as commensurate with the service entrusted to me to bring up this matter for reconsideration and to submit to higher authority the applications regarding it which have been submitted to me in the meantime.

The applicants presenting themselves as being suited for the post of Vice Chapel-Master are the following:

1. Ignaz von Seyfried, Knight,
2. Adalbert Gyrowetz,
3. Franz Schubert,
4. Konradin Kreutzer,
5. Joachim Hofmann,
6. Anselm Hüttenbrenner,
7. Wenzel Würfel,
8. Franz Gläser.

It is not to be denied that these applicants are all men of merit, more or less entitled between themselves to consideration . . .

Franz Schubert bases his claim on the services rendered by him as I. & R. choir-boy, confirmed by a certificate from the deceased Court Chapel-Master Salieri that he had learned composition under him, and asserts that he has already written five Masses with larger or smaller orchestra, which have been produced in various churches . . .

Regardless of the question arising here of the manifold deserts of Umlauf, a musician worthy in every respect, suggested by my predecessor, Count Moritz Dietrichstein, and the other applicants named above, I for my part am nevertheless of the unprejudiced

Josef von Spaun.   Oil Painting by Leopold Kupelwieser (1835)

PLATE XX

Franz von Schober. Oil Painting by Leopold Kupelwieser (1823)

In the background Schober's birthplace, Torup Castle near Malmö (Sweden), after a drawing by himself

PLATE XXI

opinion that in the circumstances of the present time the care of the most exalted Exchequer should be particularly considered, and that the problem of filling the Vice Chapel-Master's post would be best solved if an individual were found who is equal to the service of the I. & R. Court Chapel, which would relieve the most exalted Exchequer of any additional burden.

I have therefore taken pains to procure myself the decree granting his pension to the honourably known Court Theatre conductor Josef Weigl, of which I enclose a copy.

It appears from this most exalted decree, dated 29th September 1802, that he, Weigl, has been favoured with a pension of 3,000 florins, or 6,000 florins, V.C., with the additional 100 per cent, which comes to 2,400 florins, A.C.; from which is deducted, however, the salary of 800 fl., A.C., per annum he received from the theatre lessee Barbaja, so that he receives an annual increment of 1,600 fl., A.C., from the theatre accounts.

The regular salary of the Court Vice Chapel-Master amounts to 1,000 fl., A.C., per annum, plus 200 fl. for lodgings.

Since the above-mentioned most exalted decree expressly states that Weigl may be called upon to perform other duties suited to his capabilities, it appears to me that he, not being listed among the applicants, should regard it as a signal favour on the part of the most venerated Monarch to deduct the salary of 1,000 fl., A.C., from his pension if he is called upon to serve as Vice Musical Director to the Court, and, by a special most exalted grace, to be left with the enjoyment of only the 200 fl., A.C., for lodgings in consideration of his new duties, whereupon the increment in the pension of the repeatedly mentioned Weigl would amount to only 600 fl., A.C.

In submitting to Your Serene Highness this my unauthoritative view, I respectfully await the most exalted resolution concerning this matter, in order to proceed accordingly and to take the further necessary measures.

Vienna, 19th December 1826.   K., Ct. Harrach.

Cf. No. 646.—For Trauttmansdorff *see* No. 10.—For Schubert's application *see also* Nos. 77, 78, 200, 201, 203 and 204.—The post had not been formally advertised; the petitions were thus sent in spontaneously and there was nothing to prevent any Austrian musician from applying for the appointment.—Weigl was still first conductor of the court theatres.—The last-named sum of 600 florins, A.C., is arrived at by deduction of the 1,000 florins for the salary of the assistant conductor from the 1,600 florins Weigl received from the court theatre accountancy.

748. FROM FRANZ VON HARTMANN'S DIARY

19th December 1826: I went with Spax to Schober's, where I found Schwind and Bauernfeld, and we looked at Flaxman's engravings for Aeschylus. . . . Went with Fritz to Bogner's, where Derffel was. Then Spax came. Schwind too for a moment. We went to Pepi Spaun's, who took us to [Kleist's] 'Katie of Heilbronn,' where we had an extremely enjoyable evening. The Anschütz couple in particular played magnificently. She as Katie, he as Count Wetter. Then we went to the "Anchor," where we jeered at Schwind and Schober, who had been terribly bored by 'The Two Imps' ['Die beiden Spadifankerl']. Schubert and Lachner came too. We stayed there till 11.45. Pepi invited me to breakfast at Corti's to-morrow.

John Flaxman had died in London on 7th December. His series of illustrations exercised a strong influence on the contour-drawings of his German contemporaries, as for instance on Schwind's 'Freischütz' illustrations. As a sculptor he was not so well known on the Continent. His thirty illustrations for the tragedies of Aeschylus, engraved by T. Piroli and F. Howard, had appeared in London in 1795.—For Heinrich von Kleist's 'Katie of Heilbronn' ('Käthchen von Heilbronn') cf. Nos. 691 and 1118; for the Anschütz couple see note preceding No. 269. The performance took place at the Burg Theatre.—'The Two Imps' (Spadifankerl is Viennese for "little devil" or "imp") was a comic pasticcio with songs in two acts by Karl Meisl, with music by Franz Volkert, played since 1819 at the Leopoldstadt Theatre.—Peter Corti, a well-known café proprietor, kept several establishments in the inner city.

749. FROM FRANZ VON HARTMANN'S DIARY

20th December 1826: I went to the Spauns', who came with me
to Corti's (coffee-house in the Paradeisgartel) and stood me breakfast there.   Pepi went earlier.   I stayed on there with Spax for
some time.   Then I took him through the most frightful mud to
Schubert's, but did not go up with him. . . . [In the evening] I
went with Fritz to the "Anchor"; Derffel and Enk there at first.
Then Schubert and the Spauns.   Quite good fun.   Not home till
12 o'clock.

The Paradies-Gärtchen ("Paradeisgartel" is dialect) on the Löwel
Bastion, in the region of the later Burg Theatre, had a café where during
the warm season a wind band played morning and evening.   Corti's
pavilion in the nearby Volksgarten in front of the Hofburg, rebuilt later
on, became the favourite pitch of the orchestras directed by the elder
Strauss and Lanner.—The way to Schubert's new lodgings led almost
completely round the City on the bastion.

750. FROM THE PROGRAMME of the Sixth Evening Entertainment held by the Philharmonic Society, 21st December 1826 (Conductor, Herr [Vincenz] Hauschka)

4. 'The Dwarf' ['Der Zwerg'], poem by M., Edler von Collin,
set to music by Franz Schubert, performed by Herr [Johann]
Schoberlechner.

Johann Karl Schoberlechner, born in Vienna in 1800, a bass singer, was
a brother of the pianoforte player Franz Schoberlechner (see No. 290) and
later appeared under the stage-name of Schober.

751. NOTE ON THE ABOVE PROGRAMME

Sung by Schoberlechner, Frau Schmiedel.

Julie Schmiedel (née Schauff, Vienna, 1807), a soprano singer and
pianoforte player, was the wife of Johann Baptist Schmiedel (see No. 353).

752. FROM FRANZ VON HARTMANN'S DIARY

21st December 1826: I went with Fritz to Spaun's, who gave us a ticket for this evening . . . At Bogner's we saw the Spauns, Schober, Derffel, Schwind and Schubert. Then I went with Haas to the Little Society, where they did a beautiful Quintet by Beethoven, a pianoforte concerto, a ridiculous violoncello pot-pourri (although by Romberg), 'The Dwarf' (which was sung twice), an aria from Kreutzer's 'Libussa' and a duet by Rossini (from the 'Barber'); and lastly a chorus by Randhartinger (Körner's 'Drinking-Song before Battle'). Then we went with Fritz and Walcher to the "Anchor," where later on Gahy, Enderes, the Spauns (who had been to 'The Peasant as Millionaire'), Lachner, Schubert, Schober, Schwind, Enk, &c., arrived. We stayed on till after 12 o'clock. But there were too many.

"Little Society" (*Kleiner Verein*) was the name of the Philharmonic Society's private evening entertainments.—The Quintet was Beethoven's Op. 29, in C major; the pot-pourri was by Bernhard Romberg; the song from Körner's collection 'Lyre and Sword' ('Leyer und Schwert'), which Schubert had set for a single voice in 1815, was composed for double male-voice choir by Randhartinger. The programme further contained "Variations for Pianoforte with Accompaniment" by one Winkler.—Ferdinand Walcher (later Ritter von Uysdael), born in 1799 at Waidhofen-on-the-Ybbs in Lower Austria, a law student, was apprentice conveyancer in the Marine Department of the Court War Council; he had known Fritz von Hartmann since 1823. He was a high baritone.— 'The Girl from the Fairy World, or The Peasant as Millionaire' ('Das Mädchen aus der Feenwelt, oder Der Bauer als Millionär'), a magic fairy-play with songs in three acts by Ferdinand Raimund, with music by Josef Drechsler (including the still popular "Brüderlein fein" and the 'Aschen-lied'), had been produced at the Leopoldstadt Theatre on 10th November 1826.

753. FROM FRANZ VON HARTMANN'S DIARY

22nd December 1826: I went to the "Anchor," where almost the whole party was present again (except Gahy and Haas). Schwind was there too. Home at 11.30.

754. From the Official 'Wiener Zeitung,' 23rd December 1826

At the I. & R. Priv. Art and Music Establishment
of Sauer & Leidesdorf,
Kärntnerstrasse, No. 941, is just published (Pest, at K. Lichtl's):

New Dances of Gotham
['Neue Krähwinkler-Tänze']
for the Pianoforte,
by Schubert, Lachner, Lanz, Randhartinger, Fischhof, von Gyika,
Leidesdorf and others.

With a new Gothamiad as a Title-page.

Price, 1 Florin 30 Kreuzer, V.C.

———————

Modern Love-Waltzes
['Moderne Liebes-Walzer']
for the Pianoforte,
by Schubert, Lachner, Lanz, Sowinsky, Fischhof, von Gyika,
Leidesdorf and others.

With an appropriate Title-page.   Price, 1 Florin 30 Kreuzer, V.C.

For the earlier set cf. No. 611. A copy is in the British Museum, another in Mr. Anthony van Hoboken's collection at Lausanne. Schubert's contributions are Nos. 1 and 11, two waltzes which, with the one mentioned below, were reprinted in the 'Zeitschrift der Internationalen Musikgesellschaft' (Leipzig, 1902, vol. iii, pp. 319–20), but are not in the "complete" edition.—Lachner is Franz.—J. von Gyika de Désánfalva came of the family of the art patron Konstantin von Gyika, in whose house Anton Halm (see No. 379) became tutor about 1825.—Only one composer, Karl Braun, is not named in the advertisement.—For the title-page see No. 1018.—The other collection is known only by the copies in the British Museum and in the Vienna City Library. It contains one waltz by Schubert, reprinted in the journal named above. William Barclay Squire, who reissued these three dances, suspected a caricature of Schubert on the second title-page, which shows an illustration of the following verse:

> How easy heart and hand are wed
> When by dear father's dollars sped.
> [Modern Love.]

Albert Sowinsky (Sovinsky), born in 1803 at Ladizin in Ukraine, was a pianoforte virtuoso, then in Vienna and later living in Paris.

755. FROM FRANZ VON HARTMANN'S DIARY

27th December 1826: We went to the "Anchor"; Schubert, the Lachners and Randhartinger there. Schober came too, reproaching us for not having been for so long. We three sat on with Schubert for a long time. At last we saw Schober home.

The Hartmann brothers, with Josef von Spaun, had again been at the Wanderers' at Nussdorf on 25th December.

756. FROM THE PROGRAMME of the Seventh Evening Entertainment of the Philharmonic Society, 28th December 1826 (Conductor, Herr Kirchlehner)

2. 'The Young Nun' ['Die junge Nonne'], poem by Craigher, set to music by Schubert, performed by Fräulein [Karoline] Schindler.

No details are known of Karoline Schindler.

757. FROM FRANZ VON HARTMANN'S DIARY

28th December 1826: We call for the Schallhammers and the Roux's to go to the Little Society's concert. I meet there Fräulein Mertens, who was at the previous concert at Linz, and have a very lively talk with her. I also see Enderes, who stands next to me. They perform a quartet by Haydn, a Schubert song ('The Young Nun'), an insipid violin concerto, a tedious pianoforte concerto, a trio from 'Margherita d'Anjou' (by Meyerbeer) and lastly the fine chorus from [Rossini's] 'Mosè in Egitto,' while a young Miss Griesbach from London played the harp. Afterwards we see the Schallhammers and Louise Roux home.

Franz, Ritter von Schallhammer, an uncle of the Hartmanns', with his wife and his daughter Malchen (Amalie), had come from Linz to visit his son Karl, who studied law in Vienna; and so, probably, did the Roux couple, who had a daughter named Louise.—Of Fräulein Mertens nothing is known.—The programme of this evening entertainment (*see* No. 756), preserved only in manuscript by the Philharmonic Society, included

among other things a string Quartet in G major by Haydn, variations for
the violin by Stefan Franz (born 1785, leader of the Burg Theatre orchestra), a 'Rondo brillant' for pianoforte with string quartet accompaniment
by Worzischek, the prayer from Rossini's opera, sung by a Fräulein
Mayerhofer, Herren Tietze and (Johann Karl) Schoberlechner and a
choir.—Miss Griesbach is not named on the programme. Early in 1827
and at the close of 1828, as Madame Griesbach, she gave harp recitals
of her own at the County Hall, with no particular success. She is
probably identical with Eleonora Eliza Griesbach, the English governess to the two daughters—one illegitimate and the other adopted—
of the banker Johann Heinrich Adolf von Geymüller, a nephew of
the brothers Johann Heinrich (see No. 214) and Johann Jakob von
Geymüller. His proper name was Falkner, but he took his mother's
maiden name. After the death of his uncles (1824 and 1834) and his
first, frivolous wife Rosalie, née Deahna, who had formerly been governess
in the household of Count Fries (see No. 224), he married Miss Griesbach
in 1835. He was a spendthrift, and brought the bank to ruin in 1841.
He died in Switzerland, the Geymüllers' home, in 1848 and left Eleonora
mentally unhinged, with a son, Heinrich Adolf, later an art expert. Her
family came from Hanover, but she was born in England. Her father
had three musical sons; her grandmother was Sophie Elisabeth, née
Herschel, Sir William Herschel's elder sister. Geymüller's foster-
daughter, Louise Marsch, who was adopted by his younger uncle, in 1828
married Count Adolf August Friedrich Kielmannsegg, a secretary to the
Hanoverian legation in Paris, where she lived with him about 1835 and
successfully propagated Schubert's songs. Aloisia, Countess Kielmannsegg, as she then called herself, died in Paris in 1837.

758. JENGER TO FRAU PACHLER

Vienna, 29th December 1826.

. . . Friend Schubert is firmly resolved to go to Graz next
year; but if he does not get there with me, it will again come to
nothing, like this year. I kiss your hands, dear lady, for the kind
offer to let me have a room in your large new dwelling, and shall
accept it with the utmost pleasure when the time comes.

Cf. No. 685.—Dr. Pachler, the barrister, after the death of his mother,
had the apartments on the second floor of his house in the Herrengasse at
Graz restored and enlarged.

759. FROM FRANZ VON HARTMANN'S DIARY

29th December 1826: I go with Fritz to the "Anchor"; Spaun and Enderes there, later Schober too. Spaun tells us about Linz. . . . A dispute on crime then arises, very violent and entertaining, which does not end until 11.30.

760. FROM FRANZ VON HARTMANN'S DIARY

30th December 1826: We go to the "Anchor," where Schober, Schwind, Schubert, Bauernfeld and Derffel are. Spaun comes later, and Derffel and Bauernfeld leave. The talk is of chivalric novels, tall stories of the Seminary, &c. As we step out of the "Anchor," all is deeply snowed under. We itch for a game of snowballs, which we carry out immediately, at the point where the Grünangergasse leads into the Singerstrasse. Spaun is on my side, Fritz and Schober on Schwind's. Schober always hits me hard and without fail, and I him or Schwind in particular. Spaun gloriously protects himself against the shots with his open umbrella. Schubert and Haas take no part in the fight. Home, where the house-steward was rude because we rang loudly.

"Even Schober" took part in the snowball fight, as Hartmann says in his family chronicle.—Schwind made a caricature of Josef von Spaun and his umbrella, but not in this particular scene (iconographical volume, pl. 412).

761. FROM FRANZ VON HARTMANN'S DIARY

31st December 1826: Towards half-past eight we were due at Schober's, where Enderes, Schwind, Schubert and Bauernfeld went, and later on Spaun, which caused general pleasure, since it was thought that he was at Baldacci's and we feared he would not come at all. We are very merry the whole evening, smoke tobacco and read most amusing letters. Then we sit down to supper in the next room and wait for 12 o'clock to strike. Next Schober's mother appears from the adjoining room, looking like a ghost. On the stroke of 12 glasses were filled with Tokay, and we drank each other's health for the coming year, Fritz, Spaun and myself not forgetting our dear parents. Then we drank coffee, smoked again, and at 2 o'clock left at last, first Spaun and Enderes, then we others except Schwind, who slept at Schober's. Or rather we waddled off. Parted with Schubert and Bauernfeld in the Singerstrasse.

Anton, Freiherr von Baldacci, born in 1761, a councillor of state, was married to Franziska, *née* Freiin von Cothmann, who was the younger sister of Spaun's grandmother.

'Song in the Greenery' ('Das Lied im Grünen'), Op. posth. 115, No. 1 (1827). Engraved Vignette from Karl Czerny's Arrangement of Schubert's Song for Pianoforte Solo. Vienna 1838–9

Entrance to Bogner's Café. Water-colour by Moritz
von Schwind, from his Cycle, "Die Lachner-Rolle"
(1862). Schwind and Franz Lachner passing Schwind's
Picture of a Turk, painted on the Door. *See* pp.
569 f. and Plate facing p. 753

1827

Song Cycle, 'The Winter Journey' ('Die Winterreise'), Part I, February.

'Serenade' ('Ständchen') (Grillparzer) for Alto solo and Female Quartet with Pianoforte Accompaniment (xviii. 4), July.

'The Winter Journey,' Part II, October.

2 Pianoforte Trios, B flat major and E flat major (vii. 3 and 4), the latter finished November.

8 Impromptus for Pianoforte (xi. 2 and 3), finished December.

Fantasy for Pianoforte and Violin (viii. 5), December.

---

762. FROM FRANZ VON HARTMANN'S DIARY

2nd January 1827: Towards 10 o'clock we meet Schober and Schubert at the "Anchor," but unfortunately Spaun is not there. We remain until 12 o'clock, but it is not very jolly.

Schubert has a christening certificate made, 3rd January 1827.—It is quoted by Kreissle, p. 3 (German edition, No. 3), and was made out according to our No. 2, but is now lost. The purpose for which Schubert procured it is not known.

763. FROM FRANZ VON HARTMANN'S DIARY

3rd January 1827: About 9.40 we went to the "Anchor," where again Spaun was not present; only Schober; Bauernfeld, the Lachners and tall Huber were there. After 11.20 we were alone with Schober, who told us about his youth and especially of the splendid life at Schnepfental, until 12.45, when we parted at last.

Schober had been educated at Schnepfental (see note preceding No. 74).

764. From the Official 'Wiener Zeitung,' 5th January 1827

At the House of Anton Diabelli & Co.,
Art and Music Dealers in Vienna, 1133 Graben,
are newly published, and to be had of K. Lichtl in Pest
at the same price:

The Solitary
[Der Einsame]
Poem by K. Lappe.
Set to Music
for One Voice with Pianoforte Accompaniment,
by Franz Schubert

Work 41.   1 Florin 30 Kreuzer, V.C.

To the Setting Sun
[An die untergehende Sonne]
Poem by Kosegarten.
Set to Music
for One Voice with Pianoforte Accompaniment
by Franz Schubert

Work 44.   1 Florin, V.C.

Opp. 41 and 44, both without dedications, appeared after Op. 66.

765. From Fritz von Hartmann's Diary

(In French)

6th January 1827: I heard Mass at 8 o'clock in the University
church with Franz.   We then went to Spaun's, . . .

Here begins Fritz von Hartmann's diary of 1827, written in schoolboy
French.   It will hereafter be quoted only where it serves to supplement
the diary of his brother Franz, written in German.

766. From Franz von Hartmann's Diary

6th January 1827: We went to Spaun's, where we were invited
to breakfast with Gahy. It was very jolly and cosy, and Gahy
then played two magnificent sonatas by Schubert and his German

dances, which had delighted us so much on the 17th ult.   After
the first sonata Enderes and Schober joined us.   Schober showed
his displeasure with the sonatas and almost began a dispute with
Spaun.

These sonatas were presumably Op. 42, in A minor, and Op. 53, in
D major, Schubert's two "grandes sonates," both published by that time.
The German dances are those published the following month as 'Hommage
aux belles Viennoises' in Op. 67 (see No. 745).

767. From Fritz von Hartmann's Diary

7th January 1827: After dinner the four of us [Ferdinand and
Ludwig Sauter and Franz and Fritz von Hartmann] all went to
Steiner's café, where I . . . had a talk with Lachner of Munich,
a friend of Schubert's.

Ludwig Sauter was Ferdinand's youngest brother, a law student.—
Steiner's café was in the Untere Bäckerstrasse (now No. 2).

768. From Franz von Hartmann's Diary

9th January 1827: We went to the "Anchor."   Spaun alone
was there, and we chatted gaily with him.   At last Schober came,
late, when Spaun was just on the point of leaving.   But Spaun
stayed on a little, and I once again lost a coin in the most charming
way: I showed a 20-piece of this year that had been given me, and
Schober pocketed it as though it were his own.   How sadly did
I see it vanish!   We stayed on with Schober until after 12.30,
discussing Jean Paul and Goethe.

The twenty-kreuzer piece, worth a third of a florin, was a silver coin.

769. From the 'Theaterzeitung,' 11th January 1827

Published there [at Sauer & Leidesdorf's]: 'New Dances of
Gotham' ['Neue Krähwinkler-Tänze'] and 'Modern Love Waltzes'
['Moderne Liebeswalzer'] by the most popular composers in

Vienna, among whom we need but name Schubert, Lachner, Randhartinger, Leidesdorf, &c. Both books are adorned with similar, very handsomely lithographed vignettes, the first of which represents an extremely droll and wittily popular Gothamite scene.

v. S.

[? Franz von Schlechta.]

Cf. No. 754.

770. FROM THE PROGRAMME of the Ninth Evening Entertainment held by the Philharmonic Society, 11th January 1827 (Conductor, Herr Schmiedel)

4. 'Chronos the Charioteer' ['An Schwager Kronos'], Poem by Goethe, set to Music by Franz Schubert, performed by Herr Schoberlechner.

For Schmiedel cf. No. 353, for Schoberlechner No. 750.

771. JENGER TO FRAU PACHLER

Vienna, 12th January 1827.

. . . Schubert asks to kiss your hands, dear lady, though unbeknownst, and he looks forward with much pleasure to making the acquaintance of so warm an admirer of Beethoven's works.

God grant that our reciprocal wish to visit Graz this year may be fulfilled.

For the friendship between Beethoven and Frau Pachler *see* No. 685. She was for a time considered a claimant to the title of "The Immortal Beloved."

772. FROM FRANZ VON HARTMANN'S DIARY

12th January 1827: Walcher sings for us [in his lodgings at Frau Angerer's] some really beautiful Schubert songs ('Urge into the Distance') ['Drang in die Ferne'] by Leitner and 'To be Sung on the Water' by Stolberg) . . . To Spaun's, where there is a Schubertiad. The dear Witteczek couple and his mother-in-law are

there already; tall Huber too. Then, one by one, came Gahy,
Schober, Schubert, Enderes, Walcher (who however had to leave
before the music began), Moritz Pflügl (who has been in Paris),
Lachner, a certain Rieder, Perfetta; finally Vogl and his wife,
Bauernfeld, Schwind, Gross. We had a splendid sonata for four
hands, glorious variations and many magnificent songs, among them
a brand-new one (sung by Richard Cœur-de-Lion in 'Ivanhoe')
and old ones including 'Night and Dreams' and the 'Erl King.'
A specially beautiful one, 'Sunset Glow' ['Die Abendröte'] by
Lappe was sung twice by Vogl, who happened to be in an exceptionally good mood. Then we had a delicious repast, and several
toasts were drunk. Suddenly Spaun arrived and said we must
drink brotherhood, which much surprised and pleased me. Then
we had tossing in a blanket (Enderes and Huber, the latter be-
having very clumsily) and made the well-known beautiful star
with four pairs. At last we took our leave of our kind hosts and
went helter-skelter to Bogner's, where we smoked a few pipes,
and in the street Schwind, running and flapping his cloak, gave a
striking illusion of flying.

Walcher (*see* No. 752) had for years lived at Frau Angerer's, a timber
dealer on the Seilerstätte, where Fritz Hartmann too spent the winter
of 1823–4.—The two songs, which were sung by Walcher, must have
been just engraved: they appeared (separately) the following March
(No. 816).—Witteczek's mother-in-law is Professor Watteroth's widow.
—Moritz von Pflügl came from Linz.—Rieder is Wilhelm August, the
painter (*see* No. 401).—For Perfetta *see* No. 653.—Gross is Josef (*see*
No. 242).—The duet sonata may have been that in C major of June 1824,
published only in 1838 as 'Grand Duo,' Op. 140, and the variations are
the 'Andantino varié' on a French original theme, written in 1826 and
published the following July as part of Op. 84 (*see* No. 916).—The first
of the songs sung by Vogl is 'The Crusader's Return' (cf. No. 84),
usually assigned to March 1826, but actually only just then written; it
appeared as Op. 86 in March 1828 (*see* No. 1057).—Schubert wrote two
songs under the title of 'Abendröte'; but the proper title for that by
Lappe is 'Im Abendrot.'—"Tossing in a blanket" is actually "tossing
foxes" (*Füchse prellen*), an expression due to a former practice of tor-
menting captured foxes to death by tossing them in a net or cloth. The
"star" was probably some other gymnastic display taking that shape.—
Hartmann, in speaking of the "hosts," seems to refer to Spaun and

Enderes, although he had mentioned the latter among the guests (cf. No. 788).—Schwind, who had already in 1823 wished for a circular cloak, which at that time his niggardly grandmother had refused to buy him, seems to have received or bought one in the end. He had learnt to give a striking imitation of the flight of a bat with it "by throwing the collar of his cloak aloft with both arms while he ran, jumping at the same time and thus keeping his feet off the ground" (Hartmann's family chronicle).

773. From Fritz von Hartmann's Diary

12th January 1827: I have known the height of art [Schubert and Vogl] well enough these last few years to save myself a close description. Suffice it to say that nearly all the songs I heard to-day were new to me, but that they are just as fine as the earlier works by this inexhaustible composer . . . At that party I also met Rueskäfer of Linz, for the first time since his arrival . . . We finished with a few gymnastic displays and did not leave until near midnight; which was still too early for some of us, for Schober, Schubert, Schwind, Huber, Bauernfeld, Franz and I went on to Bogner's café, where we spent the first hour of the new day.

Michael Rueskäfer (*see* No. 17), born in Vienna in 1794, had been conveyancer in the customs administration at Linz and was called to Vienna as examiner of excise affairs.

774. From Franz von Hartmann's Diary

13th January 1827: We went to the "Anchor," where we found Spaun, Enderes, Gahy and Schober; Derffel too, at first. After having been there a long time and considering it time to adjourn, we went in glorious moonlight outside Bogner's café, where we danced and indulged in all kinds of childish performances. Thence we danced across the Stock-am-Eisen Square and round St. Stephen's Church, at which we gazed in astonishment. Then to the Goldschmiedgasse, where again at the café, as well as at Peter Square and at the café in the Graben, we made our demonstrations. When we came to Geringer's café on the Kohlmarkt, we wanted to push in Spaun (who is always against going late to coffee-houses).   But when we had opened the door, behold! he went in of his own accord, and we all quite calmly tripped after him.   We smoked there and had quite a jolly confabulation.   In the end we parted, however, and got home at 12.30.

Schubert was absent that evening.—The Stock-am-Eisen (or Stock-ameisen) Square, between St. Stephen's cathedral and the Graben, took its name from a legend.   The proper name is Stock im Eisen, but it is rarely so called.   The story is of a locksmith's apprentice who sold his soul to the devil in order to make a lock incapable of being opened from the tree-trunk that is said to have once marked the boundary of the Wiener Wald.   In memory of the poor youth, who of course went to hell, every locksmith who passed the tree would knock a nail into it, so long as there was room.   It still exists.—In the Goldschmiedgasse was Anton Schneider's café (next door to the Partridge Tavern), on the Peter Square that of Leopold Geringer, in the Graben that of Franziska Schweiger and in the Kohlmarkt that of Karl Geringer.

775. From Franz von Hartmann's Diary

14th January 1827: With Fritz to Spaun's, who had asked us to breakfast.   When we have breakfasted there, Gahy plays some very fine German Dances of Schubert's.   Enderes juggles beautifully with sticks, rods and the like; I try to emulate him and let a stick on which a steel hammer was balanced drop heavily on his forehead, which gives me a terrible fright.   I could no longer listen to the dances at all, but stayed with him all the time while he bathed the swelling and thus fortunately kept it down.

776. From Fritz von Hartmann's Diary

14th January 1827: Enderes too was there [at Josef von Spaun's] as well as Gahy, who played entrancing waltzes by Schubert (entitled 'Valses nobles').

For the Waltzes cf. No. 782.

777. PROBST TO SCHUBERT

[Outside:]

Franz Schubert, Esq.

Musical Artist and Composer,

Vienna.

[Inside:]

Herr Franz Schubert, Rt. Hon.

Vienna.

Leipzig, 1 5th January 1 8 2 7.

Not until late did I receive your manuscripts through Artaria & Co. Much as I should like to have the pleasure of incorporating your name in my catalogue, I must nevertheless forgo it for the present, being overburdened with work by the publication of Kalkbrenner's *Œuvres complets* [sic]. I may also confess that the fee of 80 florins, A.C., for each manuscript seemed to me a somewhat high estimate. I am holding the three works at your disposal and remain, with compliments,

Most respectfully yours,

H. A. Probst.

Cf. No. 694. Schubert's reply, probably dating from the autumn, is not preserved. It is thus not known which three works he vainly offered to Probst. The correspondence was resumed early in 1 8 2 8 (*see* No. 1 0 3 6).—Of Kalkbrenner's (*see* No. 476) works Probst published ten books entitled 'Œuvres complètes pour le Pianoforte seul et à 4 mains, édition augmentée, revue et corrigée par l'Auteur.'

778. FROM THE BERLIN 'ALLGEMEINE MUSIKALISCHE ZEITUNG,' 28th February 1 8 2 7

(Correspondence from Vienna, January 1 8 2 7.)

The "Little Society's" evening entertainments continue uninterruptedly. Among the novelties were: . . . several fine songs by Schubert.

779. FROM THE PROGRAMME of the Tenth Evening Entertainment held by the Philharmonic Society, 18th January 1827 (Conductor, Herr Schönpichler)

2. 'Longing,' poem by Schiller, set to music by Fr. Schubert, performed by Fräulein Louise Weiss.

On Schönpichler cf. No. 218.—Of Louise Weiss no details are known.

780. NOTE ON THE ABOVE PROGRAMME

Sung by Louise Weiss, badly.   Frau von Schmiedel.

For Frau Schmiedel *see* No. 751.   The "von" is merely a matter of politeness.

781. FROM FRANZ VON HARTMANN'S DIARY

18th January 1827: At 7 o'clock I went in Haas's company to the Little Society, where I nearly had to listen at the door, as I was late.   Quartet by Romberg, silly violin concerto; Schubert's song 'Longing' ['Sehnsucht'] by Schiller.   Pianoforte concerto. Trio from 'The Barber of Seville.'   Chorus from Spohr's 'Faust.' Then I met Spaun, Enderes, Gahy and Fritz.   Being in search of another ale-house, we entered the "Partridge," where however the smoke is even worse than at the "Anchor," so that we immediately took refuge there.   We performed all sorts of tricks there and, having waited vainly for Schober, went home at 11 o'clock.

Haas is Karl (*see* No. 741).—The programme consisted of a string Quartet in E major by Andreas Romberg; a Polonaise by Leopold Jansa; Adagio and Rondo with string quartet accompaniment by "Henri Herz of Paris" (born in Vienna in 1803, settled in Paris since 1816, the most famous pianoforte player at that time), with Sowinsky (*see* No. 754) at the pianoforte; a trio from Rossini's 'Barber'; an aria with chorus from Spohr's opera 'Faust.'—The Partridge Tavern, in the Goldschmiedgasse, near St. Stephen's cathedral, was next door to the Café Schneider, on the other side of the gate.—Schober had been taken ill (*see* No. 792).

782. FROM THE OFFICIAL 'WIENER ZEITUNG,' 22nd January 1827

At the House of Tobias Haslinger,

Art and Music Dealer in Vienna, in the Graben, No. 572,
in the House of the Austrian Savings Bank, are published
and to be had of K. Lichtl in Pest at the same price:

Valses nobles

pour le Pianoforte seul

par

François Schubert

Œuvre 77.   Prix 40 Kr., A.C.

Haslinger, who had been sole proprietor of the former publishing firm
of Steiner & Co. since 1826, here published his first Schubert work.
The title was, once again, the publisher's.   Like all Schubert's dances, it
bears no dedication.   It appeared before Op. 67 and several other works
with lower opus numbers, which indicates that these had already been
assigned.

783. PRINCE TRAUTTMANSDORFF TO COUNT HARRACH

According to the most exalted resolution of the 22nd inst.
His Majesty has condescended to appoint the Court Theatre conductor Josef Weigl as Vice Chapel-Master with the regular
emoluments. . . .

The report of 19th December of last year is thus liquidated and
all applications are herewith returned to the competitors.

On behalf of the I. & R. High Steward's Office.

Trauttmansdorff.   Vienna, 24th January 1827.

Freiherr von Sacken.

Cf. Nos. 747 and 787.—Weigl seems after all to have received the full
salary of 1,000 florins and the 200 florins extra for lodgings.

784. From Fritz von Hartmann's Diary

24th January 1827: At the Little Society I was present at
the rehearsal of a delicious chorus by Schubert, entitled 'Night's
Brightness' ['Nachthelle'].

The male-voice quartet with tenor solo and pianoforte accompaniment,
entitled 'Night's Brightness,' words by Seidl, was composed in September
1826 (*see* Nos. 785 and 786).

785. Ferdinand Walcher to Schubert

[Outside:]

Franz Schubert, Esq.
To be delivered in person.

[Inside:]

Cre - do   in   u - num De - um!

Not you, I know well enough, but you will believe this—that
Tietze will sing your 'Night's Brightness' * at the Little Society
to-night, to which N. Fröhlich invited you by means of the 3
enclosed tickets, which I have the honour to transmit to you by
way of the coffee-house of the "Merry Black-Pudding," on account
of the deep snow.

Vienna, 25th January 1827.

Your very affectionate
Well-wisher Walcher.

Vidi July-moulter of Freiburg.

* Night's brightness here suggests neither somnambulism, nor
clairvoyance, nor slept-off hangover, &c., but a poem by Seidl
with music by Schubert for a principal and damnably high tenor,

with chorus, for the which I am engaged as second tenor and have, to that end, already ordered a superb F from the baker of Baden, who is said to make the best buns.

N.B. Don't forget Kleyle, and to-morrow you might well come to Kiesewetter's.

Schubert did omit the words "Credo in unam sanctam catholicam et apostolicam ecclesiam" from his Masses, but of course not the "Credo" proper.—Walcher (see No. 752) had fraternized with Schubert.—The organizer of this evening entertainment given by the Philharmonic Society ("Little Society") seems to have been Nanette (Anna) Fröhlich.—Bogner's café had the jocular nickname of Zur lustigen Plunzen (blood-sausage or black-pudding), perhaps in allusion to the corpulent proprietor.—Jenger, who came from Freiburg i/B., was given the nickname of Julimauser, which is a bird moulting in July.—A master baker at Baden near Vienna was well known for his large crescents, which were called Ringeln there; a waltz by Lanner took its name from them. Walcher here supposed that this baker would accept an order for a bun in the shape of the letter F.—Franz Joachim, Ritter von Kleyle, born in 1775 at Haslach in Baden (Germany), was estate manager to Field Marshal the Archduke Karl. He lived with his beautiful wife Karoline, née Ockel, in a villa at Penzing, near the palace of Schönbrunn. They had six daughters and three sons. One of the daughters, Sophie, the friend of the ill-starred poet Lenau, married Max Löwenthal (see No. 319); Rosalie, a pupil of the poet Adalbert Stifter, married Karl, Freiherr von Schönstein (see No. 436); and Johanna became engaged to the music-lover Emanuel Mikschik, who after Schubert's death often accompanied Vogl on the pianoforte. The Kleyles' Penzing home, which still stands in its splendid park, was frequented by Schubert, Walcher, Jenger and Teltscher.

786. FROM THE PROGRAMME of the Eleventh Evening Entertainment held by the Philharmonic Society, 25th January 1827 (Conductor, Herr [Johann Baptist] Geissler)

2. 'Night's Brightness' ['Nachthelle'], poem by Seidl, set to music by Franz Schubert, performed by Herr Tietze and the choir (in manuscript).

For Geissler see No. 633.—Walcher sang among the second tenors in the quartet, which was performed by a choir. Jenger evidently accompanied at the pianoforte.

787. INTIMATION on Schubert's Petition to the Emperor

His Majesty having condescended to fill the post herein applied for, no further steps can be taken concerning it.

On behalf of the I. & R. Court Music Office.

Vienna, 27th January 1827.

This disposal is on the reverse of the petition to the emperor (No. 646), which was therefore returned to Schubert. The draft for it is preserved in the State Archives in Vienna, for all the eight applicants (Weigl, of course, did not apply). Josef von Spaun reports that Schubert said concerning this: "Much as I should have liked to receive this appointment, I shall have to make the best of the matter, since it was given to so worthy a man as Weigl.' (Cf., however, No. 149.) Bauernfeld relates that in the summer of 1827 he spoke with Schubert about the outcome of this competition. He pretends to have said to Schubert: "They have preferred an amateur to you!"—which is rather like a novelist's elaboration—and to have at that time suggested that he should give a concert of his own works (cf. No. 456).

Performance of the 'Rondo brillant' in B minor, Op. 70 (viii. 1), by Karl Maria von Bocklet (pianoforte) and Josef Slawjk (violin), at Domenico Artaria's in Schubert's presence, (?) early 1827.— Domenico Artaria, born in 1775 at Blevio on Lake Como, was the proprietor of the firm of Artaria & Co., founded in 1770, which up to the middle of the nineteenth century played a leading part in Vienna's musical life, afterwards in its art, and was liquidated only in 1934. It was on excellent terms with Mozart, Haydn and Beethoven.—The Rondo, written in 1826, was published there in April (No. 852).—Slawjk, born in Bohemia in 1806, had lived in Vienna since 1826. It was he again who, with Bocklet, played the Fantasy for pianoforte and violin (Op. posth. 159) at Schubert's concert early in 1828 (see No. 1009).

788. FROM FRANZ VON HARTMANN'S DIARY

31st January 1827: Towards 8 o'clock to Spaun's, who had invited us. Gahy, the two Rueskäfers, Enderes and Derffel were there. Gahy at first played glorious things by Schubert, then we supped and smoked splendid, genuinely American cigars, and in the end the two hosts, who were extremely lively and kind,

performed all sorts of surprising tricks.   At 12.45 we at last took
our leave and trundled home.

The two Rueskäfers were Friedrich and Michael (*see* Nos. 745 and
773).—American—which no doubt meant Havana—cigars were a
special luxury in Austria, because of the State tobacco monopoly, which
meant that foreign tobacco was heavily taxed.—The two hosts are Spaun
and Enderes.—Schubert was not present; it was his birthday.

789. From Bauernfeld's Diary

1st February 1827.

At Kriehuber's wedding yesterday.

Josef Kriehuber (cf. No. 441), born in Vienna in 1801, the highly
gifted and successful lithographer and water-colour painter of portraits,
married Marie Forstner.

790. From the Programme of the Twelfth Evening Entertainment held by the Philharmonic Society, 1st February 1827 (Conductor, Herr [Ferdinand] Piringer)

'Diana in Anger' ['Die zürnende Diana'], poem by Mayrhofer,
set to music by Schubert, performed by Herr Schoberlechner.

On Piringer *see* No. 633, on Schoberlechner No. 750.

791. Note on the above Programme

Sung by Schoberlechner two tones lower.   Jenger accomp.

'To Diana in Anger' ('Der zürnenden Diana,' which is the proper
title) was written for a tenor voice, and Schoberlechner was a bass.

792. From Franz von Hartmann's Diary

1st February 1827: I went (without finding them) to Schwind
and Schubert. . . . At 10 o'clock to the "Anchor"; Spaun,
Enderes, Schubert, Gahy, Fritz and Schober (for the first time after
an illness) already there.   Home at 11.15.

For Schober cf. No. 781.

793. FROM FRANZ VON HARTMANN'S DIARY

3rd February 1827: To the "Anchor" with Enderes; Spaun,
Schober, Schwind, Schubert and Bauernfeld there again. There
has not been such exceptionally good fun for a long time. So we
stayed on again until 11.30.

794. NINA . . . TO SCHOBER AND SCHUBERT

[Vienna, 6th February ? 1827.]

We, by the grace of God ruler of all the halberdiers and janissaries, hereby take into arrest for the 15th inst., by virtue of this
edict and in the name of a well-known, mathematically mapped-out
power allied to Ourselves (*id est* Baroness Drossdick), the two well-
nourished forms of a certain P. T. Schober and *ditto* Schubert.
The aforesaid are to collaborate according to the powers of their
minds and bodies in the glorification of a musical, declamatorical
and dancical evening entertainment.

The snowed-up nightingales of the Alleegasse will, notwithstanding all the cold bark, flute with all their might.

We exact implicit obedience on the part of our vassals.

Issued at our windy residence on St. Dorothea's Day.

Nina.

This humorous note was found among the remains of Schober's correspondence (now in the Vienna City Library). The writer's identity
remains open to conjectures, which have not so far been convincing. Her
friend, Baroness Therese Drossdick, was the wife of Wilhelm, Freiherr
von Drossdick, aulic councillor to the United Court Chancellery, who
was among the subscribers to the 'Swan Song' cycle after Schubert's
death. (As is well known, Beethoven's friend Therese Malfatti married
Wilhelm von Drossdick in 1817.) It is worthy of note that in 1827–8
Vogl lived in the Alleegasse behind the Karl church in the Wieden
suburb. His wife's name, however, was Kunigunde, not Nina.—P. T. is
short for *pleno titulo.*—The "cold bark" is not easily explained, but
Schwind wrote to Schober on 6th May 1824: "How readily would I shed
all this cold bark."—The letter is not dated, but the day is fixed by the
feast of St. Dorothea; the year, however, might have been 1828.

795. FROM THE PROGRAMME of the Thirteenth Evening Entertainment held by the Philharmonic Society, 8th February 1827 (Conductor, Herr Bogner)

4. 'Song of the Imprisoned Huntsman' from Walter Scott's 'Lady of the Lake,' set to music by Franz Schubert, performed by Herr Schoberlechner.

On Bogner cf. No. 531.

796. NOTE ON THE ABOVE PROGRAMME

Sung by Schoberlechner, v.g. Jenger acc.

797. FROM THE 'HARMONICON,' London, July 1827
(Report from Vienna.)

In our Society of Music were given two new songs, composed by the favourite Schubert, which excited general interest. The first was *Die zürnende Diana* (the Wrathful Diana), the second, the Forester's song, from Sir W. Scott's *Lady of the Lake*.

Cf. No. 790.

798. FROM THE FRANKFORT 'ALLGEMEINER MUSIKALISCHER ANZEIGER,' 10th February 1827

'Hector's Farewell' ['Hektors Abschied']. 'Emma.' 'The Maiden's Plaint' ['Des Mädchens Klage']. Poems by Friedrich von Schiller. Set to music for one voice with pianoforte accompaniment by Franz Schubert. Work 56 [*recte* 58].

'The Butterfly' ['Der Schmetterling'] and 'The Mountains' ['Die Berge']. By Friedrich von Schlegel. 'To the Moon' ['An den Mond']. By Friedrich von (?) Hölty. Set to music &c. by Franz Schubert. Work 57. Vienna, Thaddaeus Weigl. 4 Florins, A.C., & 46 Kreuzer, A.C.

Both books contain well-written music, in which however we are unable to praise any particular depth. This kind of vocal music is too artificial for genuine German song and too simple to be called dramatic. Whatever it is capable of being in such circumstances, Herr Schubert must be said to have achieved, and we might recommend both these little works in preference to many similar ones to lovers of song.

Cf. No. 645.—"Genuine German song" still meant the strophic song-form, as it had been practised by Reichardt and Zelter.

799. FROM FRANZ VON HARTMANN'S DIARY

10th February 1827: Haas accompanied Fritz and me to Schober's lodgings, where we were invited to a ball. There for once we found all the male Schobero-Spaunic acquaintances and all the Schobero-Schwindian female ones: namely 12 girls and young women of whom I did not know a single one at first. All very beautiful, except Netty Hönig, who however is all the more affectionate, and Fräulein Rinna, who was also at Conci's recently. The loveliest dancer was a certain Fräulein Grünwedel, with whom indeed Spaun was altogether enchanted. Equally glorious (and really the fairest) was the so-called "Flower of the Land." Two cotillons were danced, for which I got two very interesting partners: the famous pianoforte player Blahetka and Fräulein Grünwedel. In the intervals between the dances there was carousing and sausage-eating. I made the acquaintance of a medical student and probable brother-in-law for Karl Hönig, named Puffer. In the end we had singing and music-making. On the whole I spent a quite agreeable evening after all, though at first, as I knew so few of those present, I could have howled with Fritz from sheer boredom (like the hussar major Pauliny). At 1.15 the ball was finished. I had to see home a young lady who lives down by the Augarten all by myself. It was the most lovely moonlit night and the air felt extremely fresh. My charge was very nice, and the long distance seemed so short to me that I was very much vexed when we arrived at her home. However, I consoled myself when we wished each other a very friendly good-morning and because the

gadding about had been so pleasant.   The broad, bright and yet
wholly deserted road made a very curious impression on me.   I
went home and was almost glad that the caretaker let me ring six
times for him.   Fritz was already in, and I went to bed at 2 o'clock
(3 according to Fritz).

This was on a Saturday.—Schober had just moved with his mother
from the Obere Bäckerstrasse to the more genteel "Unter den Tuchlauben," near the Graben, to the second floor of the "Blue Hedgehog"
house, which was next door to the Philharmonic Society's "Red Hedgehog."   Schubert followed them there as their guest, for most of the
remainder of his life.   He had two rooms and a "music closet" there,
which was more than he had ever had before.—Ernst Rinna von Sarenbach,
born in 1792 (? at Görz), was court physician; he had two sons and a
daughter, Cäcilia, who was a friend of Schober's.—Karl von Conci, a doctor of law, was aulic councillor of the Supreme Law Courts.—Of Fräulein
Grünwedel nothing is known.—The "Flower of the Land" was Louise
Forstern, Kriehuber's sister-in-law (see No. 789).—Karl Hönig (see No.
391) was engaged to Therese Puffer (born 1806); the medical student was
her brother.—Michael Pauliny, Freiherr von Kovelsdam, had become a
knight of the Maria Theresa Order during the War of Liberation; but the
allusion to him cannot be explained.—The girl whom Franz saw home was
named Emilie (see No. 812); the Augarten is in the Leopold suburb.—In
Hartmann's family chronicle "a beautiful young Frau von Planer" (probably the wife of the barrister Johann Georg, Edler von Planer) is also
named among the guests who had heard Schubert play his 'Valses nobles'
(No. 782).

800. FROM FRITZ VON HARTMANN'S DIARY

10th February 1827: At 7 o'clock I went with Franz to Schober's,
following a long-standing invitation, which Josef von Spaun had
repeated when he came to fetch us this forenoon.   At Schober's I
met among others Spaun, Gahy, Enderes, Schubert, Schwind and his
brother, Bauernfeld; the ladies, little known to me, included
Netty Hönig, Fräulein Puffer, Leopoldine Blahetka (the famous
pianoforte player), Fräulein Grünwedel, &c.   Most of the ladies
were beautiful, which made a very pretty picture.   For all that
I did not enjoy myself very much at first, as I had the ill luck to
dance the first cotillon with the only ugly girl among those present,

a misfortune I had perforce to endure.   Her name was Fräulein
Rinna.   At the second cotillon I was more fortunate: I danced
with Fräulein Blahetka.   Three years ago she enchanted me, but
since then she has lost much of her beauty and still more of
her charming manners, because great attentions were paid to her
in Germany, where she toured for 18 months.   The music was
splendid, for it consisted of nothing but waltzes by Schubert,
played partly by the composer himself and partly by Gahy.   We
remained at Schober's until after 2 o'clock in the morning.   Thereupon the men took it in turns to see the ladies home.   I escorted
Therese Puffer, with whom I talked more then than I had done all
through the ball, because I did not wish to approach the girls
who were very much taken up with their close acquaintances.   In
the end I accompanied the brothers Schwind as far as the Karolinen
Gate.

Schwind's brother is August (*see* No. 515).—As Schubert was not in
the party on the way to the Karolinentor (where he had lived for a few
weeks), it must be supposed that he had already moved to Schober's, or
at least spent that night there.

801. FROM FRITZ VON HARTMANN'S DIARY

11th February 1827: [Ball at the Trieste wholesale dealer
Reyer's.]   The fourth waltz I danced after supper with a Fräulein
Gosmar, with whom I . . . talked about Schubert's music,
among other things.

Franz Thaddäus, Ritter von Reyer, born in 1761 at Malborget in
Carinthia, was a wholesale merchant and banker, not ennobled till 1826;
his son Konstantin, born in 1801 at Trieste, became a "Freiherr" and a
member of the Austrian Upper House.—Louise Gosmar, born in 1803,
later Leopold Sonnleithner's wife, was one of three daughters of a north
German Jewish commercial family settled in Vienna in 1812.   They had
been baptized Protestants at Leipzig (St. Thomas's church).   Therese
married the Trieste wholesale merchant Karl Sebastian Rosenkart; Emilia
became the wife of Andreas, Freiherr von Stifft (born 1787, cf. No. 52·).
Probably Louise is meant here, of whom we shall hear more.

802. From the Official 'Wiener Zeitung,' 12th February 1827

Latest Dance Music for the Pianoforte
for the Carnival of 1827,
which has been published by Anton Diabelli & Co.,
Art and Music Dealers, in the Graben, No. 1133, and
may be had of K. Lichtl in Pest at the same price:

. . . .

Schubert, Fr., Hommage aux belles Viennoises (Viennese Ladies'
Country Dances) [Wiener Damen-Ländler]
Op. 67.   1 Florin 30 Kreuzer.

. . . . . .

(Property of the Publishers.)

Op. 67 appeared, without an individual dedication, after Op. 77, the
'Valses nobles.' For its title cf. No. 745. Besides the sixteen country
dances it also contained two écossaises: the sub-title is thus incomplete.

803. From Franz von Hartmann's Diary

13th February 1827: We went [after 11 o'clock] to the
"Anchor"; Spaun, Gahy and Schubert still there. We remained
a short half hour.

804. From Fritz von Hartmann's Diary

14th February 1827: [Picnic at Frau von Pratty's, Derffel's
landlady.] A Herr Kandler played a good deal on the pianoforte
and also sang several songs by Schubert; Gahy played the same
composer's 'Valses nobles.'

Nothing is known of Frau Pratty.—For Kandler *see* No. 288.

805. From the Leipzig 'Allgemeine Musikalische Zeitung,' 4th April 1827

(Vienna correspondence, February 1827.)

The indefatigable song composer Schubert has again had two new vocal pieces performed at the Society's weekly evening entertainments, viz. 'Diana in Anger,' poem by Mayrhofer, and the 'Song of the Imprisoned Huntsman' from Walter Scott's 'Lady of the Lake.' He works (like Karl Czerny in his own way) almost too much at this species, and earlier excellent things are scarcely to be surpassed by the good ones that follow.

Cf. Nos. 790 and 795.

806. From Franz von Hartmann's Diary

15th February 1827: Fritz and I went to the "Anchor," whither Eli [von Spiegelfeld] accompanied us. After a long time came Enderes, Spaun, Schober and Schubert. We were very jolly, I sang German dances for Schubert. Home at 11.45.

According to Fritz von Hartmann's diary the brothers had first been to one of the Philharmonic Society's evening entertainments with Josef von Spaun.—Elias (Eli), Freiherr von Spiegelfeld, born 1811, became an officer. He was a descendant of one of two Viennese families of that name: he and three brothers were the sons of Anton, a governor at Trieste, who died in 1822; two other sons and three daughters were the children of a late councillor to the Court of Appeal.

807. From Fritz von Hartmann's Diary

15th February 1827: . . . I like these people better and better.

"These people" are the friends named in No. 806.

Anton Schindler takes to the ailing Beethoven sixty songs by Schubert, some of them in manuscript, February 1827. Cf. note preceding No. 831.

808. FROM THE REGISTER OF PROPERTY of the Viennese
Municipality

(Concerning the reservation of the house Himmelpfortgrund No. 10.)

17th February 1827—its cassation.

Cf. No. 705. The shares in the four children's inheritance, entered
in the property register after their mother's death in 1812, were now
deducted by their father from the purchase price, the second instalment
of which (3,000 florins) he had probably received already before the
term (24th April 1827). The entry was thus officially cancelled.

809. FROM FRANZ VON HARTMANN'S DIARY

17th February 1827: At 6.30 I dressed to go to the ball at
Schober's. There was almost exactly the same company as a
week ago; but there were not so many lady dancers. Spaun was
particularly nice to-day. The one I like best among the dancers is
the so-called "young nun," Betty Puffer, who is very agreeable.
We danced away busily. (I the two cotillons with Frau von
Kriehuber and Fräulein Grünwedel.) During the intervals we
had beer and sausages. August Schwind too was very nice. I
know them all better already than I did a week ago. At 2.45
everybody went home. I accompanied the Hönigs, but in the
most tedious manner, as I had to escort an aunt.

This was a Saturday again (cf. Nos. 799 and 800).—Betty (Babette)
Puffer was Therese's sister.—The Hönig's aunt is the wife of Ludwig
Hönig (see No. 591).

810. FROM FRANZ VON HARTMANN'S DIARY

21st February 1827: To the "Anchor" at 9.30, where Bauern-
feld, Lachner and Randhartinger were at first. Much later came
Spaun (hurried from a ball), Schober, Schubert and Schwind.
We stayed together until midnight.

"The Caprice" ("Der Mutwille"). Garden House of the Bruchmann Family at Hütteldorf near Vienna. Water-colour (c. 1822). See p. 278 f.

In the doorway one of the surviving daughters, Juliana or Justina von Bruchmann

PLATE XXII

Countess Karoline Esterházy in Later Life. Water-colour by Anton Hähnisch (1837)

PLATE XXIII

811. From Franz von Hartmann's Diary

22nd February 1827: We went to the "Castle of Eisenstadt" (an ale-house in the Naglergasse), where after a frightfully long time Schubert, Schober and Spaun came too.   Interesting musical discourses.   Home towards midnight.

The Castle of Eisenstadt Tavern (*Zum Schloss Eisenstadt*), named after the seat of the Esterházy princes, where Haydn had lived for a number of years, was now becoming the Schubertians' regular haunt for six months. It was near the Graben.

812. From Franz von Hartmann's Diary

24th February 1827: To the ball at Schober's, where among the male and female dancers of the other day (except Blahetka) there were the hideous Fräulein Rinna and a certain Marie Pinterics, who must be very lovely and nice, since most men fall in love with her.   I danced the first cotillon with the "Young Nun," the second with an old aunt of the Hönigs, the third with Fräulein Rinna. German dances with all of them.   Fritz was unbearably dull. I broke a cup.   What 's more, I danced frightfully badly.   Nearly fell in love with the "Flower of the Land."   Saw Fräulein Emilie home, as I did a fortnight ago.   Went back, rang more than twenty times at the front door and stood there more than three quarters of an hour before I was admitted.

A Saturday again.—Marie was a sister of Pinterics (*see* No. 492).— The "Young Nun" is Betty Puffer, the "Flower of the Land" Louise Forstern.—For Fräulein Emilie cf. No. 799.

813. From Fritz von Hartmann's Diary

24th February 1827: At 7.30 I went with my brother to Schober's where we were invited to the last little ball.   I danced several rounds of German dances, the first cotillon with Louise Forster, a girl so beautiful that she rejoices in the nickname of "the Flower of the Land,' and the second cotillon with Therese Puffer.   The rest of the time I spent in talk with Spaun, Schubert, Gahy and Netty Hönig. Before we parted we men smoked a pipe. It was 3 in the morning when I got home.

Pipe-smoking is mentioned here because it occurred during a party at which ladies were present, though evidently in a separate room.

813A. [IMPRIMATUR OF THE VIENNA CENSORSHIP for Schubert's Op. 81: 'Alinde,' 'To the Lute' ('An die Laute') and 'For Good-night' ('Zur guten Nacht'), 26th February 1827]

All songs had to be submitted to the censorship on account of their words. In this case the sanction, *Excudatur*, is written on the title-page of the manuscript, which Schubert himself had dated January 1827. Cf. No. 893:

814. FROM THE 'THEATERZEITUNG,' 27th February 1827

It is sufficiently known what a magnificent effect was made by Goethe's poem, 'Erl King,' in Schubert's masterly composition. We offer here a similar poem, which in our opinion opens up a rich field to composers and whose merit is enhanced by its brevity. [There follow five anonymous stanzas entitled 'Nina.']

The poem is the work of a bungler.

815. FROM FRITZ VON HARTMANN'S DIARY

1st March 1827: To the County Hall, where the first *Concert spirituel* was given. Mozart's C major Symphony enchanted me most. I met Spaun, Enderes and Schubert.

The *Concert spirituel*, founded by Gebauer in 1819, was now conducted by Piringer and Geissler (*see* notes preceding Nos. 275 and 634). The programme included Beethoven's 'Consecration of the House' overture and a chorus from Handel's 'Israel in Egypt' (with additional accompaniments by Mosel).

816. FROM THE OFFICIAL 'WIENER ZEITUNG,' 2nd March 1827

At the House of Anton Diabelli & Co.,
Art and Music Dealers, in the Graben, No. 1133, are just published,
and to be had of K. Lichtl in Pest at the same price:

SONGS FROM 'WILHELM MEISTER'
by Goethe,
set to Music with Pianoforte Accompaniment
and reverentially dedicated to
Mathilde, Princess of Schwarzenberg,
by FRANZ SCHUBERT.
Work 62.   Price, 1 Florin, Assimilated Coinage.

Contents:
No. 1. Duet: Mignon and the Harper ("Whoso knows longing")
No. 2. Mignon's Song: ("Bid me not speak it")
No. 3. Mignon's Song: ("Let me dissemble")
No. 4. Mignon's Song: ("Whoso knows longing")

URGE INTO THE DISTANCE
['Drang in die Ferne']
Poem by K. G. von Leitner.
Set to Music
for One Voice with Pianoforte Accompaniment
by FRANZ SCHUBERT
Work 71.   Price, 30 Kreuzer, A.C.

TO BE SUNG ON THE WATER
['Auf dem Wasser zu singen']
Poem by Leopold, Count von Stolberg.
Set to Music
for One Voice with Pianoforte Accompaniment
by FRANZ SCHUBERT
Work 72.   Price, 30 Kreuzer, A.C.
(Property of the Publishers.)

Op. 62, which appeared after Op. 77, was probably the first new work
Schubert had assigned to Diabelli's firm after his reconciliation to him.
It was written in January 1826 and dedicated to Princess Mathilde

Schwarzenberg (born 1804). She was the daughter of Prince Josef Johann Schwarzenberg (born 1769), who had been a patron of Haydn and Beethoven, and the sister of the later Prince Felix (born 1800), who became Prime Minister of Austria. Schubert may have been brought into touch with her by Barth (*see* No. 203).—Opp. 71 and 72 (without dedications) were reprints of songs first published in the 'Wiener Zeit-schrift' (*see* notes preceding No. 354 and following No. 417).

817. FROM FRANZ VON HARTMANN'S DIARY

3rd March 1827: At the "Castle of Eisenstadt" there were Spaun, Schober, Schubert and Bauernfeld. We talked of the Greeks, the Hungarians and Grillparzer. Quite lively. Home at 11.30.

During the Greek Wars of Liberation (1821–9) England, Russia and France entered into an alliance in 1827 to protect Greece against Turkey. Cf. No. 436 for the Greek songs by Wilhelm Müller, with whose work Schubert was occupied again at this time (*see* No. 819).—In Hungary the national spirit was reawakened by the reopening of Parliament, which had been closed down in 1812–24.

818. FROM FRITZ VON HARTMANN'S DIARY

3rd March 1827: Also, Turks and Lord Cochrane [were discussed.]

Thomas Cochrane, tenth Earl of Dundonald, had been in command of the Greek navy since March 1827.

819. FROM FRANZ VON HARTMANN'S DIARY

4th March 1827: I went with Fritz to Schubert's, who had invited us, but never appeared at all. Schwind sang in the mean-time; the "Flower of the Land" was there too. With Spaun, Schober, Schwind, Bauernfeld and Fritz to the "Castle of Eisen-stadt," where Schubert, Gahy and Enderes appeared as well. We talk d about the beasts of the forest. Home at 11 o'clock.

Schubert had invited his friends to his new lodgings at Schober's. His first compositions there were two songs on poems by Schober, 'Hunts- man's Love Song' ('Jägers Liebeslied') and 'Boatman's Song of Farewell' ('Schiffers Scheidelied'), and in the same month of February he also wrote the first part of the 'Winter Journey,' his second cycle on poems by Wilhelm Müller, the second part of which he set at the same place in October 1827. He evidently wished to sing these songs to his friends. Spaun reports how greatly the 'Winter Journey' songs affected Schubert, both in the process of composition and in performance. This may have been the reason for his absence from his own party. But the performance was only postponed: according to Spaun Schubert sang the whole 'Winter Journey' to his friends, which could not have happened before the autumn of 1827. Their gloomy moods caused consternation in the circle. The only song Schober liked was 'The Lime-Tree.' But Schubert was confident, and his friends were enthusiastic when Vogl sang the cycle to them later. Spaun was of the opinion that these songs contributed to Schubert's early death.

820. FROM FRITZ VON HARTMANN'S DIARY

4th March 1827: We went to Schober's, where we met Spaun, Schwind, Bauernfeld and Kriehuber with his wife and sister-in-law ("the Flower of the Land"), because Schubert, who is Schober's lodger, had invited us to hear some new compositions of his. Everybody was assembled, but friend Schubert did not come. At last Schwind undertook to sing several of Schubert's earlier songs, which enchanted us. At half-past nine we all went to the "Castle of Eisenstadt," where Schubert too arrived soon after us and won all hearts by his amiable simplicity, although he had deceived our hopes by his artist's negligence.

821. SCHUBERT TO FRANZ LACHNER

Dear Lachner,

Be so kind as to hand the bearer of this my Quartet in G major, score as well as the written-out parts, since *Slawik* promised me to visit you on Wednesday evening.

Vienna, 5th March 1827.   Frz. Schubert.

This string Quartet, Schubert's last, was written at the end of June 1826.   Lachner had probably borrowed it, or Schubert may have left it with him after a first reading through.   He probably did not write out the parts himself.   Slawjk (*see* note preceding No. 788) may have wished to play it through before performing it on 7th March with Schubert, Lachner and another.

822. FROM THE PROGRAMME of the Fifteenth Evening Entertainment held by the Philharmonic Society, 8th March 1827 (Conductor, Herr Kirchlehner)

4. Norman's Song from 'The Lady of the Lake' by Walter Scott with music by Schubert, performed by Herr Tietze, accompanied by Herr Schubert. . . .

6. 'God in Nature' ['Gott in der Natur'], poem by Gleim, music by Schubert, performed by lady pupils of the Conservatory.

For Kirchlehner *see* No. 523.—The facts that two works by Schubert were performed on the same evening and that he himself accompanied are significant.   The quartet for women's voices, the words of which were actually by Ewald Christian von Kleist, was sung by twelve students.

823. FROM FRANZ VON HARTMANN'S DIARY

8th March 1827: At 9 o'clock we three [Ferdinand Sauter, Karl von Revertera and I] went with Haas to the "Castle of Eisenstadt," where the whole former "Anchor" party, with the exception of Schwind and Bauernfeld, happened to be.   We chatted a great deal with Karl and Spaun, and in general had much fun with all the others too.   Enderes alone left earlier, we others only at 11.45.

Karl, Count Revertera, was a brother of Antoń (*see* No. 478), Hartmann's brother-in-law.

824. FROM FRANZ VON HARTMANN'S DIARY

11th March 1827: At 10 o'clock I went with Vize to his people, where we had music and food; Dini sang Schubert's 'Young Nun' very well.

The party took place at the house of Katharina, Freiin von Spiegelfeld, widow of a councillor of the Courts of Appeal, who lived in the square "Am Hof" with her children (*see* No. 846A).—Franz, Freiherr von Spiegelfeld, born in 1803, who for some unknown reason was nicknamed "Vize" (perhaps he was vice-president of some organization or held some other deputy post), was a cousin of Elias (*see* No. 806); Leopoldine (Dini), born in 1806, was his sister, nicknamed "The Oriental."

825. FROM FRITZ VON HARTMANN'S DIARY

11th March 1827: Leopoldine sang the 'Young Nun' and other songs by Schubert very well.

826. FROM THE BERLIN 'ALLGEMEINE MUSIKALISCHE ZEITUNG,' 14th March 1827

(Review of Schubert's Opp. 60 and 65.)

. . . If we . . . consider the works submitted, we cannot, to begin with, refuse Herr Schubert our approval of his choice of words, Schiller's 'Dithyramb' excepted; true, it expresses one single sentiment, but that is wholly subordinated to the rule of the idea, and this appears to us to be altogether unmusical. It therefore does not seem in the least strange to us that this very piece is the weakest of them all. In order of ascendance it is followed by No. 3 in the second collection, 'From Heliopolis' by Mayrhofer. This is allegorical and for that very reason not particularly musical; yet its underlying feeling still appears fairly clearly. The remaining three songs are quite excellent; be it understood that we are here always envisaging reference to composition, for should we be obliged to arrange the poems in question in the order of their own merit, the result might well be very different. All the songs by Schubert designated here excel by a high degree of originality, which never appears to be forced, and is thus never merely mannered. Moreover, Herr Schubert knows very well how to write for a bass; we are even of the opinion that the second collection also must have been intended, not for a female voice at all, but for a high bass. It nowhere goes above middle E.

The 'Veteran's Song' ['Greisenlied'] (in B minor) offers us the most beautiful portrait of a splendidly virile and venerable poet: he has allowed the varied and changing phases of life to go past him and surveys the world with serene and unclouded eyes; brisk outward activity is ended, but inwardly the old vigour still burgeons unimpaired. We cannot undertake to single out separate fine moments for praise, for the whole song is excellent.—The 'Dithyramb,' even though the weakest song in these collections, is not therefore bad by a long way, indeed not even mediocre. But it has not the true inward fire; its bacchic glow and swing at times seems merely forced, just as the melody in general shows an unaccustomed opposition to natural development. But we have no doubt at all that the song will greatly please in a live and accurate performance, which however will present difficulties. The 'Boatman's Song to the Dioscuri' is altogether beautiful; no one could possibly speak to the heart at once more blandly and more forcibly than it is done here. The words satisfy the [above] demands: the sentiment is reflected simply but exhaustively, and the music corresponds perfectly to this; the two are one, so that it would be impossible to imagine the latter without the former. But that is precisely the sign of the greatest perfection in song. In this, as in the following, 'The Wanderer,' Herr Schubert clearly depicts the whole scene for us. Both are night pieces. In the one we see the boatman alone on the darksome high sea; in the other we have a vaporous landscape by moonlight with all its changing shadows and misty shapes. At the close of the last-mentioned song the conduct of the melody is most original.— The *last*, 'From Heliopolis' by Mayrhofer (probably not the she-wolf of the I. & R. privileged Theater an der Wien), contains a passage, "of mankind never could I ask it," which suddenly interrupts the whole melodic flow and therefore appears unsuitable to us. Declamation must not become the chief consideration in song, since music thus sacrifices its joint rule with poetry. What seems to be admirably contrived in this song is its turn to E major, and the splendid, full harmony under the clear melody on the last pages is most lovely to hear.

We thus believe that we may be justly allowed to recommend

these songs most particularly, and we close with the sincere
wish that we shall ere long receive similar things by this excellent
author — who has before now furnished much beautiful vocal
music . . .   4.

[Heinrich Dorn.]

'The Wanderer' is the less familiar song of that name, to Schlegel's
poem.—No. 1 of Op. 65 is set for tenor, No. 2 for bass or baritone, No. 3
for mezzo-soprano or contralto.—On the animal mimic Leopold Mayerhofer, whom the critic all but confuses with the poet Johann Mayrhofer,
see No. 422.—Dorn was himself a composer.

827. From Franz von Hartmann's Diary

14th March 1827: Alone to the "Castle of Eisenstadt." Schwind,
Spaun, Schober, Schubert, Gahy, Enderes there, and Nágy for a
time.   We remained until midnight.

Kreissle mentions (p. 220) a military official named Karl Nágy as one
of Schubert's acquaintances, but Franz von Hartmann calls the "rare
Hungarian" with whom Schober had made friends not long before, a
Hungarian court conveyancer. He was probably Martin von Nágy,
registrar in the Palatine Chancellery (for the Archduke Josef, Palatine
—i.e. the Viceroy—of Hungary, *see* No. 612).

828. From Fritz von Hartmann's Diary

15th March 1827: At 4 o'clock I went with Karl Haas to the
second *Concert spirituel* in the County Hall.   They played a glorious
symphony by the Abbé Vogler, a number from Mozart's 'Davidde
penitente' and the grandiose ninth Symphony by Beethoven. . . .
After the concert I accompanied Spaun. . . .   Towards 8 o'clock
I betook myself to the Little Musical Society, where nothing of
any note was to be heard at all. . . .   After that concert I went to
the "Castle of Eisenstadt," where I remained alone for a long time;
at last came Schober, Enderes, Gahy and Schubert, and Spaun
followed after midnight.   This afternoon's concert, and art in
general, were the main topics of conversation.   At 12.30 I
went home.

The "symphony" by Vogler was the overture to his opera 'Samori,' composed as an afterthought for Darmstadt in 1811 and described by the Leipzig 'Allgemeine musikalische Zeitung' as "as masterpiece of the harmonic art." The "number" from Mozart's cantata was the trio in E minor and the final chorus in C major.

829. FROM THE PROGRAMME of a Concert given by Peregrin Feigerl, a Pupil of the Conservatory, 18th March 1827, at 12.30 p.m., in the Philharmonic Society's Hall at the "Red Hedgehog."

5. Psalm [XXIII] set to music by Schubert, performed by the lady singing-pupils of the third Conservatory class.

Feigerl, born in 1803, had appeared as a violinist as early as 1824, but did not become a pupil of Böhm's until later. He went to the Josefstadt Theatre and ended as a music teacher.—Tietze sang an aria from 'Der Freischütz' "by special courtesy towards the concert-giver," and the quartet was sung "by all the young ladies."

830. FROM THE 'THEATERZEITUNG,' 24th March 1827

There was also a fine Psalm by Schubert, performed by the lady singing-pupils of the third Conservatory class, as a pleasant indication of the progress made by that institution, under the direction of their meritorious teacher, Mlle [Anna] Fröhlich.

Another notice appeared on 28th March in the Leipzig 'Allgemeine musikalische Zeitung' (German edition, No. 844), which erroneously supposed the Psalm to have been performed for the first time the preceding autumn (see No. 696).

At this time, about 19th March, Schubert visited the dying Beethoven, probably with Schindler, Teltscher and Anselm and Josef Hüttenbrenner, Anselm having come from Graz on purpose. In February Schindler had brought the master (who then had Schwind's 'Figaro'cycle with him), some sixty of Schubert's songs, including some not yet printed, such as 'Viola.' Among them were 'Iphigenia,' 'Bounds of Mankind,' 'Omnipotence,' 'The Young Nun,' 'The Fair Maid of the Mill' and others. Beethoven, who then knew hardly five of Schubert's five hundred songs written by that time and also wished to know his operas and more of his pianoforte music, is said to have exclaimed: "Truly, in Schubert there is a divine spark!''—In those days, in March 1827, Schubert also met at Frau von Lászny's Hummel and the future pianoforte virtuoso Ferdinand Hiller (born Frankfort o/M., 1811), who were on a visit to Vienna. Hummel there improvised at the pianoforte on Schubert's song 'The Blind Boy,' which Vogl had just sung.

831. FROM FRITZ VON HARTMANN'S DIARY

21st March 1827: At 10 o'clock we went to the "Castle of Eisenstadt" to see out friends Schober, Spaun, Schubert, &c.; but none of them came.

832. FROM FRANZ VON HARTMANN'S DIARY

22nd March 1827: I went to the "Castle of Eisenstadt," where in a little while Schober appeared, and a long time afterwards Schubert. We talked quite interestingly until 11.45. As we climbed the stairs at home I was seized by some sort of slight horror, our landlord, the tailor, having died this morning, and the discussions at the "Castle of Eisenstadt" having also turned on very gruesome things.

The Hartmann brothers lived in the Riemergasse, near the Singerstrasse, at the lodgings of the tailor Watzolini, where the brothers Sauter followed them in February.

833. FROM THE OFFICIAL 'WIENER ZEITUNG,' 23rd March 1827

At the House of A. Pennauer,
Priv. Art and Music Dealer, in the Graben, in Fischer's House,
No. 1122, is just published:

Schubert, Grande Sonate pour le Pianoforte seul. Œuvre 42. Price,
4 Fl. 30 Kr.

Cf. note preceding No. 624. This was clearly a belated announcement.

834. FROM A GRAZ PROGRAMME, 25th March 1827

(Grand vocal and instrumental concert given by members of the theatre orchestra trained at the Prague Conservatory, in conjunction with Graz opera singers and the Styrian Musical Society, in the Knights' Hall.)

Part I. . . . No. 5. Vocal Quartet by Schubert; sung by Herren Marschall, Streicher, Schütze and Adolph . . .

Part II. . . . No. 10. Vocal Quartet by Schubert; sung by Herren Marschall, Streicher, Schütze and Adolph.

The Graz theatre had been managed since 1823 by Johann Stöger (actually Althaller, born Stockerau, Lower Austria, 1790) and his wife Johanna, *née* Wimmer, formerly the widow of the Prague theatre manager Liebich. Part of the orchestra had followed the management from Prague.—The two quartets were presumably 'The Little Village' and 'The Nightingale,' which had already been sung at Graz earlier (*see* Nos. 308 and 311). No details are known of the singers, two tenors and two basses.

835. FROM THE OFFICIAL 'GRAZER ZEITUNG,' 7th April 1827

The close of the first part was a vocal quartet by Schubert, quite valiantly sung . . .

The concert was concluded by a vocal quartet composed by Schubert and quite well performed . . .

Beethoven dies 26th March 1827.

836. FROM FRANZ VON HARTMANN'S DIARY

27th March 1827: To the "Castle of Eisenstadt," where Schober arrived after a long time. We talked with him about Watteroth and Byron until midnight.

Watteroth may have been the professor's elder son (*see* No. 81), Vinzenz, conveyancer in the registry of the Lower Austrian County Government, a cellist, who died soon after.

837. From Franz von Hartmann's Diary

28th March 1827: Out to the Schwarzspanierhaus, where I contemplated the body of the divine Beethoven, who died the day before yesterday, at 6 in the evening. Already on entering his room, which is large and somewhat neglected, I was moved by its desolate look. It is scantily furnished, and only the pianoforte, of which the English made him a present, as well as a very fine coffin, struck a note of beauty in it. In some places lay music and several books. No catafalque had as yet been erected, but he still lay on the mattress of his bed. A cover was spread over him, and a venerable old man, whom I would regard rather as a servant than as a watcher, uncovered him for me. There I saw his splendid face, which unhappily I had never been able to see in life. Such a heavenly dignity lay spread over him, in spite of the disfigurement he is said to have suffered, that I could scarcely look my fill. I departed full of emotion; and only when I was downstairs could I have wept for not having begged the good old man to cut me off a few of his hairs. Ferdinand Sauter, whom I had arranged to meet, but whom I missed, ran across me, and I turned back with him, telling him of my plan. The old man showed him to us once more and also uncovered the chest for us, which, like the greatly swollen abdomen, was already quite blue. The smell of corruption was very strong already. We pressed a gratuity into the old man's hand and asked him for hair from Beethoven's head. He shook his head and motioned us to be silent. So we sadly trundled down the stairs, when suddenly the old man softly called us from the banisters upstairs, asking us to wait at the gate until the three fops had departed who were viewing the dead hero, tapping their swagger-canes on their pantaloons. We then reascended the stairs and, issuing from the door and putting his finger-tips to his lips, he gave us the hair in a piece of paper and vanished. We left, sorrowfully happy about it. Fritz met us, and I told him of our errand, whereupon he did the same.—In the Kohlmarkt we looked at the latest portrait that has appeared of him and found that his corpse still resembled it very much.—Then I met Spaun, whom I told all this . . . Dispute with Haas, who maintained that the present made to the deceased by the English (1,000 florins, A.C., with the advice to claim everything that may still be required at Roth-schild's) was very shabby.

The Schwarzspanierhaus, named after the earlier holy order of the Black Spaniards in Vienna, was outside the Schottentor on the glacis, adjoining the Alsergrund suburb. It was Beethoven's last home.—The pianoforte was the six-octave instrument made by John Broadwood & Sons in London, presented to the master in 1817 by Thomas Broadwood, a member of that firm.—Teltscher drew Beethoven as he lay there dying on 26th March (iconographical volume, p. 465).—Beethoven had died of dropsy.—The portrait, evidently in the shop of Artaria & Co., was probably Danhauser's drawing of the dead man's head, made on 28th March. (For Danhauser *see* Nos. 388 and 613.)—The Philharmonic Society in London had sent Beethoven, through the Rothschilds, the sum of £100 (= 1,000 florins, A.C.), which he received in the middle of March, with a prospect of more to come if it should be needed as assistance during his illness.

838. FROM BAUERNFELD'S DIARY

29th March 1827.

On the 26th Beethoven died, 56 years of age. To-day was his funeral. I went with Schubert. Anschütz delivered a funeral oration by Grillparzer in front of the Währing cemetery.

The district cemetery of Währing, on the main thoroughfare of that suburb, was situated outside the Währinger Linie (the toll boundary), like the general Währing cemetery outside the Nussdorfer Linie, where Schubert's mother was buried and which was the older of the two. The district cemetery was consecrated in 1796, altered in 1820–30, closed in 1873 and transformed in 1925 into the so-called Schubert Park, where among the few gravestones still preserved are those of Beethoven and Schubert, whose bones, however, were transferred as early as 1888 to the famous Grove of Honour (*Ehrenhain*) for Viennese musicians at the modern Central Cemetery in the Simmering suburb.—The fine oration by Grill-parzer had to be delivered by the court actor Anschütz (*see* note following No. 268) outside the cemetery, for only priests were allowed to speak at the graves. It contains the sentence "True, he still lives, and long may he live yet, the German language and tongue's hero . . .," correctly understood to allude to Goethe by those present, but on a later occasion erroneously taken to refer to Schubert. Ferdinand Sauter allowed himself to be so far carried away as to exclaim: "Bravo Anschütz!" which made a painful impression.

839. FROM FRANZ VON HARTMANN'S DIARY

29th March 1827: Saw Beethoven's funeral with Fritz and Haas. It lasted a very long time, and there was a crowd of spectators. A Miserere of his own was sung, and many composers followed. We went out with Schober, Schwind and Karl Revertera to the cemetery where he was buried (at Währing). There we waited for an hour and a half, until at last Anschütz &c. arrived. A ring was formed round him, and when the coffin came at last, he delivered a magnificent oration (written by Grillparzer), in which he also described the glorious Beethoven as a man in a manner wholly worthy of him. Home with Enderes, Schubert, Schober and Bauernfeld. Discoursed with Ludwig Sauter and Nandi as well as Ferdinand, whom I told about it, and with Antonio later on, who was also present at the oration. Fritz went to the "Castle of Eisenstadt."

The funeral service took place in the parish church of the Alsergrund suburb, near the place of death.—Nandi was Franz von Lankmayr's nickname and Antonio that of his brother Anton; both were friends of the Hartmanns'.—Ludwig Sauter died the next day, and Ferdinand was much sympathized with by his friends.

840. FROM FRITZ VON HARTMANN'S DIARY

29th March 1827: I went to the "Castle of Eisenstadt," where I remained with Schober, Schubert and Schwind until almost 1 a.m. Needless to say, we talked of nothing but Beethoven, his works and the well-merited honours paid to his memory to-day.

This entry, published in full in the 'Neues Wiener Journal' of 17th December 1920, but adding nothing to that in Franz's diary, seems to contradict the tradition according to which Schubert is said to have gone to the Mehlgrube Inn with Franz Lachner and Randhartinger after Beethoven's funeral, and there to have raised his glass, first to the master's memory and afterwards to the one among the three who was destined first to follow him into the grave.

841. FROM THE 'SAMMLER,' 14th April 1827
(On Beethoven's funeral.)

7. On both sides columns of torch-bearers, among whom were Herren . . . Schubert. . . . All were clad in black, with gloves of the same colour and streaming crape on the left arm, except the torch-bearers, who for compensation had bunches of white lilies pinned on, whereas the torches were craped.

In the Berlin 'Allgemeine musikalische Zeitung' of 23rd May Schubert's name is spelt "Schubart."—Grillparzer and Raimund were also among the torch-bearers, the rest of whom were nearly all Viennese musicians of distinction.

842. FROM 'LUDWIG VAN BEETHOVEN'S FUNERAL; AND HISTORICAL RECORD OF THE MUSICAL WORKS PERFORMED THEREAT,' Vienna, June 1827

(Preface for the edition of the 'Dirge at Beethoven's Funeral in Vienna on 29th March 1827 . . . arranged . . . from Beethoven's Manuscript . . . by Ignaz, Ritter von Seyfried,' published by Tobias Haslinger, Vienna, June 1827.)

VII. In the files on either side, from the head of the procession back to the hearse, were the torch-bearers, thirty-six in number, consisting of . . . musicians, and among them Herren . . . Schubert . . ., all in funereal clothes with white roses and bunches of lilies tied to their arms with crape, and with burning wax torches.

The same text, "for the sake of correcting several particulars, . . . some erroneous, others incomplete," also appeared in the summer of 1827 in Haslinger's edition of Seyfried's 'Libera,' which had been sung in the church of the Alsergrund suburb, as well as with Seyfried's setting of the poem 'Beethoven's Funeral' by Alois Jeitteles, the poet of Beethoven's song-cycle 'To the Distant Beloved.'

843. FROM THE MAINZ 'CÄCILIA,' Spring 1827
['Vienna in the Year 1826.']

Among the young composers . . . Schubert writes fine songs.

This report was written on the night of New Year's Eve 1827.

844. From Franz von Hartmann's Diary

4th April 1827: To the "Castle of Eisenstadt," where Schubert and Bauernfeld were. I confabulated with them until 11 o'clock about music and Goethe.

845. From the Programme of the Concert given by Josef Merk, Member of the Court Chapel, first Violoncellist at the Kärntnertor Theatre and Professor at the Conservatory, 6th April 1827, at 7 p.m., in the Small Assembly Hall

5. Four-part Song by Schubert, performed by the singers mentioned above [Eichberger, Ruprecht, Kral and Borschitzky].

For Merk cf. No. 282.—The quartet may have been 'Grave and Moon' ('Grab und Mond') of September 1826.—Josef Eichberger, born in 1808 in Bohemia, was at that time temporarily engaged as tenor at the Kärntnertor Theatre. On Ruprecht cf. No. 306. Kral too was a professional singer. Franz Borschitzky, born in 1794 at Reisenmarkt in Lower Austria, also worked at the Court Opera.—On that evening the boy Sigismund Thalberg (born at Geneva in 1812, the natural son of Count Moritz Dietrichstein) played the first movement of Hummel's pianoforte Concerto in B minor.

846. From the 'Theaterzeitung,' 12th April 1827

Two vocal quartets by Eisenhofer and Schubert were very finely sung by singers of our German Opera.

Franz Xaver Eisenhofer, about whom nothing else is known, during those years published five instalments of male-voice quartets, containing six each, at Georg Falter's in Munich. He was thus a temporary rival of Schubert's in this branch of composition. The 'Wiener Zeitschrift' of 19th April (German edition, No. 859) says of this concert that Eisenhofer's quartet "received extraordinary applause, while Schubert's left the audience cold."

846A. Eduard Horstig to his Parents at Bückeburg

Vienna, 10th April 1827.

We gave a great evening party. Among those present were Count Salm, Prince Ferdinand of Hesse-Philippsthal, Baron Jacquin, the orientalist Baron Hammer, three Barons Boyneburg, President Count Ugarte, von Stein, Baron Spiegelfeld together with his ladies, Grillparzer, Aulic Councillor Lehmann, Baron Pereira and Aulic Councillor Weckbecker with their families, Baron Schlechta; Anselm Hüttenbrenner extemporized on the pianoforte, Tietze sang songs by Schubert and Beethoven's 'Adelaide,' accompanied by Schubert. Baron Ransonnet played the mandoline, Nina herself the harp most touchingly, and Bayer organized quartets.

Eduard Horstig (born at Bückeburg, c. 1793), son of the music-loving Consistory Councillor Karl Gottlieb Horstig and his wife Susanne, née d'Aubigny von Engelbronner, had gone to Vienna in 1814 and become a civil servant. He lived from 1825 with his aunt Nina (born at Cassel in 1777), who had remained single and, like her elder sister, was an amateur singer; she had published in 1803 a manual of singing which had appeared in a second edition in 1824, also some songs in various languages (including English), had been in London about 1804 and later in Bombay. She lived in a house belonging to Prince Paar in the Riemerstrasse. In her book, which Beethoven is said to have valued, she speaks of Eduard Horstig as a musical wonder-baby.—Hugo Franz, Count Salm-Reifferscheid-Krautheim (born 1776) had been an officer and become a naturalist; he visited England in 1801.—Prince Friedrich W. K. L. of Hesse-Philippsthal was a field marshal lieutenant of the artillery.—Josef Franz, Freiherr van Jacquin (born at Schemnitz in 1766) was professor of chemistry and director of the Botanical Gardens.—For Hammer see No. 237.—Moritz Heinrich, Freiherr Boyneburg zu Lengsfeld (born 1788), was a general of cavalry; the others were possibly his brothers.—Alois, Count von und zu Ugarte (born 1784) was president of the Upper Austrian County Government.—Emerich, Freiherr von Stein (born at Görz in 1762) was field marshal lieutenant and brigadier of the artillery. —Freiherr von Spiegelfeld was probably the officer Anton von Spiegelfeld (born 1801), with his mother Katharina and his sisters (cf. Nos. 806 and 824).—Franz Kaspar Lehmann (born in the Grand Duchy of Baden in 1769) was aulic councillor in the Court War Council and a historian.— Heinrich, Freiherr von Pereira (born 1773), a banker, was married to Henriette von Arnstein (born in Berlin, 1780).—Bernhard (later Ritter von) Weckbecker (born at Coblenz in 1778), married to Emilie Obermayer, was also an aulic councillor in the Court War Council.—Karl Freiherr von Ransonnet-Villez (born in Vienna, 1802) was an official in the Lower Austrian County Government.—Bayer cannot be identified.

847. From the Official 'Wiener Zeitung,' 11th April 1827

At the House of Tobias Haslinger,
Art and Music Dealer in Vienna, in the Graben, No. 572, in the
House of the Austrian Savings Bank, is just published:

MUSEUM FOR PIANOFORTE MUSIC
Book IX, containing:

FANTASY, *Andante* and *Allegretto*
for Pianoforte solo,
by FRANZ SCHUBERT.

Work 78. 2 Florins, A.C.

(Also to be had of K. Lichtl at Pest and of Kraer & Deyrkauf
at Graz.)

Op. 78 appeared before Opp. 73–6. For the dedication to "den
hochwohlgebornen Herrn Joseph Edlen von Spaun" cf. Nos. 737 and
740A. (A sample is here given in German of a form of address that
cannot be translated, except literally by "well-born," and has been
reproduced in this work by "Esq." as a rule.) Spaun had already received the dedication of Op. 13 (No. 330). The advertisement omits
the title of the third movement, *Menuetto* [*sic*]. The original title,
"Sonata," was avoided by the publisher, who wished to give a distinctive
name to the work; but on the inside heading it is described as "Fantasy
or Sonata." The work appeared in a collection, 'Museum für Klavier-
musik (Musée musical des Clavecinistes),' a title that appears on a fly-
leaf. The first book of this collection, published when the firm was
still Steiner & Co., had been Beethoven's A major "Hammerclavier"
Sonata, Op. 101.

848. From the Frankfort 'Allgemeiner Musikalischer Anzeiger,' 14th April 1827

6 Polonaises for the Pianoforte *à 4 mains*, composed by Franz
Schubert. Work 61. Books I and II. Vienna, Cappi & Czerny,
à 1 Florin, A.C.

Not polonaises in the true sense of the term should be expected
here, but short, most original and for the most part very richly
melodious little movements for the pianoforte in polonaise rhythm,

which however we should have preferred not maintained throughout these two books, this having resulted in undue uniformity,
hardly compensated for by the other beauties and peculiarities.
The execution is difficult at times on account of the sometimes
surprising and sometimes, it may be said, far-fetched modulations.
Thoroughly recommended.

849. From the Berlin 'Allgemeine Musikalische Zeitung,' 6th June 1827

(Vienna correspondence, April 1827.)

The weekly evening entertainments of the Little Society resemble
a pattern-card . . . For compensation Schubert once again presented us with some fruits of his very fine talent that are healthy
to the core, such as 'Diana in Anger' ['Die zürnende Diana'],
poem by Mayrhofer, the 'Song of the Imprisoned Huntsman' and
'Norman's Song' from Walter Scott's 'Lady of the Lake,' 'God
in Nature' ['Gott in der Natur'] by Gleim, &c.

Cf. Nos. 790, 795 and 822.

850. From the Programme of the Last Subscription Concert given by Ignaz Schuppanzigh (Violin I), 16th April 1827, at 4.30 p.m., in the Philharmonic Society's Little Hall at the "Red Hedgehog"

[Performers: Karl Holz (violin II), Franz Weiss (viola), Josef Linke
(violoncello), Josef Melzer (? double bass), Georg Klein (? clarinet),
Friedrich Hradezky (? horn) and August Mittag (? bassoon).]

1. New Great Octet for five String and three Wind Instruments,
by Herr Schubert.

This was Easter Monday.—For the Octet cf. No. 441 and note preceding No. 458. The players were approximately the same as in 1824 at
the private first performance at Count Troyer's, who was probably replaced by the court clarinettist Klein.—The concert further included
Beethoven's song-cycle 'To the Distant Beloved' and his E flat major
pianoforte Concerto arranged for two pianofortes and string quartet.

851. From the 'Theaterzeitung,' 26th April 1827

This musical and very respectable enterprise was brought to a close to-day with a new Octet for five string and three wind instruments by Schubert . . . Herr Schubert's composition is commensurate with the author's acknowledged talent, luminous, agreeable and interesting; only it is possible that too great a claim may be made on the hearers' attention by its long duration.   If the themes do not fail to recall familiar ideas by some distant resemblances, they are nevertheless worked out with individual originality, and Herr Schubert has proved himself, in this species as well, as a gallant and felicitous composer.

Other notices appeared in the Leipzig and the Berlin 'Allgemeine musi-kalische Zeitung' on 30th May and 1st August 1827 respectively (German edition, Nos. 865 and 866).

852. From the Official 'Wiener Zeitung,' 19th April 1827

At the House of Artaria & Co.,
Art Dealers in the Kohlmarkt, No. 1151, is quite newly published,
and also to be had of K. Lichtl in Pest:

.   .   .   .

Schubert, Fr., Rondeau brillant pour Pianof.
et Violon.   Œuvre 70.   1 Fl. 30 Kr. A.C.

Op. 70 appeared without a dedication, after Op. 78.   For the private first performance *see* note preceding No. 788.

853. From Franz von Hartmann's Diary

19th April 1827: I went to the last *Concert spirituel*, with a ticket Spaun had intended for Marl (who came too late).   They did the first movement of Beethoven's last Symphony and the glorious Coronation Mass by Cherubini (1824, for the coronation of Charles X).   I saw Spaun there, Frau von Ottenwalt, Schwind and Schubert, the last two of whom I accompanied across the Glacis.   They were very nice.

Marl is Karl Maurus Mayrhofer (*see* No. 681), who had gone to Vienna for medical examinations.—Symphonies were then usually performed with their movements separated or isolated.—Cherubini had become fairly popular in Vienna by his operas. Schubert cared only for his 'Medea.' The Mass was Cherubini's second, in D major.—Ottenwalt was in Vienna with his wife on the occasion of some examination in law; they stayed with Spaun.—Schubert evidently went to visit Schwind.

854. From Fritz von Hartmann's Diary

20th April 1827: At home we came across Josef von Spaun, who invited several of us to a Schubertiad to-morrow, including my uncle, whom we met later, on setting out to go and see Herr and Frau Arneth, who had invited the Ottenwalt couple to their home, Josef von Spaun, Karl Haas with his sister Netti, [K. M.] Mayrhofer, Moritz Pflügl and some others . . . Frau Arneth very obligingly sang several songs by Schubert and Himmel, and read a few enchanting poems by Schiller.

Hartmann's uncle is Schallhammer (*see* No. 757).—For Anna (Netti) Haas *see* No. 478, for Pflügl No. 772.

855. From Franz von Hartmann's Diary

21st April 1827: At 7 o'clock we went to Spaun's with Maurus Mayrhofer, Enk and Haas. There was a Schubertiad and an enormous attendance, including Uncle Franz in addition to the members of the party on 15th December of last year, and he was so delighted with it that he assured us he had never heard anything so magnificent. We had 'Bounds of Mankind' ['Grenzen der Menschheit'], 'Sunset Glow' ['Das Abendrot'], 'The Wayfarer and the Moon' ['Der Wanderer und der (*sic*) Mond'], 'In the Open' ['Im Freien'], 'Who dares' ['Wer wagt's'], 'Dithyramb,' Romance from 'Ivanhoe,' Romance from 'Montrose' by Walter Scott, 'Fragment from Aeschylus,' &c. Wonderful! We drank brotherhood with Ottenwalt, and so did Enk! At 12 o'clock we left there, and a large party went to Bogner's [café], where however for that very reason it was no longer particularly jolly, and the glorious impressions of the Schubertiad became somewhat effaced.

For Enk *see* No. 738.—For the other Schubertiad *see* No. 741.—The third song mentioned is properly 'The Wayfarer to the Moon' ('Der Wanderer an den Mond'). "Who dares" is the opening of the song 'The Angry Bard' ('Der zürnende Barde'). The first of the romances is that of Richard Cœur de Lion, the other is 'Annot Lyle's Song,' which Hartmann says comes "from 'Allan Macaulay.'"

856. FROM FRITZ VON HARTMANN'S DIARY

21st April 1827: At first I talked with Frau Wanderer from Nussdorf and with her daughter Betty, but after that I conversed only with my uncle, with Mayrhofer and Moritz Pflügl. Vogl sang splendidly, mostly new songs by Schubert . . . When the music was finished, we began eating and drinking, and madcap gaiety, for which spiritual enjoyments had prepared us, took hold of all those present . . . We stayed together until 11.30; then several of us, viz. Schober, Schwind, Schubert, Mayrhofer, Enk, Hönig, Franz and I, went to the Café Bogner, where we ruminated, each quite quietly to himself, over what we had heard and seen to-day. After 1 o'clock we went to bed.

Mayrhofer is Karl Maurus Mayrhofer again. Among the eight songs mentioned by Franz (in No. 855) only three date from 1826–7; but more than eight were sung.—Schwind is not mentioned in these diaries again until the middle of June (*see* No. 909).—Hönig is Karl (*see* No. 391).

857. FROM THE PROGRAMME of the Private Concert given by Josef Rudolf Lewy, jun., Horn Player at the Kärntnertor Theatre, 22nd April 1827, at the Hour of Noon, in the Philharmonic Society's Hall

7. 'Night Song in the Forest' ['Nachtgesang im Walde,' xvi. 1], poem by Herr J. G. Seidl, set to music for four male voices with four horns *obbligato* by Franz Schubert; performed by Herren Eichberger, Ruprecht, Preisinger and Borschitzky, together with Herren Janatka, Leeser and the brothers Lewy.

For the brothers Lewy cf. No. 731.—The quartet had been written for this concert in April.—Johann Janatka and (? R.) Leeser may have worked at the Kärtnertor Theatre.

858. From the 'Theaterzeitung,' 1st May 1827

Besides, much pleasure was given by a new composition by our ingenious vocal poet Franz Schubert. He set to music a poem by Johann Gabriel Seidl, 'Night Song in the Forest' ['Nachtgesang in Walde'], for four male voices, which he had accompanied by four *obbligato* horns. The difficulty of this, no doubt, lay in the distribution of effects and in the danger of either letting the vocal parts be drowned or degrading the accompaniment to a superfluous extra. The richly imaginative tone-poet successfully avoided both, and his tone-picture, performed in more suitable surroundings, at a serenade in the open air, should be enchantingly effective.

It is said that the quartet was rehearsed at the village of Dornbach near Vienna (cf. No. 891), thus probably in the open. *See* No. 934.— Another notice appeared on 3rd May in the 'Wiener Zeitschrift' (German edition, No. 874).

859. From the Official 'Wiener Zeitung,' 19th April 1827
(Announcement of the following concert.)

By gracious consent, L. Jansa, member of the I. & R. Court Chapel, will have the honour of giving a concert on Sunday, 22nd April 1827, at noon, in the Lower-Austrian County Hall, at which he will be supported by Mlle Müller and Herren Bocklet, Feigerl, Schubert and two most favourably known amateurs in the performance of his latest composition.

Jansa's concert took place at the same hour as Lewy's.—For Feigerl *see* No. 829.—The two amateurs were a singer (Tietze) and a cellist. Feigerl alone took part in one of Jansa's two compositions.—Similar announcements appeared on 21st April in the 'Wiener Zeitschrift' and the 'Sammler' (German edition, Nos. 876 and 877).

860. FROM THE PROGRAMME given by Leopold Jansa, Member
of the I. & R. Court Chapel, 22nd April 1827, at 12.30 p.m.,
in the County Hall

3. 'Norman's Song' by Walter Scott, set to music by Herr
Fr. Schubert, performed by an excellent singer, accompanied on
the pianoforte by the composer himself . . .

Mlle Müller and the gentlemen artists mentioned above have . . .
taken up their parts by special courtesy towards the concert-giver.

The programme contained Beethoven's 'Egmont' overture, conducted
by Stefan Franz (*see* No. 757); a duet for violins, played by Jansa and
Feigerl; a pianoforte Trio in E major by Hummel, with Bocklet as pianist;
declamations spoken by Sophie Müller; and violin Variations by Jansa.

861. FROM THE 'THEATERZEITUNG,' 1st May 1827

The amateur gentleman who delivered the very accomplished
composition by Schubert, 'Norman's Song,' is too generally
known to the local musical world as a capital singer of songs not
to have been expected to give the most agreeable performance of
this soulful work; but he gave so much pleasure that he had to
repeat this piece.

In another criticism in the 'Theaterzeitung' of 3rd May, as well as in
a third, published in the 'Wiener Zeitschrift' of 10th May (German
edition, Nos. 880 and 881), Tietze is named as the singer and reference
is made to his "excellent achievement" at Beethoven's funeral service.

862. FRANZISKA VON RONER TO ANTONIE OSTER

22nd April [? 1827.]

Dear Toni,

We are asked to an evening party to-morrow at Frau von
Witteczek's, and the said friend has requested me to suggest to you
whether you would not also devote to-morrow evening to her.
Vogl will sing there, accompanied by Schubert. As there will

be many Osterians at the party in question, I do not doubt that you will be importuned with the entreaty to play something. I wished to apprise you of that beforehand. In the affirmative case please come to us to-morrow towards 6 o'clock, as we should then go to the W.'s together.

Your devoted
Fanny Roner.

Franziska Roner von Ehrenwerth, born in 1795 at Innsbruck, later the wife of Josef von Spaun, came from a family of the southern Tyrol. Her father, Karl, Ritter (later Freiherr) von Roner, an aulic councillor of justice, was a keen autograph collector. Schubert presented her with the manuscript of the four Italian canzonets for contralto, set to poems by Jacopo Vitorelli and Metastasio in 1820 (xx. 575–8).—Antonie Oster, born in 1811, had already appeared as pianoforte player at the age of ten. She died in 1828, before Schubert.—Fräulein Roner lived with her sister Anna and her brother-in-law, Anton Leopold, Ritter von Roschmann, born in 1777 at Innsbruck, aulic councillor in the United Court Chancellery, retired since 1819.

863. DEDICATION OF THE SONG, 'To Music' ['An die Musik'] (xx. 314), in Albert Sowinski's Album

Vienna, 24th April 1827. For kindly remembrance.

Frz. Schubert.

This is the fourth and last autograph copy of this famous song, reproduced in Hippolyte Barbedette's Schubert biography (Paris, 1866). The song, to words by Schober, appeared the following December (No. 980).—For Sowinsky, who first went to Italy and then to Paris, see No. 754.

864. FROM FRANZ VON HARTMANN'S DIARY

24th April 1827: [K. M. Mayrhofer and the Ottenwalt couple leave for Linz.] We went to the express coach, where nearly all the participants in the last Schubertiad were, even Vogl . . . At last the coach made off, and the Eisenstadt-Castle party, including the two Memnonides friends, went to the "Castle of Eisenstadt."

It was jolly there, and we stayed until nearly 12 o'clock, Then we saw Schober and Schubert home and afterwards went four deep to the "Partridge" Coffee-house, where we drank grog until 1 o'clock and I lost two rounds of billiards to Sauter and won one.

The last Schubertiad, so far as the Hartmanns were concerned, had taken place on 21st April (*see* Nos. 855 and 856); but there may have been a musical evening at the Witteczeks' on the 23rd (*see* No. 862), as a farewell to the Ottenwalt couple.—The two "Memnonides friends" (*see* No. 739) were Karl Enk von der Burg and Ferdinand Sauter.—The Partridge Coffee-house, as it is still called in a new building to-day, was the Café Schneider (*see* No. 774), so called after the house, "The Golden Partridge," which also contained an inn (*see* No. 581).

865. From Fritz von Hartmann's Diary

24th April 1827: Part of those who remained behind, Josef von Spaun, Schober, Schubert, Enderes, Enk, Sauter, Franz and I went to the "Castle of Eisenstadt," where we revived the old tavern scenes and entertained each other with all sorts of talk, especially on swimming and on to-day's muddle among the stage-coaches.

Swimming, like gymnastics, was regarded with suspicion under Metternich's political system because it gave rise to associations that were difficult to supervise. But it was little cultivated at that time. Josef von Spaun was a pioneer of that sport.—On the departure of the express coach, which did a 23½ hours' journey from Vienna to Linz once a week, there had been trouble about a place for Countess Antonie Attems of Graz.

866. From the Leipzig 'Allgemeine Musikalische Zeitung,' 25th April 1827

Four Poems, by Rückert and Platen, set to music for one voice with pianoforte accompaniment by Franz Schubert [Op. 59]. Vienna, Sauer & Leidesdorf. (Price, 16 Groschen.)

That the better of the numerous songs and song-like vocal pieces by Herr S. show spirit and soul, and that both often express themselves in a peculiar manner (as they do here, in all the four numbers), is doubtless acknowledged by all who have taken care to know them, including even those who have many objections to make to this manner of his. This at least is true, and it is once again proved by the first two numbers in this book: Herr Schubert is far-fetched and artificial to a degree—not in his melody, but in his harmony —and in particular he modulates so oddly and often so very suddenly towards the remotest regions as no composer on earth has done, at any rate in songs and other small vocal pieces (thus, for instance, in the first song the quite short and very simple melody is dragged through pretty well all the keys of the whole gamut, and several times from one extreme to the other by a mere two progressions); but it is equally true that (as in the present cases) he does not seek in vain, that he really conjures up something which has truly much to communicate to our fancy and feeling, and does it significantly, provided that it is performed with absolute certainty and unconstraint. Let us therefore try ourselves on them, and them on us!—No. 3 and 4, on the other hand, are far simpler, without being therefore less original. To these we feel we may assure a general success, and we too like these two songs best. We gather them up into our choicest collections, the more so because their words are appealing and as yet little known, with gratitude to the poet (Rückert) and the composer; and there is no doubt that many others will do alike.

[G. W. Fink.]

Op. 59 contains the setting of Platen's 'Thou lov'st me not' and the Rückert songs 'That she hath been here,' 'Thou art repose' and 'Laughing and Weeping.'

867. DEDICATION on the Manuscript of the C Major Allegretto for Pianoforte (xi. 12) to Ferdinand Walcher

Allegretto. To my dear friend Walcher for remembrance. Frz. Schubert. Vienna, 26th April 1827.

Walcher (see No. 752) left on 5th May for Venice, where he was employed in the Austrian navy. On 3rd May there was a farewell evening for him at Tax's alehouse in the Spänglergasse.

868. From Franz von Hartmann's Diary

26th April 1827: At 9.45 to the "Castle of Eisenstadt": Spaun there; later on Schober, Enderes and Schubert also. Not home till 11.45.

869. From Fritz von Hartmann's Diary

26th April 1827: ["Castle of Eisenstadt."] Discussion on magnetism.

Vienna was the cradle of magnetism, thanks to Franz Anton Mesmer (Josef's brother, see No. 62), who had begun his career there, but was sharply opposed by the medical profession. Bruchmann too had tried his hand as a magnetist in 1826.

870. From Franz von Hartmann's Diary

28th April 1827: With Fritz to the opera, 'The White Lady,' by Boïeldieu, which is quite wonderful. We also saw Walcher and the Fröhlichs (well known to musical Vienna) in the fifth tier. After the opera Fritz and I went to the "Castle of Eisenstadt," where Enderes was present, and later on Schober and Schubert. Tedious juridical dispute until 12.30.

'La Dame blanche,' produced in Paris in 1825, had reached Vienna in 1826 in a translation by Castelli (see No. 656).

871. From the 'Sammler,' 15th May 1827

(On the concert given by the pianist Fanny Sallamon, 29th April 1827, at noon, in the County Hall.)

Instead of the Rossini aria, which Mlle Vio was unable to sing owing to sudden obstacles, we heard, most delighted with the happily effected exchange, Schubert's 'The Solitary' ['Der Einsame'], sung by our most excellent amateur, Herr Tietze, whom Herr Schubert himself accompanied on the pianoforte. Who could fail to have been deeply touched, elevated and delighted by the profound and beautiful content of this song, so soulfully performed?

A. M.

Fanny (Franziska) Sallamon was of about the same age as Antonie Oster (*see* No. 862), another pianistic wonder-child who had first appeared at the age of eleven.   She was a pupil of Josef Czerny's.—For Betty Vio *see* No. 167.—Other notices appeared in the 'Theaterzeitung' of 8th May and the 'Wiener Zeitschrift' of 10th May (German edition, Nos. 890 and 891).

872. FROM FRANZ VON HARTMANN'S DIARY

30th April 1827: Went to the "Castle of Eisenstadt" and chatted with [Josef von Spaun,] Haas, Schober and Schubert until after midnight.

873. FROM FRITZ VON HARTMANN'S DIARY

30th April 1827: ["Castle of Eisenstadt."]   Spaun gave us examples of Polish roughness.

Spaun had been in Galicia, whose inhabitants were predominantly Polish.

874. FROM THE FRANKFORT 'ALLGEMEINER MUSIKALISCHER ANZEIGER,' 5th May 1827

Valse[s] noble[s] pour le Pianoforte seul par François Schubert.   Œuvre 77. Vienne chez T. Haslinger.   10 Groschen.

The reviewer is unable to account for the adjective "*noble*" in considering these dances.   They are not bad, but neither are they more than ordinary.   Only some single traits here and there are successful and do justice to Herr F. S.'s favourably familiar manner. For the rest, the reviewer feels that a dance should never consist of two parts only, as is the case here; for its repetition, often for hours on end, must result in unendurable weariness.

Schubert's dances, written for domestic balls, are to be played in series.   Op. 77 comprises a dozen waltzes.

875. Jenger to Frau Pachler

Vienna, 5th May 1827, at noon.

. . . I consider that it would be best to start on the journey to Graz at the beginning of September. Schubert I shall most certainly bring with me this time, as well as another friend, the lithographer Teltscher.

Teltscher did not go to Graz until later.

876. From the Invitation to the Concert for the Benefit of Needy Widows and Orphans of Members of the Faculty of Jurisprudence in Vienna, 6th May 1827, 12.30 p.m., in the Large University Hall

2. 'In the Open' ['Im Freien'], song by G. Seidl, set to music and accompanied by Herr Franz Schubert, sung by Herr Tietze.

Cf. Schwind's plan of the middle of August 1825 to give Schubert's "Gmunden-Gastein" Symphony at such a concert in 1826 (see No. 581). —Preliminary announcements of this concert appeared in the official 'Wiener Zeitung' of 28th April and in the 'Oesterreichischer Beobachter' of 6th May.—The programme contained Catel's overture to 'Semiramis'; the *adagio* and rondo from Hummel's B minor pianoforte Concerto, played by Thalberg (see No. 845); Friedrich von Matthisson's poem 'Spring Ritual' ('Frühlingsfeier'), spoken by Sophie Müller; an aria from Giuseppe Niccolini's opera 'Annibale in Bitinia,' with chorus, sung by Josefine Fröhlich; and violin Variations composed and played by Georg Hellmesberger. The concert was held in the hall (*Aula*), opposite the Seminary, where Schubert had appeared as a choir-boy at the end of 1811 (see note preceding No. 32). (In the same hall, at the end of 1813, Beethoven's seventh Symphony had preceded that memorable performance of his "battle symphony," 'Wellington's Victory at Victoria,' in which the best musicians in Vienna took part as orchestral players, including Salieri, Hummel, Meyerbeer, Spohr and Moscheles.) Tickets for the concert were to be had from the dean of the faculty of law, Dr. Hönig, the barrister Dr. Kaspar Wagner, whom we are yet to meet, and the music shops of Weigl, Haslinger and Diabelli.

877. FROM THE 'SAMMLER,' 28th June 1827

No. 3. 'In the Open' ['Im Freien'], poem by Seidl, composed and accompanied at the pianoforte by Herr Schubert, sung by Herr Tietze. Beautiful as were the composition and its delivery, the reviewer is bound to say that in his opinion the place is too large for a song not the finest shades of which must be allowed to be lost. It would come off much better in a room.

M***

The order of the items had been altered.—It is quite true that the beautiful hall is acoustically unsatisfactory.

878. JOSEF VON SPAUN, JOSEF GAHY AND SCHUBERT to the Brothers Franz and Fritz von Hartmann
On a visit here
were:

Josef von Spaun, I. & R. Deputy
of the Lottery Directorate
Landowner & Councillor of Upper Austria,
Hon. Member of the Linz Musical Society,
Corresponding Member of the
Lemberg Cecilia Society,
Lord of Jägermeinleiten,
&c. &c. &c.
Josef von Gahy, Court Probationer
of the I. & R. General
Court Chamber.
Franz Schubert
Composer,
and expect you both to-night at the
"Castle of Eisenstadt." 8th May 1827.

This note, most of it in Spaun's hand, was left after a fruitless call at the Hartmanns' lodgings in the Riemergasse.—Spaun's titles are humorously exaggerated: he was no landowner, and "Jägermeinleiten" appears to be an allusion to Jägermayr's inn at Linz (*see* No. 569).

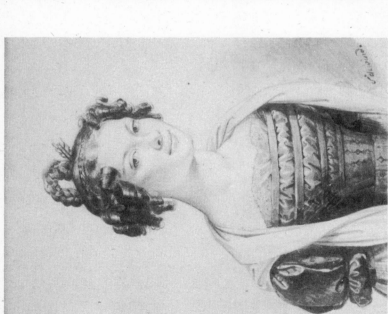

Anna Hönig.   Drawing in Indian Ink by Moritz von
Schwind (c. 1828)

Therese Hönig.   Oil Painting by Ferdinand Georg
Waldmüller (c. 1830)

PLATE XXIV

Vogl and Schubert. "Setting out to Fight and to Conquer." Caricature in Pencil, probably by Franz von Schober (c. 1825). *See* p. 928

PLATE XXV

879. From Franz von Hartmann's Diary

8th May 1827: At home we found a chit from Spaun, Schubert and Gahy summoning us to the "Castle of Eisenstadt" . . . So we went there and remained (apart from those three, Enderes and Schober were also there) until 12.15. It was particularly jolly. There was twaddle about politics, too.

880. From Franz von Hartmann's Diary

11th May 1827: At 10 o'clock to the "Castle of Eisenstadt"; Spaun there, later on Enderes and Schubert. We entertained each other excellently until 11.20.

881. From Fritz von Hartmann's Diary

11th May 1827: At 11.30 we saw Schubert home.

882. Censor's Note on one Manuscript of the Comic Trio, 'The Barristers' ['Die Advokaten'], Op. 74 (xix. 1)

Excudatur.

From the I. & R. Central Book
Censorship Office.
Vienna, 12th May 1827.
Schodl m. p.

Cf. No. 886. The title-page and part of the manuscript are in the Fitzwilliam Museum at Cambridge; the remainder, incompletely preserved, is in the Vienna City Library. The first copy, however, dated 25th–27th December 1812, is in the possession of Franz Lachner's descendants.

883. From Franz von Hartmann's Diary

14th May 1827: To Bruchmann's lecture, which was quite good
. . . To the "Castle of Eisenstadt"; only Schober and Schubert
there.   Tedious, and yet not home until 12.30.

Bruchmann attached so little importance to the theme of his dissertation
for the legal doctor's degree that he does not so much as mention it in
his contemporary letters to Senn.   The "programme" was at the Hartmanns', but has not been preserved.

884. From Fritz von Hartmann's Diary

14th May 1827: At 10 o'clock we went to the "Castle of Eisenstadt," where we met Schober and Schubert, also a few musicians,
who talked about Beethoven and other things.

885. From the Official 'Wiener Zeitung,' 16th May 1827

At the House of Tobias Haslinger,
Music Publisher in Vienna,
in the Graben, in the House of the Austrian Savings Bank, No. 572,
is just published, and also to be had of K. Lichtl in Pest:

HOMESICKNESS   —   OMNIPOTENCE
['Das Heimweh']   ['Die Allmacht']

Poems by Ladislaus von Pyrker.
Set to Music
for One Voice with Pianoforte Accompaniment
by
Franz Schubert.

Work 79.   1 Florin, A.C.

This work, like Op. 4 (*see* No. 239), is dedicated to Pyrker, the poet
of these songs composed in 1825, who however did not this time return
a present to Schubert.

886. From the Official 'Wiener Zeitung,' 16th May 1827

At the House of Anton Diabelli & Co.,
Art and Music Dealers in the Graben, No. 1133, are just published,
and to be had of K. Lichtl in Pest at the same price:

The Quail's Call (*Il canto della quaglia*).
['Der Wachtelschlag']
Set to Music
for One Voice with Pianoforte
Accompaniment
by Fr. Schubert.
Work 68. Price, 30 Kreuzer, A.C.

The Barristers.
['Die Advokaten']
Comic Trio for two Tenors and Bass, with Pianoforte
Accompaniment.
Set to Music by Fr. Schubert.
Work 74. Price, 1 Florin, A.C.

The Rose.
['Die Rose']
Poem by Friedrich Schlegel.
Set to Music
for One Voice with Pianoforte Accompaniment
by Fr. Schubert.
Work 73. Price 30 Kreuzer, A.C.

N.B. A list of all Schubert's works is printed with this song.

At least two of these three works, all without dedications, were once
again left-overs of the earlier transactions between Schubert and the firm
of (Cappi &) Diabelli. Opp. 68 and 73 had appeared already in 1822
as supplements to the 'Wiener Zeitschrift' (*see* notes preceding Nos.
302 and 287). 'The Quail's Call' (*see* note preceding No. 595) here
appeared in German and Italian (cf. No. 676). The engraved catalogue
added to 'The Rose' comprises Opp. 1–74, and thus includes Schubert's
works issued by other publishers; but all these were only a small
fraction of his output (cf. note preceding No. 1134).—Op. 74 is a
peculiar case: it is the work of another, Anton Fischer (born in 1778
at Ried in Swabia, settled in Vienna from 1798, conductor at the Theater

an der Wien in the end, died Vienna, 1808), and merely altered a little by Schubert. The original was published in Vienna *c.* 1805. As Schubert wrote down his arrangement twice (*see* No. 882), he must have used it in 1812, much as he did the guitar Quartet after Matiegka (*see* No. 56) in 1814. Seeing that Schubert had stacks of unpublished works of his own in hand, both about 1822 and about 1827, it can only be supposed that some injudicious friend, perhaps Josef Hüttenbrenner, must have given or pawned this arrangement of another composer's insignificant work to the publisher.

887. JAKOB AND JOSEFA RICKEL'S PETITION to the Magistracy of
     Vienna for Possession of the House No. 10, in the Him-
     melpfortgrund

Hon. Magistracy,

The undersigned have, according to contract A, purchased the house No. 10 in the Himmelpfortgrund of Herr Franz Schubert for 6,400 florins in silver coin and 200 florins key money, and since the vendor has now delivered them the conveyance *sub* B, they request the hon. Magistracy to grant them possession of the said house, and to issue the order to the Registry.

Vienna, 16th May 1827.   Jakob Rickel,
                                                          Josefa Rickel.

[Endorsement:]

The Registry, at which the enclosed petition is to be deposited, is charged with the grant to the applicants of the house No. 10, in the Himmelpfortgrund, sold by Franz Schubert, and the duplicate is to be remitted to Franz Schubert *ad manus*.

                                         Magistracy of Vienna.
                                         25th May 1827.
To be handed to   Schütz.
    Herr Franz Schubert,
    Official Schoolmaster   30th May 1827.
    in the Rossau,   [Illegible.]
    Grün[e]torgasse, No. 147.   Maschek.

Cf. Nos. 705 and 808.—The enclosures were retained by the Magistracy with the original.—Johann Baptist Schütz was registrar to the Magistracy of the City if Vienna; Martin Maschek was usher there.

888. Jenger to Frau Pachler

Vienna, 19th May 1827.

. . . Friend Pachler may be right in almost dreading my own and my friend's visit. We shall endeavour to make his premonitions come true, and to this we have long been looking forward . . . But the chief thing, which is to see all my dear ones at Graz again, I shall not therefore forget; and in September that pleasure shall materialize for me, whatever may occur to oppose it.

Cf. No. 875.

889. From Fritz von Hartmann's Diary

24th May 1827: We fetched Karl Haas . . . and visited the Wanderer family at Nussdorf. Frau Günther, the daughter of the house, had come from Ried. Several visitors were there, such as Haller (a medical student), Herr and Frau von Kurzrock, Josef von Spaun and others. Haas and I conversed mainly with Betty Wanderer, who played some of Schubert's dances on the pianoforte.

For the Wanderers cf. note preceding No. 595. Their daughter Josephine (Pepi) was married to her father's colleague Günther at Ried in Upper Austria.—For Haller cf. No. 745.

890. From the Official 'Wiener Zeitung,' 25th May 1827

At the House of Tobias Haslinger,
Music Publisher in Vienna,
in the Graben, in the House of the Austrian Savings Bank, No. 572,
is just published
and also to be had of K. Lichtl in Pest:

THE WAYFARER ADDRESSING THE MOON
['Der Wanderer an den Mond']

THE PASSING-BELL — IN THE OPEN
['Das Zügenglöcklein']   ['Im Freien']
Poems by J. G. Seidl.

Set to Music
for One Voice with Pianoforte Accompaniment
by
Franz Schubert

Work 80.   Price, 1 Florin, A.C.

This work is dedicated "in friendship" to Witteczek.

891. From Fritz von Hartmann's Diary

26th May 1827: Towards 10 o'clock we went to the "Castle of Eisenstadt," where we talked to Schober, Gahy and Schubert, who is now living at Dornbach.   Spaun was vainly expected.

Schubert, probably with Schober, spent a few weeks of that spring at Dornbach, where he stayed at the inn of the "Empress of Austria." Dornbach lies to the west of the city near the Wiener Wald, and the inn (now in different use) was on the main thoroughfare.

892. From Franz von Hartmann's Diary

26th May 1827: . . . But I was pretty well bored and already fell asleep on the spot, until at last we cleared out at 12.15.

893. From the Official 'Wiener Zeitung,' 28th May 1827

At the House of Tobias Haslinger,
Music Publisher in Vienna,
in the Graben, in the House of the Austrian Savings Bank, No. 572,
is just published, and also to be had of K. Lichtl in Pest:

Alinde.

To the Lute.   —   For Good-night.
['An die Laute']   ['Zur guten Nacht']
Poems by Fr. Rochlitz.

Set to Music

for One Voice with Pianoforte Accompaniment

by

Franz Schubert

Work 81.   Price, 45 Kreuzer, A.C.

Cf. No. 813A.—The fly-leaf of this work bears a dedication to the poet Rochlitz, "that author deserving so well of music and the polite sciences," signed, not by Schubert, but by the publisher.   Cf. Nos. 299, 651 and 972.

> Schubert's Overture to 'Fierabras,' Op. 76, arranged for four hands by Carl Czerny, appears at Anton Diabelli & Co.'s (? spring) 1827.—The opus number 76 was given only to this arrangement; Schubert did not use it for the overture in its original form, nor for the opera as a whole.

894. Sophie von Kleyle to Ferdinand Walcher at Venice

Penzing, 1st June 1827.

We do not lack visitors, for we have several each day; Angerer and Jenger come more often than usual, and Schubert too has given us the pleasure once already; he was most amiable and talkative, but escaped suddenly, before any one had an inkling.

For Kleyle and for Penzing see No. 785.—Fritz Angerer was the son of Walcher's landlady (see No. 772).

895. Censor's Note on the Autograph of the Male-Voice Quartet, 'Wine and Love' ('Wein und Liebe'), (xvi. 37)

Excudatur.

From the I. & R. Central Book Censorship Office.

Vienna, 2nd June 1827.

Schodl.

Cf. No. 956.

896. CENSOR's NOTE on the Autograph of the Male-Voice Quartet
'Spring Song' ('Frühlingslied') (xxi. 36a)

Excudatur.

From the I. & R. Central Book Censorship Office.

Vienna, 2nd June 1827.

Schodl.

This vocal quartet, to words by Aaron Pollak, was probably intended
at first as a companion piece to 'Wine and Love' ('Wein und Liebe') in
place of 'Grave and Moon.' In 1829 Haslinger announced it as being in
the press, together with the 'Swan Song' cycle, but never published it.

897. FROM FRANZ VON HARTMANN's DIARY

2nd June 1827: At the "[Castle of] Eisenstadt" were Kurzrock,
Spaun, Gahy and also, for a short time, Schober and an acquaintance, a merchant named Mayer from Breslau, very dull. Home
at midnight.

Antonio Mayer (*see* No. 391) was born at Trieste in 1800 an innkeeper's son, had been at Breslau from about 1820 until the end of 1826
and was now on his way home to Trieste. Karl Holtei describes him in
his reminiscences as "one of the most amiable, intelligent, merry and
at the same time good-natured people who ever lived." When Schober
in the spring of 1826 wished to try trading in Hungarian wines with
Germany, Mayer dissuaded him. Neither did an art estabishment
materialize which Schober intended to open with him in Vienna. Whether
Mayer became his collaborator in the "Lithographic Institute" (1827–8)
is uncertain. Mayer later acquired the Luna hotel at Venice.

898. FROM FRANZ VON HARTMANN's DIARY

4th June 1827: To the ["Castle of] Eisenstadt"; Spaun, Schubert, Schober and Mayer there. At 11.45 we went home at last.

899. [LOST RENEWED INVITATION from Frau Pachler to Jenger and Schubert to come to Graz, 7th June 1827]

Cf. Nos. 888 and 904.

900. From Franz von Hartmann's Diary

11th June 1827: At 9.45 with Fritz to the "Castle of Eisenstadt," where were Enderes, Spaun, Schober, Schubert.   Home at 11.30.

901. From the Index of the Philharmonic Society, (?) early June 1827

Schubert (Franz, Composer).   Election of the same as representative. Fascicle: Minutes of the Meeting. No. of Document: 183.

902. Schubert to the Philharmonic Society

> To
> the Committee of Management
> of the Philharmonic Society
> in the Austrian
> Imperial State.

The Committee of Management of the Philharmonic Society in the Austrian Imperial State having deemed me worthy of being elected a member of the body of the hon. Society's representatives, I hereby declare myself to feel greatly honoured by this election and ready with much pleasure to conform to the duties involved thereby.

Franz Schubert.

Vienna, 12th June 1827.   Composer.

903. From the Index of the Philharmonic Society, Middle of June 1827

Schubert (Franz, Composer).   Declaration of his readiness to accept the appointment. Fascicle: Act of Election. No. of the Document: 23.

There is no indication that Schubert in any way took part in the committee's functions. The fellows were only an ornament of the Philharmonic Society.

904. SCHUBERT TO FRAU PACHLER

Madam,   Vienna, 12th June 1827.

Although I cannot imagine in what way I may have deserved so kind an offer as your honour has informed me of by the letter sent to Jenger, nor whether I shall ever be able to offer anything in return, I nevertheless cannot forbear to accept an invitation whereby I shall not only set eyes at last on much-vaunted Graz, but have the privilege, moreover, of making your honour's acquaintance.

I remain,
with all respect,
your honour's
most devoted Frz. Schubert.

See Nos. 899 and 908.

905. FROM THE OFFICIAL 'WIENER ZEITUNG,' 15th June 1827

At the House of Anton Diabelli & Co.,
Art and Music Dealers, in the Graben, No. 1133, is just published, and to be had of K. Lichtl in Pest at the same price:

Continuation of the Periodical Work
THE MUSICAL COMPANION
IN LONELY HOURS
['Der Musikalische Gesellschafter
in einsamen Stunden']
arranged for a Flute
and edited
by A. Diabelli.

.   .   .   .   .   .

No. 40. Collection of favourite Viennese Dances by Lanner, Strauss, Krall, Schubert, &c., Price, 1 Florin.
N.B. To be continued.

No copy of this book is known. Which dance, or dances, by Schubert appeared there in a flute arrangement is thus uncertain. Possibly Op. 67, the 'Wiener Damen-Ländler,' was drawn upon.

906. From Franz von Hartmann's Diary

15th June 1827: At 9.30 with Fritz to the "Castle of Eisenstadt"; Schubert, Schober and Spaun also there. Home at midnight.

907. From Fritz von Hartmann's Diary

15th June 1827: ["Castle of Eisenstadt."] Talk about politics.

908. Jenger to Frau Pachler

Vienna, 16th June 1827.

. . . Friend Schubert was quite enchanted by your kind invitation; and his thanks and promise to accept this pleasant invitation is contained in the enclosed slip.

We both look forward very gladly to this excursion into dear Styria, and I also hope that you, dear lady, will be well satisfied with my travelling companion.

We shall then once again well and truly live for music, and Schubert shall weave many a new and endearing flowerlet into our musical chaplet. Friend Dr. Karl too shall be content with us in all respects; for we shall not lack valour where wine and beer flows either. If only the time of departure were here now; however, these 10 weeks too will pass, and that in agreeable hopes of happy days.

The enclosure is No. 904.—There is no longer any question of Teltscher's visit to Graz.—The brewery was actually in Dr. Pachler's house (see No. 685); the beer-garden was in the vicinity.

909. From Fritz von Hartmann's Diary

19th June 1827: We went to the "Castle of Eisenstadt," where we finished this day [at midnight] in the agreeable society of Messrs. Spaun, Schubert, Schober and Schwind.

910. From Franz von Hartmann's Diary

20th June 1827: To the "Castle of Eisenstadt," where after a long time Spaun, Schober and Schubert arrived, and we stayed until 12 o'clock.

911. From Fritz von Hartmann's Diary

20th June 1827: . . . Schober, Spaun, Schubert and a certain Herr Goldhahn.

For Goldhahn *see* No. 390.

'Wayfarer's Night Song' ('Wanderers Nachtlied'), Op. 96, No. 3 (xx. 420), and 'Consolation in Song' ('Trost im Liede') (xx. 313) appear in the 'Wiener Zeitschrift,' 23rd June 1827.—This is the "other" 'Wanderers Nachtlied' by Goethe, the famous 'Ueber allen Gipfeln ist Ruh.' Goethe placed it after the first and called it "another."

Franz von Bruchmann marries Juliana von Weyrother, 25th June 1827.—For Fräulein von Weyrother *see* No. 401. Bruchmann was now a doctor of law. The marriage service took place at St. Stephen's cathedral; it was witnessed, apart from the bride's father, by Friedrich von Schlegel (*see* No. 337).

912. From Fritz von Hartmann's Diary

29th June 1827. Franz and I visited the Wanderer family. Some played on the pianoforte. Betty sang songs by Schubert and others.

Franz von Hartmann reports that the other songs were by "bad composers," and that Josef von Spaun and the medical student Haller were also present.

912A. Ferdinand Mayerhofer von Grünbühel to Bauernfeld

Wolfsberg, 30th June 1827.

How, then, are Schober, Schubert and Schwind? Do they still recollect sometimes, I wonder, that I crossed the course of their

lives like an apparition? . . . Kraissl, a painter, is here, and sends
many greetings to Schwind, Schubert and Schober.—A good fellow.

Mayerhofer was clearly in official service in Carinthia again, where
Kraissl (*see* note preceding No. 244) had been settled since 1824. Wolfsberg is to the north-east of Klagenfurt.

913. MOSEL ON SALIERI'S TEACHING, 1827

. . . These male and female composition pupils, some past,
some still with him, were: Herren . . . Schubert . . .

This sentence appeared in 1827 in Mosel's biography of Salieri, p. 184,
footnote. Among the Salieri pupils living in 1827 Mosel mentions, for
composition, Karl von Doblhoff, Josef Weigl, Hummel, Moscheles,
Stuntz, Assmayr and Liszt; for singing, among others, Mozatti and Frau
Rosenbaum (cf. No. 89).

The words of a lost Schubert song, 'To God' ('An Gott'), by
Hohlfeld, appear in Johann Wilhelm Klein's 'Lieder für Blinde
und von Blinden' ('Songs for the Blind and by the Blind'), Vienna,
1827.—Klein, born in 1765 at Allerheim near Nördlingen, was the
founder and director of the Institute for the Blind in Vienna, where
Sechter became music master in 1811. Maylath's translation of
'The Blind Boy' by Colley Cibber (*see* No. 596) is reprinted here
and its composition by Sechter is mentioned. Unfortunately the
book contains no musical supplements, nor did the institution preserve the songs in manuscript, so that Schubert's is lost. Its poem
may have been by the Bohemian C. C. Hohlfeld. It begins with
the words "Kein Auge hat Dein Angesicht geschaut . . . Dein
Weg ist Licht," and it has three verses.

914. ANTONIO MAYER TO SCHOBER

Trieste, 1st July 1827.

You might . . . set out and come here [with Bauernfeld and
Schwind] . . . In order to complete the quadrille, Schubert
should be forced to join you.—Be good genii and come, oh come,
oh come!—

The friends in Vienna do not appear to have thought of accepting Mayer's
invitation to visit him at his home by the banks of the Adria, although in
September Schubert could easily have reached Trieste from Graz.

915. FROM THE OFFICIAL 'WIENER ZEITUNG,' 6th July 1827

At the House of Anton Diabelli & Co.,
Art and Music Dealers, in the Graben, No. 1133, are published,
and to be had of K. Lichtl in Pest at the same price:

.   .   .   .   .   .

.   .   .   .   .   .

FOUR POLONAISES
for Pianoforte four Hands.
composed by FRANZ SCHUBERT.
Work 75.   1 Florin, A.C.

Op. 75, without a dedication, appeared after Op. 81. These Polonaises, like those of Op. 61 (see No. 671), are undated, nor have their
manuscripts been preserved. The second of them was reprinted in an
arrangement for two hands while Schubert was still alive (see note
preceding No. 1149). Schubert is said to have received 60 florins, V.C.,
for Op. 75 (according to Franz von Hartmann's family chronicle, though
this mentions only Polonaises without opus numbers and names Haslinger
as their publisher).

916. FROM THE OFFICIAL 'WIENER ZEITUNG,' 6th July 1827

At the House of Thaddaeus Weigl,
Art and Music Dealer in Vienna, in the Graben, No. 1144
(next to the "King of England"), is quite newly published:

Andantino varié et Rondeau brillant
composés pour le
Pianoforte à quâtre [sic] mains
(sur des motifs origineaux [sic] Français)
par
François Schubert.
Œuvre 84.   Prix, 4 fl. V.C.

L'Andantino séparé, 1 fl. 30 kr. Le Rondeau séparé, 2 fl. 30 kr.

Cf. No. 664. The two new movements are designated (by hand)
on the title-page as Op. 84, Nos. 1 and 2. Op. 84 appeared, without a
dedication, before Op. 83.

917. From Franz von Hartmann's Diary

19th July 1827: To Bogner's, all five of us who compose the Anchorites' party. Enk played billiards with Clodi, and we saw Schober, Schubert and Bauernfeld, who made an appointment with us at the "Castle of Eisenstadt" to-night, where in fact we did go with Clodi and Enk. . . . Quite jolly at the "Eisenstadt." Schober and Schubert were there, and we stayed until 12 o'clock. Dinand was with us too.

The brothers Hartmann, Ferdinand Sauter, Karl Enk von der Burg, Anton von Lankmayr and Franz Xaver, Freiherr von Spiegelfeld, had a luncheon-table reserved for them at the Anchorite or Hermit ("Einsiedel") Tavern; Franz Clodi had also joined their company.—"Dinand" is Sauter.

918. From August Heinrich Hoffmann von Fallersleben's Diary

[Vienna, 28th July 1827.]

At 6.30 departure for Dornbach with Panofka in a stage-coach. We put up at the "Empress of Austria," but—Schubert is no longer at Dornbach.

Heinrich Hoffmann von Fallersleben, born 1789, Prussian librarian, collector of German folksongs and later the author of the words "Deutschland, Deutschland über alles" imposed on Haydn's Austrian people's hymn, had gone to Vienna on a visit with Heinrich Panofka and a merchant from Breslau. He stayed there from 30th June to the middle of August. Panofka, born in 1807 at Breslau, had originally been a law student, but became a pupil of Mayseder and a violin virtuoso. He gave a concert in Vienna in 1827, later went to Munich and Berlin, to Paris in 1834, where he worked on behalf of Schubert, and to London in 1844. Cf. No. 1090. —The two visitors had heard in the city that Schubert was spending that summer at Dornbach (see No. 891); but he had been there only from the end of May until June.

919. From Hoffmann von Fallersleben's Diary

[4th August 1827.]

"White Wolf" Inn.   Schubert is going to compose.

The "White Wolf" is in the (old) Fleischmarkt, facing Schwind's birthplace. It was there, then, that Hoffmann von Fallersleben met Schubert, having probably invited him. Schubert did not set any of his poems. *See* No. 928.

920. From the Official 'Wiener Zeitung,' 6th August 1827

At the House of A. Pennauer,

Priv. Art and Music Dealer, in Vienna, in the Graben,

No. 1122, in Fischer's House, has just been published,

and is to be had of K. Lichtl in Pest:

The Unhappy One.   Hope.

['Der Unglückliche']   ['Die Hoffnung']

The Youth by the Brook.

['Der Jüngling am Bache']

Three Poems,

set to Music for One Voice with Pianoforte Accompaniment,

by Franz Schubert

Work 84 [*recte* 87].   Price, 1 Florin, A.C.

The opus number 84 was used in error, perhaps because Thaddäus Weigl should have published the two additional movements of the work now bearing that number (*see* No. 916) as Op. 63, Nos. 2 and 3, to follow Op. 63, No. 1. On the other hand Op. 87 seems to have been already assigned to Leidesdorf, as is witnessed by the designation of Op. 92 in its page-heading (in No. 1120). Op. 87 appeared, without a dedication, before Opp. 85 and 86.

921. FROM FRANZ VON HARTMANN'S DIARY

10th August 1827: We went to the "Castle of Eisenstadt"; Schubert and Schober there. Stayed until 12.40. Unmannerly discussion!

On the same day Schober showed the Hartmann brothers and Max Clodi lithographs produced by his press.

First performance of 'Serenade' ('Ständchen') (xviii. 4) by Josefine Fröhlich with her sister Anna's lady pupils, on Louise Gosmar's birthday in the garden of the Lang house at Döbling, 11th August 1827, in the evening.—Louise Gosmar (*see* No. 801) was a pupil of Anna Fröhlich's, who had asked Grillparzer for a poem which Schubert first set for contralto solo with male-voice chorus by mistake, but of which he made a second version suited to its purpose.—The ladies were conveyed from the city in three carriages, but the pianoforte was secretly moved into the front garden to give the birthday-child a surprise. Schubert was not present. Cf. No. 1016.—The house of Josef, Freiherr von Lang, where the Gosmars lived, was on the corner of the Silbergasse and the Nussberggasse; Beethoven had lived there in 1815.

922. FROM FRANZ VON HARTMANN'S DIARY

11th August 1827: [At 10 o'clock] to the "Eisenstadt," where were Spaun, Ottenwalt, Schubert, [Enderes,] Derffel, Schober and Clax.   Home at 11.45.

The Ottenwalts were on a visit to Vienna again.—"Clax" is Max Clodi.

923. FROM FRANZ VON HARTMANN'S DIARY

12th August 1827: We dropped in at the "Eisenstadt," and there came Spaun, (the very dear) Frau von Ottenwalt, Schubert and Schober. Very jolly talk, and Frau von Ottenwalt quoted gruesome passages from my last letter to her, which I had written to Linz. At 11.45 we reached home.

924. FROM FRANZ VON HARTMANN'S DIARY

13th August 1827: At 9.45 in the evening I went to the "Castle of Eisenstadt" and saw all the Spaun and Ottenwalt acquaintances. We stayed till 11.40.　Frau von Ottenwalt very nice.　Clax dull.

925. FROM FRITZ VON HARTMANN'S DIARY

13th August 1827: Herr and Frau Ottenwalt, Josef von Spaun, Schober, Schubert, Enderes, Gahy, Derffel, Clodi and my brother came to the "Castle of Eisenstadt."

926. FROM FRITZ VON HARTMANN'S DIARY

14th August 1827: After 9 o'clock my brother and I went to the express coach office to say good-bye to Herr and Frau von Otten-walt and to Therese Haas, who drove to Linz with Weydiner. Then the whole party that had been present at the departure, namely Spaun, Enderes, Clodi, Schober, Schubert, my brother and I, betook ourselves to the ale-house "Where the Wolf preaches to the Geese," and we stayed till midnight.

For Therese Haas *see* No. 478.—Of Weydiner (? Weydinger) nothing is known.—The ale-house, named after the legend of a false preacher, which was depicted on its sign, was in the Wallnergasse near the Kohl-markt and for a time became the circle's new haunt. They had given up the Green Anchor Inn.

927. FROM FRANZ VON HARTMANN'S DIARY

14th August 1827: To the "Wolf preaching to the Geese"; Clax there and we whilom "Anchor" men.　Home at 11.45.

928. FROM HOFFMANN VON FALLERSLEBEN'S DIARY

[Grinzing, 15th August 1827.]

The old fiddler played Mozart . . . Schubert with his girl we

espied from our seat; he came to join us and did not show himself
again. Franz Lachner, the fourth Musical Director at the Kärntnertor Theatre, also came to see us.

This note in the diary of a comparative stranger is very informative. It
describes a Viennese new-wine inn (*Heuriger*) on a Monday, probably in the
evening, at which a solitary old violinist plays Mozart—a very different picture from that imagined in later times as a typical scene of that sort. And
we find Schubert without his friends and with a girl, whom the writer takes
to be "his" girl, but who was probably a casual acquaintance. He was
plainly embarrassed. Lachner seems to have been there only by accident,
or he may have left Schubert alone on account of the girl. Hoffmann,
by the way, gives the following impression of Schubert in his autobiography, 'My Life,' of 1868: "He seemed to me to have quite a healthy,
vigorous nature. He spoke Viennese, wore, like everybody in Vienna, fine
linen, a clean coat and a shiny hat, and there was nothing in his face, or
in his whole being, that resembled my Schubert."

929. FROM FRANZ VON HARTMANN'S DIARY

20th August 1827: (9 o'clock) at the "Geese preached at by the
Wolf" . . . Spaun, Schubert, Schober, Clax, Hintringer, Karl
Revertera were there. We were annoyed, then laughed again,
and so on, and went home at 12.15.

Hintringer is probably a visitor from Linz: Josef Hintringer, an official
in the Banking Administration and a member of the Musical Society.—
For Karl, Count Revertera, *see* No. 823.

930. FROM FRITZ VON HARTMANN'S DIARY

20th August 1827: [At the "Wolf."] The whole party was
much embittered over the wretched students' slavery, and we made
a great many plans to obtain a pass for my unhappy brother to-
morrow.

The vice-rector of the university would not allow Franz von Hartmann
to leave for home after his successful examination until after the thanksgiving service to be held at the university church. But he received a
permit from the police on the following day.

931. FROM THE PROGRAMME of the Examination of the Vienna Conservatory Pupils, 21st August 1827, at 4 p.m., in the County Hall

9. Chorus for 2 soprano and 2 alto voices, by Franz Schubert ['God in Nature' ('Gott in der Natur') (xviii. 3)], sung by the lady pupils of the third class.

Jenger, as deputy secretary of the Philharmonic Society, delivered the opening speech. The programme again contained a chorus from Abbé Stadler's 'Polyxena' (see No. 222) as well as the final sextet from Mozart's 'Don Giovanni' (see No. 249).

932. FROM THE 'THEATERZEITUNG,' 28th August 1827.

9. Chorus for two soprano and two alto voices by Franz Schubert, sung by the lady pupils of the third class. The name "Schubert" has a fair sound and his works, wholly enwrapped in the rosy veil of originality and feeling, stand high in the public favour. This work can only consolidate it further—this sterling composition has been altogether wrested by Schubert from nature and its inseparable companion, beauty.—The delivery was delicate and full of feeling.

Other notices appeared in the 'Sammler,' which correctly names the poet as (Ewald Christian von) Kleist, on 8th September, in the official 'Wiener Zeitung' on the 15th and in the Dresden 'Abendzeitung' on 1st October 1827 (German edition, Nos. 950–2).

933. FROM FRITZ VON HARTMANN'S DIARY

21st August 1827: Spaun, Clodi, Sauter and I went to the ale-house, which is now the order of the day; thither came Schober and Schubert later on. We amused ourselves excellently until midnight.

Franz von Hartmann, whose birthday it was, left for Linz the following day; his brother Fritz followed him on 5th September. Franz returned to Vienna University early in November with another brother, Louis.

Heinrich, Karl Schubert's second son, born 23rd August 1827 (Schubert's third nephew).

934. FROM THE 'THEATERZEITUNG,' 28th August 1827

(Remark under the title of the poem, 'Night Song in the Forest' ['Nachtgesang in Walde'] [xvi. 1] by Johann Gabriel Seidl.)

(For four male voices, with accompaniment of four horns *obbligato*, set by Franz Schubert.)

Cf. No. 857.

935. JENGER TO FRAU PACHLER

Vienna, 30th August 1827.

On the coming Sunday, 2nd September, friend Schubert and I shall leave here by express coach at 9.30 p.m. and hope, God willing, to be with you at Graz on Monday evening, at 9 o'clock, to which we look forward with profound happiness.

Now I have yet a great request to make in advance of Dr. Karl.

It is this: four dear, good Freiburg friends and acquaintances of Schneller's are here, namely Commander Baron von Reinach, two Barons von Andlau and Mayer, the administrator of the University Foundation.

By means of diplomatic intrigues I have contrived to arrange that these four compatriots should make their homeward journey by way of Graz, Obersteier, Salzburg, Innsbruck, &c., instead of Maria-Zell and the Salzkammergut.

The aforesaid are to travel by post from here to Mürzzuschlag on Sunday morning and from there to Graz on Monday, in order to be in time for the theatre on that day. On Tuesday they will remain with us at Graz, and on Wednesday they are to go on to Salzburg.

In regard to these countrymen I therefore beg Dr. Karl

1) to induce Andreas Sattinger—to whom I shall direct these Swabians—to see that they find good quarters at his house and that Reinach will be provided with a salaried servant;

2) it would be very handsome of friend Pachler if he were to use his influence to have a pretty comedy performed on Monday and, if possible, a decent opera on Tuesday, possibly 'Der

Freischütz,' &c. &c., so that the Freiburgers may take with them a good impression of Graz in this respect also. Finally, I address the request to you, dear and gracious lady, that we may see grandmamma and Schneller's family at your house or Frau von Leeb's on Tuesday, for but a short time, since the Freiburgers—if they wish to see the most remarkable sights of Graz in a single day—will not have much time left to pay visits all round . . .

To conclude, I and Schubert kiss your hands . . .

The fare was 9 florins, 20 kreuzer, A.C. Schubert may have obtained the means for this journey from the proceeds of Opp. 75 and 87 (Nos. 915 and 920).—Franz Xaver, Freiherr von Andlau-Birseck (cf. No. 606), born in 1799 at Freiburg i/B., had been in Vienna since March 1826 as a diplomat for the Duchy of Baden. In his 'Leaves of Recollection' ('Erinnerungsblätter') of 1857 he gives an unsympathetic picture of Schubert, but invalidates his judgment by naming the folksong "Ich hatt' einen Kameraden" as one of Schubert's songs. Andlau's brother Heinrich, born in 1802, became his successor in Vienna in 1830. Of Jenger's other two countrymen nothing is known. All those living round the Lake of Constance were called Swabians indiscriminately, whether they were Swiss, Germans or Austrians. The four travelled by one of the postal service's special carriages.—Sattinger was an innkeeper at Graz.—Pachler, as his son Faust was to relate later on, was the theatre manager Stöger's *alter ego* (*see* No. 834).—On Monday took place the second performance of Meyerbeer's opera 'Il crociato in Egitto' (cf. note preceding No. 939), and the following day two new comedies were given.—Frau Leeb was a friend of the Pachlers'.—Frau Pachler's mother was the widow Therese Koschak.—For Schneller, who lived at Freiburg, cf. No. 706.

936. FROM BAUERNFELD'S DIARY

31st August 1827.

Moritz to Munich on 7th August. Gap in the friendly circle. By the way—see Kotzebue's 'Philibert, or Circumstances' ['Die Verhältnisse']. What is to become of us all? Shall we stick together? . . . Schubert composes the 'Count of Gleichen.'

Schwind, who like Bauernfeld had been somewhat out of touch with the Schubert circle, had gone to Munich with a recommendation from Grillparzer to Peter Cornelius, his future master, in order to become

acquainted with the Academy of Fine Arts there.   He stayed from about
20th to 30th August.—Kotzebue's novel was published at Königsberg in
1809 and was reprinted in Vienna in 1824.   Its hero, an idealist, loses
his circle of friends through "circumstances" of various kinds and, after
many disappointments, finds a true friend in a noble woman.   On the
opera cf. No. 716; it is a fact that Schubert was occupied with it that
summer.

937. From Bauernfeld's 'Poetic Diary,' 1827

A chapter of my life ends here:
A comedy 's done; but where 's its sphere?

In trepidation and half-hearted
A second and a third I started;
And, once in train, I settled next
For Schubert on an opera-text.

The comedies were 'Frivolity and Love' ('Leichtsinn und Liebe'),
written in October–December 1826, 'The Doubter' ('Der Zweifler'),
dating from September, and 'The Wooer' ('Der Brautwerber') of July–
December 1827 (cf. No. 1145).   The libretto Bauernfeld had finished
already in 1826.   His 'Poetic Diary' ('Poetisches Tagebuch') did not
appear till 1887.

938. From the Official 'Wiener Zeitung,' 3rd September 1827

At the House of Tobias Haslinger,
Music Publisher in Vienna,
in the Graben, in the House of the First Austrian Savings Bank,
No. 572,
are just published,
and to be had of all Music Dealers in the Austrian Provinces
(in Pest at K. Lichtl's):

VARIATIONS
for Pianoforte 4 hands
on a Theme
from the Opera, 'Marie,' by Hérold.

Composed
by
Franz Schubert.

Work 82.   1 Fl. 45 Kr., A.C.

Op. 82 appeared after Opp. 84 and 87.   It is dedicated to "His Reverence Herr Kajetan Neuhaus, Professor of Theoretical and Practical Philosophy at Linz," who was on the staff of the Lyceum there and a member of the Musical Society.   Nothing else is known about his relations with Schubert.—Hérold's opera (libretto by F. A. E. de Planard) was given at the Kärntnertor Theatre, soon after its production in Paris on 18th December 1826, translated by Castelli.   The theme is the song of Lubin, the miller, Act III, Scene x, called the "miller song" in Germany, beginning "Sur la rivière, comme mon père," or "Was einst vor Jahren" in the translation.   For Hérold cf. note preceding No. 240.

> Schubert hears at the Graz County Playhouse Meyerbeer's opera, 'Il crociato in Egitto,' libretto, after Gaetano Rossi, by Josef Kupelwieser, with Johann Nestroy as the Sultan Aladdin, 5th September 1827.—Josef Kupelwieser, the librettist of 'Fierabras,' was secretary to the Graz and Pressburg theatres under Stöger's management. Meyerbeer's opera is said to have displeased Schubert; this is asserted by Anselm Hüttenbrenner, who welcomed Schubert to Graz, introduced his wife and children to him and played him his (Hüttenbrenner's) 'Erl King' song.   Teltscher, either before or after this time, made a coloured drawing of Jenger, Hüttenbrenner and Schubert in a portrait group in Vienna, having already lithographed them separately.—Nestroy (see No. 222) was engaged by the Graz theatre in 1826–9.

939. From the Official 'Grazer Zeitung,' 6th September 1827
Announcement [of the following concert].

On Saturday, 8th September of this year, the Styrian Musical Society will hold a grand concert, the whole proceeds whereof, without any deduction of costs, which an anonymous person has declared himself willing to defray, will be devoted in equal parts to the inhabitants rendered necessitous by the floods that have lately occurred in the plains and the needy widows and orphans of county schoolmasters whose annual support is incumbent on the Musical Society by statute.

The directorate of the County Theatre, in consideration of this charitable purpose, have readily granted the use of their premises for the undertaking, which will thus hold its performance in the County Theatre, whose larger space, together with the retention of the usual prices of admission, will offer the whole public an opportunity of taking part and devoting a contribution to the distressed.

A commensurate success being assured by reason of the reunion of all the capital's art-lovers, of the kind collaboration on the part of an artistic and greatly celebrated composer from the metropolis, and above all by the honourable public's frequently proved humanity, it is only requested, without any further exhortation to charity, that the subscribers' priority claims on their seats for the day of performance may be presented to the Inspectorate of the County Theatre on the ground floor of the playhouse before 12 o'clock at the latest, where all other orders for stalls will also be accepted, as well as at the box-office until 6 o'clock in the evening at the latest, whereafter all seats not disposed of will be open to the public.

From the Committee of the Styrian Musical Society.   Graz, 4th September 1827.

Pachler and Hüttenbrenner were concerned in the arrangements for this concert and in Schubert's participation. The day was that of the Nativity of the Virgin Mary (cf. No. 308).   For the country schoolmasters cf. No. 554.

940. FROM A GRAZ CONCERT PROGRAMME, 8th September 1827, 7 p.m.

Part I. . . . 2. 'Norman's Song' from Walter Scott's 'Lady of the Lake,' for tenor and pianoforte, composed and accompanied by Herr Franz Schubert, external honorary member of the Styrian Musical Society . . .

Part II. . . . 1. Chorus for 2 soprano and 2 alto voices by Franz Schubert . . .

4. 'Spirit of Love' ['Geist der Liebe'], by Matthisson, set to music for 4 male voices by Franz Schubert. . . .

The Musical Society is again devoting the receipts due to it by statute to a charitable cause, which, together with the kind colla-boration of a composer whose ingenious works are known and admired even in remote foreign countries, guarantees the numerous attendance of a generous and art-loving public.

The chorus was 'God in Nature' ('Gott in der Natur'), sung from the manuscript (cf. No. 931); Schubert may thus have brought it with him. —The male-voice quartet, in which Nestroy may have taken part once more (cf. No. 275, etc.), was also accompanied on the pianoforte by Schubert. A Graz contemporary and namesake, the cellist Franz Schubert (of whom Teltscher made a water-colour portrait), erroneously mentioned 'The Gondolier' ('Der Gondelfahrer') instead of 'Spirit of Love' in his recollections of those days written for Luib. By the way, an alleged Schubert letter published in the Stuttgart 'Neue Musikzeitung' of 7th October 1920 (vol. 42, No. 1, pp. 5–7) is by this namesake of Graz.

> Excursion of the Graz Schubert party to the castle of Wildbach, 10th to 12th September 1827.—Wildbach is near Deutsch-Lands-berg, some twenty miles south-west of Graz. It was managed by the widow Anna Massegg, née Tax, an aunt of Dr. Pachler's. She had six daughters, the eldest of whom sang Schubert songs, accom-panied by her music master, Fuchs, from the nearby Frauental, the father of Robert Fuchs, the composer, and of Johann Nepomuk Fuchs, a court musical director. Cf. No. 966. The Graz party drove out in several carriages: Schubert, Hüttenbrenner and Jenger in the first, the Pachlers in a second. The local Schilcher wine, which is pink and light, pleased Schubert particularly. The castle was already the property of the widow's children, who included a son. The musical entertainment took place in the "blue room" on the first floor, overlooking the fine garden.

941. FROM THE OFFICIAL 'WIENER ZEITUNG,' 12th September 1827

At the House of Tobias Haslinger,
Music Publisher in Vienna,
in the Graben, in the House of the First Austrian Savings Bank,
No. 572,
are just published,
and also to be had of K. Lichtl in Pest:

THREE
SONGS FOR A BASS VOICE
(*L'incanto degli occhi — Il traditor deluso — Il modo di prender moglie*)
(Italian and German),
with Pianoforte Accompaniment
by
FRANZ SCHUBERT.
Work 83.
No. 1, 24 Kreuzer; No. 2, 36 Kr.; No. 3, 36 Kr., A.C.
Complete, 1 Fl. 36 Kr., A.C.

Op. 83 appeared after Opp. 84 and 87.   It is dedicated to the famous
bass Luigi Lablache, born in 1794 at Naples, who was engaged at the
Kärntnertor Theatre.   Schubert is said to have met him at Kiesewetter's,
but he also frequented Frau von Lászny's house, where he once took the
second bass in the male-voice quartet 'The Gondolier' ('Der Gondelfahrer'), and that of Kajetan Giannatasio del Rio, who had two musical
daughters, Fanny (Franziska) and Nanni (Anna), and where 'Domestic
Warfare' ('Der häusliche Krieg') was once performed with pianoforte
accompaniment.   (Giannatasio kept a private school for boys, in which
Beethoven's nephew Karl was a pupil in 1816–18.)   Lablache, who did
not speak German, had sung Figaro in Rossini's as well as in Mozart's
opera in 1824, and later became music master to Queen Victoria.   Thalberg became his son-in-law.—The title names Metastasio as the author of
the three poems, but that of the third song is not by him: its author is
unknown.

942. FROM KARL PACHLER'S CASH-BOOK

13th September 1827: Carrier to Wildbach, with gratuity—
20 Fl., V.C., 40 Kr., A.C

943. JOCULAR PLAYBILL on Schubert's Friends at Graz,
September 1827

'The Footfall in the Haller Castle' or
'Don't pinch me so!'

Dramatis Personae:

Harengos	—	Dr. Franz Haring,
Pachleros	—	Dr. Karl Pachler,
Schwammerl	—	Franz Schubert,
Schilcherl	—	Anselm Hüttenbrenner.

Haller's Castle (*Hallerschlössel*) is at the foot of the Ruckerlberg, south-east of Graz, with a view of the nearby town. Its original name was Sparbersbach, but it was renamed after a new owner about 1800. In 1827 it belonged to the barrister Dr. Franz Haring. He had married recently and had numerous relations to stay at his summer residence. For this reason the Pachlers, who usually rented the whole house for the summer, had not moved there that year. But Haring had among his guests Dr. Josef Schweighofer, an official in the exchequer, and his wife Katharina, who later became friends of Teltscher's. A Fräulein Kathi (Katharina) Mayer von Gravenegg (cf. No. 1127) came on a visit and sang Styrian folksongs for Schubert, who was often a guest at Haller's Castle with the Pachlers during that month. This playbill for a comedy that may never have been performed was written by a handsome widow whom Jenger courted. It gives us a clue to the nicknames of some of the men of the party, including Schilcherl (derived from the Styrian wine) for Hüttenbrenner and Schwammerl (translated as "Tubby" here) for Schubert (*see* note to No. 391).

944. FROM KARL PACHLER'S CASH-BOOK

16th September 1827: 2 pipe bowls—8 Kr., A.C. . . . To wife for housekeeping—100 Fl., V.C.

Several Schubertiads were held in the Pachler house. But for the most part Schubert had to be his own singer. Among the songs he performed there was 'The Wayfarer addressing the Moon' ('Der Wanderer an den Mond'), and he frequently played pianoforte duets with Jenger. However, he also took pleasure in his hostess's pianoforte playing, for she had a special gift for "musical portraits" in which she capitally characterized or caricatured her acquaintances. Frau Pachler, by the way, had hoped until as late as the past winter that she might have Beethoven too as a guest during the year. Sophie Müller and Heinrich Anschütz had frequented her home when they appeared as guest artists at the Graz theatre.

944A. FROM THE FRANKFORT 'ALLGEMEINE MUSIKALISCHE ZEITUNG,' 19th September 1827

(Criticisms of the song-books, Opp. 81 and 80.)

[1.] Not at all badly done. Only quite simple, it is true, as the sense of the words requires, but with beautiful, pleasing melodies. No. 1, 'Alinde,' is in 6–8 time, moderate, in A major. No. 2, 'To the Lute,' in 6–8, fairly quick, in D major. No. 3, 'For Good-night,' in 4–4 time, rather slow, in D major.

F.

[2.] Quite similar to the preceding set. No. 1, 'The Wayfarer addressing the Moon,' opens in 2–4 time, fairly animated, in G minor and closes in G major. No. 2, 'The Passing-Bell,' is in 4–4 time, slow, in A♭ major. No. 3, 'In the Open,' in 2–4 time, moderate and with feeling, in E♭ major.

F.

945. SCHUBERT TO FRANZ SELLIERS DE MORANVILLE

Dear Herr von Sellier,

I came to apologize for not having kept my word recently. If you knew how impossible it had been made for me to do so, I am sure you would forgive me. Hoping that I shall not lose your goodwill, I remain,

With all respect,
Your most devoted
Graz, 19th September 1827.   Frz. Schubert.

Selliers was Chancellor at the Court War Council, formerly employed in Vienna and now, as Jenger's successor, at Graz. He was a member of the Vienna Philharmonic Society. Schubert seems to have made him a promise he was not able or willing to keep—perhaps merely a visit.

946. KEEPSAKE FOR FRAU PACHLER

20th September 1827.

To our dear hostess
for kind remembrance
Jenger.   Schubert.

Schubert and Jenger left that day, travelling by a different route from that by which they had come; *see* No. 949.

947. [LOST LETTER from Frau Pachler to Jenger asking him to remind Schubert of his promise to write a pianoforte piece for four hands for her husband's coming birthday and name-day, to be played by Faust Pachler and his mother, 20th September 1827]

Frau Pachler wrote on the very same day to make sure that Schubert would not forget. Her son was born in 1819, and was thus eight years of age. Cf. Nos. 957 and 958.

'The Blind Boy' (Der blinde Knabe'), Op. 101 (xx. 468), appears in the 'Wiener Zeitschrift,' 25th September 1827.—Cf. note preceding No. 597.

948. SCHUBERT TO FRAU PACHLER

Vienna, 27th September 1827.

Madam,

Already it becomes clear to me that I was only too happy at Graz, and I cannot as yet get accustomed to Vienna. True, it is rather large, but then it is empty of cordiality, candour, genuine thought, reasonable words, and especially of intelligent deeds. There is so much confused chatter that one hardly knows whether one is on one's head or one's heels, and one rarely or never achieves any inward contentment. 'Tis possible, of course, that the fault is largely my own, since I take a long time to warm up. At Graz I soon recognized an artless and sincere way of being together, and a longer stay would have allowed me to take to it even more readily. Above all, I shall never forget the kindly shelter, where, with its dear hostess and the sturdy "Pachleros," as well as little Faust, I spent the happiest days I have had for a long time. Hoping to be yet able to prove my gratitude in an adequate manner, I remain, with profound respect,

Most devotedly yours,
Frz. Schubert.

P.S. The opera libretto I hope to be able to send in a few days.

The two friends had arrived in Vienna on the 24th.—The opera libretto is that of 'Alfonso and Estrella,' which Pachler wished to show to the Graz theatre manager Stöger. Schubert afterwards sent the original score to Graz as well, but did not live to have the work performed. Fourteen years later Pachler returned the manuscript to Ferdinand Schubert.

949. JENGER TO FRAU PACHLER

Vienna, 27th September 1827, Noon.

Through the intermediary of our fortunate Styrian, Josef Hüttenbrenner, who is leaving here for Graz to-morrow, friend Tubby and I send you, dear lady, as well as to friend Dr. Karl, our heartiest and sincerest thanks once more for all the kindness and friendship you have shown us. We shall never forget it, the more particularly because both Schubert and I have very seldom spent such glorious days as we did recently at dear Graz and its environs, among which Wildbach and its cherished inhabitants take the first place.

Here things are not going too well as yet, especially with me, for I have again to drive the big cart with all my might, though I shall hardly be in danger of breaking the reins. Compared with the previous twenty days, it is almost insupportable; yet I suppose it is the right thing, when all is said. One must therefore make the best of it.

A short description of our return journey may not be without some interest for you, dear lady; so I will begin with Fürstenfeld. For, as friend Karrer will probably have told you, we did not take kindly to the separation from our dear, good hosts, and the heavens themselves shared our sorrow.

At Fürstenfeld, then, we found an excellent welcome at my dear old friend's, Frau Burgomaster Fritzi Wittman. The next day. (21st), having seen the sights of the town and of the neighbouring Mount Calvary in the forenoon, we left at 3 o'clock, after luncheon, and safely arrived at Hartberg by 8 in the evening, where the magistrate Herr von Zschock (a brother of Captain Baron Z.) offered us excellent quarters for the night.

On the 22nd we entered the coach early, at 5 o'clock, and arrived, at half-past 9 on the most glorious day, outside Friedberg in the Pinka, where we breakfasted.

Thence we climbed on foot to the summit of the Eselberg, which we reached at 12 o'clock and where we enjoyed the finest of views as far as down to Styria and Hungary and up into Austria —over forty hours' march in diameter, no doubt.

At the frontier on the summit we removed our caps and sent our heartiest greetings to all our dear ones in Styria, with the sincerest thanks for all we received there and the firmest resolve to come again as soon as possible.

Thereupon we went down hill along the splendid new road to Aspang, where we lunched, and at last safely arrived at 8 in the evening—after enduring some fatigues owing to the bad field paths from Seebenstein via Pitten and Walbersbach—at Schleinz, where again we found an admirable welcome. An hour later our host, the dealer Stehmann, arrived from Vienna with two acquaintances, and we remained at Schleinz, after passing a merry Sunday and Monday morning, until 3 o'clock on Monday afternoon, when we set out on the return journey to Vienna with Stehmann and the other two Viennese, arriving there safe and sound at half-past nine at night. Below the Tuchlauben, at the "Blue Hedgehog," where Schubert lives, we two parted, resolving to send our news to the dear ones at Graz as soon as possible, which I now do, together with the enclosed letter just handed me by Schubert.— We thank you especially heartily, dear, excellent lady, for the lines you so kindly wrote on the very day of our departure, which I found as soon as I arrived at my office yesterday. . . . With the

Schubert. Lithograph by Josef Teltscher (1826). *See* p. 928

PLATE XXVI

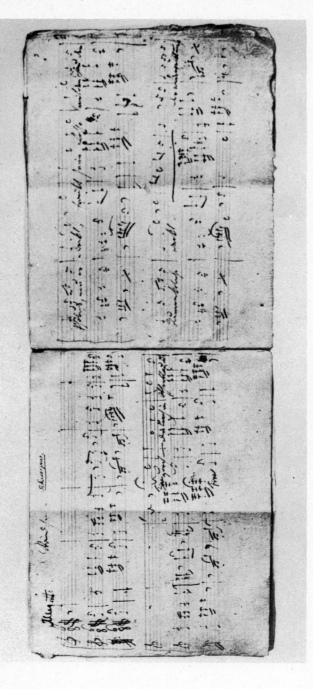

'Hark, Hark, the Lark' ('Morgenständchen'). The First Two Pages of the Autograph (1826)

PLATE XXVII

special request, dear lady, to give my very, very kindest messages to all our acquaintances—particularly at Wildbach, and there even more particularly to my darling "Netti"—I remain, with renewed heartfelt thanks and the sincerest greetings to you and friend Karl,

Your grateful friend,

Hans Jenger.

Josef Hüttenbrenner left for his home on holiday.   He took Schubert's letter (No. 948) with him as well.—"Friend Karrer" may have been the carrier.—The return journey was made through north-eastern Styria and Lower Austria, by different stages, instead of the usual post route across the Semmering, by which they had come.—Fürstenfeld is about thirty miles west of Graz.—Fritzi (Friederike) was the wife of the burgomaster of Fürstenberg, Karl Johann Wittmann.—Hartberg is about seventeen miles farther north.—Anton Zschock, born at Hartberg in 1775, was an innkeeper and a lover of the arts.   His brother was probably the officer Ludwig, Freiherr von Zschock, born in 1792.—Friedberg is about twelve miles north of Hartberg.   The Pinga, *recte* Pinggau, is the basin of the river Pinka on which Friedberg lies.—The "Eselberg," *recte* Möselberg, is a spur (3,200 feet) of the Wechsel (5,700 feet); Mönichkirchen (*c.* five miles north of Friedberg) is on the Möselberg, Aspang at its foot, about four miles to the north.—"Into Austria" means into the heart of Austria, in this case particularly Lower Austria.—From Aspang the road goes north for eleven miles to Seebenstein.   (Anton David Steiger, *see* No. 590, had been director of the romantic circle at Seebenstein Castle about 1820—"the knight of the blue earth.")   Pitten is three miles north-west of Seebenstein, and four miles farther on is Wolkersdorf, close to which, near Frohsdorf, is the castle of Schleinz, whose owner was then the merchant Stehmann (or? Rehmann).   He, like the Wittmanns and the Zschocks, was evidently acquainted with Jenger. The last part of the way probably led through Wiener Neustadt, Baden and Mödling.—Netti is Anna, Frau Massegg's second daughter.

950. ERNST VON FEUCHTERSLEBEN to Romeo Seligmann at Nikolsburg

[Vienna, Autumn 1827.]

. . . Not long ago Schubert came from Graz full of enthusiasm, but richer by only two songs.   Schwind has left Munich and is expected by his brother at Linz. Bauernfeld writes, Schober lithographs.

Seligmann, born in 1808 at Nikolsburg in Moravia, was a doctor and later professor of medical history in Vienna, a friend of Feuchtersleben's. —The songs were 'Secret Loving' ('Heimliches Lieben') to words by Helmina von Chézy's mother, Karoline Louise von Klencke, sent to Frau Pachler through Schneller, and 'An Old Scottish Ballad' ('Edward' from Percy's 'Reliques,' translated by Herder).   To these are no doubt to be added the dances Schubert had written at Graz: the 'Grätzer Walzer,' Op. 91, and the 'Grätzer Galopp' (see No. 994).—Schwind was at Salzburg early in September, at Ebenzweier Castle in the middle of the month and from the end of September to the middle of October at Linz, where Josef von Spaun was too at that time.

951. FROM THE 'WIENER ZEITSCHRIFT FÜR KUNST,'
29th September 1827

'Fantasy, Andante, Minuet and Allegretto' for Pianoforte solo. Dedicated to Josef Edler von Spaun, Esq., by Franz Schubert. Work 78.   Vienna, Tobias Haslinger.

The popular and talented song composer here gives to the musical world a Fantasy, wherein he has given free play to his imagination and offers the player harmonious enjoyment, without rendering the performance too difficult by the accumulation of excessive intricacies.   Both hands are as a rule fully occupied, and Beethoven's manner of frequently doubling the treble part an octave below, while thirds or sixths run parallel to it, seems to be also a favourite device of Herr Schubert's, who often proceeds thus in his constructions.   Passing notes, anticipations and suspensions are treated with great freedom, which frequently results in beautiful and often strange relationships.   The composer has made the whole even more interesting by well-contrived imitations.   The first piece is effective.   The Andante allows and demands a great deal of expression.   The trio of the Minuet is particularly successful.   The Allegretto is fiery and calls for brilliant performance.   Herr

Schubert keeps closely to a theme and works it out very logically; but not seldom he sacrifices variety. It is right and proper to rank this work among the good pianoforte compositions which by no means aim at being mere dancing-lessons for the fingers. It demands practised players. The engraving, like that of all the publications issued by the firm in question, is to be commended.

952. ANTON SCHINDLER to B. Schott's Court Music Establishment at Mainz

Vienna, 29th September 1827.

. . . Thus a song recently came into my hands which a Court singer of Karlsruhe, whose name is Schütz, I believe, published with the name of Herr C. van Beethoven as composer. This Herr C. van Beethoven is the immortalized master L. Beethoven's nephew, who never in his life took it into his head to write so much as a note. And what does it amount to?—two waltzes with words fitted to them: the first is by J. [sic] Schubert and the second by Hummel [Himmel], copied out note for note.—Should not the public be officially warned about such a hideous imposture?—

This was an open letter, published in Schott's periodical 'Cäcilia' (vol. vii, No. 26, pp. 91 f.) under the title of 'Small Contributions to L. van Beethoven's Characterization and to the History of his Works.' Heinrich Schütz, a singer and actor at the ducal court of Baden, had published with Schott in the spring of 1826 the so-called 'Favourite Waltz' ('Favorit-Walzer') by Beethoven (cf. No. 384), with words added to it ("O süsse Himmelslust") and with guitar or pianoforte accompaniment. It is No. 250 of a 'Selection of Songs with Pianoforte or Guitar accompaniment,' but bears the name of "L. von Beethoven." Schotts themselves at the same time brought out 'Le Désir, Valse favorite von Beethoven' for pianoforte solo. On a similar occasion, when the 'Sehnsuchtswalzer' alleged to be by Beethoven once again appeared in the shape of a song, the Leipzig 'Allgemeine musikalische Zeitung' wrote in December 1831: ". . . it is by the late Schubert, ladies, your pet!"

952A. The Rev. Father Kolumban Daigele to Schubert's
Father

Together with our greetings to our lady cousin, the gentlemen
your sons and little daughter . . . I repeat once again our good
wishes, with a good glass of wine, and remain

Your most devoted cousin and kinsman,

                                                            Kol.
Jenö, 30th September 1827.

[Postscript by Elisabeth Kleyenböck:]

I kiss and greet . . . all the children, big and little.

For Daigele *see* No. 131. He had been living since July 1818 at Telki, to
the west of Buda, as administrator for the Vienna Scottish Monastery and was
priest at the neighbouring Jenö, where (as at Buda) Anton Herbaschek held
a property. The latter was married to Franziska (Fanny) Kleyenböck,
whose sister Elisabeth (Lisi) was housekeeper to Daigele. Schubert's
stepmother and Therese Obermeyer, a baker's wife in the Himmelpfortgrund, were the other two of the four Kleyenböck sisters (*see* No. 49),
who were Daigele's cousins. Schubert's father was not related to Daigele
otherwise than by marriage. The congratulations were addressed to him
for his name-day, which fell on 4th October. The gentlemen-sons are
Schubert and his three brothers, the little daughter is probably his stepsister Josefa, while the big and little children are those of both the elder
Schubert's marriages.—The wine sent by Daigele was a Buda vintage.

The poet Wilhelm Müller (*see* No. 436) dies at Dessau, 30th September 1827.

Franz Michael Vierthaler (*see* No. 137) dies, 3rd October 1827.

953. [Lost Letter from Frau Pachler to Jenger, enclosed in a
parcel for Schubert, 5th October 1827.]

Cf. No. 967.

954. From Fritz von Hartmann's Diary

[Linz,] 5th October 1827: I went to see Schwind (who lives with
Anton von Spaun). I saw him work at the drawing for his illustration of Josef Kenner's poem, 'Stillfried und Sigunde.' Having

talked a great deal with him and my brothers, I sang songs by
Schubert, accompanied by my brother Louis.

For Schwind cf. No. 950.—The poem is preserved in the Vienna City
Library, but the drawing is lost.

955. From the Munich 'Allgemeine Musik-Zeitung,'
6th October 1827

'Alinde,' 'To the Lute' ['An die Laute'], 'For Good-night' ['Zur
guten Nacht']. Poems by Friedrich Rochlitz. Set to
Music for one Voice with Pianoforte Accompaniment by
Franz Schubert. Work 81. Vienna, Tobias Haslinger.
12 Groschen or 54 Kreuzer.

The first of these poems is not intended as a song, and it therefore
receives a somewhat more closely worked-out musical treatment.
This, however, is so characteristic and original that for this reason
alone we should be able to recommend the little work to lovers
of song, even if the following song, 'To the Lute,' were less
successful than it is. No. 3 is least individual; nevertheless, it
too makes the most delightful effect.

'The Wayfarer addressing the Moon' ['Der Wanderer an
den Mond], 'The Passing-Bell' ['Das Zügenglöcklein'],
'In the Open' ['Im Freien']. Poems by Seidl. Set to
Music for 1 Voice with Pianoforte Accompaniment by
Franz Schubert. Op. 80. Ibid. 1 Florin, A.C.

No. 1. Most excellent. Simple voice part, clear harmony, yet
alive and true in expression. No. 2. Less good, although more
choice, especially in the accompaniment, which however should
remain altogether subsidiary in a true song. The same applies
to No. 3, where a figure of accompaniment is too consistently
kept going for nine pages on end. For all that, these two little
works are among the most excellent of their kind.

Fr. St.
[Franz Stoepel.]

This was the first issue of that periodical. The notice may have been occasioned by Schwind's visit to Munich.—"Not intended as a song" no doubt means not conceived purely strophically, for 'Alinde' is a strophic song with a difference. The "true song" was that still cultivated by composers like Reichardt and Zelter, who treated the accompaniment merely as an auxiliary feature.—Stoepel, born in Prussia in 1794, a writer on music, had been in London about 1815.

956. From the Official 'Wiener Zeitung,' 8th October 1827

At the House of Tobias Haslinger,
Art and Music Dealer in Vienna,
in the Graben, in the House of the First Austrian Savings Bank,
No. 572,
are just published,
and also to be had of K. Lichtl in Pest:
The German Love Minstrels
['Die deutschen Minnesänger']
Latest Collection of Songs
for Four Male Voices.
Containing:

No. 1. 'Grave and Moon' ['Grab und Mond'].   A.C.
Words by Seidl, music by Fr. Schubert . . 15 Kr.
No. 4. 'Wine and Love ['Wein und Liebe'].
Words by Haug, music by Fr. Schubert . . 30 Kr.
(To be continued.)

This collection of excellent vocal compositions by the foremost German tone-poets will not only include the latest original works, but make a careful choice among the sterling older ones, in order to offer nothing to an art-loving public which is not likely to be welcomed by it and worthy of its particular attention.

The whole stock (of some 300 vocal pieces) ensures agreeable variety and uninterrupted continuation.

Cf. Nos. 895 and 896.—The collection began with six books.—Schubert's contributions, like the others, were given no opus numbers.—Johann Christoph Friedrich Haug was born in 1761 at Niederstotzingen in Württemberg.

957. Schubert to Frau Pachler

(Below the *secondo* and *primo* parts of the manuscript of the Children's March [ix. 7].)

I herewith send your honour the four-handed piece for little Faust. I fear I shall not earn his applause, since I do not feel that I am exactly made for this kind of composition. I hope that your honour is in better health than I, for my usual headaches are already assailing me again. Pray give Dr. Karl my heartiest good wishes for his name-day and tell him that the book of my opera, which that sloth, Herr Gottdank, has had for months to read through, has not yet been returned to me even now. For the rest, I remain,

with all respect,

your most devoted

Vienna, 12th October 1827.   Franz Schubert.

Cf. No. 947. The piece was intended for little Faust Pachler and his mother to play on Dr. Pachler's name-day, 4th November.—For Schubert's headaches cf. Nos. 961 and 971.—Gottdank (*see* No. 167), who worked at Graz off and on, had been producer at the Kärntnertor Theatre since the end of 1821. The performance of 'Alfonso and Estrella' seems thus to have been reconsidered at the Court Opera, where however it did not appear until 1882. Cf. No. 948.

958. Jenger to Faust Pachler

(On the reverse of the *primo* part of the Children's March.)

Dear little Friend,

That I did not fail to carry out your commission you will see from this sheet. Study it diligently, therefore, and think of friend Tubby and me on the 4th of the coming month. Give your father all the best messages you can think of on his name-day; we shall be with you all in spirit on that day. Write to me again soon, for your letter gave me much pleasure. But I did not receive it until the 10th of this month through friend Gomez. Many, many greetings to your highly honoured, dear parents and all other acquaintances. You, dear Faust, be heartily kissed by

Your friend

Vienna, 12th October 1827.   Hans Jenger.

Faust.Pachler seems to have written a letter to Jenger at the end of September and given it to the latter's colleague Gomez to take with him, reminding his correspondent of Schubert's promise in order to receive the march in time to practise it.—Anton Gomez von Parientos had been assistant registrar to the General Command at Graz, and was now at the Court War Council in a similar capacity; he was also a minor lyric poet.

959. FROM FRITZ VON HARTMANN'S DIARY

[Linz,] 12th October 1827: [Max von Spaun's name-day.] We breakfasted at Herr and Frau Ottenwalt's. A poem written by Schwind and my brother Franz was read, the subject of which was a comic adventure Max Spaun met with a few days ago . . . At midday I visited Schwind, who had erected a pretty throne for Max von Spaun. When the latter was on it, we formed a circle, chatting and smoking. Then we sang three- and four-part songs by Schubert . . . At 6 o'clock came Josef von Spaun, who listened to my brother as he played a glorious sonata by Schubert.

Schwind was an accomplished occasional poet. 'The Spixiad,' to which he added amusing illustrations in Vienna on 5th August 1828 (one of which is in the iconographical volume, p. 416), is a comic epic describing the story of a young Viennese lady who was sent to Belgium by her family because of a love affair with an officer, and to whom Franz von Spaun, as *postillon d'amour*, conveyed a letter to Linz at the last moment.—The Sonata may have been that in G major, Op. 78, dedicated to Josef von Spaun.

960. FROM THE 'THEATERZEITUNG,' 13th October 1827

(Remark under the poem, 'Song in the Greenery' ['Das Lied im Grünen'] [xx. 543] by Friedrich Reil.)

Was often sung in the meadows here and there this summer by a merry party to an agreeable, cheerful melody by Schubert.

Schubert had composed the song in June 1827, but it did not appear until two years later, as No. 1 of the Op. posth. 115, with three additional verses "dedicated belatedly by the poet to the transfigured one and set below the melody."—Reil, born in 1773 in the valley of Ehrenbreitstein (Rhineland), was court actor at the Burg Theatre and an occasional poet.

961. [LOST LETTER FROM SCHUBERT, 15th October 1827, regretting his inability to be present at a party, owing to his being utterly unfit for any society.]

This letter was offered at an auction on 21st October 1887 by Leo Liepmannssohn in Berlin, but is now lost sight of. An address was indicated on its reverse. Cf. No. 971.

962. SCHUBERT TO JOHANN PHILIPP NEUMANN

Most honoured Professor,   Vienna, 16th October 1827.

I duly received the 100 florins, V.C., which you sent me for the composition of the vocal pieces for Mass, and only hope that the said compositions may be commensurate with your expectations.

With all respect,

Your

most devoted

Frz. Schubert.

Neumann, born in 1774 at Trebitsch in Moravia, a cousin of the widow Anna Watteroth (*née* Rupprecht, 1776), was professor of physics at the Polytechnic Institute since its foundation in 1815, also secretary and librarian there. He was a champion of Joseph II's policy of enlightenment, had literary inclinations and in 1798 had founded the 'Neue Wiener Musenalmanach.' He was the librettist of Schubert's unfinished opera 'Sakuntala' (1820), based on Kalidasa's Indian drama, of which only two acts were sketched.—The idea of a "German Mass," to be sung by the congregation in Catholic churches, was not new. In 1782 Michael Haydn had written a "German High Mass" ("Hier liegt vor Deiner Majestät") by command of the Archbishop Hieronymus of Salzburg, which became fairly popular. Neumann's text ("Wohin soll ich mich wenden?") is said to have been already printed privately by Anton Benko of Vienna in 1826 with the title of 'Sacred Songs (for the Holy Sacrament of Mass) by Johann Philipp Neumann, set to Music by Franz Schubert,' but no copy of this is extant. In 1827 the text appeared, without the authors' names, as 'Songs for the Celebration of the Holy Sacrament of Mass. Together with an Appendix containing The Lord's Prayer'; printed by Anton von Haykul. A copy of this is in the Vienna City Library. Benko had been employed since 1824 in the printing works of his aunt, Anna von Haykul (Anton's widow), which seems to make the alleged first edition of 1826 even more questionable. It was long supposed that this

Mass was written for the students at the Polytechnic Institute and was first performed by them at the neighbouring Karl church; but the fact has been overlooked that the work was originally written for mixed chorus and that the students of the academies were exclusively male at that time. Neumann had in fact no chance to have the Mass performed in Schubert's lifetime (*see* No. 965), and he probably did not see this hope fulfilled until twenty years later.   This was about the time that one of his sons, Ludwig Gottfried (*see* No. 572), undertook to write a Schubert biography (which was never finished).—The fee Schubert received from Neumann in person was exactly the same as that which he had privately received for the 'Prometheus' cantata in 1816 (*see* No. 91).

963. From Fritz von Hartmann's Diary

[Linz,] 18th October 1827: After 8 o'clock I went with my brothers to Herr and Frau von Ottenwalt's, in order to breakfast there with Josef and Max von Spaun, Schwind and others.   Schwind and my brother Ludwig played splendid four-handed pieces by Schubert.

Schwind returned to Vienna the next day.

964. From Bauernfeld's Diary

[End of] October 1827.

Grillparzer will send us the opera to the Königstadt Theatre . . . Schwind is back.   He is well and cheerful.

The opera is 'The Count of Gleichen.'   For the Königstadt Theatre in Berlin *see* No. 564.   For the difficulties the opera had in Vienna cf. No. 716.   Grillparzer, of course, could have sent only the manuscript libretto to Berlin.

965. Note in the Censorship Register of the Viennese Archiepiscopal Consistory for the Years 1821–29

1827, 24th October [received and settled].

'Songs for the celebration of the Holy Sacrament of the Mass. Together with an appendix containing: The Lord's Prayer by

Joh. Ph. Neumann.   Set to music by Franz Schubert.'   (But without music enclosed.)   Manuscript.

admittuntur, but not for official church use.

Cf. No. 962.   Like the court theatres, the diocese of the Archbishop of
Vienna also had its own censorship, for ecclesiastical matters.   This licence
refers to the text of the printed (? second) version of the German Mass.
The music was not submitted, the words alone concerning the censorship.
In the first (complete) edition of the work its publisher, J. P. Gotthard of
Vienna, quoted from a lost diary of Neumann's in his preface, dated
December 1870.   According to this Neumann in 1827 filed a petition
with the Vienna Consistory for the introduction of the German Mass into
the Catholic church service, which however was refused.   The work was
admitted for church use only in the second half of the nineteenth century.

965A. NOTE OF CENSORSHIP on the Printer's Copy of the 'Winter
Journey,' Part I

Excudatur.

From the Central Book Censorship Office.

Vienna, 24th October 1827.   Schodl.

The first part of this cycle had to be rewritten at the publisher's before
it went to the engraver, the autograph being difficult to read.   In this
copy Schubert still made a few alterations.

966. ANNA MASSEGG, JUN., TO FRAU PACHLER

Wildbach, 25th October 1827.

If you should write to Jenger at any time, please send him many
cordial greetings from us all.—We shall never forget the day you
spent with us with the other dear company, and I have often
thought quietly to myself how gladly I should recall it and how I
wish it would last long, for we shall miss that kind of thing for
a long time to come and are quite at a loss to know why the honour
of having so delightful a party in our house should have come our
way.

Cf. note preceding No. 941 and that to No. 949.   The day Fräulein
Massegg cannot forget is 11th September 1827.

967. [Lost Letter from Schubert to Frau Pachler, 26th October
1827]

Cf. No. 968.

968. Jenger to Frau Pachler

Vienna, 26th October 1827.

Only this morning did I receive, through Menz, your few lines
of the 5th inst., as well as the small packet for friend Tubby,
which I handed to him at once and his acknowledgment for which
is enclosed.   Your favourite, Sophie Müller, and her father shall
have your greetings delivered by me to-night.   We shall have a
small musical evening there, where with a young lady who has
long been most anxious to know you—having heard so many pleasant
and good things of you from Müller's father, from friend Tubby
and from myself—I shall be playing the *Divertissement* [*à la*]
hongrois[*e*].   That lady is Irene Kiesewetter, whose name, written
by herself, you, dear lady, will find on the above-mentioned
Divertissement, which is in your hands.   There will be much talk
to-night about you, your husband and your child, which is always
the case whenever I get to the Müllers'.   Friend T[ubby] also
chimes in very gladly with this theme, and so we shall again produce
a few variations on it this evening.   What a pity, what an endless
pity, that you cannot witness it, for we should all be very heartily
glad of that, and the long-cherished wish of this most dear and
capable pianoforte player, Irene, would be fulfilled at last.—Here,
dear lady, I see you smile somewhat roguishly, and I try to imagine
what you may be thinking of it; but I tell you in advance that you
may be mistaken in this matter, as indeed I had already declared
at Graz.   Sophie Müller and Schubert could and would testify to
the truth of this; but it occurs to me at this moment that ladies,
including spinsters, could not be legally admissible witnesses, and
so we had better leave things as they were. . . . How does dear
little Faust fare with his march by T[ubby]? — Quite well by
now, no doubt . . .

Ignaz Menz, who came from Graz, was a doctor in Vienna; he lived in the
Kohlmarkt, where Jenger joined him later.—The packet may have con-

tained the first collection of poems by Leitner (*see* No. 511), published in
1825. Schubert's acknowledgment is lost.—Sophie Müller, accompanied
by her father, had appeared as a guest at the Graz theatre in the summers of
1824 and 1825.—For Irene von Kiesewetter *see* No. 598. Jenger had
evidently left her copy of the 'Divertissement a la hongroise' behind at
Graz.—For the 'Children's March' cf. No. 957.

968A. From the Frankfort 'Allgemeine Musikalische Zeitung,' 27th October 1827

(On the pianoforte Sonata in G major, Op. 78.)

Quite good work on the whole.   The pieces contained in this
book are not too difficult, and are attractive; they may thus be
recommended for practice.   The contents are indicated by the
title.

R. . .

The title was, of course, 'Fantasy, Andante, Minuet and Allegretto,'
but the notice calls the composer Schubart.

969. From Franz von Hartmann's Diary

Autumn 1827: Every Wednesday and Saturday evening we go to
the ale-house, where Enk, Schober, Schubert and Spaun are to be
met.   Nearly every day to Bogner's coffee-house, as the newspapers now interest me a great deal . . . Dinand Sauter is most
melancholy on the whole, but occasionally unrestrainedly jolly.
So there is little to be done with him.   Unfortunately Schober
cannot bear him at all, which I regret the more because it was I,
in fact, who made them acquainted and encouraged Dinand, who
is now quite well aware of not being welcome.

970. Schubert to Jenger [? 1827]

Dear Jenger,
I am unable to come to lunch.   Excuse me.   We shall meet in
the evening at 7.30 o'clock.

Schubert.

This note is written in pencil.   It may be a first, unused draft for
No. 971.

971. Schubert to Jenger

[Outside:]

Johann Jenger, Esq.

[Inside:]

Dear Friend,

I am unable to appear for lunch at Henikstein's; please forgive me. But I shall appear without fail at 7.30 o'clock in the evening.

7th November 1827.   Schubert.

This note was in the collection of the Prokesch von Osten family. Anton Prokesch (*see* No. 277) was Schneller's stepson and, with Marie Koschak (later Frau Pachler), had been his pupil at Graz. He later married Irene von Kiesewetter.—The words "at Henikstein's" were added by Schubert after completion of the letter.—Josef, Ritter von Henikstein, who is clearly meant here, was the eldest of three brothers engaged in wholesale trade; he was born in 1768, was a widower, had a daughter who painted, and had been a friend of Mozart's, later a patron of Beethoven's. He was a member of the Philharmonic Society, sang bass and played the mandoline and cello. Weekly concerts were given at his house, and he played in the string quartets. Reichardt, during his visit to Vienna in 1808, had seen Italian comic operas performed there.—In the evening Schubert may have visited Menz or Kiesewetter.

972. Rochlitz to Schubert

[Outside:]

Franz Schubert, Esq.

in

Enclosed.   Vienna.

[Inside:]

Sir,   Leipzig, 7th November 1827.

You know the respect and affection I have for you and your compositions; and Herr Haslinger has transmitted my thanks for your music to my three songs, as well as my desire that you may embellish a larger poem by your art; also your inclination to do so. Permit me, therefore, to come to this subject at once. The poem I have in mind is 'The First Sound' ['Der erste Ton']. You will

find it in Vol. V of my collected works, which Herr Haslinger
possesses.   I will set down here how I imagine the music for it;
but do not by any means think that I wish to dictate in any way
(for I have no right to do so); take what I say rather as a mere
suggestion for your consideration, and then follow whatever
may occur to you as the result of such deliberations—as you
may be inspired—whether it accords with my proposal wholly
or in part or not at all.   Overture: a single, short, plucked
chord, *ff*, and then a note sustained as long as possible, $<>$, for
clarinet or horn, with a pause.   Now a soft opening, darkly
intertwined, harmonically rather than melodically—a kind of
chaos which only gradually grows clearer and lighter.   Whether
the overture is to close here or to be followed by an *allegro* I will
not decide; if the latter is chosen, let the *allegro* be serious, but
very forceful and brilliant, yet dying down on a close derived from
the first movement.   At this point declamation without music up
to the words "Wirken gegeben."   Here the orchestra drops in
quietly with sustained chords; the words are spoken to these, with
only very short interludes between the principal sections of the
speech, up to "Erdenreich."   Here a longer, sombre interlude.
A shorter and more gentle one after "Gott."   The next sentence, as
far as "selbst gefällt," without any music whatever.   For that from
"Nun schwingen" to "soll ich sein," chords with very short
interludes at the main sections; now, however, a more developed,
gently serene interlude, after which, at the words "Nun schliesset,"
&c., everything begins to move more and more in the music and
gradually to increase.   This grows into free instrumental play
after the words "Wiederhall sie nach," and so forms a developed
preparation and introduction for the great chorus, as splendid
and brilliant as possible: "Drum Preis dir," developed as long and
as effectively as it may please the composer; but the last two lines,
and thus the close of the whole, are given a gentler and milder
music, without any change of tempo or key.   Composed in this
manner by a master of such spirit and feeling as yourself, and spoken
by an orator as worthy as your Anschütz, it promises to make a
great impression, and indeed one such as anybody, connoisseur or
otherwise, must honour and love.   However—I repeat—all this

is a mere suggestion; the choice and the decision is yours.—For the rest, I am delighted to have come a little closer to you in this manner also and to refresh your memory of me. Should a work result and should I receive it, I would take care that as finished a performance as possible is given at our concerts.—With the greatest respect and devotion,

Rochlitz.

Cf. Nos. 299, 651 and 893.—The poem 'The First Sound' had appeared already on 2nd October 1805, with the sub-heading of 'A Fantasy,' in the Leipzig 'Allgemeine musikalische Zeitung,' and in 1808 was composed by Weber, whose setting was repeatedly performed from 1810 on, though not in Vienna. It reappeared in 1822 in a 'Selection of the Best of Friedrich Rochlitz's Complete Writings' (vol. v, pp. 197 ff.). At the end of that year the poet offered it to Beethoven through Haslinger, but without success. Weber's setting was thus referred to by Rochlitz in his second letter to Haslinger: "Beethoven is . . . by no means wrong in saying that a musical treatment of 'The First Sound' should recall Haydn's 'Creation.' It is true that this, too, might be avoided by the choice of an entirely different treatment, namely the presentation of the poem as a piece of declamation (melodramatically) with instrumental interludes. However, it was set to music in this way once before, though not well, so that our artist would hardly care to repeat this procedure, although that composition has remained almost wholly unknown, and there is nobody in this wide world who has less cause to fear such a clash than he. Should he nevertheless wish to enter into this idea, the following outward shape would perhaps be the most advantageous: . . . Since there are only three instrumental interludes, these could be made into fairly extended pieces, and any painting of details, and thus even the remotest resemblance to 'The Creation,' could be avoided." In his letter to Schubert, as in his first proposal of Beethoven, Rochlitz never so much as alluded to Weber.—"Da vernahm . . ." is the opening of the second half of the poem, which extends to sixty-six lines and was again reproduced in the German edition of Thayer's 'Beethoven' (vol. iv, 2nd ed., pp. 575 f.).—For Anschütz cf. Nos. 269 and 839.

973. SCHUBERT TO ROCHLITZ, (?) November 1827

Sir,

I was much honoured by your valued letter, since it brought me into closer touch with so excellent a man.

Your proposal concerning the poem of 'The First Sound' I have carefully considered, and it is true that I believe your suggested treatment of it to be capable of making an admirable effect. But as in this way it would be a kind of melodrama rather than an oratorio or cantata, and the former being no longer favoured (perhaps with good reason), I must openly confess that I should very much prefer a poem that may be treated as an oratorio, not only because an orator like Anschütz is not always to be had, but also because it is my most ardent wish to furnish a purely musical work, without any extraneous matter apart from the elevating idea of a long poem to be set wholly to music. I need hardly say that I recognize in you the poet for such a work and that I should devote all my powers and diligence to composing it in a manner worthy of the poetry.

'The First Sound' really being so glorious a poem, I should be glad to try it, should you wish me to set it to music, but I should let the music (i.e. song) enter at the words "Da vernahm," if you agree.

With the greatest respect,

Your most devoted
Frz. Schubert.

This brought the correspondence between Schubert and Rochlitz to an end.—Cf. No. 641 (Zedlitz's 'Nocturnal Review' ['Nächtliche Heer-schau'].)

974. FROM THE PROGRAMME of the First Evening Entertainment held by the Philharmonic Society, 22nd November 1827 (Conductor, Herr Bogner)

4. 'Diana in Anger' ['Die zürnende Diana'], poem by Mayrhofer, set to music by Fr. Schubert, sung by Herr Schnitzer.

For Bogner *see* No. 531.—Kolumban Schnitzer, later von Meerau (cf. No. 598), was a violist and a tenor singer. But he had a musical son, who may have been meant here.

975. Note on the above Programme

Schnitzer.   Fröhlich.

Anna Fröhlich accompanied Schnitzer.

976. From the Leipzig 'Allgemeine Musikalische Zeitung,'
16th January 1828
(Berlin correspondence, November 1827.)

November also brought us the opening of the Bernhard Romberg quartet evenings in the beautiful hall of the Vocal Academy . . . In addition [at the third of the first three concerts] . . . Franz Schubert's composition, 'Erl King'—which in the critic's opinion matches neither Reichardt's nor Zelter's, although it is surcharged with modulation and eccentricity—was sung by Herr-Bader to the accomplished and forceful pianoforte accompaniment of young Mendelssohn-Bartholdy.

> For Bernhard Romberg, the cellist, who was then conductor in Berlin, cf. No. 325.—The Vocal Academy (*Singakademie*) there was founded by Zelter for the cultivation of choral music.—This was Romberg's third musical evening that season, held on 3rd November.—Karl Adam Bader, born in 1789 at Bamberg, was first tenor at the Berlin Opera.—The Berlin 'Allgemeine musikalische Zeitung' of 5th December 1827 also mentioned this concert, which apart from Schubert's song consisted entirely of works by Romberg.—Reichardt's setting of 'Erl King,' the second of about seventy in all, was still held much in honour to the end of Goethe's lifetime, although Karl Loewe too had brought out his Op. 1 as early as 1824.   Zelter's was not printed till 1896 and probably never sung in public in his lifetime.

> > Countess Marie Esterházy marries August, Count Breunner-Enkevoerth, 1st December 1827.—Count Breunner was born in 1796. He was aulic councillor in the Ministry of Finance, chamberlain and later a member of the Upper House.   On 1st October 1828, at Grafenegg Castle near Krems in Lower Austria, Marie gave birth to a son, August, who later became the owner of Zseliz, and whose eldest daughter married John Whitehead, an industrialist at Trieste, in 1887.

977. From Fritz von Hartmann's Diary

[Linz,] 5th December 1827: At 7 o'clock I went to the Baroness Rosenberg's, where I found my mother, my sister [Therese] and several other ladies.   I talked most with Fräulein Minna, who also sang a few songs by Schubert.

Elisabeth was the wife of Johann, Freiherr von Rosenberg, a commissioner of civil engineering, and Wilhelmine (Minna) was her daughter. The family belonged to the Linz Musical Society.—For Therese von Hartmann cf. note preceding No. 372.

978. From the Programme of the Third Evening Entertainment held by the Philharmonic Society, 6th December 1827

4. 'The Combat' ['Der Kampf'], poem by Schiller, set to music by Franz Schubert, sung by Herr Schoberlechner.

979. From the Official 'Wiener Zeitung,' 10th December 1827

At the House of Tobias Haslinger,
Music Publisher in Vienna,
in the Graben, in the House of the First Austrian Savings Bank,
No. 572,
is just published
and to be had (also of K. Lichtl in Pest):

Impromptu
pour le Pianoforte seul
par
Franç. Schubert.
Œuvre 87.   No. 1 et 2 à 45 Kr., A.C.

Op. 87, *recte* Op. 90—for the number 87 had to be used to replace the mistaken Op. 84 (*see* No. 920)—appeared, without a dedication, before Op. 89.   The title reads 'No. . Impromptu pour le Piano-Forte,' the number being left blank to be inserted (1 or 2) by hand.   This kind of lyrical pianoforte piece—described as "short lyric and narrative form" by Sir W. H. Hadow—has its forerunners, so far as Schubert is concerned, in the 'Eclogues,' 'Rhapsodies' and 'Dithyrambs' by Tomaschek (*see* No. 241), as well as in Worzischek's 'Impromptus.' It was in the latter's Op. 7, published by Mechetti of Vienna in 1822, that this title was first used for that type of work. (Czapek's Op. 6, entitled 'Impromptu brillant,' was brought out by the same publisher in 1826.) The name did thus not originate with Schubert, who took it up later for his Op. posth. 142 (cf. No. 1043). Haslinger intended to publish the other two pieces of Op. 90 as early as 1828, and he actually advertised all the four numbers in December of that year. But eventually Nos. 3 and 4 of Op. 90 were first published by his son Karl in 1857 or 1858, and No. 3 was transposed from G flat major to G major.

980. FROM THE OFFICIAL 'WIENER ZEITUNG,' 12th December 1827

At the House of Thaddaeus Weigl,
Art and Music Dealer, in Vienna, in the Graben, No. 1144 (next to the "King of England"), is quite newly published:

EVENING SONG TO THE DISTANT ONE
['Abendlied für die Entfernte']

THEKLA (a Ghostly Voice)   AT MIDNIGHT
['Thekla (eine Geisterstimme)']   ['Um Mitternacht']

TO MUSIC
['An die Musik']

Four Poems,
set to Music for One Voice with Pianoforte Accompaniment
by FRANZ SCHUBERT.

Work 88.   Price, 45 Kreuzer, A.C.

Op. 88 too appeared without any dedication.

981. FROM THE PROGRAMME of the Fourth Evening Entertainment
    held by the Philharmonic Society, 13th December 1827
    (Conductor, Herr Hauschka)

'The Dwarf' ['Der Zwerg'], poem by Collin, set to music by Schubert, performed by Herr Schoberlechner.

982. Note on the above Programme

Sung by Schoberlechner.   Fr. von Schmiedel.

Frau Schmiedel accompanied at the pianoforte.

983. From the Programme of the I. & R. Hofburg Theatre, 18th December 1827

For the first time

THE PARIAH

Tragedy in One Act by Michael Beer

[after Casimir Delavigne]

.   .   .   .

[With music by Mosel based on Mozart and Schubert (Op. 40, No. 3)].

For Beer cf. No. 707.   The performance was given at the instigation of Sophie Müller.   The play was repeated only on 19th and 21st December. —Mosel was the official director of the two court theatres.   The march is one of the two of Op. 40, which Liszt orchestrated later; Mosel's version was never published.

984. From the Leipzig 'Allgemeine Musikalische Zeitung,' 26th December 1827

Fantasy, Andante, Minuet and Allegretto, for Pianoforte solo— by Franz Schubert.   Work 78.   Vienna, Haslinger.   (Price 1 Thaler 8 Groschen.)

The composer, who has made for himself a numerous following by not a few excellent songs, is capable of doing the same by means of pianoforte pieces.   We are convinced of this by their nature, although we know only one other apart from those mentioned here: a grand Sonata dedicated to the Archduke Rudolf of Austria.   For both he has evidently chosen Beethoven as a model, and indeed his later works for that instrument, with or without accompaniment.   If that has its advantages for an artist of spirit and accomplishment such as Herr Schubert, on which we need not expatiate further, it also has its dangers.   To begin where a great master left off, a master whose striking individuality endeavoured to enlarge the confines of art as far as possible and boldly and inconsiderately to take his stand upon its extremes, that alone is fraught with peril.   Now, however, Beethoven appears to us furthermore to be in a class by himself alone, as it were, especially as he showed himself in his middle and later period, so that in truth he should not by any means be chosen as an absolute model, since any one who desired to be successful in that master's own line could only be he himself.   It is in that respect with him as with Jean Paul: his most original ways suit him alone, having proceeded from his very nature and being that nature itself; men of fine minds who imitated him neither became like him nor remained themselves, and they thus expended their best energies, whatever valuable and valued work they may still have been able to produce—witness Ernst Wagner in 'The Travelling Painters' and 'The Abecedarian.' That dullards have produced but caricatures of their models we need not mention, since we are not by any means concerned with any one of the kind here.   We are therefore of the opinion that one should accept genuises of that sort with admiration and joy just as they are, according to their quite peculiar nature and its resulting quite peculiar characteristics; be elevated, strengthened and refreshed by them; and follow them on their dizzy mountain heights with eyes as sharp as one can muster: but then, elevated, strengthened and refreshed, go one's own way, whether it leads to their neighbourhood or not, so long as it too leads upwards.

To take these utterances for censure of the work under notice would be to misunderstand us completely: they are nothing more than our thoughts, occasioned by its author and, as it seems to us, not inopportunely expressed just now—for him, if he will ponder them and accept them should he find them to be true, but also, and even more so, for others who are now following the same paths without his qualifications.   We shall now keep to the work as it is, and as we have found it.

The Fantasy, which forms the first movement (*Molto moderato e cantabile*, 12–8, G major), does not vindicate the rights of its species in the way in which masters of former times in particular, such as

the Bachs, made it do so excellently, but in that which Beethoven
too accepted (among whose fantasies that in C sharp minor
especially belongs to his least known but most wonderful pianoforte pieces), according to which within a not unusual form and
disposition all the inward things take an unaccustomed and fantastic shape.   Our author uses for his basis an extremely simple,
almost too insignificant melodious song, opposes it to a second,
also very simple one, though it shows more meaning in itself as
well as in its harmonic lay-out, and he now develops out of both
and out of their variants what is after all a closely knit whole,
besides much that is more or less related to them, interposed
between them and variously harmonized and patterned out of
them and around them.   Here and there, perhaps, he plays for
playing's sake—with the instrument, too, which is asked, for
example, to produce sustained notes and chords, like a string
quartet; he repeats too much and becomes altogether too long
for that which he intends to offer, and actually does offer.   (The
movement fills eight closely engraved pages; and if the author's
direction to repeat the first part is obeyed, they grow to eleven.)
Very well played in every respect, and also on a very good instrument, however, the movement remains interesting, although
it would be more so if it were shorter and less repetitive.—The
second movement (*Andante*, 3–8, D major and minor) begins with
a beautiful, gentle song, which is also very beautifully written in
four parts throughout.   It is at once followed by a contrasting,
vigorous second middle section of admirable effectiveness; and
out of both is spun, often with much skill and everywhere with
praiseworthy application as well as with evidences of an original
mind and disposition, a whole which again occupies seven pages,
not counting repeats.   Yet we cannot say that this *Andante*, with
its appeal to mind and emotion, strikes us as too long, and that it
contains anything we should care to miss.—The third movement
is an animated minuet (B minor) with a delightful trio (B major),
approximately in the manner of some in Beethoven's earlier
quartets; not long and, especially after what has gone before,
excellent in its effect.—The finale (*Allegretto*, 4–4, G major) is a
fiery, curious and here and there somewhat freakish bravura

movement, devised like a great, free rondo. It runs on for twelve pages, as though in a single breath, and hardly allows the player and the listener to gasp. The invention, both melodic and harmonic, much of the arrangement and development (especially the throwing together of greater or smaller thematic fragments, &c.), and even the rhythmic element, is strange; but, just as it stands, it shows a notable talent as unmistakably as a firm determination to keep to anything once chosen and a youthful fire that does not flicker out but goes on burning steadily. But then this movement, presented as it should be, is difficult to play, much more so than it looks at a first glance through. Not the finger-work alone—for what daunts the pianoforte players of to-day in that respect?—but much rather the energy, the differentiation of the parts and the bringing out of the themes or at least of the allusions to them: it is this which makes it difficult; and without these things it will merely rush past without even becoming clear to the hearer, and will scarcely leave anything behind in him.

If we have lingered longer over this composition than it is as a rule possible to do with the spate of other novelties of this kind, we regard ourselves as justified by the fact that it is by no means an ordinary one and that it comes from an artist who is still young and who has raised the most pleasurable hopes by several of his works produced so far. To such, we deem, respect should be paid in public, that they may be encouraged and fortified, and the attention of amateurs may be drawn to them; but they should not receive mere general praise and flattery, for they should hear what is thought of their work by others, to whom they too will pay attention, not only in regard to some single works of theirs, but to the path they have chosen for preference; and hear it before they have grown too much accustomed to a road along which they may sometimes have been led less by their own impulses than by outside influence, temporal or local circumstances, and the like, and from which habit prevents them from wishing to depart or, even if they wish it, being able to do so. True, this inability in itself would be no misfortune, provided the road is a good one; but it may not only bring the evil with it that other paths are disregarded which likewise lead to a goal and may be shorter, fairer and more secure, but that the familiar one too is followed more and more without looking, thinking and feeling, precisely because of its familiarity, and taken at a uniform jog-trot: that is to say, one becomes mannered, stiff and one-sided, grows more practised in that one-sidedness, but also colder and more ordinary, or in order to avoid having that appearance becomes exaggerated, eccentric and unpalatable.

[? G. W. Fink.]

This journal had noticed Op. 42 in the spring of 1826 (*see* No. 632).— Ernst Wagner, born in 1769 at Rossdorf in Saxony, had published the novel 'The Travelling Painters' ('Die reisenden Maler') in 1806 and, in 1810, as the continuation of another prose work, the 'Historical Alphabet of an Abecedarian from Henneberg aged Forty' ('Historisches A B C eines vierzigjährigen hennebergischen Fibelschützen').

985. CANTATA to Celebrate the Recovery of Irene von Kiesewetter (xvii. 15), 26th December 1827

(In Italian.)

Like to a streamlet clear and limpid
Thy life, Irene, now doth flow,
Companioned art thou by the Graces:
Faith, Virtue, Friendship with thee go.

Thy pains alone with cruel rigour
A jealous Fate would let us share,
And bitterer still because we knew them
Too many and too hard to bear.

Irene, goddess fair of peace,
Preserve in thee a tranquil heart,
And may for many years of life
Thy filial love still play its part.

Long may she live then, fair Irene,
The darling of our heart,
Long live Irene, fair Irene.

[? Schnitzer.]

Cf. No. 598.   The poet may have been inspired by Metastasio, several
of whose arias and cantatas are addressed to a "bella Irene."   The words
are rather confused.   The cantata begins with male voices in four parts
(? for solo voices) and merges into a mixed chorus, the whole accompanied by two pianofortes, 'which were probably played by Schubert
and Jenger.

986. FROM THE CHRONOLOGICAL LIST of all the . . . Matinées,
    Concerts and Musical Entertainments (Vienna, 1829)

1827. December.   On the 26th . . . In the Musical Society's
hall.   Quartets of Herr Schuppanzigh's . . . 2. New Trio [in
E flat major, Op. 100, vii. 4)] for pianoforte, violin and violoncello, by Schubert; the principal part performed by Herr C. M.
Bocklet [violin—Schuppanzigh, violoncello—Linke].

This printed list, never before quoted from in these documents, contains several concerts known from other sources (cf. No. 1006).—
Leopold von Sonnleithner told Kreissle that in the *andante* of this Trio
(November 1827) Schubert had used one of the Swedish folksongs he had
heard at the Fröhlich sisters' from the tenor Isaak Albert Berg.   Born at
Stockholm in 1803, Berg had studied with Siboni at Copenhagen in 1825–7
(*see* note preceding No. 74), went to Vienna in 1827 with a recommendation from Siboni for Josefine Fröhlich.   According to Anna Fröhlich's
reminiscences it was the *andante* of the G major string Quartet in which
Schubert used this theme; but that work was already finished by the
middle of 1826.   Another tradition has it that Schubert drew upon a
song composed by Berg himself (who was Jenny Lind's teacher later on).
What is certain is that this theme has not so far been identified.—*See*
No. 1043.

987. FROM THE 'SAMMLER,' 29th December 1827

From Haslinger's active offices, whose presses are comparable to
a *perpetuum mobile*, have issued, apart from several interesting pieces
by the favourite masters Franz Schubert and Carl Czerny, new
studies for the pianoforte [by Karl Kessler].

J. Karl Kessler was born in 1800 at Leitmeritz in Bohemia and lived in
Vienna in 1827–30.

'To Music' ('An die Musik'). Autograph Copy for the Album of Albert Sowinski (1827). *See* p. 634

Schubert at Grinzing.   Water-colour by Moritz von
Schwind, from his Cycle, "Die Lachner-Rolle" (1862)

Schubert is shown sipping new wine, with Franz Lachner
and Bauernfeld.   In the background Grinzing Church,
Kahlenberg and Leopoldsberg

1828

'Miriam's Song of Triumph' ('Mirjams Siegesgesang') for Soprano solo and Mixed Chorus with Pianoforte Accompaniment (xvii. 9), March.

Symphony in C major (i. 7), begun March.

Fantasy in F minor for Pianoforte Duet (ix. 24), finished April.

3 Impromptus for Pianoforte (xi. 13), May.

Mass in E flat major (xiii. 6), June.

Songs to poems by Heine, Rellstab and Seidl (so-called 'Swan-Song' ['Schwanengesang']), including 'Serenade' ('Ständchen') and 'The Double' ('Der Doppelgänger'), August–October.

String Quintet in C major (iv. 1), September.

Sonatas for Pianoforte in C minor, A major and B flat major (x. 13–15), finished 26th September.

Hymn for 8 Male Voices with Wind Accompaniment (xvi. 2), October.

---

988. FROM THE 'WIENER ZEITSCHRIFT FÜR KUNST,' &c., 8th January 1828

ON NEW YEAR'S EVE 1828

Roll onward, you ever revoluble seasons,
Into the abyss where we lose you for aye!
The cradle you fashion, the hearse you construct us,
You plunge us in darkness and bring us the day:
Our pleasure and pain you have both in your pow'rs
While fleeting and fast run the changeable hours.

Let happy ones cry: "Do not leave us so quickly,
O day full of glory and joyous emotion!"
Day only replies: "Ever downward I hasten,
Compelled to be lost in Time's infinite ocean;
You hold not, nor speed, if you chatter and palter:
I move to a law no mere mortal will alter."

The sufferer urges, afflicted and lonely,
In hope of some solace to come with the night:
"O day, of all days most inimical, only
Depart and conceal thy derisory light!"
Yet still the sun continues to render
His glory, and answers to tears with his splendour.

For never to human desire and longing
Will mighty, implacable Nature bow;
The sorrow of mortals to still she will venture
Alone when the Godhead's decree doth allow:
No tear will soften, no sigh will reach her,
To grasp human suffering nothing will teach her.

In youth still resplendent, thou livest in glory,
Thy head proudly bearing, luxuriant each lock;
Strong is thy courage, relentless thy purpose,
Thou know'st not the perils at which thou dost mock:
With others who share thy inordinate needs
Wouldst ride upon Helios' galloping steeds.

Yet go and stamp on the earth impatient:
It will not tremble below thy tread;
Thy voice will falter, thy breath be exhausted,
Thy courage broken and strength have fled.
Go, make like a Titan a valiant show:
Yet youth must at last to senility grow.

And you, fair maidens, so trim of figure,
So anxious to lure us with beauty's dower;
Your arts will not rescue your youth and your vigour,
Nor will you retain your enchanting power.
Not now, not to-morrow—and yet it will be:
We 'll see you all past, though no passing we see.

The spells of the poet, the pleasures of singing,
They too will be gone, be they true as they may;
No longer will songs in our party be ringing,
For the singer too will be called away.
The waters from source to the sea must throng,
The singer at last will be lost in his song.

Therefore praise and for ever cherish
Changing instants of our career:
Fortune will age and it will perish
For him who dare never retain it here.
The fruit that the spring's sun doth deploy
In springtime you may and shall enjoy.

Let us then honour the gods' decreeing,
Who gave us these fleeting hours of glee;
They grant us what 's meet, withhold the unseemly,
Which they will never allow us to see;
For in our time we must grow and mature,
To make one day the hereafter sure.

Bauernfeld.

Cf. Schober's New Year's Eve poem for 1823 (No. 338).—The present
poem, which shows Goethe's influence, is in some ways prophetic.
Unlike Schober's poem, it was published immediately.

989. FROM FRANZ VON HARTMANN'S DIARY

1st January 1828: At Schober's. On the stroke of 12 we
(Spaun, Enk, Schober, Schubert, Gahy, Eduard Rössler—a young
medical student from Pest—Bauernfeld, Schwind and we two)
drank mutually to a happy new year in Malaga. Bauernfeld then
read a poem on that time of year. At 2 o'clock we went home,
and on St. Stephen's Square we congratulated Enk on his
birthday . . . To Bogner's coffee-house, where I received a
beautiful, expensive new year's card from the markers, and where

the whole usual party was.   I drank brotherhood with Schober at his place to-day.

Rössler, the son of a man of letters at Pest, was then a boarder at Schober's and thus temporarily Schubert's neighbour.—The markers (*marqueurs*) were the waiters at the coffee-house who chalked up the points at billiards.   It was the custom for waiters to offer each regular frequenter pretty New Year's cards in order to secure correspondingly generous extra gratuities.   These cards were adorned with all sorts of little pictures and tinsel, very much like English valentines, but in later times they were replaced by pocket-books with calendars.

990. FROM FRANZ VON HARTMANN'S DIARY

2nd January 1828: To the ale-house, where Spaun and Schober argued over the duel, and Spaun at last said (quite rightly) that this conversation should stop.   Schober, who was just speaking, was so offended by this as to begin to make a fearful noise about it. Spaun, whose behaviour was exemplary, left at last.   Schober prostituted himself.   When it got somewhat jollier, it was 1.30. All went home.

Duels were prohibited by authority, but regarded in certain circles as a social obligation in cases of real or imaginary affronts.—"Schober prostituted himself" means that he exposed himself by his uncontrolled behaviour.

991. FROM THE PROGRAMME of the Sixth Evening Entertainment held by the Philharmonic Society, 3rd January 1828 (Conductor, Herr Schmiedel)

4. 'Norman's Song,' poem from Walter Scott's 'Lady of the Lake,' set to music by Schubert, performed by Herr Tietze . . .

6. New Quintet, 'Moonlight' ['Mondenschein'], poem by Schober, set to music by Franz Schubert, performed by Herren Tietze, Gross, [Karl] Greisinger, [Anton] Obermüller and Fuchs.

As in the spring of 1827 (*see* No. 822), Schubert was here exceptionally represented with two works.—The Quintet had been written two years earlier.—Gross is Karl Maria (*see* No. 524); Fuchs is Alois (*see* No. 602).

992. Note on the above Programme

Tietze.   Frau Schmiedel, rep.—Tietze, Gross, Greisinger, Ober-müller, Fuchs.   Frau Schmiedel.

Frau Schmiedel accompanied both works.   The song had to be repeated. The Quintet was published by Diabelli in 1831 as Op. posth. 102 with an apocryphal pianoforte accompaniment *ad libitum*.

993. From Franz von Hartmann's Diary

3rd January 1828: To Bogner's; the usual party there.   Spaun, on his arrival and departure, most jovially shook Schober's hand.

994. From the Official 'Wiener Zeitung,' 5th January 1828

At the House of Tobias Haslinger,
Art and Music Dealer in Vienna, in the Graben, in the House of the Austrian Savings Bank, No. 572, are just published and to be had:

Waltzes of Graz
['Grätzer-Walzer']
for Pianoforte solo
by
Franz Schubert.

36 Kreuzer, A.C.

Schubert, Fr., 'Galop of Graz' ['Grätzer-Galoppe'] for the Pianoforte.

10 Kreuzer, for 4 hands, 15 Kreuzer, A.C.

.   .   .   .   .   .

Also to be had in Pest of K. Lichtl, at Graz of Kraer & Deyrkauf and L. Greiner.

These dances were probably written at Graz in September 1827.   They appeared without any dedication: the twelve Waltzes as Op. 91, the Galop as No. 10 of sixteen 'Favorit- oder Lieblings-Galoppe,' most of which

were named after different towns and some of which were by the elder
Strauss and Lanner. The edition for pianoforte duet is by another hand.
In his list of Carnival music for 1828, on the reverse of the title-page of
Op. 91, Haslinger designated the Galop as Op. 92, but not so on the
title-page of his edition, which calls it "Galoppe" in faulty French
(cf. No. 603).

995. FROM FRANZ VON HARTMANN'S DIARY

5th January 1828: To Schober's, who finished reading the
'Funeral Wreaths' ['Totenkränze'] of Zedlitz and began 'The Story of
the Marquise von O.' (by Kleist). Then we went to the ale-house,
where Spaun and Enderes were too, and Dinand. Home at 12.30.

"Readings" had begun at Schober's in the new year once more, having
been dropped since 1824, and they were now to be held each Saturday.—
Zedlitz (see No. 641) had shortly before published his canzoni under the
title of 'Totenkränze.'—Heinrich von Kleist's novel 'Die Marquise von
O****,' had first appeared in a periodical entitled 'Phöbus.'—Dinand is
Ferdinand Sauter.—Schubert is probably not mentioned merely because
he lived in the house.

996. FROM THE BERLIN 'ALLGEMEINE MUSIKALISCHE ZEITUNG,' 9th January 1828

Quartet by F. Schubert, for the Pianoforte, 4 hands, arranged
by C. Schönberg. Halle, K. A. Kümmel.

A highly unsuccessful composition in the style of the old quartets
by Pleyel, in a mediocre pianoforte arrangement. Is Herr Schönberg a friend or an enemy of Herr Schubert's? It is, at any rate,
no proof of friendship to bring such a bungled youthful piece of
work into the light again. Herr Schubert is fortunate that he has
by this time made a better name for himself by other works. The
paper is good, the engraving is worthy of the composition, the
price for the whole work is too dear at 20 silver groats.

C. F. J. Girschner.

This criticism, like the more favourable one in the Leipzig 'Allgemeine
musikalische Zeitung' of 23rd January 1828 (German edition, No. 1030),
is due to an error. The Quartet was not by our Schubert, but by his

namesake of Dresden (*see* No. 102), who had died at the end of 1824 and had published a flute Quartet as Op. 4 in 1817, a work which Friedrich Hofmeister, in his catalogues of 1828 and 1844, attributed to the Viennese Schubert, the second time even with an indication of the key of A minor (instead of G major), which misled Nottebohm into listing this arrangement under Op. 29. The index to the Leipzig journal too gives the work under the name of Schubert of Vienna.—Ignaz Josef Pleyel, born in 1757 at Rupperstal in Lower Austria, who had lived in London in 1792–5, became a famous pianoforte manufacturer in Paris.—Karl Friedrich J. Girschner, born in 1794 at Spandau, was a pianoforte teacher in Berlin.

997. FROM THE OFFICIAL 'GRAZER ZEITUNG,' 10th January 1828

At the House of Kraer & Deyrkauf,
Art and Music Dealers at Graz, in the Herrengasse
in Freiherr von Mandell's House
are to be had at Assimilated Coinage prices:

WALTZES OF GRAZ
['Grätzer-Walzer']
for the Pianoforte
by FRANZ SCHUBERT.

Op. 91.   Price, 36 Kreuzer.

———

GALOP OF GRAZ
['Grätzer-Galoppe']
for the Pianoforte
by FRANZ SCHUBERT.

For Pianoforte solo . . . 10 Kr.
  ,,   ,,   4 hands . . 15 Kr.

998. MARIE VON PRATOBEVERA TO HER BETROTHED, JOSEF BERGMANN, AT CILLI

Vienna, 10th January 1828.

We have already begun the Carnival very agreeably, not dancing, but listening. On Twelfth Night there was a small musical party at uncle's [Dr. Kaspar Wagner] in his own honour.   True, Schubert kept us waiting for him in vain, but for compensation Tietze sang many of his songs so touchingly and soulfully that we did not feel his absence too painfully.   I could have wished, my friend, I might conjure you here, so beautiful and glorious was this feast; and I was especially enraptured by the transfiguration of Marie Wagner, who forgot all her pains and sorrows and was once again as if transported into the earliest years of fair youth from sheer musical enthusiasm.   She played quite well on the pianoforte, too, a four-handed piece by Schubert with Louise Weiss; also, Louise and Marie Weiss sang, and—marvel and wonder!—our little domestic nightingale Fanni also sang 2 songs.   She really has a very agreeable voice and feels what she sings.—My songs were silenced next to this little past-mistress . . .

Marie Elisabeth was the eldest daughter of Karl Josef and the sister of Adolf, Freiherr von Pratobevera (see note preceding No. 628).   Karl Josef's first wife was Josefine, née Raab, a daughter of Leopold Mozart's last landlord at Salzburg, the Viennese barrister Dr. Ignaz Raab, whose other daughter, Antonia, was married to his colleague Kaspar Wagner in Vienna.   Marie, born in 1804, had three sisters who were also musical: Louise, who in 1840 married Marie's widower; Franziska, who married Josef Tremier (see No. 1103A) in 1829; and Bertha, who became the wife of the later Schubert biographer Heinrich Kreissle von Hellborn.—Josef Bergmann, born in 1796 at Hüttenau in the Vorarlberg, had lived in Vienna in 1814–26 and was now professor at the grammar school of Cilli in Styria, to become later an important historian, philologist and classical scholar. The following summer he became third custodian of the Cabinet for Coins and Antiques and did distinguished work on the Ambras collection, so that he was able to marry his betrothed on 20th October 1828.—Wagner, born in 1773 at Trieste, a friend of Zacharias Werner's (died 1823), was a barrister and solicitor (see No. 876 and the present note, above); he lived in the Obere Bäckerstrasse near the old University, and had a musical daughter, Marie, also born in 1804, who had lost her betrothed c. 1825 and married a Dr. Gustav Mitterbacher only in 1842.—For Louise Weiss cf. No. 779.   Marie Weiss, possibly her sister, may have been Marie Mathilde, who sang contralto (see note preceding No. 275). —Fanni is Franziska von Pratobevera.—Marie had given up singing.

999. FROM THE PROGRAMME of the Seventh Evening Entertainment held by the Philharmonic Society, 10th January 1828 (Conductor, Herr Kirchlehner)

4. 'Good Night' ['Gute Nacht'], from the song-cycle, 'The Winter Journey' ['Die Winterreise'], by W. Müller, set to music by F. Schubert, performed by Herr Tietze.

This was the first song of the cycle to be sung at a semi-public concert.

1000. FROM FRANZ VON HARTMANN'S DIARY

12th January 1828: To Schober, where the splendid 'Story of the Marquise von O.' by Kleist was read to the end and a book, 'Travel Notions' ['Reiseideen'] by Heine, begun. Some pleasant things. Much wit. False tendencies. What pleased me most so far were the youthful recollections of Düsseldorf.—To the pub ("The Geese preached at by the Wolf"), where we stayed until after midnight.

Heinrich Heine, Schubert's exact contemporary, had published the first part of his 'Reisebilder' in May 1826, and his 'Buch der Lieder,' also containing these 'Travel Pictures,' in October 1827. The 'Heimkehr' cycle, from which Schubert took his six Heine songs, opened the 'Reisebilder' of 1826. It includes 'The Book Le Grand,' the general title of which is 'Ideas'; among its contents are the recollections of the poet's youth at Düsseldorf. The "false tendencies" are Heine's enthusiasm for Napoleon, of which Hartmann as a good German could not approve. Schubert may have found the poems for his six Heine songs, which later appeared in the 'Swan Song' cycle, in Schober's copy of the 'Travel Pictures,' although Schönstein reported that late in the summer of 1828 Schubert had given him a copy of the 'Book of Songs' with the places of these six poems dog-eared. The titles were added by Schubert in his manuscript: Heine's poems have none.—Cf. No. 1008.

On 13th January 1828, at noon, at the small assembly hall, an anonymous 'Night Song' ('Nachtgesang') for four male voices was performed, which has clearly nothing to do with Schubert's 'Night Song in the Forest' ('Nachtgesang im Walde') accompanied by four horns or pianoforte ad lib. (German edition, Nos. 1016 and 1017: announcement and criticism in the 'Wiener Zeitschrift' of 13th and 24th January 1828 respectively.)

1001. From the Official 'Wiener Zeitung,' 14th January 1828

At the House of Tobias Haslinger,

Music Publisher in Vienna,

in the Graben, in the House of the First Austrian Savings Bank,

No. 572,

is just published and to be had:

(In Pest of K. Lichtl.—At Hermannstadt of W. H. Thierry.
—At Graz of Kraer & Deyrkauf.—L. Greiner.)

Winter Journey

['Winterreise']

by

Wilhelm Müller.

Set to Music

for One Voice with Pianoforte Accompaniment

by

Franz Schubert.

Work 89.

Bound in Coloured Cover.

Price, 3 Florins, A.C.

Property of the Publisher.

Part I, containing:

No. 1. 'Good Night' ['Gute Nacht'].—2. 'The Weather Vane' ['Die Wetterfahne'].—3. 'Frozen Tears' ['Gefrorene Thränen']. —4. 'Numbness' ['Erstarrung'].—5. 'The Lime-Tree' ['Der Lindenbaum'].—6. 'Flood' ['Wasserflut'].—7. 'On the River' ['Auf dem Flusse'].—8. 'Retrospect' ['Rückblick'].—9. 'Will-o'-the-Wisp' ['Irrlicht'].—10. 'Rest' ['Rast'].—11. 'Dream of Spring' ['Frühlingstraum'].—12. 'Solitude' ['Einsamkeit'].

This cycle of songs, the first part of which is herewith submitted to the art-loving public, and whose second half will follow as soon as possible, is the latest product of the mind of a composer who is justly esteemed for his treatments of numerous poems, and who here proves anew the powers he possesses in this direction particularly. Any poet may congratulate himself who is so well understood by his composer, understood alike with warm feeling and with daring imagination, and indeed only thus has his dead letter called into active life by all-powerful sound.

The publisher may flatter himself on having neglected nothing on his side in contributing towards the outwardly pleasing appearance of so valuable a gift.

Hermannstadt (Nágy-Szében) was the capital of Transylvania in Hungary. —Op. 89 appeared without a dedication in a blue-green cover with a white vignette, the first part after Opp. 90 and 91, the second only on 30th December (thus after Schubert's death).

1002. FROM THE OFFICIAL 'GRAZER ZEITUNG,' 14th January 1828

At the Art and Music Establishment
of J. L. Greiner at Graz, in the Herrengasse, No. 198,
are to be had at Assimilated Coinage prices:

DANCE-GIFTS

WALTZES OF GRAZ.
['Grätzer Walzer']
for the Pianoforte by FR. SCHUBERT.   36 Kreuzer.

GALOPS OF GRAZ
['Grätzer Galoppe']
for the Pianoforte by FR. SCHUBERT,
for 4 hands, 15 Kr.; solo, 10 Kr.

1003. FROM THE DRESDEN 'ABENDZEITUNG,' 19th March 1828
(Vienna correspondence, early 1828.)

Musical composition too tends towards littleness. . . . An honourable exception is made by the inspired Schubert with his songs. They have cleared a path for themselves through the welter, and this characteristic composer's name already resounds honourably from all lips, just as his songs are sung wherever triplet frippery has not yet ousted all feeling for truth and beauty.

[? Höhler.]

The critic either forgot the accompaniment of 'Erl King' or did not think of it as "triplet frippery."

1004. FROM FRANZ VON HARTMANN'S DIARY

15th January 1828: To Bogner's, where I learn from Clodi that Spaun is to marry Fräulein Roner, who, it is true, is 30 years of age, but very nice, cultivated and pretty; with which I am delighted.

Schubert Serenading the Future Occupants of an Un-finished House. Water-colour by Moritz von Schwind, from his Cycle, "Die Lachner-Rolle" (1862)

Schubert is singing with Franz Lachner, Schwind and Bauernfeld

Josef von Spaun had become secretly engaged on 6th January, and this was now becoming known. For his betrothed *see* No. 862. She was actually thirty-two, but even so seven years younger than he.

1005. FROM FRANZ VON HARTMANN'S DIARY

16th January 1828: To the pub, where all the pub-crawlers got together. Spaun now no longer made a secret of his marriage to us, which occasioned the most amusing discourses. Not home till 12.15.

1006. FROM THE 'CHRONOLOGICAL LIST of all the . . . Matinées,
  Concerts and Musical Entertainments' (Vienna, 1829)

1828. January. On the 17th. In the Society's hall. Eighth Evening Entertainment. . . . 4. 'The Gondolier' ['Der Gondelfahrer'], by Schubert, performed by Herren Schnitzer, Gross, Greisinger and Tobiaschek.

There is no other evidence for this concert either (cf. No. 986). In the book published in 1829 it is erroneously dated 1827. The singers are Kolumban Schnitzer, Karl Maria Gross, Karl Greisinger and Josef Tobiaschek. This last may be identical with Josef Kalasanz Tobiaschek, born in 1792 at Slepotitz in Bohemia, settled in Vienna since about 1813, who studied with Salieri and attended Kiesewetter's lectures on harmony; later a teacher of singing at Teltsch in Moravia.

1007. SCHUBERT TO ANSELM HÜTTENBRENNER

[Outside:]   To
                      Anselm Hüttenbrenner, Esq.,
                          Landowner in the Rosental
                                          at
                                              Graz.
[Inside:]
                              Vienna, 18th January 1828.
My dear old Hüttenbrenner,
    You must be surprised at my writing for once. I too. But if I do write, it is because I have a purpose. Listen, then: there is a drawing-master's post vacant at your Graz, and the competition for it is announced. My brother Carl, whom perhaps you

know too, wishes to obtain this post.   He is greatly skilled, both as landscape painter and as draughtsman.   Now if you could do something for him in this matter, I should be infinitely obliged to you.   You are a powerful man at Graz and may know somebody in the county council or someone else who has influence.—My brother is married and has a family, and it would thus be an excellent thing for him to obtain a safe appointment.   I hope you are very well, and also your dear family and your brothers.   My heartiest greetings to all.   Recently a new Trio of mine for pianoforte, violin and violoncello was performed at Schuppanzigh's and pleased very much.   It was admirably executed by Bocklet, Schuppanzigh and Linke.   Have you done nothing new?   Apropos, why do the two songs at Greiner's, or whatever his name is, not appear?   What is the meaning of it?   The deuce!!!

I repeat my above request, and only remember that what you do for my brother, you do for me,

In expectation of agreeable news,

I remain

Your faithful friend

until death.

Frz. Schubert.

This letter is in the British Museum.   It bears the postmark "Vienna, 20th January."—The name of the property was not Rosental, but Rosenegg, and it was at Geidorf, now a suburb of Graz.   The Hüttenbrenners' other property was Rotenturm near Judenburg in Styria.—The 'Steiermärkisches Amtsblatt,' a supplement to the 'Grazer Zeitung,' had advertised a competition for the post of drawing-master in the fourth form of the training-school at Graz on 11th December 1827; examinations to be held on 31st January at Graz or Vienna.   The salary offered was 500 florins, A.C.—Karl Schubert had two sons.—Anselm's brothers at Graz were Andreas and Heinrich Hüttenbrenner (see No. 150).—For the Trio see No. 986.—Hüttenbrenner was then occupied with the opera 'Charles of England, or Woodstock Castle' (libretto by Ignaz Kollmann, after Scott), which he never finished.—The two songs were 'In the Forest' ('Im Walde') and 'On the Bruck' ('Auf der Bruck'), which were however not published by Johann Lorenz Greiner, but by Josef Andreas Kienreich at Graz (see No. 1103).—The phrase "until death" here appears for the first time in Schubert's letters, and this was the last to Anselm Hüttenbrenner, so far as we know.—Cf. No. 1022.

1008. From Franz von Hartmann's Diary

19th January 1828: To Schober's, where Heine's 'Travel Notions' were read to the end. Then to the pub, to which Ottenwalt and Spaun came too, and altogether 13 acquaintances. Not till midnight did we pack off home.

Cf. No. 1000.—Ottenwalt had gone to Vienna because of his doctor's degree (cf. No. 1019).

1009. From the Programme of Josef Slawjk's Concert, 20th January 1828, at 12.30 p.m., in the County Hall

6. Fantasy for pianoforte and violin [viii. 5], by Franz Schubert, performed by Herr Karl Maria von Bocklet and the concert-giver.

For Slawjk *see* note preceding No. 788.—The Fantasy, not published until 1850 as Op. posth. 159, contains in its third movement variations on the song 'Greetings to thee' ('Sei mir gegrüsst'). (About this time, probably as early as the summer of 1827, the song itself, sung by the Court Opera singer Ludwig Cramolini [born Vienna, 1805] and accompanied by Friedrich Kappus von Pichelstein, had been used to conciliate Kappus's betrothed, Marie von Berthold. Schubert, Merk and Schuppanzigh—evidently fee'd by Kappus, as was Cramolini—are said to have taken part in this birthday serenade in the village of Kahlenberg near Vienna.) The matinée produced among other things a new violin Concerto by Slawjk. —An announcement of this concert appeared in the 'Theaterzeitung' of 17th January (German edition, No. 1025).

1010. From the 'Theaterzeitung,' 29th January 1828

Herr Slawjk performed . . . a Fantasy for violin and pianoforte with Herr Karl Maria von Bocklet, composed by Herr Schubert. . . . How much he still lacks as a solid violinist was seen conspicuously enough in Schubert's Fantasy, a piece of music which, it is true, can be enjoyed as it deserves only in a smaller room and by an audience of true connoisseurs; even when it is performed by players wholly fitted for it, for which Bocklet is the right man.

1011. From the 'Sammler,' 7th February 1828

The Fantasy . . . occupied rather too much of the time a Viennese is prepared to devote to pleasures of the mind. The hall emptied gradually, and the writer confesses that he too is unable to say anything about the conclusion of this piece of music.

The concert took place at midday.

1012. From the Leipzig 'Allgemeine Musikalische Zeitung,' 2nd April 1828

A new Fantasy for pianoforte and violin, by Franz Schubert, refused to please in any way. The verdict that might fairly be pronounced on it is that the favourite composer has in this case positively miscomposed.

This notice reports by mistake that the concert took place at the Kärntnertor Theatre and on 5th February. The writer was obviously not present. Cf. No. 1081.

1013. From the 'Harmonicon,' London, July 1828

A new Fantasia, for pianoforte and violin, from the pen of Franz Schubert possesses merit far above the common order.

1013A. Marie von Pratobevera to her Betrothed, Josef Bergmann at Cilli

Vienna, 22nd January 1828.

Our little nightingale really does sing soulfully, especially the latest songs by Schubert, 'The Winter Journey.' A number of connected songs, a companion-piece to the 'Maid of the Mill' songs, by the same poet and also nearly identical in content. Laments over a sweetheart's faithlessness. One pleases me uncommonly well, so that I must write it down for you:

FLOOD
[4 verses follow.]

The music is equally sorrowful, it fits the words entirely, and to hear it beautifully sung makes an infinite impression. Especially in connection with the rest. I should have liked to write them all down for you, but I should have to send you books, not letters any longer, if I were to carry out this purpose.

The "nightingale" is Marie's sister Franziska. She sang songs from the first part of the 'Winter Journey.'

1014. FROM THE LEIPZIG 'ALLGEMEINE MUSIKALISCHE ZEITUNG,' 23rd January 1828

1) 'Homesickness' ['Das Heimweh']. 'Omnipotence' ['Die Allmacht']. Poems by Ladislaus Pyrker—set to music for one voice, with pianoforte accompaniment, by Franz Schubert. Work 79. Vienna, Haslinger. (Price, 16 Groschen.)

2) 'The Wayfarer Addressing the Moon' ['Der Wanderer an den Mond']. 'The Passing-Bell ['Das Zügenglöcklein']. 'In the Open' ['Im Freien']. Poems by J. G. Seidl. As above. Work 80. (Price, 16 Gr.)

3) 'Alinde.' 'To·the Lute' ['An die Laute']. 'For Goodnight' ['Zur guten Nacht']. Poems by Friedrich Rochlitz. Do. Work 81. (Price, 16 Gr.)

These are the latest books of songs and more or less developed vocal pieces by the composer mentioned, who for some time has been not a little valued and liked everywhere; and several pieces in them evidently rank with his most excellent. What has been praised or blamed in Herr S.'s songs in these pages, and elsewhere afterwards, that is to be praised and blamed in the present ones also, but with the difference that one now finds more occasion than of yore for the former and less for the latter, and that again

is praise in itself.   If those judgments, as they were pronounced
and as they here confirm themselves anew, are gathered together
in their essentials, they come to the following: Herr S. knows how
to choose poems which are really good (in themselves and for
musical treatment) and have not yet been used up either; he is
capable and usually succeeds in discovering in each what predominates emotionally and therefore for music, and above all he
places that into his generally simple melody, while he allows his
accompaniment, which however is very rarely mere accompaniment, to paint this further, and for that purpose he is fond of using
images, parables or scenic features in the poems.   In both he
often shows originality of invention and execution, sound knowledge of harmony and honest industry: on the other hand he often,
and sometimes very greatly, oversteps the species in hand, or
else that which should by rights have been developed in such and
such a piece; he likes to labour at the harmonies for the sake of
being new and piquant; and he is inordinately addicted to giving
too many notes to the pianoforte part, either at once or in succession.   Now those praiseworthy things, as the reader will readily
see, are decisive and lasting in art—as regards effect, first of all,
but not exclusively; those which we have blamed, although not
altogether negligible, yet belong to what a young artist who thinks
and who pays heed to friendly advice will gradually abandon,
especially as it is usually but adopted as a sign of the times, which
now everywhere strive towards extremes, or follows some model
which cleverly exercised them or made a sensation with them; or,
if not adopted, then it comes from within, in which case it is part
of youthfulness and will pass quickly enough with youth itself.
After which general preliminaries, let us briefly go through the
separate books.

   Work 79. Excellent poems (especially the second, a noble
psalm), each not only composed continuously, but carried out
broadly, the first so to speak scenically.   The melody of the first
is suitably and effectively based on an allusion to the Swiss *ranz
des vaches* of the Emmental, and even more so is the developed and
always important accompaniment, and its use is very successful.
It makes its deepest impression where, on p. 9, it returns after

an effective interlude and is now firmly retained to the end.   The
second is truly grand, solemn and fervent.   Properly performed
(which however requires a capable, resounding voice and a
vividly feeling heart), it can surely nowhere fail to make a profound
impression.   The voice part of this second piece, although expressive and at the same time infallibly significant in detail, is
nevertheless simple and approaches a grandiose declamatory style.
The accompaniment is not figured, but moves almost throughout
in broken chord sequences that keep closely to the voice, but in
weighty and capitally laid-out ones.   We not only praise this piece,
but gratefully wish its author good fortune with it.   Only two
remarks we will permit ourselves: the words "Blickst du flehend"
&c. (the first time, p. 16) should be more closely related to
what has gone before by metrical relationship and harmonic
modulation; and then, the antique metres, suitably as they are used
by the venerable Pyrker, would by rights allow of even fewer
repetitions than Herr S. has assigned them, especially in the first
piece.   Only generalizing, and particularly emphatic and sen-
tentious terminations should be repeated there, if it is considered
necessary or advisable at all.

Work 80.   The poems are pretty; but for the purpose of musical
composition one could wish for a more careful linguistic finish
and desire at least that they should be free of false accents and make
fewer words on that which they express; all of which has made the
avoidance of all that is long-winded and monotonous not a little
difficult for Herr S., since he wished to remain praiseworthily
faithful throughout all the verses, not only to the melody, but also
(in essentials) to the chosen accompaniment, particularly in Nos. 2
and 3.   He has achieved this avoidance, so far as it was possible
in these circumstances; but the singer and pianist must put much
variety into their delivery, if the faults are not to show through
somewhat in the last number.   In the first the poet's false accentuation has induced the composer from the first to exhibit this
falseness even more and to make it much more noticeable in his
endeavour to remain true to a melody which is entirely appropriate
to the whole.   But no doubt he ought to have made a virtue of
necessity here and might have helped things on a little, even if

he did not wish to interfere as decisively as it would have been necessary to do without regard to the other verses, viz.:

Ich   auf der Erd',   am   Him-mel   du: wir

and similarly in the corresponding line. Disregarding this and considering only the total impression on our feelings, this song, with its extremely simple melody, its slightly varying accompaniment and its transition into the major, is pretty.—'The Passing-Bell,' no doubt a provincialism for a small angelus bell, which is pulled, not trodden, touches both the strings and the heart more profoundly. This too, besides, is a well turned-out musical work of art; for the bell takes its note, E♭-in-altissimo, as the fifth of the song's keynote, and continually strikes in the same way in the accompaniment—always lying high and to be always clearly brought out in performance with the little finger—throughout all the verses (and that means for five pages, since they are continuously composed, although in essentials they remain similar to one another), while the melody and the very select harmony carry on quite freely and unconstrainedly. On pp. 8 and 10 alone is the busy sexton allowed to rest for three bars, whereafter he must be at it again. It is a delightful piece.—The third number, 'In the Open,' likewise gentle in character, is laid out in the opposite direction, although here too the melody is kept simple and the important accompaniment uniform. While in the second song the thought and the harmonic refinement was decisive, here it is the sound of the instrument itself, to be treated as discreetly and delicately as possible, which proves decisive. With such treatment the singer's simple melody will not be covered up too much; the piece, nine pages long, will in such a performance at least have as much variety as it needs, and the whole will doubtless be heard with pleasure.

Work 81. Poems by F. Rochlitz, very well chosen. Much as they resemble each other in clarity of expression and natural

representation of inward life, as musical poetry always should,
they are yet sufficiently differentiated by their genuine character.
The first is playfully serious, the second endearingly tender and the
third soulful and deeply moving. The first was not easy to treat
well musically. It is in stanzas which correspond exactly to each
other, so that each had to be given the same music. But they are
in dialogue, indeed, so to speak, scenic, so that at the same time
the very different and contrasted speakers had to be set differently
and in contrast. Nevertheless the tone of speech and the lay-out
are quite simple, and the music too had to remain so. Herr S.
did in fact treat it thus. As regards the first point, the stanzas
are certainly set out separately, and a few departures are to be
found; but only small and not disturbing ones. As to the second
(the contrast between the personages), it is contained in the music
decisively and clearly enough; and the third (the very simple
treatment) has likewise been observed, with the exception of
a few harmonic turns, which first occur on p. 3, bar 1, then in
bar 4 and the transition to 5, and which seem to us, for this
particular piece, to sound a little too abrupt and therefore too
hard. The second song is attractive: the accompaniment, since
it refers to the lute, is kept in the lutenist manner; all is as secretive
as a furtive serenade. The third is an equally simple sociable song
that will easily find access wherever people are not wont to sing
merely of wine, love and jesting. One singer introduces it; the
chorus repeats the last lines; the accompaniment merely gives
the chords for the solo and afterwards supports the *tutti*. Only the
last six repeated notes of each verse impair the seriousness of the
whole by their horn-like and commonplace close. We recommend
that they should be omitted without more ado. Although we are
bound to declare these three pieces too as well turned out and even
suspect ourselves of detecting in them a special care to do justice to
the poems according to their own nature, it yet seems to us that
Herr S.'s disposition and habit draws him more readily towards that
which demands much music as to that which needs little; and that
he therefore moves more freely in the former than in the latter.

All three little works are well engraved.

[? G. W. Fink.]

The strophic form, which was still understood by "song" (*Lied*), is here opposed to the continuously set vocal piece called *Gesang*.—The observation that Schubert made use of the Emmental *ranz des vaches* ("chanson de l'Emmental") is not convincing; the reference is evidently to the song in Swiss dialect, 'Es isch key sölige Stamme' ('There is no happier calling') in the 'Sammlung von Schweizer Kuhreigen' (Bern, 1812, p. 11; 1826, p. 10).—The passing-bell (*Zügenglöcklein*) in Austria is a small funeral bell to be found in every Catholic church and rung only when one of its own parishioners is known to be dying, as a call to prayer to the others.—Rochlitz was the founder of this periodical.—In the same issue appeared a notice of the arrangement of the spurious quartet mentioned in No. 996 (German edition, No. 1030).

1015. FROM FRANZ VON HARTMANN'S DIARY

23rd January 1828: To Schwind's, where there was some nasty bawling . . . Then to the pub, where it was quite jolly. Not home till 12 o'clock.

Schwind was still living with his mother at the Moonshine House near the Karl church.

1016. FROM THE PROGRAMME of the Ninth Evening Entertainment held by the Philharmonic Society, 24th January 1828 (Conductor, Herr Bogner)

4. 'The Serenade' ['Das Ständchen'], poem by Herr Grillparzer, set to music by Schubert, performed by Fräulein [Josefine] Fröhlich (both in manuscript).

Cf. note preceding No. 922.—This was the first semi-public performance. Bogner was Anna and Josefine Fröhlich's brother-in-law. Anna, whose pupils sang the chorus, was the organizer. She sent for Schubert, who lived next door, but very nearly missed the performance once again; Walcher and Jenger found him in Leonhard Wanner's ale-house the "Oak-Tree" on the Brandstätte, not far from the "Red Hedgehog" and the "Blue Hedgehog." (Beethoven and Grillparzer had frequented the "Oak" in 1826; cf. No. 581.) Schubert seems to have said to Anna Fröhlich after the performance: "Really, I never thought it was so beautiful."

1017. FROM THE LEIPZIG 'ALLGEMEINE MUSIKALISCHE ZEITUNG,'
26th March 1828

On the 24th [January] we heard . . . at the Society's evening
circle a new Serenade, poem by Grillparzer and set to music by
Schubert, which Fräulein Fröhlich performed with a girls' chorus
and which counts among the most charming of this favourite
composer's works.

1018. FROM THE OFFICIAL 'WIENER ZEITUNG,' 26th January 1828

At the House of M. J. Leidesdorf,
Art and Music Dealer, in the Kärntnerstrasse,
is just published and to be had:

DANCES OF GOTHAM
['Krähwinkler Tänze']
composed for the Pianoforte
by various masters.

Book I: The Gothamites are holding a ball and roister right heartily.

Book II: A citizen's wife of Gotham opens the ball with a
"German."

Book III: Domestic entertainment in a "closed circle" at Gotham;
each book à 30 Kreuzer, A.C.

After Sauer's secession Leidesdorf had become the sole owner of the
publishing house.—For the 'Dances of Gotham' see Nos. 611 and 754.
The new third book evidently contained nothing by Schubert. Its
title-page alone is preserved: it is worded 'Continuation of the Favourite
Dances of Gotham' ('Fortsetzung der beliebten Krähwinkler Tänze,'
formerly in the Georg Eckl collection in Vienna). The vignettes described in the advertisement, which illustrate puns, are anonymous
lithographs: the first (which served for two fascicles) puns on the word
"ball," for it represents a dance, but also shows the globe being held
in the shape of a large ball; the second refers to a "German dance"
(country dance), but shows a German in national costume dancing with a
Gotham lady; the third is a round dance (?) with the dancers in chains.

1019. FROM FRANZ VON HARTMANN'S DIARY

26th January 1828: At Ottenwalt's very fine lecture. To Bogner's; Marl, Schober, Clodi there. Very fine dispute about action, deed and word. To Schober's, who read us Kleist's tale of 'The Combat' ['Der Zweikampf']. Merry pub-crawling until 12.30.

The theme of Ottenwalt's legal discourse is not known. Aged nearly forty, he had taken a doctor's degree in order to become assistant in the Chamber Procuratorship in Vienna two years later.—The "dispute" may have been connected with the lecture.—"Marl" is Karl Maurus Mayrhofer.—Heinrich von Kleist's 'Combat' had appeared in 1811 in the second volume of his 'Tales.'

1020. FRANZISKA VON RONER TO ANTONIE OSTER

[? January] 28th [? 1828].

It is with pleasure that I inform you that we are, so to say, certain of the singer Vogl's collaboration in your concert. In order, however, to leave no stone unturned, I ask you in the name of my friend Frau Witteczek to be present at an evening party which is to take place at her house the day after to-morrow, as Vogl and Schubert are to be there too. If your father gives you permission for this, as I hope, I shall discuss details with him to-morrow morning.

Cf. No. 862.—Antonie Oster's concert took place on 9th March at the County Hall, with the assistance of the cellist Leopold Böhm (born Vienna, 1806) of the Theater an der Wien, who is not identical with the violinist of that name (see No. 513). Vogl did not take part. Cf. No. 1024.

1021. FROM FRANZ VON HARTMANN'S DIARY

28th January 1828: With Enk, Louis and Jérôme to Spaun's, where glorious music was made by Schuppanzigh, Bocklet, Linke, Schubert and Gahy. The Prelate of [St.] Florian and the two

Maiers, the Ottenwalts, Spaun's very nice betrothed, &c., were there, altogether fifty people. We nearly all got tipsy. We danced. I a great deal with Frau von Ottenwalt. Then we nearly all went to Bogner's, where we sat on till 2.30.

This was the last Schubertiad at Josef von Spaun's, given in honour of his betrothed in his official lodgings, the "Nag's Stables" (*Klepperställe*) in the Teinfaltstrasse. Spaun describes the evening in his recollections of Schubert, who brought Bocklet, Schuppanzigh and Linke with him for a performance of one of his pianoforte Trios (probably the one in B flat major) and played entrancingly with Bocklet a set of pianoforte duet variations on a theme of his own (perhaps those in A flat major). Bocklet is said to have kissed Schubert afterwards. Probably Schubert and Gahy then played for dancing.—Jérôme (Hieronymus) von Kleimayrn, born in 1808, was an officer.—The prelate was Michael von Arneth (*see* No. 364). —The two "Maiers" from St. Florian were Theophil Friedrich Mayr, known as "the Swede," who later became Arneth's successor, and Friedrich Gottlieb Mayer, at that time a deacon (*see* No. 681).—Marie Ottenwalt had again gone to Vienna with her husband.

1022. JENGER TO FRAU PACHLER

Vienna, 29th January 1828.

Above all I now have to discuss two affairs of our friend Tubby —who sends many compliments to you and friend Dr. Karl and dear Faust—concerning which he has himself partly written to Dr. Karl himself—if it 's true, I must add.

The thing is that at the Training School of Graz the drawing-master's post is vacant, for which a brother of our Tubby will compete and enter the competition here, and that on the 31st inst.—The required examination papers will then be immediately sent from here to the County Council at Graz, which offers this post. Who is responsible for it on the Council I do not know. So much is certain, however, that friend Pachler can do a great deal in the matter, nor will he be unwilling to do so, no doubt.

I think, therefore, that our old friend Begutter, Baron Schimmelfenning, Anselm Hüttenbrenner, will be able to do much, through Councillor Gindl, &c. &c., for the realization of friend T[ubby]'s dearest wish, if, that is, Dr. Carlos would urge them thereto, and in order that he may do this I request your kind intervention.

Success in this matter would be one more cause for T. to revisit the dear Grazers quite soon, which however may also occur sooner than he realizes at present, and for the following reason:

Irene, the daughter of my [superior,] Court Councillor Kiesewetter—the lady of whom, so far as I remember, I have often talked to you as being one of the foremost pianoforte players in Vienna—has recently recovered from a serious illness. Now her doctor has recommended her a small journey in the coming spring by way of a change of air, and upon my further suggestion a short trip into Styria might be preferentially chosen for this purpose because the mother and daughter have long desired to get to know this land of promise and its dear inhabitants—about whom I have spoken to them I don't know how often.—If this comes to pass, Tubby and I will travel with them as couriers, and thus we should see you all in a few months.

Another concern of friend T.'s is that you, dear lady, will kindly allow written permission to be sought by a fair hand for the engraving of a book of songs Schubert has dedicated to you, so that the manuscript need not be sent to Graz. I have already spoken about it to Fräulein Irene, and she will gladly take this upon herself. But this ought to be done very soon, and I therefore beg for your very speedy permission. . . .

Anselm Hüttenbrenner is a slacker and waster not to look after the two Schubert songs at Kienreich's and to see that they are engraved at last.

Cf. No. 1007.—Schubert had probably written only to Anselm Hüttenbrenner in this matter, and not to Pachler. — Franz Anselm Begutter was director of the training school at Graz; Josef, Freiherr von Schimmelfenning, was secretary to the Styrian County Government; Josef Gindl was a government councillor there and a canon at the abbey of Seckau. Begutter and Gindl, like Schubert, were honorary members of the Styrian Musical Society.—Carlos is Dr. Pachler.—Kiesewetter was Jenger's superior in the Court War Council.—"So far as I remember" is apparently said ironically, for Jenger had often raved about Irene.—For her illness cf. No. 985. Her physician was probably Dr. Menz (see No. 968). Her mother, Jakobine, née Cavallo, came from Heidelberg.—Fräulein

Kiesewetter was to be authorized by Frau Pachler to write the permission for the dedication of Op. 106 (*see* note preceding No. 1115) on its proof on her behalf, which she did.—For the two songs printed at Graz *see* Nos. 1007 and 1103.—Karl Schubert did not obtain the post.—The Kiesewetters did not go to Graz.

1023. FROM THE LEIPZIG 'ALLGEMEINE MUSIKALISCHE ZEITUNG,' 30th January 1828

No. I. *L'incanto degli occhi* ('Spell of the Eyes'). No. II. *Il traditor deluso* ('The Traitor Duped'). No. III. *Il modo di prender moglie* ('The Way to take a Wife'). Poems by Metastasio. Set to music for a bass voice with pianoforte accompaniment, &c., by Franz Schubert. Work 83. Vienna, Tobias Haslinger. Price, No. I, 1 Fl. 24 Kr. No. II, 2 Fl. 36 Kr., No. III, 3 Fl. 36 Kr.

These three developed songs by the generally lauded and favoured composer, designated as a single work, were recently published in three well-engraved books and are certainly quite as commendable on the whole as the songs by the same tone-poet which have recently been made advantageously known by detailed criticisms in these pages. It is therefore to be hoped that these songs too will shortly find numerous friends, as they deserve, the more so because the poems by the immortal Metastasio have been underlaid with a fluent German translation. It has already been observed earlier that the composer as a rule has the happy fore-sight to choose from the rich store of poetry words which, interesting in themselves, are suitable for musical treatment, a scrupulosity we cannot sufficiently recommend to young composers, especially in the domain of song, where good poetry matters far more than many musicians still appear to believe, quite erroneously.

The first song is very unassuming and melodious, yet furnished, according to the composer's predilection, with some unexpected but skilfully applied modulations, which lend one charm the more to chains of melody that are very singable, easily grasped and most advantageous to a good bass voice. If some few passing notes form insignificant false relations of the kind no longer noticed nowadays but wholly unnecessary in our opinion, they are yet not nearly so obtrusive as many of those which are now the order of the day.

The second song is kept scenic throughout. It begins with a short recitative, in which the opening of the German words, "Weh mir," is indistinct, the first syllable being made short. Everything else is treated commensurately with the despairing traitor's terror-stricken, horrified state of mind. The introductory recitative is followed by an *allegro molto* in E minor. Although some melodic repetitions almost irresistibly recall Mozart here and there, and some drastic modulations begin by appearing very daring, as many a hearer may feel, some possible slight reminiscences of the master after whose pattern the whole is organized cannot in the least impair its well-contrived characteristic expression, and the harmonic audacities, now we are accustomed to far more dreadful wolf's glens, will very soon be regarded as appropriate to the despairing subject, the more readily because the melody must be called extremely favourable to a good bass voice.

The third song is far more lightly taken than the preceding one, as the subject demands. The chief character of the whole is fresh resoluteness of a daintily playful kind, incidentally half disclosing a lightly ironic tinge, which greatly enhances one's pleasure. From the very opening the verse "Must quickly catch a woman" is very well prepared by a modulation proceeding rapidly from chord to chord. The first *allegro ma non troppo*, which fills far more than half the song, is also worked to Mozart's model. It merges into an *allegro vivace* and from 6–8 into 4–4 time, which last is provided with so brilliant a close that the singer could shine to his heart's content with that alone. Signor Luigi Lablache, to whom these three numbers are dedicated, is sure to make a furore with them.

It will be seen from these short descriptions that each of the three pieces is kept in a character wholly different from that of the others: the first is placid, the second passionately wild and the third sprightly in tone. All three are very well suited to sociable entertainments.

[? G. W. Fink.]

The poem of the third song is not by Metastasio (*see* No. 941).—The "detailed criticism" is No. 1014.—The translation may be by Craigher (*see* No. 596).—"Far more dreadful wolf's glens" is doubtless an allusion to the second scene of Act II in Weber's 'Freischütz.'

1024. From Franz von Hartmann's Diary

30th January 1828: Pepi Spaun took us, with Ottenwalt, to the Court Secretary Witteczek, where at first there was a Schubertiad, then supper, then a ball, then a drinking-bout, all very jolly. He, she and the mother-in-law were uncommonly nice already. Then the Drossdicks, the Kübecks and still others arrived. It was 2 o'clock before we left, in the seventh heaven.

Cf. No. 1020.—Josef von Spaun's betrothed and her future sister-in-law, Frau Ottenwalt, were probably also present.—Witteczek's mother-in-law is the widow Watteroth.—For Drossdick cf. No. 794.—The Kübecks are probably Karl Friedrich Kübeck, Freiherr von Kübau, born in 1780 at Iglau in Bohemia, minister of finance, and his second wife, Julie, *née* Lang in 1805, whom he had married in 1827.

1025. From the Programme of the Tenth Evening Entertainment held by the Philharmonic Society, 31st January 1828 (Conductor, Herr Fischer)

2. 'Ellen's Song,' poem from Walter Scott's 'Lady of the Lake,' set to music by F. Schubert, performed by Fräulein [Theresia] Josephi.

This was Schubert's birthday, his last.—'Ellen's Song' was probably the third, the famous 'Ave Maria.'

1026. From the Official 'Wiener Zeitung,' 31st January 1828

(Announcement of the concert given by Leopold Jansa, violinist and member of the I. & R. Court Chapel, 2nd February 1828, at noon, in the County Hall.)

. . . The remaining numbers consist of . . . a song by Franz Schubert . . .

For Jansa *see* No. 525.—Another announcement appeared on the same day in the 'Theaterzeitung' (German edition, No. 1042).—Schubert himself accompanied.

1027. FROM THE 'THEATERZEITUNG,' 9th February 1828

Herr Tietze, the most honourably known tenor singer, praise-worthy particularly in the performance of soulful German songs, sang a song from Walter Scott's 'Ivanhoe,' set by Herr Schubert, with general applause. It is the song of Richard, Cœur de Lion, a quite excellently turned-out composition. In it Schubert's genius once again soars upward in the rosy light of the romantic sphere with such graceful motion that it affords a delightful pleasure to listen to the strong and assured beating of his wings. The composition is so touchingly simple in its melody, so rich and yet so comprehensible in its modulations, and its unity is attained with such certainty by the continuous figure of the accompaniment, that this song is bound to produce a truly elevated state of mind in all those who appreciate a sensitive composition. The romantic bent of the vigorous hero Cœur de Lion is truly painted in sound.

1028. FROM THE 'WIENER ZEITSCHRIFT FÜR KUNST,' &c., 14th February 1828

The song of 'Richard, Cœur de Lion' by Franz Schubert was sung as an intermezzo by our valiant amateur, Herr Tietze, and accompanied at the pianoforte by the composer himself. The tempo was evidently too fast, that is to say for the singer, though not for the composer. The singer had too hard a fight with the syllables, but was in good voice and sang movingly. The public honoured them both with applause.

1029. FROM FRANZ VON HARTMANN'S DIARY

2nd February 1828 (Candlemas): Schober fetched us, whereupon there was a reading at his place. Kleist's 'Foundling' was read there, and the divine 'Prometheus' by Aeschylus. Afterwards we went to the pub, where there was such a to-do with the un-mannerly hostess, and therefore also with her husband, that we all

resolved never to go there again.   For all that, we stayed until
after midnight, and at last went home.

Kleist's 'Foundling' ('Der Findling') had appeared in the same volume
as his 'Combat' (*see* No. 1019).

1030. From Franz von Hartmann's Diary

4th February 1828: I went to the ale-house of the "Burgundian
Cross," where however one cannot smoke.   Consequently thence
with Schober and Dinand to the "Snail."   Such a noise as to put us
to flight, like Io, to the "Partridge," where besides those two
dear Dr. Hörwarter was also present.   Home at 11.30.

The "Burgundian Cross" was in the Obere Bräunerstrasse, the "Snail"
on the Peter Square.—Dinand is Sauter.—The comparison with Io (cf.
No. 258) probably arose from the reading of 'Prometheus Bound' two
days earlier.—The Partridge Coffee-house, in the Goldschmiedgasse
near the cathedral, now became the Schubertians' habitual haunt (cf. note
proceding No. 415, also Nos. 774 and 864).—Johann Baptist Hörwarter,
Karl Enk's friend and collaborator (*see* No. 738), born in 1784 at Kitzbühel
in the Tyrol, was a doctor of medicine and domestic physician at the
Dominican monastery; a great music-lover, he studied the old masters and
as late as 1832 still gave a musical evening at his beautiful home in the
monastery, in which Countess Revertera (*née* Hartmann) and Tietze took
part and where Schwind made fun of the absent Vogl's fopperies.

1031. From Franz von Hartmann's Diary

5th February 1828: To the express coach, where we took leave
of the Ottenwalts, and then went *in corpore pubianorum* to the
"Partridge"; Hörwarter there too.   Home at 11.40.

The Ottenwalts were returning to Linz.—Hartmann's dog-Latin is *in
corpore beiselianorum*, *Beisel* or *Beisl* being a Viennese slang word for an inn
or public-house.   He means the company of friends who had so far
frequented "The Wolf preaching to the Geese."

1032. From the Leipzig 'Allgemeine Musikalische Zeitung,'
6th February 1828

Variations for the Pianoforte, 4 Hands, on a Theme from the Opera, 'Marie,' by Hérold—composed by Franz Schubert. Work 82.   Vienna, Tobias Haslinger.   Price, 1 Thaler, 4 Groschen.

Herr Schubert's artistic products have been several times discussed in our pages recently, and in general he has always been deferentially considered; his invention and taste have been praised, anything that was pointed out as still deficient was said to be rather accidental, superficial and thus easily done away with; that it pertained rather to youth and fashion, having no cause to show itself obtrusively, and that it was already pleasantly noticeable how these faults were gradually diminishing. Neither do we hesitate to subscribe to this judgment of experts as being well founded; yet precisely because this is no mean praise, we feel urged to add this: we hope for the sake of an always estimable public that the composer will not thereby be induced immediately to regard all that he writes, and will write, as good and worthy of being printed, without careful personal examination, merely because it happens to have been set down on paper; rather should he be impelled by the most willing acknowledgment of his talent and readily expressed pleasure in the best of his creations to an all the more careful consideration of his own works and to an all the more enthusiastic production of new pieces, as it behoves a true artist. He is so well gifted by nature as to be capable of this, if only he is always keenly intent and bewares of being over-hasty. The young artist will himself confidently feel that we write this warning preamble with no other than a good intention, and one which is well disposed towards him and his cause. For we are once again obliged to praise him, and moreover quite particularly.

He has furnished a work here which must certainly be counted among the best of recent times known to us in this species. It is not very easy to write good variations: we should be richer in them if it were; indeed it is not even the business of every accomplished

musician to move successfully in this field, if one is not to be
content merely with changes of figuration in the conventional
manner, devoid of inherent spirit and living force. A quite
peculiar disposition and skill in imaginative shaping is required to
invent and to display an ingenious whole by means of a gradual
succession of variants of a given theme, and that with an increasing
heightening of the interest for both the player and the hearer, as
Haydn, Mozart and Beethoven were able to do so outstandingly
well. For that each variation must have its particular expression
and special character; all the parts must be carried out equally
and according to their position; and all these procedures must have
a certain inevitable relationship to each other: the one must not
only lead naturally and unconstrainedly to the other, but should
also elucidate and elevate it, down to a wholly satisfying and pleasing
conclusion that may be brilliant or may offer complete repose.—
And all this the composer of the present work has actually accomplished to a very great extent, even to that transparency which
beautifies and conjures up before our senses the whole wealth of
the most diversified groups, unmixed and wholly clear and free,
like a reflection in the sea, which is the precious possession of complete mastery alone, though of course it may yet fail here and there.
For that reason, however, it will seem only the more delightful
to the vast majority of amateurs, since that which befogs this
crystal clarity is precisely what is most characteristic of our time;
that is to say, frequent surprise attacks with strange chords, or
rather transitions and modulations which mostly show our tonal
beauties in confusion, and which here too are to be occasionally
found again. Disregarding what many may count among the major
beauties, that is to say among the fashionable ones, we declare
these Variations to be the best of his that has so far come our way.
The theme is at once very captivatingly treated, yet with the
greatest simplicity. All the variations built upon it (there are
eight of them, on twenty-nine well-engraved pages) are mutually
intertwined, diversified without affectation and rich without
ostentation, the modish chords excepted. But the difficulty for
the players is always on the increase, down to the last, rather long-
drawn *Allegro vivace, ma non più.* Altogether they are not easy

to perform, if too much is not to be lost in undue huddling. But they are worth being practised with accuracy.

[? G. W. Fink.]

The reference to the "judgment of experts" seems to indicate that not all the reviews of Schubert's works in this periodical were from one and the same pen—the editor's (Fink's).

1033. FROM THE PROGRAMME of the Eleventh Evening Entertainment held by the Philharmonic Society, 7th February 1828 (Conductor, Herr Chimani)

4. Psalm 23 for 4 voices by Schubert.

Chimani is Dr. Franz Chimani, a barrister, or Josef (? his son), who were both fellows of the Philharmonic Society.

1034. NOTE ON THE ABOVE PROGRAMME

8 lady pupils. Fröhlich. I. rep.

The pupils were those of Anna Fröhlich. "I" means that the writer was present; "rep." that the chorus had to be repeated.

1035. FROM THE 'THEATERZEITUNG,' 9th February 1828

NEW CARNIVAL GIFTS

Haslinger's Art Establishment . . . newly published dance music: For pianoforte solo: Waltzes by Lanner, Lickl, Adolf Müller, Strauss, Schubert; . . . Galops by Schubert; . . . further, for the pianoforte, 4 hands, by the composers mentioned; . . . from 10 Kreuzer downwards per lot . . . As regards composition the works by Herren Schubert, Lanner and Strauss distinguish themselves particularly.

Schubert's dances are the 'Graz Waltzes,' Op. 91, and the 'Graz Galop,' the latter also arranged for pianoforte duet.

1036. PROBST TO SCHUBERT

[Outside:]
Franz Schubert, Esq.,
Musician and Composer,
Vienna.

[Postal Remark:]

Does not belong to Herr Schubert [at the Theatre] on the Wien.
Graben, at Herr Haslinger's.
Opened because of similar names.

[Inside:]
Leipzig, 9th February 1828.

I was truly sorry that differences of opinion before my journey
to Vienna did not allow your valued suggestions for the publication of your compositions by my firm to be attended by success.
When, however, I had the pleasure of your personal acquaintance
last year, I took the opportunity of mentioning that it would be
most agreeable to me to receive some of the later products of your
mind, which accordingly you promised to grant me. I have since
made the acquaintance of your later songs, such as 'The Passing-
Bell,' 'On the Water' and several others, and noticed more and
more how advantageously and ever more clearly and soulfully you
give utterance to your imagination. I have further taken delight
in several four-handed works, e.g. the four Polonaises, Op. 75, and
the Variations on the miller's song, Op. 82, which convince me
more and more that it would be easy to disseminate your name
throughout the rest of Germany and the North, in which I will
gladly lend a hand, considering talents like yours.

Kindly, therefore, send me anything you have finished to your
satisfaction—songs, vocal pieces or romances which, without
sacrificing any of your individuality, are yet not difficult to grasp;
and also assign to me some pieces for four hands of a similar kind.
You may simply hand the manuscripts to Herr Lähne at Artaria &
Co.'s, who will promptly forward them to me. On the fee we
shall soon be agreed, so long as you treat me according to a reasonable scale, and you will always find me honest in that respect,
provided the works are such as to give pleasure to myself. The
Viennese publishers' terms might most readily serve us as guide in

the matter.   Herr Lähne would then see in due course that you are promptly paid.

For the rest I must ask you seriously to examine the works you may assign to me, but not to communicate them first to your publishers at home, and to keep any business arrangements between us really between us alone.   That you will not regret it if you grant me your friendly confidence and give me the opportunity of actively furthering your reputation by a careful choice of truly well-written compositions, I will vouch for with my sacred word.

And so I present you my compliments with the most sincere respect as

Your devoted

H. A. Probst.

The address was insufficient: Schubert was not known all over Vienna. This letter, like No. 1110, went to a Josef Schubert, who, although not a well-known musician, happened to be known to the post office.—For Probst cf. Nos. 688, 694 and 777.   He had visited Vienna in the spring of 1827.—'The Passing-Bell' ('Das Zügenglöcklein.') is Op. 80, No. 2, 'To be sung on the Water' ('Auf dem Wasser zu singen') Op. 72.   For the "miller's song" cf. No. 938.—The competition between Austrian and German publishers was no longer regulated by imperial privileges, as it had been from time to time in the eighteenth century, nor was it yet alleviated by any mutual association.   Ever since Beethoven, a champion of musical author's property, had frequently sold the same work to more than one publisher, there was always a good deal of rivalry on both sides of the frontier.—See No. 1077.

1037. B. SCHOTT'S SONS TO SCHUBERT

[Outside:]

Franz Schubert, Esq.,

Famous Composer in

Vienna.

[Inside:]

Mainz, 9th February, 1828.

Franz Schubert, Esq., in Vienna.

Sir,

You have been known to us for several years by your admirably contrived compositions, and we had already earlier cherished the

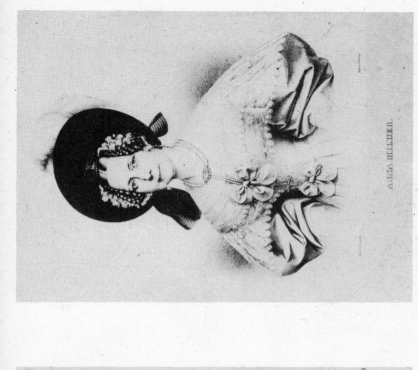

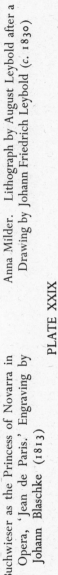

Cathinka Buchwieser as the Princess of Novarra in
Boïeldieu's Opera, 'Jean de Paris.' Engraving by
Johann Blaschke (1813)

Anna Milder. Lithograph by August Leybold after a
Drawing by Johann Friedrich Leybold (c. 1830)

PLATE XXIX

Bogner's Café, later named Café Rothaler, on the corner of Singerstrasse and Blutgassel. *See* pp. 569 f. and 586

PLATE XXX

wish to acquire some of your works for our catalogue, had not too much of our workmen's time been occupied by the works Opp. 121, 122, 123, 124, 125, 126, 127, 128 and 131 by the departed Beethoven, among which is many a very bulky *opus*.

We now take the liberty to request of you some works for publication. Pianoforte works or vocal pieces for one or several voices, with or without pianoforte accompaniment, will always be welcomed by us. Kindly fix the fee, which we shall remit to you on Vienna through Herren Franck & Co.

What we should point out to you is that we also have an establishment in Paris, where we shall likewise make your compositions known each time.

If you should have a number of things in stock and would like to send us a list of them, this would also be most agreeable to us. We remain yours respectfully,

B. Schott's Sons.

It is curious that Probst and Schott should have spontaneously written to Schubert on the very same day, the latter for the first time. Bernhard Schott's firm was founded about 1770 and went to his sons in 1817, who published most of Beethoven's last works, including the 'Missa solemnis' and the ninth Symphony.—This letter, although it too was insufficiently addressed, probably reached Schubert direct.—Franck & Co. were wholesale merchants in Vienna (*see* No. 1120).—*See* No. 1043.

1038. FROM FRANZ VON HARTMANN'S DIARY

9th February 1828: To Schober's who read Goethe's 'Pandora.' To the "Partridge," where I talked a good deal with the doctor in particular, of which I am very glad. Home at 11.45.

Goethe's festival play 'Pandora' had appeared in 1808 in the Vienna periodical 'Prometheus,' edited by Josef Ludwig Stoll (1778–1815), three of whose poems Schubert set as songs shortly after Stoll's death (xx. 149–51).—The doctor is Hörwarter.

1039. FROM FRANZ VON HARTMANN'S DIARY

14th February 1828: I visited Schubert with Enk, then went to the "Partridge," where Schober was too. Home at 10 o'clock.

. Schober had thus not been at home.

1040. From the Dresden 'Theaterzeitung,'
Middle of February 1828

(On the I. & R. Court Theatre next the Kärntnertor in Vienna.)

. . . On entering this orphaned temple of music, one can scarcely believe that it stands in a country which after all has done more for music than for any other branch of art, a country which should be proud of its Mozart, Haydn and Beethoven, where next to these stars of the first magnitude many excellent men have composed, . . . and where even now a . . . Schubert, . . . not to mention lesser lights—works and lives for the honour of German art . . . The truly great Lablache, who understands and honours German music, and highly esteems Schubert's song compositions, for instance, repeatedly expressed his astonishment at the lack of all patriotism in Vienna . . .

r—e—o—a.

The editor of this supplement to the 'Morgenzeitung' was Tieck (*see* No. 575).—The Kärntnertor Theatre, leased to Barbaja until April 1828, had newly produced five Italian, two translated French and five German operas. The champions of German opera, including this critic, had thus no cause for any special dissatisfaction, unless they found no great works among those five German operas (which included Spohr's 'Faust'). It is true that on 1st May, after the expiry of Barbaja's second lease, the house remained closed for a long time, in fact until 5th January 1829, except for Paganini's concerts in May and August 1828 and a few others.

1041. From Franz von Hartmann's Diary

15th February 1828: With Dinand and Enk to Schober's, where 'Twilight Glow' ['Die Abendröte'], a cycle of Schlegel's poems and Kleist's delicious comedy, 'The Broken Pitcher' ['Der Zerbrochene Krug'], were read. Then to the "Partridge," where it was quite jolly. At 12.30 came Ehlers and Jérôme, the latter quite tipsy. With these and Louis and Vacano we went to the Partridge Coffee-house, where Jérôme vomited; I saw him home and went back there, where we stayed until after 3 o'clock, smoking.

'Twilight Glow' is a series of poems by Friedrich von Schlegel, published in 1809 in his collected 'Poems.' Schubert had set the introductory poem to the first part of this cycle in March 1820 (xx. 376) and called it quite correctly 'Abendröte, Part I.' He made songs of others both earlier and later.—Kleist's famous comedy had appeared in 1811.— Nothing is known of Ehlers and Vacano.—Dinand is Sauter, Jérôme is von Kleimayrn.

1042. FROM FRANZ VON HARTMANN'S DIARY

16th February 1828: At 12.30 [a.m.] to Leibenfrost's coffeehouse; Dr. Hörwarter, Braun, Schubert and Bocklet also there. It was quite jolly.   Not home till 3.30.

For Leibenfrost's café *see* note preceding No. 532.—Braun may be the writer Karl Johann Braun, Ritter von Braunthal, born in 1802 at Eger in Bohemia. He related in 1840, in some rather dubious recollections, that Schubert had compared Mozart and Beethoven to Schiller and Shakespeare.

1043. SCHUBERT TO B. SCHOTT'S SONS

Vienna, 21st February 1828.

Gentlemen,

I feel much honoured by your letter of 8th February and enter with pleasure into closer relations with so reputable an art establishment, which is so fit to give my works greater currency abroad.

I have the following compositions in stock:

a) Trio for pianoforte, violin and violoncello, which has been produced here with much success.

b) Two string Quartets (G major and D minor).

c) Four Impromptus for pianoforte solo, which might be published separately or all four together.

d) Fantasy for pianoforte duet, dedicated to Countess Caroline Esterházy.

e) Fantasy for pianoforte and violin.

f) Songs for one voice with pianoforte accompaniment, poems by Schiller, Goethe, Klopstock, &c. &c., and Seidl, Schober, Leitner, Schulze, &c. &c.

g) Four-part choruses for male voices as well as for female voices with pianoforte accompaniment, two of them with a solo voice, poems by Grillparzer and Seidl.

h) A five-part song for male voices, poem by Schober.

i) 'Battle Song' by Klopstock, double chorus for eight male voices.

k) Comic Trio, 'The Wedding Roast' ['Der Hochzeitsbraten'], by Schober, for soprano, tenor and bass, which has been performed with success.

This is the list of my finished compositions, excepting three operas, a Mass and a symphony. These last compositions I mention only in order to make you acquainted with my strivings after the highest in art.

Now, if you should wish anything from the above list for publication, I shall assign it to you with pleasure against a reasonable fee.

With all respect

Franz Schubert.

My address:

Under the Tuchlauben,
at the "Blue Hedgehog,"
2nd floor.

Cf. No. 1037, which actually dates from the 9th, not the 8th, as Schubert writes.—For (a) cf. No. 986: it is the pianoforte Trio in E flat major.—(b) are the last two string Quartets.—(c) is the Op. posth. 142, then still planned as Op. 101 by Schubert (cf. No. 979).—(d) is the Fantasy in F minor, published by Diabelli in 1829 as Op. 103, according to Schubert's own reckoning, and with the French dedication to the countess, as the composer had desired. The work had been sketched in January 1828 and must have been finished in February; but a fair copy was not made until April, and it was performed privately by Schubert and Franz Lachner on 9th May (see No. 1094).—(e) is Op. posth. 159 (see No. 1009).—(f) comprises over four hundred songs.—(g) includes the 'Night Song in the Forest' ('Nachtgesang im Walde,' Op. posth. 139b), the '23rd Psalm' (Op. posth. 132), the choral 'Serenade' ('Ständchen,' Op. posth. 135) and 'Night Brightness' ('Nachthelle,' Op. posth. 134).

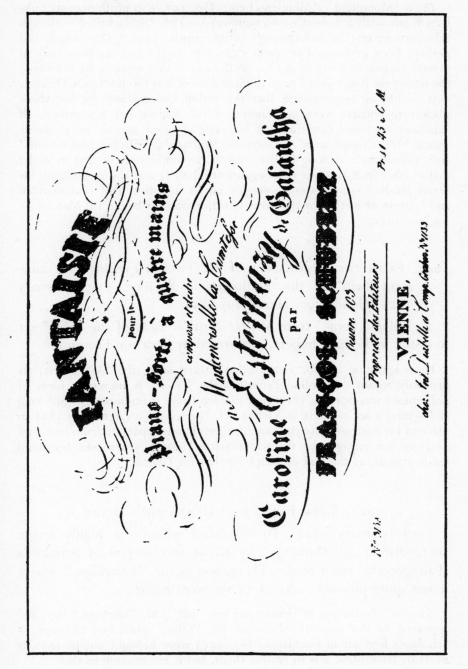

—(*h*) is 'Moonlight' ('Mondenschein,' Op. 102, also posthumously published, but with Schubert's own number).—(*i*) is 'Schlachtlied'—though Schubert writes 'Schlachtgesang'—(Op. posth. 151).—(*k*), which had perhaps been performed at Spaun's (*see* No. 1021) and certainly only in private, appeared in 1829 as Op. posth. 104 with a vignette by Schwind; the same year Roser gave a stage performance of it at the Josefstadt Theatre. —It should be remembered that the string Quintet and the last three pianoforte Sonatas were not composed till August and September.—If Schubert mentions but three of his eight finished operas, he probably means 'The Conspirators' ('Domestic Warfare'), 'Alfonso and Estrella' and 'Fierabras.' Among his five masses he thinks only of that in A flat major (that in E flat was not begun until June); and the one among his seven finished symphonies he singles out is doubtless that of Gmunden and Gastein of 1825 (for the great C major was not begun till March).— *See* No. 1051.

1044. FROM THE PROGRAMME of the Twelfth Evening Entertainment held by the Philharmonic Society, 21st February 1828 (Conductor, Herr Hauschka)

2. 'Ellen's Song,' from Walter Scott's 'Lady of the Lake,' set to music by Franz Schubert, performed by Frau von Frontini.

Here again, as in No. 1025, Ellen's third song, the 'Ave Maria,' is probably meant.—Karoline Frontini (the "von" is merely a form of politeness) was born in 1810 (her maiden name is unknown). She sang at Paganini's last concert in Vienna (cf. No. 1068) on 25th July 1828 in place of his mistress Antonia Bianchi, then already separated from him, and in 1829 was engaged by the Kärntnertor Theatre, where she remained for five years, at the end of which she left for Galicia.

1045. FROM FRANZ VON HARTMANN'S DIARY

23rd February 1828: To Schober's where the highly tragic 'Betrothal at St. Domingo' by Kleist and several of Schober's 'Palingeneses' were read. Thereupon to the "Partridge," where it was quite pleasant. At 11.15 we went home.

Kleist's 'Verlobung in [Hartmann has "auf"] St. Domingo,' too, had appeared in the second volume of his 'Tales,' published in 1811.— Schober's first set of poems (*see* No. 605) were brought out in 1826 at Breslau; Bauernfeld was to review them, but it never came to that.

1046. From Franz von Hartmann's Diary

25th February 1828: Enk fetched me [in the morning] to the Partridge Inn, where we stayed until after 12.30. In the street Schober, Enk and I met Schubert, Horzalka and Slawjk, with whom we went to the Partridge Coffee-house. I played eleven rounds of skittles with Enk there, and we stayed until 2.30, drinking grog. (Horzalka is the composer who once said: "I give my house-steward each day a groat in twenty-kreuzer pieces.")

For Horzalka *see* No. 342.—The "rounds of skittles" were a special continental game of billiards. The game was made more difficult by small cones set up in the middle of the table which the player had to aim at upsetting indirectly with one of the opponent's balls he had to hit first.—It was the custom in Vienna to give the house-steward or porter, who locked the gate at 10 p.m., a small gratuity, which gradually became his legal right. It was a sixth of a florin, i.e. 10 kreuzer, and it continued to be called a *Sechserl* long after the florin had begun to conform to the decimal system, and contained 100 kreuzer instead of 60, indeed even when the currency was turned into crowns and shillings.

1047. From Franz von Hartmann's Diary

27th February 1828: Went for a walk with Enk and Felber [to Hernals], where we ran into Schubert.

Josef Felber was a fellow-student of Hartmann's.—Hernals was an outlying place to the west of Vienna. Mayssen (*see* No. 483) lived there.

1048. From the Programme of the Thirteenth Evening Entertainment held by the Philharmonic Society, 28th February 1828 (Conductor, Herr Piringer)

2. Four-part song, 'God in Nature' ['Gott in der Natur'], poem by Gleim, set to music by Schubert.

For Piringer *see* No. 633.—The words were, as was pointed out earlier, by Ewald Christian von Kleist.—This was the Philharmonic Society's last performance of a work by Schubert in his lifetime.

1049. NOTE ON THE ABOVE PROGRAMME

Lady pupils of the Conservatory. [Anna] Fröhlich. I was not there, because of Grillparzer's play.

Grillparzer's play was the tragedy 'A Faithful Servant to his Master' ('Ein treuer Diener seines Herrn'), given for the first time that night at the Burg Theatre. Bauernfeld was there too. Cf. No. 1082.

1050. FROM FRANZ VON HARTMANN'S DIARY

28th February 1828: To the "Snail"; Marl, Enk, Schwind, Schober, Schubert, Bayer and Manschgo there. 11.45.

"Marl" is Karl Maurus Mayrhofer.—Schwind had brought two of his colleagues with him: Josef Bayer, born in Vienna in 1804 (of the same age with him), and Johann Manschgo, born in 1800 at Weyer in Upper Austria. Manschgo was an amateur pianoforte player, singer and poet, who marked a number of poems in his manuscript collection "pleased Schubert." But this may be one of those suspicious posthumous friendships of Schubert's. In any case Schubert never set a poem by Manschgo.

1051. B. SCHOTT'S SONS TO SCHUBERT

[Outside:]

Franz Schubert, Esq.,
Under the Tuchlauben at the
"Blue Hedgehog," 2nd floor, in

Vienna.

[Inside:]

Mainz, 29th February 1828.

Herr Franz Schubert in Vienna.

Sir,

You have given us the greatest pleasure by replying immediately to our letter, addressed to you on the 8th inst. We gather from this what you still have in stock at present in the way of manuscripts, and we should at once come to terms with you for all your works, were it not that we are obliged to carry out as well obligations

entered into earlier; your works are all so attractive to a publisher
that the choice is difficult.

Please be kind enough to send us the following of the works
listed:

1. Trio for pianoforte, violin and violoncello,
2. Four Impromptus for pianoforte solo,
3. Fantasy for pianoforte duet,
4. Fantasy for piano and violin,
5. Four-part choruses for male voices,
6. Five-part chorus for male voices,
7. 'Battle Song' for double chorus of 8 voices,
8. Comic Trio, 'The Wedding Roast' ['Der Hochzeitsbraten'].

We shall publish these works by degrees and as soon as possible,
and then ask you anew for later works.

You will please to fix the lowest fee possible and permit us to
remit you the fee for each work through Vienna immediately after
publication.   Kindly advise us also of how many copies you wish
to have for distribution to your friends.

Will you kindly deliver the packet for enclosure to Herr Andreas
Landschütz, pianoforte instrument maker, resident in the Mariahilf
High Road, No. 16, at the "Red Cracknel"?   For he will shortly
consign to us two grand pianofortes, and we shall save carriage
in this way.

Yet proceed as you please in the matter of the consignment.

You may also hand any packet for enclosure to Herr Ferdinand
Cammeretto, instrument maker, resident in the Laimgrube on
the Wien, at the "White Ox," No. 68, who also as a rule sends us a
consignment of pianos each month and is a very reliable man.

Looking forward to your consignment, we remain with the
highest respect.

                                                B. Schott's Sons.

Cf. No. 1043.—The firm copied Schubert's error about the date of
their former letter (No. 1037).   Their supposition that Schubert had
given them a complete list of his compositions not yet assigned to publishers (excepting operas, masses and symphonies) seems ingenuous to
those who are wise after the event.—Their No. 1 corresponds to his
letter (a); the others are 2=(c), 3=(d), 4=(e), 5=(g), 6=(h),

7 = (i), 8 = (k). They disregarded the string quartets (b) and the songs (f), as also the female-voice choruses in (g).—The Viennese pianoforte makers had their quarters mainly in the region behind the Theater an der Wien.—Manuscripts weighing more than five (continental) pounds were not allowed to be sent by letter post, but could only be transmitted by the slower parcel post, the consignment of which was troublesome.— *See* No. 1076.

1052. ANTONIO MAYER TO SCHOBER

Trieste, 29th February 1828.

. . . Most cordial greetings to Herren Bauernfeld, Schwind, Schubert, &c.

For Mayer *see* No. 897.

1053. FROM FRANZ VON HARTMANN'S DIARY

1st March 1828: To Schober's, where again several 'Palingeneses' and the first half of Tieck's splendid novel, 'The Picture Gallery,' were read. Then to the "Snail," where the painters made draw-ings from dots and Schubert made a German dance out of notes. Home at 11.30.

Tieck's novel, 'Die Gemälde' (Hartmann has 'Die Gemäldegalerie') was first published in an almanac and later (1823) separately.—The painters are doubtless Schwind, Bayer and Manschgo. The drawing from dots, of which Schwind was a master, was a game similar to that of writing verses on given words (*see* No. 244). The composition of dances on given notes was no real innovation on Kirnberger's game of dice (Berlin, 1751) and some of its imitators; but it is a pity that nothing of the kind from Schubert's hand has been preserved.

1054. FROM JOHANN VESQUE VON PÜTTLINGEN'S DIARY

5th March 1828: Evening party with Vogl, Schubert and Grillparzer.

For Vesque cf. No. 525. He is said to have been in touch with Schubert in 1827 and 1828, to have sung songs of his accompanied by the composer and to have gone with Schubert to visit Vogl, who taught him declamation.

The party may have been given at the house of his father, who was custodian of the court library, and who lived in the Hofburg.

1055. SCHUBERT'S PETITION to the Philharmonic Society with Advice by Jenger

P. N. [Protocol No.] 672   65
                                    Misc.[ellanea]

Franz Schubert, member of the
Body of Representatives of the Phil.
Society in the Aust. Imp.
   State, Vienna, on
5th, *praes.* 6th March 1828,
requests the cession   ADVICE.
of the room at the "Red   The Petitioner
   Hedgehog"   is to have the sought-for Society's
for the performance of a   room at the "Red Hedgehog"
private concert on   for the performance of his private
21st March 1828, at 7 p.m.,   concert in the evening of
with submission of the con-   21st March of the ct. yr.
sent thereto from the   assigned to him with pleasure and
two I. & R. Court Theatres.   without cost, and is for this pur-
                                  pose to present himself with this
Exp. Kiesewetter.   advice
                                  at the Society's Chancellery.

Vidi [illegible].
For the   th meeting   From the Com. of Management.
of the Committee of Manage-
   ment
of the Phil. Soc. in the   Vienna, 6th March 1828.
   Aust. Imp. State.
Document No. —   Jenger.

   This petition is not in Schubert's hand.—The concert of Schubert's works, his first and last, was at first planned for 21st March. The permission of the court theatres had actually to be sought only for functions held on church or state festival days (the so-called *Normatage*), on which those houses were closed.

1056. From Franz von Hartmann's Diary

8th March 1828: To Schober's, where the splendid novel by Tieck, begun a week ago, was read to the end. To the "Snail," where it was dull and lasted till nearly 12.30.

Cf. No. 1053.

1057. From the Official 'Wiener Zeitung,' 14th March 1828

At the House of Anton Diabelli & Co.,
Art and Music Dealers, in the Graben, No. 1133, are just published, and to be had of K. Lichtl in Pest at the same price:

ANNOT LYLE'S SONG
from Walter Scott's 'Montrose'
and
NORNA'S SONG from Walter Scott's 'Pirate'
set to Music for One Voice with Pianoforte Accompaniment
by FRANZ SCHUBERT.

Work 85.   Price, 45 Kreuzer, A.C.

ROMANCE OF RICHARD CŒUR DE LÍON
from Walter Scott's 'Ivanhoe,'
set to Music for One Voice with Pianoforte Accompaniment,
by FRANZ SCHUBERT.

Work 86.   Price, 45 Kreuzer, A.C.
(Property of the Publishers.)

Opp. 85 and 86, without dedications, appeared after Op. 91.

1058. From Franz von Hartmann's Diary

15th March 1828: To Schober's, where the beginning of Tieck's splendid novel, 'The Betrothal' ['Die Verlobung'], was read. Thereafter to the "Snail," where we stayed till 11.30.

Tieck's novel had first appeared in an almanac and later (1823) separately.

1059. From Perth's Diary

(On the concert given by the boy Josef Khayll, 16th March 1828, 4.30 p.m., in the Philharmonic Society's room at the "Red Hedgehog.")

3. 'Norman's Song,' from 'The Lady of the Lake' by Walter Scott, set to music by Franz Schubert. Sweetly and beautifully sung by Herr Tietze, and accompanied on the fortepiano by Herr Schubert.

For Perth cf. No. 146.—The boy Khayll, born c. 1815, came of a family of wind players, three brothers employed at the court theatres and in the court chapel. He was a violinist and a pupil of Jansa's. His father was probably Josef Khayll, born 1781, an oboist and teacher at the Conservatory. A Josefine Khayll had played the pianoforte at concerts at Hatwig's (see note preceding No. 100).

1060. From the Berlin 'Allgemeine Musikalische Zeitung,' 19th March 1828

(On Schubert's Op. 83: Three Italian Songs.)

Italian composers are quite content as a rule if they have only succeeded in reproducing in their music the chief sense of the words in general, although that is not always and in every case sufficient. To correct and make good the deficiencies of the declamatary expression is thus nearly always left to the singer. German composers have not so much confidence in their singers and thus often lose themselves too much in an anxious endeavour to give special meaning to each word and to enhance that expression even more by an often redundantly descriptive accompaniment, so that again the main, fundamental colour of the whole is thereby frequently obliterated. In each species, therefore, something remains to be desired: in the former always a little more, in the latter often a little less. If, however, one is confronted with a case where a composition in the Italian manner by a German comes up for judgment, like the above songs by Schubert, for instance, one finds oneself not a little embarrassed to know which side to take in order to find a standpoint for one's criticism, whether on the German or on the Italian. Each shows matter for some blame. As an Italian composer Herr S. gives too little scope to song and still too much to the accompaniment. The flow of his melodies is too intermittent, too heavy-handed; it is no glowing lava stream, but only a somewhat cold, murmuring, northern brooklet, whose merry plashing even is often drowned by the seriously dolorous rustlings of neighbouring oak forests (in the accompaniment). In short, these are not genuine, light-winged Italian song-tunes as the Italians of to-day in particular demand them. German singers might take to them more kindly, although the German art critic is bound to observe that truth of expression is often sacrificed for the sake of a pretty cantilena. We were best pleased with No. 2, 'Il traditor deluso.' No. 3, 'Il modo di prender moglie,' is too much of an imitation of the first aria of Rossini's barber, without so much as approaching it in lightness, fire, effect—in fact genius. Herr Schubert has thus not yet succeeded with these songs in bringing about an alliance, however desirable, between German and Italian music.

H. Marschner.

Heinrich Marschner, born in 1795 at Zittau in Saxony, had been in Vienna in 1817 and was now musical director at Danzig. According to the manuscript, which has been preserved, he wrote this criticism on 29th December 1827. His opera 'The Vampire' was produced at Leipzig ten days after the appearance of this notice.

1061. FROM FRANZ VON HARTMANN'S DIARY

22nd March 1828: At Schober's, where the fine Tieck novel was read to the end, as well as the 'Palingeneses.' Thereupon to the "Snail," where Spaun tried to do a trick with a pipe-stem. He made a pass with it; the upper part remained in his hands and the other piece flew at the head of a guest in the next room. We had all sorts of tricks and chatter. At 11.40 we went home.

Cf. Nos. 1058 and 1045.

1062. FROM THE 'THEATERZEITUNG,' 25th March 1828

(Announcement of Schubert's concert.)

CONCERT ANNOUNCEMENT

Among the manifold musical art exhibitions which have been offered us in the course of this *saison* and still await us, one should attract general attention the more because it offers enjoyment both new and surprising by the novelty and sterling value of the compositions and the attractive variety among the musical items as well as the sympathetic collaboration of the most celebrated local artists.—Franz Schubert, whose powerfully intellectual, enchantingly lovely and original tone-poems have made him the favourite of the whole musical public, and which may well secure their creator a more than ephemeral, nay an imperishable name by their genuine artistic value, will perform on 26th March, at a private concert (in the Austrian Philharmonic Society's room), a series of the latest products of his mind, according to the following programme: 1. First movement from a new string Quartet, performed by Herren Professor Böhm, Holz, Weiss and Linke. 2. Four new songs, performed by Herr Vogl, retired I. & R. Court Opera singer. 3. 'Serenade' ['Ständchen'] by Grillparzer: soprano solo and chorus delivered by Mlle Josefine Fröhlich and the lady pupils of the Conservatory. 4. New Trio for pianoforte, violin and violoncello, performed by Herren K. M. von Bocklet, Böhm and Linke. 5. 'On the River' ['Auf dem Strome'], song with horn and pianoforte accompaniment, performed by Herren Tietze and Lewy. 6. 'Omnipotence' ['Die Allmacht'] by Ladislaus von Pyrker, sung by Herr Vogl. 7. 'Battle Song' ['Schlachtgesang'] by Klopstock, double chorus for male voices.—May the glorious German tone-poet, then, be granted an attendance such as his modesty and unobtrusiveness would alone deserve, quite apart from his artistic eminence and the rare and great musical enjoyment which is to be expected.—Tickets, at 3 florins, V.C., are to be had at the art establishments of Herren Diabelli, Haslinger and Leidesdorf.

The forthcoming concerts were those to be given by Paganini (*see* No. 1068).—On Sunday, 23rd March, at Linke's "Private Musical

Entertainment" in memory of Beethoven (the first anniversary of whose
death was on the 26th, the day of Schubert's concert) the F major string
Quartet, Op. 135, received its first public performance at the same place
and at the hands of ? Böhm, Holz, Weiss and Linke.   Schuppanzigh
seems to have been already indisposed, otherwise he would certainly
have led Beethoven's work; he would also more than probably have taken
part in Schubert's concert, which may for that very reason have been
postponed from 21st to 26th March.   The idea of giving such a concert
dated back to 1823 and 1824 (cf. Nos. 415 and 456).   Bauernfeld
boasted later that it was he who finally decided Schubert (*see* No. 787); but
Sonnleithner's opinion is that what induced Schubert was the fact that he
had saturated the Viennese publishers with his works and could dispose of
nothing more in that way.—The string Quartet was evidently that in
G major, for if the D minor had been chosen it is certain that the movement played would have been the second, the variations on 'Death and
the Maiden.'—Of the four songs 'The Wayfarer addressing the Moon'
would not have been "new," but a substitute was found for it at the last
moment (*see* No. 1064).—The 'Serenade' has actually a contralto, not a
soprano solo.—The pianoforte Trio was again that in E flat major (*see*
No. 986).—'On the River' was written especially for this concert.

1063. From the 'Wiener Zeitschrift für Kunst,' &c., 25th March 1828

PRIVATE CONCERT.

On 26th March Herr Franz Schubert will give a private concert
in the hall of the Lower Austrian Musical Society (under the
Tuchlauben, No. 558), at which the following pieces, of his composition throughout, will be heard: . . . Four songs with pianoforte accompaniment: 'The Crusade' ['Der Kreuzzug'] by Leitner,
'The Stars' ['Die Sterne'] by the same, 'The Wayfarer addressing
the Moon' ['Der Wanderer an den Mond'] by Seidl and a Fragment
from Aeschylus. . . . Tickets, at 3 florins, V.C., are to be had at
the art establishments of Herren Haslinger, Diabelli and Leides-
dorfer [*sic*].   To commence at 7 o'clock in the evening.

The 'Sammler' of 25th March reproduced the whole programme in its
first version.

1064. PROGRAMME OF SCHUBERT'S CONCERT

Invitation
to the Private Concert which Franz Schubert
will have the honour of giving on
26th March, at 7 p.m., in the Room of the Austrian Philharmonic
Society, under the Tuchlauben, No. 558.

Pieces to appear are

1. First movement of a new string Quartet, performed by
   Herren Böhm, Holz, Weiss and Linke.

2. a) 'The Crusade' ['Der Kreuzzug'] by Leitner ⎱ Songs with
   b) 'The Stars' ['Die Sterne'] by the same   pianoforte
   c) 'Fisherman's Ditty ['Fischerweise'] by   accompani-
      Schlechta   ment, per-
   d) 'Fragment from Aeschylus'   ⎰ formed by
                           Herr Vogl, I. & R. retired
                           Court Opera singer.

3. 'Serenade' ['Ständchen'] by Grillparzer, soprano solo and
   chorus, performed by Fräulein Josefine Fröhlich and the
   lady pupils of the Conservatory.

4. New Trio for piano-forte, violin and violoncello, performed
   by Herren Karl Maria von Bocklet, Böhm and Linke.

5. 'On the River' ['Auf dem Strome'] by Rellstab, song with
   horn and piano-forte accompaniment, performed by
   Herren Tietze and Lewy, jun.

6. 'Omnipotence' ['Die Allmacht'] by Ladislaus Pyrker, song
   with pianoforte accompaniment, performed by Herr Vogl.

7. 'Battle Song' ['Schlachtgesang'] by Klopstock, double chorus
   for male voices.

All the musical pieces are composed by the concert-giver.
Tickets at 3 fl., V.C., are to be had at the art establishments of
Herren Haslinger, Diabelli and Leidesdorf.

The programme, lithographed on fine paper with the wrong date (28th, corrected by hand to 26th), is extant in two versions: the first is the rejected one containing 'The Wayfarer addressing the Moon' as No. 2c; the other contains instead the 'Fisherman's Ditty' ('Fischerweise) to a poem by Schlechta.—Schubert accompanied at the pianoforte. —The words "soprano solo" in No. 3 seem to have been copied by the newspaper from the programme; but as Josefine Fröhlich sang soprano as well as contralto at that time, the part may really have been transposed for a high voice. The chorus was again recruited from her sister Anna's pupils.—The younger Lewy was Josef Rudolf (*see* No. 731).—The male-voice choir was probably made up of members of the Philharmonic Society which repeated the whole programme on 26th March 1928 to celebrate the centenary of the concert.—The net proceeds amounted to 800 florins, V.C.

1065. From Franz von Hartmann's Diary

26th March 1828: With Louis and Enk to Schubert's concert. I shall never forget how glorious that was. What pleased me greatly, too, was to see the Schallhammers and the Witteczeks there. To the "Snail," where we jubilated until midnight.

Louis is Hartmann's brother.—For the Schallhammers *see* No. 757.

1066. From Bauernfeld's Diary

[End of] March 1828.

Schwind has wooed Netti, and came in a torn tail-coat. Betrothal party. His despair. On the 26th was Schubert's concert. Enormous applause, good receipts.

Cf. No. 685. Bauernfeld reports that he and Schubert waited at the coffee-house (? Bogner's) while Schwind went wooing. When Schwind, probably before the Schubert concert, returned in despair over the mishap with the torn frock-coat (not evening dress, but a coloured garment for festive occasions) "Schubert could not stop tittering good-naturedly." Schwind was now betrothed, but his engagement was broken off in October 1829 on account of religious differences and of his financial position (*see* No. XXXVII).

Invitation to Schubert's Concert, with the First
Version of the Programme (1828).   See pp. 753 f.

1067. From the Leipzig 'Allgemeine Musikalische Zeitung,'
7th May 1828

(Vienna correspondence.)

. . . If all these works [by Beethoven], performed to perfection
[at Josef Linke's private entertainment in the Philharmonic Society's
hall on 23rd March], afforded an indescribable aural treat, the same
must be said with hardly less emphasis in praise of that *soirée
musicale* which the excellent Schubert held in the very same place
on the 26th, giving a hearing to the following from among the
considerable number of his mostly successful works: 1. A new
string Quartet; full of spirit and originality, . . . 2. Four songs,
'The Crusade,' 'The Stars' 'Fisherman's Ditty' ['Fischerweise']
and 'Fragment from Aeschylus,' sung by the retired I. & R. Court
Opera singer Herr Vogl and accompanied on the pianoforte by the
composer; . . . 7. 'Battle Song,' by Klopstock, double chorus for
male voices; conceived with truly Germanic power and reflecting
the exalted Bard's sublime words.—Had all these artistic enjoyments not excelled to such a high degree, one might well have been
generally satisfied with that which the registrar, Herr Franz Glöggl,
offered at his annual benefit the following day, the 27th . . .

For Linke's concert *see* No. 1062.—Franz Glöggl, born *c.* 1797 at
Linz, played double bass and trombone, was keeper of the Philharmonic
Society's archives and later became a teacher at the Conservatory.

1068. From the Dresden 'Abendzeitung,' 12th June 1828

(Vienna correspondence.)

There is but one voice within our walls, and that cries: "Hear
Paganini!" . . . Now it may be quite normal that next to him
all the other executive musical artists are put into the shade.
But many are satisfied if even in the shade they are able to earn a
few florins still, and so it comes about that even next to his concerts we still see a sufficiency of musical recitals and concerts
announced. *Multum clamoris, parum lanae!* Thus I can now tell
you . . . of a private concert given by the favourite composer

Schubert . . . All these gentry and every piece they performed
were applauded more or less.   There was unquestionably much
that was good among it all, but the minor stars, paled before the
radiance of this comet in the musical heavens [Paganini] . . .

The hubbub over Paganini was probably the reason why none of the
Viennese papers published a notice of Schubert's concert.   The great
fiddler, then forty-five years of age, made Vienna his first stage on his
belated triumphal progress through Europe.   He arrived there on 16th
March, accompanied by his mistress Antonia Bianchi and their son
Achille, whom he kept with him when he dismissed his mother in Vienna
(*see* No. 1044).   On 29th March he gave his first concert in the assembly
hall.   It was poorly attended, but enthusiasm soon went to unheard-of
lengths.   Again and again Paganini was obliged to prolong his sojourn,
which in the end lasted four months, and he gave altogether fourteen
concerts, a few of them at the court theatres.   At the assembly hall the
prices were 2 florins, A.C., or 5 florins, V.C., for the stalls and twice that
in the dress-circle.   (Angelica Catalani had asked even more—5 florins,
A.C.—in 1818; yet Paganini's prices made such a sensation that from
that time the Viennese cab-drivers came to call the five-florin note in
Viennese currency *Paganinerl*.)   Paganini's receipts for each concert at
the assembly hall averaged 2,500 florins, A.C.; all in all they came to
20,000 florins, and including the concerts at the theatres he made 30,000
florins, A.C.   Schuppanzigh (*see* No. 1062) undertook the conducting of
the orchestra at these concerts only in April.   *See* No. 1095.

•1069. From the Berlin 'Allgemeine Musikalische Zeitung,' 2nd July 1828

(Vienna correspondence.)

 . . . Herr Franz Schubert, who at a private concert gave a
hearing to nothing but works of his own, chiefly vocal, a species
in which he is particularly successful.   The numerous gathering
of friends and patrons did not stint resounding applause after each
number and saw to it that several of them were repeated.

This short notice was followed by several columns on the first Paganini
concerts.

1070. From the 'Theaterzeitung,' 29th March 1828

'Winter Journey' ['Winterreise']. By Wilhelm Müller, set to music for one voice with pianoforte accompaniment by Franz Schubert. Work 89. Part I. Property of the Publisher. Vienna, Tobias Haslinger, music publisher at the house of the Savings Bank, in the Graben.

To draw attention to anything well carried out is the most agreeable business a lover of art can serve. We thus very gladly speak of the work under notice, which does honour to its origin from the point of view of the poet, the composer and the publisher. Müller is naïve, sentimental and sets against outward nature a parallel of some passionate soul-state, which takes its colour and significance from the former. Schubert has understood his poet with the kind of genius that is his own. His music is as naïve as the poet's expression; the emotions contained in the poems are as deeply reflected in his own feelings, and these are so brought out in sound that none can sing or hear them without being touched to the heart. Schubert's mind shows a bold sweep everywhere, whereby he carries every one away with him who approaches him, and he takes them through the immeasurable depth of the human heart into the far distance, where premonitions of the infinite dawn upon them longingly in a rosy radiance, but where at the same time the shuddering bliss of an inexpressible presentiment is companioned by the gentle pain of the constraining present which hems in the boundaries of human existence. Herein lies the nature of German romantic being and art, and in this sense Schubert is a German composer through and through, who does honour to our fatherland and our time. It is this spirit that is breathed by the present songs; it expresses itself through them even where the subject seems to point to entirely different paths; and in this logical establishing of harmony between outward and inward things lies the chief merit of both poets, the speaking and the singing one. An analysis of technical beauties cannot be attempted in this journal, which is not devoted to theory, but to draw attention to the viewpoint from which this beautiful and noble work may be most feelingly and fully enjoyed is an urgent necessity at this time of day, the more so since it has become almost a craze to submit only to material impressions in music.

We stand in God's fair, free nature and in fields and forests, behold the blue sky above, the luscious green, the delightful grouping of trees; we feel the enlivening warmth of spring, the sweet scent of the meadows is wafted to us, and we feel so much at ease that we do not in the least want to be disturbed in our passive enjoyment by the reminder of higher things in these impressions themselves, or at least have no active desire for them. A truly epicurean pleasure of this kind is all very well as a *medium stimulans*, but a rider who has buckled on his spurs is not therefore mounted as yet! The presentation on the publisher's part is worthy of them; it is to be hoped that the second part of the work will not fail to appear, since the number of those who take pleasure in that kind of thing cannot be small.

1070A. From the Frankfort 'Allgemeine Musikalische Zeitung,' 29th March 1828

(Review of Op. 79, 'Homesickness' ['Das Heimweh'] and 'Omnipotence' ['Die Allmacht'].)

Excellent and grandiose things must not be sought in these compositions. In this respect they range with countless others, which have nevertheless been kindly received by music-lovers. So much is deserved by this worklet also, since the composer's good intentions and knowledge are unmistakably shown therein.

S. . . . .r.

1071. From Franz von Hartmann's Diary

29th March 1828: To Schober's, who again started a splendid novel by Tieck, 'The Secretive One' ['Der Geheimnisvolle']. "Snail." Home at 11.30.

Tieck's novel had appeared in a periodical in 1822 and separately in 1823.—This was the day of Paganini's first concert, at which Schubert was probably present (*see* No. 1095).

1071A. Marie von Pratobevera to her Betrothed, Josff Bergmann at Cilli

[Vienna,] 31st March 1828.

This year, then, I made an excursion into the open before you, my Mountain Friend; not into the hills, though, but into verdant pastures, growing towards this world's hopes, as also among verdant graves, pastures for eternity. For we were at Währing, on the anniversary of the funeral of Beethoven, who died a year ago, to have a look at his tombstone and also to hear the song dedicated to his memory by his admirers. The day was heavenly fair, the song most touching, and sung among graves it could not fail to make a deep impression.—I was surprised only that not more people were there, and also at the simple monument, made of common stone. It represents a pyramid, at the top of which hangs a very clumsy lyre, and at the base is just his name in gilt letters. I admit that I much like the idea of making no verses on him, but merely to set down his name, and yet making him immortal thereby; but I do think the stone and the workmanship unworthy. But enough of graves and death: I must tell you about fresh and blossoming life, which prevailed at a concert given by Schubert on 26th March. Only compositions by *himself* were given, and *gloriously*. Everybody was lost in a frenzy of admiration and rapture. There was as much clapping and stamping as in 'King Lear' (does it hurt you, admirer of 'Lear,' to know that what is due to him alone is vouchsafed to others as well? Yet you would have been delighted, in spite of the Cillian day and night music). I saw the Baroness Wetzlar at the concert, too. They say Pauline C. [Koudelka] was also there, but unfortunately I did not see her, it was so packed. The separate pieces I shall not describe to you: in the golden autumn we shall ourselves play them all for you, kind, considerate poet.

The monument is preserved as a cenotaph in the present Schubert Park at Währing. The "funeral sounds at Beethoven's grave" were a male-voice chorus on a hymn-tune by the deceased, with words by Grill-parzer. The music, No. 2 of the three Equali for trombones written at Linz in 1812, was first printed in an arrangement for four male voices with pianoforte accompaniment in Ignaz von Seyfried's book on Beethoven's thorough-bass studies ('Ludwig van Beethovens Studien im Generalbasse,' 1832). It is said there that the chorus was sung in the cemetery "before a chosen number of friends and admirers."—Katharina, Freiin Wetzlar von Plankenstein, was the mother of Pauline, Freiin von Koudelka, born 1806, daughter of the musical Lieutenant-Field-Marshal Josef von Koudelka. Pauline had taken Greek lessons from Bergmann in Vienna.—Bergmann had shortly before sent his betrothed some poems of his own.

> Schubert presents the Philharmonic Society with his new C major Symphony (i. 7) for performance, spring 1828; this having been declined as too long and difficult, he offers the earlier C major Symphony (i. 6).—This information rests on tradition. It is a fact that in the society's catalogues, under the mark XIII. 8024, a symphony by Schubert is entered in the year 1828, the manuscript of which did not remain there. The great C major Symphony was declined on account of its length and difficulty, much as it was later in Paris (1842) and London (1844). Its manuscript probably came into the Philharmonic Society's archives in 1838. That of the earlier and smaller C major Symphony, which Schubert substituted, did not remain there after its performance by the society on 14th December 1828, soon after Schubert's death, but only reached the archives in 1900. The parts, however, copied by the society's treasurer, Josef Glöggl, bear the mark 8023, the number preceding that of the score of the great C major. This, by the way, was called No. 7 as early as 1838; i.e. it was counted without regard for the two unfinished Symphonies in E minor and B minor or the lost Gmunden-Gastein Symphony.

1072. SOPHIE MÜLLER TO HER BROTHER JOSEF
(About waltzes of his composition.)

[Vienna, Spring 1828.]

By the way, you must have a fine idea of my hand. What stretches! Even Bocklet and Schubert, the Blahetka and Oster (our most excellent pianoforte players) found these chords widely spread.

Josef was one of Sophie Müller's three brothers, an opera singer at Munich and an occasional composer. It is possible that the work in question, which was then still unprinted, was the 'Nine Waltzes with Trios, together with a Fantasy-Waltz, composed for the Pianoforte and dedicated to Fräulein Sophie Müller by A. J. Müller' (Mannheim, published for the author by K. F. Heckel, lithographed).

1073. JOHANN SCHICKH TO SCHUBERT

[Outside:]

Franz Schubert, Esq.,
Celebrated Composer,
Tuchlauben, No. 556,
2nd Floor.

[Inside:]

Dearest Friend,

The enclosed has been sent to me for insertion in the 'Wiener Zeitschrift' by a circle of great admirers of your beautiful and famous compositions.

Gladly as I associate myself, with all my heart, with that circle, both in admiration of your glorious talents and in the desire expressed in that appeal, the article nevertheless seems to me unsuited to publication, and I have no doubt that you will be as firmly convinced of that as I am.

In order, however, to further as far as possible the purposes of that circle, which is unknown to me, I have the pleasure of sending you the article in question, in the hope that I shall justify my action in the eyes of that music-loving circle in taking this course, seeing the impossibility of my carrying out the original purpose of the article; and I beg you to accept the assurance of my heartiest friendship and respect, with which I remain,

Your

most obedient friend,

3rd April 1828.   Schickh.

For Schickh cf. note following No. 199.—The complimentary article, containing a request to repeat the concert of 26th March, has unfortunately not been preserved. Schubert, by the way, was willing to give such concerts annually.

1074. FROM FRANZ VON HARTMANN'S DIARY

5th April 1828: To Schober's, where that splendid novel by
Tieck was read to the end.   Home at 9.45.

Cf. No. 1071.

> Josefine von Koller marries Franz Krackowizer, 8th April 1828.
> —For Fräulein von Koller cf. No. 154.—Krackowizer was estate-
> manager to Prince Wilhelm Auersperg at Losensteinleiten in
> Upper Austria, later head steward at Wels Castle.

1075. FROM THE LEIPZIG 'ALLGEMEINE MUSIKALISCHE ZEITUNG,' 9th April 1828

'The German Love Minstrels' ['Die deutschen Minnesänger'].
Latest Collection of songs for four male voices.   Vienna, Tobias
Haslinger.   Six books.

It is well known that four-part male-voice song has made
numerous friends everywhere in recent times; in almost every town
singing circles have formed themselves, and many of them can show
valiant song composers, the most excellent of whose gifts may well
be worthy of being made generally known.   It may seem just as
well, however, that many among them are unfit for publication;
we have for some time received many four-part songs, though they
were not always good.   Considering the accumulation of such
compositions, they cannot fail, for a number of reasons which
we do not intend to mention here, to include things mixed in form
and vocal pieces too like solo songs, as in the present instance.
That the true, glorious species of song will thereby suffer and
find less access to the majority than ever can hardly be denied,
unfortunately, unless the flood of such songs burrows them their
own grave, which indeed may easily happen.   However, the six
books to be noticed here do not inundate us, for each contains
but a single piece.

No. 1. Price, 15 Kreuzer.   'Grave and Moon' ['Grab und
Mond'] by Seidl and Schubert.

The song has its peculiarities and, well performed, will greatly appeal to all whose ears are well enough educated willingly to accept a few hitherto forbidden consecutive fifths with an old-world flavour. . . .

No. 4. Price, 30 Kreuzer. Words by Haug, composed by Fr. Schubert. 'Wine and Love' ['Wein und Liebe'].

Favoured though Herr Schubert be at present, this song will hardly make many friends. Indeed, it carries on so confusedly that the why and wherefore of it all is impossible to fathom. Sentiment gains nothing thereby. We count this among the composer's miscarried products and must again advise him not to have everything printed which he writes; he will otherwise but damage himself. . . .

[? G. W. Fink.]

Cf. No. 956.—In Vienna and the rest of Austria male-voice choirs began to be formed only after Schubert's death. Music for male voices was cultivated chiefly by solo quartets.—The warning at the end alludes to No. 1032.

1076. SCHUBERT TO B. SCHOTT'S SONS

Vienna, 10th April 1828.

Sirs,

The arrangements for and performance of my concert, at which all the musical pieces were of my composition, have prevented me so long from replying to your letter. However, I have since had copies made of the desired Trio (which was received at my concert by a tightly packed audience with such extraordinary applause that I have been urged to repeat the concert), the Impromptus and the five-part male chorus, and if the said Trio is agreeable to you for 100 fl., A.C., and the other two works together for 60 fl. coinage, I can send them off at once. All I should request is publication as soon as possible.

With all respect,

Frz. Schubert.

Cf. No. 1051.—Schubert sent only three of the desired eight works: Nos. 1, 2 and 6 of the list in that letter.—See No. 1091.

1077. SCHUBERT TO PROBST

[Outside:]

From Vienna
To the Book-Shop
of [H. A.] Probst, Esq.,
at Leipzig.

[Inside:]

Vienna, 10th April 1828.

Sir,

You have honoured me with a letter which, owing to the arrangements connected with my concert, has so far remained unanswered. It may perhaps not be without interest for you if I inform you that not only was the concert in question, at which all the pieces were of my composition, crammed full, but also that I received extraordinary approbation. A Trio for pianoforte, violin and violoncello in particular found general approval, so much so, indeed, that I have been invited to give a second concert (*quasi* as a repeat performance). For the rest, I can assign to you some works with pleasure, if you are inclined to agree to the reasonable fee of 60 florins, A.C., per sizable book. I need hardly assure you that I shall not send you anything which I do not regard as thoroughly successful, in so far as this is possible for an author and for some select circles [to judge], since, when all is said, it must be above all in my own interest to send good works abroad.

With all respect,
Your devoted
Frz. Schubert.

N.B. My address is:
Under the Tuchlauben,
"Blue Hedgehog," 2nd floor.

Cf. No. 1036.—This and the preceding letter reflect an elated mood induced by the concert—a new self-confidence.—The reference to a general desire for the repetition of the concert may be connected with No. 1073.—A "sizable book" probably meant a weightier one than those containing the four Impromptus or the male-voice quintet, for which together he asked only 60 florins, A.C. According to No. 1096 Schubert refers to a book of songs or pianoforte pieces.—The exact address was no longer needed in a letter to Schott, but still had to be given in one to Probst.—*See* No. 1081.

1078. From Franz von Hartmann's Diary

10th April 1828: To Bogner's, where Pepi Spaun told me that Spax will arrive here to-morrow.

Spax, i.e. Max von Spaun, went to Vienna for a fortnight to attend his brother's wedding.

1079. From Franz von Hartmann's Diary

11th April 1828: To Spaun's, where in fact I did meet Spaxel! . . . To the "Snail"; Spax and the jolly company there. Home at 12.30.

Spaxel is the affectionate diminutive of the nickname above.

1079A. From the Frankfort 'Allgemeine Musikalische Zeitung,' 12th April 1828

(Report on the review No. 798, concerning Opp. 57 and 58.)

Much fault found, yet recommended.

This periodical published a survey of the other published at Frankfort.

1080. From Franz von Hartmann's Diary

14th April 1828: Up at 7.30. With Marl to Spaun's marriage to dear Fanny Roner.

The marriage took place at 8 a.m. in the Peter church near the Graben. Aulic Councillor von Roschmann (see No. 862), the bride's brother-in-law, and Witteczek were the witnesses. A drive into the country planned to take place afterwards had to be given up owing to rain. Instead the wedding dinner was taken at Roschmann's. Schubert was certainly present. Kenner presented Spaun with a water-colour view of Linz painted by himself.—"Marl" is Karl Maurus Mayrhofer.

[Outside:]

Registered.

Franz Schubert, Esq.,

Musician and Composer,

Vienna.

under the Tuchlauben, at the
"Blue Hedgehog," 2nd floor.

[Inside:]

Franz Schubert, Esq., in Vienna.

Leipzig, 15th April 1828.

A violent attack of fever obliges me to answer your favour of the
10th inst. by the hand of a friend.

I accept, upon your word, the Trio kindly offered me against a
fee of (20 fl.) 60.—[A.C.], which please receive enclosed in

    (20 fl.) 25.— rent coupons No. 85548.
    (,,) 25.—   do.   No. 122305.
    (,,) 10.— Nat. treasury note.

    ———————————

    (20 fl.) 60.—;

but I still hope that you will shortly accede to my request to send
me very soon some selected trifles for the voice or for four hands,
a trio being as a rule but an honorary article and rarely capable
of bringing in anything.

Please hand the manuscript, sealed, to Herr Robert Lähne at
the establishment of Herren Artaria & Co., in Vienna, and you
may in future always choose that way of consignment to me, so
that you will incur no unnecessary postage.

I take it that the Trio mentioned above does not in any event
mean the Fantasy played at Herr Slawjk's concert at the Kärntnertor
Theatre on 5th February; for this has been unfavourably criticized
in the Leipzig 'Musikalische Zeitung,' No. 14, p. 223.

I have taken the most cordial interest in the success gained by your concert, and wish you a full measure of every deserved recognition in the future.

I now await your Trio and remain meanwhile, with compliments,

Respectfully and amicably yours,

Fl. 60.   H. A. Probst.

Cf. No. 1077.—The pianoforte Trio in E flat major had, it is true, been mentioned by Schubert in his letter to Probst, but offered the same day to Schott for 100 florins, A.C. He certainly had not thought of the books he proposed to Probst for 60 florins, A.C., as being as "sizable" as that. Probst, as .though scenting the competition, at once replied from his sick-bed, suggesting 60 florins for the Trio and even assigning him the fee there and then. The fact that he set the 20-florin currency of the assimilated coinage (*see* note after No. 27) in front of the separate amounts and the total sum induced Grove to suppose that he had paid only 20 florins 60 kreuzer for the Trio; but it would be as nonsensical to write out such a sum as it would be to write £20 20s. 0d. (Grove, in his lamentation, three times writes 20 florins 60 kreuzer and once 21 florins, as though, suspecting that there was something wrong, he had invented an Austrian guinea.) However, Probst was none too generous, for it must be remembered that Schubert, who accepted the money, and therefore the proposal, had to bear the costs of copying.—The criticism referred to is No. 1012.—*See* No. 1096.

1082. From Franz von Hartmann's Diary

16th April 1828: To Bogner's, whither Spax came too, who took me to Grillparzer's magnificent tragedy ('Banc-Banus'), 'A True Servant to his Master.' Then to the "Snail."

Cf. No. 1049.—Banc-Banus is the hero of Grillparzer's 'Ein treuer Diener seines Herrn,' and the play's Hungarian title is actually 'Bánk-Bán.'

1083. From Franz von Hartmann's Diary

17th April 1828: Up at 6.15. To Spax's, where Pepi's wife had such a fright at seeing us that she nearly dropped. I had to remain to breakfast, and admired the splendid arrangement of those lodgings. Then went with the Spauns, Witteczek, Gross and Gahy to the Löbl Bastion, and afterwards with Spax to Doblhoff's and Kupelwieser's (meeting nobody at either place) . . .

"A Schubert Evening at Josef von Spaun's" ("Ein Schubert-Abend bei Josef von Spaun"). Sepia Drawing by Moritz von Schwind (1868). The Original in the Schubert Museum of the City of Vienna. See pp. 572, 784, 927 and 958

PLATE XXXI

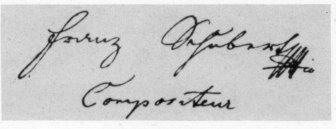

Schubert's Signature

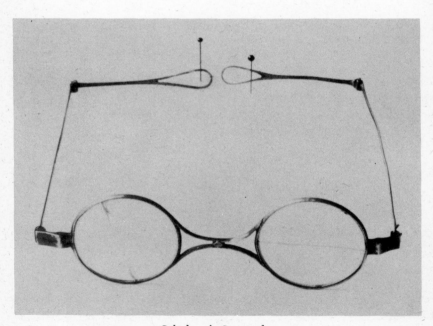

Schubert's Spectacles

PLATE XXXII

To the "Snail"; Spax also there. I saw him home with Dinand about 11.45.

Spax is Max von Spaun, Pepi his brother Josef. The couple lived in a new apartment, but clearly in the same house in the Teinfaltstrasse where Spaun's brother was now on a visit.—Gross is Josef.—The Löbl Bastion, *recte Löwelbastei*, was above the Löwel Gate leading to the Josefstadt suburb, near the Hofburg and the present Burg Theatre.—Doblhoff is Anton, Kupelwieser is Leopold, Dinand is Sauter.

1084. FROM FRANZ VON HARTMANN'S DIARY

18th April 1828: To the "Snail"; Spaxel there too. About 11.45 I betook myself home.

1085. FROM THE 'SAMMLER,' 17th April 1828

(Announcement of the concert given by Josef Rudolf Lewy, jun., member of the I. & R. Court Opera orchestra, 20th April 1828, at noon, in the Small Assembly Hall.)

5. 'On the River' ['Auf dem Strome'], by Rellstab, song with horn and pianoforte accompaniment by Schubert, performed by an excellent amateur, Herr Schubert and the concert-giver.

The singer is probably Tietze (cf. No. 1064).

1086. FROM FRANZ VON HARTMANN'S DIARY

22nd April 1828: Dear, good Max came to take leave.

Max von Spaun was returning to Linz.

1087. FROM FRANZ VON HARTMANN'S DIARY

23rd April 1828: To Schober's, where Tieck's fine story, 'The War in the Cévennes,' was begun. "Snail" . . . To bed at 11.30.

Tieck's novel, the proper title of which is 'Der Aufruhr [Revolt] in den Cevennen,' had appeared incomplete (only two of four parts) in 1826. Bauernfeld, who did not take part in these gatherings, had read it already in 1827.

1088. JENGER TO FRAU PACHLER

Vienna, 26th April 1828.

At the house of my Court Councillor von Kiesewetter died his wife's sister, which will certainly postpone the projected journey into dear Styria for a fairly long time—that is to say, Frau von Kiesewetter's and her daughter Irene's . . . Well, one star has risen for me on the musical horizon, one that stands alone and solitary in this world, and that is the greatest violin virtuoso who has ever existed and will ever be born—to wit, Paganini, whom I have heard twice already.—What you, dear lady, will read about him in all the papers—and he receives much praise—is all too little.—One can only hear, admire and wonder at him. More I cannot say. When we once again converse verbally, you shall hear more about him.

The booklet of songs by friend Schubert which he dedicates to you—and which Fräulein Irene Kiesewetter, your deputy, has accepted in your name—has already been passed for engraving. It contains the following songs:

1. 'Secret Loving' ['Heimliches Lieben']. 2. 'Weeping' ['Das Weinen']. 3. 'Before my Cradle' ['Vor meiner Wiege'] (the last two by Leitner). 4. 'Old Scottish Ballad' ['Altschottische Ballade']. The first and last composed in your house.

When Schubert and I come to you—which will doubtless be at the end of August—we shall bring some copies with us for you.

Should it happen by that time that Frau von Kiesewetter and Fräulein Irene will come to Graz with us, my only regret would be that, as *cavaliere servente* to the two ladies, I should not be able to make use of your kind offer to stay with you, as I should have to live with them at the inn.

But more about that later . . .

Cf. No. 1022.—This letter seems to indicate that the 'Old Scottish Ballad' ('Edward') was originally intended for No. 4 of Op. 106. On its appearance soon afterwards, however, the place of that song, which was perhaps considered too bloodthirsty for a delicate dedication, was taken by the Shakespeare song 'To Silvia.' The Ballad did not appear until 1863, as Op. posth. 165, No. 5.

1089. FROM FRANZ VON HARTMANN'S DIARY

26th April 1828: To Schober's, where the reading of that novel by Tieck was continued. "Snail." Home at midnight.

Cf. No. 1087.

1090. DEDICATION OF THE SONG, 'Autumn' ['Herbst'] (xx. 589), in Heinrich Panofka's Album, 28th April 1828

For kind remembrance.   Frz. Schubert.

For Panofka *see* No. 918. The song, a forerunner of the Rellstab songs in the cycle later entitled 'Swan Song' (*see* No. XVI), was preserved only in this fair copy.

1091. B. SCHOTT'S SONS TO SCHUBERT

[Outside:]

Franz Schubert, Esq.,
under the Tuchlauben at the "Blue Hedgehog,"
2nd floor

in

Vienna.

[Inside:]

Mainz, 28th April 1828.

Herr Franz Schubert in Vienna.

Sir,

Your favour of 10th April acquaints us with the fee for your manuscripts.

We note your wish to have these engraved very soon, in which case we would ask you for the moment only for the Impromptus and the five-part male chorus, the fee for which we shall settle with the amount of 60 fl., A.C.

The Trio is probably long, and as we have recently published several trios, and short of doing ourselves harm, we shall be obliged to defer that kind of composition until a little later, which might not after all be to your advantage.

As soon as we have finished printing the works described by you,
we shall take the liberty of asking you for something else again.
We salute you with respect.

B. Schott's Sons.

May we ask you to attend to the enclosed at your convenience?

Cf. No. 1076.—Schott fortunately did not ask for the pianoforte Trio,
for which Probst had paid in the meantime,   But the other two works
together came to less than the 100 florins, A.C., Schubert had asked for
the Trio.   While Probst snapped up that work for 60 florins, he too
expressed a desire for "trifles" which he, like Schott, preferred.—
What the enclosure contained is not known, for it was doubtless forwarded to one of Schott's business friends (? Haslinger).—*See* No. 1100.

1092. FROM FRANZ VON HARTMANN'S DIARY

4th May 1828: In the evening came Enk, who had gone on a
country excursion with the Schober party to-day, during which
Dinand behaved oddly and was severely talked to about it.   With
Enk to the "Snail," where Schober and Enderes were too.   When
these three had gone, Schubert came, and I sat on there with him
quite merrily until 12.20.

Whether Schubert took part in the excursion is uncertain.—Dinand is
Sauter.—There were no readings at Schober's between 3rd May and
14th June.

> Leopold von Sonnleithner marries Louise Gosmar, 6th May 1828.
> Ignaz Sonnleithner's family was ennobled in 1828, including Leopold,
> now Edler von Sonnleithner.—On Fräulein Gosmar, who now
> turned Catholic at last, *see* No. 801.—Schubert is sure to have
> attended this wedding.

1093. FROM THE PHILHARMONIC SOCIETY'S RECORDS

Meeting. 8th May 1828.   Concerning the public concerts to
be held on 29th May and 3rd June at the I. & R. Court Theatre
at the Kärntnertor.

. . . 5.   do. [Psalm] by Schubert . . .

See No. 1101.

1094. FROM BAUERNFELD'S DIARY

9th May 1828.

Heard Paganini. The admission (5 fl.) was paid for me by Schubert. . . . To-day Schubert (with Lachner) played his new, wonderful four-handed Fantasy to me.

Schubert had already attended one of Paganini's earlier concerts, perhaps with Jenger (cf. No. 1088), if not the first, then that of 13th or 20th April. Doubtless still in funds, he sat in the stalls with Bauernfeld on 4th May. This concert included the overture to Mozart's 'La clemenza di Tito'; a violin Concerto by Rodolphe Kreutzer (the second movement, *Cantabile*, with double stoppings by Paganini); a cavatina by Pacini sung by Antonia Bianchi; recitative and three airs ("Deh cari venite," "Nel cor più non mi sento," "Di certi giovani conosco l'arte") with variations, played on the G string; aria by Mercadante sung by Bianchi; variations on the witches' dance from Süssmayr's ballet 'Il noce di Benevento.'—For the Fantasy in F minor *see* No. 1043.

1095. FROM A LOST LETTER FROM SCHUBERT to Anselm Hüttenbrenner

(On Niccolo Paganini)
[Spring 1828.]

I have heard an angel sing in the *Adagio*.

Cf. No. 1007.—It is worth noting that Schubert is said to have already used a similar turn of phrase at the Seminary, when he said of the trio of the minuet in Mozart's G minor Symphony: "It is as though the angels were joining in their voices."—He is perhaps referring to an earlier Paganini concert here, not to that of 4th May. On 29th March Paganini had played for the first time his own second violin Concerto, Op. 7, in B minor. Between a wild *allegro*, with double shakes in thirds, and before the famous rondo, in which a bell accompanies the solo violin's harmonics, there is, as the third of the four movements, an *Adagio* in D major which made a particularly deep impression by its simple and expressive melody. It seems likely that this was the one Schubert referred to among several slow movements Paganini played at that time, some of them as interpolations into other composers' consertos.

1096. SCHUBERT TO PROBST

[Outside:]

[H. A.] von Probst, Esq.

[Inside:]

Vienna, 10th May 1828.

Sir,

Herewith I am sending you the desired Trio, although a song or pianoforte book was understood for the price of 60 fl., A.C., and not a trio, for which six times as much work is required. In order, however, to make a beginning at last, I would only ask for the speediest possible publication, and for the dispatch of 6 copies. The cuts indicated in the last movement are to be most scrupulously observed. Be sure to have it performed for the first time by capable people, and most particularly see to a continual uniformity of tempo at the changes of the time-signature in the last movement. The minuet at a moderate pace and *piano* throughout, the trio, on the other hand, vigorous except where *p* and *pp* are marked. In expectation of the earliest publication,

I remain,

respectfully,

your devoted

Frz. Schubert.

Cf. No. 1081.—The complete edition of Schubert's works reproduced the pianoforte Trio in E flat major, Op. 100, from Probst's first edition, which appeared in October or November 1828, the autograph not being accessible in 1886. In an appendix (vii. 4b), which is missing in most of the copies of series vii, the work was printed over again, unabridged, in 1891. The editor, Ignaz Brüll, expressed his doubts whether the two cuts in the finale were Schubert's own. This, however, is now proved, and the form in which the work is generally known is the definitive one. It appears that Schubert made the changes in the autograph and in the manuscript copy shortly before sending off the work to Probst because the work had proved too long in performance. The autograph, like other Schubert manuscripts, went to Countess Karoline Esterházy. (Brahms possessed a sketch for it.)—Schubert may have had a performance at Leipzig in mind, brought about by Probst.—*See* No. 1123.

1097. IGNAZ PAPSCH TO FRAU PACHLER

Vienna, 10th May 1828.

Augusta and Roderich send you all their kisses, and so do Jenger and Schubert.

Papsch, born in 1800, worked as an actor at Graz under the covering name of Pusch.—Heinrich Anschütz's (*see* note on p. 202) children were Roderich (born 1818 at Breslau), who had already appeared in children's parts at the Burg Theatre, and Auguste, born in 1819, whose later married names were first Koberwein and then Demuth, and who joined the same theatre in 1831.

1098. PAPSCH TO FRAU PACHLER

Vienna, 11th May 1828.

Jenger, Tubby, Müller and the Anschützes send cordial greetings.

Müller is Sophie.

1099. FERDINAND TRAWEGER, SEN., TO SCHUBERT

[Outside:]

From Gmunden on Lake Traun.
Franz Schubert, Esq.,
Composer

in

To be delivered at the "Red   Vienna.
Hedgehog" under the Tuch-
lauben on the 2nd floor.

[Inside:]

Gmunden, 19th May 1828.

Dear Friend Schubert,

Zierer told me you would like to be at Gmunden again, and that he was to ask me how much I charge for board and lodging, and I was to write to you about it. You really embarrass me; if I did not know you and your open, guileless way of thinking, and if I did not fear that in the end you might not come, I should ask nothing. But in order to get the idea out of your head that you might be a burden to any one, and so that you may stay on without constraint as long as you like, listen: for your room, which you know, including breakfast, lunch and supper, you will pay me 50 kreuzer, V.C., per day, and pay extra for what you wish to drink. I must close, else I shall miss the post. Write to me immediately whether my proposal satisfies you.

Your
sincere friend,
Ferdinand Traweger.

For Traweger cf. No. 132 and 562.—He confused Schubert's house with that of the Philharmonic Society in the address: Schubert was at the "Blue Hedgehog."—Franz Zierer, whom Schindler cited as witness in the Schechner affair (*see* No. 656), was a flautist in the orchestra of the Kärntnertor Theatre; he was then on a concert tour (*see* No. 1140), which took him to Italy. He heard of Schubert's death at Naples.—Schubert thought of the Salzkammergut as well as of Graz for his recuperation, but his hopes were in vain.

1100. SCHUBERT TO B. SCHOTT'S SONS

[Outside:]

To the Art Establishment
of Schott's Sons
at Mainz.

[Inside:]

Sirs,   Vienna, 23rd May 1828.

Herewith I send you the two desired compositions, each at the rate of 60 florins currency. I request you to publish the same as soon as possible and trust that you will do good business with them, as indeed I may hope, since both compositions have been very well received here. In expectation of the promised fee, I remain,

With respect,
Frz. Schubert.

N.B. I also beg you to let me have 6 copies of each work.

Cf. No. 1091.—The four Impromptus, which were published as Op. posth. 142 by Diabelli only in 1838, had not been played in public. For the other work in question, 'Moonlight,' *see* Nos. 991 and 992.—"All respect" (No. 1076) has now become mere "respect" (and Probst's "all respect" [No. 1077] was lowered to "respectfully" [No. 1096]).— The parcel was sent through Haslinger.—*See* No. 1151.

1101. From the Programme of the Grand Pupils' Concert of the Conservatory, 29th May 1828, at 7 p.m., in the Kärntnertor Theatre

Part II. . . . 9. Psalm 23, a vocal chorus by Herr Fr. Schubert, performed by the lady pupils of the Singing School, third section.

The concert, given for the benefit of the Conservatory, included a prologue, the overtures to Cherubini's 'Anacreon' and Catel's 'Semiramis' (but not the one to 'The Enchanted Rose' by Wolfram, which had been submitted: cf. No. 663), a duet from Gyrowetz's 'Federica ed Adolfo' and another by the same composer, both sung as female choruses, as well as, once again, the final sextet from 'Don Giovanni.'—Cf. No. 1093.

1102. From the 'Sammler,' 24th June 1828

9. Psalm 23. Vocal chorus with pianoforte accompaniment by Fr. Schubert. The singing students of the third section endeavoured to carry into their performance the profound feeling the composer brought to bear on this Psalm. How successful they were in this was proved by the general demand for its repetition.

L.

1103. From the Official 'Wiener Zeitung,' 30th May 1828

At the House of Tobias Haslinger,
Music Publisher in Vienna,
in the Graben, in the House of the First Austrian Savings Bank,
No. 572.

is to be had:

IN THE FOREST and ON THE BRUCK,

['Im Walde']   ['Auf der Brücke' (*sic*)]

two Poems by Ernst Schulze,

set to Music

for One Voice with Pianoforte Accompaniment

by

FRANZ SCHUBERT,

during his presence at Graz.

Op. 90 [*sic*].   Price, 1 Florin 20 Kreuzer, A.C.

The name of this song composer, renowned at home and abroad, guarantees the inward content of the work announced, which ranks worthily with those published earlier and will be greatly welcomed by every admirer of the Schubertian Muse. We particularly draw attention to the second song, 'On the Bridge' [*sic*], which stands there, as original as 'Erl King' and 'The Wanderer,' and may even dispute the front rank with these favourite songs.

Op. "90" *recte* 93, appeared after Op. 91, without a dedication. The number 90, perhaps suggested by Schubert while he was at Graz (cf. Nos. 1007 and 1022), had in the meantime been used for the first 'Four Impromptus' (cf. the further confusion with Opp. 87 and 84 in Nos. 979, 920 and 916; when Diabelli changed Op. 90 into Op. 93 Leidesdorf had already used the latter for the later Op. 108). The advertisement by a misprint says "absence at Graz" (*Abwesenheit* instead of *Anwesenheit*), which might have made sense, but did not appear so on the title-page, nor in later advertisements. The book had been lithographed by Josef Franz Kaiser at Graz and published there by Josef Andreas Kienreich; Haslinger was only the latter's agent in Vienna. The correct title of the second song, according to Schubert as well as the poet, Schulze, is 'Auf der Bruck,' a place near Göttingen where the poem was written. For the same reason the other poem bears the original title of 'In the Forest behind Falken-hagen' (also near Göttingen) and has as little to do with a forest as its companion has with a bridge. The corruption is due to the first publisher.

1103A. Marie von Pratobevera to her Betrothed, Josef Bergmann at Cilli

Vienna, 31st May 1828.

Tremier comes to see us very often . . . Now she [Fanni] is overwhelmed by him with sweet, touching songs by Schubert, for, do you know, he is even more enraptured by Fanni's singing than you ever were by my voice in the old days.

Josef Tremier, born in 1805, was the betrothed of Franziska von Pratobevera (see No. 998). Her album, which is now in the Vienna City Library, was evidently started by her fiancé. It contains for the most part copies of Schubert songs, some transposed for mezzo-soprano or contralto, as well as the holograph title of the song 'Death's Music' ('Todesmusik'); Beethoven's 'Evening Song under a Starlit Sky' ('Abend-lied unterm gestirnten Himmel') transposed by Schubert himself from E major to D major; and, among the copies of Schubert's own works, a copy of his own copy of Reichardt's song 'Iphigenia's Monologue' (published in 1804, copied by Schubert in 1815, his autograph in the Fitzwilliam Museum at Cambridge).

1104. Inscription on the Autograph of the Organ Fugue in E minor (ix. 28)

Baden, 3rd June 1828.

The date is written by an unknown hand. Franz Lachner arranged a competition with Schubert when they and Johann (or ? Josef Kilian) Schickh (see No. 511) spent a night in an inn at Baden.

Schubert, with J. Schickh and Franz Lachner, makes an excursion from Baden to the Heiligenkreuz Monastery, 4th June 1828. The watering-place of Baden lies south of Vienna; the Cistercian abbey of Heiligenkreuz, founded in 1135, is north-west of Baden. Lachner and Schubert played on the abbey church organ there two fugues for four hands written the day before. This was Schubert's only work for organ alone. It was published in 1844 as Op. posth. 152 by Diabelli, for organ or pianoforte duet.

1105. JOHANN THEODOR MOSEWIUS TO SCHUBERT

[Outside:]

Franz Schubert, Esq.,
Celebrated Composer in
Vienna.

[Inside:]

Very dear Sir and Friend,

I take the liberty of asking my countryman, the music teacher Herr Kühn, to hand you these lines and of recommending you the same most particularly, as he wishes to remain in Vienna for some time and intends to develop his talent for composition there. I am heartily glad to be informed of your well-being through Haslinger, and to hear that altogether things are with you as you deserve, i.e. well.—As for your continued diligence, your compositions bear witness to it, and their value continues to be more and more appreciated also in our formerly rather one-sided North. You will not set great store by the fact that I too am among your great admirers, and that your 'Maid of the Mill' songs in particular have opened up to me an understanding of your individuality. I continue to be curious about all the products of your Muse and have been truly edified by your 'Winter Journey.' —You will know by this time that I have resigned my former post; I was appointed musical director and academic music teacher at the University here, and as the exalted Ministry at the same time entrusted me with the direction of the Royal Institute for Church Music, I am very happy in that sphere of activity also.—Perhaps I may be so fortunate as to see you again very soon and to repeat to you verbally the assurance that I am and remain most respectfully and in true devotion.

Your
appreciative friend

Breslau, 4th June 1828.   Mosewius.

Mosewius, born in 1788 at Königsberg, had been an opera singer until 1825. He had appeared as a guest in Vienna in 1822, been in touch with Schober at Breslau in 1824, founded the Vocal Academy there, and was since 1827 second lecturer of music at the University and director of the

Royal Academic Institute for Church Music.—Josef Karl Kühn, born at Elbing, East Prussia, in 1803, had been a teacher of musical theory at Breslau since 1825.

1106. Mosewius to Schober

Breslau, 4th June 1828.

I take advantage of these lines to inform you of some change of heart: it concerns our Schubert, whom I have now learnt to care for very much; I take him as he is and find him not only excellent, but unexcelled. Our *objectum litis*, the 'Maid of the Mill' songs, it was which first converted me; and his 'Passing-Bell' ['Das Zügenglöcklein'], 'Wayfarer addressing the Moon' ['Der Wanderer an den Mond'] and above all the 'Winter Journey' are glorious. I am curious in advance about any of his work and keep my pupils busy singing it all, into whose hands, as you know, I place nothing that is bad, to the best of my knowledge.

The letter to Schubert was evidently enclosed in that to Schober. Mosewius may have known that the two lived together.

1107. From the 'Wiener Zeitschrift für Kunst,' &c., 7th June 1828

Rondeau brillant pour Pianoforte et Violon par François Schubert. Op. 70. Vienne, chez Artaria et Comp.

The grandiose talent of the renowned song and romance composer is many-sided and tries itself in every branch, as do all those who possess the spirit of true and upward-striving art. The work under notice shows a bold master of harmony, who gives his picture a strong, vigorous fundamental tone and within that knows how to unite his shapes and groups in such a way that they all go to the making of a beautiful whole. A fiery imagination animates this piece and draws the player to the depths and heights of harmony, borne now by a mighty hurricane, now by gentle waves.

Although the whole is brilliant, it is not indebted for its existence to mere figurations, such as grin at us in thousandfold contortions from many a composition and fatigue the soul. The inventive spirit has here often beaten its wings mightily enough and lifted us up with it. Both the pianoforte and the fiddle require a practised artist, who must be prepared for passages which have not by any means attained to their right of citizenship by endless use, but betoken a succession of new and inspired ideas. The player will feel attracted in an interesting way by a beautiful harmonic interchange.

1108. From the 'Wiener Zeitschrift für Kunst,' &c., 7th June 1828

'Winter Journey' ['Winterreise'] by Wilhelm Müller. Set to music for one voice with pianoforte accompaniment by Franz Shcubert. Work 89. [Part I.] Vienna, Tobias Haslinger.

It is with much pleasure that we undertake to announce this fine and interesting work, in which the composer's genius irradiates with true inspiration the glorious songs by the most noble of poets. The first number, 'Good Night' ['Gute Nacht'], distinguishes itself by profoundly felt melancholy, which only in the last verse takes on a consoling character, where at [the thought of] the beloved's slumber the poet's whole love reawakens.—'The Weather-Vane' ['Die Wetterfahne'] is a picture of wild despair, and very powerful; 'Numbness' ['Erstarrung'] a most impassioned painting; 'The Lime-Tree' ['Der Lindenbaum'] a song full of emotion, in which musical delineation again takes a very handsome share; how deeply felt is 'Flood' ['Wasserflut'] and 'On the River' ['Auf dem Flusse'], while in 'Retrospect' ['Rückblick'] the accompaniment takes a most wonderful share; how simple and ingenious at once is 'Will-o'-the-Wisp' ['Das Irrlicht']; how effective in 'Rest' ['Rast'] is the passage where the expression changes between loud and soft, proclaiming the agitated heart's clamorous tempest; how truly romantic is 'Dream of Spring' ['Der Frühlingstraum'], to which the sad song of sorrow, 'Solitude' ['Die Einsamkeit'] succeeds as the fairest flower of the great wreath.

We congratulate the gifted composer with all our hearts on so well-made and beautiful a work and gladly await its sequel.

1109. PAULINE DE CHOISEUL TO ANTONIE OSTER

Millotitz [Moravia], 13th June 1828.

. . . I would further ask you, dear Toni, to send me the 'Valses sentimentales' in 2 books, by Schubert. For 2 hands.

Pauline, Comtesse de Choiseul d'Aillecourt, *née* Countess Sérényi, a dame of the Order of the Starry Cross, was just awaiting a new pianoforte by Graf (*see* No. 66) on her country estate, and she also ordered, through Antonie Oster, Karl Czerny's Variations on Paganini's rondo, 'La Campanella' (cf. No. 1095), just published. Hugelmann had dedicated to her the third book of his pianoforte duet arrangement of Mozart's string quintets (*see* No. 483).

1110. KARL BRÜGGEMANN TO SCHUBERT

[Outside:]

Franz Schubert, Esq., Composer.

Vienna.

Franked.

[Postal Note:]

Does not belong to Herr Josef Schubert on the Wien.
City, to be sought out at Diabelli's.

[Inside:]

Highly honoured Sir,

I have been publishing these last few months a collection of pianoforte compositions, which appears in monthly numbers and contains one half of original and the other half of arranged items. I take the liberty, Sir, of asking most submissively whether you would be inclined to support this undertaking by contributions for pianoforte without accompaniment. The original compositions to be included must not be too difficult, but may on the

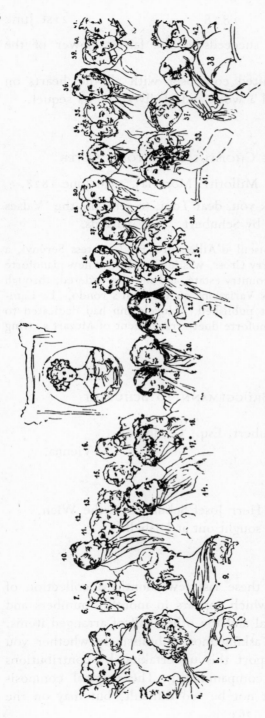

Key to Schwind's "Schubert Evening at Spaun's." Pen-and-ink Drawing by Hans Mauer (1913).

1. Karl Pinterics. 2. Josef Witteczek. 3. Franz Lachner. 4. Ignaz Lachner... 9. Franziska Pinterics (Karl's wife). 10. Karl von Schönstein. 11. Benedikt Randhartinger. 12. Josef von Gahy. 13. Johann Steiger von Amstein. 14. Johann Michael Vogl. 15. Ferdinand Mayerhofer von Grünbühel. 16. Anton von Doblhoff. 17. SCHUBERT. 18. Josef von Spaun. 19. Franz von Hartmann, 20. Anton von Spaun. . . . 22. Kunigunde Vogl. 23. Ludwig Kraissl. 24. Josef Kenner. 25. Marie Ottenwalt. 26. Ludwig Ferdinand Schnorr von Carolsfeld. 27. Moritz von Schwind. 28. Anna Hönig. 29. August Wilhelm Rieder. 30. Leopold Kupelwieser. 31. Therese Hönig. 32. Anton Dietrich. 33. Franz von Schober. 34. Romeo Franz Seligmann. 35. Ernst von Feuchtersleben. 36. Franz Grillparzer. 37. Justina von Bruchmann. 38. Eduard von Bauernfeld. 39. Franz von Bruchmann. 40. Johann Chrisostomus Senn. 41. Johann Mayrhofer. 42. Ignaz Franz Castelli. The portrait on the wall is that of Countess Karoline Esterházy, painted by Josef Teltscher. The other portraits are of later friends of Schwind's

contrary be quite easy; their form is left wholly to the honoured collaborators' discretion, except that their extent should not exceed two sheets, since each book consists of only three sheets. Smaller things, such as little rondos, dances and the like, are also quite suitable for inclusion. The editorship has been assumed by Herr Mühling, musical director at Magdeburg, whose name will warrant you that nothing is taken up which might stand unworthily side by side with your contributions.

If you are inclined, Sir, to grant the above wish, I would most respectfully ask you to give me news speedily and to fix your fee, payment of which shall always be made promptly. Should you by any chance have anything in stock to suit the above purpose, I beg you to join it at once to your valued reply. It remains for me to observe that the purpose of the undertaking makes it desirable that the contributions should consist of easily comprehensible and pleasing music.

I am, Sir, most respectfully,
Your obedient servant,

Halberstadt, 21st June 1828.   Brüggemann.

Brüggemann was the last German publisher to approach Schubert.— The letter, insufficiently addressed, once again went to that officially known but now unknown Schubert in the "an der Wien" suburb (cf. No. 1036).—The 'Museum for Pianoforte Music and Song,' edited by August Mühling (born in 1786 at Raguhn, orchestral and concert manager at Magdeburg since 1823), appeared in 1828–31, twelve books per annum. —Schubert's reply, which was not unfavourable, is lost (see No. 1122).

1111. FROM FRANZ VON HARTMANN'S DIARY

21st June 1828: To Schober's, who read us Kleist's 'Prince of Hesse-Homburg.'

Heinrich von Kleist's drama 'Der Prinz von Homburg' was published in 1821 in his 'Literary Remains' ('Hinterlassene Schriften') and produced in Vienna in 1831.

1112. From the Berlin 'Allgemeine Musikalische Zeitung,'
25th June 1828

. . . To the same category [as songs by Theodor Fröhlich, Ferdinand Stegmayer, Johann Spech and K. E. Hering] belongs, finally, the following work, which must be recommended by a special mention on account of its author's more widespread reputation, its extent and the excellence of its typographical presentation:

'Winter Journey.' ['Winterreise'] by Wilhelm Müller. For one voice and pianoforte by Franz Schubert. Work 89. Part I. Haslinger, Vienna. Price, 2 Thaler.

Schubert has talent, shows originality here and there, and would do even better work were it not for the fatal 89. Nothing leads more readily to frittering and flattening, nothing tempts more to an easy-going manner, than a glut in song composition in particular. The same might be said of our present-day poets. Their two dozen spring, three dozen love, four dozen wayfarer's, five dozen miller's and 666 dozen oriental songs recall the miser's soup, in which a single shining patch of grease floats upon an ocean. Wilhelm Müller sings in the 'Winter Journey' 1. 'Good Night,' 2. 'The Weather-Vane,' 3. 'Frozen Tears,' 4. 'Numbness,' 5. 'The Lime-Tree,' 6. 'Flood' (hear, hear!), 7. 'On the River' —in short he does not close before No. 24, 'The Hurdy-Gurdy Man' ['Der Leiermann']. Schubert has already assiduously pursued him through twelve numbers. It might have become one good song had it not become twenty-four of them. But if Goethe too had made three thousand (proportionately) out of his song

How splendidly radiant
Is Nature for me!

well, the less Goethe he.

However—there must be goods in bales too, and Müller and Schubert may be recommended!

Friedrich Theodor Fröhlich was born in 1803 at Brugg (Aargau) in Switzerland; Karl Eduard Hering in 1807 at Oschatz in Saxony.—For Stegmayer see No. 513, for Spech No. 366.—The Goethe poem quoted is the 'Mailied,' composed by Beethoven, among others.—The tone of this review is very Berlinish.

1113. FROM FRANZ VON HARTMANN'S DIARY

28th June 1828: With Enk to Schober's. Kleist's 'Prince of Homburg' read to the end. To the "Partridge"; Hörwarter there too. Schwind behaved knavishly towards Dinand. Dinand very handsome. Home about 12.45.

Cf. No. 1111.—Dinand is Ferdinand Sauter.

1114. FROM FRANZ VON HARTMANN'S DIARY

29th June 1828: To Grinzing with Enk and Louis, after having ferreted out Schubert too. All four tipsy, more or less, but Schubert especially. Home at midnight.

Hartmann supplements this entry as follows in his family chronicle: "We were tipsy, Enk especially, who began a race in the streets."—This is the only case of Schubert's being described as inebriated in any document. The stories which represent him as a drunkard are disproved— apart from the quantity of his work done during such a short span of life —by remarks written down by Spaun, his oldest friend, after the publication of Kreissle's biography: ". . . Schubert was always moderate, and if he had not been so of his own accord, his finances would have forced him thereto. . . . It is said to have happened one day that, on turning into an inn at Grinzing with his brothers and their friends on a very hot day, he drank a little beyond his thirst, being tired after a long walk; but such an accident does not justify his being accused of drunkenness, he being so temperate as a rule. . . ." The very same day may here be referred to, for as late as 1864 Spaun may easily have imperfectly remembered who the participants were.

> Schubert's Op. 96, 'The Stars' ('Die Sterne'), 'Huntsman's Love Song' ('Jägers Liebeslied'), 'Wayfarer's Night Song' ('Wanderers Nachtlied') and 'Fisherman's Ditty' ('Fischerweise'), appears with a dedication to Charlotte, Princess von Kinsky, 1828.

> Schubert's Op. 106, 'Secret Loving' ('Heimliches Lieben'), 'Weeping' ('Das Weinen'), 'Before my Cradle' ('Vor meiner Wiege') and 'To Silvia' appears with a dedication to Frau Marie Pachler, 1828.

> Opp. 96 and 106 appeared privately printed, lithographed at Schober's establishment, which however is not named on the

title-pages.   The first issue of Op. 96, with an imprint of the dedication in brown ink, is signed by Schubert, but he himself inserted the
opus number on the whole edition.   The words of 'Huntsman's
Love Song' are by Schober, who acquired the autograph; oddly
enough the same poem became a folksong in Transylvania with music
by an anonymous composer.   For No. 3 cf. note preceding No. 912.
—Marie Karoline, or Charlotte, Princess Kinsky, *née* Freiin von
Kerpen in 1782, was the widow of Prince Ferdinand Kinsky of
Wchinitz and Tettau, a patron of Beethoven, who in a letter to
Breitkopf & Härtel in 1812 called her "one of the prettiest of the
fattest women in Vienna," and who dedicated three works to her.
She was a dame of the Starry Cross and chief stewardess to the Archduchess Sophie (mother of the Emperor Francis Joseph).   She
"sang with a smooth, full, Italian tone."   In her drawing-room in
the Freiung square the following scene is said to have taken place:
the guests acclaimed only the singer of the songs (Schönstein) and
ignored the accompanist, who also happened to be the composer;
when the hostess commiserated him, Schubert said that "he was
quite accustomed to being overlooked, indeed he quite liked it, for he
thus felt less embarrassed" (Spaun's Recollections).   The fact
is that Schubert was not so easily at home in the palaces of the
Viennese nobility as Beethoven had been.—On the title-page of
Op. 106 there are, in the first issue, notes in Schubert's hand.
For this work cf. Nos. 1022 and 1088.—Op. 96 appeared probably before Opp. 92 and 94, which were not announced till
July (*see* No. 1120), and certainly before Op. 95 (No. 1133);
Op. 106, however, came out not only before Op. 97 (No. 1153), but
before the posthumously published Opp. 98, 99, 101–5 (*see* Supple-
ment, No. V, p. 943).

1115. FROM THE DRESDEN 'ABENDZEITUNG,' 8th September 1828

(Vienna correspondence, June–July 1828.)

The best of these [smaller musical compositions] may well be
Schubert's songs, of which one excels the next in characteristic
tone-painting.

1116. From Robert Schumann's Diary, 1828

In the summer of 1828 composition of a great many four-handed polonaises and songs by J. Kerner and Lord Byron. Letter to Wiedebein (and Reissiger). Also to Franz Schubert (not sent off).

The eight polonaises are preserved in the archives of the Philharmonic Society in Vienna, and they were published in 1933.—Justinus Kerner, born in 1786, was a physician and poet. Gottlob Wiedebein, born in 1799 at Eilenstadt near Halberstadt, a conductor and song composer, was a friend of Schumann's. On Reissiger *see* note preceding No. 275.— The letter to Schubert is unfortunately not extant. Schumann soon became one of the first and most ardent heralds of Schubert's art.

Katharina Lászny, *née* Buchwieser, dies 3rd July 1828.

1117. Jenger to Frau Pachler

Vienna, 4th July 1828.

The absence of two officials from my office to take the waters at Baden, and further the not very brilliant financial circumstances of friend Schubert—who sends a great many compliments to you, friend Dr. Karl and little Faust as well as all acquaintances—are the obstacles that prevent us just now from taking advantage of your kind invitation to come to Graz.—Schubert had in any case planned to spend part of the summer at Gmunden and its environs —whence he has already received several invitations—from accepting which he has however so far been prevented by the above-mentioned financial embarrassments.

He is still here at present, works diligently at a new Mass and only awaits still—wherever it may come from—the necessary money to take his flight into Upper Austria.

In these circumstances our excursion to Graz may thus take its turn at the beginning of September again, as it did last year, if on my side the Russians and the Turks do not queer my pitch, which would annoy me frightfully. . . . Above all, it is now a matter of patiently awaiting the time which will bring either roses or thorns with it . . .

As regards our accommodation, whether, that is, we are to stay with you at the Hallerschlössel or at your town house, we Viennese would certainly prefer the former.   May God only grant that we shall be allowed to settle down at the one place or the other; the rest will come of itself.   But should I really be unable to get away this year, I shall at least send you friend Schubert, who is already— as he told me to-day—looking forward to being able to spend a few weeks near you.

For Gmunden *see* No. 1099.   By its "environs" Ebenzweier is probably meant, where Anton von Spaun and his wife stayed in the late summer.— The new Mass is that in E flat major, begun in June.—During the Greek War of Liberation Russian troops occupied the Danube principalities in 1828.   Jenger was employed by the Court War Council.—The Pachlers again spent the summer of 1828 at Haller's Castle near Graz (*see* No. 943). —Schubert got neither to Gmunden nor to Styria.

1118. From Franz von Hartmann's Diary

5th July 1828: Out to Schober's, who read us the first two acts of [Kleist's] 'Katie of Heilbronn.'   Then to the "Moonshine" with him, where it was most jolly and interesting.   Home at 11.30.

Between early July and early August Hartmann uses the turn of phrase "out to Schober's," which seems to indicate that Schober and his mother (? with Schubert) again made a short summer sojourn in the environs of Vienna, e.g. at Währing as in 1826.   But nothing is known about this.—On Kleist's 'Käthchen von Heilbronn' *see* Nos. 691 and 748.— The "Moonshine" is Schwind's home.

1119. Charlotte, Princess Kinsky, to Schubert

Please receive my thanks once again, dear Herr Schubert, both for the interest you took in the success of my concert and for the dedication of the songs just received, which I look forward to admiring next winter, if your and Baron Schönstein's complaisance will afford me that delight.   Please accept the enclosed as a poor token of my gratitude, and thus greatly oblige your devoted

Charlotte, Pncs. Kinsky.

Vienna, 7th July
1828.

Cf. note preceding No. 1115.—The princess's musical evening, which must have taken place shortly before, was probably the occasion of that experience with Schönstein, who had introduced Schubert there.—The amount of the honorarium the princess sent is not known.

Antonie Oster dies, 8th July 1828.

1120. FROM THE OFFICIAL 'WIENER ZEITUNG,' 11th July 1828

At the House of M. J. Leidesdorf,

Art and Music Dealer in Vienna, Kärntnerstrasse, No. 941,

is just published and to be had (in Pest of Herr

K. Lichtl, as well as of all book and music dealers in

the Austrian Provinces):

Momens musicales [sic]
pour le Pianoforte
par François Schubert.

Œuvre 94.   Two Books, each 36 Kreuzer, A.C.

.   .   .   .

| THE MUSES' SON | ON THE LAKE | SPIRIT'S GREETING |
| ['Der Musensohn'] | ['Auf dem See'] | ['Geistes-Gruss'] |

Three Poems by Goethe,

for Voice with Pianoforte Accompaniment,

by FR. SCHUBERT.

Op. 92.   Price, 1 Florin, A.C.

According to No. 1150 Opp. 92 and 94 had already been announced for the Easter Fair (the Leipzig book-mart); but they were only now advertised in Vienna.   That such a preliminary announcement had no great significance is shown by the fact that Op. 93 (*recte* Op. 108), notified by Leidesdorf at the same fair, was not advertised in Vienna until 28th January 1829.—Op. 94 (without dedication) bears on the page-heading, as well as in the advertisement, the grammatically faulty title of 'Momens musicales,' and on the cover "musicals," a mistake that perpetuated itself for a long time.   There are six pieces, three in each book, Nos. 3 and 6 of which had already appeared in Sauer & Leidesdorf's collections (*see* Nos. 407, 510 and 608).—Op. 92 is "dedicated to the well-born Frau Josefine von Franck" (*née* von Körber, Bielitz, 1789, *see* No. 1037).

She was the widow of the wholesale merchant and art collector Josef,
Ritter von Franck, member of the Lower Austrian County Council, who
had died the preceding year.   He had a collection of original portraits of
artists of the Viennese stage, whom he would invite to lunch and reward
for their sittings with a gold coin placed under their covers at table.
Schubert's dedication to the lady was clearly due to no other reason than
that of a present made to him in return.—It was at this time, July 1828,
that Schubert wrote the 92nd Psalm (in Hebrew) for the City Temple of
the Jewish community, set for baritone solo with S.A.T.B.   The solo was
sung by Salomon Sulzer (born at Hohenems, Vorarlberg, in 1804), a re-
former of Jewish religious singing, on whom Frances Trollope wrote in
1836: "A voice, to which that of [John] Braham in his best days was not
superior."   An alleged letter from Schubert to Sulzer concerning the
song 'Omnipotence,' published by one of the cantor's descendants
('Neues Wiener Journal,' 9th March 1928), is a forgery.

1121. FROM FRANZ VON HARTMANN'S DIARY

12th July 1828: Out to Schober's, where the reading of
'Katie of Heilbronn' was finished.   Then to the "Partridge,"
where Hörwarter was, also his brother.   Home at 12 o'clock.

Cf. No. 1118.—Nothing is known about Hörwarter's brother.

1122. [LOST LETTER FROM SCHUBERT to Brüggemann, middle of July 1828.]

Cf. No. 1110; see No. 1132.

1123. PROBST TO SCHUBERT

[Outside:]

Franz Schubert, Esq.,

Musician and Composer.

Vienna.

At convenience.

[Inside:]

Franz Schubert, Esq., Musician and Composer in Vienna.

Leipzig, 18th July 1828.

Not until to-day did I receive your favour of 10th May with the Trio, and you must therefore not be surprised, my valued friend, if this work is published somewhat later than perhaps you expected. However, work on it has started immediately, and it may be ready within about six weeks. In the meantime I would ask you further to let me know

1) the title as well as the dedication, if any,

2) the opus number,

as I should like to proceed as nearly as possible in accordance with your wishes in this respect.

All your further directions concerning this work shall be followed most faithfully.

As soon as it is ready, I shall send you the stipulated six copies as an enclosure.

My opinion of it I shall have the honour of communicating to you later, until which time I remain in

respectful devotion,

H. A. Probst.

Cf. No. 1096.—Schubert seems to have chosen a roundabout way of sending the copy of the E flat major pianoforte Trio.—Probst probably kept the expression of his opinion of the work (for which he was not asked) for a time at which he would be able to hear it.—See No. 1129.

1124. FROM FRANZ VON HARTMANN'S DIARY

19th July 1828: To Schober's, who read us the strange but very fine 'Novel' by Goethe. To the "Partridge"; the doctor, Dinand, Enk, Louis there too; Schubert not till later. Home at 12.20.

Goethe's 'Novel' ('Novelle' is its actual title) had just appeared.— The doctor is Hörwarter, Dinand is Sauter, Louis is Hartmann's brother.

1125. From Franz von Hartmann's Diary

23rd July 1828: With Enk and Louis to the "Neuling," where we sat quite merrily with Schubert. Home at 9.30.

Vincenz Neuling was a music-loving burgess who exercised several callings. A pupil of Mayseder's, he was a violinist and a fellow of the Philharmonic Society, he composed, was the owner of the Gundelhof in the Bauernmarkt (where among others Ignaz von Sonnleithner lived), a court jeweller, a district almoner, a brewer (like Dr. Pachler at Graz) and the owner of a beer-garden in the Landstrasse suburb, where he regularly engaged string quartets or brass bands to play for his guests' entertainment. Bauernfeld, who lived close by at that time, frequented it with friends.

1126. From Franz von Hartmann's Diary

July 26th 1828: With Enk to Schober's, who however left us all in the lurch.

The reading at Schober's was cancelled for that Saturday.

1127. From Franz von Hartmann's Diary

27th July 1828: To Nussdorf with Potpeschnigg and Haller. Betty was very bitter and sad to-day. Thus there was nothing much to be done with her. Mayrhofer, the poet, was there too. Glorious Schubert songs were sung in chorus. We did not drive away until 10 o'clock. Then to the "Zögernitz," where we sat on until 12.15.

This visit was again paid to the Wanderer family (*see* note preceding No. 595).—Johann Potpeschnigg (a medical student who married Fräulein von Grafenegg [*see* No. 943] and an ancestor of Hugo Wolf's friend) and Adam Haller (*see* No. 745) were friends of Karl Maurus Mayrhofer's. Johann Mayrhofer had become a rare visitor to the Schubert circle.—Ferdinand Zögernitz (the founder of a "Casino" still in existence) kept an inn at Döbling on the way from the city to Grinzing or Nussdorf.

1128. From the Munich 'Allgemeine Musik-Zeitung,'
28th July 1828

'Winter Journey' ['Winterreise']. By Wilhelm Müller. Set
to music for one voice with pianoforte accompaniment by Franz
Schubert. Work 89. Part I. Vienna, Haslinger. 3 Florins, A.C.

A song cycle as to content and form of the words, with love
and tears for its main subject. That the songful W. Müller has
once again offered splendid things here, especially in details,
stands the less in need of being insisted on because we may permit
ourselves to quote a few fragments.

[The poems 'Frozen Tears' and 'Numbness' follow.]

This notwithstanding, the task of a song cycle, if it is to form a
beautiful whole, seems to us to be to carry in the detail and variety
of its parts the conditions of a continuous and increasing interest,
and therefore to be capable of being sung from beginning to end in
order to achieve its purpose completely; and this has not been
quite happily achieved. For the latter, in spite of the beauty of
the separate parts, yet appears to be impossible, for one thing
because the whole suffers from a certain monotony, and for
another because the composer in particular has spread it all rather
too much.—German song, in our opinion, should be but an overflowing of a full and deeply moved heart and, up to a certain point,
wholly exclude all that is didactic, historical or reflective. Such
deep and inward emotional life, bursting to express itself, cannot
be preserved in the glowing breast without becoming lukewarm
and growing cold; for which reason we do not on the whole
approve of song cycles. Only in the first, fairest days of life's
blossoming does true song thrive, and so it should unfold itself
only in single flowers. To wind it into wreaths is infinitely
difficult, for each one almost lives its own life. We may therefore
recommend single blossoms and leaves of this song-chaplet to
lovers of singing as thoughtful, delicate and highly artistic gifts;
for the two singers have proved themselves worthy of each other,
and in both works truth and beauty go hand in hand!

[? Franz Stoepel.]

1129. SCHUBERT TO PROBST

[Vienna, 1st August 1828.]

Sir,

The opus number of the Trio is 100. I request that the edition should be faultless and look forward to it longingly. This work is to be dedicated to nobody, save those who find pleasure in it. That is the most profitable dedication.

With all respect,

Frz. Schubert.

Cf. No. 1123.—The work appeared in October or November 1828.—This letter was the first of Schubert's to be printed: in G. W. Fink's criticism of the work in the Leipzig 'Allgemeine musikalische Zeitung' of 10th December 1828.—*See* No. 1152.

1130. FROM FRANZ VON HARTMANN'S DIARY

2nd August 1828: Out to Schober's with Enk, Schubert and Bayer, after having been at the "Moonshine" earlier. Schober read us 'Faust' up to the entry of Mephistopheles. To the "Moonshine" again. Home at 11.30.

For Bayer cf. No. 1050.—The Moonshine House was the Schwind family's home.—Only the first part of Goethe's 'Faust' was then published.

1131. FROM FRANZ VON HARTMANN'S DIARY

6th August 1828: To the "Partridge"; the doctor, Enk and Bayer there. We stayed until 11.45. (Later Schubert came.)

The doctor is Hörwarter.—The reading at Schober's on 9th August was cancelled.

1132. BRÜGGEMANN TO SCHUBERT

[Outside:]
> To the Composer
> > Franz Schubert, Esq.,
> > > in
> > > > Vienna.
> > > > Tuchlauben, "Blue Hedgehog,"

Franked.   2nd floor.

[Inside:]
Honoured Sir,

I am very glad that you, Sir, are inclined to furnish compositions for Mühling's 'Museum,' and I await your kind consignments. In order to avoid any misunderstanding, I repeat that the longest contributions must not exceed two sheets and that I can include therein nothing but things for two hands without accompaniment. As for the fee, kindly fix it with each consignment; it shall be promptly paid to you through the bookseller Herr [F.] Jasper in Vienna.   Please send manuscripts by way of the stage-coach.   As I shall publish larger compositions as well in the future, I should be greatly pleased if you would make me offers of that kind also.

> With the greatest respect,
> > I am, Sir,

Halberstadt,   Your obedient servant,
  10th August 1828.   Brüggemann.

Cf. No. 1122.—The "stage-coach" (*Fahrpost*) is here mentioned in contradistinction to the mounted post, which handled letters only.— This letter marks the end of Schubert's correspondence with Brüggemann, so far as it is extant.   Whether Schubert ever sent anything to this publisher is uncertain; but the firm counted upon a contribution from him, according to a report in the 'Theaterzeitung' of 6th January 1829, written at Pest in the autumn of 1828 and belatedly printed.   It contains the following: "We inform lovers of music of the appearance, at Pest, of the 'Museum for Pianoforte for two and four hands, and Song,' edited by A. Mühling, with contributions by K. A. von Winkhler [*see* No. 476] . . . Schubert, etc.   The names of these meritorious collaborators guarantee the quality of these compositions."   The collection never appeared at Pest: it was probably obtainable from an agent there.   But it contained nothing by Schubert.

1133. FROM THE OFFICIAL 'WIENER ZEITUNG,' 13th August 1828

At the House of Thaddäus Weigl,
Art and Music Dealer in Vienna, on the Graben, No. 1144,
(next to the "King of England"), are newly to be had
(in Pest of F. Tomala, at Brno of J. G. Gastl):

FOUR REFRAIN-SONGS
by Johann Gabriel Seidl,
set to Music for One Voice with Pianoforte Accompaniment,
and most amicably dedicated to the Poet by
FRANZ SCHUBERT.

Work 95.   Price, 54 Kreuzer, Ass. Coinage.

Published separately:

No. 1. 'The Differentiation, or Meg's Obedience'
['Die Unterscheidung, oder: Gretchens Gehorsam'] 20 Kr.

No. 2. 'With you alone!' ['Bei dir allein!']   30 Kr.

No. 3. 'Men are wicked' ['Die Männer sind *méchant*']   20 Kr.

No. 4. 'Earthly Bliss' ['Irdisches Glück']   20 Kr.

The public has long cherished the wish to have, for once, a composition of a merry, comic nature from the pen of this song composer of genius. This wish has been gratified in a surprising manner by Herr Schubert in the present four songs, which in part are truly comic and in part bear in them the character of ingenuousness and humour.

Op. 95 appeared after Opp. 96 and 106. These songs, of which no autograph is preserved, are undated. According to the advertisement they seem to have been written not long before their publication. Schubert's dealings with Thaddäus Weigl were otherwise confined to the years 1826 and 1827. Seidl's remark of August 1826 (*see* No. 692) could already have applied to these songs, since Franz Lachner too made a setting of No. 3. On the copies No. 1 is called only 'The Differentiation'; the alternative title is given only in the advertisement. In 1835 Seidl (in the almanac 'The Violet' ['Das Veilchen']) called it 'Meg's Abhorrence of Love' ('Gretchens Abscheu vor der Liebe').—A refrain-song is the setting of a poem in which each verse concludes with the same lines, which may yield dramatic or comic variants in performance.—The four songs were also sold separately.

> In Op. 95 a catalogue of the "Complete Works of Franz Schubert" is published, 13th August 1828.—The list takes up two pages, following the title-page. Cf. No. 886; the list in Op. 73 had in the meantime been increased up to Op. 87 in a second issue.

1134. FROM THE 'WIENER ZEITSCHRIFT FÜR KUNST,' &c., 14th August 1828

Première grande Sonate pour le Pianoforte composée et dédiée à Son Altesse Imp. et Roy. Eminentissime Monseigneur le Cardinal Rodolphe Archiduc d'Autriche &c. &c. par François Schubert de Vienne. Œuvre 42. Vienne chez A. Pennauer.

In this work the favourite composer of romances submits to the public a composition the serious style of which expresses itself quite imposingly at the opening as well as in the whole development. Just as Herr Schubert shows himself in his songs as a worthy connoisseur of harmony and knows how to season his melodies with beautiful chords, he is here seen in an almost martial mood, in which a well-chosen change of harmonies accompanies the march-like middle theme in manifold variants. The moderate tempo is very well suited to the course taken by the ideas, and the composer keeps logically to the virile character he has once chosen. In the second part the bass leads the theme through a variety of turns into ever-new harmonies, and beautiful allusions at last take the place of the principal figure.

The *Andante poco moto* is very well made; the melody, assigned to the middle register, gives rise to very agreeable and interesting inversions and is developed with great variety by the composer. This movement is brilliant without being exactly difficult, and demands much expression. The fiery *Scherzo* receives its true significance only from the milder trio. Both are well managed.

The *Allegro vivace* is very finely worked out and the large figures running through the upper, middle and lower parts show Herr Franz Schubert's fine inventive spirit. Performed with enough liveliness, this finale has a brilliant effect. The whole Sonata shows no artificial difficulties and offers the thinking player much opportunity to display his power of performance.

This Sonata had appeared as early as the beginning of 1826 (*see* note preceding No. 624).

1135. ANTONIO MAYER TO SCHOBER

> Ancona, 14th August 1828.

. . . A thousand cordial greetings to the Schwinds 1° and 2°, Schubert, Bauernfeld, Siegert and all friends.

Schwind's elder brother was August (*see* No. 515).—Nothing is known of Siegert.

1135A. FROM SCHUMANN'S DIARY, August 1828

Polonaises by Schubert: purely and simply thunderstorms breaking forth, with romantic rainbows over solemnly slumbering worlds.

Cf. No. 1116.—The remark refers to Opp. 61 and/or 75 for pianoforte duet; Nos. 671 and 915.—*See* No. 1147A.

1136. FROM FRANZ VON HARTMANN'S DIARY

16th August 1828: To Schober's . . . He read splendidly from 'Faust' to-day. Then we went to the "Moonshine." Home at 11.30.

Cf. No. 1130.—There was no reading at Schober's on the evening of 23rd August; by the 30th Hartmann had already left. In his family chronicle he mentions, in addition, Karl Leberecht Immermann's 'Tragedy in the Tyrol' ('Das Trauerspiel in Tirol') as having been read; it deals with Andreas Hofer and was published in 1827.

The Anchor Tavern (Gasthaus 'Zum Anker'), Grünangergasse

PLATE XXXIII

Schubert.   Oil Painting by Willibrord Josef Mähler (c. 1827).   *See* p. 928

PLATE XXXIV

1137. FROM BAUERNFELD'S DIARY

24th August 1828.

Played the comedy, 'The Unfortunates' ['Die Unglücklichen'], at Hönig's at Währing. I did the critic. Schwind looked delicious as dancing-master and miser.

The family of Ludwig Hönig, sen. (cf. Nos. 591 and 809) spent that summer at Währing.—The comedy was a one-act play by Kotzebue, whom Bauernfeld took for his model as a comic playwright.

1138. FRAU PACHLER TO ANNA MORACK IN VIENNA

[Graz,] 26th August 1828.

Next month I expect a couple of acquaintances from Vienna: Schubert, the famous song composer and another musical friend, Jenger by name, who was formerly employed at Graz and was transferred to Vienna three years ago. As they are to stay with us, that ought to make a little change in my otherwise so monotonous existence.

Frau Morack, who lived in Vienna, was an aunt of Frau Pachler's, probably the wife of Johann Morack, aulic councillor to the Supreme Court of Justice.—Cf. Nos. 1117 and 1141.

1139. FROM FRANZ VON HARTMANN'S DIARY

26th August 1828: With Enk to Wanner's, where we were most merry with Schubert and Lachner. Home at 11.50.

Wanner was the proprietor of the "Oak-Tree" (see No. 1016). According to Hartmann's chronicle the friends sat in front of the ale-house on the Brandstätte square.

1140. FROM A GRAZ CONCERT PROGRAMME, 27th August 1828
(Grand vocal and instrumental concert given by Franz Zierer in the County Playhouse.)

Part II. . . . No. 3. Song by Franz Schubert, with pianoforte accompaniment, performed by Herr Schmezer.

For Zierer, who was an honorary member of the Styrian Musical Society, cf. No. 1099.—Which song of Schubert's was sung at Graz, as the last to be performed there in his lifetime, is not known.—Friedrich Schmezer, born in 1803 at Wertheim in Baden, a tenor and song-writer, visited London in 1834 and 1840.

1141. [LOST LETTER from Frau Pachler to Jenger and Schubert, 28th August 1828.]

Cf. Nos. 1138 and 1147.

1142. FROM FRANZ VON HARTMANN'S DIARY

29th August 1828: To the ale-house in the Komödiengassel. The splendid Hörwarter, Enk (who most affectionately gave me Tyrtaeus for remembrance), Böbie, Dinand, Schober, Schubert and Jérôme were there. To Corra's. Grog. Cordial farewell. Home at 1.15.

This was the last evening spent in Vienna by the brothers Franz and Louis von Hartmann: they went home to Linz the next day.—The ale-house was near the Kärntnertor Theatre (cf. Nos. 302 and 336).—The present was perhaps K. C. H. Stock's metrical translation of the war poems of Tyrtaeus, published in 1820.—"Böbie" may be Hieronymus Bobies, court chancellor in the general court chamberlain's office. Dinand is Sauter, Jérôme is Kleimayrn.—Simon Corra was the owner of a café in the Bürgerspital apartment house, facing the theatre. It is there that Bauernfeld is said to have come across Schubert by accident and each was astonished to see the other eat six crescents with his milky coffee: neither had had any lunch.

1143. FROM THE 'THEATERZEITUNG,' 30th August 1828

'The Differentiation' ['Die Unterscheidung']—'With you alone!' ['Bei dir allein!']—'Men are wicked' ['Die Männer sind méchant']—'Earthly Bliss' ['Irdisches Glück']. Refrain songs by Johann Gabriel Seidl. Set to music and most amicably dedicated to the poet by Franz Schubert. (At Thaddaeus Weigl's.)—14 Groschen.

A splendid present for lovers of song composition in general and of our genius, Schubert, in particular. There had long been an ardent desire to have something of this kind from the author of these pieces, a species at which (with the possible exception of the vocal trio, 'The Barristers' ['Die Advokaten']) he had not yet tried his hand. But Herr Schubert has shown that every path is clear for true talent. He has hit off in these songs, which Herr Seidl seems to have shaped after the fashion of the light species of vaudeville, the character of ingenuousness, of affectionate grace, of bitter obstinacy and of humour, so well that we cannot help ranking these compositions with the most successful of his works. —Especially attractive is the third number of this set; and the last is perfectly suited to sociable amusement. We therefore recommend this latest work, which the composer has dedicated to his friend, the poet of the songs, Herr J. G. Seidl, who has already furnished so much material for composition, to all lovers of song. The presentation is neat, the engraving clear and correct. —The numbers may also be had separately.

F—f.

For 'The Barristers' see No. 886. The secret of this piece was thus not yet revealed.

> Schubert removes, on the advice of Dr. Ernst Rinna von Sarenbach, to his brother Ferdinand's in the Neue Wieden suburb, No. 694, 1st September 1828.—Schubert was ailing. He suffered from effusions of blood and fits of giddiness. The doctor thought that the air outside the city would do him good. Unfortunately, however, the house on the Neue Wieden (part of the Wieden suburb), into which his brother Ferdinand had moved in August, was new and damp, and in any case the sanitary conditions in that region were still very insufficient. The street had as yet no proper name and was officially called the "newly opened street near the archiepiscopal barn." Later it was variously named after the Archbishop of Vienna, Leopold Max, Count Firmian, after the Burgomaster Anton Lumpert and lastly "Kettenbrückengasse," after the nearby suspension bridge across the river Wien, opened on 18th September 1828. The house bore, apart from the official number 694 Auf der Wieden, the name of "Zur Stadt Ronsperg," after a place on the

Bohemian-Bavarian frontier.—Rinna (*see* No. 799) was acquainted with the Schober family; he published in 1833–6 a 'Repertory of the most excellent Spas, Remedies, Operating Methods, etc.' His children were musical.—Schubert (according to a letter from Schober to Ferdinand Schubert, 18th March 1848) left nearly all his manuscripts in the "music closet" at Schober's, which shows that his removal to Ferdinand's was not intended to be permanent.

1144. FROM THE 'THEATERZEITUNG,' 27th September 1828

(On the solemn dedication of the recast bell at the restored parish church of the Holy Trinity, Alsergrund suburb, 2nd September 1828.)

During the solemn procession the following song, 'Faith, Hope and Charity' ['Glaube, Hoffnung und Liebe'], written by the I. & R. Court actor, Herr Reil, and provided with a lovely melody by Herr Franz Schubert, was sung: [here follow the words, three verses with a refrain.]

F. H. Böckh.

The church was the same in which Beethoven's funeral service had taken place (*see* Nos. 839 and 842). Its largest bell had cracked twenty-three years earlier. It had now been recast and was brought back in procession. The abbot of the Scottish monastery, P. Andreas, consecrated it. It was raised on that day, but not rung until Sunday, 7th September.—Michael Leitermayer, born in Vienna in 1799, had been choirmaster at the church since 1827. Like Schubert he had been a pupil of Michael Holzer in the Himmelpfortgrund, and it was evidently he who asked his childhood companion to write this chorus. (The E flat major Mass too was first performed in the Alsergrund church, on 4th October 1829, it is said at Schubert's own request.)—For Reil cf. No. 960. His poem is not identical with that of the song of the same name (*see* No. 1153). It begins "Gott, lass die Glocke glücklich steigen." Schubert set it for mixed chorus with wind accompaniment (xvii. 5). The work appeared, with pianoforte accompaniment *ad lib.*, on 30th December 1828, "for a charitable purpose," privately printed, without opus number.—For Böckh cf. No. 246.

1145. FROM BAUERNFELD'S DIARY

6th September 1828.

The first performance yesterday [of my comedy, 'The Suitors' ('Die Brautwerber')].   So-called *succès d'estime*.   I was as though annihilated and from the very first verses recognized the senseless- ness of writing a long piece in Alexandrines.   Grillparzer, Schwind, Schubert, Schober and other friends expected me at the inn— I could not bring myself to see them.   Walked about the streets and met Grillparzer towards midnight.   He was most amiable.— I feel like one battered to death to-day.   A frightful awakening.

The production of this comedy took place at the theatre in the Hofburg. It had been written in the second half of 1827 and was given four times only, finishing on 15th September.   In the morning Schubert visited the author with Schwind and said: "To me the comedy was extraordinarily pleasing.   To all of us.   And yet we are no asses!"   To which Bauernfeld replied laughingly: "What's the good of that, if I am one?"   The criticisms were unfavourable, and Bauernfeld went into the country for a few weeks.

1146. FROM BAUERNFELD'S 'POETICAL DIARY,' 1828

The opening scenes.   I felt quite sick,
The verses sounded so hollow, so slick!
Lord, how the public was amused,
And Schwind and Schubert quite enthused.
Tributes from friends and praise from all!
And yet, methinks I had a fall.

For Bauernfeld's 'Poetical Diary' *see* No. 575.

1147. JENGER TO FRAU PACHLER

Vienna, 6th September 1828.

Friend Schubert and I have moved to new lodgings on the first of this month, and that is the reason why the answer to your last kind letter of the 28th ult. will not arrive at Graz within the prescribed eight days.—I could no longer find Schubert in the old lodgings, and neither did I ever find him in the new ones on the Wieden. Last night I spoke to him at last at the Burg Theatre, and I am now able to tell you, dear lady, that friend Tubby expects an improvement in his finances shortly, and confidently reckons, as soon as this has happened, to avail himself immediately of your kind invitation and to arrive at Graz with a new operetta. In any case you will receive definite news, either from him or from me, a week before his arrival at Graz.—True, he wishes that I may be able to travel with him, but—as I have already told you in my last letter—I shall not be able to get away, on account of this year's manœuvres, which are to last until the 24th inst. . . .

Should Schubert remain with you until the end of October, it may yet be possible for me to come to Graz for at any rate a week, to see all my dear ones again and to fetch Tubby . . .

I am now looking up my diary of last year day by day and take pleasure in the recollection of those happy days.

To-day it is a year since the good Swabians left Graz. I have already talked with Andlau about it to-day, who sends you all many, many kind thoughts . . .

On the 10th, 11th and 12th I shall think of the glorious trip to Wildbach.

Many, many kind wishes to all the participants and members of the family at Wildbach—but especially to my darling.

Cf. No. 1141.—Jenger had moved to Dr. Menz's (*see* No. 968).— What he means by a "new operetta" by Schubert is not clear. 'The Count of Gleichen' had not advanced beyond sketches and could not very well have been called an operetta. Neither could 'Alfonso and Estrella,' which moreover was even less new, supposing that Schubert intended to take the score to Graz with him and had not yet sent it. This may have been merely a jest on Jenger's part.—The manœuvres were those held in the autumn near Baden, which were particularly impressive that year. —Schubert wished to spend the month of October at Graz, not September, as in 1827.—The "good Swabians" were Jenger's countrymen of Freiburg i/B. (*see* No. 935).—For the excursion to Wildbach *see* note preceding No. 941.—The "darling" (*Zärterl*) is Netti (Anna) Massegg (*see* No. 949).

1147A. FROM SCHUMANN'S DIARY, September 1828

A most characteristic trait in Schubert's polonaises is, as in most
of his other compositions, that he never marks his loveliest passages
with such a direction as *dolce*; he shares this with Goethe, who
never calls anything in his tragedies "touching," "woeful," etc.
The works in which many a *dolce* occurs are certainly not sweet,
just as according to J. Paul's aesthetics the comedies which are
said on the playbill to make one "die of laughter" are apt to make
one die of weeping.

Cf. Nos. 1116 and 1135A. Schumann took particular notice of
Schubert's pianoforte duet works, so far as they were published.

'In Spring' ('Im Frühling'), Bk. 25, No. 2 (xx. 497), appears in
the 'Wiener Zeitschrift,' 16th September 1828.

1148. SCHUBERT TO JENGER

[Outside:]
                    [J. B.] von Jenger, Esq.
[Inside:]

                                    25th September 1828.

The second part of the 'Winter Journey' I have already handed
to Haslinger. Nothing will come of the journey to Graz this
year, as money and weather are wholly unfavourable. The
invitation to Dr. Menz's I accept with pleasure, for I always very
much like to hear Baron Schönstein sing. You may meet me on
Saturday afternoon at Bogner's coffee-house, Singerstrasse, between
4 and 5 o'clock.

                                    Your friend
                                        Schubert.

My address is:
    Neue Wieden, Firmiansgasse
        No. 496, 2nd floor on the right.

It is curious that Schubert only now handed the publisher the manuscript
of the second part of the 'Winter Journey,' which had been ready since
October 1827. It seems probable that Haslinger, warned by his experiences

with the first part, had returned it to him for revision. But there are no material changes in the manuscript of the second part. The fee paid for it, if indeed Schubert had not received it long before, was not sufficient to cover a journey to Graz. All the same, it is quite incredible that Schubert received only 6 florins, A.C., for six of these twelve songs, as Franz Lachner told Grove.—The party at Dr. Menz's seems to have taken place on Saturday the 27th. Schönstein sang and Schubert, it is said, played his latest sonatas of September 1828, of which the one in B flat major was finished only on the 26th. (For these Haslinger paid Ferdinand Schubert 70 florins, A.C., each, that is 210 florins in all, on 17th December 1828, and at the same time 290 florins, A.C., for thirteen of the fourteen songs in the 'Swan Song.')—By a slip Schubert writes the house number as 496 instead of 694.

> In the 'Pocket-Book for Sociable Pleasure for the Year 1829,' edited by Ferdinand Philippi and published by Leopold Voss of Leipzig, an arrangement for pianoforte solo of the Polonaise, Op. 75, No. 2, appears, autumn 1828.

1149. From the 'Quarterly Musical Magazine and Review,'
London, early 1829

State of Music in Vienna
[Autumn 1828]

. . . The other young composers who have distinguished themselves at Vienna are MM. Sechter, who is greatest in fugues; Schubert, who composes beautiful melodies; Lachner, whose sonatas are good; and some others.

1150. From the 'Intelligenzblatt zur Caecilia,' Mainz,
[Autumn] 1828

New Musical Publications
which have appeared
at the House of M. J. Leidesdorf in Vienna,
Easter Mass 1828.

Agency Depôt at Herr Wilhelm Härtel's
in Leipzig

·   ·   ·   ·   ·

For Pianoforte solo.

Schubert, Fr., *Momens musicals* [*sic*], *Œuv. 94.*

Book I—12 Groschen

Book II—12   ,,

·   ·   ·   ·   ·

For the Voice.   Gr.

Schubert, Fr., 'The Muses' Son' ['Der Musensohn']—'On
the Lake' ['Auf dem See']—'Spirit's Greeting'
['Geistes-Gruss']. 3 Poems by Goethe, for
Voice with Pianoforte Accompaniment. Op. 92   — 16

—   'Over Wildemann' ['Ueber Wildemann']—
'Death's Kiss' ['Todeskuss']—'The Apparition' ['Die Erscheinung'].—3 Poems for Voice
and Pianoforte Accompaniment. Op. 93   — 12

Cf. No. 1120.—No. 33 of 'Caecilia' containing this announcement
appeared in September or October 1828.   Opp. 92 and 94 had probably
reached Leipzig in the meantime; but hardly Op. 108 (previously Op. 94),
which does not seem to have been published before the beginning of 1829.
The book may have been printed while Schubert was still alive, but only
issued later.—Wildemann is a small mountain town in the Harz.   The
error of 'Death's Kiss,' instead of 'Death Music' ('Todesmusik'), is also
on the title-page. 'The Apparition,' now entitled 'Remembrance'
('Erinnerung'), had appeared already at the end of 1824 at Sauer &
Leidesdorf's (*see* No. 510).

1151. SCHUBERT TO B. SCHOTT'S SONS

[Outside:]

From Vienna.
To the Art Establishment of
Schott's Sons
at

Mainz.

[Inside:]

Vienna, 2nd October 1828.

Sirs,

As it is now such a long time since I last had a letter from you, and I should be very glad to know whether you have duly received the compositions I sent you, viz. 4 Impromptus and the five-part male chorus, which I dispatched to you through Haslinger, I shall be glad if you will kindly let me have a reply on the subject. I am also particularly anxious that the said compositions should appear as soon as possible. The opus number for the Impromptus is 101 and that for the [vocal] quintet 102. In anticipation of a speedy and agreeable reply,

With all respect,

My address: Frz. Schubert.

Neue Wieden, at the "City of Ronsperg,"
No. 694, 2nd floor, on the right.

Cf. No. 1100.—The Impromptus, published by Diabelli only at the end of 1838, were in the end given the opus number 142. Of No. 101 Probst made unauthorized use at the end of 1828 for the reprint of four songs, including 'The Blind Boy' from the 'Wiener Zeitschrift' (having the number inserted by hand), and in the spring of 1829 Diabelli used it for 'The Blind Boy' alone.—'Moonlight' ('Mondenschein') appeared actually as Op. 102, first at Diabelli's (about 1830).—See No. 1157.

1152. SCHUBERT TO PROBST

[Outside:]

To the Art Dealer
[H. A.] Probst, Esq.

at

Leipzig.

[Inside:]

Vienna, 2nd October 1828.

Sir,

I beg to inquire when the Trio is to appear at last. Can it be that you do not know the opus number yet? It is Op. 100. I await its appearance with longing. I have composed, among other

things, 3 Sonatas for pianoforte solo, which I should like to dedicate
to Hummel.   Moreover, I have set several songs by Heine of
Hamburg, which pleased extraordinarily here, and finally turned
out a Quintet for 2 violins, 1 viola and 2 violoncellos.   The
Sonatas I have played with much success in several places, but the
Quintet will be tried out only during the coming days.   If perchance any of these compositions would suit you, let me know.

With much respect,

I subscribe myself,

Frz. Schubert.

My address is: Neue Wieden,
No. 694, at the "City of Ronsperg,"
     2nd floor, right.

Cf. No. 1129.—This letter is like a cry of distress.   Schubert had had
a bad experience with Probst over the payment for the E flat major pianoforte Trio; yet he now offers him his latest and best works.   He exag-
gerates their claims, so far as performance and success are concerned.—
The last three Sonatas (see No. 1148), which Schubert wished to dedicate
to Hummel, were announced by Haslinger as early as 1829, but not published until 1838, by Diabelli, dedicated by the publisher to Schumann
after Hummel's death (1837) and described as "the very last compositions."—The Heine songs are the six afterwards included in the
'Swan Song' cycle.   Schubert himself had already planned to publish the
Rellstab songs (see No. XVI), beginning with 'Life's Courage' ('Lebens-
mut,' fragment, xx. 602), which was afterwards discarded, and the
Heine songs together as a cycle to be dedicated to his friends.   His offer
of the Heine songs separately was thus an act of sacrifice, due no doubt to
financial difficulties.—The string Quintet appeared only in 1853, published by C. A. Spina, Diabelli's successor.   Not even a single private
performance of this work in Schubert's lifetime is on record.   Josef Hellmesberger gave the first public performance at the chamber-music evenings
of his quartet in 1850.

Schubert, with his brother Ferdinand and two friends, makes a
three days' excursion to Unter-Waltersdorf and Eisenstadt, to visit
Joseph Haydn's grave, early October 1828.—This walking tour,
in which Josef Mayssen (see No. 496) and Johann Rieder (see No.
483) may have taken part, was perhaps undertaken by order of
Schubert's doctor, who may have wished Ferdinand to accompany
his brother.   They first went southward from Vienna for about
fifteen miles to Unter-Waltersdorf in Lower Austria, and then seven
miles farther on to Eisenstadt in Hungary (now in the Austrian
Burgenland).   It is a familiar fact that the Esterházy princes had

one of their largest castles there and that Haydn, who had spent the greater part of his life in that family's service and had welcomed Nelson at Eisenstadt in 1800, was entombed at the "Bergkirche" there since 1820. Not long before an English visitor, Adolphus Frederick, Duke of Cambridge, had reminded the reigning Prince Nicolas II by a question about the grave that Haydn was still buried at the cemetery of the Hundsturm suburb in Vienna; whereupon the prince obtained the removal of the master's bones. The skull, however, did not arrive, for it had been stolen with the connivance of Rosenbaum (*see* No. 388). It later reached the museum of the Vienna Philharmonic Society, and even the present prince, who in 1932 erected a special mausoleum for Haydn, had not yet succeeded in reuniting the skull with the rest of the skeleton.—For Schubert's visit to Michael Haydn's monument at Salzburg cf. No. 587.

1153. FROM THE OFFICIAL 'WIENER ZEITUNG,' 6th October 1828

At the House of Anton Diabelli & Co.,
Art and Music Dealers, in the Graben, No. 1133, is just published, and to be had of K. Lichtl in Pest, N. Meidinger at Pressburg and Niemirowsky at Lemberg at the same price:

FAITH, HOPE AND CHARITY.
['Glaube, Hoffnung und Liebe']
Poem by Christ[oph]. Kuffner,
set to Music for One Voice with Pianoforte Accompaniment
by FRANZ SCHUBERT.
Work 97.

Op. 97 appeared after Op. 106, without any dedication, as No. 240 of a collection entitled 'Philomele' (with pianoforte accompaniment; there is another collection with guitar accompaniment, published by Diabelli).—The price, not mentioned in the advertisement, was 30 kreuzer, A.C.—Kuffner (cf. No. 369), born in Vienna in 1780, was an official in the Court War Council and a censor. Beethoven set words of his. In the Vienna 'Jahrbücher der Literatur' he published 'The Mind and Life of the Nineteenth-Century British Poets.' The poem set by Schubert had already been used by Maximilian Stadler for a male-voice quartet. It begins "Glaube, hoffe, liebe" and must not be confused with Reil's poem of the same name composed by Schubert in that same August of 1828 (*see* No. 1144).

1154. FROM THE OFFICIAL WIENER 'ZEITUNG,' 6th October 1828

At the House of A. Pennauer,
I. & R. Privileged Art and Music Dealer in Vienna, in the Graben,
No. 1122, is just published, and to be had also of K. Lichtl in Pest,
of J. Niemirowsky at Lemberg and of W. H. Thierry at
Hermannstadt at the same price:

.   .   .   .

Schubert, Franz, 'Melancholy' ['Wehmut'] (poem by Hütten-
brenner), 'Eternal Love' ['Ewige Liebe'] by Schulze, 'Flight'
['Flucht'] by Lappe.   Set to music for 4 male voices.   Work 64.
Price, 1 Florin 45 Kreuzer, A.C.

Op. 64 (without dedication) is a belated publication of Pennauer's,
with whom Schubert had had dealings in 1825–7.   True, Nottebohm
thought that Pennauer had brought out the work already at Michaelmas
1826; but this is contradicted, not only by this advertisement, but also by
Pennauer's publication number 400, which is higher than those of the
other Schubert works published by him.—The poet of the first song is
Heinrich Hüttenbrenner (*see* No. 150).

1155. PROBST TO SCHUBERT

[Outside:]
Franz Schubert, Esq.,
Musician and Composer,
Vienna.
Neue Wieden, No. 694.
At the "City of Ronsperg," 2nd floor right.

[Inside:]
Franz Schubert, Esq.,
Vienna.

Leipzig, 6th October 1828.

In reply to your esteemed letters of August 1st and 2nd inst., I
beg to apologize for the fact that your Trio, Op. 100, is not yet
in your hands.   My travels to France and Holland have doubtless

had something to do with the delay, and moreover the work is somewhat bulky.   However, its engraving is already done, and also corrected as carefully as possible, and it will go to you, spick and span, with my next consignment to Diabelli & Co.   Of your new compositions the songs would suit me best, and I would ask you to send them.   Please communicate to me also anything easily understandable *à 4 mains* you may be writing, rather like your variations on the miller's song from 'Marie.'   Would not Himmel's theme, 'To Alexis,' be effectively workable into something of the same kind?

> With sincere respectful devotion,
>   H. A. Probst.

Cf. Nos. 1129 and 1152.—It is unlikely that Schubert lived to see a printed copy of the E flat major pianoforte Trio: Artaria & Co. announced it only on 11th December 1828, together with their own edition of the Rondo for pianoforte duet, Op. 107, as having arrived in Vienna.—The songs are those on poems by Heine, which, however, Schubert did not send to Probst.—The Variations on the miller's song from Hérold's 'Marie,' Op. 82, Probst had already mentioned earlier (*see* No. 1036).— Himmel (*see* No. 384), a Prussian, was born in 1765 and had died in 1814. His song-cycle 'Alexis and Ida' (words by Christoph August Tiedge) had appeared before Beethoven's 'To the Distant Beloved' (*see* No. 842); it contains the favourite song 'To Alexis I send thee' ('An Alexis send' ich dich'), entitled in English 'Ada to Alexis, with a Rose.'   Instead of Schubert, it was François Hünten who wrote variations on it for Probst (published in 1829 as Hünten's Op. 26).

1156. ANTON SCHINDLER TO SCHUBERT

Pest, 11th October 1828.

My dear, good friend Schubert,

Our friend Lachner is too much occupied with the production of his opera, so that not only do I undertake to invite you in his name for the important day on which that great work is to be performed, which has been fixed for the 25th or 27th inst., but my sister and I join our invitation to his and desire to receive and honour you here in our midst as a cordially well-meaning friend.

We all have plenty of room under one roof and at one table and look forward to your accepting the place reserved for you without demur, and your occupying it quite soon. See to it, then, that you leave by express coach on the 22nd inst. at the latest, and only let us know in writing two days beforehand whether we are to expect you here for certain on the morning of the 24th inst. So much for one thing: the other follows.

Sithence and whereas your name is in good repute here, we propose the following venture for you, viz. that you should decide to give a private concert here, at which for the most part only songs of yours should be performed. This promises a good success, and since it is well known that your timidity and easy-going ways will keep you from lending much of a hand in such an undertaking, I advise and inform you that you will find people here who will most readily give you their support, heavy as you are. Still, you too must contribute something, *et quidem* that you will obtain five or six letters from noble houses in Vienna to similar ones here. Lachner thinks, for instance, from Count Esterházy's household, and I think so too; say a word, for example, to our honest friend Pinterics, who will be sure to look after some of his prince's for you. But above all procure yourself a good letter to Countess Teleki, president of the Charitable Ladies Association, who is the greatest protectress of the arts here. Do not let this be a burden to you, for it will involve no trouble and no wire-pulling, but simply deliver the letters here, if we regard it as expedient, and with that *basta*! To get a few hundred florins into your pocket in this manner is a thing not to be despised, and apart from that other advantages may accrue therefrom. To it, then! Do not argue for long, and make no bones about it! You will be well and energetically supported. There is a young dilettante here who sings your songs with a fine tenor voice well, really quite well, and he is with us; the gentlemen of the theatre ditto, my sister ditto; in this way you need only deposit your fat carcass here and accompany whatever is performed. Songs for several voices cannot fail to make their effect either. Some of them are known here. Write nothing new: it is not necessary!

And so God be with you! We all expect you to act nicely and

sensibly, and not to be obstinate. To our speedy meeting, then, in the Land of Mustachios! This from your

sincere friend

Anton Schindler.

[Lost postscript from Franz Lachner, who expects Schubert in Pest on 20th October at the latest.]

Anton Schindler, Beethoven's factotum, whom we have met several times, was born in 1795 at Meedl near Neustadt in Moravia. He was in Vienna in 1813–27, in 1822–6 as leader at the Josefstadt Theatre, but went to live at Pest in September 1827 with his sister Marie, who had been engaged at the Josefstadt for only six months after him. She had been engaged at the Pest German theatre as early as 1812–14 and again worked there in 1827–9, when both went to the Kärntnertor Theatre in Vienna for a short time.—Franz Lachner had composed his first work for the stage: the opera 'The Pledge' ('Die Bürgschaft'). The libretto, based on Schiller's ballad, had been written by Ferdinand Leopold Karl, Freiherr von Biedenfeld, in 1822 to Barbaja's order. Beethoven was to compose the first and third acts, and Weigl to undertake the cheerful wedding festivities in the second. Nothing came of this, and when Lachner was at the Kärntnertor Theatre he applied himself to the forgotten book without having further recourse to the poet. Biedenfeld, born in 1788 at Karlsruhe, had lived in Vienna from May 1818 until about 1822, was a friend of Count Pálffy's and his two producers, Demmer and Küstner, and worked at that time as librettist and translator for the Theater an der Wien. In his book 'The Comic Opera of the Italians, the French and the Germans,' published in 1848, he claimed to have been acquainted with Schubert also. The latter, by the way, had himself begun an opera on that subject in 1816, the librettist of which is not known.—Although Schindler had already sent the Pest invitation to Lachner in June 1828, in a letter of 13th September to Nanette Schechner (then in Berlin) Lachner still expressed the hope that the opera would be first produced at Munich. At the end of September, however, he went to Pest, and Schubert, on bidding him farewell, is supposed to have promised to attend the production there, if possible. It took place on 30th October, for the benefit performance of Schindler's sister, but the work was not repeated. Nor was the hope fulfilled of seeing it staged in Vienna in 1829 under Gallenberg's new management. The manuscript is in the Bavarian State Library at Munich.—The stage-coach from Vienna to Buda (on the Danube bank opposite Pest) took twenty-eight hours.—The Esterházy house is that of Count Johann Karl Esterházy in Vienna, with whom Schubert was still in touch.—Pinterics (*see* No. 492) was private secretary to

Prince Josef Pálffy.—Johanna, Countess Teleki of Szák, born in 1784 a Freiin of Mécsáros, the founder and patroness of the Charitable Ladies' Association at Pest, was the second wife of Count Ladislaus Teleki, who had been in England about 1786 and was a patron of Hungarian literature. She was lady-in-waiting to the Archduchess Maria Dorothea (*see* No. 612). Her drawing-room was frequented by Pyrker and Mayláth, and among its guests from Vienna were Frau von Pichler and Grillparzer: all these had furnished Schubert with words for musical settings.—According to Lachner's recollections there was no reply from Schubert.

> Schwind removes to Munich, 22nd October 1828. Joining the academy there for the sake of his career, mainly on Netti Hönig's account, he first drove to Salzburg, then back to Linz, and went to Munich on foot by way of the Innviertel region. His term there began early in November.

1157. B. SCHOTT'S SONS TO SCHUBERT

[Outside:]

> Fr. Schubert, Esq.,
> Neue Wieden, at the "City of Lansperg [Ronsperg],"
> No. 694, 2nd floor to the right,
> Vienna.

[Inside:]

Mainz, 30th October 1828.

Herr Fr. Schubert in Vienna.

Your very much valued letters of 28th May and 2nd October have duly reached us. Our reply to the former was so much delayed because we too waited for an opportunity to send the Impromptus from here to Paris, when they arrived here.

We have received them back from there with the intimation that these works are too difficult for trifles and would find no outlet in France, and we earnestly beg your pardon for this.

The Quintet we shall publish soon; but we are bound to observe that this small *opus* is too dear at the fee fixed, for the whole occupies but six printed pages in the pianoforte part, and we assume that it is by some error that we are asked to pay 60 fl., A.C., for this.

We offer you 30 fl. for it, and shall at once settle this amount on hearing from you, or you may draw upon us.

The pianoforte work, Op. 101, we certainly do not regard as too expensive, but its impracticability for France vexed us considerably. If at any time you should write something less difficult and yet brilliant in an easier key, please send it to us without more ado.

We remain, respectfully and in friendship,

B. Schott's Sons.

P.S. In order to save any delay, we enclose a draft for 30 fl. on Herr von Heylmann's heir, together with a letter of advice, If you do not accept our proposal, return this draft to us.—The 4 Impromptus we shall enclose in our next consignment to Herr Haslinger.—

The Above.

Cf. Nos. 1100 (of 23rd, not 28th May) and 1151.—Schotts had opened a branch in Paris in 1826. In this connection it is interesting to note that there is said to have been a project in Paris in 1829 (!) to invite Schubert to go there and write an opera for the Académie Royale de Musique (Sonnleithner's letter to Luib, 1857, Philharmonic Society, Vienna).—The Impromptus, planned as Op. 101 but published as Op. posth. 142, thus came back, by the same way that they had been sent.— It does not look as though Schubert had accepted the halved fee for 'Moonlight' ('Mondenschein'); this quintet certainly was not published by Schott, but by Diabelli, though with an apocryphal pianoforte accompaniment, Schott having kept back the autograph supplement to the copy of the unaccompanied quintet.

Schubert goes to the "Red Cross" in the Himmelpfortgrund, where during the meal he disgustedly leaves a fish, 31st October 1828.— The "Red Cross" (cf. Nos. 208 and 572) was the Schubert family's regular tavern so long as they lived in the Himmelpfortgrund. The Schubert brothers still occasionally met there later.

In the morning Schubert hears at the Hernals parish church a Latin Requiem by his brother Ferdinand and afterwards goes with him and Josef Mayssen for a three hours' walk, 3rd November 1828.— The Requiem appeared at Diabelli's c. 1830 as Ferdinand's Op. 9, dedicated to the memory of Schubert and adorned with a vignette representing his gravestone. Mayssen was choirmaster at the church in the Hernals suburb.

Schubert, with Josef Lanz, enrols at Simon Sechter's as a student of fugal composition, and it is agreed that the studies should be based on Friedrich Wilhelm Marpurg s 'Dissertation on Fugue,' 4th November 1828.—For Lanz *see* No. 525. Sechter had revised Marpurg's treatise.   He was the foremost master of musical theory in Vienna after Johann Josef Fux; his most important pupil was Bruckner. Worzischek too had studied under him three months before his death. According to Schindler Schubert had intended as early as 1824 to seek Sechter's instruction, but (so the very questionable report has it) he was dissuaded by Pinterics.   The incitement to go to school with Sechter at the last is said to have come from the impression which Handel's works had made on Schubert. It is possible that Haslinger made Beethoven's copies of the Arnold edition accessible to him.   Grillparzer—who, like Schubert, set Heine's 'Fisher Maiden' ('Das Fischermädchen') to music— studied with Sechter about 1832: his exercises are preserved in the Philharmonic Society's archives.—It appears that Schubert and Lanz had a first lesson on 4th November in Sechter's dwelling at 123 Mariahilf; but at the second (? 10th November) Lanz alone was present.

Schubert takes permanently to his bed, 11th (? 14th) November 1828.—The room is a closet in the right-hand corner of the second floor.—The whole apartment, which Ferdinand left the following year, comprised no more than one room towards the street with two windows, that closet with one and a dark room towards the courtyard. Gerhard von Breuning, Beethoven's physician, thought he remembered that Schubert occupied the courtyard room; but this seems to be an error, for it is not credible that his brother would have let him lie in that black hole.   Schubert was nursed not only by Ferdinand, his wife Anna and perhaps their eldest child, the daughter Therese, aged twelve, but especially by his stepsister Josefa (*see* No. 113), who was then thirteen, and whom Spaun described as a "loving nurse."—Spaun and Bauernfeld assert that Schubert finally took to his bed on 11th November; Ferdinand says it was the 14th.

1158. SCHUBERT TO SCHOBER

[12th November 1828.]

Dear Schober,

I am ill.   I have eaten nothing for eleven days and drunk nothing, and I totter feebly and shakily from my chair to bed and back again.

Rinna is treating me.   If ever I take anything, I bring it up again
at once.

Be so kind, then, as to assist me in this desperate situation by
means of literature.   Of Cooper's I have read 'The Last of the
Mohicans,' 'The Spy,' 'The Pilot' and 'The Pioneers.'   If by any
chance you have anything else of his, I implore you to deposit it
with Frau von Bogner at the coffee-house for me.   My brother,
who is conscientiousness itself, will most faithfully pass it on to
me.   Or anything else.

Your friend

Schubert.

This last letter in Schubert's hand is undated, but it bears the note
"Received 12th November 1828.   Fr. v. Schober."—Schober stayed
away, probably from fear of infection, and did not visit Schubert that
November.   But he had evidently brought him, or sent him, a few
volumes of Fenimore Cooper from his library.   Although at Dresden in
1914 Schober's housekeeper, Frau Babette Wolf, still had a Viennese
reprint of a German translation of Cooper by *r and Wilhelmine von
Gersdorf, the edition read by Schubert seems to have been that by C. A.
Fischer, published at Frankfort o/M. in 1826–33.   In this 'The Spy'
comprises volumes 1–6, 'The Last of the Mohicans' 7–12, 'The Pioneers'
13–18 (published in 1826) and 'The Pilot' 19–24 (published in 1827–8).
If Schober sent more of that edition, it must have been the following
works published in 1828: 'Lionel Lincoln' (25–30), 'The Steppe'
(31–6) and 'The Red Rover' (37–42).   Volumes 43–75 did not appear
until after 1828.   Apart from this duodecimo edition there was an
octavo one in twelve volumes published at Leipzig in 1824–5, translated
by *r (? F. P. E. Richter), which however did not include 'The Last of
the Mohicans'; and various German publishers brought out separate
works.—It was at Bogner's café that Wilhelm von Chézy (see No. 385)
soon afterwards heard of Schubert's death.

Karl Holz, Karl Gross, Baron König and . . . play for Schubert, in
the presence of the pianoforte teacher Johann Dolezalek Beethoven's
string Quartet in C sharp minor, Op. 131, 14th November 1828.—
This very questionable information came from Holz.   He thought
the incident had occurred five days before Schubert's death,
but it could only have taken place in Schubert's own lodgings.   Op.
131 was the last but one of Beethoven's string quartets, and all these
were at that time appreciated by few even of the master's admirers.
Karl Gross may have been Karl Magnus Gross, the violinist, and
Lenau's teacher; or Karl Friedrich, the cellist, who, however, was

but an amateur.   A Baron König played the flute at the Philharmonic
Society, of which he was a member; but Leopold von Sonnleithner
also mentions a cellist of that name, who may have been the same
person.   The fourth player was not named by Holz.—Johann
Nepomuk Emanuel Dolezalek (cf. No. 525), born in 1780 at
Chotieborz in Bohemia, settled in Vienna since 1800, was cellist at
the Kärntnertor Theatre, composer and pianoforte teacher.   He
had been one of Beethoven's last visitors.

1159. [LOST ADDRESS from the Cecilia Chorus of Lemberg to
    Schubert to thank him for the copy of Psalm 23 (Op. 132,
    xviii. 2), transmitted through Josef von Spaun, autumn
    1828.]

Wolfgang Amadeus Mozart, jun. (see No. 168), had founded this association in the autumn of 1826, i.e. after Spaun's departure from Lemberg.
The document was sent through the intermediation of Spaun, who visited
Schubert in the middle of November (? at the same time as Randhartinger).
Schubert said to him: "Copy the Grillparzer 'Serenade' too and send
it to the ladies at Lemberg."   He is said to have still been able to correct
this copy and to have received a message of thanks from the choir before
he died.   His last piece of work, however, was the correction of the
proofs of Part II of the 'Winter Journey.'

Conference between Josef von Vering and Johann Baptist Wisgrill
at Schubert's sick-bed, 16th November 1828.   Josef, Ritter (later
Edler) von Vering, born in Vienna in 1793, was a nephew of Gerhard von Breuning's (see fourth note preceding No. 1158).   His sister
Julie was also buried at the Währing district cemetery (opposite
the Verings' family vault), a fact which is said to have caused
Beethoven's burial there, and thus indirectly Schubert's as well.
Vering was a friend of Rinna's, who had himself been taken ill and
asked Vering to take over Schubert's treatment.   There is thus
no connection with his becoming Schubert's doctor and the fact
that in 1821 he had published a book 'On the Healing of Syphilis
by Embrocations with Quicksilver' and in 1826 another entitled
'Syphilo-Therapy,' the latter dedicated to Rinna.   (Vering's father,
by the way, the field staff surgeon Gerhard von Vering, had
operated on Karoline, Countess Esterházy, in Vienna in the spring
of 1816.)—Johann Baptist Wisgrill, born c. 1795, had been a court
choir-boy with Schubert in 1808–11, singing alto.   In the spring
of 1809 he was at the head of the class in the academic grammar

school and after the course in philosophy he studied medicine.   Later
he became professor of surgery, published several manuals, including some on physics and chemistry, and was one of the editors
of the 'Medical Year-Books of the Austrian Imperial State' (1838 ff.).
—After this consultation Schubert's treatment seems to have been
changed.   The nurse already engaged was now joined by a male
nurse, and they doubtless performed their duties by turns (cf.
No. XII).   Schubert took his medicines punctually, with the aid
of a pocket watch that hung on a chair near his bed.

Schubert is violently and continually delirious, 17th November 1828,
in the evening.

Bauernfeld and Franz Lachner visit Schubert, 17th November 1828.
—Lachner had returned from Pest early in November (see No. 1156).
Immediately afterwards he travelled to Germany by order of the new
opera management to find singers for Vienna.   At Darmstadt a
letter from the producer Georg Friedrich Treitschke reached him,
with the news of Schubert's death.—While Bauernfeld's diary (see
No. II) merely mentions that Schubert spoke of their opera 'The
Count of Gleichen' on that day, his obituary (see No. XXXIII) says
that the composer asked for a new libretto.   In this connection
Bauernfeld's recollections of 1869 mention only 'The Count of
Gleichen,' and Lachner too recalls that work alone.—While
Schober, who received daily reports on Schubert's condition from
Vering, as well as other friends stayed away, apparently for fear of
infection, Spaun, and perhaps Josef Hüttenbrenner too, seem to have
visited Schubert once more.

Schubert is with difficulty restrained in his bed, 18th November
1828.

Rudolf von Smetana marries Justina von Bruchmann, 19th November
1828.—The marriage took place at St. Stephen's cathedral.   Smetana's brother-in-law, Streinsberg (or the latter's father), and Leopold Kupelwieser acted as witnesses.   The news of Schubert's
death reached Bruchmann's house during the wedding.

1160. Schubert's Father to his Son Ferdinand

My dear son Ferdinand,

   Days of gloom and sorrow weigh heavily upon us.   The dangerous illness of our beloved Franz acts painfully on our spirits.
Nothing remains for us in these sad days except to seek comfort

in God, and to bear any affliction that may fall on us according to God's wise dispensation with resolute submission to His holy will; and what befalls us shall convince us of God's wisdom and goodness, and give us tranquillity.

Therefore take courage and trust implicity in God; He will give you strength, that you may not succumb, and will grant you a glad future by His blessing. See to it, to the best of your ability, that our good Franz is forthwith provided with the Holy Sacraments for the dying, and I shall live in the comforting hope that God will fortify and keep him.

Sorrowfully, but strengthened by confidence in God, your father
Franz.

19th November 1828.

In the register of deaths at the church of St. Joseph in the Margareten suburb (*see* note preceding No. V) is the note "Received extreme unction only." Schubert seems to have been insufficiently conscious to take the eucharist.

1161. FROM THE FAMILY CHRONICLE OF SCHUBERT'S FATHER

[Franz Peter . . .] died Wednesday, 19th November 1828, at 3 o'clock p.m. (of typhus), buried Saturday, 22nd November 1828.

The cause of death was officially described as "nervous fever." It was typhus, or more precisely, in Schubert's case as it had been in his mother's (*see* No. 35), typhus abdominalis. Among the conditions that had helped to bring it about were Schubert's obesity, a certain inclination towards alcoholism and the bad water of the Neue Wieden district, the sanitary conditions of which were at that time still unsatisfactory. The three weeks' duration of his illness before the crisis is usual with this disease. According to Spaun's testimony Schubert died painlessly: his face remained unchanged. His age was thirty-one years, nine months, nineteen days and one and a half hours: it is possible to compute it almost to the minute, thanks to his father's very precise records.

OBITUARY NOTES

1828-39

I. ANNOUNCEMENT OF DEATH

Yesterday, Wednesday, at 3 o'clock in the afternoon, fell asleep, to wake to a better life, my most dearly beloved son Franz Schubert, musical artist and composer, after a short illness and having received the Holy Sacraments, in the 32nd year of his age.

At the same time, I and my family have to announce to our honoured friends and acquaintances that the deceased's body will be carried to the Parish Church of St. Joseph at Margareten, on Friday, 21st inst., at 2.30 p.m., from the house No. 694 on the Neu-Wieden, in the newly built street next to the so-called Bischof-Stadel, there to be consecrated.

Franz Schubert
Schoolmaster in the Rossau.

Vienna, 20th November 1828.

On Schubert's receiving the sacraments cf. No. 1160.—For the name of the street cf. note preceding No. 1144.—The Wieden suburb (including Neue Wieden) lay south of the city and the Margareten suburb west of the Wieden. The Kettenbrückengasse, as it was called later, is the boundary between the two suburbs (now districts IV and V of Greater Vienna).—The church at Margareten was the nearest. The place of interment was not yet decided on that day.

II. FROM BAUERNFELD'S DIARY

20th November 1828.

Yesterday afternoon Schubert died. On Monday I still spoke with him. On Tuesday he was delirious, on Wednesday dead. To the last he talked to me of our opera. It all seems like a dream to me. The most honest soul and the most faithful friend! I wish I lay there, in his place. For he leaves the world with fame!

Cf. second note preceding No. 1160.—The opera is 'The Count of Gleichen.'—Kenner too said he would have liked to die in Schubert's place (see No. XXV).

III. Ferdinand Schubert to his Father

Most cherished Father,

Very many are expressing the wish that the body of our good Franz should be buried in the Währing churchyard. Among those many am I too, believing myself to be induced thereto by Franz himself. For on the evening before his death, though only half conscious, he still said to me: "I implore you to transfer me to my room, not to leave me here, in this corner under the earth; do I then deserve no place above the earth?" I answered him: "Dear Franz, rest assured, believe your brother Ferdinand, whom you have always trusted, and who loves you so much. You are in the room in which you have always been so far, and lie in your bed!"—And Franz said: "No, it is not true: Beethoven does not lie here."—Could this be anything but an indication of his inmost wish to repose by the side of Beethoven, whom he so greatly revered?!—

I have therefore spoken to Rieder about it and inquired what outlay this transfer funeral would involve, and it comes to about 70 florins, A.C.—Much! Very much!—Yet surely very little for Franz!—I on my part could in such a case spare 40 fl. for the moment, having cashed 50 yesterday.—Besides, I think we may expect with certainty that all the expenses caused by his illness and his burial, &c., will soon be defrayed by what he has left.

Should you thus be of my opinion, dear Father, another great load would be removed from my mind. But you would have to decide at once and to inform me by the bearer of this, so that I may arrange for the arrival of the hearse. Also, you would have to see to it that the priest at Währing is informed before this morning is out. Your

afflicted son

21st November 1828, 6 a.m.   Ferdinand.

P.S. The women will surely not appear in black mourning? The undertaker thinks he will not have to procure any crape, as it is not usual for the unmarried, and because the bearers have red cloaks and flowers!—

The distance between the Neue Wieden and the Rossau was nearly two miles.—The churchyard is that outside the Währing boundary, the so-called Währing District Cemetery (cf. No. 838), the new gate to which bore the words "Place of Rest" (*Ort der Ruhe*) in 1827–32. The proper cemetery for the place of death should have been that at the Matzleinsdorf suburb, where Gluck was buried and where Vogl was interred later; the register of death at the Margareten church in fact records by mistake that Schubert was buried there.—For Johann Rieder cf. No. 483; he was also a district official in the Währing suburb. The distance between the Matzleinsdorf church and the Währing cemetery is about two and a half miles.—For the actual costs cf. Nos. XII and XXII. —The priest at Währing was Johann Hayek; his receipt, dated 22nd November, for 30 florins, A.C., for the grave and 44 florins 45 kreuzer, A.C., for other expenses at Währing, shows that the funeral was of the second class (there were three classes) and that the Währing school-children took part in it.—The postscript is crossed out, evidently by Ferdinand himself.—The undertaker entrusted with the arrangements was Balthasar Ausim, from whose (undated) receipt we know that there was a painted coffin and a "fine shroud," that one hundred and fifty announcements were printed (*see* No. I), that the neighbours were, as usual, informed by word of mouth, that a "handsome pall" and a "handsome cross" were provided, that "22 remainders of crape" and "2 mourning-cloaks" were supplied, and so on. As in the case of Beethoven, another bachelor, the custom of providing crape at the burial was observed. The two bearers had red cloaks. For flowers Ausim's bill shows only the item "wreath-binders' work 15 fl. 30 kr. in all."

IV. BY FRANZ SCHUBERT'S BIER

[21st November 1828]

May peace be aye with thee, thou pure angelic soul!
Amid the blooming of thy youthful flower
Death smote thee with its cruel, ruthless power,
With the eternal light to make thee whole;
The light, by which already penetrated
In life, for us thy songs thou hast created;
The light that woke thee, guided, fanned to flame
The spirit which from Heaven to thee came

Oh look, transfigured friend, down on our bitter tears,
Forgive the feeble human breast its sorrow:
'Tis we who mourn, who face an empty morrow;
Thou soarest home, released, to better spheres.
For many roses that thou gavest, living,
Fate in return but pointed thorns was giving,
But pain and sorrow, then an early tomb—
Yet they beyond for blessedness make room!

And what as heritage for us is left behind:
The works of fond affection and of power,
The sacred, noble truth we have for dower
Shall stay for ever in our heart and mind.
What music profits and what friendship gains
By thee, we hear it in celestial strains.
So let us ever follow each sweet note,
That we may meet again in worlds remote.

Franz von Schober.

Cf. note following.—The poem, written at the request of Schubert's family, is in the metre of Schober's 'Pax vobiscum' set by Schubert as a song in 1817, to the music of which it might be sung; the opening words are similar. Schober's allusions to protracted pain are curious in view of the fact that Schubert's last illness lasted only a few weeks; they must refer to life's sufferings in general.

Schubert's funeral, 21st November 1828:—He is laid in the coffin in the usual hermit's habit, with a laurel wreath about his brow. In bad weather, but with a comparatively numerous attendance, young officials and students carry the body from the house of death to St. Joseph's Church in the Margareten suburb. There a chorus, accompanied by wind instruments, sings Schubert's 'Pax vobiscum' (xx. 315) to words newly fitted to it, written by Schober at the relatives' request (No. IV), as well as a funeral motet by Johann Baptist Gänsbacher, both under the latter's direction. After the blessing of the body it is conducted to the Währing church of St. Lawrence and St. Gertrude, where a second ceremony follows, at which the 'Miserere,' a funeral song in German and the 'Libera' are sung. The coffin is then interred in the new Währing cemetery.

The hermit's habit was customary (? for men who died unmarried). Apart from the professional bearers, who probably carried the coffin only down the stairs, a number of youths bore it through the streets, since the way to the Margareten church was not long.—For Gänsbacher cf. No. 476.—The Währing church is in that suburb's main street, not far from the district cemetery; it was enlarged in 1934.—Schubert's 'Little Mourning Music' for wind instruments (cf. No. 51), dated 19th September 1813 and named by another hand on the manuscript "Franz Schubert's Funeral Ceremony," was not used on that occasion.—The elder Schubert's family chronicle erroneously gives 22nd November as the date of the funeral.   (On the elder Schubert's own grave *see* No. XLI).—Schubert's grave was given the number 323, following Beethoven's 290 in the cemetery.   Both graves are by the townward (eastern) part of the surrounding wall erected only in 1827; after Beethoven's grave came those of the Hardtmuth and Schlechta families (Schlechta's sister Therese having married Louis von Hardtmuth, a stove and later pencil manufacturer of musical proclivities); then, before Schubert's, that of Johann, Count O'Donell, who had died on 31st January 1828.   After Schubert's came that of Director Pompe (*see* No. 741), who died on 10th August 1831. In the meantime a woman had been buried in that cemetery: Constance Spencer Smith, born c. 1785 at Constantinople, daughter of the Austrian internuncio Peter Philipp Herbert, Freiherr von Rathkeal, wife of the English minister Spencer Smith (and thus a sister-in-law of Admiral Sir William Sidney Smith, who had attended the Congress of Vienna).   Her husband later went to Stuttgart and finally lived at Caen.   Byron made the acquaintance of this beautiful and politically adventurous woman at Malta in 1809 and wrote a poem on her entitled 'To Florence,' beginning "Oh Lady! . . ."   Its fifth stanza, "On thee, in whom at once conspire," was engraved on her funeral monument after her death on 21st October 1829.   Among those buried at Währing later were Rosenbaum, Lampi, Ignaz von Seyfried, Clement, Goethe's granddaughter Alma, Nestroy, Antonie von Arneth (Adamberger) and Grillparzer.

V. From Bauernfeld's Diary

22nd November 1828.

Buried our Schubert yesterday.   Schober with his art establishment is near bankruptcy, Schwind and I are discouraged: What a life is this!

Schober had kept the Lithographic Institute for about two years.— Schwind, who had taken part in the pictorial work 'Hungary's First Commanders, Dukes and Kings,' published by this press 1826–7, had written to him from Munich on 5th November that he had money enough to carry on only until the new year).

VI. FROM BAUERNFELD'S 'POETIC DIARY' (1828)

Beethoven died 26th March 1827.
Schubert died 19th November 1828.

Who gives us another "Eroica"?
Who further miller's lays?
No, music's glorious reign is o'er,
It sure has seen its fairest days!

With Schubert and Schwind in faithful unity
I shared life's pleasures with impunity.
The younger gentle was and fair,
Yet genius they had in equal share,
The last of Austria's flowers rare.

And now, dear Moritz, we have
Consigned our friend to the grave,
But need no assurance or oath:
Our friendship endures for us both.

Moritz is Schwind. The friendship between Bauernfeld and Schwind did last until the painter's death.

VII. SCHWIND TO SCHOBER

Munich, 25th November 1828.

Dear, good Schober,

Yesterday I received the letter in which Netti writes to me that Schubert is dead. You know how much I cared for him, and you may imagine that I could hardly grasp the thought of having lost him. We still have friends, dear and well-meaning ones, but there is none left who has lived that precious and memorable time with us and has not forgotten it. I have wept for him as for a brother, but now I am glad for him that he has died in his greatness and has done with his sorrows. The more I realize now what he was like, the more I see what he has suffered. You are still there, and you still have the same affection for me which in those unforgettable times bound us to our dear departed. You alone are left to be aware of that youth and that fire which, in spite of all, remains the only thing capable of giving me happiness. It is to you that I bring all the love they have not buried with him, and always to live with you and to share everything with you is my dearest prospect. The recollection of him will be with us, and all the burdens of the world will not prevent us from wholly feeling for a moment now and again what has now utterly vanished.

Your Moritz.

Write to me soon about everything you still remember of him—but quite soon. For an hour with you all I would : . . [*sic*].

Netti Hönig was still engaged to Schwind.

VIII. The Rev. Father Kolumban Daigele to Schubert's Father

Most valued Cousin and Kinsman,

First of all, myself and Lisi thank you for the congratulations received from your household. Furthermore, I am greatly pleased that little Andreas is already writing so nicely, and I have not the least doubt that he will daily progress in his diligence. His grandmother in particular sends him kisses and greetings. We are heartily grieved over the premature decease of your son Franz. Truly, he would yet have made a great sensation in the musical world. However, God resolved it so, and we may not quarrel with His all-highest will—a better life is promised to us all, and so, as God's faithful servants, we must not complain if He seems (apparently) to plunge us into sorrow. You are a father! and you should therefore reflect that you still possess tender plants whom you are enjoined to raise for the Almighty. The Lord will give you strength thereto, if only you will do away with all despondency. Other joys and pleasures will then make up to you for this blow you have suffered. Lord, Thou has given, and Thou hast taken away.—*Sit nomen Domini benedictum!* and our hearts will find comfort in this.   We shall not fail to remember the departed in our prayers.   As regards ourselves, we are, thank God, all well . . .

Ofen [near Pest], 28th November 1828.   Your

most devoted cousin and kinsman

Columban.

. . . The priest, Herr Heinrich Enderle [?], too, had already informed me of dear Franz's demise.

Cf. No. 952A.—Lisi is Elisabeth Kleyenböck.   What the two were congratulated on is not known.—Andreas is Schubert's stepbrother, aged five (*see* No. 113).—Anna Kleyenböck, the elder Schubert's second mother-in-law, was on a visit in Hungary.   All three were apparently Herbaschek's guests at Buda.—About Enderle (or ? Federle: the name is hard to decipher) nothing is known.

IX. JENGER TO FRAU PACHLER

Vienna, 30th November 1828.

. . . That I am still unable to conquer my sorrow over the demise of my good friend Schubert, and have been feeling unwell since his death, B[aron] Gr[imschitz] will likewise tell you.

I am very busy with the forthcoming performance, in St. Augustine's Church, of the Requiem for the departed [written] by his faithful friend Anselmo, and with the arrangements for a subscription for his tombstone.

He has already been given a grave to himself, three graves distant from Beethoven's, in the new Währing cemetery.

Jenger had written two detailed letters about Schubert's death earlier, but they were destroyed after the death of Dr. Pachler, to whom they were addressed, at his own request.—Anselm is Hüttenbrenner.   For the Requiem *see* No. XIX.

X. Retrospective Feelings at F. Schubert's Decease,
on 19th November 1828

(Autumn 1828)

Upon a pear-tree's branches
A little bird did tell:
The autumn leaves are falling,
'Tis time to say farewell.
Hence flutter I southward,
To warmth and to sunlight,
Far over the ocean;
The winds of the North
Destruction pour forth
With furious motion.
Then haste we to fields
Where cold winter yields
To gentle caressings
Of breezes, to blessings
Of sweet-scented flowers;
Where bliss aye doth wing us,
And undying spring us
Eternally dowers.
Oh, how I will sing there,
My voice, how 'twill ring there
In jubilant song:
When peaceful and blest
With joy-swelling breast
I greet Heaven's throng.
Happiest realms!
Sun that o'erwhelms!
To you I belong!

                                    Johann Mayrhofer.

This poem is here printed from the manuscript written down by
Mayrhofer in 1833 for Frau Franziska von Spaun (Archives of the Vienna
Philharmonic Society). Another version is in the second collection of
Mayrhofer's poems, edited by Ernst von Feuchtersleben in 1843.

Schubert's Bust in Bronze by Josef Alois Dialer (1829).
From the Tomb at the Währing Cemetery

PLATE XXXV

Schubert's Monument in the Vienna City Park, in Marble by Karl
Kundmann (1872)

PLATE XXXVI

XI. REPORT, 2nd December 1828

Case of Death on the Wieden.

Name of the Deceased: Herr Franz Schubert.

Occupation: Musician and composer.

State: Single, 32 years of age.

Domicile: No. 694, of this parish, as sub-tenant with his own brother Herr Ferdinand Schubert.

Day of Death: 19th November 1828.

Widowed Spouse: —

Orphaned Children: —

Of age, and where to be found: —

Minors, and where to be found: —

Whether a will is present: None

Where this is to be found: —

Nearest Relatives: the deceased's own father, Franz Schubert, Schoolmaster in the Rossau, No. 147; further 8 own brothers and sisters of the deceased: 1) Ferdinand, professor at St. Anna, domiciled at the place of death; 2) Ignaz, school assistant in the Himmelpfortgrund; 3) Karl, painter in the Himmelpfortgrund; 4) Theresia, married name of Schneider, wife of a professor in the I. & R. Orphanage, all of first wedlock by their mother Elisabeth; and furthermore: 5) Maria Schubert, 14; 6) Josefa, 13; 7) Andrä, 5; and 8) Anton Schubert, 3 years of age, all with the father in the Rossau and brothers and sisters of the second wedlock by their mother Anna.

Guardianship: None

Name of him who is to assume the trusteeship and in whose hands it is to be left: his own father.

Fortune—whether the same is considerable or negligible, of what main items it consists withal—and whether it is to be submitted to jurisdiction or embargo:

The aforesaid consists merely of the following, according to
the declaration of his own father and brother:

3 cloth dress coats, 3 frock coats, 10 pairs of trousers, 9 waistcoats	37 fl., A.C.
1 hat, 5 pairs shoes, 2 pairs of boots	2 fl. ,,
4 shirts, 9 neckerchiefs and pocket handkerchiefs, 13 pairs of socks, 1 sheet, 2 blankets	8 fl. ,,
1 mattress, 1 featherbed cover, 1 counterpane	6 fl. ,,
Apart from some old music besides, estimated at no belongings of the deceased are to be found	10 fl. ,,

	Total	63 fl. ,,

On the above the deceased's own father is to
demand, according to receipts held by him, for expenses due to illness and death   .   .   .   . 269 fl. 19 kr.
in Assimilated Coinage.

Submitted to jurisdiction.

	Anton Slabe, Sequestration Commissioner.
Vienna, 2nd December 1828.	Franz Schubert, Schoolmaster in the Rossau, No. 147, the deceased's own father.
	Ferd. Schubert, Teacher at the I. & R. Training School, the deceased's own brother.
Karl Wegmann, Treasurer.	Ignaz Schubert, School Assistant in the Rossau, the deceased's own brother.

Whether literature is found among the property and whether
a report has been made concerning it to the I. & R. Book-
Revision Office immediately after the assessment: None present.

[Protocol No.] 66715 pr[esented] 11th December 1828.
5 Documents.

[Outside:]

**Magistracy
of the Imperial and Royal Capital
and Residence of Vienna.
Herr Franz Schubert, No. 694,
on the Wieden.
Slabe.**

This report is, as usual, a large printed form on four pages folio, filled in by the signatories. It had to be submitted for the purpose of the official sequestration of the heritage of every deceased person until his will and his last obligations could be legally dealt with. The valuations given by the relatives were, of course, kept as low as possible, and the officials did not usually make any difficulties about them.——Schubert did not leave a will, being to the last scarcely aware of the gravity of his illness. But it was clear that his family, and especially his brother Ferdinand, were intended to benefit by what he left, and this not only on account of the expenses in which he had involved them at the end.——The description of Ignaz as being still school assistant (or assistant schoolmaster) at the Himmelpfortgrund is rectified by that added to his signature.——Karl still lived there, but no longer in the former school-house, where only the widow Maria Magdalena (*see* No. 131) remained.——Although the belongings left by the relatively well-to-do Beethoven, who owned his home, do not otherwise compare with those of Schubert, who was only a lodger, any more than does Beethoven's funeral, which was a public event, with Schubert's, held privately, a comparison of their clothes and bedding may be of interest.

Beethoven:		Schubert:	
2	cloth tail-coats	3	
2	frock coats	3	
8	pairs of trousers	10	
16	waistcoats	9	
2	hats	1	
6	pairs of boots	2	(and 5 pairs of shoes)
14	shirts	4	
20	neckerchiefs and handkerchiefs	9	
18	pairs of socks	13	
6	linen sheets	1	
4	counterpane cases	2	
4	mattresses	1	
7	bolsters	1	
3	coverlets (and 1 coarse cover)	1	

Being Ferdinand's guest, Schubert had perhaps not brought with him all the bedding he possessed, and what was left behind at Schober's may not have been listed. In Beethoven's case the valuation of the clothes and the personal and household laundry, as well as two beds and two pistols, came to only 53 florins; in Schubert's it amounted to 63 florins, A.C., although the effects were fewer.—"Some old music" (a theme for many a jeremiad) was really just a few old, used music-books, not Schubert's manuscripts, which nearly all remained at Schober's, except possibly the works of his boyhood, which his father may have kept. The valuer, by the way, would certainly not have been competent to estimate the remains of Schubert's own work; but it would have been in the interest of the heirs to assess it as low as possible if the question of its valuation had arisen at all.—For the elder Schubert's counter-claim cf. No. XXII, first part, where, it is true, no costs are shown on account of the illness, but on the other hand two tailor's bills and one shoemaker's.—Slabe was chancery clerk in the magistracy.—Schubert had probably left his books behind at Schober's also. Books left by the dead, as well as those brought by travellers, were subject to the censorship of the I. & R. Central Book-Revision Office.

XII. FERDINAND SCHUBERT'S STATEMENT FOR HIS FATHER, 6th December 1828

FRANZ'S ACCOUNT

Receipt	V.	C.	Outlay	V.	C.
	Fl.	Kr.		Fl.	Kr.
Nov. 1828.			12. XI.28 Medicine	1	5
Cash in hand 30 fl. coin and			2 Lemons	–	14
43 fl. paper	118	–	½ oz. Dutch tea	–	24
19th Nov., received from			13. Medicine	1	15
Father, 16 fl. coin	40	–	1 Lemon	–	7
20th Nov, 20 fl. coin	50	–	Bleeding	2	–
And lastly, 27th Nov., 10 fl.			14. Lemon and linseed	–	19
coin	25	–	15. Medicine	2	5
			Ointment and vesicatory		
	233	–	[plaster]	–	24
			16. To the barber	–	30
			Medicine	1	33
			½ lb. sugar	–	36
			Medicine	–	58
			Mustard powder	–	12

	Fl.	Kr.
17. Medicine	–	57
1 Lemon	–	7
the 16th for Herr von Gagstatter's carriage	2	–
18. Wine 15 kr., tea 9 kr., lemon 7 kr.	–	31
Ointment and meat	1	8
For 3 days each time 1 pt. wine	–	36
Powder	–	18
19. Medicine	–	40
On the 18th for the verger	1	–
19. A pr. pants	2	–
20. Dr. Wisgrill for consultation	5	–
For death certificate	1	40
21. For the male nurse	8	20
For the nurse	10	30
Rent for November	12	30
Heating	5	–
Laundry	5	–
For the male nurse, food and wine for 3 days	2	30
For the nurse, food and wine for 6 days	3	
21. XI. Funeral expenses as per account 84 fl. 35 kr. coin	211	27
To the undertaker for all services	5	–
Gratuity for the verger, the bearers, boy burial-attendants and grave-digger at Währing	5	50
For 2 Holy Masses	2	–
On 3rd Dec. to the shoe-maker Wudy according to settlement	22	–
For the carriage (Herr von Ponfikl's) to fetch the male nurse	5	–
	325	46

Ferd. Schubert.

Vienna, 6th December 1828.

This statement of his expenses during Schubert's illness was made out by Ferdinand for his father.   It is reckoned in Viennese currency, whereas the elder Schubert's account (No. XXII) is in assimilated coinage.—The 118 florins, V.C., shown as the first entry under receipts are clearly the money Schubert had by him when he took to his bed. The three amounts added by his father are mentioned also in the third part of No. XXII. Everything else Ferdinand defrayed out of his own pocket.— It is a pity that the medicine, ointment and powder are never specified. —Bleeding was still much in use, especially in cases of high blood pressure. The second item of 14th November appears as "hair-lentils" (*Haarlinsen*) in the original. The "vesicatory" is a blistering plaster made of cantharidin.—Gagstatter (ennobled by the writer's courtesy) was probably a liveryman who had supplied the carriage for the doctors: the consultation took place on 16th November.—The verger was required to assist at the administration of extreme unction.—The pants (*Gattie*) were newly bought for the dressing of the body.—The male nurse did not arrive until 17th November, after the woman nurse, who had come on the 14th, and he was fetched in Ponfikl's carriage (another courtesy nobleman). The male nurse cost more in salary and keep than the woman. —The money Schubert paid to his brother for food and lodging him seems to have come to 25 florins, V.C., a month.—The funeral expenses were booked by the undertaker Balthasar Ausim (*see* No. III), who also received a gratuity.—The verger and bearers came from the Margareten district; the boy attendants were the Währing gravedigger's young assistants.— The shoemaker Johann Wudy was paid something on account on 3rd December; his actual bill has not been preserved.

XIII. FROM THE 'WIENER ZEITSCHRIFT FÜR KUNST,' &c,. 9th December 1828

Franz Schubert, died, 19th November 1828.

The Muses weep, one favourite joins another:
　Wherefore thou too, so young, so full of hope?
Stern winter reigns, the nightingales to smother,
　Who do to spring in fairer lands elope!

Baron Schlechta.

This quatrain was set to music by Anselm Hüttenbrenner in 1861 and appeared with the music in the 'Lyra,' a Viennese periodical, on the hundredth anniversary of Schubert's birth, 31st January 1897.

XIV. Schubert
(December 1828)

Have e'er you seen that spring's resplendent flowers
Were withered in a single night by frost?
Knew you the roses which one morning blossomed
At eventide among the ashes tost?
And stars, which pure and bright shone in the heavens,
All of a sudden were in tempests lost?
Yea, all this saw you, and you made complaint
That all, these days, is transient, blurred and faint.

    And did you hear the song, your souls enchanted,
    And lost yourselves in his melodious strain?
    Did you not hope that it would fail you never,
    His golden sound, but e'er with you remain?
    To choose your breasts for its most favoured shrine
    And for your lives a lasting joy to gain?
    Yet he departed—and again you must
    From music into life's dark ways be thrust.

Alas! a song is transient, music fleeting:
We must endure it, must from it be weaned.
A rose will wither, and its radiance tarnish;
Yet bloom again, be loved again and gleaned.
But when the gardener and singer both
Were valiant, to their art with passion leaned,
When they far sooner than their work departed,
'Twas this that made us feared and broken-hearted.

    So vanished he, in youth and pow'r and glory,
    For whom we mourn: he vanished like his song,
    Destroyed amid the blossom-time of living,
    In youth, not left below to stay for long,
    Despair is left us, but despair is vain:
    He turns not whence for aye he will belong.
    And yet we ask it, as we dully brood:
    Was it a dream?   Can he have gone for good?

If one was worthy to succeed in life,
He was the man—a being set apart,
So true and honest, not of common clay,
So free from artifice, so skilled in art.
A single mind his guide through all his days,
Which made him thoughtful, yet did joy impart.
And though more taciturn than other mortals,
Good things in plenty traversed his heart's portals.

Above all else—how rare 'tis in our times—
He ever honoured what is truly great:
All noble things would serve him for a guide,
Nor would he to the mob capitulate;
The greatest masters would he seek for patterns
And with discrimination emulate.
The fire that glowed in him, a boon for all,
Ne'er let him into pride and envy fall.

What say I of his art?—Where do his songs
Not echo still? Whom did they leave unmoved?
You often listened, and again you hearkened,
Blessing the God who thus His bounty proved.
Spring did they waken in the hearer's heart,
The whole of Heaven seemed to earth removed.
This, sure, was art in gladness clad and splendour,
The purest and most high that Heav'n can render.

None finds us more indebted than the artist
Who lifts our burdens by his fancy's flight.
He often did it—yet he left the earth
In which his music still asserts its right.
No, never such a man shall be forgotten,
His and our country's pride and keen delight:
From land to land his fame shall ring for long
And strangers shall be friends unto his song.

But what of him? Alas! I see him wasting,
All of a sudden seized by febrile pains,

Already half enwrapt in death's dread shadow
Which fast on life and force dominion gains.
There lies your friend—the friend whom once you had!
His soul contesting what of life remains.
Till, in his fever for his art yet burning,
No longer knowing earth, to Heav'n he 's turning.

So have we cause enough for him to mourn,
His friends, his near and dear ones most of all!
Who could look coldly on the pangs of death?
Yet who 'd forget the living spirit's thrall?
For truly he 'll outlast our deepest sorrows
In realms beyond which ever to us call,
Where earlier another master went,
Whom now he may approach to his content.

For us, once pain and sorrow has abated,
He will himself in glory seem arrayed;
From ev'ry throat his praises will resound,
Into oblivion all his faults will fade;
And if some foes may once have spoken evil,
They gladly see a tribute to him made;
For this does death for the departed claim:
The world no longer grudges them their fame.

Then mourn you gently, listen to his songs,
The fairest heirloom that he left us all;
They sound as from familiar spheres afar
And into all our hearts so sweetly fall.
We raise our eyes among the stars above
And smile, no longer doubting this at all:
He is not dead in beauty's realm supernal
And in his music lives his soul eternal.

                                        Bauernfeld.

This poem, probably written for the circle of friends (cf. note preceding No. XX), was not published by Bauernfeld. But he quoted two
lines from it in his obituary (*see* No. XXXIII). The manuscript was found
in the possession of Schubert's descendants.

XV. FROM BAUERNFELD'S DIARY

December 1828.

Poem to Schubert. Good. Am also to write his obituary for the 'Modezeitung.'

Cf. No. XXXIII.

XVI. FERDINAND SCHUBERT'S LETTER OF SALE to Tobias Haslinger, 17th December 1828, with Postscript of 13th June 1829

[Outside, in Haslinger's hand:]

1828

SWAN SONG

['Schwanengesang']

3 SONATAS

Fr. Schubert

Schubert.

[Inside:]

I have to-day handed to Herr Tobias Haslinger, Art Dealer, the last thirteen songs:

1. 'Message of Love' ['Liebesbotschaft']
2. 'Warrior's Foreboding' ['Kriegers Ahnung']
3. 'Longing for Spring' ['Frühlingssehnsucht']
4. 'Serenade' ['Ständchen']   poems by
5. 'Sojourn' ['Aufenthalt']   Rellstab,
6. 'Far Away' ['In der Ferne']
7. 'Farewell' ['Abschied']
8. 'Atlas' ['Der Atlas']
9. 'Her Portrait' ['Ihr Bild']
10. 'The Fisher Girl' ['Das Fischermädchen']   poems by
11. 'The City' ['Die Stadt']   H. Heine,
12. 'By the Sea' ['Am Meer']
13. 'The Double' ['Der Doppelgänger']

and the *last three grand Sonatas* for the pianoforte, composed by my brother *Franz Schubert*, against a fee of *five hundred florins*, A.C.

This fee is to be remitted in the following instalments:

1. On the day of delivery of the manuscripts mentioned above (as it were for the first two books which together are to contain the 7 Rellstab songs):   150 fl. A.C.

2. On publication of the 3rd book (which is to contain the 8th, 9th and 10th of the songs mentioned above):   70 fl. do.

3. On publication of the 4th book (which is to contain the 11th, 12th and 13th of the songs mentioned above):   70 fl. do.

4. On publication of each of the 3 Sonatas, at 70 fl., A.C., each, and thus altogether   210 fl. do.

                     Grand Total   500 fl. A.C.

Vienna, 17th December 1828.   Ferd. Schubert.

Received by me in cash this day, the first instalment of 150 fl., A.C.

     Vienna,   Ferd. Schubert.
     17th December 1828.

Received of Herr von Haslinger in cash this day, the second instalment of 150 fl., A.C., and confirmed by

     Vienna,   Ferd. Schubert.
     13th June 1829.

This was the first sale from Schubert's remains. The song-cycle had already been planned as such by Schubert himself (*see* No. 1152). It did not appear in four books, but in two parts (*see* No. XXXI), augmented by 'The Pigeon Post' ('Die Taubenpost'), on Seidl's poem, Schubert's very last song, written in October 1828. Ludwig Rellstab, born in 1799, who in his Berlin periodical 'Iris' discussed Schubert's songs very critically after 1828, had visited Beethoven in Vienna in 1825 and given him several poems for composition. While Schindler asserted in 1857 that Schubert had obtained these unused poems from Beethoven's remains, Rellstab related in 1861 that Schubert even set them to music at Beethoven's desire. It is quite possible that both these stories are wrong and that Schubert found the Rellstab's poems he set in the latter's collection of 1827.—The three grand Sonatas, also of 1828, though advertised by Haslinger with the other works (*see* No. XVII), were handed over by him to Diabelli (*see* No. 1152).—The second payment to Ferdinand amounted to 150 florins, A.C., instead of 140 florins, no doubt because of the addition of 'The Pigeon Post.' He was never paid for the sonatas by Haslinger, who however, on 24th September 1829, acquired the song 'The Shepherd on the Rock' ('Der Hirt auf dem Felsen') with pianoforte and clarinet accompaniment, written by Schubert in October 1828 for Anna Milder as his last song but one, and sung by her at Riga in March 1830. In the same month Karoline Achten sang it in Vienna, and it was published on 1st June 1830 as Op. 129. Ferdinand had copied it on 2nd September 1829 and sent the copy to Frau Milder on the 4th by the intermediation of Vogl; the fee Ferdinand received from her through Vogl in 1830 he handed to his father.

XVII. From the Official 'Wiener Zeitung,' 2oth December 1828

For Information.
Franz Schubert's last compositions
for voice and for pianoforte

have been purchased by the undersigned for his legal property from the residuum of the recently deceased composer Franz Schubert, whose loss is sincerely mourned by all lovers of art: consisting of fourteen as yet wholly unknown songs with pianoforte accompaniment (composed in August 1828) and three new pianoforte Sonatas (composed in September 1828), and a detailed announcement of the publication of the same is to be made shortly.

Vienna, 18th December 1828.　　　　Tobias Haslinger.
　　　　　　　　　　　　　　　　　　Music Publisher.

'The Pigeon Post' seems to have been thrown in at the last moment, on the preceding day; but it was not composed as early as August 1828, like the other songs of the cycle, the title of which was agreed upon between Ferdinand and Haslinger. The Sonatas are still mentioned in the separate prospectus for the 'Swan Song' as well. This "preliminary announcement" appeared in January 1829 (and in a similar form in the official 'Wiener Zeitung' of 23rd March 1829). The price was 3 florins, A.C., to subscribers and 6 florins to other purchasers, according to the 'Wiener Zeitung' advertisement.

XVIII. Final Discharge of the Act of Inheritance, 22nd December 1828

Concerning the funeral expenses of 118 fl. 20 kr., A.C., reported as being claimed by Herr Ferdinand Schubert, *vice* his father Franz Schubert, who is prevented by illness; and further concerning the declaration by the aforesaid that his father has disbursed, besides the expenses proven by receipts, an additional 101 fl. 4 kr., A.C., and 22 fl., V.C., in settlement of divers of the deceased's debts, the estate of the late Franz Schubert, deceased on 19th November 1828, amounting to 63 fl., A.C., according to the legal inventory, is assigned *jure crediti* to his lawful father Franz Schubert after deduction of the funeral expenses claimed and other disbursements; wherefore this discharge is to be forwarded to the Sequestration Commissioner for removal of the sequestration without fee, and the case of death to be noted as settled; *et vide* protocol of death.

> From the Vienna Magistracy,
> 22nd December 1828.
> Brotkorb.

The elder Schubert was summoned on 16th December to appear before the magistracy on the 22nd. The sum of 118 florins 20 kreuzer, A.C., for the costs of Schubert's illness and funeral may be computed from Ferdinand's statement (No. XII), if the two carriage drives, the barber and the shoemaker are deducted. That of 101 florins 4 kreuzer, A.C., is represented roughly by the two tailor's bills entered in No. XXII (101 florins 11 kreuzer). The amount of 22 florins, V.C., is that of the shoemaker's receipt already mentioned (*see* No. XII). The 63 florins, A.C., are to be found in No. XI.—Joachim Brotkorb was one of the two directors of the Registry of the Civil Magistracy.

XIX. Invitation
to the
Memorial Service
for
Franz Schubert,

which is to be held on Tuesday, 23rd December 1828, at 11 o'clock in the Court and Parish Church of St. Augustine in Vienna, and at

which the Requiem for double choir by his friend, Herr Anselm
Hüttenbrenner, Musical Director of the Styrian Musical Society,
is to be performed.

The rehearsal for this Requiem will take place on 22nd December
1828 at 7 o'clock in the evening, in the concert-hall of the Philharmonic Society in the Austrian Imperial State, Tuchlauben, at
the "Red Hedgehog," 1st floor.

On behalf of the friends and admirers
of the Departed:

To Franz von Schubert, Esq.,
    School Director,
and family in Vienna.

Jos. Hüttenbrenner,
Member of the Musical Society, I. & R.
Court Functionary.

The original plan of holding the Requiem Mass in the church of St.
Joseph at Margareten having been given up for the more ambitious one of
doing so in the court church of St. Augustine near the Burg (cf. note preceding No. 67), an invitation was published in several of Vienna's newspapers on 20th December, together with an appeal for contributions
towards the gravestone. The invitation shown above is a privately
circulated one lithographed on a sheet, taken from the copy sent to the
elder Schubert. Another, addressed to Grillparzer (Philharmonic
Society archives), includes a request to take part in a choral rehearsal, to
be held with string quartet accompaniment on Sunday the 20th, at 7 p.m.,
in the Philharmonic Society's hall. Josef Hüttenbrenner, who took part
in the solos with the young tenor Josef Alois Tichatschek (later Wagner's
first Tannhäuser), had undertaken to organize the celebration in the name
of several of Schubert's friends. In a letter to Thayer of 1860 (Fitzwilliam Museum, Cambridge) he said that his brother Anselm's Requiem
had been seen by Schubert as early as 1825 and studied with admiration
for several days. This need not be accepted literally, although this
C minor Requiem really was written in 1825. It was sung at Graz
successively in honour of Salieri, Beethoven and (1835) the Emperor
Francis, and it appeared in print. The Leipzig 'Allgemeine musikalische
Zeitung,' which alone reported the music heard at Schubert's funeral
service, called it "anything rather than a *missa pro defunctis*, inasmuch as its
goings-on are far too merry for these solemn words." Numerous
musicians were present at this celebration. Similar ones had been held
in Vienna for Gluck, Haydn and—in the same church—Beethoven, but
not for Mozart.—The costs were 75 florins 6 kreuzer, A.C.

Schubertiad at Josef von Spaun's, 23rd December 1828, in the evening.—Bauernfeld's poem (No. XIV) may have been written for this occasion, which was doubtless an unusually serious one. The father of the three Hartmann brothers (*see* note preceding No. 372) was present.

XX. Schwind to Schober

Munich, Christmas Eve 1828.

Schubert is dead, and with him all that we had of the brightest and fairest . . .

XXI. Schwind to Schober

[Munich, 27th December 1828.]

As regards 'Figaro,' it was to be found in the room where I last lived, and if it is not there or in store, it must [have] got among the packets which I put together, one for Olivier and one for Schubert; *nisi hoc* it must be with the deuce . . . If he [Bauernfeld] could tear out at Schickh's those of Schubert's songs which have appeared in the 'Modezeitung,' he would do me a great service. A quite lonesome pianoforte is at my disposal.

For Schwind's pictorial cycle 'Figaro's Wedding Procession' *see* No. 544.—Ferdinand Olivier, born in 1784 at Dessau, living in Vienna from 1811 to 1830 and sharing with his brother Friedrich the nickname of "The Barons" given them by Schwind, was a landscape painter and one of the most refined representatives of the romantic school.—In the 'Modezeitung' ('Wiener Zeitschrift für Kunst, Literatur, Theater und Mode') twelve songs by Schubert had made their first appearance as musical supplements: 'The Trout' in 1820, 'To Emma' and 'The Flowers' Sorrow' in 1821, 'The Rose' and 'The Quail's Call' in 1822, 'Urge into the Distance' and 'To be Sung on the Water' in 1823, 'The Solitary' in 1825, 'Consolation in Song,' 'Wayfarer's Night Song' ("Over all the summits") and 'The Blind Boy' in 1827 and 'In Spring' in 1828 (16th September). At least five of these songs, printed on two pages in oblong folio, were also issued separately on four pages each with special titles.

XXII. List
of the Funeral Expenses and Other Outlay for
my Deceased Son Franz

		A.C.	
		Fl.	Kr.
No. 1.	Amount of funeral	84	35
No. 2.) No. 3.)	Receipts from the Parish of Währing . .	74	45
No. 4.	Master-Tailor Bartholomäus Hardt's account	60	—
No. 5.	Master-Tailor Friedrich Wendt's account .	41	11
No. 6.	Master - Cobbler Johann Wudy's account, 22 fl. V.C.	8	48
	Total	269	19

Vienna, in the Rossau, No. 147,
    27th December 1828.   Franz Schubert,
                                       Schoolmaster.

To the amount shown above of   269 fl. 19 kr., A.C.
are to be added
      to Pennauer, art dealer .   .   58 fl. 35$\frac{1}{5}$ kr., A.C.
      to Wilhelm Leschen   .   .   20 fl. — kr., A.C.
      to stone mason Wasserburger .   28 fl. — kr., A.C.
      to Herr Ritter von Schober   .   —   —   —
      to Dr. Rinna   .   .   .   25 fl. — kr., A.C.
      Amount of debts as per enclosure 202 fl. —   —

                      Total   602 fl. 54 kr., A.C.

A.C.		A.C.	
Outlay		Receipt	
74 fl. 45 kr.	to Währing	178 fl. 43 kr.	from Ferdinand.
60 fl. —	Herr Hart	7 — 14 kr.	
28 fl. —	Herr Jungbaur		
16 fl. —	on 19th Nov. to Ferdinand.		
20 fl. —	— 20th do. do.		
10 fl. —	— 27th do. do.		
Debts 202 fl. —			
410 fl. 45 kr.			

Cf. No. XII.—This statement was no longer made for the authorities.
—No. 1 represents the undertaker Ausim's bill; Nos. 2 and 3 the receipts
made out by the priest Hayek (cf. No. III). The two tailor's bills are
not preserved. (Schumann, by the way, fancied he could detect in some
of the 'Moments musicaux,' Op. 94, "tailor's bills" which Schubert
"was unable to pay"!) For the shoemaker *see* No. XII.—The publishing
firm of Pennauer seems to have paid an advance for which it could no
longer obtain a return, although it still issued and paid for Opp. 122–4
(*see* No. XXXIV).—Leschen was a pianoforte maker in the Wieden who,
in 1826, had been granted a five years' privilege for an improvement to
the tuning-pegs. He was the father of the composer Christoph Leschen,
born in 1816. The debt was probably for repairs made at an earlier
date, for Schubert no longer possessed a pianoforte, but had used that in
Schober's lodgings.—Anton Wasserburger received that amount on
12th January 1829 for the gravestone. For the funeral monument, including its inscription (cf. No. XLII), he was paid from other sources.
Both pieces of work were of "Margaretner" stone.—The debt to Schober
amounted to 191 florins 12 kreuzer; it was settled between 18th December 1828 and 9th January 1829 (*see* No. XXXIV).—Rinna's fee was
actually 25 florins 20 kreuzer.—The summary debit entry, which appears
also in the third part of this account, is not authenticated.—Among the
expenses shown in the third part are the two receipts of the priest Hayek,
the bill of the tailor Hardt (but not that of the tailor Wendt, which was
apparently still unpaid), the claim of the unknown Herr Jungbaur, the
three amounts mentioned in No. XII which the elder Schubert had given
to Ferdinand for Franz and the aforesaid summary debit entry. Among
the receipts appear so far only Haslinger's payment on account of 150
florins (*see* No. XVI) of 17th December, with another 28 florins 43
kreuzer possibly representing further gains from the musical remains;
and lastly 7 florins 14 kreuzer, which may have come from the sale of a
few of Schubert's possessions quickly disposed of by Ferdinand's (first)
wife, Anna.

XXIII FROM THE OFFICIAL 'WIENER ZEITUNG,'
31st December 1828
Information.

The undersigned having acquired by purchase from the estate
of the composer of genius, Franz Schubert, who, alas! died all too
soon, 18 songs and 1 Quartet for string instruments in E major,
with publication rights, he regards it as his duty to apprise the
music dealers as well as the deceased's numerous admirers of this

fact, with the intimation that all the musical works named above are to appear in print in the course of the year 1829.

Josef Czerny,
Art and Music Publisher.

Czerny was, after Haslinger, the first publisher to take an interest in Schubert's musical remains. He seems to have paid 100 florins, A.C., on 30th December, and on the day of Schubert's funeral he published as Op. 105 four songs previously acquired. The eighteen songs, Opp. 110–12, 117, 126 and 130, followed in 1829–30. The string Quartet in E major appeared with that in E flat major as Op. 125 at the beginning of 1830. Moreover, Czerny acquired the string Quartet in D minor ('Death and the Maiden,' published in July 1831) and the 'Trout' Quintet.

XXIV. From the 'Revue musicale,' Paris, January 1829
(In French)

On 19th November died in Vienna Schubert, the musician and composer. The Philharmonic Society of the Imperial Austrian State performed in his honour, on 23rd December, at the church of St. Augustine, the Requiem by Hüttenbrenner. A subscription was opened to erect a monument to him next to Beethoven, whose friend he was.

This was the first, though posthumous, press notice on Schubert to appear in France (cf. No. 1157).—The Requiem had not actually been organized by the Philharmonic Society, although it took a prominent part in the service indirectly.

XXV. Josef Kenner to Josef von Spaun

Linz, 27th January 1829.

. . . And indeed, had I not unmerited pleasure in my wife and children, I would gladly have died for Schubert, and would have done so unhesitatingly. For he would yet have done something unique of its kind, whereas my daily work at the office could be carried on by any mechanical being.

Cf. No. II.

XXVI. Invitation
to a
Private Concert,

which the undersigned will give on Friday, 30th January 1829, at
7 o'clock in the evening, in the Philharmonic Society's hall, one half
of the receipt for which is to be devoted to the erection of a monument for the deceased composer Franz Schubert, the other half
being intended for charitable purposes.

FORTHCOMING MUSICAL PIECES:

No. 1. 'Miriam's Song of Victory' ['Mirjams Siegessang'], poem
by Grillparzer, music by Schubert, performed by Herr
Tietze and the choir.

No. 2. Variations for the flute, by Gabrielsky, performed by Herr
Bogner.

No. 3. 'The Pigeon Post' ['Die Taubenpost'], by Seidl—'Sojourn'
['Aufenthalt'], by Rellstab, both set to music by Schubert
and performed by Herr Vogl.

No. 4. Trio for pianoforte, violin and violoncello, by Schubert,
performed by Herren von Bocklet, Professor Böhm and
Linke..

No. 5. 'Omnipotence' ['Die Allmacht'], by Pyrker, set to music
by Schubert, performed by Herr Schoberlechner.

No. 6. 'By the River' ['Am Strome'], with violoncello obbligato,
set to music by Schubert, performed by Herren Tietze
and Linke.

No. 7. First finale from the opera, 'Don Giovanni,' by Mozart,
performed by the Fräulein Kierstein, Jeckel, Sack, Herren
Tietze, Lugano, Schoberlechner, Nejebse and the choir.

Anna Fröhlich.

Admission tickets at 3 fl., V.C., are to be had at the Chancellery
of the Philharmonic Society and of all art dealers.

As early as 20th December 1828 the 'Theaterzeitung' had issued an
'Invitation to Lovers of Music' to announce the opening of a subscription
for Schubert's funeral monument: to be signed in the chancellery of the
Philharmonic Society "on specially printed sheets" before the end of

January 1829 at the latest. On the programme of the evening entertainment of 15th January, too, an invitation to this concert was issued. It took place on the eve of Schubert's birthday.—'Miriam's Song of Victory' (the invitation has 'Siegessang' instead of 'Siegesgesang'), a work in the manner of Handel, had been composed in March 1828, with pianoforte accompaniment, the orchestral accompaniment planned by Schubert being added by Franz Lachner. For the moment an accompaniment for two pianofortes was made to serve, one of them played by Anna Fröhlich. The solo is actually written for mezzo-soprano, but was on this occasion taken by a tenor. When the work appeared in 1838 Diabelli dedicated it to Aulic Councillor Witteczek.—Johann Wilhelm Gabrielski, born in 1791, was a flautist in Berlin.—The two songs sung (and repeated) by Vogl were the first from the 'Swan Song' to be heard in public.—The Trio is that in E flat major, already published.—Schoberlechner is Johann Karl. He sang No. 5 in place of Vogl, who had sung the same song at Schubert's own concert. Apart from the Trio and 'Omnipotence,' 'On the River' ('Auf dem Strom'; 'By the River' ['Am Strome'] is a mistake: it is the title of the Mayrhofer song) had also been taken from that earlier programme; but the obbligato horn was here replaced by a cello. It also appeared with alternative horn and cello parts as Op. 119 at Diabelli's in the autumn of 1829. The autograph has only the horn part.—The Mozart finale was accompanied on two pianofortes. Amalie Kierstein, whose later married name was Mick, became a professional singer. Fräulein Jeckel may have been a daughter of the Döbling apothecary (see No. 480). Karoline Sack, later married as Bauer, went to the Kärntnertor Theatre.—The concert was repeated on 5th March.

XXVII. From the Monthly Report issued by the Philharmonic Society of the Austrian Imperial State, February 1829

The Society has suffered a most painful loss by the death of Schubert, the composer of genius. A member of the body of representatives, to which Schubert had also recently belonged, has set him a small monument in the following biographical sketch:

FRANZ SCHUBERT

was born on 31st January 1797 in a remote suburb of Vienna (Himmelpfortgrund), where his father, of the same name, was a schoolmaster. The first instruction in music he received as early as the seventh year of his age from Michael Holzer, at that time choirmaster of the parish church in the neighbouring suburb of Liechtental. Since he discovered artistic talent in the boy, the

latter was destined for the I. & R. Seminary, which he entered
in his eleventh year (1808) as a Court choir-boy.   He was there
employed as solo singer for the I. & R. Court Chapel; at the same
time he learned pianoforte playing and the stringed instruments,
on which he made such rapid progress that before long, at the
orchestral practices held in the I. & R. Seminary, he conducted the
orchestra as principal violin whenever the actual leader was prevented.   Of the I. & R. Court organist of the time, Ruziczka, he
received solid instruction in thorough-bass, and later (1811–13)
of the I. & R. Court Musical Director, Salieri, in composition.
For his further education he was mainly indebted, according to his
own assertions, to his listening to the greatest and most widely
acknowledged masterpieces of Mozart, Haydn and Beethoven;
but he in no wise neglected studies properly so called, and in the
last months of his life he was still very diligently occupied, under
the guidance of his friend, the I. & R. Court organist Simon
Sechter, with contrapuntal exercises.   Five years were spent by
him in the I. & R. Seminary; when, however, his voice broke and
his artistic vocation became ever clearer to him, he left that
institution in the year 1813 and devoted himself heart and soul to
his favourite inclination.   From that time on he lived partly in
his paternal home, partly by himself, and earned his living by
teaching at first, but later exclusively by composition.   Apart
from a few excursions to Hungary, Styria and Upper Austria, he
always lived in Vienna, where his rich genius found the best nourish-
ment.   No important events mark his life, but he could thus dedicate himself to art with the greater leisure.   Unhappily his labours
were only too soon interrupted for ever, for already on 19th
November 1828, in the 32nd year of his life, a brief but virulent
inflammatory complaint snatched him away.

His death filled not only his more intimate friends but all
admirers of German art with profound sorrow.   A large number
of artists and art-lovers were present at the interment of his earthly
frame, and not only in Vienna but also in several of the provincial
capitals solemn Requiems were performed to his memory.   He
reposes by the side of Beethoven, whom he revered as his highest
ideal, and a modest but worthy tombstone will mark the spot where

he lies. Short as his career remained, it was none the less rich in superlative works of art.

Schubert was gifted with such creative genius that he could furnish the most carefully thought-out and deeply felt compositions with incredible rapidity. Already as a boy he wrote many string quartets, several symphonies and other musical pieces; but his chief predilection was to clothe in sound the verses of the most excellent poets and to render them musically in the form of songs. In this branch he matched the greatest of his precursors and by far surpassed almost all of them. The greatest originality, a deeply poetical soul, surprising truth of expression, sensitive understanding even of the poets' faintest suggestions, fiery imagination tempered by an inclination towards melancholy, charming yet simple melodies, wealth of modulation and inexhaustible novelty in the accompaniments are his foremost qualities, which find an outlet in any of his songs. Some two hundred of these songs are already known in print, and almost as many again are still available in manuscript. But he also successfully tried his hand at many other categories. We are indebted to his pen for a great number of the most favoured dances and marches, for several books of variations, many sonatas, fantasies, rondos, overtures, impromptus, trios and similar compositions for pianoforte solo and duet, some with, some without accompaniment, a large part of which is as yet unknown to the public. In addition to this came his vocal quartets, Psalms, choruses, cantatas (among which that under the title of 'Prometheus' is particularly distinguished), several string quartets, a grand Octet and three grand Symphonies and several overtures for full orchestra.

In the matter of church music he supplied three large and several smaller Masses as well as several Offertories and Graduals, and two 'Stabat Maters.' Least known are his efforts in the domain of opera, although they are important as regards number and content He wrote the following operas and dramatic works:

1) 'The Looking-Glass Knight' ['Der Spiegelritter'],

2) 'The Devil's Pleasaunce' ['Des Teufels Lustschloss'], both one-act operettas by Kotzebue;

3) 'Claudine of Villa Bella,' opera in three acts by Goethe;

4) 'The Four-Years' Sentry' ['Der vierjährige Posten'], operetta
   in one act by Körner;

5) 'The Friends of Salamanca' ['Die Freunde von Salamanka'],
   in two acts by Mayrhofer;

6) 'Don Fernando,' in one act;

7) 'The Twins' ['Die Zwillinge, recte 'Die Zwillingsbrüder'], in
   one act, first performed on 14th June 1820 at the Court
   Theatre next the Kärntnertor with success, and then
   repeated nine times;

8) 'The Magic Harp' ['Die Zauberharfe'], melodrama with songs
   and choruses, in three acts, given on 19th August 1820
   at the Theater an der Wien and several times repeated;
   the music pleased much, although the libretto failed;

9) 'Alfonso and Estrella,' grand heroic-romantic opera in three
   acts (composed in 1822);

10) 'Rosamond' ['Rosamunde'], drama with choruses in three
    acts, by Helmina von Chézy, performed at the Theater
    an der Wien on 20th December 1823 and several times
    repeated;

11) 'The Conspirators' ['Die Verschworenen'], comic operetta in
    one act, by Castelli (1824);

12) 'Fierabras,' grand opera in three acts (1824).

Apart from this there exist, unfinished:

'The Minnesinger';

'The Pledge' ['Die Bürgschaft'];

'Adrast,' by Mayrhofer; and

'Sakuntala,' by Neumann.

Moreover he wrote two numbers for Hérold's 'Magic Bell,'
which were performed with that opera at the I. & R. Court Opera
theatre. Among all these operas Schubert himself regarded
'Alfonso and Estrella,' and after that 'Fierabras,' as the best and
most suited to presentation. The fact that so few of these works

have so far reached performance can be attributed only to the
ill-will of certain persons, and in the last resort, to the changing
conditions at our opera. The revival of a German operatic
organization gives rise to the hope that they will not much longer
be withheld from the public.

   Schubert's character was simple, confiding and honest. All
aglow for art, he was at the same time a loving son, a faithful
friend, a grateful pupil. He loved mirth and sociable pleasures;
but he ever avoided those circles in which an artist is tolerated
only for fashion's sake and where, constrained by stiff formality,
he can never feel at home. Although well aware of his worth,
and acclaimed and flattered almost to excess by some enthusiasts,
he yet remained a stranger to pride and vanity, and he set so little
store by outward manifestations of applause that he often purposely
stayed away from the first productions of his works. Unlike most
young artists, he was himself the last to think of the publication
of his works. Only when some of his friends had, without his
collaboration, issued twelve of his works to his profit did he take
this task upon himself; and how great the general interest was is
proved by the fact alone that, between February 1821 and the end
of the year 1828, over a hundred of Schubert's works appeared in
print with several publishers and that a great part of his musical
remains too has already been bought up. Modest as Schubert was
in regard to his own compositions, he judged the works of others
with equal impartiality. Thus, with all his profound reverence
for the classical German music of earlier and more recent times,
he also granted full justice to Rossini's genius. It is much to be
regretted that, especially in his earlier days, Schubert chose scarcely
a single musical artist for his closest and most intimate relationships,
but for the most part only artistic practitioners in other branches,
who could indeed pay homage to his genius, but were incapable
of leading it. An excellent, experienced composer would probably have guided Schubert towards even more works of the larger
kind and have stood by him as adviser in matters of outward form,
well-planned disposition and large-scale effect.

   Schubert was a member of the Philharmonic Society of the
Austrian Imperial State; the Musical Societies of Graz and Inns-

bruck sent him diplomas of honour.   These distinctions gave him much pleasure, and he repaid them by writing several works expressly for these societies.   Among those persons who were the first to recognize and encourage his talent the retired I. & R. Court Opera singer Vogl must be particularly mentioned, who contributed very much, by the excellent declamatory delivery of his songs, towards making them known and loved, and thereby fired Schubert himself to new creativeness in that category.   The encouragements of his master, Salieri, and the friend of his youth, Anselm Hüttenbrenner, also had an enlivening effect and incited him at the beginning of his career.

The recognition and the applause of many excellent men rewarded his strivings, and among the many only the name of the ingenious Jean Paul shall still be named here, who felt himself greatly attracted towards Schubert's genius.   When that Titanic poet became blind in the last years of his life, he found consolation in having Schubert's songs sung to him, and but a few hours before his death, which he felt to be near, he demanded to hear the 'Erl King' ballad, which had attracted him above all.   Such interest could not fail to make the artist less receptive to the applause of the multitude, and indifferent to the petty attacks of some enviers.

Thus lived Schubert, and so he was.   His earthly pilgrimage was brief; but the spirit that comes from his music lives, and will live so long as German art shall endure.   His works are protected from destruction by their intrinsic value; but neither will his features be forgotten, his portrait having been repeatedly engraved and lithographed.   The I. & R. Lower-Austrian Government Councillor and Court Agent Josef Sonnleithner possesses among his collection of musicians' portraits a very good oil painting of him. The most speaking likeness which has appeared in public is that which the art and music dealer Herr Josef Czerny in the Graben has issued.

[Leopold von Sonnleithner.]

This was the first biographical obituary.   It is here translated from the Vienna Philharmonic Society's copy, with some corrections by its author, Leopold von Sonnleithner, who wrote it anonymously.   The 'Monthly Report,' which in its next number also issued a notice of Anna Fröhlich's concert for the funeral monument funds (No. XXVI), was a new periodical, which, however, lasted only a short time.

(Par. 1) In another copy of this article (a cutting) in Alois Fuchs's scrap-book, 'Schubertiana, Materials for a Biography of the Composer Franz Schubert' (later in Kreissle's possession), Anton Schindler pencilled in the following note to the passage about Salieri: "This last [the fact that Salieri gave Schubert thorough-going instruction in composition] was disproved by H[err]. Mayrhofer [see No. XXIX], and moreover we know for certain that Salieri never gave regular composition lessons. Had Schubert undergone the required studies with Salieri, it would have become superfluous for Sechter to teach him counterpoint. Salieri merely gave him advice on the treatment of the voice. A. Schindler." All this should be accepted with caution.

(3) The number of songs left unpublished (actually more than 400) had been estimated as some 200 also by the Leipzig 'Allgemeine musi-kalische Zeitung' on 24th December 1828; and by Josef L. Blahetka, the pianist's father, as "over 100" in the 'Theaterzeitung' of 27th December 1828. The former enumerated twelve grand operas, five small plays with music, eight masses, ten symphonies, several sonatas, trios and quartets; the latter six smaller and twelve grand operas, six symphonies, fourteen quartets and a large number of other compositions for pianoforte with or without accompaniment, overtures, cantatas and the like. Sonnleithner's enumeration is, of course, nearer the truth. The 'Prometheus' cantata evidently still existed at that time. By "three grand Symphonies" Sonnleithner could only have meant the unfinished, the lost Gmunden-Gastein Symphony and the great C major. (In his discussion of the smaller C major Symphony in the September 'Monthly Report' he called this a work of Schubert's early youth.)

(4) The three large masses are clearly that in C major, Op. 48, and the two in A flat and E flat, not yet printed. 'The Looking-Glass Knight' is an opera in three acts, of which however Schubert had only begun the first. 'Claudine of Villa Bella' has been incompletely preserved. Of 'The Friends of Salamanca' the music has survived without the dialogue. 'The Twins' should be 'The Twin Brothers' ('Die Zwillingsbrüder'); this was performed only six times. 'Rosamond' was repeated only once. 'The Minnesinger' has disappeared without a trace. 'The Count of Gleichen,' like 'Sakuntala,' has remained a sketch, but Sonnleithner overlooked it.

(7) Only ten books, not twelve, were published for Schubert's benefit: Opp. 1–7 and 12–14.

(8) The second city that made Schubert an honorary member of its Musical Society was Linz, not Innsbruck. We only know that the B minor (unfinished) Symphony was probably written for Graz.

(9) For Jean Paul cf. No. 631.

(10) Sonnleithner's uncle Josef (*see* No. 209) had at his apartments in the Graben a collection of musicians' portraits, most of them painted by Willibrord Josef Mähler (born in 1778 at Ehrenbreitenstein on the Rhine), a versatile amateur artist who was by profession an official in the court and state chancellery.   This collection, begun by Mähler, later went to the Philharmonic Society.   Apart from the bust on the funeral monument Mähler's portrait is the only one dating from Schubert's riper years on which he appears without spectacles.   On 28th November 1828 Josef Czerny had again advertised Rieder's Schubert portrait engraved in copper by Passini (*see* No. 607).

XXVIII. REMOVAL OF THE SEQUESTRATION ON SCHUBERT'S ESTATE

To the Magistracy,

According to Instruction A the undersigned has assigned the estate of Franz Schubert, composer, who died on 19th November 1828 on the Wieden, No. 694, the legal inventory of which amounts to 63 fl., A.C., *jure crediti* to his lawful father, Franz Schubert, on account, and has removed it free of charge from judicial sequestration.

Vienna, 1st February 1829.   Anton Slabe,
                                   Sequestration Commissioner.

Cf. No. XVIII.

XXIX. FROM THE 'NEUES ARCHIV FÜR GESCHICHTE, STAATEN-KUNDE, LITERATUR UND KUNST,' 23rd February 1829

RECOLLECTIONS OF FRANZ SCHUBERT *
by J. Mayrhofer.

Nothing is as a rule more superficially understood and less appreciated than what lies close.   Song too is subjected to this fate.   It is a general gift given to mankind; for all people sing. So does the American savage in virgin forests and by mighty rivers,

---

* This composer, who has departed this life all too soon, was born in Vienna on 31st January 1797 and died there of typhus on 19th November 1828.   Of his valued compositions 108 works have appeared in print, and with what he has left they will amount to 150.   His admirably caught likeness has appeared here in Czerny's art establishment.—EDITORIAL NOTE [in the magazine].

the Bedouin in the desert, the Finn and Laplander in the North and the son of the golden South. The mother has a song to send her child to sleep, the warrior one of encouragement for himself or his comrades in strife, and yet another has the beggar who wishes to forget his plight or to move others to pity.

Spread all over the earth, song receives a different imprint, determined by climate and by the people's disposition, history and degree of culture; it rings sadly or merrily, it is simple or artful, clear or confused, serious or playful. The people's destinies as well as their outlook come to life in their songs, for which reason choice spirits make them their concern; some have written song-poems or collected or imitated them. The German may confidently point to Herder, Goethe and Uhland. But it is only through melody that song becomes flesh and common property, as it were; here poets and composers meet and understand, join and supplement each other, and thus fused they may perhaps succeed in living on in the people.

My connection with Franz Schubert began when a friend of my youth handed him for composition my poem, 'By the Lake' ['Am See']—the fourth in the little volume published by Volke in 1824. Hand in hand with this friend Schubert, in 1814, entered the room we were to occupy jointly five years later. It is in the Wipplingerstrasse. Both the house and the room have felt the hand of time: the ceiling somewhat sunk, the daylight reduced by a large building opposite, a played-out pianoforte, a narrow book-shelf; such was the room which, together with the hours spent in it, will never be effaced from my memory.

As spring agitates the earth to bestow greenery, blossoms and gentle breezes on it, so is man shaken and endowed when he becomes aware of the creative force in him; for that is meant by Goethe's

> Wide, high, glorious the glance
> Cast around into life.
> From summit to summit
> Hovers th' eternal spirit,
> Boding life everlasting.

This fundamental feeling, combined with our love of poetry

and music, made our relationship more intimate; I wrote poetry, he composed what I had written, much of which owes its existence, its development and its popularity to his melodies. Herder is right in letting Music say to Poetry: "The dance as well as words serve me; gestures and motions as much as your verses; and indeed I hold all this—modulation, dance, rhythm—in myself.—The composer becomes a poet when he plays, just as the true poet sings when he writes."

It is well known that Schubert, as a Court choir-boy, was a pupil of the I. & R. Seminary, next door to the University. He made but moderate progress in the curriculum, the fault lying in his decided and predominant musical sense. At the evening concerts which were the rule at the Seminary he sometimes took an active share and sometimes distributed the parts among the other performers, by virtue of a kind of leadership assigned to him. Thus brought to a closer acquaintance with and understanding of the full scores, his talent was spurred on to trying itself in composition. Devoid of a more profound knowledge of texture and thorough-bass, he actually remained a natural artist. A few months before his death he began to take lessons with Sechter, which seems to indicate that the famous Salieri did not subject him to any strict schooling, although he looked through, praised or corrected Schubert's earlier essays. In consideration of the Seminary pupils' peculiarities and the classification it entailed, he was confronted with the alternatives of giving up either music or the endowment. Schubert's upright father, who was then at the head of a school in the Himmelpfortgrund, took his son back into his house as an assistant teacher, a hard lot, time-wasting, arduous and on the whole thankless, for my youthful, aspiring friend, whose life lay in melody. I believe that this was the source of the aversion to musical teaching which he expressed later. But the art of music and the interest of a few friends may have consoled and fortified him in such a depressing situation. It was in 1819, I think, that he attained to greater freedom and comfort of existence, much of which was due to a man who may be regarded as his second father: he not only took care of Schubert materially, but in truth furthered him also spiritually and artistically. To say more of this seems to me partly superfluous and partly unmanly, for there are actions one may assiduously think and feel about and emulate, but should not dilute with words.

His 'Erl King' appeared, a composition which not only elicited general admiration, but also found a ready sale. If I reflect how later on illness and monetary embarrassments beset my poor friend, it always strikes me that he failed particularly in two things which might have established his financial situation and outward independence. He thoughtlessly sacrificed, contrary to a benevolently conceived and already half-realized plan, his right of ownership in this and later works and so neglected a position favourable to the attainment of a salaried musical appointment. It may have been love of enjoyment, reinforced by earlier deprivations, as well as lack of knowledge of the world and its circumstances, which led him to such blunders.

Falsity and envy were utter strangers to him; his character was a mixture of tenderness and coarseness, sensuality and candour, sociability and melancholy. Modest, open, childlike, he had patrons and friends who devoted cordial sympathy to his fortunes and productions, a sympathy pointing to one more general that would surely have been his portion, had he lived longer, and will even more certainly be given to him who has departed in full flowering. Spiritual activity, too, is outwardly conditioned by time and space: good things need leisure, and a tree is not felled at one blow. Criticism, however, usually superficial, and beneficial neither to those who create nor to those who enjoy, in 1822 made a valiant and gratifying beginning towards a better understanding of Schubert's songs. This refers to No. 6 of the 'Allgemeine musikalische Zeitung' published by Steiner & Co.

It now seems indicated to mention two poetical works by W. Müller which form extensive cycles and permit of a more penetrating glimpse into the composer's soul. Opening with a joyful song of roaming, the 'Maid of the Mill' songs depict love in its awakening, its deceptions and hopes, its delights and sorrows. Although gloomy in some details, and especially at the end, much is offered nevertheless that is fresh, tender and pleasurable. Not so with the 'Winter Journey,' the very choice of which shows how much more serious the composer became. He had been long and seriously ill, had gone through disheartening experiences, and life for him had shed its rosy colour; winter had come for him. The poet's irony, rooted in despair, appealed to him: he expressed it in cutting tones. I was painfully moved.

If the wealth of melody he invented justly astonishes, amazement is further heightened by the clear-sightedness, the certainty and the felicity with which he penetrated into the life of the words and, I should say, into the peculiarity of each poet. How differently and yet how characteristically does he deal with Goethe, Schiller, Müller, Rückert, Schlegel, Scott, Schulze and others! Many of the poems become clear only through his music, such as the songs from 'Wilhelm Meister,' 'Memnon,' 'Chronos the Charioteer,' 'Ganymede' or 'On the Lake.' In this last the first note is an oar's stroke, and the prelude indicates the rocking of the boat by the waves in time with the rowing. The melody begins with that intimate expression of rapture and refreshment which the receptive draw from nature. The tones grow and swell on, for cloudy mountains show themselves in their sublimity. With a sure hand the transition from outward to inward contemplation is carried out; exquisite dreams throng in, but are resolutely repulsed, for "here too is love and life." And here precisely lies the key to the poem, which the composer has appropriated masterfully to himself. Vying with the poet, he now paints the manifestations of nature tenderly and lovingly. The climax of sublimity as well as the conclusion of the poem is repeated according to the musician's fair rights, and those among the given images which are emphasized most are the hovering stars that glitter over the waters. And with these highest things the song closes.

What a childlike note pours from his slumber and cradle songs, what piety from the 'Ave Maria' and 'Peace be with you,' from 'The Passing-Bell' and the 'Fragment from Aeschylus'—what tenderness from 'Suleika,' 'Greetings to thee,' 'To Silvia' and 'In the Grove'!

For me Franz Schubert was and remains a genius who faithfully accompanies me through life with appropriate melodies, agitated or quiet, changeable and enigmatic, gloomy or bright as it is.

The editors of this periodical were Johann Georg Megerle von Mühlfeld and Emerich Thomas Hohler. They assumed that two-thirds of Schubert's work had already been published, though what was printed in his lifetime represented only a small fraction. This obituary also appeared separately.

(Par. 3) Friedrich Volke published the first edition of these poems, from the subscription list for which Schubert's name is absent. The friend was Josef von Spaun. Mayrhofer's room was at Frau Sanssouci's (cf. No. 141), next door to the old town hall.

(4) The quotation is from the poem 'Chronos the Charioteer' ('An Schwager Kronos'), which Schubert had set to music.

(6) The expression "natural artist" (*Naturalist*) was greatly resented by Josef Hüttenbrenner. In Fuchs's copy (*see* No. XXVII) Schindler added the following remark to the words "Devoid of a more profound knowledge of texture and thorough-bass": ". . . of contrapuntal science is what the author means." To amplify the passage on Schubert's teaching period Ernst von Feuchtersleben, in his later edition of Mayrhofer's poems (Vienna, 1843, preface, pp. 10 f.), reproduced the following supplementary information—probably written later—from the manuscript that is now lost: "As an assistant at the school his father kept in a remote suburb, Schubert had a miserable pianoforte standing in a narrow room. How often did I seek him out there! with what emotions did I re-enter that house in November 1828, on the day the Requiem was celebrated for the departed one! The cross-currents of circumstances and society, of illness and changed views of life kept us apart later; but what had once been was no longer to be denied its rights. I often had to console Schubert's worthy father about his son's future, and I dared to prophesy that Franz would surely win through, nay that a later world would give him his due, slowly though it came to him at first. While we lived together our idiosyncrasies could not but show themselves; we were both richly endowed in that respect, and the consequences could not fail to appear. We teased each other in many different ways and turned our sharp edges on each other to our mutual amusement and pleasure. His gladsome and comfortable sensuousness and my introspective nature were thus thrown into higher relief and gave rise to names we called each other accordingly, as though we were playing parts assigned to us. Unfortunately I played my very own!" ("What keeps me [from knocking you down], you little rascal?" Mayrhofer would say in the Wipplingerstrasse, playfully making for Schubert with a stick; and the latter would answer with the magic formula of "Waldl, Waldl, thou savage author!" [Waldl = Waldmann being a south German name for a dog]. Cf. No. 258.) The "second father" is, of course, Vogl (cf. par. 18 in Spaun's obituary, No. XXX).

(8) The criticism of Schubert's songs referred to is No. 270.

(10) 'Memnon' was a song on a poem of Mayrhofer's own. Spaun relates that Mayrhofer often assured him that he only began to like his own poems when Schubert had set them to music. The quotation is from Goethe's poem 'Auf dem See': "hier auch Lieb' und Leben ist."

(11) "Peace be with you" ("Der Friede sei mit euch") is the opening of 'Pax vobiscum,' set to Schober's words (cf. No. IV).

The whole of this obituary is valuable less as an historical source than as a character-sketch of Schubert by an old friend, who wrote little prose, but here did so very sincerely.

XXX. FROM THE 'ÖSTERREICHISCHES BÜRGERBLATT FÜR VERSTAND, HERZ UND GUTE LAUNE,' Linz, 27th and 30th March and 3rd April 1829

ON FRANZ SCHUBERT *

Franz Schubert, a son of the schoolmaster Franz Schubert still living, was born in Vienna on 31st January 1797. His worthy father, who early discerned musical talent in the child, himself taught him the violin; but it was his eldest brother who gave him pianoforte lessons. This teaching was later continued by Michael Holzer, choirmaster at the parish church of Liechtental, and combined with singing-lessons. To this old and honourable master, who experienced the joy of having a Mass by his excellent pupil dedicated to him, Schubert remained gratefully devoted to his death.

A fine voice and a musical education rare for his age procured young Schubert a place as choir-boy in the I. & R. Court Chapel, in which capacity he became a pupil of the City Seminary. The

* It was the author's wish and intention to offer the public the above notices, written much earlier, which are actually extracts from an even fuller account of the very time when every one who realized so great a loss felt the need of seeking calm and elevation in the contemplation of the permanent things left us by him who was so soon torn from us. But such a loss remains ever new, for no later times, perhaps, will restore to us an original artist's spirit. On the other hand, too, a survey of his work always has the same effect, just as the products of nature, ever recurring in the same form, will always speak equally powerfully to the receptive mind. Thus the sensitive reader will not regard this essay as belated, or at least not as untimely. For the rest, it makes no other claim than that of relating experiences simply and truthfully and thus to honour the memory of the departed also in that part of the country which has so often hospitably received him and, like so many of its friendly inhabitants, was dear to and valued by him. [Josef von Spaun.]

church service was a delight to the boy; among the church works excellently performed in the I. & R. Court Chapel the very compositions which distinguished themselves more by inward content and religious exultation than by outward effect were those which made the greatest impression on his child's mind, already led by nature into the right paths.

At the same time the instrumental music at the Seminary had, by diligent collaboration among the pupils, been brought to a degree of perfection rarely to be found among such young amateurs. Daily the evening was devoted to the performance of a complete symphony and several overtures, and the young orchestra's forces sufficed for the successful performance of Haydn's, Mozart's and Beethoven's masterpieces. Schubert, scarcely twelve years of age, played second violin in the orchestra. His extraordinary interest in the masterpieces performed, however, soon drew the attention of those around him to his superior talent, and the boy was placed as leader at the head of the orchestra, where all the adults willingly submitted to him.

Above all the glorious Symphonies in G minor by Mozart and in D major by Beethoven made the profoundest impression on young Schubert every time, and even shortly before his death he still spoke of how greatly these compositions had moved and touched his youthful soul.

His musical sense was already so much developed at that time that he not only retained the melody of musical pieces once heard completely in his memory, but immediately noticed any departure and any slip in the subordinate parts.

Already at the age of 10 or 11 Schubert tried his hand at short songs, quartets and small pianoforte pieces. His first more extended work was a Fantasy for the pianoforte, written early in the year 1810. Most of this has been lost, without having ever been submitted to so much as an examination by a connoisseur. Twelve minuets with trios, written by Schubert for the pianoforte in his 14th year, which astonished all and sundry by their correct writing and their wealth of melody, seem likewise to be irretrievably lost.

Some of these small compositions drew the attention of the I. & R. Court Musical Director Salieri to young Schubert's talents.

He immediately honoured these with his warmest interest and charged the then first Court organist Ruziczka with the boy's instruction in thorough-bass. These studies, however, were confined to a few hours, for it became evident that what appears to others so difficult to learn was already innate in young Schubert, and that he already understood the nature of thorough-bass completely, needing only a knowledge of its different designations to present himself as fully instructed therein.

Young Schubert's enthusiasm for music now glowed brighter day by day, and he keenly felt that he was destined to live for art. He therefore resolved with his father's consent, having in any case already lost his soprano voice and with it his place as choir-boy, to leave the seminary and also to give up his studies, in order to follow his profession undividedly.

Even after this withdrawal from the I. & R. Court Chapel the Court Musical Director Salieri did not deprive him of his guidance: for several years he gave him almost daily instruction in composition and let him study the scores of the older Italian masters, which the young artist perused with zeal and devotion, without however finding in them the full satisfaction offered him by Mozart's operas, which he got to know from their scores at the same time, and by Beethoven's works, which most particularly aroused his enthusiasm.

This predilection of Schubert's, which Salieri did not seem to share, and the frankness with which his candid scholar declared his attitude, caused Salieri to doubt whether Schubert would pursue the path along which the master intended to educate him to opera. Added to this, Salieri wholly disapproved of the very form of composition to which his pupil was irresistibly drawn, namely German song. Goethe's and Schiller's poetry was unpalatable to the Italian and its hard language seemed to him unworthy of the composer's art. He earnestly asked Schubert not to concern himself further with essays of that kind, but rather to husband his melodies until he had become more mature, and instead to exercise himself on the short Italian stanzas Salieri submitted to him for a task. But such demands and warnings were powerless against the young artist's inward voice, and thus, of course, the teaching to which Schubert was already indebted for much could no longer

continue.   He left his great master, to whom for all that he remained gratefully devoted and for whose works, especially his
two operas, 'Axur' and 'The Danaides,' he had a high regard.

Thenceforth Schubert dedicated the first-fruits of his talent to
German song.   The first of the larger productions that has been
preserved seems to be the poem of 'Hagar's Lament in the Desert,'
set to music in 1811.   To several smaller poems by Matthisson
and Klopstock succeeded the songs 'Edone,' 'To Cidli,' and others
too are early but full expressions of his original mind already.   In
the same vein he produced the song 'To Emma' and more by
Schiller; 'Shepherd's Complaint,' 'Margaret at the Spinning-
Wheel' and others by Goethe.   At the same time the awakening
youth, receptive to all that is beautiful and great, was also fired
by Ossian, and many a splendid song testifies to the truth and profundity of those impressions.   Ballads and other larger poems on
which the fiery young tone-poet, whom no task seemed to daunt,
tried himself, such as 'The Diver,' 'Expectation' and others, also
belong to that early period.   The deeply felt and excellent ballad,
'The Minstrel,' proves that Schubert knew how to take the
measure of and find expression for this species, and that perfect
romance, Goethe's 'Erl King,' has the same early origin.

Not only countless songs, however, which all without exception
distinguish themselves already by original treatment, depth of
feeling and indescribable richness of melody, but also several larger
compositions belong to Schubert's first, incredibly fruitful period.
A grand, very melodious Symphony was composed by him as early
as 1813, a complete Mass, conducted by himself at the parish church
of Liechtental, in 1814, while again in 1815 two Symphonies
came forth; and to the same time belong the operettas, 'The
Looking-Glass Knight,' 'The Devil's Pleasaunce' and 'Claudine of
Villabella,' as well as several cantatas to which he found himself
incited by sundry occasions and quartets for string instruments at
which he tried his hand by the way.

The small public surrounding the composer during the first
years of his musical activity, consisting only of his relatives, some
of his school-fellows and a few friends, increased by degrees; and
whoever was drawn into that small circle was surprised and moved

by the impression of those daily increasing songs, which the composer still always sang himself at the time, little as he excelled in voice and delivery. To the profuse applause and lively sympathy of his friends Schubert often replied in those days: "I hope myself that something may yet be made of me," not in the least suspecting in his modesty what heights he had already reached. Even if Schubert had been torn from us at that time, he would have to be recognized as an unsurpassed composer of songs.

Schubert's rapidity in composition was extraordinary. Whoever in those days gave him a poem to set could be sure that, if the musician liked it, a well-finished composition would be ready the next day. Thus originated the glorious song, 'The Wanderer,' by Schmidt of Lübeck; thus was the reading and setting of Goethe's 'Erl King' the work of an afternoon. For his friends that time of daily precious gain will ever remain unforgettable.

Instead of becoming poorer through this lavishing of melodies, their stream seemed only to grow by its outpouring. And yet in this multiformity of the songs produced during that period a peculiar character is discernible, such as is again noticeable in the later song compositions more than once after periods of inward development. If we here single out from a multitude some more songs after those already mentioned, such as 'At Anselmo's Grave,' 'At the Grave of my Father,' by Claudius, the Harper's songs from 'Wilhelm Meister's Prentice Years,' 'The Trout,' 'On the Lake,' 'Spirit's Greeting,' 'Memnon' and others by Mayrhofer, whose friendly relationship with Schubert had the most favourable mutual influence on both the poet and the composer, it is not in order to make thereby a choice of the most excellent (for who would dare to make a selection of that kind where all are admirable and original?), but only as an attempt to indicate by examples the spirit of the songs belonging to that period.

Now, before we pursue Schubert's further achievements, it is necessary to touch upon other circumstances that had the greatest influence on his life and work.

Schubert was 15 years of age, and had already written much, before he had ever heard a good opera. Weigl's opera, 'The Orphanage,' was the first to come to his ears. It made a great

impression on the young artist; and a still greater one came from
Weigl's 'Swiss Family,' in which at that time Mme Milder, Vogl
and Weinmüller collaborated. But the impression of these two
operas, as well as that of Spontini's 'Vestal' heard later, had soon
to yield to the infinitely deeper one made on Schubert by Gluck's
'Iphigenia in Tauris.' He was moved to his depths and to tears.
That evening's effect on him he could never forget, and it was
followed by the keenest study of all Gluck's scores, which quite
enraptured Schubert for years. Again and again did he ask later
on whether the beautiful times for such enjoyment had vanished
for us for ever.

The great impression Gluck's 'Iphigeneia' made on Schubert
was further enhanced by the masterly acting and splendid singing
of the Court Opera singer Vogl. Schubert's enthusiasm for that
artist rose with every performance and nourished the ardent wish
in him to become acquainted with this master of song. A friend's
mediation fulfilled it.

At the first meeting Schubert was not unembarrassed. He first
submitted the Mayrhofer 'Eye Song,' which he had just set to music,
for judgment. Vogl, at once discerning Schubert's talent in this
song, examined with increasing interest a series of others .shown
to him by the young tone-poet, who was immensely delighted with
such approbation. Only a few weeks later Vogl was already
performing Schubert's 'Wanderer,' 'The Combat,' 'Erl King'
and others to a small but entranced circle, where the singer's
enthusiasm was the most valuable testimonial for the composer.
On the latter personally, moreover, the effect was great, lasting
and of much consequence, for that which was in his soul as hardly
so much as a wish he now saw fulfilled to perfection and beyond all
expectation. An alliance between the two artists, which became
ever closer until death severed it, resulted from that first meeting.
Vogl, with friendly advice, opened the rich treasury of his experience for his young friend, cared in a fatherly way for the
satisfaction of his needs, for which Schubert's income was insufficient in those early days, and opened him by the splendid
delivery of his songs a path to the glory he so brilliantly attained.

For indeed it was the interest Vogl showed for these songs and his unparalleled performance of them which now speedily won for them general and joyous recognition. Thenceforth some excellent amateurs here and there also began to make themselves acquainted with the spirit of these compositions; they were performed in several art-loving houses and at the concerts of the Little Philharmonic Society, and honoured with applause and decided preference by many persons distinguished by their fine cultivation as well as by their position in society, which greatly encouraged a composer who was not indifferent to the approval of the educated.

At Vogl's instigation Schubert received in 1820 the commission to set to music a small opera, 'The Twin Brothers,' for the I. & R. Court theatre at the Kärntnertor. Although the libretto left the composer entirely cold, the opera nevertheless contained a number of excellent musical pieces, and neither the treatment of the whole nor the orchestration let the work appear anywhere as that of a beginner. Yet Schubert had never before heard a performance of any larger musical piece of his composition. Much more important, however, was the music he composed soon afterwards for the melodrama of 'The Magic Harp,' which was given at the Theater an der Wien, and although that too was insignificant as regards its literary aspect, it stimulated the composer's fancy by the nature of its fairy-tale subject. And this, indeed, so wondrously dominates the composition, and there is such a dreamy tenderness in it, that one can only lament to find such a wealth of beauty lavished on a play that was incapable of maintaining itself on the stage for long. For all that, perhaps the time is not far distant when, altogether more conversant with the peculiarities of Schubert's compositions, people will seek out this work also, few as its former admirers were, and be surprised at its beauties.

Several times songs by Schubert may by now have been heard at public concerts. Before a large audience this occurred for the first time in 1821, when the 'Erl King' was performed by Vogl at the Court theatre next the Kärntnertor. Tensest attention and general tempestuous applause of the numerous public rewarded the composer and also the singer, who had at once to repeat that exhausting song almost as soon as he had finished it. Modest

Schubert had been unable at that time to find a publisher; but now
the universal success induced some of his friends to have the
'Erl King' engraved at their own expense.   In a short time the
edition was out of print, and all at once the path was clear for
general distribution by means of publication.   If only time had not
been so unpropitious to the development of our Schubert's gifts
in the matter of dramatic music!   In the year 1821 the dissolution
of the Court Opera management occurred, the best members of
the German Opera being thus lost to it; and even the ever-irre-
placeable Vogl was pensioned off.   What remained was too mediocre to maintain itself worthily next to the Italian Opera, now
introduced into the metropolis and uniting all the singing heroes
formerly scattered in the South into a whole such as can hardly
ever before have been known.   Thus seven years went by, during
which the German Opera was silenced, or made itself heard but
timidly and feebly.   And Schubert, without any prospect, nay
without even the wish to experience the performance of an opera
of his own with such inadequate means, nevertheless continued
to work at grand operas; and the hidden force of these dramatic
essays may perhaps sooner or later convince the public what we
have lost by the fact that the circumstances of the time should have
reduced an aspiring artist's soul to mere experimentation.   Even
now, these seven years being past, it looks as though here and there
national feeling, almost tired of the dazzling effect, wished to
assert its former rights, so that a better future may be dawning for
German music—and now our Schubert, who might have become
a prop and ornament of German operatic music, has so soon departed from the realm of the living.   For the lack of public performances of Schubert's larger works his friends were compensated
by his uninterrupted composition of German songs, whose source,
in spite of the adverse events just mentioned, which agitated the
artist's soul, always remained equally abundant.   'Diana in Anger,'
'Faith in Spring,' 'Hail and Farewell,' 'Bounds of Mankind,'
'Secrets,' the two "Suleikas," 'Treasure-Hunter's Desire,'
'Music of Death,' 'The Dwarf' and 'Veteran's Song' may designate
the character which predominates in Schubert's songs of the years
1820, 1821 and 1822.   In the year 1823, the same in which he

was elected an honorary member of the Musical Societies of Linz and Graz, he composed the universally favoured 'Fair Maid of the Mill,' which appeared serially in five books. The germinating and growing of passion from the first gentle premonitory stirring to its full, maddening power, from the tenderest, sweetly melancholy ecstasy to its quietly releasing sorrow and shattering pain, from the fairest rapture of hope to the consuming agony of jealousy—where has all this ever been expressed so affectingly in music?

For some years Schubert had also more frequently written musical pieces for the pianoforte, such as his first four-handed Variations, which were worthy of being dedicated to the immortal Beethoven; and ever more steadily did he progress, almost simultaneously, in such compositions and in the artistic perfection of song. In 1824 appeared the six grand Marches for four hands, among which the Funeral March, No. 5, may well be unapproached in nobly resigned sorrow, and songs, such as 'The Solitary' and 'Sunset Glow,' as genuine as they are affecting. In 1825, at Gastein, a grand Symphony for which the composer himself had a vast preference, and the very difficult Sonata, very rewarding however to a master-hand, the dedication of which H.R.H. the Archduke Rudolf graciously consented to accept; and in the same year the songs from Walter Scott's 'Lady of the Lake': 'Norman's Song,' 'The Imprisoned Huntsman' and 'Ellen's Evening Song to the Holy Virgin,' comparable only to the most splendid work produced by the great lyrist, the first two in fire and force, the last in pious emotion.

Indeed, Schubert's activity seemed ever to increase in the last years of his life. A most original Sonata for the pianoforte, dedicated by Schubert to the excellent pianist von Bocklet, a grand Funeral March and a Coronation March for four hands, an Octet for string and wind instruments, a Fantasy for the pianoforte for two and another such for four hands, two grand Trios for pianoforte, violin and violoncello, both already performed in public by Bocklet with the greatest success, the partly unfinished opera, 'The Count of Gleichen,' which Eduard von Bauernfeld, a friend of Schubert's, had written for him, a grand Mass, finished shortly before his death, and many other works space does not suffice to mention, were all composed during the last three years of Schubert's life. And at the same time new and unforgettable songs continued to come forth: 'The Blind Boy,' 'The Wayfarer addressing the Moon,' 'The Passing-Bell,' 'In the Open,' the romance of Richard Cœur de Lion from 'Ivanhoe,' these are fragrant flowers from the rich garland of song the dear departed still wove for us in the last period of his life.

More moving than anything, however, are the songs published under the title of 'Winter Journey.' They are the last of Schubert's larger works, but well worthy of closing such labour. No one, surely, could play, sing or hear without being shaken to the depths the songs contained in this work: 'Good Night,' 'Frozen Tears,' 'The Lime-Tree,' 'Will-o'-the-Wisp,' 'The Post,' 'The Crow,' 'The Inn' and a number of others.

If it was possible up to a point to give some indication in words of the fanciful, youthful emotion of the 'Maid of the Mill' songs, or at least to awaken an echo of them in the memory of those who have heard them, who could find words to describe the unnamable things the inspired artist opened up to us in song about the profoundest and most secret meaning of unhappy love?

Such triumphant progress on the artistic road could thus not fail ever to increase the number of Schubert's admirers. Vogl, who still to-day performs the Schubert songs with youthful fire and with the expression that is all his own, could scarcely sufficiently satisfy the frequent demands for this enjoyment any longer; and excellent amateurs, accustomed for years to pay homage exclusively to Italian song, returned to the home-grown which once again, thanks to the great master, reasserted its own rights with the force of innate truth; so that it seemed as though at long last the time for such well-deserved general recognition had approached—when a sorry fate tore from us the artist with whom a star of the first magnitude has set on the musical horizon.

Short as Schubert's life was, alas! the number of his works is nevertheless incredibly large. He wrote 11 operas, 2 melodramas, 6 Symphonies, several complete Masses, a large quantity of Quartets and pianoforte pieces, sometimes also unsurpassable, indeed one may say vital and spirited dances with which, no dancer himself, he merely delighted his friends occasionally and as if in play; and several cantatas, not to mention four-part and choral songs, some 400 songs, including 14 quite new ones shortly before his end, dedicated to his friends and published by Haslinger of Vienna, among which 'The Pigeon Post' was his last.

Although in none of Schubert's works do we miss his profound, original mind and his inexhaustible melodic wealth, both appear by far the most conspicuously in his songs, all the same. In this category he stands unexcelled, nay unapproached. Whatever filled the poet's breast Schubert faithfully reflected and transfigured in each of his songs, as none has done before him. Every one of his song compositions is in reality a poem on the poem he set to music; and not only for sentiment, which is doubtless at home in song, but for all the magic of fancy, for its unearthly charm and its nocturnal terrors, did he know how to find the most proper viewpoint, indeed even for high seriousness of thought had he a language. Who among those who had the felicity to hear some of his mightiest songs does not remember how this music made a long familiar poem new for him, how it was suddenly revealed to him and penetrated to his very depth as a chord or a note here and there struck into his soul, illuminating and convulsing? True, for the great masses, who are but fleetingly entertained by music, but not touched and elevated, the Schubert songs will never have more than a small attraction; but they will the more deeply affect those for whom the ear is not only the goal for sound, but merely the threshold across which they penetrate to exercise their wondrous power on the soul.

Whether Schubert's larger compositions excel equally the future will show. They are so permeated by depth and tenderness that they can be communicated in their author's spirit only if they are conceived in the same sense and performed, not with virtuosity only, but with devotion. Much of that which came before the public in conformity with these exigencies entitles us to the fairest hopes in respect of such works as well, which the death of their creator will now doubtless release from the fetters that have so far kept them in obscurity.

As regards Schubert's further personal attributes, the grief of all who stood near him over his early loss is the best testimony to follow him, who was equally excellent as a son, a brother and a friend, into the grave. He was uncommonly sincere, open, friendly, modest, grateful, sociable, communicative in joy and reserved in sorrow, yet free from all bitterness, however great the distance between achievement and recognition, between his gifts and his destiny; and his attachment to his paternal home, his friends and his native city was so great that he would have gladly sacrificed to it a more brilliant lot abroad.

The time from 9 o'clock in the morning until 2 o'clock Schubert daily and without exception devoted to composition or to his studies. But the afternoon and evening was given up to his family or his friends. No feast, no repast, no entertainment gave him pleasure if it was not seasoned by friendly intercourse. To the beauties of nature he was most receptive, and on fine summer's days he almost daily made longish excursions into the beautiful environs of Vienna in the afternoons and evenings. He had a particularly great predilection in this respect for the glorious regions of Upper Austria and Salzburg, which for several years he visited with Vogl in the summer months. At Linz, Steyr and Gmunden the delights will remain unforgettable which this pair of artists there afforded the admirers of Schubert's songs.—In the earliest times of his artistic activity, when his talent could not yet secure him a living, Schubert applied himself to teaching at his father's school. This profession, incompatible with his own inward one, he exchanged as soon as possible by endeavouring to make ends meet by pianoforte lessons. But as soon as the merest chance showed of existing on the proceeds of his compositions, he gave up teaching, preferring to live modestly on a little, so long as he could undividedly devote himself to the art he loved above all things. Even the applause of the multitude left Schubert cold, much as that of his friends pleased him; and still less was money the aim of his industry. The representations frequently made to him by art dealers that he should avoid difficulties of execution in his compositions in order to facilitate their sale he left unnoticed; indeed, he could not have heeded them, since he wrote only as his

artistic inspiration dictated, which would admit of no consideration
of difficulties, which after all might be found also in compositions
of smaller intrinsic value.

With the classical works of the great masters Schubert was
intimately acquainted, and he felt for them—for Handel, Gluck,
Mozart, Haydn and Beethoven—the most enthusiastic reverence.
He sincerely esteemed merit of any kind.   The songs by Zumsteeg,
with which he became acquainted already as a boy, may in any
case have somewhat awakened his inclination to German song and
incited his innate talent for that sort of composition to its first
utterances, and in some few [songs] of this earliest period this
influence may in fact perhaps be noticeable; but Schubert left this
path quite soon, to go his own.   Yet he never ceased to do justice
to Zumsteeg's songs, indeed he always expressed himself with
the same warmth about their value, even at the time of his own
highest accomplishment in that species of composition.   Altogether, Schubert also judged the compositions of his contemporaries
always most benevolently, although frankly.   He did not tolerate it
if his friends, in their preference for his compositions, dismissed the
works of others unjustly.   Once, when he was playing Kreutzer's
'Roaming Songs' and one of his friends spoke disparagingly about
them, he quietly replied: "I wish I had written them."   Even
shortly before his death he was highly delighted by a new pianoforte composition by Abbé Stadler, and said: "What a pleasure
it is, truly, that such things are still appearing."   He took a
joyful interest in any well-turned-out composition, no matter
from whom it came, and in truth loved art without vanity and
without envy.

On the other hand his ruthless frankness might oftentimes wound
the self-esteem of others, though his mind could see no harm.
Altogether, the world's judgment may blame him in many ways
that he was not to be constrained by the conventions of society,
where there was no intimate relationship to appeal to him, and
that he had an elastic conscience where such duties were concerned,
just as he would frequently break his promise to appear at some
function held by high-placed patrons if he saw a prospect of spending the same hours at a subsequently arranged gathering of his

friends or, more particularly, a summer's evening in the open air. This doubtless gave him the reputation here and there of having lacked social graces and education, and indeed of having been, artistic genius excepted, a quite insignificant personality. Many a circle, however, where he knew himself received with cordial sympathy and thus moved with ease, where he suspected no motives of vanity to spoil for him the practice of his art, which was sacred to him, will give the lie to calumny, and his friends recollect their loss with feelings of distress, and how he always enlivened their circle with cheerfulness, wit and sane judgment; how, in particular, he was able to account for the musical point of view in general and for the peculiarities of his works in a manner which most decisively contradicted the opinion, held here and there, that he produced his finest music as it were by inspiration pure and simple, without any conscious activity of his own.

Schubert's modesty was boundless. The loudest cheers of his friends and the greatest applause of a numerous crowd could not make him dizzy. Even the most honouring recognition on the part of great artists like K. M. von Weber, Hummel, Lablache and others did not allow him to overstep a strictly measured self-esteem. If, as so often happened in musical circles, the singer who performed his songs was overwhelmed with enthusiastic applause, and nobody thought of the little man who sat at the pianoforte and soulfully accompanied the songs of his own making, the unassuming artist did not feel in the least slighted even by such neglect, if only he could convince himself that in spite of such disregard of his person a deep sympathy with the music performed was not wanting.

Until the last year of his life Schubert made no claim on the public by any concert of his own. Only the importunity of his friends and the insufficiency of his income induced him at last, in March 1828, to give a concert for his own benefit. The extraordinary participation of a crowded audience did justice to the rare enjoyment of that evening, which will surely remain unforgettable for all who had the good fortune of partaking of this musical feast, which, alas! will recur no more. Schubert thought of giving a similar concert each year, not suspecting that his first would also

be his last, and that the next public performance of his compositions would take place only in celebration of his memory.

Enjoying robust health, Schubert paid no heed to an indisposition that had been troubling him for some time.   On 11th November he was obliged to take to his bed.   Although dangerously ill,
he did not feel painfully attacked and merely complained of weak-
ness.   From time to time he fell into delirium, during which he
sang continually.   The few lucid intervals he still devoted to the
correction of the second part of the 'Winter Journey.'   On
19th November, at 3 o'clock in the afternoon, he passed away,
and his gentle, unchanged face showed that he went to his last
home peacefully and without a struggle.

That heart of his, so rich in benevolence as in music, now
reposes in the cool of the grave prepared for the deceased next
to Beethoven's.   A memorial stone, erected by friends and
admirers, will show posterity who reposes here and how much we
loved him, so that we shall not be subjected to the same reproach
as our forbears, who neglected to mark for us the grave which
encloses the bones of Mozart.

Beyond the tomb, however, the departed is followed by our
gratitude, our longing for him and our love.

[Josef von Spaun, revised by Anton Ottenwalt.]

This is the first biography of some size, published in the form of an
obituary.   It is evident from a comparison with the even more extensive
manuscript long ascribed to Schober (who never wrote any recollections of
Schubert) and from two letters written by Ottenwalt to Spaun, dated Linz,
9th February and 17th March 1829, that Spaun sent the first version of
his essay to his brother-in-law, who edited it and published it anonymously.   This original version was published in 1936 by the Atlantis-
Verlag of Berlin and Zürich under the title of 'Recollections of Schubert:
Josef von Spaun's First Biography' ('Erinnerungen an Schubert: Josef von
Spauns erste Lebensbeschreibung'), with a comparison of the two versions
and Bauernfeld's essay (No. XXXIII), which is based on the longer of the
two.   Extracts of Ottenwalt's two letters appeared in the official 'Wiener
Zeitung' of 18th November 1928.   Spaun, by the way, wrote three more
essays on Schubert later: 'Notes on my Relations with Franz Schubert'
(1858, several times reprinted, best of all in 'Der Merker,' Vienna,
February–March 1911); 'Some Facts of my Life' in his family chronicle
(1864), also dealing with Schubert's friends (several times quoted,

e.g. in the 'Annual of the Grillparzer Society,' Vienna, 1898, but not yet correctly published); and (at the end of 1864) 'Some Observations on the Schubert Biography by Herr Ritter von Kreissle-Hellborn,' published as 'Neues um [sic] Franz Schubert' by the Vienna Schubert Association (Wiener Schubertbund) in 1934.

(Par. 1) Holzer had died as early as 1826. The Mass in C major, Op. 48, dedicated to him had appeared in 1825.

(3) The adults were the students of philosophy and theology at the Seminary.

(6) The Fantasy is written for four hands (ix. 30). The twelve minuets with trios of 1812 were shown by Spaun to Dr. Anton Schmidt (see No. 125), a friend of Mozart's, who said of them: "If it is true that these minuets were written by one still half a child, that child will grow into a master such as there have been few as yet." Schubert lent them so often that they got lost.

(9) The scores of Gluck's operas, with which Schubert became acquainted at Salieri's, are here overlooked (cf. par. 17). The scene in Hades from 'Orfeo ed Euridice' Schubert once performed from memory at the Seminary.

(10) Several exercises on words by Metastasio, written by Schubert during his student days under Salieri, have been preserved (published in Vienna in 1940). Each of the texts is repeatedly set for one and several voices. Salieri's opera 'Axur, rè d'Ormus' (libretto based on Beaumarchais by Lorenzo da Ponte) had been produced at the Burg Theatre in 1788 as a new version of 'Tarare' (Paris, 1787); the opera 'Les Danaïdes' (Paris, 1784) was never given in Vienna.

(11) 'Hagar's Lament' ('Hagars Klage in der Wüste') is the first preserved song of Schubert's; 'Edone' is already No. 230, 'To Cidli' ('An Cidli') No. 138, 'To Emma' ('An Emma') No. 26, 'Shepherd's Complaint' ('Schäfers Klagelied') No. 34, 'Margaret' ('Gretchen am Spinnrade') No. 31 in the chronological series of the complete edition. The Ossian songs range from No. 44 to No. 592, passim, and therefore over the whole of his creative lifetime. 'The Diver' ('Der Taucher') is No. 12, 'Expectation' ('Die Erwartung') No. 46, 'The Minstrel' ('Der Liedler') No. 98 and 'Erl King' ('Erlkönig') No. 178.

(12) The first Symphony is that in D major, the first Mass that in F major. The second Symphony, begun as early as the end of 1814, is in B flat major, the third again in D major. For the first operas cf. No. XXVII.

(14) 'Der Wanderer' is No. 266.

(15) 'Am Grabe Anselmos' is No. 275, 'Bei dem Grabe meines Vaters' No. 274. The Harper's and Mignon's songs from Goethe's 'Wilhelm Meister' range from No. 158 to No. 488, passim. 'The Trout' ('Die

Forelle') is No. 327, 'On the Lake' ('Auf dem See,' *see* No. XXIX)
No. 310, 'Spirit's Greeting' ('Geistesgruss') No. 174, 'Memnon'
No. 308.

(17) The dates given by Grove for Schubert's attendance at these
operas, evidently according to information from Karl Ferdinand Pohl,
are arbitrary (cf. notes preceding Nos. 29, 46 and 52).

(18) It was Schober who introduced Schubert to Vogl.

(19) 'Eye Song' ('Augenlied'), No. 171, is supposed to date back to
October 1815; the meeting, however, did not take place until the spring
of 1817. 'The Combat' ('Der Kampf') is No. 333. According to the
original version of this essay 'Ganymede,' No. 311, was also among the
first Schubert songs sung by Vogl.

(20) The concerts of the "Little Philharmonic Society" are the
evening entertainments given by the Philharmonic Society.

(22) For the concert in the Kärntnertor Theatre *see* No. 209. The
songs 'The Dwarf' ('Der Zwerg') and 'Veteran's Song' ('Greisengesang'), whose dates are uncertain, are ranged in the complete edition
as a little after 1822.

(23) The Variations, in E minor, are Op. 10, the six Marches Op. 40.
The word "appeared" (*erschienen*) used in connection with these marches
and the two songs named below them ('Der Einsame' and 'Im Abendrot')
here means that they were produced by the composer at that time, not
published. The "Gastein" (or more correctly "Gmunden-Gastein")
Symphony is unmistakably meant here (cf. Nos. 569, 581 and XXXIII,
par. 9 and list of works). The Sonata is Op. 42, in A minor; but it is
not suggested that it was written at Gastein. The Scott songs are Op. 52.

(24) The Sonata is Op. 53, in D major. Spaun does not mention the
Sonata in G major, Op. 78, dedicated to him. The Funeral March is
Op. 55, the Coronation March, *recte* 'Heroic March,' Op. 66. The
Octet is the posthumous Op. 166. The Fantasy for pianoforte solo is
the "Wanderer," Op. 15 (not of "the last years"); that for pianoforte
duet is Op. 103, in F minor. The two Trios are those in B flat major,
Op. 99 (not published till 1836) and E flat major, Op. 100. So far as
we know only the latter was performed in public in Schubert's lifetime,
and that repeatedly; the B flat may have been played at Spaun's (*see* No.
1021), but if so only in private. The Mass is that in E flat major. Among
the "other works" Spaun passed over the great C major Symphony, the
string Quintet and the last three pianoforte Sonatas. 'The Blind Boy'
('Der blinde Knabe') was written already in 1825.

(28) By the "2 melodramas" Spaun seems to mean 'The Magic Harp'
and 'Rosamond'; the latter was, of course, a play with incidental music.
It is unlikely that Spaun had in mind as a second melodrama the occasional
piece 'Farewell to the Earth' ('Abschied von der Erde') for declamation

and pianoforte (*see* note preceding No. 628). What Spaun meant by the "six symphonies," since he counted in even the "Gastein" Symphony (par. 23) can only be guessed: perhaps the fourth ("Tragic") in C minor, the fifth, in B flat major, the sixth, in C major, the unfinished, the Gmunden-Gastein and the great C major. Spaun too underestimated the number of Schubert's songs by a third by assessing them at about four hundred.

(30) For all his veneration of Schubert Spaun very much doubted whether he would ever make his way as an instrumental composer.

(33) Johann Rudolf Zumsteeg (1760–1802), born in the Odenwald and died as court musical director at Stuttgart, was Schubert's only real model in song and the ballad. Spaun related elsewhere that at the Seminary Schubert sang to him with enthusiasm from books of Zumsteeg's songs. Copies of such songs in Schubert's hand were found among Josef Hüttenbrenner's remains. The complete edition of Schubert's songs contains a couple of settings of the same words by Zumsteeg for comparison ('Ritter Toggenburg' and 'Expectation' ['Die Erwartung']). Konradin Kreutzer's 'Neun Wanderlieder,' on poems by Uhland, were his Op. 34, published *c.* 1820. Which of Abbé Georg Josef Vogler's (1749–1814) pianoforte compositions is referred to remains uncertain. His last publications were a Prelude and Fugue at Haslinger's and three Fugues at Leidesdorf's.

(35) For Schubert's being disregarded *see* note preceding No. 1115.

(36) The two Schubert concerts are those mentioned in Nos. 1064 and XXVI.

XXXI. List of the Pleno Titulo Subscribers

to

Franz Schubert's 'Swan Song' ['Schwanengesang'].

[May 1829]

Published in Vienna by Tobias Haslinger.

[Selection from the 158 Names in the Original]

Herr Tremier in Vienna.
Herr Witteczek, I. &. R. Aulic Councillor, do.
Princess Schwarzenberg, do.
Herr Schoberlechner, do.
Herr von Drossdick (Wilhelm), Freiherr, do.
Herr Frühwald, I. & R. Court Chapel singer, do.

Fräulein Fröhlich, do.

Herr Schnitzer, do.

Herr von Koller (Josef), iron merchant at Steyr.

Fräulein von Gosmar in Vienna.

Herr Enderes (Karl), do.

Herr von Spaun (Josef), do.

Herr Ottenwalt (Anton) at Linz.

Herr Hüttenbrenner (Josef) in Vienna.

  ,,   ,, (Anselm) at Graz.

Herr Förster (K.G.) at Breslau (10 copies).

Herr Vogl, retired I. & R. Court Opera singer in Vienna.

Herr von Sonnleithner, Doctor of Law, Court Judge of the Scottish Monastery, do.

Fräulein von Sonnleithner (Marie), do.

Herr Dolezalek, do.

Herr Pinterics (3 copies).

Fräulein von Lácsny (Josefine), do.

Count von Weissenwolf (Johann), do.

Herr Gottfried (Vincenz Franz), do.

Herr Obermüller (Anton), do.

Herr Walcher (Ferdinand), do.

Herr Rieder (Johann), do.

Herren Artaria & Co., do. (2 copies)

Mme Wanderer (Babette), do.

Herr von Gahy (Josef), do.

Herr Wittassek at Brno.

Herr von Liebenberg de Zsittin (K.E.), Edler, in Vienna.

Herr Greiner at Graz (3 copies).

Fräulein Kiesewetter (Irene) in Vienna.

Herr von Andlau, Freiherr, do.

Count von Esterházy (Johann Karl), do.

Herr von Schönstein (Karl), do.

Herr Menz, Dr. (Ignaz), do.

Herr Tietze (Ludwig) in Vienna.

Herr Teltscher (Josef), do.

Herr Jenger (Johann Baptist), do.

Herr Trassler (J. G.), at Brno.

Herr Berra (Marco) in Prague (4 copies).

Fräulein Hönig (Anna) in Vienna.

Herren Kraer & Deyrkauf at Graz (2 copies).

Herr Köchel, Dr. (Ludwig) in Vienna.

Herr Mikschik (Emanuel), do.

Herren Diabelli & Co., do. (2 copies).

Count von Teleki (Franz), do.

Herr Löwenthal (Max), do.

Fräulein Müller (Sophie), I. & R. Court actress, do.

Frau Pachler (Marie) at Graz.

Herr Haslinger (Kajetan), book and music dealer at Linz (3 copies).

Herr Kleindl (Josef) at Mantua.

Herr Barth (Josef), accountant to Prince Schwarzenberg, in Vienna.

In January 1829, in his announcement of the subscription in the official 'Wiener Zeitung,' and again in March 1829 in his prospectus for the 'Swan Song' (almost the same wording), Haslinger had promised that this list should "appear as a survey of Schubert's admirers and friends, indeed in a way represent a list of the mourners' names." One hundred and fifty-eight persons had ordered one hundred and eighty copies, which were adorned on the half-title with an engraved vignette depicting a swan swimming. This appeared only in the subscription copies, which also contained the list of subscribers. The names here selected, so far as they do not appear in full, are those of the following persons: Josef Tremier, Josef Wilhelm Witteczek, Mathilde Princess zu Schwarzenberg, Johann Karl Schoberlechner, Josef Frühwald, Anna Fröhlich, Kolumban Schnitzer, Therese Gosmar, the music-dealer Karl Gustav Förster, Johann Michael Vogl, Ignaz von Sonnleithner, Johann Nepomuk Dolezalek, Karl Pinterics, Johann Nepomuk August Wittasek, the music-dealer Johann Lorenz Greiner, Franz von Andlau; Trassler, Berra and Kraer & Deyrkauf were also music-dealers.

XXXII. FROM THE 'THEATERZEITUNG,' 21st May 1829

Among the numerous manuscripts which the favourite tone-poet, Franz Schubert, left and the largest part whereof the active and far-seeing music publisher Josef Czerny has acquired by purchase and with rights of publication, a grand Quintet for pianoforte, violin, viola, violoncello and double bass was to be found. This Quintet having already been performed in several circles, at the publisher's instigation, and declared to be a masterpiece by the musical con-noisseurs present, we deem it our duty to draw the musical public's attention to this latest work by the unforgettable composer; and we state at the same time that it has appeared in print not only as a quintet for the instruments indicated above, but also for piano-forte duet, very effectively arranged by the publisher, in whose art establishment it is to be had.

Czerny's assertion that he had acquired the greater part of Schubert's remains was an absurd exaggeration; but he was probably unaware of their extent.   Cf. No. XXIII.—The 'Trout' Quintet he brought out as Op. 114. Apart from the pianoforte duet arrangement by Czerny (and some others) there is also one by Gahy, the manuscript of which is in the Vienna City Library.

XXXIII. From the 'Wiener Zeitschrift für Kunst,' &c., 9th, 11th and 13th June 1829

ON FRANZ SCHUBERT *

[Abridged]

. . . Schubert, once he had left the Seminary, had lived in his paternal home and carried out an assistant's duties in his father's school for three years.   But he was no better pleased with himself as a pedagogue than he had formerly been as a scholar, although later on, whenever this phase of his life was discussed, he jestingly prided himself not a little on the severity with which he had managed to keep his young pupils in order.   Once he had renounced an educational career, he was held in bond only by a few pianoforte lessons, from which however he also freed himself before long, whereupon he lived only from the proceeds of his compositions, now well, now precariously.   Once or twice he

---

* The author of this essay owes most of the notes contained therein, partly to sketches set down by Schubert's relatives for biographical purposes, partly—and more par-ticularly—to the written communications from one of the deceased's oldest and most intimate friends, which the present writer has used, here and there word for word, having been authorized to do so by his correspondent.—B[auernfeld].

competed for a post, namely for that of Musical Director at Laibach in 1816 and for that of vice Court Musical Director in Vienna in 1826; but he secured neither of them. The function of conductor at the Court Theatre next the Kärntnertor which, if memory serves, was offered him in 1827 by the manager of that time, he did not accept.

———

. . . At the end of this essay a chronological list of those works is to follow which are not yet in the public's hands, but deserve to be so.

. . . Above all it was Goethe's poetry which fell like a fiery spark into Schubert's fresh, youthful and still quite artless soul, but also met something there that caught fire. The present writer remembers how some years ago Schubert tried to make clear for him the effect the first reading of the small poem of 'Restless Love' produced on him. We all know it, this effect, I think. . Truly, the best impression a work of art can engender is—another work of art!

. . . Ossian's world the young singer likewise absorbed into himself and endeavoured to reproduce in sound. 'The Maiden of Inistore,' 'The Spirit of Loda,' 'Colma's Plaint' and others are glorious witnesses to his enthusiasm for the melancholy heroic poet. But not only a large number of mostly superb songs, but also compositions of greater extent fall into this first, so extraordinarily fruitful period of Schubert's youth. . . . He composed quickly and was readily enthusiastic about a good song. Thus, for example, the well-known poem of 'The Wanderer' by Schmidt of Lübeck was handed to him one day in 1816, and the next morning the song was already finished, a song that doubtless is not unfamiliar to-day to any one acquainted with the name of Schubert, In the same way he composed the 'Erl King' on the same afternoon he had read it for the first time.

A supply of new and original song-poems, produced largely for the sake of his music, came to Schubert from the production of his friend, the insufficiently recognized Johann Mayrhofer, with whom he shared lodgings for several years, an association which had the most favourable mutual influence on both. 'Memnon,' 'Antigone and Oedipus,' 'Orestes,' 'Philoctetes,' 'Diana in Anger,'

'Solitude' and many other poems are equally original and excellent
as to music and poetry.   An opera too, 'The Friends of Salamanca,'
was written jointly by the two companions.

. . . Before long Schubert's songs as sung by Vogl were among
the most desirable musical enjoyments.   By means of the song-
veteran's active and effective interest in the young artist, in regard
to his outward circumstances as well, the latter was introduced
to a larger world than that which he had known so far.   At the Little
Philharmonic Society's concerts Schubertian compositions were
frequently performed from now on; also in prominent private
circles, as for instance at Dr. Josef [sic] von Sonnleithner's, at the
house of Aulic Councillor von Kiesewetter, to whom music owed
much, and at the parties given by the now deceased Government
Councillor Matthäus von Collin.   In the house of this last Schubert
became acquainted with Count Moritz von Dietrichstein, with
Aulic Councillor von Hammer, with the future Patriarch of Venice,
then Archbishop of Erlau, with Frau Karoline Pichler and with
other important persons, who all honoured and encouraged him
with the utmost acclamation.

. . . About that time Schubert succeeded in triumphing in a small
way over those who were already beginning to turn up their noses
at his songs and in particular denied him any talent for operatic
music.   For the then management of the I. & R. Court Opera
commissioned two musical pieces from Schubert for insertion into
the opera of 'The Magic Bell' by Hérold, which was in rehearsal
there at the time: a grand aria for the tenor (sung by Rosner)
and a comic duet for tenor and bass.   This circumstance had been
kept a secret from the public and even from Schubert's closest
friends.   Now, at the performance of the opera it was these very
two musical pieces which received the most decided applause;
the duet particularly was so full of capriciousness that the serious
Schubert could scarcely be recognized in it.   Everything then
seemed to justify the hope that Schubert would develop his gifts
for the stage under the protection of the Court Opera management; but this hope vanished with the suspension of the Court
Opera régime in 1821 and the leasing of the theatre building
to Barbaja.

The best members of the German Opera gradually scattered and Italian theatre music, introduced and supported by the most excellent singers, almost exclusively usurped the stage. Schubert, however, did not allow himself to be deterred from writing operas, in spite of the small prospects of seeing them performed. At the end of 1821 he composed the grand opera of 'Alfonso and Estrella' by Schober (which is understood to be in Berlin at present), about whose value distinguished artists and connoisseurs speak very favourably. The overture to this opera was received with extraordinary applause by the public when, in 1823, it was performed at the Theater an der Wien in front of the drama by Frau von Chézy, 'Rosamond,' for which Schubert had also composed a few choruses and a romance. In 1824 Schubert set Kupelwieser's opera, 'Fierabras,' to music, as well as a comic opera by Castelli. His last opera, in the year 1827, was 'The Count of Gleichen,' of which a complete but only partly scored sketch is extant.

To the larger works of the last years belongs further a Symphony written at Gastein in 1825, for which its author had a special liking, and the Mass of the year 1828 . . . his last work.

Whether the available larger compositions by Schubert are to be called excellent the future will show, perhaps, if the public is to be made acquainted with a number of them. A Symphony in C major, performed soon after his death at one of the Musical Society's grand concerts and composed as early as 1817, although counted by Schubert himself among his less successful works, certainly justified expectations, for although it is written almost throughout in the manner of a master highly esteemed by the young composer, yet that master himself would have had no cause to be ashamed to rank it among his own works. Perhaps the Society will by and by make us acquainted with one of Schubert's later symphonies, possibly with the "Gastein" Symphony. . . .

However, whether these large products of his, of which one may say in advance that they will hardly prove to be valueless, betoken a talent for instrumental and stage music or not, and though it may be debatable whether their creator would have furnished anything of excellence in the aforesaid categories in other circumstances or given a longer life, what we possess in perfection, that wherein Schubert shows himself unique and unsurpassed—his songs—is alone sufficient to confirm and maintain their creator's fame. . . .

If the composition of several hundreds of songs, distinguished by an immeasurable wealth of melody and by most original, always characteristic accompaniments, may justify claims to the fame of a great song composer, this must be due to Schubert to a great extent, indeed before all others, even the masters of the art, who perhaps, occupied with other branches of their art, paid less attention to the evolution of the song or—to say it straight out—were not after all as decidedly and predominantly gifted as Schubert was for this aspect of their art. Would that an artistic judge whose soul is capable of listening as sensitively as his ear, who could unite cultivated feeling with a critical sense and artistic technique, and both with the gift of words—would that such a one were to demonstrate in detail the value of Schubert's songs and to show from their chronology how their creator's art, gradually becoming cleansed more and more of a few little flaws, clarified itself ever more gloriously and so could not fail to become ever surer of its effect on the hearts and souls of sympathetic listeners.

———

So far as it is possible to draw conclusions as to a man's character and mind from his artistic products, those will not go astray who judge Schubert from his songs to have been a man full of affection and goodness of heart; yet few would probably have thought a major trait of his being—his enjoyment of life and his truly Austrian jollity—to be the fundamental or leading note of such countless dreamy and melancholy songs, although their creator did not fail to produce merry and vigorous melodies either, among which for instance the music for Goethe's 'The Muses' Son' and for Seidl's 'Wayfarer addressing the Moon' verily do our hearts good.

The musical author of these songs was perfectly described by the trite expression "He is like a child." Confiding, frank, incapable of treachery, sociable, communicative in joy—who knew him otherwise? His devotion to his friends and relatives was great, as was their love for him; a brother could wish for no better brother, a father for no better son than he was, and he was for each friend whatever a friend could ask.

If the serenity given him as dowry with his bride, Art, became somewhat dimmed in his last years, since his outward circumstances in no wise improved with his rising fame, he still remained always far from bitterness and worked diligently and cheerfully. As he had no sort of employment, he was able to divide his life between congenial work and pleasure, as behoves an artist, between the Muses and the Graces, as it were. The morning andtforenoon, until 2 o'clock, Schubert without exception devoted to composition or to the study of old masters. Afternoons and evenings were reserved for sociability, artistic enjoyments and above all walks in Vienna's beautiful environs, where he never lacked merry company; for the ease expressed by his whole nature and a kindly wit that proceeded from this well-being ensured that he was always joined by a large number of friends and younger companions. Several summers, already in the earlier years, he spent at Zseliz in Hungary with Count Esterházy's family. But his jolliest summers were those he spent with his elder friend Vogl in Upper Austria and at Salzburg. Like minstrels in the age of chivalry they traversed the smiling countryside and sang in the houses and to the hearts of song-loving people. Linz, Steyr (Vogl's birthplace), Gmunden, Gastein (where the then Patriarch of Venice assembled a select party) and many of Upper Austria's monasteries gladly and frequently received these amiable singers and will go on remembering them long and yearningly.

This pleasant and pleasurable life, however, neither hindered our Schubert in his industry nor did parties and manifold acquaintances make him forget the friends in whose circle he felt most at home. At the time Schubert came out into the world several young men in his native city, mostly poets and painters (e.g. the esteemed Kupelwieser), gathered together, whom genuine striving after art and similarity of views soon united in sincere friendship, and into whose circle Schubert too was drawn. The mutual communication between these youths and their artistic conversations had a great effect on him and stimulated him, if not so much to talk, at any rate to the most varied musical productivity. To several of these friends he was most cordially devoted to the end of his life, and he often expressed regret, in letters as well as conversation, that the friendly union of so many worthy young men, as will happen, became disrupted by their pursuing different careers and by other chances.

The little that has been said so far will surely convince any one, even those who do not know Schubert's songs, that such a man could not be rough or uncultivated. Yet I have often had to listen to just this reproach; indeed there are people who regarded the author of such songs, who was at the same time able to deliver them so tenderly and feelingly, as a kind of musical machine that had only to be wound up to grind out the most beautiful Mozartian (or Schubertian) melodies without itself having felt anything. But the reasons for such misunderstanding lay in those people themselves. Schubert was sometimes dragged to certain gatherings at which those present are less intent on listening than on boasting of what they have heard. At such parties, indeed, Schubert was dumb and almost embarrassed; nay, as some gentlemen assure us, even rude (although he possessed more moral politeness than any Frenchman, only not of the French kind). Another fault, however, must be mentioned which genteel and stiff society called forth in him.

That is, if an invitation to such a party had already been accepted by him and the prospect might perhaps show itself of spending the evening in a cosy circle of well-wishers and friends, or if a fine summer evening lured him out, Schubert was easily tempted to break his word, which was often taken in very bad part, although it was the only kind of bad faith of which he was capable.

As regards the other reproach made to our singer of songs, that of a lack of cultivation, some isolated thoughts which Schubert jotted down in a note-book of the year 1824 may find a place here:

[Nos. 194 and 450–3.]

These random thoughts, which may have "escaped" their author, as he says in a letter to a friend of a poem communicated therein, for the rest bear witness to many things that went on inside him,

testifying to a profound and in some respects even secretive soul;
and a poem on Schubert's death tells us truly that

> . . . though more taciturn than other mortals,
> Good things in plenty traversed his heart's portals.

That Schubert always remained modest and unassuming his
friends know as well as any one who has spoken but a few words
with him. How often did the singers of his songs at large and
small gatherings receive resounding applause while nobody thought
of the little man, their creator, who sat quite quietly at the pianoforte! But he did not resent this. Similarly kind-hearted was
Schubert in judging the compositions of others; nobody can ever
have heard a harsh verdict from his lips, but he remained frank
and candid when he found fault, and this candour did not always
yield him the best fruit. Thus, for example, Karl Maria von
Weber had made the most flattering references to Schubert's
compositions during his stay in Vienna and already before that in a
letter, and given him in person many a proof of his regard, indeed
had even promised him to stage one of his operas at Dresden.
But after the performance of 'Euryanthe' in Vienna Weber sought
Schubert's opinion of this work, when the latter told him quite
openly that although he regarded that opera as admirably worked,
there seemed to him to be a conspicuous lack of melody in it,
for which reason he was obliged to regard this new work as
greatly inferior to the splendid 'Freischütz.' This assertion was
very unfavourably received by the great artist, who never thereafter offered Schubert any further proofs of a continuance of his
goodwill. If this touchiness is felt to be excusable in a famous
man accustomed to daily homage, the good Schubert's sincerely
expressed blame, which he is sure to have uttered in all modesty,
should not be charged to him as rudeness. He was asked for his
opinion and regarded it as his duty to say what he felt. He would
probably have preferred to remain silent, for hasty judgment was
not a thing he could be reproached with; but the worldly tricks
of subtly evading the expression of definitely requested views or
of giving praise in ambiguous words were strangers to him in his
youth. and doubtless would always have remained so.

In the spring of 1828 Schubert, persuaded by his friends, gave a concert at which his compositions, performed by Fräulein Josefine Fröhlich, Herren Vogl, Tietze, von Bocklet and others, received general and thunderous applause, which spurred him to the decision to organize a larger concert the following winter. But that first one was also to be his last.

On 11th November of that year, having already been ailing for some time, he was forced by increasing exhaustion to take to a sick-bed. He felt no pains, as he himself declared, but sleeplessness and lassitude tortured the hitherto so healthy and vigorous man.

He nevertheless still made use of a few better moments to correct the proofs of the second part of the 'Winter Journey.'

On 17th November the present author found him very weak, but quiet and not without hope of recovery; he also expressed the lively wish to receive a further new opera libretto. However, on that same evening he became more violently delirious, having been but intermittently and feebly attacked before, and scarcely grew more lucid again; his illness had passed into a virulent attack of typhus, and on 19th November, at 3 o'clock in the afternoon, he passed away. A long procession of friends and admirers accompanied the cherished remains, and the sounds of Mozart's Requiem soon afterwards rose sorrowingly into the air and mourned for the lost singer.

Schubert's frame lies in the grave prepared for the departed next to that of Beethoven, the master he so greatly venerated, and a modest memorial stone will show our descendants who reposes side by side with the great master, and who it was we deemed worthy of such a resting-place.

Bauernfeld.

APPENDIX.

Chronological List of the most excellent of Franz Schubert's Works which have not hitherto become generally known.

1810. Fantasy for pianoforte duet.

1811. 'Hagar's Lament' ['Hagars Klage'] (song).

1812. Variations in E♭ for pianoforte.

1813–27. 10 string Quartets.

1813. Symphony in D major.

,,   'The Diver' ['Der Taucher'], ballad for one voice with pianoforte accompaniment.

1814. Mass in F major.

1815. 12 Viennese German Dances (for pianoforte).

,,   'Fernando,' musical play in one act.

,,   2 Symphonies, in D major and B♭ major.

,,   'The Pledge' ['Die Bürgschaft'], ballad for one voice with pianoforte accompaniment.

1816. Trio for violin, viola and violoncello.

,,   Symphony in B♭ major.

,,   Tragic Symphony, in C minor.

,,   Klopstock's 'Stabat Mater' (oratorio).

,,   3 Sonatas for pianoforte and violin.

1817. 2 Overtures in the Italian style.

,,   Sonata for pianoforte and violin in A major.

1818. Cantata for soprano, tenor and bass with pianoforte accompaniment.

1821–2. 'Alfonso and Estrella,' grand opera.

1823. 'Domestic Warfare' ['Der häusliche Krieg'], musical play.

1824. 'Fierabras,' grand opera.

,,   Mass in A♭ major.

,,   Octet for 2 violins, viola, clarinet, bassoon, horn, violoncello and double bass.

1825. Grand Symphony.

,,   3 pianoforte Sonatas.

1827. 'Serenade' ['Ständchen'] (by Grillparzer), chorus with alto solo and pianoforte accompaniment.

,,   German Mass for 4 voices and organ.

,,   'Night Brightness' ['Nachthelle'] (by Seidl), solo and male voice chorus with pianoforte accompaniment.

1828. 'Miriam's Song of Triumph' ['Mirjams Siegesgesang'] (by Grillparzer), solo and chorus with pianoforte accompaniment.

1828. Quintet for 2 violins, viola and 2 violoncellos.

,,   Fugue in E♭ minor [E minor] for organ or pianoforte, four
          hands.

,,   'Hymn to the Holy Ghost.'

,,   Last Symphony.

,,   Church solo for tenor and chorus.

,,   Mass in E♭ major (last work).

Finally, a large number of songs (both of the earlier and the later years) by Mayrhofer, Seidl, Gottfried von Leitner, Ernst Schulze, Heine, &c.

It is thought desirable to apprise the public further that two portraits and a bust of Schubert are to be had.   The portraits are:

1. A copper engraving, after Rieder's drawing, by Passini (at Josef Czerny's in the Graben, No. 1134, for the price of 1 fl. 12 kr., A.C.).

2. A lithographed portrait, drawn and lithographed by Rieder (at Artaria & Co.'s for the price of 36 kr., A.C.).   Both are of excellent workmanship and extraordinary likenesses.

The bust, of which plaster casts are to be had at the price of 12 fl., A.C., at the art establishment of Herr Tobias Haslinger, is from the hand of the young local academic sculptor Franz [*recte* Josef Alois] Dialer, and unites artistic execution with resemblance.

For this essay (cf. No. XV) Bauernfeld made use of the articles by Josef von Spaun (No. XXX) and Ferdinand Schubert (No. XLVI), both in their original version, which in the latter case is lost.   An undated letter from Spaun to Bauernfeld, written early in 1829 (formerly in the possession of Max Friedlaender in Berlin), refers to this: Bauernfeld had sent Spaun the copy-book with Ferdinand Schubert's notes to look at, and Spaun wishes to send Bauernfeld his own manuscript, which he thinks will be more useful to him.   He is of the opinion that Ferdinand's manuscript book "contains hardly anything but an enumeration of the very works by our dead friend which are less interesting and partly less successful.   For all the admiration I have given the dear departed for years, I still feel that we shall never make a Mozart or a Haydn of him in instrumental and church composition, whereas in song he is unsurpassed. . . . I think, therefore, that Schubert should be treated as a song composer by his biographers and that those things which appear as the most important in the copy-book now before us should be dealt with as being subordinate. Besides, this book contains next to nothing on his development and on the circumstances which so considerably influenced it. His relations with Salieri are misrepresented and those with Vogl not touched upon at all. . . . The best thing would be for us to go into conference with Schober, at which you could make notes of everything we should be able to tell you from our recollections." Whether this conference ever took place we do not know. Ferdinand's notes had evidently been supplemented by his father and his brother Ignaz. The passages Bauernfeld took over literally, or almost literally, from Spaun are omitted here. The essay bears a motto from Heine (in verse): "Wild and exuberant fancy is the love-minstrel's steed, art serves him for a shield and words are his sword."

(Par. 1) It is significant that there is here no question of the intention to appoint Schubert as a conductor at the Kärntnertor Theatre (*see* No. 656).

(3) 'Restless Love' ('Rastlose Liebe') was written as early as 1815.

(4) The Ossian songs named here also belong to 1815.

(6) The "Little Philharmonic Society" concerts were the Philharmonic Society's evening entertainments. The archbishop is Pyrker. Mosel seems to have made Schubert's acquaintance before the visit to Matthäus von Collin.

(8) The copy of the score of 'Alfonso and Estrella' sent to Anna Milder still lay unused at the Königstadt Theatre in Berlin in 1842, when Ferdinand discovered that the original was in the hands of Dr. Pachler at Graz. The operetta by Castelli is 'The Conspirators' ('Domestic Warfare') ['Die Verschworenen' ('Der häusliche Krieg')].

(9) For the Gmunden-Gastein Symphony cf. No. XXX, par. 23, and the appendix to this number. The Mass is that in E flat major.

(10) The fact that Schubert, if indeed he did have such a poor opinion of the small C major Symphony, nevertheless thought of it as a possible substitute for the great one in the same key, declined by the Philharmonic Society, proves that he never even considered the possibility of a performance of the unfinished B minor Symphony, though he must have cared far more for it. By the unnamed model for that sixth Symphony Beethoven in unquestionably meant; but neither he nor Mozart pointed its way so directly as the overture style of the period and Rossini (Alfred Einstein).

(20) The word "escaped" appears in No. 498. The lines are quoted from Bauernfeld's own poem, No. XIV.

(21) The opera Weber wished to take under his wing was 'Alfonso and Estrella.' For his meeting with Schubert after the first performance of 'Euryanthe' *see* note preceding No. 387.

(25) For Schubert's supposed desire for a new opera libretto *see*

second note preceding No. 1160. Mozart's Requiem was performed on
27th November 1828 at a funeral service organized by the musical society
of the Maria Trost church in the St. Ulrich suburb, situated between the
present Burggasse and Neustiftgasse. Ferdinand Schubert was associated
with that society, and he gave the second performance of the E flat major
Mass there on 15th November 1829 (cf. No. 1144).

(27, appendix) Here are the corresponding numbers in the complete
edition: ix. 30; xx. 1; the E flat Variations of 1812 are lost; v. 3–4,
6–11, 13–15 (actually eleven string quartets, written between 1813 and
1826); i. 1, xx. 12; xiii. 1; xxi. 23, xv. 3, i. 3 and 2, xx. 109; vi. 1,
i. 5 and 4, xiv. 13, viii. 2–4; ii. 5 and 6, viii. 6; xix. 3 (written in 1819);
xv. 9, 6 and 10, xiii. 5, iii. 1; Gmunden-Gastein Symphony (lost),
x. 9–11 (but 10 written already in 1819); xviii. 4, xiii. 7, xvi. 13;
xvii. 9, iv. 1, ix. 28, xvi. 42, i. 7, xxi. 33, xiii. 6. The Mass was begun
as early as June; the Offertory—here shown last but one—dates from
October, as do the second Benedictus for the C major Mass, 'The Shepherd on the Rock' and 'The Pigeon Post': the other songs of the 'Swan
Song' were written in August); the string Quintet probably from the late
summer of 1828. (The B minor Symphony is not mentioned either by
Bauernfeld, by Spaun [No. XXX] or by Ferdinand Schubert [No. XLVI].)

(30) For the copper engraving cf. Nos. 607 and XXVII.

(31) It is not known when this lithograph was published.

(32) Josef Alois Dialer, born in 1797 at Imst in the Tyrol, settled in
Vienna since 1815 and acquainted with the Schuberts, had intended this
bust for the funeral monument (see No. XXXVI). The plaster casts of
the model were advertised by Haslinger in the Vienna 'Allgemeine
musikalische Zeitung' as early as 17th January 1829.

Bauernfeld also wrote about Schubert in 1869 in 'Die Presse' (17th and
21st April) and in the 'Neue Freie Presse' (6th June), as well as repeatedly
in various essays on Schwind, Vogl, Schenk and others. The Schubert
recollections of 1869 were originally intended for the almanac of the
Viennese journalists' and authors' association 'Concordia,' and when
Bauernfeld asked Schober to contribute, the latter belatedly replied from
Pest on 6th February 1869: "A kind of love story of Schubert, which,
I believe, is not known to a soul, since I, the only confidant, never told it
to anybody, I should have gladly communicated to you, leaving it to you
to decide how much of it would be fit for publication; but of course it is
now too late." Actually there would have been time, but Schober did
not mention the matter again. No doubt this story is therefore lost
for ever.

XXXIV. FERDINAND SCHUBERT'S ACCOUNT FOR HIS FATHER,
June 1829
For my Father, Herr Franz Schubert.

Received	A.C.	Spent	A.C.
17th Dec. 1828	150 fl. —	18th Dec. 1828	
30th Dec. 1828	100 fl. —	Herr von Schober	40 fl. —
5th Jan. 1829	58 fl. 36	30th Dec. 1828	
9th Jan. 1829	120 fl. —	Herr von Czerny	14 fl. 45
25th do.	10 fl. —	31st Dec. 1828	
28th Feb.	30 fl. —	Herr von Schober	40 fl. —
2nd May	30 fl. —	5th Jan. 1829	
		Herr Pennauer	58 fl. 36
	498 fl. 36	9th Jan. 1829	
		Herr von Schober	111 fl. 12
Received	498 fl. 36	21st Jan. 1829	
Spent	309 fl. 53	Dr. von Rinna	25 fl. 20
		29th Jan. 1829	
Remains	188 fl. 43	To the pianoforte	
14th June	150 fl. —	maker Leschen	20 fl. —
	338 fl. 43		309 fl. 53

Ferdinand.

Cf. Nos. XII and XXII.—Among the receipts representing the dead composer's payment—and overpayment—of his debts the first and last amounts of 150 florins were paid by Haslinger for the 'Swan Song' (see No. XVI: the second instalment actually on 13th June). The 100 florins are evidently Josef Czerny's payment for eighteen songs and a string quartet (see No. XXIII). The debt to Pennauer seems to have been settled by Schubert's father through Ferdinand: the amount of 58 florins 36 (originally 35½) kreuzer appears on the same day under both debit and credit. The receipt of 120 florins and the payment to Schober of 111 florins 12 kreuzer may have to be taken as a similar double entry; but this, as well as the three smaller receipts following, may rather be payments from the three publishers, Pennauer (for the E flat major Sonata, Op. 122, and three songs, Opp. 123 and 124), Thaddäus Weigl (for one song, Op. 130) and Leidesdorf (for five songs, Opp. 115, 116 and 119). Among the expenditures are three instalments paid to Schober, whenever the receipts made it possible, for Schubert's total debt to him of 191 florins 12 kreuzer; this may have included the rent for the last months, although Schober was generous towards his friends and even when he was on the verge of bankruptcy in the autumn of 1828 was asked for money by Schwind, among others (*see* note to No. V). The small payment to Czerny may have been the difference between those 100 florins and the actual fee (i.e. change) or, as in Pennauer's case, an advance repaid. Rinna's doctor's fee here appears for the first time, but Leschen's bill already occurs in No. XXII.

XXXV. GRILLPARZER'S SKETCHES FOR THE INSCRIPTION ON SCHUBERT'S TOMB, Mid-September 1829

Wayfarer! Hast thou heard Schubert's Song?
Under this stone he lies. (Here lies he who sang them.)

He was placed near the best ones when he died, and yet
he was still scarcely half-way in his career.

The art of music here entombed a rich possession,
but even far fairer hopes.

He gave to poesy (art of poetry) tones (sounds) and
language (speech) to music, Neither spouse nor maiden,
it is as sisters that the two embrace above
Schubert's head (grave).

He bade poetry resound and music speak.

In the third sketch, which was that finally chosen, the word "far" (*viel*) was added later. This low estimate of Schubert's creative maturity Grillparzer shared with Josef von Spaun and others.

XXXVI. Inscription on Schubert's Tombstone, Autumn 1829

THE ART OF MUSIC HERE ENTOMBED A RICH POSSESSION,

BUT EVEN FAR FAIRER HOPES.

FRANZ SCHUBERT LIES HERE.

BORN ON XXXI JANUARY MDCCXCVII.

DIED ON XIX NOVEMBER MDCCCXXVIII.

XXXI YEARS OF AGE.

The funeral monument was not erected until the summer of 1830 (*see* No. XLIII). The funds for it and for the Requiem (*see* No. XIX) were collected by a committee on which Grillparzer, Jenger and Schober acted as administrators. They had received 69 florins 42 kreuzer from Anna Fröhlich as the net receipts of her two concerts (*see* No. XXVI), 40 florins collected by Jenger and 251 florins 48 kreuzer from Haslinger: altogether 360 florins 90 kreuzer, A.C., on 10th August 1829. Haslinger's sum may have been the profits from the sale of Teltscher's lithograph (*see* No. 621), which came into the market only in the spring of 1829 (sold at 1 florin 15 kreuzer, V.C.), and from that of the simultaneously published musical 'Obituary for Schubert in Mournful Voices at the Pianoforte' (30 kreuzer, V.C.) by Anselm Hüttenbrenner (iconographical volume, facing page 237). (Similar obituary works were Abbé Stadler's 'Fugue for the Organ or the Pianoforte on the Name of the too-soon-departed Composer Franz Schubert' and Sechter's 'Fugue in C minor for the Organ or the Piano-Forte. To the Memory of the too-soon-departed Franz Schubert'; both published by Diabelli and reproduced in the iconographical volume, facing pages 370 and 478 respectively. Sechter's Fugue appeared already on 28th November 1828.) Cf. No. XLII.

XXXVII. From Bauernfeld's Diary

[October] 1829.

Schwind's marriage has been broken off. Mayerhofer's long since. Moritz to Munich again. We still went to Währing, to Schubert's grave.

Schwind had gone to Vienna on a short visit. For the final dissolution of his engagement to Anna Hönig cf. No. 1066. Ferdinand Mayerhofer

von Grünbühel, who married her in 1832, had been first engaged to
Jeannette von Mitis (*see* No. 614).   Long after Anna had become Mayerhofer's wife Schwind remembered her as the "queen of my early years,"
and added: "I can stand a good deal in the matter of Catholicism as a rule,
but too much is too much."   Mayerhofer himself became a practising
Catholic and president of the Marian Congregation.   When in 1850 he
became chief of the Voivodina and the Banat Schwind called the former
"sweet Anne Page" the "Voivodess," and when her husband advanced
to the rank of Lieutenant-Field-Marshal, he nicknamed her the "General-
ess."—The scene at Schubert's grave was perpetuated by Schwind on
one of the leaves in his 'Lachner-Rolle,' a cycle of water-colour drawings
in honour of Franz Lachner (1862), himself exchanging parts with the
hero of this work.

XXXVIII. Ferdinand Schubert to Diabelli

[Outside:]

Anton Diabelli, Esq.
into his own hands.

In loco.

[Inside:]

29th November 1829.

Sir,

Against a fee of 2,400 fl., A.C., I assign to you all the songs for
one voice with pianoforte accompaniment composed by my brother,
and in addition to them the following musical pieces also:

1. Pianoforte Music.

1. Concerto (Adagio and Rondo) with quartet accompaniment
2. Sonata for pianoforte and arpeggione.
3. Three easy, very fine Sonatas for pianoforte and violin.
4. Sonata in A for pianoforte and violin.
5. 1 book of Variations.
6. Grand Sonata in D for pianoforte solo (written at Gastein).
7. Four Sonatas for pianoforte solo.
8. Fugue in E minor *à 4 mains* for pianoforte or organ.

2. Music for String Instruments.

1. Trio for violin, viola and violoncello.
2. Nine Quartets.
3. Grand Quintet.
4. Adagio and Rondo in A, with quartet accompaniment.
5. Concerto in D, with orchestral accompaniment.
6. And therewith all further compositions under this head, should some still be found and the same be suitable for publication.
7. Moreover the Octet for 2 violins, viola, clarinet, bassoon, horn, violoncello and double bass.

The following are therefore excepted: 1. All the operas, 2. the oratorios, 3. the cantatas with full orchestra, 4. all songs for several voices, 5. the symphonies, 6. the overtures and 7. the Masses.

Should you be inclined, or disinclined, to accept this proposal, I beg you in either case to be good enough to give me notice in the matter by the 1st or at latest the 2nd December of this year.

With particular respect

Your

devoted

Ferd. Schubert.

"All the songs" are Schubert's 'Remains of Musical Poetry' ('Nach-gelassene musikalische Dichtungen') published by Diabelli & Co. in fifty fascicles between 10th July 1830 and 1851. When the contract was signed, however, probably only forty instalments were contemplated (cf. No. XXXIX).—The pianoforte music comprises: (1) vii. 2 (properly with trio accompaniment, published only in 1866 by A. O. Witzendorf in Vienna); (2) viii. 8 (1871, J. P. Gotthard, Vienna); (3) viii. 2–4 (Op. 137, 1836); (4) viii. 6 (Op. 162, c. 1852); (5) xi. 6 (first published in the complete edition); (6) x. 11 (Op. 53, already published by Matthias Artaria in 1826 and thus offered to Diabelli by mistake); (7) x. 3 (first published in the complete edition), 5 (Op. 147, c. 1843), 6 (Op. 164, c. 1853 by Diabelli's successor, C. A. Spina), 8 (Op. 143, 1839); (8) ix. 28 (Op. 152, c. 1843).—The music for string instruments comprises: (1) xxi. 5 (first published in the complete edition); (2) 2 to 9, 15 (2–6 first published in the complete edition; 7 by C. F. Peters, Leipzig, 1871; 8 as

Op. 168 by Spina, 1863; 9 by Peters, *c.* 1871; 15, *c.* 1852); (3) iv. 1 (Op.
163, Spina, 1853); (4) xxi. 4 (published in the complete edition: *Rondo*
with an *Adagio* introduction); (5) xxi. 3 (published in the complete
edition); (6) uncertain; (7) iii. 1 (Op. 166, Spina, *c.* 1854).—Among the
works not offered are (2) 'Lazarus,' xvii. 1, and the German 'Stabat
Mater,' xiv. 13; (3) Cantata for Spendou (xvii. 2, which however appeared at Diabelli's in 1830 as Op. 128), that for the emperor's birthday
(xvii. 3, which appeared at Diabelli's in 1848 as Op. 157, with different
words) and that for Vierthaler (xvii. 4, first published in the complete
edition).—The proposal seems to have been accepted in its essentials, as
may be gathered from the agreement following (except Nos. 3, 6 and 8 of
the first group and No. 7 of the second).

XXXIX. Confirmation of Sale to Anton Diabelli & Co.,
? early 1830

(The wording, taken from Kreissle's biography, is uncertain.)

We, the undersigned heirs of Franz Schubert, deceased, composer
in Vienna, hereby confirm that the I. & R. Privileged Art and Music
Establishment of A. Diabelli & Co. in Vienna has acquired the
manuscripts of the following compositions by the aforesaid Franz
Schubert, and that accordingly the house of A. Diabelli & Co. is
to be regarded as the rightful and sole publisher of these works.
Opus 1 to *opus* 153 inclusive, with the exception of *opera* 33, 34,
36, 37, 38, 60, 61, 65, 70, 78, 79, 80, 81, 82, 83, 89, 90, 91,
100, 105, 107, 110, 111, 112, 114, 117, 118, 120, 125, 126, 129,
131 and 141. Further the first 40 fascicles of the posthumous
songs and 51 other songs, 14 vocal quartets, the canons of the
year 1813, a Cantata for 3 voices in C, the 'Hymn to the Holy
Ghost,' the 'Stabat Mater' in F minor, the great 'Hallelujah' and
'Magnificat' in C, the string Quintet in C, 4 string Quartets,
in C, G and 2 in B♭, a string Trio in B♭, two pianoforte Sonatas,
in A♭ and A minor, Variations in F, an Adagio in D♭ and Allegretto in E for pianoforte, the Sonata in A minor for pianoforte and arpeggione or cello, the Sonata in A for pianoforte
and violin, the Fantasy in C for pianoforte and violin, a Rondo in A
for violin with quartet accompaniment, an Adagio and Rondo in F
for pianoforte with quartet accompaniment, a Concert Piece

in D for violin and orchestra, an Overture in D for orchestra,
the Overture to the third act of 'The Magic Harp,' the Easter
Cantata ('Lazarus'), a 'Tantum ergo' for four voices and orchestra
in E♭ and an Offertory in B♭ for tenor solo, chorus and orchestra.

According to the footnote on p. 566 of his Schubert biography Kreissle
had the wording of this agreement, which he assigned to about the year
1830, from Diabelli's successor, C. A. Spina. The first sentence is
there quoted in inverted commas, and thus no doubt literally; the rest
approximately and probably abridged. Grove concluded that this lost
document dated from early 1830 because it included Op. 121, the
'Two Characteristic Marches' for pianoforte duet, which appeared in
February 1830. The opus numbers after 120 were clearly added afterwards, for they were not yet fixed by 1830. Diabelli and Spina also
used nearly all the opus numbers from 154 to 173 (only Op. 170 was
published by Gotthard), but these works had not yet been acquired in
1830. The following works appeared with other publishers: Opp. 33,
34, 36–8, 60, 61, 65 (Cappi and Czerny); 105, 110–12, 114, 117, 118,
120, 125, 126, 131 as well as the D minor string Quartet (Josef Czerny,
their successor); 70, 107 (Artaria & Co.); 77–83, 89–91, 129, 139b,
141, also the 'Graz Galop,' the male-voice quartets 'Grave and Moon'
and 'Wine and Love,' and the 'Swan Song' cycle (Haslinger); 93 (Kienreich, taken over by Haslinger); 100 (Probst). Opp. 77, 93 and 139b,
however, are not mentioned as exceptions in this agreement. For other
reasons the following are not exempt either: Opp. 20–30, 35, 40, 59, 69,
also 92, 94, 115, 116, 119 (Sauer & Leidesdorf or Leidesdorf alone); 31, 39,
42, 43, 55, 56, 64, 66, 87, 122–4 (Pennauer); 52–4 (Matthias Artaria);
57, 58, 63, 84, 88, 95, 130 (Thaddäus Weigl); and lastly Opp. 96 and
106, published by Schubert on his own account and taken over by Diabelli
in February 1829. Diabelli also took over the catalogues of the last
three firms, at least as far as Schubert's works were concerned; but the
Leidesdorf firm first went to Anton Berka in 1830, and only with the
latter to Diabelli c. 1835, at the same time as he acquired Pennauer's
business; Matthias Artaria and, for the greater part, Thaddäus Weigl he
took up c. 1833. From the latter he also received Op. 130, published
only on 12th July 1830, which appears to invalidate Grove's suggestion
that the present document dates from early 1830—but see No. XL. It is
possible, too, that the whole document was so much altered by Kreissle
that no conclusions as to any dates had better be drawn from it; he may not
have counted among the opus numbers which the agreement expressly
named as belonging to other publishers those which only went to Diabelli
later by right of succession.—The "first forty fascicles" of the remains
were surely not enumerated under that title in the agreement. Of the

works named thereafter only a part had appeared even by 1865, according to Kreissle. The fifty-one songs, most of them published in fascicles 41–50, cannot be identified in detail. Of the fourteen vocal quartets at least a dozen, between the opus numbers 132 and 170, were issued by Diabelli or Spina. The canons of 1813 were published in the complete edition as xix. 9–14, 22, 23 and xxi. 37–43. The Cantata is xix. 3 (Op. 158, published in 1848), the 'Hymn' xvi. 2 (Op. 154, c. 1847), the 'Stabat Mater' xiv. 13, the 'Hallelujah xx. 227 (c. 1846 in fascicle 41 of 'Remains of Musical Poetry'), the 'Magnificat' xiv. 11, the string Quintet iv. 1 (Op. 163, Spina, 1853), the string Quartets v. 4, 15, 5 and 8 (of which only the second appeared at Diabelli's, as Op. 161 c. 1852); the string Trio xxi. 5, the pianoforte Sonatas x. 3 and 8 (the latter published in 1839 as Op. 143), the Variations xi. 6, the Adagio and Allegretto xi. 5 (Op. 145, c. 1845), the Sonata for arpeggione viii. 8 (Gotthard, 1871), the violin Sonata viii. 6 (Op. 162, c. 1852), the violin Fantasy viii. 5 (Op. 159, 1850), the violin Rondo xxi. 4 (first published in the complete edition), the Adagio and Rondo (properly with trio accompaniment) vii. 2 (A. O. Witzendorf, Czerny's successor, 1866), the Concert Piece xxi. 3 (first published in the complete edition), the Overture in D major probably ii. 4 (first published in the complete edition), the second 'Magic Harp' overture in xv. 7 (first published in the complete edition), 'Lazarus' xvii. 1 (fragment only preserved, complete edition; first performed on Easter Sunday, 11th April 1830 at the church of St. Anna), the 'Tantum ergo' xxi. 32 (C. F. Peters, Leipzig, 1890), the Offertory xxi. 33 (C. F. Peters, Leipzig, 1890).—Whether Ferdinand Schubert received those 2,400 florins, A.C. (see No. XXXVIII), from Diabelli, who was still to acquire the three great pianoforte Sonatas in C minor, A major and B flat major, or whether he was paid more or less, is not known. When Schindler ostensibly occupied himself with the MSS at Diabelli's in 1831, the latter estimated the number of songs and partsongs, including sacred ones, as 570.

XL. From the Vienna 'Allgemeiner Musikalischer Anzeiger,' 6th February 1830

The local art establishment of Diabelli & Co. has acquired for itself the whole of the remains of Franz Schubert's compositions. Among these remains, they understand, some 400 songs of different dimensions are still to be found. How desirable would it not be for the numerous admirers of this composer of genius to possess a uniformly produced complete edition of his work, so widely scattered by publication! And this is a point not now expressed for the first time, since we recollect that a voice deserving of attention has already made itself heard to this effect abroad.

> Cf. No. XXXII; *see* Nos. XXXVIII and XXXIX.—The 'Remains of Musical Poetry' issued in their fifty fascicles about one hundred and thirty-five songs and partsongs.—No Austrian or foreign press opinion is known to have uttered a desire for a complete Schubert edition before the year 1830. C. S. Richault in Paris, who had made a beginning with an edition of the songs with French translations in 1834, entertained such a project about 1835; C. A. Spina in Vienna, Diabelli's successor, made similar plans about 1865; and L. Holle at Wolfenbüttel pretended to be issuing "the first complete and authentic edition" in the ten volumes of 'Collective Compositions' published about 1870. The complete edition, however, did not materialize until towards the end of the century, when Breitkopf & Härtel between 1884 and 1897 brought out nearly all Schubert's known works for the centenary of his birth in twenty-one series comprising thirty-nine folio volumes. (Brahms prevented the publication of a few works.)

> Wilhelmine Schröder-Devrient, accompanied by Frau Christine Genast, sings the 'Erl King' to Goethe at Weimar, 24th April 1830. —After the performance Goethe kissed her forehead, saying: "I have heard this composition once before, when it did not appeal to me at all; but sung in this way, the whole shapes itself into a visible picture." Another remark, however, made three weeks later, shows that Goethe—even two years before his death—was by no means converted to Schubert, of whose songs, indeed, he may never have heard another. Schröder-Devrient went to Paris as a guest artist in 1830 and to London in 1831 and 1833.

XLI. From the Schuberts' Family Chronicle
(Entry by the stepmother.)

On 9th July 1830, at 6.30 p.m., died my [our] most dearly beloved and valued husband, and father respectively.

This entry is similar in style to that of the elder Schubert's note on the death of his own father (*see* note before B4). Franz Schubert, sen., died two days before his sixty-seventh birthday, "after a long and painful illness." The school in the Rossau, where his son Ignaz succeeded him as master, had at that time six assistant teachers and about five hundred pupils. The elder Schubert was buried next to his first wife in the general Währing cemetery outside the Nussdorf boundary, and thus near his earlier sphere in the Himmelpfortgrund.

XLII. GRILLPARZER'S SKETCH for an Announcement concerning the Completion of Schubert's Tombstone, July 1830

All Schubert's friends and admirers, but especially those who have actively shown their feelings for him by contributions to his memorial, are informed that this memorial, very successfully executed by a skilled hand and adorned with a good likeness of the deceased in the form of a cast-iron bust, has just been completed and erected in the churchyard at Währing, where it is open to general inspection.

The authentication of the use made of the amounts paid in by subscription is to be published later.

Cf. Nos. XXXIII (par. 33) and XXXVI.—This announcement never appeared; neither did the accounts.—The costs of the Requiem (*see* No. XIX) were 75 florins 6 kreuzer, A.C.   For the plaster cast of the bust, which Dialer had modelled free of charge, 16 florins had been paid. The bust itself had been cast at the ironworks at Blansko in Moravia for 72 florins.   Wasserburger (*see* No. XXII) received 195 florins 40 kreuzer for the funeral monument, "a monument of Margaretner stone based on a drawn model," with an inscription of a hundred and sixty letters, etc. The draft was by Schober, made with the aid of the architect Ludwig Förster (born in 1797 at Bayreuth, since 1820 co-rector at the Vienna Academy).   Including some incidental expenses the funeral monument including the bust cost about 300 florins, so that by 10th August 1829 nearly all the expenditure had already been recovered, including that for the funeral service at St. Augustine's church.   While Beethoven's grave bore no effigy, Schubert's was adorned with the speakingly lifelike bust by Dialer, an unusual thing at that time and place.   (In all Vienna there was only one public monument, to the Emperor Josef II, and in the cemeteries there was hardly any portrait sculpture.)

XLIII. FROM THE VIENNA 'ALLGEMEINER MUSIKALISCHER ANZEIGER,' 6th November 1830

. . . The tombstone is simple—as simple as his songs, but it conceals a profound soul, as they do.

Beethoven's and Schubert's graves were renewed in 1863.   During the exhumation and reinterment photographs of the skulls were taken and measurements of the other remains were made (cf. iconographical

volume, plates 58–61 and App., pp. 8–13). In 1888 the remains of
both masters were disinterred once more, this time in order to be
transferred to the musicians' Grove of Honour in Vienna's new central
cemetery in the south-eastern suburb of Simmering. A new gravestone
was there erected for Schubert, who in 1872 had been the first musician
to be given a monument in Vienna (Stadtpark). When the Währing
district cemetery finally fell into disuse as such in 1925 and was turned into
the Schubert Park the two cenotaphs for Beethoven and Schubert were
preserved.

XLIV. From the Leipzig 'Neue Zeitschrift für Musik,' 3rd April 1835

('Gazette musicale,' Paris, 26th April 1835)

CONCERNING FRANZ SCHUBERT'S LARGER POSTHUMOUS WORKS

We hasten to bring the following announcement to our readers'
notice and to request them urgently to disseminate this information
and to do their best in the interests of the matter itself.

Franz Schubert, the composer of genius and soulful song-writer
who departed this life all too soon, has left behind a number of
musical works remaining in his brother's hands, which the latter,
partly in order not to deprive the world of these works, and partly
also to make use for his own benefit of his brother's spiritual
heritage according to the deceased's wish, is willing to assign for
performance to theatre managements and musicians at moderate
fees. These works are: I. *Operas:* 'The Devil's Pleasaunce,' in
2 acts (completed in 1814)—'Fernando,' in 1 act (1815)—'The
Friends of Salamanca,' in 2 acts, by Mayrhofer (1815)—'The
Four-Years' Sentry,' in 1 act (1815)—'The Pledge,' in 3 acts
(1816)—'The Twin Brothers,' in 1 act—'The Magic Harp,'
melodrama in 3 acts (1820)—'Domestic Warfare,' in 1 act, by
Castelli (1823)—'Fierabras,' in 3 acts, by Schober [*sic*] (1823).
II. *Symphonies:* in D major (1813), in D major (1815), in B♭
major (1815), in C minor (1816), in B♭ major (1816), in C
major (1818), in C minor [*sic*] (his last). III. *Masses:* in F major,
for 4 voices and full orchestra (1814)—in G major, for 4 voices
and small orchestra (1815)—in B♭ major, for 4 voices and medium

orchestra—in A♭ major and E♭ major, both for 4 voices and full orchestra (1822 and 1828).

Whoever desires anything of the above is requested to get into touch with Herr Ferdinand Schubert, Teacher at the I. & R. Training School in Vienna.

Ferdinand had sent this appeal, which had no practical success, to Schumann as the editor of the 'Neue Zeitschrift.' It was afterwards reprinted in Paris. It is, of course, concerned with the works not acquired by Diabelli (*see* No. XXXIX). The introductory sentences seem to indicate that Ferdinand regarded himself as Schubert's sole heir, and no doubt he was right from the moral point of view, although Schubert had left no will (*see* No. XI). The works mentioned are the following, according to the complete edition. Operas: xv. 1, 3, 4, 2, 13, 5, 7, 6, 10 (actually Josef Kupelwieser's libretto). The following stage works are missing from the list: 'Alfonso and Estrella' (not then accessible, *see* No. XLVI, par. 16), the 'Rosamond' music (the rights in which were perhaps held by Helmina von Chézy), 'Claudine of Villa Bella' (at that time with Josef Hüttenbrenner, probably still complete) and the other fragments—apart from 'The Pledge'—viz. 'The Looking-Glass Knight' and 'Adrast' (the libretto of which was then still extant in Mayrhofer's hands).—Symphonies: i. 1, 3, 2, 4, 5, 6 and 7 (actually in C major). The B minor Symphony, preserved at Graz by Anselm Hüttenbrenner, is thus not enumerated.—Masses: xiii. 1, 2, 3 (of 1815), 5 and 6. The Mass in C major, Op. 48, of 1816 (already published in 1825) and the 'German Mass' (for which Neumann held the rights) are missing.

XLV. FERDINAND SCHUBERT TO BREITKOPF & HÄRTEL

Vienna, 31st January 1839.

Sirs,

Through Herr Schumann it has come to my knowledge that you would not be disinclined to acquire by purchase some of the compositions by my late brother (*Franz Schubert*), symphonies in particular; but that you would like first to examine the manuscripts. I hasten therefore to inform you that I shall have the honour of sending you immediately two of the *seven* extant *symphonies* by my brother through Herren Diabelli & Co., with the next consignment of their publications. Of the sixth Symphony you will receive not only the score but also the orchestral parts, this work having been already performed once in Vienna with great success ·(in 1829 by the Philharmonic Society in the Imperial Assembly Hall), and so that you may perhaps be good enough to cause this composition to be produced by the honoured Dr. *Mendelssohn* at Leipzig before this year is out. Of the seventh Symphony you will receive only a faithful copy of the original score (copied by myself), the manuscript itself being preserved as an authentic memento in the archives of the Austrian Philharmonic Society.

For convenience of checking a list of these seven symphonies is appended, and I intend to assign them to you altogether for 700 fl., A.C.; separately the prices are:

for the 1st Symphony	100 fl. A.C.	
—— 2nd do.	100 fl. A.C.	
—— 3rd do.	150 fl. A.C.	
—— 4th do.	150 fl. A.C.	
—— 5th do.	100 fl. A.C.	
—— 6th do.	150 fl. A.C.	
—— 7th do.	200 fl. A.C.	

I politely request you to let me have your kind reply as early as possible, and remain, with all respect,

Your devoted

Ferd. Schubert,

Teacher at the I. & R. Training School,
1st Administrator of the Society for the
Widows of Schoolmasters,

Professor of Organ Playing at the Conservatory,
School Commissioner of the Society for the
Promotion of True Church Music.

(Resident in the Alsergrund suburb, Wicken-burggasse, No. 12, 2nd floor.)

Schumann spent the winter of 1838–9 in Vienna and on New Year's day visited Ferdinand Schubert, where he saw with astonishment and admiration what an enormous number of manuscripts still remained after

Diabelli's purchase. He wrote to Breitkopf & Härtel on 6th January 1839 that he had found there four masses, four or five symphonies and —among other things—eight children. The publishers at once offered to suggest one of the symphonies for performance at Leipzig during the current season. Ferdinand therefore sent, together with this letter, the little C major Symphony in its original score with the copied parts and the great C major Symphony in a full score copied by himself. It was not till 1838 that the autograph of this "No. 7" seems to have come into the possession of the Philharmonic Society, for whom it had originally been written, according to Alois Fuchs. Ferdinand at first only thought of the possibility of having No. 6 performed at Leipzig. As the publishers and Mendelssohn too mentioned only one symphony in their letters, it looks as though Schumann himself had not at first thought of suggesting the "seventh." It was only when Mendelssohn had seen both works that he came to a decision and gave the first performance of the great C major Symphony at Leipzig on 21st March 1839. It is worthy of note that already at that time, in the spring of 1839, he had proposed this work and even sent the orchestral parts used at Leipzig to the Philharmonic Society in London, who as late as 1844 still disdained to accept it even from him. (Prince Albert then gave a performance of it with his domestic orchestra at Windsor Castle.) On the day after the Leipzig performance the publishers offered, through the intermediation of Schumann, 180 florins instead of the 250 florins asked for, and Ferdinand, on Schumann's advice, accepted this on 10th April 1839. Mendelssohn returned the copy to the publishers on 23rd April, and the work appeared in 1840, in parts at first, the score being published only in 1849. Ferdinand's proposal, written on Schubert's birthday, thus had a practical result. His low valuation of the fifth Symphony is explained by the fact that it is the smallest of these works in size. The first Symphony takes up ninety-one sheets, the second ninety-four, the third fifty-six, the fourth ninety-four, the fifth twenty-seven, the sixth eighty-two, (the unfinished thirty-nine) and the great C major a hundred and thirty in manuscript. All are in oblong folio, except the fourth, which is in upright folio.—Diabelli had not shown any interest in the symphonies. The seven are those listed in No. XLIV, without the unfinished. The little C major Symphony was first performed in Vienna on 14th December 1828 (see note preceding No. 1072); but Ferdinand overlooked the fact that it was repeated on 12th March 1829 at a *Concert spirituel* in the County Hall, "with incomparably better effect," as the Leipzig 'Allgemeine musikalische Zeitung,' Breitkopf & Härtel's domestic organ, reported.—Ferdinand in 1848 offered Breitkopf & Härtel the first six Symphonies, together with the still unprinted masses and operas, for 3,000 fl., A.C.; but nothing came of this.

XLVI. From the Leipzig 'Neue Zeitschriift für Musik,' 23rd April–3rd May 1839

from franz schubert's life
by
Ferdinand Schubert.

Franz (Peter) Schubert was born in 1797, on 31st January, in Vienna (Himmelpfortgrund suburb, parish of Liechtental).

His father, Franz Schubert, was the son of a peasant from Neudorf in Moravia, who studied in Vienna and in 1784 went to the Leopoldstadt as school assistant to his brother. His schoolmaster's talent, supported by an honest and noble character, secured him in 1786 the post of schoolmaster in the parish of "the 14 Holy Friends in Need" at Liechtental. Married to Elisabeth Vietz, he begot 14 children, of whom however only 5 remained alive: Ignaz, Ferdinand, Karl, our Franz and Theresia. Married a second time, he begot 5 more children, of whom 4—Marie, Josefa, Andreas and Anton—still survive.

In Franz his father, who earlier had given their first lessons in violin playing also to Ignaz and Ferdinand, and afterwards to Franz himself, perceived great talent for music from early childhood. Dear, good Franz now received lessons in pianoforte playing from his brother Ignaz. Later he was taught violin and pianoforte playing, as well as singing, by the choirmaster *Michael Holzer*, who several times asserted with tears in his eyes that he had never yet had such a pupil: "For," said he, "whenever I wished to impart something new to him, he always knew it already. I often looked at him in silent wonder."

Schubert was then some 10 years old, and in his 11th year he was a first soprano in the Liechtental church. Already at that time he delivered everything with the most appropriate expression; in those days he also played a violin solo in the organ-loft of the church and already composed small songs, string quartets and pianoforte pieces.

His rapid progress in music astonished his father, who was intent on affording him the opportunity of further education and entering him at the I. & R. Seminary for that purpose.

In October 1808 our Schubert was thus presented to the I. & R. Seminary directorate and had to *sing for his trial*. The boy wore a light blue, whitish coat, so that the other people, including the remaining children who were also to be admitted to the Seminary, made fun of him among themselves with such remarks as "That is doubtless a miller's son; he won't fail," &c. However, the schoolmaster's son made a sensation, not only by his white frock coat, but also with the Court Musical Directors *Salieri* and *Eybler* and with the singing-master *Korner*, as well as by his certainty in sight-reading the trial songs submitted to him. He was accordingly admitted. He parted most sorrowfully with his father, mother, brothers and sisters; but the *gold* braid on his uniform seemed to make him calm and confident again.

At the Imperial Seminary he now had the opportunity of being present at certain musical performances. The great zeal he showed at the domestic music-making, where in the absence of the music master Ruzicka he conducted the symphonies and overtures, as well as his compositions (such as 'Hagar's Lament,' the 'Corpse Fantasy,' a fantasy for pianoforte duet, string quartets, &c.), induced the first Court Musical Director Salieri to give him lessons in composition. There again Schubert showed his extraordinary gifts to his master's astonishment, so that the latter, asked how Schubert was faring, replied: "That one knows everything; he composes operas, songs, quartets, symphonies and whatever you will."

For his father and his elder brothers it was a uncommon pleasure to play *quartets* with him. This happened chiefly in the holiday months. The youngest of them all was the most sensitive there. Whenever a mistake was made, were it never so small, he would look the guilty one in the face, either seriously or sometimes with a smile; if Papa, who played the cello, was in the wrong, he would say nothing at first, but if the mistake was repeated, he would say quite shyly and smilingly: "*Sir, there must be a mistake somewhere!*", and our good father would gladly be taught by him. In these quartets Franz always played the viola, his brother Ignaz second violin, Ferdinand (whom Franz favoured most among his brothers) first, and Papa the violoncello.

To induce Schubert to *compose for his brothers* was an easy matter.

Thus he wrote 30 minuets [1] for Ignaz, together with trios, in a very easy style for the pianoforte; for Ferdinand a quintet Overture, a violin Concerto, a congratulatory cantata,[2] and so on. In 1820 he wrote for the same brother 6 antiphons for Palm Sunday, in not more than 30 minutes (the manuscript of which, written in black chalk, still exists). For his father's name-day he composed a trio [2] for male voices with guitar accompaniment, the words for this having been written by himself as well. In the same way he showed himself a poet and composer in a work that was given the following title by him: 'Contributions to the Jubilee for the 50th Anniversary of the first I. & R. Court Musical Director Salieri, by his pupil Franz Schubert.' [2] Altogether his rapidity in writing down his compositions was amazing. Schubert's *very first piano-forte composition* (1810) was a Fantasy for 4 hands in which more than twelve different movements occur, and indeed each with a character of its own: it consists of 32 very closely written pages. This was followed by two further, smaller ones. A peculiarity is that each of these Fantasies closes in a key different from that in which it began. A book of *pianoforte Variations*, which he played to his father as the first product of his composer's skill, also bears his own imprint already. All these compositions—still un-published—are in the possession of his brother Ferdinand.

Soon the little master tried his hand also at *string quartets*, of which some 12 or 15 gradually appeared.

Songs he composed with particular pleasure, even as a boy. The first seems to have been 'Hagar's Lament.' How this small minstrel, young as he still was, knew how to accompany with his music the poems of such great minds is incomprehensible.

And so, during the 5 years of training in the I. & R. Seminary, he progressed ever more rapidly, and soon composed *overtures* and *symphonies* too.

When at last he left the Seminary owing to his extraordinary attachment to music, and later on was three times summoned by conscription to register as a soldier, he decided in the end to serve as an *assistant schoolmaster*.

And indeed he did considerable service for three years at his

---

[1] They are lost.   [2] Still in the possession of Ferdinand Schubert.

father's school, where he kept strict order. During that time he was again active in the choir of the Liechtental Church each Sunday and holiday, and it was doubtless this which induced him to compose a *grand Mass* (1814), which made not a little sensation at Liechtental and was also performed 10 days later at St. Augustine's Church in Vienna.

It was a touching sight to see young Schubert, who was then the most youthful of all the acting musicians present, conduct his composition. How seriously he did it, and with what foresight, so that the old gentlemen would say: "He might have been Court Musical Director for the last 30 years, he could not do better." But it will be long before any music is again performed with such enthusiasm as this first Mass of his was. For his first teacher was choirmaster, his brother Ferdinand organist, an excellent friend and his favourite singer the first soprano, and the remaining musicians consisted of none but friends of his youth or people among whom he had grown up. In his heart's joy his father at that time presented him with a five-octave pianoforte.

Operas Schubert composed in considerable numbers; but only the little musical play, 'The Twin Brothers,' and the melodrama, 'The Magic Harp,' reached the public, and none of the larger ones. 'Alfonso and Estrella,' too, still lies in Berlin unperformed.

His manner of writing, owing to its peculiarity, found but little response at first. What quickly paved him his way afterwards was the publication of the 'Erl King,' which soon made the round of Germany. Thenceforward his fame grew more and more, and if he had seen how much he is honoured now, he would certainly have created even more glorious things.[1]

Although Schubert never represented himself as a [pianoforte] virtuoso, any connoisseur who had the chance of hearing him in private circles will nevertheless attest that he knew how to treat this instrument with *mastery* and in a quite *peculiar manner*, so that a great specialist in music, to whom he once played his last sonatas, exclaimed: "Schubert, I almost admire your playing even more

---

[1] A Symphony, performed for the first time at Leipzig not long ago, is among the most remarkable things created since Beethoven; it is to be published shortly by Breitkopf & Härtel.   ED. [Robert Schumann.]

than your compositions!''—*Beethoven*, whom he held sacred and who often expressed himself with great appreciation, especially about his songs, he met frequently, although he could not for that reason be called Beethoven's pupil, as has often been done.

In his intercourse Schubert was amiable and urbane, and he had many friends. A proof of this last was given by the concert organized by him shortly before his death, which had a following such as is rarely to be found. It is hardly to be believed how much Schubert wrote. A complete list of his *published* works has been printed by Herren Diabelli & Co. But these publishers, and especially Ferdinand Schubert, possess such a large amount of still unpublished works besides, that it might be worth the trouble to mention at least the more important of them here, listed according to the years of composition.

The compositions marked D. in the following list are still in the hands of Herren Diabelli & Co.; those marked Sch. still in Ferdinand Schubert's possession. *The Editor will gladly act as mediator in the case of inquiries concerning the possible acquisition of this or that composition for publication.*

1810. In that year, his 13th, Schubert composed his first Fantasy for pianoforte, 4 hands (Sch.).

1811. He dedicated to his brother Ferdinand a quintet Overture (Sch.). Furthermore he composed a string Quartet (D.), the second pianoforte Fantasy for 4 hands (Sch.) and many songs (D.). .

1812. He composed: String Quartets in C and B♭ (D.), Sonata for pianoforte, violin and cello (D.), quartet Overture in B♭ (Sch.), Overture for orchestra in D (Sch.), Variations in E♭ (Sch.), Andante for pianoforte (Sch.) and many songs. A 'Salve Regina' and 'Kyrie,' composed in the same year, appeared in print.

1813. Octet for wind instruments [Harmonie-Oktett] (Sch.), 3 Minuets and Trios for orchestra (Sch.), string Quartets in. C, B♭, E♭ and D (D.), three 'Kyries' (Sch.), 30 Minuets and Trios for pianoforte (lost), Symphony in D (Sch.), the third pianoforte Fantasy for 4 hands (Sch.), Trios and Canons (D.) and many songs.

1814. String Quartets in C minor, D and B♭ (D.), 5 Minuets and 6 German Dances with Trios for quartet and 2 horns (Sch.), song and chorus with orchestral accompaniment, 'Who may be great?' (Sch.), grand Mass in F (Sch.), 'Salve Regina' (D.), many songs.

1815. 12 German Dances with coda for pianoforte (Sch.), 10 Variations for pianoforte (Sch.), grand 'Magnificat' (D.), 'The Friends of Salamanca,' comic musical play in 2 acts (Sch.), 'The Four-Years' Sentry,' musical play in 1 act (Sch.), 'Salve Regina' (D.), Offertory (D.), 'Fernando,' musical play in 1 act (Sch.), two Symphonies, in D and B♭ (Sch.), second 'Dona nobis' for the Mass in F (Sch.), Sonatas for pianoforte in F and C (D.), Quartet in G minor (D.), Mass in G (Sch.), a large number of songs.

1816. Trio for violin, viola and violoncello (D.), Quartet in F (D.), violin Concerto in D (Sch.), 'The Pledge,' opera in 3 acts (unfinished) (Sch.), Symphony in B (Sch.), Tragic Symphony, in C minor (Sch.), oratorio: Klopstock's 'Stabat Mater' (D.), pianoforte Sonata in F (Sch.), chorus of angels, 'Christ is arisen,' for 4 voices (Sch.), 'Salve Regina' (D.).

That year he competed for a musical director's post at Laibach, which however was not granted to him.

1817. Polonaise for violin (Sch.), Trio for violin, viola and cello (D.), Symphony in C (Sch.), two Overtures in the Italian style (D.), pianoforte Sonatas in E♭, F minor, A minor and A♭ (D.), Sonata for pianoforte and violin in A (D.), many songs.

1818. Sonatas for pianoforte in C and F, a large number of songs.

In the summer of this year Schubert travelled to Hungary, to the country seat of Count J. Esterházy, by whom he was engaged as singing and pianoforte master.

1819. 'The Twin Brothers,' farce in 1 act (Sch.), Overture in E (Sch.), Cantata (D.), many songs.

917

1820. Quartet in C minor, 'Resurrection' [Auferstehung], oratorio by Niemeyer (first section only) (D.), many songs.

1821. 'Song of the Spirits over the Waters' for 8 male voices &c. (D.), many songs.

In this year Herren Court Musical Directors *Salieri* and *Weigl*, Herr Aulic Councillor von *Mosel* and the Court Musical Intendant Count *Dietrichstein* gave him certificates on his musical talent, such as can rarely have fallen to the lot of artists.

From the then Patriarch of Venice, Pyrker von Felső-Eör, he received the following letter: [here follows No. 237].

1822. The opera 'Alfonso and Estrella,' which lies in Berlin, 'Tantum ergo' in D (D.), songs.

In this year Schubert dedicated the 12th of his published works to the Bishop of St. Pölten, and in return was honoured with the following letter: [here follows No. 331].

1823. 'Fierabras,' heroic-romantic opera in 3 acts (Sch.), 'Domestic Warfare' (originally 'The Conspirators'), opera in 1 act by Castelli (Sch.), Sonata for pianoforte in A minor (D.), do. for pianoforte and arpeggione in A minor (D.), many songs.

This year he was elected an *honorary member* by the Graz as well as the Linz Musical Society.

1824. Octet for 2 violins, viola, clarinet, bassoon, horn, violoncello and double bass (D.), 'Salve Regina' in C for four male voices (D.), songs.

1825. Sonata in C (D.).

In this year Schubert, in the company of the I. & R. Court Opera singer Vogl, made a pleasure trip to Gastein. Their stay at that mountain spa counted among the fairest days of his life, which intercourse with the Patriarch Pyrker and other worthy men had made so pleasant for him.

1826 and 1827. He composed: 'Battle Song' by Klopstock for 8 male voices (D.), chorus with alto solo and pianoforte accompaniment (D.), 'German Mass' for 4 voices and organ

(D.), Quartet in G major (D.), 'Night Brightness,' solo and chorus for male voices with pianoforte accompaniment (D.), a mass of songs.

In the year 1826 he sought for the post of vice Court Musical Director. But the conductor of the Court Opera, *Weigl*, was placed in it. Schubert, however, remarked on that occasion: "*Since so worthy a man as Weigl has received it, I shall have to rest content.*"

That same year he received from the Committee of Management of the Philharmonic Society of the Austrian Imperial State a letter of thanks (together with 100 fl., A.C.): [here follows No. 713].

In the year 1828, in the month of March, Schubert yielded to general persuasion to give a private concert at the hall of the Austrian Philharmonic Society. Never had this hall been crowded with more people than it was on this occasion.

1828. The year of Schubert's death is particularly notable on account of his creation of many beautiful works
 He laboured incessantly at a grand Mass in E♭, one of his most profound and perfect works.
 The following compositions belong to that same year: a Quintet for 2 violins, 1 viola and 2 cellos (D.), the three grand pianoforte Sonatas (which he wished to dedicate to Hummel, the same which, recently printed, were dedicated to Herr R. Schumann by the publishers, Herren Diabelli & Co.), many songs by Rellstab, by Heine and Seidl, the second part of the 'Winter Journey' (the proof correction of which was the last stroke of his pen) (Haslinger), a Duo in A minor for pianoforte (D.), a pianoforte Sonata in E♭ minor for 4 hands (D.), a Fugue for 4 hands in E minor (D.), the 'Hymn to the Holy Ghost' for 8 male voices and wind accompaniment *ad libitum* (D.), a 'Tantum ergo' in E♭ (Sch.) and a tenor aria with chorus (Sch.).

In September already Schubert *ailed* and *doctored*. However, his indisposition again decreased somewhat. At the beginning of October he therefore made, in the company of his brother Ferdinand and two other friends, a little pleasure trip to Unter-Waltersdorf, and thence an excursion to Eisenstadt, where he sought out

Josef Haydn's tomb and remained at its side for a fairly long time. He ate and drank most moderately during these three days of travel, but was very bright withal and had many merry notions.

But once he was back in Vienna, his indisposition increased once more.

Then, on the last day of October, when he wished to eat a fish in the evening, he suddenly threw his knife and fork on the plate as soon as he had tasted the first morsel, suggesting that he found this food immensely repellent and felt just as though he had taken poison. From that moment Schubert hardly ate or drank anything more, taking nothing but medicines. He also tried to find relief by moving in the fresh air, and therefore still took a few walks. On 3rd November, in the early morning, he yet made his way from the Neu-Wieden to Hernals, *to hear the Latin Requiem composed by his brother Ferdinand.*—He called it simple, yet effectively made at the same time, and altogether signified his pleasure in it. The Requiem was the last music to which he listened. After the service he again took exercise for three hours. But on his way home he complained greatly of lassitude. In the course of a few days he grew ever more helpless and weak, until at last he wholly took to a sick-bed. It was 14th November when he became bedridden, although he sat up for a few hours each day and still corrected the second part of the 'Winter Journey.' On the 19th of that month, at 3 o'clock in the afternoon, death overtook him, however.

On the eve of his demise he called his brother to his bedside in these words: "Ferdinand! put your ear to my mouth," and then said quite mysteriously: "You, what is the matter with me?" —Ferdinand replied: "Dear Franz! we are all very anxious to make you well again, and the doctor assures us, too, that you will soon be restored to health; only you must be good and keep in bed!"— All day long he wanted to get up, and he continued to imagine that he was in a strange room.

A few hours later the doctor appeared, who persuaded him in similar words. But Schubert looked fixedly into the doctor's eyes, grasped at the wall with a feeble hand, and said slowly and seriously:

"Here, here is my end!"

The first version of this sketch was probably that which Bauernfeld had received from the Schubert family in 1829 for use for his obituary (No. XXXIII). Perhaps there were a few notes by Schubert's father and his brother Ignaz in it, as quoted by Kreissle on pages 4 and 5 of his biography: "In his fifth year," the father writes, "I prepared him for elementary instruction, and in his sixth I let him go to school, where he always distinguished himself as the first among his schoolfellows. Even in his earliest youth he was fond of society, and he was never merrier than when he was able to spend his leisure hours among a circle of cheerful friends. In his eighth year I imparted to him the necessary preliminary knowledge of violin playing and practised him until he was able to play easy duets fairly well; then I sent him to the singing-lessons of Herr Michael Holzer, the choirmaster in the Liechtental." Ignaz had given the boy his first instruction in pianoforte playing, and he wrote about this as follows: "I was much astonished when, after only a few months he informed me that he had now no further use for my teaching and would be quite able to get on by himself. And indeed he went so far in a short time that I had myself to acknowledge him as a master far surpassing me and no longer to be caught up [by me]."—Ferdinand's article was clearly written at the instigation of Schumann, who published it in his periodical with a few footnotes of his own.

(Par. 3) Schubert's father thus supplements Holzer's remark: "It follows that actually I did not give him any lessons, but merely conversed with him and looked at him in silent wonder."

(7) The compositions named are xx. 1, 3 (recte 'A Corpse Fantasy' ['Eine Leichenphantasie'], words by Schiller); ix. 30; the three string quartets in mixed keys, of which (owing to Brahms's veto) only the second, v. 1, was printed and the others have been lost in the meantime.

(9) The minuets dated from 1813; the Overture for string quintet of 1811, which is also missing from the complete edition, has been preserved by the publisher A. Cranz at Leipzig, the successor of Diabelli, Spina and Friedrich Schreiber of Vienna. The "violin Concerto" is the Concert Piece in D major of 1816, xxi. 3. The "congratulatory cantata" is probably that entitled 'Namensfeier' of 1815, written for Vierthaler, xvii. 4 (generally said by mistake to have been written for his father). The "antiphons" are xiv. 18. The trio is xix. 4 (No. 56). The cantata for Salieri is xix. 5 (No. 89). The pianoforte fantasies are ix. 30–2 (cf. par. 7). The variations are probably the unpublished six (originally seven, but No. 4 is missing) in F major, now somewhere in the United States.

(10) The number of string quartets is actually nineteen; but if the three in mixed keys of 1811–12 (see par. 7) and the lost one in E flat major of 1813 are deducted, then the remaining ones really number fifteen.

(12) The overtures ii. 1, 2 and xxi. 1, 2 certainly belong to this time. The second of these was intended for a comedy, 'The Devil as Hydraulicus,' and the third probably appertains to the operetta 'The Looking-Glass Knight' (xv. 12, fragment). The D major Symphony of the autumn of 1813 (i. 1) may also have been written when Schubert was still at the Seminary.

(13) Cf. No. 113. Schubert became liable to military duty in 1815 at the earliest, that is at the age of eighteen. As he attended the preparatory course already in 1813–14, in order to become assistant schoolmaster in the autumn of 1814, the three conscription summonses could no longer directly influence this decision. They had to be expected, it is true, but after his first examination Schubert knew himself to be ineligible. He was, however, examined, for all that he was a school assistant.

(14) The mass is xiii. 1; for the performances, his friend Therese Grob and the pianoforte given to him by his father, cf. notes preceding No. 67.

(16) 'The Twin Brothers' and 'The **Magic** Harp' were printed as xv. 5 and 7 (cf. Nos. 167 and 180). 'Alfonso and Estrella' was in Berlin, at the Königstadt Theatre, only in the manuscript copy Schubert had sent to Anna Milder in 1825; the original was at Dr. Pachler's at Graz.

(17) The 'Erl King' was twice reprinted in Germany during Schubert's lifetime, 'Margaret at the Spinning-Wheel' and 'The Wanderer' each once; 'Suleika's Second Song' twice; 'The Trout' and Op. 60 ('Veteran's Song' and 'Dithyramb') each three times; 'The Quail's Call' once.—The Symphony mentioned in Schumann's footnote is, of course, Schubert's last. Breitkopf & Härtel had already acquired it (*see* No. XLV).

(18). The "specialist in music," according to Kreissle (p. 128), was Horzalka (*see* No. 342). The passage referring to Schubert's frequently meeting Beethoven bears a note in Schindler's hand in Alois Fuchs's 'Schubertiana' collection (*see* note to No. XXVII, par. 1): "This is untrue. A. Schindler."

(19) At the earliest in 1851 A. Diabelli & Co. published a 'Thematic Catalogue of Printed Compositions by Franz Schubert,' which was, of course, even less complete than Gustav Nottebohm's catalogue published by Diabelli's successor, Friedrich Schreiber, in 1874—that is long before the complete edition. The works in the list that follows, which is incomplete and disfigured by misprints, correspond to the numbers in the complete edition given hereunder:

(1810) ix. 30.

(1811) For the quintet Overture cf. above, par. 9; the string Quartet in "D major" is lost; ix. 31; among the songs the first preserved one is 'Hagar's Lament,' xx. 1.

(1812) v. 2, 3; the "Sonata" was published only in 1923, in Vienna; the quartet Overture was lost owing to Brahms's veto; ii. 2; the Variations (*see* note to No. XXXIII, par. 28) also disappeared; xi. 9; the 'Salve Regina' was published only in 1928, in Vienna; xiv. 14. The two pieces of church music had not yet appeared at that time: there must be a mistake here.

(1813) iii. 2; ii. 8 (actually five minuets with six trios); v. 4, 5, 10, 6; xiv. 15, 16, 21 (the third Kyrie was used by Ferdinand in his Pastoral Mass, Op. 13, in 1833); for the thirty minuets *see* above, par. 9, and note to No. XXX, par. 6; i. 1; ix. 32; xix. 9–14, 22, 23 and xxi. 37–43.

(1814) The first string Quartet is preserved only in part: its *grave* movement was published in Vienna in 1939; v. 7, 8; for the five minuets with six trios *see* 1813; the five (not six) preserved German dances with coda and seven trios also date from 1813, ii. 9; xvi. 43; xiii. 1; xiv. 9.

(1815) xxi. 23; xi. 6; xiv. 11 (written in 1816); xv. 4, 2; xiv. 2, 4; xv. 3; i. 3, 2 (No. 2 of 1814); xiii. 1 (supp.); x. 1 (in E major) and 2; v. 9; xiii. 2.

(1816) vi. 1; v. 11 (in E major); xxi. 3 (*see* above, par. 9); xv. 13; i. 5, 4; xiv. 13; xi. 14 (in E major, known as 'Five Pianoforte Pieces'); xvii. 18; xiv. 17.

(1817) The Polonaise was published only in 1928, in Vienna; xxi. 5; i. 6 (October 1817–February 1818); ii. 5, 6; x. 7 (Op. 122), 4 (in E minor), 6 (Op. 164), 3; viii. 6 (Op. 162).

(1818) xxi. 11, 12 (in F minor), both incompletely preserved.

(1819) xv. 5; ii. 7 (in E minor); xix. 3 (cantata for Vogl's birthday, Op. 158).

(1820) v. 12 (the *allegro* alone complete); xvii. 1 ('Lazarus').

(1821) xvi. 3 (Op. 167).

(1822) xv. 9 (between autumn 1821 and spring 1823, *see* above, par. 16); xiv. 8.

(1823) xv. 10, 6; x. 8 (Op. 143); viii. 8 (1824).

(1824) iii. 1 (Op. 166); xiv. 19 (Op. 149).

(1825) x. 9 (in A minor, Op. 42); but Op. 42 had long been published, so that Ferdinand may have been thinking of the second of the three A minor Sonatas (x. 8, Op. 143), which however dates from 1823.

(1826 and 1827) xvi. 28 (Op. 151, 1827); xviii. 4 (Op. 135, 'Serenade,' 1827); xiii. 7 (1826 or 1827); v. 15 (Op. 161, 1826); xvi. 13 (Op. 156, 1826).

(1828) xiii. 6; iv. 1 (Op. 163); x. 13–15; most of the songs are in the
'Swan Song' cycle; xx. 529–40 (Op. 89, Part II); ix. 23 (called
'Life's Tempests' ['Lebensstürme'], Op. 144); probably
xi. 13 (called 'Three Pianoforte Pieces,' for two hands, E flat
minor, E flat major, C flat major); ix. 28 (Op. 152); xvi. 2
(Op. 154); xxi. 32, 33.

(Par. 33) The date of 14th November for the day on which Schubert
took to his bed seems to be wrong: Spaun and Bauernfeld agree in giving
the 11th.—On 12th August 1841 Ferdinand Schubert sent Anton Schindler two and a half sheets of manuscript, 'Sketches for Franz Schubert's
Biography,' two-thirds of which comprised a catalogue of all the works
with the exception of songs and partsongs. This manuscript, evidently
Ferdinand's best, is unfortunately not extant; but Schindler made use of
it in 1857 for his 'Recollections of Franz Schubert' ('Niederrheinische
Musikzeitung,' Cologne, 7th and 14th March). Apart from songs and
partsongs, which he too mentions only summarily, Schindler's list (in
which the misprints of 1839 are for the most part corrected) contains
a few interesting additions, as follows: 1812. The Variations in E flat are
here said to have been written for pianoforte, that is to say for two hands,
and their number is given as six; this again points to the manuscript in
the United States (*see above*, par. 9), where six out of seven variations in F are
preserved, undated.—1814. 'Tantum ergo' in C, probably one of the two
of August 1816 (xiv. 7 and that published in Vienna in 1935).—1815.
'Name-Day Celebration ['Namensfeier'], little Cantata,' written for
Vierthaler, xvii. 4.—1816. Rondo in A for violin, xxi. 4; 'Cantata by
Hoheisel,' written for Spendou, xvii. 2 (Op. 128); three sonatas for
pianoforte and violin, viii. 2–4; 'Pianoforte Concerto,' *recte* 'Adagio and
Rondo concertante' for pianoforte, violin, viola and cello, vii. 2; 'Requiem
(first movement only, up to the fugue)' in E flat, unpublished (Vienna
Philharmonic Society); 'Duetto for soprano and tenor,' xiv. 10; Mass in C
major, xiii. 4 (Op. 48).—1817. Quintet for pianoforte, violin, viola, cello
and double bass, vii. 1 (the 'Trout' Quintet, written in 1819, Op. 114).—
1818. Rondo for pianoforte duet, ix. 14; 'Variations for four hands
(dedicated to Beethoven),' ix. 15 (Op. 10); Sonata for four hands in
B flat, ix. 11 (Op. 30).—1820. Six Antiphons for Palm Sunday, xiv. 18.
—1823. 'Seventeen Germans [dances] for Pianoforte,' so called also at
the sale to Diabelli on 26th November 1829, probably the seventeen
Country Dances ('Ländler'), xii. 10, part of which at least were not
written until July 1824 at Zseliz, and which were published only in 1869
by J. P. Gotthard of Vienna.—1824. Quartet in D minor, v. 14 ('Death
and the Maiden,' finished in 1826).—1825. 'Three Sonatas, A major,
C major and D major, the last composed at Gastein' (the one in C is
mentioned also in Ferdinand's list of 1839), x. 10 (Op. 120, of 1819), 9

(Op. 42), 11 (Op. 53).—1827. Trio in E flat for pianoforte, violin and cello, vii. 4 (Op. 100).—1828. A second Benedictus for the Mass in C major, xiii. 4, supplement (published by Diabelli already in 1829). It will be seen that several works already printed were included in this list. The manuscripts, with the exception of the Symphonies, for the most part went gradually to the Vienna City Library. The autographs of the Symphonies are in the archives of the Philharmonic Society of Vienna, except that of No. 5, which is in the Prussian State Library in Berlin.

* * *

Other documents dating from the period covered by Nos. I—XLVI, following Schubert's death, are known, but they have been purposely omitted. A list may, however, be added of the poems and obituaries to be found among them.

POEMS. 'Franz Schubert's Funeral Service' ('Franz Schuberts Totenfeier') by Eduard Duller (single sheet).—'Friendship's Feelings at the Grave of Herr F. S., too soon departed for Art and his Friends' ('Freundesgefühle am Grabe des für die Kunst und seine Freunde zu früh entschlafenen Herrn F. S.') by Josef Müller, assistant teacher at the elder Schubert's school (manuscript).—'At Schubert's Grave' ('An Schuberts Grabe') by K—s ('Theaterzeitung,' 6th December 1828).— 'To my Friend F. S.' ('Meinem Freunde F. S.!') by Johann Gabriel Seidl ('Wiener Zeitschrift,' 6th December 1828).—'Allegory' ('Allegorie') by Franz Stelzhamer ('Theaterzeitung,' 13th December 1828).— 'Dedicated to Schubert's Memory' ('Dem Andenken Schuberts geweiht') by E. Khier ('Der Sammler,' 16th December 1828).—'Weeping Willow, planted by the Grave of the unforgettable Composer F. S.' ('Trauerweide, gepflanzt an dem Grabe des unvergesslichen Tondichters F. Sch.') by Peter Bleich ('Der Sammler,' 18th December 1828).—'Farewell. At Schubert's Grave' ('Nachruf. An Schuberts Grabe') by Andreas Schumacher ('Theaterzeitung,' 20th December 1828).—Prologue for the funeral celebration held on 27th December 1828 at the house of Professor Abbé Luigi Tomazolli at Linz, by Karl Adam Kaltenbrunner ('Oesterreichisches Bürgerblatt,' Linz, 10th April 1829).—Epilogue to 'Song in the Greenery' ('Das Lied im Grünen') by Friedrich Reil (first edition of Op. 115, 16th June 1829).

OBITUARIES. 'Obituary Notice' ('Nekrologische Notiz') by Josef Christian, Freiherr von Zedlitz ('Wiener Zeitschrift,' 25th November 1828).—'Schubert's Shade' ('Schuberts Manen') anonymous ('Wiener Zeitschrift,' 11th December 1828).—Obituary by J. L. Blahetka ('Theaterzeitung,' 27th December 1828).—Introduction to a review of the 'Winter Journey' and 'Swan Song' cycles by Gottfried Wilhelm Fink ('Allgemeine musikalische Zeitung,' Leipzig, 7th October 1829).

APPENDICES

I. ICONOGRAPHY

SCHUBERT'S APPEARANCE AND THE AUTHENTIC PORTRAITS

THERE are several descriptions of Schubert's personal appearance, all of them reprinted in the preface to the portfolio 'Die historischen Bildnisse Franz Schuberts in getreuen Nachbildungen' (Vienna, 1922). The most important of them are probably the following two:

Georg Franz Eckel, a contemporary of Schubert's youth and later a physician, wrote thus to Ferdinand Luib in 1858:

> The figure short, but sturdy, with well-developed solid bones and firm muscles; not angular, but rather rounded. The neck short and strong; shoulders, chest and pelvis broad, finely curved; arms and thighs rounded; hands and feet small; his walk lively and vigorous. The fairly large, round and powerful skull was surrounded by brown, abundantly growing locks. The face, in which the forehead and chin were particularly well developed, showed traits that were not so much actually beautiful as expressive and forceful. The mild eyes, light brown if I am not mistaken, which could flash fire when he was excited, were strongly overshadowed by fairly prominent and bushy brows, and thus seemed smaller than they really were, especially as he often narrowed them, as short-sighted people will. The nose was of medium size, blunt and tilted up a little, and joined by a gentle inward sweep to his full, abundant, firmly set lips, which he generally kept closed. His chin was deeply dimpled. The complexion was pale, but vital, as is usual with genius. The play of his features proclaimed the workings of creative genius, stern when he frowned mightily and compressed his lips, sweet when the eye shone and the mouth smiled. Altogether Schubert's appearance showed an Olympian's classic expression of harmony between vigour and urbanity.

There is no more precise information about the colour of his eyes. His height, already pretty correctly estimated by Grove at 5 ft. 1 in. (1·50 m.), is now officially attested by the measurement shown in the conscription list (No. 113) as 1·57 m.

Karl Langer, Ritter von Edenberg, a Viennese anatomist, thus described his findings at his examination of the skulls of Haydn, Beethoven and Schubert in 1887 (that of the last having been first exhumed in 1863):

> Schubert's skull is distinguished from the others by its ample form, impaired neither by age nor by disease, and by the thick build of its bones: it is plainly that of a man who died at an age of full vigour. . . . The denture is absolutely intact but for the upper incisor on the extreme right, and strongly developed.

The tooth had probably fallen out only in the grave. At the second exhumation of 1888 the left lower incisor towards the centre was also missing. The teeth were then described by the anatomist Karl Toldt as 'very large, with broad, not blunted crowns, entirely intact.'

. . . .

To the fact that Schubert's friends included several plastic artists we owe a larger number of portraits than the brevity and the confined setting of his life would otherwise have permitted. Unfortunately no portrait by Moritz von Schwind made during those years has been preserved, apart from the small figure in the group No. 2. The gifted and prolific lithographer Josef Kriehuber, too, produced only a posthumous likeness. A group of the circle at the "Hungarian Crown" by Ludwig Ferdinand von Schnorr is said to have been lost. Whether Josef Alois Dialer, who made the bust for Schubert's funeral monument, was able to do so from the direct model we do not know. The following ten authentic portraits therefore remain:

1. SILHOUETTE. Indian ink. 1¾ in. by 1¼ in. Anonymous. Marked 1817. From Anton Holzapfel's remains. (The ten concentric rings framing it are not reproduced.) Schubert is shown without spectacles, although he wore them already in the Seminary, i.e. before 1814.

2. GAME OF BALL AT ATZENBRUGG ('The Feast at Atzenbrugg'). Etching. 4 in. by 6½ in. Landscape and architecture drawn by Franz von Schober, figures by Moritz von Schwind, the whole etched by Ludwig Mohn, c. 1820. Schubert (with Vogl and Schwind) is shown sitting on the grass in shirt-sleeves and smoking a long pipe. In the background is Atzenbrugg Castle, which Schwind also represented on the wall of his 'Schubert Evening at Spaun's.' (Three pictures are seen there: on the left Atzenbrugg, on the right probably Lake Traun, in the centre Countess Karoline Esterházy, after Teltscher's portrait.) A coloured print once belonging to Schober is in the possession of the Vienna Philharmonic Society.

3. EXCURSION OF THE SCHUBERTIANS (from Atzenbrugg to Aumühl). Water-colour. 9 in. by 1 ft. ½ in. Painted for Schober by Leopold Kupelwieser in 1820. Schubert (with the painter) represented as walking behind the carriage. The Aumühle is visible in the background.

4. PARTY GAME OF THE SCHUBERTIANS (at Atzenbrugg). Water-colour. 1 ft. 1¼ in. by 1 ft. 5¼ in. Painted for Schober by Kupelwieser in 1821. Drawing-room in the castle. The party acting and solving a charade, the word being "Rheinfall." represented by two syllables: "rein" for "Rhein" and "Fall." The solution is a pun on the converse "Sündenfall," i.e. the first fall of man. Schubert

is seated at the pianoforte, evidently after having accompanied the tableau vivant with improvised music.

5. FULL-FACE DRAWING. Pencil. 8¼ in. by 6¼ in. Drawn by Kupelwieser on 10th July 1821, probably at Atzenbrugg.

6. "MICHAEL VOGL AND FRANZ SCHUBERT setting out to fight and to conquer." Caricature in pencil. Size of the original unknown. Probably drawn by Schober about 1825. The original was lost about fifty years ago. Formerly in Schober's possession. A sketch for it is extant.

7. WATER-COLOUR. 8 in. by 10 in. By Wilhelm August Rieder, painted in May 1825. Three-quarter length. The best-known of the contemporary portraits.—Engraved by Johann Passini in 1825. Lithographed by Rieder himself in 1828.

8. LITHOGRAPH. 1 ft. 5¾ in. by 11¾ in. Drawn by Josef Teltscher in 1826.—There are two later states; all three are rare.

9. JENGER, ANSELM HÜTTENBRENNER AND SCHUBERT. Coloured drawing. 8 in. by 6½ in. Drawn by Teltscher about 1827. Heads and shoulders. Formerly in Karl von Schönstein's possession.

10. OIL PORTRAIT. 1 ft. 10 in. by 1 ft. 5¼ in. Painted by Willibrord Josef Mähler about 1827 for Josef Sonnleithner's collection of musicians' portraits. Without spectacles.

Schober declared the portrait in the group No. 4 (which belonged to him) to be the most faithful. Schwind called it an excellent likeness and said that the full-face drawing, No. 5, and the lithograph, No. 8, also deserved attention; but he agreed with the judgment of other friends that the water-colour, No. 7, was the best portrait. The oil painting, No. 10, which may not have been known to Schober and Schwind, or at any rate not intimately, was regarded as very successful by Leopold von Sonnleithner.

It remains to mention three alleged Schubert portraits which have been given undeserved prominence in recent times:

(a) A chalk drawing of 1813 (Liechtenstein Gallery, Vienna), attributed to Leopold Kupelwieser, who had not yet made Schubert's acquaintance that year. Not only is this sheet not by him, but the youth it represents shows no sort of likeness to Schubert.

(b) A miniature by Robert Theer, 1829 (Kestner Museum, Hanover). A genuine Theer, but not even a posthumous Schubert.

(c) An oil portrait by Ferdinand Robert Kettner, 1816 (auctioned at Graz in 1934). Probably a genuine Kettner, since nobody would trouble to forge him, but not so much as a pretended Schubert.

II. SCHUBERT'S LODGINGS IN VIENNA

Early 1797 to Spring 1801 :

Suburb of Himmelpfortgrund (north-west), Upper High Road, No. 72, "The Red Crayfish." Owner, Matthias Schmidtgruber. Now municipal district No. IX, 54 Nussdorferstrasse. Commemorative tablet with bust. Schubert Museum of the City of Vienna on the first floor. House, courtyard and garden largely unchanged. "Trout Fountain" in the courtyard. View from the garden down to the Liechtental parish church.

Spring 1801 to Autumn 1808 :

Suburb of Himmelpfortgrund, No. 10, "The Red Crayfish," dia-gonally facing the birthplace. Owners, Schubert's father and mother. School on the ground floor, dwelling-place on the first floor. House and courtyard preserved (no garden). Now Vienna IX, 3 Säulengasse. Commemorative tablet.

Autumn 1808 to Autumn 1813 :

Inner City, No. 796, I. & R. City Seminary, situated within the old university, between the Academic Grammar School (right) and the Jesuit or University church (left), facing the great hall of the University (now Academy of Science). Now Vienna I, 1 Universitätsplatz. Commemorative tablet.

Autumn 1813 to Autumn 1816 :

School house at Himmelpfortgrund, as above. Owners, Franz Schubert, sen., and his children of the first marriage (except Ignaz).

Spring 1816 (interim) :

Suburb of Landstrasse (south-east), No. 97. Owner, Professor Heinrich Josef Watteroth, of the University. House, courtyard and garden preserved. Now Vienna III, 17 Erdbergerstrasse. Schubert lived there temporarily with Josef von Spaun, who had a room in the house. Commemorative tablet.

Autumn 1816 to August 1817 :

Inner City, No. 592, "Winter." Owner, Karl Edler von Bartenfeld. Stone figure of "Sir Winter" at the corner. Demolished. New building, Vienna I, 26 Tuchlauben, corner of Landskrongasse. Schubert lived there as the Schober family's guest.

End of 1817 :

School house at Himmelpfortgrund, as above.

Early 1818 :

Suburb of Rossau (north-west, closer to the Inner City), No. 147, new school house. Owner, Community of Rossau. Demolished. New building, Vienna IX, 11 Grünetorgasse, "Schubert School," the staircase adorned with scenes from Schubert's life. Commemorative tablet.

(Summer 1818: Zseliz Castle, Hungary, in the service of Count Johann Karl Esterházy.)

Autumn 1818 to end of 1820 :

Inner City, No. 420, between the old town hall and the Hoher Markt. Owner, Johann Irrsa. The third floor sublet by Frau Anna Sanssouci. Schubert lived in Johann Mayrhofer's room. Demolished, later "Liebighaus," finally converted into a corner block with two neighbouring houses. Now Vienna I, 2 Wipplingerstrasse.

(Summer 1819: Upper Austria.)

1821 :

Inner City, No. 380, near the preceding lodgings; formerly the Theatine monastery. Owner, Maria Josefa Desprez, Freiin von Neufmanil. Subletting tenant unknown. Schubert lived alone there for the first time, as an independent lodger. Demolished. New building, Vienna I, 21 Wipplingerstrasse, corner of Tiefer Graben.

(Autumn 1821: St. Pölten, Lower Austria.)

1822 to Summer 1823 :

Inner City, No. 1155, "Göttweigerhof." Owner, Göttweig Monastery (Lower Austria). Schubert was there the Schober family's guest again. Altered by the addition of a story in 1828. Now Vienna I, 9 Spiegelgasse, corner of Göttweigergasse. Commemorative tablet.

Autumn 1822 to Spring 1823 (interim) :

School house in the Rossau, as above.

(Summer 1823: Upper Austria.)

Autumn 1823 to Spring 1824 :

Inner City, No. 1187. Owner, Johann Schmid. Schubert lived with Josef Huber on the first floor. Demolished. New building, Vienna I, 14 Stubentorbastei, the second house towards the Liebenberggasse.

(Summer 1824: Zseliz Castle.)

October 1824 to February 1825 :

School house in the Rossau, as above.

February 1825 to Summer 1826 :

Suburb of Wieden (south), No. 100. Owner, Johann Fruhwirth. The house is situated between the Karl church and the house "The

Holy Trinity," next to which was the Moonshine House (the Schwind family's residence). Subletting tenant of the apartment No. 26, Georg Kellner. Schubert lived, alone for the second time, in a room on the second floor, above the gate on the left. The low and rambling house has a picturesque courtyard. Now Vienna IV, 9 Technikerstrasse.

(Summer 1825: Upper Austria and Salzburg.)

Spring and Summer 1826 (interim):

Village of Währing (north-west). No details known. Schubert lived there intermittently with Schwind at Schober's.

Autumn 1826:

Inner City, No. 765. Owner, Anton, Freiherr von Sala. Demolished. New building, Vienna I, 6 Bäckerstrasse, second house before the Essiggasse. Schubert lived there with Schober again.

End of 1826 to February 1827:

Inner City (No. ?), on the bastion near the Karolinentor.' Demolished Facing the present Stadtpark. Schubert lived there alone once more.

March 1827 to August 1828:

Inner City, Nos. 556 and 557, "The Blue Hedgehog" (house with a passage through to the Wildpretmarkt, next door to the "Red Hedgehog," the Philharmonic Society's quarters, not far from the Winter House). Owners, Kajetan Franz Wenzel and Franz Anton, Edle von Sternegg. Demolished. New building, Vienna I, 18 Tuchlauben. Schubert again lived with Schober, on the second floor, where he had two rooms and a music closet at his disposal.

May to June 1827 (interim):

Village of Dornbach (west-north-west), main street, inn "The Empress of Austria." Owner, Paul Konrath. Schubert's room is said to have been on the second floor. Now used for other purposes, Vienna XVII, 101 Dornbacherstrasse. Commemorative tablet.

(September 1827: Graz.)

September to November 1828:

Suburb of Wieden, No. 694, "The City of Ronsperg." Owner, Johann Kiffmann. Schubert lived there with his brother Ferdinand, on the second floor to the right, in a closet facing the street. Now Vienna V, 6 Kettenbrückengasse. Commemorative tablet.

NOTE. The period spent at the General Hospital (4 Alserstrasse, Vienna IX) in 1823 and the excursions to Atzenbrugg Castle in Lower Austria about 1820–1, being of uncertain date, have not been considered here.

931

COMPARATIVE NOTE. Gluck and Haydn, who moved only once or twice during their residence in Vienna, both owned their own houses in the end.

Mozart, who, like them, was married, changed house seventeen times during his sixteen years in Vienna, living at sixteen different addresses, one of them being repeated.

Beethoven, during his thirty-five years in Vienna, occupied about forty-four different lodgings, returning to earlier ones fourteen times.

Schubert, who was a lodger only three times on his own account, had seventeen addresses during his thirty-one years, three of them being repeated, so that there were twenty changes. If we subtract the first twenty years to bring him into line with the other masters mentioned here, he occupied fourteen (sixteen) different lodgings in eleven years.

III. SCHUBERT'S INCOME

Year.	Source.	V.C. Fl.	A.C. Fl.
1816.	'Prometheus' Cantata	100	24
1818–28.	15 contributions to almanacs and periodicals	300	72*
1818–28.	[7] appearances as pianoforte player and accompanist (not always remunerated) .		120*
1818.	Music lessons at Zseliz (four months at 75 florins, A.C., each)		300*
c. 1820.	Music lessons at the Esterházys' in Vienna (2 florins, A.C., per lesson) . . .		100*
1820–1, 1824.	Music for 3 stage works and 2 extra numbers for an opera ('The Twin Brothers,' 'The Magic Harp,' 'The Magic Bell,' 'Rosamond')		160*
1820–8.	Repeated accompanying at noble private houses		100*
1821–2.	Opp. 1–7 and 10–12 (disposal on sale or return and settlement) [Cappi & Diabelli]	2,000	480
1821.	Present for the dedication of Op. 2 (20 ducats)		80
1821.	Present for Op. 4 (12 ducats) . . .		50
1822–8.	For about half of 16 other dedications to patrons (at 16 ducats each) . . .		520*
1822–8.	c. 70 op. numbers (at 50 florins, A.C., each)		3,500*
1822.	Composer's fee for the mixed-voice Quartet, xvii. 11 (Op. posth. 146) . . .	50	12

Year.	Source.	V.C. Fl.	A.C. Fl.
1822.	Composer's fee for xvii. 3 (Op. posth. 157)	25	6*
1823–6.	16 contributions to collective works . .		80*
1823–6.	Opp. 20–30, 35, 40, 59, 69 (at 200 florins, V.C., each) [Sauer & Leidesdorf] . .	3,000	720*
1823.	Op. 15 ('Wanderer' Fantasy) . . .	50	12
1824.	'Rosamond' music: rights of performance outside Vienna (no such performances given)		100*
1824.	Music lessons at Zseliz (5 months at 100 florins., A.C., each)		500*
1825.	Op. 52 (songs from Walter Scott's 'Lady of the Lake') [Matthias Artaria] . .		200
1826.	Opp. 53 and 54 [Matthias Artaria] . .	300	72
1826.	Composer's fee for the melodrama 'Farewell to Earth' (xx. 603)	25	6*
1826.	Present from the Philharmonic Society .		100
1827.	Share in the sale of the family house (mother's heirloom)	204	48
1827.	Composer's fee for the 'German' Mass .	100	24
1828.	Proceeds of his concert (own compositions) .	800	192
1828.	Op. 100 (Pianoforte Trio in E flat major) .		60
			7,638

The items marked * are conjectural, some as to their amounts and some altogether.

The total amount was about £760, earned in the space of a dozen years an average of about £63 per annum. In Austria this meant 636 florins 30 kreuzer, A.C., a year, or 53 florins a month. In order to estimate these amounts properly it should be recalled that from the autumn of 1814 to the autumn of 1816, while Schubert lived at home, he received an annual remuneration of 80 florins, A.C., from his father as a school assistant, and that in 1816 he competed for the official post of music-master at Laibach, which should have brought him in 500 florins, A.C., per annum. The second court organist in Vienna received the same amount, nor did the second court musical director earn more than 800 florins, A.C. Schubert's furnished room near the Karl church cost 25 florins, V.C., or 6 florins, A.C., a month, which was considered dear; on the other hand he generally lived rent free with friends. Food with the normal drinks came to about 1 florin, A.C., a day. But the irregularity of his income would have made any sort of sound economical management difficult even for a more practical nature.

Living in Vienna between the two world wars of the twentieth century was undoubtedly at least three times as expensive as it had been before the 1848 revolution. About 1925 the value of 50 florins, A.C., would have been equivalent to £15 rather than to £5; and Schubert's income of those 7,600 florins would have been, not £760, but more than £2,000. Even that seems to us little enough for him to make out of his work during his lifetime. There is but one consolation we may derive from the foregoing, partly speculative statement: Schubert never starved.

IV. FIRST PERFORMANCES OF WORKS BY SCHUBERT IN HIS LIFETIME

(Performances given in private and those of uncertain date are omitted.)

1814.	16th Oct.	Mass in F major (xiii. 1).	Liechtental Church.
1817.	22nd Jan.	Cantata for Spendou (xvii. 2) with Overture (ii. 3).	Orphanage.
1818.	1st Mar.	Overture in the Italian Style (ii. 5 or 6).	Roman Emperor Inn.
	12th Mar.	Overture in the Italian Style arranged for pianoforte 8 hands.	,,
	Sept.	German Requiem.	Orphanage.
	29th Sept.	Polonaise in B flat major for violin and orchestra.	,,
1819.	28th Feb.	'Shepherd's Complaint' ('Schäfers Klagelied').	Roman Emperor Inn.
1820,	28th Mar.	Antiphons (xiv. 18).	Altlerchenfeld Church.
	14th June.	'The Twin Brothers' ('Die Zwillingsbrüder') (xv. 5).	Kärntnertor Theatre.
	19th Aug.	'The Magic Harp' ('Die Zauberharfe') (xv. 7).	Theater an der Wien.
1821.	25th Jan.	'Erl King' ('Erlkönig').	Philharmonic Society (Gundelhof).
	8th Feb.	'Longing' ('Die Sehnsucht') (xx. 357).	,,

1821.	7th Mar.	'Song of the Spirits over the Waters' ('Gesang der Geister über den Wassern') (xvi. 3).	Kärntnertor Theatre.
	7th Mar.	'The Little Village' ('Das Dörfchen') (xvi. 4).	,,
	8th Mar.	'Group from Tartarus' ('Gruppe aus dem Tartarus').	Philharmonic Society (Gundelhof).
	22nd Apr.	'The Nightingale' ('Die Nachtigall') (xvi. 5).	Kärntnertor Theatre.
	20th June	Aria and duet added to Hérold's opera 'La Cloehette' (xv. 15).	,,
	30th Aug.	Psalm XXIII (xviii. 2).	Philharmonic Society (Gundelhof).
	18th Nov.	Overture in E minor (ii. 7).	Large Assembly Hall.
	18th Nov.	'The Wanderer' (xx. 266).	Roman Emperor Inn
	2nd Dec.	'The Youth on the Hill' ('Der Jüngling auf dem Hügel').	,,
1822.	11th Feb.	'On the Emperor's Birthday' ('Am Geburtstag des Kaisers') (xvii. 3).	Theresianum.
	3rd Mar.	'Spirit of Love' ('Geist der Liebe') (xvi. 6).	Large Assembly Hall.
	7th Apr.	'Spring Song' ('Frühlingsgesang') (xvi. 7).	Kärntnertor Theatre.
1823.	20th Feb.	'Margaret at the Spinning-Wheel' ('Gretchen am Spinnrade').	Philharmonic Society ("Red Hedgehog").
	6th Mar.	'The Overblown Lime-Tree' ('Die abgeblühte Linde').	,,
	20th Dec.	'Rosamond' ('Rosamunde'), with the overture to 'Alfonso and Estrella.'	Theater an der Wien.
1824.	14th Mar.	String Quartet in A minor (v. 13).	Philharmonic Society ("Red Hedgehog").

1825.	3rd Feb.	'The Flowers' Sorrow' ('Der Blumen Schmerz').	Philharmonic Society ("Red Hedgehog").
	24th Feb.	'To Diana in Anger' ('Der zürnenden Diana').	,,
	20th Mar.	'The Flight' ('Die Flucht') (xvi. 26).	County Hall.
	10th Apr.	'The Alpine Hunter' ('Der Alpenjäger') (xx. 332).	Philharmonic Society ("Red Hedgehog").
	9th June.	'Suleika's Second Song.'	Jagor's Hall, Berlin.
	8th Sept.	Offertory No. 1 ('Totus in corde,' xiv. 1).	Maria Trost (St. Ulric's) Church.
	8th Sept.	Offertory No. 2 ('Salve Regina,' xiv. 2).	,,
	8th Sept.	'Tantum ergo' in C major (xiv. 6).	,,
	8th Sept.	Mass in C major (xiii. 4).	,,
	17th Nov.	'The Gondolier' ('Der Gondelfahrer') (xvi. 9).	Philharmonic Society ("Red Hedgehog").
1826.	6th Jan.	Galop and (8) Écossaises (xii. 23) arranged for orchestra.	"Seven Electors" Hall, Pest.
	12th Jan.	'Restless Love' ('Rastlose Liebe').	Philharmonic Society ("Red Hedgehog").
	23rd Nov.	'The Solitary' ('Der Einsame').	,,
	21st Dec.	'The Dwarf' ('Der Zwerg').	,,
	28th Dec.	'The Young Nun' ('Die junge Nonne').	,,
1827.	11th Jan.	'Chronos the Charioteer' ('An Schwager Kronos').	,,
	25th Jan.	'Night Brightness' ('Nachthelle').	,,
	8th Feb.	'Lay of the Imprisoned Huntsman' ('Lied des gefangenen Jägers').	,,
	8th Mar.	'God in Nature' ('Gott in der Natur') (xviii. 3).	,,
	8th Mar.	'Norman's Song'	,,

1827.	16th Apr.	Octet (iii. 1).	Philharmonic Society ("Red Hedgehog").
	22nd Apr.	'Night Song in the Forest' ('Nachtgesang im Walde') (xvi. 1).	,,
	6th May.	'In the Open' ('Im Freien').	Hall of the University.
	6th Dec.	'The Combat' ('Der Kampf').	Philharmonic Society ("Red Hedgehog").
	26th Dec.	Pianoforte Trio in E flat major (vii. 4).	,,
1828.	3rd Jan.	'Moonlight' ('Mondenschein') (xvi. 27).	,,
	10th Jan.	'Good Night!' ('Gute Nacht!').	,,
	20th Jan.	Fantasy for Pianoforte and Violin in C major (viii. 5).	County Hall.
	24th Jan.	'Serenade' ('Ständchen') (xviii. 4).	Philharmonic Society ("Red Hedgehog").
	31st Jan.	'Ellen's (third) Song.'	,,
	2nd Feb.	'Romance of Richard Cœur de Lion.'	County Hall.
	26th Mar.	String Quartet in G major (v. 15), first movement. 'Battle Song' ('Schlachtlied') (xvi. 28). 'Fragment from Aeschylus.' 'Fisherman's Ditty' ('Fischerweise'). 'The Crusade' ('Der Kreuzzug'). 'The Stars' ('Die Sterne') (xx. 552). 'On the River' ('Auf dem Strome').	Philharmonic Society ("Red Hedgehog"). Schubert's own concert.
	Summer.	Psalm XCII (xvii. 19).	Jewish Temple.
	2nd Sept.	'Faith, Hope and Charity' ('Glaube, Hoffnung und Liebe') (xvii. 5).	Trinity Church.

Schubert was several times present as conductor, performer or accompanist at the pianoforte.   The following is a summary of all his public appearances:

1814, 16th October—Mass in F major—Liechtental Church; repeated 26th October—Court Church of St. Augustine (conductor).

1818, 12th March—one of the two Overtures in the Italian Style, arr. for 8 hands—Roman Emperor Inn (performer).

1827, 8th March—'Norman's Song'—Philharmonic Society (accompanist).

1827, 22nd April—'Norman's Song'—County Hall.

1827, 29th April—'The Solitary'—County Hall.

1827, 8th September—'Norman's Song'—County Theatre, Graz.

1828, 16th March—'Norman's Song'—Philharmonic Society.

1828, 26th March (Schubert's own concert)—accompaniments of 7 works—Philharmonic Society.

1828, 20th April—'On the River' (accompaniment)—Small Assembly Hall.

Schubert thus appeared in public twice as conductor, once as pianoforte player and seven times as accompanist.

V. LIST OF WORKS
PUBLISHED IN SCHUBERT'S LIFETIME
(a) WORKS WITH OPUS NUMBERS
(in numerical order)

(Numbers in brackets are those wrongly used for the first issues.)

1. 'Erl King' ('Erlkönig').   2nd April 1821 (on sale or return).

2. 'Margaret at the Spinning-wheel' ('Gretchen am Spinnrade'). 30th April 1821 (on sale or return).

3. 4 Goethe songs (including 'The Hedgerose' ['Heidenröslein']). 29th May 1821 (on sale or return).

4. 3 Songs (including Schmidt's 'Wanderer').   29th May 1821 (on sale or return).

5. 5 Goethe songs (including 'Restless Love' ['Rastlose Liebe']). 9th July 1821 (on sale or return).

6. 3 Songs (including 'Antigone and Oedipus' ['Antigone und Oedip']). 23rd August 1821 (on sale or return).

7. 3 Songs (including 'Death and the Maiden' ['Der Tod und das Mädchen']). 27th November 1821 (on sale or return).

8. 4 Songs (including 'Erlaf Lake' ['Erlafsee']). 9th May 1822.

9. 'Original Dances' ('Original-Tänze') (36 waltzes in two books) for pianoforte. 29th November 1821.

10. 8 'Variations on a French Song' ('Variationen über ein französisches Lied') for pianoforte duet. 19th April 1822.

11. 3 Male-voice Quartets (including 'The Little Village' ['Das Dörfchen']). 12th June 1822.

12. 3 'Songs of the Harper' ('Gesänge des Harfners') (Goethe). 13th December 1822 (on sale or return).

13. 3 Songs (including Mayrhofer's 'Alpine Hunter' ['Der Alpenjäger']). 13th December 1822 (on sale or return).

14. 'Suleika' (I) and 'Secrets' ('Geheimes') (Goethe). 13th December 1822 (on sale or return).

15. Fantasy for pianoforte ('Wanderer'). 24th February 1823.

16. 'Spring Song' ('Frühlingslied') (Schober) and 'Enjoyment of Nature' ('Naturgenuss'), male-voice quartets. 9th October 1823.

17. 4 Male-voice Quartets (including 'Night' ['Die Nacht']). 9th October 1823.

18. 'Waltzes, Country Dances and Écossaises' ('Walzer, Ländler und Ecossaisen') (38 dances in 2 books) for pianoforte. 5th February 1823.

19. 3 Goethe songs (including 'Chronos the Charioteer' ['An Schwager Kronos']). 6th June 1825.

20. 3 Songs (including 'Greetings to thee' ['Sei mir gegrüsst']). 10th April 1823.

21. 3 Songs (including Mayrhofer's 'The Boatman' ['Der Schiffer']). 19th June 1823.

22. M. von Collin's 'The Dwarf' ('Der Zwerg') and 'Melancholy' ('Wehmut'). 27th May 1823.

23. 4 Songs (including 'Love hath lied' ['Die Liebe hat gelogen']). 4th August 1823.

24. 'Group from Tartarus' ('Gruppe aus dem Tartarus') and 'Slumber Song' ('Schlummerlied'). 27th October 1823.

25. Song-cycle 'The Fair Maid of the Mill' ('Die schöne Müllerin') (20 songs in 5 books). I. 17th February 1824; II. 24th March 1824; III—V. 12th August 1824.

26. Vocal numbers for the drama 'Rosamond' ('Rosamunde') (1 song and 3 choruses, in 4 books). 24th March ff. 1824.

27. 'Trois Marches héroïques' for pianoforte duet. 18th December 1824.

28. 'The Gondolier' ('Der Gondelfahrer'), male-voice quartet. 12th August 1824.

29. (No. 1) String Quartet in A minor. 7th September 1824. (Nos. 2 and 3 not published.)

30. Sonata in B flat major for pianoforte duet. 30th December 1823.

31. 'Suleika's Second Song' ('Suleikas zweiter Gesang') (Goethe). 12th August 1825.

32 (–). 'The Trout' ('Die Forelle'). 13th January 1825. (No opus number until the third issue.)

33. 'German and Écossaises' ('Deutsche Tänze und Ecossaisen') (18 dances) for pianoforte. 8th January 1825.

34. Overture in F major for pianoforte duet. 28th February 1825.

35. 8 'Variations sur un thème original' for pianoforte duet. 9th February 1825.

36 (35). 'Diana in Anger' ('Die zürnende Diana') and 'Night Piece' ('Nachtstück'). 11th February 1825.

37. Schiller's 'The Pilgrim' ('Der Pilgrim') and 'Alpine Hunter' ('Der Alpenjäger'). 28th February 1825.

38. 'The Minstrel' ('Der Liedler'). 9th May 1825.

39. 'Longing' ('Die Sehnsucht') (Schiller). 8th February 1826.

40. 'Six Grandes Marches et Trios' (in 2 books) for pianoforte duet. 7th May and 21st September 1825.

41. 'The Solitary' ('Der Einsame'). 5th January 1827.

42. 'Première Grande Sonate,' A minor, for pianoforte. Early 1826.

43. 'The Young Nun' ('Die junge Nonne') and 'Night and Dreams' ('Nacht und Träume'). 25th July 1825.

44. 'To the Setting Sun' ('An die untergehende Sonne'). 5th January 1827.

45. 'Tantum ergo' in C major. Early September 1825.

46. Offertory No. 1 ('Totus in corde langueo') in C major. Mid September 1825.

47. Offertory No. 2 ('Salve Regina') in F major. 4th August 1825.

48. 'Missa' in C major. 3rd September 1825.

49. 'Galoppe [sic] et Écossaises' (8 dances) for pianoforte. 21st November 1825.

50. 'Valses sentimentales' (34 in 2 books) for pianoforte. 21st November 1825.

51. '3 Marches militaires' for pianoforte duet. 7th August 1826.

52. 'Seven Songs from Walter Scott's "Lady of the Lake"' ('Sieben Gesänge aus Walter Scotts Fräulein vom See') (in 2 books). 5th April 1826.

53. 'Seconde Grande Sonate,' D major, for pianoforte. 8th April 1826.

54. 'Divertissement à la hongroise' for pianoforte duet. 8th April 1826.

55. 'Grande Marche funèbre à l'occasion de la mort de S. M. Alexandre I' for pianoforte duet. 8th February 1826.

56. 3 Songs (including 'Hail and Farewell' ['Willkommen und Abschied'] (2 books). 14th July 1826.

57. 3 Songs (including Hölty's 'To the Moon' ['An den Mond']). 6th April 1826.

58 (56). 3 Schiller songs (including 'Hector's Farewell' ['Hektors Abschied']). 6th April 1826.

59. 4 Songs (including 'Thou art repose' ['Du bist die Ruh']). 21st September 1826. (The opus number added by hand.)

60. 'Veteran's Song' ('Greisengesang') and 'Dithyramb.' 10th June 1826.

61. 6 Polonaises for pianoforte duet. 8th July 1826.

62. 'Songs from "Wilhelm Meister"' ('Gesänge aus Wilhelm Meister') (4 Goethe songs). 2nd March 1827.

63 (No. 1). 'Divertissement en forme d'une marche brillante et raisonnée, composé sur des motifs originaux français' for pianoforte duet. 17th June 1826. (Nos. 2 and 3: Op. 84.)

64. 3 Male-voice Quartets (including 'Flight' ['Flucht']). 6th October 1828.

65. 3 Songs (including 'A Boatman's Song to the Dioscuri' ['Lied eines Schiffers an die Dioskuren']). 24th November 1826.

66. 'Grande Marche héroïque, composée à l'occasion du Sacre de Sa Majesté Nicolas I' for pianoforte duet. 14th September 1826.

67. 'Hommage aux belles Viennoises, Viennese Ladies' Country Dances [and Écossaises]' ('. . ., Wiener Damen-Ländler [und Ecossaisen']) (18 dances for pianoforte). 12th February 1827.

68. 'The Quail's Call' ('Der Wachtelschlag'). 16th May 1827.

69 (52). Overture to the Opera 'Alfonso and Estrella' (arranged) for pianoforte duet. 20th February 1826.

70. 'Rondeau brillant' in B minor for pianoforte and violin. 19th April 1827.

71. 'Urge into the Distance' ('Drang in die Ferne'). 2nd March 1827.

72. 'To be sung on the Water' ('Auf dem Wasser zu singen'). 2nd March 1827.

73. 'The Rose' ('Die Rose).' 16th May 1827.

74. 'The Barristers' ('Die Advokaten') for 2 tenors and bass. 16th May 1827.

75. 4 Polonaises for pianoforte duet. 6th July 1827.

76. Overture to the Opera 'Fierabras,' arranged for pianoforte duet by Karl Czerny. 1827.

77. 'Valses nobles' (12) for pianoforte. 22nd January 1827.

78. 'Fantasy, Andante, Minuet and Allegretto' ('Fantasie, . . . Menuetto und . . .') (Sonata in G major) for pianoforte. 11th April 1827.

79. Pyrker's 'Homesickness' ('Das Heimweh') and 'Omnipotence' ('Die Allmacht'). 16th May 1827.

80. 3 Seidl songs (including 'The Wayfarer addressing the Moon' ['Der Wanderer an den Mond']). 25th May 1827.

81. 3 Rochlitz songs (including 'To the Lute' ['An die Laute']). 28th May 1827.

82. 8 Variations on a Theme from Hérold's Opera 'Marie' for pianoforte duet. 3rd September 1827. (Republished at Hamburg in 1860 as Op. 82, No. 1, together with ix. 18 as No. 2.)

83. 3 Italian songs. 12th September 1827.

84. 'Andantino varié et Rondeau brillant, composés sur des motifs originaux français' (2 books) for pianoforte duet. 6th July 1827 (*see* Op. 63).

85. Scott's 'Annot Lyle's Song' ('Lied der Anne Lyle') and 'Norna's Song' ('Gesang der Norna'). 14th March 1828.

86. 'Romance of Richard Cœur de Lion' ('Romanze des Richard Löwenherz') (Scott). 14th March 1828.

87 (84). 3 Songs (including 'The Youth at the Brook' ['Der Jüngling am Bache']). 6th August 1827.

88. 4 Songs (including 'To Music' ['An die Musik']). 12th December 1827.

89. Song-cycle 'Winter Journey' ('Winterreise') (24 songs in 2 parts) (Vol. II posthumous). 14th January and 30th December 1828.

90 (87). 'Impromptu,' Nos. 1 and 2, for pianoforte. 10th December 1827. (Nos. 3 and 4 not published till 1857 or 1858.)

91. 12 'Waltzes of Graz' ('Graetzer Walzer') for pianoforte. 5th January 1828. (The 'Graz Galop' ['Graetzer Galoppe'] appeared at the same time without opus number.)

92. 3 Goethe songs (including 'The Muses' Son' ['Der Musensohn']). 11th July 1828.

93 (90). 'In the Forest' ('Im Walde') and 'On the Bruck' ('Auf der Brücke' [*recte* Bruck]). 30th May 1828.

94. 'Momens musicals' (*sic*) (6 in 2 books) for pianoforte. 11th July 1828.

95. 'Four Refrain-Songs' ('Vier Refrain-Lieder') (Seidl). 13th August 1828.

96 (–). 4 Songs (including 'Wayfarer's Night Song' ['Wanderers Nachtlied'] II). Summer 1828 (privately printed). (No opus number on the first issue.)

97. Song 'Faith, Hope and Charity' ('Glaube, Hoffnung und Liebe'). 6th October 1828.

100. 'Grand Trio pour Pianoforte, Violon et Violoncelle' in E flat major. October-November 1828 (Leipzig).

106 (–). 4 Songs (including 'Who is Silvia?' ['An Sylvia']). Summer 1828 (privately printed). (No opus number on the first issue.)

108 (93). 3 Songs (including 'Recollection' ['Erinnerung']). Autumn 1828.

Posthumous Works with Opus Numbers assigned by Schubert

98. 3 Songs (including Claudius's 'Cradle Song' ['Wiegenlied']). 10th July 1829.

99. 'Premier Grand Trio pour Piano Forte, Violon et Violoncelle,' in B flat major. 1836.

101. 'The Blind Boy' ('Der blinde Knabe'). 16th March 1829. (The opus number, originally intended by Schubert for the Impromptus, Op. 142, had already been wrongly used at Leipzig on 12th December 1828 for four reprints of songs, the present one included.)

102. 'Moonlight' ('Mondenschein') for male-voice quintet. About 1830.

103. Fantasy in F minor for pianoforte duet. 16th March 1829.

104. 'The Wedding Roast' ('Der Hochzeitsbraten') for soprano, tenor and bass. 1829.

105. 4 Seidl songs (including 'Contradiction' ['Widerspruch']). 21st November 1828 (the day of Schubert's funeral).

(b) WORKS WITHOUT OPUS NUMBERS
(in chronological order)

6th February 1818. At the Erlaf Lake' ('Am Erlafsee') (Op. 8, No. 3).—Supplement to the 'Mahlerisches Taschenbuch für Freunde interessanter Gegenden, etc.,' vol. vi. Vienna, 1818.

28th September 1820. 'Reflection' ('Widerschein) (xx. 535, 1st version).—Supplement to the 'Taschenbuch zum geselligen Vergnügen,' edited by F. Kind, vol. 31. Leipzig, 1821.

9th December 1820. 'The Trout' ('Die Forelle') (Op. 32).—Supplement to the 'Wiener Zeitschrift für Kunst, Literatur, Theater und Mode.'

30th June 1821. 'To Emma' ('An Emma') (Op. 58, No. 2). Supplement to the 'Wiener Zeitschrift.'

8th December 1821. 'The Flowers' Sorrow' ('Der Blumen Schmerz') (Op. 173, No. 4).—Supplement to the 'Wiener Zeitschrift.'

11th February 1822. 'For the Birthday of His Majesty the Emperor' ('Am Geburtstag Ihrer Majestät des Kaisers') (Op. 157).—Privately printed.

7th May 1822. 'The Rose' ('Die Rose') (Op. 73).—Supplement to the 'Wiener Zeitschrift.'

30th July 1822. 'The Quail's Call' ('Der Wachtelschlag') (Op. 68).—Supplement to the 'Wiener Zeitschrift.'

10th January 1823. 3 German Dances (xii. 14).—'Carneval 1823,' Book II.

25th March 1823. 'Urge into the Distance' ('Drang in die Ferne') (Op. 71).—Supplement to the 'Wiener Zeitschrift.'

19th December 1823. 'Air russe' (Op. 94, No. 3) and Waltz (xii. 18, No. 2).—'Album musical,' Year I.

30th December 1823. 'To be sung on the Water' ('Auf dem Wasser zu singen') (Op. 72).—Supplement to the 'Wiener Zeitschrift.'

21st February 1824. 2 Country Dances ('Ländler') (Op. 127, No. 2, and xii. 10, No. 6).—'Halt's enk z'samm!', Book II.

21st February 1824. 3 Écossaises (xii. 25, Nos. 3 and 6; 'Die Musik,' Berlin, 1st September 1912).—'Nouvelles Galoppes favorites et Écossaises.'

9th June 1824. Variation on a Waltz by Anton Diabelli (xi. 8).—'Vaterländischer Künstlerverein,' Part II.

26th June 1824. 'Song to Death' ('Lied and den Tod') (xx. 326).— Supplement to the 'Allgemeine musikalische Zeitung mit besonderer Rücksicht auf den österreichischen Kaiserstaat,' Vienna.

11th December 1824. 'Plaintes d'un Troubadour' (Op. 94, No. 6) and 'The Apparition' ('Die Erscheinung') (later called 'Recollection' ['Erinnerung'], Op. 108, No. 3).—'Album musical,' Year II.

22nd December 1824. Waltz (xii. 10, No. 17).—'Musikalisches Angebinde zum neuen Jahre.'

7th February 1825. German Dance (?).—'Terpsichore' (lost).

12th March 1825. 'The Solitary' ('Der Einsame') (Op. 41).—Supplement to the 'Wiener Zeitschrift.'

29th December 1825. Waltz ('Moderne Welt,' Vienna, 1st December 1925).—'Seid uns zum zweiten Mal willkommen!'

29th December 1825. Cotillon (xii. 22).—'Ernst und Tändelei.'

23rd December 1826. Waltz ('Zeitschrift der Internationalen Musikgesellschaft,' vol. iii. Leipzig, 1902, p. 319).—'Moderne Liebes-Walzer.'

23rd December 1826. 2 Waltzes ('Zeitschrift der Internationalen Musikgesellschaft,' vol. iii. Leipzig, 1902, pp. 319–20).—'Neue Krähwinkler Tänze.'

23rd June 1827. 'Consolation in Song' ('Trost im Liede') (xx. 313). Supplement to the 'Wiener Zeitschrift.'

23rd June 1827. 'Wayfarer's Night Song' ('Wanderers Nachtlied') II (Op. 96, No. 3).—Supplement to the 'Wiener Zeitschrift.'

25th September 1827. 'The Blind Boy' ('Der blinde Knabe') (Op. 101). —Supplement to the 'Wiener Zeitschrift.'

8th October 1827. 'Grave and Moon' ('Grab und Mond') (xvi. 41).— 'Die deutschen Minnesänger,' vol. i.

8th October 1827. 'Wine and Song' ('Wein und Liebe') (xvi. 37).— 'Die deutschen Minnesänger,' vol. iv.

5th January 1828. 'Graz Galop' ('Graetzer Galoppe') (xii. 24).— No. 10 of the 'Favorit-Galoppe.'

16th September 1828. 'In Spring' ('Im Frühling') (xx. 497).—Supplement to the 'Wiener Zeitschrift.'

SUMMARY OF WORKS PUBLISHED DURING SCHUBERT'S LIFETIME

  3 Chamber works (1 string quartet, 1 pianoforte trio, 1 duet for pianoforte and violin).

 56 Pieces for pianoforte duet (including 1 sonata, 3 divertimenti, 1 overture, 14 marches, 10 polonaises).

 13 Pieces for pianoforte solo (including 3 sonatas, 1 fantasy, 2 impromptus, 6 moments musicaux).

193 Dances for pianoforte solo.

  4 Church works (including 1 mass).

 22 Works for several voices.

187 Songs.

———

478 numbers.

In order to appreciate this amount properly it should be borne in mind that, although it appears to represent about one-third of Schubert's complete works, a single dance or variation (the Diabelli variation) or song is counted as a unit and thus appears as weighty as a mass, an opera or a symphony.

In actual fact the summary includes not a single one of the nine symphonies, neither of the two quintets, only one of nineteen string quartets, three of twenty-one pianoforte sonatas, one of seven masses, none of the ten operas, only twenty-two of over a hundred songs for several voices and but 187 of about 600 songs.

Schubert's greatest success was with his songs, but the market could not keep pace with his production of them, even during the last years, when it was much reduced.

Here is a list of Schubert's publishers with indications of the works issued by them:

(a) WITH OPUS NUMBERS

Cappi & Diabelli (Anton Diabelli & Co.): Opp. 1–18, 19, 32, 41, 44–51, 62, 67–8, 71–6, 85–6, 97 and 1 pianoforte piece in a collection.

Sauer & Leidesdorf (M. J. Leidesdorf): Opp. 20–30, 35, 40, 59, 69, 92, 94, 108 and 12 dances, 2 pianoforte pieces and 1 song in 7 collections.

Anton Pennauer: Opp. 31, 39, 42–3, 55–6, 64, 66, 87.

Cappi & Co. (Cappi & Czerny): Opp. 33–4, 36–8, 60–1, 65.

Matthias Artaria: Opp. 52–4.

Thaddäus Weigl: Opp. 57–8, 63, 84, 88, 95.

Artaria & Co.: Opp. 70, 107.

Tobias Haslinger: Opp. 77–83, 89–91 and 1 dance and 2 partsongs in 2 collections.
J. A. Kienreich, Graz: Op. 93.
Schubert himself: Opp. 96, 106.
H. A. Probst, Leipzig: Op. 100.

(b) WITHOUT OPUS NUMBERS

Anton Doll: 1 song in an almanac.
Anton Strauss: 12 songs as supplements to the 'Wiener Zeitschrift.'
G. J. Göschen, Leipzig: 1 song in an almanac.
Theresianum: 1 partsong (privately printed).
Lithographisches Institut: 1 song as supplement to the Vienna 'Allgemeine musikalische Zeitung.'
K. F. Müller: 3 dances in 3 collections.
Pietro Mechetti: 1 dance in a collection.

VI. DEDICATIONS

LIST OF PERSONS TO WHOM SCHUBERT ADDRESSED DEDICATIONS IN PRINT

Name	Op.	Work
Barth, Josef (friendship)	11	3 male-voice quartets.
Beethoven (veneration and admiration)	10	Variations in E minor for pianoforte duet.
Berchtold, Anton, Count	35	Variations in A flat major for pianoforte duet.
Bernhardt, J. (gratitude and friendship)	40	6 Marches for pianoforte duet.
Bocklet, Karl Maria von	53	Sonata in D major for pianoforte.
Bruchmann, Frau Justine von	20	3 Songs.
Collin, Matthäus von	22	2 Songs (Collin).
Dankesreither, Johann Nepomuk, Ritter von (respect)	12	3 Songs.
Dietrichstein, Moritz, Count (respect)	1	'Erl King.'
Esterházy, Johann, Count (respect)	8	4 Songs.
Esterházy, Karoline, Countess	103	Fantasy in F minor for pianoforte duet.
Franck, Frau Josefine von	92	3 Songs.

Name	Op.	Work
Fries, Moritz, Count of the Realm (respect)	2	'Margaret at the Spinning-wheel.'
Goethe (veneration)	19	3 Songs (Goethe).
Hönig, Fräulein Anna	69 (52)	Overture to 'Alfonso and Estrella' arranged for pianoforte duet.
Holzer, Michael (remembrance)	48	Mass in C major.
Hummel, Johann Nepomuk (see Note)	—	Sonatas in C minor, A major and B flat major (published posthumously).
Hüttenbrenner, Josef (friendship)	116	'Expectation' (published posthumously).
Kenner, Josef	38	'The Minstrel' (Kenner).
Kinsky, Karoline, Princess (respect)	96	4 Songs.
Lablache, Luigi	83	3 Italian Songs.
Lászny, Frau Katharina von	36 54	2 Songs. 'Divertissement à la hongroise' for pianoforte duet.
Liebenberg, Emanuel Karl, Edler von	15	Fantasy in C major ('Wanderer') for pianoforte.
Mayrhofer, Johann (friendship)	21	3 Songs (Mayrhofer).
Milder-Hauptmann, Frau Anna	31	'Suleika's Second Song.'
Mosel, lgnaz, Edler von (high regard)	3	4 Songs.
Neuhaus, Kajetan	82	Variations in C major for pianoforte duet.
Pachler, Frau Marie Leopoldine	106	4 Songs.
Pálffy, Ferdinand, Count	30	Sonata in B flat major for pianoforte duet.
Pinterics, Karl (friendship)	56	3 Songs.
Pyrker, Johann Ladislaus von (respect)	4 79	3 Songs. 2 Songs (Pyrker).
Rudolf, Archduke	42	Sonata in A minor for pianoforte.
Salieri, Antonio	5	5 Songs.
Schnorr, Ludwig Ferdinand von (friendship)	37	2 Songs.

Name	Op.	Work
Schober, Franz, Ritter von	14	2 Songs.
Schönstein, Karl, Freiherr von	25	'The Fair Maid of the Mill.'
Schuppanzigh, Ignaz (friendship)	29	String Quartet in A minor.
Schwarzenberg, Mathilde, Princess (respect)	62	4 Songs.
Seidl, Johann Gabriel (friendship)	95	4 Refrain Songs (Seidl).
Spaun, Josef, Edler von (friendship)	{ 13	3 Songs.
	{ 78	Sonata in G major for pianoforte.
Széchényi, Louis, Count (high regard)	7	3 Songs (2 to words by Széchényi.
Tietze, Ludwig (friendship)	46	Offertory No. 1, in C major.
Vogl, Michael (high regard)	6	3 Songs.
Weissenwolff, Sophie, Countess (high regard)	52	7 Songs from 'The Lady of the Lake.'
Witteczek, Josef (friendship)	80	3 Songs.

NOTE. The Sonatas intended for Hummel were afterwards dedicated to Schumann by the publisher. The dedication of Op. 81, three songs to poems by Rochlitz, to the poet is also the publisher's. The posthumously published thirteen Variations in A minor for pianoforte (without opus number) bear the printed dedication to the "friend and fellow-student" Anselm Hüttenbrenner, from whose first string Quartet (Op. 3) the theme is taken; but this dedication is not on Schubert's manuscript. The same may be true of the dedication of Op. 116 to Josef Hüttenbrenner; but in that case the manuscript is not extant.

VII. PERSONALIA

LATER DATA CONCERNING THE SCHUBERT CIRCLE

(Facts contemporary with Schubert's life are given in the Commentary and may be found by means of the Index.)

Assmayr, Ignaz (1790–1862), became vice chapel master at the court chapel in 1838.

Bauernfeld, Eduard von (1802–90), remained unmarried, was an official in the Lottery Administration under Josef von Spaun until 1848, a successful author of comedies for the Burg Theatre and a champion of the freedom of the press. In 1844 he translated four of Dickens's chief works for a Viennese complete edition that was never finished, sponsored by the musician Julius Becher, who was shot in 1848, and a Mr. Bird, the Vienna correspondent of 'The Times.' In 1845 he visited England. His recollections of Schubert are mentioned in No. XXXIII.

Bocklet, Karl Maria von (1801–81), founded a private school for pianoforte duet playing, which was later taken over by his son.

Bogner, Ferdinand (1786–1846), lived on bad terms with his wife, the intractable Barbara (see Fröhlich), and retained his professorship of the flute at the Conservatory.

Bruchmann, Franz Seraph, Ritter von (1798–1867), went after the death of his wife, Juliana, née von Weyrother, who died in her first childbed in 1830, into the Redemptorist Order, like his brother-in-law Smetana. He died at its college of Gars-on-the-Inn (Bavaria), where he was provincial of the German province of the Order until 1865.—His father, Johann Christian (1768–1849), survived the mother, Justine, née Weis (1774–1840). His sister Isabella (1801–36), who married Streinsberg, died in her third childbed; Justina (1805–29), who married Smetana, in her first.

Castelli, Ignaz Franz (1781–1862), became librarian and secretary to the Lower Austrian County Council and remained a prolific author. When he heard a concert performance of 'Domestic Warfare' for the first time in 1861 he remarked that he had been told at the time that Schubert had made a gloomy tone-picture of 'The Conspirators,' as the opera was originally called. Incidentally, Henry Hiles (1826–1904) made new use of the libretto in an English translation entitled 'War in the Household.' Castelli published amusing reminiscences, in which, however, Schubert is scarcely mentioned.

Chézy, Wilhelmine (Helmina) Christine, née Klencke (1783–1856), remained in Austria until 1833, revised her drama of 'Rosamunde' and as late as 1837 tried once more to have it performed at Munich with Schubert's music, before it was lost for good. She died at Geneva.—Her son Wilhelm Theodor (1806–56), the first male author in the family for four generations, last lived in Vienna; Max, the painter (1808–46), died at Heidelberg. Both Helmina and Wilhelm mention Schubert in their memoirs.

Clodi, Therese (before 1804–after 1847), remained unmarried. After the death of her father, Florian Maximilian (1740–26th October 1828), the children sold the castle of Ebenzweier to the Archduke Maximilian d'Este (1782–1863), quartermaster-general, who died there, and they bought a property at the nearby Traunkirchen. Therese, who became impoverished soon after, went to Vienna, supporting herself first by needlework and later as head of the girls' institute at Penzing near Vienna. Her brother Max (1804–54) became director of the registry in the Upper Austrian County Council; Josef (1806–49) died as an officer at Venice; Franz (b. 1808) became director of the field dispensary at Hermannstadt in Transylvania.

Craigher de Jachelutta, Jakob Nikolaus, Reichsfreiherr von (1797–1855), became Belgian consul at Trieste, travelled in the east in 1843 and died at Cormons near Görz.

Diabelli, Anton (1781–1858), continued to direct the firm of A. Diabelli & Co. until 1853; he was succeeded by his partner Karl Anton Spina (q.v.).

Doblhoff, Anton, Freiherr von (1800–72), became Minister of Commerce in 1848, later Minister of the Interior and finally Minister of Education. He was also a writer on agriculture.—His betrothed, Jeannette Cuny de Pierron, had died in 1828.

Doppler, Josef, became manager at C. A. Spina's, the successor to the music-publishing firm of A. Diabelli & Co., where Sir George Grove met him as late as 1867.

Ebner, Johann Leopold (1791–1870), who was married to Seraphine Schellmann (d. 1857), became court chamber councillor at Innsbruck. He left the collection of copies of Schubert's songs (*see* Albert Stadler), made until 1817, to his brother Johann Ebner, Ritter von Rofenstein, whose daughter, Frau Marie Kerner von Marilaun in Vienna, inherited it.

Eckel, Georg Franz, M.D., became director of the Veterinary Institute in Vienna (now Veterinary High School), but before 1860 began to work as physician again.

Enderes, Karl, Ritter von (1787–1861), became court councillor in the Ministry of Finance, married the love of his youth, Kamilla Ellmauer, a pupil of Vogl's, after the death of her first husband, Josef Gross (d. 1834). In 1840 he became the guardian of Vogl's daughter Henriette, aged twelve.

Enk von der Burg, Karl (1800–85), became inspector of grammar-schools. in Lower Austria, translated Epictetus in 1866–7 and died as court councillor at Salzburg.

Esterházy, Karoline, Countess (1805–51), in 1844 married at Pressburg (Bratislava) Count Karl Folliot de Crenneville-Poutet, chamberlain and retired major. The marriage was, however, soon annulled. She died at Pressburg and was buried at Zseliz.—Her father, Count Johann Karl (1775–1834), was survived by his wife, the Countess Rosine (1779–1854). Karoline's sister Marie, Countess Breunner-Enkevoerth

(1802–37), predeceased her. Her brother, Count Albert (1813–1845), married Marie, Countess Apponyi, in 1843 and died in Paris. Count Folliot and Countess Marie Esterházy (*née* Apponyi) both married a second time.

Fröhlich, Anna (1793–1880), continued to teach singing at the Conservatory.—Her sister Barbara (1798–1878), who married Bogner (q.v.), became drawing-mistress at the civilian girls' boarding school at Hernals near Vienna. Josefine Fröhlich (1808–78) became a private teacher of the pianoforte and singing. Katharina (1800–79), Grillparzer's "eternal betrothed," remained single, like two of her three sisters. The four sisters all died at a great age and close together. Their parents, who are nowhere mentioned, died about 1842.

Gahy, Josef von (1793–1864), became department councillor. When the third and fourth fingers of his right hand became paralysed he made special arrangements for pianoforte duet of many of Schubert's works in order to be able to play them with Marie von Stohl, a good pianist (MSS in the Vienna City Library).

Grillparzer, Franz (1791–1872), remained single, became director of the Court Chamber Archives, visited England in 1836 and died greatly honoured as dramatist and poet.

Grob, Therese, married Bergmann (1798–1875), died childless.—Her brother Heinrich (1800–55), a merchant, married to Barbara Müllner since 1826, had two sons. The daughter of one of them, Frau Marianne Meangya at Mödling near Vienna, inherited Therese's collection of early Schubert songs in autographs.

Hartmann, Franz von (1808–75), married Rosalie, Freiin von Talatzko, and became president of the District Council at Graz.—His father, Friedrich Ludwig (1773–1844), died at Kirchschlag (Upper Austria) a few years after his wife, Maria Anna (b. 1779).—His brother Fritz (1805–1850) became district captain at Braunau (Upper Austria), and Ludwig (1810–81) director of finance at Salzburg.—Their sister Anna (b. 1797) was the wife of Anton, Count Revertera von Salandra, an officer; Therese (b. 1812) married in 1836—immediately after a proposal from Schwind—Eduard, Ritter von Arbter, last heard of as councillor to the Supreme County Courts at Brno. Schwind allegorically represented his unhappy love in a water-colour, 'The Strange Saint.'

Hellmesberger, Johann Georg (1800–73), was leader of the orchestra at the Kärntnertor Theatre in 1830–67 and professor of the violin at the Conservatory. The quartet founded by his son, Josef, gave the first public performances of several of Schubert's works, including the string Quintet.

Hönig, Anna (1803–88), married in 1832 Ferdinand Mayerhofer von Grünbühel (q.v.) and went into a convent after his death.—Her father, Franz (1766–1852), court judge of the cathedral chapter of St. Stephen's, was succeeded in that office by Franz Xaver Gutherz (1802–65), the second husband of Therese Puffer (1806–67). Her brother, Karl Hönig, Therese's first husband, had died in 1836 after a long illness.

Holzapfel, Anton (1792–1868), became a municipal councillor in Vienna. On being pensioned off in 1850 he moved with his family to Aistersheim near Wels in Upper Austria.

Huber, Josef (1794–1870), became an official in the Court War Accountancy. Having lost his first betrothed, Rosalie Kranzbichler, he married Maria Schmidt.

Hüttenbrenner, Anselm (1794–1868), remained artistic director of the Styrian Musical Society until 1839. He burnt his diary in 1841, lived a more and more retired life after the death of his wife Elise, née von Pichler (1800–48), composed among other things a funeral march for Major-General Sir Henry Havelock in 1858, presented Johann Herbeck with the manuscript of Schubert's unfinished B minor Symphony for performance in 1865 and died a discontented pietist on his property of Strasserhof near Graz. His recollections of Schubert, written for Liszt and for Luib, appeared in the Grillparzer Society's almanac for 1906.—His brother Josef (1796–1882) remained unmarried, became an assistant in the Ministry of the Interior and in 1860, in a letter to the Beethoven biographer A. W. Thayer, called himself "Schubert's prophet, singer, friend and pupil," but was rather Anselm's prophet in the end. Of the brothers Andreas (1797–1868) and Heinrich (1799–1830), the former was burgomaster of Graz in 1848 and became councillor to the Supreme County Council; the latter was a few years before his early death provisional professor of law at Graz University.

Jenger, Johann Baptist (1792–1856), remained single and became an official in the Court War Council of the Lower Austrian General Command.

Kenner, Josef (1794–1868), married Anna Kreil, became district captain at Freistadt in Upper Austria, later at Ischl, and died there with a pension and with the title of Statthaltereirat.

Kiesewetter von Wiesenbrunn, Irene (1811–72), married in 1832 Julius Schneller's adopted son, Anton Prokesch (1795–1876), who became Freiherr and Count von Osten, lieutenant-field-marshal and internuncio. She died at Graz.—Her father, Rafael Georg (1773–1850), remained vice-president of the Philharmonic Society until 1843. Her elder brother Karl died as chamber councillor at Milan in 1854.

Kleindl, Josef (1796–1882), became aulic councillor to the Supreme Court of Law and Cassation. In his will he left to the Wiener Schubertbund, a male-voice choir founded in 1863, a considerable sum "for the cultivation of the Schubertian Muse."

Koller, Josefine von (1801–74), was married since the spring of 1828 to Franz Krackowizer, later head supervisor at the castle of Wels in Upper Austria. She died at Türnitz (Lower Austria).—Her father, Josef (1780–1864), and her mother, Therese, née von Horalek (1783–1853), both died at Steyr. The emblems which adorned their music-room later went to the Vienna Schubert Association (Wiener Schubertbund).

Korner, Philipp (1761–1831), died as choirmaster of the children in the court chapel.

Kreil, Josef (1792–1855), was last councillor of administration to the Archbishop of Prague.—His brother, Franz Sales, Ritter von Kreil, died in 1867 as vice-president of the government representation at Linz. Another brother, Karl (1798–1862), became director of the Imperial Meteorological Institute in Vienna. For the sister Anna *see* Kenner.

Kupelwieser, Leopold (1796–1862), became a distinguished portrait and ecclesiastical painter (he decorated the Liechtental and University churches, among others), and in 1836 professor at the Academy of Fine Arts.—His wife, Johanna, née Lutz (b. 1803), died in 1883. His brother Josef (1791–1866), who was twice married, was last secretary to the Josefstadt Theatre.

Lachner, Franz (1803–90), was first conductor at the Kärntnertor Theatre in 1829–34 and in 1852 became General Musical Director at Munich. He was an opponent of Wagner, like Schwind, who, in 1862, humorously commemorated Lachner's career in a series of water-colours.—His brother Ignaz (1807–95), who succeeded him in 1824 as organist of the Protestant church in Vienna, also became a theatre conductor and died at Hanover. Vincenz (1811–93), who succeeded Ignaz in 1831, visited London in 1842 and finally taught at the Conservatory of Karlsruhe.

Leidesdorf, Maximilian Josef (1788–1840), migrated to Florence about 1830, where he published the 'Rivista musicale' and became chamber pianist to the ducal court of Tuscany and professor at the Conservatorio. —His daughter Louise was married for the second time to the journalist Michael Étienne, a son of Claude Étienne (*see* No. 108).

Leitermayer, Michael (1799–1867), became singing-master at the Josefstadt Theatre in 1834 and in 1835 organized at the hall of the Philharmonic Society a concert "to the memory of the friend of his youth, Franz Schubert."

Löwenthal, Max (1799–1872), was ennobled in 1863 and was last Post-master-General for Austria. Among his poems printed privately in 1871 there is one entitled 'Nemo Propheta in Patria,' which may refer to Schubert. In 1829 he married Sophie von Kleyle (1810–89), who, like himself, was a friend of the poet Nikolaus Lenau.

Mayerhofer, Ferdinand, Freiherr von Grünbühel (1798–1869), married Anna Hönig (q.v.) in 1832, having broken off his engagement to Jeannette von Mitis in 1829, was provisional head of the Voivodina and the Banat in 1849–51 and died as a lieutenant-field-marshal.

Mayrhofer, Johann (1787–1836), attempted suicide already in 1831 after the fall of Warsaw, and during a cholera epidemic in Vienna he leapt to his death from a third-floor window of the Book Revision Office. His friend, the legal scholar Franz Alois, Edler von Zeiller (1751–summer 1828), whom Schubert and Anselm Hüttenbrenner had frequented, had preceded him by a suicidal fall into the Danube.

Milder, Pauline Anna, married Hauptmann (1785–1838), the Berlin Court Opera singer, was pensioned off in 1831, but gave a concert in Vienna as late as 1836 and sang Schubert's 'Hermann and Thusnelda' at one of the Philharmonic Society's evening entertainments, lived there for two years with her married daughter and died in Berlin.

Mosel, Ignaz Franz, Edler von (1772–1844), became first custodian of the Court Library in 1829 and married once more after the death of his second wife, Katharina, née Lambert (1789–1832).

Müller, Sophie (1803–30), the actress, was mourned by the whole of Vienna at her early death.

Nestroy, Johann (1801–62), returned to Vienna in 1830 and was active there, first as singer, then as comedian and lastly as director, at the theatre in the Leopoldstadt, already called Carl Theatre at that time. He died at Graz as a famous author of comedies.

Ottenwalt, Anton (1789–1845), became in 1830 assistant in the Chamber Procuratorship in Vienna and died there with the title of Imperial Coun-cillor.—His wife, Marie, née von Spaun (b. 1795), followed him in 1847. Their only child, Karl, died at the age of eight in 1837.

Pachler, Marie, née Koschak (1794–1855), never received a copy of the privately printed book of songs (Op. 106) dedicated to her and was obliged to buy Diabelli's new issue at Graz in 1829.—Her husband, Karl (1789–1850) predeceased her. Their son, Faust (1819–91), a poet in a modest way, became custodian of the Court Library.

Paumgartner, Sylvester (c. 1763–1841), organized a concert for the benefit of the Salzburg Mozart monument in his music-room at Steyr in 1839.

Pinterics, Karl (d. 1831), left a collection of Schubert songs, which went to Witteczek, and a catalogue of 505 of those songs which also benefited Witteczek's (q.v.) collection.

Pyrker von Felsö-Eör, Johann Ladislaus (1773–1847), the archbishop, wrote a 'Folk Hymn' for the Salzburg Mozart Festival of 1842 in which occur the lines:

Auch lasst uns Schubert preisen	And let us Schubert praise
Ob seiner Zauberweisen!	And his enchanting lays!

Randhartinger, Benedikt (1802–93), was chapel master of the court chapel in 1862–6, in succession to Assmayr. About 1830 he dedicated to the memory of Schubert his vocal quartet with pianoforte accompaniment, 'Ins stille Land' (poem by J. G. von Salis, set by Schubert as a song in 1816 and entitled 'Lied'). About 1860 he revised the 'Fair Maid of the Mill' cycle for Diabelli's successor, Spina.

Rieder, Wilhelm August (1796–1880), a good portrait and historical painter, became custodian of the imperial picture gallery (1857–78). His father, Ambros (1771–1857), who, like Josef Sonnleithner and Dr. Anton Schmidt (*see* No. 125), had known Haydn, Mozart, Beethoven and Schubert, died at Perchtoldsdorf near Vienna. His brother Johann (*see* No. 483) and his sister Magdalena, whose later married name was Rupp, had also been acquainted with Schubert.

Rinna von Sarenbach, Ernst (*c.* 1792–1837), died as court physician in Vienna.

Rueskäfer, Michael, Freiherr von Wellenthal (1794–1872), became representative of the Ministry of Finance, received the title of Excellency, was ennobled and in 1862 retired with a pension. After the death of his first wife, Anna, he married Marie von Hintermayr of Steyr, and after her death her sister.

Sauter, Ferdinand (1804–54), became an insurance official in 1839 and died a drunkard, a degenerated poetic genius.

Schellmann, Albert, jun. (1798–1854), followed his father of the same name (1759–1844) as a barrister to the mining and county courts at Steyr. His mother, Barbara, *née* Reutter (b. 1770), died a year after her husband. For Seraphine, one of his numerous sisters, *see* Ebner.

Schlechta, Franz, Freiherr von Wssehrd (1796–1875), became head of a department in the Ministry of Finance. Heinrich Hollpein, Ignaz Schubert's stepson, painted his portrait in 1835. A fairly extensive poem on Schubert, written by Schlechta about 1840 and read by him at a club, has been lost.

Schnorr von Carolsfeld, Ludwig Ferdinand (1788–1853), a distinguished historical painter, preceded Rieder as custodian of the imperial picture gallery. His mystical leanings disappeared after the death of his friend Friedrich von Schlegel (1829), but he remained a devout Catholic to the end.

Schober, Franz, Ritter von (1796–1882), lost his lithographic establishment in 1829 and, as the last of the unhappy family, was bereft of his mother, Katharina, *née* Derffel (1764–1833), four years later. After a lawsuit against his uncle, Franz Derffel, for the property of Chorherrn in Lower Austria, he went to Hungary as companion and major-domo to various noble families, showed an interest in Therese, Countess Brunsvik's, nurseries there and for a time acted as Liszt's secretary. He then went to Weimar, where he became chamberlain and councillor of legation, or at any rate held those titles, and very nearly that of general intendant. At Dresden, where he made friends with the concert-master François Schubert, the old beau, who had once vainly wooed Marie von Spaun and had talked of Justina von Smetana as his last love in 1836, in 1856 married the literary blue-stocking Thekla von Gumpert, the originator of the immortal 'Töchter-Album,' an annual for flappers. The marriage lasted barely eight years and its course is illustrated by the traditional cry "Thekla, I shall strangle you!" He remained at Dresden to the end, though with some interruptions, living among furniture designed by himself and over a thousand books, including a single volume of his own poems (in three different stages) and a pamphlet on Liszt. He never had the energy to write down his recollections of Schubert. A projected journey to London fell through. His housekeeper, Frau Babette Wolf, lived on at his old dwelling as late as 1915.

Schönstein, Karl, Freiherr von (1797–1876), married Rosalie von Kleyle in 1845, one of Aulic Councillor Joachim von Kleyle's numerous daughters, but lost his wife within a year; in 1849 he took a second wife, Amalia von Winther of Munich (d. 1860), was pensioned off as councillor to the Ministry of Finance in 1856 and died at Aussee in Upper Austria. In 1838 he moved Liszt to tears with his performance of 'The Fair Maid of the Mill,' and in 1866 Schwind still addressed him as "Baron Schönstein, Journeyman Miller."

Schubert, Ferdinand (1794–1859), was married for the second time in 1832 to Therese Spazierer (1803–82), in 1851 became director of the chief training-school and left a dozen children. At a time when he had even more, he was obliged to farm out some of them, and so it sometimes came about that the schoolmaster, who was occupied with so many other people's children, failed to recognize his own when he met them in the street.—Ignaz (1785–1844) succeeded his father in

1830 as schoolmaster in the Rossau suburb.—Karl (1795–1855) remained a teacher of calligraphy; his sons Ferdinand (1824–53) and Heinrich (1827–97) became painters.—Maria Theresia (1801–78) survived her husband, the teacher Matthias Schneider (1788–1851).— The stepmother Anna, née Kleyenböck (1783–1860), about 1830 supervised the needlework lessons given at the Rossau school by her daughters: Maria (1814–35) and Josefa (1815–61), whose later married names were first Zant and then Bitthan. Anna's son, Andreas (1823–1893), became a councillor of accountancy; the other, Anton Eduard (1826–92), known as Father Hermann in the Vienna Scottish monastery, was an excellent preacher.

Schwind, Moritz von (1804–71), who had renounced Anna Hönig and vainly proposed to Therese von Hartmann, at last married Louise Sachs, the daughter of a major of Baden, with whom he lived very happily. He returned to Munich for good after a period at Karlsruhe and another at Frankfort o/M., and became the foremost German painter of fairy tales and legends. But he also delighted in large and small illustrations of all kinds of literary works, as well as in conceits of his own—his "occasional poems." He was a master of drawing and composition (especially in the matter of synchronizing successive scenes seen side by side), but not so much a master of colour. Schubert and other friends of his he often used as figures for his pictures. A plan to paint a music-room illustrated with scenes from Schubert's works unfortunately did not proceed beyond some pencil and water-colour sketches. One of the lunettes in the loggia of the Vienna Opera is dedicated to Schubert, whom, however, and the bygone time of his own youth, he glorified chiefly in his large sepia-drawing 'A Schubert Evening at Josef von Spaun's,' whose execution in oil of c. 1870 unhappily did not go beyond a sketch. Music accompanied him all his life, but he was a quarrelsome opponent of Wagner and Liszt. In 1857, when on an official visit to Manchester for the Exhibition, he also visited London. For Glasgow Cathedral he drew ten cartoons in 1858–9, which were executed in stained glass among many other windows made at Munich. With Schober he quarrelled irremediably, though not until the former had procured for him the commission for the frescoes in the Wartburg: an enthusiastic attachment of their youth turned into open enmity.

Seidl, Johann Gabriel (1804–75), became professor at the grammar-school of Cilli in Styria, in 1840 custodian of the collection of coins and antiques in Vienna, and also a censor. His portrait, painted by Teltscher (1829) shows on the pianoforte the music of several of his poems set by Schubert: 'The Wayfarer addressing the Moon,' 'In the Open' and 'Pigeon Post.' Seidl's son married a daughter of Ferdinand Schubert.

Senn, Johann Chrisostomus (1795–1857), became a teacher at a cadet school in the Tyrol, was pensioned off in 1832 and then continued to make a living as a clerk in various lawyers' offices.

Smetana, Rudolf, Ritter von (1802–71), joined the Redemptorist Order after the death of his wife, Justina (see Bruchmann) in 1829, and was last vicar-general of that Order. In 1851 he visited Liverpool officially, in 1857 he was pensioned off and, like his brother-in-law Bruchmann, he died at Gars in Bavaria. Another of the brethren, Alois Pichler, edited some poems of his in 1904 under the title of 'Gott und — wir,' sonnets on Holy Writ, specimens of which had already been published in Karl Dilgskron's biography of Smetana (1902).

Sonnleithner, Leopold, Edler von (1797–1873), became court judge at the Scottish Endowment and also a barrister in 1842, like his father Ignaz (1770–1831), with whom he had been ennobled in 1828. His diary, kept from 1812 onwards, is lost; but he published valuable essays on the domestic musical life of Vienna in the first half of the nineteenth century.—His wife, Louise, née Gosmar, 1803, died in 1858. His uncle, Josef (1766–1835), anticipated him in collecting material for musical history. Leopold collected particularly facts for a history of the Viennese opera. His recollections of Schubert he wrote down for Ferdinand Luib in 1857–8 ('Zeitschrift für Musikwissenschaft,' Leipzig, May 1919, vol. i, No. 8, pp. 466–83).

Spaun, Josef, Freiherr von (1788–1865), became lottery director and aulic councillor in 1841, Freiherr in 1859 and was pensioned in 1861. He bequeathed the Schubert collection left to him by Witteczek (q.v.) to the Philharmonic Society. He died on his country estate of Traun-kirchen in Upper Austria. On the drawing of an ideal gravestone made by Schwind (iconographical vol., Plate 413), showing the mourning water-nymphs of Lake Traun, a panel bears a verse from Mayrhofer's 'Night Piece.' For Spaun's recollections of Schubert see No. XXX. His wife, Franziska, née Roner von Ehrenwerth, 1795, died at Görz in 1890; her son, Hermann, became an Austrian admiral.—Spaun's mother, Josefa (1757–1835), died as the result of a street accident in Vienna. His brother, Anton (1790–1849), became a syndic of the Upper Austrian county council, a scholar in history and literature and a collector of Austrian folksongs; the latter's wife, Henriette, née Vogelsang, 1798, survived him until 1870. The brother Franz (1792–1829) died early as district commissioner at Steyr; his wife, Louise, née Wanderer, survived him. The brother Max (1797–1844) married Marie Zach at Laibach in 1833 and became court secretary at the General Court Chamber in Vienna. For the sister Marie see Otten-walt.

Spina, Karl Anton, Diabelli's partner since 1824, in 1853 took over the firm of that name, which had become Schubert's chief publisher. In 1872 it went to Friedrich Schreiber and in 1876 to August Cranz of Hamburg and Leipzig. Before the change-over, on 28th February 1851, Spina opened A. Diabelli & Co.'s "Schubert Salon" at No. 2 Seilerstätte (near the Hungarian Crown Inn) with a celebration introduced with a prologue by Bauernfeld. On 25th November 1853 Spina again held a celebration there for the twenty-fifth anniversary of Schubert's death. Schwind's hope of decorating that room with his Schubert pictures did not materialize; but the house was demolished as early as 1860.

Stadler, Albert (1794–1888), published a few songs of his own at Linz c. 1835, including two on poems by Karl Gottfried von Leitner already set by Schubert. He migrated to Salzburg in 1845, where his wife, Antonie, *née* Weilnböck (*see* No. 154), died in 1863. He was pensioned off in 1876 as Lower Austrian government councillor in Vienna. His copies of Schubert songs composed up to 1817 were, not unlike Ebner's (q.v.), an important source for the complete edition.—His sister Katharina (1798–1861) died as the wife of a teacher at a model school, Franz Xaver Kojeder, at Schwanenstadt in Upper Austria.

Streinsberg, Josef Ludwig von (1798–1862), died as departmental councillor of one of the ministries. For his wife, Isabella, *see* Bruchmann.

Teltscher, Josef (1801–37), a highly gifted portraitist (lithographer, water-colour painter and miniaturist), later lived at Graz and was drowned during a journey in Greece in the harbour of the Piraeus. He lost his life bathing; the assertion that he did so in attempting to save another has not been proved.

Tietze, Ludwig (1797–1850), became proctor's man at the University, tenor in the court chapel and a member of the committee of the *Concert spirituel*.

Traweger, Ferdinand (d. 1832), left a son, Eduard (1820–1909), who became captain in the police force and was the last person who had known Schubert.

Umlauff, Johann Karl, Ritter von Frankwell (1796–1861), became president of the Supreme County Court at Pressburg (Bratislava) and died in Vienna.

Unger, Johann Karl (1771–1836), had to part with his daughter Karoline (1803–77) when she was only twenty-two, for she left Vienna in 1825. In 1839–40 she was once more engaged at the Kärntnertor Theatre, but she left the stage in 1843, when she married the French scholar François Sabatier. She died at Florence.

Vering, Josef, Edler von (1793–1862), later became a specialist in nervous complaints, ear troubles, scrofula and gout.

Vesque von Püttlingen, Johann, Ritter von (1803–83), who composed under the pseudonym of J. Hoven, became head of a department in the Ministry of the Exterior and vice-president of the Philharmonic Society.

Vogl, Johann Michael (1768–1840), sang the 'Erl King' for the last time in public in 1834, but still performed the whole of the 'Winter Journey' at Karl von Enderes's when he was over seventy, greatly moving the whole company. In his lost diary, quoted by Bauernfeld in his obituary of Vogl in 1841, the singer spoke of Schubert's somnambulistic way of working. In the copies of Schubert's songs from which he sang all kinds of vocal ornaments are marked; some of these books are preserved in the Philharmonic Society's archives. His treatise on singing remained unfinished. Vogl's wife was still living at Steyr in 1865, having retired there after his death.

Walcher, Ferdinand, Ritter von Uysdael (1799–1873), became aulic councillor and head of the chancellery in the Lord High Steward's office of the Archduke Karl, later Archduke Albrecht. He married Hermine Sartorius.

Weisse, Maximilian, Ritter von (1798–1863), married to Karoline Lierhammer of Nuremberg since 1826, was director of the observatory at Cracow in 1825–61 and became a famous astronomer, corresponding member of the Royal Astronomical Society in London in 1848. He died in retirement at Wels in Upper Austria.

Weissenwolff, Johann Nepomuk Ungnad, Count (1779–1855), steward of the patrimonial dominions and lieutenant-colonel, survived his wife, Sophie Gabriele, *née* Countess Breuner (1794–1847).

Witteczek, Josef Wilhelm (1787–1859), became aulic councillor in the Exchequer in 1828. In 1831 he acquired Pinterics's (q.v.) collection of Schubert songs and collected all Schubert's works published up to 1850, mostly in first editions, as well as all the unpublished ones in fair copies made by one Weiser, with the exception of the symphonies, masses and operas: eighty-eight volumes in all, which also include indices, copies of criticisms and portraits of Schubert and his performers. He bequeathed this collection to Josef von Spaun, who left it to the Philharmonic Society. It was an important source for the complete edition of Schubert's works. Witteczek's wife, Wilhelmine, *née* Watteroth (1800–47), died after biting her cheek during a repast. Witteczek left a large library and a considerable fortune, both for the benefit of the public.

VIII. BIBLIOGRAPHY

(a) THE MOST IMPORTANT BOOKS ON SCHUBERT
(in chronological order)

Kreissle von Hellborn, Heinrich, 'Franz Schubert.' (Vienna, 1865.) Translated by Arthur Duke Coleridge, London, 1869, with an Appendix, by George Grove, on Schubert's symphonies.

Reissmann, August, 'Franz Schubert: sein Leben und seine Werke.' (Berlin, 1873.)

Nottebohm, Gustav, 'Thematisches Verzeichnis der im Druck erschienenen Werke von Franz Schubert.' (Vienna, 1874.)

Grove, George, Article in his 'Dictionary of Music and Musicians,' vol. iii, pp. 319–82, with additions in vol. iv, pp. 786 f. (London, 1883.) (The article is slightly altered in the later editions, with some additions in the 1940 Supplement, by W. H. Hadow, H. C. Colles and K. Geiringer.)

Friedlaender, Max, 'Beiträge zur Biographie Franz Schuberts.' Rostock Dissertation. (Berlin, 1887.) (Latest version, 'Franz Schubert: Skizze seines Lebens und Wirkens.' Leipzig, 1928.)

Schubert-Ausstellung der k. k. Reichshaupt- und Residenzstadt Wien, 1897 (catalogue).

Mandyczewski, Eusebius (and others), 'Franz Schubert. Kritisch durchgesehene Gesamtausgabe. Revisionsbericht.' (Leipzig, 1897.) (The report for Series II is by Johann Nepomuk Fuchs, that for Series VII and VIII by Ignaz Brüll and that for Series X, XI, XII by Julius Epstein.)

Heuberger, Richard, 'Franz Schubert.' (Berlin, 1902; second edition, 1908; third edition, revised by Hermann, Freiherr von der Pfordten, 1920.)

Dahms, Walter, 'Schubert.' (Berlin, 1912.) (Based on materials collected by Alois Fellner; the second and later editions, without illustrations, based on the following work.)

Deutsch, Otto Erich, 'Franz Schubert: die Dokumente seines Lebens und Schaffens,' vol. ii, part i, 'Die Dokumente seines Lebens' (Munich, 1913); vol. iii, 'Sein Leben in Bildern' (Munich, 1914). (Thematic Catalogue and Recollections of Schubert unpublished.)

Bauer, Moritz, 'Die Lieder Franz Schuberts,' vol. i. (Leipzig, 1915.) (Vol. ii. unpublished.)

Költzsch, Hans, 'Franz Schuberts Klaviersonaten.' Erlangen Dissertation. (Leipzig, 1927.)

BIBLIOGRAPHY

Capell, Richard, 'Schubert's Songs.' (London, 1928.)

Mies, Paul, 'Schubert, der Meister des Liedes.' (Berlin, 1928.)

Katalog der Schubert-Zentenar-Ausstellung der Stadt Wien, 1928.

Laaff, Ernst, 'Franz Schuberts Sinfonien.' Frankfort o/M. Dissertation. (Wiesbaden, 1933.)

Vetter, Walter, 'Franz Schubert.' (Potsdam, 1934.)

Kahl, Willi, 'Verzeichnis des Schrifttums über Franz Schubert, 1828–1928.' (Ratisbon, 1938.)

(b) Selection from the Author's Works on Schubert

Schubert-Brevier. (Berlin, 1905.)

Anselm Hüttenbrenner's Erinnerungen an Schubert. 'Jahrbuch der Grillparzer-Gesellschaft,' Year XVI, Vienna, 1906, pp. 99 ff.

Schuberts Aufenthalt in Graz 1827. 'Die Musik,' Year VI, Berlin, 1st and 15th January 1907, pp. 10 ff. and 91 ff.

Das Schuberthaus in der Rossau (Grünetorgasse). 'Neues Wiener Tagblatt,' 22nd August 1913.

Das Schubert'sche Familienhaus (Säulengasse). 'Neue Freie Presse,' Vienna, 19th November 1913.

Schubert in Ungarn. 'Pester Lloyd,' Budapest, 13th January 1914. (Final version, unpublished, radio lecture, Budapest, 15th November 1935.)

Das Urbild der 'Schönen Müllerin.' 'Alt-Wiener Kalender,' Year I, Vienna, 1917, pp. 48 ff.

Franz Schuberts Briefe und Schriften. (Munich, 1919.) (Second edition, Munich, 1922; third, in English, London, 1928.)

Ein Schuberthaus in Erdberg [recte auf der Landstrasse] (Erdbergergasse). 'Der Merker,' Year X, Vienna, July 1919, pp. 478 ff.

Schubert im Fruhwirth-Haus (Technikerstrasse). 'Blätter des Opern-theaters,' Year I, Vienna, 1921, pp. 26 ff.

Schuberts Krankheit. 'Zeitschrift für Musikwissenschaft,' Year IV, Leipzig, November 1921, pp. 100 ff. (Cf. Year III, June–July 1921, pp. 552 ff.)

Die historischen Bildnisse Franz Schuberts in getreuen Nachbildungen. (Vienna, 1922.) (Second edition, privately printed, Vienna, 1928.)

Schuberts Erstlinge: Vorwort zu 'Franz Schuberts fünf erste Lieder,' in Faksimile-Reproduktion herausgegeben. (Vienna, 1922, pp. iii ff.)

BIBLIOGRAPHY

Schuberts Vater. 'Alt-Wiener Kalender,' Year IV, Vienna, 1924, pp. 134 ff.

Schuberts Gasteiner Sinfonie. 'Neue Freie Presse,' Vienna, 11th July 1925. (Final version, unpublished, in the radio lecture 'Schuberts sinfonisches Schaffen,' Basle, 5th May 1934.)

Der intime Schubert. Special number of 'Die moderne Welt,' vol. vii, No. 13, Vienna, 1st December 1925. (With some contributions by other authors.)

Schuberts Einkommen. 'Frankfurter Zeitung,' 4th August 1926. (Supplement in 'Zeitschrift für Musikwissenschaft,' Year IX, Leipzig, October 1926, pp. 61 f.)

Die Originalausgaben von Schuberts Goethe-Liedern (Bibliography). (Vienna, 1926.)

Franz von Schober, Schuberts schwedischer Freund (unpublished). Lecture, Stockholm, 25th January 1927.

Schubert ohne Guitarre. 'Schubert-Gabe' of the 'Österreichische Guitarre-Zeitschrift,' Year II, Vienna, 1928, pp. 18 ff. (Cf. 'Zeitschrift für Musikwissenschaft,' Year XI, Leipzig, November 1928, pp. 124 ff., and Year XIV, August-September 1932, pp. 476 ff.)

Schwinds Schubertzimmer. 'Österreichische Guitarre - Zeitschrift,' Year II, Vienna, 1928, pp. 46 ff. (on the sketches for a music-room with pictures illustrating Schubert's works).

Einführung zu 'Rosamunde,' Textbuch von Hugo Engelbrecht (sc. Schwarz) für Konzertaufführungen. (Vienna, 1928, pp. 3 ff.)

Schubert unter den Wiener Sängerknaben. 'Schubert-Zentenarfeier der Wiener Sängerknaben,' Vienna, 1928, pp. 3 ff.

Das k. k. Stadtkonvikt zu Schuberts Zeit. 'Die Quelle,' Year LXXVIII, April 1928, pp. 477 ff.

Franz Schuberts Tagebuch (von 1816, Faksimile mit Vorwort und Transkription). (Vienna, 1928.) (New York, 1928, without the preface and with transcription in English.)

Ferdinand Schuberts 'Deutsches Requiem' von Franz Schubert: Vorwort zur Neuausgabe der 'Deutschen Trauermesse.' (Vienna, 1928, pp. 1 ff.; cf. 'Zeitschrift für Musikwissenschaft,' Year XI, Leipzig, November 1928, pp. 126 f.)

Schuberts Verleger. 'Der Bär,' Year V, Leipzig, 1928, pp. 13 ff.

Schuberts zwei Liederhefte für Goethe (fair copies). 'Die Musik,' Year XXI, Berlin, October 1928, pp. 31 ff.

Das 'Advokaten'-Terzett [a plagiarism] von Schubert. 'Zeitschrift für Musikwissenschaft,' Year XI, Leipzig, November 1928, pp. 65 ff.

Schuberts Popularität einst und jetzt (Lecture, Basle, 5th May 1934). 'National-Zeitung,' Basle, Sunday Supplement, 1st July 1934.

Goethe und Schubert (Lecture, Vienna, 27th April 1935). 'Chronik des Wiener Goethe-Vereins,' Year XLI, Vienna, 1936, pp. 13 ff.

Grillparzer und Schubert (unpublished). Lecture delivered before the Grillparzer-Gesellschaft, Vienna, 20th January 1936.

The Riddle of Schubert's Unfinished Symphony. 'The Music Review,' vol. i, Cambridge, February 1940, pp. 36 ff. (cf. vol. ii, February 1941, pp. 63 ff.; vol. ii, May 1941, p. 184, and vol. iii, February 1942, pp. 10 ff.).

The Chronology of Schubert's String Quartets. 'Music & Letters,' vol. xxiv, January 1943, pp. 25 ff.

The Reception of Schubert's Works in England (unpublished). Lecture delivered in Bedford College for Women, London, 28th November 1945.

IX. SUMMARY COMPARISON

BETWEEN THE FIRST EDITION (IN GERMAN) AND THE FINAL EDITION (IN ENGLISH)

The German edition contains 1,183 numbers and 4 "a" numbers: 1,187 documents all told.

The English edition contains 1,161 numbers and 22 "A" numbers: 1,183 documents. To these are added, however, the 5 pre-natal documents, marked A to E, and the 46 posthumous documents, numbered I to XLVI: 51 in all. The total number of documents in the English edition is thus 1,234.

Of the 1,187 numbers in the German edition about 76 have now been dropped as being of small importance. They are for the most part criticisms of works already dealt with in other notices, at least one of which has been retained for each work discussed. None of the criticisms omitted contains anything new or of special interest. They are, however, all referred to in the commentary.

Furthermore about 91 facts have been taken over from the German edition; but they are no longer numbered, actual documents only being now included in the enumeration. About 77 new facts have moreover been added.

Documents published here for the first time number about 155, and to these must be added 9 documents previously regarded as lost, which have been recovered or rediscovered since the publication of the German edition.

Some of the documents have been more extensively quoted, others have been abridged; many have been corrected.

If the number of facts mentioned be counted, the English edition contains some 1,400 items as compared with the 1,187 in the German edition—an increase of about 213 in spite of the 76 omissions.

.   .   .   .   .   .

Both editions giving the documents in chronological order, it will be easy for those who for some reason wish to refer to the original texts, to identify those in the German edition by means of the dates, in spite of the different enumeration. In only a few cases a reversal of the order was found to be necessary, and in three a division, as the following concordance will show:

English German		German English	
8 =	10	10 =	8
141 =	155	155 =	141
158 =	664, supp. A		
163 =	166	166 =	163
242 =	285	285 =	242
253 =	307	295 =	265
265 =	295	307 =	253
296 =	345	345 =	296
345 =	369a	369a=	345
433 =	451, part 1	451 =	433 and 435
435 =	451, part 2		
544 =	564, part 1	564 =	544 and 548A
548A=	564, part 2	664, supp. A=	158
654 =	672	672 =	654
655 =	673	673 =	655
693 =	702	702 =	693
fact between			
721 and 722 =	728	728 =	fact between 721 and 722
725A=	769	769 =	725A
926 =	945	945 =	926

The documents thought to have been lost are the following in the English edition (numbers in brackets are those of the headings referring in the German edition to these documents, which were known to have existed, but could not then be traced): 55 (55), 322 (351), 369 (390), 562 (586), 655 (673), 986 (1,003, substitute), 1,077 (1,092), 1,096 (1,110), 1,152 (1,164).

LIST OF SCHUBERT'S WORKS MENTIONED
IN THE BOOK

GENERAL INDEX OF NAMES, PLACES, TITLES, AND SELECTED SUBJECTS

'Swan Song' ('Schwanengesang'), Song Cycle (1828). Engraved Vignette
for Subscribers' Copies of the First Edition (1829).   See pp. 882–4